AMERICA VOTES 20

A HANDBOOK OF CONTEMPORARY

AMERICAN ELECTION STATISTICS

COMPILED AND EDITED BY

RICHARD M. SCAMMON

and

ALICE V. McGILLIVRAY

1992

ELECTIONS RESEARCH CENTER

CONGRESSIONAL QUARTERLY   WASHINGTON   1993

© 1993 ELECTIONS RESEARCH CENTER
5508 Greystone Street
Chevy Chase, Maryland 20815

Copies available from: Congressional Quarterly Inc., 1414 22nd St. N.W., Washington, D.C. 20037

Printed in the United States of America

Library of Congress Catalog Card Number: 56-10132
International Standard Book Number: 0-87187-784-4

CONTENTS

Chicago, Detroit, Harris county (Texas), Los Angeles county, New York City and Philadelphia data will be found in the appropriate state sections.

INTRODUCTION

The twentieth volume of AMERICA VOTES follows the general pattern used in previous editions of the handbook. The state chapter system is continued, with a profile sheet listing the current Governor, Senators and Representatives along with tables of the post-World War II statewide vote for President, Governor and Senator. In the Presidential table, the plurality figures are calculated on a first-second party basis and are not limited to a Republican-Democratic plurality as in the Senator and Governor tables.

Following this information is a map of the state by congressional districts and county-by-county tables of the 1992 vote for President, Governor and Senator. The 1991 vote for Governor in Kentucky, Louisiana and Mississippi is also included along with the 1991 special Senatorial election in Pennsylvania. The vote cast for congressional candidates is presented by congressional district. The implementation of the 1990 Census for redistricting purposes led to changes in the congressional district lines in all multi-member states except Maine which redistricted in 1993; therefore, past data are included only for states with one at-large member and for the two districts in Maine. For earlier election results (and earlier boundaries) previous volumes of AMERICA VOTES should be consulted.

The note section which completes each state chapter contains the distribution of the non-major party vote, minor party ballot designations, discrepancies or corrections in the canvassed returns, special state situations and the primary elections data. Included within the appropriate state chapters are voting data and voting division maps for Chicago, Detroit, Harris county (Texas), New York City, Philadelphia and Los Angeles county. In the chapters for New England states, tables are included which list the voting by larger cities and towns except for Rhode Island which lists all cities and towns.

Attention of AMERICA VOTES 20 users is directed to the format of the Presidential vote statistics in each state. The data are presented in a four-column tabulation (Republican, Democratic, Perot and Other) and the plurality figures are calculated on a first-second party basis.

In line with suggestions from our readers, new features in *AMERICA VOTES 20* include county-by-county voter registration data, a summary by state of the vote for each minor party candidate and a voter turnout table. In the minor-party table, the write-in vote for a candidate is designated by an asterisk. Using this table, the reader is able to determine in which states a minor party candidate was on the ballot. The 1992 state-by-state turnout chart gives the Census estimate of the resident voting-age population, the statewide registration and the total valid vote for President. Using the valid vote for President, calculations include the percent of the voting-age population registered and the percent turnout of the voting-age population and the registered voters.

In the front section of AMERICA VOTES 20, the reader will find historical data for Presidential elections from 1920 through 1992 and data for the Presidential preference primaries from 1968 through 1992 by state and/or summary table. This section also includes special elections held between the general elections of 1990 and 1992 to fill vacancies in the 102nd Congress and changes which occurred after the 1992 general election up to publication date.

The AMERICA VOTES series is compiled from the final, official results obtained from the election authorities in each state. From this raw material is built a set of national reference volumes on American elections. To make these reference volumes of maximum efficiency in meeting the needs of its users, suggestions as to new materials, together with any corrections of data, are welcome.

Richard M. Scammon
Alice V. McGillivray

Washington, D.C.
July 1993

UNITED STATES

POST ELECTION CHANGES

Following the 1992 General Election, and prior to July 31, 1993, there were seven changes in the membership of the 103rd Congress.

SENATORS

Tennessee — Albert Gore, Jr. resigned January 1993 to become Vice-President of the United States; Harland Mathews (D) was appointed January 1993 to fill out the remaining two years of the term.

Texas — Lloyd Bentsen (D) resigned January 1993 to become Secretary of the Treasury; Bob Krueger (D) was appointed January 1993 to fill the seat until a special election in June 1993 for the remaining year and a half of the term. Kay Bailey Hutchison (R) was elected in the June 1993 special election.

REPRESENTATIVES

17th CD California — Leon E. Panetta (D) resigned January 1993 to become Director of the Office of Management and Budget; Sam Farr (D) was elected June 1993 to succeed him.

3rd CD Michigan — Paul Henry (R) died July 1993. As of publication, the date for a special election to fill the seat had not been set.

2nd CD Mississippi — Mike Espy (D) resigned January 1993 to become Secretary of Agriculture; Bennie Thompson (D) was elected April 1993 to succeed him.

2nd CD Ohio — Willis D. Gradison (R) retired March 1993 to become president of the Health Insurance Association of America; Rob Portman (R) was elected May 1993 to succeed him.

1st CD Wisconsin — Les Aspin (D) resigned January 1993 to become Secretary of Defense; Peter W. Barca (D) was elected May 1993 to succeed him.

UNITED STATES

SPECIAL ELECTIONS TO THE 102ND CONGRESS

Between the General Elections of 1990 and 1992, one appointment was made to the Senate and nine special elections were held to fill vacancies in the 102nd Congress. Results of these elections are listed below.

SENATORS

CALIFORNIA

Pete Wilson (R) resigned November 1990 upon being elected Governor of California; John Seymour (R) was appointed December 1990 to fill the vacancy until a special election in November 1992 for the remaining two years of the term.

PENNSYLVANIA

H. John Heinz (R) died April 1991; Harris Wofford (D) was elected November 1991 to fill out the remaining three years of the term; had been appointed May 1991 to fill the vacancy until the November 1991 Special Election.

Candidates were nominated by state party committees.

November 5, 1991 Special Election

1,860,760 Harris Wofford (D); 1,521,986 Richard L. Thornburgh (R). The county-by-county returns can be found in the Pennsylvania section of this volume.

REPRESENTATIVES

ARIZONA 2ND CD

Morris K. Udall (D) resigned May 1991; Ed Pastor (D) was elected September 1991 to fill out the remaining term for the 102nd Congress.

August 13, 1991 Special Republican Primary

4,259 Pat Conner; 3,826 John P. Kaites; 2,731 Don Shooter; 1,529 Al Rodriguez; 713 Elliott Glasser.

August 13, 1991 Special Democratic Primary

12,374 Ed Pastor; 10,575 Tom Volgy; 8,874 Virginia Yrun; 787 Joseph D. Sweeney; 503 Craig Runyon.

September 24, 1991 Special Election

32,289 Ed Pastor (D); 25,814 Pat Conner (R); 33 Bruce A. Friedemann (write-in).

ILLINOIS 15TH CD

Edward R. Madigan (R) resigned March 1991 upon being sworn in as Secretary of Agriculture; Thomas Ewing (R) was elected July 1991 to fill out the remaining term for the 102nd Congress.

May 21, 1991 Special Democratic Primary

2,464 Gerald Bradley; 1,701 Tim L. Hall.

May 21, 1991 Special Republican Primary

Thomas Ewing, unopposed.

UNITED STATES

July 2, 1991 Special Election

25,675 Thomas Ewing (R); 13,011 Gerald Bradley (D); 24 Lloyd Metz (write-in).

MASSACHUSETTS 1ST CD

Silvio O. Conte (R) died February 1991; John Olver (D) was elected June 1991 to fill out the remaining term for the 102nd Congress.

April 30, 1991 Special Republican Primary

14,564 Steven D. Pierce; 8,613 Donald A. Thurston; 1,538 Janelyn Patashnick; 43 scattered write-in.

April 30, 1991 Special Democratic Primary
18,426 John Olver; 11,053 Linda J. Melconian; 10,479 Christopher J. Hodgkins; 8,343 Sherwood Guernsey; 6,515 James G. Collins; 2,182 Leonard J. Collamore; 1,787 Donald L. Robinson; 474 John R. Arden; 278 Lisa Baskin; 128 Stephen I. Bloomfield; 72 scattered write-in.

June 4, 1991 Special Election

70,022 John Olver (D); 68,052 Steven D. Pierce (R); 1,859 Patrick J. Armstrong (Independent); 880 Dennis M. Kelly (Pro-Democracy Reform); 250 Thomas Boynton (no party); 86 scattered write-in.

NEW YORK 8TH CD

Theodore S. Weiss (D) died one day before the September 15 Democratic primary in which he won the nomination. Jerrold Nadler (D) was substituted after the primary by the local party committee. The September Republican and Democratic primaries and the November general election results listed in the New York chapter filled both the remaining months of Mr. Weiss' term in the 102nd Congress and the full term for the 103rd Congress.

NORTH CAROLINA 1ST CD

Walter B. Jones (D) died September 1992; Eva Clayton (D) was elected November 1992 to fill our the remaining months of the term for the 102nd Congress. This election was held using the old (pre 1992) congressional district boundaries.

Candidates were nominated by local party committees.

November 3, 1992 Special Election

118,324 Eva Clayton (D); 86,273 Ted Tyler (R); 4,121 C. Barry Williams (Libertarian).

PENNSYLVANIA 2ND CD

William H. Gray (D) resigned September 1991 to become president of the United Negro College Fund; Lucien E. Blackwell (D) was elected November 1991 to fill out the remaining term for the 102nd Congress.

Candidates were nominated by local party committees.

November 5, 1991 Special Election

51,820 Lucien E. Blackwell (D); 37,068 Chaka Fattah (Consumer); 36,469 John F. White (Independent); 6,928 Nadine G. Smith-Bulford (R).

UNITED STATES

TEXAS 3RD CD

Steve Bartlett (R) resigned March 1991 to run for Mayor of Dallas; Sam Johnson (R) was elected May 1991 to fill out the remaining term for the 102nd Congress.

May 4, 1991 Special All-Party Primary

15,018 Tom Pauken (R); 10,855 Sam Johnson (R); 6,756 Bill Hammond (R); 5,909 Paul Z. Pilzer (R); 5,484 Dan Branch (R); 5,156 Pete Sessions (R); 2,324 Wayne E. Putman (D); 1,139 Farrell Ray (R); 806 Robert E. Lyle (R); 802 Mel Richardson (Independent); 238 Rufus Higginbotham (Independent); 168 David Corley (R); 9 Phil Allen (write-in); 1 Mitch Whatley (write-in); 1 Noel Kopola (write-in).

May 18, 1991 Special Run-Off Election

24,004 Sam Johnson(R); 21,647 Tom Pauken (R).

VIRGINIA 7TH CD

D. French Slaughter (R) resigned August 1991; George F. Allen was elected November 1991 to fill out the remaining term for the 102nd Congress.

Candidates were nominated by local party conventions.

November 5, 1991 Special Election

106,745 George F. Allen (R); 59,655 Kay Slaughter (D); 5,566 John A. Torrice (Independent); 89 scattered write-in.

UNITED STATES

POPULAR VOTE FOR PRESIDENT 1920 TO 1992

Year	Total Vote	Republican		Democratic		Other Vote	Plurality	Percentage			
								Total Vote		Major Vote	
		Vote	Candidate	Vote	Candidate			Rep.	Dem.	Rep.	Dem.
1992	104,425,014	39,103,882	Bush, George	44,909,326	Clinton, Bill	20,411,806	5,805,444 D	37.4%	43.0%	46.5%	53.5%
1988	91,594,809	48,886,097	Bush, George	41,809,074	Dukakis, Michael S.	899,638	7,077,023 R	53.4%	45.6%	53.9%	46.1%
1984	92,652,842	54,455,075	Reagan, Ronald	37,577,185	Mondale, Walter F.	620,582	16,877,890 R	58.8%	40.6%	59.2%	40.8%
1980	86,515,221	43,904,153	Reagan, Ronald	35,483,883	Carter, Jimmy	7,127,185	8,420,270 R	50.7%	41.0%	55.3%	44.7%
1976	81,555,889	39,147,793	Ford, Gerald R.	40,830,763	Carter, Jimmy	1,577,333	1,682,970 D	48.0%	50.1%	48.9%	51.1%
1972	77,718,554	47,169,911	Nixon, Richard M.	29,170,383	McGovern, George S.	1,378,260	17,999,528 R	60.7%	37.5%	61.8%	38.2%
1968	73,211,875	31,785,480	Nixon, Richard M.	31,275,166	Humphrey, Hubert H.	10,151,229	510,314 R	43.4%	42.7%	50.4%	49.6%
1964	70,644,592	27,178,188	Goldwater, Barry M.	43,129,566	Johnson, Lyndon B.	336,838	15,951,378 D	38.5%	61.1%	38.7%	61.3%
1960	68,838,219	34,108,157	Nixon, Richard M.	34,226,731	Kennedy, John F.	503,331	118,574 D	49.5%	49.7%	49.9%	50.1%
1956	62,026,908	35,590,472	Eisenhower, Dwight D.	26,022,752	Stevenson, Adlai E.	413,684	9,567,720 R	57.4%	42.0%	57.8%	42.2%
1952	61,550,918	33,936,234	Eisenhower, Dwight D.	27,314,992	Stevenson, Adlai E.	299,692	6,621,242 R	55.1%	44.4%	55.4%	44.6%
1948	48,793,826	21,991,291	Dewey, Thomas E.	24,179,345	Truman, Harry S.	2,623,190	2,188,054 D	45.1%	49.6%	47.6%	52.4%
1944	47,976,670	22,017,617	Dewey, Thomas E.	25,612,610	Roosevelt, Franklin D.	346,443	3,594,993 D	45.9%	53.4%	46.2%	53.8%
1940	49,900,418	22,348,480	Willkie, Wendell	27,313,041	Roosevelt, Franklin D.	238,897	4,964,561 D	44.8%	54.7%	45.0%	55.0%
1936	45,654,763	16,684,231	Landon, Alfred M.	27,757,333	Roosevelt, Franklin D.	1,213,199	11,073,102 D	36.5%	60.8%	37.5%	62.5%
1932	39,758,759	15,760,684	Hoover, Herbert C.	22,829,501	Roosevelt, Franklin D.	1,168,574	7,068,817 D	39.6%	57.4%	40.8%	59.2%
1928	36,805,951	21,437,277	Hoover, Herbert C.	15,007,698	Smith, Alfred E.	360,976	6,429,579 R	58.2%	40.8%	58.8%	41.2%
1924	29,095,023	15,719,921	Coolidge, Calvin	8,386,704	Davis, John W.	4,988,398	7,333,217 R	54.0%	28.8%	65.2%	34.8%
1920	26,768,613	16,153,115	Harding, Warren G.	9,133,092	Cox, James M.	1,482,406	7,020,023 R	60.3%	34.1%	63.9%	36.1%

For detail of other vote see note section included with each U.S. summary table that follows.

ELECTORAL COLLEGE VOTE 1920 TO 1992

Year	Total	Republican	Democratic	Other	
1992	538	168	370	—	
1988	538	426	111	1	BENTSEN
1984	538	525	13	—	
1980	538	489	49	—	
1976	538	240	297	1	REAGAN
1972	538	520	17	1	LIBERTARIAN
1968	538	301	191	46	AIP
1964	538	52	486	—	
1960	537	219	303	15	BYRD
1956	531	457	73	1	JONES
1952	531	442	89	—	
1948	531	189	303	39	SR
1944	531	99	432	—	
1940	531	82	449	—	
1936	531	8	523	—	
1932	531	59	472	—	
1928	531	444	87	—	
1924	531	382	136	13	PROGRESSIVE
1920	531	404	127	—	

PRESIDENT 1992

In New York the Republican figures include Conservative and Right to Life votes and the Democratic figures include Liberal votes.

In Minnesota, the Republican candidates appear on the ballot as Independent-Republican, the Democratic as Democratic-Farmer-Labor. In many states various non-major party candidates appeared on the ballot with variations of the party designations, were carried with entirely different party labels or listed as "Independent". The state note sections list the party labels used by the minor-party candidates. In several states minor party Vice-Presidential candidates were different from those listed below.

The candidates listed below include all those who appeared on the ballot in at least one state. Where identified by state authorities, write-in votes for minor party candidates are credited to their total below. See the minor party vote chart which follows the United States table for details.

44,909,326	Bill Clinton and Albert Gore, Jr., Democratic.
39,103,882	George Bush and J. Danforth Quayle, Republican.
19,741,657	Ross Perot and James Stockdale, Independent.
291,627	Andre V. Marrou and Nancy Lord, Libertarian.
107,014	James Gritz and Cyril Minett, America First.
73,714	Lenora B. Fulani and Maria E. Munoz, New Alliance.
43,434	Howard Phillips and Albion W. Knight, Taxpayers.
39,179	John Hagelin and Mike Tompkins, Natural Law.
27,961	Ron Daniels and Asiba Tupahache, Peace and Freedom.
26,333	Lyndon H. LaRouche and James L. Bevel, Economic Recovery.
23,096	James Warren and Willie Mae Reid, Socialist Workers.
4,749	Drew Bradford and no Vice Presidential candidate, Independent.
3,875	Jack Herer and Derrick P. Grimmer, Grassroots.
3,057	J. Quinn Brisben and Barbara Garson, Socialist.
3,050	Helen Halyard and Fred Mazelis, Workers League.
2,199	John Yiamouyiannas and Allen C. McCone, Take Back America.
1,149	Delbert L. Ehlers and Rick Wendt, Independent.
961	Earl F. Dodge and George Ormsby, Prohibition.
956	Jim Boren and Will Weidman, Apathy.
405	Eugene A. Hem and Joanne Roland, Third Party.
339	Isabell Masters and Walter Masters, Looking Back.
292	Robert J. Smith and Doris Feimer, American.
181	Gloria LaRiva and Larry Holmes, Workers World.

In addition to the votes listed above, 14,041 scattered write-in votes were reported from various states and 2,537 votes were cast for "None of these Candidates" in Nevada.

UNITED STATES

PRESIDENT 1992

State	Electoral Vote Rep.	Dem.	Other	Total Vote	Republican	Democratic	Perot	Other	Plurality	Rep.	Dem.	Perot
Alabama	9			1,688,060	804,283	690,080	183,109	10,588	114,203 R	47.6%	40.9%	10.8%
Alaska	3			258,506	102,000	78,294	73,481	4,731	23,706 R	39.5%	30.3%	28.4%
Arizona	8			1,486,975	572,086	543,050	353,741	18,098	29,036 R	38.5%	36.5%	23.8%
Arkansas		6		950,653	337,324	505,823	99,132	8,374	168,499 D	35.5%	53.2%	10.4%
California		54		11,131,721	3,630,574	5,121,325	2,296,006	83,816	1,490,751 D	32.6%	46.0%	20.6%
Colorado		8		1,569,180	562,850	629,681	366,010	10,639	66,831 D	35.9%	40.1%	23.3%
Connecticut		8		1,616,332	578,313	682,318	348,771	6,930	104,005 D	35.8%	42.2%	21.6%
Delaware		3		289,735	102,313	126,054	59,213	2,155	23,741 D	35.3%	43.5%	20.4%
Florida	25			5,314,392	2,173,310	2,072,698	1,053,067	15,317	100,612 R	40.9%	39.0%	19.8%
Georgia		13		2,321,125	995,252	1,008,966	309,657	7,250	13,714 D	42.9%	43.5%	13.3%
Hawaii		4		372,842	136,822	179,310	53,003	3,707	42,488 D	36.7%	48.1%	14.2%
Idaho	4			482,142	202,645	137,013	130,395	12,089	65,632 R	42.0%	28.4%	27.0%
Illinois		22		5,050,157	1,734,096	2,453,350	840,515	22,196	719,254 D	34.3%	48.6%	16.6%
Indiana	12			2,305,871	989,375	848,420	455,934	12,142	140,955 R	42.9%	36.8%	19.8%
Iowa		7		1,354,607	504,891	586,353	253,468	9,895	81,462 D	37.3%	43.3%	18.7%
Kansas	6			1,157,335	449,951	390,434	312,358	4,592	59,517 R	38.9%	33.7%	27.0%
Kentucky		8		1,492,900	617,178	665,104	203,944	6,674	47,926 D	41.3%	44.6%	13.7%
Louisiana		9		1,790,017	733,386	815,971	211,478	29,182	82,585 D	41.0%	45.6%	11.8%
Maine		4		679,499	206,504	263,420	206,820	2,755	56,600 D	30.4%	38.8%	30.4%
Maryland		12		1,985,046	707,094	988,571	281,414	7,967	281,477 D	35.6%	49.8%	14.2%
Massachusetts		10		2,773,700	805,049	1,318,662	630,731	19,258	513,613 D	29.0%	47.5%	22.7%
Michigan		18		4,274,673	1,554,940	1,871,182	824,813	23,738	316,242 D	36.4%	43.8%	19.3%
Minnesota		10		2,347,948	747,841	1,020,997	562,506	16,604	273,156 D	31.9%	43.5%	24.0%
Mississippi	7			981,793	487,793	400,258	85,626	8,116	87,535 R	49.7%	40.8%	8.7%
Missouri		11		2,391,565	811,159	1,053,873	518,741	7,792	242,714 D	33.9%	44.1%	21.7%
Montana		3		410,611	144,207	154,507	107,225	4,672	10,300 D	35.1%	37.6%	26.1%
Nebraska	5			737,546	343,678	216,864	174,104	2,900	126,814 R	46.6%	29.4%	23.6%
Nevada		4		506,318	175,828	189,148	132,580	8,762	13,320 D	34.7%	37.4%	26.2%
New Hampshire		4		537,943	202,484	209,040	121,337	5,082	6,556 D	37.6%	38.9%	22.6%
New Jersey		15		3,343,594	1,356,865	1,436,206	521,829	28,694	79,341 D	40.6%	43.0%	15.6%
New Mexico		5		569,986	212,824	261,617	91,895	3,650	48,793 D	37.3%	45.9%	16.1%
New York		33		6,926,925	2,346,649	3,444,450	1,090,721	45,105	1,097,801 D	33.9%	49.7%	15.7%
North Carolina	14			2,611,850	1,134,661	1,114,042	357,864	5,283	20,619 R	43.4%	42.7%	13.7%
North Dakota	3			308,133	136,244	99,168	71,084	1,637	37,076 R	44.2%	32.2%	23.1%
Ohio		21		4,939,967	1,894,310	1,984,942	1,036,426	24,289	90,632 D	38.3%	40.2%	21.0%
Oklahoma	8			1,390,359	592,929	473,066	319,878	4,486	119,863 R	42.6%	34.0%	23.0%
Oregon		7		1,462,643	475,757	621,314	354,091	11,481	145,557 D	32.5%	42.5%	24.2%
Pennsylvania		23		4,959,810	1,791,841	2,239,164	902,667	26,138	447,323 D	36.1%	45.1%	18.2%
Rhode Island		4		453,477	131,601	213,299	105,045	3,532	81,698 D	29.0%	47.0%	23.2%
South Carolina	8			1,202,527	577,507	479,514	138,872	6,634	97,993 R	48.0%	39.9%	11.5%
South Dakota	3			336,254	136,718	124,888	73,295	1,353	11,830 R	40.7%	37.1%	21.8%
Tennessee		11		1,982,638	841,300	933,521	199,968	7,849	92,221 D	42.4%	47.1%	10.1%
Texas	32			6,154,018	2,496,071	2,281,815	1,354,781	21,351	214,256 R	40.6%	37.1%	22.0%
Utah	5			743,999	322,632	183,429	203,400	34,538	119,232 R	43.4%	24.7%	27.3%
Vermont		3		289,701	88,122	133,592	65,991	1,996	45,470 D	30.4%	46.1%	22.8%
Virginia	13			2,558,665	1,150,517	1,038,650	348,639	20,859	111,867 R	45.0%	40.6%	13.6%
Washington		11		2,288,230	731,234	993,037	541,780	22,179	261,803 D	32.0%	43.4%	23.7%
West Virginia		5		683,762	241,974	331,001	108,829	1,958	89,027 D	35.4%	48.4%	15.9%
Wisconsin		11		2,531,114	930,855	1,041,066	544,479	14,714	110,211 D	36.8%	41.1%	21.5%
Wyoming	3			200,598	79,347	68,160	51,263	1,828	11,187 R	39.6%	34.0%	25.6%
Dist. of Col.		3		227,572	20,698	192,619	9,681	4,574	171,921 D	9.1%	84.6%	4.3%
United States	168	370		104,425,014	39,103,882	44,909,326	19,741,657	670,149	5,805,444 D	37.4%	43.0%	18.9%

UNITED STATES

PRESIDENT 1992 MINOR PARTIES

State	Other	Marrou	Gritz	Fulani	Phillips	Hagelin	Daniels	LaRouche	Warren	Other Candidates and Scattered
Alabama	10,588	5,737	—	2,161	—	495	—	641	831	723
Alaska	4,731	1,378	1,379	330	377	433	—	469	—	365
Arizona	18,098	6,759	8,141	923	—	2,267	—	8*	—	—
Arkansas	8,374	1,261	819	1,022	1,437	764	—	762	—	2,309
California	83,816	48,139	3,077*	—	12,711	836*	18,597	180*	115*	161
Colorado	10,639	8,669	274*	1,608	—	47*	—	20*	—	21
Connecticut	6,930	5,391	72*	1,363	20*	75*	—	4*	5*	—
Delaware	2,155	935	9*	1,105	2*	6*	—	9*	3*	86
Florida	15,317	15,079	—	—	—	214*	—	—	—	24
Georgia	7,250	7,110	78*	44*	7*	—	—	—	9*	2
Hawaii	3,707	1,119	1,452	720	—	416	—	—	—	—
Idaho	12,089	1,167	10,281	613	—	24*	—	1*	—	3
Illinois	22,196	9,218	3,577	5,267	—	2,751	—	—	1,361	22
Indiana	12,142	7,936	1,467*	2,583	—	126*	—	14*	—	16
Iowa	9,895	1,076	1,177	197	480	3,079	212	238	273	3,163
Kansas	4,592	4,314	79*	10*	55*	77*	—	—	—	57
Kentucky	6,674	4,513	47*	430	989	695	—	—	—	—
Louisiana	29,182	3,155	18,545	1,434	1,552	889	1,663	1,136	—	808
Maine	2,755	1,681	—	519	464	—	—	—	—	91
Maryland	7,967	4,715	41*	2,786	22*	191*	167*	18*	25*	2
Massachusetts	19,258	9,024	—	3,172	2,218	1,812	—	1,027	—	2,005
Michigan	23,738	10,175	168*	21*	8,263	2,954	—	14*	—	2,143
Minnesota	16,604	3,374	3,363	958	733	1,406	—	622	990	5,158
Mississippi	8,116	2,154	545	2,625	1,652	1,140	—	—	—	—
Missouri	7,792	7,497	180*	17*	—	64*	12*	13*	6*	3
Montana	4,672	986	3,658	8*	—	20*	—	—	—	—
Nebraska	2,900	1,340	—	846	—	714	—	—	—	—
Nevada	8,762	1,835	2,892	483	677	338	—	—	—	2,537
New Hampshire	5,082	3,548	—	512	—	292	—	—	—	730
New Jersey	28,694	6,822	1,867	3,513	2,670	1,353	1,996	2,095	2,011	6,367
New Mexico	3,650	1,615	—	369	620	562	—	—	183	301
New York	45,105	13,451	23*	11,318	—	4,420	385*	20*	15,472	16
North Carolina	5,283	5,171	—	59*	—	41*	—	—	12*	—
North Dakota	1,637	416	—	143	—	240	—	642	193	3
Ohio	24,289	7,252	4,699	6,413	—	3,437	—	2,446	32*	10
Oklahoma	4,486	4,486	—	—	—	—	—	—	—	—
Oregon	11,481	4,277	1,470*	3,030	—	91*	—	—	—	2,613
Pennsylvania	26,138	21,477	—	4,661	—	—	—	—	—	—
Rhode Island	3,532	571	3*	1,878	215	262	1*	494	—	108
South Carolina	6,634	2,719	—	1,235	2,680	—	—	—	—	—
South Dakota	1,353	814	—	110	—	429	—	—	—	—
Tennessee	7,849	1,847	756	727	579	599	511	460	277	2,093
Texas	21,351	19,699	505*	301*	359*	217*	—	169*	—	101
Utah	34,538	1,900	28,602	414	393	1,319	177	1,089	200	444
Vermont	1,996	501	—	429	124	315	—	57	82	488
Virginia	20,859	5,730	—	3,192	—	—	—	11,937	—	—
Washington	22,179	7,533	4,854	1,776	2,354	2,456	1,171	855	515	665
West Virginia	1,958	1,873	34*	6*	2*	2*	—	—	6*	35
Wisconsin	14,714	2,877	2,311	654	1,772	1,070	1,883	633	390	3,124
Wyoming	1,828	844	569*	270	7*	11*	—	—	—	127
Dist. of Col.	4,574	467	—	1,459	—	230	1,186	260	105	867
United States	670,149	291,627	107,014	73,714	43,434	39,179	27,961	26,333	23,096	37,791

An asterisk to the right of a candidate's vote indicates write-in.

The vote, including write-ins, for minor party candidates who received less than 5,000 votes is as follows: 4,749 Bradford (on the ballot in New Jersey); 3,875 Herer (on the ballot in Iowa, Minnesota and Wisconsin); 3,057 Brisben (on the ballot in Tennessee, Utah, Wisconsin and DC); 3,050 Halyard (on the ballot in Michigan and New Jersey); 2,199 Yiamouyiannis (on the ballot in Arkansas, Iowa, Louisiana and Tennessee); 1,149 Ehlers (on the ballot in Iowa); 961 Dodge (on the ballot in Arkansas, New Mexico and Tennessee); 956 Boren (on the ballot in Arkansas); 405 Hem (on the ballot in Wisconsin); 339 Masters (on the ballot in Arkansas); 292 Smith (on the ballot in Utah); 181 LaRiva (on the ballot in New Mexico). The other vote column also includes 2,537 votes cast in Nevada for "None of these Candidates" and 14,041 scattered write-ins.

UNITED STATES

1992 TURNOUT

State	Resident Voting Age Population	November 1992 Registration	Total Valid Vote President	Percentage Voting Age Registered	Percentage Voting Age Voted	Percentage Registered Voted
Alabama	3,056,000	2,367,972	1,688,060	77.5%	55.2%	71.3%
Alaska	395,000	315,058	258,506	79.8%	65.4%	82.1%
Arizona	2,749,000	1,964,949	1,486,975	71.5%	54.1%	75.7%
Arkansas	1,768,000	1,317,944	950,653	74.5%	53.8%	72.1%
California	22,668,000	15,101,473	11,131,721	66.6%	49.1%	73.7%
Colorado	2,501,000	2,003,375	1,569,180	80.1%	62.7%	78.3%
Connecticut	2,535,000	1,955,268	1,616,332	77.1%	63.8%	82.7%
Delaware	525,000	342,088	289,735	65.2%	55.2%	84.7%
Florida	10,586,000	6,541,825	5,314,392	61.8%	50.2%	81.2%
Georgia	4,950,000	3,177,061	2,321,125	64.2%	46.9%	73.1%
Hawaii	889,000	464,495	372,842	52.2%	41.9%	80.3%
Idaho	740,000	611,121	482,142	82.6%	65.2%	78.9%
Illinois	8,568,000	6,600,358	5,050,157	77.0%	58.9%	76.5%
Indiana	4,176,000	3,180,157	2,305,871	76.2%	55.2%	72.5%
Iowa	2,075,000	1,703,532	1,354,607	82.1%	65.3%	79.5%
Kansas	1,836,000	1,365,849	1,157,335	74.4%	63.0%	84.7%
Kentucky	2,779,000	2,076,263	1,492,900	74.7%	53.7%	71.9%
Louisiana	2,992,000	2,292,129	1,790,017	76.6%	59.8%	78.1%
Maine	944,000	974,605	679,499	103.2%	72.0%	69.7%
Maryland	3,719,000	2,463,010	1,985,046	66.2%	53.4%	80.6%
Massachusetts	4,607,000	3,351,918	2,773,700	72.8%	60.2%	82.7%
Michigan	6,923,000	6,147,083	4,274,673	88.8%	61.7%	69.5%
Minnesota	3,278,000	3,138,901	2,347,948	95.8%	71.6%	74.8%
Mississippi	1,861,000	1,640,150	981,793	88.1%	52.8%	59.9%
Missouri	3,858,000	3,067,955	2,391,565	79.5%	62.0%	78.0%
Montana	586,000	529,822	410,611	90.4%	70.1%	77.5%
Nebraska	1,167,000	951,395	737,546	81.5%	63.2%	77.5%
Nevada	1,013,000	649,913	506,318	64.2%	50.0%	77.9%
New Hampshire	852,000	660,985	537,943	77.6%	63.1%	81.4%
New Jersey	5,943,000	4,059,472	3,343,594	68.3%	56.3%	82.4%
New Mexico	1,104,000	706,966	569,986	64.0%	51.6%	80.6%
New York	13,609,000	9,193,391	6,926,925	67.6%	50.9%	75.3%
North Carolina	5,217,000	3,817,380	2,611,850	73.2%	50.1%	68.4%
North Dakota *	458,000	—	308,133	—	67.3%	—
Ohio	8,146,000	6,542,931	4,939,967	80.3%	60.6%	75.5%
Oklahoma	2,328,000	2,302,279	1,390,359	98.9%	59.7%	60.4%
Oregon	2,226,000	1,774,449	1,462,643	79.7%	65.7%	82.4%
Pennsylvania	9,129,000	5,993,002	4,959,810	65.6%	54.3%	82.8%
Rhode Island	776,000	554,664	453,477	71.5%	58.4%	81.8%
South Carolina	2,672,000	1,537,140	1,202,527	57.5%	45.0%	78.2%
South Dakota	502,000	448,292	336,254	89.3%	67.0%	75.0%
Tennessee	3,783,000	2,726,449	1,982,638	72.1%	52.4%	72.7%
Texas	12,524,000	8,440,143	6,154,018	67.4%	49.1%	72.9%
Utah	1,142,000	965,211	743,999	84.5%	65.1%	77.1%
Vermont	429,000	383,371	289,701	89.4%	67.5%	75.6%
Virginia	4,842,000	3,054,662	2,558,665	63.1%	52.8%	83.8%
Washington	3,818,000	2,814,680	2,288,230	73.7%	59.9%	81.3%
West Virginia	1,350,000	956,172	683,762	70.8%	50.6%	71.5%
Wisconsin *	3,669,000	—	2,531,114	—	69.0%	—
Wyoming	322,000	234,260	200,598	72.8%	62.3%	85.6%
Dist. of Col.	459,000	340,953	227,572	74.3%	49.6%	66.7%
United States	189,044,000	133,802,521	104,425,014	70.8%	55.2%	78.0%

* North Dakota has no formal registration system; Wisconsin has no statewide registration system.

PRESIDENT 1988

In West Virginia, one Democratic elector voted in the Electoral College for Lloyd Bentsen for President and Michael S. Dukakis for Vice-President.

In New York the Republican figures include Conservative votes and the Democratic figures include Liberal votes.

In Minnesota, the Republican candidates appear on the ballot as Independent-Republican, the Democratic as Democratic-Farmer-Labor. In many states various non-major party candidates appeared on the ballot with variations of the party designations given here, were listed as "Independent" or were carried with entirely different party labels.

In several states minor party Vice-Presidential candidates were different from those listed below.

The full list of candidates for President and Vice-President was:

48,886,097	George Bush and J. Danforth Quayle, *Republican*.
41,809,074	Michael S. Dukakis and Lloyd Bentsen, *Democratic*.
432,179	Ron Paul and Andre V. Marrou, *Libertarian*.
217,219	Lenora B. Fulani and Joyce Dattner, *New Alliance*.
47,047	David E. Duke and Floyd C. Parker, *Populist*.
30,905	Eugene J. McCarthy and Florence Rice, *Consumer*.
27,818	James C. Griffin and Charles J. Morsa, *American Independent*.
25,562	Lyndon H. LaRouche and Debra H. Freeman, *National Economic Recovery*.
20,504	William A. Marra and Joan Andrews, *Right to Life*.
18,693	Ed Winn and Barry Porster, *Workers League*.
15,604	James Warren and Kathleen Mickells, *Socialist Workers*.
10,370	Herbert Lewin and Vikki Murdock, *Peace and Freedom*.
8,002	Earl F. Dodge and George Ormsby, *Prohibition*.
7,846	Larry Holmes and Gloria LaRiva, *Workers World*.
3,882	Willa Kenoyer and Ron Ehrenreich, *Socialist*.
3,475	Delmar Dennis and Earl Jeppson, *American*.
1,949	Jack Herer and Dana Beal, *Grassroots*.
372	Louie G. Youngkeit with no Vice-Presidential candidate, *Independent*.
236	John G. Martin and Cleveland Sparrow, *Third World Assembly*.

The candidates listed above include all those who appeared on the ballot in at least one state. Republican, Democratic and New Alliance candidates appeared on the ballot in all fifty-one jurisdictions. The Libertarian nominees were on the ballot in all save four. Where identified by state authorities, write-in votes for minor party candidates are credited to their total above and listed in the individual state note sections. In addition to the votes listed, 21,041 scattered write-in votes were reported from various states and 6,934 votes were cast for "None of these Candidates" in Nevada.

UNITED STATES

PRESIDENT 1988

State	Electoral Vote Rep.	Dem.	Other	Total Vote	Republican	Democratic	Other	Plurality	Percentage Total Vote Rep.	Dem.	Major Vote Rep.	Dem
Alabama	9			1,378,476	815,576	549,506	13,394	266,070 R	59.2%	39.9%	59.7%	40.3%
Alaska	3			200,116	119,251	72,584	8,281	46,667 R	59.6%	36.3%	62.2%	37.8%
Arizona	7			1,171,873	702,541	454,029	15,303	248,512 R	60.0%	38.7%	60.7%	39.3%
Arkansas	6			827,738	466,578	349,237	11,923	117,341 R	56.4%	42.2%	57.2%	42.8%
California	47			9,887,065	5,054,917	4,702,233	129,915	352,684 R	51.1%	47.6%	51.8%	48.2%
Colorado	8			1,372,394	728,177	621,453	22,764	106,724 R	53.1%	45.3%	54.0%	46.0%
Connecticut	8			1,443,394	750,241	676,584	16,569	73,657 R	52.0%	46.9%	52.6%	47.4%
Delaware	3			249,891	139,639	108,647	1,605	30,992 R	55.9%	43.5%	56.2%	43.8%
Florida	21			4,302,313	2,618,885	1,656,701	26,727	962,184 R	60.9%	38.5%	61.3%	38.7%
Georgia	12			1,809,672	1,081,331	714,792	13,549	366,539 R	59.8%	39.5%	60.2%	39.8%
Hawaii		4		354,461	158,625	192,364	3,472	33,739 D	44.8%	54.3%	45.2%	54.8%
Idaho	4			408,968	253,881	147,272	7,815	106,609 R	62.1%	36.0%	63.3%	36.7%
Illinois	24			4,559,120	2,310,939	2,215,940	32,241	94,999 R	50.7%	48.6%	51.0%	49.0%
Indiana	12			2,168,621	1,297,763	860,643	10,215	437,120 R	59.8%	39.7%	60.1%	39.9%
Iowa		8		1,225,614	545,355	670,557	9,702	125,202 D	44.5%	54.7%	44.9%	55.1%
Kansas	7			993,044	554,049	422,636	16,359	131,413 R	55.8%	42.6%	56.7%	43.3%
Kentucky	9			1,322,517	734,281	580,368	7,868	153,913 R	55.5%	43.9%	55.9%	44.1%
Louisiana	10			1,628,202	883,702	717,460	27,040	166,242 R	54.3%	44.1%	55.2%	44.8%
Maine	4			555,035	307,131	243,569	4,335	63,562 R	55.3%	43.9%	55.8%	44.2%
Maryland	10			1,714,358	876,167	826,304	11,887	49,863 R	51.1%	48.2%	51.5%	48.5%
Massachusetts		13		2,632,805	1,194,635	1,401,415	36,755	206,780 D	45.4%	53.2%	46.0%	54.0%
Michigan	20			3,669,163	1,965,486	1,675,783	27,894	289,703 R	53.6%	45.7%	54.0%	46.0%
Minnesota		10		2,096,790	962,337	1,109,471	24,982	147,134 D	45.9%	52.9%	46.4%	53.6%
Mississippi	7			931,527	557,890	363,921	9,716	193,969 R	59.9%	39.1%	60.5%	39.5%
Missouri	11			2,093,713	1,084,953	1,001,619	7,141	83,334 R	51.8%	47.8%	52.0%	48.0%
Montana	4			365,674	190,412	168,936	6,326	21,476 R	52.1%	46.2%	53.0%	47.0%
Nebraska	5			661,465	397,956	259,235	4,274	138,721 R	60.2%	39.2%	60.6%	39.4%
Nevada	4			350,067	206,040	132,738	11,289	73,302 R	58.9%	37.9%	60.8%	39.2%
New Hampshire	4			451,074	281,537	163,696	5,841	117,841 R	62.4%	36.3%	63.2%	36.8%
New Jersey	16			3,099,553	1,743,192	1,320,352	36,009	422,840 R	56.2%	42.6%	56.9%	43.1%
New Mexico	5			521,287	270,341	244,497	6,449	25,844 R	51.9%	46.9%	52.5%	47.5%
New York		36		6,485,683	3,081,871	3,347,882	55,930	266,011 D	47.5%	51.6%	47.9%	52.1%
North Carolina	13			2,134,370	1,237,258	890,167	6,945	347,091 R	58.0%	41.7%	58.2%	41.8%
North Dakota	3			297,261	166,559	127,739	2,963	38,820 R	56.0%	43.0%	56.6%	43.4%
Ohio	23			4,393,699	2,416,549	1,939,629	37,521	476,920 R	55.0%	44.1%	55.5%	44.5%
Oklahoma	8			1,171,036	678,367	483,423	9,246	194,944 R	57.9%	41.3%	58.4%	41.6%
Oregon		7		1,201,694	560,126	616,206	25,362	56,080 D	46.6%	51.3%	47.6%	52.4%
Pennsylvania	25			4,536,251	2,300,087	2,194,944	41,220	105,143 R	50.7%	48.4%	51.2%	48.8%
Rhode Island		4		404,620	177,761	225,123	1,736	47,362 D	43.9%	55.6%	44.1%	55.9%
South Carolina	8			986,009	606,443	370,554	9,012	235,889 R	61.5%	37.6%	62.1%	37.9%
South Dakota	3			312,991	165,415	145,560	2,016	19,855 R	52.8%	46.5%	53.2%	46.8%
Tennessee	11			1,636,250	947,233	679,794	9,223	267,439 R	57.9%	41.5%	58.2%	41.8%
Texas	29			5,427,410	3,036,829	2,352,748	37,833	684,081 R	56.0%	43.3%	56.3%	43.7%
Utah	5			647,008	428,442	207,343	11,223	221,099 R	66.2%	32.0%	67.4%	32.6%
Vermont	3			243,328	124,331	115,775	3,222	8,556 R	51.1%	47.6%	51.8%	48.2%
Virginia	12			2,191,609	1,309,162	859,799	22,648	449,363 R	59.7%	39.2%	60.4%	39.6%
Washington		10		1,865,253	903,835	933,516	27,902	29,681 D	48.5%	50.0%	49.2%	50.8%
West Virginia		5	1	653,311	310,065	341,016	2,230	30,951 D	47.5%	52.2%	47.6%	52.4%
Wisconsin		11		2,191,608	1,047,499	1,126,794	17,315	79,295 D	47.8%	51.4%	48.2%	51.8%
Wyoming	3			176,551	106,867	67,113	2,571	39,754 R	60.5%	38.0%	61.4%	38.6%
Dist. of Col.		3		192,877	27,590	159,407	5,880	131,817 D	14.3%	82.6%	14.8%	85.2%
United States	426	111	1	91,594,809	48,886,097	41,809,074	899,638	7,077,023 R	53.4%	45.6%	53.9%	46.1%

PRESIDENT 1984

In New York the Republican figures include Conservative votes and the Democratic figures include Liberal votes.

In Minnesota, the Republican candidates appear on the ballot as Independent-Republican, the Democratic as Democratic-Farmer-Labor. In many states various non-major party candidates appeared on the ballot with variations of the party designations given here, were listed as "Independent" or "Non-Party", or were carried with entirely different party labels.

The Workers World candidate for President was Gavrielle Holmes in Ohio and Rhode Island; in several states minor party Vice-Presidential candidates were different from those listed below.

The full list of candidates for President and Vice-President was:

54,455,075	Ronald Reagan and George Bush,	*Republican.*
37,577,185	Walter F. Mondale and Geraldine A. Ferraro,	*Democratic.*
228,314	David Bergland and James A. Lewis,	*Libertarian.*
78,807	Lyndon H. LaRouche and Billy M. Davis,	*Independent.*
72,200	Sonia Johnson and Richard Walton,	*Citizens.*
66,336	Bob Richards and Maureen Salaman,	*Populist.*
46,868	Dennis L. Serrette and Nancy Ross,	*Alliance.*
36,386	Gus Hall and Angela Davis,	*Communist.*
24,706	Mel Mason and Matilde Zimmermann,	*Socialist Workers.*
17,985	Larry Holmes and Gloria LaRiva,	*Workers World.*
13,161	Delmar Dennis and Traves Brownlee,	*American.*
10,801	Ed Winn and Helen Halyard,	*Workers League.*
4,242	Earl F. Dodge and Warren C. Martin,	*Prohibition.*
1,486	John B. Anderson and Grace Pierce,	*National Unity.*
892	Gerald Baker and Ferris Alger,	*Big Deal.*
825	Arthur J. Lowery and Raymond L. Garland,	*United Sovreign Citizens.*

The candidates listed above are those who appeared on the ballot in at least one state. Where identified by state authorities, write-in votes for minor party candidates are credited to their total above and listed in the individual state note sections. In addition to the votes listed, 13,623 scattered write-in votes were reported from various states and 3,950 votes were cast for "None of these Candidates" in Nevada.

UNITED STATES

PRESIDENT 1984

State	Electoral Vote Rep.	Dem.	Other	Total Vote	Republican	Democratic	Other	Plurality	Total Vote Rep.	Dem.	Major Vote Rep.	Dem.
Alabama	9			1,441,713	872,849	551,899	16,965	320,950 R	60.5%	38.3%	61.3%	38.7%
Alaska	3			207,605	138,377	62,007	7,221	76,370 R	66.7%	29.9%	69.1%	30.9%
Arizona	7			1,025,897	681,416	333,854	10,627	347,562 R	66.4%	32.5%	67.1%	32.9%
Arkansas	6			884,406	534,774	338,646	10,986	196,128 R	60.5%	38.3%	61.2%	38.8%
California	47			9,505,423	5,467,009	3,922,519	115,895	1,544,490 R	57.5%	41.3%	58.2%	41.8%
Colorado	8			1,295,380	821,817	454,975	18,588	366,842 R	63.4%	35.1%	64.4%	35.6%
Connecticut	8			1,466,900	890,877	569,597	6,426	321,280 R	60.7%	38.8%	61.0%	39.0%
Delaware	3			254,572	152,190	101,656	726	50,534 R	59.8%	39.9%	60.0%	40.0%
Florida	21			4,180,051	2,730,350	1,448,816	885	1,281,534 R	65.3%	34.7%	65.3%	34.7%
Georgia	12			1,776,120	1,068,722	706,628	770	362,094 R	60.2%	39.8%	60.2%	39.8%
Hawaii	4			335,846	185,050	147,154	3,642	37,896 R	55.1%	43.8%	55.7%	44.3%
Idaho	4			411,144	297,523	108,510	5,111	189,013 R	72.4%	26.4%	73.3%	26.7%
Illinois	24			4,819,088	2,707,103	2,086,499	25,486	620,604 R	56.2%	43.3%	56.5%	43.5%
Indiana	12			2,233,069	1,377,230	841,481	14,358	535,749 R	61.7%	37.7%	62.1%	37.9%
Iowa	8			1,319,805	703,088	605,620	11,097	97,468 R	53.3%	45.9%	53.7%	46.3%
Kansas	7			1,021,991	677,296	333,149	11,546	344,147 R	66.3%	32.6%	67.0%	33.0%
Kentucky	9			1,369,345	821,702	539,539	8,104	282,163 R	60.0%	39.4%	60.4%	39.6%
Louisiana	10			1,706,822	1,037,299	651,586	17,937	385,713 R	60.8%	38.2%	61.4%	38.6%
Maine	4			553,144	336,500	214,515	2,129	121,985 R	60.8%	38.8%	61.1%	38.9%
Maryland	10			1,675,873	879,918	787,935	8,020	91,983 R	52.5%	47.0%	52.8%	47.2%
Massachusetts	13			2,559,453	1,310,936	1,239,606	8,911	71,330 R	51.2%	48.4%	51.4%	48.6%
Michigan	20			3,801,658	2,251,571	1,529,638	20,449	721,933 R	59.2%	40.2%	59.5%	40.5%
Minnesota		10		2,084,449	1,032,603	1,036,364	15,482	3,761 D	49.5%	49.7%	49.9%	50.1%
Mississippi	7			941,104	582,377	352,192	6,535	230,185 R	61.9%	37.4%	62.3%	37.7%
Missouri	11			2,122,783	1,274,188	848,583	12	425,605 R	60.0%	40.0%	60.0%	40.0%
Montana	4			384,377	232,450	146,742	5,185	85,708 R	60.5%	38.2%	61.3%	38.7%
Nebraska	5			652,090	460,054	187,866	4,170	272,188 R	70.6%	28.8%	71.0%	29.0%
Nevada	4			286,667	188,770	91,655	6,242	97,115 R	65.8%	32.0%	67.3%	32.7%
New Hampshire	4			389,066	267,051	120,395	1,620	146,656 R	68.6%	30.9%	68.9%	31.1%
New Jersey	16			3,217,862	1,933,630	1,261,323	22,909	672,307 R	60.1%	39.2%	60.5%	39.5%
New Mexico	5			514,370	307,101	201,769	5,500	105,332 R	59.7%	39.2%	60.3%	39.7%
New York	36			6,806,810	3,664,763	3,119,609	22,438	545,154 R	53.8%	45.8%	54.0%	46.0%
North Carolina	13			2,175,361	1,346,481	824,287	4,593	522,194 R	61.9%	37.9%	62.0%	38.0%
North Dakota	3			308,971	200,336	104,429	4,206	95,907 R	64.8%	33.8%	65.7%	34.3%
Ohio	23			4,547,619	2,678,560	1,825,440	43,619	853,120 R	58.9%	40.1%	59.5%	40.5%
Oklahoma	8			1,255,676	861,530	385,080	9,066	476,450 R	68.6%	30.7%	69.1%	30.9%
Oregon	7			1,226,527	685,700	536,479	4,348	149,221 R	55.9%	43.7%	56.1%	43.9%
Pennsylvania	25			4,844,903	2,584,323	2,228,131	32,449	356,192 R	53.3%	46.0%	53.7%	46.3%
Rhode Island	4			410,492	212,080	197,106	1,306	14,974 R	51.7%	48.0%	51.8%	48.2%
South Carolina	8			968,529	615,539	344,459	8,531	271,080 R	63.6%	35.6%	64.1%	35.9%
South Dakota	3			317,867	200,267	116,113	1,487	84,154 R	63.0%	36.5%	63.3%	36.7%
Tennessee	11			1,711,994	990,212	711,714	10,068	278,498 R	57.8%	41.6%	58.2%	41.8%
Texas	29			5,397,571	3,433,428	1,949,276	14,867	1,484,152 R	63.6%	36.1%	63.8%	36.2%
Utah	5			629,656	469,105	155,369	5,182	313,736 R	74.5%	24.7%	75.1%	24.9%
Vermont	3			234,561	135,865	95,730	2,966	40,135 R	57.9%	40.8%	58.7%	41.3%
Virginia	12			2,146,635	1,337,078	796,250	13,307	540,828 R	62.3%	37.1%	62.7%	37.3%
Washington	10			1,883,910	1,051,670	807,352	24,888	244,318 R	55.8%	42.9%	56.6%	43.4%
West Virginia	6			735,742	405,483	328,125	2,134	77,358 R	55.1%	44.6%	55.3%	44.7%
Wisconsin	11			2,211,689	1,198,584	995,740	17,365	202,844 R	54.2%	45.0%	54.6%	45.4%
Wyoming	3			188,968	133,241	53,370	2,357	79,871 R	70.5%	28.2%	71.4%	28.6%
Dist. of Col.		3		211,288	29,009	180,408	1,871	151,399 D	13.7%	85.4%	13.9%	86.1%
United States	525	13	—	92,652,842	54,455,075	37,577,185	620,582	16,877,890 R	58.8%	40.6%	59.2%	40.8%

PRESIDENT 1980

In New York the Republican figures include Conservative votes and in a number of states candidates appeared on the ballot with variants of the party designations listed below, without any party designation, or with entirely different party names.

In several cases, Vice-Presidential nominees were different from those listed for most states and the Socialist Workers party nominee for President varied from state to state.

43,904,153	Ronald Reagan and George Bush, <u>Republican.</u>
35,483,883	Jimmy Carter and Walter F. Mondale, <u>Democratic.</u>
5,720,060	John B. Anderson and Patrick J. Lucey, <u>Independent.</u>
921,299	Edward E. Clark and David Koch, <u>Libertarian.</u>
234,294	Barry Commoner and LaDonna Harris, <u>Citizens.</u>
45,023	Gus Hall and Angela Davis, <u>Communist.</u>
41,268	John R. Rarick and Eileen M. Shearer, <u>American Independent.</u>
38,737	Clifton DeBerry and Matilde Zimmermann, <u>Socialist Workers.</u>
32,327	Ellen McCormack and Carroll Driscoll, <u>Right to Life.</u>
18,116	Maureen Smith and Elizabeth Barron, <u>Peace and Freedom.</u>
13,300	Deirdre Griswold and Larry Holmes, <u>Workers World.</u>
7,212	Benjamin C. Bubar and Earl F. Dodge, <u>Statesman.</u>
6,898	David McReynolds and Diane Drufenbrock, <u>Socialist.</u>
6,647	Percy L. Greaves and Frank L. Varnum, <u>American.</u>
6,272	Andrew Pulley and Matilde Zimmermann, <u>Socialist Workers.</u>
4,029	Richard Congress and Matilde Zimmermann, <u>Socialist Workers.</u>
3,694	Kurt Lynen and Harry Kieve, <u>Middle Class.</u>
1,718	Bill Gahres and J. F. Loughlin, <u>Down With Lawyers.</u>
1,555	Frank W. Shelton and George E. Jackson, <u>American.</u>
923	Martin E. Wendelken with no Vice-Presidential candidate, <u>Independent.</u>
296	Harley McLain and Jewelie Goeller, <u>Natural Peoples.</u>

In addition to these votes, 13,185 scattered write-in votes were reported from various states, 6,139 votes were cast in Minnesota for American party electors without designated national nominees, and 4,193 votes were cast for "None of these Candidates" in Nevada.

UNITED STATES

PRESIDENT 1980

State	Electoral Vote Rep.	Electoral Vote Dem.	Electoral Vote Other	Total Vote	Republican	Democratic	Other	Plurality	Percentage Total Vote Rep.	Percentage Total Vote Dem.	Percentage Major Vote Rep.	Percentage Major Vote Dem.
Alabama	9			1,341,929	654,192	636,730	51,007	17,462 R	48.8%	47.4%	50.7%	49.3%
Alaska	3			158,445	86,112	41,842	30,491	44,270 R	54.3%	26.4%	67.3%	32.7%
Arizona	6			873,945	529,688	246,843	97,414	282,845 R	60.6%	28.2%	68.2%	31.8%
Arkansas	6			837,582	403,164	398,041	36,377	5,123 R	48.1%	47.5%	50.3%	49.7%
California	45			8,587,063	4,524,858	3,083,661	978,544	1,441,197 R	52.7%	35.9%	59.5%	40.5%
Colorado	7			1,184,415	652,264	367,973	164,178	284,291 R	55.1%	31.1%	63.9%	36.1%
Connecticut	8			1,406,285	677,210	541,732	187,343	135,478 R	48.2%	38.5%	55.6%	44.4%
Delaware	3			235,900	111,252	105,754	18,894	5,498 R	47.2%	44.8%	51.3%	48.7%
Florida	17			3,686,930	2,046,951	1,419,475	220,504	627,476 R	55.5%	38.5%	59.1%	40.9%
Georgia		12		1,596,695	654,168	890,733	51,794	236,565 D	41.0%	55.8%	42.3%	57.7%
Hawaii		4		303,287	130,112	135,879	37,296	5,767 D	42.9%	44.8%	48.9%	51.1%
Idaho	4			437,431	290,699	110,192	36,540	180,507 R	66.5%	25.2%	72.5%	27.5%
Illinois	26			4,749,721	2,358,049	1,981,413	410,259	376,636 R	49.6%	41.7%	54.3%	45.7%
Indiana	13			2,242,033	1,255,656	844,197	142,180	411,459 R	56.0%	37.7%	59.8%	40.2%
Iowa	8			1,317,661	676,026	508,672	132,963	167,354 R	51.3%	38.6%	57.1%	42.9%
Kansas	7			979,795	566,812	326,150	86,833	240,662 R	57.9%	33.3%	63.5%	36.5%
Kentucky	9			1,294,627	635,274	616,417	42,936	18,857 R	49.1%	47.6%	50.8%	49.2%
Louisiana	10			1,548,591	792,853	708,453	47,285	84,400 R	51.2%	45.7%	52.8%	47.2%
Maine	4			523,011	238,522	220,974	63,515	17,548 R	45.6%	42.3%	51.9%	48.1%
Maryland		10		1,540,496	680,606	726,161	133,729	45,555 D	44.2%	47.1%	48.4%	51.6%
Massachusetts	14			2,524,298	1,057,631	1,053,802	412,865	3,829 R	41.9%	41.7%	50.1%	49.9%
Michigan	21			3,909,725	1,915,225	1,661,532	332,968	253,693 R	49.0%	42.5%	53.5%	46.5%
Minnesota		10		2,051,980	873,268	954,174	224,538	80,906 D	42.6%	46.5%	47.8%	52.2%
Mississippi	7			892,620	441,089	429,281	22,250	11,808 R	49.4%	48.1%	50.7%	49.3%
Missouri	12			2,099,824	1,074,181	931,182	94,461	142,999 R	51.2%	44.3%	53.6%	46.4%
Montana	4			363,952	206,814	118,032	39,106	88,782 R	56.8%	32.4%	63.7%	36.3%
Nebraska	5			640,854	419,937	166,851	54,066	253,086 R	65.5%	26.0%	71.6%	28.4%
Nevada	3			247,885	155,017	66,666	26,202	88,351 R	62.5%	26.9%	69.9%	30.1%
New Hampshire	4			383,990	221,705	108,864	53,421	112,841 R	57.7%	28.4%	67.1%	32.9%
New Jersey	17			2,975,684	1,546,557	1,147,364	281,763	399,193 R	52.0%	38.6%	57.4%	42.6%
New Mexico	4			456,971	250,779	167,826	38,366	82,953 R	54.9%	36.7%	59.9%	40.1%
New York	41			6,201,959	2,893,831	2,728,372	579,756	165,459 R	46.7%	44.0%	51.5%	48.5%
North Carolina	13			1,855,833	915,018	875,635	65,180	39,383 R	49.3%	47.2%	51.1%	48.9%
North Dakota	3			301,545	193,695	79,189	28,661	114,506 R	64.2%	26.3%	71.0%	29.0%
Ohio	25			4,283,603	2,206,545	1,752,414	324,644	454,131 R	51.5%	40.9%	55.7%	44.3%
Oklahoma	8			1,149,708	695,570	402,026	52,112	293,544 R	60.5%	35.0%	63.4%	36.6%
Oregon	6			1,181,516	571,044	456,890	153,582	114,154 R	48.3%	38.7%	55.6%	44.4%
Pennsylvania	27			4,561,501	2,261,872	1,937,540	362,089	324,332 R	49.6%	42.5%	53.9%	46.1%
Rhode Island		4		416,072	154,793	198,342	62,937	43,549 D	37.2%	47.7%	43.8%	56.2%
South Carolina	8			894,071	441,841	430,385	21,845	11,456 R	49.4%	48.1%	50.7%	49.3%
South Dakota	4			327,703	198,343	103,855	25,505	94,488 R	60.5%	31.7%	65.6%	34.4%
Tennessee	10			1,617,616	787,761	783,051	46,804	4,710 R	48.7%	48.4%	50.1%	49.9%
Texas	26			4,541,636	2,510,705	1,881,147	149,784	629,558 R	55.3%	41.4%	57.2%	42.8%
Utah	4			604,222	439,687	124,266	40,269	315,421 R	72.8%	20.6%	78.0%	22.0%
Vermont	3			213,299	94,628	81,952	36,719	12,676 R	44.4%	38.4%	53.6%	46.4%
Virginia	12			1,866,032	989,609	752,174	124,249	237,435 R	53.0%	40.3%	56.8%	43.2%
Washington	9			1,742,394	865,244	650,193	226,957	215,051 R	49.7%	37.3%	57.1%	42.9%
West Virginia		6		737,715	334,206	367,462	36,047	33,256 D	45.3%	49.8%	47.6%	52.4%
Wisconsin	11			2,273,221	1,088,845	981,584	202,792	107,261 R	47.9%	43.2%	52.6%	47.4%
Wyoming	3			176,713	110,700	49,427	16,586	61,273 R	62.6%	28.0%	69.1%	30.9%
Dist. of Col.		3		175,237	23,545	131,113	20,579	107,568 D	13.4%	74.8%	15.2%	84.8%
United States	489	49	—	86,515,221	43,904,153	35,483,883	7,127,185	8,420,270 R	50.7%	41.0%	55.3%	44.7%

PRESIDENT 1976

In Washington, one Republican elector voted in the Electoral College for Ronald Reagan for President and Robert Dole for Vice-President.

In New York the Republican figures include Conservative votes and the Democratic figures include Liberal votes; in Vermont the Democratic figures include votes cast on the Independent Vermonters party ticket.

In a number of states candidates appeared on the ballot with variants of the party designations listed below and in several cases with entirely different party names.

The ballot designations for electors for Eugene J. McCarthy for President varied from state to state, as did the names of Vice-Presidential candidates running with him. In New Jersey, the Maddox Vice-Presidential candidate was Edmund O. Matzal.

The full list of candidates for President and Vice-President was:

40,830,763	Jimmy Carter and Walter F. Mondale, Democratic.
39,147,793	Gerald R. Ford and Robert Dole, Republican.
756,691	Eugene J. McCarthy with various Vice-Presidential candidates, Independent.
173,011	Roger L. MacBride and David D. Bergland, Libertarian.
170,531	Lester G. Maddox and William D. Dyke, American Independent.
160,773	Thomas J. Anderson and Rufus Shackelford, American.
91,314	Peter Camejo and Willie Mae Reid, Socialist Workers.
58,992	Gus Hall and Jarvis Tyner, Communist.
49,024	Margaret Wright and Benjamin Spock, People's.
40,043	Lyndon H. LaRouche and R. W. Evans, United States Labor.
15,934	Benjamin C. Bubar and Earl F. Dodge, Prohibition.
9,616	Julius Levin and Constance Blomen, Socialist Labor.
6,038	Frank P. Zeidler and J. Q. Brisben, Socialist.
361	Ernest L. Miller and Roy N. Eddy, Restoration.
36	Frank Taylor and Henry Swan, United American.

In addition to these votes, 39,861 scattered write-in votes were reported from various states and 5,108 votes were cast for "None of these Candidates" in Nevada.

UNITED STATES

PRESIDENT 1976

State	Electoral Vote Rep.	Dem.	Other	Total Vote	Republican	Democratic	Other	Plurality	Total Vote Rep.	Dem.	Major Vote Rep.	Dem.
Alabama		9		1,182,850	504,070	659,170	19,610	155,100 D	42.6%	55.7%	43.3%	56.7%
Alaska	3			123,574	71,555	44,058	7,961	27,497 R	57.9%	35.7%	61.9%	38.1%
Arizona	6			742,719	418,642	295,602	28,475	123,040 R	56.4%	39.8%	58.6%	41.4%
Arkansas		6		767,535	267,903	498,604	1,028	230,701 D	34.9%	65.0%	35.0%	65.0%
California	45			7,867,117	3,882,244	3,742,284	242,589	139,960 R	49.3%	47.6%	50.9%	49.1%
Colorado	7			1,081,554	584,367	460,353	36,834	124,014 R	54.0%	42.6%	55.9%	44.1%
Connecticut	8			1,381,526	719,261	647,895	14,370	71,366 R	52.1%	46.9%	52.6%	47.4%
Delaware		3		235,834	109,831	122,596	3,407	12,765 D	46.6%	52.0%	47.3%	52.7%
Florida		17		3,150,631	1,469,531	1,636,000	45,100	166,469 D	46.6%	51.9%	47.3%	52.7%
Georgia		12		1,467,458	483,743	979,409	4,306	495,666 D	33.0%	66.7%	33.1%	66.9%
Hawaii		4		291,301	140,003	147,375	3,923	7,372 D	48.1%	50.6%	48.7%	51.3%
Idaho	4			344,071	204,151	126,549	13,371	77,602 R	59.3%	36.8%	61.7%	38.3%
Illinois	26			4,718,914	2,364,269	2,271,295	83,350	92,974 R	50.1%	48.1%	51.0%	49.0%
Indiana	13			2,220,362	1,183,958	1,014,714	21,690	169,244 R	53.3%	45.7%	53.8%	46.2%
Iowa	8			1,279,306	632,863	619,931	26,512	12,932 R	49.5%	48.5%	50.5%	49.5%
Kansas	7			957,845	502,752	430,421	24,672	72,331 R	52.5%	44.9%	53.9%	46.1%
Kentucky		9		1,167,142	531,852	615,717	19,573	83,865 D	45.6%	52.8%	46.3%	53.7%
Louisiana		10		1,278,439	587,446	661,365	29,628	73,919 D	46.0%	51.7%	47.0%	53.0%
Maine	4			483,216	236,320	232,279	14,617	4,041 R	48.9%	48.1%	50.4%	49.6%
Maryland		10		1,439,897	672,661	759,612	7,624	86,951 D	46.7%	52.8%	47.0%	53.0%
Massachusetts		14		2,547,558	1,030,276	1,429,475	87,807	399,199 D	40.4%	56.1%	41.9%	58.1%
Michigan	21			3,653,749	1,893,742	1,696,714	63,293	197,028 R	51.8%	46.4%	52.7%	47.3%
Minnesota		10		1,949,931	819,395	1,070,440	60,096	251,045 D	42.0%	54.9%	43.4%	56.6%
Mississippi		7		769,361	366,846	381,309	21,206	14,463 D	47.7%	49.6%	49.0%	51.0%
Missouri		12		1,953,600	927,443	998,387	27,770	70,944 D	47.5%	51.1%	48.2%	51.8%
Montana	4			328,734	173,703	149,259	5,772	24,444 R	52.8%	45.4%	53.8%	46.2%
Nebraska	5			607,668	359,705	233,692	14,271	126,013 R	59.2%	38.5%	60.6%	39.4%
Nevada	3			201,876	101,273	92,479	8,124	8,794 R	50.2%	45.8%	52.3%	47.7%
New Hampshire	4			339,618	185,935	147,635	6,048	38,300 R	54.7%	43.5%	55.7%	44.3%
New Jersey	17			3,014,472	1,509,688	1,444,653	60,131	65,035 R	50.1%	47.9%	51.1%	48.9%
New Mexico	4			418,409	211,419	201,148	5,842	10,271 R	50.5%	48.1%	51.2%	48.8%
New York		41		6,534,170	3,100,791	3,389,558	43,821	288,767 D	47.5%	51.9%	47.8%	52.2%
North Carolina		13		1,678,914	741,960	927,365	9,589	185,405 D	44.2%	55.2%	44.4%	55.6%
North Dakota	3			297,188	153,470	136,078	7,640	17,392 R	51.6%	45.8%	53.0%	47.0%
Ohio		25		4,111,873	2,000,505	2,011,621	99,747	11,116 D	48.7%	48.9%	49.9%	50.1%
Oklahoma	8			1,092,251	545,708	532,442	14,101	13,266 R	50.0%	48.7%	50.6%	49.4%
Oregon	6			1,029,876	492,120	490,407	47,349	1,713 R	47.8%	47.6%	50.1%	49.9%
Pennsylvania		27		4,620,787	2,205,604	2,328,677	86,506	123,073 D	47.7%	50.4%	48.6%	51.4%
Rhode Island		4		411,170	181,249	227,636	2,285	46,387 D	44.1%	55.4%	44.3%	55.7%
South Carolina		8		802,583	346,149	450,807	5,627	104,658 D	43.1%	56.2%	43.4%	56.6%
South Dakota	4			300,678	151,505	147,068	2,105	4,437 R	50.4%	48.9%	50.7%	49.3%
Tennessee		10		1,476,345	633,969	825,879	16,497	191,910 D	42.9%	55.9%	43.4%	56.6%
Texas		26		4,071,884	1,953,300	2,082,319	36,265	129,019 D	48.0%	51.1%	48.4%	51.6%
Utah	4			541,198	337,908	182,110	21,180	155,798 R	62.4%	33.6%	65.0%	35.0%
Vermont	3			187,765	102,085	80,954	4,726	21,131 R	54.4%	43.1%	55.8%	44.2%
Virginia	12			1,697,094	836,554	813,896	46,644	22,658 R	49.3%	48.0%	50.7%	49.3%
Washington	8		1	1,555,534	777,732	717,323	60,479	60,409 R	50.0%	46.1%	52.0%	48.0%
West Virginia		6		750,964	314,760	435,914	290	121,154 D	41.9%	58.0%	41.9%	58.1%
Wisconsin		11		2,104,175	1,004,987	1,040,232	58,956	35,245 D	47.8%	49.4%	49.1%	50.9%
Wyoming	3			156,343	92,717	62,239	1,387	30,478 R	59.3%	39.8%	59.8%	40.2%
Dist. of Col.		3		168,830	27,873	137,818	3,139	109,945 D	16.5%	81.6%	16.8%	83.2%
United States	240	297	1	81,555,889	39,147,793	40,830,763	1,577,333	1,682,970 D	48.0%	50.1%	48.9%	51.1%

PRESIDENT 1972

In Virginia one Republican elector voted in the Electoral College for the Libertarian candidates for President and Vice-President.

In New York the Republican figures include Conservative votes and the Democratic figures include Liberal votes. In Alabama the Democratic figures include votes cast on the National Democratic Party of Alabama ticket, and in South Carolina include United Citizens Party votes.

In certain states candidates appeared on the ballot under party names other than those used below; for the Socialist Workers party the votes listed for Jenness and Pulley were actually cast for substitute candidates (Reed and DeBerry) or without named candidates in several states.

The Democratic Vice-Presidential candidate originally was Senator Thomas F. Eagleton; on his withdrawal shortly after the party convention, R. Sargent Shriver was named by the Democratic National Committee as candidate.

The full list of candidates for President and Vice-President was:

47,169,911	Richard M. Nixon and Spiro T. Agnew, Republican.
29,170,383	George S. McGovern and R. Sargent Shriver, Democratic.
1,099,482	John G. Schmitz and Thomas J. Anderson, American.
78,756	Benjamin Spock and Julius Hobson, People's.
66,677	Linda Jenness and Andrew Pulley, Socialist Workers.
53,814	Louis Fisher and Genevieve Gunderson, Socialist Labor.
25,595	Gus Hall and Jarvis Tyner, Communist.
13,505	E. Harold Munn and Marshall E. Uncapher, Prohibition.
3,673	John Hospers and Theodora Nathan, Libertarian.
1,743	John V. Mahalchik and Irving Homer, America First.
220	Gabriel Green and Daniel Fry, Universal.

In addition to the above, 34,795 scattered votes were reported from various states.

Vice-President Agnew resigned in October 1973 and Representative Gerald R. Ford of Michigan was nominated by President Nixon to fill the vacancy. In November (Senate) and December (House of Representatives) this action was approved by Congress.

In August 1974 President Nixon resigned and was succeeded by Vice-President Ford. In the same month Nelson A. Rockefeller, former Governor of New York, was nominated to be Vice-President and was confirmed by Congress in December 1974.

UNITED STATES

PRESIDENT 1972

State	Electoral Vote Rep.	Electoral Vote Dem.	Electoral Vote Other	Total Vote	Republican	Democratic	Other	Plurality	% Total Vote Rep.	% Total Vote Dem.	% Major Vote Rep.	% Major Vote Dem.
Alabama	9			1,006,111	728,701	256,923	20,487	471,778 R	72.4%	25.5%	73.9%	26.1%
Alaska	3			95,219	55,349	32,967	6,903	22,382 R	58.1%	34.6%	62.7%	37.3%
Arizona	6			622,926	402,812	198,540	21,574	204,272 R	64.7%	31.9%	67.0%	33.0%
Arkansas	6			651,320	448,541	199,892	2,887	248,649 R	68.9%	30.7%	69.2%	30.8%
California	45			8,367,862	4,602,096	3,475,847	289,919	1,126,249 R	55.0%	41.5%	57.0%	43.0%
Colorado	7			953,884	597,189	329,980	26,715	267,209 R	62.6%	34.6%	64.4%	35.6%
Connecticut	8			1,384,277	810,763	555,498	18,016	255,265 R	58.6%	40.1%	59.3%	40.7%
Delaware	3			235,516	140,357	92,283	2,876	48,074 R	59.6%	39.2%	60.3%	39.7%
Florida	17			2,583,283	1,857,759	718,117	7,407	1,139,642 R	71.9%	27.8%	72.1%	27.9%
Georgia	12			1,174,772	881,496	289,529	3,747	591,967 R	75.0%	24.6%	75.3%	24.7%
Hawaii	4			270,274	168,865	101,409		67,456 R	62.5%	37.5%	62.5%	37.5%
Idaho	4			310,379	199,384	80,826	30,169	118,558 R	64.2%	26.0%	71.2%	28.8%
Illinois	26			4,723,236	2,788,179	1,913,472	21,585	874,707 R	59.0%	40.5%	59.3%	40.7%
Indiana	13			2,125,529	1,405,154	708,568	11,807	696,586 R	66.1%	33.3%	66.5%	33.5%
Iowa	8			1,225,944	706,207	496,206	23,531	210,001 R	57.6%	40.5%	58.7%	41.3%
Kansas	7			916,095	619,812	270,287	25,996	349,525 R	67.7%	29.5%	69.6%	30.4%
Kentucky	9			1,067,499	676,446	371,159	19,894	305,287 R	63.4%	34.8%	64.6%	35.4%
Louisiana	10			1,051,491	686,852	298,142	66,497	388,710 R	65.3%	28.4%	69.7%	30.3%
Maine	4			417,042	256,458	160,584		95,874 R	61.5%	38.5%	61.5%	38.5%
Maryland	10			1,353,812	829,305	505,781	18,726	323,524 R	61.3%	37.4%	62.1%	37.9%
Massachusetts		14		2,458,756	1,112,078	1,332,540	14,138	220,462 D	45.2%	54.2%	45.5%	54.5%
Michigan	21			3,489,727	1,961,721	1,459,435	68,571	502,286 R	56.2%	41.8%	57.3%	42.7%
Minnesota	10			1,741,652	898,269	802,346	41,037	95,923 R	51.6%	46.1%	52.8%	47.2%
Mississippi	7			645,963	505,125	126,782	14,056	378,343 R	78.2%	19.6%	79.9%	20.1%
Missouri	12			1,855,803	1,153,852	697,147	4,804	456,705 R	62.2%	37.6%	62.3%	37.7%
Montana	4			317,603	183,976	120,197	13,430	63,779 R	57.9%	37.8%	60.5%	39.5%
Nebraska	5			576,289	406,298	169,991		236,307 R	70.5%	29.5%	70.5%	29.5%
Nevada	3			181,766	115,750	66,016		49,734 R	63.7%	36.3%	63.7%	36.3%
New Hampshire	4			334,055	213,724	116,435	3,896	97,289 R	64.0%	34.9%	64.7%	35.3%
New Jersey	17			2,997,229	1,845,502	1,102,211	49,516	743,291 R	61.6%	36.8%	62.6%	37.4%
New Mexico	4			386,241	235,606	141,084	9,551	94,522 R	61.0%	36.5%	62.5%	37.5%
New York	41			7,165,919	4,192,778	2,951,084	22,057	1,241,694 R	58.5%	41.2%	58.7%	41.3%
North Carolina	13			1,518,612	1,054,889	438,705	25,018	616,184 R	69.5%	28.9%	70.6%	29.4%
North Dakota	3			280,514	174,109	100,384	6,021	73,725 R	62.1%	35.8%	63.4%	36.6%
Ohio	25			4,094,787	2,441,827	1,558,889	94,071	882,938 R	59.6%	38.1%	61.0%	39.0%
Oklahoma	8			1,029,900	759,025	247,147	23,728	511,878 R	73.7%	24.0%	75.4%	24.6%
Oregon	6			927,946	486,686	392,760	48,500	93,926 R	52.4%	42.3%	55.3%	44.7%
Pennsylvania	27			4,592,106	2,714,521	1,796,951	80,634	917,570 R	59.1%	39.1%	60.2%	39.8%
Rhode Island	4			415,808	220,383	194,645	780	25,738 R	53.0%	46.8%	53.1%	46.9%
South Carolina	8			673,960	477,044	186,824	10,092	290,220 R	70.8%	27.7%	71.9%	28.1%
South Dakota	4			307,415	166,476	139,945	994	26,531 R	54.2%	45.5%	54.3%	45.7%
Tennessee	10			1,201,182	813,147	357,293	30,742	455,854 R	67.7%	29.7%	69.5%	30.5%
Texas	26			3,471,281	2,298,896	1,154,289	18,096	1,144,607 R	66.2%	33.3%	66.6%	33.4%
Utah	4			478,476	323,643	126,284	28,549	197,359 R	67.6%	26.4%	71.9%	28.1%
Vermont	3			186,947	117,149	68,174	1,624	48,975 R	62.7%	36.5%	63.2%	36.8%
Virginia	11		1	1,457,019	988,493	438,887	29,639	549,606 R	67.8%	30.1%	69.3%	30.7%
Washington	9			1,470,847	837,135	568,334	65,378	268,801 R	56.9%	38.6%	59.6%	40.4%
West Virginia	6			762,399	484,964	277,435		207,529 R	63.6%	36.4%	63.6%	36.4%
Wisconsin	11			1,852,890	989,430	810,174	53,286	179,256 R	53.4%	43.7%	55.0%	45.0%
Wyoming	3			145,570	100,464	44,358	748	56,106 R	69.0%	30.5%	69.4%	30.6%
Dist. of Col.		3		163,421	35,226	127,627	568	92,401 D	21.6%	78.1%	21.6%	78.4%
United States	520	17	1	77,718,554	47,169,911	29,170,383	1,378,260	17,999,528 R	60.7%	37.5%	61.8%	38.2%

PRESIDENT 1968

In North Carolina one Republican elector voted in the Electoral College for the American Independent candidates for President and Vice-President.

In New York the Democratic figure includes Liberal votes and in Alabama the Democratic vote is the total of the Alabama Independent Democratic and National Democratic Party of Alabama vote. In certain states candidates appeared under variants of the party name used below and in most states the Vice-Presidential candidate of the American Independent party was listed as Marvin Griffin rather than Curtis E. LeMay.

The full list of candidates for President and Vice-President was:

31,785,480	Richard M. Nixon and Spiro T. Agnew, Republican.
31,275,166	Hubert H. Humphrey and Edmund S. Muskie, Democratic.
9,906,473	George C. Wallace and Curtis E. LeMay, American Independent.
52,588	Henning A. Blomen and George S. Taylor, Socialist Labor.
47,133	Dick Gregory, Peace and Freedom, with various Vice-Presidential candidates.
41,388	Fred Halstead and Paul Boutelle, Socialist Workers.
36,563	Eldridge Cleaver, Peace and Freedom, with various Vice-Presidential candidates.
25,552	Eugene J. McCarthy, under various titles and written-in, but without indication of Vice-Presidential candidates.
15,123	E. Harold Munn and Rolland E. Fisher, Prohibition.
1,519	Ventura Chavez and Adelicio Moya, People's Constitutional.
1,075	Charlene Mitchell and Michael Zagarell, Communist.
142	James Hensley and Roscoe B. MacKenna, Universal.
34	Richard K. Troxell and Merle Thayer, Constitution.
17	Kent M. Soeters and James P. Powers, Berkeley Defense Group.

In the vote listed above for Eldridge Cleaver, two states are included (California and Utah) in which only the party Vice-Presidential candidate appeared on the ballot.

In addition to these votes, 12,430 were cast for elector tickets for which there were no formal Presidential or Vice-Presidential candidates, and 11,192 scattered votes were reported from various states.

UNITED STATES

PRESIDENT 1968

State	Electoral Vote Rep.	Dem.	AIP	Total Vote	Republican	Democratic	AIP	Other	Plurality	Percentage Total Vote Rep.	Dem.	AIP
Alabama			10	1,049,922	146,923	196,579	691,425	14,995	494,846 A	14.0%	18.7%	65.9%
Alaska	3			83,035	37,600	35,411	10,024		2,189 R	45.3%	42.6%	12.1%
Arizona	5			486,936	266,721	170,514	46,573	3,128	96,207 R	54.8%	35.0%	9.6%
Arkansas			6	619,969	190,759	188,228	240,982		50,223 A	30.8%	30.4%	38.9%
California	40			7,251,587	3,467,664	3,244,318	487,270	52,335	223,346 R	47.8%	44.7%	6.7%
Colorado	6			811,199	409,345	335,174	60,813	5,867	74,171 R	50.5%	41.3%	7.5%
Connecticut		8		1,256,232	556,721	621,561	76,650	1,300	64,840 D	44.3%	49.5%	6.1%
Delaware	3			214,367	96,714	89,194	28,459		7,520 R	45.1%	41.6%	13.3%
Florida	14			2,187,805	886,804	676,794	624,207		210,010 R	40.5%	30.9%	28.5%
Georgia			12	1,250,266	380,111	334,440	535,550	165	155,439 A	30.4%	26.7%	42.8%
Hawaii		4		236,218	91,425	141,324	3,469		49,899 D	38.7%	59.8%	1.5%
Idaho	4			291,183	165,369	89,273	36,541		76,096 R	56.8%	30.7%	12.5%
Illinois	26			4,619,749	2,174,774	2,039,814	390,958	14,203	134,960 R	47.1%	44.2%	8.5%
Indiana	13			2,123,597	1,067,885	806,659	243,108	5,945	261,226 R	50.3%	38.0%	11.4%
Iowa	9			1,167,931	619,106	476,699	66,422	5,704	142,407 R	53.0%	40.8%	5.7%
Kansas	7			872,783	478,674	302,996	88,921	2,192	175,678 R	54.8%	34.7%	10.2%
Kentucky	9			1,055,893	462,411	397,541	193,098	2,843	64,870 R	43.8%	37.6%	18.3%
Louisiana			10	1,097,450	257,535	309,615	530,300		220,685 A	23.5%	28.2%	48.3%
Maine		4		392,936	169,254	217,312	6,370		48,058 D	43.1%	55.3%	1.6%
Maryland		10		1,235,039	517,995	538,310	178,734		20,315 D	41.9%	43.6%	14.5%
Massachusetts		14		2,331,752	766,844	1,469,218	87,088	8,602	702,374 D	32.9%	63.0%	3.7%
Michigan		21		3,306,250	1,370,665	1,593,082	331,968	10,535	222,417 D	41.5%	48.2%	10.0%
Minnesota		10		1,588,506	658,643	857,738	68,931	3,194	199,095 D	41.5%	54.0%	4.3%
Mississippi			7	654,509	88,516	150,644	415,349		264,705 A	13.5%	23.0%	63.5%
Missouri	12			1,809,502	811,932	791,444	206,126		20,488 R	44.9%	43.7%	11.4%
Montana	4			274,404	138,835	114,117	20,015	1,437	24,718 R	50.6%	41.6%	7.3%
Nebraska	5			536,851	321,163	170,784	44,904		150,379 R	59.8%	31.8%	8.4%
Nevada	3			154,218	73,188	60,598	20,432		12,590 R	47.5%	39.3%	13.2%
New Hampshire	4			297,298	154,903	130,589	11,173	633	24,314 R	52.1%	43.9%	3.8%
New Jersey	17			2,875,395	1,325,467	1,264,206	262,187	23,535	61,261 R	46.1%	44.0%	9.1%
New Mexico	4			327,350	169,692	130,081	25,737	1,840	39,611 R	51.8%	39.7%	7.9%
New York		43		6,791,688	3,007,932	3,378,470	358,864	46,422	370,538 D	44.3%	49.7%	5.3%
North Carolina	12		1	1,587,493	627,192	464,113	496,188		131,004 R	39.5%	29.2%	31.3%
North Dakota	4			247,882	138,669	94,769	14,244	200	43,900 R	55.9%	38.2%	5.7%
Ohio	26			3,959,698	1,791,014	1,700,586	467,495	603	90,428 R	45.2%	42.9%	11.8%
Oklahoma	8			943,086	449,697	301,658	191,731		148,039 R	47.7%	32.0%	20.3%
Oregon	6			819,622	408,433	358,866	49,683	2,640	49,567 R	49.8%	43.8%	6.1%
Pennsylvania		29		4,747,928	2,090,017	2,259,405	378,582	19,924	169,388 D	44.0%	47.6%	8.0%
Rhode Island		4		385,000	122,359	246,518	15,678	445	124,159 D	31.8%	64.0%	4.1%
South Carolina	8			666,978	254,062	197,486	215,430		38,632 R	38.1%	29.6%	32.3%
South Dakota	4			281,264	149,841	118,023	13,400		31,818 R	53.3%	42.0%	4.8%
Tennessee	11			1,248,617	472,592	351,233	424,792		47,800 R	37.8%	28.1%	34.0%
Texas		25		3,079,216	1,227,844	1,266,804	584,269	299	38,960 D	39.9%	41.1%	19.0%
Utah	4			422,568	238,728	156,665	26,906	269	82,063 R	56.5%	37.1%	6.4%
Vermont	3			161,404	85,142	70,255	5,104	903	14,887 R	52.8%	43.5%	3.2%
Virginia	12			1,361,491	590,319	442,387	321,833	6,952	147,932 R	43.4%	32.5%	23.6%
Washington		9		1,304,281	588,510	616,037	96,990	2,744	27,527 D	45.1%	47.2%	7.4%
West Virginia		7		754,206	307,555	374,091	72,560		66,536 D	40.8%	49.6%	9.6%
Wisconsin	12			1,691,538	809,997	748,804	127,835	4,902	61,193 R	47.9%	44.3%	7.6%
Wyoming	3			127,205	70,927	45,173	11,105		25,754 R	55.8%	35.5%	8.7%
Dist. of Col.		3		170,578	31,012	139,566			108,554 D	18.2%	81.8%	
United States	301	191	46	73,211,875	31,785,480	31,275,166	9,906,473	244,756	510,314 R	43.4%	42.7%	13.5%

PRESIDENT 1964

In New York the Democratic figure includes Liberal votes.

The full list of candidates for President and Vice-President was:

43,129,566	Lyndon B. Johnson and Hubert H. Humphrey, <u>Democratic.</u>
27,178,188	Barry M. Goldwater and William E. Miller, <u>Republican.</u>
45,219	Eric Hass and Henning A. Blomen, <u>Socialist Labor.</u>
32,720	Clifton DeBerry and Edward Shaw, <u>Socialist Workers.</u>
23,267	E. Harold Munn and Mark R. Shaw, <u>Prohibition.</u>
6,953	John Kasper and J. B. Stoner, <u>National States Rights.</u>
5,060	Joseph B. Lightburn and T. C. Billings, <u>Constitution.</u>
19	James Hensley and John O. Hopkins, <u>Universal.</u>

In addition, 210,732 votes were cast in Alabama for an unpledged Democratic elector ticket and 12,868 scattered votes were reported from various states.

UNITED STATES

PRESIDENT 1964

State	Electoral Vote Rep.	Electoral Vote Dem.	Electoral Vote Other	Total Vote	Republican	Democratic	Other	Plurality	Total Vote Rep.	Total Vote Dem.	Major Vote Rep.	Major Vote Dem.
Alabama	10			689,818	479,085		210,733	268,353 R	69.5%		100.0%	
Alaska		3		67,259	22,930	44,329		21,399 D	34.1%	65.9%	34.1%	65.9%
Arizona	5			480,770	242,535	237,753	482	4,782 R	50.4%	49.5%	50.5%	49.5%
Arkansas		6		560,426	243,264	314,197	2,965	70,933 D	43.4%	56.1%	43.6%	56.4%
California		40		7,057,586	2,879,108	4,171,877	6,601	1,292,769 D	40.8%	59.1%	40.8%	59.2%
Colorado		6		776,986	296,767	476,024	4,195	179,257 D	38.2%	61.3%	38.4%	61.6%
Connecticut		8		1,218,578	390,996	826,269	1,313	435,273 D	32.1%	67.8%	32.1%	67.9%
Delaware		3		201,320	78,078	122,704	538	44,626 D	38.8%	60.9%	38.9%	61.1%
Florida		14		1,854,481	905,941	948,540		42,599 D	48.9%	51.1%	48.9%	51.1%
Georgia	12			1,139,335	616,584	522,556	195	94,028 R	54.1%	45.9%	54.1%	45.9%
Hawaii		4		207,271	44,022	163,249		119,227 D	21.2%	78.8%	21.2%	78.8%
Idaho		4		292,477	143,557	148,920		5,363 D	49.1%	50.9%	49.1%	50.9%
Illinois		26		4,702,841	1,905,946	2,796,833	62	890,887 D	40.5%	59.5%	40.5%	59.5%
Indiana		13		2,091,606	911,118	1,170,848	9,640	259,730 D	43.6%	56.0%	43.8%	56.2%
Iowa		9		1,184,539	449,148	733,030	2,361	283,882 D	37.9%	61.9%	38.0%	62.0%
Kansas		7		857,901	386,579	464,028	7,294	77,449 D	45.1%	54.1%	45.4%	54.6%
Kentucky		9		1,046,105	372,977	669,659	3,469	296,682 D	35.7%	64.0%	35.8%	64.2%
Louisiana	10			896,293	509,225	387,068		122,157 R	56.8%	43.2%	56.8%	43.2%
Maine		4		380,965	118,701	262,264		143,563 D	31.2%	68.8%	31.2%	68.8%
Maryland		10		1,116,457	385,495	730,912	50	345,417 D	34.5%	65.5%	34.5%	65.5%
Massachusetts		14		2,344,798	549,727	1,786,422	8,649	1,236,695 D	23.4%	76.2%	23.5%	76.5%
Michigan		21		3,203,102	1,060,152	2,136,615	6,335	1,076,463 D	33.1%	66.7%	33.2%	66.8%
Minnesota		10		1,554,462	559,624	991,117	3,721	431,493 D	36.0%	63.8%	36.1%	63.9%
Mississippi	7			409,146	356,528	52,618		303,910 R	87.1%	12.9%	87.1%	12.9%
Missouri		12		1,817,879	653,535	1,164,344		510,809 D	36.0%	64.0%	36.0%	64.0%
Montana		4		278,628	113,032	164,246	1,350	51,214 D	40.6%	58.9%	40.8%	59.2%
Nebraska		5		584,154	276,847	307,307		30,460 D	47.4%	52.6%	47.4%	52.6%
Nevada		3		135,433	56,094	79,339		23,245 D	41.4%	58.6%	41.4%	58.6%
New Hampshire		4		288,093	104,029	184,064		80,035 D	36.1%	63.9%	36.1%	63.9%
New Jersey		17		2,847,663	964,174	1,868,231	15,258	904,057 D	33.9%	65.6%	34.0%	66.0%
New Mexico		4		328,645	132,838	194,015	1,792	61,177 D	40.4%	59.0%	40.6%	59.4%
New York		43		7,166,275	2,243,559	4,913,102	9,614	2,669,543 D	31.3%	68.6%	31.3%	68.7%
North Carolina		13		1,424,983	624,844	800,139		175,295 D	43.8%	56.2%	43.8%	56.2%
North Dakota		4		258,389	108,207	149,784	398	41,577 D	41.9%	58.0%	41.9%	58.1%
Ohio		26		3,969,196	1,470,865	2,498,331		1,027,466 D	37.1%	62.9%	37.1%	62.9%
Oklahoma		8		932,499	412,665	519,834		107,169 D	44.3%	55.7%	44.3%	55.7%
Oregon		6		786,305	282,779	501,017	2,509	218,238 D	36.0%	63.7%	36.1%	63.9%
Pennsylvania		29		4,822,690	1,673,657	3,130,954	18,079	1,457,297 D	34.7%	64.9%	34.8%	65.2%
Rhode Island		4		390,091	74,615	315,463	13	240,848 D	19.1%	80.9%	19.1%	80.9%
South Carolina	8			524,779	309,048	215,723	8	93,325 R	58.9%	41.1%	58.9%	41.1%
South Dakota		4		293,118	130,108	163,010		32,902 D	44.4%	55.6%	44.4%	55.6%
Tennessee		11		1,143,946	508,965	634,947	34	125,982 D	44.5%	55.5%	44.5%	55.5%
Texas		25		2,626,811	958,566	1,663,185	5,060	704,619 D	36.5%	63.3%	36.6%	63.4%
Utah		4		401,413	181,785	219,628		37,843 D	45.3%	54.7%	45.3%	54.7%
Vermont		3		163,089	54,942	108,127	20	53,185 D	33.7%	66.3%	33.7%	66.3%
Virginia		12		1,042,267	481,334	558,038	2,895	76,704 D	46.2%	53.5%	46.3%	53.7%
Washington		9		1,258,556	470,366	779,881	8,309	309,515 D	37.4%	62.0%	37.6%	62.4%
West Virginia		7		792,040	253,953	538,087		284,134 D	32.1%	67.9%	32.1%	67.9%
Wisconsin		12		1,691,815	638,495	1,050,424	2,896	411,929 D	37.7%	62.1%	37.8%	62.2%
Wyoming		3		142,716	61,998	80,718		18,720 D	43.4%	56.6%	43.4%	56.6%
Dist. of Col.		3		198,597	28,801	169,796		140,995 D	14.5%	85.5%	14.5%	85.5%
United States	52	486	—	70,644,592	27,178,188	43,129,566	336,838	15,951,378 D	38.5%	61.1%	38.7%	61.3%

PRESIDENT 1960

Senator Harry Flood Byrd received 15 votes for President in the Electoral College; these were the votes of 6 of the 11 Democratic electors in Alabama, all 8 unpledged Democratic electors in Mississippi, and one of the 8 Republican electors in Oklahoma. The Alabama and Mississippi electors also cast 14 votes for Senator Strom Thurmond for Vice-President; the single Oklahoma elector voted for Senator Barry M. Goldwater for Vice-President.

In New York the Democratic figure includes Liberal votes.

The full list of candidates for President and Vice-President was:

34,226,731	John F. Kennedy and Lyndon B. Johnson, Democratic.
34,108,157	Richard M. Nixon and Henry Cabot Lodge, Republican.
47,522	Eric Hass and Georgia Cozzini, Socialist Labor.
46,203	Rutherford L. Decker and E. Harold Munn, Prohibition.
44,977	Orval E. Faubus and John G. Crommelin, National States Rights.
40,165	Farrell Dobbs and Myra Tanner Weiss, Socialist Workers.
18,162	Charles L. Sullivan and Merritt B. Curtis, Constitution.
8,708	J. Bracken Lee and Kent H. Courtney, Conservative.
4,204	C. Benton Coiner and Edward J. Silverman, Conservative.
1,767	Lar Daly and B. M. Miller, Tax Cut.
1,485	Clennon King and Reginald Carter, Independent Afro-American.
1,401	Merritt B. Curtis and B. M. Miller, Constitution.

In addition, 169,572 votes were cast in Louisiana for Independent electors and 116,248 in Mississippi for an unpledged Democratic elector ticket. 539 votes were cast in Michigan for an Independent American ticket and 2,378 scattered votes were reported from various states.

UNITED STATES

PRESIDENT 1960

State	Electoral Vote Rep.	Electoral Vote Dem.	Electoral Vote Other	Total Vote	Republican	Democratic	Other	Plurality	Total Vote Rep.	Total Vote Dem.	Major Vote Rep.	Major Vote Dem.
Alabama		5	6	570,225	237,981	324,050	8,194	86,069 D	41.7%	56.8%	42.3%	57.7%
Alaska	3			60,762	30,953	29,809		1,144 R	50.9%	49.1%	50.9%	49.1%
Arizona	4			398,491	221,241	176,781	469	44,460 R	55.5%	44.4%	55.6%	44.4%
Arkansas		8		428,509	184,508	215,049	28,952	30,541 D	43.1%	50.2%	46.2%	53.8%
California	32			6,506,578	3,259,722	3,224,099	22,757	35,623 R	50.1%	49.6%	50.3%	49.7%
Colorado	6			736,236	402,242	330,629	3,365	71,613 R	54.6%	44.9%	54.9%	45.1%
Connecticut		8		1,222,883	565,813	657,055	15	91,242 D	46.3%	53.7%	46.3%	53.7%
Delaware		3		196,683	96,373	99,590	720	3,217 D	49.0%	50.6%	49.2%	50.8%
Florida	10			1,544,176	795,476	748,700		46,776 R	51.5%	48.5%	51.5%	48.5%
Georgia		12		733,349	274,472	458,638	239	184,166 D	37.4%	62.5%	37.4%	62.6%
Hawaii		3		184,705	92,295	92,410		115 D	50.0%	50.0%	50.0%	50.0%
Idaho	4			300,450	161,597	138,853		22,744 R	53.8%	46.2%	53.8%	46.2%
Illinois		27		4,757,409	2,368,988	2,377,846	10,575	8,858 D	49.8%	50.0%	49.9%	50.1%
Indiana	13			2,135,360	1,175,120	952,358	7,882	222,762 R	55.0%	44.6%	55.2%	44.8%
Iowa	10			1,273,810	722,381	550,565	864	171,816 R	56.7%	43.2%	56.7%	43.3%
Kansas	8			928,825	561,474	363,213	4,138	198,261 R	60.4%	39.1%	60.7%	39.3%
Kentucky	10			1,124,462	602,607	521,855		80,752 R	53.6%	46.4%	53.6%	46.4%
Louisiana		10		807,891	230,980	407,339	169,572	176,359 D	28.6%	50.4%	36.2%	63.8%
Maine	5			421,767	240,608	181,159		59,449 R	57.0%	43.0%	57.0%	43.0%
Maryland		9		1,055,349	489,538	565,808	3	76,270 D	46.4%	53.6%	46.4%	53.6%
Massachusetts		16		2,469,480	976,750	1,487,174	5,556	510,424 D	39.6%	60.2%	39.6%	60.4%
Michigan		20		3,318,097	1,620,428	1,687,269	10,400	66,841 D	48.8%	50.9%	49.0%	51.0%
Minnesota		11		1,541,887	757,915	779,933	4,039	22,018 D	49.2%	50.6%	49.3%	50.7%
Mississippi			8	298,171	73,561	108,362	116,248	7,886 U	24.7%	36.3%	40.4%	59.6%
Missouri		13		1,934,422	962,221	972,201		9,980 D	49.7%	50.3%	49.7%	50.3%
Montana	4			277,579	141,841	134,891	847	6,950 R	51.1%	48.6%	51.3%	48.7%
Nebraska	6			613,095	380,553	232,542		148,011 R	62.1%	37.9%	62.1%	37.9%
Nevada		3		107,267	52,387	54,880		2,493 D	48.8%	51.2%	48.8%	51.2%
New Hampshire	4			295,761	157,989	137,772		20,217 R	53.4%	46.6%	53.4%	46.6%
New Jersey		16		2,773,111	1,363,324	1,385,415	24,372	22,091 D	49.2%	50.0%	49.6%	50.4%
New Mexico		4		311,107	153,733	156,027	1,347	2,294 D	49.4%	50.2%	49.6%	50.4%
New York		45		7,291,079	3,446,419	3,830,085	14,575	383,666 D	47.3%	52.5%	47.4%	52.6%
North Carolina		14		1,368,556	655,420	713,136		57,716 D	47.9%	52.1%	47.9%	52.1%
North Dakota	4			278,431	154,310	123,963	158	30,347 R	55.4%	44.5%	55.5%	44.5%
Ohio	25			4,161,859	2,217,611	1,944,248		273,363 R	53.3%	46.7%	53.3%	46.7%
Oklahoma	7		1	903,150	533,039	370,111		162,928 R	59.0%	41.0%	59.0%	41.0%
Oregon	6			776,421	408,060	367,402	959	40,658 R	52.6%	47.3%	52.6%	47.4%
Pennsylvania		32		5,006,541	2,439,956	2,556,282	10,303	116,326 D	48.7%	51.1%	48.8%	51.2%
Rhode Island		4		405,535	147,502	258,032	1	110,530 D	36.4%	63.6%	36.4%	63.6%
South Carolina		8		386,688	188,558	198,129	1	9,571 D	48.8%	51.2%	48.8%	51.2%
South Dakota	4			306,487	178,417	128,070		50,347 R	58.2%	41.8%	58.2%	41.8%
Tennessee	11			1,051,792	556,577	481,453	13,762	75,124 R	52.9%	45.8%	53.6%	46.4%
Texas		24		2,311,084	1,121,310	1,167,567	22,207	46,257 D	48.5%	50.5%	49.0%	51.0%
Utah	4			374,709	205,361	169,248	100	36,113 R	54.8%	45.2%	54.8%	45.2%
Vermont	3			167,324	98,131	69,186	7	28,945 R	58.6%	41.3%	58.6%	41.4%
Virginia	12			771,449	404,521	362,327	4,601	42,194 R	52.4%	47.0%	52.8%	47.2%
Washington	9			1,241,572	629,273	599,298	13,001	29,975 R	50.7%	48.3%	51.2%	48.8%
West Virginia		8		837,781	395,995	441,786		45,791 D	47.3%	52.7%	47.3%	52.7%
Wisconsin	12			1,729,082	895,175	830,805	3,102	64,370 R	51.8%	48.0%	51.9%	48.1%
Wyoming	3			140,782	77,451	63,331		14,120 R	55.0%	45.0%	55.0%	45.0%
United States	219	303	15	68,838,219	34,108,157	34,226,731	503,331	118,574 D	49.5%	49.7%	49.9%	50.1%

PRESIDENT 1956

One of the 11 Democratic electors chosen in Alabama cast his Electoral College vote for Walter B. Jones and Herman Talmadge rather than for the national Democratic candidates.

The Republican figure in Mississippi includes votes cast for two elector tickets. In New York the Democratic figure includes Liberal votes.

The full list of candidates for President and Vice-President was:

35,590,472	Dwight D. Eisenhower and Richard M. Nixon, Republican.
26,022,752	Adlai E. Stevenson and Estes Kefauver, Democratic.
111,178	T. Coleman Andrews and Thomas H. Werdel, States Rights.
44,450	Eric Hass and Georgia Cozzini, Socialist Labor.
41,937	Enoch A. Holtwick and Edwin M. Cooper, Prohibition.
7,797	Farrell Dobbs and Myra Tanner Weiss, Socialist Workers.
2,657	Harry Flood Byrd and William E. Jenner, States Rights.
2,126	Darlington Hoopes and Samuel H. Friedman, Socialist.
1,829	Henry B. Krajewski and Anne Marie Yezo, American Third Party.
8	Gerald L. K. Smith and Charles F. Robertson, Christian Nationalist.

In addition, 196,318 votes were cast in Alabama, Louisiana, Mississippi, and South Carolina for Independent electors or for States Rights elector tickets not officially pledged to any candidate, and 5,384 scattered votes were reported from various states.

UNITED STATES

PRESIDENT 1956

State	Electoral Vote Rep.	Electoral Vote Dem.	Electoral Vote Other	Total Vote	Republican	Democratic	Other	Plurality	Total Vote Rep.	Total Vote Dem.	Major Vote Rep.	Major Vote Dem.
Alabama		10	1	496,861	195,694	280,844	20,323	85,150 D	39.4%	56.5%	41.1%	58.9%
Alaska												
Arizona	4			290,173	176,990	112,880	303	64,110 R	61.0%	38.9%	61.1%	38.9%
Arkansas		8		406,572	186,287	213,277	7,008	26,990 D	45.8%	52.5%	46.6%	53.4%
California	32			5,466,355	3,027,668	2,420,135	18,552	607,533 R	55.4%	44.3%	55.6%	44.4%
Colorado	6			657,074	394,479	257,997	4,598	136,482 R	60.0%	39.3%	60.5%	39.5%
Connecticut	8			1,117,121	711,837	405,079	205	306,758 R	63.7%	36.3%	63.7%	36.3%
Delaware	3			177,988	98,057	79,421	510	18,636 R	55.1%	44.6%	55.3%	44.7%
Florida	10			1,125,762	643,849	480,371	1,542	163,478 R	57.2%	42.7%	57.3%	42.7%
Georgia		12		669,655	222,778	444,688	2,189	221,910 D	33.3%	66.4%	33.4%	66.6%
Hawaii												
Idaho	4			272,989	166,979	105,868	142	61,111 R	61.2%	38.8%	61.2%	38.8%
Illinois	27			4,407,407	2,623,327	1,775,682	8,398	847,645 R	59.5%	40.3%	59.6%	40.4%
Indiana	13			1,974,607	1,182,811	783,908	7,888	398,903 R	59.9%	39.7%	60.1%	39.9%
Iowa	10			1,234,564	729,187	501,858	3,519	227,329 R	59.1%	40.7%	59.2%	40.8%
Kansas	8			866,243	566,878	296,317	3,048	270,561 R	65.4%	34.2%	65.7%	34.3%
Kentucky	10			1,053,805	572,192	476,453	5,160	95,739 R	54.3%	45.2%	54.6%	45.4%
Louisiana	10			617,544	329,047	243,977	44,520	85,070 R	53.3%	39.5%	57.4%	42.6%
Maine	5			351,706	249,238	102,468		146,770 R	70.9%	29.1%	70.9%	29.1%
Maryland	9			932,827	559,738	372,613	476	187,125 R	60.0%	39.9%	60.0%	40.0%
Massachusetts	16			2,348,506	1,393,197	948,190	7,119	445,007 R	59.3%	40.4%	59.5%	40.5%
Michigan	20			3,080,468	1,713,647	1,359,898	6,923	353,749 R	55.6%	44.1%	55.8%	44.2%
Minnesota	11			1,340,005	719,302	617,525	3,178	101,777 R	53.7%	46.1%	53.8%	46.2%
Mississippi		8		248,104	60,685	144,453	42,966	83,768 D	24.5%	58.2%	29.6%	70.4%
Missouri		13		1,832,562	914,289	918,273		3,984 D	49.9%	50.1%	49.9%	50.1%
Montana	4			271,171	154,933	116,238		38,695 R	57.1%	42.9%	57.1%	42.9%
Nebraska	6			577,137	378,108	199,029		179,079 R	65.5%	34.5%	65.5%	34.5%
Nevada	3			96,689	56,049	40,640		15,409 R	58.0%	42.0%	58.0%	42.0%
New Hampshire	4			266,994	176,519	90,364	111	86,155 R	66.1%	33.8%	66.1%	33.9%
New Jersey	16			2,484,312	1,606,942	850,337	27,033	756,605 R	64.7%	34.2%	65.4%	34.6%
New Mexico	4			253,926	146,788	106,098	1,040	40,690 R	57.8%	41.8%	58.0%	42.0%
New York	45			7,095,971	4,345,506	2,747,944	2,521	1,597,562 R	61.2%	38.4%	61.3%	38.7%
North Carolina		14		1,165,592	575,062	590,530		15,468 D	49.3%	50.7%	49.3%	50.7%
North Dakota	4			253,991	156,766	96,742	483	60,024 R	61.7%	38.1%	61.8%	38.2%
Ohio	25			3,702,265	2,262,610	1,439,655		822,955 R	61.1%	38.9%	61.1%	38.9%
Oklahoma	8			859,350	473,769	385,581		88,188 R	55.1%	44.9%	55.1%	44.9%
Oregon	6			736,132	406,393	329,204	535	77,189 R	55.2%	44.7%	55.2%	44.8%
Pennsylvania	32			4,576,503	2,585,252	1,981,769	9,482	603,483 R	56.5%	43.3%	56.6%	43.4%
Rhode Island	4			387,609	225,819	161,790		64,029 R	58.3%	41.7%	58.3%	41.7%
South Carolina		8		300,583	75,700	136,372	88,511	47,863 D	25.2%	45.4%	35.7%	64.3%
South Dakota	4			293,857	171,569	122,288		49,281 R	58.4%	41.6%	58.4%	41.6%
Tennessee	11			939,404	462,288	456,507	20,609	5,781 R	49.2%	48.6%	50.3%	49.7%
Texas	24			1,955,168	1,080,619	859,958	14,591	220,661 R	55.3%	44.0%	55.7%	44.3%
Utah	4			333,995	215,631	118,364		97,267 R	64.6%	35.4%	64.6%	35.4%
Vermont	3			152,978	110,390	42,549	39	67,841 R	72.2%	27.8%	72.2%	27.8%
Virginia	12			697,978	386,459	267,760	43,759	118,699 R	55.4%	38.4%	59.1%	40.9%
Washington	9			1,150,889	620,430	523,002	7,457	97,428 R	53.9%	45.4%	54.3%	45.7%
West Virginia	8			830,831	449,297	381,534		67,763 R	54.1%	45.9%	54.1%	45.9%
Wisconsin	12			1,550,558	954,844	586,768	8,946	368,076 R	61.6%	37.8%	61.9%	38.1%
Wyoming	3			124,127	74,573	49,554		25,019 R	60.1%	39.9%	60.1%	39.9%
United States	457	73	1	62,026,908	35,590,472	26,022,752	413,684	9,567,720 R	57.4%	42.0%	57.8%	42.2%

PRESIDENT 1952

The Republican figure in South Carolina includes votes cast for two elector tickets; in Mississippi the Republican total is the vote cast for an Independent elector ticket "pledged to vote for the nominees of the National Republican Party". In New York the Democratic figure includes Liberal votes.

The full list of candidates for President and Vice-President was:

33,936,234	Dwight D. Eisenhower and Richard M. Nixon, <u>Republican.</u>
27,314,992	Adlai E. Stevenson and John J. Sparkman, <u>Democratic.</u>
140,023	Vincent Hallinan and Charlotta Bass, <u>Progressive.</u>
72,949	Stuart Hamblen and Enoch A. Holtwick, <u>Prohibition.</u>
30,267	Eric Hass and Stephen Emery, <u>Socialist Labor.</u>
20,203	Darlington Hoopes and Samuel H. Friedman, <u>Socialist.</u>
10,312	Farrell Dobbs and Myra Tanner Weiss, <u>Socialist Workers.</u>
4,203	Henry B. Krajewski and Frank Jenkins, <u>Poor Man's Party.</u>

In addition, 17,205 votes were cast for various elector tickets filed on behalf of General Douglas MacArthur, including Christian Nationalist (with Jack B. Tenney as candidate for Vice-President), Constitution (with Vivien Kellems), and America First (with Senator Harry Flood Byrd). In California, Missouri, and Texas the MacArthur vote was cast for two elector tickets. 4,530 scattered votes were reported from various states.

UNITED STATES

PRESIDENT 1952

State	Electoral Vote Rep.	Electoral Vote Dem.	Electoral Vote Other	Total Vote	Republican	Democratic	Other	Plurality	Percentage Total Vote Rep.	Percentage Total Vote Dem.	Percentage Major Vote Rep.	Percentage Major Vote Dem.
Alabama		11		426,120	149,231	275,075	1,814	125,844 D	35.0%	64.6%	35.2%	64.8%
Alaska												
Arizona	4			260,570	152,042	108,528		43,514 R	58.3%	41.7%	58.3%	41.7%
Arkansas		8		404,800	177,155	226,300	1,345	49,145 D	43.8%	55.9%	43.9%	56.1%
California	32			5,141,849	2,897,310	2,197,548	46,991	699,762 R	56.3%	42.7%	56.9%	43.1%
Colorado	6			630,103	379,782	245,504	4,817	134,278 R	60.3%	39.0%	60.7%	39.3%
Connecticut	8			1,096,911	611,012	481,649	4,250	129,363 R	55.7%	43.9%	55.9%	44.1%
Delaware	3			174,025	90,059	83,315	651	6,744 R	51.8%	47.9%	51.9%	48.1%
Florida	10			989,337	544,036	444,950	351	99,086 R	55.0%	45.0%	55.0%	45.0%
Georgia		12		655,785	198,961	456,823	1	257,862 D	30.3%	69.7%	30.3%	69.7%
Hawaii												
Idaho	4			276,254	180,707	95,081	466	85,626 R	65.4%	34.4%	65.5%	34.5%
Illinois	27			4,481,058	2,457,327	2,013,920	9,811	443,407 R	54.8%	44.9%	55.0%	45.0%
Indiana	13			1,955,049	1,136,259	801,530	17,260	334,729 R	58.1%	41.0%	58.6%	41.4%
Iowa	10			1,268,773	808,906	451,513	8,354	357,393 R	63.8%	35.6%	64.2%	35.8%
Kansas	8			896,166	616,302	273,296	6,568	343,006 R	68.8%	30.5%	69.3%	30.7%
Kentucky		10		993,148	495,029	495,729	2,390	700 D	49.8%	49.9%	50.0%	50.0%
Louisiana		10		651,952	306,925	345,027		38,102 D	47.1%	52.9%	47.1%	52.9%
Maine	5			351,786	232,353	118,806	627	113,547 R	66.0%	33.8%	66.2%	33.8%
Maryland	9			902,074	499,424	395,337	7,313	104,087 R	55.4%	43.8%	55.8%	44.2%
Massachusetts	16			2,383,398	1,292,325	1,083,525	7,548	208,800 R	54.2%	45.5%	54.4%	45.6%
Michigan	20			2,798,592	1,551,529	1,230,657	16,406	320,872 R	55.4%	44.0%	55.8%	44.2%
Minnesota	11			1,379,483	763,211	608,458	7,814	154,753 R	55.3%	44.1%	55.6%	44.4%
Mississippi		8		285,532	112,966	172,566		59,600 D	39.6%	60.4%	39.6%	60.4%
Missouri	13			1,892,062	959,429	929,830	2,803	29,599 R	50.7%	49.1%	50.8%	49.2%
Montana	4			265,037	157,394	106,213	1,430	51,181 R	59.4%	40.1%	59.7%	40.3%
Nebraska	6			609,660	421,603	188,057		233,546 R	69.2%	30.8%	69.2%	30.8%
Nevada	3			82,190	50,502	31,688		18,814 R	61.4%	38.6%	61.4%	38.6%
New Hampshire	4			272,950	166,287	106,663		59,624 R	60.9%	39.1%	60.9%	39.1%
New Jersey	16			2,418,554	1,373,613	1,015,902	29,039	357,711 R	56.8%	42.0%	57.5%	42.5%
New Mexico	4			238,608	132,170	105,661	777	26,509 R	55.4%	44.3%	55.6%	44.4%
New York	45			7,128,239	3,952,813	3,104,601	70,825	848,212 R	55.5%	43.6%	56.0%	44.0%
North Carolina		14		1,210,910	558,107	652,803		94,696 D	46.1%	53.9%	46.1%	53.9%
North Dakota	4			270,127	191,712	76,694	1,721	115,018 R	71.0%	28.4%	71.4%	28.6%
Ohio	25			3,700,758	2,100,391	1,600,367		500,024 R	56.8%	43.2%	56.8%	43.2%
Oklahoma	8			948,984	518,045	430,939		87,106 R	54.6%	45.4%	54.6%	45.4%
Oregon	6			695,059	420,815	270,579	3,665	150,236 R	60.5%	38.9%	60.9%	39.1%
Pennsylvania	32			4,580,969	2,415,789	2,146,269	18,911	269,520 R	52.7%	46.9%	53.0%	47.0%
Rhode Island	4			414,498	210,935	203,293	270	7,642 R	50.9%	49.0%	50.9%	49.1%
South Carolina		8		341,087	168,082	173,004	1	4,922 D	49.3%	50.7%	49.3%	50.7%
South Dakota	4			294,283	203,857	90,426		113,431 R	69.3%	30.7%	69.3%	30.7%
Tennessee	11			892,553	446,147	443,710	2,696	2,437 R	50.0%	49.7%	50.1%	49.9%
Texas	24			2,075,946	1,102,878	969,228	3,840	133,650 R	53.1%	46.7%	53.2%	46.8%
Utah	4			329,554	194,190	135,364		58,826 R	58.9%	41.1%	58.9%	41.1%
Vermont	3			153,557	109,717	43,355	485	66,362 R	71.5%	28.2%	71.7%	28.3%
Virginia	12			619,689	349,037	268,677	1,975	80,360 R	56.3%	43.4%	56.5%	43.5%
Washington	9			1,102,708	599,107	492,845	10,756	106,262 R	54.3%	44.7%	54.9%	45.1%
West Virginia		8		873,548	419,970	453,578		33,608 D	48.1%	51.9%	48.1%	51.9%
Wisconsin	12			1,607,370	979,744	622,175	5,451	357,569 R	61.0%	38.7%	61.2%	38.8%
Wyoming	3			129,253	81,049	47,934	270	33,115 R	62.7%	37.1%	62.8%	37.2%
United States	442	89	—	61,550,918	33,936,234	27,314,992	299,692	6,621,242 R	55.1%	44.4%	55.4%	44.6%

PRESIDENT 1948

The electoral votes of Alabama, Louisiana, Mississippi, and South Carolina were cast for the States Rights nominees. In addition, one of the 12 Democratic electors chosen in Tennessee cast his Electoral College vote for the States Rights nominees rather than for the national Democratic candidates.

In Alabama the Democratic electors were pledged to the States Rights candidates. There were no national Democratic electors on the ballot in that state.

The Republican figure in Mississippi includes votes cast for two elector tickets. In New York the Democratic figure includes Liberal votes.

The full list of candidates for President and Vice-President was:

24,179,345	Harry S. Truman and Alben W. Barkley, Democratic.
21,991,291	Thomas E. Dewey and Earl Warren, Republican.
1,176,125	Strom Thurmond and Fielding L. Wright, States Rights.
1,157,326	Henry A. Wallace and Glen H. Taylor, Progressive.
139,572	Norman Thomas and Tucker P. Smith, Socialist.
103,900	Claude A. Watson and Dale H. Learn, Prohibition.
29,241	Edward A. Teichert and Stephen Emery, Socialist Labor.
13,614	Farrell Dobbs and Grace Carlson, Socialist Workers.

In addition, 3,412 scattered votes were reported from various states.

UNITED STATES

PRESIDENT 1948

State	Electoral Vote Rep.	Electoral Vote Dem.	Electoral Vote Other	Total Vote	Republican	Democratic	Other	Plurality	Pct Total Vote Rep.	Pct Total Vote Dem.	Pct Major Vote Rep.	Pct Major Vote Dem.
Alabama			11	214,980	40,930		174,050	130,513 SR	19.0%		100.0%	
Alaska												
Arizona		4		177,065	77,597	95,251	4,217	17,654 D	43.8%	53.8%	44.9%	55.1%
Arkansas		9		242,475	50,959	149,659	41,857	98,700 D	21.0%	61.7%	25.4%	74.6%
California		25		4,021,538	1,895,269	1,913,134	213,135	17,865 D	47.1%	47.6%	49.8%	50.2%
Colorado		6		515,237	239,714	267,288	8,235	27,574 D	46.5%	51.9%	47.3%	52.7%
Connecticut	8			883,518	437,754	423,297	22,467	14,457 R	49.5%	47.9%	50.8%	49.2%
Delaware	3			139,073	69,588	67,813	1,672	1,775 R	50.0%	48.8%	50.6%	49.4%
Florida		8		577,643	194,280	281,988	101,375	87,708 D	33.6%	48.8%	40.8%	59.2%
Georgia		12		418,844	76,691	254,646	87,507	169,511 D	18.3%	60.8%	23.1%	76.9%
Hawaii												
Idaho		4		214,816	101,514	107,370	5,932	5,856 D	47.3%	50.0%	48.6%	51.4%
Illinois		28		3,984,046	1,961,103	1,994,715	28,228	33,612 D	49.2%	50.1%	49.6%	50.4%
Indiana	13			1,656,212	821,079	807,831	27,302	13,248 R	49.6%	48.8%	50.4%	49.6%
Iowa		10		1,038,264	494,018	522,380	21,866	28,362 D	47.6%	50.3%	48.6%	51.4%
Kansas	8			788,819	423,039	351,902	13,878	71,137 R	53.6%	44.6%	54.6%	45.4%
Kentucky		11		822,658	341,210	466,756	14,692	125,546 D	41.5%	56.7%	42.2%	57.8%
Louisiana			10	416,336	72,657	136,344	207,335	67,946 SR	17.5%	32.7%	34.8%	65.2%
Maine	5			264,787	150,234	111,916	2,637	38,318 R	56.7%	42.3%	57.3%	42.7%
Maryland	8			596,748	294,814	286,521	15,413	8,293 R	49.4%	48.0%	50.7%	49.3%
Massachusetts		16		2,107,146	909,370	1,151,788	45,988	242,418 D	43.2%	54.7%	44.1%	55.9%
Michigan	19			2,109,609	1,038,595	1,003,448	67,566	35,147 R	49.2%	47.6%	50.9%	49.1%
Minnesota		11		1,212,226	483,617	692,966	35,643	209,349 D	39.9%	57.2%	41.1%	58.9%
Mississippi			9	192,190	5,043	19,384	167,763	148,154 SR	2.6%	10.1%	20.6%	79.4%
Missouri		15		1,578,628	655,039	917,315	6,274	262,276 D	41.5%	58.1%	41.7%	58.3%
Montana		4		224,278	96,770	119,071	8,437	22,301 D	43.1%	53.1%	44.8%	55.2%
Nebraska	6			488,940	264,774	224,165	1	40,609 R	54.2%	45.8%	54.2%	45.8%
Nevada		3		62,117	29,357	31,291	1,469	1,934 D	47.3%	50.4%	48.4%	51.6%
New Hampshire	4			231,440	121,299	107,995	2,146	13,304 R	52.4%	46.7%	52.9%	47.1%
New Jersey	16			1,949,555	981,124	895,455	72,976	85,669 R	50.3%	45.9%	52.3%	47.7%
New Mexico		4		187,063	80,303	105,464	1,296	25,161 D	42.9%	56.4%	43.2%	56.8%
New York	47			6,177,337	2,841,163	2,780,204	555,970	60,959 R	46.0%	45.0%	50.5%	49.5%
North Carolina		14		791,209	258,572	459,070	73,567	200,498 D	32.7%	58.0%	36.0%	64.0%
North Dakota	4			220,716	115,139	95,812	9,765	19,327 R	52.2%	43.4%	54.6%	45.4%
Ohio		25		2,936,071	1,445,684	1,452,791	37,596	7,107 D	49.2%	49.5%	49.9%	50.1%
Oklahoma		10		721,599	268,817	452,782		183,965 D	37.3%	62.7%	37.3%	62.7%
Oregon	6			524,080	260,904	243,147	20,029	17,757 R	49.8%	46.4%	51.8%	48.2%
Pennsylvania	35			3,735,348	1,902,197	1,752,426	80,725	149,771 R	50.9%	46.9%	52.0%	48.0%
Rhode Island		4		327,702	135,787	188,736	3,179	52,949 D	41.4%	57.6%	41.8%	58.2%
South Carolina			8	142,571	5,386	34,423	102,762	68,184 SR	3.8%	24.1%	13.5%	86.5%
South Dakota	4			250,105	129,651	117,653	2,801	11,998 R	51.8%	47.0%	52.4%	47.6%
Tennessee		11	1	550,283	202,914	270,402	76,967	67,488 D	36.9%	49.1%	42.9%	57.1%
Texas		23		1,249,577	303,467	824,235	121,875	520,768 D	24.3%	66.0%	26.9%	73.1%
Utah		4		276,306	124,402	149,151	2,753	24,749 D	45.0%	54.0%	45.5%	54.5%
Vermont	3			123,382	75,926	45,557	1,899	30,369 R	61.5%	36.9%	62.5%	37.5%
Virginia		11		419,256	172,070	200,786	46,400	28,716 D	41.0%	47.9%	46.1%	53.9%
Washington		8		905,058	386,314	476,165	42,579	89,851 D	42.7%	52.6%	44.8%	55.2%
West Virginia		8		748,750	316,251	429,188	3,311	112,937 D	42.2%	57.3%	42.4%	57.6%
Wisconsin		12		1,276,800	590,959	647,310	38,531	56,351 D	46.3%	50.7%	47.7%	52.3%
Wyoming		3		101,425	47,947	52,354	1,124	4,407 D	47.3%	51.6%	47.8%	52.2%
United States	189	303	39	48,793,826	21,991,291	24,179,345	2,623,190	2,188,054 D	45.1%	49.6%	47.6%	52.4%

PRESIDENT 1944

The Republican figures in Georgia, Mississippi and South Carolina include votes cast for two elector tickets. The Democratic figure in Mississippi includes votes cast for two elector tickets and in New York includes American Labor and Liberal votes.

In South Carolina an uncommitted Southern Democratic elector ticket ran in second place ahead of the Republican candidates.

The full list of candidates for President and Vice-President was:

25,612,610	Franklin D. Roosevelt and Harry S. Truman, <u>Democratic</u>.
22,017,617	Thomas E. Dewey and John W. Bricker, <u>Republican</u>.
79,003	Norman Thomas and Darlington Hoopes, <u>Socialist</u>.
74,799	Claude A. Watson and Andrew Johnson, <u>Prohibition</u>.
45,191	Edward A. Teichert and Arla A. Albaugh, <u>Socialist Labor</u>.
1,780	Gerald L. K. Smith and Harry Romer, <u>American First</u>.

In addition, 135,444 votes were cast in Texas for a Texas Regulars elector ticket and 7,799 in South Carolina for an uncommitted Southern Democratic elector ticket. There were 2,447 scattered votes reported from various states.

UNITED STATES

PRESIDENT 1944

State	Electoral Vote Rep.	Dem.	Other	Total Vote	Republican	Democratic	Other	Plurality	Percentage Total Vote Rep.	Dem.	Major Vote Rep.	Dem.
Alabama		11		244,743	44,540	198,918	1,285	154,378 D	18.2%	81.3%	18.3%	81.7%
Alaska												
Arizona		4		137,634	56,287	80,926	421	24,639 D	40.9%	58.8%	41.0%	59.0%
Arkansas		9		212,954	63,551	148,965	438	85,414 D	29.8%	70.0%	29.9%	70.1%
California		25		3,520,875	1,512,965	1,988,564	19,346	475,599 D	43.0%	56.5%	43.2%	56.8%
Colorado	6			505,039	268,731	234,331	1,977	34,400 R	53.2%	46.4%	53.4%	46.6%
Connecticut		8		831,990	390,527	435,146	6,317	44,619 D	46.9%	52.3%	47.3%	52.7%
Delaware		3		125,361	56,747	68,166	448	11,419 D	45.3%	54.4%	45.4%	54.6%
Florida		8		482,803	143,215	339,377	211	196,162 D	29.7%	70.3%	29.7%	70.3%
Georgia		12		328,129	59,900	268,187	42	208,287 D	18.3%	81.7%	18.3%	81.7%
Hawaii												
Idaho		4		208,321	100,137	107,399	785	7,262 D	48.1%	51.6%	48.3%	51.7%
Illinois		28		4,036,061	1,939,314	2,079,479	17,268	140,165 D	48.0%	51.5%	48.3%	51.7%
Indiana	13			1,672,091	875,891	781,403	14,797	94,488 R	52.4%	46.7%	52.9%	47.1%
Iowa	10			1,052,599	547,267	499,876	5,456	47,391 R	52.0%	47.5%	52.3%	47.7%
Kansas	8			733,776	442,096	287,458	4,222	154,638 R	60.2%	39.2%	60.6%	39.4%
Kentucky		11		867,924	392,448	472,589	2,887	80,141 D	45.2%	54.5%	45.4%	54.6%
Louisiana		10		349,383	67,750	281,564	69	213,814 D	19.4%	80.6%	19.4%	80.6%
Maine	5			296,400	155,434	140,631	335	14,803 R	52.4%	47.4%	52.5%	47.5%
Maryland		8		608,439	292,949	315,490		22,541 D	48.1%	51.9%	48.1%	51.9%
Massachusetts		16		1,960,665	921,350	1,035,296	4,019	113,946 D	47.0%	52.8%	47.1%	52.9%
Michigan		19		2,205,223	1,084,423	1,106,899	13,901	22,476 D	49.2%	50.2%	49.5%	50.5%
Minnesota		11		1,125,504	527,416	589,864	8,224	62,448 D	46.9%	52.4%	47.2%	52.8%
Mississippi		9		180,234	11,613	168,621		157,008 D	6.4%	93.6%	6.4%	93.6%
Missouri		15		1,571,697	761,175	807,356	3,166	46,181 D	48.4%	51.4%	48.5%	51.5%
Montana		4		207,355	93,163	112,556	1,636	19,393 D	44.9%	54.3%	45.3%	54.7%
Nebraska	6			563,126	329,880	233,246		96,634 R	58.6%	41.4%	58.6%	41.4%
Nevada		3		54,234	24,611	29,623		5,012 D	45.4%	54.6%	45.4%	54.6%
New Hampshire		4		229,625	109,916	119,663	46	9,747 D	47.9%	52.1%	47.9%	52.1%
New Jersey		16		1,963,761	961,335	987,874	14,552	26,539 D	49.0%	50.3%	49.3%	50.7%
New Mexico		4		152,225	70,688	81,389	148	10,701 D	46.4%	53.5%	46.5%	53.5%
New York		47		6,316,790	2,987,647	3,304,238	24,905	316,591 D	47.3%	52.3%	47.5%	52.5%
North Carolina		14		790,554	263,155	527,399		264,244 D	33.3%	66.7%	33.3%	66.7%
North Dakota	4			220,182	118,535	100,144	1,503	18,391 R	53.8%	45.5%	54.2%	45.8%
Ohio	25			3,153,056	1,582,293	1,570,763		11,530 R	50.2%	49.8%	50.2%	49.8%
Oklahoma		10		722,636	319,424	401,549	1,663	82,125 D	44.2%	55.6%	44.3%	55.7%
Oregon		6		480,147	225,365	248,635	6,147	23,270 D	46.9%	51.8%	47.5%	52.5%
Pennsylvania		35		3,794,793	1,835,054	1,940,479	19,260	105,425 D	48.4%	51.1%	48.6%	51.4%
Rhode Island		4		299,276	123,487	175,356	433	51,869 D	41.3%	58.6%	41.3%	58.7%
South Carolina		8		103,382	4,617	90,601	8,164	82,802 D	4.5%	87.6%	4.8%	95.2%
South Dakota	4			232,076	135,365	96,711		38,654 R	58.3%	41.7%	58.3%	41.7%
Tennessee		12		510,692	200,311	308,707	1,674	108,396 D	39.2%	60.4%	39.4%	60.6%
Texas		23		1,150,334	191,423	821,605	137,306	630,182 D	16.6%	71.4%	18.9%	81.1%
Utah		4		248,319	97,891	150,088	340	52,197 D	39.4%	60.4%	39.5%	60.5%
Vermont	3			125,361	71,527	53,820	14	17,707 R	57.1%	42.9%	57.1%	42.9%
Virginia		11		388,485	145,243	242,276	966	97,033 D	37.4%	62.4%	37.5%	62.5%
Washington		8		856,328	361,689	486,774	7,865	125,085 D	42.2%	56.8%	42.6%	57.4%
West Virginia		8		715,596	322,819	392,777		69,958 D	45.1%	54.9%	45.1%	54.9%
Wisconsin	12			1,339,152	674,532	650,413	14,207	24,119 R	50.4%	48.6%	50.9%	49.1%
Wyoming	3			101,340	51,921	49,419		2,502 R	51.2%	48.8%	51.2%	48.8%
United States	99	432	—	47,976,670	22,017,617	25,612,610	346,443	3,594,993 D	45.9%	53.4%	46.2%	53.8%

PRESIDENT 1940

The Republican figures in Connecticut, Georgia, Mississippi and South Carolina include votes cast for two or three elector tickets. In New York the Democratic figure includes American Labor votes.

The full list of candidates for President and Vice-President was:

27,313,041	Franklin D. Roosevelt and Henry A. Wallace, <u>Democratic</u>.
22,348,480	Wendell Willkie and Charles L. McNary, <u>Republican</u>.
116,410	Norman Thomas and Maynard C. Krueger, <u>Socialist</u>.
58,708	Roger Babson and Edgar V. Moorman, <u>Prohibition</u>.
46,259	Earl Browder and James W. Ford, <u>Communist</u>.
14,892	John W. Aiken and Aaron M. Orange, <u>Socialist Labor</u>.

In addition, 545 votes were cast in North Dakota for the individual candidacy of Alfred Knutson and 2,083 scattered votes were reported from various states.

UNITED STATES

PRESIDENT 1940

State	Electoral Vote Rep.	Dem.	Other	Total Vote	Republican	Democratic	Other	Plurality	Percentage Total Vote Rep.	Dem.	Major Vote Rep.	Dem.
Alabama		11		294,219	42,184	250,726	1,309	208,542 D	14.3%	85.2%	14.4%	85.6%
Alaska												
Arizona		3		150,039	54,030	95,267	742	41,237 D	36.0%	63.5%	36.2%	63.8%
Arkansas		9		200,429	42,122	157,213	1,094	115,091 D	21.0%	78.4%	21.1%	78.9%
California		22		3,268,791	1,351,419	1,877,618	39,754	526,199 D	41.3%	57.4%	41.9%	58.1%
Colorado	6			549,004	279,576	265,554	3,874	14,022 R	50.9%	48.4%	51.3%	48.7%
Connecticut		8		781,502	361,819	417,621	2,062	55,802 D	46.3%	53.4%	46.4%	53.6%
Delaware		3		136,374	61,440	74,599	335	13,159 D	45.1%	54.7%	45.2%	54.8%
Florida		7		485,640	126,158	359,334	148	233,176 D	26.0%	74.0%	26.0%	74.0%
Georgia		12		312,686	46,495	265,194	997	218,699 D	14.9%	84.8%	14.9%	85.1%
Hawaii												
Idaho		4		235,168	106,553	127,842	773	21,289 D	45.3%	54.4%	45.5%	54.5%
Illinois		29		4,217,935	2,047,240	2,149,934	20,761	102,694 D	48.5%	51.0%	48.8%	51.2%
Indiana	14			1,782,747	899,466	874,063	9,218	25,403 R	50.5%	49.0%	50.7%	49.3%
Iowa	11			1,215,432	632,370	578,802	4,260	53,568 R	52.0%	47.6%	52.2%	47.8%
Kansas	9			860,297	489,169	364,725	6,403	124,444 R	56.9%	42.4%	57.3%	42.7%
Kentucky		11		970,163	410,384	557,322	2,457	146,938 D	42.3%	57.4%	42.4%	57.6%
Louisiana		10		372,305	52,446	319,751	108	267,305 D	14.1%	85.9%	14.1%	85.9%
Maine	5			320,840	163,951	156,478	411	7,473 R	51.1%	48.8%	51.2%	48.8%
Maryland		8		660,104	269,534	384,546	6,024	115,012 D	40.8%	58.3%	41.2%	58.8%
Massachusetts		17		2,026,993	939,700	1,076,522	10,771	136,822 D	46.4%	53.1%	46.6%	53.4%
Michigan	19			2,085,929	1,039,917	1,032,991	13,021	6,926 R	49.9%	49.5%	50.2%	49.8%
Minnesota		11		1,251,188	596,274	644,196	10,718	47,922 D	47.7%	51.5%	48.1%	51.9%
Mississippi		9		175,824	7,364	168,267	193	160,903 D	4.2%	95.7%	4.2%	95.8%
Missouri		15		1,833,729	871,009	958,476	4,244	87,467 D	47.5%	52.3%	47.6%	52.4%
Montana		4		247,873	99,579	145,698	2,596	46,119 D	40.2%	58.8%	40.6%	59.4%
Nebraska	7			615,878	352,201	263,677		88,524 R	57.2%	42.8%	57.2%	42.8%
Nevada		3		53,174	21,229	31,945		10,716 D	39.9%	60.1%	39.9%	60.1%
New Hampshire		4		235,419	110,127	125,292		15,165 D	46.8%	53.2%	46.8%	53.2%
New Jersey		16		1,972,552	945,475	1,016,808	10,269	71,333 D	47.9%	51.5%	48.2%	51.8%
New Mexico		3		183,258	79,315	103,699	244	24,384 D	43.3%	56.6%	43.3%	56.7%
New York		47		6,301,596	3,027,478	3,251,918	22,200	224,440 D	48.0%	51.6%	48.2%	51.8%
North Carolina		13		822,648	213,633	609,015		395,382 D	26.0%	74.0%	26.0%	74.0%
North Dakota	4			280,775	154,590	124,036	2,149	30,554 R	55.1%	44.2%	55.5%	44.5%
Ohio		26		3,319,912	1,586,773	1,733,139		146,366 D	47.8%	52.2%	47.8%	52.2%
Oklahoma		11		826,212	348,872	474,313	3,027	125,441 D	42.2%	57.4%	42.4%	57.6%
Oregon		5		481,240	219,555	258,415	3,270	38,860 D	45.6%	53.7%	45.9%	54.1%
Pennsylvania		36		4,078,714	1,889,848	2,171,035	17,831	281,187 D	46.3%	53.2%	46.5%	53.5%
Rhode Island		4		321,152	138,654	182,181	317	43,527 D	43.2%	56.7%	43.2%	56.8%
South Carolina		8		99,830	4,360	95,470		91,110 D	4.4%	95.6%	4.4%	95.6%
South Dakota	4			308,427	177,065	131,362		45,703 R	57.4%	42.6%	57.4%	42.6%
Tennessee		11		522,823	169,153	351,601	2,069	182,448 D	32.4%	67.3%	32.5%	67.5%
Texas		23		1,124,437	212,692	909,974	1,771	697,282 D	18.9%	80.9%	18.9%	81.1%
Utah		4		247,819	93,151	154,277	391	61,126 D	37.6%	62.3%	37.6%	62.4%
Vermont	3			143,062	78,371	64,269	422	14,102 R	54.8%	44.9%	54.9%	45.1%
Virginia		11		346,608	109,363	235,961	1,284	126,598 D	31.6%	68.1%	31.7%	68.3%
Washington		8		793,833	322,123	462,145	9,565	140,022 D	40.6%	58.2%	41.1%	58.9%
West Virginia		8		868,076	372,414	495,662		123,248 D	42.9%	57.1%	42.9%	57.1%
Wisconsin		12		1,405,522	679,206	704,821	21,495	25,615 D	48.3%	50.1%	49.1%	50.9%
Wyoming		3		112,240	52,633	59,287	320	6,654 D	46.9%	52.8%	47.0%	53.0%
United States	82	449	—	49,900,418	22,348,480	27,313,041	238,897	4,964,561 D	44.8%	54.7%	45.0%	55.0%

PRESIDENT 1936

The Republican figures in Delaware, Mississippi, and South Carolina include votes cast for two elector tickets. In New York the Democratic figure includes American Labor votes.

The full list of candidates for President and Vice-President was:

27,757,333	Franklin D. Roosevelt and John N. Garner, <u>Democratic</u>.
16,684,231	Alfred M. Landon and Frank Knox, <u>Republican</u>.
892,267	William Lemke and Thomas C. O'Brien, <u>Union</u>.
187,833	Norman Thomas and George A. Nelson, <u>Socialist</u>.
80,171	Earl Browder and James W. Ford, <u>Communist</u>.
37,677	D. Leigh Colvin and Claude A. Watson, <u>Prohibition</u>.
12,829	John W. Aiken and Emil F. Teichert, <u>Socialist Labor</u>.
1,598	William Dudley Pelley and Willard W. Kemp, <u>Christian</u>.

In addition, 824 scattered votes were reported from various states.

UNITED STATES

PRESIDENT 1936

State	Electoral Vote Rep.	Electoral Vote Dem.	Electoral Vote Other	Total Vote	Republican	Democratic	Other	Plurality	Pct Total Vote Rep.	Pct Total Vote Dem.	Pct Major Vote Rep.	Pct Major Vote Dem.
Alabama		11		275,744	35,358	238,196	2,190	202,838 D	12.8%	86.4%	12.9%	87.1%
Alaska												
Arizona		3		124,163	33,433	86,722	4,008	53,289 D	26.9%	69.8%	27.8%	72.2%
Arkansas		9		179,431	32,049	146,765	617	114,716 D	17.9%	81.8%	17.9%	82.1%
California		22		2,638,882	836,431	1,766,836	35,615	930,405 D	31.7%	67.0%	32.1%	67.9%
Colorado		6		488,685	181,267	295,021	12,397	113,754 D	37.1%	60.4%	38.1%	61.9%
Connecticut		8		690,723	278,685	382,129	29,909	103,444 D	40.3%	55.3%	42.2%	57.8%
Delaware		3		127,603	57,236	69,702	665	12,466 D	44.9%	54.6%	45.1%	54.9%
Florida		7		327,436	78,248	249,117	71	170,869 D	23.9%	76.1%	23.9%	76.1%
Georgia		12		293,170	36,943	255,363	864	218,420 D	12.6%	87.1%	12.6%	87.4%
Hawaii												
Idaho		4		199,617	66,256	125,683	7,678	59,427 D	33.2%	63.0%	34.5%	65.5%
Illinois		29		3,956,522	1,570,393	2,282,999	103,130	712,606 D	39.7%	57.7%	40.8%	59.2%
Indiana		14		1,650,897	691,570	934,974	24,353	243,404 D	41.9%	56.6%	42.5%	57.5%
Iowa		11		1,142,737	487,977	621,756	33,004	133,779 D	42.7%	54.4%	44.0%	56.0%
Kansas		9		865,507	397,727	464,520	3,260	66,793 D	46.0%	53.7%	46.1%	53.9%
Kentucky		11		926,214	369,702	541,944	14,568	172,242 D	39.9%	58.5%	40.6%	59.4%
Louisiana		10		329,778	36,791	292,894	93	256,103 D	11.2%	88.8%	11.2%	88.8%
Maine	5			304,240	168,823	126,333	9,084	42,490 R	55.5%	41.5%	57.2%	42.8%
Maryland		8		624,896	231,435	389,612	3,849	158,177 D	37.0%	62.3%	37.3%	62.7%
Massachusetts		17		1,840,357	768,613	942,716	129,028	174,103 D	41.8%	51.2%	44.9%	55.1%
Michigan		19		1,805,098	699,733	1,016,794	88,571	317,061 D	38.8%	56.3%	40.8%	59.2%
Minnesota		11		1,129,975	350,461	698,811	80,703	348,350 D	31.0%	61.8%	33.4%	66.6%
Mississippi		9		162,142	4,467	157,333	342	152,866 D	2.8%	97.0%	2.8%	97.2%
Missouri		15		1,828,635	697,891	1,111,043	19,701	413,152 D	38.2%	60.8%	38.6%	61.4%
Montana		4		230,502	63,598	159,690	7,214	96,092 D	27.6%	69.3%	28.5%	71.5%
Nebraska		7		608,023	247,731	347,445	12,847	99,714 D	40.7%	57.1%	41.6%	58.4%
Nevada		3		43,848	11,923	31,925		20,002 D	27.2%	72.8%	27.2%	72.8%
New Hampshire		4		218,114	104,642	108,460	5,012	3,818 D	48.0%	49.7%	49.1%	50.9%
New Jersey		16		1,820,437	720,322	1,083,850	16,265	363,528 D	39.6%	59.5%	39.9%	60.1%
New Mexico		3		169,135	61,727	106,037	1,371	44,310 D	36.5%	62.7%	36.8%	63.2%
New York		47		5,596,398	2,180,670	3,293,222	122,506	1,112,552 D	39.0%	58.8%	39.8%	60.2%
North Carolina		13		839,475	223,294	616,141	40	392,847 D	26.6%	73.4%	26.6%	73.4%
North Dakota		4		273,716	72,751	163,148	37,817	90,397 D	26.6%	59.6%	30.8%	69.2%
Ohio		26		3,012,660	1,127,855	1,747,140	137,665	619,285 D	37.4%	58.0%	39.2%	60.8%
Oklahoma		11		749,740	245,122	501,069	3,549	255,947 D	32.7%	66.8%	32.8%	67.2%
Oregon		5		414,021	122,706	266,733	24,582	144,027 D	29.6%	64.4%	31.5%	68.5%
Pennsylvania		36		4,138,105	1,690,300	2,353,788	94,017	663,488 D	40.8%	56.9%	41.8%	58.2%
Rhode Island		4		310,278	125,031	164,338	20,909	39,307 D	40.3%	53.0%	43.2%	56.8%
South Carolina		8		115,437	1,646	113,791		112,145 D	1.4%	98.6%	1.4%	98.6%
South Dakota		4		296,452	125,977	160,137	10,338	34,160 D	42.5%	54.0%	44.0%	56.0%
Tennessee		11		477,086	147,055	328,083	1,948	181,028 D	30.8%	68.8%	30.9%	69.1%
Texas		23		849,701	104,661	739,952	5,088	635,291 D	12.3%	87.1%	12.4%	87.6%
Utah		4		216,679	64,555	150,248	1,876	85,693 D	29.8%	69.3%	30.1%	69.9%
Vermont	3			143,689	81,023	62,124	542	18,899 R	56.4%	43.2%	56.6%	43.4%
Virginia		11		334,590	98,336	234,980	1,274	136,644 D	29.4%	70.2%	29.5%	70.5%
Washington		8		692,338	206,892	459,579	25,867	252,687 D	29.9%	66.4%	31.0%	69.0%
West Virginia		8		829,945	325,358	502,582	2,005	177,224 D	39.2%	60.6%	39.3%	60.7%
Wisconsin		12		1,258,560	380,828	802,984	74,748	422,156 D	30.3%	63.8%	32.2%	67.8%
Wyoming		3		103,382	38,739	62,624	2,019	23,885 D	37.5%	60.6%	38.2%	61.8%
United States	8	523	—	45,654,763	16,684,231	27,757,333	1,213,199	11,073,102 D	36.5%	60.8%	37.5%	62.5%

PRESIDENT 1932

The Republican figure in Mississippi includes votes cast for two elector tickets.

The full list of candidates for President and Vice-President was:

22,829,501	Franklin D. Roosevelt and John N. Garner, <u>Democratic</u>.
15,760,684	Herbert C. Hoover and Charles Curtis, <u>Republican</u>.
884,649	Norman Thomas and James H. Maurer, <u>Socialist</u>.
103,253	William Z. Foster and James W. Ford, <u>Communist</u>.
81,872	William D. Upshaw and Frank S. Regan, <u>Prohibition</u>.
53,247	William H. Harvey and Frank Hemenway, <u>Liberty</u>.
34,043	Verne L. Reynolds and John W. Aiken, <u>Socialist Labor</u>.
7,431	Jacob S. Coxey and Julius J. Reiter, <u>Farmer-Labor</u>.
1,645	John Zahnd and Florence Garvin, <u>National</u>.
740	James R. Cox and Victor C. Tisdal, <u>Jobless</u>.

In addition, 157 votes were cast for a Jacksonian elector ticket in Texas and 9 in Arizona for an Arizona Progressive Democratic Ticket. There were 1,528 scattered votes reported from various states.

UNITED STATES

PRESIDENT 1932

State	Electoral Vote Rep.	Dem.	Other	Total Vote	Republican	Democratic	Other	Plurality	Percentage Total Vote Rep.	Dem.	Major Vote Rep.	Dem.
Alabama		11		245,303	34,675	207,910	2,718	173,235 D	14.1%	84.8%	14.3%	85.7%
Alaska												
Arizona		3		118,251	36,104	79,264	2,883	43,160 D	30.5%	67.0%	31.3%	68.7%
Arkansas		9		216,569	27,465	186,829	2,275	159,364 D	12.7%	86.3%	12.8%	87.2%
California		22		2,266,972	847,902	1,324,157	94,913	476,255 D	37.4%	58.4%	39.0%	61.0%
Colorado		6		457,696	189,617	250,877	17,202	61,260 D	41.4%	54.8%	43.0%	57.0%
Connecticut	8			594,183	288,420	281,632	24,131	6,788 R	48.5%	47.4%	50.6%	49.4%
Delaware	3			112,901	57,073	54,319	1,509	2,754 R	50.6%	48.1%	51.2%	48.8%
Florida		7		276,943	69,170	206,307	1,466	137,137 D	25.0%	74.5%	25.1%	74.9%
Georgia		12		255,590	19,863	234,118	1,609	214,255 D	7.8%	91.6%	7.8%	92.2%
Hawaii												
Idaho		4		186,520	71,312	109,479	5,729	38,167 D	38.2%	58.7%	39.4%	60.6%
Illinois		29		3,407,926	1,432,756	1,882,304	92,866	449,548 D	42.0%	55.2%	43.2%	56.8%
Indiana		14		1,576,927	677,184	862,054	37,689	184,870 D	42.9%	54.7%	44.0%	56.0%
Iowa		11		1,036,687	414,433	598,019	24,235	183,586 D	40.0%	57.7%	40.9%	59.1%
Kansas		9		791,978	349,498	424,204	18,276	74,706 D	44.1%	53.6%	45.2%	54.8%
Kentucky		11		983,059	394,716	580,574	7,769	185,858 D	40.2%	59.1%	40.5%	59.5%
Louisiana		10		268,804	18,853	249,418	533	230,565 D	7.0%	92.8%	7.0%	93.0%
Maine	5			298,444	166,631	128,907	2,906	37,724 R	55.8%	43.2%	56.4%	43.6%
Maryland		8		511,054	184,184	314,314	12,556	130,130 D	36.0%	61.5%	36.9%	63.1%
Massachusetts		17		1,580,114	736,959	800,148	43,007	63,189 D	46.6%	50.6%	47.9%	52.1%
Michigan		19		1,664,765	739,894	871,700	53,171	131,806 D	44.4%	52.4%	45.9%	54.1%
Minnesota		11		1,002,843	363,959	600,806	38,078	236,847 D	36.3%	59.9%	37.7%	62.3%
Mississippi		9		146,034	5,180	140,168	686	134,988 D	3.5%	96.0%	3.6%	96.4%
Missouri		15		1,609,894	564,713	1,025,406	19,775	460,693 D	35.1%	63.7%	35.5%	64.5%
Montana		4		216,479	78,078	127,286	11,115	49,208 D	36.1%	58.8%	38.0%	62.0%
Nebraska		7		570,135	201,177	359,082	9,876	157,905 D	35.3%	63.0%	35.9%	64.1%
Nevada		3		41,430	12,674	28,756		16,082 D	30.6%	69.4%	30.6%	69.4%
New Hampshire	4			205,520	103,629	100,680	1,211	2,949 R	50.4%	49.0%	50.7%	49.3%
New Jersey		16		1,630,063	775,684	806,630	47,749	30,946 D	47.6%	49.5%	49.0%	51.0%
New Mexico		3		151,606	54,217	95,089	2,300	40,872 D	35.8%	62.7%	36.3%	63.7%
New York		47		4,688,614	1,937,963	2,534,959	215,692	596,996 D	41.3%	54.1%	43.3%	56.7%
North Carolina		13		711,498	208,344	497,566	5,588	289,222 D	29.3%	69.9%	29.5%	70.5%
North Dakota		4		256,290	71,772	178,350	6,168	106,578 D	28.0%	69.6%	28.7%	71.3%
Ohio		26		2,609,728	1,227,319	1,301,695	80,714	74,376 D	47.0%	49.9%	48.5%	51.5%
Oklahoma		11		704,633	188,165	516,468		328,303 D	26.7%	73.3%	26.7%	73.3%
Oregon		5		368,751	136,019	213,871	18,861	77,852 D	36.9%	58.0%	38.9%	61.1%
Pennsylvania	36			2,859,021	1,453,540	1,295,948	109,533	157,592 R	50.8%	45.3%	52.9%	47.1%
Rhode Island		4		266,170	115,266	146,604	4,300	31,338 D	43.3%	55.1%	44.0%	56.0%
South Carolina		8		104,407	1,978	102,347	82	100,369 D	1.9%	98.0%	1.9%	98.1%
South Dakota		4		288,438	99,212	183,515	5,711	84,303 D	34.4%	63.6%	35.1%	64.9%
Tennessee		11		390,273	126,752	259,473	4,048	132,721 D	32.5%	66.5%	32.8%	67.2%
Texas		23		874,382	98,218	771,109	5,055	672,891 D	11.2%	88.2%	11.3%	88.7%
Utah		4		206,578	84,795	116,750	5,033	31,955 D	41.0%	56.5%	42.1%	57.9%
Vermont	3			136,980	78,984	56,266	1,730	22,718 R	57.7%	41.1%	58.4%	41.6%
Virginia		11		297,942	89,637	203,979	4,326	114,342 D	30.1%	68.5%	30.5%	69.5%
Washington		8		614,814	208,645	353,260	52,909	144,615 D	33.9%	57.5%	37.1%	62.9%
West Virginia		8		743,774	330,731	405,124	7,919	74,393 D	44.5%	54.5%	44.9%	55.1%
Wisconsin		12		1,114,814	347,741	707,410	59,663	359,669 D	31.2%	63.5%	33.0%	67.0%
Wyoming		3		96,962	39,583	54,370	3,009	14,787 D	40.8%	56.1%	42.1%	57.9%
United States	59	472	—	39,758,759	15,760,684	22,829,501	1,168,574	7,068,817 D	39.6%	57.4%	40.8%	59.2%

PRESIDENT 1928

The Republican figures in Georgia, Mississippi, and South Carolina include votes cast for two or three elector tickets; in Pennsylvania the Communist total includes votes cast for two elector tickets.

The full list of candidates for President and Vice-President was:

21,437,277	Herbert C. Hoover and Charles Curtis, <u>Republican</u>.
15,007,698	Alfred E. Smith and Joseph T. Robinson, <u>Democratic</u>.
265,583	Norman Thomas and James H. Maurer, <u>Socialist</u>.
46,896	William Z. Foster and Benjamin Gitlow, <u>Communist</u>.
21,586	Verne L. Reynolds and Jeremiah D. Crowley, <u>Socialist Labor</u>.
20,101	William F. Varney and James A. Edgerton, <u>Prohibition</u>.
6,390	Frank E. Webb and L. R. Tillman, <u>Farmer-Labor</u>.

In addition, 420 scattered votes were reported from various states.

UNITED STATES

PRESIDENT 1928

State	Electoral Vote Rep.	Dem.	Other	Total Vote	Republican	Democratic	Other	Plurality	Percentage Total Vote Rep.	Dem.	Major Vote Rep.	Dem.
Alabama		12		248,981	120,725	127,796	460	7,071 D	48.5%	51.3%	48.6%	51.4%
Alaska												
Arizona	3			91,254	52,533	38,537	184	13,996 R	57.6%	42.2%	57.7%	42.3%
Arkansas		9		197,726	77,784	119,196	746	41,412 D	39.3%	60.3%	39.5%	60.5%
California	13			1,796,656	1,162,323	614,365	19,968	547,958 R	64.7%	34.2%	65.4%	34.6%
Colorado	6			392,242	253,872	133,131	5,239	120,741 R	64.7%	33.9%	65.6%	34.4%
Connecticut	7			553,118	296,641	252,085	4,392	44,556 R	53.6%	45.6%	54.1%	45.9%
Delaware	3			104,602	68,860	35,354	388	33,506 R	65.8%	33.8%	66.1%	33.9%
Florida	6			252,068	145,860	101,764	4,444	44,096 R	57.9%	40.4%	58.9%	41.1%
Georgia		14		231,592	101,800	129,604	188	27,804 D	44.0%	56.0%	44.0%	56.0%
Hawaii												
Idaho	4			151,541	97,322	52,926	1,293	44,396 R	64.2%	34.9%	64.8%	35.2%
Illinois	29			3,107,489	1,769,141	1,313,817	24,531	455,324 R	56.9%	42.3%	57.4%	42.6%
Indiana	15			1,421,314	848,290	562,691	10,333	285,599 R	59.7%	39.6%	60.1%	39.9%
Iowa	13			1,009,189	623,570	379,011	6,608	244,559 R	61.8%	37.6%	62.2%	37.8%
Kansas	10			713,200	513,672	193,003	6,525	320,669 R	72.0%	27.1%	72.7%	27.3%
Kentucky	13			940,521	558,064	381,070	1,387	176,994 R	59.3%	40.5%	59.4%	40.6%
Louisiana		10		215,833	51,160	164,655	18	113,495 D	23.7%	76.3%	23.7%	76.3%
Maine	6			262,170	179,923	81,179	1,068	98,744 R	68.6%	31.0%	68.9%	31.1%
Maryland	8			528,348	301,479	223,626	3,243	77,853 R	57.1%	42.3%	57.4%	42.6%
Massachusetts		18		1,577,823	775,566	792,758	9,499	17,192 D	49.2%	50.2%	49.5%	50.5%
Michigan	15			1,372,082	965,396	396,762	9,924	568,634 R	70.4%	28.9%	70.9%	29.1%
Minnesota	12			970,976	560,977	396,451	13,548	164,526 R	57.8%	40.8%	58.6%	41.4%
Mississippi		10		151,568	27,030	124,538		97,508 D	17.8%	82.2%	17.8%	82.2%
Missouri	18			1,500,845	834,080	662,684	4,081	171,396 R	55.6%	44.2%	55.7%	44.3%
Montana	4			194,108	113,300	78,578	2,230	34,722 R	58.4%	40.5%	59.0%	41.0%
Nebraska	8			547,128	345,745	197,950	3,433	147,795 R	63.2%	36.2%	63.6%	36.4%
Nevada	3			32,417	18,327	14,090		4,237 R	56.5%	43.5%	56.5%	43.5%
New Hampshire	4			196,757	115,404	80,715	638	34,689 R	58.7%	41.0%	58.8%	41.2%
New Jersey	14			1,549,381	926,050	616,517	6,814	309,533 R	59.8%	39.8%	60.0%	40.0%
New Mexico	3			118,077	69,708	48,211	158	21,497 R	59.0%	40.8%	59.1%	40.9%
New York	45			4,405,626	2,193,344	2,089,863	122,419	103,481 R	49.8%	47.4%	51.2%	48.8%
North Carolina	12			635,150	348,923	286,227		62,696 R	54.9%	45.1%	54.9%	45.1%
North Dakota	5			239,845	131,419	106,648	1,778	24,771 R	54.8%	44.5%	55.2%	44.8%
Ohio	24			2,508,346	1,627,546	864,210	16,590	763,336 R	64.9%	34.5%	65.3%	34.7%
Oklahoma	10			618,427	394,046	219,174	5,207	174,872 R	63.7%	35.4%	64.3%	35.7%
Oregon	5			319,942	205,341	109,223	5,378	96,118 R	64.2%	34.1%	65.3%	34.7%
Pennsylvania	38			3,150,612	2,055,382	1,067,586	27,644	987,796 R	65.2%	33.9%	65.8%	34.2%
Rhode Island		5		237,194	117,522	118,973	699	1,451 D	49.5%	50.2%	49.7%	50.3%
South Carolina		9		68,605	5,858	62,700	47	56,842 D	8.5%	91.4%	8.5%	91.5%
South Dakota	5			261,857	157,603	102,660	1,594	54,943 R	60.2%	39.2%	60.6%	39.4%
Tennessee	12			353,192	195,388	157,143	661	38,245 R	55.3%	44.5%	55.4%	44.6%
Texas	20			717,733	372,324	344,542	867	27,782 R	51.9%	48.0%	51.9%	48.1%
Utah	4			176,603	94,618	80,985	1,000	13,633 R	53.6%	45.9%	53.9%	46.1%
Vermont	4			135,191	90,404	44,440	347	45,964 R	66.9%	32.9%	67.0%	33.0%
Virginia	12			305,364	164,609	140,146	609	24,463 R	53.9%	45.9%	54.0%	46.0%
Washington	7			500,840	335,844	156,772	8,224	179,072 R	67.1%	31.3%	68.2%	31.8%
West Virginia	8			642,752	375,551	263,784	3,417	111,767 R	58.4%	41.0%	58.7%	41.3%
Wisconsin	13			1,016,831	544,205	450,259	22,367	93,946 R	53.5%	44.3%	54.7%	45.3%
Wyoming	3			82,835	52,748	29,299	788	23,449 R	63.7%	35.4%	64.3%	35.7%
United States	444	87	—	36,805,951	21,437,277	15,007,698	360,976	6,429,579 R	58.2%	40.8%	58.8%	41.2%

PRESIDENT 1924

Wisconsin's 13 electoral votes were cast for the Progressive nominees, and in eleven other states in the Midwest and West the Progressive candidates ran second. In several states the Progressive total includes votes cast for two or three elector tickets.

The full list of candidates for President and Vice-President was:

15,719,921	Calvin Coolidge and Charles G. Dawes, Republican.
8,386,704	John W. Davis and Charles W. Bryan, Democratic.
4,832,532	Robert M. LaFollette and Burton K. Wheeler, Progressive.
56,292	Herman P. Faris and Marie Caroline Brehm, Prohibition.
34,174	Frank T. Johns and Verne L. Reynolds, Socialist Labor.
33,360	William Z. Foster and Benjamin Gitlow, Communist.
24,340	Gilbert O. Nations and Leander L. Pickett, American.
2,948	William J. Wallace and John C. Lincoln, Commonwealth Land.

In addition, 4,752 scattered votes were reported from various states.

UNITED STATES

PRESIDENT 1924

State	Electoral Vote Rep.	Dem.	Other	Total Vote	Republican	Democratic	Progressive	Other	Plurality	Percentage Total Vote Rep.	Dem.	Prog.
Alabama		12		164,563	42,823	113,138	8,040	562	70,315 D	26.0%	68.8%	4.9%
Alaska												
Arizona	3			73,961	30,516	26,235	17,210		4,281 R	41.3%	35.5%	23.3%
Arkansas		9		138,540	40,583	84,790	13,167		44,207 D	29.3%	61.2%	9.5%
California	13			1,281,778	733,250	105,514	424,649	18,365	308,601 R	57.2%	8.2%	33.1%
Colorado	6			342,261	195,171	75,238	69,946	1,906	119,933 R	57.0%	22.0%	20.4%
Connecticut	7			400,396	246,322	110,184	42,416	1,474	136,138 R	61.5%	27.5%	10.6%
Delaware	3			90,885	52,441	33,445	4,979	20	18,996 R	57.7%	36.8%	5.5%
Florida		6		109,158	30,633	62,083	8,625	7,817	31,450 D	28.1%	56.9%	7.9%
Georgia		14		166,635	30,300	123,262	12,687	386	92,962 D	18.2%	74.0%	7.6%
Hawaii												
Idaho	4			147,690	69,791	23,951	53,948		15,843 R	47.3%	16.2%	36.5%
Illinois	29			2,470,067	1,453,321	576,975	432,027	7,744	876,346 R	58.8%	23.4%	17.5%
Indiana	15			1,272,390	703,042	492,245	71,700	5,403	210,797 R	55.3%	38.7%	5.6%
Iowa	13			976,770	537,458	160,382	274,448	4,482	263,010 R	55.0%	16.4%	28.1%
Kansas	10			662,456	407,671	156,320	98,461	4	251,351 R	61.5%	23.6%	14.9%
Kentucky	13			813,843	396,758	375,593	38,465	3,027	21,165 R	48.8%	46.2%	4.7%
Louisiana		10		121,951	24,670	93,218		4,063	68,548 D	20.2%	76.4%	
Maine	6			192,192	138,440	41,964	11,382	406	96,476 R	72.0%	21.8%	5.9%
Maryland	8			358,630	162,414	148,072	47,157	987	14,342 R	45.3%	41.3%	13.1%
Massachusetts	18			1,129,837	703,476	280,831	141,225	4,305	422,645 R	62.3%	24.9%	12.5%
Michigan	15			1,160,419	874,631	152,359	122,014	11,415	722,272 R	75.4%	13.1%	10.5%
Minnesota	12			822,146	420,759	55,913	339,192	6,282	81,567 R	51.2%	6.8%	41.3%
Mississippi		10		112,442	8,494	100,474	3,474		91,980 D	7.6%	89.4%	3.1%
Missouri	18			1,310,095	648,488	574,962	83,996	2,649	73,526 R	49.5%	43.9%	6.4%
Montana	4			174,425	74,138	33,805	66,124	358	8,014 R	42.5%	19.4%	37.9%
Nebraska	8			463,559	218,985	137,299	105,681	1,594	81,686 R	47.2%	29.6%	22.8%
Nevada	3			26,921	11,243	5,909	9,769		1,474 R	41.8%	21.9%	36.3%
New Hampshire	4			164,769	98,575	57,201	8,993		41,374 R	59.8%	34.7%	5.5%
New Jersey	14			1,088,054	676,277	298,043	109,028	4,706	378,234 R	62.2%	27.4%	10.0%
New Mexico	3			112,830	54,745	48,542	9,543		6,203 R	48.5%	43.0%	8.5%
New York	45			3,263,939	1,820,058	950,796	474,913	18,172	869,262 R	55.8%	29.1%	14.6%
North Carolina		12		481,608	190,754	284,190	6,651	13	93,436 D	39.6%	59.0%	1.4%
North Dakota	5			199,081	94,931	13,858	89,922	370	5,009 R	47.7%	7.0%	45.2%
Ohio	24			2,016,296	1,176,130	477,887	358,008	4,271	698,243 R	58.3%	23.7%	17.8%
Oklahoma		10		527,828	225,756	255,798	46,274		30,042 D	42.8%	48.5%	8.8%
Oregon	5			279,488	142,579	67,589	68,403	917	74,176 R	51.0%	24.2%	24.5%
Pennsylvania	38			2,144,850	1,401,481	409,192	307,567	26,610	992,289 R	65.3%	19.1%	14.3%
Rhode Island	5			210,115	125,286	76,606	7,628	595	48,680 R	59.6%	36.5%	3.6%
South Carolina		9		50,755	1,123	49,008	623	1	47,885 D	2.2%	96.6%	1.2%
South Dakota	5			203,868	101,299	27,214	75,355		25,944 R	49.7%	13.3%	37.0%
Tennessee		12		301,030	130,831	159,339	10,666	194	28,508 D	43.5%	52.9%	3.5%
Texas		20		657,054	130,794	483,381	42,879		352,587 D	19.9%	73.6%	6.5%
Utah	4			156,990	77,327	47,001	32,662		30,326 R	49.3%	29.9%	20.8%
Vermont	4			102,917	80,498	16,124	5,964	331	64,374 R	78.2%	15.7%	5.8%
Virginia		12		223,603	73,328	139,717	10,369	189	66,389 D	32.8%	62.5%	4.6%
Washington	7			421,549	220,224	42,842	150,727	7,756	69,497 R	52.2%	10.2%	35.8%
West Virginia	8			583,662	288,635	257,232	36,723	1,072	31,403 R	49.5%	44.1%	6.3%
Wisconsin			13	840,827	311,614	68,115	453,678	7,420	142,064 P	37.1%	8.1%	54.0%
Wyoming	3			79,900	41,858	12,868	25,174		16,684 R	52.4%	16.1%	31.5%
United States	382	136	13	29,095,023	15,719,921	8,386,704	4,832,532	155,866	7,333,217 R	54.0%	28.8%	16.6%

PRESIDENT 1920

The Republican figure in South Carolina includes votes cast for two elector tickets; the figure in Florida is the vote cast for the one elector candidate who ran on both Republican tickets in that state. In Washington, the total vote for minor party candidates exceeded that for the Democratic candidates, but the Democratic total was greater than that for any one of the minor party nominees.

The full list of candidates for President and Vice-President was:

16,153,115	Warren G. Harding and Calvin Coolidge, <u>Republican</u>.
9,133,092	James M. Cox and Franklin D. Roosevelt, <u>Democratic</u>.
915,490	Eugene V. Debs and Seymour Stedman, <u>Socialist</u>.
265,229	Parley P. Christensen and Max S. Hayes, <u>Farmer-Labor</u>.
189,339	Aaron S. Watkins and D. Leigh Colvin, <u>Prohibition</u>.
48,098	James Ferguson and William J. Hough, <u>American</u>.
30,594	William W. Cox and August Gillhaus, <u>Socialist Labor</u>.
5,833	Robert C. Macauley and Richard C. Barnum, <u>Single Tax</u>.

In addition, 27,309 votes were cast in Texas for a Black-and-Tan Republican elector ticket and 514 scattered votes were reported from various states.

UNITED STATES

PRESIDENT 1920

State	Electoral Vote Rep.	Dem.	Other	Total Vote	Republican	Democratic	Other	Plurality	% Total Vote Rep.	Dem.	% Major Vote Rep.	Dem.
Alabama		12		233,951	74,719	156,064	3,168	81,345 D	31.9%	66.7%	32.4%	67.6%
Alaska												
Arizona	3			66,803	37,016	29,546	241	7,470 R	55.4%	44.2%	55.6%	44.4%
Arkansas		9		183,871	72,316	106,427	5,128	34,111 D	39.3%	57.9%	40.5%	59.5%
California	13			943,463	624,992	229,191	89,280	395,801 R	66.2%	24.3%	73.2%	26.8%
Colorado	6			292,053	173,248	104,936	13,869	68,312 R	59.3%	35.9%	62.3%	37.7%
Connecticut	7			365,518	229,238	120,721	15,559	108,517 R	62.7%	33.0%	65.5%	34.5%
Delaware	3			94,875	52,858	39,911	2,106	12,947 R	55.7%	42.1%	57.0%	43.0%
Florida		6		145,684	44,853	90,515	10,316	45,662 D	30.8%	62.1%	33.1%	66.9%
Georgia		14		149,558	42,981	106,112	465	63,131 D	28.7%	71.0%	28.8%	71.2%
Hawaii												
Idaho	4			138,281	91,351	46,930		44,421 R	66.1%	33.9%	66.1%	33.9%
Illinois	29			2,094,714	1,420,480	534,395	139,839	886,085 R	67.8%	25.5%	72.7%	27.3%
Indiana	15			1,262,974	696,370	511,364	55,240	185,006 R	55.1%	40.5%	57.7%	42.3%
Iowa	13			894,959	634,674	227,804	32,481	406,870 R	70.9%	25.5%	73.6%	26.4%
Kansas	10			570,243	369,268	185,464	15,511	183,804 R	64.8%	32.5%	66.6%	33.4%
Kentucky		13		918,636	452,480	456,497	9,659	4,017 D	49.3%	49.7%	49.8%	50.2%
Louisiana		10		126,397	38,539	87,519	339	48,980 D	30.5%	69.2%	30.6%	69.4%
Maine	6			197,840	136,355	58,961	2,524	77,394 R	68.9%	29.8%	69.8%	30.2%
Maryland	8			428,443	236,117	180,626	11,700	55,491 R	55.1%	42.2%	56.7%	43.3%
Massachusetts	18			993,718	681,153	276,691	35,874	404,462 R	68.5%	27.8%	71.1%	28.9%
Michigan	15			1,048,411	762,865	233,450	52,096	529,415 R	72.8%	22.3%	76.6%	23.4%
Minnesota	12			735,838	519,421	142,994	73,423	376,427 R	70.6%	19.4%	78.4%	21.6%
Mississippi		10		82,351	11,576	69,136	1,639	57,560 D	14.1%	84.0%	14.3%	85.7%
Missouri	18			1,332,140	727,252	574,699	30,189	152,553 R	54.6%	43.1%	55.9%	44.1%
Montana	4			179,006	109,430	57,372	12,204	52,058 R	61.1%	32.1%	65.6%	34.4%
Nebraska	8			382,743	247,498	119,608	15,637	127,890 R	64.7%	31.3%	67.4%	32.6%
Nevada	3			27,194	15,479	9,851	1,864	5,628 R	56.9%	36.2%	61.1%	38.9%
New Hampshire	4			159,092	95,196	62,662	1,234	32,534 R	59.8%	39.4%	60.3%	39.7%
New Jersey	14			910,251	615,333	258,761	36,157	356,572 R	67.6%	28.4%	70.4%	29.6%
New Mexico	3			105,412	57,634	46,668	1,110	10,966 R	54.7%	44.3%	55.3%	44.7%
New York	45			2,898,513	1,871,167	781,238	246,108	1,089,929 R	64.6%	27.0%	70.5%	29.5%
North Carolina		12		538,649	232,819	305,367	463	72,548 D	43.2%	56.7%	43.3%	56.7%
North Dakota	5			205,786	160,082	37,422	8,282	122,660 R	77.8%	18.2%	81.1%	18.9%
Ohio	24			2,021,653	1,182,022	780,037	59,594	401,985 R	58.5%	38.6%	60.2%	39.8%
Oklahoma	10			485,678	243,840	216,122	25,716	27,718 R	50.2%	44.5%	53.0%	47.0%
Oregon	5			238,522	143,592	80,019	14,911	63,573 R	60.2%	33.5%	64.2%	35.8%
Pennsylvania	38			1,851,248	1,218,215	503,202	129,831	715,013 R	65.8%	27.2%	70.8%	29.2%
Rhode Island	5			167,981	107,463	55,062	5,456	52,401 R	64.0%	32.8%	66.1%	33.9%
South Carolina		9		66,808	2,610	64,170	28	61,560 D	3.9%	96.1%	3.9%	96.1%
South Dakota	5			182,237	110,692	35,938	35,607	74,754 R	60.7%	19.7%	75.5%	24.5%
Tennessee	12			428,036	219,229	206,558	2,249	12,671 R	51.2%	48.3%	51.5%	48.5%
Texas		20		486,109	114,658	287,920	83,531	173,262 D	23.6%	59.2%	28.5%	71.5%
Utah	4			145,828	81,555	56,639	7,634	24,916 R	55.9%	38.8%	59.0%	41.0%
Vermont	4			89,961	68,212	20,919	830	47,293 R	75.8%	23.3%	76.5%	23.5%
Virginia		12		231,000	87,456	141,670	1,874	54,214 D	37.9%	61.3%	38.2%	61.8%
Washington	7			398,715	223,137	84,298	91,280	138,839 R	56.0%	21.1%	72.6%	27.4%
West Virginia	8			509,936	282,007	220,785	7,144	61,222 R	55.3%	43.3%	56.1%	43.9%
Wisconsin	13			701,281	498,576	113,422	89,283	385,154 R	71.1%	16.2%	81.5%	18.5%
Wyoming	3			56,253	35,091	17,429	3,733	17,662 R	62.4%	31.0%	66.8%	33.2%
United States	404	127	—	26,768,613	16,153,115	9,133,092	1,482,406	7,020,023 R	60.3%	34.1%	63.9%	36.1%

1992 PRESIDENTIAL PRIMARIES

In 1992 thirty-eight states and the District of Columbia held Presidential primaries, though there was no Republican preference vote in New York.

In some jurisdictions balloting was for delegate slates linked to specific Presidential candidates; in others, electors indicated only a personal preference as to their party's nominee.

The chronologic tables, included at the end of this section, give the major party primary vote in each state for those candidates who received at least 150,000 votes nationwide.

Republican candidates on the ballot in at least one state were Sharon Anderson, Jack J. H. Beemont, Norm Bertasavage, Richard P. Bosa, Emmanuel L. Branch, Patrick J. Buchanan, George Bush, Billy Joe Clegg, Paul B. Conley, Paul C. Daugherty, Georgiana H. Doerschuck, Charles R. Doty, David E. Duke, Oscar A. Erickson, Thomas S. Fabish, Jack Fellure, Maurice Horton, Paul S. Jensen, F. Dean Johnson, Stephen A. Koczak, Vincent A. Latchford, James P. Lennane, Michael S. Levinson, Isabell Masters, John D. Merwin, Stephen D. Michael, Beatrice J. Mooney, Hubert D. Patty, Pat Paulsen, Richard F. Reber, Tennie Rogers, Conrad A. Ryden, Terrance R. Scott, Philip P. Skow, Harold E. Stassen, Jack Trinsey, George A. Zimmermann.

Democratic candidates on the ballot in at least one state were Lawrence A. Agran, Nathan J. Averick, George H. Ballard, John A. Barnes, Don Beamgard, George W. Benns, Frank J. Bona, Edmund G. Brown Jr.,Stephen Burke, John P. Cahill, Bill Clinton, Bob Cunningham, Dean A. Curtis, Barry J. Deutsch, Susan C. Fey, Paul Fisher, Lenora B. Fulani, James B. Gay, Robert F. Hanson, Tom Harkin, Gary Hauptli, Tod H. Hawks, Jim Hayes, Karl J. Hegger, Rufus T. Higginbotham, Gilbert H. Holmes, William Horrigan, Bob Kerrey, Caroline P. Killeen, Ron Kovic, William P. Kreml, Lyndon H. LaRouche, Tom Laughlin, Patrick J. Mahoney, Jeffrey F. Marsh, J. Louis McAlpine, Eugene J. McCarthy, Angus W. McDonald, Fanny R. Z. Monyek, Ralph Nader, Chris Norton, Edward T. O'Donnell, William D. Pawley, Mary Jane Rachner, John D. Rigazio, Ray Rollinson, Cyril E. Sagan, Stephen H. Schwartz, Tom Siekman, Ralph Spelbring, John J. Staradumsky, Louis Stokes, Leonard D. Talbow, Curly Thornton, Paul E. Tsongas, Raymond J. Vanskiver, L. Douglas Wilder, Charles Woods.

ALABAMA JUNE 2

Republican   122,703 Bush; 29,830 Uncommitted; 12,588 Buchanan.

Democratic   307,621 Clinton; 90,863 Uncommitted; 30,626 Brown; 15,247 Woods; 6,542 LaRouche.

ARKANSAS MAY 26

Republican   45,590 Bush; 6,551 Buchanan.

Democratic   342,017 Clinton; 90,710 Uncommitted; 55,234 Brown; 14,656 LaRouche.

CALIFORNIA JUNE 2

Republican   1,587,369 Bush; 568,892 Buchanan; 203 scattered write-ins.

Democratic   1,359,112 Clinton; 1,150,460 Brown; 212,522 Tsongas; 60,635 McCarthy; 33,935 Kerrey; 24,784 Agran; 21,971 LaRouche; 190 scattered write-ins.

American Independent   15,456 Howard Phillips; 13 scattered write-ins.

Libertarian   15,002 Andre V. Marrou; 12 scattered write-ins.

Peace & Freedom   4,586 Lenora B. Fulani; 2,868 Ron Daniels; 1,434 R. Alison Star-Martinez; 6 scattered write-ins.

1992 PRESIDENTIAL PRIMARIES

COLORADO MARCH 3

Republican   132,100 Bush; 58,753 Buchanan; 1,592 Zimmermann; 1,332 Jensen; 719 Scott; 659 Koczak; 535 Rogers.

Democratic   69,073 Brown; 64,470 Clinton; 61,360 Tsongas; 29,572 Kerrey; 5,866 Harkin; 5,356 Noncommitted; 1,051 Woods; 672 Agran; 532 Burke; 488 McCarthy; 328 LaRouche; 279 Hayes; 202 Talbow; 165 Hawks; 76 Shiekman; 59 Marsh; 48 McAlpine; 46 Rollinson.

CONNECTICUT MARCH 24

Republican   66,356 Bush; 21,815 Buchanan; 9,008 Uncommitted; 2,294 Duke.

Democratic   64,472 Brown; 61,698 Clinton; 33,811 Tsongas; 5,430 Uncommitted; 2,688 Agran; 1,919 Harkin; 1,169 Kerrey; 1,036 McCarthy; 896 LaRouche.

FLORIDA MARCH 10

Republican   608,077 Bush; 285,386 Buchanan.

Democratic   570,566 Clinton; 388,124 Tsongas; 139,569 Brown; 13,587 Harkin; 12,011 Kerrey.

GEORGIA MARCH 3

Republican   291,905 Bush; 162,085 Buchanan.

Democratic   259,907 Clinton; 109,148 Tsongas; 36,808 Brown; 22,033 Kerrey; 17,256 Uncommitted; 9,479 Harkin.

IDAHO MAY 26

Republican   73,297 Bush; 27,038 "None of the Names Shown; 15,167 Buchanan.

Democratic   27,004 Clinton; 16,029 "None of the Names Shown; 9,212 Brown; 2,011 LaRouche; 868 Agran.

ILLINOIS MARCH 17

Republican   634,588 Bush; 186,915 Buchanan; 9,637 Horton.

Democratic   776,829 Clinton; 387,891 Tsongas; 220,346 Brown; 67,612 Uncommitted; 30,710 Harkin; 10,916 Kerrey; 6,599 LaRouche; 3,227 Agran.

INDIANA MAY 5

Republican   374,666 Bush; 92,949 Buchanan.

Democratic   301,905 Clinton; 102,379 Brown; 58,215 Tsongas; 14,350 Kerrey.

KANSAS APRIL 7

Republican   132,131 Bush; 35,450 "None of the Names Shown; 31,494 Buchanan; 5,105 Paulsen; 3,837 Duke; 1,303 Masters; 1,105 Skow; 766 Zimmermann; 735 Beemont; 417 Doty; 262 Koczak; 236 Daugherty; 164 Fellure; 85 Rogers; 62 Patty; 44 Fabish.

Democratic   82,145 Clinton; 24,413 Tsongas; 22,159 "None of the Names Shown; 20,811 Brown; 2,215 Kerrey; 1,303 Hauptli; 1,119 Woods; 1,009 Beamgard; 940 Harkin; 892 Barnes; 765 Hawks; 631 LaRouche; 537 Spelbring; 510 Vanskiver; 364 Pawley; 160 Marsh; 147 Agran; 131 McAlpine.

1992 PRESIDENTIAL PRIMARIES

KENTUCKY MAY 26

Republican 75,371 Bush; 25,748 Uncommitted.

Democratic 207,804 Clinton; 103,590 Uncommitted; 30,709 Brown; 18,097 Tsongas; 7,136 Harkin; 3,242 Kerrey.

LOUISIANA MARCH 10

Republican 83,744 Bush; 36,525 Buchanan; 11,955 Duke; 1,186 Paulsen; 1,111 Rogers; 474 Zimmermann; 114 Fabish.

Democratic 267,002 Clinton; 42,508 Tsongas; 25,480 Brown; 15,129 McCarthy; 8,989 Woods; 4,294 Burke; 4,033 Harkin; 3,511 Agran; 3,082 LaRouche; 2,984 Kerrey; 2,120 Marsh; 1,857 Laughlin; 1,469 Hawks; 1,069 Rollinson; 870 McAlpine.

MARYLAND MARCH 3

Republican 168,374 Bush; 71,647 Buchanan.

Democratic 230,490 Tsongas; 189,905 Clinton; 46,500 Brown; 36,155 Uncommitted; 32,899 Harkin; 27,035 Kerrey; 4,259 LaRouche.

MASSACHUSETTS MARCH 10

Republican 176,868 Bush; 74,797 Buchanan; 10,132 No Preference; 5,557 Duke; 2,347 scattered write-ins.

Democratic 526,297 Tsongas; 115,746 Brown; 86,817 Clinton; 32,881 Nader; 12,198 No Preference; 5,409 Kerrey; 3,764 Harkin; 3,127 McCarthy; 2,224 Agran; 2,167 LaRouche; 2,255 scattered write-ins.

Independent 352 Howard Phillips; 269 No Preference; 177 Bo Gritz; 54 Robert J. Smith; 36 Darcy G. Richardson; 35 Erik Thompson; 26 Earl F. Dodge; 24 J. Quinn Brisben; 21 Michael S. Levinson; 391 scattered write-ins.

MICHIGAN MARCH 17

Republican 301,948 Bush; 112,122 Buchanan; 23,809 Uncommitted; 10,688 Duke; 566 scattered write-ins.

Democratic 297,280 Clinton; 151,400 Brown; 97,017 Tsongas; 27,836 Uncommitted; 6,265 Harkin; 3,219 Kerrey; 2,049 LaRouche; 906 scattered write-ins.

MINNESOTA APRIL 7

Republican 84,841 Bush; 32,094 Buchanan; 4,098 Uncommitted; 4,074 Stassen; 300 Anderson; 196 Mooney; 135 Zimmermann; 61 Rogers; 3,558 Ross Perot (write-in); 3,399 scattered write-ins.

Democratic 63,584 Clinton; 62,474 Brown; 43,588 Tsongas; 11,366 Uncommitted; 4,077 Harkin; 3,704 McCarthy; 1,191 Kerrey; 1,042 Agran; 990 Woods; 620 Rachner; 532 LaRouche; 348 Burke; 183 McAlpine; 111 Hawks; 106 Marsh; 105 Averick; 4,250 Ross Perot (write-in); 5,899 scattered write-ins.

MISSISSIPPI MARCH 10

Republican 111,794 Bush; 25,891 Buchanan; 16,426 Duke; 408 Clegg; 189 Rogers.

Democratic 139,893 Clinton; 18,396 Brown; 15,538 Tsongas; 11,796 Uncommitted; 2,509 Harkin; 1,660 Kerrey; 1,394 LaRouche; 171 scattered write-ins.

1992 PRESIDENTIAL PRIMARIES

MONTANA JUNE 2

Republican   65,176 Bush; 15,098 No Preference; 10,701 Buchanan.

Democratic   54,989 Clinton; 28,164 No Preference; 21,704 Brown; 12,614 Tsongas.

NEBRASKA MAY 12

Republican   156,346 Bush; 25,847 Buchanan; 2,808 Duke; 1,313 Zimmermann; 751 Rogers; 5,033 scattered write-ins.

Democratic   68,562 Clinton; 31,673 Brown; 24,714 Uncommitted; 10,707 Tsongas; 4,239 Harkin; 1,520 McCarthy; 1,148 LaRouche; 485 Woods; 280 Agran; 7,259 scattered write-ins.

NEW HAMPSHIRE FEBRUARY 18

Republican   92,233 Bush; 65,087 Buchanan; 1,684 Lennane; 600 Paulsen; 349 Bosa; 223 Merwin; 206 Stassen; 115 Conley; 110 Clegg; 57 Doerschuck; 53 Daugherty; 44 Levinson; 36 Fellure; 32 Latchford; 31 Patty; 31 Zimmermann; 29 Koczak; 25 Fabish; 24 Johnson; 23 Bertasavage; 22 Trinsey; 20 Rogers; 20 Ryden; 16 Erickson; 14 Reber; 13,081 scattered write-ins.

Democratic   55,638 Tsongas; 41,522 Clinton; 18,575 Kerrey; 17,057 Harkin; 13,654 Brown; 3,251 Laughlin; 2,862 Woods; 402 Fulani; 332 Agran; 303 Mahoney; 211 McCarthy; 186 Rigazio; 125 Thornton; 115 LaRouche; 103 Wilder; 93 Killeen; 83 Cahill; 82 Fisher; 65 Bona; 61 Hegger; 53 Horrigan; 43 Curtis; 39 Burke; 39 Holmes; 36 Kovic; 31 Higginbotham; 31 Norton; 29 Monyek; 28 Gay; 26 Deutsch; 26 Sagan; 24 O'Donnell; 23 Shiekman; 17 Schwartz; 11 Benns; 7 Averick; 12,636 scattered write-ins.

Libertarian   3,219 Andre V. Marrou; 168 scattered write-ins.

NEW JERSEY JUNE 2

Republican   240,535 Bush; 46,432 Buchanan; 23,303 Ross Perot (write-in).

Democratic   243,741 Clinton; 79,877 Brown; 45,191 Tsongas; 12,478 Ross Perot (write-in); 7,799 LaRouche; 2,067 Ballard; 1,473 Hanson.

NEW MEXICO JUNE 2

Republican   55,522 Bush; 23,574 Uncommitted; 7,871 Buchanan.

Democratic   95,933 Clinton; 35,269 Uncommitted; 30,705 Brown; 11,315 Tsongas; 3,233 Harkin; 2,573 Agran; 2,415 LaRouche.

NEW YORK APRIL 7

Republican   No Presidential preference vote held.

Democratic   412,349 Clinton; 288,330 Tsongas; 264,278 Brown; 11,535 Harkin; 11,147 Kerrey; 10,733 Agran; 9,354 McCarthy.

NORTH CAROLINA MAY 5

Republican   200,387 Bush; 55,420 Buchanan; 27,764 No Preference.

Democratic   443,498 Clinton; 106,697 No Preference; 71,984 Brown; 57,589 Tsongas; 6,216 Kerrey; 5,891 Harkin.

1992 PRESIDENTIAL PRIMARIES

NORTH DAKOTA JUNE 9

Republican   39,863 Bush; 4,093 Paulsen; 3,852 Ross Perot (write-in).

Democratic   9,516 Ross Perot (write-in); 7,003 LaRouche; 6,641 Woods; 4,866 Shiekman; 4,760 Clinton (write-in).

OHIO JUNE 2

Republican   716,766 Bush; 143,687 Buchanan.

Democratic   638,347 Clinton; 197,449 Brown; 110,773 Tsongas; 29,983 Stokes; 25,395 Harkin; 22,976 Kerrey; 17,412 LaRouche.

OKLAHOMA MARCH 10

Republican   151,612 Bush; 57,933 Buchanan; 5,672 Duke; 1,830 Masters; 674 Rogers.

Democratic   293,266 Clinton; 69,624 Brown; 16,828 Woods; 14,015 Harkin; 13,252 Kerrey; 6,474 LaRouche; 2,670 McAlpine.

OREGON MAY 19

Republican   203,957 Bush; 57,730 Buchanan; 6,667 Duke; 35,805 scattered write-ins.

Democratic   159,802 Clinton; 110,494 Brown; 37,139 Tsongas; 6,714 McCarthy; 3,096 LaRouche; 1,895 Woods; 1,652 Agran; 33,540 scattered write-ins.

PENNSYLVANIA APRIL 28

Republican   774,865 Bush; 233,912 Buchanan.

Democratic   715,031 Clinton; 325,543 Brown; 161,572 Tsongas; 21,534 LaRouche; 21,013 Harkin; 20,802 Kerrey.

RHODE ISLAND MARCH 10

Republican   9,853 Bush; 4,967 Buchanan; 444 Uncommitted; 326 Duke; 46 scattered write-ins.

Democratic   26,825 Tsongas; 10,762 Clinton; 9,541 Brown; 703 Uncommitted; 469 Kerrey; 408 Woods; 319 Harkin; 308 Fey; 300 LaRouche; 235 McCarthy; 168 Staradumsky; 94 Laughlin; 91 Rollinson; 79 Agran; 52 Thornton; 48 Burke; 307 scattered write-ins.

SOUTH CAROLINA MARCH 7

Republican   99,558 Bush; 38,247 Buchanan; 10,553 Duke; 482 Daugherty.

Democratic   73,221 Clinton; 21,338 Tsongas; 7,657 Harkin; 6,961 Brown; 3,640 Uncommitted; 1,369 Cunningham; 854 Woods; 566 Kerrey; 336 Kreml; 268 McDonald; 204 LaRouche.

SOUTH DAKOTA FEBRUARY 25

Republican   30,964 Bush; 13,707 Uncommitted.

Democratic   23,892 Kerrey; 15,023 Harkin; 11,375 Clinton; 5,729 Tsongas; 2,300 Brown; 606 Agran; 441 LaRouche; 137 Wilder.

1992 PRESIDENTIAL PRIMARIES

TENNESSEE MARCH 10

Republican   178,219 Bush; 54,585 Buchanan; 7,709 Duke; 5,022 Uncommitted; 118 scattered write-ins.

Democratic   214,485 Clinton; 61,717 Tsongas; 25,560 Brown; 12,551 Uncommitted; 2,099 Harkin; 1,638 Kerrey; 432 scattered write-ins.

TEXAS MARCH 10

Republican   556,280 Bush; 190,572 Buchanan; 27,936 Uncommitted; 20,255 Duke; 1,349 Zimmermann; 754 Rogers.

Democratic   972,151 Clinton; 285,191 Tsongas; 118,923 Brown; 30,092 Woods; 20,298 Kerrey; 19,617 Harkin; 12,220 LaRouche; 7,876 Benns; 7,674 Higginbotham; 4,924 Hawks; 4,009 McAlpine.

WASHINGTON MAY 19

Republican   86,839 Bush; 25,423 Ross Perot (write-in); 13,273 Buchanan; 2,619 Michael; 1,501 Duke.

Democratic   62,171 Clinton; 34,111 Brown; 28,311 Ross Perot (write-in); 18,981 Tsongas; 1,858 Harkin; 1,489 Kerrey; 1,060 LaRouche.

WEST VIRGINIA MAY 12

Republican   99,994 Bush; 18,067 Buchanan; 6,096 Fellure.

Democratic   227,815 Clinton; 36,505 Brown; 21,271 Tsongas; 9,632 McDonald; 3,152 Kerrey; 3,141 LaRouche; 2,774 Harkin; 1,487 Woods; 1,089 Spelbring.

WISCONSIN APRIL 7

Republican   364,507 Bush; 78,516 Buchanan; 12,867 Duke; 8,725 Uninstructed; 3,819 Stassen; 1,013 Branch; 12,801 scattered write-ins.

Democratic   287,356 Clinton; 266,207 Brown; 168,619 Tsongas; 15,487 Uninstructed; 6,525 McCarthy; 5,395 Harkin; 3,193 Agran; 3,120 LaRouche; 3,044 Kerrey; 13,650 scattered write-ins.

DISTRICT OF COLUMBIA MAY 5

Republican   4,265 Bush; 970 Buchanan.

Democratic   45,716 Clinton; 6,452 Tsongas; 5,292 Uncommitted; 4,444 Brown.

1992 REPUBLICAN PREFERENCE PRIMARIES

Date		State	Total Vote	Buchanan	Bush	Duke	Uncommitted	Other
Feb.	18	New Hampshire	174,165	65,087	92,233	—	—	16,845
	25	South Dakota	44,671	—	30,964	—	13,707	—
March	3	Colorado	195,690	58,753	132,100	—	—	4,837
	3	Georgia	453,990	162,085	291,905	—	—	—
	3	Maryland	240,021	71,647	168,374	—	—	—
	7	South Carolina	148,840	38,247	99,558	10,553	—	482
	10	Florida	893,463	285,386	608,077	—	—	—
	10	Louisiana	135,109	36,525	83,744	11,955	—	2,885
	10	Massachusetts	269,701	74,797	176,868	5,557	10,132	2,347
	10	Mississippi	154,708	25,891	111,794	16,426	—	597
	10	Oklahoma	217,721	57,933	151,612	5,672	—	2,504
	10	Rhode Island	15,636	4,967	9,853	326	444	46
	10	Tennessee	245,653	54,585	178,219	7,709	5,022	118
	10	Texas	797,146	190,572	556,280	20,255	27,936	2,103
	17	Illinois	831,140	186,915	634,588	—	—	9,637
	17	Michigan	449,133	112,122	301,948	10,688	23,809	566
	24	Connecticut	99,473	21,815	66,356	2,294	9,008	
April	7	Kansas	213,196	31,494	132,131	3,837	35,450	10,284
	7	Minnesota	132,756	32,094	84,841	—	4,098	11,723
	7	New York	No Presidential Preference Vote Held					
	7	Wisconsin	482,248	78,516	364,507	12,867	8,725	17,633
	28	Pennsylvania	1,008,777	233,912	774,865	—	—	—
May	5	Dist. of Col.	5,235	970	4,265	—	—	—
	5	Indiana	467,615	92,949	374,666	—	—	—
	5	North Carolina	283,571	55,420	200,387	—	27,764	—
	12	Nebraska	192,098	25,847	156,346	2,808	—	7,097
	12	West Virginia	124,157	18,067	99,994	—	—	6,096
	19	Oregon	304,159	57,730	203,957	6,667	—	35,805
	19	Washington	129,655	13,273	86,839	1,501	—	28,042
	26	Arkansas	52,141	6,551	45,590	—	—	—
	26	Idaho	115,502	15,167	73,297	—	27,038	—
	26	Kentucky	101,119	—	75,371	—	25,748	—
June	2	Alabama	165,121	12,588	122,703	—	29,830	—
	2	California	2,156,464	568,892	1,587,369	—	—	203
	2	Montana	90,975	10,701	65,176	—	15,098	—
	2	New Jersey	310,270	46,432	240,535	—	—	23,303
	2	New Mexico	86,967	7,871	55,522	—	23,574	—
	2	Ohio	860,453	143,687	716,766	—	—	—
	9	North Dakota	47,808	—	39,863	—	—	7,945
		Total	12,696,547	2,899,488	9,199,463	119,115	287,383	191,098

The Uncommitted column above includes votes cast on the following ballot lines: Uncommitted, No Preference, Uninstructed and "None of the Names Shown."

Other vote includes 56,136 Perot(write-in); 10,984 Paulsen; 9,637 Horton; 8,099 Stassen; 6,296 Fellure; 5,660 Zimmermann; 4,180 Rogers; 3,133 Masters; 2,619 Michael; 1,684 Lennane; 1,332 Jensen; 1,105 Skow; 1,013 Branch; 950 Koczak; 771 Daugherty; 735 Beemont; 719 Scott; 518 Clegg; 417 Doty; 349 Bosa; 300 Anderson; 223 Merwin; 196 Mooney; 183 Fabish; 115 Conley; 93 Patty; 57 Doerschuck; 44 Levinson; 32 Latchford; 24 Johnson; 23 Bertasavage; 22 Trinsey; 20 Ryden; 16 Erickson; 14 Reber and 73,399 scattered write-ins.

1992 DEMOCRATIC PREFERENCE PRIMARIES

Date		State	Total Vote	Brown	Clinton	Harkin	Kerrey	Tsongas	Uncommitted	Other
Feb.	18	New Hampshire	167,819	13,654	41,522	17,057	18,575	55,638	—	21,373
	25	South Dakota	59,503	2,300	11,375	15,023	23,892	5,729	—	1,184
March	3	Colorado	239,643	69,073	64,470	5,866	29,572	61,360	5,356	3,946
	3	Georgia	454,631	36,808	259,907	9,479	22,033	109,148	17,256	
	3	Maryland	567,243	46,500	189,905	32,899	27,035	230,490	36,155	4,259
	7	South Carolina	116,414	6,961	73,221	7,657	566	21,338	3,640	3,031
	10	Florida	1,123,857	139,569	570,566	13,587	12,011	388,124	—	—
	10	Louisiana	384,397	25,480	267,002	4,033	2,984	42,508	—	42,390
	10	Massachusetts	792,885	115,746	86,817	3,764	5,409	526,297	12,198	42,654
	10	Mississippi	191,357	18,396	139,893	2,509	1,660	15,538	11,796	1,565
	10	Oklahoma	416,129	69,624	293,266	14,015	13,252	—	—	25,972
	10	Rhode Island	50,709	9,541	10,762	319	469	26,825	703	2,090
	10	Tennessee	318,482	25,560	214,485	2,099	1,638	61,717	12,551	432
	10	Texas	1,482,975	118,923	972,151	19,617	20,298	285,191	—	66,795
	17	Illinois	1,504,130	220,346	776,829	30,710	10,916	387,891	67,612	9,826
	17	Michigan	585,972	151,400	297,280	6,265	3,219	97,017	27,836	2,955
	24	Connecticut	173,119	64,472	61,698	1,919	1,169	33,811	5,430	4,620
April	7	Kansas	160,251	20,811	82,145	940	2,215	24,413	22,159	7,568
	7	Minnesota	204,170	62,474	63,584	4,077	1,191	43,588	11,366	17,890
	7	New York	1,007,726	264,278	412,349	11,535	11,147	288,330	—	20,087
	7	Wisconsin	772,596	266,207	287,356	5,395	3,044	168,619	15,487	26,488
	28	Pennsylvania	1,265,495	325,543	715,031	21,013	20,802	161,572	—	21,534
May	5	Dist. of Col.	61,904	4,444	45,716	—		6,452	5,292	—
	5	Indiana	476,849	102,379	301,905	—	14,350	58,215	—	—
	5	North Carolina	691,875	71,984	443,498	5,891	6,216	57,589	106,697	—
	12	Nebraska	150,587	31,673	68,562	4,239	—	10,707	24,714	10,692
	12	West Virginia	306,866	36,505	227,815	2,774	3,152	21,271	—	15,349
	19	Oregon	354,332	110,494	159,802	—	—	37,139	—	46,897
	19	Washington	147,981	34,111	62,171	1,858	1,489	18,981	—	29,371
	26	Arkansas	502,617	55,234	342,017	—	—	—	90,710	14,656
	26	Idaho	55,124	9,212	27,004	—	—	—	16,029	2,879
	26	Kentucky	370,578	30,709	207,804	7,136	3,242	18,097	103,590	—
June	2	Alabama	450,899	30,626	307,621	—	—	—	90,863	21,789
	2	California	2,863,609	1,150,460	1,359,112	—	33,935	212,522	—	107,580
	2	Montana	117,471	21,704	54,989	—	—	12,614	28,164	—
	2	New Jersey	392,626	79,877	243,741	—	—	45,191	—	23,817
	2	New Mexico	181,443	30,705	95,933	3,233	—	11,315	35,269	4,988
	2	Ohio	1,042,335	197,449	638,347	25,395	22,976	110,773	—	47,395
	9	North Dakota	32,786	—	4,760	—	—	—	—	28,026
		TOTAL	20,239,385	4,071,232	10,482,411	280,304	318,457	3,656,010	750,873	680,098

The Uncommitted column above includes votes cast on the following ballot lines: Uncommitted, Noncommitted, No Preference, Uninstructed and "None of the Names Shown".

Other vote includes 154,599 LaRouche; 108,678 McCarthy; 88,948 Woods; 58,611 Agran; 54,755 Perot (write-ins); 32,881 Nader; 29,983 Stokes; 9,900 McDonald; 7,911 McAlpine; 7,887 Benns; 7,705 Higginbotham; 7,434 Hawks; 5,261 Burke; 5,202 Laughlin; 4,965 Shiekman; 2,445 Marsh; 2,067 Ballard; 1,626 Spelbring; 1,473 Hanson; 1,369 Cunningham; 1,303 Hauptli; 1,206 Rollinson; 1,009 Beamgard; 892 Barnes; 620 Rachner; 510 Vanskiver; 402 Fulani; 364 Pawley; 336 Kreml; 308 Fey; 303 Mahoney; 279 Hayes; 240 Wilder; 202 Talbow; 186 Rigazio; 177 Thornton; 168 Staradumsky; 112 Averick; 93 Killeen; 83 Cahill; 82 Fisher; 65 Bona; 61 Hegger; 53 Horrigan; 43 Curtis; 39 Holmes; 36 Kovic; 31 Norton; 29 Monyek; 28 Gay; 26 Deutsch; 26 Sagan; 24 O'Donnell; 17 Schwartz and 77,045 scattered write-ins.

1988 PRESIDENTIAL PRIMARIES

In 1988 thirty-six states and the District of Columbia held Presidential primaries though there was no Republican voting in New York and no Democratic voting in South Carolina.

In some jurisdictions balloting was for delegate slates linked to specific Presidential candidates; in others, electors indicated only a personal preference as to their party's nominee.

The tables included here give the major party primary vote in each state for those candidates on the ballot in at least twenty states. An asterisk in the table indicates votes written-in for a candidate not on the ballot.

Republican candidates on the ballot in at least one state were George Bush, Paul B. Conley, Robert Dole, Robert F. Drucker, Pierre duPont, Alexander M. Haig, William Horrigan, Jack F. Kemp, Michael S. Levinson, Isabell Masters, Mary Jane Rachner, Pat Robertson and Harold E. Stassen.

Democratic candidates on the ballot in at least one state were Frank Ahern, Douglas Applegate, Bruce Babbitt, Norbert G. Dennerll, Florenzo DiDonato, Charles R. Doty, Michael S. Dukakis, David E. Duke, William J. duPont, Richard A. Gephardt, Albert Gore, Jr., Gary W. Hart, Jesse L. Jackson, Richard B. Kay, William King, Claude R. Kirk, Stephen A. Koczak, Lyndon H. LaRouche, Stanley Lock, Angus W. McDonald, William A. Marra, Anthony R. Martin-Trigona, Edward T. O'Donnell, Conrad W. Roy, Cyril E. Sagan, Paul Simon, Frank L. Thomas, Osie Thorpe, James A. Traficant, A. A. VanPetten, Jennifer Alden Wesner, W. A. Williams and Irwin Zucker.

ALABAMA MARCH 8

Republican   137,807 Bush; 34,733 Dole; 29,772 Robertson; 10,557 Kemp; 392 duPont; 300 Haig.

Democratic   176,764 Jackson; 151,739 Gore; 31,306 Dukakis; 30,214 Gephardt; 7,530 Hart; 3,063 Simon; 2,410 Babbitt; 1,771 Uncommitted; 845 LaRouche.

ARKANSAS MARCH 8

Republican   32,114 Bush, 17,667 Dole; 12,918 Robertson; 3,499 Kemp; 1,402 Uncommitted; 359 duPont; 346 Haig.

Democratic   185,758 Gore; 94,103 Dukakis; 85,003 Jackson; 59,711 Gephardt; 35,553 Uncommitted; 18,630 Hart; 9,020 Simon; 4,805 Duke; 2,614 Babbitt; 2,347 LaRouche.

CALIFORNIA JUNE 7

Republican   1,856,273 Bush; 289,220 Dole; 94,779 Robertson; 115 scattered write-in.

Democratic   1,910,808 Dukakis; 1,102,093 Jackson; 56,645 Gore; 43,771 Simon; 25,417 LaRouche.

American Independent   9,792 James C. Griffin; 5,401 James Gritz; 3 scattered write-in.

Peace & Freedom   2,117 Lenora B. Fulani; 1,222 Shirley Isaacson; 1,042 Larry Holmes; 778 Herb Lewin; 411 Willa Kenoyer; 353 Al Hamburg; 6 scattered write-in.

CONNECTICUT MARCH 29

Republican   73,501 Bush; 21,005 Dole; 3,281 Kemp; 3,193 Uncommitted; 3,191 Robertson.

Democratic   140,291 Dukakis; 68,372 Jackson; 18,501 Gore; 5,761 Hart; 3,140 Simon; 2,370 Babbitt; 1,951 Uncommitted; 1,009 Gephardt.

1988 PRESIDENTIAL PRIMARIES

FLORIDA MARCH 8

Republican 559,820 Bush; 191,197 Dole; 95,826 Robertson; 41,795 Kemp; 6,726 duPont; 5,858 Haig.

Democratic 521,041 Dukakis; 254,912 Jackson; 182,861 Gephardt; 161,165 Gore; 79,088 Undecided; 36,315 Hart; 27,620 Simon; 10,296 Babbitt.

GEORGIA MARCH 8

Republican 215,516 Bush; 94,749 Dole; 65,163 Robertson; 23,409 Kemp; 1,309 duPont; 782 Haig.

Democratic 247,831 Jackson; 201,490 Gore; 97,179 Dukakis; 41,489 Gephardt; 15,852 Hart; 8,388 Simon; 7,276 Uncommitted; 3,247 Babbitt.

IDAHO MAY 24

Republican 55,464 Bush; 6,935 None of the Names Shown; 5,876 Robertson.

Democratic 37,696 Dukakis; 8,066 Jackson; 2,308 "None of the Names Shown"; 1,891 Gore; 1,409 Simon.

ILLINOIS MARCH 15

Republican 469,151 Bush; 309,253 Dole; 59,087 Robertson; 12,687 Kemp; 4,653 duPont; 3,806 Haig.

Democratic 635,219 Simon; 484,233 Jackson; 245,289 Dukakis; 77,265 Gore; 35,108 Gephardt; 12,769 Hart; 6,094 LaRouche; 4,953 Babbitt.

Solidarity 170 Lenora B. Fulani.

INDIANA MAY 3

Republican 351,829 Bush; 42,878 Dole; 28,712 Robertson; 14,236 Kemp.

Democratic 449,495 Dukakis; 145,021 Jackson; 21,865 Gore; 16,777 Gephardt; 12,550 Simon.

KENTUCKY MARCH 8

Republican 72,020 Bush; 27,868 Dole; 13,526 Robertson; 4,020 Kemp; 2,245 Uncommitted; 844 Stassen; 457 duPont; 422 Haig.

Democratic 145,988 Gore; 59,433 Dukakis; 49,667 Jackson; 28,982 Gephardt; 11,798 Hart; 10,465 Uncommitted; 9,393 Simon; 1,290 Babbitt; 681 LaRouche; 537 Martin-Trigona; 487 Kay.

LOUISIANA MARCH 8

Republican 83,687 Bush; 26,295 Robertson; 25,626 Dole; 7,722 Kemp; 853 duPont; 598 Haig.

Democratic 221,532 Jackson; 174,974 Gore; 95,667 Dukakis; 66,434 Gephardt; 26,442 Hart; 23,390 Duke; 5,155 Simon; 3,701 Ahern; 3,076 Babbitt; 1,681 LaRouche; 1,575 Dennerll; 823 Kay.

MARYLAND MARCH 8

Republican 107,026 Bush; 64,987 Dole; 12,860 Robertson; 11,909 Kemp; 2,551 duPont; 1,421 Haig.

Democratic 242,479 Dukakis; 152,642 Jackson; 46,063 Gore; 42,059 Gephardt; 16,513 Simon; 14,948 Uncommitted; 9,732 Hart; 4,750 Babbitt; 2,149 LaRouche.

1988 PRESIDENTIAL PRIMARIES

MASSACHUSETTS MARCH 8

Republican   141,113 Bush; 63,392 Dole; 16,791 Kemp; 10,891 Robertson; 3,522 duPont; 3,416 No Preference; 1,705 Haig; 351 scattered write-in.

Democratic   418,256 Dukakis; 133,141 Jackson; 72,944 Gephardt; 31,631 Gore; 26,176 Simon; 11,866 No Preference; 10,837 Hart; 4,222 Babbitt; 1,971 DiDonato; 998 LaRouche; 1,405 scattered write-in.

MISSISSIPPI MARCH 8

Republican   104,814 Bush; 26,855 Dole; 21,378 Robertson; 5,479 Kemp.

Democratic   160,651 Jackson; 120,364 Gore; 29,941 Dukakis; 19,693 Gephardt; 13,934 Hart; 9,384 Uncommitted; 2,118 Simon; 2,037 Babbitt; 1,295 LaRouche. Data given are for the amended returns.

MISSOURI MARCH 8

Republican   168,812 Bush; 164,394 Dole; 44,705 Robertson; 14,180 Kemp; 5,563 Uncommitted; 1,788 duPont; 858 Haig.

Democratic   305,287 Gephardt; 106,386 Jackson; 61,303 Dukakis; 21,433 Simon; 14,549 Gore; 7,607 Hart; 6,635 Uncommitted; 1,760 Duke; 1,377 Babbitt; 664 LaRouche; 372 Kay; 241 Koczak; 191 Dennerll.

MONTANA JUNE 7

Republican   63,098 Bush; 16,762 Dole; 6,520 No Preference.

Democratic   83,684 Dukakis; 26,908 Jackson; 4,083 No Preference; 3,369 Gephardt; 2,261 Gore; 1,566 Simon.

NEBRASKA MAY 10

Republican   138,784 Bush; 45,572 Dole; 10,334 Robertson; 8,423 Kemp; 936 scattered write-in.

Democratic   106,334 Dukakis; 43,380 Jackson; 4,948 Gephardt; 4,763 Uncommitted; 4,220 Hart; 2,519 Gore; 2,104 Simon; 416 LaRouche; 324 scattered write-in.

New Alliance   10 Lenora B. Fulani.

NEW HAMPSHIRE FEBRUARY 16

Republican   59,290 Bush; 44,797 Dole; 20,114 Kemp; 15,885 duPont; 14,775 Robertson; 481 Haig; 130 Stassen; 107 Conley; 107 Rachner; 83 Drucker; 76 Horrigan; 43 Levinson; 1,756 scattered write-in.

Democratic   44,112 Dukakis; 24,513 Gephardt; 21,094 Simon; 9,615 Jackson; 8,400 Gore; 5,644 Babbitt; 4,888 Hart; 1,349 William J. duPont; 264 Duke; 188 LaRouche; 142 Marra; 122 Roy; 84 DiDonato; 61 Martin-Trigona; 47 Koczak; 36 King; 33 O'Donnell; 33 Sagan; 28 Thomas; 25 Kirk; 22 Zucker; 18 Dennerll; 16 Thorpe; 10 VanPetten; 9 Lock; 2,759 scattered write-in.

NEW JERSEY JUNE 7

Republican   241,033 Bush.

Democratic   414,829 Dukakis; 213,705 Jackson; 18,062 Gore; 2,621 LaRouche; 2,594 Marra; 2,491 Duke.

1988 PRESIDENTIAL PRIMARIES

NEW MEXICO JUNE 7

Republican   69,359 Bush; 9,305 Dole; 5,350 Robertson; 2,569 Uncommitted; 2,161 Haig.

Democratic   114,968 Dukakis; 52,988 Jackson; 6,898 Hart; 4,747 Gore; 3,275 Uncommitted; 2,913 Babbitt; 2,821 Simon.

NEW YORK APRIL 19

Republican   No Presidential primary held.

Democratic   801,457 Dukakis; 585,076 Jackson; 157,559 Gore; 17,011 Simon; 10,258 Uncommitted; 2,672 Gephardt; 1,153 LaRouche.

NORTH CAROLINA MARCH 8

Republican   124,260 Bush; 107,032 Dole; 26,861 Robertson; 11,361 Kemp; 2,797 No Preference; 944 duPont; 546 Haig.

Democratic   235,669 Gore; 224,177 Jackson; 137,993 Dukakis; 37,553 Gephardt; 16,381 Hart; 16,337 No Preference; 8,032 Simon; 3,816 Babbitt.

NORTH DAKOTA JUNE 14

Republican   37,062 Bush; 2,372 Rachner.

Democratic   No candidate names appeared on the ballot. Tallied write-in votes were 2,890 Dukakis; 515 Jackson.

Libertarian   985 Ron Paul.

OHIO MAY 3

Republican   643,907 Bush slate; 94,650 Dole slate; 56,347 Robertson slate. The data given here are for the state-wide at-large slates pledged to the candidates indicated.

Democratic   869,792 Dukakis slates; 378,866 Jackson slates; 29,931 Gore slates; 29,912 Traficant slates; 28,414 Hart slates; 25,068 Applegate slate; 15,524 Simon slates; 6,065 LaRouche slates. The data given here are the sum of the votes cast for delegate slates by Congressional District pledged to the candidates indicated. Only Dukakis and Gore had delegate slates in all twenty-one Congressional Districts.

OKLAHOMA MARCH 8

Republican   78,224 Bush; 73,016 Dole; 44,067 Robertson; 11,439 Kemp; 938 duPont; 715 Haig; 539 Masters.

Democratic   162,584 Gore; 82,596 Gephardt; 66,278 Dukakis; 52,417 Jackson; 14,336 Hart; 6,901 Simon; 2,388 Duke; 1,601 Babbitt; 1,078 LaRouche; 1,068 Koczak; 1,005 Doty; 475 Dennerll.

OREGON MAY 17

Republican   199,938 Bush; 49,128 Dole; 21,212 Robertson; 4,208 scattered write-in.

Democratic   221,048 Dukakis; 148,207 Jackson; 6,772 Gephardt; 5,445 Gore; 4,757 Simon; 1,562 LaRouche; 1,141 scattered write-in.

1988 PRESIDENTIAL PRIMARIES

PENNSYLVANIA APRIL 26

Republican 687,323 Bush; 103,763 Dole; 79,463 Robertson.

Democratic 1,002,480 Dukakis; 411,260 Jackson; 44,542 Gore; 20,473 Hart; 9,692 Simon; 7,546 Wesner; 7,254 Gephardt; 4,443 LaRouche.

RHODE ISLAND MARCH 8

Republican 10,401 Bush; 3,628 Dole; 911 Robertson; 792 Kemp; 174 Uncommitted; 80 duPont; 49 Haig.

Democratic 34,211 Dukakis; 7,445 Jackson; 2,028 Gephardt; 1,939 Gore; 1,395 Simon; 809 Uncommitted; 733 Hart; 469 Babbitt.

SOUTH CAROLINA MARCH 5

Republican 94,738 Bush; 40,265 Dole; 37,261 Robertson; 22,431 Kemp; 316 duPont; 177 Haig; 104 Stassen.

Democratic No Presidential primary held.

SOUTH DAKOTA FEBRUARY 23

Republican 51,599 Dole slate; 18,310 Robertson slate; 17,404 Bush slate; 4,290 Kemp slate; 1,226 Uncommitted slate; 576 duPont slate.

Democratic 31,184 Gephardt; 22,349 Dukakis; 5,993 Gore; 3,992 Simon; 3,875 Hart; 3,867 Jackson; 346 Babbitt.

TENNESSEE MARCH 8

Republican 152,515 Bush; 55,027 Dole; 32,015 Robertson; 10,911 Kemp; 2,340 Uncommitted; 777 Haig; 646 duPont; 21 scattered write-in.

Democratic 416,861 Gore; 119,248 Jackson; 19,348 Dukakis; 8,470 Gephardt; 4,706 Hart; 3,032 Uncommitted; 2,647 Simon; 1,946 Babbitt; 56 scattered write-in.

TEXAS MARCH 8

Republican 648,178 Bush; 155,449 Robertson; 140,795 Dole; 50,586 Kemp; 12,563 Uncommitted; 4,245 duPont; 3,140 Haig.

Democratic 579,713 Dukakis; 433,335 Jackson; 357,764 Gore; 240,158 Gephardt; 82,199 Hart; 34,499 Simon; 11,618 Babbitt; 9,013 LaRouche; 8,808 Duke; 6,238 Williams; 3,700 Dennerll.

VERMONT MARCH 1

Republican 23,565 Bush; 18,655 Dole; 2,452 Robertson; 1,877 Kemp; 808 duPont; 324 Haig; 151 scattered write-in.

Democratic 28,353 Dukakis; 13,044 Jackson; 3,910 Gephardt; 2,620 Simon; 2,055 Hart; 809 scattered write-in.

Liberty
Union 199 Willa Kenoyer; 65 Herb Lewin; 25 scattered write-in.

1988 PRESIDENTIAL PRIMARIES

VIRGINIA MARCH 8

Republican   124,738 Bush; 60,921 Dole; 32,173 Robertson; 10,809 Kemp; 3,675 Uncommitted; 1,229 duPont; 597 Haig.

Democratic   164,709 Jackson; 81,419 Gore; 80,183 Dukakis; 15,935 Gephardt; 7,045 Simon; 6,266 Hart; 6,142 Uncommitted; 2,454 Babbitt; 746 LaRouche.

WEST VIRGINIA MAY 10

Republican   110,705 Bush; 15,600 Dole; 10,417 Robertson; 3,820 Kemp; 1,604 Stassen; 994 Conley.

Democratic   254,289 Dukakis; 45,788 Jackson; 11,573 Gore; 9,284 Hart; 6,130 Gephardt; 3,604 McDonald; 2,280 Simon; 1,978 Babbitt; 1,482 LaRouche; 1,383 Duke; 1,339 Dennerll; 967 Traficant.

WISCONSIN APRIL 5

Republican   295,295 Bush; 28,460 Dole; 24,798 Robertson; 4,915 Kemp; 2,372 Uninstructed Delegation; 1,554 Haig; 1,504 duPont; 396 scattered write-in.

Democratic   483,172 Dukakis; 285,995 Jackson; 176,712 Gore; 48,419 Simon; 7,996 Gephardt; 7,068 Hart; 2,554 Uninstructed Delegation; 2,353 Babbitt; 513 scattered write-in.

DISTRICT OF COLUMBIA MAY 3

Republican   5,890 Bush; 469 Dole; 268 Robertson; 93 scattered write-in.

Democratic   68,840 Jackson; 15,415 Dukakis; 769 Simon; 648 Gore; 300 Gephardt; 80 Thorpe.

1988 REPUBLICAN PREFERENCE PRIMARIES

Date		State	Total Vote	Bush	Dole	duPont	Haig	Kemp	Robertson	Other
Feb.	16	New Hampshire	157,644	59,290	44,797	15,885	481	20,114	14,775	2,302
	23	South Dakota	93,405	17,404	51,599	576		4,290	18,310	1,226
Mar.	1	Vermont	47,832	23,565	18,655	808	324	1,877	2,452	151
	5	South Carolina	195,292	94,738	40,265	316	177	22,431	37,261	104
	8	Alabama	213,561	137,807	34,733	392	300	10,557	29,772	
	8	Arkansas	68,305	32,114	17,667	359	346	3,499	12,918	1,402
	8	Florida	901,222	559,820	191,197	6,726	5,858	41,795	95,826	
	8	Georgia	400,928	215,516	94,749	1,309	782	23,409	65,163	
	8	Kentucky	121,402	72,020	27,868	457	422	4,020	13,526	3,089
	8	Louisiana	144,781	83,687	25,626	853	598	7,722	26,295	
	8	Maryland	200,754	107,026	64,987	2,551	1,421	11,909	12,860	
	8	Massachusetts	241,181	141,113	63,392	3,522	1,705	16,791	10,891	3,767
	8	Mississippi	158,526	104,814	26,855			5,479	21,378	
	8	Missouri	400,300	168,812	164,394	1,788	858	14,180	44,705	5,563
	8	North Carolina	273,801	124,260	107,032	944	546	11,361	26,861	2,797
	8	Oklahoma	208,938	78,224	73,016	938	715	11,439	44,067	539
	8	Rhode Island	16,035	10,401	3,628	80	49	792	911	174
	8	Tennessee	254,252	152,515	55,027	646	777	10,911	32,015	2,361
	8	Texas	1,014,956	648,178	140,795	4,245	3,140	50,586	155,449	12,563
	8	Virginia	234,142	124,738	60,921	1,229	597	10,809	32,173	3,675
	15	Illinois	858,637	469,151	309,253	4,653	3,806	12,687	59,087	
	29	Connecticut	104,171	73,501	21,005			3,281	3,191	3,193
April	5	Wisconsin	359,294	295,295	28,460	1,504	1,554	4,915	24,798	2,768
	19	New York	No Primary held							
	26	Pennsylvania	870,549	687,323	103,763				79,463	
May	3	Indiana	437,655	351,829	42,878			14,236	28,712	
	3	Ohio	794,904	643,907	94,650				56,347	
	3	District of Columbia	6,720	5,890	469				268	93
	10	Nebraska	204,049	138,784	45,572			8,423	10,334	936
	10	West Virginia	143,140	110,705	15,600			3,820	10,417	2,598
	17	Oregon	274,486	199,938	49,128				21,212	4,208
	24	Idaho	68,275	55,464					5,876	6,935
June	7	California	2,240,387	1,856,273	289,220				94,779	115
	7	Montana	86,380	63,098	16,762					6,520
	7	New Jersey	241,033	241,033						
	7	New Mexico	88,744	69,359	9,305		2,161		5,350	2,569
	14	North Dakota	39,434	37,062						2,372
			12,165,115	8,254,654	2,333,268	49,781	26,617	331,333	1,097,442	72,020

Other vote includes 34,950 Uncommitted; 12,733 No Preference; 6,935 "None of the Names Shown"; 2,682 Stassen; 2,479 Rachner; 2,372 Uninstructed Delegation; 1,101 Conley; 539 Masters; 83 Drucker; 76 Horrigan; 43 Levinson; 8,027 scattered.

1988 DEMOCRATIC PREFERENCE PRIMARIES

Date		State	Total Vote	Babbitt	Dukakis	Gephardt	Gore	Hart	Jackson	LaRouche	Simon	Other
Feb.	16	New Hampshire	123,512	5,644	44,112	24,513	8,400	4,888	9,615	188	21,094	5,058
	23	South Dakota	71,606	346	22,349	31,184	5,993	3,875	3,867		3,992	
Mar.	1	Vermont	50,791		28,353	3,910		2,055	13,044		2,620	809
	5	South Carolina	No Primary held									
	8	Alabama	405,642	2,410	31,306	30,214	151,739	7,530	176,764	845	3,063	1,771
	8	Arkansas	497,544	2,614	94,103	59,711	185,758	18,630	85,003	2,347	9,020	40,358
	8	Florida	1,273,298	10,296	521,041	182,861	161,165	36,315	254,912		27,620	79,088
	8	Georgia	622,752	3,247	97,179	41,489	201,490	15,852	247,831		8,388	7,276
	8	Kentucky	318,721	1,290	59,433	28,982	145,988	11,798	49,667	681	9,393	11,489
	8	Louisiana	624,450	3,076	95,667	66,434	174,974	26,442	221,532	1,681	5,155	29,489
	8	Maryland	531,335	4,750	242,479	42,059	46,063	9,732	152,642	2,149	16,513	14,948
	8	Massachusetts	713,447	4,222	418,256	72,944	31,631	10,837	133,141	998	26,176	15,242
	8	Mississippi	359,417	2,037	29,941	19,693	120,364	13,934	160,651	1,295	2,118	9,384
	8	Missouri	527,805	1,377	61,303	305,287	14,549	7,607	106,386	664	21,433	9,199
	8	North Carolina	679,958	3,816	137,993	37,553	235,669	16,381	224,177		8,032	16,337
	8	Oklahoma	392,727	1,601	66,278	82,596	162,584	14,336	52,417	1,078	6,901	4,936
	8	Rhode Island	49,029	469	34,211	2,028	1,939	733	7,445		1,395	809
	8	Tennessee	576,314	1,946	19,348	8,470	416,861	4,706	119,248		2,647	3,088
	8	Texas	1,767,045	11,618	579,713	240,158	357,764	82,199	433,335	9,013	34,499	18,746
	8	Virginia	364,899	2,454	80,183	15,935	81,419	6,266	164,709	746	7,045˙	6,142
	15	Illinois	1,500,930	4,953	245,289	35,108	77,265	12,769	484,233	6,094	635,219	
	29	Connecticut	241,395	2,370	140,291	1,009	18,501	5,761	68,372		3,140	1,951
April	5	Wisconsin	1,014,782	2,353	483,172	7,996	176,712	7,068	285,995		48,419	3,067
	19	New York	1,575,186		801,457	2,672	157,559		585,076	1,153	17,011	10,258
	26	Pennsylvania	1,507,690		1,002,480	7,254	44,542	20,473	411,260	4,443	9,692	7,546
May	3	Indiana	645,708		449,495	16,777	21,865		145,021		12,550	
	3	Ohio	1,383,572		869,792		29,931	28,414	378,866	6,065	15,524	54,980
	3	District of Columbia	86,052		15,415	300	648		68,840		769	80
	10	Nebraska	169,008		106,334	4,948	2,519	4,220	43,380	416	2,104	5,087
	10	West Virginia	340,097	1,978	254,289	6,130	11,573	9,284	45,788	1,482	2,280	7,293
	17	Oregon	388,932		221,048	6,772	5,445		148,207	1,562	4,757	1,141
	24	Idaho	51,370		37,696		1,891		8,066		1,409	2,308
June	7	California	3,138,734		1,910,808		56,645		1,102,093	25,417	43,771	
	7	Montana	121,871		83,684	3,369	2,261		26,908		1,566	4,083
	7	New Jersey	654,302		414,829		18,062		213,705	2,621		5,085
	7	New Mexico	188,610	2,913	114,968		4,747	6,898	52,988		2,821	3,275
	14	North Dakota	3,405		2,890				515			
			22,961,936	77,780	9,817,185	1,388,356	3,134,516	389,003	6,685,699	70,938	1,018,136	380,323

Other vote includes 116,262 Uncommitted; 79,088 Undecided; 45,289 Duke; 32,286 No Preference; 30,879 Traficant; 25,068 Applegate; 7,298 Dennerll; 7,546 Wesner; 6,238 Williams; 3,701 Ahern; 3,604 McDonald; 2,736 Marra; 2,554 Uninstructed Delegation; 2,308 "None of the Names Shown"; 2,055 DiDonato; 1,682 Kay; 1,356 Koczak; 1,349 duPont; 1,005 Doty; 598 Martin-Trigona; 122 Roy; 96 Thorpe; 36 King; 33 O'Donnell; 33 Sagan; 28 Thomas; 25 Kirk; 22 Zucker; 10 VanPetter; 9 Lock; 7,007 scattered.

1984 REPUBLICAN PREFERENCE PRIMARIES

Date		State	Total Vote	Reagan	Other
Feb.	28	New Hampshire	75,570	65,033	10,537
Mar.	6	Vermont	33,643	33,218	425
	13	Alabama	No Primary Held		
	13	Florida	344,150	344,150	—
	13	Georgia	50,793	50,793	—
	13	Massachusetts	65,937	58,996	6,941
	13	Rhode Island	2,235	2,028	207
	20	Illinois	595,078	594,742	336
	27	Connecticut	No Primary Held		
April	3	New York	No Primary Held		
	3	Wisconsin	294,813	280,608	14,205
	10	Pennsylvania	621,206	616,916	4,290
May	1	District of Columbia	5,692	5,692	—
	1	Tennessee	82,921	75,367	7,554
	5	Louisiana	16,687	14,964	1,723
	5	Texas	319,839	308,713	11,126
	8	Indiana	428,559	428,559	—
	8	Maryland	73,663	73,663	—
	8	North Carolina	No Primary Held		
	8	Ohio	658,169	658,169	—
	15	Nebraksa	146,648	145,245	1,403
	15	Oregon	243,346	238,594	4,752
	22	Idaho	105,687	97,450	8,237
June	5	California	1,874,975	1,874,897	78
	5	Montana	71,887	66,432	5,455
	5	New Jersey	240,054	240,054	—
	5	New Mexico	42,994	40,805	2,189
	5	South Dakota	No Primary Held		
	5	West Virginia	136,996	125,790	11,206
	12	North Dakota	44,109	44,109	
			6,575,651	6,484,987	90,664

Other vote includes 22,791 Uncommitted; 14,047 "Ronald Reagan No"; 12,749 Stassen; 10,383 No Preference; 8,237 "None of the Names Shown"; 360 Kelley; 252 Arnold; 202 Fernandez; 21,643 scattered.

1984 DEMOCRATIC PREFERENCE PRIMARIES

Date		State	Total Vote	Glenn	Hart	Jackson	LaRouche	McGovern	Mondale	Other
Feb.	28	New Hampshire	101,131	12,088	37,702	5,311	—	5,217	28,173	12,640
Mar.	6	Vermont	74,059	—	51,873	5,761	—	—	14,834	1,591
	13	Alabama	428,283	89,286	88,465	83,787	—	—	148,165	18,580
	13	Florida	1,182,190	128,209	463,799	144,263	—	17,614	394,350	33,955
	13	Georgia	684,541	122,744	186,903	143,730	—	11,321	208,588	11,255
	13	Massachusetts	630,962	45,456	245,943	31,824	—	134,341	160,893	12,505
	13	Rhode Island	44,511	2,249	20,011	3,875	—	2,146	15,338	892
	20	Illinois	1,659,425	19,800	584,579	348,843	—	25,336	670,951	9,916
	27	Connecticut	220,842	955	116,286	26,395	—	2,426	64,230	10,550
April	3	New York	1,387,950	15,941	380,564	355,541	—	4,547	621,581	9,776
	3	Wisconsin	635,768	6,398	282,435	62,524	—	10,166	261,374	12,871
	10	Pennsylvania	1,656,294	22,605	551,335	264,463	19,180	13,139	747,267	38,305
May	1	District of Columbia	102,731	—	7,305	69,106	—	—	26,320	—
	1	Tennessee	322,063	4,198	93,710	81,418	—	3,824	132,201	6,712
	5	Louisiana	318,810	—	79,593	136,707	4,970	3,158	71,162	23,220
	5	Texas	No Primary held							
	8	Indiana	716,955	16,046	299,491	98,190	—	—	293,413	9,815
	8	Maryland	506,886	6,238	123,365	129,387	7,836	5,796	215,222	19,042
	8	North Carolina	960,857	17,659	289,877	243,945	—	10,149	342,324	56,903
	8	Ohio	1,447,236	—	608,528	237,133	4,336	8,991	583,595	4,653
	15	Nebraska	148,855	—	86,582	13,495	1,227	1,561	39,635	6,355
	15	Oregon	399,679	10,831	233,638	37,106	5,943	—	110,374	1,787
	22	Idaho	54,722	—	31,737	3,104	1,196	—	16,460	2,225
June	5	California	2,970,903	96,770	1,155,499	546,693	52,647	69,926	1,049,342	26
	5	Montana	34,214	—	3,080*	388*	—	—	2,026*	28,720
	5	New Jersey	676,561	—	200,948	159,788	10,309	—	305,516	—
	5	New Mexico	187,403	—	87,610	22,168	3,330	5,143	67,675	1,477
	5	South Dakota	52,561	—	26,641	2,738	1,383	—	20,495	1,304
	5	West Virginia	369,245	—	137,866	24,697	7,274	—	198,776	632
	12	North Dakota	33,555	—	28,603	—	4,018	—	934	—
			18,009,192	617,473	6,503,968	3,282,380	123,649	334,801	6,811,214	335,707

Other vote includes 77,697 No Preference; 59,254 Uncommitted; 52,759 Askew; 51,437 Cranston; 33,684 Hollings; 9,815 Brewster; 9,261 "None of the Names Shown"; 8,014 Griser; 7,957 Willis; 4,847 Williams; 2,699 Kay; 1,855 Koczak; 632 Timinski; 132 Buchanan; 127 Beckman; 74 O'Donnell; 34 King; 25 Kreml; 24 Bagley; 24 Kirk; 21 Rudnicki; 20 Clendenan; 20 Sagan; 19 Caplette; 15,276 scattered.

1980 REPUBLICAN PREFERENCE PRIMARIES

Date		State	Total Vote	Anderson	Baker	Bush	Connally	Crane	Reagan	Other
Feb.	26	New Hampshire	147,157	14,458	18,943	33,443	2,239	2,618	72,983	2,473
Mar.	4	Massachusetts	400,826	122,987	19,366	124,365	4,714	4,669	115,334	9,391
	4	Vermont	65,611	19,030	8,055	14,226	884	1,238	19,720	2,458
	8	South Carolina	145,501	—	773	21,569	43,113	—	79,549	497
	11	Alabama	211,353	—	1,963	54,730	1,077	5,099	147,352	1,132
	11	Florida	614,995	56,636	6,345	185,996	4,958	12,000	345,699	3,361
	11	Georgia	200,171	16,853	1,571	25,293	2,388	6,308	146,500	1,258
	18	Illinois	1,130,081	415,193	7,051	124,057	4,548	24,865	547,355	7,012
	25	Connecticut	182,284	40,354	2,446	70,367	598	1,887	61,735	4,897
	25	New York	No Primary Held							
April	1	Kansas	285,398	51,924	3,603	35,838	2,067	1,367	179,739	10,860
	1	Wisconsin	907,853	248,623	3,298	276,164	2,312	2,951	364,898	9,607
	5	Louisiana	41,683	—	—	7,818	—	—	31,212	2,653
	22	Pennsylvania	1,241,411	26,890	30,846	626,759	10,656	—	527,916	18,344
May	3	Texas	526,769	—	—	249,819	—	—	268,798	8,152
	6	Indiana	568,313	56,342	—	92,955	—	—	419,016	—
	6	North Carolina	168,391	8,542	2,543	36,631	1,107	547	113,854	5,167
	6	Tennessee	195,210	8,722	—	35,274	—	1,574	144,625	5,015
	6	District of Columbia	7,529	2,025	—	4,973	—	270	—	261
	13	Maryland	167,303	16,244	—	68,389	—	2,113	80,557	—
	13	Nebraska	205,203	11,879	—	31,380	—	1,062	155,995	4,887
	20	Michigan	595,176	48,947	—	341,998	—	—	189,184	15,047
	20	Oregon	315,366	32,118	—	109,210	—	2,324	170,449	1,265
	27	Arkansas	No Primary Held							
	27	Idaho	134,879	13,130	5,416	—	—	1,024	111,868	3,441
	27	Kentucky	94,795	4,791	—	6,861	—	—	78,072	5,071
	27	Nevada	47,395	—	—	3,078	—	—	39,352	4,965
June	3	California	2,564,072	349,315	—	125,113	—	21,465	2,057,923	10,256
	3	Mississippi	25,751	—	—	2,105	—	—	23,028	618
	3	Montana	79,423	—	—	7,665	—	—	68,744	3,014
	3	New Jersey	277,977	—	—	47,447	—	—	225,959	4,571
	3	New Mexico	59,546	7,171	—	5,892	—	4,412	37,982	4,089
	3	Ohio	856,773	—	—	164,485	—	—	692,288	—
	3	Rhode Island	5,335	—	—	993	—	—	3,839	503
	3	South Dakota	82,905	—	—	3,691	—	—	72,861	6,353
	3	West Virginia	138,016	—	—	19,509	—	—	115,407	3,100
			12,690,451	1,572,174	112,219	2,958,093	80,661	97,793	7,709,793	159,718

Other vote includes 38,708 Uncommitted; 24,753 Stassen; 23,423 Fernandez; 15,161 No Preference; 9,321 "None of the Names Shown"; 7,298 Dole; 4,965 "None of These Candidates"; 4,357 Jacobson; 3,757 Kelley; 1,063 Yeager; 483 Carris; 355 Belluso; 311 Carlson; 244 Badgley; 67 Pickett; 25,452 scattered.

1980 DEMOCRATIC PREFERENCE PRIMARIES

Date		State	Total Vote	Brown	Carter	Kennedy	LaRouche	Other
Feb.	26	New Hampshire	111,930	10,743	52,692	41,745	2,326	4,424
Mar.	4	Massachusetts	907,323	31,498	260,401	590,393	—	25,031
	4	Vermont	39,703	—	29,015	10,135	—	553
	8	South Carolina	No Primary Held					
	11	Alabama	237,464	9,529	193,734	31,382	—	2,819
	11	Florida	1,098,003	53,474	666,321	254,727	—	123,481
	11	Georgia	384,780	7,255	338,772	32,315	513	5,925
	18	Illinois	1,201,067	39,168	780,787	359,875	19,192	2,045
	25	Connecticut	210,275	5,386	87,207	98,662	5,617	13,403
	25	New York	989,062	—	406,305	582,757	—	—
April	1	Kansas	193,918	9,434	109,807	61,318	—	13,359
	1	Wisconsin	629,619	74,496	353,662	189,520	6,896	5,045
	5	Louisiana	358,741	16,774	199,956	80,797	—	61,214
	22	Pennsylvania	1,613,551	37,669	732,332	736,854	—	106,696
May	3	Texas	1,377,354	35,585	770,390	314,129	—	257,250
	6	Indiana	589,441	—	398,949	190,492	—	—
	6	North Carolina	737,262	21,420	516,778	130,684	—	68,380
	6	Tennessee	294,680	5,612	221,658	53,258	925	13,227
	6	District of Columbia	64,150	—	23,697	39,561	892	—
	13	Maryland	477,090	14,313	226,528	181,091	4,388	50,770
	13	Nebraska	153,881	5,478	72,120	57,826	1,169	17,288
	20	Michigan	78,424	23,043	—	—	8,948	46,433
	20	Oregon	368,322	34,409	208,693	114,651	—	10,569
	27	Arkansas	448,290	—	269,375	78,542	—	100,373
	27	Idaho	50,482	2,078	31,383	11,087	—	5,934
	27	Kentucky	240,331	—	160,819	55,167	—	24,345
	27	Nevada	66,948	—	25,159	19,296	—	22,493
June	3	California	3,363,969	135,962	1,266,276	1,507,142	71,779	382,810
	3	Mississippi	No Primary Held					
	3	Montana	130,059	—	66,922	47,671	—	15,466
	3	New Jersey	560,908	—	212,387	315,109	13,913	19,499
	3	New Mexico	159,364	—	66,621	73,721	4,798	14,224
	3	Ohio	1,186,410	—	605,744	523,874	35,268	21,524
	3	Rhode Island	38,327	310	9,907	26,179	1,160	771
	3	South Dakota	68,763	—	31,251	33,418	—	4,094
	3	West Virginia	317,934	—	197,687	120,247	—	—
			18,747,825	573,636	9,593,335	6,963,625	177,784	1,439,445

Other vote includes 950,378 Uncommitted; 301,695 No Preference; 48,061 Kay; 48,032 Finch; 22,493 "None of These Candidates"; 13,857 "None of the Names Shown"; 4,002 Maddox; 2,255 Reaux; 609 Nuckols; 571 Ahern; 364 Rollinson; 47,128 Scattered.

1976 REPUBLICAN PREFERENCE PRIMARIES

Date		State	Total Vote	Ford	Reagan	Other
February	24	New Hampshire	111,674	55,156	53,569	2,949
March	2	Massachusetts	188,449	115,375	63,555	9,519
	2	Vermont	32,157	27,014	4,892	251
	9	Florida	609,819	321,982	287,837	—
	16	Illinois	775,893	456,750	311,295	7,848
	23	North Carolina	193,727	88,897	101,468	3,362
April	6	Wisconsin	591,812	326,869	262,126	2,817
	27	Pennsylvania	796,660	733,472	40,510	22,678
May	4	District of Columbia	No Primary			
	4	Georgia	188,472	59,801	128,671	—
	4	Indiana	631,292	307,513	323,779	—
	11	Nebraska	208,414	94,542	113,493	379
	11	West Virginia	155,692	88,386	67,306	—
	18	Maryland	165,971	96,291	69,680	—
	18	Michigan	1,062,814	690,180	364,052	8,582
	25	Arkansas	32,541	11,430	20,628	483
	25	Idaho	89,793	22,323	66,743	727
	25	Kentucky	133,528	67,976	62,683	2,869
	25	Nevada	47,749	13,747	31,637	2,365
	25	Oregon	298,535	150,181	136,691	11,663
	25	Tennessee	242,535	120,685	118,997	2,853
June	1	Montana	89,779	31,100	56,683	1,996
	1	Rhode Island	14,352	9,365	4,480	507
	1	South Dakota	84,077	36,976	43,068	4,033
	8	California	2,450,511	845,655	1,604,836	20
	8	New Jersey	242,122	242,122	—	—
	8	Ohio	935,757	516,111	419,646	—
			10,374,125	5,529,899	4,758,325	85,901

Other vote includes 7,582 Daly; 1,088 Klein; 42,514 scattered write-ins; 15,391 No Preference; 14,727 Uncommitted; 2,365 "None of These Candidates"; 2,234 "None of the Names Shown".

1976 DEMOCRATIC PREFERENCE PRIMARIES

Date	State	Total Vote	Bayh	Brown	Byrd	Carter	Church	Harris	Jackson	McCormack	Shriver	Udall	Wallace	Other
February 24	New Hampshire	82,381	12,510	—	—	23,373	—	8,863	1,857	1,007	6,743	18,710	1,061	8,257
March 2	Massachusetts	735,821	34,963	—	—	101,948	—	55,701	164,393	25,772	53,252	130,440	123,112	46,240
March 2	Vermont	38,714	—	—	—	16,335	—	4,893	—	3,324	10,699	—	—	3,463
March 9	Florida	1,300,330	8,750	—	5,042	448,844	4,906	5,397	310,944	7,595	7,084	27,235	396,820	77,713
March 16	Illinois	1,311,914	—	—	—	630,915	—	98,862	—	—	214,024	—	361,798	6,315
March 23	North Carolina	604,832	—	—	—	324,437	—	5,923	25,749	—	—	14,032	210,166	24,525
April 6	Wisconsin	740,528	1,255	—	—	271,220	—	8,185	47,605	26,982	5,097	263,771	92,460	23,953
April 27	Pennsylvania	1,385,042	15,320	—	—	511,905	—	13,067	340,340	38,800	—	259,166	155,902	50,542
May 4	District of Columbia	33,291	—	—	—	10,521	—	461	—	—	—	6,999	—	15,310
May 4	Georgia	502,471	824	—	3,628	419,272	2,477	699	3,358	635	1,378	9,755	57,594	2,851
May 4	Indiana	614,389	—	—	—	417,480	—	—	72,080	31,708	—	—	93,121	—
May 11	Nebraska	175,013	407	—	—	65,833	67,297	811	2,642	6,033	384	4,688	5,567	21,351
May 11	West Virginia	372,577	—	—	331,639	—	—	—	—	—	—	—	40,938	—
May 18	Maryland	591,746	—	286,672	—	219,404	—	6,841	13,956	7,907	—	32,790	24,176	—
May 18	Michigan	708,666	—	—	—	307,559	—	4,081	10,332	7,623	5,738	305,134	49,204	18,995
May 25	Arkansas	501,800	—	—	—	314,306	—	—	9,554	—	—	37,783	83,005	57,152
May 25	Idaho	74,405	—	1,453	—	8,818	58,570	319	485	—	—	981	1,115	2,664
May 25	Kentucky	306,006	—	—	—	181,690	—	—	8,186	17,061	—	33,262	51,540	14,267
May 25	Nevada	75,242	—	39,671	—	17,567	6,778	—	1,896	—	—	2,237	2,490	4,603
May 25	Oregon	432,632	743	106,812	—	115,310	145,394	1,344	5,298	3,753	—	11,747	5,797	36,434
May 25	Tennessee	334,078	—	1,556	—	259,243	8,026	1,628	5,672	1,782	—	12,420	36,495	7,256
June 1	Montana	106,841	—	—	—	26,329	63,448	—	2,856	—	—	6,708	3,680	3,820
June 1	Rhode Island	60,348	247	—	—	18,237	16,423	—	756	2,468	—	2,543	507	19,167
June 1	South Dakota	58,671	—	—	—	24,186	—	573	558	4,561	—	19,510	1,412	7,871
June 8	California	3,409,701	11,419	2,013,210	—	697,092	250,581	16,920	38,634	29,242	—	171,501	102,292	78,810
June 8	New Jersey	360,839	—	—	—	210,655	49,034	—	31,820	21,774	—	—	31,183	16,373
June 8	Ohio	1,134,374	—	—	—	593,130	157,884	—	35,404	—	—	240,342	63,953	43,661
		16,052,652	86,438	2,449,374	340,309	6,235,609	830,818	234,568	1,134,375	238,027	304,399	1,611,754	1,995,388	591,593

Other vote includes 88,254 Shapp; 61,992 Humphrey; 43,661 Donahey; 19,805 Kennedy; 8,717 Blessitt; 4,046 Bentsen; 3,935 Lunger; 3,574 Gray; 3,555 Lomento; 3,021 Rollinson; 2,305 Fifi Rockefeller; 2,288 Gonas; 1,829 Kelleher; 1,487 Ahern; 404 Sanford; 398 Bona; 371 Arnold; 351 Eisenman; 174 Clegg; 173 Schechter; 153 Roden; 49 Loewenherz; 205,019 Uncommitted; 81,971 No Preference; 42,304 scattered write-ins; 7,154 "None of the Names Shown"; 4,603 "None of These Candidates".

1972 REPUBLICAN PREFERENCE PRIMARIES

Date		State	Total Vote	Ashbrook	McCloskey	Nixon	Other
March	7	New Hampshire	117,208	11,362	23,190	79,239	3,417
	14	Florida	414,207	36,617	17,312	360,278	—
	21	Illinois	33,569	170	47	32,550	802
April	4	Wisconsin	286,444	2,604	3,651	277,601	2,588
	25	Massachusetts	122,139	4,864	16,435	99,150	1,690
	25	Pennsylvania	184,801	—	—	153,886	30,915
May	2	District of Columbia	No Slates Entered				
	2	Indiana	417,069	—	—	417,069	—
	2	Ohio	692,828	—	—	692,828	—
	4	Tennessee	114,489	2,419	2,370	109,696	4
	6	North Carolina	167,899	—	8,732	159,167	—
	9	Nebraska	194,272	4,996	9,011	179,464	801
	9	West Virginia	No Candidates Entered				
	16	Maryland	115,249	6,718	9,223	99,308	—
	16	Michigan	336,743	—	9,691	321,652	5,400
	23	Rhode Island	5,611	175	337	4,953	146
	23	Oregon	282,010	16,696	29,365	231,151	4,798
June	6	California	2,283,922	224,922	—	2,058,825	175
	6	New Jersey	No Candidates Entered				
	6	New Mexico	55,469	—	3,367	49,067	3,035
	6	South Dakota	52,820	—	—	52,820	—
			5,876,749	311,543	132,731	5,378,704	53,771

Other vote includes 1,211 Paulsen; 52,559 Uncommitted, None, and scattered.

1972 DEMOCRATIC PREFERENCE PRIMARIES

Date		State	Total Vote	Chisholm	Humphrey	Jackson	McCarthy	McGovern	Muskie	Wallace	Other
March	7	New Hampshire	88,854	—	348	197	—	33,007	41,235	175	13,892
	14	Florida	1,264,554	43,989	234,658	170,156	5,847	78,232	112,523	526,651	92,498
	21	Illinois	1,225,144	777	1,476	442	444,260	3,687	766,914	7,017	571
April	4	Wisconsin	1,128,584	9,198	233,748	88,068	15,543	333,528	115,811	248,676	84,012
	25	Massachusetts	618,516	22,398	48,929	8,499	8,736	325,673	131,709	45,807	26,765
	25	Pennsylvania	1,374,839	306	481,900	38,767	—	280,861	279,983	292,437	585
May	2	District of Columbia	29,560	—	—	—	—	—	—	—	29,560
	2	Indiana	751,458	—	354,244	—	—	—	87,719	309,495	—
	2	Ohio	1,212,330	—	499,680	98,498	26,026	480,320	107,806	—	—
	4	Tennessee	492,721	18,809	78,350	5,896	2,267	35,551	9,634	335,858	6,356
	6	North Carolina	821,410	61,723	—	9,416	—	—	30,739	413,518	306,014
	9	Nebraska	192,137	1,763	65,968	5,276	3,194	79,309	6,886	23,912	5,829
	9	West Virginia	368,484	—	246,596	—	—	—	—	121,888	—
	16	Maryland	568,131	12,602	151,981	17,728	4,691	126,978	13,363	219,687	21,101
	16	Michigan	1,588,073	44,090	249,798	6,938	—	425,694	38,701	809,239	13,613
	23	Rhode Island	37,864	—	7,701	138	245	15,603	7,838	5,802	537
	23	Oregon	408,644	2,975	51,163	22,042	8,943	205,328	10,244	81,868	26,081
June	6	California	3,564,518	157,435	1,375,064	28,901	34,203	1,550,652	72,701	268,551	77,011
	6	New Jersey	76,834	51,433	—	—	—	—	—	—	25,401
	6	New Mexico	153,293	3,205	39,768	4,236	—	51,011	6,411	44,843	3,819
	6	South Dakota	28,017	—	—	—	—	28,017	—	—	—
			15,993,965	430,703	4,121,372	505,198	553,955	4,053,451	1,840,217	3,755,424	733,645

Other vote includes 331,415 Sanford; 196,406 Lindsay; 79,446 Yorty; 37,401 Mills; 21,217 Fauntroy; 16,693 Kennedy; 11,798 Hartke; 8,286 Mink; 869 Coll; 30,114 Uncommitted, None, and scattered.

1968 REPUBLICAN PREFERENCE PRIMARIES

Date		State	Total Vote	Nixon	Reagan	Other
March	12	New Hampshire	103,938	80,666	—	23,272
April	2	Wisconsin	489,853	390,368	50,727	48,758
	23	Pennsylvania	287,573	171,815	7,934	107,824
	30	Massachusetts	106,521	27,447	1,770	77,304
May	7	Indiana	508,362	508,362	—	—
	7	Ohio	614,492	—	—	614,492
	14	Nebraska	200,476	140,336	42,703	17,437
	28	Florida	51,509	—	—	51,509
	28	Oregon	312,159	203,037	63,707	45,415
June	4	California	1,525,091	—	1,525,091	—
	4	New Jersey	88,592	71,809	2,737	14,046
	4	South Dakota	68,113	68,113	—	—
	11	Illinois	22,403	17,490	1,601	3,312
			4,379,082	1,679,443	1,696,270	1,003,369

Other vote includes 614,492 Rhodes; 164,340 Rockefeller; 31,598 Stassen; 31,465 Volpe; 3,830 Romney; 1,302 Americus; 1,223 Shafer; 527 Stone; 247 Hoover; 161 Watumull; 151 Evans; 73 Coy; 39 DuMont; 58,272 No Preference and 95,649 scattered.

1968 DEMOCRATIC PREFERENCE PRIMARIES

Date		State	Total Vote	McCarthy	Kennedy	Johnson	Humphrey	Other
March	12	New Hampshire	55,464	23,263	—	27,520	—	4,681
April	2	Wisconsin	733,002	412,160	46,507	253,696	3,605	17,034
	23	Pennsylvania	597,089	428,259	65,430	21,265	51,998	30,137
	30	Massachusetts	248,903	122,697	68,604	6,890	44,156	6,556
May	7	Indiana	776,513	209,695	328,118	—	—	238,700
	7	Ohio	549,140	—	—	549,140		
	14	Nebraska	162,611	50,655	84,102	9,187	12,087	6,580
	28	Florida	512,357	147,216	—	—	—	365,141
	28	Oregon	373,070	163,990	141,631	45,174	12,421	9,854
June	4	California	3,181,753	1,329,301	1,472,166	—	—	380,286
	4	New Jersey	27,446	9,906	8,603	—	5,578	3,359
	4	South Dakota	64,287	13,145	31,826	19,316	—	—
	11	Illinois	12,038	4,646	—	—	2,059	5,333
			7,293,673	2,914,933	2,246,987	383,048	131,904	1,616,801

Other vote includes 549,140 Young; 238,700 Branigin; 236,242 Smathers; 33,520 Wallace; 4,052 Edward M. Kennedy; 186 Crommelin; 170 Lee; 77 Gordon; 521,046 No Preference and 33,668 scattered.

ALABAMA

GOVERNOR

James E. Folsom, Jr. (D). Elected Lt. Governor 1990; became Governor April 1993 upon the conviction of Governor Guy Hunt (R).

SENATORS

Howell Heflin (D). Re-elected 1990 to a six-year term. Previously elected 1984, 1978.

Richard C. Shelby (D). Re-elected 1992 to a six-year term. Previously elected 1986.

REPRESENTATIVES

1. H. L. Callahan (R)
2. Terry Everett (R)
3. Glen Browder (D)
4. Tom Bevill (D)
5. Bud Cramer (D)
6. Spencer Bachus (R)
7. Earl F. Hilliard (D)

POSTWAR VOTE FOR PRESIDENT

| | | Republican | | Democratic | | Other | | Percentage | | | |
| | Total | | | | | | | Total Vote | | Major Vote | |
Year	Vote	Vote	Candidate	Vote	Candidate	Vote	Plurality	Rep.	Dem.	Rep.	Dem.
1992 **	1,688,060	804,283	Bush, George	690,080	Clinton, Bill	193,697	114,203 R	47.6%	40.9%	53.8%	46.2%
1988	1,378,476	815,576	Bush, George	549,506	Dukakis, Michael S.	13,394	266,070 R	59.2%	39.9%	59.7%	40.3%
1984	1,441,713	872,849	Reagan, Ronald	551,899	Mondale, Walter F.	16,965	320,950 R	60.5%	38.3%	61.3%	38.7%
1980	1,341,929	654,192	Reagan, Ronald	636,730	Carter, Jimmy	51,007	17,462 R	48.8%	47.4%	50.7%	49.3%
1976	1,182,850	504,070	Ford, Gerald R.	659,170	Carter, Jimmy	19,610	155,100 D	42.6%	55.7%	43.3%	56.7%
1972	1,006,111	728,701	Nixon, Richard M.	256,923	McGovern, George S.	20,487	471,778 R	72.4%	25.5%	73.9%	26.1%
1968 **	1,049,922	146,923	Nixon, Richard M.	196,579	Humphrey, Hubert H.	706,420	494,846 A	14.0%	18.7%	42.8%	57.2%
1964 **	689,818	479,085	Goldwater, Barry M.		Johnson, Lyndon B.	210,733	268,353 R	69.5%		100.0%	
1960	570,225	237,981	Nixon, Richard M.	324,050	Kennedy, John F.	8,194	86,069 D	41.7%	56.8%	42.3%	57.7%
1956	496,861	195,694	Eisenhower, Dwight D.	280,844	Stevenson, Adlai E.	20,323	85,150 D	39.4%	56.5%	41.1%	58.9%
1952	426,120	149,231	Eisenhower, Dwight D.	275,075	Stevenson, Adlai E.	1,814	125,844 D	35.0%	64.6%	35.2%	64.8%
1948 **	214,980	40,930	Dewey, Thomas E.		Truman, Harry S.	174,050	130,513 SR	19.0%		100.0%	

In 1992 the other vote column includes 183,109 votes cast for Perot. In 1968 other vote was 691,425 American Independent (Wallace); 10,960 American Independent of Alabama; 4,022 Prohibition and 13 scattered. In 1964 and 1948 the national Democratic candidates were not represented on the ballot. In 1964 other vote was 210,732 Unpledged Democratic and 1 scattered. In 1948 other vote was 171,443 States Rights; 1,522 Progressive and 1,085 Prohibition.

POSTWAR VOTE FOR GOVERNOR

| | | Republican | | Democratic | | Other | Rep.-Dem. | Percentage | | | |
| | Total | | | | | | | Total Vote | | Major Vote | |
Year	Vote	Vote	Candidate	Vote	Candidate	Vote	Plurality	Rep.	Dem.	Rep.	Dem.
1990	1,216,250	633,519	Hunt, Guy	582.106	Hubbert, Paul R.	625	51,413 R	52.1%	47.9%	52.1%	47.9%
1986	1,236,230	696,203	Hunt, Guy	537,163	Baxley, Bill	2,864	159,040 R	56.3%	43.5%	56.4%	43.6%
1982	1,128,725	440,815	Folmar, Emory	650,538	Wallace, George C.	37,372	209,723 D	39.1%	57.6%	40.4%	59.6%
1978	760,474	196,963	Hunt, Guy	551,886	James, Forrest H.	11,625	354,923 D	25.9%	72.6%	26.3%	73.7%
1974	598,305	88,381	McCary, Elvin	497,574	Wallace, George C.	12,350	409,193 D	14.8%	83.2%	15.1%	84.9%
1970 **	854,952		—	637,046	Wallace, George C.	217,906	637,046 D		74.5%		100.0%
1966	848,101	262,943	Martin, James D.	537,505	Wallace, Mrs. George C.	47,653	274,562 D	31.0%	63.4%	32.8%	67.2%
1962	315,776		—	303,987	Wallace, George C.	11,789	303,987 D		96.3%		100.0%
1958	270,952	30,415	Longshore, W. L.	239,633	Patterson, John	904	209,218 D	11.2%	88.4%	11.3%	88.7%
1954	333,090	88,688	Amernethy, Tom	244,401	Folsom, James E.	1	155,713 D	26.6%	73.4%	26.6%	73.4%
1950	170,541	15,127	Crowder, John S.	155,414	Persons, Gordon		140,287 D	8.9%	91.1%	8.9%	91.1%
1946	197,324	22,362	Ward, Lyman	174,962	Folsom, James E.		152,600 D	11.3%	88.7%	11.3%	88.7%

In 1970 other vote was 125,491 National Democratic Party of Alabama (Cashin); 75,679 Independent (Shelton); 9,705 Prohibition (Couch); 3,534 Independent (Walter) and 3,497 Whig (Watts).

ALABAMA

POSTWAR VOTE FOR SENATOR

Year	Total Vote	Republican		Democratic		Other Vote	Rep.-Dem. Plurality	Percentage			
								Total Vote		Major Vote	
		Vote	Candidate	Vote	Candidate			Rep.	Dem.	Rep.	Dem.
1992	1,577,799	522,015	Sellers, Richard	1,022,698	Shelby, Richard C.	33,086	500,683 D	33.1%	64.8%	33.8%	66.2%
1990	1,185,563	467,190	Cabaniss, Bill	717,814	Heflin, Howell	559	250,624 D	39.4%	60.5%	39.4%	60.6%
1986	1,211,953	602,537	Denton, Jeremiah	609,360	Shelby, Richard C.	56	6,823 D	49.7%	50.3%	49.7%	50.3%
1984	1,371,238	498,508	Smith, Albert L.	860,535	Heflin, Howell	12,195	362,027 D	36.4%	62.8%	36.7%	63.3%
1980	1,296,757	650,362	Denton, Jeremiah	610,175	Folsom, James E., Jr.	36,220	40,187 R	50.2%	47.1%	51.6%	48.4%
1978	582,025		—	547,054	Heflin, Howell	34,971	547,054 D		94.0%		100.0%
1978 S	731,614	316,170	Martin, James D.	401,852	Stewart, Donald W.	13,592	85,682 D	43.2%	54.9%	44.0%	56.0%
1974	523,290		—	501,541	Allen, James B.	21,749	501,541 D		95.8%		100.0%
1972	1,051,099	347,523	Blount, Winston M.	654,491	Sparkman, John J.	49,085	306,968 D	33.1%	62.3%	34.7%	65.3%
1968	912,708	201,227	Hooper, Perry	638,774	Allen, James B.	72,707	437,547 D	22.0%	70.0%	24.0%	76.0%
1966	802,608	313,018	Grenier, John	482,138	Sparkman, John J.	7,452	169,120 D	39.0%	60.1%	39.4%	60.6%
1962	397,079	195,134	Martin, James D.	201,937	Hill, Lister	8	6,803 D	49.1%	50.9%	49.1%	50.9%
1960	554,081	164,868	Elgin, Julian	389,196	Sparkman, John J.	17	224,328 D	29.8%	70.2%	29.8%	70.2%
1956	330,191		—	330,182	Hill, Lister	9	330,182 D		100.0%		100.0%
1954	314,459	55,110	Guin, J. Foy	259,348	Sparkman, John J.	1	204,238 D	17.5%	82.5%	17.5%	82.5%
1950	164,011		—	125,534	Hill, Lister	38,477	125,534 D		76.5%		100.0%
1948	220,875	35,341	Parsons, Paul G.	185,534	Sparkman, John J.		150,193 D	16.0%	84.0%	16.0%	84.0%
1946 S	163,217		—	163,217	Sparkman, John J.		163,217 D		100.0%		100.0%

The 1946 election and one of the 1978 elections were for short terms to fill vacancies.

ALABAMA

Districts Established March 27, 1992

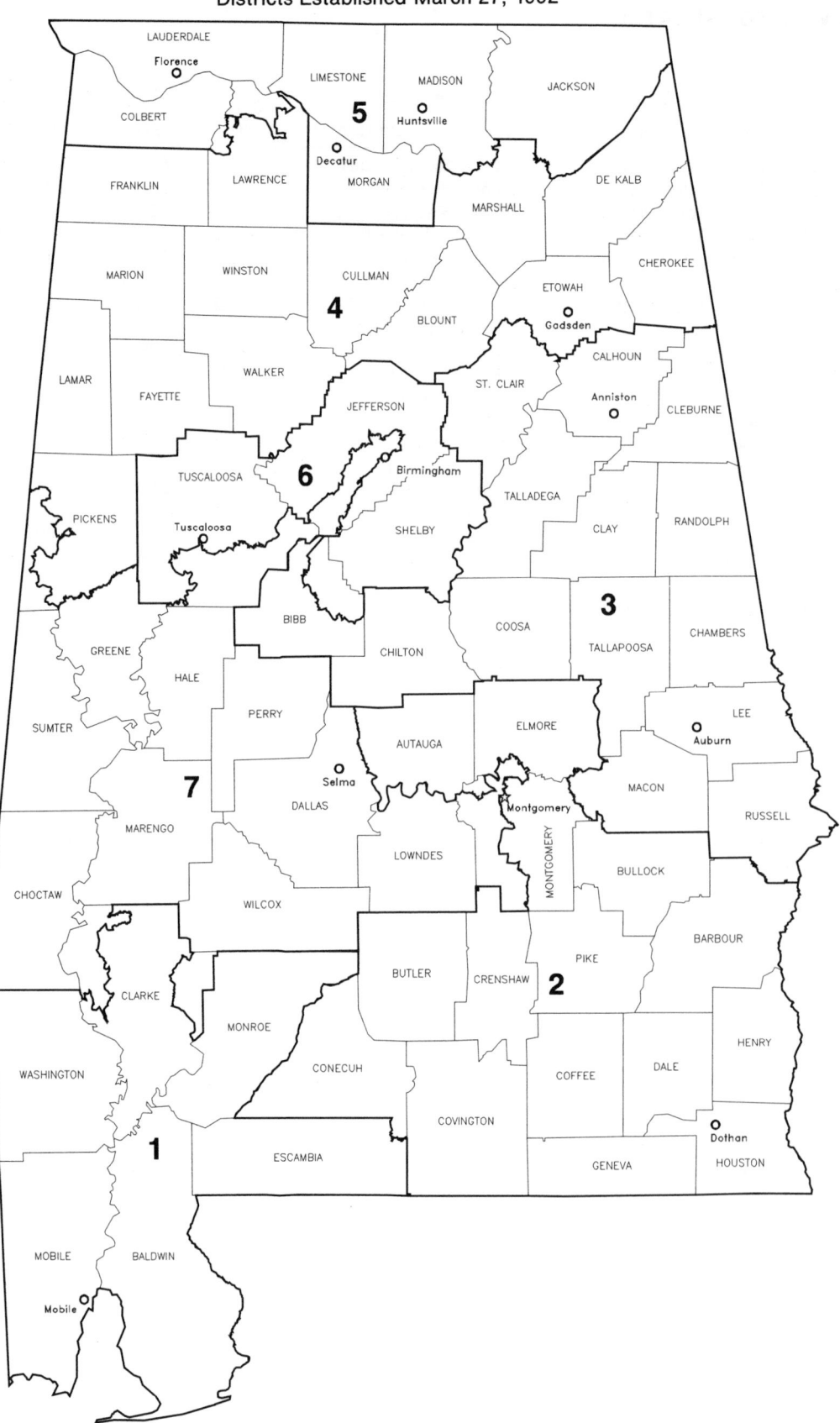

ALABAMA

PRESIDENT 1992

Registration	County	Total Vote	Republican	Democratic	Perot	Other	Plurality	Percentage Total Vote Rep.	Dem.	Perot
21,157	AUTAUGA	15,585	8,715	4,819	1,916	135	3,896 R	55.9%	30.9%	12.3%
66,931	BALDWIN	46,476	26,270	12,195	7,656	355	14,075 R	56.5%	26.2%	16.5%
17,239	BARBOUR	10,431	4,475	4,836	1,020	100	361 D	42.9%	46.4%	9.8%
8,477	BIBB	6,720	3,124	2,900	686	10	224 R	46.5%	43.2%	10.2%
24,865	BLOUNT	16,505	8,882	5,433	1,949	241	3,449 R	53.8%	32.9%	11.8%
6,517	BULLOCK	4,816	1,253	3,259	266	38	2,006 D	26.0%	67.7%	5.5%
10,767	BUTLER	8,478	3,494	4,021	867	96	527 D	41.2%	47.4%	10.2%
64,999	CALHOUN	42,800	20,623	16,453	4,717	1,007	4,170 R	48.2%	38.4%	11.0%
24,696	CHAMBERS	13,091	5,682	5,938	1,427	44	256 D	43.4%	45.4%	10.9%
12,413	CHEROKEE	7,876	2,745	4,222	846	63	1,477 D	34.9%	53.6%	10.7%
22,536	CHILTON	14,468	8,126	4,946	1,363	33	3,180 R	56.2%	34.2%	9.4%
7,643	CHOCTAW	7,560	3,069	3,941	489	61	872 D	40.6%	52.1%	6.5%
16,423	CLARKE	11,717	5,495	5,023	872	327	472 R	46.9%	42.9%	7.4%
7,817	CLAY	5,755	2,859	2,073	652	171	786 R	49.7%	36.0%	11.3%
8,821	CLEBURNE	5,237	2,425	2,144	630	38	281 R	46.3%	40.9%	12.0%
25,137	COFFEE	15,533	7,591	5,776	2,021	145	1,815 R	48.9%	37.2%	13.0%
24,187	COLBERT	22,439	8,073	12,206	2,098	62	4,133 D	36.0%	54.4%	9.3%
10,199	CONECUH	6,307	2,463	3,155	552	137	692 D	39.1%	50.0%	8.8%
6,908	COOSA	4,798	1,973	2,330	476	19	357 D	41.1%	48.6%	9.9%
27,572	COVINGTON	13,962	6,840	5,004	1,880	238	1,836 R	49.0%	35.8%	13.5%
8,645	CRENSHAW	5,290	2,339	2,404	485	62	65 D	44.2%	45.4%	9.2%
41,430	CULLMAN	29,043	14,411	10,451	4,113	68	3,960 R	49.6%	36.0%	14.2%
25,664	DALE	15,787	8,123	5,098	2,423	143	3,025 R	51.5%	32.3%	15.3%
36,708	DALLAS	19,604	7,394	11,053	1,110	47	3,659 D	37.7%	56.4%	5.7%
21,224	DE KALB	21,585	10,519	8,245	2,741	80	2,274 R	48.7%	38.2%	12.7%
30,153	ELMORE	20,388	11,356	6,223	2,765	44	5,133 R	55.7%	30.5%	13.6%
16,082	ESCAMBIA	12,824	5,955	4,809	1,616	444	1,146 R	46.4%	37.5%	12.6%
61,342	ETOWAH	42,451	17,467	20,558	4,277	149	3,091 D	41.1%	48.4%	10.1%
11,834	FAYETTE	8,470	3,604	3,830	1,012	24	226 D	42.6%	45.2%	11.9%
19,026	FRANKLIN	11,858	4,794	5,953	1,075	36	1,159 D	40.4%	50.2%	9.1%
15,905	GENEVA	9,867	4,843	3,622	1,323	79	1,221 R	49.1%	36.7%	13.4%
6,854	GREENE	4,881	805	3,865	194	17	3,060 D	16.5%	79.2%	4.0%
9,768	HALE	6,023	2,001	3,481	486	55	1,480 D	33.2%	57.8%	8.1%
9,280	HENRY	6,499	2,970	2,804	667	58	166 R	45.7%	43.1%	10.3%
36,922	HOUSTON	29,760	17,360	8,857	3,492	51	8,503 R	58.3%	29.8%	11.7%
22,939	JACKSON	18,916	5,711	10,628	2,462	115	4,917 D	30.2%	56.2%	13.0%
386,343	JEFFERSON	298,884	149,832	125,889	22,191	972	23,943 R	50.1%	42.1%	7.4%
11,198	LAMAR	6,898	3,262	2,849	763	24	413 R	47.3%	41.3%	11.1%
37,662	LAUDERDALE	33,756	13,728	15,936	4,009	83	2,208 D	40.7%	47.2%	11.9%
18,026	LAWRENCE	11,589	3,576	6,364	1,624	25	2,788 D	30.9%	54.9%	14.0%
57,270	LEE	35,490	16,885	13,770	4,572	263	3,115 R	47.6%	38.8%	12.9%
30,542	LIMESTONE	21,597	9,862	8,087	3,584	64	1,775 R	45.7%	37.4%	16.6%
8,375	LOWNDES	5,148	1,328	3,500	284	36	2,172 D	25.8%	68.0%	5.5%
12,544	MACON	8,762	1,134	7,253	283	92	6,119 D	12.9%	82.8%	3.2%
139,594	MADISON	107,834	51,444	38,974	16,989	427	12,470 R	47.7%	36.1%	15.8%
18,619	MARENGO	11,244	4,470	5,632	919	223	1,162 D	39.8%	50.1%	8.2%
19,119	MARION	13,270	5,692	6,167	1,389	22	475 D	42.9%	46.5%	10.5%
43,977	MARSHALL	26,717	12,249	10,421	3,795	252	1,828 R	45.8%	39.0%	14.2%
212,078	MOBILE	143,788	72,935	54,962	15,105	786	17,973 R	50.7%	38.2%	10.5%
14,377	MONROE	9,745	4,919	3,872	759	195	1,047 R	50.5%	39.7%	7.8%
107,041	MONTGOMERY	86,152	40,742	37,342	7,647	421	3,400 R	47.3%	43.3%	8.9%
61,419	MORGAN	43,978	21,073	15,091	7,683	131	5,982 R	47.9%	34.3%	17.5%
8,947	PERRY	5,813	1,829	3,712	213	59	1,883 D	31.5%	63.9%	3.7%
12,969	PICKENS	8,142	3,634	3,783	690	35	149 D	44.6%	46.5%	8.5%
18,024	PIKE	11,193	5,423	4,688	1,024	58	735 R	48.4%	41.9%	9.1%
11,319	RANDOLPH	8,152	3,813	3,318	919	102	495 R	46.8%	40.7%	11.3%
17,224	RUSSELL	15,689	5,587	8,647	1,360	95	3,060 D	35.6%	55.1%	8.7%
28,538	ST. CLAIR	21,624	12,447	6,517	2,614	46	5,930 R	57.6%	30.1%	12.1%
70,167	SHELBY	48,165	32,736	10,317	5,022	90	22,419 R	68.0%	21.4%	10.4%
10,127	SUMTER	7,025	1,807	4,810	388	20	3,003 D	25.7%	68.5%	5.5%

ALABAMA

PRESIDENT 1992

Registration	County	Total Vote	Republican	Democratic	Perot	Other	Plurality	Percentage Total Vote		
								Rep.	Dem.	Perot
33,338	TALLADEGA	26,264	12,661	10,695	2,629	279	1,966 R	48.2%	40.7%	10.0%
27,268	TALLAPOOSA	15,456	8,140	5,703	1,562	51	2,437 R	52.7%	36.9%	10.1%
81,087	TUSCALOOSA	58,073	27,454	23,495	7,011	113	3,959 R	47.3%	40.5%	12.1%
44,427	WALKER	29,534	11,301	14,831	3,344	58	3,530 D	38.3%	50.2%	11.3%
9,812	WASHINGTON	8,162	3,270	4,046	829	17	776 D	40.1%	49.6%	10.2%
10,811	WILCOX	5,304	1,671	3,439	174	20	1,768 D	31.5%	64.8%	3.3%
16,650	WINSTON	10,089	5,550	3,415	1,110	14	2,135 R	55.0%	33.8%	11.0%
2,367,972	TOTAL	1,688,060	804,283	690,080	183,109	10,588	114,203 R	47.6%	40.9%	10.8%

ALABAMA

SENATOR 1992

Registration	County	Total Vote	Republican	Democratic	Other	Rep.-Dem. Plurality	Percentage Total Vote Rep.	Dem.	Major Vote Rep.	Dem.
21,157	AUTAUGA	13,533	4,279	9,012	242	4,733 D	31.6%	66.6%	32.2%	67.8%
66,931	BALDWIN	41,388	19,258	21,036	1,094	1,778 D	46.5%	50.8%	47.8%	52.2%
17,239	BARBOUR	8,015	2,087	5,783	145	3,696 D	26.0%	72.2%	26.5%	73.5%
8,477	BIBB	6,653	1,698	4,877	78	3,179 D	25.5%	73.3%	25.8%	74.2%
24,865	BLOUNT	14,706	5,974	8,311	421	2,337 D	40.6%	56.5%	41.8%	58.2%
6,517	BULLOCK	4,087	480	3,564	43	3,084 D	11.7%	87.2%	11.9%	88.1%
10,767	BUTLER	7,059	1,655	5,305	99	3,650 D	23.4%	75.2%	23.8%	76.2%
64,999	CALHOUN	37,958	14,190	22,735	1,033	8,545 D	37.4%	59.9%	38.4%	61.6%
24,696	CHAMBERS	12,398	3,942	8,187	269	4,245 D	31.8%	66.0%	32.5%	67.5%
12,413	CHEROKEE	6,542	1,372	5,004	166	3,632 D	21.0%	76.5%	21.5%	78.5%
22,536	CHILTON	14,219	4,409	9,636	174	5,227 D	31.0%	67.8%	31.4%	68.6%
7,643	CHOCTAW	6,294	1,195	5,069	30	3,874 D	19.0%	80.5%	19.1%	80.9%
16,423	CLARKE	10,030	3,260	6,655	115	3,395 D	32.5%	66.4%	32.9%	67.1%
7,817	CLAY	4,512	1,309	3,061	142	1,752 D	29.0%	67.8%	30.0%	70.0%
8,821	CLEBURNE	4,033	1,354	2,560	119	1,206 D	33.6%	63.5%	34.6%	65.4%
25,137	COFFEE	13,878	3,420	10,222	236	6,802 D	24.6%	73.7%	25.1%	74.9%
24,187	COLBERT	21,875	4,965	16,589	321	11,624 D	22.7%	75.8%	23.0%	77.0%
10,199	CONECUH	4,755	980	3,679	96	2,699 D	20.6%	77.4%	21.0%	79.0%
6,908	COOSA	4,704	1,142	3,452	110	2,310 D	24.3%	73.4%	24.9%	75.1%
27,572	COVINGTON	10,906	2,703	7,835	368	5,132 D	24.8%	71.8%	25.7%	74.3%
8,645	CRENSHAW	4,350	777	3,484	89	2,707 D	17.9%	80.1%	18.2%	81.8%
41,430	CULLMAN	28,385	10,380	17,366	639	6,986 D	36.6%	61.2%	37.4%	62.6%
25,664	DALE	13,686	4,341	9,096	249	4,755 D	31.7%	66.5%	32.3%	67.7%
36,708	DALLAS	18,915	3,275	15,493	147	12,218 D	17.3%	81.9%	17.4%	82.6%
21,224	DE KALB	19,168	7,515	11,176	477	3,661 D	39.2%	58.3%	40.2%	59.8%
30,153	ELMORE	19,744	6,078	13,288	378	7,210 D	30.8%	67.3%	31.4%	68.6%
16,082	ESCAMBIA	10,442	3,874	6,268	300	2,394 D	37.1%	60.0%	38.2%	61.8%
61,342	ETOWAH	41,323	11,289	29,183	851	17,894 D	27.3%	70.6%	27.9%	72.1%
11,834	FAYETTE	8,256	1,960	6,184	112	4,224 D	23.7%	74.9%	24.1%	75.9%
19,026	FRANKLIN	11,444	3,021	8,215	208	5,194 D	26.4%	71.8%	26.9%	73.1%
15,905	GENEVA	7,735	1,802	5,629	304	3,827 D	23.3%	72.8%	24.2%	75.8%
6,854	GREENE	4,546	371	4,155	20	3,784 D	8.2%	91.4%	8.2%	91.8%
9,768	HALE	5,151	861	4,227	63	3,366 D	16.7%	82.1%	16.9%	83.1%
9,280	HENRY	4,775	1,162	3,533	80	2,371 D	24.3%	74.0%	24.7%	75.3%
36,922	HOUSTON	28,953	9,651	18,918	384	9,267 D	33.3%	65.3%	33.8%	66.2%
22,939	JACKSON	15,724	3,973	11,396	355	7,423 D	25.3%	72.5%	25.9%	74.1%
386,343	JEFFERSON	292,770	109,615	178,070	5,085	68,455 D	37.4%	60.8%	38.1%	61.9%
11,198	LAMAR	6,459	2,015	4,318	126	2,303 D	31.2%	66.9%	31.8%	68.2%
37,662	LAUDERDALE	32,614	8,509	23,521	584	15,012 D	26.1%	72.1%	26.6%	73.4%
18,026	LAWRENCE	11,248	1,971	9,103	174	7,132 D	17.5%	80.9%	17.8%	82.2%
57,270	LEE	30,592	13,684	15,983	925	2,299 D	44.7%	52.2%	46.1%	53.9%
30,542	LIMESTONE	20,848	6,657	13,703	488	7,046 D	31.9%	65.7%	32.7%	67.3%
8,375	LOWNDES	4,400	597	3,748	55	3,151 D	13.6%	85.2%	13.7%	86.3%
12,544	MACON	7,739	700	6,818	221	6,118 D	9.0%	88.1%	9.3%	90.7%
139,594	MADISON	104,925	35,311	66,537	3,077	31,226 D	33.7%	63.4%	34.7%	65.3%
18,619	MARENGO	9,846	1,747	8,019	80	6,272 D	17.7%	81.4%	17.9%	82.1%
19,119	MARION	12,837	3,650	8,946	241	5,296 D	28.4%	69.7%	29.0%	71.0%
43,977	MARSHALL	23,090	7,790	14,665	635	6,875 D	33.7%	63.5%	34.7%	65.3%
212,078	MOBILE	134,391	50,731	80,566	3,094	29,835 D	37.7%	59.9%	38.6%	61.4%
14,377	MONROE	8,500	3,084	5,276	140	2,192 D	36.3%	62.1%	36.9%	63.1%
107,041	MONTGOMERY	79,611	22,838	55,442	1,331	32,604 D	28.7%	69.6%	29.2%	70.8%
61,419	MORGAN	42,855	15,645	26,110	1,100	10,465 D	36.5%	60.9%	37.5%	62.5%
8,947	PERRY	5,270	992	4,215	63	3,223 D	18.8%	80.0%	19.1%	80.9%
12,969	PICKENS	7,703	1,980	5,616	107	3,636 D	25.7%	72.9%	26.1%	73.9%
18,024	PIKE	9,456	2,073	7,278	105	5,205 D	21.9%	77.0%	22.2%	77.8%
11,319	RANDOLPH	6,485	2,219	4,079	187	1,860 D	34.2%	62.9%	35.2%	64.8%
17,224	RUSSELL	13,180	3,831	9,066	283	5,235 D	29.1%	68.8%	29.7%	70.3%
28,538	ST. CLAIR	21,255	9,318	11,528	409	2,210 D	43.8%	54.2%	44.7%	55.3%
70,167	SHELBY	47,343	24,470	22,118	755	2,352 R	51.7%	46.7%	52.5%	47.5%
10,127	SUMTER	6,812	785	5,980	47	5,195 D	11.5%	87.8%	11.6%	88.4%

ALABAMA

SENATOR 1992

Registration	County	Total Vote	Republican	Democratic	Other	Rep.-Dem. Plurality	Percentage Total Vote Rep.	Percentage Total Vote Dem.	Percentage Major Vote Rep.	Percentage Major Vote Dem.
33,338	TALLADEGA	22,379	8,319	13,594	466	5,275 D	37.2%	60.7%	38.0%	62.0%
27,268	TALLAPOOSA	15,107	4,839	10,042	226	5,203 D	32.0%	66.5%	32.5%	67.5%
81,087	TUSCALOOSA	57,093	15,136	40,937	1,020	25,801 D	26.5%	71.7%	27.0%	73.0%
44,427	WALKER	28,789	7,037	21,262	490	14,225 D	24.4%	73.9%	24.9%	75.1%
9,812	WASHINGTON	7,879	1,541	6,209	129	4,668 D	19.6%	78.8%	19.9%	80.1%
10,811	WILCOX	5,135	844	4,269	22	3,425 D	16.4%	83.1%	16.5%	83.5%
16,650	WINSTON	9,771	4,085	5,497	189	1,412 D	41.8%	56.3%	42.6%	57.4%
2,367,972	TOTAL	1,577,799	522,015	1,022,698	33,086	500,683 D	33.1%	64.8%	33.8%	66.2%

ALABAMA

CONGRESS

CD	Year	Total Vote	Republican		Democratic		Other Vote	Rep.-Dem. Plurality	Percentage			
			Vote	Candidate	Vote	Candidate			Total Vote		Major Vote	
									Rep.	Dem.	Rep.	Dem.
1	1992	214,204	128,874	CALLAHAN, H. L.	78,742	BREWER, WILLLIAM A.	6,588	50,132 R	60.2%	36.8%	62.1%	37.9%
2	1992	228,160	112,906	EVERETT, TERRY	109,335	WALLACE, GEORGE C., JR.	5,919	3,571 R	49.5%	47.9%	50.8%	49.2%
3	1992	197,604	73,800	SLEDGE, DON	119,175	BROWDER, GLEN	4,629	45,375 D	37.3%	60.3%	38.2%	61.8%
4	1992	230,523	66,934	STRICKLAND, MICKEY	157,907	BEVILL, TOM	5,682	90,973 D	29.0%	68.5%	29.8%	70.2%
5	1992	244,133	77,951	SMITH, TERRY	160,060	CRAMER, BUD	6,122	82,109 D	31.9%	65.6%	32.8%	67.2%
6	1992	280,139	146,599	BACHUS, SPENCER	126,062	ERDREICH, BEN	7,478	20,537 R	52.3%	45.0%	53.8%	46.2%
7	1992	207,773	36,086	JONES, KERVIN	144,320	HILLIARD, EARL F.	27,367	108,234 D	17.4%	69.5%	20.0%	80.0%

ALABAMA

1992 GENERAL ELECTION

President Other vote was 5,737 Libertarian (Marrou); 2,161 Independent (Fulani); 831 Independent (Warren); 641 Independent (LaRouche); 495 Independent (Hagelin) and 723 scattered write-ins. The total of the other vote column includes the 723 write-in votes not available by county.

Senator Other vote was 31,811 Libertarian (Shockley) and 1,275 scattered write-ins. The total of the other vote column includes the 1,375 write-in votes not available by county.

Congress Other vote was 6,548 Libertarian (Garrett) and 40 scattered write-ins in CD 1; 3,150 Libertarian (Reeves), 1,426 Independent (Brassell), 1,330 Independent (Boone) and 13 scattered write-ins in CD 2; 4,570 Libertarian (Templeton) and 59 scattered write-ins in CD 3; 5,646 Libertarian (King) and 36 scattered write-ins in CD 4; 6,006 Libertarian (Seibert) and 116 scattered write-ins in CD 5; 4,521 Independent (Cloum), 2,836 Libertarian (Bodenhausen) and 121 scattered write-ins in CD 6; 12,461 Independent (Lewis), 11,466 Independent (Chambliss), 2,135 Libertarian (Mayer), 1,165 Socialist Workers (Hawkins) and 140 scattered write-ins in CD 7.

1992 PRIMARIES

JUNE 2 REPUBLICAN

Senator Richard Sellers, unopposed.

Congress Unopposed in three CD's. Contested as follows:

CD 2 9,619 Terry Everett; 6,883 Larry Dixon.
CD 3 3,967 Don Sledge; 2,776 Ted McLaughlin.
CD 6 28,043 Spencer Bachus; 26,221 Marty Connors; 11,190 Jim Gunter; 7,075 Mike King.
CD 7 2,629 Jonathan McPherson; 2,323 Kervin Jones; 1,007 Alfred J. Middleton.

JUNE 2 DEMOCRATIC

Senator 304,957 Richard C. Shelby; 136,836 Chris McNair; 28,432 Bob Miller; 25,956 Mrs. Frank Ross Stewart.

Congress Unopposed in five CD's. Contested as follows:

CD 2 41,135 George C. Wallace, Jr.; 26,502 Faye Baggiano; 15,311 Larry Lee.
CD 7 36,005 Earl F. Hilliard; 28,156 Hank Sanders; 23,385 John Knight; 13,595 Sam Taylor; 8,317 Edward B. McClain; 6,364 James L. Thomas.

JUNE 30 REPUBLICAN RUN-OFF

Congress

CD 6 20,114 Spencer Bachus; 13,856 Marty Connors.
CD 7 844 Kervin Jones; 591 Jonathan McPherson.

JUNE 30 DEMOCRATIC RUN-OFF

Congress

CD 2 37,498 George C. Wallace, Jr.; 28,157 Faye Baggiano.
CD 7 35,914 Earl F. Hilliard; 35,244 Hank Sanders.

ALASKA

GOVERNOR
Walter J. Hickel (Alaskan Independence). Elected 1990 to a four-year term. Previously elected 1966 as a Republican.

SENATORS
Frank H. Murkowski (R). Re-elected 1992 to a six-year term. Previously elected 1986, 1980.

Ted Stevens (R). Re-elected 1990 to a six-year term. Previously elected 1984, 1978, 1972, and in 1970 to fill out term vacated by the death of Senator E. L. Bartlett; had been appointed December 1968 to fill this vacancy.

REPRESENTATIVE
At-Large. Don Young (R)

POSTWAR VOTE FOR PRESIDENT

| | | Republican | | Democratic | | Other | | Percentage | | | |
| | Total | | | | | | | Total Vote | | Major Vote | |
Year	Vote	Vote	Candidate	Vote	Candidate	Vote	Plurality	Rep.	Dem.	Rep.	Dem.
1992 **	258,506	102,000	Bush, George	78,294	Clinton, Bill	78,212	23,706 R	39.5%	30.3%	56.6%	43.4%
1988	200,116	119,251	Bush, George	72,584	Dukakis, Michael S.	8,281	46,667 R	59.6%	36.3%	62.2%	37.8%
1984	207,605	138,377	Reagan, Ronald	62,007	Mondale, Walter F.	7,221	76,370 R	66.7%	29.9%	69.1%	30.9%
1980	158,445	86,112	Reagan, Ronald	41,842	Carter, Jimmy	30,491	44,270 R	54.3%	26.4%	67.3%	32.7%
1976	123,574	71,555	Ford, Gerald R.	44,058	Carter, Jimmy	7,961	27,497 R	57.9%	35.7%	61.9%	38.1%
1972	95,219	55,349	Nixon, Richard M.	32,967	McGovern, George S.	6,903	22,382 R	58.1%	34.6%	62.7%	37.3%
1968	83,035	37,600	Nixon, Richard M.	35,411	Humphrey, Hubert H.	10,024	2,189 R	45.3%	42.6%	51.5%	48.5%
1964	67,259	22,930	Goldwater, Barry M.	44,329	Johnson, Lyndon B.		21,399 D	34.1%	65.9%	34.1%	65.9%
1960	60,762	30,953	Nixon, Richard M.	29,809	Kennedy, John F.		1,144 R	50.9%	49.1%	50.9%	49.1%

In 1992 the other vote column includes 73,481 votes for Perot. Alaska was formally admitted to statehood in January 1959.

POSTWAR VOTE FOR GOVERNOR

| | | Republican | | Democratic | | Other | Rep.-Dem. | Percentage | | | |
| | Total | | | | | | | Total Vote | | Major Vote | |
Year	Vote	Vote	Candidate	Vote	Candidate	Vote	Plurality	Rep.	Dem.	Rep.	Dem.
1990 **	194,750	50,991	Sturgulewski, Arliss	60,201	Knowles, Tony	83,558	9,210 D	26.2%	30.9%	45.9%	54.1%
1986	179,555	76,515	Sturgulewski, Arliss	84,943	Cowper, Steve	18,097	8,428 D	42.6%	47.3%	47.4%	52.6%
1982	194,885	72,291	Fink, Tom	89,918	Sheffield, Bill	32,676	17,627 D	37.1%	46.1%	44.6%	55.4%
1978 **	126,910	49,580	Hammond, Jay S.	25,656	Croft, Chancy	51,674	23,924 R	39.1%	20.2%	65.9%	34.1%
1974	96,163	45,840	Hammond, Jay S.	45,553	Egan, William A.	4,770	287 R	47.7%	47.4%	50.2%	49.8%
1970	80,779	37,264	Miller, Keith	42,309	Egan, William A.	1,206	5,045 D	46.1%	52.4%	46.8%	53.2%
1966	66,294	33,145	Hickel, Walter J.	32,065	Egan, William A.	1,084	1,080 R	50.0%	48.4%	50.8%	49.2%
1962	56,681	27,054	Stepovich, Mike	29,627	Egan, William A.		2,573 D	47.7%	52.3%	47.7%	52.3%
1958	48,968	19,299	Butrovich, John	29,189	Egan, William A.	480	9,890 D	39.4%	59.6%	39.8%	60.2%

In 1978 other vote was 33,555 Walter J. Hickel (write-in); 15,656 Tom Kelly (Alaskans for Kelly) and 2,463 Donald R. Wright (Alaskan Independence). In 1990 Walter J. Hickel, the Alaskan Independence candidate, polled 75,721 votes (38.9% of the total vote) and won the election with a 15,520 plurality.

ALASKA

POSTWAR VOTE FOR SENATOR

Year	Total Vote	Republican		Democratic		Other Vote	Rep.-Dem. Plurality	Percentage			
								Total Vote		Major Vote	
		Vote	Candidate	Vote	Candidate			Rep.	Dem.	Rep.	Dem.
1992	239,714	127,163	Murkowski, Frank H.	92,065	Smith, Tony	20,486	35,098 R	53.0%	38.4%	58.0%	42.0%
1990	189,957	125,806	Stevens, Ted	61,152	Beasley, Michael	2,999	64,654 R	66.2%	32.2%	67.3%	32.7%
1986	180,801	97,674	Murkowski, Frank H.	79,727	Olds, Glenn	3,400	17,947 R	54.0%	44.1%	55.1%	44.9%
1984	206,438	146,919	Stevens, Ted	58,804	Havelock, John E.	715	88,115 R	71.2%	28.5%	71.4%	28.6%
1980	156,762	84,159	Murkowski, Frank H.	72,007	Gruening, Clark S.	596	12,152 R	53.7%	45.9%	53.9%	46.1%
1978	122,741	92,783	Stevens, Ted	29,574	Hobbs, Donald W.	384	63,209 R	75.6%	24.1%	75.8%	24.2%
1974	93,275	38,914	Lewis, C. R.	54,361	Gravel, Mike		15,447 D	41.7%	58.3%	41.7%	58.3%
1972	96,007	74,216	Stevens, Ted	21,791	Guess, Gene		52,425 R	77.3%	22.7%	77.3%	22.7%
1970 S	80,364	47,908	Stevens, Ted	32,456	Kay, Wendell P.		15,452 R	59.6%	40.4%	59.6%	40.4%
1968	80,931	30,286	Rasmuson, Elmer	36,527	Gravel, Mike	14,118	6,241 D	37.4%	45.1%	45.3%	54.7%
1966	65,250	15,961	McKinley, Lee L.	49,289	Bartlett, E. L.		33,328 D	24.5%	75.5%	24.5%	75.5%
1962	58,181	24,354	Stevens, Ted	33,827	Gruening, Ernest		9,473 D	41.9%	58.1%	41.9%	58.1%
1960	59,978	21,937	McKinley, Lee L.	38,041	Bartlett, E. L.		16,104 D	36.6%	63.4%	36.6%	63.4%
1958 S	49,525	23,462	Stepovich, Mike	26,063	Gruening, Ernest		2,601 D	47.4%	52.6%	47.4%	52.6%
1958 S	48,837	7,299	Robertson, R. E.	40,939	Bartlett, E. L.	599	33,640 D	14.9%	83.8%	15.1%	84.9%

The two 1958 elections were held to indeterminate terms and the Senate later determined by lot that Senator Gruening would serve four years, Senator Bartlett two. The 1970 election was for a short term to fill a vacancy.

ALASKA
One At Large
Election Districts Established June 29, 1992

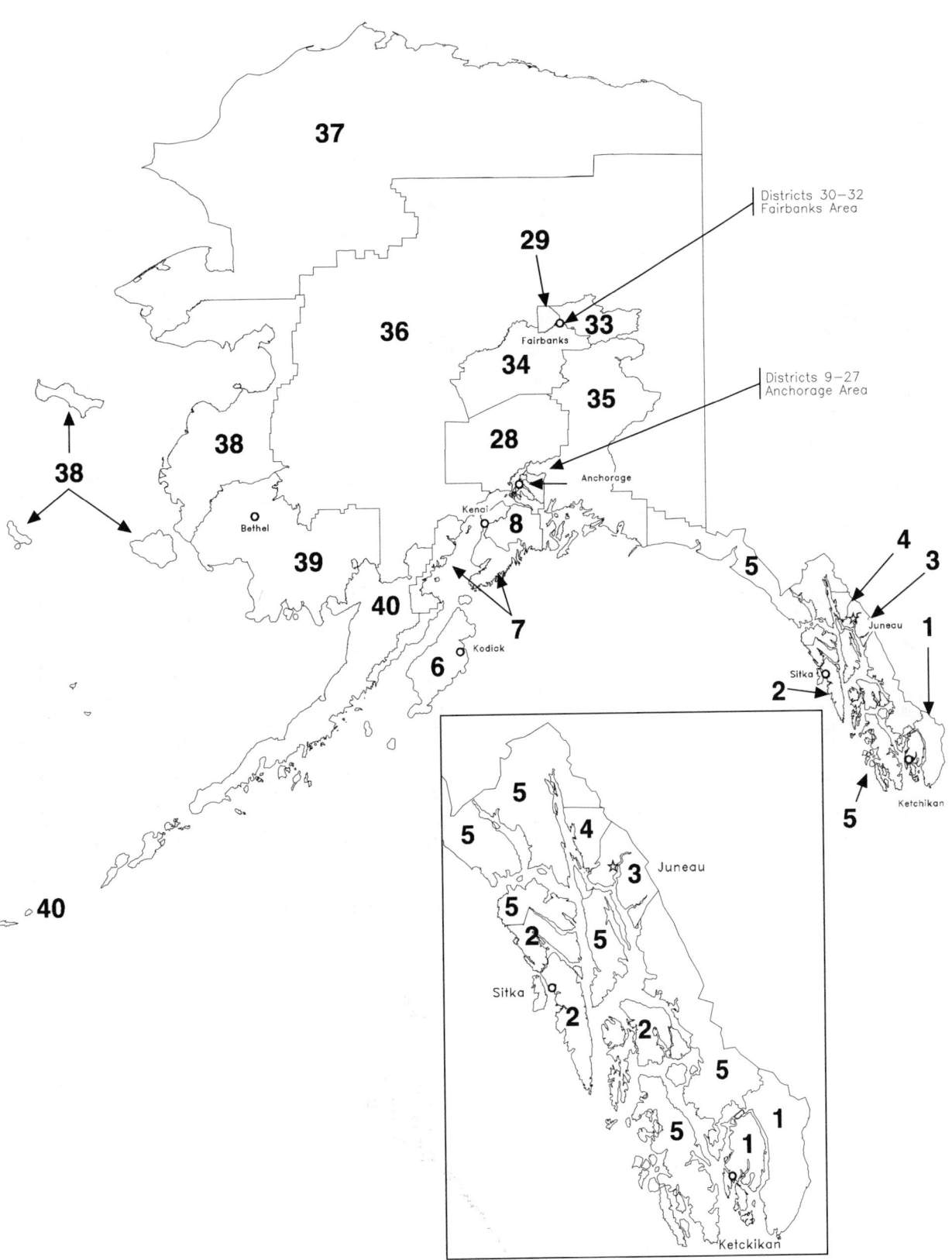

ALASKA

PRESIDENT 1992

Registration	District	Total Vote	Republican	Democratic	Perot	Other	Plurality	Percentage Total Vote		
								Rep.	Dem.	Perot
8,454	DISTRICT 1	6,760	2,495	2,055	2,120	90	375 R	36.9%	30.4%	31.4%
9,298	DISTRICT 2	7,719	2,916	2,565	2,137	101	351 R	37.8%	33.2%	27.7%
9,490	DISTRICT 3	8,042	2,447	4,064	1,424	107	1,617 D	30.4%	50.5%	17.7%
8,416	DISTRICT 4	7,238	2,894	2,688	1,561	95	206 R	40.0%	37.1%	21.6%
7,948	DISTRICT 5	5,742	1,844	2,095	1,684	119	251 D	32.1%	36.5%	29.3%
7,148	DISTRICT 6	5,711	2,345	1,546	1,748	72	597 R	41.1%	27.1%	30.6%
7,858	DISTRICT 7	6,704	2,173	2,088	2,244	199	71 P	32.4%	31.1%	33.5%
7,420	DISTRICT 8	6,449	2,499	1,509	2,325	116	174 R	38.8%	23.4%	36.1%
7,224	DISTRICT 9	6,414	2,349	1,540	2,368	157	19 P	36.6%	24.0%	36.9%
8,698	DISTRICT 10	7,493	3,548	1,947	1,899	99	1,601 R	47.4%	26.0%	25.3%
8,274	DISTRICT 11	6,920	2,730	2,009	2,081	100	649 R	39.5%	29.0%	30.1%
7,978	DISTRICT 12	6,963	2,999	1,831	2,039	94	960 R	43.1%	26.3%	29.3%
9,454	DISTRICT 13	7,989	2,963	3,001	1,907	118	38 D	37.1%	37.6%	23.9%
7,600	DISTRICT 14	6,124	3,013	1,423	1,599	89	1,414 R	49.2%	23.2%	26.1%
7,642	DISTRICT 15	5,941	1,842	2,389	1,591	119	547 D	31.0%	40.2%	26.8%
6,599	DISTRICT 16	4,633	1,375	1,814	1,320	124	439 D	29.7%	39.2%	28.5%
7,807	DISTRICT 17	6,423	2,623	1,749	1,958	93	665 R	40.8%	27.2%	30.5%
9,495	DISTRICT 18	8,357	3,629	2,483	2,134	111	1,146 R	43.4%	29.7%	25.5%
7,562	DISTRICT 19	6,419	2,539	1,931	1,840	109	608 R	39.6%	30.1%	28.7%
8,677	DISTRICT 20	7,225	2,914	2,383	1,823	105	531 R	40.3%	33.0%	25.2%
8,002	DISTRICT 21	6,632	2,437	2,386	1,693	116	51 R	36.7%	36.0%	25.5%
8,649	DISTRICT 22	7,233	3,164	2,253	1,713	103	911 R	43.7%	31.1%	23.7%
6,287	DISTRICT 23	4,550	2,127	1,139	1,217	67	910 R	46.7%	25.0%	26.7%
8,626	DISTRICT 24	7,338	3,441	1,876	1,930	91	1,511 R	46.9%	25.6%	26.3%
8,020	DISTRICT 25	6,927	3,197	1,513	2,122	95	1,075 R	46.2%	21.8%	30.6%
7,442	DISTRICT 26	6,686	2,675	1,439	2,419	153	256 R	40.0%	21.5%	36.2%
8,050	DISTRICT 27	6,970	2,757	1,625	2,401	187	356 R	39.6%	23.3%	34.4%
7,901	DISTRICT 28	7,034	2,459	1,522	2,825	228	366 P	35.0%	21.6%	40.2%
8,674	DISTRICT 29	7,623	2,205	3,216	2,026	176	1,011 D	28.9%	42.2%	26.6%
7,682	DISTRICT 30	6,333	2,434	1,860	1,912	127	522 R	38.4%	29.4%	30.2%
7,720	DISTRICT 31	6,340	2,223	1,969	1,992	156	231 R	35.1%	31.1%	31.4%
6,660	DISTRICT 32	5,293	2,339	1,150	1,724	80	615 R	44.2%	21.7%	32.6%
8,524	DISTRICT 33	7,252	3,100	1,712	2,278	162	822 R	42.7%	23.6%	31.4%
9,037	DISTRICT 34	7,183	3,408	1,455	2,201	119	1,207 R	47.4%	20.3%	30.6%
8,152	DISTRICT 35	6,415	2,525	1,572	2,139	179	386 R	39.4%	24.5%	33.3%
7,280	DISTRICT 36	5,284	2,081	1,748	1,322	133	333 R	39.4%	33.1%	25.0%
6,564	DISTRICT 37	4,543	1,689	1,822	925	107	133 D	37.2%	40.1%	20.4%
6,705	DISTRICT 38	4,864	2,011	1,897	850	106	114 R	41.3%	39.0%	17.5%
6,221	DISTRICT 39	4,516	1,777	1,797	860	82	20 D	39.3%	39.8%	19.0%
5,820	DISTRICT 40	4,166	1,786	1,211	1,122	47	575 R	42.9%	29.1%	26.9%
	FEDERAL ABSENTEE	58	28	22	8		6 R	48.3%	37.9%	13.8%
315,058	TOTAL	258,506	102,000	78,294	73,481	4,731	23,706 R	39.5%	30.3%	28.4%

ALASKA

SENATOR 1992

Registration	District	Total Vote	Republican	Democratic	Other	Rep.-Dem. Plurality	Percentage			
							Total Vote		Major Vote	
							Rep.	Dem.	Rep.	Dem.
8,454	DISTRICT 1	6,227	3,576	2,233	418	1,343 R	57.4%	35.9%	61.6%	38.4%
9,298	DISTRICT 2	7,168	3,990	2,642	536	1,348 R	55.7%	36.9%	60.2%	39.8%
9,490	DISTRICT 3	7,704	3,143	3,805	756	662 D	40.8%	49.4%	45.2%	54.8%
8,416	DISTRICT 4	6,915	3,485	2,929	501	556 R	50.4%	42.4%	54.3%	45.7%
7,948	DISTRICT 5	5,379	2,461	2,483	435	22 D	45.8%	46.2%	49.8%	50.2%
7,148	DISTRICT 6	5,125	2,426	2,204	495	222 R	47.3%	43.0%	52.4%	47.6%
7,858	DISTRICT 7	6,207	2,964	2,298	945	666 R	47.8%	37.0%	56.3%	43.7%
7,420	DISTRICT 8	5,859	3,189	2,157	513	1,032 R	54.4%	36.8%	59.7%	40.3%
7,224	DISTRICT 9	5,773	3,013	2,215	545	798 R	52.2%	38.4%	57.6%	42.4%
8,698	DISTRICT 10	7,116	4,358	2,217	541	2,141 R	61.2%	31.2%	66.3%	33.7%
8,274	DISTRICT 11	6,397	3,441	2,409	547	1,032 R	53.8%	37.7%	58.8%	41.2%
7,978	DISTRICT 12	6,466	3,743	2,188	535	1,555 R	57.9%	33.8%	63.1%	36.9%
9,454	DISTRICT 13	7,567	3,849	2,951	767	898 R	50.9%	39.0%	56.6%	43.4%
7,600	DISTRICT 14	5,475	3,268	1,727	480	1,541 R	59.7%	31.5%	65.4%	34.6%
7,642	DISTRICT 15	5,414	2,416	2,332	666	84 R	44.6%	43.1%	50.9%	49.1%
6,599	DISTRICT 16	4,075	1,753	1,860	462	107 D	43.0%	45.6%	48.5%	51.5%
7,807	DISTRICT 17	5,928	3,365	2,070	493	1,295 R	56.8%	34.9%	61.9%	38.1%
9,495	DISTRICT 18	8,008	4,596	2,696	716	1,900 R	57.4%	33.7%	63.0%	37.0%
7,562	DISTRICT 19	5,885	3,206	2,165	514	1,041 R	54.5%	36.8%	59.7%	40.3%
8,677	DISTRICT 20	6,754	3,645	2,498	611	1,147 R	54.0%	37.0%	59.3%	40.7%
8,002	DISTRICT 21	6,127	3,129	2,402	596	727 R	51.1%	39.2%	56.6%	43.4%
8,649	DISTRICT 22	6,833	3,944	2,390	499	1,554 R	57.7%	35.0%	62.3%	37.7%
6,287	DISTRICT 23	3,753	2,126	1,296	331	830 R	56.6%	34.5%	62.1%	37.9%
8,626	DISTRICT 24	6,775	4,048	2,176	551	1,872 R	59.7%	32.1%	65.0%	35.0%
8,020	DISTRICT 25	6,377	3,816	1,997	564	1,819 R	59.8%	31.3%	65.6%	34.4%
7,442	DISTRICT 26	6,148	3,494	2,063	591	1,431 R	56.8%	33.6%	62.9%	37.1%
8,050	DISTRICT 27	6,524	3,653	2,285	586	1,368 R	56.0%	35.0%	61.5%	38.5%
7,901	DISTRICT 28	6,391	3,393	2,234	764	1,159 R	53.1%	35.0%	60.3%	39.7%
8,674	DISTRICT 29	7,198	3,090	3,428	680	338 D	42.9%	47.6%	47.4%	52.6%
7,682	DISTRICT 30	5,916	3,080	2,476	360	604 R	52.1%	41.9%	55.4%	44.6%
7,720	DISTRICT 31	5,932	2,953	2,624	355	329 R	49.8%	44.2%	52.9%	47.1%
6,660	DISTRICT 32	4,619	2,750	1,562	307	1,188 R	59.5%	33.8%	63.8%	36.2%
8,524	DISTRICT 33	6,880	4,039	2,422	419	1,617 R	58.7%	35.2%	62.5%	37.5%
9,037	DISTRICT 34	6,671	3,988	2,182	501	1,806 R	59.8%	32.7%	64.6%	35.4%
8,152	DISTRICT 35	6,081	3,213	2,296	572	917 R	52.8%	37.8%	58.3%	41.7%
7,280	DISTRICT 36	5,020	2,628	2,056	336	572 R	52.4%	41.0%	56.1%	43.9%
6,564	DISTRICT 37	4,336	1,918	2,214	204	296 D	44.2%	51.1%	46.4%	53.6%
6,705	DISTRICT 38	4,644	2,137	2,272	235	135 D	46.0%	48.9%	48.5%	51.5%
6,221	DISTRICT 39	4,268	1,872	2,131	265	259 D	43.9%	49.9%	46.8%	53.2%
5,820	DISTRICT 40	3,743	1,992	1,462	289	530 R	53.2%	39.1%	57.7%	42.3%
	FEDERAL ABSENTEE	36	13	18	5	5 D	36.1%	50.0%	41.9%	58.1%
315,058	TOTAL	239,714	127,163	92,065	20,486	35,098 R	53.0%	38.4%	58.0%	42.0%

ALASKA

CONGRESS

CD	Year	Total Vote	Republican		Democratic		Other Vote	Rep.-Dem. Plurality	Percentage			
									Total Vote		Major Vote	
			Vote	Candidate	Vote	Candidate			Rep.	Dem.	Rep.	Dem.
AL	1992	239,116	111,849	YOUNG, DON	102,378	DEVENS, JOHN S.	24,889	9,471 R	46.8%	42.8%	52.2%	47.8%
AL	1990	191,647	99,003	YOUNG, DON	91,677	DEVENS, JOHN S.	967	7,326 R	51.7%	47.8%	51.9%	48.1%
AL	1988	192,955	120,595	YOUNG, DON	71,881	GRUENSTEIN, PETER	479	48,714 R	62.5%	37.3%	62.7%	37.3%
AL	1986	180,277	101,799	YOUNG, DON	74,053	BEGICH, PEGGE	4,425	27,746 R	56.5%	41.1%	57.9%	42.1%
AL	1984	206,437	113,582	YOUNG, DON	86,052	BEGICH, PEGGE	6,803	27,530 R	55.0%	41.7%	56.9%	43.1%
AL	1982	181,084	128,274	YOUNG, DON	52,011	CARLSON, DAVE	799	76,263 R	70.8%	28.7%	71.2%	28.8%
AL	1980	154,618	114,089	YOUNG, DON	39,922	PARNELL, KEVIN	607	74,167 R	73.8%	25.8%	74.1%	25.9%
AL	1978	124,187	68,811	YOUNG, DON	55,176	RODEY, PATRICK	200	13,635 R	55.4%	44.4%	55.5%	44.5%
AL	1976	118,208	83,722	YOUNG, DON	34,194	HOPSON, EBEN	292	49,528 R	70.8%	28.9%	71.0%	29.0%
AL	1974	95,921	51,641	YOUNG, DON	44,280	HENSLEY, WILLIAM L.		7,361 R	53.8%	46.2%	53.8%	46.2%
AL	1972	95,401	41,750	YOUNG, DON	53,651	BEGICH, N. J.		11,901 D	43.8%	56.2%	43.8%	56.2%
AL	1970	80,084	35,947	MURKOWSKI, FRANK H.	44,137	BEGICH, N. J.		8,190 D	44.9%	55.1%	44.9%	55.1%
AL	1968	80,362	43,577	POLLOCK, HOWARD W.	36,785	BEGICH, N. J.		6,792 R	54.2%	45.8%	54.2%	45.8%
AL	1966	65,907	34,040	POLLOCK, HOWARD W.	31,867	RIVERS, RALPH J.		2,173 R	51.6%	48.4%	51.6%	48.4%
AL	1964	67,146	32,556	THOMAS, LOWELL	34,590	RIVERS, RALPH J.		2,034 D	48.5%	51.5%	48.5%	51.5%
AL	1962	58,591	26,638	THOMAS, LOWELL	31,953	RIVERS, RALPH J.		5,315 D	45.5%	54.5%	45.5%	54.5%
AL	1960	59,063	25,517	RETTIG, R. L.	33,546	RIVERS, RALPH J.		8,029 D	43.2%	56.8%	43.2%	56.8%
AL	1958	48,647	20,699	BENSON, HENRY A.	27,948	RIVERS, RALPH J.		7,249 D	42.5%	57.5%	42.5%	57.5%
AL	1956	28,266	9,332	GILLAM, BYRON A.	18,934	BARTLETT, E. L.		9,602 D	33.0%	67.0%	33.0%	67.0%
AL	1954	26,999	7,083	DIMOCK, BARBARA D.	19,916	BARTLETT, E. L.		12,833 D	26.2%	73.8%	26.2%	73.8%
AL	1952	25,112	10,893	REEVE, ROBERT C.	14,219	BARTLETT, E. L.		3,326 D	43.4%	56.6%	43.4%	56.6%
AL	1950	18,726	5,138	PETERSON, ALMER J.	13,588	BARTLETT, E. L.		8,450 D	27.4%	72.6%	27.4%	72.6%
AL	1948	22,309	4,789	STOCK, R. H.	17,520	BARTLETT, E. L.		12,731 D	21.5%	78.5%	21.5%	78.5%
AL	1946	16,384	4,868	PETERSON, ALMER J.	11,516	BARTLETT, E. L.		6,648 D	29.7%	70.3%	29.7%	70.3%

ALASKA

1992 GENERAL ELECTION

President   Other vote was 1,379 America First (Gritz); 1,378 Libertarian (Marrou); 469 Independents for Economic Recovery (LaRouche); 433 Natural Law (Hagelin); 377 Taxpayers(Phillips); 330 New Alliance (Fulani); 365 scattered write-ins.

Senator   Other vote was 20,019 Green (Jordan) and 467 scattered write-ins.

Congress   Other vote was 15,049 Alaskan Independence (States); 9,529 Green (Milligan) and 311 scattered write-in.

1992 PRIMARIES

In 1992 the Republican primary was a closed primary with only candidates from that party on the ballot. All other parties ran on a multi-party ballot with nominations going to the candidate with the highest vote in each party.

SEPTEMBER 8 REPUBLICAN

Senator   37,486 Frank H. Murkowski; 9,065 Jed Whittaker.

Congress   Contested as follows:

AL   24,869 Don Young; 19,774 Virginia Collins; 1,671 William L. Holton; 630 Larry A. Seip.

SEPTEMBER 8 DEMOCRATIC

Senator   33,162 Tony Smith; 29,586 William L. Hensley; 2,657 Michael Beasley; 1,607 Joseph A. Sonneman; 1,000 Frank Vondersaar.

Congress   Contested as follows:

AL   37,587 John S. Devens; 25,970 Patrick Rodey.

SEPTEMBER 8 ALASKAN INDEPENDENCE

Senator   No candidate.

Congress   Contested as follows:

AL   3,510 Michael A. States; 2,901 Tom Taggart.

SEPTEMBER 8 GREEN

Senator   Mary E. Jodan, unopposed.

Congress   Unopposed at-large.

ARIZONA

GOVERNOR
Fife Symington (R). Elected February 1991, in a special run-off election, to a four year term.

SENATORS
Dennis DeConcini (D). Re-elected 1988 to a six-year term. Previously elected 1982, 1976.

John McCain (R). Re-elected 1992 to a six-year term. Previously elected 1986.

REPRESENTATIVES
1. Sam Coopersmith (D)
2. Ed Pastor (D)
3. Bob Stump (R)
4. Jon Kyl (R)
5. Jim Kolbe (R)
6. Karan English (D)

POSTWAR VOTE FOR PRESIDENT

Year	Total Vote	Republican		Democratic		Other Vote	Plurality	Percentage			
								Total Vote		Major Vote	
		Vote	Candidate	Vote	Candidate			Rep.	Dem.	Rep.	Dem.
1992 **	1,486,975	572,086	Bush, George	543,050	Clinton, Bill	371,839	29,036 R	38.5%	36.5%	51.3%	48.7%
1988	1,171,873	702,541	Bush, George	454,029	Dukakis, Michael S.	15,303	248,512 R	60.0%	38.7%	60.7%	39.3%
1984	1,025,897	681,416	Reagan, Ronald	333,854	Mondale, Walter F.	10,627	347,562 R	66.4%	32.5%	67.1%	32.9%
1980	873,945	529,688	Reagan, Ronald	246,843	Carter, Jimmy	97,414	282,845 R	60.6%	28.2%	68.2%	31.8%
1976	742,719	418,642	Ford, Gerald R.	295,602	Carter, Jimmy	28,475	123,040 R	56.4%	39.8%	58.6%	41.4%
1972	622,926	402,812	Nixon, Richard M.	198,540	McGovern, George S.	21,574	204,272 R	64.7%	31.9%	67.0%	33.0%
1968	486,936	266,721	Nixon, Richard M.	170,514	Humphrey, Hubert H.	49,701	96,207 R	54.8%	35.0%	61.0%	39.0%
1964	480,770	242,535	Goldwater, Barry M.	237,753	Johnson, Lyndon B.	482	4,782 R	50.4%	49.5%	50.5%	49.5%
1960	398,491	221,241	Nixon, Richard M.	176,781	Kennedy, John F.	469	44,460 R	55.5%	44.4%	55.6%	44.4%
1956	290,173	176,990	Eisenhower, Dwight D.	112,880	Stevenson, Adlai E.	303	64,110 R	61.0%	38.9%	61.1%	38.9%
1952	260,570	152,042	Eisenhower, Dwight D.	108,528	Stevenson, Adlai E.		43,514 R	58.3%	41.7%	58.3%	41.7%
1948	177,065	77,597	Dewey, Thomas E.	95,251	Truman, Harry S.	4,217	17,654 D	43.8%	53.8%	44.9%	55.1%

In 1992 the other vote column includes 353,741 votes cast for Perot.

ARIZONA

POSTWAR VOTE FOR GOVERNOR

Year	Total Vote	Republican		Democratic		Other Vote	Rep.-Dem. Plurality	Percentage			
								Total Vote		Major Vote	
		Vote	Candidate	Vote	Candidate			Rep.	Dem.	Rep.	Dem.
1990 * *	940,737	492,569	Symington, Fife	448,168	Goddard, Terry		44,401 R	52.4%	47.6%	52.4%	47.6%
1986 * *	866,984	343,913	Mecham, Evan	298,986	Warner, Carolyn	224,085	44,927 R	39.7%	34.5%	53.5%	46.5%
1982	726,364	235,877	Corbet, Leo	453,795	Babbitt, Bruce	36,692	217,918 D	32.5%	62.5%	34.2%	65.8%
1978	538,556	241,093	Mecham, Evan	282,605	Babbitt, Bruce	14,858	41,512 D	44.8%	52.5%	46.0%	54.0%
1974	552,202	273,674	Williams, Russell	278,375	Castro, Raul H.	153	4,701 D	49.6%	50.4%	49.6%	50.4%
1970 * *	411,409	209,522	Williams, John R.	201,887	Castro, Raul H.		7,635 R	50.9%	49.1%	50.9%	49.1%
1968	483,998	279,923	Williams, John R.	204,075	Goddard, Sam		75,848 R	57.8%	42.2%	57.8%	42.2%
1966	378,342	203,438	Williams, John R.	174,904	Goddard, Sam		28,534 R	53.8%	46.2%	53.8%	46.2%
1964	473,502	221,404	Kleindienst, Richard	252,098	Goddard, Sam		30,694 D	46.8%	53.2%	46.8%	53.2%
1962	365,841	200,578	Fannin, Paul	165,263	Goddard, Sam		35,315 R	54.8%	45.2%	54.8%	45.2%
1960	397,107	235,502	Fannin, Paul	161,605	Ackerman, Lee		73,897 R	59.3%	40.7%	59.3%	40.7%
1958	290,465	160,136	Fannin, Paul	130,329	Morrison, Robert		29,807 R	55.1%	44.9%	55.1%	44.9%
1956	288,592	116,744	Griffen, Horace B.	171,848	McFarland, Ernest W.		55,104 D	40.5%	59.5%	40.5%	59.5%
1954	243,970	115,866	Pyle, Howard	128,104	McFarland, Ernest W.		12,238 D	47.5%	52.5%	47.5%	52.5%
1952	260,285	156,592	Pyle, Howard	103,693	Haldiman, Joe C.		52,899 R	60.2%	39.8%	60.2%	39.8%
1950	195,227	99,109	Pyle, Howard	96,118	Frohmiller, Ana		2,991 R	50.8%	49.2%	50.8%	49.2%
1948	175,767	70,419	Brockett, Bruce	104,008	Garvey, Dan E.	1,340	33,589 D	40.1%	59.2%	40.4%	59.6%
1946	122,462	48,867	Brockett, Bruce	73,595	Osborn, Sidney P.		24,728 D	39.9%	60.1%	39.9%	60.1%

The term of office for Arizona's Governor was increased from two to four years effective with the 1970 election. In 1986 other vote was Bill Schulz (Independent). In 1990 neither major-party candidate won an absolute majority, therefore a run-off election was held Feburary 26, 1991; the vote above is for the Feburary run-off.

POSTWAR VOTE FOR SENATOR

Year	Total Vote	Republican		Democratic		Other Vote	Rep.-Dem. Plurality	Percentage			
								Total Vote		Major Vote	
		Vote	Candidate	Vote	Candidate			Rep.	Dem.	Rep.	Dem.
1992	1,382,051	771,395	McCain, John	436,321	Sargent, Claire	174,335	335,074 R	55.8%	31.6%	63.9%	36.1%
1988	1,164,539	478,060	DeGreen, Keith	660,403	DeConcini, Dennis	26,076	182,343 D	41.1%	56.7%	42.0%	58.0%
1986	862,921	521,850	McCain, John	340,965	Kimball, Richard	106	180,885 R	60.5%	39.5%	60.5%	39.5%
1982	723,885	291,749	Dunn, Pete	411,970	DeConcini, Dennis	20,166	120,221 D	40.3%	56.9%	41.5%	58.5%
1980	874,238	432,371	Goldwater, Barry M.	422,972	Schulz, Bill	18,895	9,399 R	49.5%	48.4%	50.5%	49.5%
1976	741,210	321,236	Steiger, Sam	400,334	DeConcini, Dennis	19,640	79,098 D	43.3%	54.0%	44.5%	55.5%
1974	549,919	320,396	Goldwater, Barry M.	229,523	Marshall, Jonathan		90,873 R	58.3%	41.7%	58.3%	41.7%
1970	407,796	228,284	Fannin, Paul	179,512	Grossman, Sam		48,772 R	56.0%	44.0%	56.0%	44.0%
1968	479,945	274,607	Goldwater, Barry M.	205,338	Elson, Roy L.		69,269 R	57.2%	42.8%	57.2%	42.8%
1964	468,801	241,089	Fannin, Paul	227,712	Elson, Roy L.		13,377 R	51.4%	48.6%	51.4%	48.6%
1962	362,605	163,388	Mecham, Evan	199,217	Hayden, Carl		35,829 D	45.1%	54.9%	45.1%	54.9%
1958	293,623	164,593	Goldwater, Barry M.	129,030	McFarland, Ernest W.		35,563 R	56.1%	43.9%	56.1%	43.9%
1956	278,263	107,447	Jones, Ross F.	170,816	Hayden, Carl		63,369 D	38.6%	61.4%	38.6%	61.4%
1952	257,401	132,063	Goldwater, Barry M.	125,338	McFarland, Ernest W.		6,725 R	51.3%	48.7%	51.3%	48.7%
1950	185,092	68,846	Brockett, Bruce	116,246	Hayden, Carl		47,400 D	37.2%	62.8%	37.2%	62.8%
1946	116,239	35,022	Powers, Ward S.	80,415	McFarland, Ernest W.	802	45,393 D	30.1%	69.2%	30.3%	69.7%

ARIZONA

Districts Established May 6, 1992

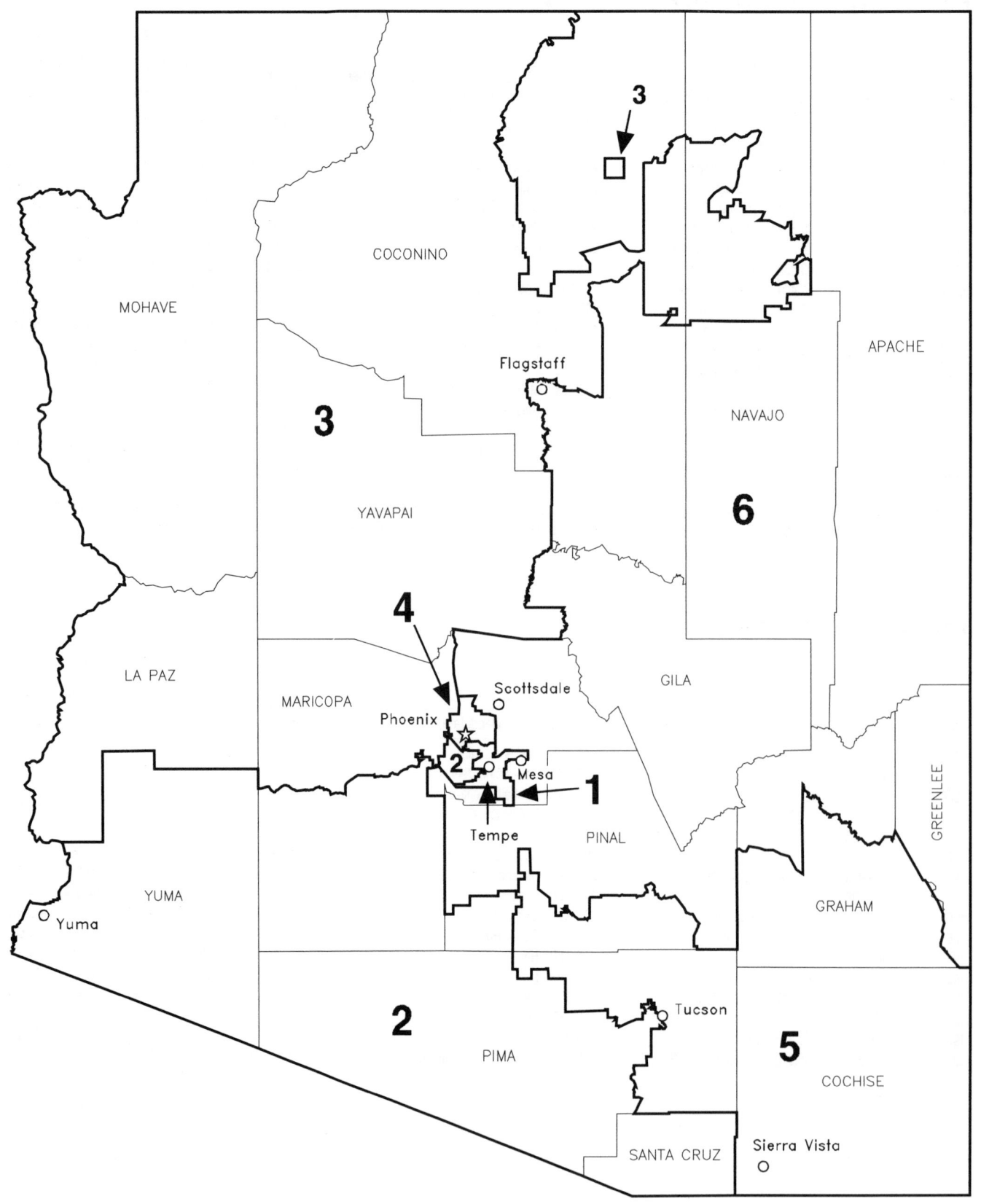

ARIZONA

PRESIDENT 1992

Registration	County	Total Vote	Republican	Democratic	Perot	Other	Plurality	Percentage Total Vote		
								Rep.	Dem.	Perot
28,397	APACHE	18,258	4,588	11,218	1,979	473	6,630 D	25.1%	61.4%	10.8%
44,985	COCHISE	33,150	12,202	12,701	7,857	390	499 D	36.8%	38.3%	23.7%
54,649	COCONINO	42,618	13,769	18,888	9,363	598	5,119 D	32.3%	44.3%	22.0%
24,311	GILA	18,478	5,781	7,571	4,694	432	1,790 D	31.3%	41.0%	25.4%
12,883	GRAHAM	9,699	4,169	3,391	1,860	279	778 R	43.0%	35.0%	19.2%
5,108	GREENLEE	3,962	1,451	1,695	794	22	244 D	36.6%	42.8%	20.0%
6,557	LA PAZ	4,961	1,599	1,808	1,488	66	209 D	32.2%	36.4%	30.0%
1,147,672	MARICOPA	876,832	360,049	285,457	221,475	9,851	74,592 R	41.1%	32.6%	25.3%
55,009	MOHAVE	40,616	13,684	13,255	12,706	971	429 R	33.7%	32.6%	31.3%
36,431	NAVAJO	24,638	7,994	10,882	4,787	975	2,888 D	32.4%	44.2%	19.4%
375,942	PIMA	281,484	97,036	128,569	53,925	1,954	31,533 D	34.5%	45.7%	19.2%
51,143	PINAL	36,739	11,669	15,468	9,231	371	3,799 D	31.8%	42.1%	25.1%
11,268	SANTA CRUZ	8,080	3,024	3,512	1,447	97	488 D	37.4%	43.5%	17.9%
70,202	YAVAPAI	59,415	23,419	18,268	16,409	1,319	5,151 R	39.4%	30.7%	27.6%
40,392	YUMA	28,045	11,652	10,367	5,726	300	1,285 R	41.5%	37.0%	20.4%
1,964,949	TOTAL	1,486,975	572,086	543,050	353,741	18,098	29,036 R	38.5%	36.5%	23.8%

ARIZONA

SENATOR 1992

Registration	County	Total Vote	Republican	Democratic	Other	Rep.-Dem. Plurality	Percentage			
							Total Vote		Major Vote	
							Rep.	Dem.	Rep.	Dem.
28,397	APACHE	18,081	7,564	8,543	1,974	979 D	41.8%	47.2%	47.0%	53.0%
44,985	COCHISE	32,857	19,166	10,304	3,387	8,862 R	58.3%	31.4%	65.0%	35.0%
54,649	COCONINO	41,797	23,766	14,414	3,617	9,352 R	56.9%	34.5%	62.2%	37.8%
24,311	GILA	18,346	9,007	6,011	3,328	2,996 R	49.1%	32.8%	60.0%	40.0%
12,883	GRAHAM	9,727	4,766	2,659	2,302	2,107 R	49.0%	27.3%	64.2%	35.8%
5,108	GREENLEE	3,957	2,086	1,375	496	711 R	52.7%	34.7%	60.3%	39.7%
6,557	LA PAZ	4,910	2,641	1,465	804	1,176 R	53.8%	29.8%	64.3%	35.7%
1,147,672	MARICOPA	790,649	443,607	234,584	112,458	209,023 R	56.1%	29.7%	65.4%	34.6%
55,009	MOHAVE	39,771	21,190	12,513	6,068	8,677 R	53.3%	31.5%	62.9%	37.1%
36,431	NAVAJO	24,498	12,601	7,949	3,948	4,652 R	51.4%	32.4%	61.3%	38.7%
375,942	PIMA	267,194	153,015	95,789	18,390	57,226 R	57.3%	35.8%	61.5%	38.5%
51,143	PINAL	36,505	19,095	12,011	5,399	7,084 R	52.3%	32.9%	61.4%	38.6%
11,268	SANTA CRUZ	7,770	4,591	2,614	565	1,977 R	59.1%	33.6%	63.7%	36.3%
70,202	YAVAPAI	58,525	32,053	17,073	9,399	14,980 R	54.8%	29.2%	65.2%	34.8%
40,392	YUMA	27,464	16,247	9,017	2,200	7,230 R	59.2%	32.8%	64.3%	35.7%
1,964,949	TOTAL	1,382,051	771,395	436,321	174,335	335,074 R	55.8%	31.6%	63.9%	36.1%

ARIZONA

CONGRESS

| CD | Year | Total Vote | Republican | | Democratic | | Other Vote | Rep.-Dem. Plurality | Percentage | | | |
| | | | Vote | Candidate | Vote | Candidate | | | Total Vote | | Major Vote | |
									Rep.	Dem.	Rep.	Dem.
1	1992	254,789	113,613	RHODES, JOHN J., III	130,715	COOPERSMITH, SAM	10,461	17,102 D	44.6%	51.3%	46.5%	53.5%
2	1992	137,378	41,257	SHOOTER, DON	90,693	PASTOR, ED	5,428	49,436 D	30.0%	66.0%	31.3%	68.7%
3	1992	258,503	158,906	STUMP, BOB	88,830	HARTSTONE, ROGER	10,767	70,076 R	61.5%	34.4%	64.1%	35.9%
4	1992	264,066	156,330	KYL, JON	70,572	MYBECK, WALTER R.	37,164	85,758 R	59.2%	26.7%	68.9%	31.1%
5	1992	259,813	172,867	KOLBE, JIM	77,256	TOEVS, JIM	9,690	95,611 R	66.5%	29.7%	69.1%	30.9%
6	1992	234,372	97,074	WEAD, DOUG	124,251	ENGLISH, KARAN	13,047	27,177 D	41.4%	53.0%	43.9%	56.1%

ARIZONA

1992 GENERAL ELECTION

President   Other vote was 8,141 Independent (Gritz); 6,759 Libertarian (Marrou); 2,267 Natural Law (Hagelin); 923 New Alliance (Fulani); 8 LaRouche (write-in).

Senator   Other vote was 145,361 Independent (Mecham); 22,613 Libertarian (DeLamare); 6,335 National Alliance (Finkelstein); 26 Winn (write-in).

Congress   Other vote was Natural Law (Goldstein) in CD 1; 5,423 Libertarian (Detaranto) and 5 scattered write-ins in CD 2; Natural Law (Volponi) in CD 3; 25,553 Independent (Collings), 11,611 Libertarian (McDermott) in CD 4; Libertarian (Willis) in CD 5; Independent (Stannard) in CD 6.

1992 PRIMARIES

SEPTEMBER 8 REPUBLICAN

Senator   John McCain, unopposed.

Congress   Unopposed in two CD's. Contested as follows:

CD 1   15,601 John J. Rhodes, III; 14,194 Stan Barnes; 11,464 Bill Mundell; 3,968 Trace Bartlett; 2,162 John C. Lincoln.
CD 3   38,634 Bob Stump; 18,603 Barbara Keough.
CD 5   37,140 Jim Kolbe; 19,921 Mike Beehler.
CD 6   17,948 Doug Wead; 12,190 Phil MacDonnell; 9,948 Mike Meyer.

SEPTEMBER 8 DEMOCRATIC

Senator   124,174 Claire Sargent; 94,326 Truman Spangrud.

Congress   Unopposed in four CD's. Contested as follows:

CD 1   17,420 Sam Coopersmith; 6,269 David J. Sanson.
CD 6   23,389 Karan English; 15,710 Alan Stephens; 14,102 Albert Hale.

ARKANSAS

GOVERNOR
Jim Guy Tucker (D). Elected Lt. Governor in 1990; became Governor in December 1992 upon the resignation of Governor Bill Clinton (D) who was elected President November 1992. Next Election November 1994.

SENATORS
Dale Bumpers (D). Re-elected 1992 to a six-year term. Previously elected 1986, 1980, 1974.

David H. Pryor (D). Re-elected 1990 to a six-year term. Previously elected 1984, 1978.

REPRESENTATIVES
1. Blanche Lambert (D)
2. Ray Thornton (D)
3. Tim Hutchinson (R)
4. Jay Dickey (R)

POSTWAR VOTE FOR PRESIDENT

		Republican		Democratic		Other		Total Vote		Major Vote	
Year	Total Vote	Vote	Candidate	Vote	Candidate	Vote	Plurality	Rep.	Dem.	Rep.	Dem.
1992 **	950,653	337,324	Bush, George	505,823	Clinton, Bill	107,506	168,499 D	35.5%	53.2%	40.0%	60.0%
1988	827,738	466,578	Bush, George	349,237	Dukakis, Michael S.	11,923	117,341 R	56.4%	42.2%	57.2%	42.8%
1984	884,406	534,774	Reagan, Ronald	338,646	Mondale, Walter F.	10,986	196,128 R	60.5%	38.3%	61.2%	38.8%
1980	837,582	403,164	Reagan, Ronald	398,041	Carter, Jimmy	36,377	5,123 R	48.1%	47.5%	50.3%	49.7%
1976	767,535	267,903	Ford, Gerald R.	498,604	Carter, Jimmy	1,028	230,701 D	34.9%	65.0%	35.0%	65.0%
1972	651,320	448,541	Nixon, Richard M.	199,892	McGovern, George S.	2,887	248,649 R	68.9%	30.7%	69.2%	30.8%
1968 **	619,969	190,759	Nixon, Richard M.	188,228	Humphrey, Hubert H.	240,982	50,223 A	30.8%	30.4%	50.3%	49.7%
1964	560,426	243,264	Goldwater, Barry M.	314,197	Johnson, Lyndon B.	2,965	70,933 D	43.4%	56.1%	43.6%	56.4%
1960	428,509	184,508	Nixon, Richard M.	215,049	Kennedy, John F.	28,952	30,541 D	43.1%	50.2%	46.2%	53.8%
1956	406,572	186,287	Eisenhower, Dwight D.	213,277	Stevenson, Adlai E.	7,008	26,990 D	45.8%	52.5%	46.6%	53.4%
1952	404,800	177,155	Eisenhower, Dwight D.	226,300	Stevenson, Adlai E.	1,345	49,145 D	43.8%	55.9%	43.9%	56.1%
1948 **	242,475	50,959	Dewey, Thomas E.	149,659	Truman, Harry S.	41,857	98,700 D	21.0%	61.7%	25.4%	74.6%

In 1992 the other vote column includes 99,132 votes cast for Perot. In 1968 other vote was American (Wallace). In 1948 other vote was 40,068 States Rights; 1,037 Socialist; 751 Progressive and 1 Prohibition.

ARKANSAS

POSTWAR VOTE FOR GOVERNOR

Year	Total Vote	Republican Vote	Republican Candidate	Democratic Vote	Democratic Candidate	Other Vote	Rep.-Dem. Plurality	Percentage Total Vote Rep.	Percentage Total Vote Dem.	Percentage Major Vote Rep.	Percentage Major Vote Dem.
1990	696,412	295,925	Nelson, Sheffield	400,386	Clinton, Bill	101	104,461 D	42.5%	57.5%	42.5%	57.5%
1986 **	688,551	248,427	White, Frank D.	439,882	Clinton, Bill	242	191,455 D	36.1%	63.9%	36.1%	63.9%
1984	886,548	331,987	Freeman, Woody	554,561	Clinton, Bill		222,574 D	37.4%	62.6%	37.4%	62.6%
1982	789,351	357,496	White, Frank D.	431,855	Clinton, Bill		74,359 D	45.3%	54.7%	45.3%	54.7%
1980	838,925	435,684	White, Frank D.	403,241	Clinton, Bill		32,443 R	51.9%	48.1%	51.9%	48.1%
1978	528,912	193,746	Lowe, A. Lynn	335,101	Clinton, Bill	65	141,355 D	36.6%	63.4%	36.6%	63.4%
1976	726,949	121,716	Griffith, Leon	605,083	Pryor, David H.	150	483,367 D	16.7%	83.2%	16.7%	83.3%
1974	545,974	187,872	Coon, Ken	358,018	Pryor, David H.	84	170,146 D	34.4%	65.6%	34.4%	65.6%
1972	648,069	159,177	Blaylock, Len E.	488,892	Bumpers, Dale		329,715 D	24.6%	75.4%	24.6%	75.4%
1970	609,198	197,418	Rockefeller, Winthrop	375,648	Bumpers, Dale	36,132	178,230 D	32.4%	61.7%	34.4%	65.6%
1968	615,595	322,782	Rockefeller, Winthrop	292,813	Crank, Marion		29,969 R	52.4%	47.6%	52.4%	47.6%
1966	563,527	306,324	Rockefeller, Winthrop	257,203	Johnson, James D.		49,121 R	54.4%	45.6%	54.4%	45.6%
1964	592,113	254,561	Rockefeller, Winthrop	337,489	Faubus, Orval E.	63	82,928 D	43.0%	57.0%	43.0%	57.0%
1962	308,092	82,349	Ricketts, Willis	225,743	Faubus, Orval E.		143,394 D	26.7%	73.3%	26.7%	73.3%
1960	421,985	129,921	Britt, Henry M.	292,064	Faubus, Orval E.		162,143 D	30.8%	69.2%	30.8%	69.2%
1958	286,886	50,288	Johnson, George W.	236,598	Faubus, Orval E.		186,310 D	17.5%	82.5%	17.5%	82.5%
1956	399,012	77,215	Mitchell, Roy	321,797	Faubus, Orval E.		244,582 D	19.4%	80.6%	19.4%	80.6%
1954	335,176	127,004	Remmel, Pratt C.	208,121	Faubus, Orval E.	51	81,117 D	37.9%	62.1%	37.9%	62.1%
1952	391,592	49,292	Speck, Jefferson W.	342,292	Cherry, Francis	8	293,000 D	12.6%	87.4%	12.6%	87.4%
1950	317,087	50,309	Speck, Jefferson W.	266,778	McMath, Sidney S.		216,469 D	15.9%	84.1%	15.9%	84.1%
1948	249,301	26,500	Black, Charles R.	222,801	McMath, Sidney S.		196,301 D	10.6%	89.4%	10.6%	89.4%
1946	152,162	24,133	Mills, W. T.	128,029	Laney, Ben T.		103,896 D	15.9%	84.1%	15.9%	84.1%

The term of office for Arkansas' Governor was increased from two to four years effective with the 1986 election.

POSTWAR VOTE FOR SENATOR

Year	Total Vote	Republican Vote	Republican Candidate	Democratic Vote	Democratic Candidate	Other Vote	Rep.-Dem. Plurality	Percentage Total Vote Rep.	Percentage Total Vote Dem.	Percentage Major Vote Rep.	Percentage Major Vote Dem.
1992	920,008	366,373	Huckabee, Mike	553,635	Bumpers, Dale		187,262 D	39.8%	60.2%	39.8%	60.2%
1990 **	494,735		—	493,910	Pryor, David H.	825	493,910 D		99.8%		100.0%
1986	695,487	262,313	Hutchinson, Asa	433,122	Bumpers, Dale	52	170,809 D	37.7%	62.3%	37.7%	62.3%
1984	875,956	373,615	Bethune, Ed	502,341	Pryor, David H.		128,726 D	42.7%	57.3%	42.7%	57.3%
1980	808,812	330,576	Clark, Bill	477,905	Bumpers, Dale	331	147,329 D	40.9%	59.1%	40.9%	59.1%
1978	522,239	84,722	Kelly, Tom	399,916	Pryor, David H.	37,601	315,194 D	16.2%	76.6%	17.5%	82.5%
1974	543,082	82,026	Jones, John H.	461,056	Bumpers, Dale		379,030 D	15.1%	84.9%	15.1%	84.9%
1972	634,636	248,238	Babbitt, Wayne H.	386,398	McClellan, John L.		138,160 D	39.1%	60.9%	39.1%	60.9%
1968	591,704	241,739	Bernard, Charles T.	349,965	Fulbright, J. W.		108,226 D	40.9%	59.1%	40.9%	59.1%
1966 **			—		McClellan, John L.						
1962	312,880	98,013	Jones, Kenneth	214,867	Fulbright, J. W.		116,854 D	31.3%	68.7%	31.3%	68.7%
1960 **			—		McClellan, John L.						
1956	399,695	68,016	Henley, Ben C.	331,679	Fulbright, J. W.		263,663 D	17.0%	83.0%	17.0%	83.0%
1954	291,058		—	291,058	McClellan, John L.		291,058 D		100.0%		100.0%
1950	302,582		—	302,582	Fulbright, J. W.		302,582 D		100.0%		100.0%
1948	216,401		—	216,401	McClellan, John L.		216,401 D		100.0%		100.0%

Senator McClellan was re-elected in 1966 and in 1960, but his vote was not canvassed in many counties. In 1990 Senator Pryor's vote was not canvassed in seven counties due to the fact that he was unopposed.

ARKANSAS

Districts Established April 10, 1991

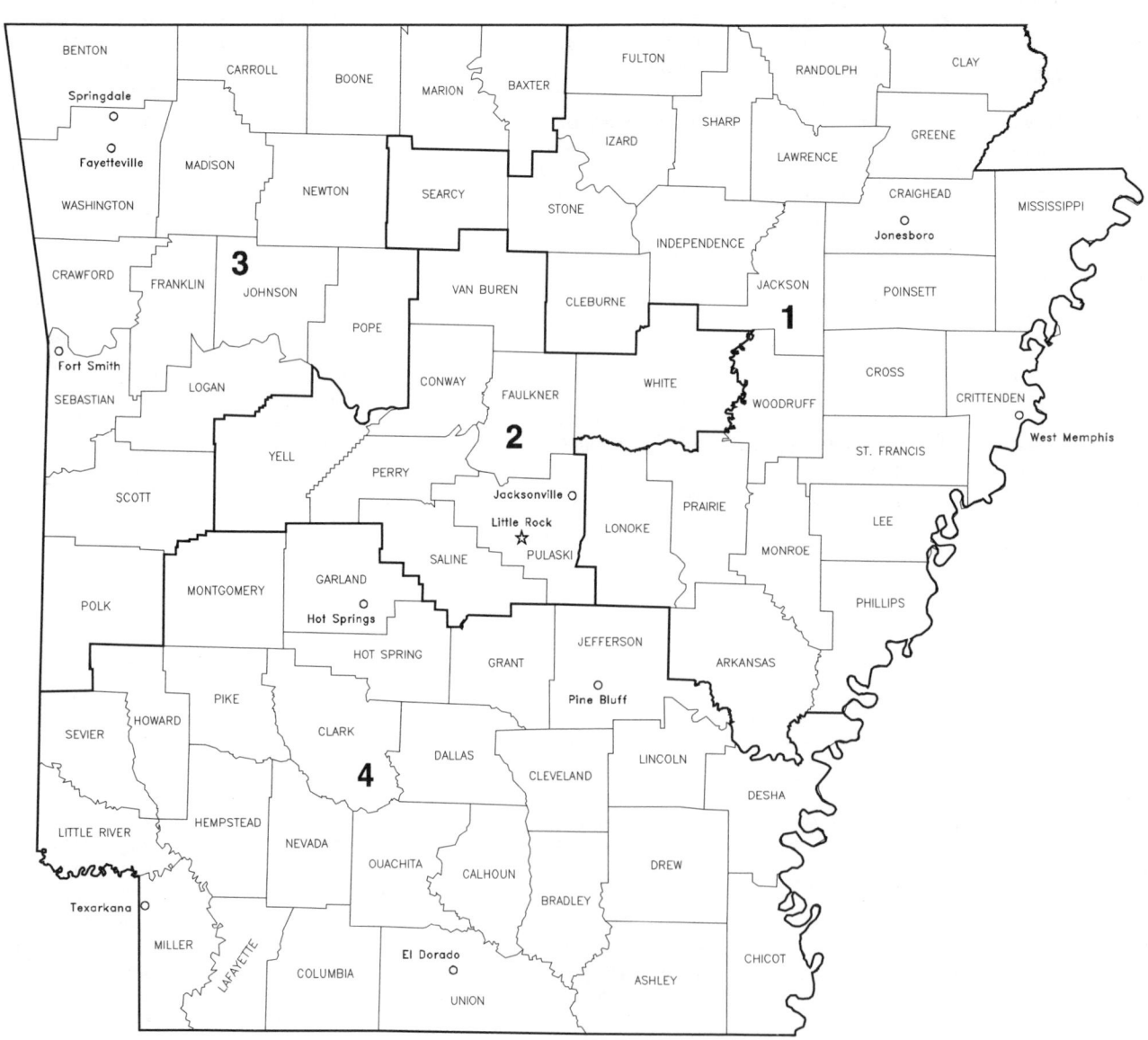

ARKANSAS

PRESIDENT 1992

Registration	County	Total Vote	Republican	Democratic	Perot	Other	Plurality	Percentage Total Vote		
								Rep.	Dem.	Perot
10,650	ARKANSAS	7,980	2,594	4,709	639	38	2,115 D	32.5%	59.0%	8.0%
13,105	ASHLEY	9,567	2,686	5,876	931	74	3,190 D	28.1%	61.4%	9.7%
21,472	BAXTER	15,732	5,640	6,991	2,938	163	1,351 D	35.9%	44.4%	18.7%
55,984	BENTON	43,279	21,126	15,774	6,128	251	5,352 R	48.8%	36.4%	14.2%
18,674	BOONE	14,437	6,094	6,128	2,079	136	34 D	42.2%	42.4%	14.4%
6,542	BRADLEY	4,837	1,482	2,954	391	10	1,472 D	30.6%	61.1%	8.1%
3,914	CALHOUN	2,702	1,047	1,389	257	9	342 D	38.7%	51.4%	9.5%
11,784	CARROLL	8,857	3,535	3,769	1,500	53	234 D	39.9%	42.6%	16.9%
8,170	CHICOT	5,099	1,242	3,504	347	6	2,262 D	24.4%	68.7%	6.8%
11,783	CLARK	8,922	2,403	5,767	714	38	3,364 D	26.9%	64.6%	8.0%
9,952	CLAY	7,080	1,647	4,848	568	17	3,201 D	23.3%	68.5%	8.0%
12,907	CLEBURNE	9,980	3,580	5,090	1,263	47	1,510 D	35.9%	51.0%	12.7%
5,115	CLEVELAND	3,378	1,127	1,893	337	21	766 D	33.4%	56.0%	10.0%
12,884	COLUMBIA	9,819	3,702	4,747	1,090	280	1,045 D	37.7%	48.3%	11.1%
12,882	CONWAY	8,481	2,719	4,898	803	61	2,179 D	32.1%	57.8%	9.5%
34,014	CRAIGHEAD	25,596	9,104	13,931	2,274	287	4,827 D	35.6%	54.4%	8.9%
21,350	CRAWFORD	16,165	6,882	6,656	2,442	185	226 R	42.6%	41.2%	15.1%
25,110	CRITTENDEN	17,108	5,910	9,683	848	667	3,773 D	34.5%	56.6%	5.0%
9,445	CROSS	6,986	2,303	4,058	602	23	1,755 D	33.0%	58.1%	8.6%
6,057	DALLAS	3,925	1,458	2,107	345	15	649 D	37.1%	53.7%	8.8%
8,080	DESHA	5,621	1,279	3,815	392	135	2,536 D	22.8%	67.9%	7.0%
8,975	DREW	6,298	1,938	3,748	596	16	1,810 D	30.8%	59.5%	9.5%
33,860	FAULKNER	25,215	9,491	13,000	2,437	287	3,509 D	37.6%	51.6%	9.7%
10,210	FRANKLIN	6,736	2,495	3,217	987	37	722 D	37.0%	47.8%	14.7%
7,631	FULTON	4,736	1,258	2,827	631	20	1,569 D	26.6%	59.7%	13.3%
48,900	GARLAND	35,995	12,886	18,811	3,475	823	5,925 D	35.8%	52.3%	9.7%
8,122	GRANT	6,198	2,272	3,190	702	34	918 D	36.7%	51.5%	11.3%
16,962	GREENE	12,322	3,510	7,541	1,213	58	4,031 D	28.5%	61.2%	9.8%
12,005	HEMPSTEAD	8,922	2,387	5,476	1,022	37	3,089 D	26.8%	61.4%	11.5%
15,266	HOT SPRING	10,616	3,036	6,308	1,209	63	3,272 D	28.6%	59.4%	11.4%
6,697	HOWARD	4,975	1,728	2,764	466	17	1,036 D	34.7%	55.6%	9.4%
16,588	INDEPENDENCE	12,840	4,232	7,083	1,444	81	2,851 D	33.0%	55.2%	11.2%
7,567	IZARD	5,588	1,532	3,419	606	31	1,887 D	27.4%	61.2%	10.8%
10,594	JACKSON	7,524	1,864	4,944	673	43	3,080 D	24.8%	65.7%	8.9%
44,526	JEFFERSON	31,692	7,525	21,819	2,067	281	14,294 D	23.7%	68.8%	6.5%
10,397	JOHNSON	7,578	2,563	3,951	1,013	51	1,388 D	33.8%	52.1%	13.4%
5,257	LAFAYETTE	3,979	1,188	2,273	504	14	1,085 D	29.9%	57.1%	12.7%
9,553	LAWRENCE	6,929	2,124	4,146	636	23	2,022 D	30.7%	59.8%	9.2%
7,809	LEE	5,066	1,293	3,436	308	29	2,143 D	25.5%	67.8%	6.1%
6,122	LINCOLN	4,347	1,142	2,805	390	10	1,663 D	26.3%	64.5%	9.0%
7,938	LITTLE RIVER	5,718	1,483	3,327	890	18	1,844 D	25.9%	58.2%	15.6%
11,651	LOGAN	8,687	3,408	3,995	1,220	64	587 D	39.2%	46.0%	14.0%
19,225	LONOKE	15,824	6,253	7,963	1,554	54	1,710 D	39.5%	50.3%	9.8%
7,328	MADISON	5,277	2,238	2,415	598	26	177 D	42.4%	45.8%	11.3%
8,293	MARION	6,245	2,023	2,757	1,327	138	734 D	32.4%	44.1%	21.2%
19,543	MILLER	14,623	5,273	7,050	2,249	51	1,777 D	36.1%	48.2%	15.4%
26,675	MISSISSIPPI	15,962	4,697	10,046	981	238	5,349 D	29.4%	62.9%	6.1%
5,959	MONROE	4,272	1,324	2,578	355	15	1,254 D	31.0%	60.3%	8.3%
5,252	MONTGOMERY	3,712	1,205	1,904	576	27	699 D	32.5%	51.3%	15.5%
6,827	NEVADA	3,948	1,217	2,242	455	34	1,025 D	30.8%	56.8%	11.5%
5,775	NEWTON	4,144	1,730	1,765	608	41	35 D	41.7%	42.6%	14.7%
19,550	OUACHITA	12,415	3,711	7,411	1,238	55	3,700 D	29.9%	59.7%	10.0%
5,401	PERRY	3,504	1,162	1,906	412	24	744 D	33.2%	54.4%	11.8%
16,732	PHILLIPS	9,837	2,695	6,456	634	52	3,761 D	27.4%	65.6%	6.4%
6,014	PIKE	4,232	1,577	2,168	472	15	591 D	37.3%	51.2%	11.2%
12,520	POINSETT	8,571	2,425	5,341	761	44	2,916 D	28.3%	62.3%	8.9%
9,905	POLK	7,217	2,757	3,162	1,225	73	405 D	38.2%	43.8%	17.0%
24,173	POPE	17,862	8,056	7,704	1,989	113	352 R	45.1%	43.1%	11.1%
5,418	PRAIRIE	3,956	1,154	2,366	434	2	1,212 D	29.2%	59.8%	11.0%
196,596	PULASKI	136,957	47,789	79,482	8,751	935	31,693 D	34.9%	58.0%	6.4%

ARKANSAS

PRESIDENT 1992

Registration	County	Total Vote	Republican	Democratic	Perot	Other	Plurality	Percentage Total Vote		
								Rep.	Dem.	Perot
8,426	RANDOLPH	6,314	1,766	3,921	578	49	2,155 D	28.0%	62.1%	9.2%
16,040	ST. FRANCIS	10,635	3,289	6,548	766	32	3,259 D	30.9%	61.6%	7.2%
36,252	SALINE	25,661	10,105	12,671	2,751	134	2,566 D	39.4%	49.4%	10.7%
6,394	SCOTT	4,562	1,695	2,228	610	29	533 D	37.2%	48.8%	13.4%
5,455	SEARCY	3,984	1,772	1,679	503	30	93 R	44.5%	42.1%	12.6%
52,500	SEBASTIAN	39,659	16,817	16,570	6,023	249	247 R	42.4%	41.8%	15.2%
6,926	SEVIER	5,011	1,592	2,558	643	218	966 D	31.8%	51.0%	12.8%
9,550	SHARP	7,196	2,486	3,761	921	28	1,275 D	34.5%	52.3%	12.8%
6,789	STONE	5,039	1,672	2,622	697	48	950 D	33.2%	52.0%	13.8%
24,734	UNION	18,580	7,305	8,786	1,919	570	1,481 D	39.3%	47.3%	10.3%
9,630	VAN BUREN	7,361	2,612	3,819	888	42	1,207 D	35.5%	51.9%	12.1%
62,508	WASHINGTON	47,880	20,292	22,029	5,304	255	1,737 D	42.4%	46.0%	11.1%
29,195	WHITE	21,563	8,538	10,494	2,366	165	1,956 D	39.6%	48.7%	11.0%
5,174	WOODRUFF	3,495	676	2,589	227	3	1,913 D	19.3%	74.1%	6.5%
10,681	YELL	7,643	2,506	4,165	940	32	1,659 D	32.8%	54.5%	12.3%
1,317,944	TOTAL	950,653	337,324	505,823	99,132	8,374	168,499 D	35.5%	53.2%	10.4%

ARKANSAS

SENATOR 1992

| | | | | | | | | Percentage | | | |
| | | | | | | Rep.-Dem. | | Total Vote | | Major Vote | |
Registration	County	Total Vote	Republican	Democratic	Other	Plurality		Rep.	Dem.	Rep.	Dem.
10,650	ARKANSAS	6,922	1,859	5,063		3,204	D	26.9%	73.1%	26.9%	73.1%
13,105	ASHLEY	8,604	3,186	5,418		2,232	D	37.0%	63.0%	37.0%	63.0%
21,472	BAXTER	14,978	7,071	7,907		836	D	47.2%	52.8%	47.2%	52.8%
55,984	BENTON	43,541	24,597	18,944		5,653	R	56.5%	43.5%	56.5%	43.5%
18,674	BOONE	13,335	6,364	6,971		607	D	47.7%	52.3%	47.7%	52.3%
6,542	BRADLEY	4,897	1,533	3,364		1,831	D	31.3%	68.7%	31.3%	68.7%
3,914	CALHOUN	2,713	1,055	1,658		603	D	38.9%	61.1%	38.9%	61.1%
11,784	CARROLL	8,878	4,437	4,441		4	D	50.0%	50.0%	50.0%	50.0%
8,170	CHICOT	5,155	1,228	3,927		2,699	D	23.8%	76.2%	23.8%	76.2%
11,783	CLARK	8,964	2,652	6,312		3,660	D	29.6%	70.4%	29.6%	70.4%
9,952	CLAY	7,009	1,724	5,285		3,561	D	24.6%	75.4%	24.6%	75.4%
12,907	CLEBURNE	10,098	3,867	6,231		2,364	D	38.3%	61.7%	38.3%	61.7%
5,115	CLEVELAND	3,450	1,164	2,286		1,122	D	33.7%	66.3%	33.7%	66.3%
12,884	COLUMBIA	8,828	4,852	3,976		876	R	55.0%	45.0%	55.0%	45.0%
12,882	CONWAY	8,332	2,914	5,418		2,504	D	35.0%	65.0%	35.0%	65.0%
34,014	CRAIGHEAD	24,408	9,117	15,291		6,174	D	37.4%	62.6%	37.4%	62.6%
21,350	CRAWFORD	15,844	8,371	7,473		898	R	52.8%	47.2%	52.8%	47.2%
25,110	CRITTENDEN	14,355	5,596	8,759		3,163	D	39.0%	61.0%	39.0%	61.0%
9,445	CROSS	6,880	2,268	4,612		2,344	D	33.0%	67.0%	33.0%	67.0%
6,057	DALLAS	4,179	1,351	2,828		1,477	D	32.3%	67.7%	32.3%	67.7%
8,080	DESHA	5,263	1,277	3,986		2,709	D	24.3%	75.7%	24.3%	75.7%
8,975	DREW	6,241	1,880	4,361		2,481	D	30.1%	69.9%	30.1%	69.9%
33,860	FAULKNER	24,064	9,601	14,463		4,862	D	39.9%	60.1%	39.9%	60.1%
10,210	FRANKLIN	6,739	2,739	4,000		1,261	D	40.6%	59.4%	40.6%	59.4%
7,631	FULTON	4,638	1,452	3,186		1,734	D	31.3%	68.7%	31.3%	68.7%
48,900	GARLAND	31,163	14,910	16,253		1,343	D	47.8%	52.2%	47.8%	52.2%
8,122	GRANT	6,230	2,362	3,868		1,506	D	37.9%	62.1%	37.9%	62.1%
16,962	GREENE	12,764	3,860	8,904		5,044	D	30.2%	69.8%	30.2%	69.8%
12,005	HEMPSTEAD	8,727	4,170	4,557		387	D	47.8%	52.2%	47.8%	52.2%
15,266	HOT SPRING	11,290	3,642	7,648		4,006	D	32.3%	67.7%	32.3%	67.7%
6,697	HOWARD	4,752	2,086	2,666		580	D	43.9%	56.1%	43.9%	56.1%
16,588	INDEPENDENCE	12,935	4,420	8,515		4,095	D	34.2%	65.8%	34.2%	65.8%
7,567	IZARD	5,628	1,763	3,865		2,102	D	31.3%	68.7%	31.3%	68.7%
10,594	JACKSON	7,495	1,920	5,575		3,655	D	25.6%	74.4%	25.6%	74.4%
44,526	JEFFERSON	29,248	8,368	20,880		12,512	D	28.6%	71.4%	28.6%	71.4%
10,397	JOHNSON	7,747	3,011	4,736		1,725	D	38.9%	61.1%	38.9%	61.1%
5,257	LAFAYETTE	3,955	1,640	2,315		675	D	41.5%	58.5%	41.5%	58.5%
9,553	LAWRENCE	6,854	1,955	4,899		2,944	D	28.5%	71.5%	28.5%	71.5%
7,809	LEE	4,995	1,018	3,977		2,959	D	20.4%	79.6%	20.4%	79.6%
6,122	LINCOLN	4,330	1,160	3,170		2,010	D	26.8%	73.2%	26.8%	73.2%
7,938	LITTLE RIVER	5,677	2,345	3,332		987	D	41.3%	58.7%	41.3%	58.7%
11,651	LOGAN	8,494	3,685	4,809		1,124	D	43.4%	56.6%	43.4%	56.6%
19,225	LONOKE	15,612	6,018	9,594		3,576	D	38.5%	61.5%	38.5%	61.5%
7,328	MADISON	5,261	2,419	2,842		423	D	46.0%	54.0%	46.0%	54.0%
8,293	MARION	5,429	2,569	2,860		291	D	47.3%	52.7%	47.3%	52.7%
19,543	MILLER	14,663	7,945	6,718		1,227	R	54.2%	45.8%	54.2%	45.8%
26,675	MISSISSIPPI	13,805	4,311	9,494		5,183	D	31.2%	68.8%	31.2%	68.8%
5,959	MONROE	4,305	1,089	3,216		2,127	D	25.3%	74.7%	25.3%	74.7%
5,252	MONTGOMERY	3,745	1,522	2,223		701	D	40.6%	59.4%	40.6%	59.4%
6,827	NEVADA	4,058	1,527	2,531		1,004	D	37.6%	62.4%	37.6%	62.4%
5,775	NEWTON	4,040	1,958	2,082		124	D	48.5%	51.5%	48.5%	51.5%
19,550	OUACHITA	12,523	4,475	8,048		3,573	D	35.7%	64.3%	35.7%	64.3%
5,401	PERRY	3,470	1,240	2,230		990	D	35.7%	64.3%	35.7%	64.3%
16,732	PHILLIPS	9,426	2,150	7,276		5,126	D	22.8%	77.2%	22.8%	77.2%
6,014	PIKE	4,254	1,830	2,424		594	D	43.0%	57.0%	43.0%	57.0%
12,520	POINSETT	8,740	2,562	6,178		3,616	D	29.3%	70.7%	29.3%	70.7%
9,905	POLK	7,232	3,713	3,519		194	R	51.3%	48.7%	51.3%	48.7%
24,173	POPE	18,845	9,029	9,816		787	D	47.9%	52.1%	47.9%	52.1%
5,418	PRAIRIE	4,025	1,091	2,934		1,843	D	27.1%	72.9%	27.1%	72.9%
196,596	PULASKI	133,285	46,864	86,421		39,557	D	35.2%	64.8%	35.2%	64.8%

ARKANSAS

SENATOR 1992

Registration	County	Total Vote	Republican	Democratic	Other	Rep.-Dem. Plurality	Percentage			
							Total Vote		Major Vote	
							Rep.	Dem.	Rep.	Dem.
8,426	RANDOLPH	6,001	1,813	4,188		2,375 D	30.2%	69.8%	30.2%	69.8%
16,040	ST. FRANCIS	10,516	3,234	7,282		4,048 D	30.8%	69.2%	30.8%	69.2%
36,252	SALINE	27,688	11,474	16,214		4,740 D	41.4%	58.6%	41.4%	58.6%
6,394	SCOTT	4,558	2,076	2,482		406 D	45.5%	54.5%	45.5%	54.5%
5,455	SEARCY	3,658	1,716	1,942		226 D	46.9%	53.1%	46.9%	53.1%
52,500	SEBASTIAN	35,871	18,974	16,897		2,077 R	52.9%	47.1%	52.9%	47.1%
6,926	SEVIER	5,036	2,109	2,927		818 D	41.9%	58.1%	41.9%	58.1%
9,550	SHARP	7,246	2,831	4,415		1,584 D	39.1%	60.9%	39.1%	60.9%
6,789	STONE	3,903	1,351	2,552		1,201 D	34.6%	65.4%	34.6%	65.4%
24,734	UNION	17,611	8,238	9,373		1,135 D	46.8%	53.2%	46.8%	53.2%
9,630	VAN BUREN	7,192	2,954	4,238		1,284 D	41.1%	58.9%	41.1%	58.9%
62,508	WASHINGTON	47,562	21,474	26,088		4,614 D	45.1%	54.9%	45.1%	54.9%
29,195	WHITE	19,143	8,124	11,019		2,895 D	42.4%	57.6%	42.4%	57.6%
5,174	WOODRUFF	3,048	548	2,500		1,952 D	18.0%	82.0%	18.0%	82.0%
10,681	YELL	7,658	2,675	4,983		2,308 D	34.9%	65.1%	34.9%	65.1%
1,317,944	TOTAL	920,008	366,373	553,635		187,262 D	39.8%	60.2%	39.8%	60.2%

ARKANSAS

CONGRESS

CD	Year	Total Vote	Republican		Democratic		Other Vote	Rep.-Dem. Plurality	Percentage			
			Vote	Candidate	Vote	Candidate			Total Vote		Major Vote	
									Rep.	Dem.	Rep.	Dem.
1	1992	214,176	64,618	HAYES, TERRY	149,558	LAMBERT, BLANCHE		84,940 D	30.2%	69.8%	30.2%	69.8%
2	1992	208,924	53,978	SCOTT, DENNIS	154,946	THORNTON, RAY		100,968 D	25.8%	74.2%	25.8%	74.2%
3	1992	249,494	125,295	HUTCHINSON, TIM	117,775	VAN WINKLE, JOHN	6,424	7,520 R	50.2%	47.2%	51.5%	48.5%
4	1992	215,927	113,009	DICKEY, JAY	102,918	MCCUEN, W. J.		10,091 R	52.3%	47.7%	52.3%	47.7%

ARKANSAS

1992 GENERAL ELECTION

President   Other vote was 1,437 Taxpayers (Phillips); 1,261 Libertarian (Marrou); 1,022 New Alliance (Fulani); 956 Apathy (Boren); 819 America First (Gritz); 764 Natural Law (Hagelin); 762 Justice, Industry, Agriculture (LaRouche); 554 Take Back America (Yiamouyiannis); 472 Prohibition (Dodge); 327 Looking Back (Masters).

Senator

Congress   Other vote was Independent (Forbes) in CD 3.

1992 PRIMARIES

MAY 26 REPUBLICAN

Senator   41,346 Mike Huckabee; 10,892 David Busby.

Congress   Unopposed in three CD's. Contested as follows:

CD 3   17,380 Tim Hutchinson; 10,534 Dick Barclay; 4,879 Dryden Pence.

MAY 26 DEMOCRATIC

Senator   322,458 Dale Bumpers; 177,273 Julia H. Jones.

Congress   Unopposed in CD 2. Contested as follows:

CD 1   86,142 Blanche Lambert; 54,686 William Alexander.
CD 3   34,781 John VanWinkle; 23,044 Don Nelms; 14,838 Bill Harrison; 14,294 Dan Ivy.
CD 4   60,854 Beryl F. Anthony; 46,451 W. J. McCuen; 45,018 Pat Pappas.

JUNE 9 DEMOCRATIC RUN-OFF

Congress   Contested as follows:

CD 3   30,135 John VanWinkle; 21,418 Don Nelms.
CD 4   44,743 W. J. McCuen; 43,003 Beryl F. Anthony.

CALIFORNIA

GOVERNOR

Pete Wilson (R). Elected 1990 to a four-year term.

SENATORS

Barbara Boxer (D). Elected 1992 to a six-year term.

Dianne Feinstein (D). Elected 1992 to fill the remaining two years of the term vacated when Senator Pete Wilson (R) was elected Governor in November 1990.

REPRESENTATIVES

1. Dan Hamburg (D)
2. Wally Herger (R)
3. Vic Fazio (D)
4. John T. Doolittle (R)
5. Robert T. Matsui (D)
6. Lynn Woolsey (D)
7. George Miller (D)
8. Nancy Pelosi (D)
9. Ronald V. Dellums (D)
10. Bill Baker (R)
11. Richard W. Pombo (R)
12. Tom Lantos (D)
13. Fortney Stark (D)
14. Anna G. Eshoo (D)
15. Norman Y. Mineta (D)
16. Don Edwards (D)
17. Leon E. Panetta (D)
(see page 1)
18. Gary A. Condit (D)
19. Richard Lehman (D)
20. Calvin Dooley (D)
21. William M. Thomas (R)
22. Michael Huffington (R)
23. Elton Gallegly (R)
24. Anthony C. Beilenson (D)
25. Howard P. McKeon (R)
26. Howard L. Berman (D)
27. Carlos J. Moorhead (R)
28. David Dreier (R)
29. Henry A. Waxman (D)
30. Xavier Becerra (D)
31. Mathew G. Martinez (D)
32. Julian C. Dixon (D)
33. Lucille Roybal-Allard (D)
34. Esteban Torres (D)
35. Maxine Waters (D)
36. Jane Harman (D)
37. Walter R. Tucker (D)
38. Steve Horn (R)
39. Ed Royce (R)
40. Jerry Lewis (R)
41. Jay C. Kim (R)
42. George E. Brown (D)
43. Ken Calvert (R)
44. Al McCandless (R)
45. Dana Rohrabacher (R)
46. Robert K. Dornan (R)
47. Christopher Cox (R)
48. Ron Packard (R)
49. Lynn Schenk (D)
50. Bob Filner (D)
51. Randy Cunningham (R)
52. Duncan L. Hunter (R)

POSTWAR VOTE FOR PRESIDENT

Year	Total Vote	Republican Vote	Republican Candidate	Democratic Vote	Democratic Candidate	Other Vote	Plurality	Total Vote Rep.	Total Vote Dem.	Major Vote Rep.	Major Vote Dem.
1992 **	11,131,721	3,630,574	Bush, George	5,121,325	Clinton, Bill	2,379,822	1,490,751 D	32.6%	46.0%	41.5%	58.5%
1988	9,887,065	5,054,917	Bush, George	4,702,233	Dukakis, Michael S.	129,915	352,684 R	51.1%	47.6%	51.8%	48.2%
1984	9,505,423	5,467,009	Reagan, Ronald	3,922,519	Mondale, Walter F.	115,895	1,544,490 R	57.5%	41.3%	58.2%	41.8%
1980	8,587,063	4,524,858	Reagan, Ronald	3,083,661	Carter, Jimmy	978,544	1,441,197 R	52.7%	35.9%	59.5%	40.5%
1976	7,867,117	3,882,244	Ford, Gerald R.	3,742,284	Carter, Jimmy	242,589	139,960 R	49.3%	47.6%	50.9%	49.1%
1972	8,367,862	4,602,096	Nixon, Richard M.	3,475,847	McGovern, George S.	289,919	1,126,249 R	55.0%	41.5%	57.0%	43.0%
1968	7,251,587	3,467,664	Nixon, Richard M.	3,244,318	Humphrey, Hubert H.	539,605	223,346 R	47.8%	44.7%	51.7%	48.3%
1964	7,057,586	2,879,108	Goldwater, Barry M.	4,171,877	Johnson, Lyndon B.	6,601	1,292,769 D	40.8%	59.1%	40.8%	59.2%
1960	6,506,578	3,259,722	Nixon, Richard M.	3,224,099	Kennedy, John F.	22,757	35,623 R	50.1%	49.6%	50.3%	49.7%
1956	5,466,355	3,027,668	Eisenhower, Dwight D.	2,420,135	Stevenson, Adlai E.	18,552	607,533 R	55.4%	44.3%	55.6%	44.4%
1952	5,141,849	2,897,310	Eisenhower, Dwight D.	2,197,548	Stevenson, Adlai E.	46,991	699,762 R	56.3%	42.7%	56.9%	43.1%
1948	4,021,538	1,895,269	Dewey, Thomas E.	1,913,134	Truman, Harry S.	213,135	17,865 D	47.1%	47.6%	49.8%	50.2%

In 1992 the other vote column includes 2,296,006 votes cast for Perot.

CALIFORNIA

POSTWAR VOTE FOR GOVERNOR

Year	Total Vote	Republican		Democratic		Other Vote	Rep.-Dem. Plurality	Percentage			
								Total Vote		Major Vote	
		Vote	Candidate	Vote	Candidate			Rep.	Dem.	Rep.	Dem.
1990	7,699,467	3,791,904	Wilson, Pete	3,525,197	Feinstein, Dianne	382,366	266,707 R	49.2%	45.8%	51.8%	48.2%
1986	7,443,551	4,506,601	Deukmejian, George	2,781,714	Bradley, Tom	155,236	1,724,887 R	60.5%	37.4%	61.8%	38.2%
1982	7,876,698	3,881,014	Deukmejian, George	3,787,669	Bradley, Tom	208,015	93,345 R	49.3%	48.1%	50.6%	49.4%
1978	6,922,378	2,526,534	Younger, Evelle J.	3,878,812	Brown, Edmund G., Jr.	517,032	1,352,278 D	36.5%	56.0%	39.4%	60.6%
1974	6,248,070	2,952,954	Flournoy, Houston I.	3,131,648	Brown, Edmund G., Jr.	163,468	178,694 D	47.3%	50.1%	48.5%	51.5%
1970	6,510,072	3,439,664	Reagan, Ronald	2,938,607	Unruh, Jess	131,801	501,057 R	52.8%	45.1%	53.9%	46.1%
1966	6,503,445	3,742,913	Reagan, Ronald	2,749,174	Brown, Edmund G.	11,358	993,739 R	57.6%	42.3%	57.7%	42.3%
1962	5,853,270	2,740,351	Nixon, Richard M.	3,037,109	Brown, Edmund G.	75,810	296,758 D	46.8%	51.9%	47.4%	52.6%
1958	5,255,777	2,110,911	Knowland, William F.	3,140,076	Brown, Edmund G.	4,790	1,029,165 D	40.2%	59.7%	40.2%	59.8%
1954	4,030,368	2,290,519	Knight, Goodwin J.	1,739,368	Graves, Richard P.	481	551,151 R	56.8%	43.2%	56.8%	43.2%
1950	3,796,090	2,461,754	Warren, Earl	1,333,856	Roosevelt, James	480	1,127,898 R	64.8%	35.1%	64.9%	35.1%
1946 **	2,558,399	2,344,542	Warren, Earl	—		213,857	2,344,542 R	91.6%		100.0%	

In 1946 the Republican candidate won both major party nominations.

POSTWAR VOTE FOR SENATOR

Year	Total Vote	Republican		Democratic		Other Vote	Rep.-Dem. Plurality	Percentage			
								Total Vote		Major Vote	
		Vote	Candidate	Vote	Candidate			Rep.	Dem.	Rep.	Dem.
1992	10,799,703	4,644,182	Herschensohn, Bruce	5,173,467	Boxer, Barbara	982,054	529,285 D	43.0%	47.9%	47.3%	52.7%
1992 S	10,782,743	4,093,501	Seymour, John	5,853,651	Feinstein, Dianne	835,591	1,760,150 D	38.0%	54.3%	41.2%	58.8%
1988	9,743,598	5,143,409	Wilson, Pete	4,287,253	McCarthy, Leo	312,936	856,156 R	52.8%	44.0%	54.5%	45.5%
1986	7,398,549	3,541,804	Zschau, Ed	3,646,672	Cranston, Alan	210,073	104,868 D	47.9%	49.3%	49.3%	50.7%
1982	7,805,538	4,022,565	Wilson, Pete	3,494,968	Brown, Edmund G., Jr.	288,005	527,597 R	51.5%	44.8%	53.5%	46.5%
1980	8,327,481	3,093,426	Gann, Paul	4,705,399	Cranston, Alan	528,656	1,611,973 D	37.1%	56.5%	39.7%	60.3%
1976	7,472,268	3,748,973	Hayakawa, S. I.	3,502,862	Tunney, John V.	220,433	246,111 R	50.2%	46.9%	51.7%	48.3%
1974	6,102,432	2,210,267	Richardson, H. L.	3,693,160	Cranston, Alan	199,005	1,482,893 D	36.2%	60.5%	37.4%	62.6%
1970	6,492,157	2,877,617	Murphy, George	3,496,558	Tunney, John V.	117,982	618,941 D	44.3%	53.9%	45.1%	54.9%
1968	7,102,465	3,329,148	Rafferty, Max	3,680,352	Cranston, Alan	92,965	351,204 D	46.9%	51.8%	47.5%	52.5%
1964	7,041,821	3,628,555	Murphy, George	3,411,912	Salinger, Pierre	1,354	216,643 R	51.5%	48.5%	51.5%	48.5%
1962	5,647,952	3,180,483	Kuchel, Thomas H.	2,452,839	Richards, Richard	14,630	727,644 R	56.3%	43.4%	56.5%	43.5%
1958	5,135,221	2,204,337	Knight, Goodwin J.	2,927,693	Engle, Clair	3,191	723,356 D	42.9%	57.0%	43.0%	57.0%
1956	5,361,467	2,892,918	Kuchel, Thomas H.	2,445,816	Richards, Richard	22,733	447,102 R	54.0%	45.6%	54.2%	45.8%
1954 S	3,929,668	2,090,836	Kuchel, Thomas H.	1,788,071	Yorty, Samuel W.	50,761	302,765 R	53.2%	45.5%	53.9%	46.1%
1952 **	4,542,548	3,982,448	Knowland, William F.	—		560,100	3,982,448 R	87.7%		100.0%	
1950	3,686,315	2,183,454	Nixon, Richard M.	1,502,507	Douglas, Helen	354	680,947 R	59.2%	40.8%	59.2%	40.8%
1946	2,639,465	1,428,067	Knowland, William F.	1,167,161	Rogers, Will	44,237	260,906 R	54.1%	44.2%	55.0%	45.0%

One of the 1992 elections was for a short term to fill a vacancy. The 1954 election was for a short term to fill a vacancy. In 1952 the Republican candidate won both major party nominations.

CALIFORNIA

Districts Established January 28, 1992

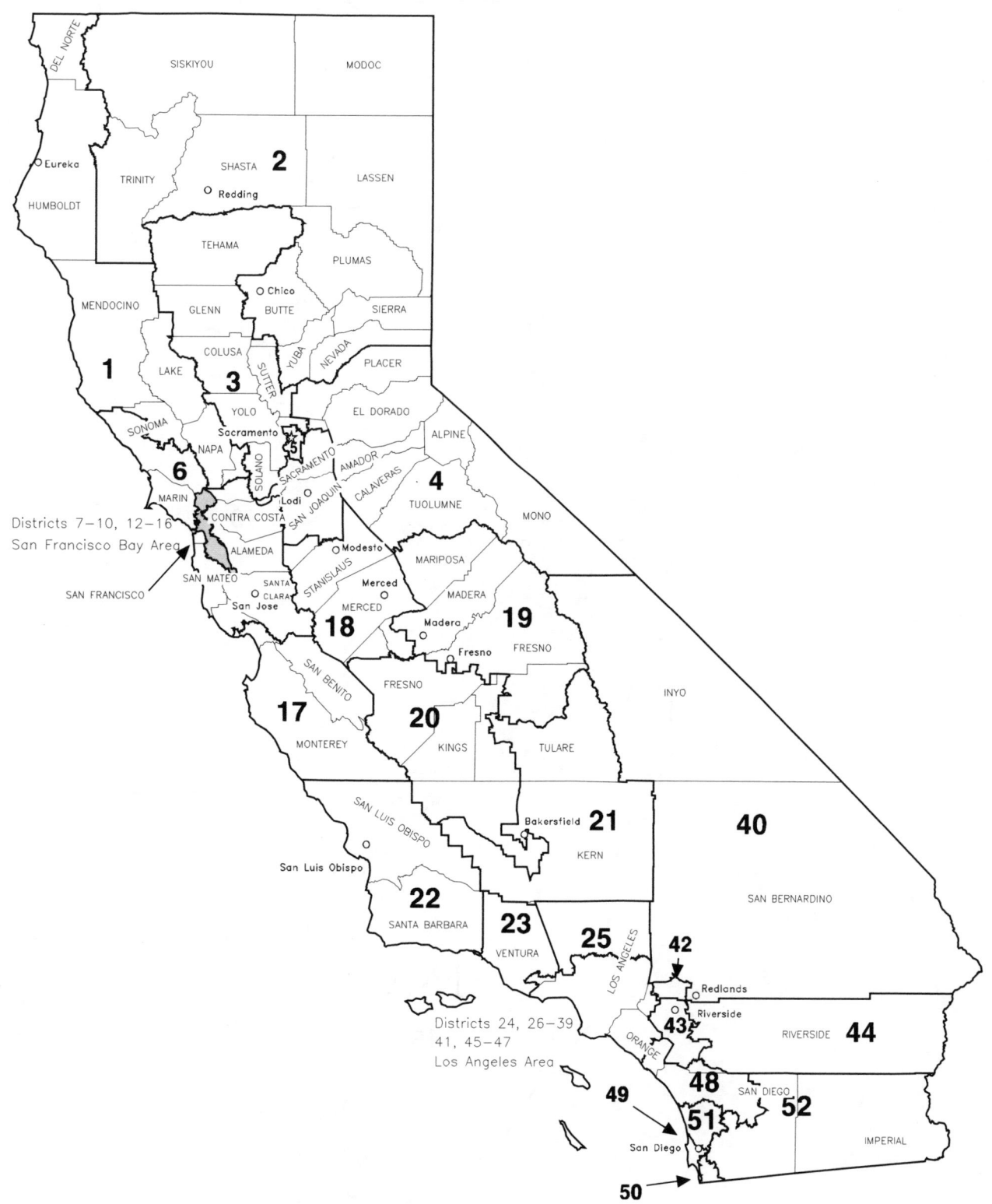

SAN FRANCISCO BAY AREA

CONGRESSIONAL DISTRICTS

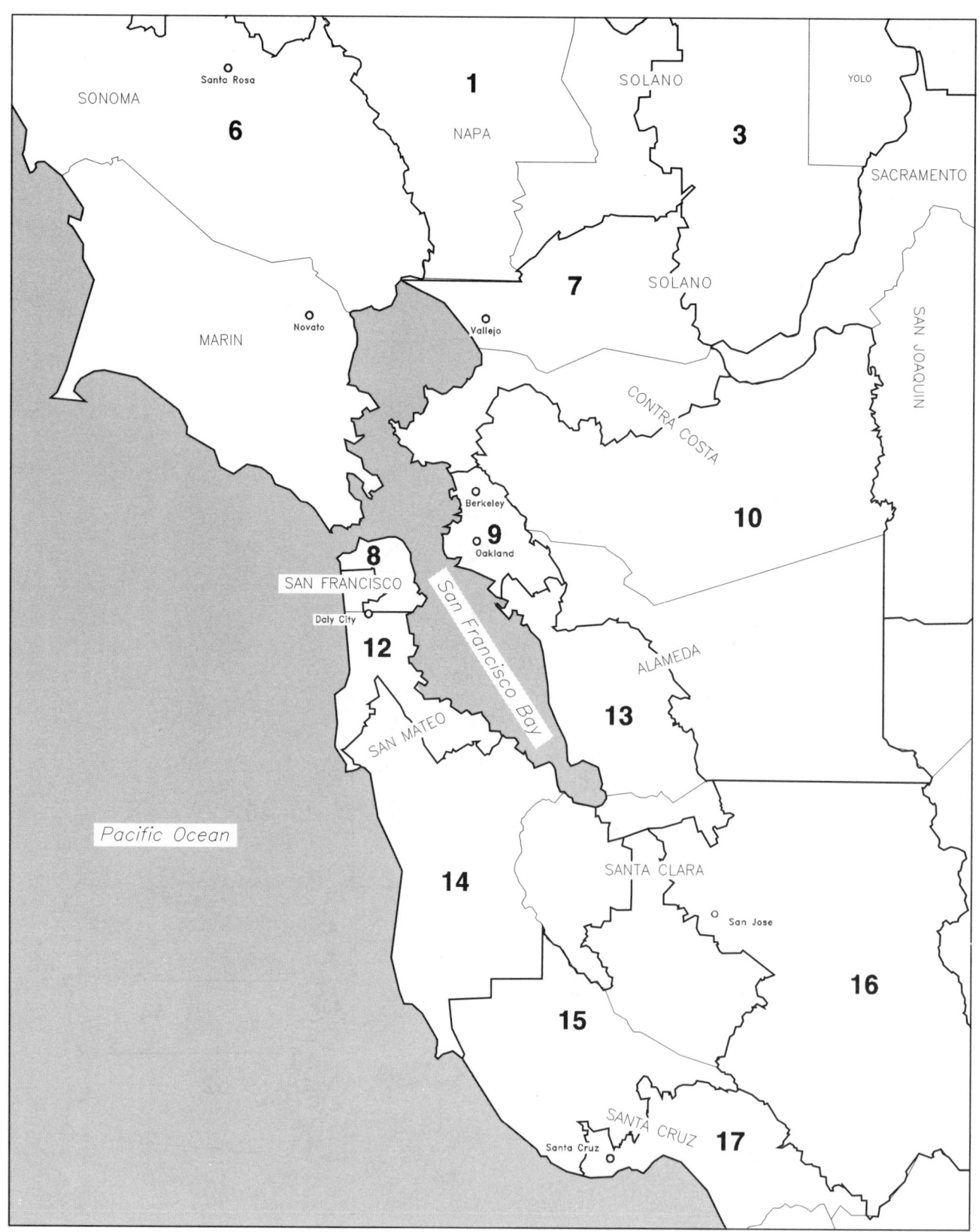

LOS ANGELES COUNTY AREA

CONGRESSIONAL DISTRICTS

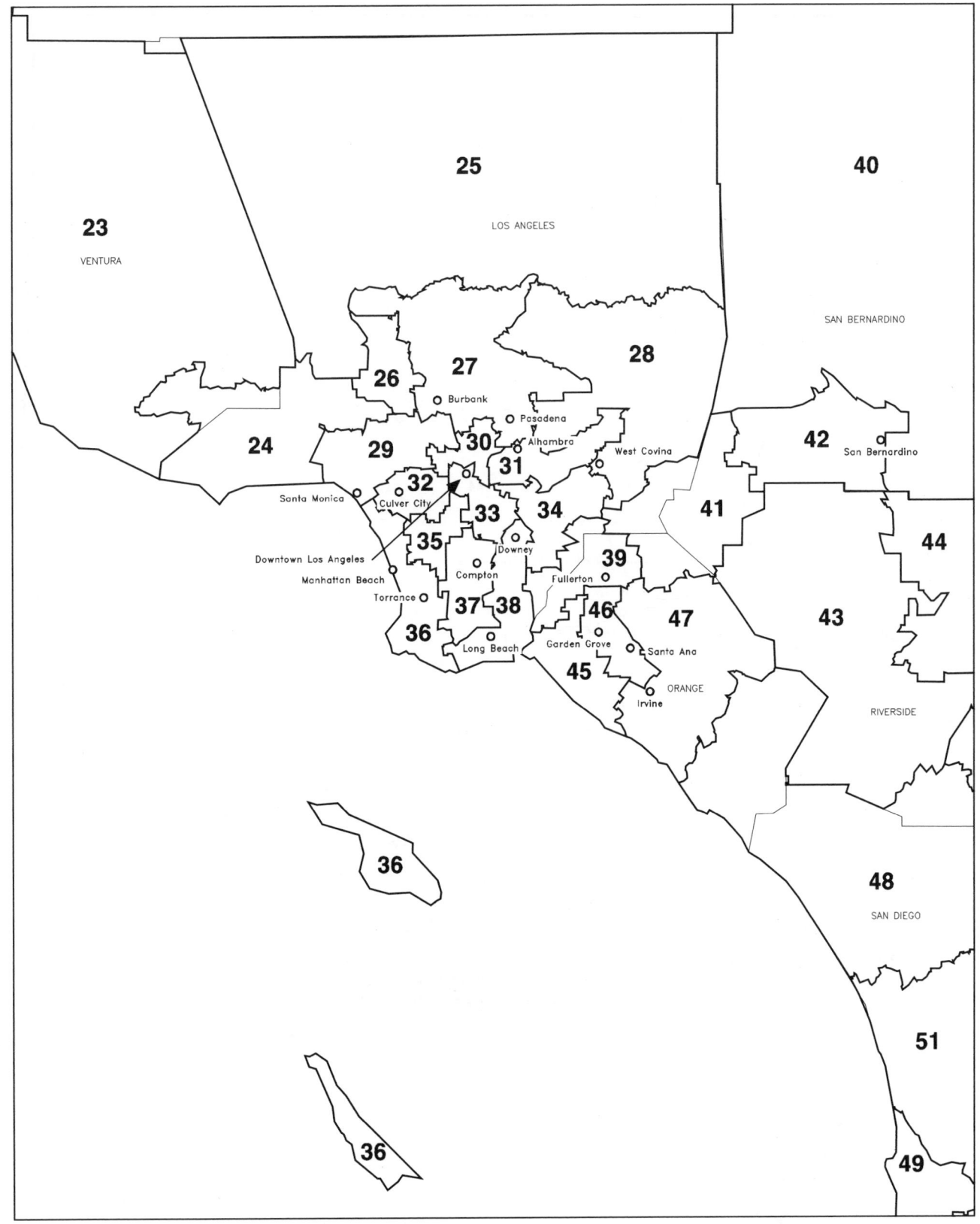

Los Angeles County

Assembly District Boundaries

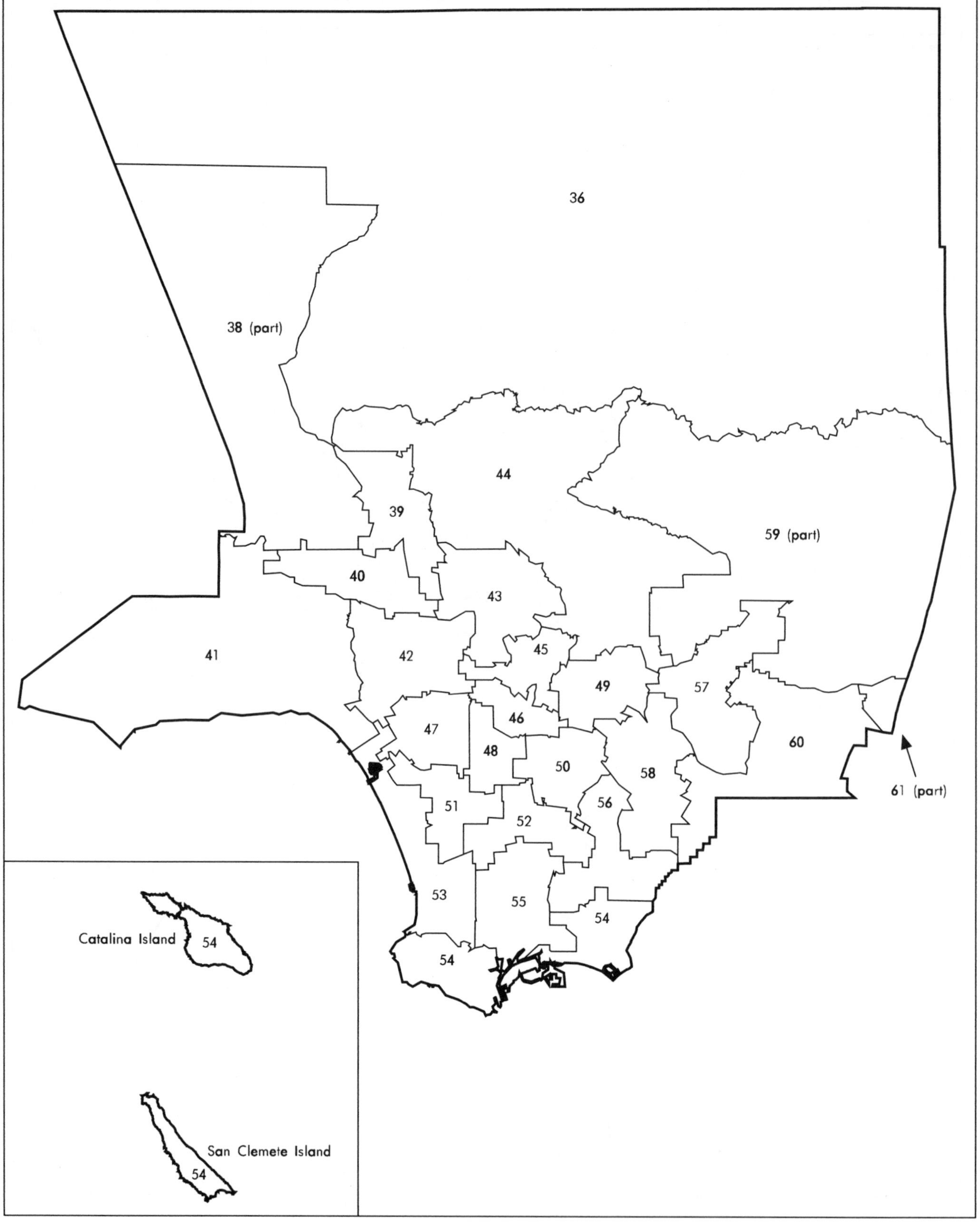

36

38 (part)

44

39

40

59 (part)

43

41

42

45

49

57

47

46

48

50

58

60

51

56

52

61 (part)

53

55

54

Catalina Island   54

54

San Clemete Island   54

CALIFORNIA

PRESIDENT 1992

Registration	County	Total Vote	Republican	Democratic	Perot	Other	Plurality	Percentage Total Vote		
								Rep.	Dem.	Perot
758,435	ALAMEDA	530,145	109,292	334,224	81,643	4,986	224,932 D	20.6%	63.0%	15.4%
733	ALPINE	631	222	215	186	8	7 R	35.2%	34.1%	29.5%
17,915	AMADOR	15,434	5,477	5,286	4,553	118	191 R	35.5%	34.2%	29.5%
112,424	BUTTE	85,014	31,608	32,489	20,231	686	881 D	37.2%	38.2%	23.8%
20,823	CALAVERAS	16,991	6,006	5,989	4,848	148	17 R	35.3%	35.2%	28.5%
7,173	COLUSA	5,635	2,589	1,798	1,206	42	791 R	45.9%	31.9%	21.4%
507,451	CONTRA COSTA	382,823	112,965	194,960	72,518	2,380	81,995 D	29.5%	50.9%	18.9%
12,272	DEL NORTE	9,353	3,083	3,639	2,575	56	556 D	33.0%	38.9%	27.5%
81,200	EL DORADO	64,887	25,906	21,012	17,503	466	4,894 R	39.9%	32.4%	27.0%
311,952	FRESNO	219,161	89,137	92,418	36,299	1,307	3,281 D	40.7%	42.2%	16.6%
11,145	GLENN	8,816	3,812	2,666	2,278	60	1,146 R	43.2%	30.2%	25.8%
76,796	HUMBOLDT	60,021	18,299	28,854	12,340	528	10,555 D	30.5%	48.1%	20.6%
39,797	IMPERIAL	25,318	9,759	11,109	4,247	203	1,350 D	38.5%	43.9%	16.8%
10,518	INYO	8,464	3,689	2,695	1,999	81	994 R	43.6%	31.8%	23.6%
252,324	KERN	179,263	80,762	60,510	36,891	1,100	20,252 R	45.1%	33.8%	20.6%
36,690	KINGS	25,651	10,673	9,982	4,899	97	691 R	41.6%	38.9%	19.1%
29,470	LAKE	23,213	6,678	10,548	5,797	190	3,870 D	28.8%	45.4%	25.0%
12,509	LASSEN	10,362	3,836	3,388	3,004	134	448 R	37.0%	32.7%	29.0%
3,744,096	LOS ANGELES	2,753,403	799,607	1,446,529	488,624	18,643	646,922 D	29.0%	52.5%	17.7%
43,869	MADERA	30,245	13,066	10,863	6,156	160	2,203 R	43.2%	35.9%	20.4%
153,338	MARIN	130,707	30,479	76,158	22,986	1,084	45,679 D	23.3%	58.3%	17.6%
10,139	MARIPOSA	8,287	2,982	3,023	2,211	71	41 D	36.0%	36.5%	26.7%
47,038	MENDOCINO	36,538	7,958	18,344	9,753	483	8,591 D	21.8%	50.2%	26.7%
69,659	MERCED	49,284	17,981	20,133	10,914	256	2,152 D	36.5%	40.9%	22.1%
5,936	MODOC	4,625	1,803	1,489	1,269	64	314 R	39.0%	32.2%	27.4%
5,687	MONO	4,355	1,570	1,489	1,248	48	81 R	36.1%	34.2%	28.7%
160,821	MONTEREY	116,689	36,461	54,861	24,472	895	18,400 D	31.2%	47.0%	21.0%
65,171	NAPA	53,455	15,662	24,215	13,150	428	8,553 D	29.3%	45.3%	24.6%
54,739	NEVADA	44,201	17,343	15,433	11,072	353	1,910 R	39.2%	34.9%	25.0%
1,240,778	ORANGE	972,549	426,613	306,930	232,394	6,612	119,683 R	43.9%	31.6%	23.9%
113,122	PLACER	91,366	38,298	30,783	21,741	544	7,515 R	41.9%	33.7%	23.8%
12,460	PLUMAS	9,949	3,599	3,742	2,551	57	143 D	36.2%	37.6%	25.6%
597,020	RIVERSIDE	430,275	159,457	166,241	102,233	2,344	6,784 D	37.1%	38.6%	23.8%
629,200	SACRAMENTO	453,512	160,366	197,540	91,412	4,194	37,174 D	35.4%	43.6%	20.2%
17,299	SAN BENITO	12,739	4,112	5,354	3,182	91	1,242 D	32.3%	42.0%	25.0%
682,980	SAN BERNARDINO	474,070	176,563	183,634	109,183	4,690	7,071 D	37.2%	38.7%	23.0%
1,382,383	SAN DIEGO	986,646	352,125	367,397	259,249	7,875	15,272 D	35.7%	37.2%	26.3%
477,740	SAN FRANCISCO	322,207	57,352	233,263	29,018	2,574	175,911 D	17.8%	72.4%	9.0%
230,858	SAN JOAQUIN	154,210	58,355	63,655	31,205	995	5,300 D	37.8%	41.3%	20.2%
128,898	SAN LUIS OBISPO	104,619	36,384	40,136	27,314	785	3,752 D	34.8%	38.4%	26.1%
347,694	SAN MATEO	276,508	75,080	149,232	50,465	1,731	74,152 D	27.2%	54.0%	18.3%
209,998	SANTA BARBARA	162,756	57,375	69,215	35,105	1,061	11,840 D	35.3%	42.5%	21.6%
820,028	SANTA CLARA	602,055	170,870	296,265	128,895	6,025	125,395 D	28.4%	49.2%	21.4%
148,281	SANTA CRUZ	113,992	24,916	66,183	21,615	1,278	41,267 D	21.9%	58.1%	19.0%
84,450	SHASTA	68,359	28,190	21,605	17,990	574	6,585 R	41.2%	31.6%	26.3%
2,331	SIERRA	1,875	691	653	519	12	38 R	36.9%	34.8%	27.7%
25,645	SISKIYOU	20,679	6,660	8,254	5,567	198	1,594 D	32.2%	39.9%	26.9%
173,167	SOLANO	132,111	38,883	64,320	27,851	1,057	25,437 D	29.4%	48.7%	21.1%
245,538	SONOMA	197,691	47,619	104,334	43,859	1,879	56,715 D	24.1%	52.8%	22.2%
179,471	STANISLAUS	128,005	47,275	52,415	27,651	664	5,140 D	36.9%	40.9%	21.6%
34,418	SUTTER	25,860	12,956	7,883	4,881	140	5,073 R	50.1%	30.5%	18.9%
27,129	TEHAMA	20,979	7,419	7,508	5,884	168	89 D	35.4%	35.8%	28.0%
8,248	TRINITY	6,029	1,886	1,967	2,092	84	125 P	31.3%	32.6%	34.7%
125,167	TULARE	88,553	40,482	31,188	16,430	453	9,294 R	45.7%	35.2%	18.6%
29,932	TUOLUMNE	24,178	8,525	9,216	6,294	143	691 D	35.3%	38.1%	26.0%
359,236	VENTURA	267,647	94,911	99,011	71,844	1,881	4,100 D	35.5%	37.0%	26.8%
84,116	YOLO	62,436	17,574	33,297	11,073	492	15,723 D	28.1%	53.3%	17.7%
23,766	YUBA	16,895	7,333	5,785	3,637	140	1,548 R	43.4%	34.2%	21.5%
15,101,473	TOTAL	11,131,721	3,630,574	5,121,325	2,296,006	83,816	1,490,751 D	32.6%	46.0%	20.6%

CALIFORNIA

SENATOR 1992
(FULL TERM)

Registration	County	Total Vote	Republican	Democratic	Other	Rep.-Dem. Plurality	Percentage Total Vote Rep.	Dem.	Major Vote Rep.	Dem.
758,435	ALAMEDA	512,393	128,489	343,020	40,884	214,531 D	25.1%	66.9%	27.3%	72.7%
733	ALPINE	602	260	272	70	12 D	43.2%	45.2%	48.9%	51.1%
17,915	AMADOR	15,061	7,366	6,082	1,613	1,284 R	48.9%	40.4%	54.8%	45.2%
112,424	BUTTE	84,207	43,338	31,505	9,364	11,833 R	51.5%	37.4%	57.9%	42.1%
20,823	CALAVERAS	16,693	8,269	6,402	2,022	1,867 R	49.5%	38.4%	56.4%	43.6%
7,173	COLUSA	5,538	3,112	1,859	567	1,253 R	56.2%	33.6%	62.6%	37.4%
507,451	CONTRA COSTA	368,952	131,923	203,563	33,466	71,640 D	35.8%	55.2%	39.3%	60.7%
12,272	DEL NORTE	9,186	4,289	3,891	1,006	398 R	46.7%	42.4%	52.4%	47.6%
81,200	EL DORADO	63,636	32,368	24,601	6,667	7,767 R	50.9%	38.7%	56.8%	43.2%
311,952	FRESNO	212,059	117,891	78,321	15,847	39,570 R	55.6%	36.9%	60.1%	39.9%
11,145	GLENN	8,644	5,373	2,271	1,000	3,102 R	62.2%	26.3%	70.3%	29.7%
76,796	HUMBOLDT	57,402	24,757	27,916	4,729	3,159 D	43.1%	48.6%	47.0%	53.0%
39,797	IMPERIAL	26,008	11,389	11,614	3,005	225 D	43.8%	44.7%	49.5%	50.5%
10,518	INYO	8,273	4,847	2,563	863	2,284 R	58.6%	31.0%	65.4%	34.6%
252,324	KERN	175,366	106,916	53,141	15,309	53,775 R	61.0%	30.3%	66.8%	33.2%
36,690	KINGS	24,636	14,079	8,151	2,406	5,928 R	57.1%	33.1%	63.3%	36.7%
29,470	LAKE	23,080	9,357	10,805	2,918	1,448 D	40.5%	46.8%	46.4%	53.6%
12,509	LASSEN	9,873	4,823	3,761	1,289	1,062 R	48.9%	38.1%	56.2%	43.8%
3,744,096	LOS ANGELES	2,684,066	1,062,974	1,410,423	210,669	347,449 D	39.6%	52.5%	43.0%	57.0%
43,869	MADERA	29,475	17,609	9,401	2,465	8,208 R	59.7%	31.9%	65.2%	34.8%
153,338	MARIN	127,472	37,150	80,902	9,420	43,752 D	29.1%	63.5%	31.5%	68.5%
10,139	MARIPOSA	8,110	4,211	2,989	910	1,222 R	51.9%	36.9%	58.5%	41.5%
47,038	MENDOCINO	35,397	11,718	19,818	3,861	8,100 D	33.1%	56.0%	37.2%	62.8%
69,659	MERCED	45,519	22,360	17,848	5,311	4,512 R	49.1%	39.2%	55.6%	44.4%
5,936	MODOC	4,378	2,367	1,429	582	938 R	54.1%	32.6%	62.4%	37.6%
5,687	MONO	4,310	2,034	1,820	456	214 R	47.2%	42.2%	52.8%	47.2%
160,821	MONTEREY	111,810	45,903	54,400	11,507	8,497 D	41.1%	48.7%	45.8%	54.2%
65,171	NAPA	51,878	20,655	25,746	5,477	5,091 D	39.8%	49.6%	44.5%	55.5%
54,739	NEVADA	43,328	21,609	17,091	4,628	4,518 R	49.9%	39.4%	55.8%	44.2%
1,240,778	ORANGE	950,977	550,502	317,740	82,735	232,762 R	57.9%	33.4%	63.4%	36.6%
113,122	PLACER	88,740	44,813	34,905	9,022	9,908 R	50.5%	39.3%	56.2%	43.8%
12,460	PLUMAS	9,960	4,728	4,032	1,200	696 R	47.5%	40.5%	54.0%	46.0%
597,020	RIVERSIDE	422,134	218,778	160,630	42,726	58,148 R	51.8%	38.1%	57.7%	42.3%
629,200	SACRAMENTO	439,717	179,844	215,853	44,020	36,009 D	40.9%	49.1%	45.4%	54.6%
17,299	SAN BENITO	12,396	5,527	5,415	1,454	112 R	44.6%	43.7%	50.5%	49.5%
682,980	SAN BERNARDINO	446,114	231,143	164,620	50,351	66,523 R	51.8%	36.9%	58.4%	41.6%
1,382,383	SAN DIEGO	946,429	448,181	399,087	99,161	49,094 R	47.4%	42.2%	52.9%	47.1%
477,740	SAN FRANCISCO	304,372	56,972	233,068	14,332	176,096 D	18.7%	76.6%	19.6%	80.4%
230,858	SAN JOAQUIN	157,728	75,032	66,484	16,212	8,548 R	47.6%	42.2%	53.0%	47.0%
128,898	SAN LUIS OBISPO	101,437	49,945	41,824	9,668	8,121 R	49.2%	41.2%	54.4%	45.6%
347,694	SAN MATEO	266,885	87,209	158,490	21,186	71,281 D	32.7%	59.4%	35.5%	64.5%
209,998	SANTA BARBARA	157,394	72,793	70,998	13,603	1,795 R	46.2%	45.1%	50.6%	49.4%
820,028	SANTA CLARA	581,983	206,913	314,884	60,186	107,971 D	35.6%	54.1%	39.7%	60.3%
148,281	SANTA CRUZ	110,971	32,482	67,927	10,562	35,445 D	29.3%	61.2%	32.3%	67.7%
84,450	SHASTA	66,467	39,507	18,868	8,092	20,639 R	59.4%	28.4%	67.7%	32.3%
2,331	SIERRA	1,822	878	705	239	173 R	48.2%	38.7%	55.5%	44.5%
25,645	SISKIYOU	19,989	9,568	8,115	2,306	1,453 R	47.9%	40.6%	54.1%	45.9%
173,167	SOLANO	129,175	47,148	67,007	15,020	19,859 D	36.5%	51.9%	41.3%	58.7%
245,538	SONOMA	192,026	62,696	108,991	20,339	46,295 D	32.6%	56.8%	36.5%	63.5%
179,471	STANISLAUS	123,681	55,875	55,688	12,118	187 R	45.2%	45.0%	50.1%	49.9%
34,418	SUTTER	25,040	14,783	7,719	2,538	7,064 R	59.0%	30.8%	65.7%	34.3%
27,129	TEHAMA	21,005	11,893	6,450	2,662	5,443 R	56.6%	30.7%	64.8%	35.2%
8,248	TRINITY	6,431	3,184	2,261	986	923 R	49.5%	35.2%	58.5%	41.5%
125,167	TULARE	86,573	53,856	25,311	7,406	28,545 R	62.2%	29.2%	68.0%	32.0%
29,932	TUOLUMNE	22,915	10,596	9,811	2,508	785 R	46.2%	42.8%	51.9%	48.1%
359,236	VENTURA	263,309	133,274	104,335	25,700	28,939 R	50.6%	39.6%	56.1%	43.9%
84,116	YOLO	60,113	19,900	35,006	5,207	15,106 D	33.1%	58.2%	36.2%	63.8%
23,766	YUBA	16,568	8,726	5,638	2,204	3,088 R	52.7%	34.0%	60.7%	39.3%
15,101,473	TOTAL	10,799,703	4,644,182	5,173,467	982,054	529,285 D	43.0%	47.9%	47.3%	52.7%

CALIFORNIA

SENATOR 1992
(SHORT TERM)

Registration	County	Total Vote	Republican	Democratic	Other	Rep.-Dem. Plurality	Percentage Total Vote Rep.	Dem.	Major Vote Rep.	Dem.
758,435	ALAMEDA	516,367	113,223	374,675	28,469	261,452 D	21.9%	72.6%	23.2%	76.8%
733	ALPINE	599	252	287	60	35 D	42.1%	47.9%	46.8%	53.2%
17,915	AMADOR	15,157	6,463	7,319	1,375	856 D	42.6%	48.3%	46.9%	53.1%
112,424	BUTTE	83,630	38,111	37,396	8,123	715 R	45.6%	44.7%	50.5%	49.5%
20,823	CALAVERAS	16,807	7,059	7,839	1,909	780 D	42.0%	46.6%	47.4%	52.6%
7,173	COLUSA	5,543	3,014	2,083	446	931 R	54.4%	37.6%	59.1%	40.9%
507,451	CONTRA COSTA	365,298	115,507	229,988	19,803	114,481 D	31.6%	63.0%	33.4%	66.6%
12,272	DEL NORTE	9,223	3,658	4,696	869	1,038 D	39.7%	50.9%	43.8%	56.2%
81,200	EL DORADO	63,870	29,101	28,957	5,812	144 R	45.6%	45.3%	50.1%	49.9%
311,952	FRESNO	210,751	102,172	94,988	13,591	7,184 R	48.5%	45.1%	51.8%	48.2%
11,145	GLENN	8,652	4,908	2,864	880	2,044 R	56.7%	33.1%	63.1%	36.9%
76,796	HUMBOLDT	58,817	19,513	35,178	4,126	15,665 D	33.2%	59.8%	35.7%	64.3%
39,797	IMPERIAL	25,494	11,070	12,433	1,991	1,363 D	43.4%	48.8%	47.1%	52.9%
10,518	INYO	8,199	4,318	3,067	814	1,251 R	52.7%	37.4%	58.5%	41.5%
252,324	KERN	175,334	95,483	63,661	16,190	31,822 R	54.5%	36.3%	60.0%	40.0%
36,690	KINGS	24,091	12,115	9,805	2,171	2,310 R	50.3%	40.7%	55.3%	44.7%
29,470	LAKE	23,106	8,096	12,732	2,278	4,636 D	35.0%	55.1%	38.9%	61.1%
12,509	LASSEN	9,916	4,724	4,005	1,187	719 R	47.6%	40.4%	54.1%	45.9%
3,744,096	LOS ANGELES	2,643,495	899,656	1,552,223	191,616	652,567 D	34.0%	58.7%	36.7%	63.3%
43,869	MADERA	29,360	15,309	11,682	2,369	3,627 R	52.1%	39.8%	56.7%	43.3%
153,338	MARIN	129,401	31,846	92,205	5,350	60,359 D	24.6%	71.3%	25.7%	74.3%
10,139	MARIPOSA	8,112	3,568	3,681	863	113 D	44.0%	45.4%	49.2%	50.8%
47,038	MENDOCINO	36,310	10,993	22,000	3,317	11,007 D	30.3%	60.6%	33.3%	66.7%
69,659	MERCED	46,233	20,246	22,010	3,977	1,764 D	43.8%	47.6%	47.9%	52.1%
5,936	MODOC	4,395	2,327	1,572	496	755 R	52.9%	35.8%	59.7%	40.3%
5,687	MONO	4,281	1,911	1,931	439	20 D	44.6%	45.1%	49.7%	50.3%
160,821	MONTEREY	112,774	39,182	66,417	7,175	27,235 D	34.7%	58.9%	37.1%	62.9%
65,171	NAPA	52,398	18,539	29,875	3,984	11,336 D	35.4%	57.0%	38.3%	61.7%
54,739	NEVADA	43,538	19,476	20,044	4,018	568 D	44.7%	46.0%	49.3%	50.7%
1,240,778	ORANGE	946,081	481,810	377,170	87,101	104,640 R	50.9%	39.9%	56.1%	43.9%
113,122	PLACER	88,555	40,497	40,511	7,547	14 D	45.7%	45.7%	50.0%	50.0%
12,460	PLUMAS	10,007	4,367	4,647	993	280 D	43.6%	46.4%	48.4%	51.6%
597,020	RIVERSIDE	420,935	191,258	187,548	42,129	3,710 R	45.4%	44.6%	50.5%	49.5%
629,200	SACRAMENTO	442,098	168,318	237,722	36,058	69,404 D	38.1%	53.8%	41.5%	58.5%
17,299	SAN BENITO	12,498	4,637	6,938	923	2,301 D	37.1%	55.5%	40.1%	59.9%
682,980	SAN BERNARDINO	453,136	206,969	200,979	45,188	5,990 R	45.7%	44.4%	50.7%	49.3%
1,382,383	SAN DIEGO	942,868	411,362	442,855	88,651	31,493 D	43.6%	47.0%	48.2%	51.8%
477,740	SAN FRANCISCO	311,361	49,165	250,972	11,224	201,807 D	15.8%	80.6%	16.4%	83.6%
230,858	SAN JOAQUIN	156,665	67,531	76,607	12,527	9,076 D	43.1%	48.9%	46.9%	53.1%
128,898	SAN LUIS OBISPO	101,902	44,775	48,376	8,751	3,601 D	43.9%	47.5%	48.1%	51.9%
347,694	SAN MATEO	270,605	75,470	181,990	13,145	106,520 D	27.9%	67.3%	29.3%	70.7%
209,998	SANTA BARBARA	156,965	67,043	77,900	12,022	10,857 D	42.7%	49.6%	46.3%	53.7%
820,028	SANTA CLARA	586,933	181,858	364,997	40,078	183,139 D	31.0%	62.2%	33.3%	66.7%
148,281	SANTA CRUZ	112,449	28,562	76,327	7,560	47,765 D	25.4%	67.9%	27.2%	72.8%
84,450	SHASTA	66,417	34,192	25,111	7,114	9,081 R	51.5%	37.8%	57.7%	42.3%
2,331	SIERRA	1,813	808	818	187	10 D	44.6%	45.1%	49.7%	50.3%
25,645	SISKIYOU	20,210	9,180	8,963	2,067	217 R	45.4%	44.3%	50.6%	49.4%
173,161	SOLANO	129,936	41,970	77,739	10,227	35,769 D	32.3%	59.8%	35.1%	64.9%
245,538	SONOMA	193,314	56,793	121,471	15,050	64,678 D	29.4%	62.8%	31.9%	68.1%
179,471	STANISLAUS	123,953	51,549	62,110	10,294	10,561 D	41.6%	50.1%	45.4%	54.6%
34,418	SUTTER	25,079	13,427	9,135	2,517	4,292 R	53.5%	36.4%	59.5%	40.5%
27,129	TEHAMA	20,992	10,116	8,253	2,623	1,863 R	48.2%	39.3%	55.1%	44.9%
8,248	TRINITY	6,468	2,824	2,743	901	81 R	43.7%	42.4%	50.7%	49.3%
125,167	TULARE	85,884	48,493	30,665	6,726	17,828 R	56.5%	35.7%	61.3%	38.7%
29,932	TUOLUMNE	23,527	9,550	11,895	2,082	2,345 D	40.6%	50.6%	44.5%	55.5%
359,236	VENTURA	263,499	122,064	119,366	22,069	2,698 R	46.3%	45.3%	50.6%	49.4%
84,116	YOLO	60,538	19,191	37,340	4,007	18,149 D	31.7%	61.7%	33.9%	66.1%
23,766	YUBA	16,904	7,882	6,890	2,132	992 R	46.6%	40.8%	53.4%	46.6%
15,101,473	TOTAL	10,782,743	4,093,501	5,853,651	835,591	1,760,150 D	38.0%	54.3%	41.2%	58.8%

LOS ANGELES COUNTY

PRESIDENT 1992

Registration	Assembly District	Total Vote	Republican	Democratic	Perot	Other	Plurality	Percentage Total Vote		
								Rep.	Dem.	Perot
190,118	DISTRICT 36	146,120	61,104	45,690	38,575	751	15,414 R	41.8%	31.3%	26.4%
122,602	DISTRICT 38 (PART)	97,705	32,567	42,840	21,714	584	10,273 D	33.3%	43.8%	22.2%
101,656	DISTRICT 39	69,167	17,342	38,079	13,280	466	20,737 D	25.1%	55.1%	19.2%
159,286	DISTRICT 40	123,377	28,256	70,809	23,410	902	42,553 D	22.9%	57.4%	19.0%
241,034	DISTRICT 41	195,953	53,237	105,203	36,217	1,296	51,966 D	27.2%	53.7%	18.5%
235,448	DISTRICT 42	187,570	34,677	128,155	23,630	1,108	93,478 D	18.5%	68.3%	12.6%
158,390	DISTRICT 43	124,016	42,542	56,981	23,656	837	14,439 D	34.3%	45.9%	19.1%
206,757	DISTRICT 44	160,218	58,553	71,403	29,034	1,228	12,850 D	36.5%	44.6%	18.1%
91,448	DISTRICT 45	62,385	13,971	39,655	8,176	583	25,684 D	22.4%	63.6%	13.1%
58,913	DISTRICT 46	32,829	7,578	21,490	3,437	324	13,912 D	23.1%	65.5%	10.5%
193,994	DISTRICT 47	142,858	18,267	110,135	13,356	1,100	91,868 D	12.8%	77.1%	9.3%
120,631	DISTRICT 48	68,540	3,890	61,354	2,980	316	57,464 D	5.7%	89.5%	4.3%
119,695	DISTRICT 49	82,771	26,212	44,557	11,590	412	18,345 D	31.7%	53.8%	14.0%
65,255	DISTRICT 50	38,734	9,099	23,872	5,493	270	14,773 D	23.5%	61.6%	14.2%
151,440	DISTRICT 51	101,593	18,940	68,475	13,539	639	49,535 D	18.6%	67.4%	13.3%
127,725	DISTRICT 52	74,828	10,259	57,026	7,004	539	46,767 D	13.7%	76.2%	9.4%
235,601	DISTRICT 53	188,074	62,627	80,520	43,497	1,430	17,893 D	33.3%	42.8%	23.1%
207,740	DISTRICT 54	160,320	54,738	69,305	35,180	1,097	14,567 D	34.1%	43.2%	21.9%
131,610	DISTRICT 55	85,538	18,804	54,239	11,992	503	35,435 D	22.0%	63.4%	14.0%
178,633	DISTRICT 56	133,842	49,977	54,499	28,526	840	4,522 D	37.3%	40.7%	21.3%
112,946	DISTRICT 57	76,836	25,194	36,731	14,545	366	11,537 D	32.8%	47.8%	18.9%
147,717	DISTRICT 58	103,732	30,877	53,558	18,692	605	22,681 D	29.8%	51.6%	18.0%
194,234	DISTRICT 59	152,160	63,123	55,741	32,256	1,040	7,382 R	41.5%	36.6%	21.2%
171,033	DISTRICT 60	131,182	54,269	49,658	26,656	599	4,611 R	41.4%	37.9%	20.3%
20,190	DISTRICT 61 (PART)	12,335	3,504	6,554	2,189	88	3,050 D	28.4%	53.1%	17.7%
3,744,096	TOTAL	2,753,403	799,607	1,446,529	488,624	18,643	646,922 D	29.0%	52.5%	17.7%

LOS ANGELES COUNTY

SENATOR 1992
(FULL TERM)

Registration	Assembly District	Total Vote	Republican	Democratic	Other	Rep.-Dem. Plurality	Percentage Total Vote Rep.	Dem.	Major Vote Rep.	Dem.
190,118	DISTRICT 36	143,165	82,098	45,848	15,219	36,250 R	57.3%	32.0%	64.2%	35.8%
122,602	DISTRICT 38 (PART)	95,687	45,755	42,560	7,372	3,195 R	47.8%	44.5%	51.8%	48.2%
101,656	DISTRICT 39	67,634	25,083	35,951	6,600	10,868 D	37.1%	53.2%	41.1%	58.9%
159,286	DISTRICT 40	120,428	41,202	69,654	9,572	28,452 D	34.2%	57.8%	37.2%	62.8%
241,034	DISTRICT 41	191,907	73,161	107,450	11,296	34,289 D	38.1%	56.0%	40.5%	59.5%
235,448	DISTRICT 42	182,804	46,750	127,598	8,456	80,848 D	25.6%	69.8%	26.8%	73.2%
158,390	DISTRICT 43	120,834	54,981	56,259	9,594	1,278 D	45.5%	46.6%	49.4%	50.6%
206,757	DISTRICT 44	156,900	74,346	71,118	11,436	3,228 R	47.4%	45.3%	51.1%	48.9%
91,448	DISTRICT 45	60,553	17,324	37,955	5,274	20,631 D	28.6%	62.7%	31.3%	68.7%
58,913	DISTRICT 46	31,678	8,622	20,531	2,525	11,909 D	27.2%	64.8%	29.6%	70.4%
193,994	DISTRICT 47	138,835	25,594	106,040	7,201	80,446 D	18.4%	76.4%	19.4%	80.6%
120,631	DISTRICT 48	65,400	5,533	56,400	3,467	50,867 D	8.5%	86.2%	8.9%	91.1%
119,695	DISTRICT 49	79,857	31,127	41,154	7,576	10,027 D	39.0%	51.5%	43.1%	56.9%
65,255	DISTRICT 50	37,566	11,684	21,323	4,559	9,639 D	31.1%	56.8%	35.4%	64.6%
151,440	DISTRICT 51	98,967	26,216	65,904	6,847	39,688 D	26.5%	66.6%	28.5%	71.5%
127,725	DISTRICT 52	72,837	14,084	53,658	5,095	39,574 D	19.3%	73.7%	20.8%	79.2%
235,601	DISTRICT 53	183,511	82,620	86,566	14,325	3,946 D	45.0%	47.2%	48.8%	51.2%
207,740	DISTRICT 54	157,021	74,073	71,088	11,860	2,985 R	47.2%	45.3%	51.0%	49.0%
131,610	DISTRICT 55	82,929	24,656	51,025	7,248	26,369 D	29.7%	61.5%	32.6%	67.4%
178,633	DISTRICT 56	130,556	66,213	53,385	10,958	12,828 R	50.7%	40.9%	55.4%	44.6%
112,946	DISTRICT 57	74,814	33,339	33,378	8,097	39 D	44.6%	44.6%	50.0%	50.0%
147,717	DISTRICT 58	101,487	41,506	48,697	11,284	7,191 D	40.9%	48.0%	46.0%	54.0%
194,234	DISTRICT 59	148,986	82,881	54,070	12,035	28,811 R	55.6%	36.3%	60.5%	39.5%
171,033	DISTRICT 60	127,667	69,526	46,759	11,382	22,767 R	54.5%	36.6%	59.8%	40.2%
20,190	DISTRICT 61 (PART)	11,978	4,600	6,052	1,326	1,452 D	38.4%	50.5%	43.2%	56.8%
3,744,096	TOTAL	2,684,066	1,062,974	1,410,423	210,669	347,449 D	39.6%	52.5%	43.0%	57.0%

LOS ANGELES COUNTY

SENATOR 1992
(SHORT TERM)

Registration	Assembly District	Total Vote	Republican	Democratic	Other	Rep.-Dem. Plurality	Percentage			
							Total Vote		Major Vote	
							Rep.	Dem.	Rep.	Dem.
190,118	DISTRICT 36	140,655	72,541	53,684	14,430	18,857 R	51.6%	38.2%	57.5%	42.5%
122,602	DISTRICT 38 (PART)	93,783	38,919	48,370	6,494	9,451 D	41.5%	51.6%	44.6%	55.4%
101,656	DISTRICT 39	66,203	20,578	39,520	6,105	18,942 D	31.1%	59.7%	34.2%	65.8%
159,286	DISTRICT 40	118,703	34,516	75,689	8,498	41,173 D	29.1%	63.8%	31.3%	68.7%
241,034	DISTRICT 41	190,950	62,483	119,107	9,360	56,624 D	32.7%	62.4%	34.4%	65.6%
235,448	DISTRICT 42	181,158	39,402	135,221	6,535	95,819 D	21.8%	74.6%	22.6%	77.4%
158,390	DISTRICT 43	118,004	47,767	61,708	8,529	13,941 D	40.5%	52.3%	43.6%	56.4%
206,757	DISTRICT 44	154,351	64,330	79,039	10,982	14,709 D	41.7%	51.2%	44.9%	55.1%
91,448	DISTRICT 45	59,352	14,514	40,445	4,393	25,931 D	24.5%	68.1%	26.4%	73.6%
58,913	DISTRICT 46	31,145	7,466	21,650	2,029	14,184 D	24.0%	69.5%	25.6%	74.4%
193,994	DISTRICT 47	137,362	21,047	110,557	5,758	89,510 D	15.3%	80.5%	16.0%	84.0%
120,631	DISTRICT 48	63,727	4,422	56,691	2,614	52,269 D	6.9%	89.0%	7.2%	92.8%
119,695	DISTRICT 49	77,771	24,584	46,994	6,193	22,410 D	31.6%	60.4%	34.3%	65.7%
65,255	DISTRICT 50	36,749	9,781	23,681	3,287	13,900 D	26.6%	64.4%	29.2%	70.8%
151,440	DISTRICT 51	98,197	22,232	70,037	5,928	47,805 D	22.6%	71.3%	24.1%	75.9%
127,725	DISTRICT 52	71,506	11,550	55,499	4,457	43,949 D	16.2%	77.6%	17.2%	82.8%
235,601	DISTRICT 53	180,954	72,502	95,436	13,016	22,934 D	40.1%	52.7%	43.2%	56.8%
207,740	DISTRICT 54	154,748	63,043	79,041	12,664	15,998 D	40.7%	51.1%	44.4%	55.6%
131,610	DISTRICT 55	81,527	19,964	55,033	6,530	35,069 D	24.5%	67.5%	26.6%	73.4%
178,633	DISTRICT 56	129,142	56,237	60,752	12,153	4,515 D	43.5%	47.0%	48.1%	51.9%
112,946	DISTRICT 57	73,563	27,237	39,644	6,682	12,407 D	37.0%	53.9%	40.7%	59.3%
147,717	DISTRICT 58	99,283	32,838	56,322	10,123	23,484 D	33.1%	56.7%	36.8%	63.2%
194,234	DISTRICT 59	146,791	70,462	64,354	11,975	6,108 R	48.0%	43.8%	52.3%	47.7%
171,033	DISTRICT 60	126,077	57,417	56,993	11,667	424 R	45.5%	45.2%	50.2%	49.8%
20,190	DISTRICT 61 (PART)	11,774	3,824	6,756	1,194	2,932 D	32.5%	57.4%	36.1%	63.9%
3,744,096	TOTAL	2,643,495	899,656	1,552,223	191,616	652,567 D	34.0%	58.7%	36.7%	63.3%

CALIFORNIA

CONGRESS

CD	Year	Total Vote	Republican		Democratic		Other Vote	Rep.-Dem. Plurality	Percentage			
									Total Vote		Major Vote	
			Vote	Candidate	Vote	Candidate			Rep.	Dem.	Rep.	Dem.
1	1992	251,206	113,266	RIGGS, FRANK	119,676	HAMBURG, DAN	18,264	6,410 D	45.1%	47.6%	48.6%	51.4%
2	1992	256,556	167,247	HERGER, WALLY	71,780	FREEDMAN, ELLIOT R.	17,529	95,467 R	65.2%	28.0%	70.0%	30.0%
3	1992	238,685	96,092	RICHARDSON, H. L.	122,149	FAZIO, VIC	20,444	26,057 D	40.3%	51.2%	44.0%	56.0%
4	1992	283,365	141,155	DOOLITTLE, JOHN T.	129,489	MALBERG, PATRICIA	12,721	11,666 R	49.8%	45.7%	52.2%	47.8%
5	1992	230,560	58,698	DINSMORE, ROBERT S.	158,250	MATSUI, ROBERT T.	13,612	99,552 D	25.5%	68.6%	27.1%	72.9%
6	1992	291,786	98,171	FILANTE, BILL	190,322	WOOLSEY, LYNN	3,293	92,151 D	33.6%	65.2%	34.0%	66.0%
7	1992	217,982	54,822	SCHOLL, DAVE	153,320	MILLER, GEORGE	9,840	98,498 D	25.1%	70.3%	26.3%	73.7%
8	1992	232,691	25,693	WOLIN, MARC	191,906	PELOSI, NANCY	15,092	166,213 D	11.0%	82.5%	11.8%	88.2%
9	1992	228,467	53,707	HUNTER, G. WILLIAM	164,265	DELLUMS, RONALD V.	10,495	110,558 D	23.5%	71.9%	24.6%	75.4%
10	1992	280,429	145,702	BAKER, BILL	134,635	WILLIAMS, WENDELL H.	92	11,067 R	52.0%	48.0%	52.0%	48.0%
11	1992	198,490	94,453	POMBO, RICHARD W.	90,539	GARAMENDI, PATRICIA	13,498	3,914 R	47.6%	45.6%	51.1%	48.9%
12	1992	228,407	53,278	TOMLIN, JIM	157,205	LANTOS, TOM	17,924	103,927 D	23.3%	68.8%	25.3%	74.7%
13	1992	205,516	64,953	TEYLER, VERNE	123,795	STARK, FORTNEY	16,768	58,842 D	31.6%	60.2%	34.4%	65.6%
14	1992	259,222	101,202	HUENING, TOM	146,873	ESHOO, ANNA G.	11,147	45,671 D	39.0%	56.7%	40.8%	59.2%
15	1992	265,370	82,875	WICK, ROBERT	168,617	MINETA, NORMAN Y.	13,878	85,742 D	31.2%	63.5%	33.0%	67.0%
16	1992	155,883	49,843	BUNDESEN, TED	96,661	EDWARDS, DON	9,379	46,818 D	32.0%	62.0%	34.0%	66.0%
17	1992	210,367	49,947	MCCAMPBELL, BILL	151,565	PANETTA, LEON E.	8,855	101,618 D	23.7%	72.0%	24.8%	75.2%
18	1992	165,011			139,704	CONDIT, GARY A.	25,307	139,704 D		84.7%		100.0%
19	1992	216,640	100,590	CLOUD, TAL L.	101,619	LEHMAN, RICHARD	14,431	1,029 D	46.4%	46.9%	49.7%	50.3%
20	1992	112,067	39,388	HUNT, ED	72,679	DOOLEY, CALVIN		33,291 D	35.1%	64.9%	35.1%	64.9%
21	1992	195,965	127,758	THOMAS, WILLIAM M.	68,058	VOLLMER, DEBORAH	149	59,700 R	65.2%	34.7%	65.2%	34.8%
22	1992	249,924	131,242	HUFFINGTON, MICHAEL	87,328	OCHOA, GLORIA	31,354	43,914 R	52.5%	34.9%	60.0%	40.0%
23	1992	212,881	115,504	GALLEGLY, ELTON	88,225	FERGUSON, ANITA P.	9,152	27,279 R	54.3%	41.4%	56.7%	43.3%
24	1992	255,267	99,835	MCCLINTOCK, TOM	141,742	BEILENSON, ANTHONY C.	13,690	41,907 D	39.1%	55.5%	41.3%	58.7%
25	1992	218,715	113,611	MCKEON, HOWARD P.	72,233	GILMARTIN, JAMES H.	32,871	41,378 R	51.9%	33.0%	61.1%	38.9%
26	1992	120,908	36,453	FROSCH, GARY E.	73,807	BERMAN, HOWARD L.	10,648	37,354 D	30.1%	61.0%	33.1%	66.9%
27	1992	212,450	105,521	MOORHEAD, CARLOS J.	83,805	KAHN, DOUG	23,124	21,716 R	49.7%	39.4%	55.7%	44.3%
28	1992	209,382	122,353	DREIER, DAVID	76,525	WACHTEL, AL	10,504	45,828 R	58.4%	36.5%	61.5%	38.5%
29	1992	261,486	67,141	ROBBINS, MARK A.	160,312	WAXMAN, HENRY A.	34,033	93,171 D	25.7%	61.3%	29.5%	70.5%
30	1992	83,543	20,034	WAKSBERG, MORRY	48,800	BECERRA, XAVIER	14,709	28,766 D	24.0%	58.4%	29.1%	70.9%

CALIFORNIA

CONGRESS

CD	Year	Total Vote	Republican Vote	Republican Candidate	Democratic Vote	Democratic Candidate	Other Vote	Rep.-Dem. Plurality	Total Vote Rep.	Total Vote Dem.	Major Vote Rep.	Major Vote Dem.
31	1992	109,197	40,873	FRANCO, REUBEN D.	68,324	MARTINEZ, MATTHEW G.		27,451 D	37.4%	62.6%	37.4%	62.6%
32	1992	172,812			150,644	DIXON, JULIAN C.	22,168	150,644 D		87.2%		100.0%
33	1992	50,779	15,428	GUZMAN, ROBERT	32,010	ROYBAL-ALLARD, LUCILLE	3,341	16,582 D	30.4%	63.0%	32.5%	67.5%
34	1992	149,718	50,907	HERNANDEZ, JAY	91,738	TORRES, ESTEBAN	7,073	40,831 D	34.0%	61.3%	35.7%	64.3%
35	1992	124,776	17,417	TRUMAN, NATE	102,941	WATERS, MAXINE	4,418	85,524 D	14.0%	82.5%	14.5%	85.5%
36	1992	259,757	109,684	FLORES, JOAN M.	125,751	HARMAN, JANE	24,322	16,067 D	42.2%	48.4%	46.6%	53.4%
37	1992	113,337			97,159	TUCKER, WALTER R.	16,178	97,159 D		85.7%		100.0%
38	1992	189,321	92,038	HORN, STEVE	82,108	BRAUDE, EVAN A.	15,175	9,930 R	48.6%	43.4%	52.9%	47.1%
39	1992	213,684	122,472	ROYCE, ED	81,728	MCCLANAHAN, MOLLY	9,484	40,744 R	57.3%	38.2%	60.0%	40.0%
40	1992	205,283	129,563	LEWIS, JERRY	63,881	RUSK, DONALD M.	11,839	65,682 R	63.1%	31.1%	67.0%	33.0%
41	1992	170,666	101,753	KIM, JAY C.	58,777	BAKER, BOB	10,136	42,976 R	59.6%	34.4%	63.4%	36.6%
42	1992	157,455	69,251	RUTAN, RICHARD B.	79,780	BROWN, GEORGE E.	8,424	10,529 D	44.0%	50.7%	46.5%	53.5%
43	1992	190,639	88,987	CALVERT, KEN	88,468	TAKANO, MARK A.	13,184	519 R	46.7%	46.4%	50.1%	49.9%
44	1992	203,541	110,333	MCCANDLESS, AL	81,693	SMITH, GEORGIA	11,515	28,640 R	54.2%	40.1%	57.5%	42.5%
45	1992	227,016	123,731	ROHRABACHER, DANA	88,508	MCCABE, PATRICIA	14,777	35,223 R	54.5%	39.0%	58.3%	41.7%
46	1992	110,806	55,659	DORNAN, ROBERT K.	45,435	BANUELOS, ROBERT J.	9,712	10,224 R	50.2%	41.0%	55.1%	44.9%
47	1992	254,257	165,004	COX, CHRISTOPHER	76,924	ANWILER, JOHN F.	12,329	88,080 R	64.9%	30.3%	68.2%	31.8%
48	1992	230,495	140,935	PACKARD, RON	67,415	FARBER, MICHAEL	22,145	73,520 R	61.1%	29.2%	67.6%	32.4%
49	1992	248,898	106,170	JARVIS, JUDY	127,280	SCHENK, LYNN	15,448	21,110 D	42.7%	51.1%	45.5%	54.5%
50	1992	136,626	39,531	VALENCIA, TONY	77,293	FILNER, BOB	19,802	37,762 D	28.9%	56.6%	33.8%	66.2%
51	1992	252,995	141,890	CUNNINGHAM, RANDY	85,148	HERBERT, BEA	25,957	56,742 R	56.1%	33.7%	62.5%	37.5%
52	1992	213,784	112,995	HUNTER, DUNCAN L.	88,076	GASTIL, JANET M.	12,713	24,919 R	52.9%	41.2%	56.2%	43.8%

CALIFORNIA

1992 GENERAL ELECTION

President   Other vote was 48,139 Libertarian (Marrou); 18,597 Peace and Freedom (Daniels); 12,711 American Independent (Phillips); 3,077 Gritz (write-in); 836 Hagelin (write-in); 180 LaRouche (write-in); 115 Warren (write-in); 12 Masters (write-in); 149 scattered write-in.

Senator Full Term   Other vote was 373,051 American Independent (McCready); Peace and Freedom (Torres); 235,919 Libertarian (Genis); scattered write-in.

Senator Short Term   Other vote was 305,697 Peace and Freedom (Horne); 281,973 American Independent (Meeuwenberg); 247,799 Libertarian (Boddie); 122 scattered write-in.

Congress   Other vote was 10,764 Peace and Freedom (Baldwin) and 7,500 Libertarian (Howard) in CD 1; Libertarian (Pendery) in CD 2; Libertarian (Crain) in CD 3; 12,705 Libertarian (McHargue) and 16 Brooksher (write-in) in CD 4; 4,745 American Independent (Mors), 4,547 Libertarian (Rufer), 4,316 Green (Harter) and 4 Bergeron (write-in) in CD 5; 3,141 Heater (write-in) and 152 Beary (write-in) in CD 6; Peace and Freedom (Franklin) in CD 7; 7,572 Peace and Freedom (Cadabes), 7,511 Libertarian (Elwood) and 9 Goldwater (write-in) in CD 8; 10,472 Peace and Freedom (Linn) and 23 Musa (write-in) in CD 9; 55 Williams (write-in) and 37 Janlois (write-in) in CD 10; Libertarian (Roberts) in CD 11; 10,142 Peace and Freedom (Weldon) and 7,782 Libertarian (O'Brien) in CD 12; Peace and Freedom (Allen) in CD 13; 7,220 Libertarian (Olson), 3,912 Peace and Freedom (Wald), 12 Sims (write-in) and 3 Maginnis (write-in) in CD 14; 13,293 Libertarian (Dieterly) and 585 Futrell (write-in) in CD 15; 9,370 Peace and Freedom (Kuumba), 5 Hunt (write-in), 3 Loeber (write-in) and 1 James (write-in) in CD 16; 4,804 Peace and Freedom (Smith) and 4,051 Libertarian (Wilkes) in CD 17; Libertarian (Almstrom) in CD 18; 13,334 Peace and Freedom (Wells) and 1,097 Williams (write-in) in CD 19; Hodges (write-in) in CD 21; 23,699 Green (Lorenz), 7,553 Libertarian (Dilbeck) and 102 Bialosky (write-in) in CD 22; 9,091 Libertarian (Wood) and 61 Dunbar (write-in) in CD 23; Peace and Freedom (Lindblad) in CD 24; 13,930 Independent (Pamplin), 6,932 Libertarian (Christensen), 6,919 Green (Wilken) and 5,090 Peace and Freedom (Lawrence) in CD 25; 7,180 Peace and Freedom (Hinds) and 3,468 Libertarian (Zimring) in CD 26; 11,003 Green (Moorman), 7,329 Peace and Freedom (Edwards), 4,790 Libertarian (Decherd) and 2 Ballantyne (write-in) in CD 27; 6,233 Green (Sheasby) and 4,271 Libertarian (Dominy) in CD 28; 15,445 Independent (Davis), 13,888 Peace and Freedom (Davies), 4,699 Libertarian (Rogin) and 1 Vann (write-in) in CD 29; 6,315 Green (Bonpane), 6,173 Peace and Freedom (Nakano) and 2,221 Libertarian (Consalvo) in CD 30; 12,384 Libertarian (Weber), 9,782 Peace and Freedom (Williams) and 2 Lesnick-Beltran (write-in) in CD 32; 2,135 Peace and Freedom (Delia) and 1,206 Libertarian (Olvera) in CD 33; 7,072 Libertarian (Swinney) and 1 Worland (write-in) in CD 34; 2,797 Peace and Freedom (Miles), 1,618 Libertarian (Rogers) and 3 Mego (write-in) in CD 35; 13,297 Green (Greene), 5,519 Peace and Freedom (Stanley), 5,504 Libertarian (Denny) and 2 Martz (write-in) in CD 36; Peace and Freedom (Duren) in CD 37; 8,391 Peace and Freedom (Burton), 6,756 Libertarian (Ashley), 14 Brown (write-in) and 14 Venable (write-in) in CD 38; Libertarian (Dean) in CD 39; Peace and Freedom (Akin) in CD 40; Peace and Freedom (Noonan) in CD 41; Libertarian (Ward) in CD 42; 6,095 American Independent (Odom), 4,989 Libertarian (Berkman) and 2,100 Schwab (write-in) in CD 43; Libertarian (Turner) in CD 44; Libertarian (Copeland) in CD 45; Libertarian (Newhouse) in CD 46; 12,297 Peace and Freedom (Quirk) and 32 Charles (write-in) in CD 47; 13,396 Peace and Freedom (White) and 8,749 Libertarian (Lowe) in CD 48; 10,706 Libertarian (Wallner), 4,738 Peace and Freedom (Zaslow) and 4 Thompson (write-in) in CD 49; 15,489 Libertarian (Hutchinson), 4,250 Peace and Freedom (Batchlder) and 63 Pickard (write-in) in CD 50; 10,309 Libertarian (Holmes), 10,307 Peace and Freedom (Clark), 5,328 Green (Roe) and 13 Johnson (write-in) in CD 51; 6,977 Libertarian (Shea), 5,734 Peace and Freedom (Gretsinger) and 2 Marmon (write-in)in CD 52.

CALIFORNIA

LOS ANGELES COUNTY

President   Other vote was 9,711 Libertarian (Marrou); 5,058 Peace and Freedom (Daniels); 3,094 American Independent (Phillips); 483 Gritz (write-in); 146 Hagelin (write-in); 60 LaRouche (write-in); 26 Warren (write-in); 2 Masters (write-in); 3 scattered write-in. The total of the other vote column includes the 720 write-in votes not available by assembly district.

Senator
Full Term   Other vote was 95,779 Peace and Freedom (Torres); 68,630 American Independent (McCready); 46,195 Libertarian (Genis); 65 scattered write-in. The total of the other vote column includes the 65 write-in votes not available by assembly district.

Senator
Short Term   Other vote was 84,093 Peace and Freedom (Horne); 55,380 American Independent (Meeuwenberg); 52,123 Libertarian (Boodie); 20 scattered write-in. The total of the other vote column includes the 20 write-in votes not available by assembly district.

1992 PRIMARIES

JUNE 2 REPUBLICAN

Senator
Full Term   956,146 Bruce Herschensohn; 895,970 Tom Campbell; 417,848 Sonny Bono; 94,623 Isaac P. Yonker; 60,104 Alexander Justice; 54,941 John W. Spring; 20,810 John M. Brown.

Senator
Short Term   1,216,096 John Seymour; 638,279 William E. Dannemeyer; 306,182 Jim Trinity; 216,177 William B. Allen.

Congress   Unopposed in fourteen CD's. No candidate in CD's 9, 18, 32 and 37. In CD 9, G. William Hunter received 1,424 write-in votes and qualified for the general election ballot. In CD 32, write-in votes were 530 Andrew D. Milder and 25 Timothy J. Vrieling; neither candidate qualified for the general election ballot. In CD 37, Anna L. Jessen received 64 write-in votes but did not qualify for the general election ballot. Contested as follows:

CD 1   41,097 Frank Riggs; 15,010 Terrance J. Brown.
CD 2   67,389 Wally Herger; 8,467 Steve Kunelis.
CD 3   40,835 H. L. Richardson; 16,319 Jacqueline J. Carpenter.
CD 4   57,631 John T. Doolittle; 23,404 Don Brooksher.
CD 6   35,815 Bill Filante; 13,687 Derek Coyle; 7,036 Claude Heater.
CD 10   46,786 Bill Baker; 26,387 Dave Williams.
CD 11   16,704 Richard W. Pombo; 12,482 Sandy Smoley; 11,029 Jack A. Sieglock; 4,455 Frank W. Hauck; 1,703 Cleo N. Robinson; 341 Ivaldo Lenci.
CD 14   23,475 Tom Huening; 9,453 Dixon Arnett; 8,947 Michael C. Mailbach; 7,473 Paul L. Biddle; 4,735 Bill Quraishi.
CD 15   33,708 Robert Wick; 21,564 Douglas B. Allen.
CD 17   22,492 Bill McCampbell; 12,846 Louis Darrigo.
CD 19   16,963 Tal L. Cloud; 15,728 George P. Radanovich; 10,322 Mark Johnson; 8,880 Richard Morgan.
CD 20   11,366 Ed Hunt; 10,038 Paul Young.
CD 21   37,657 William M. Thomas; 19,684 Carlos Murillo; 105 John J. Varela (write-in).
CD 22   38,406 Michael Huffington; 33,844 Robert J. Lagomarsino; 5,570 Gordon Klemm; 1,292 Dick Pauly.
CD 23   34,666 Elton Gallegly; 15,518 Daphne Becker; 4,597 Robert Shakman.
CD 24   20,163 Tom McClintock; 13,884 Sang R. Korman; 10,679 Bill Spillane; 4,382 Jim Salomon; 2,889 Rob Meyer; 2,238 Stephen M. Weiss; 1,805 Nicholas T. Hariton; 1,582 Robert Colaco; 902 Harry Wachtel.
CD 25   24,509 Howard P. McKeon; 23,804 Phillip D. Wyman; 4,568 Larry Logsdon; 4,438 John H. Rousselot; 3,366 John J. Lynch; 1,242 Tom McVarish.
CD 26   9,327 Gary E. Forsch; 9,172 Bill Glass.
CD 27   37,172 Carlos J. Moorhead; 10,354 Louis Morelli; 6,622 Barry L. Hatch; 6,141 Lionel Allen.
CD 31   10,023 Reuben D. Franco; 5,280 Nick Hai.

CALIFORNIA

CD 36   23,407 Joan M. Flores; 21,027 Maureen Reagan; 7,812 Bill Beverly; 6,633 Bill Fahey; 3,352 John Barbieri; 2,538 Wayne T. McDonald; 1,300 Bart Swanson; 878 John Stevenson; 796 Wayne Westling, 466 Don Karg; 338 Parker R. Herriott.

CD 38   13,423 Steve Horn; 13,318 Dennis Brown; 5,747 Tom Poe; 4,556 Andrew J. Hopwood; 3,418 William A. Ward; 2,177 Jerry Bakke; 1,428 Sanford W. Kahn; 1,032 John C. Brogdon.

CD 41   13,399 Jay C. Kim; 12,510 Charles W. Bader; 12,070 James V. Lacy; 2,966 George H. Margolis; 1,868 John Hoover; 1,753 James Todhunter.

CD 42   11,137 Richard B. Rutan; 8,716 Bob Hammock; 7,930 Chuck Williams; 2,091 Robert B. Westerman.

CD 43   13,387 Ken Calvert; 10,624 S. Joseph Khoury; 8,784 Bob Lynn; 8,750 Larry P. Arnn; 2,694 Bill Franklin; 2,270 Daniel Hantman; 1,958 William E. Jones.

CD 44   33,738 Al McCandless; 11,323 Bud Mathewson; 10,113 Lewis A. Silva.

CD 45   30,649 Dana Rohrabacher; 17,748 Peter Buffa; 15,592 Peter Green; 7 Dwayne B. Smith (write-in).

CD 46   17,558 Robert K. Dornan; 11,893 Judith M. Ryan.

CD 47   53,628 Christopher Cox; 15,633 Robert L. Moore; 9,873 Steven J. Forque.

CD 48   45,217 Ron Packard; 13,632 Stephen Todd; 12,077 Ed Mayerhofer.

CD 49   12,733 Judy Jarvis; 10,396 Alan Uke; 7,161 Ray Saatjian; 7,105 Skip Cox; 5,230 Dave Pierce; 4,997 Bill Mitchell; 4,213 Roy Moeller; 3,770 John C. Weil; 3,550 Ron Hecker; 2,191 Bob Tatum.

CD 50   9,019 Tony Valencia; 7,406 Lou A. Monge; 7,286 Luis Acle.

CD 51   40,645 Randy Cunningham; 14,514 William Davis; 12,039 Bill Lowery; 6,227 Michael Perdue; 5,003 Adelito M. Gale. Mr. Lowery announced his retirement on April 14, but his name remained on the primary ballot.

CD 52   35,681 Duncan L. Hunter; 13,604 Eric Epifano; 10,337 Robert E. Krysak; 80 Janet M. Gastil (write-in); 1 Delecia Holt (write-in).

JUNE 2 DEMOCRATIC

Senator Full Term   1,339,126 Barbara Boxer; 935,209 Leo McCarthy; 667,359 Mel Levine; 122,954 Charles Greene.

Senator Short Term   1,775,730 Dianne Feinstein; 1,009,761 Gray Davis; 149,918 David Kearns; 139,410 Joseph M. Alioto.

Congress   Unopposed in twenty-three CD's. No candidate in CD 21. In CD 21, write-in votes were 1,537 Deborah Vollmer and 429 John L. Evans; Ms Vollmer qualified for the general election ballot. Contested as follows:

CD 6   25,484 Lynn Woolsey; 18,090 Eric J. Koenigshofer; 16,979 Denis Rice; 13,202 Bennett Johnston; 7,872 Anna Nevenic; 5,666 David N. Strand; 4,140 William H. Morrison; 3,772 Joe Nation; 2,565 Howell Hurst.

CD 10   25,192 Wendell H. Williams; 22,090 Ayn Wieskamp; 18,125 John Staley.

CD 11   34,427 Patricia Garamendi; 10,719 George L. Barber; 4,951 Mike Garey; 3,520 Craig Wischhusen.

CD 12   62,397 Tom Lantos; 8,200 Glenn Tenney; 5,696 Jim Dunlap; 5 Chris Hoffman (write-in).

CD 14   32,001 Anna G. Eshoo; 28,858 Ted Lempert; 11,574 Tom Nolan; 1,800 Thomas R. Harney; 1,655 Gerry B. Andeen; 1,445 Robert Palmer; 1,242 Gary Bond; 530 John Yusken.

CD 16   37,833 Don Edwards; 15,105 Edward R. Dykes.

CD 17   52,580 Leon E. Panetta; 8,631 Art Dunn.

CD 19   39,846 Richard Lehman; 12,728 Curtis Youngs.

CD 22   42,487 Gloria Ochoa; 6,823 Ron Olmstead; 5,626 Michael A. Thomas; 3,252 Jon A. LeSage; 1,586 Jack Theimer.

CD 23   30,265 Anita P. Ferguson; 18,004 Kevin Sweeney.

CD 27   21,014 Doug Kahn; 20,288 John Grula.

CD 28   20,511 Al Wachtel; 12,009 Tommy L. Randle; 8,956 Kevin Dockery.

CD 29   72,283 Henry A. Waxman; 13,350 Scott M. Gaulke.

CD 30   10,417 Xavier Becerra; 7,089 Leticia Quezada; 5,128 Albert C. Lum; 4,136 Jeff J. Penichet; 2,320 Gonzalo Molina; 1,908 Helen Hernandez; 611 Roland R. Mora; 444 Esca W. Smith; 336 Mark Calney; 325 Ysidro Molina.

CD 31   20,248 Matthew G. Martinez; 8,678 Bonifacio Garcia; 3,188 Louis A. M. Ritchie; 3,136 A. Gus Hernandez.

CALIFORNIA

CD 33	14,112 Lucille Roybal-Allard; 3,138 Frank Fernandez; 1,685 Lucy F. Kihm.
CD 35	51,534 Maxine Waters; 6,252 Roger A. Young.
CD 36	26,812 Jane Harman; 9,216 Ada Unruh; 6,952 Charlene A. Richards; 5,200 Bryan W. Stevens; 4,107 Paul P. Kamm; 4,027 Gregory Stock; 2,940 Colin K. O'Brien.
CD 37	22,536 Walter R. Tucker; 21,433 Lynn Dymally; 6,491 Vera R. Dewitt; 4,804 Joe Mendez; 2,307 Lawrence A. Grigsby.
CD 38	20,210 Evan A. Braude; 13,204 Peter Mathews; 6,104 Ray O'Neal; 5,476 Bill Glazewski; 4,034 Clarence Gregory.
CD 39	29,399 Molly McClanahan; 12,071 Garry Hamud.
CD 43	11,193 Mark A. Takano; 8,000 Raven L. Workman; 5,543 Tom Jameson; 4,845 Harley L. Ross; 3,097 Dom F. Betro; 3,080 Art Cassel; 2,774 James R. Covell.
CD 44	17,368 Georgia Smith; 12,714 Clark McCartney; 10,419 Joel Simpson.
CD 45	20,235 Patricia McCabe; 6,750 B. H. Sarker; 6,294 Jim Foley; 4,322 Steve Olim.
CD 46	5,574 Robert J. Banuelos; 5,136 Ricardo Nicol; 4,787 Jeff LeTourneau; 3,560 Nazeer Ahmed; 3,382 Norman Z. Eckenrode.
CD 49	32,303 Lynn Schenk; 14,879 Byron Georgiou; 6,811 Bill Winston; 4,594 Carol J. Lucke; 2,066 Troy X. Kelley.
CD 50	10,932 Bob Filner; 9,846 Wadie P. Deddeh; 8,416 Jim Bates; 7,868 Juan C. Vargas; 4,120 Greg Akili; 843 Lincoln Pickard.
CD 51	14,043 Bea Herbert; 9,529 Steve Thorne; 8,666 Jeff Schwartz; 5,606 Steve Posner; 2,992 Brian J. Dunlea; 15 John J. Leone (write-in).

JUNE 2 AMERICAN INDEPENDENT

Senator Full Term	Jerome McCready, unopposed.
Senator Short Term	Paul Meeuwenberg, unopposed.
Congress	Unopposed in all CD's in which candidates were entered.

JUNE 2 GREEN

Senator Full Term	No candidate.
Senator Short Term	No candidate.
Congress	Unopposed in all CD's in which candidates were entered.

JUNE 2 LIBERTARIAN

Senator Full Term	June R. Genis, unopposed
Senator Short Term	Richard B. Boddie, unopposed.
Congress	Unopposed in all CD's in which candidates were entered.

CALIFORNIA

JUNE 2 PEACE AND FREEDOM

Senator
Full Term
5,492 Genevieve Torres; 3,610 Shirley Lee.

Senator
Short Term
5,681 Gerald Horne; 3,195 Jamie Mangia.

Congress Unopposed in all CD's in which candidates were entered except the four CD's listed below.

CD 9	257 Dave Linn; 255 Helen R. Abel.
CD 29	193 Susan C. Davies; 183 Maggie Phair.
CD 30	143 Elizabeth A. Nakano; 132 Maria Munoz.
CD 33	48 Tim Delia; 29 Frank Boeheim.

COLORADO

GOVERNOR
Roy Romer (D). Re-elected 1990 to a four-year term. Previously elected 1986.

SENATORS
Hank Brown (R). Elected 1990 to a six-year term.

Ben N. Campbell (D). Elected 1992 to a six-year term.

REPRESENTATIVES
1. Patricia Schroeder (D)
2. David Skaggs (D)
3. Scott McInnis (R)
4. Wayne Allard (R)
5. Joel Hefley (R)
6. Daniel L. Schaefer (R)

POSTWAR VOTE FOR PRESIDENT

Year	Total Vote	Republican Vote	Candidate	Democratic Vote	Candidate	Other Vote	Plurality	Total Vote Rep.	Total Vote Dem.	Major Vote Rep.	Major Vote Dem.
1992 **	1,569,180	562,850	Bush, George	629,681	Clinton, Bill	376,649	66,831 D	35.9%	40.1%	47.2%	52.8%
1988	1,372,394	728,177	Bush, George	621,453	Dukakis, Michael S.	22,764	106,724 R	53.1%	45.3%	54.0%	46.0%
1984	1,295,380	821,817	Reagan, Ronald	454,975	Mondale, Walter F.	18,588	366,842 R	63.4%	35.1%	64.4%	35.6%
1980	1,184,415	652,264	Reagan, Ronald	367,973	Carter, Jimmy	164,178	284,291 R	55.1%	31.1%	63.9%	36.1%
1976	1,081,554	584,367	Ford, Gerald R.	460,353	Carter, Jimmy	36,834	124,014 R	54.0%	42.6%	55.9%	44.1%
1972	953,884	597,189	Nixon, Richard M.	329,980	McGovern, George S.	26,715	267,209 R	62.6%	34.6%	64.4%	35.6%
1968	811,199	409,345	Nixon, Richard M.	335,174	Humphrey, Hubert H.	66,680	74,171 R	50.5%	41.3%	55.0%	45.0%
1964	776,986	296,767	Goldwater, Barry M.	476,024	Johnson, Lyndon B.	4,195	179,257 D	38.2%	61.3%	38.4%	61.6%
1960	736,236	402,242	Nixon, Richard M.	330,629	Kennedy, John F.	3,365	71,613 R	54.6%	44.9%	54.9%	45.1%
1956	657,074	394,479	Eisenhower, Dwight D.	257,997	Stevenson, Adlai E.	4,598	136,482 R	60.0%	39.3%	60.5%	39.5%
1952	630,103	379,782	Eisenhower, Dwight D.	245,504	Stevenson, Adlai E.	4,817	134,278 R	60.3%	39.0%	60.7%	39.3%
1948	515,237	239,714	Dewey, Thomas E.	267,288	Truman, Harry S.	8,235	27,574 D	46.5%	51.9%	47.3%	52.7%

In 1992 the other vote column includes 366,010 votes cast for Perot.

POSTWAR VOTE FOR GOVERNOR

Year	Total Vote	Republican Vote	Candidate	Democratic Vote	Candidate	Other Vote	Rep.-Dem. Plurality	Total Vote Rep.	Total Vote Dem.	Major Vote Rep.	Major Vote Dem.
1990	1,011,272	358,403	Andrews, John	626,032	Romer, Roy	26,837	267,629 D	35.4%	61.9%	36.4%	63.6%
1986	1,058,928	434,420	Strickland, Ted	616,325	Romer, Roy	8,183	181,905 D	41.0%	58.2%	41.3%	58.7%
1982	956,021	302,740	Fuhr, John D.	627,960	Lamm, Richard D.	25,321	325,220 D	31.7%	65.7%	32.5%	67.5%
1978	823,807	317,292	Strickland, Ted	483,985	Lamm, Richard D.	22,530	166,693 D	38.5%	58.7%	39.6%	60.4%
1974	828,968	378,698	Vanderhoof, John D.	441,408	Lamm, Richard D.	8,862	62,710 D	45.7%	53.2%	46.2%	53.8%
1970	668,496	350,690	Love, John A.	302,432	Hogan, Mark	15,374	48,258 R	52.5%	45.2%	53.7%	46.3%
1966	660,063	356,730	Love, John A.	287,132	Knous, Robert L.	16,201	69,598 R	54.0%	43.5%	55.4%	44.6%
1962	616,481	349,342	Love, John A.	262,890	McNichols, Stephen	4,249	86,452 R	56.7%	42.6%	57.1%	42.9%
1958 **	549,808	228,643	Burch, Palmer L.	321,165	McNichols, Stephen		92,522 D	41.6%	58.4%	41.6%	58.4%
1956	645,233	313,950	Brotzman, Donald G.	331,283	McNichols, Stephen		17,333 D	48.7%	51.3%	48.7%	51.3%
1954	489,540	227,335	Brotzman, Donald G.	262,205	Johnson, Ed C.		34,870 D	46.4%	53.6%	46.4%	53.6%
1952	613,034	349,924	Thornton, Dan	260,044	Metzger, John W.	3,066	89,880 R	57.1%	42.4%	57.4%	42.6%
1950	450,994	236,472	Thornton, Dan	212,976	Johnson, Walter	1,546	23,496 R	52.4%	47.2%	52.6%	47.4%
1948	501,680	168,928	Hamil, David A.	332,752	Knous, William Lee		163,824 D	33.7%	66.3%	33.7%	66.3%
1946	335,087	160,483	Lavington, Leon E.	174,604	Knous, William Lee		14,121 D	47.9%	52.1%	47.9%	52.1%

The term of office of Colorado's Governor was increased from two to four years effective with the 1958 election.

COLORADO

POSTWAR VOTE FOR SENATOR

Year	Total Vote	Republican		Democratic		Other Vote	Rep.-Dem. Plurality	Percentage			
								Total Vote		Major Vote	
		Vote	Candidate	Vote	Candidate			Rep.	Dem.	Rep.	Dem.
1992	1,552,289	662,893	Considine, Terry	803,725	Campbell, Ben N.	85,671	140,832 D	42.7%	51.8%	45.2%	54.8%
1990	1,022,027	569,048	Brown, Hank	425,746	Heath, Josie	27,233	143,302 R	55.7%	41.7%	57.2%	42.8%
1986	1,060,765	512,994	Kramer, Ken	529,449	Wirth, Timothy E.	18,322	16,455 D	48.4%	49.9%	49.2%	50.8%
1984	1,297,809	833,821	Armstrong, William L.	449,327	Dick, Nancy	14,661	384,494 R	64.2%	34.6%	65.0%	35.0%
1980	1,173,646	571,295	Buchanan, Mary E.	590,501	Hart, Gary W.	11,850	19,206 D	48.7%	50.3%	49.2%	50.8%
1978	819,150	480,596	Armstrong, William L.	330,247	Haskell, Floyd K.	8,307	150,349 R	58.7%	40.3%	59.3%	40.7%
1974	824,166	325,508	Dominick, Peter H.	471,691	Hart, Gary W.	26,967	146,183 D	39.5%	57.2%	40.8%	59.2%
1972	926,093	447,957	Allott, Gordon	457,545	Haskell, Floyd K.	20,591	9,588 D	48.4%	49.4%	49.5%	50.5%
1968	785,536	459,952	Dominick, Peter H.	325,584	McNichols, Stephen		134,368 R	58.6%	41.4%	58.6%	41.4%
1966	634,898	368,307	Allott, Gordon	266,259	Romer, Roy	332	102,048 R	58.0%	41.9%	58.0%	42.0%
1962	613,444	328,655	Dominick, Peter H.	279,586	Carroll, John A.	5,203	49,069 R	53.6%	45.6%	54.0%	46.0%
1960	727,633	389,428	Allott, Gordon	334,854	Knous, Robert L.	3,351	54,574 R	53.5%	46.0%	53.8%	46.2%
1956	636,974	317,102	Thornton, Dan	319,872	Carroll, John A.		2,770 D	49.8%	50.2%	49.8%	50.2%
1954	484,188	248,502	Allott, Gordon	235,686	Carroll, John A.		12,816 R	51.3%	48.7%	51.3%	48.7%
1950	450,176	239,734	Millikin, Eugene D.	210,442	Carroll, John A.		29,292 R	53.3%	46.7%	53.3%	46.7%
1948	510,121	165,069	Nicholson, W. F.	340,719	Johnson, Ed C.	4,333	175,650 D	32.4%	66.8%	32.6%	67.4%

COLORADO

Districts Established March 24, 1992

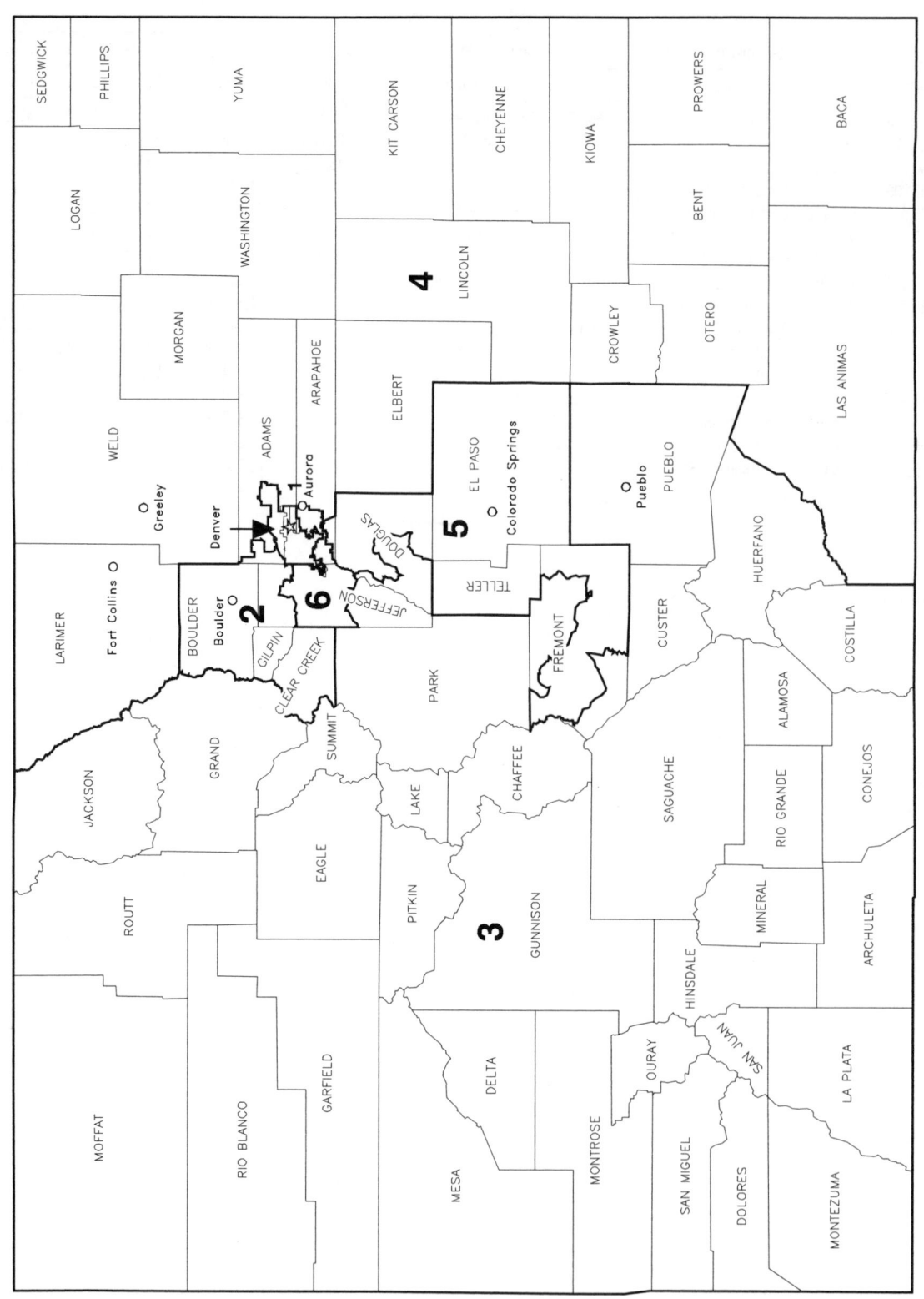

COLORADO

PRESIDENT 1992

Registration	County	Total Vote	Republican	Democratic	Perot	Other	Plurality	Percentage Total Vote		
								Rep.	Dem.	Perot
135,594	ADAMS	103,077	30,856	45,357	26,379	485	14,501 D	29.9%	44.0%	25.6%
6,624	ALAMOSA	4,617	1,572	1,928	1,089	28	356 D	34.0%	41.8%	23.6%
245,088	ARAPAHOE	183,935	72,221	66,607	44,363	744	5,614 R	39.3%	36.2%	24.1%
3,651	ARCHULETA	2,816	1,242	819	741	14	423 R	44.1%	29.1%	26.3%
3,046	BACA	2,622	1,240	726	647	9	514 R	47.3%	27.7%	24.7%
2,800	BENT	2,257	759	985	506	7	226 D	33.6%	43.6%	22.4%
157,074	BOULDER	126,771	33,553	64,567	27,762	889	31,014 D	26.5%	50.9%	21.9%
7,636	CHAFFEE	6,282	2,419	2,284	1,549	30	135 R	38.5%	36.4%	24.7%
1,433	CHEYENNE	1,212	615	301	292	4	314 R	50.7%	24.8%	24.1%
5,475	CLEAR CREEK	4,460	1,356	1,744	1,308	52	388 D	30.4%	39.1%	29.3%
4,411	CONEJOS	3,465	1,160	1,705	578	22	545 D	33.5%	49.2%	16.7%
2,323	COSTILLA	1,753	366	1,180	199	8	814 D	20.9%	67.3%	11.4%
1,813	CROWLEY	1,458	602	570	276	10	32 R	41.3%	39.1%	18.9%
1,755	CUSTER	1,375	651	343	368	13	283 R	47.3%	24.9%	26.8%
12,641	DELTA	10,494	4,359	3,424	2,627	84	935 R	41.5%	32.6%	25.0%
288,879	DENVER	217,919	55,418	121,961	37,298	3,242	66,543 D	25.4%	56.0%	17.1%
1,035	DOLORES	846	315	242	285	4	30 R	37.2%	28.6%	33.7%
51,547	DOUGLAS	40,060	18,592	9,991	11,329	148	7,263 R	46.4%	24.9%	28.3%
13,777	EAGLE	10,870	3,100	3,870	3,821	79	49 D	28.5%	35.6%	35.2%
6,682	ELBERT	5,045	2,205	1,237	1,567	36	638 R	43.7%	24.5%	31.1%
208,331	EL PASO	167,169	86,044	45,827	34,346	952	40,217 R	51.5%	27.4%	20.5%
19,765	FREMONT	15,131	5,961	5,356	3,709	105	605 R	39.4%	35.4%	24.5%
16,809	GARFIELD	13,976	4,404	5,082	4,408	82	674 D	31.5%	36.4%	31.5%
2,300	GILPIN	1,759	462	726	545	26	181 D	26.3%	41.3%	31.0%
6,507	GRAND	4,918	1,763	1,678	1,454	23	85 R	35.8%	34.1%	29.6%
7,079	GUNNISON	5,759	1,662	2,389	1,671	37	718 D	28.9%	41.5%	29.0%
588	HINSDALE	476	188	151	136	1	37 R	39.5%	31.7%	28.6%
3,870	HUERFANO	2,313	685	1,224	385	19	539 D	29.6%	52.9%	16.6%
1,149	JACKSON	966	422	216	326	2	96 R	43.7%	22.4%	33.7%
281,880	JEFFERSON	223,203	82,705	80,834	58,404	1,260	1,871 R	37.1%	36.2%	26.2%
1,244	KIOWA	1,030	472	290	267	1	182 R	45.8%	28.2%	25.9%
4,461	KIT CARSON	3,658	1,801	925	919	13	876 R	49.2%	25.3%	25.1%
3,613	LAKE	2,923	605	1,426	863	29	563 D	20.7%	48.8%	29.5%
19,081	LA PLATA	15,613	5,522	5,913	4,083	95	391 D	35.4%	37.9%	26.2%
122,170	LARIMER	99,660	35,995	38,232	24,879	554	2,237 D	36.1%	38.4%	25.0%
8,335	LAS ANIMAS	6,569	1,739	3,847	953	30	2,108 D	26.5%	58.6%	14.5%
2,738	LINCOLN	2,306	1,079	640	581	6	439 R	46.8%	27.8%	25.2%
9,949	LOGAN	8,345	3,420	2,718	2,184	23	702 R	41.0%	32.6%	26.2%
56,063	MESA	44,067	18,169	15,162	10,474	262	3,007 R	41.2%	34.4%	23.8%
573	MINERAL	449	159	171	117	2	12 D	35.4%	38.1%	26.1%
7,012	MOFFAT	5,095	1,809	1,386	1,875	25	66 P	35.5%	27.2%	36.8%
9,466	MONTEZUMA	7,638	3,124	2,270	2,205	39	854 R	40.9%	29.7%	28.9%
14,041	MONTROSE	11,723	4,847	3,713	3,093	70	1,134 R	41.3%	31.7%	26.4%
10,934	MORGAN	8,930	3,724	2,985	2,175	46	739 R	41.7%	33.4%	24.4%
10,527	OTERO	8,313	3,120	3,485	1,590	118	365 D	37.5%	41.9%	19.1%
1,876	OURAY	1,583	653	461	466	3	187 R	41.3%	29.1%	29.4%
5,453	PARK	4,276	1,530	1,307	1,396	43	134 R	35.8%	30.6%	32.6%
2,734	PHILLIPS	2,303	1,075	692	525	11	383 R	46.7%	30.0%	22.8%
9,687	PITKIN	7,469	1,686	3,820	1,907	56	1,913 D	22.6%	51.1%	25.5%
6,853	PROWERS	5,377	2,371	1,770	1,184	52	601 R	44.1%	32.9%	22.0%
70,402	PUEBLO	56,438	16,120	30,261	9,841	216	14,141 D	28.6%	53.6%	17.4%
3,881	RIO BLANCO	2,850	1,231	778	794	47	437 R	43.2%	27.3%	27.9%
5,652	RIO GRANDE	4,533	1,927	1,541	1,043	22	386 R	42.5%	34.0%	23.0%
10,413	ROUTT	8,161	2,358	3,188	2,564	51	624 D	28.9%	39.1%	31.4%
2,747	SAGUACHE	2,174	675	1,011	471	17	336 D	31.0%	46.5%	21.7%
572	SAN JUAN	453	118	147	183	5	36 P	26.0%	32.5%	40.4%
3,319	SAN MIGUEL	2,663	628	1,380	634	21	746 D	23.6%	51.8%	23.8%
1,735	SEDGWICK	1,146	447	397	295	7	50 R	39.0%	34.6%	25.7%
10,633	SUMMIT	8,370	2,256	3,344	2,715	55	629 D	27.0%	40.0%	32.4%
9,111	TELLER	6,914	3,050	1,873	1,927	64	1,123 R	44.1%	27.1%	27.9%

COLORADO

PRESIDENT 1992

Registration	County	Total Vote	Republican	Democratic	Perot	Other	Plurality	Percentage Total Vote		
								Rep.	Dem.	Perot
3,121	WASHINGTON	2,613	1,266	660	671	16	595 R	48.5%	25.3%	25.7%
68,075	WELD	54,029	20,958	19,295	13,571	205	1,663 R	38.8%	35.7%	25.1%
5,342	YUMA	4,505	2,019	1,269	1,197	20	750 R	44.8%	28.2%	26.6%
2,003,375	TOTAL	1,569,180	562,850	629,681	366,010	10,639	66,831 D	35.9%	40.1%	23.3%

COLORADO

SENATOR 1992

Registration	County	Total Vote	Republican	Democratic	Other	Rep.-Dem. Plurality	Percentage			
							Total Vote		Major Vote	
							Rep.	Dem.	Rep.	Dem.
135,594	ADAMS	101,960	37,843	57,395	6,722	19,552 D	37.1%	56.3%	39.7%	60.3%
6,624	ALAMOSA	4,611	1,462	2,963	186	1,501 D	31.7%	64.3%	33.0%	67.0%
245,088	ARAPAHOE	181,133	85,953	86,474	8,706	521 D	47.5%	47.7%	49.8%	50.2%
3,651	ARCHULETA	2,810	1,181	1,452	177	271 D	42.0%	51.7%	44.9%	55.1%
3,046	BACA	2,602	1,469	1,024	109	445 R	56.5%	39.4%	58.9%	41.1%
2,800	BENT	2,257	1,043	1,135	79	92 D	46.2%	50.3%	47.9%	52.1%
157,074	BOULDER	128,359	41,118	79,437	7,804	38,319 D	32.0%	61.9%	34.1%	65.9%
7,636	CHAFFEE	6,232	2,651	3,231	350	580 D	42.5%	51.8%	45.1%	54.9%
1,433	CHEYENNE	1,207	692	474	41	218 R	57.3%	39.3%	59.3%	40.7%
5,475	CLEAR CREEK	4,410	1,553	2,543	314	990 D	35.2%	57.7%	37.9%	62.1%
4,411	CONEJOS	3,460	970	2,357	133	1,387 D	28.0%	68.1%	29.2%	70.8%
2,323	COSTILLA	1,676	322	1,291	63	969 D	19.2%	77.0%	20.0%	80.0%
1,813	CROWLEY	1,469	750	673	46	77 R	51.1%	45.8%	52.7%	47.3%
1,755	CUSTER	1,392	723	571	98	152 R	51.9%	41.0%	55.9%	44.1%
12,641	DELTA	10,427	4,464	5,412	551	948 D	42.8%	51.9%	45.2%	54.8%
288,879	DENVER	209,639	63,524	135,430	10,685	71,906 D	30.3%	64.6%	31.9%	68.1%
1,035	DOLORES	828	314	454	60	140 D	37.9%	54.8%	40.9%	59.1%
51,547	DOUGLAS	39,919	22,087	15,552	2,280	6,535 R	55.3%	39.0%	58.7%	41.3%
13,777	EAGLE	10,716	3,163	6,928	625	3,765 D	29.5%	64.7%	31.3%	68.7%
6,682	ELBERT	5,281	2,652	2,271	358	381 R	50.2%	43.0%	53.9%	46.1%
208,331	EL PASO	166,250	106,106	51,130	9,014	54,976 R	63.8%	30.8%	67.5%	32.5%
19,765	FREMONT	15,090	7,728	6,511	851	1,217 R	51.2%	43.1%	54.3%	45.7%
16,809	GARFIELD	13,939	4,793	8,259	887	3,466 D	34.4%	59.3%	36.7%	63.3%
2,300	GILPIN	1,745	511	1,086	148	575 D	29.3%	62.2%	32.0%	68.0%
6,507	GRAND	4,904	1,874	2,745	285	871 D	38.2%	56.0%	40.6%	59.4%
7,079	GUNNISON	5,731	1,694	3,763	274	2,069 D	29.6%	65.7%	31.0%	69.0%
588	HINSDALE	478	177	275	26	98 D	37.0%	57.5%	39.2%	60.8%
3,870	HUERFANO	3,016	877	2,047	92	1,170 D	29.1%	67.9%	30.0%	70.0%
1,149	JACKSON	955	330	571	54	241 D	34.6%	59.8%	36.6%	63.4%
281,880	JEFFERSON	220,895	98,091	108,708	14,096	10,617 D	44.4%	49.2%	47.4%	52.6%
1,244	KIOWA	1,028	534	457	37	77 R	51.9%	44.5%	53.9%	46.1%
4,461	KIT CARSON	3,640	1,768	1,672	200	96 R	48.6%	45.9%	51.4%	48.6%
3,613	LAKE	2,887	670	2,016	201	1,346 D	23.2%	69.8%	24.9%	75.1%
19,081	LA PLATA	15,448	4,844	9,833	771	4,989 D	31.4%	63.7%	33.0%	67.0%
122,170	LARIMER	98,374	42,897	50,373	5,104	7,476 D	43.6%	51.2%	46.0%	54.0%
8,335	LAS ANIMAS	6,549	2,530	3,749	270	1,219 D	38.6%	57.2%	40.3%	59.7%
2,738	LINCOLN	2,295	1,199	974	122	225 R	52.2%	42.4%	55.2%	44.8%
9,949	LOGAN	8,291	3,831	4,001	459	170 D	46.2%	48.3%	48.9%	51.1%
56,063	MESA	43,899	20,290	21,375	2,234	1,085 D	46.2%	48.7%	48.7%	51.3%
573	MINERAL	450	126	312	12	186 D	28.0%	69.3%	28.8%	71.2%
7,012	MOFFAT	5,086	1,695	3,010	381	1,315 D	33.3%	59.2%	36.0%	64.0%
9,466	MONTEZUMA	7,572	3,051	4,022	499	971 D	40.3%	53.1%	43.1%	56.9%
14,041	MONTROSE	11,662	5,101	5,977	584	876 D	43.7%	51.3%	46.0%	54.0%
10,934	MORGAN	8,550	4,211	3,808	531	403 R	49.3%	44.5%	52.5%	47.5%
10,527	OTERO	8,099	4,033	3,628	438	405 R	49.8%	44.8%	52.6%	47.4%
1,876	OURAY	1,586	700	798	88	98 D	44.1%	50.3%	46.7%	53.3%
5,453	PARK	4,190	1,710	2,119	361	409 D	40.8%	50.6%	44.7%	55.3%
2,734	PHILLIPS	2,289	1,203	993	93	210 R	52.6%	43.4%	54.8%	45.2%
9,687	PITKIN	7,280	1,589	5,313	378	3,724 D	21.8%	73.0%	23.0%	77.0%
6,853	PROWERS	5,173	2,801	2,068	304	733 R	54.1%	40.0%	57.5%	42.5%
70,402	PUEBLO	56,594	20,571	34,253	1,770	13,682 D	36.3%	60.5%	37.5%	62.5%
3,881	RIO BLANCO	2,723	1,056	1,511	156	455 D	38.8%	55.5%	41.1%	58.9%
5,652	RIO GRANDE	4,547	1,617	2,733	197	1,116 D	35.6%	60.1%	37.2%	62.8%
10,413	ROUTT	8,096	2,185	5,525	386	3,340 D	27.0%	68.2%	28.3%	71.7%
2,747	SAGUACHE	2,177	623	1,457	97	834 D	28.6%	66.9%	30.0%	70.0%
572	SAN JUAN	451	123	285	43	162 D	27.3%	63.2%	30.1%	69.9%
3,319	SAN MIGUEL	2,628	625	1,880	123	1,255 D	23.8%	71.5%	25.0%	75.0%
1,735	SEDGWICK	1,121	528	551	42	23 D	47.1%	49.2%	48.9%	51.1%
10,633	SUMMIT	8,282	2,415	5,376	491	2,961 D	29.2%	64.9%	31.0%	69.0%
9,111	TELLER	6,839	3,743	2,595	501	1,148 R	54.7%	37.9%	59.1%	40.9%

COLORADO

SENATOR 1992

Registration	County	Total Vote	Republican	Democratic	Other	Rep.-Dem. Plurality		Percentage			
								Total Vote		Major Vote	
								Rep.	Dem.	Rep.	Dem.
3,121	WASHINGTON	2,588	1,336	1,097	155	239	R	51.6%	42.4%	54.9%	45.1%
68,075	WELD	54,042	25,093	25,641	3,308	548	D	46.4%	47.4%	49.5%	50.5%
5,342	YUMA	4,462	2,080	2,161	221	81	D	46.6%	48.4%	49.0%	51.0%
2,003,375	TOTAL	1,552,289	662,893	803,725	85,671	140,832	D	42.7%	51.8%	45.2%	54.8%

COLORADO

CONGRESS

CD	Year	Total Vote	Republican		Democratic		Other Vote	Rep.-Dem. Plurality	Percentage			
									Total Vote		Major Vote	
			Vote	Candidate	Vote	Candidate			Rep.	Dem.	Rep.	Dem.
1	1992	227,531	70,902	ARAGON, RAYMOND D.	156,629	SCHROEDER, PATRICIA		85,727 D	31.2%	68.8%	31.2%	68.8%
2	1992	271,361	88,470	DAY, BRYAN	164,790	SKAGGS, DAVID	18,101	76,320 D	32.6%	60.7%	34.9%	65.1%
3	1992	261,964	143,293	MCINNIS, SCOTT	114,480	CALLIHAN, MIKE	4,191	28,813 R	54.7%	43.7%	55.6%	44.4%
4	1992	241,841	139,884	ALLARD, WAYNE	101,957	REDDER, TOM		37,927 R	57.8%	42.2%	57.8%	42.2%
5	1992	243,415	173,096	HEFLEY, JOEL	62,550	ORIEZ, CHARLES A.	7,769	110,546 R	71.1%	25.7%	73.5%	26.5%
6	1992	233,097	142,021	SCHAEFER, DANIEL L.	91,073	KOLBE, TOM	3	50,948 R	60.9%	39.1%	60.9%	39.1%

COLORADO

1992 GENERAL ELECTION

President Other vote was 8,669 Libertarian (Marrou); 1,608 New Alliance (Fulani); 274 Gritz (write-in); 47 Hagelin (write-in); 21 Dodge (write-in); 20 LaRouche (write-in).

Senator Other vote was 42,455 Perot's Independents (Grimes); 22,846 Christian Pro Life (Noah); 20,347 Independent (Winters); 23 scattered write-in.

Congress Other vote was American Grassroots Alternative (Tharp) in CD 2; 4,189 Colorado Populist (Nelson) and 2 Hayes (write-in) in CD 3; Libertarian (Hamburger) in CD 5; Higgerson (write-in) in CD 6.

1992 PRIMARIES

AUGUST 11 REPUBLICAN

Senator Terry Considine, unopposed.

Congress Unopposed in five CD's. Contested as follows:

  CD 2 10,084 Bryan Day; 9,668 Sharon Klusman.

AUGUST 11 DEMOCRATIC

Senator 117,634 Ben N. Campbell; 93,599 Richard D. Lamm; 47,418 Josie Heath.

Congress Unopposed in five CD's. Contested as follows:

  CD 2 35,248 David Skaggs; 9,164 James L. Harrington.

CONNECTICUT

GOVERNOR
Lowell P. Weicker (Connecticut Party). Elected 1990 to a four-year term.

SENATORS
Christopher J. Dodd (D). Re-elected 1992 to a six-year term. Previously elected 1986, 1980.

Joseph I. Lieberman (D). Elected 1988 to a six-year term.

REPRESENTATIVES
1. Barbara B. Kennelly (D)
2. Samuel Gejdenson (D)
3. Rosa L. DeLauro (D)
4. Christopher Shays (R)
5. Gary A. Franks (R)
6. Nancy L. Johnson (R)

POSTWAR VOTE FOR PRESIDENT

		Republican		Democratic		Other		Percentage Total Vote		Major Vote	
Year	Total Vote	Vote	Candidate	Vote	Candidate	Vote	Plurality	Rep.	Dem.	Rep.	Dem.
1992 **	1,616,332	578,313	Bush, George	682,318	Clinton, Bill	355,701	104,005 D	35.8%	42.2%	45.9%	54.1%
1988	1,443,394	750,241	Bush, George	676,584	Dukakis, Michael S.	16,569	73,657 R	52.0%	46.9%	52.6%	47.4%
1984	1,466,900	890,877	Reagan, Ronald	569,597	Mondale, Walter F.	6,426	321,280 R	60.7%	38.8%	61.0%	39.0%
1980	1,406,285	677,210	Reagan, Ronald	541,732	Carter, Jimmy	187,343	135,478 R	48.2%	38.5%	55.6%	44.4%
1976	1,381,526	719,261	Ford, Gerald R.	647,895	Carter, Jimmy	14,370	71,366 R	52.1%	46.9%	52.6%	47.4%
1972	1,384,277	810,763	Nixon, Richard M.	555,498	McGovern, George S.	18,016	255,265 R	58.6%	40.1%	59.3%	40.7%
1968	1,256,232	556,721	Nixon, Richard M.	621,561	Humphrey, Hubert H.	77,950	64,840 D	44.3%	49.5%	47.2%	52.8%
1964	1,218,578	390,996	Goldwater, Barry M.	826,269	Johnson, Lyndon B.	1,313	435,273 D	32.1%	67.8%	32.1%	67.9%
1960	1,222,883	565,813	Nixon, Richard M.	657,055	Kennedy, John F.	15	91,242 D	46.3%	53.7%	46.3%	53.7%
1956	1,117,121	711,837	Eisenhower, Dwight D.	405,079	Stevenson, Adlai E.	205	306,758 R	63.7%	36.3%	63.7%	36.3%
1952	1,096,911	611,012	Eisenhower, Dwight D.	481,649	Stevenson, Adlai E.	4,250	129,363 R	55.7%	43.9%	55.9%	44.1%
1948	883,518	437,754	Dewey, Thomas E.	423,297	Truman, Harry S.	22,467	14,457 R	49.5%	47.9%	50.8%	49.2%

In 1992 the other vote column includes 348,771 votes cast for Perot.

POSTWAR VOTE FOR GOVERNOR

		Republican		Democratic		Other	Rep.-Dem.	Percentage Total Vote		Major Vote	
Year	Total Vote	Vote	Candidate	Vote	Candidate	Vote	Plurality	Rep.	Dem.	Rep.	Dem.
1990 **	1,141,122	427,840	Rowland, John G.	236,641	Morrison, Bruce A.	476,641	191,199 R	37.5%	20.7%	64.4%	35.6%
1986	993,692	408,489	Belaga, Julie D.	575,638	O'Neill, William A.	9,565	167,149 D	41.1%	57.9%	41.5%	58.5%
1982	1,084,156	497,773	Rome, Lewis B.	578,264	O'Neill, William A.	8,119	80,491 D	45.9%	53.3%	46.3%	53.7%
1978	1,036,608	422,316	Sarasin, Ronald A.	613,109	Grasso, Ella T.	1,183	190,793 D	40.7%	59.1%	40.8%	59.2%
1974	1,102,773	440,169	Steele, Robert H.	643,490	Grasso, Ella T.	19,114	203,321 D	39.9%	58.4%	40.6%	59.4%
1970	1,082,797	582,160	Meskill, Thomas J.	500,561	Daddario, Emilio	76	81,599 R	53.8%	46.2%	53.8%	46.2%
1966	1,008,557	446,536	Gengras, E. Clayton	561,599	Dempsey, John N.	422	115,063 D	44.3%	55.7%	44.3%	55.7%
1962	1,031,902	482,852	Alsop, John	549,027	Dempsey, John N.	23	66,175 D	46.8%	53.2%	46.8%	53.2%
1958	974,509	360,644	Zeller, Fred R.	607,012	Ribicoff, Abraham A.	6,853	246,368 D	37.0%	62.3%	37.3%	62.7%
1954	936,753	460,528	Lodge, John D.	463,643	Ribicoff, Abraham A.	12,582	3,115 D	49.2%	49.5%	49.8%	50.2%
1950 **	878,735	436,418	Lodge, John D.	419,404	Bowles, Chester	22,913	17,014 R	49.7%	47.7%	51.0%	49.0%
1948	875,170	429,071	Shannon, James C.	431,296	Bowles, Chester	14,803	2,225 D	49.0%	49.3%	49.9%	50.1%
1946	683,831	371,852	McConaughy, J. L.	276,335	Snow, Wilbert	35,644	95,517 R	54.4%	40.4%	57.4%	42.6%

The term of office for Connecticut's Governor was increased from two to four years effective with the 1950 election. In 1990 Lowell P. Weicker, the Connecticut Party candidate, polled 460,576 votes (40.4% of the total vote) and won the election with a 32,736 plurality.

CONNECTICUT

POSTWAR VOTE FOR SENATOR

Year	Total Vote	Republican Vote	Republican Candidate	Democratic Vote	Democratic Candidate	Other Vote	Rep.-Dem. Plurality	Percentage Total Vote Rep.	Total Vote Dem.	Major Vote Rep.	Major Vote Dem.
1992	1,500,709	572,036	Johnson, Brook	882,569	Dodd, Christopher J.	46,104	310,533 D	38.1%	58.8%	39.3%	60.7%
1988	1,383,526	678,454	Weicker, Lowell P.	688,499	Lieberman, Joseph I.	16,573	10,045 D	49.0%	49.8%	49.6%	50.4%
1986	976,933	340,438	Eddy, Roger W.	632,695	Dodd, Christopher J.	3,800	292,257 D	34.8%	64.8%	35.0%	65.0%
1982	1,083,613	545,987	Weicker, Lowell P.	499,146	Moffett, Anthony T.	38,480	46,841 R	50.4%	46.1%	52.2%	47.8%
1980	1,356,075	581,884	Buckley, James L.	763,969	Dodd, Christopher J.	10,222	182,085 D	42.9%	56.3%	43.2%	56.8%
1976	1,361,666	785,683	Weicker, Lowell P.	561,018	Schaffer, Gloria	14,965	224,665 R	57.7%	41.2%	58.3%	41.7%
1974	1,084,918	372,055	Brannen, James H.	690,820	Ribicoff, Abraham A.	22,043	318,765 D	34.3%	63.7%	35.0%	65.0%
1970	1,089,353	454,721	Weicker, Lowell P.	368,111	Duffey, Joseph D.	266,521	86,610 R	41.7%	33.8%	55.3%	44.7%
1968	1,206,537	551,455	May, Edwin H.	655,043	Ribicoff, Abraham A.	39	103,588 D	45.7%	54.3%	45.7%	54.3%
1964	1,208,163	426,939	Lodge, John D.	781,008	Dodd, Thomas J.	216	354,069 D	35.3%	64.6%	35.3%	64.7%
1962	1,029,301	501,694	Seely-Brown, Horace	527,522	Ribicoff, Abraham A.	85	25,828 D	48.7%	51.3%	48.7%	51.3%
1958	965,463	410,622	Purtell, William A.	554,841	Dodd, Thomas J.		144,219 D	42.5%	57.5%	42.5%	57.5%
1956	1,113,819	610,829	Bush, Prescott	479,460	Dodd, Thomas J.	23,530	131,369 R	54.8%	43.0%	56.0%	44.0%
1952	1,093,467	573,854	Purtell, William A.	485,066	Benton, William	34,547	88,788 R	52.5%	44.4%	54.2%	45.8%
1952 S	1,093,268	559,465	Bush, Prescott	530,505	Ribicoff, Abraham A.	3,298	28,960 R	51.2%	48.5%	51.3%	48.7%
1950	877,827	409,053	Talbot, Joseph E.	453,646	McMahon, Brien	15,128	44,593 D	46.6%	51.7%	47.4%	52.6%
1950 S	877,135	430,311	Bush, Prescott	431,413	Benton, William	15,411	1,102 D	49.1%	49.2%	49.9%	50.1%
1946	682,921	381,328	Baldwin, Raymond	276,424	Tone, Joseph M.	25,169	104,904 R	55.8%	40.5%	58.0%	42.0%

One each of the 1952 and 1950 elections was for a short term to fill a vacancy.

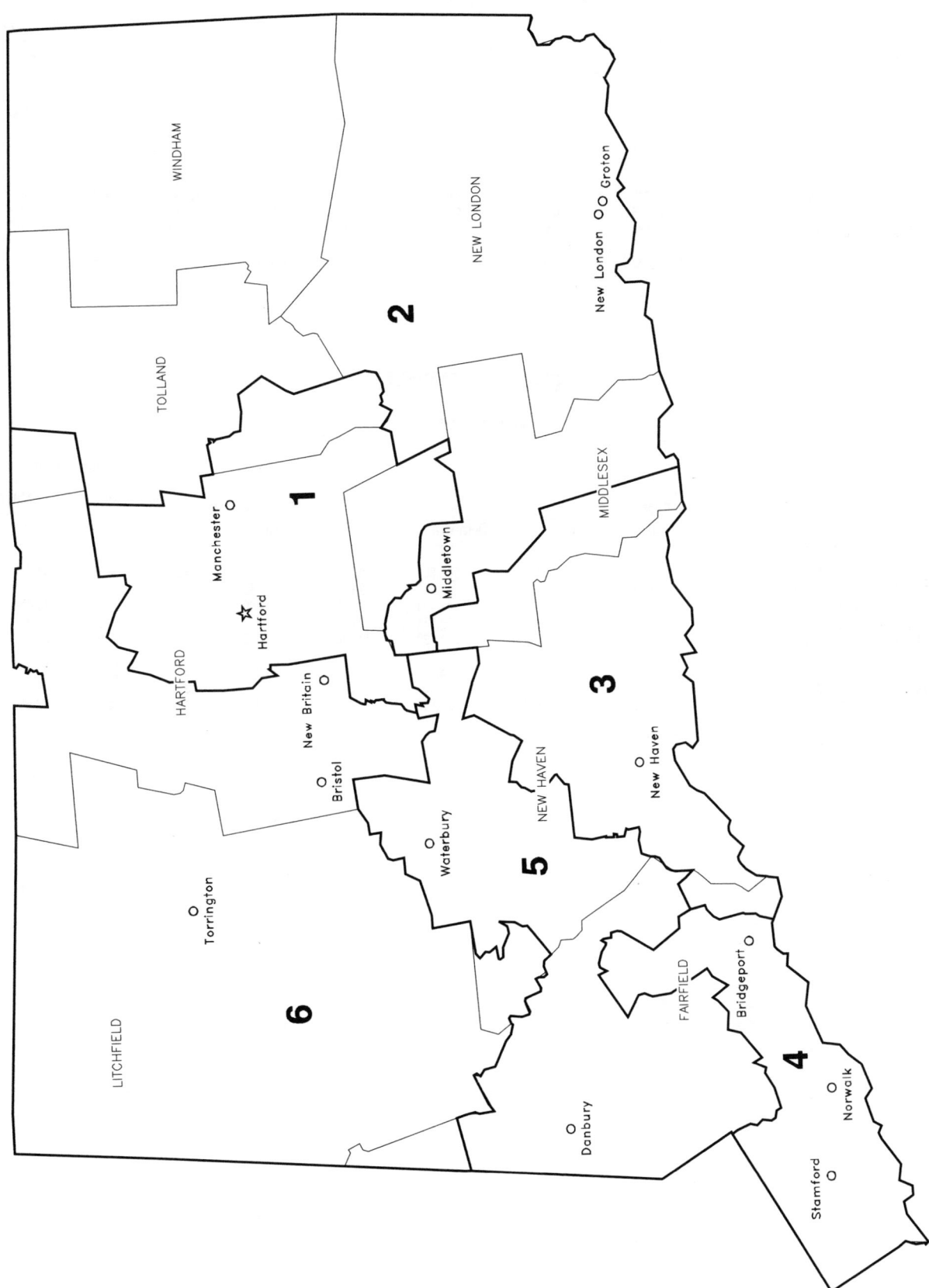

CONNECTICUT

Districts Established November 27, 1991

CONNECTICUT

PRESIDENT 1992

Registration	County	Total Vote	Republican	Democratic	Perot	Other	Plurality	Percentage Total Vote		
								Rep.	Dem.	Perot
486,441	FAIRFIELD	409,410	175,158	160,202	72,532	1,518	14,956 R	42.8%	39.1%	17.7%
507,216	HARTFORD	414,804	132,591	195,495	85,005	1,713	62,904 D	32.0%	47.1%	20.5%
107,764	LITCHFIELD	93,213	34,492	33,686	24,639	396	806 R	37.0%	36.1%	26.4%
93,971	MIDDLESEX	81,027	24,646	34,707	21,306	368	10,061 D	30.4%	42.8%	26.3%
484,616	NEW HAVEN	385,132	141,264	161,374	80,817	1,677	20,110 D	36.7%	41.9%	21.0%
142,824	NEW LONDON	117,767	34,567	49,808	32,736	656	15,241 D	29.4%	42.3%	27.8%
74,743	TOLLAND	66,215	20,632	27,425	17,930	228	6,793 D	31.2%	41.4%	27.1%
57,693	WINDHAM	48,588	14,963	19,621	13,806	198	4,658 D	30.8%	40.4%	28.4%
1,955,268	TOTAL	1,616,332	578,313	682,318	348,771	6,930	104,005 D	35.8%	42.2%	21.6%

CONNECTICUT

SENATOR 1992

Registration	County	Total Vote	Republican	Democratic	Other	Rep.-Dem. Plurality	Percentage			
							Total Vote		Major Vote	
							Rep.	Dem.	Rep.	Dem.
486,441	FAIRFIELD	375,509	162,912	203,801	8,796	40,889 D	43.4%	54.3%	44.4%	55.6%
507,216	HARTFORD	390,190	134,365	243,148	12,677	108,783 D	34.4%	62.3%	35.6%	64.4%
107,764	LITCHFIELD	87,184	36,335	47,431	3,418	11,096 D	41.7%	54.4%	43.4%	56.6%
93,971	MIDDLESEX	76,199	27,362	46,634	2,203	19,272 D	35.9%	61.2%	37.0%	63.0%
484,616	NEW HAVEN	354,850	127,992	214,520	12,338	86,528 D	36.1%	60.5%	37.4%	62.6%
142,824	NEW LONDON	109,959	41,246	65,524	3,189	24,278 D	37.5%	59.6%	38.6%	61.4%
74,743	TOLLAND	62,151	23,497	36,707	1,947	13,210 D	37.8%	59.1%	39.0%	61.0%
57,693	WINDHAM	44,619	18,327	24,804	1,488	6,477 D	41.1%	55.6%	42.5%	57.5%
1,955,268	TOTAL	1,500,709	572,036	882,569	46,104	310,533 D	38.1%	58.8%	39.3%	60.7%

CONNECTICUT

PRESIDENT 1992

Registration	City/Town	Total Vote	Republican	Democratic	Perot	Other	Plurality	Percentage Total Vote		
								Rep.	Dem.	Perot
11,123	ANSONIA	8,481	3,277	3,273	1,883	48	4 R	38.6%	38.6%	22.2%
13,004	BLOOMFIELD	10,572	2,341	6,914	1,266	51	4,573 D	22.1%	65.4%	12.0%
18,080	BRANFORD	15,263	5,622	6,575	3,018	48	953 D	36.8%	43.1%	19.8%
61,629	BRIDGEPORT	41,956	13,149	22,321	6,263	223	9,172 D	31.3%	53.2%	14.9%
34,311	BRISTOL	28,274	8,407	11,872	7,890	105	3,465 D	29.7%	42.0%	27.9%
16,210	CHESHIRE	14,556	6,484	5,096	2,935	41	1,388 R	44.5%	35.0%	20.2%
31,822	DANBURY	25,840	10,310	9,909	5,517	104	401 R	39.9%	38.3%	21.4%
12,243	DARIEN	10,987	6,396	3,089	1,463	39	3,307 R	58.2%	28.1%	13.3%
27,543	EAST HARTFORD	23,512	6,472	11,450	5,478	112	4,978 D	27.5%	48.7%	23.3%
17,874	EAST HAVEN	13,640	4,747	5,645	3,196	52	898 D	34.8%	41.4%	23.4%
27,242	ENFIELD	22,036	7,043	9,248	5,646	99	2,205 D	32.0%	42.0%	25.6%
36,354	FAIRFIELD	32,120	13,968	12,099	5,941	112	1,869 R	43.5%	37.7%	18.5%
14,065	FARMINGTON	12,374	4,893	4,917	2,520	44	24 D	39.5%	39.7%	20.4%
19,163	GLASTONBURY	17,586	6,840	6,976	3,707	63	136 D	38.9%	39.7%	21.1%
37,437	GREENWICH	32,476	15,885	11,893	4,584	114	3,992 R	48.9%	36.6%	14.1%
19,096	GROTON	15,202	4,795	6,350	3,965	92	1,555 D	31.5%	41.8%	26.1%
13,535	GUILFORD	11,714	4,164	4,933	2,584	33	769 D	35.5%	42.1%	22.1%
34,981	HAMDEN	28,487	10,273	13,484	4,645	85	3,211 D	36.1%	47.3%	16.3%
66,444	HARTFORD	36,797	6,180	26,971	3,390	256	20,791 D	16.8%	73.3%	9.2%
33,086	MANCHESTER	28,271	9,132	12,266	6,759	114	3,134 D	32.3%	43.4%	23.9%
8,731	MANSFIELD	7,900	1,754	4,677	1,440	29	2,923 D	22.2%	59.2%	18.2%
31,438	MERIDEN	25,979	8,198	11,318	6,318	145	3,120 D	31.6%	43.6%	24.3%
25,264	MIDDLETOWN	21,114	5,092	11,338	4,598	86	6,246 D	24.1%	53.7%	21.8%
32,793	MILFORD	26,708	10,686	9,278	6,681	63	1,408 R	40.0%	34.7%	25.0%
16,209	NAUGATUCK	13,883	5,371	4,410	4,021	81	961 R	38.7%	31.8%	29.0%
31,788	NEW BRITAIN	26,317	7,040	14,159	4,983	135	7,119 D	26.8%	53.8%	18.9%
71,204	NEW HAVEN	43,261	8,931	29,774	4,130	426	20,843 D	20.6%	68.8%	9.5%
13,672	NEW LONDON	9,738	2,368	5,520	1,796	54	3,152 D	24.3%	56.7%	18.4%
13,326	NEW MILFORD	11,760	4,650	3,807	3,270	33	843 R	39.5%	32.4%	27.8%
19,733	NEWINGTON	16,823	5,598	7,687	3,482	56	2,089 D	33.3%	45.7%	20.7%
12,633	NEWTOWN	11,410	4,940	3,783	2,646	41	1,157 R	43.3%	33.2%	23.2%
15,554	NORTH HAVEN	13,518	5,649	5,027	2,801	41	622 R	41.8%	37.2%	20.7%
43,850	NORWALK	37,455	14,743	16,488	6,046	178	1,745 D	39.4%	44.0%	16.1%
18,977	NORWICH	15,850	4,081	7,412	4,287	70	3,125 D	25.7%	46.8%	27.0%
15,002	RIDGEFIELD	13,291	6,166	4,729	2,328	68	1,437 R	46.4%	35.6%	17.5%
22,008	SHELTON	18,899	8,963	5,354	4,546	36	3,609 R	47.4%	28.3%	24.1%
15,591	SIMSBURY	13,776	5,788	5,440	2,520	28	348 R	42.0%	39.5%	18.3%
14,456	SOUTH WINDSOR	13,084	4,702	5,333	3,012	37	631 D	35.9%	40.8%	23.0%
23,781	SOUTHINGTON	20,210	7,346	7,740	5,038	86	394 D	36.3%	38.3%	24.9%
59,876	STAMFORD	49,926	19,809	23,185	6,763	169	3,376 D	39.7%	46.4%	13.5%
31,917	STRATFORD	26,769	10,914	9,796	5,986	73	1,118 R	40.8%	36.6%	22.4%
19,601	TORRINGTON	16,995	5,508	6,882	4,528	77	1,374 D	32.4%	40.5%	26.6%
23,502	TRUMBULL	19,974	9,486	6,353	4,067	68	3,133 R	47.5%	31.8%	20.4%
16,779	VERNON	14,893	4,905	6,241	3,699	48	1,336 D	32.9%	41.9%	24.8%
25,257	WALLINGFORD	22,011	7,942	8,539	5,445	85	597 D	36.1%	38.8%	24.7%
56,498	WATERBURY	41,896	16,155	16,366	9,188	187	211 D	38.6%	39.1%	21.9%
12,964	WATERTOWN	11,088	4,937	3,130	2,977	44	1,807 R	44.5%	28.2%	26.8%
43,618	WEST HARTFORD	37,046	12,266	19,623	5,017	140	7,357 D	33.1%	53.0%	13.5%
31,242	WEST HAVEN	25,599	8,742	11,523	5,249	85	2,781 D	34.1%	45.0%	20.5%
18,159	WESTPORT	16,216	6,166	7,799	2,196	55	1,633 D	38.0%	48.1%	13.5%
18,241	WETHERSFIELD	16,305	6,187	7,035	3,035	48	848 D	37.9%	43.1%	18.6%
11,520	WINDHAM	9,512	2,506	4,744	2,222	40	2,238 D	26.3%	49.9%	23.4%
17,517	WINDSOR	15,046	4,633	7,456	2,898	59	2,823 D	30.8%	49.6%	19.3%

CONNECTICUT

SENATOR 1992

Registration	City/Town	Total Vote	Republican	Democratic	Other	Rep.-Dem. Plurality	Total Vote Rep.	Total Vote Dem.	Major Vote Rep.	Major Vote Dem.
11,123	ANSONIA	8,092	2,731	5,040	321	5,040 D	33.7%	62.3%	35.1%	64.9%
13,004	BLOOMFIELD	10,018	2,468	7,259	291	7,259 D	24.6%	72.5%	25.4%	74.6%
18,080	BRANFORD	14,152	5,212	8,693	247	8,693 D	36.8%	61.4%	37.5%	62.5%
61,629	BRIDGEPORT	36,663	10,930	24,578	1,155	24,578 D	29.8%	67.0%	30.8%	69.2%
34,311	BRISTOL	26,201	8,842	16,385	974	16,385 D	33.7%	62.5%	35.0%	65.0%
16,210	CHESHIRE	13,748	5,816	7,539	393	7,539 D	42.3%	54.8%	43.5%	56.5%
31,822	DANBURY	23,150	9,124	13,273	753	13,273 D	39.4%	57.3%	40.7%	59.3%
12,243	DARIEN	10,348	6,208	4,007	133	6,208 R	60.0%	38.7%	60.8%	39.2%
27,543	EAST HARTFORD	21,913	6,679	14,434	800	14,434 D	30.5%	65.9%	31.6%	68.4%
17,874	EAST HAVEN	11,973	4,183	7,500	290	7,500 D	34.9%	62.6%	35.8%	64.2%
27,242	ENFIELD	20,509	7,095	12,525	889	12,525 D	34.6%	61.1%	36.2%	63.8%
36,354	FAIRFIELD	30,160	13,214	16,347	599	16,347 D	43.8%	54.2%	44.7%	55.3%
14,065	FARMINGTON	11,655	4,898	6,444	313	6,444 D	42.0%	55.3%	43.2%	56.8%
19,163	GLASTONBURY	16,819	7,504	8,914	401	8,914 D	44.6%	53.0%	45.7%	54.3%
37,437	GREENWICH	30,097	15,175	14,494	428	15,175 R	50.4%	48.2%	51.1%	48.9%
19,096	GROTON	13,996	5,339	8,253	404	8,253 D	38.1%	59.0%	39.3%	60.7%
13,535	GUILFORD	10,984	4,455	6,313	216	6,313 D	40.6%	57.5%	41.4%	58.6%
34,981	HAMDEN	26,442	8,711	17,179	552	17,179 D	32.9%	65.0%	33.6%	66.4%
66,444	HARTFORD	34,502	5,565	27,679	1,258	27,679 D	16.1%	80.2%	16.7%	83.3%
33,086	MANCHESTER	26,742	9,484	16,387	871	16,387 D	35.5%	61.3%	36.7%	63.3%
8,731	MANSFIELD	7,464	1,956	5,314	194	5,314 D	26.2%	71.2%	26.9%	73.1%
31,438	MERIDEN	23,675	7,681	15,039	955	15,039 D	32.4%	63.5%	33.8%	66.2%
25,264	MIDDLETOWN	19,626	5,591	13,447	588	13,447 D	28.5%	68.5%	29.4%	70.6%
32,793	MILFORD	24,164	9,831	13,706	627	13,706 D	40.7%	56.7%	41.8%	58.2%
16,209	NAUGATUCK	12,751	5,010	7,184	557	7,184 D	39.3%	56.3%	41.1%	58.9%
31,788	NEW BRITAIN	23,912	7,183	15,826	903	15,826 D	30.0%	66.2%	31.2%	68.8%
71,204	NEW HAVEN	40,193	7,140	30,353	2,700	30,353 D	17.8%	75.5%	19.0%	81.0%
13,672	NEW LONDON	8,665	2,385	6,017	263	6,017 D	27.5%	69.4%	28.4%	71.6%
13,326	NEW MILFORD	10,818	4,669	5,768	381	5,768 D	43.2%	53.3%	44.7%	55.3%
19,733	NEWINGTON	15,911	5,672	9,692	547	9,692 D	35.6%	60.9%	36.9%	63.1%
12,633	NEWTOWN	10,440	4,458	5,701	281	5,701 D	42.7%	54.6%	43.9%	56.1%
15,554	NORTH HAVEN	12,335	5,053	7,011	271	7,011 D	41.0%	56.8%	41.9%	58.1%
43,850	NORWALK	34,220	13,369	19,883	968	19,883 D	39.1%	58.1%	40.2%	59.8%
18,977	NORWICH	14,790	4,677	9,677	436	9,677 D	31.6%	65.4%	32.6%	67.4%
15,002	RIDGEFIELD	12,476	6,147	6,101	228	6,147 R	49.3%	48.9%	50.2%	49.8%
22,008	SHELTON	17,976	8,223	9,176	577	9,176 D	45.7%	51.0%	47.3%	52.7%
15,591	SIMSBURY	13,285	5,772	7,203	310	7,203 D	43.4%	54.2%	44.5%	55.5%
14,456	SOUTH WINDSOR	12,474	4,940	7,240	294	7,240 D	39.6%	58.0%	40.6%	59.4%
23,781	SOUTHINGTON	19,034	6,805	11,485	744	11,485 D	35.8%	60.3%	37.2%	62.8%
59,876	STAMFORD	45,090	17,188	26,962	940	26,962 D	38.1%	59.8%	38.9%	61.1%
31,917	STRATFORD	24,278	10,214	13,492	572	13,492 D	42.1%	55.6%	43.1%	56.9%
19,601	TORRINGTON	15,896	5,729	9,386	781	9,386 D	36.0%	59.0%	37.9%	62.1%
23,502	TRUMBULL	18,497	8,928	9,191	378	9,191 D	48.3%	49.7%	49.3%	50.7%
16,779	VERNON	13,947	5,299	8,236	412	8,236 D	38.0%	59.1%	39.2%	60.8%
25,257	WALLINGFORD	20,175	7,377	12,219	579	12,219 D	36.6%	60.6%	37.6%	62.4%
56,498	WATERBURY	39,072	14,307	22,938	1,827	22,938 D	36.6%	58.7%	38.4%	61.6%
12,964	WATERTOWN	10,171	4,775	5,027	369	5,027 D	46.9%	49.4%	48.7%	51.3%
43,618	WEST HARTFORD	35,490	11,966	22,850	674	22,850 D	33.7%	64.4%	34.4%	65.6%
31,242	WEST HAVEN	22,715	7,152	14,909	654	14,909 D	31.5%	65.6%	32.4%	67.6%
18,159	WESTPORT	15,088	6,050	8,818	220	8,818 D	40.1%	58.4%	40.7%	59.3%
18,241	WETHERSFIELD	15,362	6,044	8,910	408	8,910 D	39.3%	58.0%	40.4%	59.6%
11,520	WINDHAM	8,672	2,855	5,599	218	5,599 D	32.9%	64.6%	33.8%	66.2%
17,517	WINDSOR	14,173	4,716	9,032	425	9,032 D	33.3%	63.7%	34.3%	65.7%

CONNECTICUT

CONGRESS

CD	Year	Total Vote	Republican		Democratic		Other Vote	Rep.-Dem. Plurality	Percentage			
									Total Vote		Major Vote	
			Vote	Candidate	Vote	Candidate			Rep.	Dem.	Rep.	Dem.
1	1992	245,430	75,113	STEELE, PHILIP L.	164,735 * KENNELLY, BARBARA B.		5,582	89,622 D	30.6%	67.1%	31.3%	68.7%
2	1992	242,707	119,416	MUNSTER, EDWARD W.	123,291 * GEJDENSON, SAMUEL			3,875 D	49.2%	50.8%	49.2%	50.8%
3	1992	247,531	84,952	SCOTT, THOMAS	162,568 * DELAURO, ROSA L.		11	77,616 D	34.3%	65.7%	34.3%	65.7%
4	1992	219,615	147,816	SHAYS, CHRISTOPHER	58,666 SCHROPFER, DAVE		13,133	89,150 R	67.3%	26.7%	71.6%	28.4%
5	1992	240,283	104,891	FRANKS, GARY A.	74,791 LAWLOR, JAMES J.		60,601	30,100 R	43.7%	31.1%	58.4%	41.6%
6	1992	239,597	166,967	JOHNSON, NANCY L.	60,373 SLASON, EUGENE F.		12,257	106,594 R	69.7%	25.2%	73.4%	26.6%

CONNECTICUT

1992 GENERAL ELECTION

In addition to the county-by-county figures, data are presented for selected Connecticut communities. Since not all jurisdictions of the state are listed in this special tabulation, state-wide totals are shown only with the county-by-county statistics.

President   Other vote was 5,391 Libertarian (Marrou); 1,363 New Alliance (Fulani); 75 Hagelin (write-in); 72 Gritz (write-in); 20 Phillips (write-in); 5 Warren (write-in); 4 LaRouche (write-in). The total for the other vote column includes the 176 write-in votes not available by county or city/town.

Senator   Other vote was 35,315 Concerned Citizens (Gregory); 10,741 Libertarian (Grayson); 48 scattered write-in. The total for the other vote column includes the 48 scattered write-in votes not available by county or city/town. The Democratic candidate was also the Connecticut Party nominee and 304,907 of his votes were received as the Connecticut Party candidate.

Congress   As asterisk in the Congressional vote table indicates a candidate received votes as the nominee of an additional party. Other vote was 5,577 Concerned Citizens (Garneau) and 5 Hall (write-in) in CD 1; 9 Russell (write-in) and 2 Krala (write-in) in CD 3; 11,679 Connecticut Party (Smith), 1,445 Natural Law (Fried) and 9 Tonkin (write-in) in CD 4; 54,022 Connecticut Party (Taborsak), 5,090 Concerned Citizens (Rodriguez), 864 Natural Law (Nevas), 625 Independent (LaPointe) in CD 5; 9,544 Concerned Citizens (Plawecki), 1,677 Independent (Pearl), 1,036 Independent (Economu) in CD 6.

1992 PRIMARIES

Party conventions nominate Connecticut candidates, subject to a system of "challenge" primaries. Any candidate who receives 20% or more of the convention vote in entitled to challenge the endorsed candidate in a primary.

SEPTEMBER 15 REPUBLICAN

Senator   50,305 Brook Johnson; 40,542 Christopher Burnham.

Congress   Challenge primaries were held in two of the six CD's as follows:

CD 1   9,723 Philip L. Steele; 4,406 Robert F. Ludgin.
CD 2   8,928 Edward W. Munster; 7,709 Glenn Carberry.

SEPTEMBER 15 DEMOCRATIC

Senator   Christopher J. Dodd, nominated by convention.

Congress   Challenge primaries were held in two of the six CD's as follows:

CD 5   13,623 James J. Lawlor; 12,858 Lynn H. Taborsak.
CD 6   5,002 Eugene F. Slason; 3,593 Alan R. DiCara.

DELAWARE

GOVERNOR
Thomas R. Carper (D). Elected 1992 to a four-year term.

SENATORS
Joseph R. Biden (D). Re-elected 1990 to a six-year term. Previously elected 1984, 1978, 1972.

William V. Roth (R). Re-elected 1988 to a six-year term. Previously elected 1982, 1976, 1970.

REPRESENTATIVE
At-Large. Michael N. Castle (R)

POSTWAR VOTE FOR PRESIDENT

| | | Republican | | Democratic | | Other | | Percentage | | | |
| | | | | | | | | Total Vote | | Major Vote | |
Year	Total Vote	Vote	Candidate	Vote	Candidate	Vote	Plurality	Rep.	Dem.	Rep.	Dem.
1992	289,735	102,313	Bush, George	126,054	Clinton, Bill	61,368	23,741 D	35.3%	43.5%	44.8%	55.2%
1988	249,891	139,639	Bush, George	108,647	Dukakis, Michael S.	1,605	30,992 R	55.9%	43.5%	56.2%	43.8%
1984	254,572	152,190	Reagan, Ronald	101,656	Mondale, Walter F.	726	50,534 R	59.8%	39.9%	60.0%	40.0%
1980	235,900	111,252	Reagan, Ronald	105,754	Carter, Jimmy	18,894	5,498 R	47.2%	44.8%	51.3%	48.7%
1976	235,834	109,831	Ford, Gerald R.	122,596	Carter, Jimmy	3,407	12,765 D	46.6%	52.0%	47.3%	52.7%
1972	235,516	140,357	Nixon, Richard M.	92,283	McGovern, George S.	2,876	48,074 R	59.6%	39.2%	60.3%	39.7%
1968	214,367	96,714	Nixon, Richard M.	89,194	Humphrey, Hubert H.	28,459	7,520 R	45.1%	41.6%	52.0%	48.0%
1964	201,320	78,078	Goldwater, Barry M.	122,704	Johnson, Lyndon B.	538	44,626 D	38.8%	60.9%	38.9%	61.1%
1960	196,683	96,373	Nixon, Richard M.	99,590	Kennedy, John F.	720	3,217 D	49.0%	50.6%	49.2%	50.8%
1956	177,988	98,057	Eisenhower, Dwight D.	79,421	Stevenson, Adlai E.	510	18,636 R	55.1%	44.6%	55.3%	44.7%
1952	174,025	90,059	Eisenhower, Dwight D.	83,315	Stevenson, Adlai E.	651	6,744 R	51.8%	47.9%	51.9%	48.1%
1948	139,073	69,588	Dewey, Thomas E.	67,813	Truman, Harry S.	1,672	1,775 R	50.0%	48.8%	50.6%	49.4%

In 1992 the other vote column includes 59,213 votes cast for Perot.

POSTWAR VOTE FOR GOVERNOR

| | | Republican | | Democratic | | Other | Rep.-Dem. | Percentage | | | |
| | | | | | | | | Total Vote | | Major Vote | |
Year	Total Vote	Vote	Candidate	Vote	Candidate	Vote	Plurality	Rep.	Dem.	Rep.	Dem.
1992	277,058	90,725	Scott, B. Gary	179,365	Carper, Thomas R.	6,968	88,640 D	32.7%	64.7%	33.6%	66.4%
1988	239,969	169,733	Castle, Michael N.	70,236	Kreshtoll, Jacob		99,497 R	70.7%	29.3%	70.7%	29.3%
1984	243,565	135,250	Castle, Michael N.	108,315	Quillen, William T.		26,935 R	55.5%	44.5%	55.5%	44.5%
1980	225,081	159,004	duPont, Pierre	64,217	Gordy, William J.	1,860	94,787 R	70.6%	28.5%	71.2%	28.8%
1976	229,563	130,531	duPont, Pierre	97,480	Tribbitt, Sherman W.	1,552	33,051 R	56.9%	42.5%	57.2%	42.8%
1972	228,722	109,583	Peterson, Russell W.	117,274	Tribbitt, Sherman W.	1,865	7,691 D	47.9%	51.3%	48.3%	51.7%
1968	206,834	104,474	Peterson, Russell W.	102,360	Terry, Charles L.		2,114 R	50.5%	49.5%	50.5%	49.5%
1964	200,171	97,374	Buckson, David P.	102,797	Terry, Charles L.		5,423 D	48.6%	51.4%	48.6%	51.4%
1960	194,835	94,043	Rollins, John W.	100,792	Carvel, Elbert N.		6,749 D	48.3%	51.7%	48.3%	51.7%
1956	177,012	91,965	Boggs, J. Caleb	85,047	McConnell, J. H. T.		6,918 R	52.0%	48.0%	52.0%	48.0%
1952	170,749	88,977	Boggs, J. Caleb	81,772	Carvel, Elbert N.		7,205 R	52.1%	47.9%	52.1%	47.9%
1948	140,335	64,996	George, Hyland P.	75,339	Carvel, Elbert N.		10,343 D	46.3%	53.7%	46.3%	53.7%

DELAWARE

POSTWAR VOTE FOR SENATOR

Year	Total Vote	Republican		Democratic		Other Vote	Rep.-Dem. Plurality	Percentage			
								Total Vote		Major Vote	
		Vote	Candidate	Vote	Candidate			Rep.	Dem.	Rep.	Dem.
1990	180,152	64,554	Brady, M. Jane	112,918	Biden, Joseph R.	2,680	48,364 D	35.8%	62.7%	36.4%	63.6%
1988	243,493	151,115	Roth, William V.	92,378	Woo, S. B.		58,737 R	62.1%	37.9%	62.1%	37.9%
1984	245,932	98,101	Burris, John M.	147,831	Biden, Joseph R.		49,730 D	39.9%	60.1%	39.9%	60.1%
1982	190,960	105,357	Roth, William V.	84,413	Levinson, David N.	1,190	20,944 R	55.2%	44.2%	55.5%	44.5%
1978	162,072	66,479	Baxter, James H.	93,930	Biden, Joseph R.	1,663	27,451 D	41.0%	58.0%	41.4%	58.6%
1976	224,859	125,502	Roth, William V.	98,055	Maloney, Thomas C.	1,302	27,447 R	55.8%	43.6%	56.1%	43.9%
1972	229,828	112,844	Boggs, J. Caleb	116,006	Biden, Joseph R.	978	3,162 D	49.1%	50.5%	49.3%	50.7%
1970	161,439	94,979	Roth, William V.	64,740	Zimmerman, Jacob	1,720	30,239 R	58.8%	40.1%	59.5%	40.5%
1966	164,549	97,268	Boggs, J. Caleb	67,281	Tunnell, James M., Jr.		29,987 R	59.1%	40.9%	59.1%	40.9%
1964	200,703	103,782	Williams, John J.	96,850	Carvel, Elbert N.	71	6,932 R	51.7%	48.3%	51.7%	48.3%
1960	194,964	98,874	Boggs, J. Caleb	96,090	Frear, J. Allen		2,784 R	50.7%	49.3%	50.7%	49.3%
1958	154,432	82,280	Williams, John J.	72,152	Carvel, Elbert N.		10,128 R	53.3%	46.7%	53.3%	46.7%
1954	144,900	62,389	Warburton, H. B.	82,511	Frear, J. Allen		20,122 D	43.1%	56.9%	43.1%	56.9%
1952	170,705	93,020	Williams, John J.	77,685	Bayard, A. I. duP.		15,335 R	54.5%	45.5%	54.5%	45.5%
1948	141,362	68,246	Buck, C. Douglas	71,888	Frear, J. Allen	1,228	3,642 D	48.3%	50.9%	48.7%	51.3%
1946	113,513	62,603	Williams, John J.	50,910	Tunnell, James M.		11,693 R	55.2%	44.8%	55.2%	44.8%

DELAWARE

One At Large

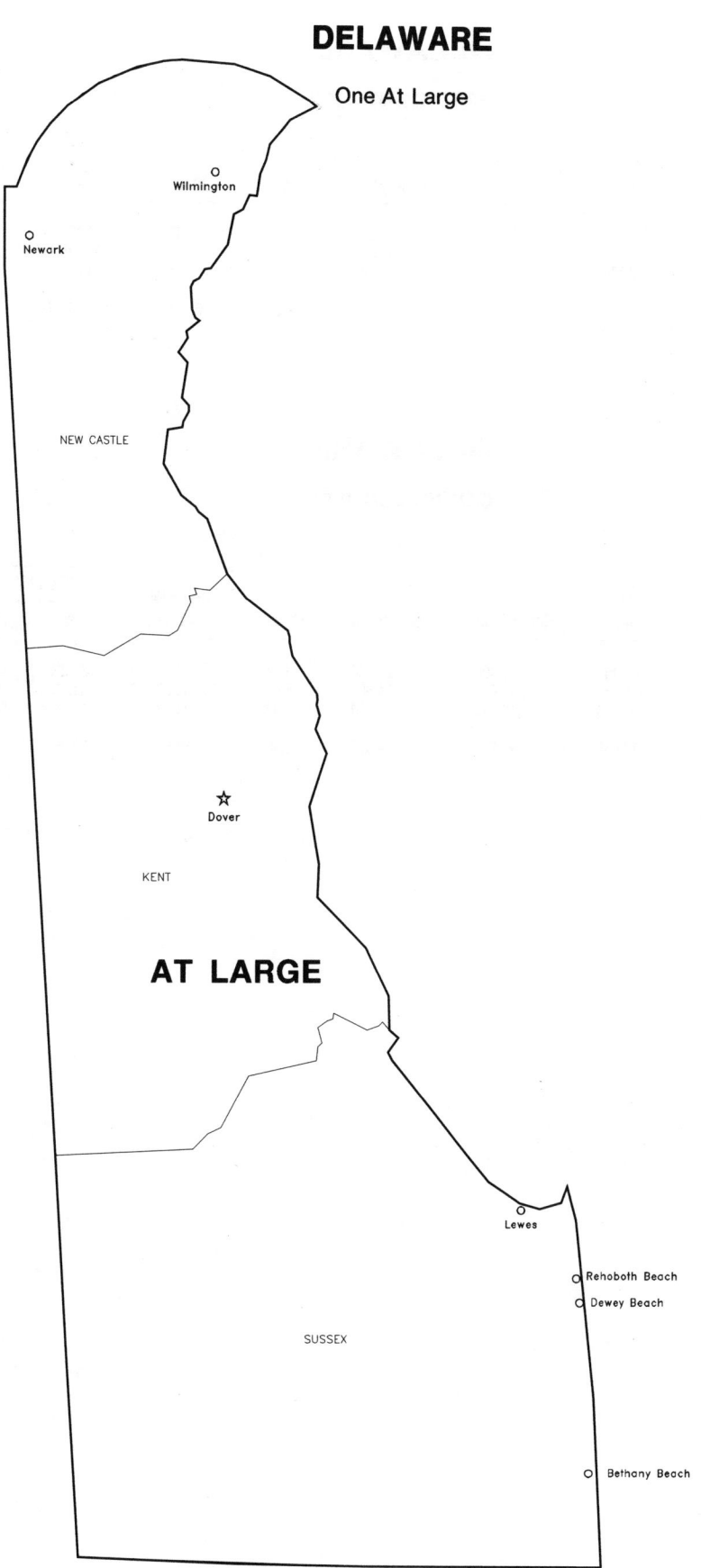

Wilmington

Newark

NEW CASTLE

☆
Dover

KENT

AT LARGE

Lewes

Rehoboth Beach

Dewey Beach

SUSSEX

Bethany Beach

DELAWARE

PRESIDENT 1992

Registration	County	Total Vote	Republican	Democratic	Perot	Other	Plurality	Percentage Total Vote		
								Rep.	Dem.	Perot
46,814	KENT	40,255	15,562	15,364	8,916	413	198 R	38.7%	38.2%	22.1%
234,121	NEW CASTLE	196,904	66,311	91,516	37,581	1,496	25,205 D	33.7%	46.5%	19.1%
61,153	SUSSEX	52,576	20,440	19,174	12,716	246	1,266 R	38.9%	36.5%	24.2%
342,088	TOTAL	289,735	102,313	126,054	59,213	2,155	23,741 D	35.3%	43.5%	20.4%

DELAWARE

GOVERNOR 1992

Registration	County	Total Vote	Republican	Democratic	Other	Rep.-Dem. Plurality	Percentage			
							Total Vote		Major Vote	
							Rep.	Dem.	Rep.	Dem.
46,814	KENT	39,158	13,406	24,734	1,018	11,328 D	34.2%	63.2%	35.1%	64.9%
234,121	NEW CASTLE	188,257	58,609	124,601	5,047	65,992 D	31.1%	66.2%	32.0%	68.0%
61,153	SUSSEX	49,643	18,710	30,030	903	11,320 D	37.7%	60.5%	38.4%	61.6%
342,088	TOTAL	277,058	90,725	179,365	6,968	88,640 D	32.7%	64.7%	33.6%	66.4%

DELAWARE

CONGRESS

CD	Year	Total Vote	Republican		Democratic		Other Vote	Rep.-Dem. Plurality	Percentage			
			Vote	Candidate	Vote	Candidate			Total Vote		Major Vote	
									Rep.	Dem.	Rep.	Dem.
AL	1992	276,157	153,037	CASTLE, MICHAEL N.	117,426	WOO, S. B.	5,694	35,611 R	55.4%	42.5%	56.6%	43.4%
AL	1990	177,432	58,037	WILLIAMS, RALPH O.	116,274	CARPER, THOMAS R.	3,121	58,237 D	32.7%	65.5%	33.3%	66.7%
AL	1988	234,517	76,179	KRAPF, JAMES P.	158,338	CARPER, THOMAS R.		82,159 D	32.5%	67.5%	32.5%	67.5%
AL	1986	160,757	53,767	NEUBERGER, THOMAS S.	106,351	CARPER, THOMAS R.	639	52,584 D	33.4%	66.2%	33.6%	66.4%
AL	1984	243,014	100,650	DUPONT, ELISE	142,070	CARPER, THOMAS R.	294	41,420 D	41.4%	58.5%	41.5%	58.5%
AL	1982	188,064	87,153	EVANS, THOMAS B.	98,533	CARPER, THOMAS R.	2,378	11,380 D	46.3%	52.4%	46.9%	53.1%
AL	1980	216,629	133,842	EVANS, THOMAS B.	81,227	MAXWELL, ROBERT L.	1,560	52,615 R	61.8%	37.5%	62.2%	37.8%
AL	1978	157,566	91,689	EVANS, THOMAS B.	64,863	HINDES, GARY E.	1,014	26,826 R	58.2%	41.2%	58.6%	41.4%
AL	1976	214,799	110,677	EVANS, THOMAS B.	102,431	SHIPLEY, SAMUEL L.	1,691	8,246 R	51.5%	47.7%	51.9%	48.1%
AL	1974	160,328	93,826	DUPONT, PIERRE	63,490	SOLES, JAMES	3,012	30,336 R	58.5%	39.6%	59.6%	40.4%
AL	1972	225,851	141,237	DUPONT, PIERRE	83,230	HANDLOFF, NORMA	1,384	58,007 R	62.5%	36.9%	62.9%	37.1%
AL	1970	160,313	86,125	DUPONT, PIERRE	71,429	DANIELLO, JOHN D.	2,759	14,696 R	53.7%	44.6%	54.7%	45.3%
AL	1968	200,820	117,827	ROTH, WILLIAM V.	82,993	MCDOWELL, HARRIS B.		34,834 R	58.7%	41.3%	58.7%	41.3%
AL	1966	163,103	90,961	ROTH, WILLIAM V.	72,142	MCDOWELL, HARRIS B.		18,819 R	55.8%	44.2%	55.8%	44.2%
AL	1964	198,691	86,254	SNOWDEN, JAMES H.	112,361	MCDOWELL, HARRIS B.	76	26,107 D	43.4%	56.6%	43.4%	56.6%
AL	1962	153,356	71,934	WILLIAMS, WILMER F.	81,166	MCDOWELL, HARRIS B.	256	9,232 D	46.9%	52.9%	47.0%	53.0%
AL	1960	194,564	96,337	MCKINSTRY, JAMES T.	98,227	MCDOWELL, HARRIS B.		1,890 D	49.5%	50.5%	49.5%	50.5%
AL	1958	152,896	76,099	HASKELL, HARRY G.	76,797	MCDOWELL, HARRIS B.		698 D	49.8%	50.2%	49.8%	50.2%
AL	1956	176,182	91,538	HASKELL, HARRY G.	84,644	MCDOWELL, HARRIS B.		6,894 R	52.0%	48.0%	52.0%	48.0%
AL	1954	144,236	65,035	MARTIN, LILLIAN	79,201	MCDOWELL, HARRIS B.		14,166 D	45.1%	54.9%	45.1%	54.9%
AL	1952	170,015	88,285	WARBURTON, H. B.	81,730	SCANNELL, JOSEPH S.		6,555 R	51.9%	48.1%	51.9%	48.1%
AL	1950	129,404	73,313	BOGGS, J. CALEB	56,091	WINCHESTER, H. M.		17,222 R	56.7%	43.3%	56.7%	43.3%
AL	1948	140,535	71,127	BOGGS, J. CALEB	68,909	MCGUIGAN, J. CARL	499	2,218 R	50.6%	49.0%	50.8%	49.2%
AL	1946	112,621	63,516	BOGGS, J. CALEB	49,105	TRAYNOR, PHILIP A.		14,411 R	56.4%	43.6%	56.4%	43.6%

DELAWARE

1992 GENERAL ELECTION

President   Other vote was 1,105 New Alliance (Fulani); 935 Libertarian (Marrou); 9 Gritz (write-in); 9 LaRouche (write-in); 6 Hagelin (write-in); 3 Warren (write-in); 2 Phillips (write-in); 86 scattered write-in.

Governor   Other vote was 3,779 Delaware Party (McDowell); 3,165 Libertarian (Cohen); 24 scattered write-in.

Congress   Other vote at-large was 5,661 Libertarian (Schmitt) and 33 scattered write-in.

1992 PRIMARIES

SEPTEMBER 12 REPUBLICAN

Governor   23,994 B. Gary Scott; 5,346 Wilfred Plomis.

Congress   Contested as follows:

AL   18,377 Michael N. Castle; 9,812 Janet C. Rzewnicki; 4,411 Bryant L. Richardson; 441 James R. Withrow.

SEPTEMBER 12 DEMOCRATIC

Governor   36,600 Thomas R. Carper; 4,434 Daniel D. Rappa.

Congress   Contested as follows:

AL   28,732 S. B. Woo; 10,329 Ernest L. Ercole.

FLORIDA

GOVERNOR
Lawton Chiles (D). Elected 1990 to a four-year term.

SENATORS
Robert Graham (D). Re-elected 1992 to a six-year term. Previously elected 1986.

Connie Mack (R). Elected 1988 to a six-year term.

REPRESENTATIVES

1. Earl D. Hutto (D)
2. Pete Peterson (D)
3. Corrine Brown (D)
4. Tillie Fowler (R)
5. Karen Thurman (D)
6. Clifford B. Stearns (R)
7. John Mica (R)
8. Bill McCollum (R)
9. Michael Bilirakis (R)
10. C. W. Young (R)
11. Sam M. Gibbons (D)
12. Charles T. Canady (R)
13. Dan Miller (R)
14. Porter J. Goss (R)
15. Jim Bacchus (D)
16. Tom Lewis (R)
17. Carrie Meek (D)
18. Ileana Ros-Lehtinen (R)
19. Harry Johnston (D)
20. Peter Deutsch (D)
21. Lincoln Diaz-Balart (R)
22. Clay Shaw (R)
23. Alcee Hastings (D)

POSTWAR VOTE FOR PRESIDENT

| | | Republican | | Democratic | | | | Percentage | | | |
| | Total | | | | | Other | | Total Vote | | Major Vote | |
Year	Vote	Vote	Candidate	Vote	Candidate	Vote	Plurality	Rep.	Dem.	Rep.	Dem.
1992 **	5,314,392	2,173,310	Bush, George	2,072,698	Clinton, Bill	1,068,384	100,612 R	40.9%	39.0%	51.2%	48.8%
1988	4,302,313	2,618,885	Bush, George	1,656,701	Dukakis, Michael S.	26,727	962,184 R	60.9%	38.5%	61.3%	38.7%
1984	4,180,051	2,730,350	Reagan, Ronald	1,448,816	Mondale, Walter F.	885	1,281,534 R	65.3%	34.7%	65.3%	34.7%
1980	3,686,930	2,046,951	Reagan, Ronald	1,419,475	Carter, Jimmy	220,504	627,476 R	55.5%	38.5%	59.1%	40.9%
1976	3,150,631	1,469,531	Ford, Gerald R.	1,636,000	Carter, Jimmy	45,100	166,469 D	46.6%	51.9%	47.3%	52.7%
1972	2,583,283	1,857,759	Nixon, Richard M.	718,117	McGovern, George S.	7,407	1,139,642 R	71.9%	27.8%	72.1%	27.9%
1968 **	2,187,805	886,804	Nixon, Richard M.	676,794	Humphrey, Hubert H.	624,207	210,010 R	40.5%	30.9%	56.7%	43.3%
1964	1,854,481	905,941	Goldwater, Barry M.	948,540	Johnson, Lyndon B.		42,599 D	48.9%	51.1%	48.9%	51.1%
1960	1,544,176	795,476	Nixon, Richard M.	748,700	Kennedy, John F.		46,776 R	51.5%	48.5%	51.5%	48.5%
1956	1,125,762	643,849	Eisenhower, Dwight D.	480,371	Stevenson, Adlai E.	1,542	163,478 R	57.2%	42.7%	57.3%	42.7%
1952	989,337	544,036	Eisenhower, Dwight D.	444,950	Stevenson, Adlai E.	351	99,086 R	55.0%	45.0%	55.0%	45.0%
1948	577,643	194,280	Dewey, Thomas E.	281,988	Truman, Harry S.	101,375	87,708 D	33.6%	48.8%	40.8%	59.2%

In 1992 the other vote column includes 1,053,067 votes cast for Perot. In 1968 other vote was George Wallace party.

FLORIDA

POSTWAR VOTE FOR GOVERNOR

Year	Total Vote	Republican		Democratic		Other Vote	Rep.-Dem. Plurality	Percentage			
		Vote	Candidate	Vote	Candidate			Total Vote		Major Vote	
								Rep.	Dem.	Rep.	Dem.
1990	3,530,871	1,535,068	Martinez, Bob	1,995,206	Chiles, Lawton	597	460,138 D	43.5%	56.5%	43.5%	56.5%
1986	3,386,171	1,847,525	Martinez, Bob	1,538,620	Pajcic, Steve	26	308,905 R	54.6%	45.4%	54.6%	45.4%
1982	2,688,566	949,013	Bafalis, L. A.	1,739,553	Graham, Robert		790,540 D	35.3%	64.7%	35.3%	64.7%
1978	2,530,468	1,123,888	Eckerd, Jack M.	1,406,580	Graham, Robert		282,692 D	44.4%	55.6%	44.4%	55.6%
1974	1,828,392	709,438	Thomas, Jerry	1,118,954	Askew, Reubin		409,516 D	38.8%	61.2%	38.8%	61.2%
1970	1,730,813	746,243	Kirk, Claude R.	984,305	Askew, Reubin	265	238,062 D	43.1%	56.9%	43.1%	56.9%
1966	1,489,661	821,190	Kirk, Claude R.	668,233	High, Robert King	238	152,957 R	55.1%	44.9%	55.1%	44.9%
1964 S	1,663,481	686,297	Holley, Charles R.	933,554	Burns, Haydon	43,630	247,257 D	41.3%	56.1%	42.4%	57.6%
1960	1,419,343	569,936	Petersen, George C.	849,407	Bryant, Farris		279,471 D	40.2%	59.8%	40.2%	59.8%
1956	1,014,733	266,980	Washburne, W. A.	747,753	Collins, LeRoy		480,773 D	26.3%	73.7%	26.3%	73.7%
1954 S	357,783	69,852	Watson, J. Tom	287,769	Collins, LeRoy	162	217,917 D	19.5%	80.4%	19.5%	80.5%
1952	834,518	210,009	Swan, Harry S.	624,463	McCarty, Dan	46	414,454 D	25.2%	74.8%	25.2%	74.8%
1948	457,638	76,153	Acker, Bert Lee	381,459	Warren, Fuller	26	305,306 D	16.6%	83.4%	16.6%	83.4%

The 1954 election was for a short term to fill a vacancy. The 1964 election was for a two-year term to permit shifting the vote for Governor to non-Presidential years.

POSTWAR VOTE FOR SENATOR

Year	Total Vote	Republican		Democratic		Other Vote	Rep.-Dem. Plurality	Percentage			
		Vote	Candidate	Vote	Candidate			Total Vote		Major Vote	
								Rep.	Dem.	Rep.	Dem.
1992	4,962,290	1,716,505	Grant, Bill	3,245,565	Graham, Robert	220	1,529,060 D	34.6%	65.4%	34.6%	65.4%
1988	4,068,209	2,051,071	Mack, Connie	2,016,553	MacKay, Buddy	585	34,518 R	50.4%	49.6%	50.4%	49.6%
1986	3,429,996	1,552,376	Hawkins, Paula	1,877,543	Graham, Robert	77	325,167 D	45.3%	54.7%	45.3%	54.7%
1982	2,653,419	1,015,330	Poole, Van B.	1,637,667	Chiles, Lawton	422	622,337 D	38.3%	61.7%	38.3%	61.7%
1980	3,528,028	1,822,460	Hawkins, Paula	1,705,409	Gunter, Bill	159	117,051 R	51.7%	48.3%	51.7%	48.3%
1976	2,857,534	1,057,886	Grady, John	1,799,518	Chiles, Lawton	130	741,632 D	37.0%	63.0%	37.0%	63.0%
1974	1,800,539	736,674	Eckerd, Jack M.	781,031	Stone, Richard	282,834	44,357 D	40.9%	43.4%	48.5%	51.5%
1970	1,675,378	772,817	Cramer, William C.	902,438	Chiles, Lawton	123	129,621 D	46.1%	53.9%	46.1%	53.9%
1968	2,024,136	1,131,499	Gurney, Edward J.	892,637	Collins, LeRoy		238,862 R	55.9%	44.1%	55.9%	44.1%
1964	1,560,337	562,212	Kirk, Claude R.	997,585	Holland, Spessard L.	540	435,373 D	36.0%	63.9%	36.0%	64.0%
1962	939,207	281,381	Rupert, Emerson H.	657,633	Smathers, George A.	193	376,252 D	30.0%	70.0%	30.0%	70.0%
1958	542,069	155,956	Hyzer, Leland	386,113	Holland, Spessard L.		230,157 D	28.8%	71.2%	28.8%	71.2%
1956	655,418		—	655,418	Smathers, George A.		655,418 D		100.0%		100.0%
1952	617,800		—	616,665	Holland, Spessard L.	1,135	616,665 D		99.8%		100.0%
1950	313,487	74,228	Booth, John P.	238,987	Smathers, George A.	272	164,759 D	23.7%	76.2%	23.7%	76.3%
1946	198,640	42,408	Schad, J. Harry	156,232	Holland, Spessard L.		113,824 D	21.3%	78.7%	21.3%	78.7%

FLORIDA

Districts Established May 14, 1992

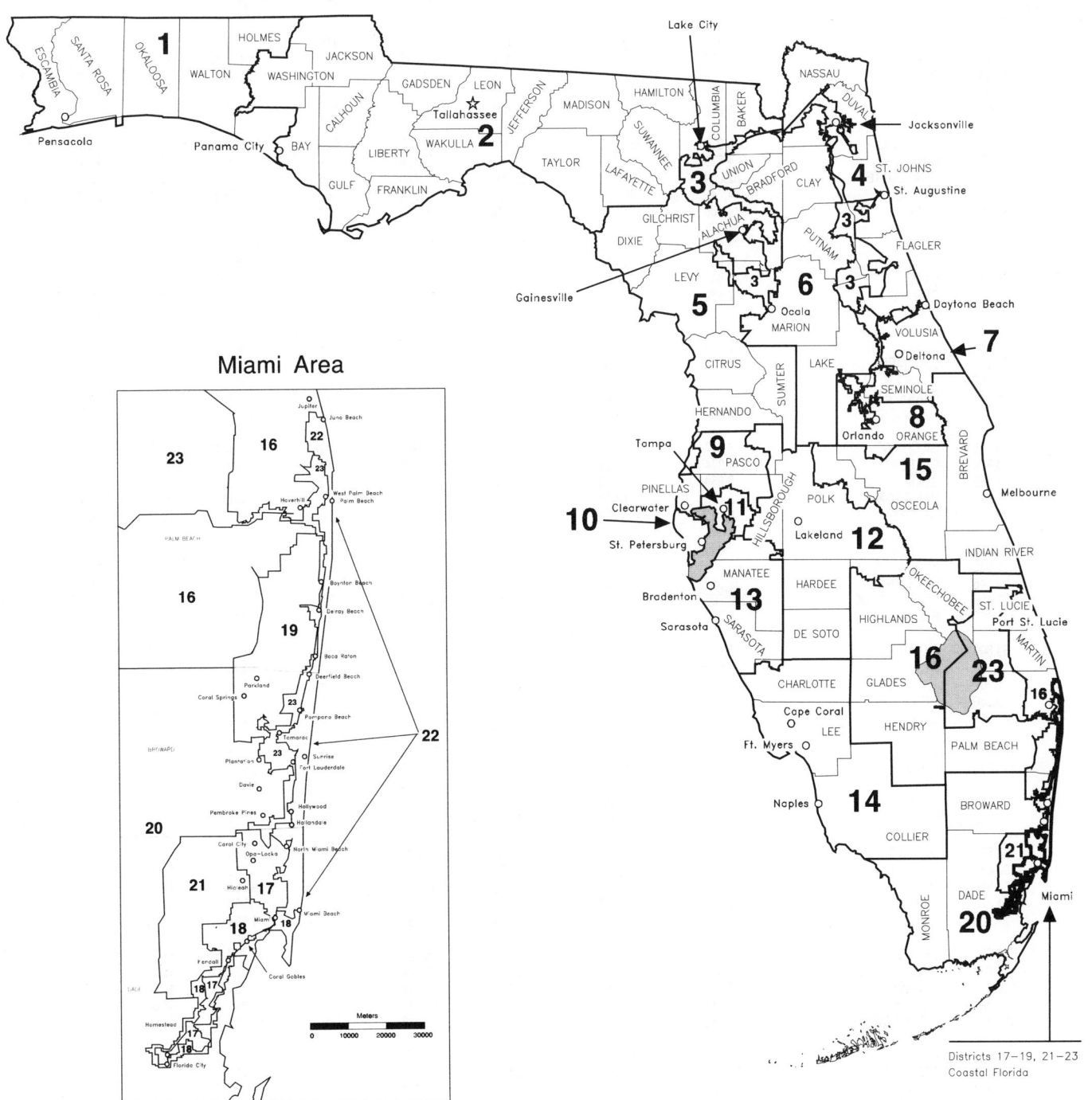

Lake City

HOLMES
JACKSON
SANTA ROSA
ESCAMBIA
OKALOOSA
WALTON
WASHINGTON
NASSAU

1

GADSDEN LEON
CALHOUN
☆ Tallahassee
Panama City BAY
LIBERTY WAKULLA **2**
GULF FRANKLIN
JEFFERSON
MADISON
HAMILTON
TAYLOR
LAFAYETTE
SUWANNEE
DIXIE
GILCHRIST
LEVY
COLUMBIA
BAKER
UNION
BRADFORD
ALACHUA
3
5
MARION
Ocala
3
6
Gainesville
Pensacola

DUVAL
Jacksonville
ST. JOHNS
4
St. Augustine
3
CLAY
PUTNAM
FLAGLER
3
Daytona Beach
VOLUSIA
7
Deltona
SEMINOLE
8
ORANGE
Orlando
BREVARD
Melbourne

CITRUS
SUMTER
LAKE
HERNANDO
Tampa
9
PASCO
PINELLAS
Clearwater
10
11
HILLSBOROUGH
St. Petersburg
POLK
Lakeland
15
OSCEOLA
INDIAN RIVER
12
MANATEE
Bradenton
13
HARDEE
Sarasota
SARASOTA
DE SOTO
HIGHLANDS
OKEECHOBEE
ST. LUCIE
Port St. Lucie
MARTIN
16
23
16
CHARLOTTE
GLADES
Cape Coral
LEE
HENDRY
PALM BEACH
Ft. Myers
14
BROWARD
Naples
COLLIER
21
DADE
Miami
MONROE
20

Districts 17–19, 21–23
Coastal Florida

Miami Area

23
Jupiter
June Beach
16
22
23
West Palm Beach
Palm Beach
Haverhill
PALM BEACH
16
Boynton Beach
Delray Beach
19
Boca Raton
Deerfield Beach
Parkland
Coral Springs
23
Pompano Beach
Tamarac
23
Sunrise
Plantation
Fort Lauderdale
BROWARD
Davie
Hollywood
Pembroke Pines
Hallandale
20
Coral City
North Miami Beach
Opa-Locka
21
Hialeah
17
Miami
18
18
Miami Beach
DADE
Kendall
18
17
Coral Gables
Homestead
17
18
Florida City
22

Meters
0   10000   20000   30000

FLORIDA

PRESIDENT 1992

Registration	County	Total Vote	Republican	Democratic	Perot	Other	Plurality	Percentage Total Vote		
								Rep.	Dem.	Perot
89,559	ALACHUA	76,372	22,813	37,888	15,296	375	15,075 D	29.9%	49.6%	20.0%
9,870	BAKER	6,756	3,418	1,976	1,315	47	1,442 R	50.6%	29.2%	19.5%
59,696	BAY	45,689	22,842	12,846	9,712	289	9,996 R	50.0%	28.1%	21.3%
10,049	BRADFORD	8,341	3,672	3,041	1,574	54	631 R	44.0%	36.5%	18.9%
228,514	BREVARD	195,860	84,585	61,091	49,509	675	23,494 R	43.2%	31.2%	25.3%
657,548	BROWARD	533,050	164,832	276,361	90,937	920	111,529 D	30.9%	51.8%	17.1%
6,126	CALHOUN	4,579	1,721	1,665	1,176	17	56 R	37.6%	36.4%	25.7%
80,696	CHARLOTTE	62,064	24,311	22,907	14,720	126	1,404 R	39.2%	36.9%	23.7%
57,216	CITRUS	44,746	16,412	15,937	12,314	83	475 R	36.7%	35.6%	27.5%
53,042	CLAY	45,485	26,360	10,610	8,423	92	15,750 R	58.0%	23.3%	18.5%
76,187	COLLIER	71,944	38,448	18,796	14,518	182	19,652 R	53.4%	26.1%	20.2%
19,379	COLUMBIA	14,954	6,492	5,528	2,906	28	964 R	43.4%	37.0%	19.4%
675,286	DADE	544,843	235,313	254,609	54,003	918	19,296 D	43.2%	46.7%	9.9%
10,610	DESOTO	7,429	3,070	2,646	1,687	26	424 R	41.3%	35.6%	22.7%
7,526	DIXIE	4,373	1,401	1,855	1,094	23	454 D	32.0%	42.4%	25.0%
349,984	DUVAL	249,926	123,631	92,098	33,388	809	31,533 R	49.5%	36.9%	13.4%
125,098	ESCAMBIA	105,221	52,868	32,045	19,923	385	20,823 R	50.2%	30.5%	18.9%
19,264	FLAGLER	16,355	6,246	6,693	3,390	26	447 D	38.2%	40.9%	20.7%
6,371	FRANKLIN	4,380	1,664	1,535	1,144	37	129 R	38.0%	35.0%	26.1%
18,571	GADSDEN	14,394	3,975	8,486	1,871	62	4,511 D	27.6%	59.0%	13.0%
5,455	GILCHRIST	4,017	1,395	1,511	1,090	21	116 D	34.7%	37.6%	27.1%
4,974	GLADES	3,374	1,185	1,305	878	6	120 D	35.1%	38.7%	26.0%
7,959	GULF	5,854	2,651	1,938	1,245	20	713 R	45.3%	33.1%	21.3%
5,800	HAMILTON	3,725	1,402	1,622	695	6	220 D	37.6%	43.5%	18.7%
8,235	HARDEE	6,433	2,900	2,018	1,499	16	882 R	45.1%	31.4%	23.3%
10,252	HENDRY	8,016	3,279	2,691	2,032	14	588 R	40.9%	33.6%	25.3%
74,036	HERNANDO	49,086	17,902	19,174	11,848	162	1,272 D	36.5%	39.1%	24.1%
38,246	HIGHLANDS	32,391	14,499	11,237	6,593	62	3,262 R	44.8%	34.7%	20.4%
372,439	HILLSBOROUGH	310,502	130,643	115,282	63,054	1,523	15,361 R	42.1%	37.1%	20.3%
8,405	HOLMES	6,528	3,196	1,877	1,427	28	1,319 R	49.0%	28.8%	21.9%
53,800	INDIAN RIVER	43,962	19,140	12,360	12,375	87	6,765 R	43.5%	28.1%	28.1%
19,119	JACKSON	14,676	6,725	5,482	2,450	19	1,243 R	45.8%	37.4%	16.7%
6,002	JEFFERSON	4,678	1,506	2,271	895	6	765 D	32.2%	48.5%	19.1%
3,360	LAFAYETTE	2,525	1,039	867	612	7	172 R	41.1%	34.3%	24.2%
79,947	LAKE	69,787	30,825	23,200	15,614	148	7,625 R	44.2%	33.2%	22.4%
190,625	LEE	166,002	73,436	53,660	38,452	454	19,776 R	44.2%	32.3%	23.2%
116,033	LEON	97,294	31,983	47,791	17,212	308	15,808 D	32.9%	49.1%	17.7%
14,356	LEVY	10,936	3,796	4,330	2,784	26	534 D	34.7%	39.6%	25.5%
3,292	LIBERTY	2,576	1,126	820	617	13	306 R	43.7%	31.8%	24.0%
7,762	MADISON	5,838	2,007	2,648	1,174	9	641 D	34.4%	45.4%	20.1%
128,875	MANATEE	100,220	42,725	33,841	23,290	364	8,884 R	42.6%	33.8%	23.2%
106,681	MARION	86,989	35,442	30,829	20,529	189	4,613 R	40.7%	35.4%	23.6%
64,048	MARTIN	53,184	24,800	14,802	13,442	140	9,998 R	46.6%	27.8%	25.3%
41,373	MONROE	28,789	9,898	10,450	8,314	127	552 D	34.4%	36.3%	28.9%
21,923	NASSAU	18,174	9,367	5,503	3,255	49	3,864 R	51.5%	30.3%	17.9%
76,622	OKALOOSA	61,769	32,818	12,038	16,671	242	16,147 R	53.1%	19.5%	27.0%
13,991	OKEECHOBEE	9,370	3,298	3,418	2,647	7	120 D	35.2%	36.5%	28.2%
267,878	ORANGE	237,011	108,788	82,683	44,844	696	26,105 R	45.9%	34.9%	18.9%
58,382	OSCEOLA	45,267	19,143	15,010	11,021	93	4,133 R	42.3%	33.2%	24.3%
484,440	PALM BEACH	405,251	140,350	187,869	76,243	789	47,519 D	34.6%	46.4%	18.8%
169,753	PASCO	135,962	47,735	53,130	34,654	443	5,395 D	35.1%	39.1%	25.5%
504,465	PINELLAS	422,851	159,121	160,528	101,257	1,945	1,407 D	37.6%	38.0%	23.9%
172,251	POLK	145,900	65,963	51,450	28,204	283	14,513 R	45.2%	35.3%	19.3%
40,299	PUTNAM	25,661	8,910	10,709	5,979	63	1,799 D	34.7%	41.7%	23.3%
51,628	ST. JOHNS	39,986	20,188	12,291	7,400	107	7,897 R	50.5%	30.7%	18.5%
89,539	ST. LUCIE	68,233	24,400	23,876	19,817	140	524 R	35.8%	35.0%	29.0%
54,695	SANTA ROSA	32,777	17,339	6,556	8,788	94	8,551 R	52.9%	20.0%	26.8%
184,437	SARASOTA	156,352	66,855	54,552	34,289	656	12,303 R	42.8%	34.9%	21.9%
139,451	SEMINOLE	117,560	57,101	35,660	24,487	312	21,441 R	48.6%	30.3%	20.8%
14,907	SUMTER	12,329	4,366	5,027	2,901	35	661 D	35.4%	40.8%	23.5%

FLORIDA

PRESIDENT 1992

Registration	County	Total Vote	Republican	Democratic	Perot	Other	Plurality	Percentage Total Vote		
								Rep.	Dem.	Perot
14,300	SUWANNEE	11,374	4,576	3,988	2,791	19	588 R	40.2%	35.1%	24.5%
9,036	TAYLOR	7,213	2,693	2,568	1,929	23	125 R	37.3%	35.6%	26.7%
4,871	UNION	3,571	1,546	1,248	770	7	298 R	43.3%	34.9%	21.6%
201,509	VOLUSIA	155,499	59,172	65,223	30,823	281	6,051 D	38.1%	41.9%	19.8%
8,708	WAKULLA	6,714	2,586	2,320	1,790	18	266 R	38.5%	34.6%	26.7%
16,730	WALTON	13,554	5,726	3,888	3,890	50	1,836 R	42.2%	28.7%	28.7%
10,344	WASHINGTON	7,871	3,695	2,544	1,596	36	1,151 R	46.9%	32.3%	20.3%
6,541,825	TOTAL	5,314,392	2,173,310	2,072,698	1,053,067	15,317	100,612 R	40.9%	39.0%	19.8%

FLORIDA

SENATOR 1992

Registration	County	Total Vote	Republican	Democratic	Other	Rep.-Dem. Plurality	Percentage			
							Total Vote		Major Vote	
							Rep.	Dem.	Rep.	Dem.
89,559	ALACHUA	74,985	20,018	54,963	4	34,945 D	26.7%	73.3%	26.7%	73.3%
9,870	BAKER	7,336	2,647	4,689		2,042 D	36.1%	63.9%	36.1%	63.9%
59,696	BAY	40,341	18,410	21,930	1	3,520 D	45.6%	54.4%	45.6%	54.4%
10,049	BRADFORD	8,192	2,401	5,791		3,390 D	29.3%	70.7%	29.3%	70.7%
228,514	BREVARD	192,658	82,168	110,490		28,322 D	42.6%	57.4%	42.6%	57.4%
657,548	BROWARD	446,872	107,432	339,439	1	232,007 D	24.0%	76.0%	24.0%	76.0%
6,126	CALHOUN	4,153	1,263	2,890		1,627 D	30.4%	69.6%	30.4%	69.6%
80,696	CHARLOTTE	61,056	24,674	36,382		11,708 D	40.4%	59.6%	40.4%	59.6%
57,216	CITRUS	45,386	17,705	27,680	1	9,975 D	39.0%	61.0%	39.0%	61.0%
53,042	CLAY	44,928	21,204	23,724		2,520 D	47.2%	52.8%	47.2%	52.8%
76,187	COLLIER	70,215	33,826	36,389		2,563 D	48.2%	51.8%	48.2%	51.8%
19,379	COLUMBIA	15,043	5,565	9,478		3,913 D	37.0%	63.0%	37.0%	63.0%
675,286	DADE	522,231	111,475	410,754	2	299,279 D	21.3%	78.7%	21.3%	78.7%
10,610	DESOTO	7,676	2,655	5,021		2,366 D	34.6%	65.4%	34.6%	65.4%
7,526	DIXIE	4,731	1,385	3,346		1,961 D	29.3%	70.7%	29.3%	70.7%
349,984	DUVAL	216,559	79,999	136,552	8	56,553 D	36.9%	63.1%	36.9%	63.1%
125,098	ESCAMBIA	100,842	43,757	57,085		13,328 D	43.4%	56.6%	43.4%	56.6%
19,264	FLAGLER	15,872	5,789	10,083		4,294 D	36.5%	63.5%	36.5%	63.5%
6,371	FRANKLIN	3,860	1,409	2,450	1	1,041 D	36.5%	63.5%	36.5%	63.5%
18,571	GADSDEN	12,815	2,328	10,487		8,159 D	18.2%	81.8%	18.2%	81.8%
5,455	GILCHRIST	4,305	1,315	2,990		1,675 D	30.5%	69.5%	30.5%	69.5%
4,974	GLADES	3,407	1,057	2,350		1,293 D	31.0%	69.0%	31.0%	69.0%
7,959	GULF	5,722	2,231	3,491		1,260 D	39.0%	61.0%	39.0%	61.0%
5,800	HAMILTON	3,709	1,040	2,669		1,629 D	28.0%	72.0%	28.0%	72.0%
8,235	HARDEE	6,339	2,208	4,131		1,923 D	34.8%	65.2%	34.8%	65.2%
10,252	HENDRY	7,868	2,370	5,498		3,128 D	30.1%	69.9%	30.1%	69.9%
74,036	HERNANDO	54,948	19,634	35,314		15,680 D	35.7%	64.3%	35.7%	64.3%
38,246	HIGHLANDS	31,888	13,077	18,811		5,734 D	41.0%	59.0%	41.0%	59.0%
372,439	HILLSBOROUGH	304,925	117,636	187,287	2	69,651 D	38.6%	61.4%	38.6%	61.4%
8,405	HOLMES	6,234	2,494	3,740		1,246 D	40.0%	60.0%	40.0%	60.0%
53,800	INDIAN RIVER	43,431	20,121	23,310		3,189 D	46.3%	53.7%	46.3%	53.7%
19,119	JACKSON	14,723	5,137	9,586		4,449 D	34.9%	65.1%	34.9%	65.1%
6,002	JEFFERSON	4,714	1,082	3,632		2,550 D	23.0%	77.0%	23.0%	77.0%
3,360	LAFAYETTE	2,549	800	1,749		949 D	31.4%	68.6%	31.4%	68.6%
79,947	LAKE	68,784	25,839	42,945		17,106 D	37.6%	62.4%	37.6%	62.4%
190,625	LEE	150,709	62,424	88,282	3	25,858 D	41.4%	58.6%	41.4%	58.6%
116,033	LEON	95.974	22,525	73,423	26	50,898 D	23.5%	76.5%	23.5%	76.5%
14,356	LEVY	10,902	3,643	7,259		3,616 D	33.4%	66.6%	33.4%	66.6%
3,292	LIBERTY	2,398	695	1,703		1,008 D	29.0%	71.0%	29.0%	71.0%
7,762	MADISON	6,018	1,627	4,390	1	2,763 D	27.0%	72.9%	27.0%	73.0%
128,875	MANATEE	98,499	39,913	58,583	3	18,670 D	40.5%	59.5%	40.5%	59.5%
106,681	MARION	28,214	10,015	18,199		8,184 D	35.5%	64.5%	35.5%	64.5%
64,048	MARTIN	85,268	32,395	52,873		20,478 D	38.0%	62.0%	38.0%	62.0%
41,373	MONROE	50,441	22,075	28,366		6,291 D	43.8%	56.2%	43.8%	56.2%
21,923	NASSAU	17,956	7,022	10,934		3,912 D	39.1%	60.9%	39.1%	60.9%
76,622	OKALOOSA	59,903	30,102	29,801		301 R	50.3%	49.7%	50.3%	49.7%
13,991	OKEECHOBEE	9,301	3,143	6,158		3,015 D	33.8%	66.2%	33.8%	66.2%
267,878	ORANGE	233,025	89,965	143,057	3	53,092 D	38.6%	61.4%	38.6%	61.4%
58,382	OSCEOLA	42,322	15,928	26,394		10,466 D	37.6%	62.4%	37.6%	62.4%
484,440	PALM BEACH	355,188	105,968	249,219	1	143,251 D	29.8%	70.2%	29.8%	70.2%
169,753	PASCO	122,821	44,307	78,514		34,207 D	36.1%	63.9%	36.1%	63.9%
504,465	PINELLAS	376,855	133,415	243,410	30	109,995 D	35.4%	64.6%	35.4%	64.6%
172,251	POLK	145,824	55,478	90,346		34,868 D	38.0%	62.0%	38.0%	62.0%
40,299	PUTNAM	25,234	7,009	18,224	1	11,215 D	27.8%	72.2%	27.8%	72.2%
51,628	ST. JOHNS	39,151	17,075	22,076		5,001 D	43.6%	56.4%	43.6%	56.4%
89,539	ST. LUCIE	62,663	22,569	40,091	3	17,522 D	36.0%	64.0%	36.0%	64.0%
54,695	SANTA ROSA	35,524	16,076	19,448		3,372 D	45.3%	54.7%	45.3%	54.7%
184,437	SARASOTA	123,705	52,968	70,709	28	17,741 D	42.8%	57.2%	42.8%	57.2%
139,451	SEMINOLE	114,185	48,249	65,932	4	17,683 D	42.3%	57.7%	42.3%	57.7%
14,907	SUMTER	10,324	2,987	7,337		4,350 D	28.9%	71.1%	28.9%	71.1%

FLORIDA

SENATOR 1992

Registration	County	Total Vote	Republican	Democratic	Other	Rep.-Dem. Plurality	Percentage			
							Total Vote		Major Vote	
							Rep.	Dem.	Rep.	Dem.
14,300	SUWANNEE	11,355	3,934	7,421		3,487 D	34.6%	65.4%	34.6%	65.4%
9,036	TAYLOR	7,058	2,162	4,896		2,734 D	30.6%	69.4%	30.6%	69.4%
4,871	UNION	3,606	982	2,624		1,642 D	27.2%	72.8%	27.2%	72.8%
201,509	VOLUSIA	151,324	49,863	101,365	96	51,502 D	33.0%	67.0%	33.0%	67.0%
8,708	WAKULLA	6,705	1,771	4,934		3,163 D	26.4%	73.6%	26.4%	73.6%
16,730	WALTON	12,936	5,212	7,723	1	2,511 D	40.3%	59.7%	40.3%	59.7%
10,344	WASHINGTON	7,605	2,857	4,748		1,891 D	37.6%	62.4%	37.6%	62.4%
6,541,825	TOTAL	4,962,290	1,716,505	3,245,565	220	1,529,060 D	34.6%	65.4%	34.6%	65.4%

FLORIDA

CONGRESS

			Republican		Democratic				Percentage			
									Total Vote		Major Vote	
CD	Year	Total Vote	Vote	Candidate	Vote	Candidate	Other Vote	Rep.-Dem. Plurality	Rep.	Dem.	Rep.	Dem.
1	1992	228,632	100,349	KETCHEL, TERRY	118,941	HUTTO, EARL D.	9,342	18,592 D	43.9%	52.0%	45.8%	54.2%
2	1992	152,426	60,425	WAGNER, RAY	167,215	PETERSON, PETE	86	106,790 D	39.6%	60.3%	39.7%	60.3%
3	1992	166,646	63,115	WEIDNER, DON	91,915	BROWN, CORRINE		28,800 D	37.9%	62.1%	37.9%	62.1%
4	1992	239,471	135,883	FOWLER, TILLIE	103,531	HAIR, MATTOX	57	32,352 R	56.7%	43.2%	56.8%	43.2%
5	1992	263,549	114,356	HOGAN, TOM	129,698	THURMAN, KAREN	19,495	15,342 D	43.4%	49.2%	46.9%	53.1%
6	1992	220,614	144,195	STEARNS, CLIFFORD B.	76,419	DENTON, PHIL		67,776 R	65.4%	34.6%	65.4%	34.6%
7	1992	223,023	125,823	MICA, JOHN	96,945	WEBSTER, DAN	255	28,878 R	56.4%	43.5%	56.5%	43.5%
8	1992	207,122	141,977	MCCOLLUM, BILL	65,145	KOVALESKI, CHUCK		76,832 R	68.5%	31.5%	68.5%	31.5%
9	1992	268,163	158,028	BILIRAKIS, MICHAEL	110,135	KNAPP, CHERYL D.		47,893 R	58.9%	41.1%	58.9%	41.1%
10	1992	264,415	149,606	YOUNG, C. W.	114,809	MOFFITT, KAREN		34,797 R	56.6%	43.4%	56.6%	43.4%
11	1992	191,354	77,640	SHARPE, MARK	100,984	GIBBONS, SAM M.	12,730	23,344 D	40.6%	52.8%	43.5%	56.5%
12	1992	192,830	100,484	CANADY, CHARLES T.	92,346	MIMS, TOM		8,138 R	52.1%	47.9%	52.1%	47.9%
13	1992	274,648	158,881	MILLER, DAN	115,767	SNELL, RAND		43,114 R	57.8%	42.2%	57.8%	42.2%
14	1992	268,511	220,351	GOSS, PORTER J.			48,160	220,351 R	82.1%		100.0%	
15	1992	261,285	128,873	TOLLEY, BILL	132,412	BACCHUS, JIM		3,539 D	49.3%	50.7%	49.3%	50.7%
16	1992	258,559	157,322	LEWIS, TOM	101,237	COMERFORD, JOHN P.		56,085 R	60.8%	39.2%	60.8%	39.2%
17	1992	102,799			102,784	MEEK, CARRIE	15	102,784 D		100.0%		100.0%
18	1992	156,897	104,755	ROS-LEHTINEN, ILEANA	52,142	DAVIS, MAGDA M.		52,613 R	66.8%	33.2%	66.8%	33.2%
19	1992	281,294	103,867	METZ, LARRY	177,423	JOHNSTON, HARRY	4	73,556 D	36.9%	63.1%	36.9%	63.1%
20	1992	237,889	91,589	KENNEDY, BEVERLY	130,959	DEUTSCH, PETER	15,341	39,370 D	38.5%	55.1%	41.2%	58.8%
21	1992			DIAZ-BALART, LINCOLN								
22	1992	247,088	128,400	SHAW, CLAY	91,625	MARGOLIS, GWEN	27,063	36,775 R	52.0%	37.1%	58.4%	41.6%
23	1992	143,935	44,807	FIELDING, ED	84,249	HASTINGS, ALCEE	14,879	39,442 D	31.1%	58.5%	34.7%	65.3%

FLORIDA

1992 GENERAL ELECTION

President   The county-by-county table includes the federal absentee votes which were not reported on earlier returns. Other vote was 15,079 Libertarian (Marrou); 214 Hagelin (write-in); 16 Brisben (write-in); 8 scattered write-in.

Senator   The county-by-county table includes the federal absentee votes which were not reported on earlier returns. Other vote was 86 Evans (write-in); 71 Wiechart (write-in); 63 Dan Fein (write-in).

Congress   According to state law, votes are not required to be tabulated for unopposed candidates. In 1992, the Republican candidate in CD 21 was unopposed. The congressional district tables include the federal absentee votes which were not reported on earlier returns. The Democratic (Brown) vote in CD 3 was corrected from 91,918. The Republican (Lewis) vote in CD 16 was corrected from 157,422. Other vote was Green (Rodgers-Hendricks) in CD 1; Prescott (write-in) in CD 2; Taylor (write-in) in CD 4; 19,462 Independent (Munkittrick) and 33 Noah (write-in) in CD 5; 213 McCarthy (write-in) and 42 Davis (write-in) in CD 7; Independent (DeMinico) in CD 11; Independent (King) in CD 14; Jill Fein (write-in) in CD 17; Hemmerle (write-in) in CD 19; Independent (Blackburn) in CD 20; 15,469 Independent (Stephens), 5,274 Independent (Anscher), 6,312 Independent (Petrie) and 8 Lambert (write-in) in CD 22; Independent (Woods) in CD 23.

1992 PRIMARIES

Primary voting was delayed in Dade county until September 8 due to the devastation caused by Hurricane Andrew which hit the area a week before the primary. The data below includes these votes cast a week after the primary date.

SEPTEMBER 1 REPUBLICAN

Senator   413,457 Bill Grant; 196,524 Rob Quartel; 126,878 Hugh Brotherton.

Congress   Unopposed in nine CD's. No candidate in CD 17. Contested as follows:

CD 1   22,080 Terry Ketchel; 18,602 Tom Banjanin.
CD 3   3,828 Don Weidner; 3,774 Steve Kelley; 1,911 George Grimsley; 1,377 Bob Harms.
CD 5   23,606 Tom Hogan; 15,802 Gene Keith; 5,711 Anthony Martin.
CD 7   24,350 John Mica; 15,768 Dick Graham; 6,073 Vaughn Forrest.
CD 8   33,482 Bill McCollum; 8,621 Lew Oliver.
CD 9   34,593 Michael Bilirakis; 17,295 Patricia Muscarella.
CD 11   11,660 Mark Sharpe; 6,455 Kevin Gowen.
CD 13   22,055 Brad Baker; 21,912 Dan Miller; 15,827 Dave Thomas; 13,828 Rick Louis; 5,127 Jim Thorpe.
CD 15   33,863 Bill Tolley; 28,834 Dixie Sansom.
CD 16   29,716 Tom Lewis; 16,621 John Anastasio.
CD 20   6,423 Beverly Kennedy; 5,396 Marilyn Bonilla; 4,103 W. Phil McConaghey.
CD 21   15,192 Lincoln Diaz-Balart; 6,941 Javier Souto.
CD 23   3,091 Ed Fielding; 3,084 Oliver Parker; 2,042 Jerome Gray.

SEPTEMBER 1 DEMOCRATIC

Senator   968,618 Robert Graham; 180,405 Jim Mahorner.

Congress   Unopposed in eight CD's. No candidate in CD's 14 and 21. Contested as follows:

CD 1   60,346 Earl D. Hutto; 17,373 Ernie Padgett; 10,411 Harry Keller.
CD 2   96,909 Pete Peterson; 43,891 Buster Smith.
CD 3   25,374 Corrine Brown; 18,209 Andrew Johnson; 10,746 Arnett Girardeau; 4,383 Glennie Mills.

FLORIDA

CD 5   60,144 Karen Thurman; 19,141 Mario Rivera.
CD 6   24,852 Phil Denton; 24,623 Richard Olsen.
CD 7   20,144 Dan Webster; 15,300 Adrienne Perry.
CD 10   30,020 Karen Moffitt; 5,148 Ted Savitskas; 3,500 Darrell DiGrazia.
CD 12   37,656 Tom Mims; 18,179 Frank O'Reilly.
CD 13   20,823 Rand Snell; 19,277 Stephanie Slavin.
CD 15   31,216 Jim Bacchus; 16,371 Larry Bessinger.
CD 17   31,262 Carrie Meek; 3,499 Darryl Reaves; 3,122 Donald Jones.
CD 20   28,753 Peter Deutsch; 17,211 Nicki Grossman.
CD 23   12,556 Lois Frankel; 10,237 Alcee Hastings; 9,881 Bill Clark; 1,872 Kenneth Cooper; 1,711 William Washington.

OCTOBER 1 REPUBLICAN RUN-OFF

Congress   Contested as follows:

CD 3   4,491 Don Weidner; 3,286 Steve Kelley.
CD 13   33,965 Dan Miller; 30,527 Brad Baker.
CD 20   3,592 Beverly Kennedy; 3,265 Marilyn Bonilla.
CD 23   2,423 Ed Fielding; 2,035 Oliver Parker.

OCTOBER 1 DEMOCRATIC RUN-OFF

Congress   Contested as follows:

CD 3   29,006 Corrine Brown; 16,427 Andrew Johnson.
CD 23   22,046 Alcee Hastings; 16,294 Lois Frankel.

GEORGIA

GOVERNOR
Zell Miller (D). Elected 1990 to a four-year term.

SENATORS
Paul Coverdell (R). Elected November 24, 1992 in a special run-off election to a six-year term.

Sam Nunn (D). Re-elected 1990 to a six-year term. Previously elected 1984, 1978, 1972.

REPRESENTATIVES
1. Jack Kingston (R)
2. Sanford Bishop (D)
3. Mac Collins (R)
4. John Linder (R)
5. John Lewis (D)
6. Newt Gingrich (R)
7. George Darden (D)
8. J. Roy Rowland (D)
9. Nathan Deal (D)
10. Don Johnson (D)
11. Cynthia McKinney (D)

POSTWAR VOTE FOR PRESIDENT

Year	Total Vote	Republican Vote	Republican Candidate	Democratic Vote	Democratic Candidate	Other Vote	Plurality	Total Vote Rep.	Total Vote Dem.	Major Vote Rep.	Major Vote Dem.
1992 **	2,321,125	995,252	Bush, George	1,008,966	Clinton, Bill	316,907	13,714 D	42.9%	43.5%	49.7%	50.3%
1988	1,809,672	1,081,331	Bush, George	714,792	Dukakis, Michael S.	13,549	366,539 R	59.8%	39.5%	60.2%	39.8%
1984	1,776,120	1,068,722	Reagan, Ronald	706,628	Mondale, Walter F.	770	362,094 R	60.2%	39.8%	60.2%	39.8%
1980	1,596,695	654,168	Reagan, Ronald	890,733	Carter, Jimmy	51,794	236,565 D	41.0%	55.8%	42.3%	57.7%
1976	1,467,458	483,743	Ford, Gerald R.	979,409	Carter, Jimmy	4,306	495,666 D	33.0%	66.7%	33.1%	66.9%
1972	1,174,772	881,496	Nixon, Richard M.	289,529	McGovern, George S.	3,747	591,967 R	75.0%	24.6%	75.3%	24.7%
1968 **	1,250,266	380,111	Nixon, Richard M.	334,440	Humphrey, Hubert H.	535,715	155,439 A	30.4%	26.7%	53.2%	46.8%
1964	1,139,335	616,584	Goldwater, Barry M.	522,556	Johnson, Lyndon B.	195	94,028 R	54.1%	45.9%	54.1%	45.9%
1960	733,349	274,472	Nixon, Richard M.	458,638	Kennedy, John F.	239	184,166 D	37.4%	62.5%	37.4%	62.6%
1956	669,655	222,778	Eisenhower, Dwight D.	444,688	Stevenson, Adlai E.	2,189	221,910 D	33.3%	66.4%	33.4%	66.6%
1952	655,785	198,961	Eisenhower, Dwight D.	456,823	Stevenson, Adlai E.	1	257,862 D	30.3%	69.7%	30.3%	69.7%
1948 **	418,844	76,691	Dewey, Thomas E.	254,646	Truman, Harry S.	87,507	169,511 D	18.3%	60.8%	23.1%	76.9%

In 1992 the other vote column includes 309,657 votes cast for Perot. In 1968 other vote was 535,550 American (Wallace) and 165 scattered. In 1948 other vote was 85,135 States Rights; 1,636 Progressive; 732 Prohibition; 3 Socialist and 1 scattered.

POSTWAR VOTE FOR GOVERNOR

Year	Total Vote	Republican Vote	Republican Candidate	Democratic Vote	Democratic Candidate	Other Vote	Rep.-Dem. Plurality	Total Vote Rep.	Total Vote Dem.	Major Vote Rep.	Major Vote Dem.
1990	1,449,682	645,625	Isakson, Johnny	766,662	Miller, Zell	37,395	121,037 D	44.5%	52.9%	45.7%	54.3%
1986	1,175,114	346,512	Davis, Guy	828,465	Harris, Joe Frank	137	481,953 D	29.5%	70.5%	29.5%	70.5%
1982	1,169,041	434,496	Bell, Robert H.	734,090	Harris, Joe Frank	455	299,594 D	37.2%	62.8%	37.2%	62.8%
1978	662,862	128,139	Cook, Rodney M.	534,572	Busbee, George	151	406,433 D	19.3%	80.6%	19.3%	80.7%
1974	936,438	289,113	Thompson, Ronnie	646,777	Busbee, George	548	357,664 D	30.9%	69.1%	30.9%	69.1%
1970	1,046,663	424,983	Suit, Hal	620,419	Carter, Jimmy	1,261	195,436 D	40.6%	59.3%	40.7%	59.3%
1966 **	975,019	453,665	Callaway, Howard H.	450,626	Maddox, Lester	70,728	3,039 R	46.5%	46.2%	50.2%	49.8%
1962	311,691		—	311,524	Sanders, Carl E.	167	311,524 D		99.9%		100.0%
1958	168,497		—	168,414	Vandiver, Ernest	83	168,414 D		100.0%		100.0%
1954	331,966		—	331,899	Griffin, Marvin	67	331,899 D		100.0%		100.0%
1950	234,430		—	230,771	Talmadge, Herman	3,659	230,771 D		98.4%		100.0%
1948 S	363,763		—	354,711	Talmadge, Herman	9,052	354,711 D		97.5%		100.0%
1946	145,403		—	143,279	Talmadge, Herman	2,124	143,279 D		98.5%		100.0%

The 1948 election was for a short term to fill a vacancy. In 1966, in the absence of a majority for any candidate, the State Legislature elected Lester Maddox to a four-year term.

GEORGIA

POSTWAR VOTE FOR SENATOR

Year	Total Vote	Republican		Democratic		Other Vote	Rep.-Dem. Plurality	Percentage			
								Total Vote		Major Vote	
		Vote	Candidate	Vote	Candidate			Rep.	Dem.	Rep.	Dem.
1992 **	1,253,991	635,114	Coverdell, Paul	618,877	Fowler, Wyche		16,237 R	50.6%	49.4%	50.6%	49.4%
1990	1,033,517		—	1,033,439	Nunn, Sam	78	1,033,439 D		100.0%		100.0%
1986	1,225,008	601,241	Mattingly, Mack	623,707	Fowler, Wyche	60	22,466 D	49.1%	50.9%	49.1%	50.9%
1984	1,681,344	337,196	Hicks, Jon Michael	1,344,104	Nunn, Sam	44	1,006,908 D	20.1%	79.9%	20.1%	79.9%
1980	1,580,340	803,686	Mattingly, Mack	776,143	Talmadge, Herman	511	27,543 R	50.9%	49.1%	50.9%	49.1%
1978	645,164	108,808	Stokes, John W.	536,320	Nunn, Sam	36	427,512 D	16.9%	83.1%	16.9%	83.1%
1974	874,555	246,866	Johnson, Jerry R.	627,376	Talmadge, Herman	313	380,510 D	28.2%	71.7%	28.2%	71.8%
1972	1,178,708	542,331	Thompson, Fletcher	635,970	Nunn, Sam	407	93,639 D	46.0%	54.0%	46.0%	54.0%
1968	1,141,889	256,796	Patton, E. Earl	885,093	Talmadge, Herman		628,297 D	22.5%	77.5%	22.5%	77.5%
1966	622,371		—	622,043	Russell, Richard B.	328	622,043 D		99.9%		100.0%
1962	306,250		—	306,250	Talmadge, Herman		306,250 D		100.0%		100.0%
1960	576,495		—	576,140	Russell, Richard B.	355	576,140 D		99.9%		100.0%
1956	541,267		—	541,094	Talmadge, Herman	173	541,094 D		100.0%		100.0%
1954	333,936		—	333,917	Russell, Richard B.	19	333,917 D		100.0%		100.0%
1950	261,293		—	261,290	George, Walter F.	3	261,290 D		100.0%		100.0%
1948	362,504		—	362,104	Russell, Richard B.	400	362,104 D		99.9%		100.0%

In 1992 the figures in the table are for the run-off election held November 24 as no candidate received a majority of the vote in the November 3 General Election. The vote in the November 3 election was 1,073,282 (47.7%) Republican (Coverdell); 1,108,416 (49.2%) Democratic (Fowler) and 69,889 (3.1%) other.

GEORGIA

Districts Established April 3, 1992

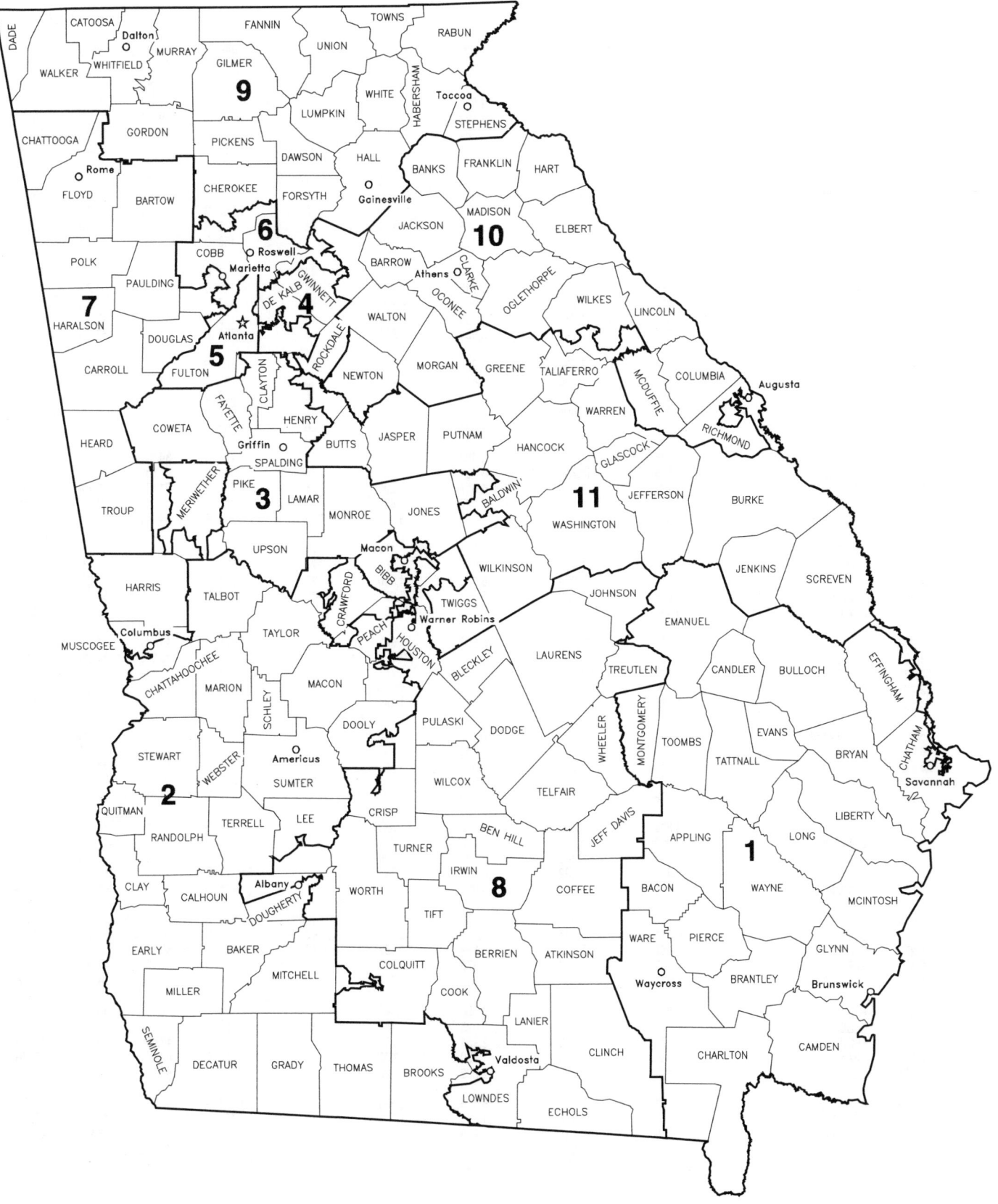

GEORGIA

PRESIDENT 1992

Registration	County	Total Vote	Republican	Democratic	Perot	Other	Plurality		Percentage Total Vote Rep.	Dem.	Perot
9,193	APPLING	6,027	2,514	2,455	1,047	11	59	R	41.7%	40.7%	17.4%
3,862	ATKINSON	2,185	779	1,056	342	8	277	D	35.7%	48.3%	15.7%
5,033	BACON	3,335	1,301	1,423	604	7	122	D	39.0%	42.7%	18.1%
2,409	BAKER	1,468	391	864	210	3	473	D	26.6%	58.9%	14.3%
15,534	BALDWIN	11,788	4,262	5,813	1,679	34	1,551	D	36.2%	49.3%	14.2%
5,019	BANKS	3,671	1,551	1,530	583	7	21	R	42.3%	41.7%	15.9%
13,497	BARROW	9,982	4,328	3,991	1,633	30	337	R	43.4%	40.0%	16.4%
22,923	BARTOW	16,990	7,742	6,675	2,500	73	1,067	R	45.6%	39.3%	14.7%
7,573	BEN HILL	4,464	1,476	2,348	619	21	872	D	33.1%	52.6%	13.9%
6,958	BERRIEN	4,543	1,637	2,103	796	7	466	D	36.0%	46.3%	17.5%
72,042	BIBB	54,049	19,847	28,070	6,021	111	8,223	D	36.7%	51.9%	11.1%
5,743	BLECKLEY	3,956	1,570	1,710	662	14	140	D	39.7%	43.2%	16.7%
6,593	BRANTLEY	4,274	1,541	1,883	840	10	342	D	36.1%	44.1%	19.7%
6,232	BROOKS	4,315	1,779	1,895	630	11	116	D	41.2%	43.9%	14.6%
8,644	BRYAN	5,928	2,789	2,031	1,095	13	758	R	47.0%	34.3%	18.5%
18,691	BULLOCH	12,644	5,690	4,903	2,020	31	787	R	45.0%	38.8%	16.0%
10,259	BURKE	6,859	2,390	3,647	807	15	1,257	D	34.8%	53.2%	11.8%
7,024	BUTTS	4,851	1,768	2,448	619	16	680	D	36.4%	50.5%	12.8%
2,935	CALHOUN	2,018	464	1,301	248	5	837	D	23.0%	64.5%	12.3%
10,906	CAMDEN	7,572	3,517	2,952	1,077	26	565	R	46.4%	39.0%	14.2%
4,137	CANDLER	2,755	1,014	1,192	541	8	178	D	36.8%	43.3%	19.6%
29,871	CARROLL	22,586	10,750	8,404	3,358	74	2,346	R	47.6%	37.2%	14.9%
19,607	CATOOSA	14,731	7,599	4,817	2,290	25	2,782	R	51.6%	32.7%	15.5%
4,373	CHARLTON	2,892	1,333	1,127	427	5	206	R	46.1%	39.0%	14.8%
97,549	CHATHAM	72,069	31,925	31,533	8,269	342	392	R	44.3%	43.8%	11.5%
2,002	CHATTAHOOCHEE	1,198	413	604	177	4	191	D	34.5%	50.4%	14.8%
10,060	CHATTOOGA	6,404	2,439	2,976	965	24	537	D	38.1%	46.5%	15.1%
42,301	CHEROKEE	29,214	16,054	8,113	4,950	97	7,941	R	55.0%	27.8%	16.9%
39,609	CLARKE	28,998	10,459	15,403	2,987	149	4,944	D	36.1%	53.1%	10.3%
1,826	CLAY	1,197	264	778	155		514	D	22.1%	65.0%	12.9%
75,280	CLAYTON	57,989	23,965	25,890	7,942	192	1,925	D	41.3%	44.6%	13.7%
3,801	CLINCH	1,837	790	759	286	2	31	R	43.0%	41.3%	15.6%
250,422	COBB	197,129	103,734	63,960	28,747	688	39,774	R	52.6%	32.4%	14.6%
13,277	COFFEE	8,339	3,778	3,275	1,256	30	503	R	45.3%	39.3%	15.1%
14,556	COLQUITT	10,276	4,680	3,891	1,682	23	789	R	45.5%	37.9%	16.4%
35,488	COLUMBIA	28,200	16,657	7,115	4,379	49	9,542	R	59.1%	25.2%	15.5%
6,000	COOK	3,605	1,318	1,731	537	19	413	D	36.6%	48.0%	14.9%
25,844	COWETA	20,552	9,814	7,093	3,587	58	2,721	R	47.8%	34.5%	17.5%
4,263	CRAWFORD	3,183	974	1,648	549	12	674	D	30.6%	51.8%	17.2%
8,530	CRISP	5,709	2,253	2,610	823	23	357	D	39.5%	45.7%	14.4%
6,695	DADE	4,804	2,191	1,782	823	8	409	R	45.6%	37.1%	17.1%
4,851	DAWSON	3,892	1,696	1,399	790	7	297	R	43.6%	35.9%	20.3%
10,981	DECATUR	7,419	3,142	3,198	1,068	11	56	D	42.4%	43.1%	14.4%
289,933	DE KALB	215,433	70,282	124,559	19,741	851	54,277	D	32.6%	57.8%	9.2%
10,251	DODGE	6,278	2,287	3,002	978	11	715	D	36.4%	47.8%	15.6%
4,838	DOOLY	3,387	1,034	1,993	350	10	959	D	30.5%	58.8%	10.3%
42,569	DOUGHERTY	30,931	12,455	15,236	3,178	62	2,781	D	40.3%	49.3%	10.3%
33,275	DOUGLAS	26,657	13,349	8,869	4,362	77	4,480	R	50.1%	33.3%	16.4%
5,519	EARLY	4,143	1,457	1,970	652	64	513	D	35.2%	47.6%	15.7%
1,439	ECHOLS	911	361	312	238		49	R	39.6%	34.2%	26.1%
11,193	EFFINGHAM	7,963	3,814	2,690	1,443	16	1,124	R	47.9%	33.8%	18.1%
8,895	ELBERT	6,167	2,372	3,025	757	13	653	D	38.5%	49.1%	12.3%
9,962	EMANUEL	6,425	2,662	2,951	755	57	289	D	41.4%	45.9%	11.8%
4,564	EVANS	2,960	1,244	1,230	480	6	14	R	42.0%	41.6%	16.2%
9,961	FANNIN	7,195	3,255	2,902	1,028	10	353	R	45.2%	40.3%	14.3%
38,466	FAYETTE	31,687	17,576	8,430	5,598	83	9,146	R	55.5%	26.6%	17.7%
35,475	FLOYD	27,860	12,378	11,614	3,779	89	764	R	44.4%	41.7%	13.6%
21,517	FORSYTH	17,086	8,652	4,936	3,453	45	3,716	R	50.6%	28.9%	20.2%
8,837	FRANKLIN	5,923	2,391	2,505	1,014	13	114	D	40.4%	42.3%	17.1%
367,710	FULTON	257,406	85,451	147,459	23,578	918	62,008	D	33.2%	57.3%	9.2%

GEORGIA

PRESIDENT 1992

Registration	County	Total Vote	Republican	Democratic	Perot	Other	Plurality	Percentage Total Vote Rep.	Dem.	Perot
8,043	GILMER	5,888	2,661	2,311	879	37	350 R	45.2%	39.2%	14.9%
1,517	GLASCOCK	1,013	516	316	180	1	200 R	50.9%	31.2%	17.8%
33,156	GLYNN	22,932	11,242	8,581	3,053	56	2,661 R	49.0%	37.4%	13.3%
18,688	GORDON	11,213	5,265	4,103	1,818	27	1,162 R	47.0%	36.6%	16.2%
8,598	GRADY	6,033	2,370	2,520	1,126	17	150 D	39.3%	41.8%	18.7%
5,718	GREENE	4,058	1,307	2,259	483	9	952 D	32.2%	55.7%	11.9%
188,754	GWINNETT	150,576	81,822	44,253	23,926	575	37,569 R	54.3%	29.4%	15.9%
11,811	HABERSHAM	9,134	4,569	3,098	1,444	23	1,471 R	50.0%	33.9%	15.8%
41,087	HALL	32,433	16,108	11,214	5,043	68	4,894 R	49.7%	34.6%	15.5%
5,329	HANCOCK	3,157	506	2,461	189	1	1,955 D	16.0%	78.0%	6.0%
11,350	HARALSON	7,621	3,142	3,281	1,167	31	139 D	41.2%	43.1%	15.3%
9,702	HARRIS	6,960	3,316	2,679	954	11	637 R	47.6%	38.5%	13.7%
10,442	HART	7,609	2,607	3,614	1,376	12	1,007 D	34.3%	47.5%	18.1%
4,749	HEARD	3,273	1,190	1,456	617	10	266 D	36.4%	44.5%	18.9%
30,658	HENRY	24,284	12,634	7,817	3,769	64	4,817 R	52.0%	32.2%	15.5%
42,601	HOUSTON	32,748	14,119	12,270	6,263	96	1,849 R	43.1%	37.5%	19.1%
4,044	IRWIN	2,820	973	1,366	465	16	393 D	34.5%	48.4%	16.5%
13,340	JACKSON	9,165	3,976	3,792	1,381	16	184 R	43.4%	41.4%	15.1%
4,318	JASPER	3,023	1,153	1,485	373	12	332 D	38.1%	49.1%	12.3%
6,760	JEFF DAVIS	4,952	1,947	2,031	958	16	84 D	39.3%	41.0%	19.3%
8,754	JEFFERSON	5,989	2,077	3,220	685	7	1,143 D	34.7%	53.8%	11.4%
4,436	JENKINS	2,728	929	1,401	394	4	472 D	34.1%	51.4%	14.4%
4,907	JOHNSON	3,295	1,314	1,473	502	6	159 D	39.9%	44.7%	15.2%
10,862	JONES	7,279	2,770	3,338	1,159	12	568 D	38.1%	45.9%	15.9%
6,434	LAMAR	4,410	1,707	2,065	600	38	358 D	38.7%	46.8%	13.6%
2,875	LANIER	1,713	600	811	298	4	211 D	35.0%	47.3%	17.4%
18,796	LAURENS	14,059	6,146	6,184	1,602	127	38 D	43.7%	44.0%	11.4%
8,080	LEE	5,908	3,061	1,811	1,024	12	1,250 R	51.8%	30.7%	17.3%
11,041	LIBERTY	7,895	2,832	3,853	1,176	34	1,021 D	35.9%	48.8%	14.9%
4,555	LINCOLN	2,958	1,149	1,327	479	3	178 D	38.8%	44.9%	16.2%
2,875	LONG	1,957	719	874	355	9	155 D	36.7%	44.7%	18.1%
30,564	LOWNDES	22,192	10,276	9,019	2,864	33	1,257 R	46.3%	40.6%	12.9%
6,988	LUMPKIN	5,036	1,972	2,010	1,035	19	38 D	39.2%	39.9%	20.6%
9,848	MCDUFFIE	6,468	2,955	2,640	860	13	315 R	45.7%	40.8%	13.3%
5,103	MCINTOSH	3,517	1,027	1,925	550	15	898 D	29.2%	54.7%	15.6%
6,692	MACON	3,806	944	2,491	363	8	1,547 D	24.8%	65.4%	9.5%
9,056	MADISON	6,893	3,351	2,393	1,129	20	958 R	48.6%	34.7%	16.4%
3,051	MARION	2,056	711	1,145	198	2	434 D	34.6%	55.7%	9.6%
10,910	MERIWETHER	7,320	2,364	4,002	942	12	1,638 D	32.3%	54.7%	12.9%
3,296	MILLER	2,217	826	934	455	2	108 D	37.3%	42.1%	20.5%
8,873	MITCHELL	5,795	1,917	3,052	818	8	1,135 D	33.1%	52.7%	14.1%
8,476	MONROE	6,168	2,423	2,774	949	22	351 D	39.3%	45.0%	15.4%
4,176	MONTGOMERY	2,617	1,009	1,185	416	7	176 D	38.6%	45.3%	15.9%
7,228	MORGAN	4,455	1,797	2,057	596	5	260 D	40.3%	46.2%	13.4%
10,977	MURRAY	7,214	3,256	2,764	1,186	8	492 R	45.1%	38.3%	16.4%
71,038	MUSCOGEE	51,280	21,386	25,476	4,327	91	4,090 D	41.7%	49.7%	8.4%
17,635	NEWTON	13,659	5,804	5,811	1,998	46	7 D	42.5%	42.5%	14.6%
10,020	OCONEE	8,076	4,125	2,745	1,182	24	1,380 R	51.1%	34.0%	14.6%
4,921	OGLETHORPE	3,703	1,590	1,491	620	2	99 R	42.9%	40.3%	16.7%
19,160	PAULDING	15,088	7,180	5,212	2,654	42	1,968 R	47.6%	34.5%	17.6%
9,508	PEACH	6,973	2,327	3,677	947	22	1,350 D	33.4%	52.7%	13.6%
7,428	PICKENS	5,748	2,332	2,359	1,037	20	27 D	40.6%	41.0%	18.0%
6,726	PIERCE	4,472	1,899	1,852	708	13	47 R	42.5%	41.4%	15.8%
5,304	PIKE	4,104	1,822	1,651	623	8	171 R	44.4%	40.2%	15.2%
14,221	POLK	10,668	4,158	4,872	1,598	40	714 D	39.0%	45.7%	15.0%
4,920	PULASKI	3,451	1,075	1,756	614	6	681 D	31.2%	50.9%	17.8%
6,657	PUTNAM	4,694	1,756	2,149	775	14	393 D	37.4%	45.8%	16.5%
1,406	QUITMAN	922	284	523	113	2	239 D	30.8%	56.7%	12.3%
6,401	RABUN	4,622	1,902	1,878	825	17	24 R	41.2%	40.6%	17.8%
4,492	RANDOLPH	2,959	887	1,756	315	1	869 D	30.0%	59.3%	10.6%

GEORGIA

PRESIDENT 1992

Registration	County	Total Vote	Republican	Democratic	Perot	Other	Plurality	Percentage Total Vote		
								Rep.	Dem.	Perot
84,215	RICHMOND	59,523	24,227	28,910	6,290	96	4,683 D	40.7%	48.6%	10.6%
28,980	ROCKDALE	22,690	11,945	7,003	3,664	78	4,942 R	52.6%	30.9%	16.1%
1,839	SCHLEY	1,296	511	601	180	4	90 D	39.4%	46.4%	13.9%
7,633	SCREVEN	4,366	1,705	1,940	709	12	235 D	39.1%	44.4%	16.2%
5,121	SEMINOLE	2,519	850	1,193	468	8	343 D	33.7%	47.4%	18.6%
22,989	SPALDING	15,734	7,262	6,392	2,044	36	870 R	46.2%	40.6%	13.0%
11,846	STEPHENS	8,493	4,047	2,976	1,448	22	1,071 R	47.7%	35.0%	17.0%
3,727	STEWART	2,909	1,186	1,540	175	8	354 D	40.8%	52.9%	6.0%
14,655	SUMTER	9,168	3,616	4,489	1,046	17	873 D	39.4%	49.0%	11.4%
4,677	TALBOT	2,682	671	1,768	238	5	1,097 D	25.0%	65.9%	8.9%
1,553	TALIAFERRO	1,106	269	755	80	2	486 D	24.3%	68.3%	7.2%
9,156	TATTNALL	5,942	2,566	2,360	996	20	206 R	43.2%	39.7%	16.8%
4,501	TAYLOR	2,872	1,078	1,508	281	5	430 D	37.5%	52.5%	9.8%
6,493	TELFAIR	4,192	1,324	2,238	613	17	914 D	31.6%	53.4%	14.6%
5,866	TERRELL	3,474	1,143	1,942	384	5	799 D	32.9%	55.9%	11.1%
17,122	THOMAS	11,948	5,500	4,841	1,591	16	659 R	46.0%	40.5%	13.3%
12,683	TIFT	9,569	4,485	3,930	1,139	15	555 R	46.9%	41.1%	11.9%
11,239	TOOMBS	7,490	3,609	2,648	1,210	23	961 R	48.2%	35.4%	16.2%
4,878	TOWNS	3,704	1,674	1,487	537	6	187 R	45.2%	40.1%	14.5%
3,837	TREUTLEN	2,344	898	1,116	318	12	218 D	38.3%	47.6%	13.6%
23,372	TROUP	17,039	8,118	6,412	2,488	21	1,706 R	47.6%	37.6%	14.6%
4,000	TURNER	3,024	936	1,669	370	49	733 D	31.0%	55.2%	12.2%
5,290	TWIGGS	3,392	853	2,097	432	10	1,244 D	25.1%	61.8%	12.7%
7,769	UNION	5,656	2,533	2,304	804	15	229 R	44.8%	40.7%	14.2%
13,372	UPSON	9,001	4,053	3,740	1,186	22	313 R	45.0%	41.6%	13.2%
23,368	WALKER	17,488	8,489	6,217	2,748	34	2,272 R	48.5%	35.6%	15.7%
17,053	WALTON	12,391	5,619	4,821	1,923	28	798 R	45.3%	38.9%	15.5%
14,733	WARE	10,424	4,573	4,573	1,263	15		43.9%	43.9%	12.1%
3,375	WARREN	2,175	751	1,239	180	5	488 D	34.5%	57.0%	8.3%
9,538	WASHINGTON	6,725	2,384	3,508	820	13	1,124 D	35.4%	52.2%	12.2%
10,736	WAYNE	7,552	3,381	3,052	1,107	12	329 R	44.8%	40.4%	14.7%
1,287	WEBSTER	911	208	600	103		392 D	22.8%	65.9%	11.3%
3,701	WHEELER	1,699	601	880	214	4	279 D	35.4%	51.8%	12.6%
7,193	WHITE	5,229	2,477	1,756	981	15	721 R	47.4%	33.6%	18.8%
29,186	WHITFIELD	22,239	12,003	7,335	2,866	35	4,668 R	54.0%	33.0%	12.9%
4,519	WILCOX	2,723	916	1,365	433	9	449 D	33.6%	50.1%	15.9%
5,359	WILKES	3,962	1,535	1,955	464	8	420 D	38.7%	49.3%	11.7%
5,468	WILKINSON	4,072	1,232	2,286	520	34	1,054 D	30.3%	56.1%	12.8%
8,580	WORTH	5,837	2,344	2,578	905	10	234 D	40.2%	44.2%	15.5%
3,177,061	TOTAL	2,321,125	995,252	1,008,966	309,657	7,250	13,714 D	42.9%	43.5%	13.3%

GEORGIA

SENATOR 1992
(NOVEMBER GENERAL ELECTION)

| | | | | | | | Percentage | | | |
| | | | | | | | Total Vote | | Major Vote | |
Registration	County	Total Vote	Republican	Democratic	Other	Rep.-Dem. Plurality	Rep.	Dem.	Rep.	Dem.
9,193	APPLING	5,192	2,616	2,413	163	203 R	50.4%	46.5%	52.0%	48.0%
3,862	ATKINSON	1,665	533	1,059	73	526 D	32.0%	63.6%	33.5%	66.5%
5,033	BACON	2,706	1,129	1,441	136	312 D	41.7%	53.3%	43.9%	56.1%
2,409	BAKER	1,229	308	881	40	573 D	25.1%	71.7%	25.9%	74.1%
15,534	BALDWIN	10,319	4,006	5,956	357	1,950 D	38.8%	57.7%	40.2%	59.8%
5,019	BANKS	3,712	1,729	1,814	169	85 D	46.6%	48.9%	48.8%	51.2%
13,497	BARROW	10,007	5,027	4,473	507	554 R	50.2%	44.7%	52.9%	47.1%
22,923	BARTOW	15,195	7,986	6,657	552	1,329 R	52.6%	43.8%	54.5%	45.5%
7,573	BEN HILL	4,332	1,404	2,796	132	1,392 D	32.4%	64.5%	33.4%	66.6%
6,958	BERRIEN	4,755	1,771	2,797	187	1,026 D	37.2%	58.8%	38.8%	61.2%
72,042	BIBB	53,688	19,779	32,778	1,131	12,999 D	36.8%	61.1%	37.6%	62.4%
5,743	BLECKLEY	3,393	1,272	1,995	126	723 D	37.5%	58.8%	38.9%	61.1%
6,593	BRANTLEY	3,564	1,437	2,000	127	563 D	40.3%	56.1%	41.8%	58.2%
6,232	BROOKS	3,680	1,418	2,163	99	745 D	38.5%	58.8%	39.6%	60.4%
8,644	BRYAN	5,267	2,933	2,207	127	726 R	55.7%	41.9%	57.1%	42.9%
18,691	BULLOCH	12,536	6,349	5,839	348	510 R	50.6%	46.6%	52.1%	47.9%
10,259	BURKE	5,903	2,853	2,866	184	13 D	48.3%	48.6%	49.9%	50.1%
7,024	BUTTS	4,814	1,894	2,781	139	887 D	39.3%	57.8%	40.5%	59.5%
2,935	CALHOUN	2,085	434	1,617	34	1,183 D	20.8%	77.6%	21.2%	78.8%
10,906	CAMDEN	6,147	3,041	2,970	136	71 R	49.5%	48.3%	50.6%	49.4%
4,137	CANDLER	2,348	1,052	1,224	72	172 D	44.8%	52.1%	46.2%	53.8%
29,871	CARROLL	22,526	11,742	10,009	775	1,733 R	52.1%	44.4%	54.0%	46.0%
19,607	CATOOSA	14,603	9,322	4,867	414	4,455 R	63.8%	33.3%	65.7%	34.3%
4,373	CHARLTON	1,953	790	1,043	120	253 D	40.5%	53.4%	43.1%	56.9%
97,549	CHATHAM	67,303	32,633	33,189	1,481	556 D	48.5%	49.3%	49.6%	50.4%
2,002	CHATTAHOOCHEE	965	403	525	37	122 D	41.8%	54.4%	43.4%	56.6%
10,060	CHATTOOGA	6,434	3,064	3,114	256	50 D	47.6%	48.4%	49.6%	50.4%
42,301	CHEROKEE	28,714	18,203	9,639	872	8,564 R	63.4%	33.6%	65.4%	34.6%
39,609	CLARKE	27,597	10,881	15,444	1,272	4,563 D	39.4%	56.0%	41.3%	58.7%
1,826	CLAY	1,093	295	769	29	474 D	27.0%	70.4%	27.7%	72.3%
75,280	CLAYTON	57,639	26,766	28,682	2,191	1,916 D	46.4%	49.8%	48.3%	51.7%
3,801	CLINCH	1,383	440	892	51	452 D	31.8%	64.5%	33.0%	67.0%
250,422	COBB	195,375	115,558	73,213	6,604	42,345 R	59.1%	37.5%	61.2%	38.8%
13,277	COFFEE	6,947	2,996	3,582	369	586 D	43.1%	51.6%	45.5%	54.5%
14,556	COLQUITT	9,535	4,463	4,779	293	316 D	46.8%	50.1%	48.3%	51.7%
35,488	COLUMBIA	28,159	19,686	7,639	834	12,047 R	69.9%	27.1%	72.0%	28.0%
6,000	COOK	3,788	1,364	2,327	97	963 D	36.0%	61.4%	37.0%	63.0%
25,844	COWETA	20,525	11,405	8,404	716	3,001 R	55.6%	40.9%	57.6%	42.4%
4,263	CRAWFORD	2,779	939	1,745	95	806 D	33.8%	62.8%	35.0%	65.0%
8,530	CRISP	5,123	1,899	3,050	174	1,151 D	37.1%	59.5%	38.4%	61.6%
6,695	DADE	3,796	2,459	1,208	129	1,251 R	64.8%	31.8%	67.1%	32.9%
4,851	DAWSON	3,799	2,013	1,704	82	309 R	53.0%	44.9%	54.2%	45.8%
10,981	DECATUR	6,436	2,650	3,566	220	916 D	41.2%	55.4%	42.6%	57.4%
289,933	DE KALB	214,586	77,573	130,372	6,641	52,799 D	36.2%	60.8%	37.3%	62.7%
10,251	DODGE	5,204	1,705	3,313	186	1,608 D	32.8%	63.7%	34.0%	66.0%
4,838	DOOLY	2,799	702	2,004	93	1,302 D	25.1%	71.6%	25.9%	74.1%
42,569	DOUGHERTY	31,215	13,225	17,355	635	4,130 D	42.4%	55.6%	43.2%	56.8%
33,275	DOUGLAS	26,563	14,931	10,626	1,006	4,305 R	56.2%	40.0%	58.4%	41.6%
5,519	EARLY	3,925	1,111	2,718	96	1,607 D	28.3%	69.2%	29.0%	71.0%
1,439	ECHOLS	690	227	439	24	212 D	32.9%	63.6%	34.1%	65.9%
11,193	EFFINGHAM	7,468	4,197	3,070	201	1,127 R	56.2%	41.1%	57.8%	42.2%
8,895	ELBERT	5,853	2,227	3,549	77	1,322 D	38.0%	60.6%	38.6%	61.4%
9,962	EMANUEL	5,272	2,676	2,480	116	196 R	50.8%	47.0%	51.9%	48.1%
4,564	EVANS	2,655	1,296	1,281	78	15 R	48.8%	48.2%	50.3%	49.7%
9,961	FANNIN	7,200	4,248	2,764	188	1,484 R	59.0%	38.4%	60.6%	39.4%
38,466	FAYETTE	31,548	20,375	10,149	1,024	10,226 R	64.6%	32.2%	66.8%	33.2%
35,475	FLOYD	27,846	13,484	13,595	767	111 D	48.4%	48.8%	49.8%	50.2%
21,517	FORSYTH	17,099	10,133	6,314	652	3,819 R	59.3%	36.9%	61.6%	38.4%
8,837	FRANKLIN	5,998	2,544	3,222	232	678 D	42.4%	53.7%	44.1%	55.9%
367,710	FULTON	257,825	95,001	155,975	6,849	60,974 D	36.8%	60.5%	37.9%	62.1%

GEORGIA

SENATOR 1992
(NOVEMBER GENERAL ELECTION)

Registration	County	Total Vote	Republican	Democratic	Other	Rep.-Dem. Plurality	Percentage Total Vote Rep.	Dem.	Major Vote Rep.	Dem.
8,043	GILMER	5,127	2,911	1,998	218	913 R	56.8%	39.0%	59.3%	40.7%
1,517	GLASCOCK	820	476	310	34	166 R	58.0%	37.8%	60.6%	39.4%
33,156	GLYNN	22,904	12,299	10,100	505	2,199 R	53.7%	44.1%	54.9%	45.1%
18,688	GORDON	9,925	5,291	4,323	311	968 R	53.3%	43.6%	55.0%	45.0%
8,598	GRADY	5,072	2,050	2,851	171	801 D	40.4%	56.2%	41.8%	58.2%
5,718	GREENE	4,050	1,454	2,464	132	1,010 D	35.9%	60.8%	37.1%	62.9%
188,754	GWINNETT	149,400	92,467	51,543	5,390	40,924 R	61.9%	34.5%	64.2%	35.8%
11,811	HABERSHAM	8,740	4,709	3,819	212	890 R	53.9%	43.7%	55.2%	44.8%
41,087	HALL	32,746	17,298	14,476	972	2,822 R	52.8%	44.2%	54.4%	45.6%
5,329	HANCOCK	2,396	398	1,875	123	1,477 D	16.6%	78.3%	17.5%	82.5%
11,350	HARALSON	7,675	3,493	3,859	323	366 D	45.5%	50.3%	47.5%	52.5%
9,702	HARRIS	6,278	3,294	2,805	179	489 R	52.5%	44.7%	54.0%	46.0%
10,442	HART	6,193	2,329	3,503	361	1,174 D	37.6%	56.6%	39.9%	60.1%
4,749	HEARD	3,242	1,369	1,721	152	352 D	42.2%	53.1%	44.3%	55.7%
30,658	HENRY	24,610	14,381	9,424	805	4,957 R	58.4%	38.3%	60.4%	39.6%
42,601	HOUSTON	32,503	15,035	16,426	1,042	1,391 D	46.3%	50.5%	47.8%	52.2%
4,044	IRWIN	2,606	853	1,688	65	835 D	32.7%	64.8%	33.6%	66.4%
13,340	JACKSON	9,120	4,328	4,405	387	77 D	47.5%	48.3%	49.6%	50.4%
4,318	JASPER	2,797	1,191	1,509	97	318 D	42.6%	54.0%	44.1%	55.9%
6,760	JEFF DAVIS	4,060	2,056	1,862	142	194 R	50.6%	45.9%	52.5%	47.5%
8,754	JEFFERSON	5,014	2,256	2,603	155	347 D	45.0%	51.9%	46.4%	53.6%
4,436	JENKINS	2,419	1,195	1,133	91	62 R	49.4%	46.8%	51.3%	48.7%
4,907	JOHNSON	2,782	928	1,821	33	893 D	33.4%	65.5%	33.8%	66.2%
10,862	JONES	6,771	2,617	3,964	190	1,347 D	38.7%	58.5%	39.8%	60.2%
6,434	LAMAR	4,160	1,774	2,293	93	519 D	42.6%	55.1%	43.6%	56.4%
2,875	LANIER	1,355	429	870	56	441 D	31.7%	64.2%	33.0%	67.0%
18,796	LAURENS	11,627	4,375	6,858	394	2,483 D	37.6%	59.0%	38.9%	61.1%
8,080	LEE	5,803	3,167	2,466	170	701 R	54.6%	42.5%	56.2%	43.8%
11,041	LIBERTY	6,778	2,935	3,565	278	630 D	43.3%	52.6%	45.2%	54.8%
4,555	LINCOLN	3,019	1,527	1,378	114	149 R	50.6%	45.6%	52.6%	47.4%
2,875	LONG	1,660	745	838	77	93 D	44.9%	50.5%	47.1%	52.9%
30,564	LOWNDES	22,031	10,289	11,300	442	1,011 D	46.7%	51.3%	47.7%	52.3%
6,988	LUMPKIN	5,044	2,430	2,395	219	35 R	48.2%	47.5%	50.4%	49.6%
9,848	MCDUFFIE	5,925	3,119	2,579	227	540 R	52.6%	43.5%	54.7%	45.3%
5,103	MCINTOSH	3,061	1,120	1,858	83	738 D	36.6%	60.7%	37.6%	62.4%
6,692	MACON	3,418	967	2,322	129	1,355 D	28.3%	67.9%	29.4%	70.6%
9,056	MADISON	6,256	3,138	2,696	422	442 R	50.2%	43.1%	53.8%	46.2%
3,051	MARION	1,928	698	1,165	65	467 D	36.2%	60.4%	37.5%	62.5%
10,910	MERIWETHER	7,476	2,731	4,532	213	1,801 D	36.5%	60.6%	37.6%	62.4%
3,296	MILLER	1,850	590	1,206	54	616 D	31.9%	65.2%	32.9%	67.1%
8,873	MITCHELL	6,016	1,778	4,095	143	2,317 D	29.6%	68.1%	30.3%	69.7%
8,476	MONROE	6,236	2,554	3,420	262	866 D	41.0%	54.8%	42.8%	57.2%
4,176	MONTGOMERY	2,330	1,033	1,265	32	232 D	44.3%	54.3%	45.0%	55.0%
7,228	MORGAN	4,495	1,969	2,369	157	400 D	43.8%	52.7%	45.4%	54.6%
10,977	MURRAY	7,119	4,075	2,789	255	1,286 R	57.2%	39.2%	59.4%	40.6%
71,038	MUSCOGEE	51,011	21,568	28,164	1,279	6,596 D	42.3%	55.2%	43.4%	56.6%
17,635	NEWTON	13,479	6,468	6,498	513	30 D	48.0%	48.2%	49.9%	50.1%
10,020	OCONEE	7,976	4,410	3,222	344	1,188 R	55.3%	40.4%	57.8%	42.2%
4,921	OGLETHORPE	3,627	1,848	1,573	206	275 R	51.0%	43.4%	54.0%	46.0%
19,160	PAULDING	14,995	8,350	6,027	618	2,323 R	55.7%	40.2%	58.1%	41.9%
9,508	PEACH	6,479	2,204	4,061	214	1,857 D	34.0%	62.7%	35.2%	64.8%
7,428	PICKENS	5,194	2,459	2,521	214	62 D	47.3%	48.5%	49.4%	50.6%
6,726	PIERCE	4,002	1,659	2,241	102	582 D	41.5%	56.0%	42.5%	57.5%
5,304	PIKE	4,036	2,071	1,822	143	249 R	51.3%	45.1%	53.2%	46.8%
14,221	POLK	9,763	4,350	5,141	272	791 D	44.6%	52.7%	45.8%	54.2%
4,920	PULASKI	2,991	893	2,005	93	1,112 D	29.9%	67.0%	30.8%	69.2%
6,657	PUTNAM	4,347	1,830	2,354	163	524 D	42.1%	54.2%	43.7%	56.3%
1,406	QUITMAN	653	217	417	19	200 D	33.2%	63.9%	34.2%	65.8%
6,401	RABUN	4,274	2,092	2,059	123	33 R	48.9%	48.2%	50.4%	49.6%
4,492	RANDOLPH	2,768	762	1,979	27	1,217 D	27.5%	71.5%	27.8%	72.2%

GEORGIA

SENATOR 1992
(NOVEMBER GENERAL ELECTION)

| | | | | | | | Percentage | | | |
| | | | | | | | Total Vote | | Major Vote | |
Registration	County	Total Vote	Republican	Democratic	Other	Rep.-Dem. Plurality	Rep.	Dem.	Rep.	Dem.
84,215	RICHMOND	59,718	28,439	29,608	1,671	1,169 D	47.6%	49.6%	49.0%	51.0%
28,980	ROCKDALE	22,680	13,544	8,362	774	5,182 R	59.7%	36.9%	61.8%	38.2%
1,839	SCHLEY	1,154	491	618	45	127 D	42.5%	53.6%	44.3%	55.7%
7,633	SCREVEN	3,453	1,765	1,569	119	196 R	51.1%	45.4%	52.9%	47.1%
5,121	SEMINOLE	2,791	923	1,783	85	860 D	33.1%	63.9%	34.1%	65.9%
22,989	SPALDING	14,779	8,019	6,292	468	1,727 R	54.3%	42.6%	56.0%	44.0%
11,846	STEPHENS	7,562	3,971	3,371	220	600 R	52.5%	44.6%	54.1%	45.9%
3,727	STEWART	1,808	556	1,183	69	627 D	30.8%	65.4%	32.0%	68.0%
14,655	SUMTER	8,133	3,202	4,717	214	1,515 D	39.4%	58.0%	40.4%	59.6%
4,677	TALBOT	1,939	590	1,274	75	684 D	30.4%	65.7%	31.7%	68.3%
1,553	TALIAFERRO	1,064	374	676	14	302 D	35.2%	63.5%	35.6%	64.4%
9,156	TATTNALL	5,138	2,338	2,649	151	311 D	45.5%	51.6%	46.9%	53.1%
4,501	TAYLOR	2,861	1,000	1,789	72	789 D	35.0%	62.5%	35.9%	64.1%
6,493	TELFAIR	3,316	1,031	2,160	125	1,129 D	31.1%	65.1%	32.3%	67.7%
5,866	TERRELL	3,013	907	2,024	82	1,117 D	30.1%	67.2%	30.9%	69.1%
17,122	THOMAS	11,980	5,913	5,840	227	73 R	49.4%	48.7%	50.3%	49.7%
12,683	TIFT	9,181	4,387	4,575	219	188 D	47.8%	49.8%	49.0%	51.0%
11,239	TOOMBS	6,482	3,737	2,584	161	1,153 R	57.7%	39.9%	59.1%	40.9%
4,878	TOWNS	3,458	1,732	1,660	66	72 R	50.1%	48.0%	51.1%	48.9%
3,837	TREUTLEN	1,868	728	1,123	17	395 D	39.0%	60.1%	39.3%	60.7%
23,372	TROUP	17,171	8,744	7,981	446	763 R	50.9%	46.5%	52.3%	47.7%
4,000	TURNER	2,873	836	1,978	59	1,142 D	29.1%	68.8%	29.7%	70.3%
5,290	TWIGGS	3,452	830	2,517	105	1,687 D	24.0%	72.9%	24.8%	75.2%
7,769	UNION	5,467	2,781	2,526	160	255 R	50.9%	46.2%	52.4%	47.6%
13,372	UPSON	9,234	4,290	4,682	262	392 D	46.5%	50.7%	47.8%	52.2%
23,368	WALKER	16,886	10,546	5,856	484	4,690 R	62.5%	34.7%	64.3%	35.7%
17,053	WALTON	11,726	5,973	5,250	503	723 R	50.9%	44.8%	53.2%	46.8%
14,733	WARE	9,194	3,741	5,224	229	1,483 D	40.7%	56.8%	41.7%	58.3%
3,375	WARREN	1,756	722	986	48	264 D	41.1%	56.2%	42.3%	57.7%
9,538	WASHINGTON	5,829	2,020	3,609	200	1,589 D	34.7%	61.9%	35.9%	64.1%
10,736	WAYNE	7,660	4,019	3,399	242	620 R	52.5%	44.4%	54.2%	45.8%
1,287	WEBSTER	697	172	502	23	330 D	24.7%	72.0%	25.5%	74.5%
3,701	WHEELER	1,442	524	912	6	388 D	36.3%	63.2%	36.5%	63.5%
7,193	WHITE	5,187	2,922	2,067	198	855 R	56.3%	39.8%	58.6%	41.4%
29,186	WHITFIELD	22,129	13,815	7,782	532	6,033 R	62.4%	35.2%	64.0%	36.0%
4,519	WILCOX	2,413	696	1,678	39	982 D	28.8%	69.5%	29.3%	70.7%
5,359	WILKES	3,384	1,518	1,749	117	231 D	44.9%	51.7%	46.5%	53.5%
5,468	WILKINSON	3,346	1,087	2,166	93	1,079 D	32.5%	64.7%	33.4%	66.6%
8,580	WORTH	6,176	2,500	3,527	149	1,027 D	40.5%	57.1%	41.5%	58.5%
3,177,061	TOTAL	2,251,587	1,073,282	1,108,416	69,889	35,134 D	47.7%	49.2%	49.2%	50.8%

GEORGIA

SENATOR 1992
(NOVEMBER 24 RUN-OFF ELECTION)

Registration	County	Total Vote	Republican	Democratic	Other	Rep.-Dem. Plurality	Percentage			
							Total Vote		Major Vote	
							Rep.	Dem.	Rep.	Dem.
9,193	APPLING	2,748	1,493	1,255		238 R	54.3%	45.7%	54.3%	45.7%
3,862	ATKINSON	1,024	413	611		198 D	40.3%	59.7%	40.3%	59.7%
5,033	BACON	1,301	665	636		29 R	51.1%	48.9%	51.1%	48.9%
2,409	BAKER	874	205	669		464 D	23.5%	76.5%	23.5%	76.5%
15,534	BALDWIN	6,474	2,982	3,492		510 D	46.1%	53.9%	46.1%	53.9%
5,019	BANKS	1,758	902	856		46 R	51.3%	48.7%	51.3%	48.7%
13,497	BARROW	4,812	2,491	2,321		170 R	51.8%	48.2%	51.8%	48.2%
22,923	BARTOW	8,039	4,192	3,847		345 R	52.1%	47.9%	52.1%	47.9%
7,573	BEN HILL	2,067	733	1,334		601 D	35.5%	64.5%	35.5%	64.5%
6,958	BERRIEN	2,242	851	1,391		540 D	38.0%	62.0%	38.0%	62.0%
72,042	BIBB	33,786	14,098	19,688		5,590 D	41.7%	58.3%	41.7%	58.3%
5,743	BLECKLEY	1,987	947	1,040		93 D	47.7%	52.3%	47.7%	52.3%
6,593	BRANTLEY	1,914	932	982		50 D	48.7%	51.3%	48.7%	51.3%
6,232	BROOKS	2,342	1,045	1,297		252 D	44.6%	55.4%	44.6%	55.4%
8,644	BRYAN	2,890	1,714	1,176		538 R	59.3%	40.7%	59.3%	40.7%
18,691	BULLOCH	6,951	3,790	3,161		629 R	54.5%	45.5%	54.5%	45.5%
10,259	BURKE	4,101	2,049	2,052		3 D	50.0%	50.0%	50.0%	50.0%
7,024	BUTTS	2,637	1,093	1,544		451 D	41.4%	58.6%	41.4%	58.6%
2,935	CALHOUN	1,270	221	1,049		828 D	17.4%	82.6%	17.4%	82.6%
10,906	CAMDEN	3,064	1,817	1,247		570 R	59.3%	40.7%	59.3%	40.7%
4,137	CANDLER	1,463	752	711		41 R	51.4%	48.6%	51.4%	48.6%
29,871	CARROLL	12,076	6,570	5,506		1,064 R	54.4%	45.6%	54.4%	45.6%
19,607	CATOOSA	7,802	5,563	2,239		3,324 R	71.3%	28.7%	71.3%	28.7%
4,373	CHARLTON	1,076	681	395		286 R	63.3%	36.7%	63.3%	36.7%
97,549	CHATHAM	42,567	21,143	21,424		281 D	49.7%	50.3%	49.7%	50.3%
2,002	CHATTAHOOCHEE	446	196	250		54 D	43.9%	56.1%	43.9%	56.1%
10,060	CHATTOOGA	3,266	1,704	1,562		142 R	52.2%	47.8%	52.2%	47.8%
42,301	CHEROKEE	15,649	10,147	5,502		4,645 R	64.8%	35.2%	64.8%	35.2%
39,609	CLARKE	16,991	7,118	9,873		2,755 D	41.9%	58.1%	41.9%	58.1%
1,826	CLAY	630	137	493		356 D	21.7%	78.3%	21.7%	78.3%
75,280	CLAYTON	29,230	14,111	15,119		1,008 D	48.3%	51.7%	48.3%	51.7%
3,801	CLINCH	751	357	394		37 D	47.5%	52.5%	47.5%	52.5%
250,422	COBB	99,540	62,071	37,469		24,602 R	62.4%	37.6%	62.4%	37.6%
13,277	COFFEE	3,845	1,870	1,975		105 D	48.6%	51.4%	48.6%	51.4%
14,556	COLQUITT	5,748	2,701	3,047		346 D	47.0%	53.0%	47.0%	53.0%
35,488	COLUMBIA	16,549	13,041	3,508		9,533 R	78.8%	21.2%	78.8%	21.2%
6,000	COOK	1,991	690	1,301		611 D	34.7%	65.3%	34.7%	65.3%
25,844	COWETA	10,541	6,303	4,238		2,065 R	59.8%	40.2%	59.8%	40.2%
4,263	CRAWFORD	1,762	733	1,029		296 D	41.6%	58.4%	41.6%	58.4%
8,530	CRISP	2,818	1,172	1,646		474 D	41.6%	58.4%	41.6%	58.4%
6,695	DADE	2,135	1,557	578		979 R	72.9%	27.1%	72.9%	27.1%
4,851	DAWSON	1,748	977	771		206 R	55.9%	44.1%	55.9%	44.1%
10,981	DECATUR	3,824	1,903	1,921		18 D	49.8%	50.2%	49.8%	50.2%
289,933	DE KALB	124,015	47,702	76,313		28,611 D	38.5%	61.5%	38.5%	61.5%
10,251	DODGE	3,078	1,310	1,768		458 D	42.6%	57.4%	42.6%	57.4%
4,838	DOOLY	2,261	549	1,712		1,163 D	24.3%	75.7%	24.3%	75.7%
42,569	DOUGHERTY	19,347	8,660	10,687		2,027 D	44.8%	55.2%	44.8%	55.2%
33,275	DOUGLAS	12,334	7,129	5,205		1,924 R	57.8%	42.2%	57.8%	42.2%
5,519	EARLY	1,900	586	1,314		728 D	30.8%	69.2%	30.8%	69.2%
1,439	ECHOLS	312	158	154		4 R	50.6%	49.4%	50.6%	49.4%
11,193	EFFINGHAM	4,146	2,473	1,673		800 R	59.6%	40.4%	59.6%	40.4%
8,895	ELBERT	2,925	1,586	1,339		247 R	54.2%	45.8%	54.2%	45.8%
9,962	EMANUEL	3,096	1,772	1,324		448 R	57.2%	42.8%	57.2%	42.8%
4,564	EVANS	1,517	796	721		75 R	52.5%	47.5%	52.5%	47.5%
9,961	FANNIN	3,552	2,151	1,401		750 R	60.6%	39.4%	60.6%	39.4%
38,466	FAYETTE	18,307	12,542	5,765		6,777 R	68.5%	31.5%	68.5%	31.5%
35,475	FLOYD	18,316	8,917	9,399		482 D	48.7%	51.3%	48.7%	51.3%
21,517	FORSYTH	8,411	5,105	3,306		1,799 R	60.7%	39.3%	60.7%	39.3%
8,837	FRANKLIN	2,561	1,428	1,133		295 R	55.8%	44.2%	55.8%	44.2%
367,710	FULTON	143,987	53,965	90,022		36,057 D	37.5%	62.5%	37.5%	62.5%

GEORGIA

SENATOR 1992
(NOVEMBER 24 RUN-OFF ELECTION)

Registration	County	Total Vote	Republican	Democratic	Other	Rep.-Dem. Plurality	Percentage Total Vote Rep.	Dem.	Major Vote Rep.	Dem.
8,043	GILMER	3,722	1,988	1,734		254 R	53.4%	46.6%	53.4%	46.6%
1,517	GLASCOCK	528	379	149		230 R	71.8%	28.2%	71.8%	28.2%
33,156	GLYNN	13,049	7,888	5,161		2,727 R	60.4%	39.6%	60.4%	39.6%
18,688	GORDON	5,240	2,899	2,341		558 R	55.3%	44.7%	55.3%	44.7%
8,598	GRADY	3,046	1,362	1,684		322 D	44.7%	55.3%	44.7%	55.3%
5,718	GREENE	2,113	814	1,299		485 D	38.5%	61.5%	38.5%	61.5%
188,754	GWINNETT	73,728	47,523	26,205		21,318 R	64.5%	35.5%	64.5%	35.5%
11,811	HABERSHAM	5,015	2,830	2,185		645 R	56.4%	43.6%	56.4%	43.6%
41,087	HALL	16,488	9,310	7,178		2,132 R	56.5%	43.5%	56.5%	43.5%
5,329	HANCOCK	1,475	275	1,200		925 D	18.6%	81.4%	18.6%	81.4%
11,350	HARALSON	3,824	1,836	1,988		152 D	48.0%	52.0%	48.0%	52.0%
9,702	HARRIS	3,840	2,338	1,502		836 R	60.9%	39.1%	60.9%	39.1%
10,442	HART	3,070	1,711	1,359		352 R	55.7%	44.3%	55.7%	44.3%
4,749	HEARD	1,471	617	854		237 D	41.9%	58.1%	41.9%	58.1%
30,658	HENRY	13,001	7,936	5,065		2,871 R	61.0%	39.0%	61.0%	39.0%
42,601	HOUSTON	18,186	10,311	7,875		2,436 R	56.7%	43.3%	56.7%	43.3%
4,044	IRWIN	1,571	470	1,101		631 D	29.9%	70.1%	29.9%	70.1%
13,340	JACKSON	5,017	2,523	2,494		29 R	50.3%	49.7%	50.3%	49.7%
4,318	JASPER	1,898	872	1,026		154 D	45.9%	54.1%	45.9%	54.1%
6,760	JEFF DAVIS	1,848	1,074	774		300 R	58.1%	41.9%	58.1%	41.9%
8,754	JEFFERSON	3,569	1,768	1,801		33 D	49.5%	50.5%	49.5%	50.5%
4,436	JENKINS	1,307	696	611		85 R	53.3%	46.7%	53.3%	46.7%
4,907	JOHNSON	2,055	1,045	1,010		35 R	50.9%	49.1%	50.9%	49.1%
10,862	JONES	4,365	2,096	2,269		173 D	48.0%	52.0%	48.0%	52.0%
6,434	LAMAR	2,595	1,198	1,397		199 D	46.2%	53.8%	46.2%	53.8%
2,875	LANIER	737	287	450		163 D	38.9%	61.1%	38.9%	61.1%
18,796	LAURENS	7,505	3,667	3,838		171 D	48.9%	51.1%	48.9%	51.1%
8,080	LEE	3,301	1,929	1,372		557 R	58.4%	41.6%	58.4%	41.6%
11,041	LIBERTY	3,719	1,602	2,117		515 D	43.1%	56.9%	43.1%	56.9%
4,555	LINCOLN	1,467	890	577		313 R	60.7%	39.3%	60.7%	39.3%
2,875	LONG	861	370	491		121 D	43.0%	57.0%	43.0%	57.0%
30,564	LOWNDES	12,280	6,372	5,908		464 R	51.9%	48.1%	51.9%	48.1%
6,988	LUMPKIN	2,437	1,232	1,205		27 R	50.6%	49.4%	50.6%	49.4%
9,848	MCDUFFIE	3,873	2,521	1,352		1,169 R	65.1%	34.9%	65.1%	34.9%
5,103	MCINTOSH	1,834	739	1,095		356 D	40.3%	59.7%	40.3%	59.7%
6,692	MACON	2,427	705	1,722		1,017 D	29.0%	71.0%	29.0%	71.0%
9,056	MADISON	3,699	2,340	1,359		981 R	63.3%	36.7%	63.3%	36.7%
3,051	MARION	1,162	435	727		292 D	37.4%	62.6%	37.4%	62.6%
10,910	MERIWETHER	3,926	1,486	2,440		954 D	37.9%	62.1%	37.9%	62.1%
3,296	MILLER	915	351	564		213 D	38.4%	61.6%	38.4%	61.6%
8,873	MITCHELL	3,643	955	2,688		1,733 D	26.2%	73.8%	26.2%	73.8%
8,476	MONROE	3,714	1,790	1,924		134 D	48.2%	51.8%	48.2%	51.8%
4,176	MONTGOMERY	1,323	731	592		139 R	55.3%	44.7%	55.3%	44.7%
7,228	MORGAN	2,602	1,190	1,412		222 D	45.7%	54.3%	45.7%	54.3%
10,977	MURRAY	2,757	1,709	1,048		661 R	62.0%	38.0%	62.0%	38.0%
71,038	MUSCOGEE	29,633	13,860	15,773		1,913 D	46.8%	53.2%	46.8%	53.2%
17,635	NEWTON	7,553	3,574	3,979		405 D	47.3%	52.7%	47.3%	52.7%
10,020	OCONEE	4,866	2,828	2,038		790 R	58.1%	41.9%	58.1%	41.9%
4,921	OGLETHORPE	2,092	1,230	862		368 R	58.8%	41.2%	58.8%	41.2%
19,160	PAULDING	6,607	3,816	2,791		1,025 R	57.8%	42.2%	57.8%	42.2%
9,508	PEACH	4,477	1,842	2,635		793 D	41.1%	58.9%	41.1%	58.9%
7,428	PICKENS	4,345	1,999	2,346		347 D	46.0%	54.0%	46.0%	54.0%
6,726	PIERCE	2,172	1,072	1,100		28 D	49.4%	50.6%	49.4%	50.6%
5,304	PIKE	2,277	1,276	1,001		275 R	56.0%	44.0%	56.0%	44.0%
14,221	POLK	5,524	2,483	3,041		558 D	44.9%	55.1%	44.9%	55.1%
4,920	PULASKI	1,898	653	1,245		592 D	34.4%	65.6%	34.4%	65.6%
6,657	PUTNAM	2,579	1,167	1,412		245 D	45.3%	54.7%	45.3%	54.7%
1,406	QUITMAN	367	150	217		67 D	40.9%	59.1%	40.9%	59.1%
6,401	RABUN	2,369	1,308	1,061		247 R	55.2%	44.8%	55.2%	44.8%
4,492	RANDOLPH	1,628	402	1,226		824 D	24.7%	75.3%	24.7%	75.3%

GEORGIA

SENATOR 1992
(NOVEMBER 24 RUN-OFF ELECTION)

Registration	County	Total Vote	Republican	Democratic	Other	Rep.-Dem. Plurality	Percentage			
							Total Vote		Major Vote	
							Rep.	Dem.	Rep.	Dem.
84,215	RICHMOND	35,826	19,627	16,199		3,428 R	54.8%	45.2%	54.8%	45.2%
28,980	ROCKDALE	12,512	7,650	4,862		2,788 R	61.1%	38.9%	61.1%	38.9%
1,839	SCHLEY	648	307	341		34 D	47.4%	52.6%	47.4%	52.6%
7,633	SCREVEN	2,172	1,174	998		176 R	54.1%	45.9%	54.1%	45.9%
5,121	SEMINOLE	1,168	427	741		314 D	36.6%	63.4%	36.6%	63.4%
22,989	SPALDING	8,449	5,069	3,380		1,689 R	60.0%	40.0%	60.0%	40.0%
11,846	STEPHENS	4,081	2,463	1,618		845 R	60.4%	39.6%	60.4%	39.6%
3,727	STEWART	1,298	370	928		558 D	28.5%	71.5%	28.5%	71.5%
14,655	SUMTER	4,580	1,841	2,739		898 D	40.2%	59.8%	40.2%	59.8%
4,677	TALBOT	1,305	431	874		443 D	33.0%	67.0%	33.0%	67.0%
1,553	TALIAFERRO	527	172	355		183 D	32.6%	67.4%	32.6%	67.4%
9,156	TATTNALL	2,821	1,384	1,437		53 D	49.1%	50.9%	49.1%	50.9%
4,501	TAYLOR	1,606	728	878		150 D	45.3%	54.7%	45.3%	54.7%
6,493	TELFAIR	1,814	653	1,161		508 D	36.0%	64.0%	36.0%	64.0%
5,866	TERRELL	2,018	620	1,398		778 D	30.7%	69.3%	30.7%	69.3%
17,122	THOMAS	6,812	3,638	3,174		464 R	53.4%	46.6%	53.4%	46.6%
12,683	TIFT	5,352	2,505	2,847		342 D	46.8%	53.2%	46.8%	53.2%
11,239	TOOMBS	4,156	2,735	1,421		1,314 R	65.8%	34.2%	65.8%	34.2%
4,878	TOWNS	1,669	883	786		97 R	52.9%	47.1%	52.9%	47.1%
3,837	TREUTLEN	1,192	492	700		208 D	41.3%	58.7%	41.3%	58.7%
23,372	TROUP	8,716	5,096	3,620		1,476 R	58.5%	41.5%	58.5%	41.5%
4,000	TURNER	1,427	388	1,039		651 D	27.2%	72.8%	27.2%	72.8%
5,290	TWIGGS	2,020	628	1,392		764 D	31.1%	68.9%	31.1%	68.9%
7,769	UNION	2,742	1,472	1,270		202 R	53.7%	46.3%	53.7%	46.3%
13,372	UPSON	4,309	2,190	2,119		71 R	50.8%	49.2%	50.8%	49.2%
23,368	WALKER	9,395	6,589	2,806		3,783 R	70.1%	29.9%	70.1%	29.9%
17,053	WALTON	6,785	3,498	3,287		211 R	51.6%	48.4%	51.6%	48.4%
14,733	WARE	5,827	2,986	2,841		145 R	51.2%	48.8%	51.2%	48.8%
3,375	WARREN	1,281	609	672		63 D	47.5%	52.5%	47.5%	52.5%
9,538	WASHINGTON	3,827	1,588	2,239		651 D	41.5%	58.5%	41.5%	58.5%
10,736	WAYNE	4,042	2,082	1,960		122 R	51.5%	48.5%	51.5%	48.5%
1,287	WEBSTER	471	125	346		221 D	26.5%	73.5%	26.5%	73.5%
3,701	WHEELER	725	326	399		73 D	45.0%	55.0%	45.0%	55.0%
7,193	WHITE	2,726	1,612	1,114		498 R	59.1%	40.9%	59.1%	40.9%
29,186	WHITFIELD	10,491	7,093	3,398		3,695 R	67.6%	32.4%	67.6%	32.4%
4,519	WILCOX	1,326	451	875		424 D	34.0%	66.0%	34.0%	66.0%
5,359	WILKES	2,345	1,181	1,164		17 R	50.4%	49.6%	50.4%	49.6%
5,468	WILKINSON	2,500	906	1,594		688 D	36.2%	63.8%	36.2%	63.8%
8,580	WORTH	3,646	1,446	2,200		754 D	39.7%	60.3%	39.7%	60.3%
3,177,061	TOTAL	1,253,991	635,114	618,877		16,237 R	50.6%	49.4%	50.6%	49.4%

GEORGIA

CONGRESS

| CD | Year | Total Vote | Republican | | Democratic | | Other Vote | Rep.-Dem. Plurality | Percentage | | | |
| | | | Vote | Candidate | Vote | Candidate | | | Total Vote | | Major Vote | |
									Rep.	Dem.	Rep.	Dem.
1	1992	179,740	103,932	KINGSTON, JACK	75,808	CHRISTMAS, BARBARA		28,124 R	57.8%	42.2%	57.8%	42.2%
2	1992	150,382	54,593	DUDLEY, JIM	95,789	BISHOP, SANFORD		41,196 D	36.3%	63.7%	36.3%	63.7%
3	1992	208,378	114,107	COLLINS, MAC	94,271	RAY, RICHARD		19,836 R	54.8%	45.2%	54.8%	45.2%
4	1992	250,314	126,495	LINDER, JOHN	123,819	STEINBERG, CATHEY		2,676 R	50.5%	49.5%	50.5%	49.5%
5	1992	204,407	56,960	STABLER, PAUL	147,445	LEWIS, JOHN	2	90,485 D	27.9%	72.1%	27.9%	72.1%
6	1992	274,957	158,761	GINGRICH, NEWT	116,196	CENTER, TONY		42,565 R	57.7%	42.3%	57.7%	42.3%
7	1992	194,289	82,915	BEVERLY, AL	111,374	DARDEN, GEORGE		28,459 D	42.7%	57.3%	42.7%	57.3%
8	1992	194,692	86,220	CUNNINGHAM, ROBERT F.	108,472	ROWLAND, J. ROY		22,252 D	44.3%	55.7%	44.3%	55.7%
9	1992	190,943	77,919	BECKER, DANIEL	113,024	DEAL, NATHAN		35,105 D	40.8%	59.2%	40.8%	59.2%
10	1992	201,485	93,059	HUDGENS, RALPH	108,426	JOHNSON, DON		15,367 D	46.2%	53.8%	46.2%	53.8%
11	1992	164,400	44,221	LOVETT, WOODROW	120,168	MCKINNEY, CYNTHIA	11	75,947 D	26.9%	73.1%	26.9%	73.1%

GEORGIA

1992 GENERAL ELECTION

President   Other vote was 7,110 Libertarian (Marrou); 78 Gritz (write-in); 44 Fulani (write-in); 9 Warren (write-in); 7 Phillips (write-in) 2 scattered write-in.

Senator   As no candidate received a clear majority in the November 3 general election, a run-off election was held on November 24 between the top to finishers. Both of these elections are carried in this volume. Other vote in the November 3 election was 69,878 Libertarian (Hudson); 11 scattered write-in.

Congress   Other vote was scattered write-in in CD's 5 and 11.

1992 PRIMARIES

JULY 21 REPUBLICAN

Senator   100,016 Paul Coverdell; 65,471 Bob Barr; 64,514 John Knox; 32,590 Charles Tanksley; 7,352 Dean Parkison.

Congress   Contested as follows:

CD 1   14,799 Jack Kingston; 3,401 Bill Jolley.
CD 2   1,585 Jim Dudley; 838 Thomas H. McGinley; 602 Dan Menefee; 372 Joseph T. Williams.
CD 3   17,484 Mac Collins; 14,546 Paul Brown.
CD 4   17,628 John Linder; 14,381 Emory L. Morsberger; 5,847 Jimmy Fisher; 5,587 Richard Robinson; 5,455 Tom Phillips; 2,480 Ray Miller.
CD 5   7,626 Paul Stabler; 5,558 Barbara Brock; 963 J. W. Tibbs.
CD 6   35,699 Newt Gingrich; 34,719 Herman Clark.
CD 7   10,255 Al Beverly; 8,040 Brenda Fitzgerald.
CD 8   5,771 Robert F. Cunningham; 2,901 Saxby Chambliss.
CD 9   7,683 Daniel Becker; 6,778 Ben N. Whitaker; 4,941 Judy Grammer; 1,288 Lane A. Bohannon.
CD 10   9,171 Ralph Hudgens; 7,883 Frank Albert; 4,673 Mark Myers; 4,213 Curtis McGill; 2,357 Thomas E. Simpson.
CD 11   2,422 Woodrow Lovett; 2,150 Michael Pratt; 955 O. A. Smith.

JULY 21 DEMOCRATIC

Senator   Wyche Fowler, unopposed.

Congress   Unopposed in CD 7. Contested as follows:

CD 1   25,835 Barbara Christmas; 24,250 Buddy DeLoach; 21,254 Bryan Ginn; 13,251 Ron Fennel; 6,298 John Scardino; 6,003 Al Jones; 4,750 Mack Armstrong.
CD 2   40,833 Charles Hatcher; 21,692 Sanford Bishop; 19,363 Mary Y. Cummings; 11,819 Lonzy Edwards; 4,762 Phil Whigham; 4,253 Stephanie A. Kaigler.
CD 3   38,971 Richard Ray; 24,551 David Worley; 7,788 Jim Friday; 4,509 Robert Hobbs.
CD 4   25,202 Cathey Steinberg; 21,484 Bob Wilson.
CD 5   43,971 John Lewis; 13,686 Mable Thomas.
CD 6   5,813 Leonard B. Brown; 4,404 Tony Center; 3,560 Ron Sifen; 1,898 Gary Pelphrey.
CD 8   85,689 J. Roy Rowland; 41,153 Bill Lightle.
CD 9   40,634 Nathan Deal; 31,058 Tom Ramsey; 17,725 Wyc Orr.
CD 10   45,891 Don Johnson; 25,924 Ben Jones; 5,250 Marc Wetherhorn; 5,018 Doug Bower; 4,848 Chuck Pardue.
CD 11   26,160 Cynthia McKinney; 21,122 George L. DeLoach; 18,805 Gene Walker; 13,313 Michael Thurmond; 4,468 Verdree Lockhart.

GEORGIA

AUGUST 11 REPUBLICAN RUN-OFF

Senator   80,435 Paul Coverdell; 78,887 Bob Barr.

Congress   Contested as follows:

CD 2   1,080 Jim Dudley; 649 Thomas H. McGinley.
CD 4   21,807 John Linder; 13,370 Emory L. Morsberger.
CD 9   7,156 Daniel Becker; 6,392 Ben N. Whitaker.
CD 10   8,562 Ralph Hudgens; 7,182 Frank Albert.
CD 11   1,849 Woodrow Lovett; 1,571 Michael Pratt.

AUGUST 11 DEMOCRATIC RUN-OFF

Congress   Contested as follows:

CD 1   42,683 Barbara Christmas; 36,341 Buddy DeLoach.
CD 2   41,593 Sanford Bishop; 36,778 Charles Hatcher.
CD 6   4,894 Tony Center; 2,929 Leonard B. Brown.
CD 9   43,275 Nathan Deal; 35,213 Tom Ramsey.
CD 11   39,301 Cynthia McKinney; 30,389 George L. DeLoach.

HAWAII

GOVERNOR
John Waihee (D). Re-elected 1990 to a four-year term. Previously elected 1986.

SENATORS
Daniel K. Akaka (D). Elected 1990 to fill out the remaining four years of the term vacated by the death of Senator Spark M. Matsunaga (D); had previously been appointed May 1990 to fill this vacancy.

Daniel K. Inouye (D). Re-elected 1992 to a six-year term. Previously elected 1986, 1980, 1974, 1968, 1962.

REPRESENTATIVES
1. Neil Abercrombie (D)   2. Patsy T. Mink (D)

POSTWAR VOTE FOR PRESIDENT

| | | Republican | | Democratic | | | | Percentage | | | |
| | | | | | | | | Total Vote | | Major Vote | |
Year	Total Vote	Vote	Candidate	Vote	Candidate	Other Vote	Plurality	Rep.	Dem.	Rep.	Dem.
1992 **	372,842	136,822	Bush, George	179,310	Clinton, Bill	56,710	42,488 D	36.7%	48.1%	43.3%	56.7%
1988	354,461	158,625	Bush, George	192,364	Dukakis, Michael S.	3,472	33,739 D	44.8%	54.3%	45.2%	54.8%
1984	335,846	185,050	Reagan, Ronald	147,154	Mondale, Walter F.	3,642	37,896 R	55.1%	43.8%	55.7%	44.3%
1980	303,287	130,112	Reagan, Ronald	135,879	Carter, Jimmy	37,296	5,767 D	42.9%	44.8%	48.9%	51.1%
1976	291,301	140,003	Ford, Gerald R.	147,375	Carter, Jimmy	3,923	7,372 D	48.1%	50.6%	48.7%	51.3%
1972	270,274	168,865	Nixon, Richard M.	101,409	McGovern, George S.		67,456 R	62.5%	37.5%	62.5%	37.5%
1968	236,218	91,425	Nixon, Richard M.	141,324	Humphrey, Hubert H.	3,469	49,899 D	38.7%	59.8%	39.3%	60.7%
1964	207,271	44,022	Goldwater, Barry M.	163,249	Johnson, Lyndon B.		119,227 D	21.2%	78.8%	21.2%	78.8%
1960	184,705	92,295	Nixon, Richard M.	92,410	Kennedy, John F.		115 D	50.0%	50.0%	50.0%	50.0%

In 1992 the other vote column includes 53,003 votes cast for Perot. Hawaii was formally admitted to statehood in August 1959.

POSTWAR VOTE FOR GOVERNOR

| | | Republican | | Democratic | | | | Percentage | | | |
| | | | | | | | | Total Vote | | Major Vote | |
Year	Total Vote	Vote	Candidate	Vote	Candidate	Other Vote	Rep.-Dem. Plurality	Rep.	Dem.	Rep.	Dem.
1990	340,132	131,310	Hemmings, Fred	203,491	Waihee, John	5,331	72,181 D	38.6%	59.8%	39.2%	60.8%
1986	334,115	160,460	Anderson, D. G.	173,655	Waihee, John		13,195 D	48.0%	52.0%	48.0%	52.0%
1982 **	311,853	81,507	Anderson, D. G.	141,043	Ariyoshi, George R.	89,303	59,536 D	26.1%	45.2%	36.6%	63.4%
1978	281,587	124,610	Leopold, John	153,394	Ariyoshi, George R.	3,583	28,784 D	44.3%	54.5%	44.8%	55.2%
1974	249,650	113,388	Crossley, Randolph	136,262	Ariyoshi, George R.		22,874 D	45.4%	54.6%	45.4%	54.6%
1970	239,061	101,249	King, Samuel P.	137,812	Burns, John A.		36,563 D	42.4%	57.6%	42.4%	57.6%
1966	213,164	104,324	Crossley, Randolph	108,840	Burns, John A.		4,516 D	48.9%	51.1%	48.9%	51.1%
1962	196,015	81,707	Quinn, William F.	114,308	Burns, John A.		32,601 D	41.7%	58.3%	41.7%	58.3%
1959 S	168,662	86,213	Quinn, William F.	82,074	Burns, John A.	375	4,139 R	51.1%	48.7%	51.2%	48.8%

The 1959 election was for a short term pending the regular vote in 1962. In 1982 other vote was Independent Democrat (Frank F. Fasi) who ran second.

HAWAII

POSTWAR VOTE FOR SENATOR

Year	Total Vote	Republican		Democratic		Other Vote	Rep.-Dem. Plurality	Percentage			
								Total Vote		Major Vote	
		Vote	Candidate	Vote	Candidate			Rep.	Dem.	Rep.	Dem.
1992	363,662	97,928	Reed, Rick	208,266	Inouye, Daniel K.	57,468	110,338 D	26.9%	57.3%	32.0%	68.0%
1990 S	349,666	155,978	Saiki, Patricia	188,901	Akaka, Daniel K.	4,787	32,923 D	44.6%	54.0%	45.2%	54.8%
1988	323,876	66,987	Hustace, Maria M.	247,941	Matsunaga, Spark M.	8,948	180,954 D	20.7%	76.6%	21.3%	78.7%
1986	328,797	86,910	Hutchinson, Frank	241,887	Inouye, Daniel K.		154,977 D	26.4%	73.6%	26.4%	73.6%
1982	306,410	52,071	Brown, Clarence J.	245,386	Matsunaga, Spark M.	8,953	193,315 D	17.0%	80.1%	17.5%	82.5%
1980	288,006	53,068	Brown, Cooper	224,485	Inouye, Daniel K.	10,453	171,417 D	18.4%	77.9%	19.1%	80.9%
1976	302,092	122,724	Quinn, William F.	162,305	Matsunaga, Spark M.	17,063	39,581 D	40.6%	53.7%	43.1%	56.9%
1974	250,221		—	207,454	Inouye, Daniel K.	42,767	207,454 D		82.9%		100.0%
1970	240,760	124,163	Fong, Hiram L.	116,597	Heftel, Cecil		7,566 R	51.6%	48.4%	51.6%	48.4%
1968	226,927	34,008	Thiessen, Wayne C.	189,248	Inouye, Daniel K.	3,671	155,240 D	15.0%	83.4%	15.2%	84.8%
1964	208,814	110,747	Fong, Hiram L.	96,789	Gill, Thomas P.	1,278	13,958 R	53.0%	46.4%	53.4%	46.6%
1962	196,361	60,067	Dillingham, Ben F.	136,294	Inouye, Daniel K.		76,227 D	30.6%	69.4%	30.6%	69.4%
1959 **	164,808	87,161	Fong, Hiram L.	77,647	Fasi, Frank F.		9,514 R	52.9%	47.1%	52.9%	47.1%
1959 S	163,875	79,123	Tsukiyama, W. C.	83,700	Long, Oren E.	1,052	4,577 D	48.3%	51.1%	48.6%	51.4%

The two 1959 elections were held to indeterminate terms and the Senate later determined by lot that Senator Long would serve a short term, Senator Fong a long term. The 1990 election was for a short term to fill a vacancy.

HAWAII

Districts Established July 27, 1991

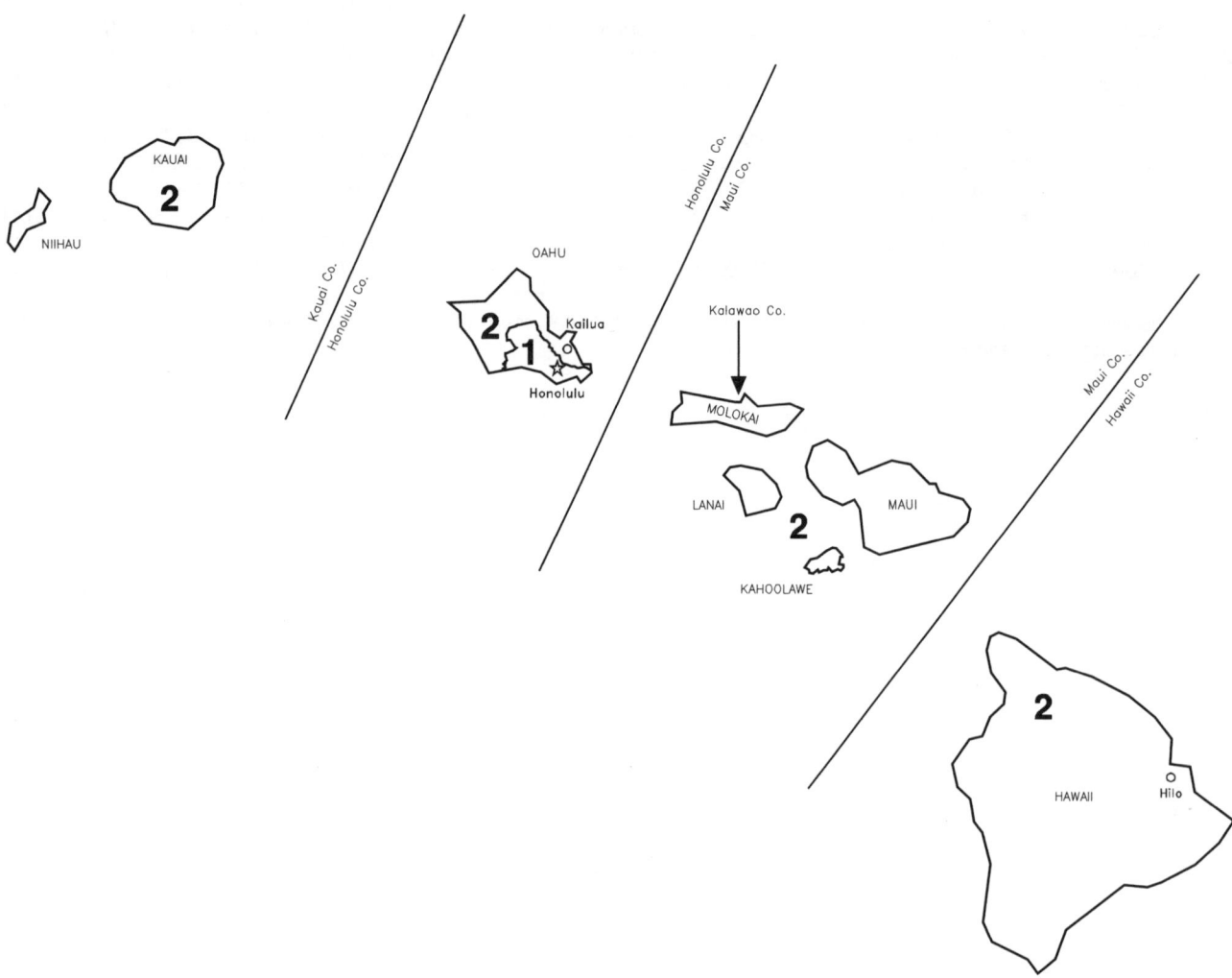

HAWAII

PRESIDENT 1992

Registration	County	Total Vote	Republican	Democratic	Perot	Other	Plurality	Percentage Total Vote		
								Rep.	Dem.	Perot
62,023	HAWAII	50,916	15,460	25,725	8,889	842	10,265 D	30.4%	50.5%	17.5%
328,463	HONOLULU	265,841	103,937	123,908	35,728	2,268	19,971 D	39.1%	46.6%	13.4%
26,771	KAUAI	18,960	6,274	10,715	1,756	215	4,441 D	33.1%	56.5%	9.3%
47,238	MAUI	37,125	11,151	18,962	6,630	382	7,811 D	30.0%	51.1%	17.9%
464,495	TOTAL	372,842	136,822	179,310	53,003	3,707	42,488 D	36.7%	48.1%	14.2%

HAWAII

SENATOR 1992

Registration	County	Total Vote	Republican	Democratic	Other	Rep.-Dem. Plurality	Percentage			
							Total Vote		Major Vote	
							Rep.	Dem.	Rep.	Dem.
62,023	HAWAII	50,231	15,130	27,461	7,640	12,331 D	30.1%	54.7%	35.5%	64.5%
328,463	HONOLULU	258,407	66,094	148,831	43,482	82,737 D	25.6%	57.6%	30.8%	69.2%
26,771	KAUAI	18,602	4,058	13,213	1,331	9,155 D	21.8%	71.0%	23.5%	76.5%
47,238	MAUI	36,422	12,646	18,761	5,015	6,115 D	34.7%	51.5%	40.3%	59.7%
464,495	TOTAL	363,662	97,928	208,266	57,468	110,338 D	26.9%	57.3%	32.0%	68.0%

HAWAII

CONGRESS

| CD | Year | Total Vote | Republican | | Democratic | | Other Vote | Rep.-Dem. Plurality | Percentage | | | |
| | | | Vote | Candidate | Vote | Candidate | | | Total Vote | | Major Vote | |
									Rep.	Dem.	Rep.	Dem.
1	1992	177,476	41,575	SUTTON, WARNER C. K.	129,332	ABERCROMBIE, NEIL	6,569	87,757 D	23.4%	72.9%	24.3%	75.7%
2	1992	180,955	40,070	PRICE, KAMUELA	131,454	MINK, PATSY T.	9,431	91,384 D	22.1%	72.6%	23.4%	76.6%

HAWAII

Kalawao county, an area of 14 square miles on Molokai Island, consists entirely of the Kalaupapa Hansen's disease settlement. The voting data for this settlement are included in the Maui county statistics.

1992 GENERAL ELECTION

President   Other vote was 1,452 Independent (Gritz); 1,119 Libertarian (Marrou); 720 National Alliance (Fulani); 416 Natural Law (Hagelin).

Senator   Other vote was 49,921 Green (Martin); 7,547 Libertarian (Rowland).

Congress   Other vote was Libertarian (Johnson) in CD 1; Libertarian (Mallan) in CD 2.

1992 PRIMARIES

SEPTEMBER 19 REPUBLICAN

Senator   33,250 Rick Reed; 9,348 Maria M. Hustace; 2,250 John James.

Congress   Contested as follows:

CD 1   12,911 Warner C. K. Sutton; 9,321 Nalani Rees.
CD 2   5,175 Kamuela Price; 5,124 Bonnie Heim; 3,015 Stuart T. Gregory; 2,341 James DeLuze; 913 Jose S. Pillos.

SEPTEMBER 19 DEMOCRATIC

Senator   141,273 Daniel K. Inouye; 44,505 Wayne K. Nishiki.

Congress   Unopposed in CD 1. Contested as follows:

CD 2   80,570 Patsy T. Mink; 16,441 David L. Bourgoin.

SEPTEMBER 19 GREEN

Senator   Linda B. Martin, unopposed.

Congress   No candidate in either district.

SEPTEMBER 19 LIBERTARIAN

Senator   Richard O. Rowland, unopposed.

Congress   Unopposed in both districts.

IDAHO

GOVERNOR
Cecil D. Andrus (D). Re-elected 1990 to a four-year term. Previously elected 1986, 1974, 1970.

SENATORS
Larry Craig (R). Elected 1990 to a six-year term.

Dirk Kempthorne (R). Elected 1992 to a six-year term.

REPRESENTATIVES
1. Larry LaRocco (D)   2. Michael D. Crapo (R)

POSTWAR VOTE FOR PRESIDENT

Year	Total Vote	Republican Vote	Republican Candidate	Democratic Vote	Democratic Candidate	Other Vote	Plurality	Total Vote Rep.	Total Vote Dem.	Major Vote Rep.	Major Vote Dem.
1992 **	482,142	202,645	Bush, George	137,013	Clinton, Bill	142,484	65,632 R	42.0%	28.4%	59.7%	40.3%
1988	408,968	253,881	Bush, George	147,272	Dukakis, Michael S.	7,815	106,609 R	62.1%	36.0%	63.3%	36.7%
1984	411,144	297,523	Reagan, Ronald	108,510	Mondale, Walter F.	5,111	189,013 R	72.4%	26.4%	73.3%	26.7%
1980	437,431	290,699	Reagan, Ronald	110,192	Carter, Jimmy	36,540	180,507 R	66.5%	25.2%	72.5%	27.5%
1976	344,071	204,151	Ford, Gerald R.	126,549	Carter, Jimmy	13,371	77,602 R	59.3%	36.8%	61.7%	38.3%
1972	310,379	199,384	Nixon, Richard M.	80,826	McGovern, George S.	30,169	118,558 R	64.2%	26.0%	71.2%	28.8%
1968	291,183	165,369	Nixon, Richard M.	89,273	Humphrey, Hubert H.	36,541	76,096 R	56.8%	30.7%	64.9%	35.1%
1964	292,477	143,557	Goldwater, Barry M.	148,920	Johnson, Lyndon B.		5,363 D	49.1%	50.9%	49.1%	50.9%
1960	300,450	161,597	Nixon, Richard M.	138,853	Kennedy, John F.		22,744 R	53.8%	46.2%	53.8%	46.2%
1956	272,989	166,979	Eisenhower, Dwight D.	105,868	Stevenson, Adlai E.	142	61,111 R	61.2%	38.8%	61.2%	38.8%
1952	276,254	180,707	Eisenhower, Dwight D.	95,081	Stevenson, Adlai E.	466	85,626 R	65.4%	34.4%	65.5%	34.5%
1948	214,816	101,514	Dewey, Thomas E.	107,370	Truman, Harry S.	5,932	5,856 D	47.3%	50.0%	48.6%	51.4%

In 1992 the other vote column includes 130,395 votes cast for Perot.

POSTWAR VOTE FOR GOVERNOR

Year	Total Vote	Republican Vote	Republican Candidate	Democratic Vote	Democratic Candidate	Other Vote	Rep.-Dem. Plurality	Total Vote Rep.	Total Vote Dem.	Major Vote Rep.	Major Vote Dem.
1990	320,610	101,937	Fairchild, Roger	218,673	Andrus, Cecil D.		116,736 D	31.8%	68.2%	31.8%	68.2%
1986	387,426	189,794	Leroy, David H.	193,429	Andrus, Cecil D.	4,203	3,635 D	49.0%	49.9%	49.5%	50.5%
1982	326,522	161,157	Batt, Philip	165,365	Evans, John V.		4,208 D	49.4%	50.6%	49.4%	50.6%
1978	288,566	114,149	Larsen, Allan	169,540	Evans, John V.	4,877	55,391 D	39.6%	58.8%	40.2%	59.8%
1974	259,632	68,731	Murphy, Jack M.	184,142	Andrus, Cecil D.	6,759	115,411 D	26.5%	70.9%	27.2%	72.8%
1970	245,112	117,108	Samuelson, Don	128,004	Andrus, Cecil D.		10,896 D	47.8%	52.2%	47.8%	52.2%
1966	252,593	104,586	Samuelson, Don	93,744	Andrus, Cecil D.	54,263	10,842 R	41.4%	37.1%	52.7%	47.3%
1962	255,454	139,578	Smylie, Robert E.	115,876	Smith, Vernon K.		23,702 R	54.6%	45.4%	54.6%	45.4%
1958	239,046	121,810	Smylie, Robert E.	117,236	Derr, A. M.		4,574 R	51.0%	49.0%	51.0%	49.0%
1954	228,685	124,038	Smylie, Robert E.	104,647	Hamilton, Clark		19,391 R	54.2%	45.8%	54.2%	45.8%
1950	204,792	107,642	Jordan, Len B.	97,150	Wright, Calvin E.		10,492 R	52.6%	47.4%	52.6%	47.4%
1946	181,364	102,233	Robins, C. A.	79,131	Williams, Arnold		23,102 R	56.4%	43.6%	56.4%	43.6%

IDAHO

POSTWAR VOTE FOR SENATOR

Year	Total Vote	Republican Vote	Republican Candidate	Democratic Vote	Democratic Candidate	Other Vote	Rep.-Dem. Plurality	Percentage Total Vote Rep.	Percentage Total Vote Dem.	Percentage Major Vote Rep.	Percentage Major Vote Dem.
1992	478,522	270,468	Kempthorne, Dirk	208,036	Stallings, Richard	18	62,432 R	56.5%	43.5%	56.5%	43.5%
1990	315,936	193,641	Craig, Larry	122,295	Twilegar, Ron J.		71,346 R	61.3%	38.7%	61.3%	38.7%
1986	382,024	196,958	Symms, Steven D.	185,066	Evans, John V.		11,892 R	51.6%	48.4%	51.6%	48.4%
1984	406,168	293,193	McClure, James A.	105,591	Busch, Peter M.	7,384	187,602 R	72.2%	26.0%	73.5%	26.5%
1980	439,647	218,701	Symms, Steven D.	214,439	Church, Frank	6,507	4,262 R	49.7%	48.8%	50.5%	49.5%
1978	284,047	194,412	McClure, James A.	89,635	Jensen, Dwight		104,777 R	68.4%	31.6%	68.4%	31.6%
1974	258,847	109,072	Smith, Robert L.	145,140	Church, Frank	4,635	36,068 D	42.1%	56.1%	42.9%	57.1%
1972	309,602	161,804	McClure, James A.	140,913	Davis, William E.	6,885	20,891 R	52.3%	45.5%	53.5%	46.5%
1968	287,876	114,394	Hansen, George V.	173,482	Church, Frank		59,088 D	39.7%	60.3%	39.7%	60.3%
1966	252,456	139,819	Jordan, Len B.	112,637	Harding, Ralph R.		27,182 R	55.4%	44.6%	55.4%	44.6%
1962	258,786	117,129	Hawley, Jack	141,657	Church, Frank		24,528 D	45.3%	54.7%	45.3%	54.7%
1962 S	257,677	131,279	Jordan, Len B.	126,398	Pfost, Gracie		4,881 R	50.9%	49.1%	50.9%	49.1%
1960	292,096	152,648	Dworshak, Henry C.	139,448	McLaughlin, Bob		13,200 R	52.3%	47.7%	52.3%	47.7%
1956	265,292	102,781	Welker, Herman	149,096	Church, Frank	13,415	46,315 D	38.7%	56.2%	40.8%	59.2%
1954	226,408	142,269	Dworshak, Henry C.	84,139	Taylor, Glen H.		58,130 R	62.8%	37.2%	62.8%	37.2%
1950	201,417	124,237	Welker, Herman	77,180	Clark, D. Worth		47,057 R	61.7%	38.3%	61.7%	38.3%
1950 S	201,970	104,068	Dworshak, Henry C.	97,902	Burtenshaw, Claude		6,166 R	51.5%	48.5%	51.5%	48.5%
1948	214,188	103,868	Dworshak, Henry C.	107,000	Miller, Bert H.	3,320	3,132 D	48.5%	50.0%	49.3%	50.7%
1946 S	180,152	105,523	Dworshak, Henry C.	74,629	Donart, George E.		30,894 R	58.6%	41.4%	58.6%	41.4%

The 1946 election and one each of the 1962 and 1950 elections were for short terms to fill vacancies.

IDAHO

Districts Established March 2, 1991

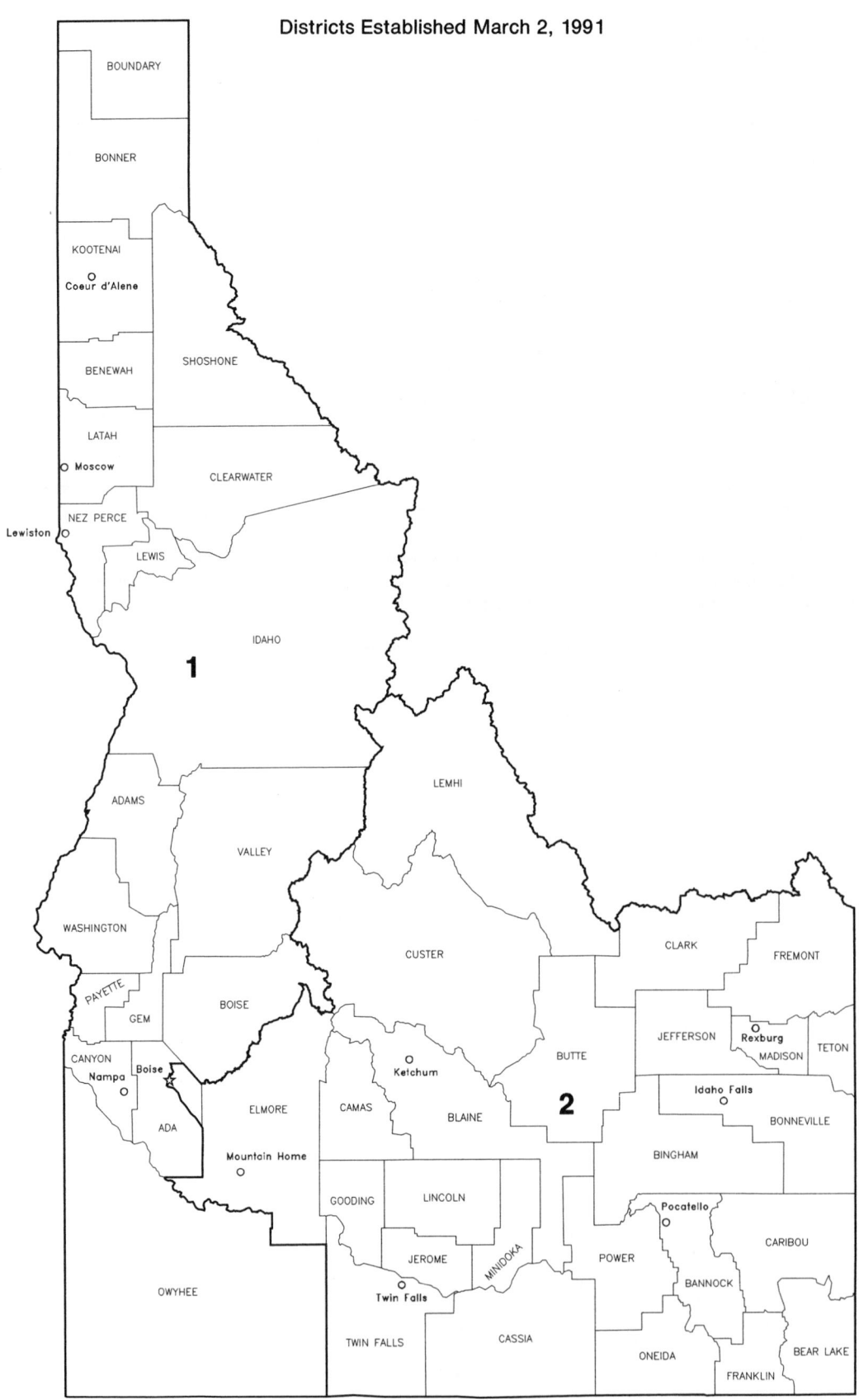

IDAHO

PRESIDENT 1992

Registration	County	Total Vote	Republican	Democratic	Perot	Other	Plurality	Percentage Total Vote		
								Rep.	Dem.	Perot
136,808	ADA	110,166	49,000	31,941	28,192	1,033	17,059 R	44.5%	29.0%	25.6%
2,396	ADAMS	1,937	754	457	695	31	59 R	38.9%	23.6%	35.9%
40,942	BANNOCK	32,211	12,016	11,091	8,116	988	925 R	37.3%	34.4%	25.2%
3,593	BEAR LAKE	2,854	1,419	562	684	189	735 R	49.7%	19.7%	24.0%
4,788	BENEWAH	3,703	1,223	1,270	1,165	45	47 D	33.0%	34.3%	31.5%
20,304	BINGHAM	15,991	7,333	3,565	4,144	949	3,189 R	45.9%	22.3%	25.9%
10,261	BLAINE	8,022	2,243	2,865	2,831	83	34 D	28.0%	35.7%	35.3%
2,759	BOISE	2,320	912	623	754	31	158 D	39.3%	26.9%	32.5%
17,419	BONNER	13,821	3,937	4,995	4,645	244	350 D	28.5%	36.1%	33.6%
43,408	BONNEVILLE	35,376	16,557	7,014	10,241	1,564	6,316 R	46.8%	19.8%	28.9%
4,946	BOUNDARY	3,774	1,479	1,095	1,136	64	343 R	39.2%	29.0%	30.1%
1,829	BUTTE	1,503	602	433	392	76	169 R	40.1%	28.8%	26.1%
584	CAMAS	486	202	134	145	5	57 R	41.6%	27.6%	29.8%
48,013	CANYON	37,849	19,220	9,095	8,974	560	10,125 R	50.8%	24.0%	23.7%
3,900	CARIBOU	3,236	1,350	562	1,088	236	262 R	41.7%	17.4%	33.6%
9,485	CASSIA	7,622	4,052	1,351	1,785	434	2,267 R	53.2%	17.7%	23.4%
555	CLARK	423	195	95	119	14	76 R	46.1%	22.5%	28.1%
5,093	CLEARWATER	3,732	1,152	1,433	1,098	49	281 D	30.9%	38.4%	29.4%
2,679	CUSTER	2,164	829	564	729	42	100 R	38.3%	26.1%	33.7%
9,128	ELMORE	6,890	3,087	1,858	1,867	78	1,220 R	44.8%	27.0%	27.1%
5,022	FRANKLIN	4,050	2,115	524	890	521	1,225 R	52.2%	12.9%	22.0%
6,045	FREMONT	4,954	2,333	903	1,349	369	984 R	47.1%	18.2%	27.2%
7,287	GEM	5,723	2,455	1,609	1,555	104	846 R	42.9%	28.1%	27.2%
6,961	GOODING	5,564	2,178	1,530	1,591	265	587 R	39.1%	27.5%	28.6%
8,392	IDAHO	6,734	2,709	1,974	1,900	151	735 R	40.2%	29.3%	28.2%
8,654	JEFFERSON	7,116	3,471	978	2,164	503	1,307 R	48.8%	13.7%	30.4%
8,501	JEROME	6,720	2,972	1,739	1,768	241	1,204 R	44.2%	25.9%	26.3%
46,971	KOOTENAI	36,328	13,065	11,553	11,261	449	1,512 R	36.0%	31.8%	31.0%
22,516	LATAH	16,330	5,353	7,233	3,602	142	1,880 D	32.8%	44.3%	22.1%
4,847	LEMHI	3,821	1,540	996	1,175	110	365 R	40.3%	26.1%	30.8%
2,250	LEWIS	1,778	593	674	491	20	81 D	33.4%	37.9%	27.6%
1,986	LINCOLN	1,699	656	514	441	88	142 R	38.6%	30.3%	26.0%
9,631	MADISON	7,763	4,591	741	1,920	511	2,671 R	59.1%	9.5%	24.7%
9,401	MINIDOKA	7,417	3,304	1,815	1,875	423	1,429 R	44.5%	24.5%	25.3%
21,906	NEZ PERCE	16,974	5,431	7,069	4,363	111	1,638 D	32.0%	41.6%	25.7%
2,220	ONEIDA	1,866	713	351	590	212	123 R	38.2%	18.8%	31.6%
3,866	OWYHEE	3,072	1,469	686	862	55	607 R	47.8%	22.3%	28.1%
8,682	PAYETTE	6,745	2,895	1,656	2,055	139	840 R	42.9%	24.6%	30.5%
3,870	POWER	2,977	1,352	837	697	91	515 R	45.4%	28.1%	23.4%
8,948	SHOSHONE	6,548	1,441	3,182	1,878	47	1,304 D	22.0%	48.6%	28.7%
2,326	TETON	1,918	762	472	608	76	154 R	39.7%	24.6%	31.7%
31,257	TWIN FALLS	23,503	10,335	6,593	6,043	532	3,742 R	44.0%	28.1%	25.7%
5,402	VALLEY	4,153	1,548	1,259	1,313	33	235 R	37.3%	30.3%	31.6%
5,290	WASHINGTON	4,281	1,802	1,122	1,204	153	598 R	42.1%	26.2%	28.1%
611,121	TOTAL	482,142	202,645	137,013	130,395	12,089	65,632 R	42.0%	28.4%	27.0%

IDAHO

SENATOR 1992

Registration	County	Total Vote	Republican	Democratic	Other	Rep.-Dem. Plurality	Percentage Total Vote Rep.	Percentage Total Vote Dem.	Percentage Major Vote Rep.	Percentage Major Vote Dem.
136,808	ADA	110,392	67,517	42,875		24,642 R	61.2%	38.8%	61.2%	38.8%
2,396	ADAMS	1,908	1,272	636		636 R	66.7%	33.3%	66.7%	33.3%
40,942	BANNOCK	32,418	14,465	17,953		3,488 D	44.6%	55.4%	44.6%	55.4%
3,593	BEAR LAKE	2,857	1,995	862		1,133 R	69.8%	30.2%	69.8%	30.2%
4,788	BENEWAH	3,551	1,789	1,762		27 R	50.4%	49.6%	50.4%	49.6%
20,304	BINGHAM	16,060	8,408	7,652		756 R	52.4%	47.6%	52.4%	47.6%
10,261	BLAINE	7,976	3,667	4,309		642 D	46.0%	54.0%	46.0%	54.0%
2,759	BOISE	2,278	1,458	820		638 R	64.0%	36.0%	64.0%	36.0%
17,419	BONNER	13,282	6,541	6,741		200 D	49.2%	50.8%	49.2%	50.8%
43,408	BONNEVILLE	35,400	20,767	14,633		6,134 R	58.7%	41.3%	58.7%	41.3%
4,946	BOUNDARY	3,605	2,005	1,600		405 R	55.6%	44.4%	55.6%	44.4%
1,829	BUTTE	1,501	708	793		85 D	47.2%	52.8%	47.2%	52.8%
584	CAMAS	482	250	232		18 R	51.9%	48.1%	51.9%	48.1%
48,013	CANYON	37,987	26,168	11,819		14,349 R	68.9%	31.1%	68.9%	31.1%
3,900	CARIBOU	3,235	1,970	1,265		705 R	60.9%	39.1%	60.9%	39.1%
9,485	CASSIA	7,696	3,981	3,715		266 R	51.7%	48.3%	51.7%	48.3%
555	CLARK	419	257	162		95 R	61.3%	38.7%	61.3%	38.7%
5,093	CLEARWATER	3,690	1,717	1,973		256 D	46.5%	53.5%	46.5%	53.5%
2,679	CUSTER	2,122	1,279	843		436 R	60.3%	39.7%	60.3%	39.7%
9,128	ELMORE	6,456	3,982	2,474		1,508 R	61.7%	38.3%	61.7%	38.3%
5,022	FRANKLIN	4,067	2,634	1,433		1,201 R	64.8%	35.2%	64.8%	35.2%
6,045	FREMONT	4,916	2,875	2,041		834 R	58.5%	41.5%	58.5%	41.5%
7,287	GEM	5,827	3,611	2,216		1,395 R	62.0%	38.0%	62.0%	38.0%
6,961	GOODING	5,306	2,678	2,628		50 R	50.5%	49.5%	50.5%	49.5%
8,392	IDAHO	6,504	3,975	2,529		1,446 R	61.1%	38.9%	61.1%	38.9%
8,654	JEFFERSON	7,159	4,487	2,672		1,815 R	62.7%	37.3%	62.7%	37.3%
8,501	JEROME	6,496	3,297	3,199		98 R	50.8%	49.2%	50.8%	49.2%
46,971	KOOTENAI	35,605	20,403	15,202		5,201 R	57.3%	42.7%	57.3%	42.7%
22,516	LATAH	16,222	7,905	8,317		412 D	48.7%	51.3%	48.7%	51.3%
4,847	LEMHI	3,600	2,328	1,272		1,056 R	64.7%	35.3%	64.7%	35.3%
2,250	LEWIS	1,722	862	860		2 R	50.1%	49.9%	50.1%	49.9%
1,986	LINCOLN	1,675	691	984		293 D	41.3%	58.7%	41.3%	58.7%
9,631	MADISON	7,633	4,352	3,281		1,071 R	57.0%	43.0%	57.0%	43.0%
9,401	MINIDOKA	7,512	3,387	4,125		738 D	45.1%	54.9%	45.1%	54.9%
21,906	NEZ PERCE	16,900	7,851	9,049		1,198 D	46.5%	53.5%	46.5%	53.5%
2,220	ONEIDA	1,756	857	899		42 D	48.8%	51.2%	48.8%	51.2%
3,866	OWYHEE	3,023	2,046	977		1,069 R	67.7%	32.3%	67.7%	32.3%
8,682	PAYETTE	6,751	4,506	2,245		2,261 R	66.7%	33.3%	66.7%	33.3%
3,870	POWER	2,937	1,337	1,600		263 D	45.5%	54.5%	45.5%	54.5%
8,948	SHOSHONE	6,464	2,329	4,135		1,806 D	36.0%	64.0%	36.0%	64.0%
2,326	TETON	1,891	902	989		87 D	47.7%	52.3%	47.7%	52.3%
31,257	TWIN FALLS	22,959	11,708	11,251		457 R	51.0%	49.0%	51.0%	49.0%
5,402	VALLEY	4,069	2,568	1,501		1,067 R	63.1%	36.9%	63.1%	36.9%
5,290	WASHINGTON	4,195	2,683	1,512		1,171 R	64.0%	36.0%	64.0%	36.0%
611,121	TOTAL	478,522	270,468	208,036	18	62,432 R	56.5%	43.5%	56.5%	43.5%

IDAHO

CONGRESS

CD	Year	Total Vote	Republican		Democratic		Other Vote	Rep.-Dem. Plurality	Percentage			
									Total Vote		Major Vote	
			Vote	Candidate	Vote	Candidate			Rep.	Dem.	Rep.	Dem.
1	1992	242,790	90,983	GILBERT, RACHEL S.	140,985	LAROCCO, LARRY	10,822	50,002 D	37.5%	58.1%	39.2%	60.8%
2	1992	229,957	139,783	CRAPO, MICHAEL D.	81,450	WILLIAMS, J. D.	8,724	58,333 R	60.8%	35.4%	63.2%	36.8%

IDAHO

1992 GENERAL ELECTION

President   Other vote was 10,281 Independent (Gritz); 1,167 Libertarian (Marrou); 613 Independent (Fulani); 24 Hagelin (write-in); 3 Brisben (write-in); 1 LaRouche (write-in). The total of the other vote column includes the 28 write-in votes not available by county.

Senator   Other vote was scattered write-in. The total of the other vote column represents the 18 scattered write-in votes not available by county.

Congress   Other vote was 6,255 Independent (Abel) and 4,567 Independent (Kinsey) in CD 1; 4,917 Independent (Kauer) and 3,807 Independent (Mansfield) in CD 2.

1992 PRIMARIES

MAY 26 REPUBLICAN

Senator   67,001 Dirk Kempthorne; 26,977 Rodney W. Beck; 22,682 Milton E. Erhart.

Congress   Contested as follows:

CD 1   35,743 Rachel S. Gilbert; 12,851 David Doremus.
CD 2   45,462 Michael D. Crapo; 21,443 Gary Glenn.

MAY 26 DEMOCRATIC

Senator   40,102 Richard Stallings; 8,976 Matt Schaffer; 6,882 David W. Shepherd.

Congress   Unopposed in CD 1. Contested as follows:

CD 2   15,195 J. D. Williams; 6,079 Jerry Seiffert.

ILLINOIS

GOVERNOR
Jim Edgar (R). Elected 1990 to a four-year term.

SENATORS
Carol M. Braun (D). Elected 1992 to a six-year term.

Paul Simon (D). Re-elected 1990 to a six-year term. Previously elected 1984.

REPRESENTATIVES

1. Bobby L. Rush (D)
2. Melvin J. Reynolds (D)
3. William O. Lipinski (D)
4. Luis V. Gutierrez (D)
5. Daniel Rostenkowski (D)
6. Henry J. Hyde (R)
7. Cardiss Collins (D)
8. Philip M. Crane (R)
9. Sindey R. Yates (D)
10. John E. Porter (R)
11. George E. Sangmeister (D)
12. Jerry F. Costello (D)
13. Harris W. Fawell (R)
14. J. Dennis Hastert (R)
15. Thomas Ewing (R)
16. Donald Manzullo (R)
17. Lane Evans (D)
18. Robert H. Michel (R)
19. Glenn Poshard (D)
20. Richard J. Durbin (D)

POSTWAR VOTE FOR PRESIDENT

Year	Total Vote	Republican Vote	Republican Candidate	Democratic Vote	Democratic Candidate	Other Vote	Plurality	Total Vote Rep.	Total Vote Dem.	Major Vote Rep.	Major Vote Dem.
1992 **	5,050,157	1,734,096	Bush, George	2,453,350	Clinton, Bill	862,711	719,254 D	34.3%	48.6%	41.4%	58.6%
1988	4,559,120	2,310,939	Bush, George	2,215,940	Dukakis, Michael S.	32,241	94,999 R	50.7%	48.6%	51.0%	49.0%
1984	4,819,088	2,707,103	Reagan, Ronald	2,086,499	Mondale, Walter F.	25,486	620,604 R	56.2%	43.3%	56.5%	43.5%
1980	4,749,721	2,358,049	Reagan, Ronald	1,981,413	Carter, Jimmy	410,259	376,636 R	49.6%	41.7%	54.3%	45.7%
1976	4,718,914	2,364,269	Ford, Gerald R.	2,271,295	Carter, Jimmy	83,350	92,974 R	50.1%	48.1%	51.0%	49.0%
1972	4,723,236	2,788,179	Nixon, Richard M.	1,913,472	McGovern, George S.	21,585	874,707 R	59.0%	40.5%	59.3%	40.7%
1968	4,619,749	2,174,774	Nixon, Richard M.	2,039,814	Humphrey, Hubert H.	405,161	134,960 R	47.1%	44.2%	51.6%	48.4%
1964	4,702,841	1,905,946	Goldwater, Barry M.	2,796,833	Johnson, Lyndon B.	62	890,887 D	40.5%	59.5%	40.5%	59.5%
1960	4,757,409	2,368,988	Nixon, Richard M.	2,377,846	Kennedy, John F.	10,575	8,858 D	49.8%	50.0%	49.9%	50.1%
1956	4,407,407	2,623,327	Eisenhower, Dwight D.	1,775,682	Stevenson, Adlai E.	8,398	847,645 R	59.5%	40.3%	59.6%	40.4%
1952	4,481,058	2,457,327	Eisenhower, Dwight D.	2,013,920	Stevenson, Adlai E.	9,811	443,407 R	54.8%	44.9%	55.0%	45.0%
1948	3,984,046	1,961,103	Dewey, Thomas E.	1,994,715	Truman, Harry S.	28,228	33,612 D	49.2%	50.1%	49.6%	50.4%

In 1992 the other vote column includes 840,515 votes cast for Perot.

ILLINOIS

POSTWAR VOTE FOR GOVERNOR

Year	Total Vote	Republican		Democratic		Other Vote	Rep.-Dem. Plurality	Percentage			
		Vote	Candidate	Vote	Candidate			Total Vote		Major Vote	
								Rep.	Dem.	Rep.	Dem.
1990	3,257,410	1,653,126	Edgar, Jim	1,569,217	Hartigan, Neil F.	35,067	83,909 R	50.7%	48.2%	51.3%	48.7%
1986 **	3,143,978	1,655,849	Thompson, James R.	208,830	[See note below]	1,279,299	1,447,019 R	52.7%	6.6%	88.8%	11.2%
1982	3,673,681	1,816,101	Thompson, James R.	1,811,027	Stevenson, Adlai E., III	46,553	5,074 R	49.4%	49.3%	50.1%	49.9%
1978	3,150,095	1,859,684	Thompson, James R.	1,263,134	Bakalis, Michael	27,277	596,550 R	59.0%	40.1%	59.6%	40.4%
1976 S	4,638,997	3,000,395	Thompson, James R.	1,610,258	Howlett, Michael J.	28,344	1,390,137 R	64.7%	34.7%	65.1%	34.9%
1972	4,678,804	2,293,809	Ogilvie, Richard B.	2,371,303	Walker, Daniel	13,692	77,494 D	49.0%	50.7%	49.2%	50.8%
1968	4,506,000	2,307,295	Ogilvie, Richard B.	2,179,501	Shapiro, Samuel H.	19,204	127,794 R	51.2%	48.4%	51.4%	48.6%
1964	4,657,500	2,239,095	Percy, Charles H.	2,418,394	Kerner, Otto	11	179,299 D	48.1%	51.9%	48.1%	51.9%
1960	4,674,187	2,070,479	Stratton, William G.	2,594,731	Kerner, Otto	8,977	524,252 D	44.3%	55.5%	44.4%	55.6%
1956	4,314,611	2,171,786	Stratton, William G.	2,134,909	Austin, Richard B.	7,916	36,877 R	50.3%	49.5%	50.4%	49.6%
1952	4,415,864	2,317,363	Stratton, William G.	2,089,721	Dixon, Sherwood	8,780	227,642 R	52.5%	47.3%	52.6%	47.4%
1948	3,940,257	1,678,007	Green, Dwight H.	2,250,074	Stevenson, Adlai E.	12,176	572,067 D	42.6%	57.1%	42.7%	57.3%

The 1976 vote was for a two-year term to permit shifting the vote for Governor to non-Presidential years. In 1986 there was no Democratic candidate for Governor on the ballot, Mark Fairchild being the "paired" Democrat for Lt. Governor and the Democratic vote above was cast for this ticket of "no name" and Fairchild. Other vote in this election was 1,256,626 Adlai E. Stevenson III (Solidarity) who received 40.0% of the total vote and came in second; 15,646 Gary L. Shilts (Libertarian); 6,843 Diane Roling (Socialist Workers) and 184 scattered.

POSTWAR VOTE FOR SENATOR

Year	Total Vote	Republican		Democratic		Other Vote	Rep.-Dem. Plurality	Percentage			
		Vote	Candidate	Vote	Candidate			Total Vote		Major Vote	
								Rep.	Dem.	Rep.	Dem.
1992	4,939,558	2,126,833	Williamson, Richard S.	2,631,229	Braun, Carol M.	181,496	504,396 D	43.1%	53.3%	44.7%	55.3%
1990	3,251,005	1,135,628	Martin, Lynn	2,115,377	Simon, Paul		979,749 D	34.9%	65.1%	34.9%	65.1%
1986	3,122,883	1,053,734	Koehler, Judy	2,033,783	Dixon, Alan J.	35,366	980,049 D	33.7%	65.1%	34.1%	65.9%
1984	4,787,473	2,308,039	Percy, Charles H.	2,397,303	Simon, Paul	82,131	89,264 D	48.2%	50.1%	49.1%	50.9%
1980	4,580,029	1,946,296	O'Neal, David C.	2,565,302	Dixon, Alan J.	68,431	619,006 D	42.5%	56.0%	43.1%	56.9%
1978	3,184,764	1,698,711	Percy, Charles H.	1,448,187	Seith, Alex	37,866	250,524 R	53.3%	45.5%	54.0%	46.0%
1974	2,914,666	1,084,884	Burditt, George M.	1,811,496	Stevenson, Adlai E., III	18,286	726,612 D	37.2%	62.2%	37.5%	62.5%
1972	4,608,380	2,867,078	Percy, Charles H.	1,721,031	Pucinski, Roman C.	20,271	1,146,047 R	62.2%	37.3%	62.5%	37.5%
1970 S	3,599,272	1,519,718	Smith, Ralph T.	2,065,054	Stevenson, Adlai E., III	14,500	545,336 D	42.2%	57.4%	42.4%	57.6%
1968	4,449,757	2,358,947	Dirksen, Everett M.	2,073,242	Clark, William G.	17,568	285,705 R	53.0%	46.6%	53.2%	46.8%
1966	3,822,725	2,100,449	Percy, Charles H.	1,678,147	Douglas, Paul H.	44,129	422,302 R	54.9%	43.9%	55.6%	44.4%
1962	3,709,216	1,961,202	Dirksen, Everett M.	1,748,007	Yates, Sidney R.	7	213,195 R	52.9%	47.1%	52.9%	47.1%
1960	4,632,796	2,093,846	Witwer, Samuel W.	2,530,943	Douglas, Paul H.	8,007	437,097 D	45.2%	54.6%	45.3%	54.7%
1956	4,264,830	2,307,352	Dirksen, Everett M.	1,949,883	Stengel, Richard	7,595	357,469 R	54.1%	45.7%	54.2%	45.8%
1954	3,368,025	1,563,683	Meek, Joseph T.	1,804,338	Douglas, Paul H.	4	240,655 D	46.4%	53.6%	46.4%	53.6%
1950	3,622,673	1,951,984	Dirksen, Everett M.	1,657,630	Lucas, Scott W.	13,059	294,354 R	53.9%	45.8%	54.1%	45.9%
1948	3,900,285	1,740,026	Brooks, C. Wayland	2,147,754	Douglas, Paul H.	12,505	407,728 D	44.6%	55.1%	44.8%	55.2%

The 1970 election was for a short term to fill a vacancy.

ILLINOIS

Districts Established November 6, 1991

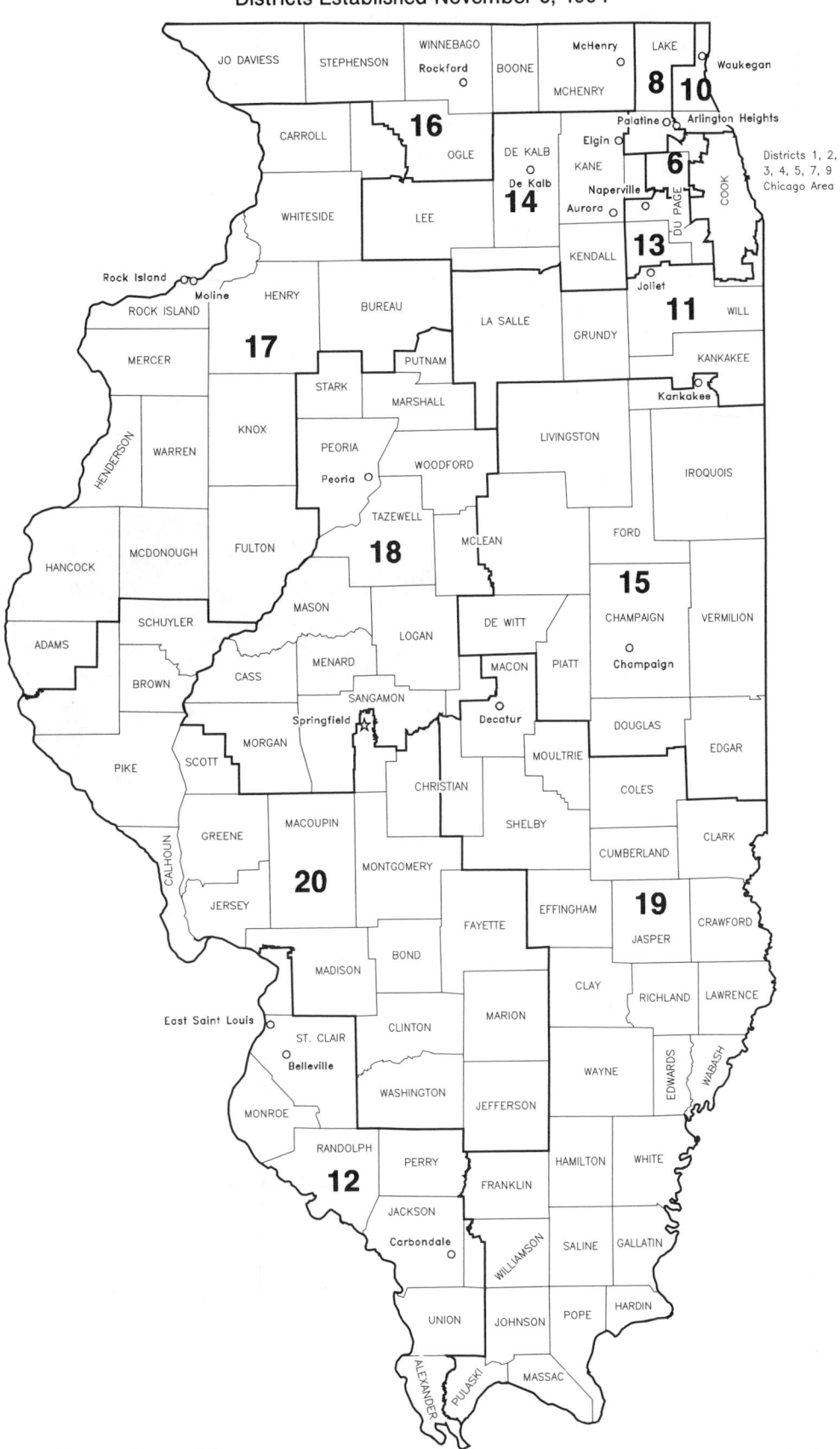

Districts 1, 2, 3, 4, 5, 7, 9 Chicago Area

COOK/DU PAGE COUNTY

CONGRESSIONAL DISTRICTS

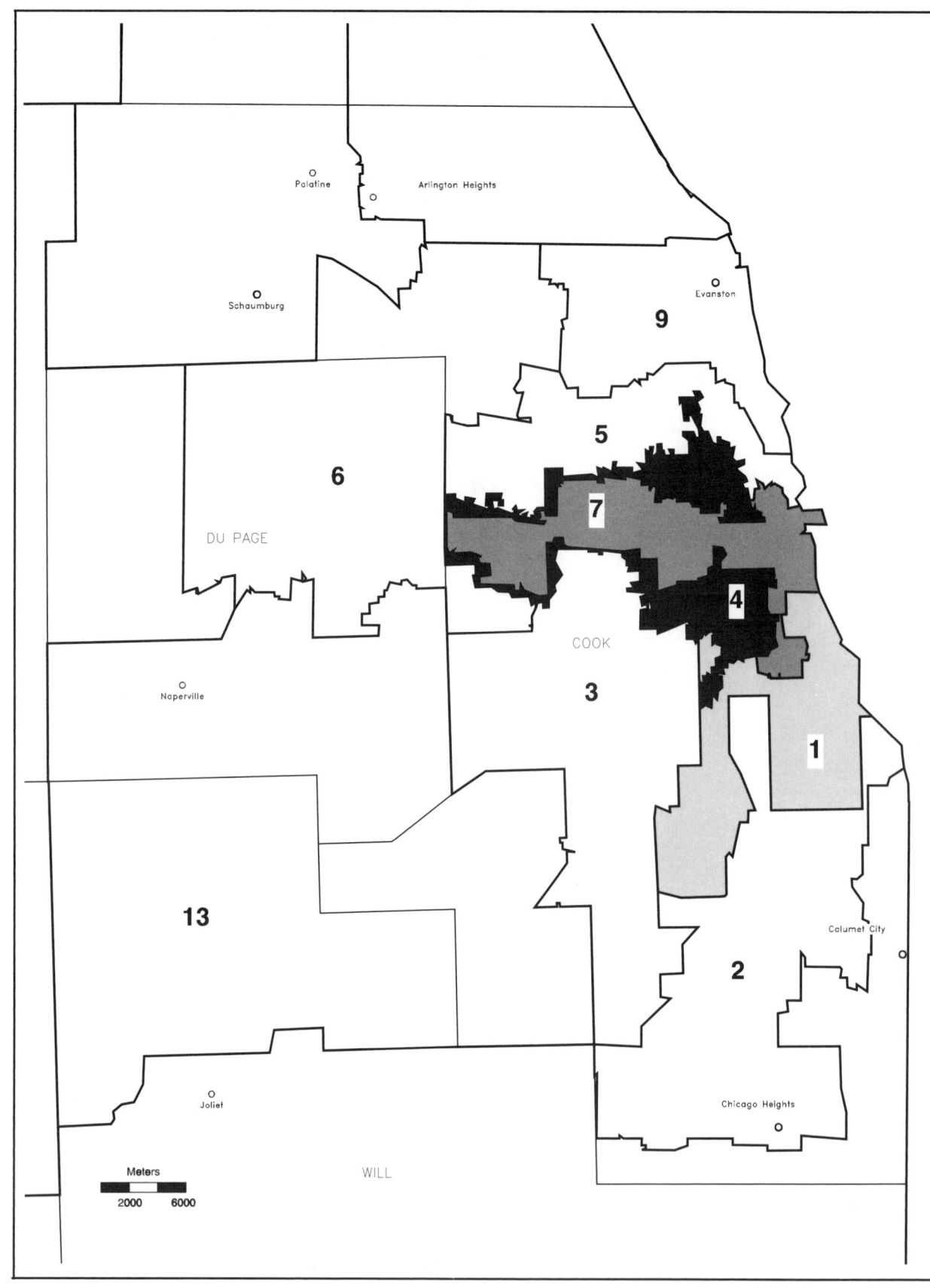

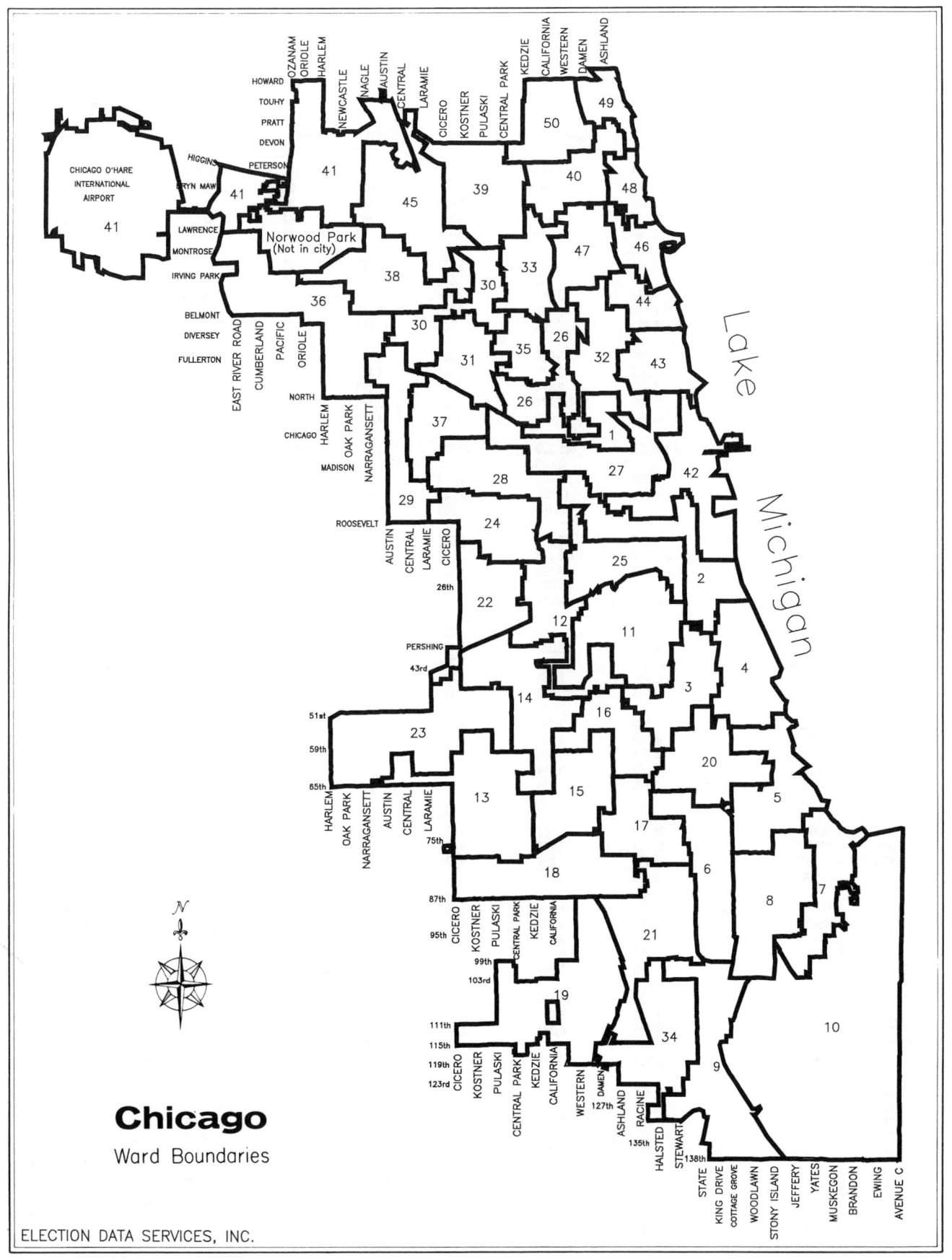

Chicago
Ward Boundaries

ILLINOIS

PRESIDENT 1992

Registration	County	Total Vote	Republican	Democratic	Perot	Other	Plurality	Percentage Total Vote		
								Rep.	Dem.	Perot
39,956	ADAMS	31,579	13,529	11,748	6,157	145	1,781 R	42.8%	37.2%	19.5%
8,046	ALEXANDER	4,362	1,301	2,566	474	21	1,265 D	29.8%	58.8%	10.9%
10,575	BOND	7,548	2,715	3,428	1,373	32	713 D	36.0%	45.4%	18.2%
15,540	BOONE	13,627	5,589	5,114	2,880	44	475 R	41.0%	37.5%	21.1%
3,604	BROWN	2,689	1,029	1,146	504	10	117 D	38.3%	42.6%	18.7%
22,306	BUREAU	17,907	6,836	7,551	3,465	55	715 D	38.2%	42.2%	19.3%
3,726	CALHOUN	2,803	745	1,519	532	7	774 D	26.6%	54.2%	19.0%
9,696	CARROLL	7,679	3,297	2,854	1,502	26	443 R	42.9%	37.2%	19.6%
9,601	CASS	6,447	2,162	3,200	1,072	13	1,038 D	33.5%	49.6%	16.6%
91,710	CHAMPAIGN	76,092	27,096	35,003	13,571	422	7,907 D	35.6%	46.0%	17.8%
23,579	CHRISTIAN	17,590	5,087	9,042	3,401	60	3,955 D	28.9%	51.4%	19.3%
10,634	CLARK	7,979	3,175	3,338	1,450	16	163 D	39.8%	41.8%	18.2%
9,379	CLAY	6,652	2,471	2,962	1,193	26	491 D	37.1%	44.5%	17.9%
19,309	CLINTON	15,822	5,771	6,686	3,315	50	915 D	36.5%	42.3%	21.0%
30,165	COLES	22,300	8,098	9,402	4,707	93	1,304 D	36.3%	42.2%	21.1%
2,924,493	COOK	2,146,655	605,300	1,249,533	281,999	9,823	644,233 D	28.2%	58.2%	13.1%
12,205	CRAWFORD	9,671	3,606	3,964	2,062	39	358 D	37.3%	41.0%	21.3%
8,226	CUMBERLAND	5,202	1,860	2,111	1,209	22	251 D	35.8%	40.6%	23.2%
40,618	DE KALB	34,232	12,655	13,744	7,680	153	1,089 D	37.0%	40.1%	22.4%
9,969	DE WITT	7,759	3,164	3,009	1,543	43	155 R	40.8%	38.8%	19.9%
10,798	DOUGLAS	8,276	3,309	3,341	1,600	26	32 D	40.0%	40.4%	19.3%
431,876	DU PAGE	370,987	178,271	114,564	76,839	1,313	63,707 R	48.1%	30.9%	20.7%
12,222	EDGAR	9,776	3,790	4,014	1,930	42	224 D	38.8%	41.1%	19.7%
4,766	EDWARDS	3,552	1,601	1,299	634	18	302 R	45.1%	36.6%	17.8%
16,853	EFFINGHAM	14,981	6,329	5,221	3,354	77	1,108 R	42.2%	34.9%	22.4%
12,048	FAYETTE	10,118	3,508	4,833	1,730	47	1,325 D	34.7%	47.8%	17.1%
7,788	FORD	6,481	3,046	2,175	1,222	38	871 R	47.0%	33.6%	18.9%
29,785	FRANKLIN	21,481	5,504	12,744	3,180	53	7,240 D	25.6%	59.3%	14.8%
24,018	FULTON	17,701	5,062	9,725	2,874	40	4,663 D	28.6%	54.9%	16.2%
4,944	GALLATIN	3,944	990	2,371	568	15	1,381 D	25.1%	60.1%	14.4%
9,130	GREENE	7,032	2,391	3,164	1,461	16	773 D	34.0%	45.0%	20.8%
19,487	GRUNDY	16,265	6,346	6,122	3,724	73	224 R	39.0%	37.6%	22.9%
6,160	HAMILTON	4,974	1,521	2,582	862	9	1,061 D	30.6%	51.9%	17.3%
13,502	HANCOCK	10,069	3,714	4,213	2,091	51	499 D	36.9%	41.8%	20.8%
3,866	HARDIN	3,173	985	1,665	515	8	680 D	31.0%	52.5%	16.2%
5,089	HENDERSON	4,048	1,310	2,013	715	10	703 D	32.4%	49.7%	17.7%
33,254	HENRY	24,371	8,989	11,077	4,231	74	2,088 D	36.9%	45.5%	17.4%
17,696	IROQUOIS	14,530	6,948	4,440	3,073	69	2,508 R	47.8%	30.6%	21.1%
35,604	JACKSON	24,434	6,899	13,373	3,995	167	6,474 D	28.2%	54.7%	16.4%
7,013	JASPER	5,480	1,996	2,284	1,160	40	288 D	36.4%	41.7%	21.2%
21,800	JEFFERSON	17,597	5,497	8,665	3,403	32	3,168 D	31.2%	49.2%	19.3%
12,757	JERSEY	10,093	2,933	4,749	2,363	48	1,816 D	29.1%	47.1%	23.4%
12,882	JO DAVIESS	10,454	4,249	4,044	2,102	59	205 R	40.6%	38.7%	20.1%
6,601	JOHNSON	5,391	2,124	2,299	944	24	175 D	39.4%	42.6%	17.5%
158,611	KANE	127,938	55,684	44,568	27,179	507	11,116 R	43.5%	34.8%	21.2%
48,955	KANKAKEE	40,071	15,411	17,229	7,264	167	1,818 D	38.5%	43.0%	18.1%
22,972	KENDALL	18,406	8,521	5,423	4,394	68	3,098 R	46.3%	29.5%	23.9%
31,559	KNOX	25,296	8,331	12,524	4,357	84	4,193 D	32.9%	49.5%	17.2%
271,375	LAKE	223,987	99,000	81,693	42,384	910	17,307 R	44.2%	36.5%	18.9%
61,394	LA SALLE	49,931	16,078	23,276	10,434	143	7,198 D	32.2%	46.6%	20.9%
9,675	LAWRENCE	7,488	2,681	3,270	1,498	39	589 D	35.8%	43.7%	20.0%
18,808	LEE	15,417	6,652	5,530	3,191	44	1,122 R	43.1%	35.9%	20.7%
20,254	LIVINGSTON	17,098	8,004	6,007	3,029	58	1,997 R	46.8%	35.1%	17.7%
20,770	LOGAN	14,195	6,567	5,169	2,420	39	1,398 R	46.3%	36.4%	17.0%
17,124	MCDONOUGH	13,922	5,297	5,814	2,770	41	517 D	38.0%	41.8%	19.9%
113,358	MCHENRY	88,294	41,356	24,783	21,817	338	16,573 R	46.8%	28.1%	24.7%
73,273	MCLEAN	59,285	25,726	23,090	10,282	187	2,636 R	43.4%	38.9%	17.3%
71,855	MACON	55,580	18,684	27,449	9,236	211	8,765 D	33.6%	49.4%	16.6%
31,811	MACOUPIN	23,661	6,518	12,050	5,018	75	5,532 D	27.5%	50.9%	21.2%
141,321	MADISON	114,095	32,167	58,484	23,110	334	26,317 D	28.2%	51.3%	20.3%

ILLINOIS

PRESIDENT 1992

Registration	County	Total Vote	Republican	Democratic	Perot	Other	Plurality	Percentage Total Vote		
								Rep.	Dem.	Perot
25,810	MARION	18,883	5,764	9,669	3,407	43	3,905 D	30.5%	51.2%	18.0%
8,070	MARSHALL	6,496	2,491	2,819	1,169	17	328 D	38.3%	43.4%	18.0%
9,680	MASON	7,702	2,473	3,969	1,245	15	1,496 D	32.1%	51.5%	16.2%
10,370	MASSAC	7,056	2,754	3,347	892	63	593 D	39.0%	47.4%	12.6%
7,462	MENARD	6,299	2,834	2,264	1,179	22	570 R	45.0%	35.9%	18.7%
11,074	MERCER	8,540	2,983	3,990	1,535	32	1,007 D	34.9%	46.7%	18.0%
15,329	MONROE	12,542	4,807	4,894	2,813	28	87 D	38.3%	39.0%	22.4%
18,208	MONTGOMERY	14,837	4,407	7,424	2,956	50	3,017 D	29.7%	50.0%	19.9%
20,121	MORGAN	16,297	6,566	6,351	3,317	63	215 R	40.3%	39.0%	20.4%
7,958	MOULTRIE	6,465	2,065	3,056	1,322	22	991 D	31.9%	47.3%	20.4%
26,870	OGLE	20,109	9,008	6,512	4,455	134	2,496 R	44.8%	32.4%	22.2%
98,304	PEORIA	81,328	30,718	38,099	12,195	316	7,381 D	37.8%	46.8%	15.0%
14,939	PERRY	11,086	3,105	6,009	1,955	17	2,904 D	28.0%	54.2%	17.6%
10,047	PIATT	8,447	3,076	3,520	1,822	29	444 D	36.4%	41.7%	21.6%
12,061	PIKE	9,037	3,342	4,016	1,643	36	674 D	37.0%	44.4%	18.2%
3,117	POPE	2,411	951	1,063	391	6	112 D	39.4%	44.1%	16.2%
5,119	PULASKI	3,549	1,169	1,987	379	14	818 D	32.9%	56.0%	10.7%
4,232	PUTNAM	3,308	969	1,574	752	13	605 D	29.3%	47.6%	22.7%
21,559	RANDOLPH	16,565	4,899	8,529	3,092	45	3,630 D	29.6%	51.5%	18.7%
10,963	RICHLAND	8,061	3,053	3,286	1,689	33	233 D	37.9%	40.8%	21.0%
91,938	ROCK ISLAND	72,039	23,212	37,412	10,416	999	14,200 D	32.2%	51.9%	14.5%
148,101	ST. CLAIR	107,541	31,951	57,625	17,592	373	25,674 D	29.7%	53.6%	16.4%
16,705	SALINE	13,254	3,667	7,258	2,302	27	3,591 D	27.7%	54.8%	17.4%
121,873	SANGAMON	96,860	39,641	40,052	16,861	306	411 D	40.9%	41.4%	17.4%
5,479	SCHUYLER	3,995	1,512	1,650	815	18	138 D	37.8%	41.3%	20.4%
3,746	SCOTT	2,783	1,132	1,057	588	6	75 R	40.7%	38.0%	21.1%
13,761	SHELBY	11,175	3,631	5,101	2,401	42	1,470 D	32.5%	45.6%	21.5%
4,155	STARK	3,351	1,384	1,336	625	6	48 R	41.3%	39.9%	18.7%
26,826	STEPHENSON	21,656	9,005	7,899	4,677	75	1,106 R	41.6%	36.5%	21.6%
79,136	TAZEWELL	59,994	23,469	26,428	9,927	170	2,959 D	39.1%	44.1%	16.5%
12,483	UNION	9,083	3,003	4,681	1,373	26	1,678 D	33.1%	51.5%	15.1%
47,246	VERMILION	38,461	11,703	18,383	8,162	213	6,680 D	30.4%	47.8%	21.2%
8,704	WABASH	6,240	2,485	2,436	1,302	17	49 R	39.8%	39.0%	20.9%
11,908	WARREN	8,446	3,325	3,661	1,436	24	336 D	39.4%	43.3%	17.0%
9,642	WASHINGTON	7,555	3,003	2,986	1,542	24	17 R	39.7%	39.5%	20.4%
12,143	WAYNE	8,872	3,809	3,332	1,702	29	477 R	42.9%	37.6%	19.2%
12,102	WHITE	8,811	3,057	4,308	1,428	18	1,251 D	34.7%	48.9%	16.2%
32,555	WHITESIDE	27,153	10,146	12,329	4,589	89	2,183 D	37.4%	45.4%	16.9%
219,528	WILL	152,123	58,337	59,633	32,788	1,365	1,296 D	38.3%	39.2%	21.6%
40,968	WILLIAMSON	28,760	9,462	14,361	4,779	158	4,899 D	32.9%	49.9%	16.6%
144,016	WINNEBAGO	112,215	42,221	48,298	21,227	469	6,077 D	37.6%	43.0%	18.9%
19,659	WOODFORD	16,305	8,032	5,490	2,733	50	2,542 R	49.3%	33.7%	16.8%
6,600,358	TOTAL	5,050,157	1,734,096	2,453,350	840,515	22,196	719,254 D	34.3%	48.6%	16.6%

ILLINOIS

SENATOR 1992

Registration	County	Total Vote	Republican	Democratic	Other	Rep.-Dem. Plurality	Percentage Total Vote Rep.	Dem.	Major Vote Rep.	Dem.
39,956	ADAMS	30,697	15,759	13,473	1,465	2,286 R	51.3%	43.9%	53.9%	46.1%
8,046	ALEXANDER	4,182	1,576	2,517	89	941 D	37.7%	60.2%	38.5%	61.5%
10,575	BOND	7,171	3,137	3,723	311	586 D	43.7%	51.9%	45.7%	54.3%
15,540	BOONE	13,392	6,830	5,648	914	1,182 R	51.0%	42.2%	54.7%	45.3%
3,604	BROWN	2,591	1,331	1,160	100	171 R	51.4%	44.8%	53.4%	46.6%
22,306	BUREAU	17,434	8,326	8,438	670	112 D	47.8%	48.4%	49.7%	50.3%
3,726	CALHOUN	2,663	953	1,654	56	701 D	35.8%	62.1%	36.6%	63.4%
9,696	CARROLL	7,521	4,140	3,064	317	1,076 R	55.0%	40.7%	57.5%	42.5%
9,601	CASS	6,253	2,654	3,361	238	707 D	42.4%	53.8%	44.1%	55.9%
91,710	CHAMPAIGN	73,854	32,236	38,103	3,515	5,867 D	43.6%	51.6%	45.8%	54.2%
23,579	CHRISTIAN	17,263	6,951	9,561	751	2,610 D	40.3%	55.4%	42.1%	57.9%
10,634	CLARK	7,724	3,815	3,636	273	179 R	49.4%	47.1%	51.2%	48.8%
9,379	CLAY	6,440	3,014	3,157	269	143 D	46.8%	49.0%	48.8%	51.2%
19,309	CLINTON	15,163	7,068	7,467	628	399 D	46.6%	49.2%	48.6%	51.4%
30,165	COLES	21,878	10,300	10,704	874	404 D	47.1%	48.9%	49.0%	51.0%
2,924,493	COOK	2,105,233	754,945	1,294,440	55,848	539,495 D	35.9%	61.5%	36.8%	63.2%
12,205	CRAWFORD	9,336	4,965	4,106	265	859 R	53.2%	44.0%	54.7%	45.3%
8,226	CUMBERLAND	5,064	2,444	2,359	261	85 R	48.3%	46.6%	50.9%	49.1%
40,618	DE KALB	33,602	15,596	16,133	1,873	537 D	46.4%	48.0%	49.2%	50.8%
9,969	DE WITT	7,538	3,872	3,299	367	573 R	51.4%	43.8%	54.0%	46.0%
10,798	DOUGLAS	8,083	4,095	3,708	280	387 R	50.7%	45.9%	52.5%	47.5%
431,876	DU PAGE	364,557	210,818	139,402	14,337	71,416 R	57.8%	38.2%	60.2%	39.8%
12,222	EDGAR	9,427	5,000	4,187	240	813 R	53.0%	44.4%	54.4%	45.6%
4,766	EDWARDS	3,319	1,711	1,478	130	233 R	51.6%	44.5%	53.7%	46.3%
16,853	EFFINGHAM	14,525	7,639	5,896	990	1,743 R	52.6%	40.6%	56.4%	43.6%
12,048	FAYETTE	9,836	4,452	4,977	407	525 D	45.3%	50.6%	47.2%	52.8%
7,788	FORD	6,315	3,530	2,431	354	1,099 R	55.9%	38.5%	59.2%	40.8%
29,785	FRANKLIN	20,640	7,438	12,391	811	4,953 D	36.0%	60.0%	37.5%	62.5%
24,018	FULTON	17,399	6,325	10,393	681	4,068 D	36.4%	59.7%	37.8%	62.2%
4,944	GALLATIN	3,674	1,118	2,442	114	1,324 D	30.4%	66.5%	31.4%	68.6%
9,130	GREENE	6,704	2,994	3,444	266	450 D	44.7%	51.4%	46.5%	53.5%
19,487	GRUNDY	15,898	8,406	6,759	733	1,647 R	52.9%	42.5%	55.4%	44.6%
6,160	HAMILTON	4,433	2,066	2,285	82	219 D	46.6%	51.5%	47.5%	52.5%
13,502	HANCOCK	9,720	4,610	4,651	459	41 D	47.4%	47.8%	49.8%	50.2%
3,866	HARDIN	2,933	1,232	1,616	85	384 D	42.0%	55.1%	43.3%	56.7%
5,089	HENDERSON	3,928	1,627	2,178	123	551 D	41.4%	55.4%	42.8%	57.2%
33,254	HENRY	23,757	11,197	11,690	870	493 D	47.1%	49.2%	48.9%	51.1%
17,696	IROQUOIS	14,180	8,368	5,066	746	3,302 R	59.0%	35.7%	62.3%	37.7%
35,604	JACKSON	24,009	9,342	13,665	1,002	4,323 D	38.9%	56.9%	40.6%	59.4%
7,013	JASPER	5,249	2,353	2,430	466	77 D	44.8%	46.3%	49.2%	50.8%
21,800	JEFFERSON	16,964	7,783	8,435	746	652 D	45.9%	49.7%	48.0%	52.0%
12,757	JERSEY	9,741	3,729	5,572	440	1,843 D	38.3%	57.2%	40.1%	59.9%
12,882	JO DAVIESS	10,051	5,136	4,493	422	643 R	51.1%	44.7%	53.3%	46.7%
6,601	JOHNSON	5,180	2,780	2,234	166	546 R	53.7%	43.1%	55.4%	44.6%
158,611	KANE	125,631	65,092	53,407	7,132	11,685 R	51.8%	42.5%	54.9%	45.1%
48,955	KANKAKEE	39,450	18,924	18,795	1,731	129 R	48.0%	47.6%	50.2%	49.8%
22,972	KENDALL	18,245	10,582	6,740	923	3,842 R	58.0%	36.9%	61.1%	38.9%
31,559	KNOX	24,702	10,877	13,001	824	2,124 D	44.0%	52.6%	45.6%	54.4%
271,375	LAKE	216,211	113,541	93,996	8,674	19,545 R	52.5%	43.5%	54.7%	45.3%
61,394	LA SALLE	48,702	21,993	24,556	2,153	2,563 D	45.2%	50.4%	47.2%	52.8%
9,675	LAWRENCE	7,142	3,286	3,612	244	326 D	46.0%	50.6%	47.6%	52.4%
18,808	LEE	15,090	8,179	6,240	671	1,939 R	54.2%	41.4%	56.7%	43.3%
20,254	LIVINGSTON	16,788	9,321	6,776	691	2,545 R	55.5%	40.4%	57.9%	42.1%
20,770	LOGAN	13,802	7,469	5,558	775	1,911 R	54.1%	40.3%	57.3%	42.7%
17,124	MCDONOUGH	13,504	6,490	6,430	584	60 R	48.1%	47.6%	50.2%	49.8%
113,358	MCHENRY	86,560	49,057	32,339	5,164	16,718 R	56.7%	37.4%	60.3%	39.7%
73,273	MCLEAN	58,487	29,619	26,585	2,283	3,034 R	50.6%	45.5%	52.7%	47.3%
71,855	MACON	54,833	23,421	28,897	2,515	5,476 D	42.7%	52.7%	44.8%	55.2%
31,811	MACOUPIN	23,016	8,361	13,842	813	5,481 D	36.3%	60.1%	37.7%	62.3%
141,321	MADISON	110,950	40,243	66,228	4,479	25,985 D	36.3%	59.7%	37.8%	62.2%

ILLINOIS

SENATOR 1992

Registration	County	Total Vote	Republican	Democratic	Other	Rep.-Dem. Plurality	Percentage			
							Total Vote		Major Vote	
							Rep.	Dem.	Rep.	Dem.
25,810	MARION	18,302	7,216	10,372	714	3,156 D	39.4%	56.7%	41.0%	59.0%
8,070	MARSHALL	6,370	2,883	3,211	276	328 D	45.3%	50.4%	47.3%	52.7%
9,680	MASON	7,524	3,018	4,205	301	1,187 D	40.1%	55.9%	41.8%	58.2%
10,370	MASSAC	6,792	3,198	3,348	246	150 D	47.1%	49.3%	48.9%	51.1%
7,462	MENARD	6,147	3,274	2,565	308	709 R	53.3%	41.7%	56.1%	43.9%
11,074	MERCER	8,337	4,045	4,033	259	12 R	48.5%	48.4%	50.1%	49.9%
15,329	MONROE	12,076	6,109	5,461	506	648 R	50.6%	45.2%	52.8%	47.2%
18,208	MONTGOMERY	14,410	5,659	8,104	647	2,445 D	39.3%	56.2%	41.1%	58.9%
20,121	MORGAN	16,046	8,351	7,104	591	1,247 R	52.0%	44.3%	54.0%	46.0%
7,958	MOULTRIE	6,317	2,697	3,369	251	672 D	42.7%	53.3%	44.5%	55.5%
26,870	OGLE	19,622	10,664	7,565	1,393	3,099 R	54.3%	38.6%	58.5%	41.5%
98,304	PEORIA	79,495	34,541	41,204	3,750	6,663 D	43.5%	51.8%	45.6%	54.4%
14,939	PERRY	10,699	4,327	5,820	552	1,493 D	40.4%	54.4%	42.6%	57.4%
10,047	PIATT	8,247	3,908	3,953	386	45 D	47.4%	47.9%	49.7%	50.3%
12,061	PIKE	8,719	4,145	4,277	297	132 D	47.5%	49.1%	49.2%	50.8%
3,117	POPE	2,306	1,194	1,043	69	151 R	51.8%	45.2%	53.4%	46.6%
5,119	PULASKI	3,427	1,429	1,924	74	495 D	41.7%	56.1%	42.6%	57.4%
4,232	PUTNAM	3,203	1,290	1,823	90	533 D	40.3%	56.9%	41.4%	58.6%
21,559	RANDOLPH	16,188	6,569	9,033	586	2,464 D	40.6%	55.8%	42.1%	57.9%
10,963	RICHLAND	7,776	3,764	3,601	411	163 R	48.4%	46.3%	51.1%	48.9%
91,938	ROCK ISLAND	70,504	30,072	37,465	2,967	7,393 D	42.7%	53.1%	44.5%	55.5%
148,101	ST. CLAIR	104,370	39,200	61,508	3,662	22,308 D	37.6%	58.9%	38.9%	61.1%
16,705	SALINE	12,650	5,044	7,230	376	2,186 D	39.9%	57.2%	41.1%	58.9%
121,873	SANGAMON	95,308	47,743	44,248	3,317	3,495 R	50.1%	46.4%	51.9%	48.1%
5,479	SCHUYLER	3,883	1,867	1,837	179	30 R	48.1%	47.3%	50.4%	49.6%
3,746	SCOTT	2,710	1,450	1,150	110	300 R	53.5%	42.4%	55.8%	44.2%
13,761	SHELBY	10,896	4,801	5,510	585	709 D	44.1%	50.6%	46.6%	53.4%
4,155	STARK	3,237	1,584	1,508	145	76 R	48.9%	46.6%	51.2%	48.8%
26,826	STEPHENSON	21,016	10,936	8,820	1,260	2,116 R	52.0%	42.0%	55.4%	44.6%
79,136	TAZEWELL	58,822	26,387	29,362	3,073	2,975 D	44.9%	49.9%	47.3%	52.7%
12,483	UNION	8,787	3,658	4,837	292	1,179 D	41.6%	55.0%	43.1%	56.9%
47,246	VERMILION	37,558	16,079	19,990	1,489	3,911 D	42.8%	53.2%	44.6%	55.4%
8,704	WABASH	5,957	2,635	3,048	274	413 D	44.2%	51.2%	46.4%	53.6%
11,908	WARREN	8,277	4,080	3,958	239	122 R	49.3%	47.8%	50.8%	49.2%
9,642	WASHINGTON	7,214	3,719	3,247	248	472 R	51.6%	45.0%	53.4%	46.6%
12,143	WAYNE	8,397	4,545	3,306	546	1,239 R	54.1%	39.4%	57.9%	42.1%
12,102	WHITE	8,360	3,437	4,656	267	1,219 D	41.1%	55.7%	42.5%	57.5%
32,555	WHITESIDE	26,619	12,003	13,650	966	1,647 D	45.1%	51.3%	46.8%	53.2%
219,528	WILL	150,328	77,550	66,660	6,118	10,890 R	51.6%	44.3%	53.8%	46.2%
40,968	WILLIAMSON	28,042	12,587	14,037	1,418	1,450 D	44.9%	50.1%	47.3%	52.7%
144,016	WINNEBAGO	110,105	50,404	51,962	7,739	1,558 D	45.8%	47.2%	49.2%	50.8%
19,659	WOODFORD	15,881	8,655	6,397	829	2,258 R	54.5%	40.3%	57.5%	42.5%
6,600,358	TOTAL	4,939,558	2,126,833	2,631,229	181,496	504,396 D	43.1%	53.3%	44.7%	55.3%

CHICAGO

PRESIDENT 1992

Registration	Ward	Total Vote	Republican	Democratic	Perot	Other	Plurality	Percentage Total Vote		
								Rep.	Dem.	Perot
21,302	WARD 1	12,705	2,073	9,329	1,189	114	7,256 D	16.3%	73.4%	9.4%
33,144	WARD 2	20,923	1,558	18,304	934	127	16,746 D	7.4%	87.5%	4.5%
32,707	WARD 3	18,104	408	17,237	345	114	16,829 D	2.3%	95.2%	1.9%
34,902	WARD 4	24,974	1,121	22,974	722	157	21,853 D	4.5%	92.0%	2.9%
34,269	WARD 5	25,814	1,209	23,609	816	180	22,400 D	4.7%	91.5%	3.2%
40,626	WARD 6	29,225	639	27,795	660	131	27,135 D	2.2%	95.1%	2.3%
33,761	WARD 7	23,745	844	22,080	725	96	21,236 D	3.6%	93.0%	3.1%
41,270	WARD 8	30,371	639	28,959	644	129	28,315 D	2.1%	95.4%	2.1%
36,006	WARD 9	24,109	612	22,837	563	97	22,225 D	2.5%	94.7%	2.3%
29,683	WARD 10	20,249	4,776	12,392	2,970	111	7,616 D	23.6%	61.2%	14.7%
26,853	WARD 11	21,438	5,343	12,881	3,127	87	7,538 D	24.9%	60.1%	14.6%
12,035	WARD 12	7,268	1,688	4,553	994	33	2,865 D	23.2%	62.6%	13.7%
32,494	WARD 13	28,170	9,401	13,453	5,205	111	4,052 D	33.4%	47.8%	18.5%
22,515	WARD 14	17,993	5,506	9,443	2,949	95	3,937 D	30.6%	52.5%	16.4%
31,248	WARD 15	20,038	1,591	17,402	924	121	15,811 D	7.9%	86.8%	4.6%
26,747	WARD 16	15,606	781	14,187	543	95	13,406 D	5.0%	90.9%	3.5%
37,129	WARD 17	23,417	398	22,480	421	118	22,059 D	1.7%	96.0%	1.8%
39,215	WARD 18	29,838	6,099	20,649	2,986	104	14,550 D	20.4%	69.2%	10.0%
39,884	WARD 19	32,330	10,916	16,111	5,168	135	5,195 D	33.8%	49.8%	16.0%
34,775	WARD 20	21,786	476	20,778	419	113	20,302 D	2.2%	95.4%	1.9%
43,260	WARD 21	30,219	620	28,833	654	112	28,179 D	2.1%	95.4%	2.2%
14,985	WARD 22	8,983	996	7,360	568	59	6,364 D	11.1%	81.9%	6.3%
34,430	WARD 23	29,227	9,684	14,083	5,345	115	4,399 D	33.1%	48.2%	18.3%
34,941	WARD 24	20,449	349	19,641	358	101	19,283 D	1.7%	96.0%	1.8%
14,356	WARD 25	8,801	1,936	5,940	872	53	4,004 D	22.0%	67.5%	9.9%
22,783	WARD 26	14,044	2,493	10,165	1,289	97	7,672 D	17.8%	72.4%	9.2%
34,339	WARD 27	20,833	2,344	17,182	1,168	139	14,838 D	11.3%	82.5%	5.6%
38,216	WARD 28	21,187	404	20,343	328	112	19,939 D	1.9%	96.0%	1.5%
34,563	WARD 29	21,613	1,414	19,156	948	95	17,742 D	6.5%	88.6%	4.4%
22,301	WARD 30	16,883	5,413	8,678	2,701	91	3,265 D	32.1%	51.4%	16.0%
20,145	WARD 31	12,702	3,191	8,074	1,360	77	4,883 D	25.1%	63.6%	10.7%
29,935	WARD 32	23,114	4,983	14,818	3,130	183	9,835 D	21.6%	64.1%	13.5%
19,936	WARD 33	15,124	3,842	9,032	2,169	81	5,190 D	25.4%	59.7%	14.3%
41,251	WARD 34	27,799	550	26,558	593	98	25,965 D	2.0%	95.5%	2.1%
19,719	WARD 35	12,717	2,838	8,498	1,281	100	5,660 D	22.3%	66.8%	10.1%
33,559	WARD 36	26,455	9,657	12,245	4,447	106	2,588 D	36.5%	46.3%	16.8%
33,951	WARD 37	20,322	707	18,992	526	97	18,285 D	3.5%	93.5%	2.6%
30,803	WARD 38	24,180	8,641	11,017	4,414	108	2,376 D	35.7%	45.6%	18.3%
23,043	WARD 39	18,648	6,394	9,486	2,676	92	3,092 D	34.3%	50.9%	14.4%
23,217	WARD 40	18,463	4,789	11,273	2,274	127	6,484 D	25.9%	61.1%	12.3%
38,013	WARD 41	30,820	13,196	11,820	5,714	90	1,376 R	42.8%	38.4%	18.5%
38,964	WARD 42	33,211	11,136	17,889	4,021	165	6,753 D	33.5%	53.9%	12.1%
38,576	WARD 43	32,970	10,744	18,119	3,944	163	7,375 D	32.6%	55.0%	12.0%
37,140	WARD 44	32,112	7,184	21,308	3,453	167	14,124 D	22.4%	66.4%	10.8%
33,834	WARD 45	27,492	10,293	11,891	5,201	107	1,598 D	37.4%	43.3%	18.9%
28,242	WARD 46	21,051	3,839	15,204	1,883	125	11,365 D	18.2%	72.2%	8.9%
27,097	WARD 47	22,210	4,850	14,209	3,014	137	9,359 D	21.8%	64.0%	13.6%
25,475	WARD 48	19,629	3,717	14,011	1,785	116	10,294 D	18.9%	71.4%	9.1%
21,105	WARD 49	16,518	2,355	12,534	1,461	168	10,179 D	14.3%	75.9%	8.8%
25,863	WARD 50	20,436	4,190	14,350	1,796	100	10,160 D	20.5%	70.2%	8.8%
	ABSENTEE	4,703	1,145	3,110	427	21	1,965 D	24.3%	66.1%	9.1%
1,524,607	TOTAL	1,101,018	199,972	793,272	102,104	5,670	593,300 D	18.2%	72.0%	9.3%

CHICAGO

SENATOR 1992

| | | | | | | | Percentage | | | |
| | | | | | | | Total Vote | | Major Vote | |
Registration	Ward	Total Vote	Republican	Democratic	Other	Rep.-Dem. Plurality	Rep.	Dem.	Rep.	Dem.
21,302	WARD 1	12,346	2,285	9,725	336	7,440 D	18.5%	78.8%	19.0%	81.0%
33,144	WARD 2	20,758	1,579	18,950	229	17,371 D	7.6%	91.3%	7.7%	92.3%
32,707	WARD 3	17,980	300	17,531	149	17,231 D	1.7%	97.5%	1.7%	98.3%
34,902	WARD 4	24,766	1,045	23,494	227	22,449 D	4.2%	94.9%	4.3%	95.7%
34,269	WARD 5	25,710	1,107	24,405	198	23,298 D	4.3%	94.9%	4.3%	95.7%
40,626	WARD 6	29,151	291	28,743	117	28,452 D	1.0%	98.6%	1.0%	99.0%
33,761	WARD 7	23,707	745	22,831	131	22,086 D	3.1%	96.3%	3.2%	96.8%
41,270	WARD 8	30,308	341	29,843	124	29,502 D	1.1%	98.5%	1.1%	98.9%
36,006	WARD 9	24,012	503	23,382	127	22,879 D	2.1%	97.4%	2.1%	97.9%
29,683	WARD 10	19,809	7,423	11,929	457	4,506 D	37.5%	60.2%	38.4%	61.6%
26,853	WARD 11	20,880	7,540	12,787	553	5,247 D	36.1%	61.2%	37.1%	62.9%
12,035	WARD 12	7,104	2,182	4,658	264	2,476 D	30.7%	65.6%	31.9%	68.1%
32,494	WARD 13	27,486	13,703	12,951	832	752 R	49.9%	47.1%	51.4%	48.6%
22,515	WARD 14	17,547	7,866	9,074	607	1,208 D	44.8%	51.7%	46.4%	53.6%
31,248	WARD 15	19,813	1,943	17,642	228	15,699 D	9.8%	89.0%	9.9%	90.1%
26,747	WARD 16	15,551	890	14,499	162	13,609 D	5.7%	93.2%	5.8%	94.2%
37,129	WARD 17	23,295	215	22,963	117	22,748 D	0.9%	98.6%	0.9%	99.1%
39,215	WARD 18	29,491	8,295	20,668	528	12,373 D	28.1%	70.1%	28.6%	71.4%
39,884	WARD 19	31,645	14,343	16,502	800	2,159 D	45.3%	52.1%	46.5%	53.5%
34,775	WARD 20	21,733	271	21,350	112	21,079 D	1.2%	98.2%	1.3%	98.7%
43,260	WARD 21	30,143	276	29,724	143	29,448 D	0.9%	98.6%	0.9%	99.1%
14,985	WARD 22	8,888	1,055	7,656	177	6,601 D	11.9%	86.1%	12.1%	87.9%
34,430	WARD 23	28,212	14,529	12,867	816	1,662 R	51.5%	45.6%	53.0%	47.0%
34,941	WARD 24	20,321	194	20,016	111	19,822 D	1.0%	98.5%	1.0%	99.0%
14,356	WARD 25	8,616	2,273	6,116	227	3,843 D	26.4%	71.0%	27.1%	72.9%
22,783	WARD 26	13,677	2,475	10,812	390	8,337 D	18.1%	79.1%	18.6%	81.4%
34,339	WARD 27	20,522	2,450	17,693	379	15,243 D	11.9%	86.2%	12.2%	87.8%
38,216	WARD 28	21,010	226	20,659	125	20,433 D	1.1%	98.3%	1.1%	98.9%
34,563	WARD 29	21,408	1,653	19,547	208	17,894 D	7.7%	91.3%	7.8%	92.2%
22,301	WARD 30	16,389	7,190	8,564	635	1,374 D	43.9%	52.3%	45.6%	54.4%
20,145	WARD 31	12,238	3,504	8,335	399	4,831 D	28.6%	68.1%	29.6%	70.4%
29,935	WARD 32	22,567	6,119	15,787	661	9,668 D	27.1%	70.0%	27.9%	72.1%
19,936	WARD 33	14,777	4,936	9,373	468	4,437 D	33.4%	63.4%	34.5%	65.5%
41,251	WARD 34	27,690	297	27,259	134	26,962 D	1.1%	98.4%	1.1%	98.9%
19,719	WARD 35	12,332	2,973	8,958	401	5,985 D	24.1%	72.6%	24.9%	75.1%
33,559	WARD 36	25,730	13,233	11,797	700	1,436 R	51.4%	45.8%	52.9%	47.1%
33,951	WARD 37	20,192	615	19,413	164	18,798 D	3.0%	96.1%	3.1%	96.9%
30,803	WARD 38	23,434	11,920	10,729	785	1,191 R	50.9%	45.8%	52.6%	47.4%
23,043	WARD 39	18,059	8,013	9,471	575	1,458 D	44.4%	52.4%	45.8%	54.2%
23,217	WARD 40	17,962	5,941	11,470	551	5,529 D	33.1%	63.9%	34.1%	65.9%
38,013	WARD 41	29,792	17,272	11,664	856	5,608 R	58.0%	39.2%	59.7%	40.3%
38,964	WARD 42	32,238	12,701	18,892	645	6,191 D	39.4%	58.6%	40.2%	59.8%
38,576	WARD 43	32,021	11,328	20,040	653	8,712 D	35.4%	62.6%	36.1%	63.9%
37,140	WARD 44	31,399	8,121	22,629	649	14,508 D	25.9%	72.1%	26.4%	73.6%
33,834	WARD 45	26,734	13,670	12,187	877	1,483 R	51.1%	45.6%	52.9%	47.1%
28,242	WARD 46	20,666	4,306	15,816	544	11,510 D	20.8%	76.5%	21.4%	78.6%
27,097	WARD 47	21,690	6,241	14,829	620	8,588 D	28.8%	68.4%	29.6%	70.4%
25,475	WARD 48	19,225	4,514	14,288	423	9,774 D	23.5%	74.3%	24.0%	76.0%
21,105	WARD 49	16,246	2,853	12,954	439	10,101 D	17.6%	79.7%	18.0%	82.0%
25,863	WARD 50	19,859	6,346	13,006	507	6,660 D	32.0%	65.5%	32.8%	67.2%
	ABSENTEE	4,521	1,312	3,143	66	1,831 D	29.0%	69.5%	29.5%	70.5%
1,524,607	TOTAL	1,081,650	251,403	809,621	20,626	558,218 D	23.2%	74.9%	23.7%	76.3%

ILLINOIS

CONGRESS

CD	Year	Total Vote	Republican Vote	Republican Candidate	Democratic Vote	Democratic Candidate	Other Vote	Rep.-Dem. Plurality	Percentage Total Vote Rep.	Dem.	Major Vote Rep.	Dem.
1	1992	252,711	43,453	WALKER, JAY	209,258	RUSH, BOBBY L.		165,805 D	17.2%	82.8%	17.2%	82.8%
2	1992	233,864	31,957	BLACKSTONE, RON	182,614	REYNOLDS, MELVIN J.	19,293	150,657 D	13.7%	78.1%	14.9%	85.1%
3	1992	255,293	93,128	LEPINSKE, HARRY C.	162,165	LIPINSKI, WILLIAM O.		69,037 D	36.5%	63.5%	36.5%	63.5%
4	1992	116,606	26,154	RODRIGUEZ-SCHEIMAN, H.	90,452	GUTIERREZ, LUIS V.		64,298 D	22.4%	77.6%	22.4%	77.6%
5	1992	232,083	90,738	ZENKICH, ELIAS R.	132,889	ROSTENKOWSKI, DANIEL	8,456	42,151 D	39.1%	57.3%	40.6%	59.4%
6	1992	251,904	165,009	HYDE, HENRY J.	86,891	WATKINS, BARRY W.	4	78,118 R	65.5%	34.5%	65.5%	34.5%
7	1992	225,281	35,346	BOCCIO, NORMAN G.	182,811	COLLINS, CARDISS	7,124	147,465 D	15.7%	81.1%	16.2%	83.8%
8	1992	238,633	132,887	CRANE, PHILIP M.	96,419	SMITH, SHEILA A.	9,327	36,468 R	55.7%	40.4%	58.0%	42.0%
9	1992	239,703	64,760	SOHN, HERBERT	162,942	YATES, SIDNEY R.	12,001	98,182 D	27.0%	68.0%	28.4%	71.6%
10	1992	240,630	155,230	PORTER, JOHN E.	85,400	KENNEDY, MICHAEL J.		69,830 R	64.5%	35.5%	64.5%	35.5%
11	1992	243,247	107,860	HERBOLSHEIMER, ROBERT T.	135,387	SANGMEISTER, GEORGE E.		27,527 D	44.3%	55.7%	44.3%	55.7%
12	1992	236,877	68,115	STARR, MIKE	168,762	COSTELLO, JERRY F.		100,647 D	28.8%	71.2%	28.8%	71.2%
13	1992	262,255	179,257	FAWELL, HARRIS W.	82,985	TEMPLE, DENNIS M.	13	96,272 R	68.4%	31.6%	68.4%	31.6%
14	1992	230,624	155,271	HASTERT, J. DENNIS	75,294	REICH, JONATHAN A.	59	79,977 R	67.3%	32.6%	67.3%	32.7%
15	1992	239,586	142,167	EWING, THOMAS	97,190	MATTIS, CHARLES D.	229	44,977 R	59.3%	40.6%	59.4%	40.6%
16	1992	255,943	142,388	MANZULLO, DONALD	113,555	COX, JOHN W.		28,833 R	55.6%	44.4%	55.6%	44.4%
17	1991	259,952	103,719	SCHLOEMER, KEN	156,233	EVANS, LANE		52,514 D	39.9%	60.1%	39.9%	60.1%
18	1992	270,976	156,533	MICHEL, ROBERT H.	114,413	HAWKINS, RONALD C.	30	42,120 R	57.8%	42.2%	57.8%	42.2%
19	1992	270,685	83,526	LEE, DOUGLAS E.	187,156	POSHARD, GLENN	3	103,630 D	30.9%	69.1%	30.9%	69.1%
20	1992	274,088	119,219	SHIMKUS, JOHN M.	154,869	DURBIN, RICHARD J.		35,650 D	43.5%	56.5%	43.5%	56.5%

ILLINOIS

1992 GENERAL ELECTION

President   Other vote was 9,218 Libertarian (Marrou); 5,267 New Alliance (Fulani); 3,577 Populist (Gritz); 2,751 Natural Law (Hagelin); 1,361 Socialist Workers (Warren); 22 scattered write-in.

Senator   Other vote was 100,422 Conservative of Illinois (Koppie); 34,527 Libertarian (Spiegel); 15,118 Natural Law (Winter); 12,689 New Alliance (Port); 10,056 Socialist Workers (Kaku); 8,656 Populist (Justice); 28 scattered write-in.

Congress   Other vote was Louanner Peters Party (Peters) in CD 2; Libertarian (Grenke) in CD 5; Petropoulos (write-in) in CD 6; 4,711 Economic Recovery (Love) and 2,413 Natural Law (McLauchlan) in CD 7; Independent Congressional (Dillier) in CD 8; Economic Recovery (Jones) in CD 9; Miron (write-in) in CD 13; Dinwiddie (write-in) in CD 14; Archibald (write-in) in CD 15; Gifford (write-in) in CD 18; Riker (write-in) in CD 19.

CHICAGO

President   Other vote was 2,185 Libertarian (Marrou); 1,456 New Alliance (Fulani); 554 Socialist Workers (Warren); 637 Populist (Gritz); 838 Natural Law (Hagelin).

Senator   Other vote was 6,928 Libertarian (Spiegel); 6,803 Conservative of Illinois (Koppie); 2,617 Natural Law (Winter); 1,938 Socialist Workers (Kaku); 1,244 Populist (Justice); 1,096 New Alliance (Port).

1992 PRIMARIES

MARCH 17 REPUBLICAN

Senator   Richard S. Williamson, unopposed.

Congress   Unopposed in nine CD's. No candidate in CD's 2, 7 and 12. In CD 2 write-in votes were 101 Ron Blackstone and 76 Ron Taylor; Mr. Blackstone qualified for the general election ballot. In CD 7, Norman G. Boccio was nominated after the primary by the local party committee. In CD 12, Mike Starr was nominated after the primary by the local party committee. Contested as follows:

CD 3   8,852 Harry C. Lepinske; 8,708 John O'Connor; 7,419 Bill O'Connor; 4,389 Barbara K. Purdy; 795 Arthur J. Jones.
CD 8   31,396 Philip M. Crane; 25,296 Gary J. Skoien.
CD 9   7,397 Herbert Sohn; 5,800 George E. Larney.
CD 10   32,959 John E. Porter; 21,895 Kathleen M. Sullivan.
CD 11   9,325 Robert T. Herbolsheimer; 8,972 Samuel Panayotovich; 7,731 Samuel J. Andreano; 4,990 Chester L. Evers; 4,135 Lloyd Chapman; 1,897 George K. Durand.
CD 13   46,417 Harris W. Fawell; 17,202 Stuart A. Wesbury.
CD 16   41,055 Donald Manzullo; 31,705 Jack Schaffer.
CD 19   19,779 Douglas E. Lee; 19,257 Paul E. Jurgens.

MARCH 17 DEMOCRATIC

Senator   557,694 Carol M. Braun; 504,077 Alan J. Dixon; 394,497 Albert F. Hofeld.

Congress   Unopposed in six CD's. No candidate in CD's 8, 10 and 13. In CD 8, Sheila A. Smith was nominated after the primary by the local party committee. In CD 10, Michael J. Kennedy was nominated after the primary by the local party committee. In CD 13, Dennis M. Temple was nominated after the primary by the local party committee. Contested as follows:

CD 1   54,231 Bobby L. Rush; 50,191 Charles A. Hayes; 14,094 Anna R. Langford; 4,256 Roosevelt Thomas; 3,486 Allen Smith; 2,219 Smith Wiiams; 13 Babette Peyton (write-in).
CD 2   61,450 Melvin J. Reynolds; 36,865 Gus Savage; 1 Ernest Thompson (write-in).

ILLINOIS

CD 3 61,124 William O. Lipinski; 38,802 Martin A. Russo; 3,551 Aloysius A. Majerczyk; 1,773 Paul J. Del Debbio.

CD 4 36,377 Luis V. Gutierrez; 24,609 Juan M. Soliz.

CD 5 56,059 Daniel Rostenkowski; 41,956 Dick Simpson.

CD 7 66,976 Cardiss Collins; 8,980 Clarence D. Clemons.

CD 9 63,211 Sidney R. Yates; 22,450 Glenn T. Sugiyama; 12,329 William M. McTighe.

CD 15 19,702 Charles D. Mattis; 17,781 Mark Weisbrot; 29 John Huber (write-in).

CD 17 47,351 Lane Evans; 10,545 Richard E. Maynard.

CD 18 20,696 Ronald C. Hawkins; 14,148 Elsie Speck; 5,604 Edward M. Cornish; 46 John Penn (write-in).

CD 19 57,566 Glenn Poshard; 35,574 Terry L. Bruce.

INDIANA

GOVERNOR
Evan Bayh (D). Re-elected 1992 to a four-year term. Previously elected 1988.

SENATORS
Daniel R. Coats (R). Re-elected 1992 to a six- year term. Had been elected 1990 to fill out the remaining two years of the term vacated when Senator J. Danforth Quayle (R) resigned to become Vice-President; had previously been appointed January 1989 to fill this vacancy.

Richard G. Lugar (R). Re-elected 1988 to a six-year term. Previously elected 1982, 1976.

REPRESENTATIVES
1. Peter J. Visclosky (D)
2. Philip R. Sharp (D)
3. Timothy J. Roemer (D)
4. Jill L. Long (D)
5. Steve Buyer (R)
6. Dan Burton (R)
7. John T. Myers (R)
8. Francis McCloskey (D)
9. Lee H. Hamilton (D)
10. Andrew Jacobs, Jr. (D)

POSTWAR VOTE FOR PRESIDENT

Year	Total Vote	Republican Vote	Republican Candidate	Democratic Vote	Democratic Candidate	Other Vote	Plurality	Total Vote Rep.	Total Vote Dem.	Major Vote Rep.	Major Vote Dem.
1992 **	2,305,871	989,375	Bush, George	848,420	Clinton, Bill	468,076	140,955 R	42.9%	36.8%	53.8%	46.2%
1988	2,168,621	1,297,763	Bush, George	860,643	Dukakis, Michael S.	10,215	437,120 R	59.8%	39.7%	60.1%	39.9%
1984	2,233,069	1,377,230	Reagan, Ronald	841,481	Mondale, Walter F.	14,358	535,749 R	61.7%	37.7%	62.1%	37.9%
1980	2,242,033	1,255,656	Reagan, Ronald	844,197	Carter, Jimmy	142,180	411,459 R	56.0%	37.7%	59.8%	40.2%
1976	2,220,362	1,183,958	Ford, Gerald R.	1,014,714	Carter, Jimmy	21,690	169,244 R	53.3%	45.7%	53.8%	46.2%
1972	2,125,529	1,405,154	Nixon, Richard M.	708,568	McGovern, George S.	11,807	696,586 R	66.1%	33.3%	66.5%	33.5%
1968	2,123,597	1,067,885	Nixon, Richard M.	806,659	Humphrey, Hubert H.	249,053	261,226 R	50.3%	38.0%	57.0%	43.0%
1964	2,091,606	911,118	Goldwater, Barry M.	1,170,848	Johnson, Lyndon B.	9,640	259,730 D	43.6%	56.0%	43.8%	56.2%
1960	2,135,360	1,175,120	Nixon, Richard M.	952,358	Kennedy, John F.	7,882	222,762 R	55.0%	44.6%	55.2%	44.8%
1956	1,974,607	1,182,811	Eisenhower, Dwight D.	783,908	Stevenson, Adlai E.	7,888	398,903 R	59.9%	39.7%	60.1%	39.9%
1952	1,955,049	1,136,259	Eisenhower, Dwight D.	801,530	Stevenson, Adlai E.	17,260	334,729 R	58.1%	41.0%	58.6%	41.4%
1948	1,656,212	821,079	Dewey, Thomas E.	807,831	Truman, Harry S.	27,302	13,248 R	49.6%	48.8%	50.4%	49.6%

In 1992 the other vote column includes 455,934 votes cast for Perot.

POSTWAR VOTE FOR GOVERNOR

Year	Total Vote	Republican Vote	Republican Candidate	Democratic Vote	Democratic Candidate	Other Vote	Rep.-Dem. Plurality	Total Vote Rep.	Total Vote Dem.	Major Vote Rep.	Major Vote Dem.
1992	2,229,116	822,533	Pearson, Linley E.	1,382,151	Bayh, Evan	24,432	559,618 D	36.9%	62.0%	37.3%	62.7%
1988	2,140,781	1,002,207	Mutz, John M.	1,138,574	Bayh, Evan		136,367 D	46.8%	53.2%	46.8%	53.2%
1984	2,197,988	1,146,497	Orr, Robert D.	1,036,922	Townsend, W. Wayne	14,569	109,575 R	52.2%	47.2%	52.5%	47.5%
1980	2,178,403	1,257,383	Orr, Robert D.	913,116	Hillenbrand, John A.	7,904	344,267 R	57.7%	41.9%	57.9%	42.1%
1976	2,175,324	1,236,555	Bowen, Otis R.	927,243	Conrad, Larry A.	11,526	309,312 R	56.8%	42.6%	57.1%	42.9%
1972	2,120,847	1,203,903	Bowen, Otis R.	900,489	Welsh, Matthew E.	16,455	303,414 R	56.8%	42.5%	57.2%	42.8%
1968	2,049,072	1,080,271	Whitcomb, Edgar D.	965,816	Rock, Robert L.	2,985	114,455 R	52.7%	47.1%	52.8%	47.2%
1964	2,072,915	901,342	Ristine, Richard O.	1,164,620	Branigin, Roger D.	6,953	263,278 D	43.5%	56.2%	43.6%	56.4%
1960	2,128,965	1,049,540	Parker, Crawford F.	1,072,717	Welsh, Matthew E.	6,708	23,177 D	49.3%	50.4%	49.5%	50.5%
1956	1,954,290	1,086,868	Handley, Harold W.	859,393	Tucker, Ralph	8,029	227,475 R	55.6%	44.0%	55.8%	44.2%
1952	1,931,869	1,075,685	Craig, George N.	841,984	Watkins, John A.	14,200	233,701 R	55.7%	43.6%	56.1%	43.9%
1948	1,652,321	745,892	Creighton, Hobart	884,995	Schricker, Henry F.	21,434	139,103 D	45.1%	53.6%	45.7%	54.3%

INDIANA

POSTWAR VOTE FOR SENATOR

Year	Total Vote	Republican		Democratic		Other Vote	Rep.-Dem. Plurality	Percentage			
		Vote	Candidate	Vote	Candidate			Total Vote		Major Vote	
								Rep.	Dem.	Rep.	Dem.
1992	2,211,426	1,267,972	Coats, Daniel R.	900,148	Hogsett, Joseph H.	43,306	367,824 R	57.3%	40.7%	58.5%	41.5%
1990 S	1,504,302	806,048	Coats, Daniel R.	696,639	Hill, Baron P.	1,615	109,409 R	53.6%	46.3%	53.6%	46.4%
1988	2,099,303	1,430,525	Lugar, Richard G.	668,778	Wickes, Jack		761,747 R	68.1%	31.9%	68.1%	31.9%
1986	1,545,563	936,143	Quayle, J. Danforth	595,192	Long, Jill L.	14,228	340,951 R	60.6%	38.5%	61.1%	38.9%
1982	1,817,287	978,301	Lugar, Richard G.	828,400	Fithian, Floyd	10,586	149,901 R	53.8%	45.6%	54.1%	45.9%
1980	2,198,376	1,182,414	Quayle, J. Danforth	1,015,962	Bayh, Birch		166,452 R	53.8%	46.2%	53.8%	46.2%
1976	2,171,187	1,275,833	Lugar, Richard G.	878,522	Hartke, R. Vance	16,832	397,311 R	58.8%	40.5%	59.2%	40.8%
1974	1,752,978	814,117	Lugar, Richard G.	889,269	Bayh, Birch	49,592	75,152 D	46.4%	50.7%	47.8%	52.2%
1970	1,737,697	866,707	Roudebush, Richard	870,990	Hartke, R. Vance		4,283 D	49.9%	50.1%	49.9%	50.1%
1968	2,053,118	988,571	Ruckelshaus, William	1,060,456	Bayh, Birch	4,091	71,885 D	48.1%	51.7%	48.2%	51.8%
1964	2,076,963	941,519	Bontrager, D. Russell	1,128,505	Hartke, R. Vance	6,939	186,986 D	45.3%	54.3%	45.5%	54.5%
1962	1,800,038	894,547	Capehart, Homer E.	905,491	Bayh, Birch		10,944 D	49.7%	50.3%	49.7%	50.3%
1958	1,724,598	731,635	Handley, Harold W.	973,636	Hartke, R. Vance	19,327	242,001 D	42.4%	56.5%	42.9%	57.1%
1956	1,963,986	1,084,262	Capehart, Homer E.	871,781	Wickard, Claude	7,943	212,481 R	55.2%	44.4%	55.4%	44.6%
1952	1,946,118	1,020,605	Jenner, William E.	911,169	Schricker, Henry F.	14,344	109,436 R	52.4%	46.8%	52.8%	47.2%
1950	1,598,724	844,303	Capehart, Homer E.	741,025	Campbell, Alex M.	13,396	103,278 R	52.8%	46.4%	53.3%	46.7%
1946	1,347,434	739,809	Jenner, William E.	584,288	Townsend, M. Clifford	23,337	155,521 R	54.9%	43.4%	55.9%	44.1%

The 1990 election was for a short term to fill a vacancy.

INDIANA

Districts Established June 13, 1991

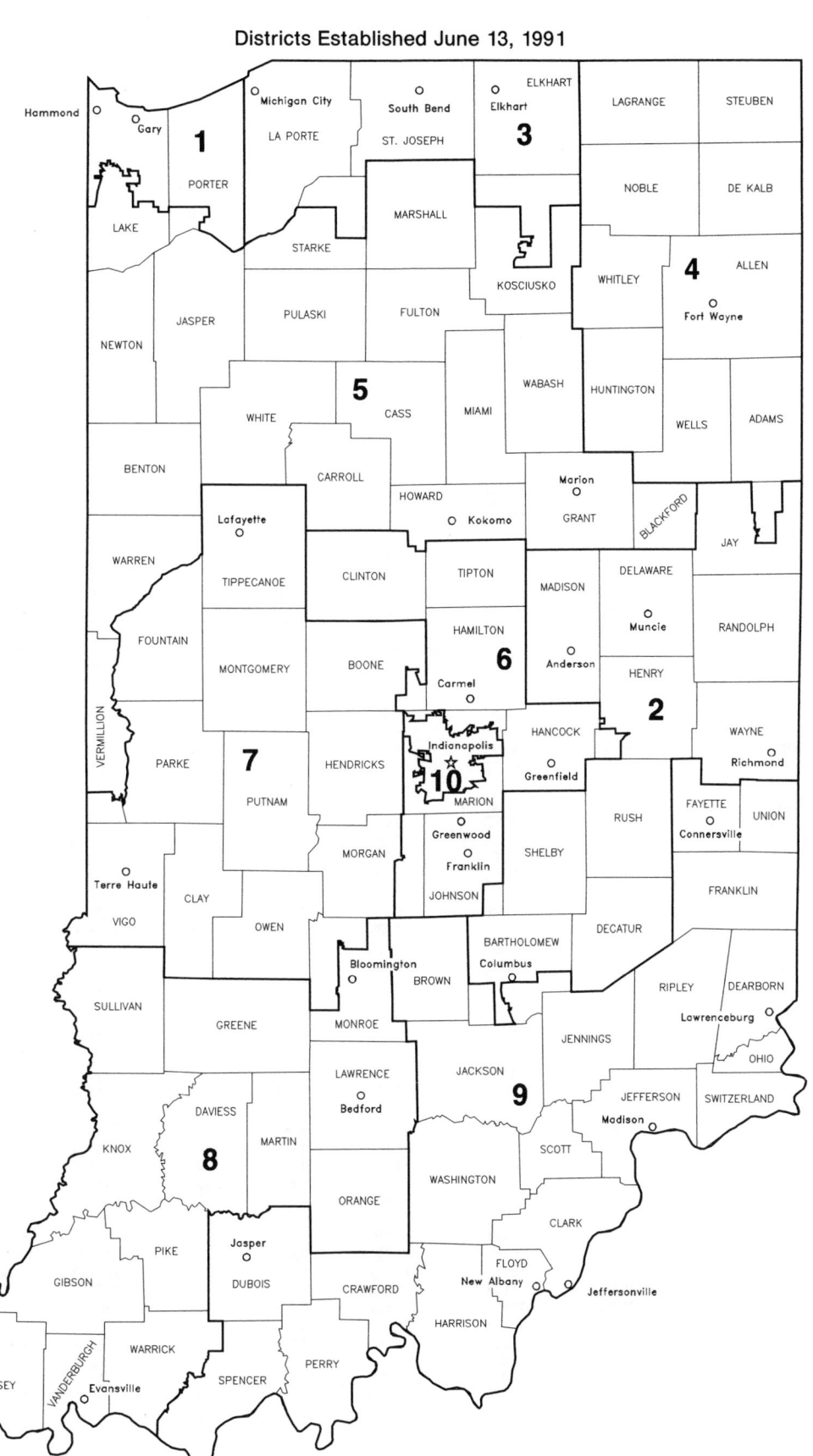

INDIANA

PRESIDENT 1992

Registration	County	Total Vote	Republican	Democratic	Perot	Other	Plurality	Percentage Total Vote		
								Rep.	Dem.	Perot
15,851	ADAMS	12,708	6,078	3,708	2,865	57	2,370 R	47.8%	29.2%	22.5%
170,307	ALLEN	121,577	55,003	39,629	25,809	1,136	15,374 R	45.2%	32.6%	21.2%
36,368	BARTHOLOMEW	27,440	13,146	8,284	5,882	128	4,862 R	47.9%	30.2%	21.4%
5,477	BENTON	4,323	2,030	1,221	1,056	16	809 R	47.0%	28.2%	24.4%
7,782	BLACKFORD	5,778	2,347	2,088	1,319	24	259 R	40.6%	36.1%	22.8%
22,578	BOONE	17,358	9,485	3,982	3,826	65	5,503 R	54.6%	22.9%	22.0%
8,732	BROWN	6,325	2,633	2,029	1,635	28	604 R	41.6%	32.1%	25.8%
10,961	CARROLL	8,562	3,800	2,561	2,173	28	1,239 R	44.4%	29.9%	25.4%
22,567	CASS	16,237	7,421	4,757	3,944	115	2,664 R	45.7%	29.3%	24.3%
50,144	CLARK	36,694	13,333	17,460	5,653	248	4,127 D	36.3%	47.6%	15.4%
13,857	CLAY	10,164	4,696	3,306	2,134	28	1,390 R	46.2%	32.5%	21.0%
17,669	CLINTON	12,224	6,141	3,490	2,535	58	2,651 R	50.2%	28.6%	20.7%
7,139	CRAWFORD	4,994	1,903	2,260	819	12	357 D	38.1%	45.3%	16.4%
14,387	DAVIESS	10,520	5,591	3,201	1,695	33	2,390 R	53.1%	30.4%	16.1%
20,029	DEARBORN	15,567	6,974	5,116	3,384	93	1,858 R	44.8%	32.9%	21.7%
13,846	DECATUR	10,291	5,195	2,774	2,299	23	2,421 R	50.5%	27.0%	22.3%
19,657	DE KALB	15,022	6,682	4,652	3,554	134	2,030 R	44.5%	31.0%	23.7%
72,681	DELAWARE	50,721	20,473	19,556	10,453	239	917 R	40.4%	38.6%	20.6%
21,050	DUBOIS	15,989	6,785	5,878	3,195	131	907 R	42.4%	36.8%	20.0%
71,380	ELKHART	52,184	27,920	14,660	9,450	154	13,260 R	53.5%	28.1%	18.1%
15,773	FAYETTE	10,710	4,376	3,969	2,299	66	407 R	40.9%	37.1%	21.5%
39,683	FLOYD	29,651	11,932	13,166	4,421	132	1,234 D	40.2%	44.4%	14.9%
11,041	FOUNTAIN	8,410	3,391	2,829	2,162	28	562 R	40.3%	33.6%	25.7%
10,885	FRANKLIN	8,167	3,831	2,456	1,858	22	1,375 R	46.9%	30.1%	22.8%
10,784	FULTON	8,527	3,982	2,552	1,963	30	1,430 R	46.7%	29.9%	23.0%
20,523	GIBSON	14,800	5,172	6,909	2,680	39	1,737 D	34.9%	46.7%	18.1%
41,445	GRANT	28,738	13,806	9,211	5,597	124	4,595 R	48.0%	32.1%	19.5%
18,095	GREENE	13,608	5,410	5,431	2,610	157	21 D	39.8%	39.9%	19.2%
73,004	HAMILTON	55,434	34,622	10,215	10,365	232	24,257 R	62.5%	18.4%	18.7%
27,063	HANCOCK	20,639	11,072	4,752	4,752	63	6,320 R	53.6%	23.0%	23.0%
17,814	HARRISON	13,671	5,403	5,768	2,469	31	365 D	39.5%	42.2%	18.1%
43,609	HENDRICKS	33,136	18,373	7,071	7,519	173	10,854 R	55.4%	21.3%	22.7%
27,677	HENRY	19,989	8,720	6,794	4,416	59	1,926 R	43.6%	34.0%	22.1%
46,293	HOWARD	34,340	15,306	10,288	8,575	171	5,018 R	44.6%	30.0%	25.0%
21,016	HUNTINGTON	16,013	9,093	3,855	2,967	98	5,238 R	56.8%	24.1%	18.5%
21,814	JACKSON	16,170	7,246	5,663	3,148	113	1,583 R	44.8%	35.0%	19.5%
13,512	JASPER	9,890	4,809	3,033	2,019	29	1,776 R	48.6%	30.7%	20.4%
10,302	JAY	8,836	3,609	3,208	1,994	25	401 R	40.8%	36.3%	22.6%
17,751	JEFFERSON	13,191	4,937	5,510	2,565	179	573 D	37.4%	41.8%	19.4%
13,690	JENNINGS	10,295	4,392	3,471	2,370	62	921 R	42.7%	33.7%	23.0%
50,912	JOHNSON	37,438	20,353	8,712	8,246	127	11,641 R	54.4%	23.3%	22.0%
23,028	KNOX	17,284	6,683	6,718	3,719	164	35 D	38.7%	38.9%	21.5%
32,725	KOSCIUSKO	24,683	14,179	5,307	5,115	82	8,872 R	57.4%	21.5%	20.7%
9,903	LAGRANGE	7,444	3,584	2,093	1,736	31	1,491 R	48.1%	28.1%	23.3%
271,911	LAKE	186,298	53,867	102,778	28,635	1,018	48,911 D	28.9%	55.2%	15.4%
57,770	LA PORTE	42,463	14,962	17,717	9,641	143	2,755 D	35.2%	41.7%	22.7%
24,328	LAWRENCE	16,781	7,712	5,557	3,452	60	2,155 R	46.0%	33.1%	20.6%
82,053	MADISON	59,058	23,479	22,276	13,100	203	1,203 R	39.8%	37.7%	22.2%
468,408	MARION	323,790	141,369	122,234	57,878	2,309	19,135 R	43.7%	37.8%	17.9%
22,052	MARSHALL	16,567	8,048	4,912	3,522	85	3,136 R	48.6%	29.6%	21.3%
7,374	MARTIN	5,438	2,523	2,018	883	14	505 R	46.4%	37.1%	16.2%
18,916	MIAMI	13,918	6,416	3,967	3,428	107	2,449 R	46.1%	28.5%	24.6%
63,695	MONROE	43,587	16,661	19,712	6,943	271	3,051 D	38.2%	45.2%	15.9%
19,726	MONTGOMERY	14,564	7,602	3,371	3,511	80	4,091 R	52.2%	23.1%	24.1%
29,531	MORGAN	21,107	10,939	4,690	5,375	103	5,564 R	51.8%	22.2%	25.5%
6,937	NEWTON	5,344	2,295	1,757	1,274	18	538 R	42.9%	32.9%	23.8%
17,982	NOBLE	13,713	5,883	4,411	3,328	91	1,472 R	42.9%	32.2%	24.3%
3,468	OHIO	2,514	1,009	970	527	8	39 R	40.1%	38.6%	21.0%
12,006	ORANGE	8,015	3,738	2,948	1,296	33	790 R	46.6%	36.8%	16.2%
9,213	OWEN	6,555	2,753	2,207	1,563	32	546 R	42.0%	33.7%	23.8%

INDIANA

PRESIDENT 1992

Registration	County	Total Vote	Republican	Democratic	Perot	Other	Plurality	Percentage Total Vote		
								Rep.	Dem.	Perot
9,553	PARKE	7,099	2,953	2,429	1,696	21	524 R	41.6%	34.2%	23.9%
12,757	PERRY	9,382	2,973	4,829	1,560	20	1,856 D	31.7%	51.5%	16.6%
8,802	PIKE	6,371	2,156	2,960	1,238	17	804 D	33.8%	46.5%	19.4%
67,601	PORTER	57,067	22,644	21,022	13,096	305	1,622 R	39.7%	36.8%	22.9%
14,778	POSEY	11,453	4,435	4,632	2,357	29	197 D	38.7%	40.4%	20.6%
7,545	PULASKI	5,916	2,712	1,950	1,214	40	762 R	45.8%	33.0%	20.5%
16,464	PUTNAM	12,048	5,341	3,487	3,174	46	1,854 R	44.3%	28.9%	26.3%
15,192	RANDOLPH	11,784	4,937	3,870	2,939	38	1,067 R	41.9%	32.8%	24.9%
14,500	RIPLEY	10,937	5,033	3,480	2,406	18	1,553 R	46.0%	31.8%	22.0%
11,258	RUSH	8,008	3,873	2,168	1,948	19	1,705 R	48.4%	27.1%	24.3%
139,554	ST. JOSEPH	104,465	38,934	46,203	18,828	500	7,269 D	37.3%	44.2%	18.0%
11,695	SCOTT	7,859	2,649	4,085	1,092	33	1,436 D	33.7%	52.0%	13.9%
21,966	SHELBY	16,211	8,075	4,560	3,521	55	3,515 R	49.8%	28.1%	21.7%
13,259	SPENCER	9,579	3,789	4,301	1,464	25	512 D	39.6%	44.9%	15.3%
12,151	STARKE	8,758	3,100	3,695	1,885	78	595 D	35.4%	42.2%	21.5%
14,207	STEUBEN	11,469	4,868	3,630	2,896	75	1,238 R	42.4%	31.7%	25.3%
12,477	SULLIVAN	9,168	3,052	4,211	1,857	48	1,159 D	33.3%	45.9%	20.3%
4,776	SWITZERLAND	3,388	1,211	1,535	636	6	324 D	35.7%	45.3%	18.8%
68,985	TIPPECANOE	50,334	23,050	17,343	9,684	257	5,707 R	45.8%	34.5%	19.2%
10,964	TIPTON	7,883	3,906	2,125	1,816	36	1,781 R	49.5%	27.0%	23.0%
3,815	UNION	2,968	1,394	898	664	12	496 R	47.0%	30.3%	22.4%
108,858	VANDERBURGH	76,840	30,271	33,799	12,513	257	3,528 D	39.4%	44.0%	16.3%
10,742	VERMILLION	7,832	2,360	3,652	1,794	26	1,292 D	30.1%	46.6%	22.9%
63,456	VIGO	42,161	15,834	18,050	8,141	136	2,216 D	37.6%	42.8%	19.3%
19,494	WABASH	15,101	7,062	4,518	3,424	97	2,544 R	46.8%	29.9%	22.7%
5,256	WARREN	4,003	1,601	1,367	1,020	15	234 R	40.0%	34.1%	25.5%
27,539	WARRICK	20,614	8,087	8,612	3,862	53	525 D	39.2%	41.8%	18.7%
13,631	WASHINGTON	10,057	4,043	4,092	1,846	76	49 D	40.2%	40.7%	18.4%
37,871	WAYNE	27,346	12,221	9,960	5,095	70	2,261 R	44.7%	36.4%	18.6%
15,576	WELLS	12,039	5,799	3,282	2,890	68	2,517 R	48.2%	27.3%	24.0%
13,524	WHITE	10,221	4,622	2,988	2,582	29	1,634 R	45.2%	29.2%	25.3%
15,737	WHITLEY	12,056	5,217	3,569	3,195	75	1,648 R	43.3%	29.6%	26.5%
3,180,157	TOTAL	2,305,871	989,375	848,420	455,934	12,142	140,955 R	42.9%	36.8%	19.8%

INDIANA

GOVERNOR 1992

Registration	County	Total Vote	Republican	Democratic	Other	Rep.-Dem. Plurality	Percentage			
							Total Vote		Major Vote	
							Rep.	Dem.	Rep.	Dem.
15,851	ADAMS	12,602	4,533	7,906	163	3,373 D	36.0%	62.7%	36.4%	63.6%
170,307	ALLEN	118,506	46,056	71,007	1,443	24,951 D	38.9%	59.9%	39.3%	60.7%
36,368	BARTHOLOMEW	26,832	10,183	16,355	294	6,172 D	38.0%	61.0%	38.4%	61.6%
5,477	BENTON	4,281	1,743	2,457	81	714 D	40.7%	57.4%	41.5%	58.5%
7,782	BLACKFORD	5,651	1,807	3,770	74	1,963 D	32.0%	66.7%	32.4%	67.6%
22,578	BOONE	16,991	8,365	8,568	58	203 D	49.2%	50.4%	49.4%	50.6%
8,732	BROWN	6,097	2,094	3,941	62	1,847 D	34.3%	64.6%	34.7%	65.3%
10,961	CARROLL	8,435	3,474	4,919	42	1,445 D	41.2%	58.3%	41.4%	58.6%
22,567	CASS	15,702	6,720	8,932	50	2,212 D	42.8%	56.9%	42.9%	57.1%
50,144	CLARK	33,330	9,384	23,825	121	14,441 D	28.2%	71.5%	28.3%	71.7%
13,857	CLAY	10,080	3,230	6,744	106	3,514 D	32.0%	66.9%	32.4%	67.6%
17,669	CLINTON	12,029	6,640	5,309	80	1,331 R	55.2%	44.1%	55.6%	44.4%
7,139	CRAWFORD	4,782	1,765	3,005	12	1,240 D	36.9%	62.8%	37.0%	63.0%
14,387	DAVIESS	10,260	4,439	5,755	66	1,316 D	43.3%	56.1%	43.5%	56.5%
20,029	DEARBORN	14,069	6,265	7,699	105	1,434 D	44.5%	54.7%	44.9%	55.1%
13,846	DECATUR	10,200	3,713	6,328	159	2,615 D	36.4%	62.0%	37.0%	63.0%
19,657	DE KALB	13,981	6,357	7,565	59	1,208 D	45.5%	54.1%	45.7%	54.3%
72,681	DELAWARE	49,656	15,932	32,802	922	16,870 D	32.1%	66.1%	32.7%	67.3%
21,050	DUBOIS	15,070	5,151	9,884	35	4,733 D	34.2%	65.6%	34.3%	65.7%
71,380	ELKHART	51,569	22,616	28,271	682	5,655 D	43.9%	54.8%	44.4%	55.6%
15,773	FAYETTE	10,080	3,778	6,257	45	2,479 D	37.5%	62.1%	37.6%	62.4%
39,683	FLOYD	27,892	8,875	18,956	61	10,081 D	31.8%	68.0%	31.9%	68.1%
11,041	FOUNTAIN	8,347	3,215	4,989	143	1,774 D	38.5%	59.8%	39.2%	60.8%
10,885	FRANKLIN	7,693	2,974	4,564	155	1,590 D	38.7%	59.3%	39.5%	60.5%
10,784	FULTON	8,434	3,428	4,877	129	1,449 D	40.6%	57.8%	41.3%	58.7%
20,523	GIBSON	14,147	4,153	9,832	162	5,679 D	29.4%	69.5%	29.7%	70.3%
41,445	GRANT	27,902	11,043	16,566	293	5,523 D	39.6%	59.4%	40.0%	60.0%
18,095	GREENE	13,081	4,440	8,594	47	4,154 D	33.9%	65.7%	34.1%	65.9%
73,004	HAMILTON	54,125	26,040	27,499	586	1,459 D	48.1%	50.8%	48.6%	51.4%
27,063	HANCOCK	20,386	8,604	11,434	348	2,830 D	42.2%	56.1%	42.9%	57.1%
17,814	HARRISON	13,524	3,726	9,581	217	5,855 D	27.6%	70.8%	28.0%	72.0%
43,609	HENDRICKS	32,301	15,412	16,453	436	1,041 D	47.7%	50.9%	48.4%	51.6%
27,677	HENRY	19,806	7,174	12,323	309	5,149 D	36.2%	62.2%	36.8%	63.2%
46,293	HOWARD	33,011	12,730	19,824	457	7,094 D	38.6%	60.1%	39.1%	60.9%
21,016	HUNTINGTON	15,354	6,756	8,455	143	1,699 D	44.0%	55.1%	44.4%	55.6%
21,814	JACKSON	15,323	5,919	9,352	52	3,433 D	38.6%	61.0%	38.8%	61.2%
13,512	JASPER	9,580	4,781	4,671	128	110 R	49.9%	48.8%	50.6%	49.4%
10,302	JAY	8,697	3,147	5,413	137	2,266 D	36.2%	62.2%	36.8%	63.2%
17,751	JEFFERSON	12,559	4,841	7,637	81	2,796 D	38.5%	60.8%	38.8%	61.2%
13,690	JENNINGS	9,762	4,292	5,399	71	1,107 D	44.0%	55.3%	44.3%	55.7%
50,912	JOHNSON	36,657	15,587	20,391	679	4,804 D	42.5%	55.6%	43.3%	56.7%
23,028	KNOX	16,564	6,109	10,264	191	4,155 D	36.9%	62.0%	37.3%	62.7%
32,725	KOSCIUSKO	24,462	11,897	12,258	307	361 D	48.6%	50.1%	49.3%	50.7%
9,903	LAGRANGE	7,230	3,291	3,936	3	645 D	45.5%	54.4%	45.5%	54.5%
271,911	LAKE	178,945	53,720	122,861	2,364	69,141 D	30.0%	68.7%	30.4%	69.6%
57,770	LA PORTE	41,192	13,547	26,963	682	13,416 D	32.9%	65.5%	33.4%	66.6%
24,328	LAWRENCE	16,215	6,650	9,418	147	2,768 D	41.0%	58.1%	41.4%	58.6%
82,053	MADISON	58,462	19,294	38,130	1,038	18,836 D	33.0%	65.2%	33.6%	66.4%
468,408	MARION	308,491	117,400	189,575	1,516	72,175 D	38.1%	61.5%	38.2%	61.8%
22,052	MARSHALL	15,914	6,844	9,007	63	2,163 D	43.0%	56.6%	43.2%	56.8%
7,374	MARTIN	5,291	1,918	3,354	19	1,436 D	36.3%	63.4%	36.4%	63.6%
18,916	MIAMI	13,292	5,652	7,586	54	1,934 D	42.5%	57.1%	42.7%	57.3%
63,695	MONROE	41,893	12,834	28,193	866	15,359 D	30.6%	67.3%	31.3%	68.7%
19,726	MONTGOMERY	14,368	6,216	7,859	293	1,643 D	43.3%	54.7%	44.2%	55.8%
29,531	MORGAN	20,540	9,911	10,325	304	414 D	48.3%	50.3%	49.0%	51.0%
6,937	NEWTON	5,275	2,394	2,776	105	382 D	45.4%	52.6%	46.3%	53.7%
17,982	NOBLE	13,354	5,451	7,717	186	2,266 D	40.8%	57.8%	41.4%	58.6%
3,468	OHIO	2,454	957	1,449	48	492 D	39.0%	59.0%	39.8%	60.2%
12,006	ORANGE	7,915	3,513	4,294	108	781 D	44.4%	54.3%	45.0%	55.0%
9,213	OWEN	6,382	2,319	3,972	91	1,653 D	36.3%	62.2%	36.9%	63.1%

INDIANA

GOVERNOR 1992

Registration	County	Total Vote	Republican	Democratic	Other	Rep.-Dem. Plurality	Percentage Total Vote Rep.	Dem.	Major Vote Rep.	Dem.
9,553	PARKE	7,056	2,497	4,445	114	1,948 D	35.4%	63.0%	36.0%	64.0%
12,757	PERRY	9,189	2,827	6,338	24	3,511 D	30.8%	69.0%	30.8%	69.2%
8,802	PIKE	6,314	1,969	4,264	81	2,295 D	31.2%	67.5%	31.6%	68.4%
67,601	PORTER	56,322	21,658	33,533	1,131	11,875 D	38.5%	59.5%	39.2%	60.8%
14,778	POSEY	11,343	3,324	7,827	192	4,503 D	29.3%	69.0%	29.8%	70.2%
7,545	PULASKI	5,705	2,306	3,383	16	1,077 D	40.4%	59.3%	40.5%	59.5%
16,464	PUTNAM	11,605	4,653	6,797	155	2,144 D	40.1%	58.6%	40.6%	59.4%
15,192	RANDOLPH	11,681	4,612	6,861	208	2,249 D	39.5%	58.7%	40.2%	59.8%
14,500	RIPLEY	10,281	4,401	5,828	52	1,427 D	42.8%	56.7%	43.0%	57.0%
11,258	RUSH	7,940	3,100	4,745	95	1,645 D	39.0%	59.8%	39.5%	60.5%
139,554	ST. JOSEPH	99,212	29,164	69,742	306	40,578 D	29.4%	70.3%	29.5%	70.5%
11,695	SCOTT	6,713	1,990	4,694	29	2,704 D	29.6%	69.9%	29.8%	70.2%
21,966	SHELBY	15,785	6,324	9,322	139	2,998 D	40.1%	59.1%	40.4%	59.6%
13,259	SPENCER	9,266	3,561	5,695	10	2,134 D	38.4%	61.5%	38.5%	61.5%
12,151	STARKE	8,226	2,855	5,322	49	2,467 D	34.7%	64.7%	34.9%	65.1%
14,207	STEUBEN	10,965	4,706	6,201	58	1,495 D	42.9%	56.6%	43.1%	56.9%
12,477	SULLIVAN	8,692	2,159	6,488	45	4,329 D	24.8%	74.6%	25.0%	75.0%
4,776	SWITZERLAND	3,039	1,075	1,950	14	875 D	35.4%	64.2%	35.5%	64.5%
68,985	TIPPECANOE	49,482	18,742	29,840	900	11,098 D	37.9%	60.3%	38.6%	61.4%
10,964	TIPTON	7,683	3,157	4,450	76	1,293 D	41.1%	57.9%	41.5%	58.5%
3,815	UNION	2,832	1,339	1,457	36	118 D	47.3%	51.4%	47.9%	52.1%
108,858	VANDERBURGH	75,004	20,782	53,240	982	32,458 D	27.7%	71.0%	28.1%	71.9%
10,742	VERMILLION	7,797	1,746	5,924	127	4,178 D	22.4%	76.0%	22.8%	77.2%
63,456	VIGO	41,600	10,030	31,036	534	21,006 D	24.1%	74.6%	24.4%	75.6%
19,494	WABASH	14,250	6,080	8,124	46	2,044 D	42.7%	57.0%	42.8%	57.2%
5,256	WARREN	3,885	1,471	2,359	55	888 D	37.9%	60.7%	38.4%	61.6%
27,539	WARRICK	20,453	6,202	13,951	300	7,749 D	30.3%	68.2%	30.8%	69.2%
13,631	WASHINGTON	9,359	3,619	5,685	55	2,066 D	38.7%	60.7%	38.9%	61.1%
37,871	WAYNE	26,714	11,106	15,261	347	4,155 D	41.6%	57.1%	42.1%	57.9%
15,576	WELLS	11,964	5,111	6,694	159	1,583 D	42.7%	56.0%	43.3%	56.7%
13,524	WHITE	9,819	3,862	5,800	157	1,938 D	39.3%	59.1%	40.0%	60.0%
15,737	WHITLEY	11,917	4,806	6,849	262	2,043 D	40.3%	57.5%	41.2%	58.8%
3,180,157	TOTAL	2,229,116	822,533	1,382,151	24,432	559,618 D	36.9%	62.0%	37.3%	62.7%

INDIANA

SENATOR 1992

Registration	County	Total Vote	Republican	Democratic	Other	Rep.-Dem. Plurality	Percentage Total Vote Rep.	Percentage Total Vote Dem.	Percentage Major Vote Rep.	Percentage Major Vote Dem.
15,851	ADAMS	12,668	8,345	4,149	174	4,196 R	65.9%	32.8%	66.8%	33.2%
170,307	ALLEN	119,697	75,991	41,499	2,207	34,492 R	63.5%	34.7%	64.7%	35.3%
36,368	BARTHOLOMEW	26,843	17,034	9,178	631	7,856 R	63.5%	34.2%	65.0%	35.0%
5,477	BENTON	4,130	2,442	1,590	98	852 R	59.1%	38.5%	60.6%	39.4%
7,782	BLACKFORD	5,685	3,253	2,342	90	911 R	57.2%	41.2%	58.1%	41.9%
22,578	BOONE	16,633	12,043	4,360	230	7,683 R	72.4%	26.2%	73.4%	26.6%
8,732	BROWN	5,843	3,591	2,103	149	1,488 R	61.5%	36.0%	63.1%	36.9%
10,961	CARROLL	8,346	4,752	3,477	117	1,275 R	56.9%	41.7%	57.7%	42.3%
22,567	CASS	15,486	8,759	6,470	257	2,289 R	56.6%	41.8%	57.5%	42.5%
50,144	CLARK	32,291	14,200	17,716	375	3,516 D	44.0%	54.9%	44.5%	55.5%
13,857	CLAY	10,077	5,890	4,026	161	1,864 R	58.4%	40.0%	59.4%	40.6%
17,669	CLINTON	11,944	7,514	4,186	244	3,328 R	62.9%	35.0%	64.2%	35.8%
7,139	CRAWFORD	4,638	2,109	2,489	40	380 D	45.5%	53.7%	45.9%	54.1%
14,387	DAVIESS	10,313	6,395	3,809	109	2,586 R	62.0%	36.9%	62.7%	37.3%
20,029	DEARBORN	13,777	7,882	5,573	322	2,309 R	57.2%	40.5%	58.6%	41.4%
13,846	DECATUR	10,200	6,481	3,500	219	2,981 R	63.5%	34.3%	64.9%	35.1%
19,657	DE KALB	14,427	9,117	5,099	211	4,018 R	63.2%	35.3%	64.1%	35.9%
72,681	DELAWARE	49,072	28,811	18,982	1,279	9,829 R	58.7%	38.7%	60.3%	39.7%
21,050	DUBOIS	14,834	8,359	6,254	221	2,105 R	56.4%	42.2%	57.2%	42.8%
71,380	ELKHART	50,358	34,644	14,949	765	19,695 R	68.8%	29.7%	69.9%	30.1%
15,773	FAYETTE	9,963	5,334	4,481	148	853 R	53.5%	45.0%	54.3%	45.7%
39,683	FLOYD	27,301	12,847	14,181	273	1,334 D	47.1%	51.9%	47.5%	52.5%
11,041	FOUNTAIN	8,328	4,565	3,578	185	987 R	54.8%	43.0%	56.1%	43.9%
10,885	FRANKLIN	7,819	4,546	3,061	212	1,485 R	58.1%	39.1%	59.8%	40.2%
10,784	FULTON	8,210	4,874	3,175	161	1,699 R	59.4%	38.7%	60.6%	39.4%
20,523	GIBSON	14,535	6,936	7,424	175	488 D	47.7%	51.1%	48.3%	51.7%
41,445	GRANT	28,071	17,696	9,930	445	7,766 R	63.0%	35.4%	64.1%	35.9%
18,095	GREENE	12,841	6,637	5,954	250	683 R	51.7%	46.4%	52.7%	47.3%
73,004	HAMILTON	54,513	43,173	10,145	1,195	33,028 R	79.2%	18.6%	81.0%	19.0%
27,063	HANCOCK	20,421	14,267	5,648	506	8,619 R	69.9%	27.7%	71.6%	28.4%
17,814	HARRISON	13,451	6,256	6,982	213	726 D	46.5%	51.9%	47.3%	52.7%
43,609	HENDRICKS	32,469	23,938	7,863	668	16,075 R	73.7%	24.2%	75.3%	24.7%
27,677	HENRY	19,742	11,465	7,873	404	3,592 R	58.1%	39.9%	59.3%	40.7%
46,293	HOWARD	33,694	19,306	13,412	976	5,894 R	57.3%	39.8%	59.0%	41.0%
21,016	HUNTINGTON	15,430	10,511	4,750	169	5,761 R	68.1%	30.8%	68.9%	31.1%
21,814	JACKSON	14,972	8,590	6,151	231	2,439 R	57.4%	41.1%	58.3%	41.7%
13,512	JASPER	9,613	5,877	3,602	134	2,275 R	61.1%	37.5%	62.0%	38.0%
10,302	JAY	8,477	5,195	3,141	141	2,054 R	61.3%	37.1%	62.3%	37.7%
17,751	JEFFERSON	12,149	5,835	6,067	247	232 D	48.0%	49.9%	49.0%	51.0%
13,690	JENNINGS	9,382	5,224	3,936	222	1,288 R	55.7%	42.0%	57.0%	43.0%
50,912	JOHNSON	35,075	25,069	9,131	875	15,938 R	71.5%	26.0%	73.3%	26.7%
23,028	KNOX	16,386	8,683	7,239	464	1,444 R	53.0%	44.2%	54.5%	45.5%
32,725	KOSCIUSKO	24,532	17,624	6,533	375	11,091 R	71.8%	26.6%	73.0%	27.0%
9,903	LAGRANGE	7,160	4,792	2,240	128	2,552 R	66.9%	31.3%	68.1%	31.9%
271,911	LAKE	177,933	66,132	108,174	3,627	42,042 D	37.2%	60.8%	37.9%	62.1%
57,770	LA PORTE	41,438	20,525	20,082	831	443 R	49.5%	48.5%	50.5%	49.5%
24,328	LAWRENCE	16,296	9,315	6,706	275	2,609 R	57.2%	41.2%	58.1%	41.9%
82,053	MADISON	58,418	31,709	25,279	1,430	6,430 R	54.3%	43.3%	55.6%	44.4%
468,408	MARION	303,993	179,213	118,781	5,999	60,432 R	59.0%	39.1%	60.1%	39.9%
22,052	MARSHALL	15,790	10,268	5,357	165	4,911 R	65.0%	33.9%	65.7%	34.3%
7,374	MARTIN	5,189	2,685	2,450	54	235 R	51.7%	47.2%	52.3%	47.7%
18,916	MIAMI	13,078	7,638	5,248	192	2,390 R	58.4%	40.1%	59.3%	40.7%
63,695	MONROE	41,748	23,409	16,685	1,654	6,724 R	56.1%	40.0%	58.4%	41.6%
19,726	MONTGOMERY	13,950	9,718	3,860	372	5,858 R	69.7%	27.7%	71.6%	28.4%
29,531	MORGAN	20,594	14,260	5,807	527	8,453 R	69.2%	28.2%	71.1%	28.9%
6,937	NEWTON	5,072	3,021	1,931	120	1,090 R	59.6%	38.1%	61.0%	39.0%
17,982	NOBLE	13,563	8,646	4,692	225	3,954 R	63.7%	34.6%	64.8%	35.2%
3,468	OHIO	2,454	1,244	1,164	46	80 R	50.7%	47.4%	51.7%	48.3%
12,006	ORANGE	7,870	4,280	3,459	131	821 R	54.4%	44.0%	55.3%	44.7%
9,213	OWEN	6,393	3,716	2,450	227	1,266 R	58.1%	38.3%	60.3%	39.7%

INDIANA

SENATOR 1992

Registration	County	Total Vote	Republican	Democratic	Other	Rep.-Dem. Plurality	Percentage			
							Total Vote		Major Vote	
							Rep.	Dem.	Rep.	Dem.
9,553	PARKE	7,069	3,962	2,958	149	1,004 R	56.0%	41.8%	57.3%	42.7%
12,757	PERRY	9,017	3,759	5,167	91	1,408 D	41.7%	57.3%	42.1%	57.9%
8,802	PIKE	6,288	3,104	3,084	100	20 R	49.4%	49.0%	50.2%	49.8%
67,601	PORTER	56,159	30,862	24,109	1,188	6,753 R	55.0%	42.9%	56.1%	43.9%
14,778	POSEY	11,367	6,433	4,720	214	1,713 R	56.6%	41.5%	57.7%	42.3%
7,545	PULASKI	5,584	3,176	2,353	55	823 R	56.9%	42.1%	57.4%	42.6%
16,464	PUTNAM	11,813	7,639	3,864	310	3,775 R	64.7%	32.7%	66.4%	33.6%
15,192	RANDOLPH	11,685	7,086	4,372	227	2,714 R	60.6%	37.4%	61.8%	38.2%
14,500	RIPLEY	9,856	5,977	3,754	125	2,223 R	60.6%	38.1%	61.4%	38.6%
11,258	RUSH	7,965	4,090	3,719	156	371 R	51.3%	46.7%	52.4%	47.6%
139,554	ST. JOSEPH	98,040	53,260	43,785	995	9,475 R	54.3%	44.7%	54.9%	45.1%
11,695	SCOTT	6,920	2,778	4,061	81	1,283 D	40.1%	58.7%	40.6%	59.4%
21,966	SHELBY	15,770	10,227	5,299	244	4,928 R	64.9%	33.6%	65.9%	34.1%
13,259	SPENCER	9,220	4,630	4,549	41	81 R	50.2%	49.3%	50.4%	49.6%
12,151	STARKE	7,968	4,014	3,816	138	198 R	50.4%	47.9%	51.3%	48.7%
14,207	STEUBEN	10,331	6,611	3,573	147	3,038 R	64.0%	34.6%	64.9%	35.1%
12,477	SULLIVAN	8,069	3,649	4,282	138	633 D	45.2%	53.1%	46.0%	54.0%
4,776	SWITZERLAND	2,808	1,279	1,500	29	221 D	45.5%	53.4%	46.0%	54.0%
68,985	TIPPECANOE	48,557	29,129	17,867	1,561	11,262 R	60.0%	36.8%	62.0%	38.0%
10,964	TIPTON	7,776	5,063	2,584	129	2,479 R	65.1%	33.2%	66.2%	33.8%
3,815	UNION	2,859	1,705	1,097	57	608 R	59.6%	38.4%	60.8%	39.2%
108,858	VANDERBURGH	74,802	41,079	32,300	1,423	8,779 R	54.9%	43.2%	56.0%	44.0%
10,742	VERMILLION	7,757	3,293	4,286	178	993 D	42.5%	55.3%	43.4%	56.6%
63,456	VIGO	40,043	19,436	19,659	948	223 D	48.5%	49.1%	49.7%	50.3%
19,494	WABASH	14,280	8,992	5,099	189	3,893 R	63.0%	35.7%	63.8%	36.2%
5,256	WARREN	3,928	2,051	1,793	84	258 R	52.2%	45.6%	53.4%	46.6%
27,539	WARRICK	20,415	11,194	8,850	371	2,344 R	54.8%	43.4%	55.8%	44.2%
13,631	WASHINGTON	9,219	4,661	4,433	125	228 R	50.6%	48.1%	51.3%	48.7%
37,871	WAYNE	26,684	15,246	10,914	524	4,332 R	57.1%	40.9%	58.3%	41.7%
15,576	WELLS	11,946	7,834	3,926	186	3,908 R	65.6%	32.9%	66.6%	33.4%
13,524	WHITE	10,037	5,893	3,895	249	1,998 R	58.7%	38.8%	60.2%	39.8%
15,737	WHITLEY	11,619	7,229	4,107	283	3,122 R	62.2%	35.3%	63.8%	36.2%
3,180,157	TOTAL	2,211,426	1,267,972	900,148	43,306	367,824 R	57.3%	40.7%	58.5%	41.5%

INDIANA

CONGRESS

CD	Year	Total Vote	Republican		Democratic		Other Vote	Rep.-Dem. Plurality	Percentage			
			Vote	Candidate	Vote	Candidate			Total Vote		Major Vote	
									Rep.	Dem.	Rep.	Dem.
1	1992	211,824	64,770	VUCICH, DAVID J.	147,054	VISCLOSKY, PETER J.		82,284 D	30.6%	69.4%	30.6%	69.4%
2	1992	229,295	90,593	FRAZIER, WILLIAM G.	130,881	SHARP, PHILIP R.	7,821	40,288 D	39.5%	57.1%	40.9%	59.1%
3	1992	211,103	89,834	BAXMEYER, CARL H.	121,269	ROEMER, TIMOTHY J.		31,435 D	42.6%	57.4%	42.6%	57.4%
4	1992	217,375	82,468	PIERSON, CHARLES W.	134,907	LONG, JILL L.		52,439 D	37.9%	62.1%	37.9%	62.1%
5	1992	220,465	112,492	BUYER, STEVE	107,973	JONTZ, JIM		4,519 R	51.0%	49.0%	51.0%	49.0%
6	1992	258,455	186,499	BURTON, DAN	71,952	BRUNER, NATALIE M.	4	114,547 R	72.2%	27.8%	72.2%	27.8%
7	1992	217,194	129,189	MYERS, JOHN T.	88,005	WEDUM, ELLEN E.		41,184 R	59.5%	40.5%	59.5%	40.5%
8	1992	238,397	108,054	MOURDOCK, RICHARD	125,244	MCCLOSKEY, FRANCIS	5,099	17,190 D	45.3%	52.5%	46.3%	53.7%
9	1992	231,037	70,057	BAILEY, MICHAEL E.	160,980	HAMILTON, LEE H.		90,923 D	30.3%	69.7%	30.3%	69.7%
10	1992	183,831	64,378	HORVATH, JANOS	117,604	JACOBS, ANDREW, JR.	1,849	53,226 D	35.0%	64.0%	35.4%	64.6%

INDIANA

1992 GENERAL ELECTION

President   Other vote was 7,936 Libertarian (Marrou); 2,583 New Alliance (Fulani); 1,467 Gritz (write-in); 126 Hagelin (write-in); 16 Brisben (write-in); 14 LaRouche (write-in).

Governor   Other vote was 24,378 New Alliance (Barton); 36 Montgomery (write-in); 18 Galanti (write-in).

Senator   Other vote was 35,733 Libertarian (Dillon); 7,474 New Alliance (Tirado); 78 Plemons (write-in); 21 Irey (write-in).

Congress   Other vote was Independent (Shaver) in CD 2; Peterson (write-in) in CD 6; 3,098 Independent (Taylor) and 2,001 Libertarian (Funkhouser) in CD 8; New Alliance (Sackett) in CD 10.

1992 PRIMARIES

MAY 5 REPUBLICAN

Governor   223,373 Linley E. Pearson; 153,089 H. Dean Evans; 80,784 John A. Johnson.

Senator   Daniel R. Coats, unopposed.

Congress   Unopposed in two CD's. Contested as follows:

CD 1   7,307 David J. Vucich; 7,273 Cresley W. Walker; 6,628 William J. Glennon.
CD 2   25,223 William G. Frazier; 11,015 Jerrell S. Simmerman; 10,384 Tom Sprague.
CD 3   18,174 Carl H. Baxmeyer; 15,147 Doug A. Bernacchi; 1,980 David W. Shaw; 1,584 Allan L. White.
CD 4   13,710 Charles W. Pierson; 12,654 Phillip J. Troyer; 11,973 Dennis L. Wright; 3,079 David C. Roach.
CD 6   64,128 Dan Burton; 8,700 George B. Tintera; 6,852 William R. Sparks.
CD 7   32,238 John T. Myers; 20,382 Charles J. Metzger.
CD 9   18,022 Michael E. Bailey; 11,876 Charles D. Loos.
CD 10   15,724 Janos Horvath; 8,103 F. Perry Ray.

MAY 5 DEMOCRATIC

Governor   Evan Bayh, unopposed.

Senator   Joseph H. Hogsett, unopposed.

Congress   Unopposed in four CD's. Contested as follows:

CD 1   53,383 Peter J. Visclosky; 10,148 George T. Jancosek; 7,426 Albert J. LaMere; 3,389 Cyril B. Huerter.
CD 3   39,540 Timothy J. Roemer; 3,110 Christopher A. Mikulak; 2,420 Anthony V. Sims.
CD 4   30,603 Jill L. Long; 4,724 J. Carolyn Williams.
CD 6   11,812 Natalie M. Bruner; 5,376 Robert F. Williams; 2,782 Ralph Spelbring.
CD 7   9,613 Ellen E. Wedum; 9,371 Donald E. Wilson; 8,895 Mark C. Spelbring; 8,069 John W. Riley.
CD 10   31,710 Andrew Jacobs, Jr.; 2,349 Joe L.Turner; 1,551 Fred Ray.

IOWA

GOVERNOR
Terry E. Branstad (R). Re-elected 1990 to a four-year term. Previously elected 1986, 1982.

SENATORS
Charles E. Grassley (R). Re-elected 1992 to a six-year term. Previously elected 1986, 1980.

Tom Harkin (D). Re-elected 1990 to a six-year term. Previously elected 1984.

REPRESENTATIVES
1. James A. Leach (R)
2. Jim Nussle (R)
3. Jim R. Lightfood (R)
4. Neal Smith (D)
5. Fred Grandy (R)

POSTWAR VOTE FOR PRESIDENT

Year	Total Vote	Republican		Democratic		Other Vote	Plurality	Percentage			
								Total Vote		Major Vote	
		Vote	Candidate	Vote	Candidate			Rep.	Dem.	Rep.	Dem.
1992 **	1,354,607	504,891	Bush, George	586,353	Clinton, Bill	263,363	81,462 D	37.3%	43.3%	46.3%	53.7%
1988	1,225,614	545,355	Bush, George	670,557	Dukakis, Michael S.	9,702	125,202 D	44.5%	54.7%	44.9%	55.1%
1984	1,319,805	703,088	Reagan, Ronald	605,620	Mondale, Walter F.	11,097	97,468 R	53.3%	45.9%	53.7%	46.3%
1980	1,317,661	676,026	Reagan, Ronald	508,672	Carter, Jimmy	132,963	167,354 R	51.3%	38.6%	57.1%	42.9%
1976	1,279,306	632,863	Ford, Gerald R.	619,931	Carter, Jimmy	26,512	12,932 R	49.5%	48.5%	50.5%	49.5%
1972	1,225,944	706,207	Nixon, Richard M.	496,206	McGovern, George S.	23,531	210,001 R	57.6%	40.5%	58.7%	41.3%
1968	1,167,931	619,106	Nixon, Richard M.	476,699	Humphrey, Hubert H.	72,126	142,407 R	53.0%	40.8%	56.5%	43.5%
1964	1,184,539	449,148	Goldwater, Barry M.	733,030	Johnson, Lyndon B.	2,361	283,882 D	37.9%	61.9%	38.0%	62.0%
1960	1,273,810	722,381	Nixon, Richard M.	550,565	Kennedy, John F.	864	171,816 R	56.7%	43.2%	56.7%	43.3%
1956	1,234,564	729,187	Eisenhower, Dwight D.	501,858	Stevenson, Adlai E.	3,519	227,329 R	59.1%	40.7%	59.2%	40.8%
1952	1,268,773	808,906	Eisenhower, Dwight D.	451,513	Stevenson, Adlai E.	8,354	357,393 R	63.8%	35.6%	64.2%	35.8%
1948	1,038,264	494,018	Dewey, Thomas E.	522,380	Truman, Harry S.	21,866	28,362 D	47.6%	50.3%	48.6%	51.4%

In 1992 the other vote column includes 253,468 votes cast for Perot.

IOWA

POSTWAR VOTE FOR GOVERNOR

Year	Total Vote	Republican Vote	Republican Candidate	Democratic Vote	Democratic Candidate	Other Vote	Rep.-Dem. Plurality	Percentage Total Vote Rep.	Percentage Total Vote Dem.	Percentage Major Vote Rep.	Percentage Major Vote Dem.
1990	976,483	591,852	Branstad, Terry E.	379,372	Avenson, Donald D.	5,259	212,480 R	60.6%	38.9%	60.9%	39.1%
1986	910,623	472,712	Branstad, Terry E.	436,987	Junkins, Lowell L.	924	35,725 R	51.9%	48.0%	52.0%	48.0%
1982	1,038,229	548,313	Branstad, Terry E.	483,291	Conlin, Roxanne	6,625	65,022 R	52.8%	46.5%	53.2%	46.8%
1978	843,190	491,713	Ray, Robert	345,519	Fitzgerald, Jerome D.	5,958	146,194 R	58.3%	41.0%	58.7%	41.3%
1974 **	920,458	534,518	Ray, Robert	377,553	Schaben, James, F.	8,387	156,965 R	58.1%	41.0%	58.6%	41.4%
1972	1,210,222	707,177	Ray, Robert	487,282	Franzenburg, Paul	15,763	219,895 R	58.4%	40.3%	59.2%	40.8%
1970	791,241	403,394	Ray, Robert	368,911	Fulton, Robert	18,936	34,483 R	51.0%	46.6%	52.2%	47.8%
1968	1,136,489	614,328	Ray, Robert	521,216	Franzenburg, Paul	945	93,112 R	54.1%	45.9%	54.1%	45.9%
1966	893,175	394,518	Murray, William G.	494,259	Hughes, Harold E.	4,398	99,741 D	44.2%	55.3%	44.4%	55.6%
1964	1,167,734	365,131	Hultman, Evan	794,610	Hughes, Harold E.	7,993	429,479 D	31.3%	68.0%	31.5%	68.5%
1962	819,854	388,955	Erbe, Norman A.	430,899	Hughes, Harold E.		41,944 D	47.4%	52.6%	47.4%	52.6%
1960	1,237,089	645,026	Erbe, Norman A.	592,063	McManus, E. J.		52,963 R	52.1%	47.9%	52.1%	47.9%
1958	859,095	394,071	Murray, William G.	465,024	Loveless, Herschel C.		70,953 D	45.9%	54.1%	45.9%	54.1%
1956	1,204,235	587,383	Hoegh, Leo A.	616,852	Loveless, Herschel C.		29,469 D	48.8%	51.2%	48.8%	51.2%
1954	848,592	435,944	Hoegh, Leo A.	410,255	Herring, Clyde E.	2,393	25,689 R	51.4%	48.3%	51.5%	48.5%
1952	1,230,045	638,388	Beardsley, William	587,671	Loveless, Herschel C.	3,986	50,717 R	51.9%	47.8%	52.1%	47.9%
1950	857,213	506,642	Beardsley, William	347,176	Gillette, Lester S.	3,395	159,466 R	59.1%	40.5%	59.3%	40.7%
1948	994,833	553,900	Beardsley, William	434,432	Switzer, Carroll O.	6,501	119,468 R	55.7%	43.7%	56.0%	44.0%
1946	631,681	362,592	Blue, Robert D.	266,190	Miles, Frank	2,899	96,402 R	57.4%	42.1%	57.7%	42.3%

The term of office of Iowa's Governor was increased from two to four years effective with the 1974 election.

POSTWAR VOTE FOR SENATOR

Year	Total Vote	Republican Vote	Republican Candidate	Democratic Vote	Democratic Candidate	Other Vote	Rep.-Dem. Plurality	Percentage Total Vote Rep.	Percentage Total Vote Dem.	Percentage Major Vote Rep.	Percentage Major Vote Dem.
1992	1,292,494	899,761	Grassely, Charles E.	351,561	Lloyd-Jones, Jean	41,172	548,200 R	69.6%	27.2%	71.9%	28.1%
1990	983,933	446,869	Tauke, Tom	535,975	Harkin, Tom	1,089	89,106 D	45.4%	54.5%	45.5%	54.5%
1986	891,762	588,880	Grassley, Charles E.	299,406	Roehrick, John P.	3,476	289,474 R	66.0%	33.6%	66.3%	33.7%
1984	1,292,700	564,381	Jepsen, Roger W.	716,883	Harkin, Tom	11,436	152,502 D	43.7%	55.5%	44.0%	56.0%
1980	1,277,034	683,014	Grassley, Charles E.	581,545	Culver, John C.	12,475	101,469 R	53.5%	45.5%	54.0%	46.0%
1978	824,654	421,598	Jepsen, Roger W.	395,066	Clark, Richard	7,990	26,532 R	51.1%	47.9%	51.6%	48.4%
1974	889,561	420,546	Stanley, David M.	462,947	Culver, John C.	6,068	42,401 D	47.3%	52.0%	47.6%	52.4%
1972	1,203,333	530,525	Miller, Jack	662,637	Clark, Richard	10,171	132,112 D	44.1%	55.1%	44.5%	55.5%
1968	1,144,086	568,469	Stanley, David M.	574,884	Hughes, Harold E.	733	6,415 D	49.7%	50.2%	49.7%	50.3%
1966	857,496	522,339	Miller, Jack	324,114	Smith, E. B.	11,043	198,225 R	60.9%	37.8%	61.7%	38.3%
1962	807,972	431,364	Hickenlooper, Bourke B.	376,602	Smith, E. B.	6	54,762 R	53.4%	46.6%	53.4%	46.6%
1960	1,237,582	642,463	Miller, Jack	595,119	Loveless, Herschel C.		47,344 R	51.9%	48.1%	51.9%	48.1%
1956	1,178,655	635,499	Hickenlooper, Bourke B.	543,156	Evans, R. M.		92,343 R	53.9%	46.1%	53.9%	46.1%
1954	847,355	442,409	Martin, Thomas E.	402,712	Gillette, Guy	2,234	39,697 R	52.2%	47.5%	52.3%	47.7%
1950	858,523	470,613	Hickenlooper, Bourke B.	383,766	Loveland, A. J.	4,144	86,847 R	54.8%	44.7%	55.1%	44.9%
1948	1,000,412	415,778	Wilson, George A.	578,226	Gillette, Guy	6,408	162,448 D	41.6%	57.8%	41.8%	58.2%

IOWA

Districts Established May 30, 1991

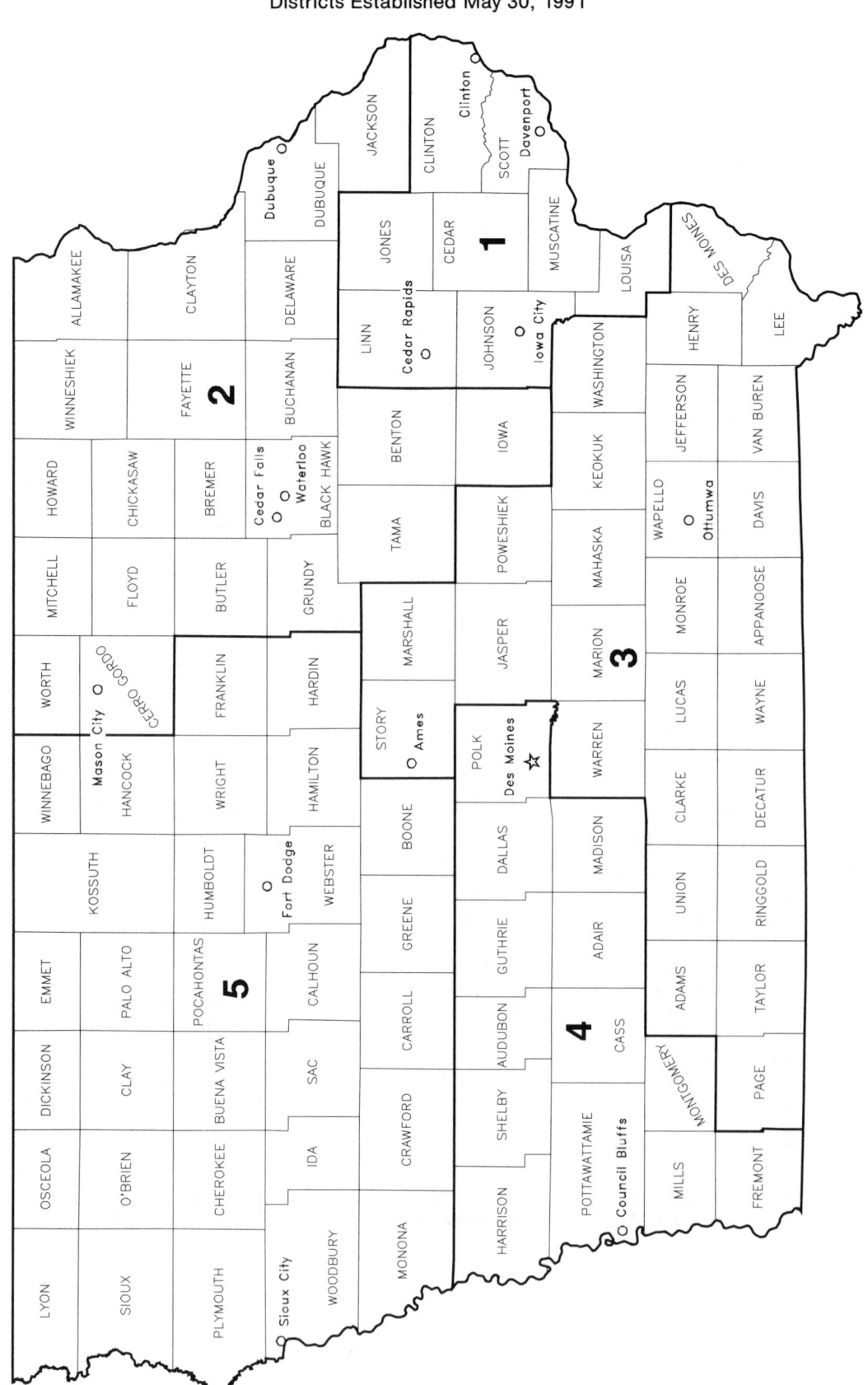

IOWA

PRESIDENT 1992

Registration	County	Total Vote	Republican	Democratic	Perot	Other	Plurality	Percentage Total Vote		
								Rep.	Dem.	Perot
5,170	ADAIR	4,194	1,713	1,655	814	12	58 R	40.8%	39.5%	19.4%
3,122	ADAMS	2,596	863	1,034	679	20	171 D	33.2%	39.8%	26.2%
8,398	ALLAMAKEE	6,679	2,627	2,362	1,543	147	265 R	39.3%	35.4%	23.1%
8,163	APPANOOSE	6,373	2,346	2,810	1,161	56	464 D	36.8%	44.1%	18.2%
4,390	AUDUBON	3,873	1,373	1,589	887	24	216 D	35.5%	41.0%	22.9%
13,502	BENTON	10,439	3,469	4,467	2,454	49	998 D	33.2%	42.8%	23.5%
77,931	BLACK HAWK	61,550	21,398	29,584	10,182	386	8,186 D	34.8%	48.1%	16.5%
15,739	BOONE	12,219	4,148	5,913	2,070	88	1,765 D	33.9%	48.4%	16.9%
14,742	BREMER	11,714	4,482	4,774	2,338	120	292 D	38.3%	40.8%	20.0%
12,024	BUCHANAN	9,654	3,313	4,166	2,126	49	853 D	34.3%	43.2%	22.0%
11,757	BUENA VISTA	9,257	3,863	3,374	1,955	65	489 R	41.7%	36.4%	21.1%
8,919	BUTLER	7,137	3,209	2,548	1,333	47	661 R	45.0%	35.7%	18.7%
6,921	CALHOUN	5,274	2,169	2,140	946	19	29 R	41.1%	40.6%	17.9%
12,390	CARROLL	9,475	3,439	3,800	2,192	44	361 D	36.3%	40.1%	23.1%
9,531	CASS	7,058	3,176	2,231	1,608	43	945 R	45.0%	31.6%	22.8%
10,277	CEDAR	8,240	2,965	3,296	1,945	34	331 D	36.0%	40.0%	23.6%
31,045	CERRO GORDO	24,293	8,250	11,415	4,498	130	3,165 D	34.0%	47.0%	18.5%
8,696	CHEROKEE	6,893	2,768	2,590	1,503	32	178 R	40.2%	37.6%	21.8%
8,184	CHICKASAW	6,640	2,129	2,913	1,566	32	784 D	32.1%	43.9%	23.6%
5,530	CLARKE	4,260	1,417	1,921	899	23	504 D	33.3%	45.1%	21.1%
10,466	CLAY	8,380	3,011	3,346	1,964	59	335 D	35.9%	39.9%	23.4%
11,495	CLAYTON	9,190	3,044	3,742	2,309	95	698 D	33.1%	40.7%	25.1%
32,325	CLINTON	24,960	8,746	11,683	4,414	117	2,937 D	35.0%	46.8%	17.7%
9,822	CRAWFORD	7,672	2,693	3,004	1,905	70	311 D	35.1%	39.2%	24.8%
18,774	DALLAS	14,861	5,587	6,554	2,665	55	967 D	37.6%	44.1%	17.9%
4,997	DAVIS	4,041	1,344	1,962	718	17	618 D	33.3%	48.6%	17.8%
5,215	DECATUR	3,986	1,316	1,866	786	18	550 D	33.0%	46.8%	19.7%
10,560	DELAWARE	8,492	3,195	3,093	2,144	60	102 R	37.6%	36.4%	25.2%
26,692	DES MOINES	21,190	6,378	11,309	3,386	117	4,931 D	30.1%	53.4%	16.0%
10,330	DICKINSON	8,304	3,196	3,106	1,974	28	90 R	38.5%	37.4%	23.8%
50,866	DUBUQUE	42,968	14,007	20,539	8,208	214	6,532 D	32.6%	47.8%	19.1%
6,402	EMMET	5,032	1,749	2,239	1,010	34	490 D	34.8%	44.5%	20.1%
13,496	FAYETTE	10,861	3,879	4,412	2,493	77	533 D	35.7%	40.6%	23.0%
10,283	FLOYD	7,750	2,404	3,688	1,611	47	1,284 D	31.0%	47.6%	20.8%
6,396	FRANKLIN	5,266	2,137	2,049	1,045	35	88 R	40.6%	38.9%	19.8%
5,125	FREMONT	3,911	1,459	1,422	1,003	27	37 R	37.3%	36.4%	25.6%
6,636	GREENE	5,353	1,952	2,422	956	23	470 D	36.5%	45.2%	17.9%
7,476	GRUNDY	6,156	3,160	1,895	1,069	32	1,265 R	51.3%	30.8%	17.4%
6,964	GUTHRIE	5,453	1,962	2,234	1,216	41	272 D	36.0%	41.0%	22.3%
9,661	HAMILTON	7,681	3,031	3,262	1,348	40	231 D	39.5%	42.5%	17.5%
7,341	HANCOCK	5,806	2,428	2,175	1,170	33	253 R	41.8%	37.5%	20.2%
12,429	HARDIN	8,979	3,590	3,792	1,547	50	202 D	40.0%	42.2%	17.2%
8,679	HARRISON	6,868	2,763	2,349	1,691	65	414 R	40.2%	34.2%	24.6%
11,386	HENRY	8,628	3,435	3,544	1,522	127	109 D	39.8%	41.1%	17.6%
5,995	HOWARD	4,862	1,516	2,099	1,193	54	583 D	31.2%	43.2%	24.5%
6,635	HUMBOLDT	5,185	2,299	1,765	1,093	28	534 R	44.3%	34.0%	21.1%
5,224	IDA	4,239	1,714	1,449	1,061	15	265 R	40.4%	34.2%	25.0%
8,934	IOWA	6,965	2,656	2,560	1,709	40	96 R	38.1%	36.8%	24.5%
11,721	JACKSON	9,305	2,673	4,421	2,096	115	1,748 D	28.7%	47.5%	22.5%
22,429	JASPER	18,012	6,866	8,120	2,972	54	1,254 D	38.1%	45.1%	16.5%
10,723	JEFFERSON	8,341	2,541	2,562	1,241	1,997	21 D	30.5%	30.7%	14.9%
71,612	JOHNSON	51,774	14,041	28,656	8,625	452	14,615 D	27.1%	55.3%	16.7%
11,128	JONES	8,900	3,071	3,508	2,306	15	437 D	34.5%	39.4%	25.9%
7,002	KEOKUK	5,577	1,981	2,329	1,238	29	348 D	35.5%	41.8%	22.2%
11,410	KOSSUTH	9,059	3,464	3,660	1,906	29	196 D	38.2%	40.4%	21.0%
23,577	LEE	17,152	4,777	9,366	2,920	89	4,589 D	27.9%	54.6%	17.0%
102,628	LINN	88,885	30,215	38,567	19,643	460	8,352 D	34.0%	43.4%	22.1%
6,361	LOUISA	4,844	1,691	2,091	1,044	18	400 D	34.9%	43.2%	21.6%
5,826	LUCAS	4,674	1,734	2,072	848	20	338 D	37.1%	44.3%	18.1%
7,340	LYON	5,726	3,272	1,331	1,068	55	1,941 R	57.1%	23.2%	18.7%

IOWA

PRESIDENT 1992

Registration	County	Total Vote	Republican	Democratic	Perot	Other	Plurality	Percentage Total Vote		
								Rep.	Dem.	Perot
8,030	MADISON	6,149	2,421	2,525	1,168	35	104 D	39.4%	41.1%	19.0%
12,493	MAHASKA	10,247	4,953	3,714	1,508	72	1,239 R	48.3%	36.2%	14.7%
18,458	MARION	13,533	6,062	5,531	1,896	44	531 R	44.8%	40.9%	14.0%
23,720	MARSHALL	18,289	6,784	8,303	3,100	102	1,519 D	37.1%	45.4%	17.0%
7,917	MILLS	6,166	2,699	1,798	1,638	31	901 R	43.8%	29.2%	26.6%
6,882	MITCHELL	5,347	1,933	2,177	1,199	38	244 D	36.2%	40.7%	22.4%
6,187	MONONA	4,849	1,660	1,939	1,231	19	279 D	34.2%	40.0%	25.4%
4,976	MONROE	3,782	1,323	1,829	612	18	506 D	35.0%	48.4%	16.2%
7,102	MONTGOMERY	5,369	2,404	1,599	1,341	25	805 R	44.8%	29.8%	25.0%
22,234	MUSCATINE	16,864	6,087	7,089	3,583	105	1,002 D	36.1%	42.0%	21.2%
9,246	O'BRIEN	7,578	3,869	2,122	1,557	30	1,747 R	51.1%	28.0%	20.5%
4,405	OSCEOLA	3,600	1,756	990	813	41	766 R	48.8%	27.5%	22.6%
9,456	PAGE	7,310	3,670	1,951	1,669	20	1,719 R	50.2%	26.7%	22.8%
6,761	PALO ALTO	5,379	1,789	2,374	1,186	30	585 D	33.3%	44.1%	22.0%
12,838	PLYMOUTH	10,484	5,196	3,171	2,039	78	2,025 R	49.6%	30.2%	19.4%
6,099	POCAHONTAS	4,669	1,743	1,919	942	65	176 D	37.3%	41.1%	20.2%
195,906	POLK	167,258	63,708	78,585	24,155	810	14,877 D	38.1%	47.0%	14.4%
46,496	POTTAWATTAMIE	37,115	15,671	13,228	8,035	181	2,443 R	42.2%	35.6%	21.6%
12,021	POWESHIEK	9,047	3,245	4,056	1,680	66	811 D	35.9%	44.8%	18.6%
3,634	RINGGOLD	2,869	967	1,341	551	10	374 D	33.7%	46.7%	19.2%
7,100	SAC	5,215	2,138	1,896	1,157	24	242 R	41.0%	36.4%	22.2%
93,736	SCOTT	74,662	28,844	33,765	11,423	630	4,921 D	38.6%	45.2%	15.3%
8,180	SHELBY	6,544	2,809	2,094	1,614	27	715 R	42.9%	32.0%	24.7%
17,911	SIOUX	14,730	10,637	2,226	1,771	96	8,411 R	72.2%	15.1%	12.0%
52,133	STORY	36,311	12,702	17,118	6,275	216	4,416 D	35.0%	47.1%	17.3%
10,494	TAMA	8,330	2,948	3,573	1,748	61	625 D	35.4%	42.9%	21.0%
4,572	TAYLOR	3,551	1,200	1,430	910	11	230 D	33.8%	40.3%	25.6%
7,908	UNION	6,102	2,224	2,565	1,280	33	341 D	36.4%	42.0%	21.0%
4,644	VAN BUREN	3,710	1,418	1,464	811	17	46 D	38.2%	39.5%	21.9%
22,409	WAPELLO	16,083	4,852	8,670	2,513	48	3,818 D	30.2%	53.9%	15.6%
23,022	WARREN	19,157	7,242	8,612	3,217	86	1,370 D	37.8%	45.0%	16.8%
11,248	WASHINGTON	9,018	3,576	3,384	1,994	64	192 R	39.7%	37.5%	22.1%
4,487	WAYNE	3,584	1,299	1,632	642	11	333 D	36.2%	45.5%	17.9%
23,645	WEBSTER	18,921	6,992	8,562	3,272	95	1,570 D	37.0%	45.3%	17.3%
7,483	WINNEBAGO	6,078	2,407	2,322	1,329	20	85 R	39.6%	38.2%	21.9%
13,203	WINNESHIEK	9,624	3,331	3,791	2,416	86	460 D	34.6%	39.4%	25.1%
54,399	WOODBURY	42,864	18,148	17,398	7,182	136	750 R	42.3%	40.6%	16.8%
5,132	WORTH	4,448	1,382	2,009	1,044	13	627 D	31.1%	45.2%	23.5%
8,173	WRIGHT	6,665	2,708	2,776	1,151	30	68 D	40.6%	41.7%	17.3%
1,703,532	TOTAL	1,354,607	504,891	586,353	253,468	9,895	81,462 D	37.3%	43.3%	18.7%

IOWA

SENATOR 1992

Registration	County	Total Vote	Republican	Democratic	Other	Rep.-Dem. Plurality	Percentage Total Vote Rep.	Dem.	Percentage Major Vote Rep.	Dem.
5,170	ADAIR	3,706	2,741	875	90	1,866 R	74.0%	23.6%	75.8%	24.2%
3,122	ADAMS	2,419	1,798	569	52	1,229 R	74.3%	23.5%	76.0%	24.0%
8,398	ALLAMAKEE	5,815	4,370	1,273	172	3,097 R	75.2%	21.9%	77.4%	22.6%
8,163	APPANOOSE	5,543	3,573	1,790	180	1,783 R	64.5%	32.3%	66.6%	33.4%
4,390	AUDUBON	3,300	2,364	824	112	1,540 R	71.6%	25.0%	74.2%	25.8%
13,502	BENTON	10,785	8,073	2,416	296	5,657 R	74.9%	22.4%	77.0%	23.0%
77,931	BLACK HAWK	56,717	38,192	16,958	1,567	21,234 R	67.3%	29.9%	69.3%	30.7%
15,739	BOONE	11,941	8,268	3,338	335	4,930 R	69.2%	28.0%	71.2%	28.8%
14,742	BREMER	11,286	8,819	2,263	204	6,556 R	78.1%	20.1%	79.6%	20.4%
12,024	BUCHANAN	9,652	7,329	2,075	248	5,254 R	75.9%	21.5%	77.9%	22.1%
11,757	BUENA VISTA	8,254	6,366	1,628	260	4,738 R	77.1%	19.7%	79.6%	20.4%
8,919	BUTLER	6,945	5,486	1,322	137	4,164 R	79.0%	19.0%	80.6%	19.4%
6,921	CALHOUN	5,388	4,051	1,175	162	2,876 R	75.2%	21.8%	77.5%	22.5%
12,390	CARROLL	9,565	7,049	2,228	288	4,821 R	73.7%	23.3%	76.0%	24.0%
9,531	CASS	7,298	5,588	1,471	239	4,117 R	76.6%	20.2%	79.2%	20.8%
10,277	CEDAR	8,127	6,079	1,831	217	4,248 R	74.8%	22.5%	76.9%	23.1%
31,045	CERRO GORDO	21,753	15,405	5,818	530	9,587 R	70.8%	26.7%	72.6%	27.4%
8,696	CHEROKEE	7,172	5,692	1,289	191	4,403 R	79.4%	18.0%	81.5%	18.5%
8,184	CHICKASAW	6,563	5,094	1,323	146	3,771 R	77.6%	20.2%	79.4%	20.6%
5,530	CLARKE	4,222	2,875	1,179	168	1,696 R	68.1%	27.9%	70.9%	29.1%
10,466	CLAY	7,101	5,034	1,772	295	3,262 R	70.9%	25.0%	74.0%	26.0%
11,495	CLAYTON	7,899	5,944	1,659	296	4,285 R	75.3%	21.0%	78.2%	21.8%
32,325	CLINTON	21,658	14,203	6,760	695	7,443 R	65.6%	31.2%	67.8%	32.2%
9,822	CRAWFORD	6,378	4,800	1,240	338	3,560 R	75.3%	19.4%	79.5%	20.5%
18,774	DALLAS	14,766	10,209	4,006	551	6,203 R	69.1%	27.1%	71.8%	28.2%
4,997	DAVIS	3,861	2,586	1,225	50	1,361 R	67.0%	31.7%	67.9%	32.1%
5,215	DECATUR	3,894	2,694	1,051	149	1,643 R	69.2%	27.0%	71.9%	28.1%
10,560	DELAWARE	7,509	5,888	1,420	201	4,468 R	78.4%	18.9%	80.6%	19.4%
26,692	DES MOINES	18,177	10,261	7,387	529	2,874 R	56.5%	40.6%	58.1%	41.9%
10,330	DICKINSON	7,341	5,477	1,593	271	3,884 R	74.6%	21.7%	77.5%	22.5%
50,866	DUBUQUE	41,952	28,334	12,713	905	15,621 R	67.5%	30.3%	69.0%	31.0%
6,402	EMMET	5,098	3,567	1,399	132	2,168 R	70.0%	27.4%	71.8%	28.2%
13,496	FAYETTE	9,813	7,063	2,455	295	4,608 R	72.0%	25.0%	74.2%	25.8%
10,283	FLOYD	7,652	5,542	1,684	426	3,858 R	72.4%	22.0%	76.7%	23.3%
6,396	FRANKLIN	4,893	3,886	896	111	2,990 R	79.4%	18.3%	81.3%	18.7%
5,125	FREMONT	3,865	2,777	954	134	1,823 R	71.8%	24.7%	74.4%	25.6%
6,636	GREENE	5,175	3,830	1,266	79	2,564 R	74.0%	24.5%	75.2%	24.8%
7,476	GRUNDY	5,733	4,708	895	130	3,813 R	82.1%	15.6%	84.0%	16.0%
6,964	GUTHRIE	5,126	3,656	1,316	154	2,340 R	71.3%	25.7%	73.5%	26.5%
9,661	HAMILTON	7,951	5,805	1,912	234	3,893 R	73.0%	24.0%	75.2%	24.8%
7,341	HANCOCK	5,778	4,762	921	95	3,841 R	82.4%	15.9%	83.8%	16.2%
12,429	HARDIN	9,246	6,856	2,182	208	4,674 R	74.2%	23.6%	75.9%	24.1%
8,679	HARRISON	6,236	4,371	1,703	162	2,668 R	70.1%	27.3%	72.0%	28.0%
11,386	HENRY	8,743	6,390	2,111	242	4,279 R	73.1%	24.1%	75.2%	24.8%
5,995	HOWARD	4,806	3,727	985	94	2,742 R	77.5%	20.5%	79.1%	20.9%
6,635	HUMBOLDT	5,305	4,191	986	128	3,205 R	79.0%	18.6%	81.0%	19.0%
5,224	IDA	3,557	2,840	593	124	2,247 R	79.8%	16.7%	82.7%	17.3%
8,934	IOWA	7,227	5,769	1,298	160	4,471 R	79.8%	18.0%	81.6%	18.4%
11,721	JACKSON	8,395	6,041	2,152	202	3,889 R	72.0%	25.6%	73.7%	26.3%
22,429	JASPER	17,966	12,115	5,345	506	6,770 R	67.4%	29.8%	69.4%	30.6%
10,723	JEFFERSON	8,416	4,404	1,464	2,548	2,940 R	52.3%	17.4%	75.1%	24.9%
71,612	JOHNSON	51,029	29,663	19,494	1,872	10,169 R	58.1%	38.2%	60.3%	39.7%
11,128	JONES	8,903	6,806	1,855	242	4,951 R	76.4%	20.8%	78.6%	21.4%
7,002	KEOKUK	4,857	3,541	1,130	186	2,411 R	72.9%	23.3%	75.8%	24.2%
11,410	KOSSUTH	8,880	6,889	1,806	185	5,083 R	77.6%	20.3%	79.2%	20.8%
23,577	LEE	17,602	9,204	7,812	586	1,392 R	52.3%	44.4%	54.1%	45.9%
102,628	LINN	88,394	61,450	24,077	2,867	37,373 R	69.5%	27.2%	71.8%	28.2%
6,361	LOUISA	4,813	3,483	1,199	131	2,284 R	72.4%	24.9%	74.4%	25.6%
5,826	LUCAS	4,497	3,253	1,156	88	2,097 R	72.3%	25.7%	73.8%	26.2%
7,340	LYON	4,999	4,195	710	94	3,485 R	83.9%	14.2%	85.5%	14.5%

IOWA

SENATOR 1992

Registration	County	Total Vote	Republican	Democratic	Other	Rep.-Dem. Plurality	Percentage			
							Total Vote		Major Vote	
							Rep.	Dem.	Rep.	Dem.
8,030	MADISON	6,379	4,450	1,675	254	2,775 R	69.8%	26.3%	72.7%	27.3%
12,493	MAHASKA	9,230	6,946	2,059	225	4,887 R	75.3%	22.3%	77.1%	22.9%
18,458	MARION	13,103	9,241	3,567	295	5,674 R	70.5%	27.2%	72.2%	27.8%
23,720	MARSHALL	18,818	13,087	5,295	436	7,792 R	69.5%	28.1%	71.2%	28.8%
7,917	MILLS	5,232	3,811	1,140	281	2,671 R	72.8%	21.8%	77.0%	23.0%
6,882	MITCHELL	5,576	4,384	1,094	98	3,290 R	78.6%	19.6%	80.0%	20.0%
6,187	MONONA	4,437	3,329	976	132	2,353 R	75.0%	22.0%	77.3%	22.7%
4,976	MONROE	3,926	2,707	1,075	144	1,632 R	69.0%	27.4%	71.6%	28.4%
7,102	MONTGOMERY	5,537	4,230	1,124	183	3,106 R	76.4%	20.3%	79.0%	21.0%
22,234	MUSCATINE	14,792	10,128	4,066	598	6,062 R	68.5%	27.5%	71.4%	28.6%
9,246	O'BRIEN	7,393	6,177	1,018	198	5,159 R	83.6%	13.8%	85.9%	14.1%
4,405	OSCEOLA	3,151	2,596	469	86	2,127 R	82.4%	14.9%	84.7%	15.3%
9,456	PAGE	7,361	5,978	1,227	156	4,751 R	81.2%	16.7%	83.0%	17.0%
6,761	PALO ALTO	4,475	3,283	1,058	134	2,225 R	73.4%	23.6%	75.6%	24.4%
12,838	PLYMOUTH	8,864	6,969	1,570	325	5,399 R	78.6%	17.7%	81.6%	18.4%
6,099	POCAHONTAS	4,760	3,733	878	149	2,855 R	78.4%	18.4%	81.0%	19.0%
195,906	POLK	166,631	110,972	50,318	5,341	60,654 R	66.6%	30.2%	68.8%	31.2%
46,496	POTTAWATTAMIE	32,766	21,343	10,278	1,145	11,065 R	65.1%	31.4%	67.5%	32.5%
12,021	POWESHIEK	8,235	5,552	2,453	230	3,099 R	67.4%	29.8%	69.4%	30.6%
3,634	RINGGOLD	2,861	2,180	609	72	1,571 R	76.2%	21.3%	78.2%	21.8%
7,100	SAC	5,428	4,338	936	154	3,402 R	79.9%	17.2%	82.3%	17.7%
93,736	SCOTT	66,226	43,640	20,354	2,232	23,286 R	65.9%	30.7%	68.2%	31.8%
8,180	SHELBY	5,357	3,953	1,183	221	2,770 R	73.8%	22.1%	77.0%	23.0%
17,911	SIOUX	13,483	12,253	1,051	179	11,202 R	90.9%	7.8%	92.1%	7.9%
52,133	STORY	34,973	22,953	10,869	1,151	12,084 R	65.6%	31.1%	67.9%	32.1%
10,494	TAMA	8,526	6,496	1,841	189	4,655 R	76.2%	21.6%	77.9%	22.1%
4,572	TAYLOR	3,283	2,526	704	53	1,822 R	76.9%	21.4%	78.2%	21.8%
7,908	UNION	5,491	3,882	1,436	173	2,446 R	70.7%	26.2%	73.0%	27.0%
4,644	VAN BUREN	3,317	2,316	927	74	1,389 R	69.8%	27.9%	71.4%	28.6%
22,409	WAPELLO	16,919	9,679	6,674	566	3,005 R	57.2%	39.4%	59.2%	40.8%
23,022	WARREN	17,357	11,537	5,228	592	6,309 R	66.5%	30.1%	68.8%	31.2%
11,248	WASHINGTON	8,551	6,368	1,969	214	4,399 R	74.5%	23.0%	76.4%	23.6%
4,487	WAYNE	3,413	2,359	1,001	53	1,358 R	69.1%	29.3%	70.2%	29.8%
23,645	WEBSTER	17,032	11,443	5,045	544	6,398 R	67.2%	29.6%	69.4%	30.6%
7,483	WINNEBAGO	5,059	3,519	1,063	477	2,456 R	69.6%	21.0%	76.8%	23.2%
13,203	WINNESHIEK	9,896	7,381	2,187	328	5,194 R	74.6%	22.1%	77.1%	22.9%
54,399	WOODBURY	42,026	30,415	10,575	1,036	19,840 R	72.4%	25.2%	74.2%	25.8%
5,132	WORTH	4,354	3,408	890	56	2,518 R	78.3%	20.4%	79.3%	20.7%
8,173	WRIGHT	6,334	4,773	1,452	109	3,321 R	75.4%	22.9%	76.7%	23.3%
1,703,532	TOTAL	1,292,494	899,761	351,561	41,172	548,200 R	69.6%	27.2%	71.9%	28.1%

IOWA

CONGRESS

CD	Year	Total Vote	Republican		Democratic		Other Vote	Rep.-Dem. Plurality	Percentage			
			Vote	Candidate	Vote	Candidate			Total Vote		Major Vote	
									Rep.	Dem.	Rep.	Dem.
1	1992	261,309	178,042	LEACH, JAMES A.	81,600	ZONNEVELD, JAN J.	1,667	96,442 R	68.1%	31.2%	68.6%	31.4%
2	1992	267,892	134,536	NUSSLE, JIM	131,570	NAGLE, DAVID R.	1,786	2,966 R	50.2%	49.1%	50.6%	49.4%
3	1992	257,276	125,931	LIGHTFOOT, JIM R.	121,063	BAXTER, ELAINE	10,282	4,868 R	48.9%	47.1%	51.0%	49.0%
4	1992	257,593	94,045	LUNDE, PAUL	158,610	SMITH, NEAL	4,938	64,565 D	36.5%	61.6%	37.2%	62.8%
5	1992	198,366	196,942	GRANDY, FRED			1,424	196,942 R	99.3%		100.0%	

214

IOWA

1992 GENERAL ELECTION

President   Other vote was 3,079 Natural Law (Hagelin); 1,177 America First (Gritz); 1,149 Independent (Ehlers); 1,076 Libertarian (Marrou); 669 Grassroots (Herer); 604 Independent (Yiamouyiannis); 480 Taxpayers (Phillips); 273 Socialist Workers (Warren); 238 Economic Recovery (LaRouche); 212 Campaign for a New Tomorrow (Daniels); 197 New Alliance (Fulani); 741 scattered write-in.

Senator   Other vote was 16,403 Natural Law (Zimmerman); 6,277 Independent (Atkinson); 5,508 Independent (Boring); 4,999 Independent (Freeburg); 3,404 Grassroots (Olsen); 2,918 Independent (Hughes); 1,370 Socialist Workers (Pulley); 293 scattered write-in.

Congress   Other vote was scattered write-in in CD 1; 1,757 Grassroots (Schoeman) and 29 scattered write-in in CD 2; 10,181 Natural Law (Chroman) and 101 scattered write-in in CD 3; 2,427 Natural Law (Yellin), 2,359 Grassroots (Oviatt) and 152 scattered write-in in CD 4; scattered write-in in CD 5.

1992 PRIMARIES

JUNE 2 REPUBLICAN

Senator   Charles E. Grassley, unopposed.

Congress   Unopposed in three CD's. Contested as follows:

CD 3   15,757 Jim R. Lightfoot; 11,251 Ronald J. Long; 28 scattered write-in.
CD 4   10,261 Paul Lunde; 8,589 R. Dean Arbuckle; 72 scattered write-in.

JUNE 2 DEMOCRATIC

Senator   60,615 Jean Lloyd-Jones; 38,774 Rosanne Freeburg; 307 scattered write-in.

Congress   Unopposed in CD's 1, 2, 3 and 4. No candidate in CD 5.

KANSAS

GOVERNOR
Joan Finney (D). Elected 1990 to a four-year term.

SENATORS
Robert Dole (R). Re-elected 1992 to a six-year term. Previously elected 1986, 1980, 1974, 1968.

Nancy Landon Kassebaum (R). Re-elected 1990 to a six-year term. Previously elected 1984, 1978.

REPRESENTATIVES
1. Pat Roberts (R)
2. Jim Slattery (D)
3. Jan Meyers (R)
4. Dan Glickman (D)

POSTWAR VOTE FOR PRESIDENT

Year	Total Vote	Republican Vote	Candidate	Democratic Vote	Candidate	Other Vote	Plurality	Percentage Total Vote Rep.	Dem.	Major Vote Rep.	Dem.
1992 **	1,157,335	449,951	Bush, George	390,434	Clinton, Bill	316,950	59,517 R	38.9%	33.7%	53.5%	46.5%
1988	993,044	554,049	Bush, George	422,636	Dukakis, Michael S.	16,359	131,413 R	55.8%	42.6%	56.7%	43.3%
1984	1,021,991	677,296	Reagan, Ronald	333,149	Mondale, Walter F.	11,546	344,147 R	66.3%	32.6%	67.0%	33.0%
1980	979,795	566,812	Reagan, Ronald	326,150	Carter, Jimmy	86,833	240,662 R	57.9%	33.3%	63.5%	36.5%
1976	957,845	502,752	Ford, Gerald R.	430,421	Carter, Jimmy	24,672	72,331 R	52.5%	44.9%	53.9%	46.1%
1972	916,095	619,812	Nixon, Richard M.	270,287	McGovern, George S.	25,996	349,525 R	67.7%	29.5%	69.6%	30.4%
1968	872,783	478,674	Nixon, Richard M.	302,996	Humphrey, Hubert H.	91,113	175,678 R	54.8%	34.7%	61.2%	38.8%
1964	857,901	386,579	Goldwater, Barry M.	464,028	Johnson, Lyndon B.	7,294	77,449 D	45.1%	54.1%	45.4%	54.6%
1960	928,825	561,474	Nixon, Richard M.	363,213	Kennedy, John F.	4,138	198,261 R	60.4%	39.1%	60.7%	39.3%
1956	866,243	566,878	Eisenhower, Dwight D.	296,317	Stevenson, Adlai E.	3,048	270,561 R	65.4%	34.2%	65.7%	34.3%
1952	896,166	616,302	Eisenhower, Dwight D.	273,296	Stevenson, Adlai E.	6,568	343,006 R	68.8%	30.5%	69.3%	30.7%
1948	788,819	423,039	Dewey, Thomas E.	351,902	Truman, Harry S.	13,878	71,137 R	53.6%	44.6%	54.6%	45.4%

In 1992 the other vote column includes 312,358 votes cast for Perot.

KANSAS

POSTWAR VOTE FOR GOVERNOR

Year	Total Vote	Republican		Democratic		Other Vote	Rep.-Dem. Plurality	Percentage			
								Total Vote		Major Vote	
		Vote	Candidate	Vote	Candidate			Rep.	Dem.	Rep.	Dem.
1990	783,325	333,589	Hayden, Mike	380,609	Finney, Joan	69,127	47,020 D	42,6%	48.6%	46.7%	53.3%
1986	840,605	436,267	Hayden, Mike	404,338	Docking, Thomas R.		31,929 R	51.9%	48.1%	51.9%	48.1%
1982	763,263	339,356	Hardage, Sam	405,772	Carlin, John	18,135	66,416 D	44.5%	53.2%	45.5%	54.5%
1978	736,246	348,015	Bennett, Robert F.	363,835	Carlin, John	24,396	15,820 D	47.3%	49.4%	48.9%	51.1%
1974 **	783,875	387,792	Bennett, Robert F.	384,115	Miller, Vern	11,968	3,677 R	49.5%	49.0%	50.2%	49.8%
1972	921,552	341,440	Kay, Morris	571,256	Docking, Robert	8,856	229,816 D	37.1%	62.0%	37.4%	62.6%
1970	745,196	333,227	Frizzell, Kent	404,611	Docking, Robert	7,358	71,384 D	44.7%	54.3%	45.2%	54.8%
1968	862,473	410,673	Harman, Rick	447,269	Docking, Robert	4,531	36,596 D	47.6%	51.9%	47.9%	52.1%
1966	692,955	304,325	Avery, William H.	380,030	Docking, Robert	8,600	75,705 D	43.9%	54.8%	44.5%	55.5%
1964	850,414	432,667	Avery, William H.	400,264	Wiles, Harry G.	17,483	32,403 R	50.9%	47.1%	51.9%	48.1%
1962	638,798	341,257	Anderson, John	291,285	Saffels, Dale E.	6,256	49,972 R	53.4%	45.6%	54.0%	46.0%
1960	922,522	511,534	Anderson, John	402,261	Docking, George	8,727	109,273 R	55.4%	43.6%	56.0%	44.0%
1958	735,939	313,036	Reed, Clyde M.	415,506	Docking, George	7,397	102,470 D	42.5%	56.5%	43.0%	57.0%
1956	864,935	364,340	Shaw, Warren W.	479,701	Docking, George	20,894	115,361 D	42.1%	55.5%	43.2%	56.8%
1954	622,633	329,868	Hall, Fred	286,218	Docking, George	6,547	43,650 R	53.0%	46.0%	53.5%	46.5%
1952	872,139	491,338	Arn, Edward F.	363,482	Rooney, Charles	17,319	127,856 R	56.3%	41.7%	57.5%	42.5%
1950	619,310	333,001	Arn, Edward F.	275,494	Anderson, Kenneth	10,815	57,507 R	53.8%	44.5%	54.7%	45.3%
1948	760,407	433,396	Carlson, Frank	307,485	Carpenter, Randolph	19,526	125,911 R	57.0%	40.4%	58.5%	41.5%
1946	577,694	309,064	Carlson, Frank	254,283	Woodring, Harry H.	14,347	54,781 R	53.5%	44.0%	54.9%	45.1%

The term of office of Kansas' Governor was increased from two to four years effective with the 1974 election.

POSTWAR VOTE FOR SENATOR

Year	Total Vote	Republican		Democratic		Other Vote	Rep.-Dem. Plurality	Percentage			
								Total Vote		Major Vote	
		Vote	Candidate	Vote	Candidate			Rep.	Dem.	Rep.	Dem.
1992	1,126,447	706,246	Dole, Robert	349,525	O'Dell, Gloria	70,676	356,721 R	62.7%	31.0%	66.9%	33.1%
1990	786,235	578,605	Kassebaum, Nancy Landon	207,491	Williams, Dick	139	371,114 R	73.6%	26.4%	73.6%	26.4%
1986	823,566	576,902	Dole, Robert	246,664	MacDonald, Guy		330,238 R	70.0%	30.0%	70.0%	30.0%
1984	996,729	757,402	Kassebaum, Nancy Landon	211,664	Maher, James	27,663	545,738 R	76.0%	21.2%	78.2%	21.8%
1980	938,957	598,686	Dole, Robert	340,271	Simpson, John		258,415 R	63.8%	36.2%	63.8%	36.2%
1978	748,839	403,354	Kassebaum, Nancy Landon	317,602	Roy, William R.	27,883	85,752 R	53.9%	42.4%	55.9%	44.1%
1974	794,437	403,983	Dole, Robert	390,451	Roy, William R.	3	13,532 R	50.9%	49.1%	50.9%	49.1%
1972	871,722	622,591	Pearson, James B.	200,764	Tetzlaff, Arch O.	48,367	421,827 R	71.4%	23.0%	75.6%	24.4%
1968	817,096	490,911	Dole, Robert	315,911	Robinson, William I.	10,274	175,000 R	60.1%	38.7%	60.8%	39.2%
1966	671,345	350,077	Pearson, James B.	303,223	Breeding, J. Floyd	18,045	46,854 R	52.1%	45.2%	53.6%	46.4%
1962	622,232	388,500	Carlson, Frank	223,630	Smith, K. L.	10,102	164,870 R	62.4%	35.9%	63.5%	36.5%
1962 S	613,250	344,689	Pearson, James B.	260,756	Aylward, Paul L.	7,805	83,933 R	56.2%	42.5%	56.9%	43.1%
1960	888,592	485,499	Schoeppel, Andrew F.	388,895	Theis, Frank	14,198	96,604 R	54.6%	43.8%	55.5%	44.5%
1956	825,280	477,822	Carlson, Frank	333,939	Hart, George	13,519	143,883 R	57.9%	40.5%	58.9%	41.1%
1954	618,063	348,144	Schoeppel, Andrew F.	258,575	McGill, George	11,344	89,569 R	56.3%	41.8%	57.4%	42.6%
1950	619,104	335,880	Carlson, Frank	271,365	Aiken, Paul	11,859	64,515 R	54.3%	43.8%	55.3%	44.7%
1948	716,342	393,412	Schoeppel, Andrew F.	305,987	McGill, George	16,943	87,425 R	54.9%	42.7%	56.3%	43.7%

One of the 1962 elections was for a short term to fill a vacancy.

KANSAS

Districts Established June 3, 1991

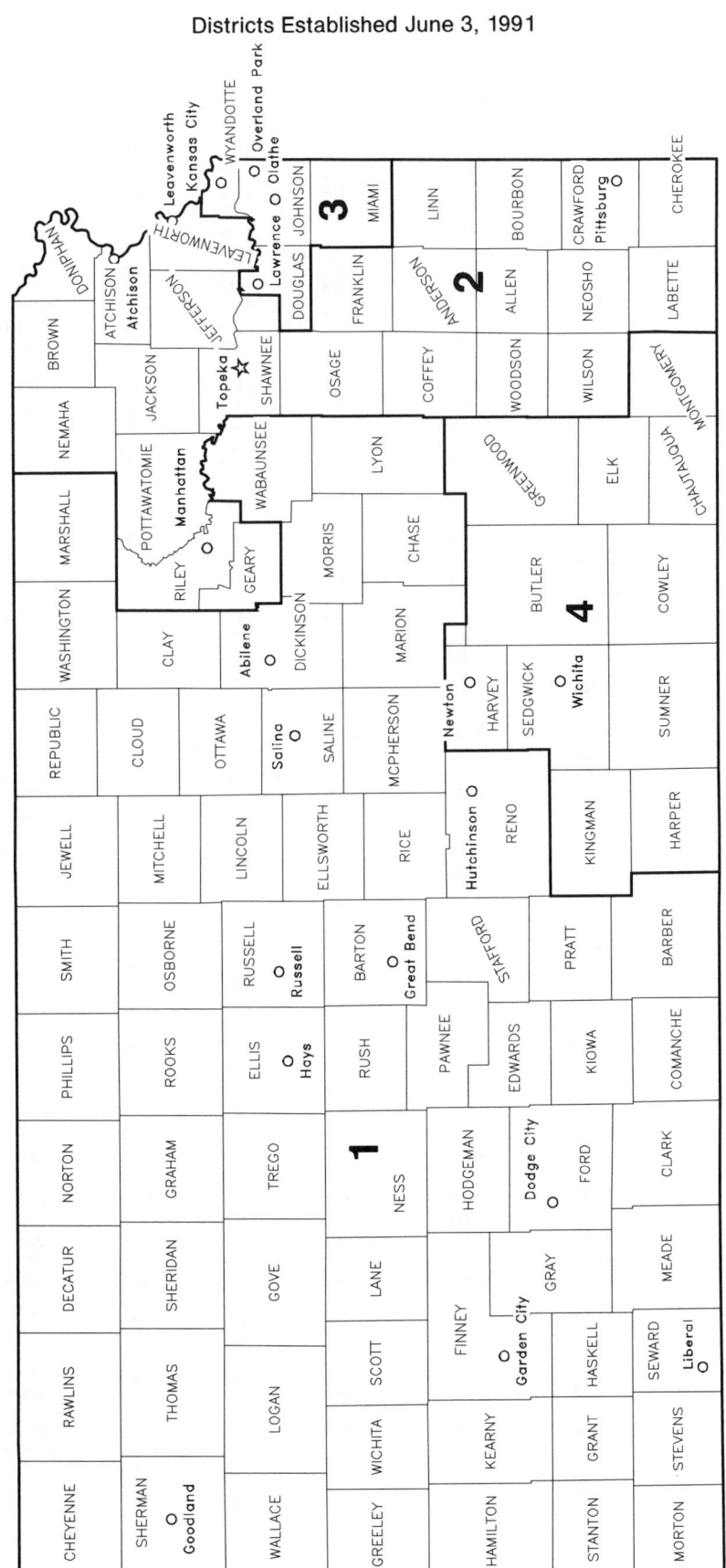

KANSAS

PRESIDENT 1992

Registration	County	Total Vote	Republican	Democratic	Perot	Other	Plurality	Percentage Total Vote		
								Rep.	Dem.	Perot
7,538	ALLEN	6,430	2,351	2,312	1,746	21	39 R	36.6%	36.0%	27.2%
4,415	ANDERSON	3,687	1,218	1,178	1,282	9	64 P	33.0%	32.0%	34.8%
8,276	ATCHISON	7,533	2,521	2,959	2,020	33	438 D	33.5%	39.3%	26.8%
3,625	BARBER	2,881	1,225	759	893	4	332 R	42.5%	26.3%	31.0%
15,369	BARTON	13,582	5,113	3,846	4,574	49	539 R	37.6%	28.3%	33.7%
8,626	BOURBON	7,162	2,876	2,509	1,763	14	367 R	40.2%	35.0%	24.6%
6,385	BROWN	5,294	2,203	1,476	1,603	12	600 R	41.6%	27.9%	30.3%
28,809	BUTLER	23,629	9,166	7,029	7,355	79	1,811 R	38.8%	29.7%	31.1%
1,915	CHASE	1,685	610	470	600	5	10 R	36.2%	27.9%	35.6%
2,601	CHAUTAUQUA	2,073	853	598	607	15	246 R	41.1%	28.8%	29.3%
11,843	CHEROKEE	9,757	3,589	4,083	2,067	18	494 D	36.8%	41.8%	21.2%
2,097	CHEYENNE	1,755	863	407	477	8	386 R	49.2%	23.2%	27.2%
1,514	CLARK	1,315	676	293	341	5	335 R	51.4%	22.3%	25.9%
5,556	CLAY	4,590	2,198	947	1,434	11	764 R	47.9%	20.6%	31.2%
6,554	CLOUD	5,448	2,131	1,720	1,578	19	411 R	39.1%	31.6%	29.0%
5,347	COFFEY	4,300	1,824	1,021	1,443	12	381 R	42.4%	23.7%	33.6%
1,490	COMANCHE	1,285	636	325	324		311 R	49.5%	25.3%	25.2%
18,668	COWLEY	15,784	5,422	5,405	4,911	46	17 R	34.4%	34.2%	31.1%
20,715	CRAWFORD	16,591	5,468	7,366	3,706	51	1,898 D	33.0%	44.4%	22.3%
2,551	DECATUR	2,089	940	576	565	8	364 R	45.0%	27.6%	27.0%
10,716	DICKINSON	9,222	3,851	2,518	2,833	20	1,018 R	41.8%	27.3%	30.7%
4,975	DONIPHAN	3,976	1,579	1,177	1,200	20	379 R	39.7%	29.6%	30.2%
49,628	DOUGLAS	42,265	12,949	19,439	9,630	247	6,490 D	30.6%	46.0%	22.8%
2,342	EDWARDS	1,925	769	567	584	5	185 R	39.9%	29.5%	30.3%
2,061	ELK	1,742	748	485	503	6	245 R	42.9%	27.8%	28.9%
15,366	ELLIS	12,453	3,985	4,544	3,887	37	559 D	32.0%	36.5%	31.2%
4,094	ELLSWORTH	3,239	1,197	1,010	1,020	12	177 R	37.0%	31.2%	31.5%
12,955	FINNEY	10,933	5,278	2,612	3,011	32	2,267 R	48.3%	23.9%	27.5%
12,816	FORD	10,358	4,342	2,635	3,341	40	1,001 R	41.9%	25.4%	32.3%
11,266	FRANKLIN	9,883	3,699	2,968	3,184	32	515 R	37.4%	30.0%	32.2%
9,906	GEARY	7,556	2,928	2,559	2,057	12	369 R	38.8%	33.9%	27.2%
1,996	GOVE	1,706	792	379	532	3	260 R	46.4%	22.2%	31.2%
2,328	GRAHAM	1,912	752	554	603	3	149 R	39.3%	29.0%	31.5%
3,825	GRANT	3,019	1,561	619	835	4	726 R	51.7%	20.5%	27.7%
2,587	GRAY	2,173	1,039	443	686	5	353 R	47.8%	20.4%	31.6%
1,037	GREELEY	873	504	191	175	3	313 R	57.7%	21.9%	20.0%
4,827	GREENWOOD	3,853	1,411	1,262	1,167	13	149 R	36.6%	32.8%	30.3%
1,649	HAMILTON	1,378	716	386	271	5	330 R	52.0%	28.0%	19.7%
4,023	HARPER	3,378	1,371	845	1,151	11	220 R	40.6%	25.0%	34.1%
18,269	HARVEY	15,012	6,259	5,047	3,653	53	1,212 R	41.7%	33.6%	24.3%
2,015	HASKELL	1,826	1,023	336	462	5	561 R	56.0%	18.4%	25.3%
1,416	HODGEMAN	1,229	625	258	343	3	282 R	50.9%	21.0%	27.9%
6,924	JACKSON	5,552	1,970	1,639	1,927	16	43 R	35.5%	29.5%	34.7%
9,259	JEFFERSON	7,781	2,569	2,538	2,642	32	73 P	33.0%	32.6%	34.0%
2,825	JEWELL	2,300	1,050	546	698	6	352 R	45.7%	23.7%	30.3%
222,815	JOHNSON	194,924	85,418	59,573	49,136	797	25,845 R	43.8%	30.6%	25.2%
2,108	KEARNY	1,709	943	384	376	6	559 R	55.2%	22.5%	22.0%
5,123	KINGMAN	4,163	1,680	1,100	1,370	13	310 R	40.4%	26.4%	32.9%
2,386	KIOWA	1,891	1,057	355	475	4	582 R	55.9%	18.8%	25.1%
12,991	LABETTE	10,177	3,368	4,196	2,577	36	828 D	33.1%	41.2%	25.3%
1,451	LANE	1,299	674	265	356	4	318 R	51.9%	20.4%	27.4%
26,157	LEAVENWORTH	23,177	7,738	8,077	7,306	56	339 R	33.4%	34.8%	31.5%
2,589	LINCOLN	2,172	893	612	657	10	236 R	41.1%	28.2%	30.2%
5,182	LINN	4,134	1,413	1,353	1,358	10	55 R	34.2%	32.7%	32.8%
1,999	LOGAN	1,709	905	355	446	3	459 R	53.0%	20.8%	26.1%
18,294	LYON	14,656	5,090	4,811	4,717	38	279 R	34.7%	32.8%	32.2%
15,035	MCPHERSON	12,991	5,745	3,645	3,561	40	2,100 R	44.2%	28.1%	27.4%
7,790	MARION	6,351	3,142	1,627	1,557	25	1,515 R	49.5%	25.6%	24.5%
6,900	MARSHALL	5,858	2,030	2,022	1,786	20	8 R	34.7%	34.5%	30.5%
2,576	MEADE	2,164	1,135	430	592	7	543 R	52.4%	19.9%	27.4%

KANSAS

PRESIDENT 1992

Registration	County	Total Vote	Republican	Democratic	Perot	Other	Plurality	Percentage Total Vote Rep.	Dem.	Perot
13,109	MIAMI	11,096	3,528	3,835	3,701	32	134 D	31.8%	34.6%	33.4%
4,377	MITCHELL	3,650	1,601	938	1,098	13	503 R	43.9%	25.7%	30.1%
19,719	MONTGOMERY	15,912	6,848	5,453	3,570	41	1,395 R	43.0%	34.3%	22.4%
3,585	MORRIS	3,111	1,071	957	1,071	12		34.4%	30.8%	34.4%
1,973	MORTON	1,670	915	398	350	7	517 R	54.8%	23.8%	21.0%
6,581	NEMAHA	5,619	2,220	1,580	1,804	15	416 R	39.5%	28.1%	32.1%
9,341	NEOSHO	7,893	2,926	2,799	2,136	32	127 R	37.1%	35.5%	27.1%
2,516	NESS	2,218	967	565	678	8	289 R	43.6%	25.5%	30.6%
3,519	NORTON	3,068	1,469	779	815	5	654 R	47.9%	25.4%	26.6%
8,692	OSAGE	7,421	2,561	2,297	2,532	31	29 R	34.5%	31.0%	34.1%
3,149	OSBORNE	2,607	1,003	779	819	6	184 R	38.5%	29.9%	31.4%
3,536	OTTAWA	2,820	1,284	764	762	10	520 R	45.5%	27.1%	27.0%
4,887	PAWNEE	3,585	1,357	1,118	1,097	13	239 R	37.9%	31.2%	30.6%
4,081	PHILLIPS	3,388	1,579	843	955	11	624 R	46.6%	24.9%	28.2%
9,728	POTTAWATOMIE	8,016	3,106	2,099	2,759	52	347 R	38.7%	26.2%	34.4%
5,700	PRATT	4,786	1,779	1,466	1,528	13	251 R	37.2%	30.6%	31.9%
2,354	RAWLINS	1,935	1,023	393	517	2	506 R	52.9%	20.3%	26.7%
35,223	RENO	28,379	11,377	9,257	7,636	109	2,120 R	40.1%	32.6%	26.9%
4,251	REPUBLIC	3,806	1,767	939	1,084	16	683 R	46.4%	24.7%	28.5%
6,127	RICE	5,271	2,158	1,555	1,543	15	603 R	40.9%	29.5%	29.3%
25,579	RILEY	21,797	8,394	7,933	5,387	83	461 R	38.5%	36.4%	24.7%
3,824	ROOKS	3,090	1,249	771	1,063	7	186 R	40.4%	25.0%	34.4%
2,590	RUSH	2,118	756	689	665	8	67 R	35.7%	32.5%	31.4%
4,580	RUSSELL	4,015	1,434	1,178	1,395	8	39 R	35.7%	29.3%	34.7%
27,450	SALINE	23,623	8,565	7,890	7,108	60	675 R	36.3%	33.4%	30.1%
2,958	SCOTT	2,535	1,426	480	621	8	805 R	56.3%	18.9%	24.5%
216,089	SEDGWICK	186,574	75,577	62,670	47,238	1,089	12,907 R	40.5%	33.6%	25.3%
8,192	SEWARD	6,806	3,477	1,488	1,818	23	1,659 R	51.1%	21.9%	26.7%
96,014	SHAWNEE	82,294	29,344	31,972	20,653	325	2,628 D	35.7%	38.9%	25.1%
1,858	SHERIDAN	1,636	739	347	546	4	193 R	45.2%	21.2%	33.4%
3,729	SHERMAN	3,278	1,630	810	828	10	802 R	49.7%	24.7%	25.3%
3,548	SMITH	2,852	1,236	789	816	11	420 R	43.3%	27.7%	28.6%
3,271	STAFFORD	2,760	1,064	777	910	9	154 R	38.6%	28.2%	33.0%
1,155	STANTON	998	556	224	214	4	332 R	55.7%	22.4%	21.4%
3,165	STEVENS	2,477	1,408	390	674	5	734 R	56.8%	15.7%	27.2%
13,672	SUMNER	11,589	4,087	3,564	3,887	51	200 R	35.3%	30.8%	33.5%
4,607	THOMAS	3,923	1,849	932	1,129	13	720 R	47.1%	23.8%	28.8%
2,307	TREGO	1,912	727	608	574	3	119 R	38.0%	31.8%	30.0%
4,105	WABAUNSEE	3,386	1,254	851	1,258	23	4 P	37.0%	25.1%	37.2%
1,243	WALLACE	1,066	679	164	219	4	460 R	63.7%	15.4%	20.5%
4,428	WASHINGTON	3,702	1,740	893	1,054	15	686 R	47.0%	24.1%	28.5%
1,396	WICHITA	1,230	681	241	303	5	378 R	55.4%	19.6%	24.6%
5,693	WILSON	4,635	1,925	1,331	1,365	14	560 R	41.5%	28.7%	29.4%
2,220	WOODSON	1,866	662	590	604	10	58 R	35.5%	31.6%	32.4%
73,333	WYANDOTTE	61,133	12,872	34,397	13,620	244	20,777 D	21.1%	56.3%	22.3%
1,365,849	TOTAL	1,157,335	449,951	390,434	312,358	4,592	59,517 R	38.9%	33.7%	27.0%

KANSAS

SENATOR 1992

Registration	County	Total Vote	Republican	Democratic	Other	Rep.-Dem. Plurality	Percentage			
							Total Vote		Major Vote	
							Rep.	Dem.	Rep.	Dem.
7,538	ALLEN	6,363	3,615	2,196	552	1,419 R	56.8%	34.5%	62.2%	37.8%
4,415	ANDERSON	3,638	1,729	1,568	341	161 R	47.5%	43.1%	52.4%	47.6%
8,276	ATCHISON	7,483	4,472	2,600	411	1,872 R	59.8%	34.7%	63.2%	36.8%
3,625	BARBER	2,830	1,781	850	199	931 R	62.9%	30.0%	67.7%	32.3%
15,369	BARTON	13,404	8,360	4,122	922	4,238 R	62.4%	30.8%	67.0%	33.0%
8,626	BOURBON	7,071	4,067	2,610	394	1,457 R	57.5%	36.9%	60.9%	39.1%
6,385	BROWN	5,245	3,206	1,720	319	1,486 R	61.1%	32.8%	65.1%	34.9%
28,809	BUTLER	23,462	15,220	6,713	1,529	8,507 R	64.9%	28.6%	69.4%	30.6%
1,915	CHASE	1,671	934	600	137	334 R	55.9%	35.9%	60.9%	39.1%
2,601	CHAUTAUQUA	2,022	1,289	569	164	720 R	63.7%	28.1%	69.4%	30.6%
11,843	CHEROKEE	9,681	5,333	3,748	600	1,585 R	55.1%	38.7%	58.7%	41.3%
2,097	CHEYENNE	1,747	1,228	395	124	833 R	70.3%	22.6%	75.7%	24.3%
1,514	CLARK	1,305	829	397	79	432 R	63.5%	30.4%	67.6%	32.4%
5,556	CLAY	4,482	3,069	1,186	227	1,883 R	68.5%	26.5%	72.1%	27.9%
6,554	CLOUD	5,397	3,233	1,750	414	1,483 R	59.9%	32.4%	64.9%	35.1%
5,347	COFFEY	4,276	2,679	1,301	296	1,378 R	62.7%	30.4%	67.3%	32.7%
1,490	COMANCHE	1,286	840	367	79	473 R	65.3%	28.5%	69.6%	30.4%
18,668	COWLEY	15,688	9,414	5,267	1,007	4,147 R	60.0%	33.6%	64.1%	35.9%
20,715	CRAWFORD	16,381	8,830	6,634	917	2,196 R	53.9%	40.5%	57.1%	42.9%
2,551	DECATUR	2,066	1,399	555	112	844 R	67.7%	26.9%	71.6%	28.4%
10,716	DICKINSON	9,120	5,603	3,024	493	2,579 R	61.4%	33.2%	64.9%	35.1%
4,975	DONIPHAN	3,900	2,545	1,058	297	1,487 R	65.3%	27.1%	70.6%	29.4%
49,628	DOUGLAS	41,625	24,740	14,380	2,505	10,360 R	59.4%	34.5%	63.2%	36.8%
2,342	EDWARDS	1,916	1,143	650	123	493 R	59.7%	33.9%	63.7%	36.3%
2,061	ELK	1,717	1,101	502	114	599 R	64.1%	29.2%	68.7%	31.3%
15,366	ELLIS	12,362	7,181	4,627	554	2,554 R	58.1%	37.4%	60.8%	39.2%
4,094	ELLSWORTH	3,184	2,017	1,057	110	960 R	63.3%	33.2%	65.6%	34.4%
12,955	FINNEY	10,849	7,265	3,054	530	4,211 R	67.0%	28.2%	70.4%	29.6%
12,816	FORD	10,291	6,911	2,855	525	4,056 R	67.2%	27.7%	70.8%	29.2%
11,266	FRANKLIN	9,766	5,480	3,586	700	1,894 R	56.1%	36.7%	60.4%	39.6%
9,906	GEARY	7,490	4,858	2,299	333	2,559 R	64.9%	30.7%	67.9%	32.1%
1,996	GOVE	1,693	1,057	550	86	507 R	62.4%	32.5%	65.8%	34.2%
2,328	GRAHAM	1,901	1,086	732	83	354 R	57.1%	38.5%	59.7%	40.3%
3,825	GRANT	3,024	2,229	655	140	1,574 R	73.7%	21.7%	77.3%	22.7%
2,587	GRAY	2,152	1,527	515	110	1,012 R	71.0%	23.9%	74.8%	25.2%
1,037	GREELEY	874	582	237	55	345 R	66.6%	27.1%	71.1%	28.9%
4,827	GREENWOOD	3,839	2,291	1,301	247	990 R	59.7%	33.9%	63.8%	36.2%
1,649	HAMILTON	1,359	911	389	59	522 R	67.0%	28.6%	70.1%	29.9%
4,023	HARPER	3,361	2,283	880	198	1,403 R	67.9%	26.2%	72.2%	27.8%
18,269	HARVEY	14,943	9,781	4,309	853	5,472 R	65.5%	28.8%	69.4%	30.6%
2,015	HASKELL	1,806	1,338	397	71	941 R	74.1%	22.0%	77.1%	22.9%
1,416	HODGEMAN	1,222	875	300	47	575 R	71.6%	24.5%	74.5%	25.5%
6,924	JACKSON	5,515	3,047	2,213	255	834 R	55.2%	40.1%	57.9%	42.1%
9,259	JEFFERSON	7,680	4,099	3,078	503	1,021 R	53.4%	40.1%	57.1%	42.9%
2,825	JEWELL	2,259	1,486	660	113	826 R	65.8%	29.2%	69.2%	30.8%
222,815	JOHNSON	188,396	132,067	45,537	10,792	86,530 R	70.1%	24.2%	74.4%	25.6%
2,108	KEARNY	1,691	1,208	401	82	807 R	71.4%	23.7%	75.1%	24.9%
5,123	KINGMAN	4,108	2,690	1,156	262	1,534 R	65.5%	28.1%	69.9%	30.1%
2,386	KIOWA	1,867	1,357	405	105	952 R	72.7%	21.7%	77.0%	23.0%
12,991	LABETTE	10,049	6,116	3,345	588	2,771 R	60.9%	33.3%	64.6%	35.4%
1,451	LANE	1,279	942	277	60	665 R	73.7%	21.7%	77.3%	22.7%
26,157	LEAVENWORTH	22,928	13,206	7,979	1,743	5,227 R	57.6%	34.8%	62.3%	37.7%
2,589	LINCOLN	2,126	1,420	617	89	803 R	66.8%	29.0%	69.7%	30.3%
5,182	LINN	4,091	2,458	1,375	258	1,083 R	60.1%	33.6%	64.1%	35.9%
1,999	LOGAN	1,686	1,156	435	95	721 R	68.6%	25.8%	72.7%	27.3%
18,294	LYON	14,579	8,013	5,632	934	2,381 R	55.0%	38.6%	58.7%	41.3%
15,035	MCPHERSON	12,926	8,550	3,748	628	4,802 R	66.1%	29.0%	69.5%	30.5%
7,790	MARION	6,292	4,238	1,791	263	2,447 R	67.4%	28.5%	70.3%	29.7%
6,900	MARSHALL	5,771	2,948	2,514	309	434 R	51.1%	43.6%	54.0%	46.0%
2,576	MEADE	2,119	1,434	560	125	874 R	67.7%	26.4%	71.9%	28.1%

KANSAS

SENATOR 1992

Registration	County	Total Vote	Republican	Democratic	Other	Rep.-Dem. Plurality	Percentage Total Vote Rep.	Dem.	Major Vote Rep.	Dem.
13,109	MIAMI	11,005	6,410	3,838	757	2,572 R	58.2%	34.9%	62.5%	37.5%
4,377	MITCHELL	3,590	2,345	1,027	218	1,318 R	65.3%	28.6%	69.5%	30.5%
19,719	MONTGOMERY	15,738	8,983	5,622	1,133	3,361 R	57.1%	35.7%	61.5%	38.5%
3,585	MORRIS	3,068	1,672	1,230	166	442 R	54.5%	40.1%	57.6%	42.4%
1,973	MORTON	1,644	1,136	430	78	706 R	69.1%	26.2%	72.5%	27.5%
6,581	NEMAHA	5,403	3,079	2,066	258	1,013 R	57.0%	38.2%	59.8%	40.2%
9,341	NEOSHO	7,465	4,152	2,748	565	1,404 R	55.6%	36.8%	60.2%	39.8%
2,516	NESS	2,187	1,420	652	115	768 R	64.9%	29.8%	68.5%	31.5%
3,519	NORTON	3,039	1,878	889	272	989 R	61.8%	29.3%	67.9%	32.1%
8,692	OSAGE	7,361	3,876	3,066	419	810 R	52.7%	41.7%	55.8%	44.2%
3,149	OSBORNE	2,560	1,581	874	105	707 R	61.8%	34.1%	64.4%	35.6%
3,536	OTTAWA	2,803	1,765	894	144	871 R	63.0%	31.9%	66.4%	33.6%
4,887	PAWNEE	3,520	2,245	1,113	162	1,132 R	63.8%	31.6%	66.9%	33.1%
4,081	PHILLIPS	3,333	2,213	901	219	1,312 R	66.4%	27.0%	71.1%	28.9%
9,728	POTTAWATOMIE	7,936	4,864	2,677	395	2,187 R	61.3%	33.7%	64.5%	35.5%
5,700	PRATT	4,723	3,055	1,418	250	1,637 R	64.7%	30.0%	68.3%	31.7%
2,354	RAWLINS	1,797	1,325	374	98	951 R	73.7%	20.8%	78.0%	22.0%
35,223	RENO	27,986	16,669	9,600	1,717	7,069 R	59.6%	34.3%	63.5%	36.5%
4,251	REPUBLIC	3,757	2,424	1,076	257	1,348 R	64.5%	28.6%	69.3%	30.7%
6,127	RICE	5,253	3,411	1,621	221	1,790 R	64.9%	30.9%	67.8%	32.2%
25,579	RILEY	21,508	14,325	6,294	889	8,031 R	66.6%	29.3%	69.5%	30.5%
3,824	ROOKS	3,049	1,884	1,018	147	866 R	61.8%	33.4%	64.9%	35.1%
2,590	RUSH	2,111	1,254	742	115	512 R	59.4%	35.1%	62.8%	37.2%
4,580	RUSSELL	3,993	2,761	1,092	140	1,669 R	69.1%	27.3%	71.7%	28.3%
27,450	SALINE	23,481	14,435	7,940	1,106	6,495 R	61.5%	33.8%	64.5%	35.5%
2,958	SCOTT	2,517	1,786	620	111	1,166 R	71.0%	24.6%	74.2%	25.8%
216,089	SEDGWICK	175,030	119,486	42,842	12,702	76,644 R	68.3%	24.5%	73.6%	26.4%
8,192	SEWARD	6,591	4,676	1,462	453	3,214 R	70.9%	22.2%	76.2%	23.8%
96,014	SHAWNEE	81,095	42,020	34,905	4,170	7,115 R	51.8%	43.0%	54.6%	45.4%
1,858	SHERIDAN	1,619	1,043	494	82	549 R	64.4%	30.5%	67.9%	32.1%
3,729	SHERMAN	3,189	2,181	833	175	1,348 R	68.4%	26.1%	72.4%	27.6%
3,548	SMITH	2,827	1,761	953	113	808 R	62.3%	33.7%	64.9%	35.1%
3,271	STAFFORD	2,726	1,769	822	135	947 R	64.9%	30.2%	68.3%	31.7%
1,155	STANTON	986	678	252	56	426 R	68.8%	25.6%	72.9%	27.1%
3,165	STEVENS	2,402	1,688	548	166	1,140 R	70.3%	22.8%	75.5%	24.5%
13,672	SUMNER	11,551	7,020	3,772	759	3,248 R	60.8%	32.7%	65.0%	35.0%
4,607	THOMAS	3,902	2,569	1,163	170	1,406 R	65.8%	29.8%	68.8%	31.2%
2,307	TREGO	1,906	1,110	699	97	411 R	58.2%	36.7%	61.4%	38.6%
4,105	WABAUNSEE	3,351	1,908	1,270	173	638 R	56.9%	37.9%	60.0%	40.0%
1,243	WALLACE	1,051	787	208	56	579 R	74.9%	19.8%	79.1%	20.9%
4,428	WASHINGTON	3,634	2,406	1,043	185	1,363 R	66.2%	28.7%	69.8%	30.2%
1,396	WICHITA	1,221	852	311	58	541 R	69.8%	25.5%	73.3%	26.7%
5,693	WILSON	4,571	2,661	1,539	371	1,122 R	58.2%	33.7%	63.4%	36.6%
2,220	WOODSON	1,845	1,049	637	159	412 R	56.9%	34.5%	62.2%	37.8%
73,333	WYANDOTTE	56,869	28,868	21,722	6,279	7,146 R	50.8%	38.2%	57.1%	42.9%
1,365,849	TOTAL	1,126,447	706,246	349,525	70,676	356,721 R	62.7%	31.0%	66.9%	33.1%

KANSAS

CONGRESS

CD	Year	Total Vote	Republican		Democratic		Other Vote	Rep.-Dem. Plurality	Percentage			
			Vote	Candidate	Vote	Candidate			Total Vote		Major Vote	
									Rep.	Dem.	Rep.	Dem.
1	1992	283,278	194,912	ROBERTS, PAT	83,620	WEST, DUANE	6,765	109,628 R	68.2%	29.5%	69.8%	30.2%
2	1992	268,476	109,801	VAN SLYKE, JIM	151,019	SLATTERY, JIM	7,986	41,170 D	40.9%	56.2%	42.1%	57.9%
3	1992	292,142	169,929	MEYERS, JAN	110,076	LOVE, TOM	12,791	59,778 R	58.1%	37.6%	60.7%	39.3%
4	1992	277,202	117,070	YOST, ERIC R.	143,671	GLICKMAN, DAN	17,275	26,505 D	42.1%	51.7%	44.9%	55.1%

KANSAS

1992 GENERAL ELECTION

President   Other vote was 4,314 Libertarian (Marrou); 79 Gritz (write-in); 77 Hagelin (write-in); 55 Phillips (write-in); 10 Fulani (write-in); 57 scattered write-in.

Senator   Other vote was 25,253 Libertarian (Kirk); 45,423 Independent (Campbell-Cline).

Congress   Other vote was Libertarian (Rosile) in CD 1; Libertarian (Clack) in CD 2; Libertarian (Kaul) in CD 3; Libertarian (Warren) in CD 4.

1992 PRIMARIES

AUGUST 4 REPUBLICAN

Senator   244,480 Robert Dole; 59,589 Richard W. Rodewald.

Congress   Unopposed in two CD's. Contested as follows:

CD 3   35,911 Jan Meyers; 20,953 Kerry Patrick; 3,947 Jim Hall; 3,014 Gary Adams.
CD 4   35,727 Eric R. Yost; 26,567 Dick Nichols; 16,858 Richard LaMunyon.

AUGUST 4 DEMOCRATIC

Senator   111,015 Gloria O'Dell; 49,416 Fred Phelps.

Congress   Unopposed in two CD's. Contested as follows:

CD 1   18,064 Duane West; 16,431 John Divine; 7,678 Jerry Molstad.
CD 3   22,538 Tom Love; 14,279 George E. Davis.

KENTUCKY

GOVERNOR
Brereton C. Jones (D). Elected 1991 to a four-year term.

SENATORS
Wendell H. Ford (D). Re-elected 1992 to a six-year term. Previously elected 1986, 1980, 1974.

Mitch McConnell (R). Re-elected 1990 to a six-year term. Previously elected 1984.

REPRESENTATIVES
1. Tom Barlow (D)
2. William H. Natcher (D)
3. Romano L. Mazzoli (D)
4. Jim Bunning (R)
5. Harold Rogers (R)
6. Scott Baesler (D)

POSTWAR VOTE FOR PRESIDENT

| | | Republican | | Democratic | | Other | | Percentage Total Vote | | Major Vote | |
| | Total | | | | | | | | | | |
Year	Vote	Vote	Candidate	Vote	Candidate	Vote	Plurality	Rep.	Dem.	Rep.	Dem.
1992 **	1,492,900	617,178	Bush, George	665,104	Clinton, Bill	210,618	47,926 D	41.3%	44.6%	48.1%	51.9%
1988	1,322,517	734,281	Bush, George	580,368	Dukakis, Michael S.	7,868	153,913 R	55.5%	43.9%	55.9%	44.1%
1984	1,369,345	821,702	Reagan, Ronald	539,539	Mondale, Walter F.	8,104	282,163 R	60.0%	39.4%	60.4%	39.6%
1980	1,294,627	635,274	Reagan, Ronald	616,417	Carter, Jimmy	42,936	18,857 R	49.1%	47.6%	50.8%	49.2%
1976	1,167,142	531,852	Ford, Gerald R.	615,717	Carter, Jimmy	19,573	83,865 D	45.6%	52.8%	46.3%	53.7%
1972	1,067,499	676,446	Nixon, Richard M.	371,159	McGovern, George S.	19,894	305,287 R	63.4%	34.8%	64.6%	35.4%
1968	1,055,893	462,411	Nixon, Richard M.	397,541	Humphrey, Hubert H.	195,941	64,870 R	43.8%	37.6%	53.8%	46.2%
1964	1,046,105	372,977	Goldwater, Barry M.	669,659	Johnson, Lyndon B.	3,469	296,682 D	35.7%	64.0%	35.8%	64.2%
1960	1,124,462	602,607	Nixon, Richard M.	521,855	Kennedy, John F.		80,752 R	53.6%	46.4%	53.6%	46.4%
1956	1,053,805	572,192	Eisenhower, Dwight D.	476,453	Stevenson, Adlai E.	5,160	95,739 R	54.3%	45.2%	54.6%	45.4%
1952	993,148	495,029	Eisenhower, Dwight D.	495,729	Stevenson, Adlai E.	2,390	700 D	49.8%	49.9%	50.0%	50.0%
1948	822,658	341,210	Dewey, Thomas E.	466,756	Truman, Harry S.	14,692	125,546 D	41.5%	56.7%	42.2%	57.8%

In 1992 the other vote column includes 203,944 votes cast for Perot.

POSTWAR VOTE FOR GOVERNOR

| | | Republican | | Democratic | | Other | Rep.-Dem. | Percentage Total Vote | | Major Vote | |
| | Total | | | | | | | | | | |
Year	Vote	Vote	Candidate	Vote	Candidate	Vote	Plurality	Rep.	Dem.	Rep.	Dem.
1991	834,920	294,452	Hopkins, Larry J.	540,468	Jones, Brereton C.		246,016 D	35.3%	64.7%	35.3%	64.7%
1987	777,815	273,141	Harper, John	504,674	Wilkinson, Wallace G.		231,533 D	35.1%	64.9%	35.1%	64.9%
1983	1,030,671	454,650	Bunning, Jim	561,674	Collins, Martha Layne	14,347	107,024 D	44.1%	54.5%	44.7%	55.3%
1979	939,366	381,278	Nunn, Louie B.	558,088	Brown, J. Y., Jr.		176,810 D	40.6%	59.4%	40.6%	59.4%
1975	748,157	277,998	Gable, Robert E.	470,159	Carroll, Julian		192,161 D	37.2%	62.8%	37.2%	62.8%
1971	930,790	412,653	Emberton, Thomas	470,720	Ford, Wendell H.	47,417	58,067 D	44.3%	50.6%	46.7%	53.3%
1967	886,946	454,123	Nunn, Louie B.	425,674	Ward, Henry	7,149	28,449 R	51.2%	48.0%	51.6%	48.4%
1963	886,047	436,496	Nunn, Louie B.	449,551	Breathitt, Edward T.		13,055 D	49.3%	50.7%	49.3%	50.7%
1959	853,005	336,456	Robsion, John M.	516,549	Combs, Bert T.		180,093 D	39.4%	60.6%	39.4%	60.6%
1955	778,488	322,671	Denney, Edwin R.	451,647	Chandler, Albert B.	4,170	128,976 D	41.4%	58.0%	41.7%	58.3%
1951	634,359	288,014	Siler, Eugene	346,345	Wetherby, Lawrence		58,331 D	45.4%	54.6%	45.4%	54.6%
1947	672,372	287,130	Dummit, Eldon S.	385,242	Clements, Earle C.		98,112 D	42.7%	57.3%	42.7%	57.3%

KENTUCKY

POSTWAR VOTE FOR SENATOR

Year	Total Vote	Republican Vote	Republican Candidate	Democratic Vote	Democratic Candidate	Other Vote	Rep.-Dem. Plurality	Percentage Total Vote Rep.	Percentage Total Vote Dem.	Percentage Major Vote Rep.	Percentage Major Vote Dem.
1992	1,330,858	476,604	Williams, David L.	836,888	Ford, Wendell H.	17,366	360,284 D	35.8%	62.9%	36.3%	63.7%
1990	916,010	478,034	McConnell, Mitch	437,976	Sloane, Harvey		40,058 R	52.2%	47.8%	52.2%	47.8%
1986	677,280	173,330	Andrews, Jackson M.	503,775	Ford, Wendell H.	175	330,445 D	25.6%	74.4%	25.6%	74.4%
1984	1,292,407	644,990	McConnell, Mitch	639,721	Huddleston, Walter	7,696	5,269 R	49.9%	49.5%	50.2%	49.8%
1980	1,106,890	386,029	Foust, Mary Louise	720,861	Ford, Wendell H.		334,832 D	34.9%	65.1%	34.9%	65.1%
1978	476,783	175,766	Guenthner, Louie	290,730	Huddleston, Walter	10,287	114,964 D	36.9%	61.0%	37.7%	62.3%
1974	745,994	328,982	Cook, Marlow W.	399,406	Ford, Wendell H.	17,606	70,424 D	44.1%	53.5%	45.2%	54.8%
1972	1,037,861	494,337	Nunn, Louie B.	528,550	Huddleston, Walter	14,974	34,213 D	47.6%	50.9%	48.3%	51.7%
1968	942,865	484,260	Cook, Marlow W.	448,960	Peden, Katherine	9,645	35,300 R	51.4%	47.6%	51.9%	48.1%
1966	749,884	483,805	Cooper, John Sherman	266,079	Brown, J. Y.		217,726 R	64.5%	35.5%	64.5%	35.5%
1962	820,088	432,648	Morton, Thruston B.	387,440	Wyatt, Wilson W.		45,208 R	52.8%	47.2%	52.8%	47.2%
1960	1,088,377	644,087	Cooper, John Sherman	444,290	Johnson, Keen		199,797 R	59.2%	40.8%	59.2%	40.8%
1956	1,006,825	506,903	Morton, Thruston B.	499,922	Clements, Earle C.		6,981 R	50.3%	49.7%	50.3%	49.7%
1956 S	1,011,645	538,505	Cooper, John Sherman	473,140	Wetherby, Lawrence		65,365 R	53.2%	46.8%	53.2%	46.8%
1954	797,057	362,948	Cooper, John Sherman	434,109	Barkley, Alben W.		71,161 D	45.5%	54.5%	45.5%	54.5%
1952 S	960,228	494,576	Cooper, John Sherman	465,652	Underwood, Thomas R.		28,924 R	51.5%	48.5%	51.5%	48.5%
1950	612,617	278,368	Dawson, Charles L.	334,249	Clements, Earle C.		55,881 D	45.4%	54.6%	45.4%	54.6%
1948	794,469	383,776	Cooper, John Sherman	408,256	Chapman, Virgil	2,437	24,480 D	48.3%	51.4%	48.5%	51.5%
1946 S	615,119	327,652	Cooper, John Sherman	285,829	Brown, J. Y.	1,638	41,823 R	53.3%	46.5%	53.4%	46.6%

One of the 1956 elections and those in 1952 and 1946 were for short terms to fill vacancies.

226

KENTUCKY

Districts Established December 20, 1991

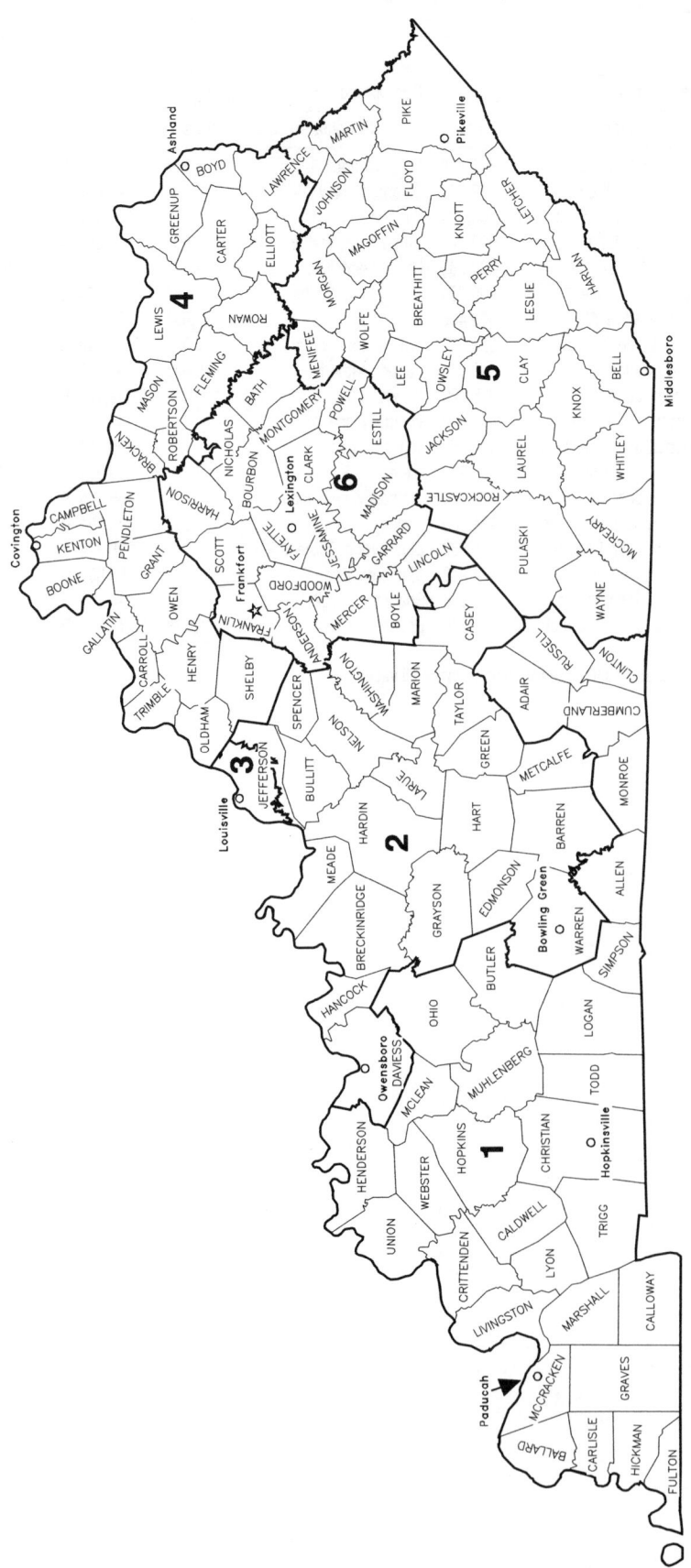

KENTUCKY

PRESIDENT 1992

Registration	County	Total Vote	Republican	Democratic	Perot	Other	Plurality	Percentage Total Vote		
								Rep.	Dem.	Perot
9,857	ADAIR	6,424	3,740	2,044	617	23	1,696 R	58.2%	31.8%	9.6%
8,413	ALLEN	5,415	2,747	2,040	606	22	707 R	50.7%	37.7%	11.2%
8,770	ANDERSON	6,472	2,731	2,491	1,219	31	240 R	42.2%	38.5%	18.8%
5,196	BALLARD	3,880	1,108	2,268	500	4	1,160 D	28.6%	58.5%	12.9%
19,549	BARREN	12,973	5,467	5,688	1,778	40	221 D	42.1%	43.8%	13.7%
7,113	BATH	4,204	1,259	2,229	694	22	970 D	29.9%	53.0%	16.5%
19,874	BELL	11,575	4,501	5,745	1,193	136	1,244 D	38.9%	49.6%	10.3%
30,111	BOONE	23,575	12,306	6,514	4,676	79	5,792 R	52.2%	27.6%	19.8%
10,102	BOURBON	6,920	2,707	2,895	1,290	28	188 D	39.1%	41.8%	18.6%
28,524	BOYD	21,147	7,387	10,496	3,195	69	3,109 D	34.9%	49.6%	15.1%
13,110	BOYLE	9,278	4,019	3,894	1,335	30	125 R	43.3%	42.0%	14.4%
4,109	BRACKEN	2,932	1,162	1,259	500	11	97 D	39.6%	42.9%	17.1%
11,021	BREATHITT	5,336	1,303	3,496	515	22	2,193 D	24.4%	65.5%	9.7%
9,731	BRECKINRIDGE	7,013	2,941	3,113	945	14	172 D	41.9%	44.4%	13.5%
25,962	BULLITT	18,969	7,745	7,830	3,333	61	85 D	40.8%	41.3%	17.6%
6,936	BUTLER	4,806	2,729	1,468	596	13	1,261 R	56.8%	30.5%	12.4%
7,646	CALDWELL	5,651	1,966	3,000	670	15	1,034 D	34.8%	53.1%	11.9%
18,158	CALLOWAY	12,740	4,654	6,181	1,853	52	1,527 D	36.5%	48.5%	14.5%
41,771	CAMPBELL	32,840	16,382	10,673	5,659	126	5,709 R	49.9%	32.5%	17.2%
3,506	CARLISLE	2,545	844	1,383	309	9	539 D	33.2%	54.3%	12.1%
5,742	CARROLL	3,746	1,046	2,119	566	15	1,073 D	27.9%	56.6%	15.1%
13,761	CARTER	8,560	3,305	4,224	989	42	919 D	38.6%	49.3%	11.6%
8,728	CASEY	5,302	3,317	1,409	542	34	1,908 R	62.6%	26.6%	10.2%
23,768	CHRISTIAN	16,288	7,737	6,709	1,789	53	1,028 R	47.5%	41.2%	11.0%
15,533	CLARK	11,517	4,625	4,892	1,955	45	267 D	40.2%	42.5%	17.0%
13,510	CLAY	7,427	4,747	2,012	648	20	2,735 R	63.9%	27.1%	8.7%
6,980	CLINTON	4,436	2,830	1,241	348	17	1,589 R	63.8%	28.0%	7.8%
5,086	CRITTENDEN	3,820	1,576	1,740	495	9	164 D	41.3%	45.5%	13.0%
4,726	CUMBERLAND	3,061	1,866	917	268	10	949 R	61.0%	30.0%	8.8%
47,366	DAVIESS	36,929	14,936	16,592	5,112	289	1,656 D	40.4%	44.9%	13.8%
6,830	EDMONSON	4,585	2,486	1,653	438	8	833 R	54.2%	36.1%	9.6%
4,492	ELLIOTT	2,525	444	1,796	273	12	1,352 D	17.6%	71.1%	10.8%
8,723	ESTILL	5,039	2,453	1,837	736	13	616 R	48.7%	36.5%	14.6%
115,672	FAYETTE	95,534	41,908	38,306	14,215	1,105	3,602 R	43.9%	40.1%	14.9%
7,643	FLEMING	5,135	2,045	2,257	815	18	212 D	39.8%	44.0%	15.9%
29,025	FLOYD	18,674	3,540	13,351	1,723	60	9,811 D	19.0%	71.5%	9.2%
27,068	FRANKLIN	21,031	7,591	9,896	3,340	204	2,305 D	36.1%	47.1%	15.9%
4,821	FULTON	3,204	1,073	1,813	306	12	740 D	33.5%	56.6%	9.6%
3,231	GALLATIN	2,329	699	1,171	445	14	472 D	30.0%	50.3%	19.1%
7,160	GARRARD	4,797	2,359	1,730	697	11	629 R	49.2%	36.1%	14.5%
7,377	GRANT	5,395	2,128	2,097	1,149	21	31 R	39.4%	38.9%	21.3%
19,540	GRAVES	15,341	5,311	8,001	1,943	86	2,690 D	34.6%	52.2%	12.7%
12,428	GRAYSON	8,507	4,533	2,909	993	72	1,624 R	53.3%	34.2%	11.7%
7,432	GREEN	4,986	2,709	1,760	500	17	949 R	54.3%	35.3%	10.0%
20,366	GREENUP	14,414	4,975	7,214	2,188	37	2,239 D	34.5%	50.0%	15.2%
4,778	HANCOCK	3,605	1,261	1,714	551	79	453 D	35.0%	47.5%	15.3%
36,387	HARDIN	25,958	12,299	9,417	4,026	216	2,882 R	47.4%	36.3%	15.5%
21,519	HARLAN	12,203	3,970	6,796	1,391	46	2,826 D	32.5%	55.7%	11.4%
8,791	HARRISON	6,189	2,148	2,795	1,225	21	647 D	34.7%	45.2%	19.8%
9,464	HART	5,858	2,401	2,852	579	26	451 D	41.0%	48.7%	9.9%
21,974	HENDERSON	16,126	5,125	8,270	2,678	53	3,145 D	31.8%	51.3%	16.6%
7,218	HENRY	5,219	1,640	2,838	720	21	1,198 D	31.4%	54.4%	13.8%
3,264	HICKMAN	2,457	861	1,296	294	6	435 D	35.0%	52.7%	12.0%
25,592	HOPKINS	17,531	6,032	8,881	2,565	53	2,849 D	34.4%	50.7%	14.6%
8,138	JACKSON	4,533	3,398	776	341	18	2,622 R	75.0%	17.1%	7.5%
379,521	JEFFERSON	309,793	116,566	152,728	39,822	677	36,162 D	37.6%	49.3%	12.9%
18,113	JESSAMINE	12,339	6,474	3,764	2,059	42	2,710 R	52.5%	30.5%	16.7%
14,918	JOHNSON	8,436	3,614	3,669	1,118	35	55 D	42.8%	43.5%	13.3%
68,007	KENTON	53,135	27,261	16,344	9,336	194	10,917 R	51.3%	30.8%	17.6%
12,065	KNOTT	7,328	1,243	5,500	560	25	4,257 D	17.0%	75.1%	7.6%

KENTUCKY

PRESIDENT 1992

Registration	County	Total Vote	Republican	Democratic	Perot	Other	Plurality	Percentage Total Vote		
								Rep.	Dem.	Perot
18,020	KNOX	9,825	5,011	3,787	972	55	1,224 R	51.0%	38.5%	9.9%
7,396	LARUE	4,930	2,154	2,190	582	4	36 D	43.7%	44.4%	11.8%
24,239	LAUREL	15,050	8,583	4,560	1,859	48	4,023 R	57.0%	30.3%	12.4%
8,650	LAWRENCE	5,057	2,084	2,400	557	16	316 D	41.2%	47.5%	11.0%
5,138	LEE	3,158	1,617	1,170	356	15	447 R	51.2%	37.0%	11.3%
8,775	LESLIE	4,936	2,879	1,591	450	16	1,288 R	58.3%	32.2%	9.1%
16,028	LETCHER	10,090	3,011	5,817	1,206	56	2,806 D	29.8%	57.7%	12.0%
7,687	LEWIS	4,904	2,493	1,713	673	25	780 R	50.8%	34.9%	13.7%
10,135	LINCOLN	5,946	2,624	2,532	762	28	92 R	44.1%	42.6%	12.8%
5,582	LIVINGSTON	4,312	1,339	2,386	578	9	1,047 D	31.1%	55.3%	13.4%
13,914	LOGAN	8,849	3,710	4,064	1,043	32	354 D	41.9%	45.9%	11.8%
3,921	LYON	2,703	820	1,583	293	7	763 D	30.3%	58.6%	10.8%
35,367	MCCRACKEN	27,153	10,657	13,341	3,077	78	2,684 D	39.2%	49.1%	11.3%
10,061	MCCREARY	6,210	3,588	1,934	624	64	1,654 R	57.8%	31.1%	10.0%
5,706	MCLEAN	4,129	1,355	2,223	529	22	868 D	32.8%	53.8%	12.8%
29,879	MADISON	19,841	8,719	8,005	3,038	79	714 R	43.9%	40.3%	15.3%
9,748	MAGOFFIN	5,711	1,992	3,261	440	18	1,269 D	34.9%	57.1%	7.7%
9,635	MARION	6,324	2,091	3,403	805	25	1,312 D	33.1%	53.8%	12.7%
16,220	MARSHALL	12,749	4,368	6,576	1,773	32	2,208 D	34.3%	51.6%	13.9%
8,173	MARTIN	4,095	1,961	1,715	393	26	246 R	47.9%	41.9%	9.6%
8,731	MASON	6,029	2,432	2,657	916	24	225 D	40.3%	44.1%	15.2%
10,666	MEADE	7,365	2,641	3,387	1,298	39	746 D	35.9%	46.0%	17.6%
3,303	MENIFEE	2,145	557	1,311	254	23	754 D	26.0%	61.1%	11.8%
10,901	MERCER	7,653	3,211	3,010	1,298	134	201 R	42.0%	39.3%	17.0%
5,967	METCALFE	3,813	1,683	1,703	409	18	20 D	44.1%	44.7%	10.7%
8,756	MONROE	5,803	3,776	1,515	480	32	2,261 R	65.1%	26.1%	8.3%
11,105	MONTGOMERY	7,611	2,590	3,686	1,308	27	1,096 D	34.0%	48.4%	17.2%
7,291	MORGAN	4,411	1,239	2,655	498	19	1,416 D	28.1%	60.2%	11.3%
18,827	MUHLENBERG	13,114	3,551	7,901	1,624	38	4,350 D	27.1%	60.2%	12.4%
15,235	NELSON	11,672	4,495	5,437	1,638	102	942 D	38.5%	46.6%	14.0%
4,210	NICHOLAS	2,789	894	1,341	513	41	447 D	32.1%	48.1%	18.4%
12,702	OHIO	8,865	3,385	4,022	1,423	35	637 D	38.2%	45.4%	16.1%
20,422	OLDHAM	16,639	8,263	5,457	2,855	64	2,806 R	49.7%	32.8%	17.2%
4,980	OWEN	3,569	1,108	1,830	613	18	722 D	31.0%	51.3%	17.2%
3,822	OWSLEY	2,342	1,437	678	209	18	759 R	61.4%	28.9%	8.9%
6,539	PENDLETON	4,669	1,810	1,740	1,086	33	70 R	38.8%	37.3%	23.3%
19,586	PERRY	12,103	4,128	6,619	1,308	48	2,491 D	34.1%	54.7%	10.8%
43,642	PIKE	28,082	8,212	17,358	2,444	68	9,146 D	29.2%	61.8%	8.7%
7,733	POWELL	5,041	1,809	2,323	874	35	514 D	35.9%	46.1%	17.3%
28,249	PULASKI	19,414	11,423	5,465	2,449	77	5,958 R	58.8%	28.1%	12.6%
1,323	ROBERTSON	945	329	439	170	7	110 D	34.8%	46.5%	18.0%
8,517	ROCKCASTLE	4,897	3,287	1,144	446	20	2,143 R	67.1%	23.4%	9.1%
11,643	ROWAN	7,274	2,469	3,558	1,212	35	1,089 D	33.9%	48.9%	16.7%
10,893	RUSSELL	7,285	4,641	1,950	673	21	2,691 R	63.7%	26.8%	9.2%
12,684	SCOTT	9,273	3,810	3,639	1,800	24	171 R	41.1%	39.2%	19.4%
14,026	SHELBY	10,445	4,550	4,398	1,451	46	152 R	43.6%	42.1%	13.9%
8,522	SIMPSON	5,840	2,280	2,834	708	18	554 D	39.0%	48.5%	12.1%
4,465	SPENCER	3,167	1,305	1,383	466	13	78 D	41.2%	43.7%	14.7%
13,322	TAYLOR	8,920	4,319	3,518	1,044	39	801 R	48.4%	39.4%	11.7%
6,080	TODD	4,202	1,691	1,858	612	41	167 D	40.2%	44.2%	14.6%
6,599	TRIGG	4,855	1,820	2,438	573	24	618 D	37.5%	50.2%	11.8%
3,820	TRIMBLE	2,631	789	1,413	413	16	624 D	30.0%	53.7%	15.7%
8,086	UNION	5,739	1,605	3,325	794	15	1,720 D	28.0%	57.9%	13.8%
41,847	WARREN	29,896	14,748	11,529	3,533	86	3,219 R	49.3%	38.6%	11.8%
6,757	WASHINGTON	4,695	2,098	2,008	542	47	90 R	44.7%	42.8%	11.5%
11,344	WAYNE	6,507	3,412	2,516	560	19	896 R	52.4%	38.7%	8.6%
8,027	WEBSTER	5,665	1,408	3,380	854	23	1,972 D	24.9%	59.7%	15.1%
18,786	WHITLEY	12,167	5,998	4,600	1,533	36	1,398 R	49.3%	37.8%	12.6%
4,947	WOLFE	2,684	697	1,674	297	16	977 D	26.0%	62.4%	11.1%
11,418	WOODFORD	8,725	3,992	3,161	1,535	37	831 R	45.8%	36.2%	17.6%
2,076,263	TOTAL	1,492,900	617,178	665,104	203,944	6,674	47,926 D	41.3%	44.6%	13.7%

KENTUCKY

GOVERNOR 1991

Registration	County	Total Vote	Republican	Democratic	Other	Rep.-Dem. Plurality	Percentage Total Vote Rep.	Total Vote Dem.	Major Vote Rep.	Major Vote Dem.
9,795	ADAIR	3,921	2,094	1,827		267 R	53.4%	46.6%	53.4%	46.6%
7,998	ALLEN	2,559	1,242	1,317		75 D	48.5%	51.5%	48.5%	51.5%
8,006	ANDERSON	4,636	1,664	2,972		1,308 D	35.9%	64.1%	35.9%	64.1%
5,088	BALLARD	2,197	539	1,658		1,119 D	24.5%	75.5%	24.5%	75.5%
18,485	BARREN	6,490	2,363	4,127		1,764 D	36.4%	63.6%	36.4%	63.6%
6,869	BATH	3,853	1,010	2,843		1,833 D	26.2%	73.8%	26.2%	73.8%
19,047	BELL	5,496	2,048	3,448		1,400 D	37.3%	62.7%	37.3%	62.7%
24,400	BOONE	9,840	4,081	5,759		1,678 D	41.5%	58.5%	41.5%	58.5%
9,295	BOURBON	4,419	1,811	2,608		797 D	41.0%	59.0%	41.0%	59.0%
25,591	BOYD	12,485	4,043	8,442		4,399 D	32.4%	67.6%	32.4%	67.6%
11,989	BOYLE	5,994	2,505	3,489		984 D	41.8%	58.2%	41.8%	58.2%
3,895	BRACKEN	1,891	836	1,055		219 D	44.2%	55.8%	44.2%	55.8%
10,737	BREATHITT	3,134	540	2,594		2,054 D	17.2%	82.8%	17.2%	82.8%
9,248	BRECKINRIDGE	4,365	1,611	2,754		1,143 D	36.9%	63.1%	36.9%	63.1%
22,118	BULLITT	9,366	2,938	6,428		3,490 D	31.4%	68.6%	31.4%	68.6%
6,717	BUTLER	2,404	1,240	1,164		76 R	51.6%	48.4%	51.6%	48.4%
7,284	CALDWELL	3,902	1,092	2,810		1,718 D	28.0%	72.0%	28.0%	72.0%
15,986	CALLOWAY	5,525	1,790	3,735		1,945 D	32.4%	67.6%	32.4%	67.6%
36,200	CAMPBELL	16,832	6,596	10,236		3,640 D	39.2%	60.8%	39.2%	60.8%
3,514	CARLISLE	1,583	496	1,087		591 D	31.3%	68.7%	31.3%	68.7%
5,489	CARROLL	2,022	461	1,561		1,100 D	22.8%	77.2%	22.8%	77.2%
13,076	CARTER	4,098	1,417	2,681		1,264 D	34.6%	65.4%	34.6%	65.4%
8,511	CASEY	3,414	2,032	1,382		650 R	59.5%	40.5%	59.5%	40.5%
20,721	CHRISTIAN	7,396	2,596	4,800		2,204 D	35.1%	64.9%	35.1%	64.9%
13,935	CLARK	7,159	2,766	4,393		1,627 D	38.6%	61.4%	38.6%	61.4%
12,957	CLAY	4,010	1,779	2,231		452 D	44.4%	55.6%	44.4%	55.6%
6,801	CLINTON	3,219	2,102	1,117		985 R	65.3%	34.7%	65.3%	34.7%
4,792	CRITTENDEN	2,093	878	1,215		337 D	41.9%	58.1%	41.9%	58.1%
4,678	CUMBERLAND	1,565	888	677		211 R	56.7%	43.3%	56.7%	43.3%
42,139	DAVIESS	20,568	7,856	12,712		4,856 D	38.2%	61.8%	38.2%	61.8%
6,513	EDMONSON	2,636	1,436	1,200		236 R	54.5%	45.5%	54.5%	45.5%
4,395	ELLIOTT	1,173	170	1,003		833 D	14.5%	85.5%	14.5%	85.5%
8,440	ESTILL	3,545	1,412	2,133		721 D	39.8%	60.2%	39.8%	60.2%
91,976	FAYETTE	52,732	22,669	30,063		7,394 D	43.0%	57.0%	43.0%	57.0%
7,472	FLEMING	3,286	1,138	2,148		1,010 D	34.6%	65.4%	34.6%	65.4%
27,666	FLOYD	11,736	1,442	10,294		8,852 D	12.3%	87.7%	12.3%	87.7%
25,428	FRANKLIN	17,118	4,321	12,797		8,476 D	25.2%	74.8%	25.2%	74.8%
4,439	FULTON	1,842	512	1,330		818 D	27.8%	72.2%	27.8%	72.2%
3,018	GALLATIN	984	251	733		482 D	25.5%	74.5%	25.5%	74.5%
6,782	GARRARD	2,761	1,359	1,402		43 D	49.2%	50.8%	49.2%	50.8%
6,655	GRANT	2,874	923	1,951		1,028 D	32.1%	67.9%	32.1%	67.9%
17,808	GRAVES	7,857	2,660	5,197		2,537 D	33.9%	66.1%	33.9%	66.1%
11,840	GRAYSON	4,779	2,331	2,448		117 D	48.8%	51.2%	48.8%	51.2%
7,338	GREEN	2,793	1,370	1,423		53 D	49.1%	50.9%	49.1%	50.9%
18,361	GREENUP	8,277	2,899	5,378		2,479 D	35.0%	65.0%	35.0%	65.0%
4,555	HANCOCK	1,922	633	1,289		656 D	32.9%	67.1%	32.9%	67.1%
31,653	HARDIN	13,901	4,918	8,983		4,065 D	35.4%	64.6%	35.4%	64.6%
19,981	HARLAN	6,008	1,876	4,132		2,256 D	31.2%	68.8%	31.2%	68.8%
8,345	HARRISON	3,859	1,374	2,485		1,111 D	35.6%	64.4%	35.6%	64.4%
8,887	HART	3,040	1,101	1,939		838 D	36.2%	63.8%	36.2%	63.8%
19,285	HENDERSON	9,712	2,210	7,502		5,292 D	22.8%	77.2%	22.8%	77.2%
6,719	HENRY	3,226	777	2,449		1,672 D	24.1%	75.9%	24.1%	75.9%
3,191	HICKMAN	1,675	723	952		229 D	43.2%	56.8%	43.2%	56.8%
22,800	HOPKINS	9,795	2,460	7,335		4,875 D	25.1%	74.9%	25.1%	74.9%
7,921	JACKSON	2,303	1,489	814		675 R	64.7%	35.3%	64.7%	35.3%
332,036	JEFFERSON	172,582	57,062	115,520		58,458 D	33.1%	66.9%	33.1%	66.9%
16,022	JESSAMINE	6,812	2,943	3,869		926 D	43.2%	56.8%	43.2%	56.8%
14,239	JOHNSON	4,232	1,554	2,678		1,124 D	36.7%	63.3%	36.7%	63.3%
57,619	KENTON	27,699	11,639	16,060		4,421 D	42.0%	58.0%	42.0%	58.0%
11,600	KNOTT	5,098	805	4,293		3,488 D	15.8%	84.2%	15.8%	84.2%

KENTUCKY

GOVERNOR 1991

Registration	County	Total Vote	Republican	Democratic	Other	Rep.-Dem. Plurality	Percentage Total Vote Rep.	Dem.	Major Vote Rep.	Dem.
16,966	KNOX	5,415	2,271	3,144		873 D	41.9%	58.1%	41.9%	58.1%
7,052	LARUE	2,566	794	1,772		978 D	30.9%	69.1%	30.9%	69.1%
21,376	LAUREL	9,388	4,837	4,551		286 R	51.5%	48.5%	51.5%	48.5%
8,361	LAWRENCE	2,600	885	1,715		830 D	34.0%	66.0%	34.0%	66.0%
4,945	LEE	2,750	1,206	1,544		338 D	43.9%	56.1%	43.9%	56.1%
8,442	LESLIE	2,422	1,175	1,247		72 D	48.5%	51.5%	48.5%	51.5%
14,930	LETCHER	6,955	1,602	5,353		3,751 D	23.0%	77.0%	23.0%	77.0%
7,434	LEWIS	3,070	1,829	1,241		588 R	59.6%	40.4%	59.6%	40.4%
9,569	LINCOLN	3,603	1,439	2,164		725 D	39.9%	60.1%	39.9%	60.1%
5,538	LIVINGSTON	2,663	778	1,885		1,107 D	29.2%	70.8%	29.2%	70.8%
13,267	LOGAN	3,957	940	3,017		2,077 D	23.8%	76.2%	23.8%	76.2%
3,532	LYON	1,951	521	1,430		909 D	26.7%	73.3%	26.7%	73.3%
30,072	MCCRACKEN	14,882	4,810	10,072		5,262 D	32.3%	67.7%	32.3%	67.7%
9,409	MCCREARY	2,018	984	1,034		50 D	48.8%	51.2%	48.8%	51.2%
5,471	MCLEAN	2,300	623	1,677		1,054 D	27.1%	72.9%	27.1%	72.9%
25,833	MADISON	11,250	4,603	6,647		2,044 D	40.9%	59.1%	40.9%	59.1%
9,333	MAGOFFIN	4,365	1,032	3,333		2,301 D	23.6%	76.4%	23.6%	76.4%
9,534	MARION	3,544	944	2,600		1,656 D	26.6%	73.4%	26.6%	73.4%
14,735	MARSHALL	6,612	1,794	4,818		3,024 D	27.1%	72.9%	27.1%	72.9%
7,764	MARTIN	1,525	641	884		243 D	42.0%	58.0%	42.0%	58.0%
8,221	MASON	3,770	1,298	2,472		1,174 D	34.4%	65.6%	34.4%	65.6%
9,742	MEADE	3,847	1,188	2,659		1,471 D	30.9%	69.1%	30.9%	69.1%
3,114	MENIFEE	1,323	310	1,013		703 D	23.4%	76.6%	23.4%	76.6%
10,092	MERCER	5,111	2,115	2,996		881 D	41.4%	58.6%	41.4%	58.6%
5,803	METCALFE	2,114	938	1,176		238 D	44.4%	55.6%	44.4%	55.6%
8,574	MONROE	2,591	1,645	946		699 R	63.5%	36.5%	63.5%	36.5%
10,541	MONTGOMERY	5,810	1,929	3,881		1,952 D	33.2%	66.8%	33.2%	66.8%
7,111	MORGAN	2,157	376	1,781		1,405 D	17.4%	82.6%	17.4%	82.6%
17,700	MUHLENBERG	6,179	1,414	4,765		3,351 D	22.9%	77.1%	22.9%	77.1%
13,829	NELSON	6,007	1,711	4,296		2,585 D	28.5%	71.5%	28.5%	71.5%
4,192	NICHOLAS	1,814	679	1,135		456 D	37.4%	62.6%	37.4%	62.6%
11,803	OHIO	4,439	1,769	2,670		901 D	39.9%	60.1%	39.9%	60.1%
17,268	OLDHAM	8,049	3,284	4,765		1,481 D	40.8%	59.2%	40.8%	59.2%
4,761	OWEN	2,437	532	1,905		1,373 D	21.8%	78.2%	21.8%	78.2%
3,613	OWSLEY	1,294	721	573		148 R	55.7%	44.3%	55.7%	44.3%
6,147	PENDLETON	2,618	880	1,738		858 D	33.6%	66.4%	33.6%	66.4%
18,397	PERRY	9,088	2,230	6,858		4,628 D	24.5%	75.5%	24.5%	75.5%
39,932	PIKE	12,705	2,554	10,151		7,597 D	20.1%	79.9%	20.1%	79.9%
7,125	POWELL	2,747	788	1,959		1,171 D	28.7%	71.3%	28.7%	71.3%
26,159	PULASKI	9,521	4,278	5,243		965 D	44.9%	55.1%	44.9%	55.1%
1,395	ROBERTSON	698	258	440		182 D	37.0%	63.0%	37.0%	63.0%
8,284	ROCKCASTLE	2,617	1,375	1,242		133 R	52.5%	47.5%	52.5%	47.5%
10,314	ROWAN	4,751	1,420	3,331		1,911 D	29.9%	70.1%	29.9%	70.1%
9,844	RUSSELL	4,776	2,726	2,050		676 R	57.1%	42.9%	57.1%	42.9%
11,162	SCOTT	5,799	2,094	3,705		1,611 D	36.1%	63.9%	36.1%	63.9%
12,934	SHELBY	6,312	2,169	4,143		1,974 D	34.4%	65.6%	34.4%	65.6%
7,660	SIMPSON	2,833	891	1,942		1,051 D	31.5%	68.5%	31.5%	68.5%
4,106	SPENCER	1,664	526	1,138		612 D	31.6%	68.4%	31.6%	68.4%
12,753	TAYLOR	4,481	1,772	2,709		937 D	39.5%	60.5%	39.5%	60.5%
5,890	TODD	1,695	404	1,291		887 D	23.8%	76.2%	23.8%	76.2%
6,216	TRIGG	2,846	777	2,069		1,292 D	27.3%	72.7%	27.3%	72.7%
3,627	TRIMBLE	1,384	472	912		440 D	34.1%	65.9%	34.1%	65.9%
7,700	UNION	3,494	731	2,763		2,032 D	20.9%	79.1%	20.9%	79.1%
37,218	WARREN	16,663	5,956	10,707		4,751 D	35.7%	64.3%	35.7%	64.3%
6,686	WASHINGTON	2,784	950	1,834		884 D	34.1%	65.9%	34.1%	65.9%
11,055	WAYNE	4,199	1,899	2,300		401 D	45.2%	54.8%	45.2%	54.8%
7,862	WEBSTER	3,568	633	2,935		2,302 D	17.7%	82.3%	17.7%	82.3%
17,396	WHITLEY	6,606	3,025	3,581		556 D	45.8%	54.2%	45.8%	54.2%
4,733	WOLFE	1,555	375	1,180		805 D	24.1%	75.9%	24.1%	75.9%
10,403	WOODFORD	6,045	1,881	4,164		2,283 D	31.1%	68.9%	31.1%	68.9%
1,873,270	TOTAL	834,920	294,452	540,468		246,016 D	35.3%	64.7%	35.3%	64.7%

KENTUCKY

SENATOR 1992

| | | | | | | | Percentage | | | |
| | | | | | | | Total Vote | | Major Vote | |
Registration	County	Total Vote	Republican	Democratic	Other	Rep.-Dem. Plurality	Rep.	Dem.	Rep.	Dem.
9,857	ADAIR	5,703	3,280	2,378	45	902 R	57.5%	41.7%	58.0%	42.0%
8,413	ALLEN	4,658	2,417	2,203	38	214 R	51.9%	47.3%	52.3%	47.7%
8,770	ANDERSON	5,768	2,145	3,543	80	1,398 D	37.2%	61.4%	37.7%	62.3%
5,196	BALLARD	3,741	579	3,128	34	2,549 D	15.5%	83.6%	15.6%	84.4%
19,549	BARREN	11,450	4,375	6,990	85	2,615 D	38.2%	61.0%	38.5%	61.5%
7,113	BATH	3,375	724	2,616	35	1,892 D	21.5%	77.5%	21.7%	78.3%
19,874	BELL	8,412	2,901	5,364	147	2,463 D	34.5%	63.8%	35.1%	64.9%
30,111	BOONE	21,261	9,525	11,372	364	1,847 D	44.8%	53.5%	45.6%	54.4%
10,102	BOURBON	6,055	1,777	4,188	90	2,411 D	29.3%	69.2%	29.8%	70.2%
28,524	BOYD	19,516	6,076	13,256	184	7,180 D	31.1%	67.9%	31.4%	68.6%
13,110	BOYLE	8,308	3,210	5,025	73	1,815 D	38.6%	60.5%	39.0%	61.0%
4,109	BRACKEN	2,387	609	1,740	38	1,131 D	25.5%	72.9%	25.9%	74.1%
11,021	BREATHITT	4,873	931	3,910	32	2,979 D	19.1%	80.2%	19.2%	80.8%
9,731	BRECKINRIDGE	6,468	2,112	4,314	42	2,202 D	32.7%	66.7%	32.9%	67.1%
25,962	BULLITT	17,375	6,205	10,954	216	4,749 D	35.7%	63.0%	36.2%	63.8%
6,936	BUTLER	4,098	2,255	1,817	26	438 R	55.0%	44.3%	55.4%	44.6%
7,646	CALDWELL	5,305	1,626	3,644	35	2,018 D	30.7%	68.7%	30.9%	69.1%
18,158	CALLOWAY	11,632	4,058	7,452	122	3,394 D	34.9%	64.1%	35.3%	64.7%
41,771	CAMPBELL	27,477	11,181	15,765	531	4,584 D	40.7%	57.4%	41.5%	58.5%
3,506	CARLISLE	2,253	480	1,760	13	1,280 D	21.3%	78.1%	21.4%	78.6%
5,742	CARROLL	3,169	664	2,449	56	1,785 D	21.0%	77.3%	21.3%	78.7%
13,761	CARTER	7,657	2,628	4,973	56	2,345 D	34.3%	64.9%	34.6%	65.4%
8,728	CASEY	4,466	2,581	1,832	53	749 D	57.8%	41.0%	58.5%	41.5%
23,768	CHRISTIAN	14,328	6,210	7,982	136	1,772 D	43.3%	55.7%	43.8%	56.2%
15,533	CLARK	9,655	3,442	6,106	107	2,664 D	35.6%	63.2%	36.0%	64.0%
13,510	CLAY	5,513	3,210	2,250	53	960 R	58.2%	40.8%	58.8%	41.2%
6,980	CLINTON	3,561	2,222	1,297	42	925 R	62.4%	36.4%	63.1%	36.9%
5,086	CRITTENDEN	3,351	1,210	2,120	21	910 D	36.1%	63.3%	36.3%	63.7%
4,726	CUMBERLAND	2,855	1,804	1,041	10	763 R	63.2%	36.5%	63.4%	36.6%
47,366	DAVIESS	33,046	10,374	22,194	478	11,820 D	31.4%	67.2%	31.9%	68.1%
6,830	EDMONSON	3,886	2,082	1,782	22	300 R	53.6%	45.9%	53.9%	46.1%
4,492	ELLIOTT	2,237	268	1,944	25	1,676 D	12.0%	86.9%	12.1%	87.9%
8,723	ESTILL	4,687	2,013	2,623	51	610 D	42.9%	56.0%	43.4%	56.6%
115,672	FAYETTE	81,609	34,047	45,941	1,621	11,894 D	41.7%	56.3%	42.6%	57.4%
7,643	FLEMING	4,281	1,321	2,909	51	1,588 D	30.9%	68.0%	31.2%	68.8%
29,025	FLOYD	15,516	2,223	13,138	155	10,915 D	14.3%	84.7%	14.5%	85.5%
27,068	FRANKLIN	18,065	4,986	12,717	362	7,731 D	27.6%	70.4%	28.2%	71.8%
4,821	FULTON	2,644	616	1,999	29	1,383 D	23.3%	75.6%	23.6%	76.4%
3,231	GALLATIN	1,888	432	1,419	37	987 D	22.9%	75.2%	23.3%	76.7%
7,160	GARRARD	4,289	1,901	2,359	29	458 D	44.3%	55.0%	44.6%	55.4%
7,377	GRANT	4,719	1,338	3,297	84	1,959 D	28.4%	69.9%	28.9%	71.1%
19,540	GRAVES	12,848	3,115	9,596	137	6,481 D	24.2%	74.7%	24.5%	75.5%
12,428	GRAYSON	7,535	3,694	3,753	88	59 D	49.0%	49.8%	49.6%	50.4%
7,432	GREEN	4,518	2,394	2,100	24	294 R	53.0%	46.5%	53.3%	46.7%
20,366	GREENUP	12,903	4,096	8,691	116	4,595 D	31.7%	67.4%	32.0%	68.0%
4,778	HANCOCK	3,082	855	2,141	86	1,286 D	27.7%	69.5%	28.5%	71.5%
36,387	HARDIN	23,907	8,728	14,858	321	6,130 D	36.5%	62.1%	37.0%	63.0%
21,519	HARLAN	9,965	2,500	7,370	95	4,870 D	25.1%	74.0%	25.3%	74.7%
8,791	HARRISON	5,710	1,567	4,084	59	2,517 D	27.4%	71.5%	27.7%	72.3%
9,464	HART	5,128	1,744	3,351	33	1,607 D	34.0%	65.3%	34.2%	65.8%
21,974	HENDERSON	14,957	3,912	10,891	154	6,979 D	26.2%	72.8%	26.4%	73.6%
7,218	HENRY	4,611	1,065	3,483	63	2,418 D	23.1%	75.5%	23.4%	76.6%
3,264	HICKMAN	2,338	493	1,808	37	1,315 D	21.1%	77.3%	21.4%	78.6%
25,592	HOPKINS	15,973	4,127	11,672	174	7,545 D	25.8%	73.1%	26.1%	73.9%
8,138	JACKSON	3,590	2,543	1,011	36	1,532 R	70.8%	28.2%	71.6%	28.4%
379,521	JEFFERSON	300,588	100,956	195,253	4,379	94,297 D	33.6%	65.0%	34.1%	65.9%
18,113	JESSAMINE	10,996	5,101	5,778	117	677 D	46.4%	52.5%	46.9%	53.1%
14,918	JOHNSON	7,410	2,650	4,672	88	2,022 D	35.8%	63.0%	36.2%	63.8%
68,007	KENTON	47,116	21,040	24,978	1,098	3,938 D	44.7%	53.0%	45.7%	54.3%
12,065	KNOTT	6,171	799	5,299	73	4,500 D	12.9%	85.9%	13.1%	86.9%

KENTUCKY

SENATOR 1992

Registration	County	Total Vote	Republican	Democratic	Other	Rep.-Dem. Plurality	Percentage			
							Total Vote		Major Vote	
							Rep.	Dem.	Rep.	Dem.
18,020	KNOX	8,119	3,443	4,594	82	1,151 D	42.4%	56.6%	42.8%	57.2%
7,396	LARUE	4,462	1,412	3,006	44	1,594 D	31.6%	67.4%	32.0%	68.0%
24,239	LAUREL	13,448	7,127	6,202	119	925 D	53.0%	46.1%	53.5%	46.5%
8,650	LAWRENCE	4,453	1,601	2,813	39	1,212 D	36.0%	63.2%	36.3%	63.7%
5,138	LEE	2,631	1,207	1,395	29	188 D	45.9%	53.0%	46.4%	53.6%
8,775	LESLIE	3,958	2,171	1,766	21	405 R	54.9%	44.6%	55.1%	44.9%
16,028	LETCHER	7,390	1,775	5,488	127	3,713 D	24.0%	74.3%	24.4%	75.6%
7,687	LEWIS	4,180	2,122	2,001	57	121 R	50.8%	47.9%	51.5%	48.5%
10,135	LINCOLN	5,598	2,049	3,501	48	1,452 D	36.6%	62.5%	36.9%	63.1%
5,582	LIVINGSTON	3,812	876	2,886	50	2,010 D	23.0%	75.7%	23.3%	76.7%
13,914	LOGAN	7,938	2,953	4,903	82	1,950 D	37.2%	61.8%	37.6%	62.4%
3,921	LYON	2,623	596	1,998	29	1,402 D	22.7%	76.2%	23.0%	77.0%
35,367	MCCRACKEN	25,278	7,262	17,841	175	10,579 D	28.7%	70.6%	28.9%	71.1%
10,061	MCCREARY	3,897	1,948	1,853	96	95 R	50.0%	47.5%	51.2%	48.8%
5,706	MCLEAN	3,773	967	2,759	47	1,792 D	25.6%	73.1%	26.0%	74.0%
29,879	MADISON	18,086	6,914	10,976	196	4,062 D	38.2%	60.7%	38.6%	61.4%
9,748	MAGOFFIN	4,640	1,327	3,256	57	1,929 D	28.6%	70.2%	29.0%	71.0%
9,635	MARION	5,339	1,125	4,149	65	3,024 D	21.1%	77.7%	21.3%	78.7%
16,220	MARSHALL	11,934	3,199	8,648	87	5,449 D	26.8%	72.5%	27.0%	73.0%
8,173	MARTIN	3,610	1,466	2,097	47	631 D	40.6%	58.1%	41.1%	58.9%
8,731	MASON	5,345	1,737	3,552	56	1,815 D	32.5%	66.5%	32.8%	67.2%
10,666	MEADE	6,765	1,891	4,776	98	2,885 D	28.0%	70.6%	28.4%	71.6%
3,303	MENIFEE	1,831	391	1,423	17	1,032 D	21.4%	77.7%	21.6%	78.4%
10,901	MERCER	6,153	2,195	3,829	129	1,634 D	35.7%	62.2%	36.4%	63.6%
5,967	METCALFE	3,309	1,377	1,895	37	518 D	41.6%	57.3%	42.1%	57.9%
8,756	MONROE	4,129	2,618	1,464	47	1,154 R	63.4%	35.5%	64.1%	35.9%
11,105	MONTGOMERY	6,475	1,669	4,719	87	3,050 D	25.8%	72.9%	26.1%	73.9%
7,291	MORGAN	3,584	620	2,928	36	2,308 D	17.3%	81.7%	17.5%	82.5%
18,827	MUHLENBERG	11,654	2,870	8,685	99	5,815 D	24.6%	74.5%	24.8%	75.2%
15,235	NELSON	9,607	2,827	6,617	163	3,790 D	29.4%	68.9%	29.9%	70.1%
4,210	NICHOLAS	2,142	492	1,597	53	1,105 D	23.0%	74.6%	23.6%	76.4%
12,702	OHIO	8,155	2,985	5,106	64	2,121 D	36.6%	62.6%	36.9%	63.1%
20,422	OLDHAM	15,175	7,425	7,612	138	187 D	48.9%	50.2%	49.4%	50.6%
4,980	OWEN	3,220	765	2,418	37	1,653 D	23.8%	75.1%	24.0%	76.0%
3,822	OWSLEY	1,591	717	854	20	137 D	45.1%	53.7%	45.6%	54.4%
6,539	PENDLETON	3,613	1,047	2,480	86	1,433 D	29.0%	68.6%	29.7%	70.3%
19,586	PERRY	9,503	2,768	6,656	79	3,888 D	29.1%	70.0%	29.4%	70.6%
43,642	PIKE	24,557	6,372	18,032	153	11,660 D	25.9%	73.4%	26.1%	73.9%
7,733	POWELL	3,831	1,174	2,586	71	1,412 D	30.6%	67.5%	31.2%	68.8%
28,249	PULASKI	15,719	7,964	7,623	132	341 R	50.7%	48.5%	51.1%	48.9%
1,323	ROBERTSON	809	217	582	10	365 D	26.8%	71.9%	27.2%	72.8%
8,517	ROCKCASTLE	4,396	2,533	1,839	24	694 R	57.6%	41.8%	57.9%	42.1%
11,643	ROWAN	6,458	1,819	4,572	67	2,753 D	28.2%	70.8%	28.5%	71.5%
10,893	RUSSELL	6,561	3,953	2,560	48	1,393 R	60.2%	39.0%	60.7%	39.3%
12,684	SCOTT	8,315	2,913	5,305	97	2,392 D	35.0%	63.8%	35.4%	64.6%
14,026	SHELBY	9,425	3,577	5,754	94	2,177 D	38.0%	61.1%	38.3%	61.7%
8,522	SIMPSON	4,818	1,789	2,991	38	1,202 D	37.1%	62.1%	37.4%	62.6%
4,465	SPENCER	2,684	793	1,862	29	1,069 D	29.5%	69.4%	29.9%	70.1%
13,322	TAYLOR	8,239	3,780	4,413	46	633 D	45.9%	53.6%	46.1%	53.9%
6,080	TODD	3,019	1,050	1,893	76	843 D	34.8%	62.7%	35.7%	64.3%
6,599	TRIGG	4,151	1,283	2,804	64	1,521 D	30.9%	67.5%	31.4%	68.6%
3,820	TRIMBLE	2,514	583	1,905	26	1,322 D	23.2%	75.8%	23.4%	76.6%
8,086	UNION	5,308	981	4,286	41	3,305 D	18.5%	80.7%	18.6%	81.4%
41,847	WARREN	28,008	13,558	14,177	273	619 D	48.4%	50.6%	48.9%	51.1%
6,757	WASHINGTON	3,889	1,315	2,502	72	1,187 D	33.8%	64.3%	34.5%	65.5%
11,344	WAYNE	5,314	2,590	2,675	49	85 D	48.7%	50.3%	49.2%	50.8%
8,027	WEBSTER	5,197	894	4,240	63	3,346 D	17.2%	81.6%	17.4%	82.6%
18,786	WHITLEY	9,150	4,404	4,610	136	206 D	48.1%	50.4%	48.9%	51.1%
4,947	WOLFE	2,200	441	1,730	29	1,289 D	20.0%	78.6%	20.3%	79.7%
11,418	WOODFORD	7,993	3,270	4,624	99	1,354 D	40.9%	57.9%	41.4%	58.6%
2,076,263	TOTAL	1,330,858	476,604	836,888	17,366	360,284 D	35.8%	62.9%	36.3%	63.7%

KENTUCKY

CONGRESS

CD	Year	Total Vote	Republican Vote	Republican Candidate	Democratic Vote	Democratic Candidate	Other Vote	Rep.-Dem. Plurality	Percentage Total Vote Rep.	Percentage Total Vote Dem.	Percentage Major Vote Rep.	Percentage Major Vote Dem.
1	1992	212,574	83,088	HAMRICK, STEVE	128,524	BARLOW, TOM	962	45,436 D	39.1%	60.5%	39.3%	60.7%
2	1992	206,578	79,684	BARTLEY, BRUCE R.	126,894	NATCHER, WILLIAM H.		47,210 D	38.6%	61.4%	38.6%	61.4%
3	1992	280,770	132,689	STOKES, SUSAN B.	148,066	MAZZOLI, RAMANO L.	15	15,377 D	47.3%	52.7%	47.3%	52.7%
4	1992	226,524	139,634	BUNNING, JIM	86,890	POORE, FLOYD G.		52,744 R	61.6%	38.4%	61.6%	38.4%
5	1992	211,015	115,255	ROGERS, HAROLD	95,760	HAYS, JOHN D.		19,495 R	54.6%	45.4%	54.6%	45.4%
6	1992	223,450	87,816	ELLINGER, CHARLES W.	135,613	BAESLER, SCOTT	21	47,797 D	39.3%	60.7%	39.3%	60.7%

234

KENTUCKY

1991 GENERAL ELECTION

Governor

1992 GENERAL ELECTION

President   Other vote was 4,513 Libertarian (Marrou); 989 Taxpayers (Phillips); 695 Natural Law (Hagelin); 430 New Alliance (Fulani); 47 Gritz (write-in).

Senator   Other vote was Libertarian (Ridenour).

Congress   Other vote was Reform Party (Seat) in CD 1; Metten (write-in) in CD 3; Gailey (write-in) in CD 6.

1991 PRIMARIES

MAY 28 REPUBLICAN

Governor   81,526 Larry J. Hopkins; 79,581 Lawrence E. Forgy.

MAY 28 DEMOCRATIC

Governor   184,703 Brereton C. Jones; 149,352 Scott Baesler; 132,060 Floyd G. Poore; 25,834 Gatewood Galbraith.

1992 PRIMARIES

MAY 26 REPUBLICAN

Senator   49,880 David L. Williams; 25,026 Philip Thompson; 7,066 Denny Ormerod.

Congress   Unopposed in five CD's. Contested as follows:

  CD 3   13,200 Susan B. Stokes; 4,685 Richard A. Lewis; 1,526 Larry J. West; 579 Tommy Klein.

MAY 26 DEMOCRATIC

Senator   Wendell H. Ford, unopposed.

Congress   Unopposed in CD 4. Contested as follows:

  CD 1   40,014 Tom Barlow; 37,188 Carroll Hubbard; 6,019 Charles T. Banken.
  CD 2   35,351 William H. Natcher; 10,072 Bob Evans; 4,428 Paul D. Hamm.
  CD 3   52,748 Romano L. Mazzoli; 16,758 Ron Greene.
  CD 5   18,454 John D. Hays; 10,586 Ned Pillersdorf; 10,453 Carol B. Hubbard; 10,452 Robert Rowe; 5,091 Jerry Cecil; 4,910 Nelson P. Bingham; 1,398 Logan Turner; 722 Steven Maynard.
  CD 6   49,954 Scott Baesler; 4,701 Roy Tudor; 2,627 J. T. Underwood; 2,425 Harvey Carroll; 1,438 Christopher Bush.

LOUISIANA

GOVERNOR
Edwin W. Edwards (D). Elected 1991 to a four-year term. Previously elected 1983, 1975, 1972.

SENATORS
John B. Breaux (D). Re-elected 1992 to a six-year term. Previously elected 1986.

J. Bennett Johnston (D). Re-elected 1990 to a six-year term. Previously elected 1984, 1978, 1972.

REPRESENTATIVES
1. Bob Livingston (R)
2. William J. Jefferson (D)
3. W. J. Tauzin (D)
4. Cleo Fields (D)
5. Jim McCrery (R)
6. Richard H. Baker (R)
7. James A. Hayes (D)

POSTWAR VOTE FOR PRESIDENT

Year	Total Vote	Republican Vote	Candidate	Democratic Vote	Candidate	Other Vote	Plurality	Total Vote Rep.	Total Vote Dem.	Major Vote Rep.	Major Vote Dem.
1992 **	1,790,017	733,386	Bush, George	815,971	Clinton, Bill	240,660	82,585 D	41.0%	45.6%	47.3%	52.7%
1988	1,628,202	883,702	Bush, George	717,460	Dukakis, Michael S.	27,040	166,242 R	54.3%	44.1%	55.2%	44.8%
1984	1,706,822	1,037,299	Reagan, Ronald	651,586	Mondale, Walter F.	17,937	385,713 R	60.8%	38.2%	61.4%	38.6%
1980	1,548,591	792,853	Reagan, Ronald	708,453	Carter, Jimmy	47,285	84,400 R	51.2%	45.7%	52.8%	47.2%
1976	1,278,439	587,446	Ford, Gerald R.	661,365	Carter, Jimmy	29,628	73,919 D	46.0%	51.7%	47.0%	53.0%
1972	1,051,491	686,852	Nixon, Richard M.	298,142	McGovern, George S.	66,497	388,710 R	65.3%	28.4%	69.7%	30.3%
1968 **	1,097,450	257,535	Nixon, Richard M.	309,615	Humphrey, Hubert H.	530,300	220,685 A	23.5%	28.2%	45.4%	54.6%
1964	896,293	509,225	Goldwater, Barry M.	387,068	Johnson, Lyndon B.		122,157 R	56.8%	43.2%	56.8%	43.2%
1960	807,891	230,980	Nixon, Richard M.	407,339	Kennedy, John F.	169,572	176,359 D	28.6%	50.4%	36.2%	63.8%
1956	617,544	329,047	Eisenhower, Dwight D.	243,977	Stevenson, Adlai E.	44,520	85,070 R	53.3%	39.5%	57.4%	42.6%
1952	651,952	306,925	Eisenhower, Dwight D.	345,027	Stevenson, Adlai E.		38,102 D	47.1%	52.9%	47.1%	52.9%
1948 **	416,336	72,657	Dewey, Thomas E.	136,344	Truman, Harry S.	207,335	67,946 SR	17.5%	32.7%	34.8%	65.2%

In 1992 the other vote column includes 211,478 votes cast for Perot. In 1968 other vote was American (Wallace). In 1948 other vote was 204,290 States Rights; 3,035 Progressive and 10 scattered.

POSTWAR VOTE FOR GOVERNOR

Year	Total Vote	Republican Vote	Candidate	Democratic Vote	Candidate	Other Vote	Rep.-Dem. Plurality	Total Vote Rep.	Total Vote Dem.	Major Vote Rep.	Major Vote Dem.
1991	1,728,040	671,009	Duke, David E.	1,057,031	Edwards, Edwin W.		386,022 D	38.8%	61.2%	38.8%	61.2%
1987 **		—			Roemer, Charles						
1983 **		—			Edwards, Edwin W.						
1979	1,371,825	690,691	Treen, David C.	681,134	Lambert, Louis		9,557 R	50.3%	49.7%	50.3%	49.7%
1975	430,095	—		430,095	Edwards, Edwin W.		430,095 D		100.0%		100.0%
1972	1,121,570	480,424	Treen, David C.	641,146	Edwards, Edwin W.		160,722 D	42.8%	57.2%	42.8%	57.2%
1968	372,762	—		372,762	McKeithen, John J.		372,762 D		100.0%		100.0%
1964	773,390	297,753	Lyons, C. H.	469,589	McKeithen, John J.	6,048	171,836 D	38.5%	60.7%	38.8%	61.2%
1960	506,562	86,135	Grevemberg, F. C.	407,907	Davis, Jimmie H.	12,520	321,772 D	17.0%	80.5%	17.4%	82.6%
1956	172,291	—		172,291	Long, Earl K.		172,291 D		100.0%		100.0%
1952	123,681	4,958	Bagwell, Harrison G.	118,723	Kennon, Robert F.		113,765 D	4.0%	96.0%	4.0%	96.0%
1948	76,566	—		76,566	Long, Earl K.		76,566 D		100.0%		100.0%

For the 1987 and 1983 elections, no run-off general election was required (see note section).

LOUISIANA

POSTWAR VOTE FOR SENATOR

Year	Total Vote	Republican Vote	Republican Candidate	Democratic Vote	Democratic Candidate	Other Vote	Rep.-Dem. Plurality	Percentage Total Vote Rep.	Percentage Total Vote Dem.	Percentage Major Vote Rep.	Percentage Major Vote Dem.
1992 * *		—			Breaux, John B.						
1990 * *		—			Johnston, J. Bennett						
1986	1,369,897	646,311	Moore, W. Henson	723,586	Breaux, John B.		77,275 D	47.2%	52.8%	47.2%	52.8%
1984 * *		—			Johnston, J. Bennett						
1980 * *		—			Long, Russell B.						
1978 * *		—			Johnston, J. Bennett						
1974	434,643		—	434,643	Long, Russell B.		434,643 D		100.0%		100.0%
1972	1,084,904	206,846	Toledano, Ben C.	598,987	Johnston, J. Bennett	279,071	392,141 D	19.1%	55.2%	25.7%	74.3%
1968	518,586		—	518,586	Long, Russell B.		518,586 D		100.0%		100.0%
1966	437,695		—	437,695	Ellender, Allen J.		437,695 D		100.0%		100.0%
1962	421,904	103,066	O'Hearn, Taylor W.	318,838	Long, Russell B.		215,772 D	24.4%	75.6%	24.4%	75.6%
1960	541,928	109,698	Reese, George W.	432,228	Ellender, Allen J.	2	322,530 D	20.2%	79.8%	20.2%	79.8%
1956	335,564		—	335,564	Long, Russell B.		335,564 D		100.0%		100.0%
1954	207,115		—	207,115	Ellender, Allen J.		207,115 D		100.0%		100.0%
1950	251,838	30,931	Gerth, Charles S.	220,907	Long, Russell B.		189,976 D	12.3%	87.7%	12.3%	87.7%
1948	330,124		—	330,115	Ellender, Allen J.	9	330,115 D		100.0%		100.0%
1948 S	408,667	102,331	Clarke, Clem S.	306,336	Long, Russell B.		204,005 D	25.0%	75.0%	25.0%	75.0%

For the 1992, 1990, 1984, 1980 and 1978 elections, no run-off election was required (see note section). One of the 1948 elections was for a short term to fill a vacancy.

LOUISIANA

Districts Established June 1, 1992

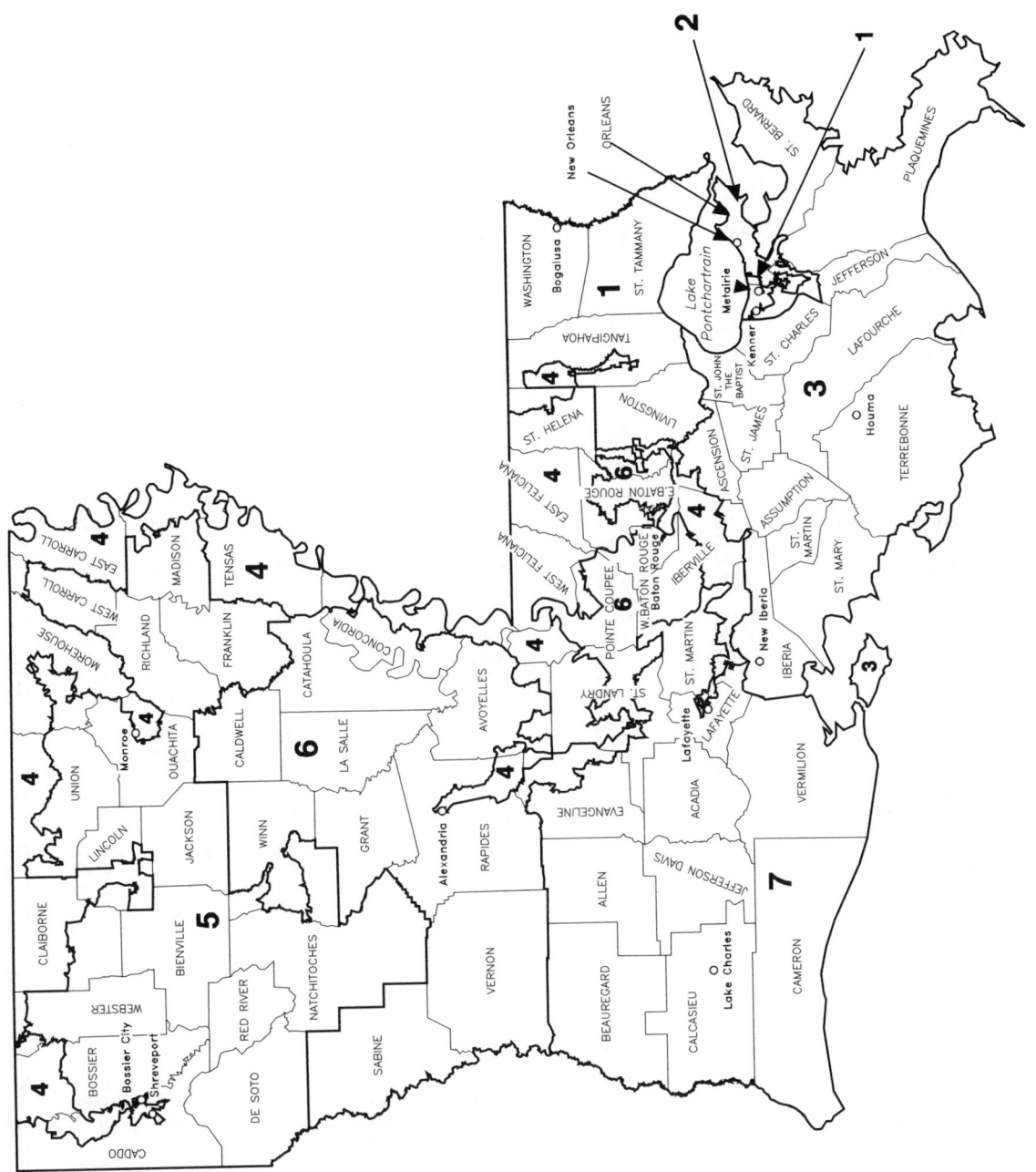

LOUISIANA

PRESIDENT 1992

Registration	Parish	Total Vote	Republican	Democratic	Perot	Other	Plurality	Percentage Total Vote Rep.	Dem.	Perot
33,230	ACADIA	24,568	9,017	12,276	3,145	130	3,259 D	36.7%	50.0%	12.8%
13,189	ALLEN	10,017	3,069	5,626	1,245	77	2,557 D	30.6%	56.2%	12.4%
34,571	ASCENSION	27,748	10,275	13,036	4,295	142	2,761 D	37.0%	47.0%	15.5%
13,938	ASSUMPTION	10,453	2,928	5,639	1,358	528	2,711 D	28.0%	53.9%	13.0%
23,175	AVOYELLES	16,549	4,851	8,696	2,139	863	3,845 D	29.3%	52.5%	12.9%
16,506	BEAUREGARD	12,551	5,119	5,037	2,103	292	82 R	40.8%	40.1%	16.8%
10,202	BIENVILLE	7,432	2,412	3,899	832	289	1,487 D	32.5%	52.5%	11.2%
40,353	BOSSIER	32,801	15,628	11,313	4,863	997	4,315 R	47.6%	34.5%	14.8%
127,562	CADDO	102,678	42,665	47,733	11,830	450	5,068 D	41.6%	46.5%	11.5%
86,206	CALCASIEU	69,862	24,847	33,570	10,980	465	8,723 D	35.6%	48.1%	15.7%
6,814	CALDWELL	4,684	1,752	2,061	653	218	309 D	37.4%	44.0%	13.9%
6,149	CAMERON	4,338	1,329	1,985	995	29	656 D	30.6%	45.8%	22.9%
7,722	CATAHOULA	5,471	1,976	2,570	773	152	594 D	36.1%	47.0%	14.1%
9,489	CLAIBORNE	6,996	2,599	3,263	926	208	664 D	37.1%	46.6%	13.2%
12,296	CONCORDIA	9,148	3,223	4,283	1,317	325	1,060 D	35.2%	46.8%	14.4%
14,652	DE SOTO	11,021	3,643	5,671	1,358	349	2,028 D	33.1%	51.5%	12.3%
202,253	EAST BATON ROUGE	166,691	81,072	68,622	16,102	895	12,450 R	48.6%	41.2%	9.7%
5,678	EAST CARROLL	3,375	1,142	1,835	283	115	693 D	33.8%	54.4%	8.4%
10,957	EAST FELICIANA	7,895	2,813	4,093	932	57	1,280 D	35.6%	51.8%	11.8%
21,862	EVANGELINE	16,376	5,147	8,564	2,124	541	3,417 D	31.4%	52.3%	13.0%
13,409	FRANKLIN	9,653	3,889	4,127	1,311	326	238 D	40.3%	42.8%	13.6%
10,755	GRANT	7,878	3,214	3,122	1,174	368	92 R	40.8%	39.6%	14.9%
38,862	IBERIA	30,530	11,905	13,040	4,337	1,248	1,135 D	39.0%	42.7%	14.2%
20,362	IBERVILLE	15,594	5,211	8,218	1,543	622	3,007 D	33.4%	52.7%	9.9%
9,527	JACKSON	7,566	3,072	3,370	882	242	298 D	40.6%	44.5%	11.7%
227,468	JEFFERSON	187,038	100,493	64,302	21,278	965	36,191 R	53.7%	34.4%	11.4%
17,931	JEFFERSON DAVIS	13,838	4,513	7,022	2,221	82	2,509 D	32.6%	50.7%	16.1%
90,052	LAFAYETTE	71,762	32,406	28,583	9,124	1,649	3,823 R	45.2%	39.8%	12.7%
44,346	LAFOURCHE	35,645	12,744	16,182	5,077	1,642	3,438 D	35.8%	45.4%	14.2%
9,214	LA SALLE	6,723	3,068	2,389	993	273	679 R	45.6%	35.5%	14.8%
21,655	LINCOLN	16,561	7,220	7,205	1,751	385	15 R	43.6%	43.5%	10.6%
40,236	LIVINGSTON	31,421	14,808	11,499	4,971	143	3,309 R	47.1%	36.6%	15.8%
7,769	MADISON	5,106	1,702	2,773	469	162	1,071 D	33.3%	54.3%	9.2%
17,395	MOREHOUSE	13,463	5,364	6,013	1,727	359	649 D	39.8%	44.7%	12.8%
20,615	NATCHITOCHES	14,779	5,694	6,974	1,606	505	1,280 D	38.5%	47.2%	10.9%
262,258	ORLEANS	197,349	52,019	133,261	10,889	1,180	81,242 D	26.4%	67.5%	5.5%
72,307	OUACHITA	56,502	27,600	20,835	6,612	1,455	6,765 R	48.8%	36.9%	11.7%
14,935	PLAQUEMINES	11,257	5,018	4,467	1,729	43	551 R	44.6%	39.7%	15.4%
14,557	POINTE COUPEE	11,322	3,563	6,512	1,157	90	2,949 D	31.5%	57.5%	10.2%
70,133	RAPIDES	51,882	22,783	20,873	6,599	1,627	1,910 R	43.9%	40.2%	12.7%
6,190	RED RIVER	4,680	1,649	2,360	566	105	711 D	35.2%	50.4%	12.1%
11,876	RICHLAND	8,903	3,808	3,706	1,054	335	102 R	42.8%	41.6%	11.8%
13,658	SABINE	9,348	3,586	4,173	1,219	370	587 D	38.4%	44.6%	13.0%
40,051	ST. BERNARD	32,938	16,131	12,305	4,308	194	3,826 R	49.0%	37.4%	13.1%
25,412	ST. CHARLES	20,877	9,158	8,810	2,593	316	348 R	43.9%	42.2%	12.4%
7,908	ST. HELENA	5,618	1,515	3,416	589	98	1,901 D	27.0%	60.8%	10.5%
13,910	ST. JAMES	11,186	3,339	6,609	993	245	3,270 D	29.8%	59.1%	8.9%
22,679	ST. JOHN THE BAPTIST	17,851	6,730	8,977	1,922	222	2,247 D	37.7%	50.3%	10.8%
48,945	ST. LANDRY	36,815	11,882	20,383	4,266	284	8,501 D	32.3%	55.4%	11.6%
25,897	ST. MARTIN	20,426	5,909	11,252	2,573	692	5,343 D	28.9%	55.1%	12.6%
31,730	ST. MARY	23,440	8,792	10,648	3,257	743	1,856 D	37.5%	45.4%	13.9%
81,885	ST. TAMMANY	66,921	37,839	19,735	9,005	342	18,104 R	56.5%	29.5%	13.5%
46,308	TANGIPAHOA	34,245	14,128	15,194	4,612	311	1,066 D	41.3%	44.4%	13.5%
4,597	TENSAS	3,266	1,153	1,666	353	94	513 D	35.3%	51.0%	10.8%
43,858	TERREBONNE	34,664	14,662	13,325	5,505	1,172	1,337 R	42.3%	38.4%	15.9%
13,044	UNION	10,069	4,434	4,005	1,209	421	429 R	44.0%	39.8%	12.0%
30,466	VERMILION	23,444	7,062	12,324	3,127	931	5,262 D	30.1%	52.6%	13.3%
20,507	VERNON	14,767	5,912	6,005	2,313	537	93 D	40.0%	40.7%	15.7%
25,111	WASHINGTON	18,753	7,227	9,095	2,303	128	1,868 D	38.5%	48.5%	12.3%
22,368	WEBSTER	18,264	6,640	8,380	2,629	615	1,740 D	36.4%	45.9%	14.4%

LOUISIANA

PRESIDENT 1992

Registration	Parish	Total Vote	Republican	Democratic	Perot	Other	Plurality	Percentage Total Vote		
								Rep.	Dem.	Perot
12,269	WEST BATON ROUGE	9,976	3,522	5,131	1,249	74	1,609 D	35.3%	51.4%	12.5%
6,883	WEST CARROLL	5,120	2,082	2,068	771	199	14 R	40.7%	40.4%	15.1%
5,691	WEST FELICIANA	4,374	1,501	2,328	516	29	827 D	34.3%	53.2%	11.8%
10,296	WINN	7,549	2,932	3,537	843	237	605 D	38.8%	46.9%	11.2%
2,292,129	TOTAL	1,790,017	733,386	815,971	211,478	29,182	82,585 D	41.0%	45.6%	11.8%

LOUISIANA

GOVERNOR 1991

							Percentage			
							Total Vote		Major Vote	
Registration	Parish	Total Vote	Republican	Democratic	Other	Rep.-Dem. Plurality	Rep.	Dem.	Rep.	Dem.
31,966	ACADIA	24,700	9,772	14,928		5,156 D	39.6%	60.4%	39.6%	60.4%
12,989	ALLEN	10,207	4,036	6,171		2,135 D	39.5%	60.5%	39.5%	60.5%
32,681	ASCENSION	27,659	12,867	14,792		1,925 D	46.5%	53.5%	46.5%	53.5%
13,581	ASSUMPTION	10,873	4,385	6,488		2,103 D	40.3%	59.7%	40.3%	59.7%
22,755	AVOYELLES	16,836	7,792	9,044		1,252 D	46.3%	53.7%	46.3%	53.7%
15,884	BEAUREGARD	11,916	6,351	5,565		786 R	53.3%	46.7%	53.3%	46.7%
10,028	BIENVILLE	7,901	3,216	4,685		1,469 D	40.7%	59.3%	40.7%	59.3%
36,717	BOSSIER	28,993	14,457	14,536		79 D	49.9%	50.1%	49.9%	50.1%
118,138	CADDO	93,524	33,591	59,933		26,342 D	35.9%	64.1%	35.9%	64.1%
82,023	CALCASIEU	61,810	21,193	40,617		19,424 D	34.3%	65.7%	34.3%	65.7%
6,787	CALDWELL	5,702	3,590	2,112		1,478 R	63.0%	37.0%	63.0%	37.0%
6,197	CAMERON	4,122	1,453	2,669		1,216 D	35.2%	64.8%	35.2%	64.8%
7,672	CATAHOULA	6,285	3,470	2,815		655 R	55.2%	44.8%	55.2%	44.8%
9,302	CLAIBORNE	7,503	3,174	4,329		1,155 D	42.3%	57.7%	42.3%	57.7%
12,151	CONCORDIA	9,584	5,040	4,544		496 R	52.6%	47.4%	52.6%	47.4%
14,247	DE SOTO	11,178	4,571	6,607		2,036 D	40.9%	59.1%	40.9%	59.1%
187,893	EAST BATON ROUGE	150,794	50,656	100,138		49,482 D	33.6%	66.4%	33.6%	66.4%
5,844	EAST CARROLL	4,374	1,357	3,017		1,660 D	31.0%	69.0%	31.0%	69.0%
10,559	EAST FELICIANA	8,311	3,362	4,949		1,587 D	40.5%	59.5%	40.5%	59.5%
21,584	EVANGELINE	16,417	7,470	8,947		1,477 D	45.5%	54.5%	45.5%	54.5%
13,013	FRANKLIN	10,589	6,179	4,410		1,769 R	58.4%	41.6%	58.4%	41.6%
10,447	GRANT	8,016	4,500	3,516		984 R	56.1%	43.9%	56.1%	43.9%
37,653	IBERIA	29,408	12,814	16,594		3,780 D	43.6%	56.4%	43.6%	56.4%
20,016	IBERVILLE	16,563	5,870	10,693		4,823 D	35.4%	64.6%	35.4%	64.6%
9,296	JACKSON	7,518	4,173	3,345		828 R	55.5%	44.5%	55.5%	44.5%
210,969	JEFFERSON	172,444	70,183	102,261		32,078 D	40.7%	59.3%	40.7%	59.3%
17,490	JEFFERSON DAVIS	13,451	4,870	8,581		3,711 D	36.2%	63.8%	36.2%	63.8%
83,500	LAFAYETTE	63,152	22,336	40,816		18,480 D	35.4%	64.6%	35.4%	64.6%
41,916	LAFOURCHE	36,001	14,655	21,346		6,691 D	40.7%	59.3%	40.7%	59.3%
9,094	LA SALLE	7,342	4,910	2,432		2,478 R	66.9%	33.1%	66.9%	33.1%
19,466	LINCOLN	15,325	5,943	9,382		3,439 D	38.8%	61.2%	38.8%	61.2%
38,028	LIVINGSTON	30,706	18,554	12,152		6,402 R	60.4%	39.6%	60.4%	39.6%
7,661	MADISON	5,868	2,286	3,582		1,296 D	39.0%	61.0%	39.0%	61.0%
16,673	MOREHOUSE	13,778	7,261	6,517		744 R	52.7%	47.3%	52.7%	47.3%
19,950	NATCHITOCHES	15,230	6,360	8,870		2,510 D	41.8%	58.2%	41.8%	58.2%
245,028	ORLEANS	199,665	25,921	173,744		147,823 D	13.0%	87.0%	13.0%	87.0%
67,374	OUACHITA	52,859	26,722	26,137		585 R	50.6%	49.4%	50.6%	49.4%
14,504	PLAQUEMINES	11,990	5,301	6,689		1,388 D	44.2%	55.8%	44.2%	55.8%
14,426	POINTE COUPEE	12,117	4,687	7,430		2,743 D	38.7%	61.3%	38.7%	61.3%
68,636	RAPIDES	49,400	21,762	27,638		5,876 D	44.1%	55.9%	44.1%	55.9%
6,007	RED RIVER	5,013	2,339	2,674		335 D	46.7%	53.3%	46.7%	53.3%
11,523	RICHLAND	9,149	5,179	3,970		1,209 R	56.6%	43.4%	56.6%	43.4%
13,455	SABINE	9,886	5,251	4,635		616 R	53.1%	46.9%	53.1%	46.9%
38,688	ST. BERNARD	32,547	18,153	14,394		3,759 R	55.8%	44.2%	55.8%	44.2%
23,907	ST. CHARLES	20,565	7,885	12,680		4,795 D	38.3%	61.7%	38.3%	61.7%
7,709	ST. HELENA	6,148	2,448	3,700		1,252 D	39.8%	60.2%	39.8%	60.2%
13,845	ST. JAMES	12,102	4,074	8,028		3,954 D	33.7%	66.3%	33.7%	66.3%
21,529	ST. JOHN THE BAPTIST	18,678	6,685	11,993		5,308 D	35.8%	64.2%	35.8%	64.2%
47,957	ST. LANDRY	38,087	14,725	23,362		8,637 D	38.7%	61.3%	38.7%	61.3%
24,834	ST. MARTIN	19,821	7,095	12,726		5,631 D	35.8%	64.2%	35.8%	64.2%
30,750	ST. MARY	24,486	9,447	15,039		5,592 D	38.6%	61.4%	38.6%	61.4%
72,664	ST. TAMMANY	58,478	25,800	32,678		6,878 D	44.1%	55.9%	44.1%	55.9%
43,193	TANGIPAHOA	35,248	16,469	18,779		2,310 D	46.7%	53.3%	46.7%	53.3%
4,447	TENSAS	3,387	1,394	1,993		599 D	41.2%	58.8%	41.2%	58.8%
41,746	TERREBONNE	33,461	13,662	19,799		6,137 D	40.8%	59.2%	40.8%	59.2%
12,589	UNION	10,049	6,020	4,029		1,991 R	59.9%	40.1%	59.9%	40.1%
29,937	VERMILION	22,359	7,882	14,477		6,595 D	35.3%	64.7%	35.3%	64.7%
19,542	VERNON	13,532	6,856	6,676		180 R	50.7%	49.3%	50.7%	49.3%
23,572	WASHINGTON	19,734	10,577	9,157		1,420 R	53.6%	46.4%	53.6%	46.4%
21,776	WEBSTER	17,430	8,406	9,024		618 D	48.2%	51.8%	48.2%	51.8%

LOUISIANA

GOVERNOR 1991

Registration	Parish	Total Vote	Republican	Democratic	Other	Rep.-Dem. Plurality	Percentage			
							Total Vote		Major Vote	
							Rep.	Dem.	Rep.	Dem.
11,440	WEST BATON ROUGE	10,108	4,092	6,016		1,924 D	40.5%	59.5%	40.5%	59.5%
6,730	WEST CARROLL	5,221	3,596	1,625		1,971 R	68.9%	31.1%	68.9%	31.1%
5,451	WEST FELICIANA	4,492	1,596	2,896		1,300 D	35.5%	64.5%	35.5%	64.5%
10,124	WINN	7,948	4,288	3,660		628 R	54.0%	46.0%	54.0%	46.0%
2,167,553	TOTAL	1,728,040	671,009	1,057,031		386,022 D	38.8%	61.2%	38.8%	61.2%

LOUISIANA

SENATOR 1992
(PRIMARY ELECTION)

Registration	Parish	Total Vote	Republican	Democratic	Independent	Other	Plurality	Percentage Total Vote		
								Rep.	Dem.	Ind.
32,885	ACADIA	10,581	1,290	7,882	457	952	6,592 D	12.2%	74.5%	4.3%
13,117	ALLEN	5,876	311	4,880	208	477	4,569 D	5.3%	83.0%	3.5%
34,243	ASCENSION	11,299	1,147	8,401	568	1,183	7,254 D	10.2%	74.4%	5.0%
13,886	ASSUMPTION	3,348	122	2,684	182	360	2,502 D	3.6%	80.2%	5.4%
23,124	AVOYELLES	8,483	300	6,770	431	982	6,339 D	3.5%	79.8%	5.1%
16,280	BEAUREGARD	4,479	304	3,430	210	535	3,126 D	6.8%	76.6%	4.7%
10,114	BIENVILLE	4,371	193	3,405	215	558	3,190 D	4.4%	77.9%	4.9%
38,938	BOSSIER	16,338	1,586	11,670	1,337	1,745	10,084 D	9.7%	71.4%	8.2%
122,711	CADDO	55,372	4,927	42,176	4,375	3,894	37,249 D	8.9%	76.2%	7.9%
83,092	CALCASIEU	31,769	2,903	24,585	1,462	2,819	21,682 D	9.1%	77.4%	4.6%
6,821	CALDWELL	2,379	114	1,848	165	252	1,683 D	4.8%	77.7%	6.9%
6,128	CAMERON	1,721	97	1,426	38	160	1,329 D	5.6%	82.9%	2.2%
7,724	CATAHOULA	2,691	137	2,108	111	335	1,971 D	5.1%	78.3%	4.1%
9,407	CLAIBORNE	3,071	175	2,375	161	360	2,200 D	5.7%	77.3%	5.2%
12,248	CONCORDIA	4,090	308	3,129	210	443	2,821 D	7.5%	76.5%	5.1%
14,472	DE SOTO	6,635	298	5,319	377	641	4,942 D	4.5%	80.2%	5.7%
197,155	EAST BATON ROUGE	93,035	13,083	67,013	5,793	7,146	53,930 D	14.1%	72.0%	6.2%
5,645	EAST CARROLL	2,039	58	1,649	86	246	1,563 D	2.8%	80.9%	4.2%
10,889	EAST FELICIANA	3,461	398	2,605	151	307	2,207 D	11.5%	75.3%	4.4%
21,684	EVANGELINE	10,846	500	8,367	622	1,357	7,745 D	4.6%	77.1%	5.7%
13,293	FRANKLIN	6,089	242	4,829	294	724	4,535 D	4.0%	79.3%	4.8%
10,666	GRANT	5,466	290	4,019	504	653	3,515 D	5.3%	73.5%	9.2%
38,554	IBERIA	15,952	1,577	11,568	1,205	1,602	9,991 D	9.9%	72.5%	7.6%
20,174	IBERVILLE	12,668	625	10,093	459	1,491	9,468 D	4.9%	79.7%	3.6%
9,435	JACKSON	5,594	212	4,556	220	606	4,336 D	3.8%	81.4%	3.9%
222,156	JEFFERSON	85,709	8,035	53,341	15,405	8,928	37,936 D	9.4%	62.2%	18.0%
17,720	JEFFERSON DAVIS	7,096	538	5,746	197	615	5,208 D	7.6%	81.0%	2.8%
87,396	LAFAYETTE	30,616	3,637	21,257	2,818	2,904	17,620 D	11.9%	69.4%	9.2%
43,931	LAFOURCHE	12,306	689	9,052	1,369	1,196	7,683 D	5.6%	73.6%	11.1%
9,144	LA SALLE	3,008	157	2,161	217	473	1,944 D	5.2%	71.8%	7.2%
20,941	LINCOLN	9,249	545	7,360	501	843	6,815 D	5.9%	79.6%	5.4%
39,628	LIVINGSTON	13,939	1,682	9,933	834	1,490	8,251 D	12.1%	71.3%	6.0%
7,731	MADISON	3,372	141	2,726	99	406	2,585 D	4.2%	80.8%	2.9%
17,251	MOREHOUSE	6,699	387	5,075	413	824	4,662 D	5.8%	75.8%	6.2%
20,454	NATCHITOCHES	7,507	449	5,757	367	934	5,308 D	6.0%	76.7%	4.9%
254,769	ORLEANS	82,063	3,140	63,305	9,772	5,846	53,533 D	3.8%	77.1%	11.9%
71,006	OUACHITA	32,695	2,476	24,464	2,643	3,112	21,821 D	7.6%	74.8%	8.1%
14,846	PLAQUEMINES	5,089	912	3,362	500	315	2,450 D	17.9%	66.1%	9.8%
14,551	POINTE COUPEE	5,492	358	4,574	187	373	4,216 D	6.5%	83.3%	3.4%
69,315	RAPIDES	25,168	1,359	18,108	2,935	2,766	15,173 D	5.4%	71.9%	11.7%
6,120	RED RIVER	2,789	140	2,219	158	272	2,061 D	5.0%	79.6%	5.7%
11,782	RICHLAND	5,980	231	4,697	394	658	4,303 D	3.9%	78.5%	6.6%
13,562	SABINE	4,312	276	3,351	192	493	3,075 D	6.4%	77.7%	4.5%
39,764	ST. BERNARD	8,529	526	5,585	1,616	802	3,969 D	6.2%	65.5%	18.9%
25,018	ST. CHARLES	4,610	433	3,131	558	488	2,573 D	9.4%	67.9%	12.1%
7,909	ST. HELENA	2,243	229	1,676	110	228	1,447 D	10.2%	74.7%	4.9%
13,900	ST. JAMES	3,517	162	2,542	169	644	2,373 D	4.6%	72.3%	4.8%
22,377	ST. JOHN THE BAPTIST	6,804	545	3,913	600	1,746	3,313 D	8.0%	57.5%	8.8%
48,774	ST. LANDRY	18,524	1,681	14,337	831	1,675	12,656 D	9.1%	77.4%	4.5%
25,740	ST. MARTIN	7,436	556	5,713	403	764	5,157 D	7.5%	76.8%	5.4%
31,553	ST. MARY	10,584	468	7,398	803	1,915	6,595 D	4.4%	69.9%	7.6%
78,837	ST. TAMMANY	17,672	2,964	9,206	3,583	1,919	5,623 D	16.8%	52.1%	20.3%
45,654	TANGIPAHOA	13,655	1,387	9,359	1,268	1,641	7,972 D	10.2%	68.5%	9.3%
4,577	TENSAS	2,353	113	1,895	72	273	1,782 D	4.8%	80.5%	3.1%
43,354	TERREBONNE	17,916	977	13,289	1,971	1,679	11,318 D	5.5%	74.2%	11.0%
12,970	UNION	5,471	329	4,270	311	561	3,941 D	6.0%	78.0%	5.7%
30,212	VERMILION	8,376	532	6,138	732	974	5,406 D	6.4%	73.3%	8.7%
20,038	VERNON	6,894	308	5,487	328	771	5,159 D	4.5%	79.6%	4.8%
24,919	WASHINGTON	10,327	977	7,505	847	998	6,528 D	9.5%	72.7%	8.2%
21,933	WEBSTER	11,403	473	8,749	1,007	1,174	7,742 D	4.1%	76.7%	8.8%

LOUISIANA

SENATOR 1992
(PRIMARY ELECTION)

Registration	Parish	Total Vote	Republican	Democratic	Independent	Other	Plurality	Percentage Total Vote		
								Rep.	Dem.	Ind.
12,044	WEST BATON ROUGE	6,542	446	5,385	235	476	4,939 D	6.8%	82.3%	3.6%
6,854	WEST CARROLL	2,330	93	1,690	150	397	1,540 D	4.0%	72.5%	6.4%
5,663	WEST FELICIANA	2,104	207	1,644	63	190	1,437 D	9.8%	78.1%	3.0%
10,218	WINN	5,005	231	3,834	286	654	3,548 D	4.6%	76.6%	5.7%
2,247,296	TOTAL	843,037	69,986	616,021	74,785	82,245	541,236 D	8.3%	73.1%	8.9%

LOUISIANA

CONGRESS

CD	Year	Total Vote	Republican Vote	Republican Candidate	Democratic Vote	Democratic Candidate	Other Vote	Rep.-Dem. Plurality	Percentage Total Vote Rep.	Percentage Total Vote Dem.	Major Vote Rep.	Major Vote Dem.
1	1992			LIVINGSTON, BOB								
2	1992					JEFFERSON, WILLIAM J.						
3	1992					TAUZIN, W. J.						
4	1992	194,831			194,831	FIELDS/JONES		194,831 D		100.0%		100.0%
5	1992	243,580	153,501	MCCRERY, JIM	90,079	HUCKABY, JERRY		63,422 R	63.0%	37.0%	63.0%	37.0%
6	1992	245,178	245,178	BAKER/HOLLOWAY				245,178 R	100.0%		100.0%	
7	1992					HAYES, JAMES A.						

LOUISIANA

1991 GENERAL ELECTION

Governor   Election held November 16, 1991.

1992 GENERAL ELECTION

President   Other vote was 18,545 America First (Gritz); 3,155 Libertarian (Marrou); 1,663 Equal Justice & Opportunity (Daniels); 1,552 Taxpayers (Phillips); 1,434 More Perfect Democracy (Fulani); 1,136 Justice, Liberty, Agriculture (LaRouche); 889 Natural Law (Hagelin); 808 Independent (Yiamonyiannis).

Senator   Since the primary election decided the Senatorial race, the data carried in the table for Senator 1992 are for the primary contest between the candidates listed below. The vote by parish is presented in four columns (Republican (Stockstill), Democratic (Breaux), Independent Ned (Khachaturian) and Other (Accardo and Strong). The plurality figures are calculated on a first-second party basis.

Congress   See primary note section below. Since candidates who are unopposed in the primary or who receive a majority in the primary are elected unopposed, run-off elections were held in only three districts (CD's 4, 5 and 6). In CD 4 the run-off was between two Democratic candidates: Cleo Fields received 143,980 votes and Charles Jones received 50,851 giving Fields the election with 73.9% of the vote and a plurality of 93,129. In CD 6 the run-off was between two Republican candidates: Richard H. Baker received 123,953 votes and Clyde C. Holloway received 121,225 votes giving Baker the election with 50.6% of the vote and a plurality of 2,728.

PRIMARIES

Louisiana holds an open primary election with candidates from all parties running on the same ballot. Any candidate who receives a majority is elected. If no candidate receives 50 percent or more, a run-off election is held in November between the top two finishers, without regard to party affiliation.

OCTOBER 19, 1991 OPEN PRIMARY

Governor   523,195 Edwin W. Edwards (D); 491,342 David E. Duke (R); 410,690 Charles Roemer (R); 82,683 Clyde C. Holloway (R); 11,847 Sam Jones (D); 9,663 Ed Karst (Ind.); 7,385 Fred Dent (D); 4,118 Annie L. Thompson (R); 4,000 Jim Crowley (D); 2,053 Albert H. Powell (D); 1,372 Ronnie G. Johnson (Ind.); 1,006 Ken Lewis (D).

OCTOBER 3, 1992 OPEN PRIMARY

Senator   616,021 John B. Breaux (D); 74,785 John Khachturian (Ind.); 69,986 Lyle Stockstill (R); 45,839 Nick J. Accardo (D); 36,406 Fred C. Strong (R).

Congress   Contested as follows:

CD 1   83,685 Bob Livingston (R); 11,620 Annie L. Thompson (R); 7,874 Vincent J. Bruno (R); 4,789 Richie Martin (R); 4,442 Jules W. Hillery (Ind.); 2,641 Greg V. Reinhard (Ind.).

CD 2   67,030 William J. Jefferson (D); 14,121 Wilma K. Irvin (D); 10,090 Roger C. Johnson (Ind.).

CD 3   82,047 W. J. Tauzin (D); 18,402 Paul I. Boynton (R).

CD 4   62,697 Cleo Fields (D); 18,305 Charles Jones (D); 14,157 Joe Shyne (D); 11,264 Faye Williams (D); 10,275 Steve Myers (R); 8,982 Emile K. Ventre (R); 2,791 James Ross (D); 2,675 Ralph Hall (D).

CD 5   69,511 Jim McCrery (R); 46,386 Jerry Huckaby (D); 35,306 Robert Thompson (D); 3,369 L. D. Knox (Ind.); 2,971 Donal A. Milton (R).

CD 6   52,012 Clyde C. Holloway (R); 46,990 Richard H. Baker (R); 42,819 Ned Randolph (D).

CD 7   84,149 James A. Hayes (D); 23,870 Fredric Hayes (R); 7,184 Robert J. Nain (R).

MAINE

GOVERNOR
John R. McKernan (R). Re-elected 1990 to a four-year term. Previously elected 1986.

SENATORS
William S. Cohen (R). Re-elected 1990 to a six-year term. Previously elected 1984, 1978.

George J. Mitchell (D). Re-elected 1988 to a six-year term. Previously elected 1982. Appointed May 1980 to fill our the term vacated by the resignation of Senator Edmund S. Muskie to become Secretary of State.

REPRESENTATIVES
1. Thomas H. Andrews (D)   2. Olympia J. Snowe (R)

POSTWAR VOTE FOR PRESIDENT

| Year | Total Vote | Republican | | Democratic | | Other Vote | Plurality | Percentage | | | |
| | | Vote | Candidate | Vote | Candidate | | | Total Vote | | Major Vote | |
								Rep.	Dem.	Rep.	Dem.
1992 * *	679,499	206,504	Bush, George	263,420	Clinton, Bill	209,575	56,600 D	30.4%	38.8%	43.9%	56.1%
1988	555,035	307,131	Bush, George	243,569	Dukakis, Michael S.	4,335	63,562 R	55.3%	43.9%	55.8%	44.2%
1984	553,144	336,500	Reagan, Ronald	214,515	Mondale, Walter F.	2,129	121,985 R	60.8%	38.8%	61.1%	38.9%
1980	523,011	238,522	Reagan, Ronald	220,974	Carter, Jimmy	63,515	17,548 R	45.6%	42.3%	51.9%	48.1%
1976	483,216	236,320	Ford, Gerald R.	232,279	Carter, Jimmy	14,617	4,041 R	48.9%	48.1%	50.4%	49.6%
1972	417,042	256,458	Nixon, Richard M.	160,584	McGovern, George S.		95,874 R	61.5%	38.5%	61.5%	38.5%
1968	392,936	169,254	Nixon, Richard M.	217,312	Humphrey, Hubert H.	6,370	48,058 D	43.1%	55.3%	43.8%	56.2%
1964	380,965	118,701	Goldwater, Barry M.	262,264	Johnson, Lyndon B.		143,563 D	31.2%	68.8%	31.2%	68.8%
1960	421,767	240,608	Nixon, Richard M.	181,159	Kennedy, John F.		59,449 R	57.0%	43.0%	57.0%	43.0%
1956	351,706	249,238	Eisenhower, Dwight D.	102,468	Stevenson, Adlai E.		146,770 R	70.9%	29.1%	70.9%	29.1%
1952	351,786	232,353	Eisenhower, Dwight D.	118,806	Stevenson, Adlai E.	627	113,547 R	66.0%	33.8%	66.2%	33.8%
1948	264,787	150,234	Dewey, Thomas E.	111,916	Truman, Harry S.	2,637	38,318 R	56.7%	42.3%	57.3%	42.7%

In 1992 the other vote column includes 206,820 votes cast for Perot who came in second statewide.

MAINE

POSTWAR VOTE FOR GOVERNOR

Year	Total Vote	Republican		Democratic		Other Vote	Rep.-Dem. Plurality	Percentage			
								Total Vote		Major Vote	
		Vote	Candidate	Vote	Candidate			Rep.	Dem.	Rep.	Dem.
1990	522,492	243,766	McKernan, John R.	230,038	Brennan, Joseph E.	48,688	13,728 R	46.7%	44.0%	51.4%	48.6%
1986 **	426,861	170,312	McKernan, John R.	128,744	Tierney, James	127,805	41,568 R	39.9%	30.2%	56.9%	43.1%
1982	460,295	172,949	Cragin, Charles L.	281,066	Brennan, Joseph E.	6,280	108,117 D	37.6%	61.1%	38.1%	61.9%
1978	370,258	126,862	Palmer, Linwood E.	176,493	Brennan, Joseph E.	66,903	49,631 D	34.3%	47.7%	41.8%	58.2%
1974 **	363,945	84,176	Erwin, James S.	132,219	Mitchell, George J.	147,550	48,043 D	23.1%	36.3%	38.9%	61.1%
1970	325,386	162,248	Erwin, James S.	163,138	Curtis, Kenneth M.		890 D	49.9%	50.1%	49.9%	50.1%
1966	323,838	151,802	Reed, John H.	172,036	Curtis, Kenneth M.		20,234 D	46.9%	53.1%	46.9%	53.1%
1962	292,725	146,604	Reed, John H.	146,121	Dolloff, Maynard C.		483 R	50.1%	49.9%	50.1%	49.9%
1960 S	417,315	219,768	Reed, John H.	197,547	Coffin, Frank M.		22,221 R	52.7%	47.3%	52.7%	47.3%
1958 **	280,295	134,572	Hildreth, Horace A.	145,723	Clauson, Clinton A.		11,151 D	48.0%	52.0%	48.0%	52.0%
1956	304,649	124,395	Trafton, Willis A.	180,254	Muskie, Edmund S.		55,859 D	40.8%	59.2%	40.8%	59.2%
1954	248,971	113,298	Cross, Burton M.	135,673	Muskie, Edmund S.		22,375 D	45.5%	54.5%	45.5%	54.5%
1952	248,441	128,532	Cross, Burton M.	82,538	Oliver, James C.	37,371	45,994 R	51.7%	33.2%	60.9%	39.1%
1950	241,177	145,823	Payne, Frederick G.	94,304	Grant, Earl S.	1,050	51,519 R	60.5%	39.1%	60.7%	39.3%
1948	222,500	145,956	Payne, Frederick G.	76,544	Lausier, Louis B.		69,412 R	65.6%	34.4%	65.6%	34.4%
1946	179,951	110,327	Hildreth, Horace A.	69,624	Clark, F. Davis		40,703 R	61.3%	38.7%	61.3%	38.7%

The term of office of Maine's Governor was increased from two to four years effective with the 1958 election. The 1960 election was for a short term to fill a vacancy. In 1974 James B. Longley, an Independent candidate, polled 142,464 votes (39.1% of the total vote) and won the election with a 10,245 plurality. In 1986 other vote was 64,317 Sherry F. Huber (Independent); 63,474 John E. Menario (Independent) and 14 scattered.

POSTWAR VOTE FOR SENATOR

Year	Total Vote	Republican		Democratic		Other Vote	Rep.-Dem. Plurality	Percentage			
								Total Vote		Major Vote	
		Vote	Candidate	Vote	Candidate			Rep.	Dem.	Rep.	Dem.
1990	520,320	319,167	Cohen, William S.	201,053	Rolde, Neil	100	118,114 R	61.3%	38.6%	61.4%	38.6%
1988	557,375	104,758	Wyman, Jasper S.	452,590	Mitchell, George J.	27	347,832 D	18.8%	81.2%	18.8%	81.2%
1984	551,406	404,414	Cohen, William S.	142,626	Mitchell, Elizabeth H.	4,366	261,788 R	73.3%	25.9%	73.9%	26.1%
1982	459,715	179,882	Emery, David F.	279,819	Mitchell, George J.	14	99,937 D	39.1%	60.9%	39.1%	60.9%
1978	375,172	212,294	Cohen, William S.	127,327	Hathaway, William D.	35,551	84,967 R	56.6%	33.9%	62.5%	37.5%
1976	486,254	193,489	Monks, Robert A. G.	292,704	Muskie, Edmund S.	61	99,215 D	39.8%	60.2%	39.8%	60.2%
1972	421,310	197,040	Smith, Margaret Chase	224,270	Hathaway, William D.		27,230 D	46.8%	53.2%	46.8%	53.2%
1970	323,860	123,906	Bishop, Neil S.	199,954	Muskie, Edmund S.		76,048 D	38.3%	61.7%	38.3%	61.7%
1966	319,535	188,291	Smith, Margaret Chase	131,136	Violette, Elmer H.	108	57,155 R	58.9%	41.0%	58.9%	41.1%
1964	380,551	127,040	McIntire, Clifford	253,511	Muskie, Edmund S.		126,471 D	33.4%	66.6%	33.4%	66.6%
1960	416,699	256,890	Smith, Margaret Chase	159,809	Cormier, Lucia M.		97,081 R	61.6%	38.4%	61.6%	38.4%
1958	284,226	111,522	Payne, Frederick G.	172,704	Muskie, Edmund S.		61,182 D	39.2%	60.8%	39.2%	60.8%
1954	246,605	144,530	Smith, Margaret Chase	102,075	Fullam, Paul A.		42,455 R	58.6%	41.4%	58.6%	41.4%
1952	237,164	139,205	Payne, Frederick G.	82,665	Dube, Roger P.	15,294	56,540 R	58.7%	34.9%	62.7%	37.3%
1948	223,256	159,182	Smith, Margaret Chase	64,074	Scolten, Adrian H.		95,108 R	71.3%	28.7%	71.3%	28.7%
1946	175,014	111,215	Brewster, Owen	63,799	MacDonald, Peter		47,416 R	63.5%	36.5%	63.5%	36.5%

MAINE

Districts Established March 28, 1983

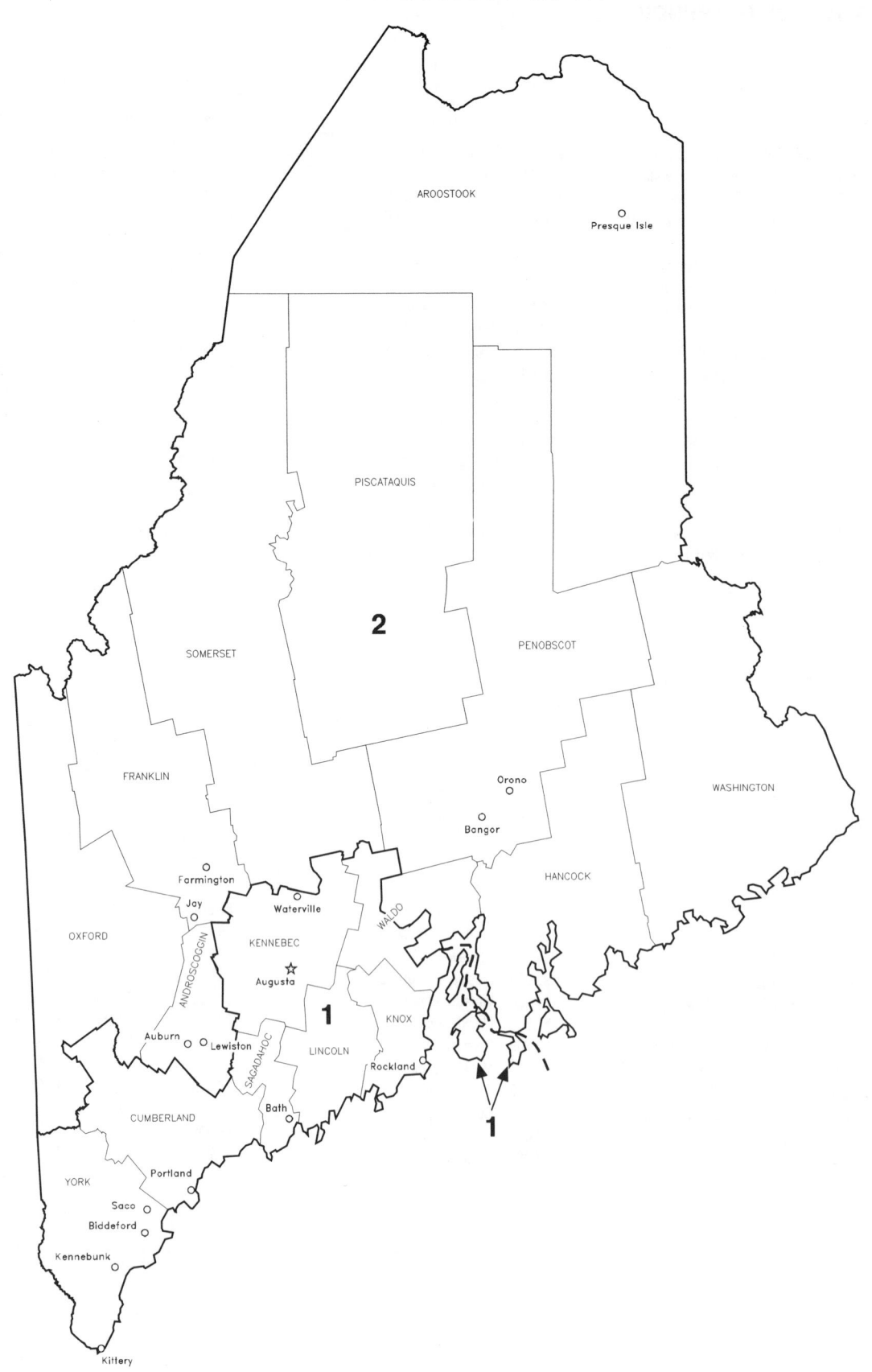

MAINE

PRESIDENT 1992

Registration	County	Total Vote	Republican	Democratic	Perot	Other	Plurality		Percentage Total Vote		
									Rep.	Dem.	Perot
79,816	ANDROSCOGGIN	55,144	14,174	22,247	18,518	205	3,729	D	25.7%	40.3%	33.6%
59,169	AROOSTOOK	38,585	12,409	15,682	10,376	118	3,273	D	32.2%	40.6%	26.9%
205,903	CUMBERLAND	141,522	45,752	60,781	34,443	546	15,029	D	32.3%	42.9%	24.3%
24,503	FRANKLIN	16,523	4,608	6,739	5,115	61	1,624	D	27.9%	40.8%	31.0%
40,498	HANCOCK	28,805	8,657	10,126	9,865	157	261	D	30.1%	35.2%	34.2%
90,687	KENNEBEC	63,921	17,135	25,125	21,436	225	3,689	D	26.8%	39.3%	33.5%
30,564	KNOX	20,338	6,310	7,631	6,303	94	1,321	D	31.0%	37.5%	31.0%
26,144	LINCOLN	19,036	6,405	6,714	5,808	109	309	D	33.6%	35.3%	30.5%
41,741	OXFORD	29,356	8,194	11,202	9,815	145	1,387	D	27.9%	38.2%	33.4%
111,175	PENOBSCOT	80,444	24,218	29,485	26,437	304	3,048	D	30.1%	36.7%	32.9%
13,962	PISCATAQUIS	10,031	2,970	3,323	3,688	50	365	P	29.6%	33.1%	36.8%
25,159	SAGADAHOC	18,513	5,917	6,828	5,705	63	911	D	32.0%	36.9%	30.8%
38,797	SOMERSET	26,424	6,780	9,274	10,293	77	1,019	P	25.7%	35.1%	39.0%
27,066	WALDO	18,529	5,241	6,472	6,702	114	230	P	28.3%	34.9%	36.2%
26,190	WASHINGTON	17,765	5,493	6,284	5,894	94	390	D	30.9%	35.4%	33.2%
133,231	YORK	94,563	32,241	35,507	26,422	393	3,266	D	34.1%	37.5%	27.9%
974,605	TOTAL	679,499	206,504	263,420	206,820	2,755	56,600	D	30.4%	38.8%	30.4%

MAINE

PRESIDENT 1992

Registration	City/Town	Total Vote	Republican	Democratic	Perot	Other	Plurality	Percentage Total Vote		
								Rep.	Dem.	Perot
16,610	AUBURN	12,693	3,653	5,025	3,964	51	1,061 D	28.8%	39.6%	31.2%
15,190	AUGUSTA	10,702	3,003	4,657	3,002	40	1,654 D	28.1%	43.5%	28.1%
22,066	BANGOR	16,771	5,185	6,826	4,689	71	1,641 D	30.9%	40.7%	28.0%
7,095	BATH	5,093	1,630	1,988	1,458	17	358 D	32.0%	39.0%	28.6%
5,113	BELFAST	3,214	993	1,180	1,024	17	156 D	30.9%	36.7%	31.9%
3,598	BERWICK	2,746	1,006	865	861	14	141 R	36.6%	31.5%	31.4%
16,092	BIDDEFORD	10,225	2,533	4,945	2,717	30	2,228 D	24.8%	48.4%	26.6%
6,905	BREWER	5,349	1,907	1,788	1,625	29	119 R	35.7%	33.4%	30.4%
14,272	BRUNSWICK	10,060	3,058	4,686	2,282	34	1,628 D	30.4%	46.6%	22.7%
5,509	BUXTON	4,028	1,253	1,401	1,356	18	45 D	31.1%	34.8%	33.7%
4,367	CAMDEN	3,239	883	1,549	798	9	666 D	27.3%	47.8%	24.6%
7,518	CAPE ELIZABETH	5,885	2,418	2,368	1,082	17	50 R	41.1%	40.2%	18.4%
7,847	CARIBOU	4,025	1,256	1,577	1,185	7	321 D	31.2%	39.2%	29.4%
5,229	CUMBERLAND TOWN	4,140	1,763	1,473	884	20	290 R	42.6%	35.6%	21.4%
4,612	ELIOT	3,273	1,335	1,115	816	7	220 R	40.8%	34.1%	24.9%
5,217	ELLSWORTH	3,526	1,303	1,050	1,159	14	144 R	37.0%	29.8%	32.9%
6,091	FAIRFIELD	3,578	738	1,260	1,573	7	313 P	20.6%	35.2%	44.0%
7,055	FALMOUTH	5,321	2,240	2,002	1,066	13	238 R	42.1%	37.6%	20.0%
6,752	FARMINGTON	3,707	1,126	1,492	1,073	16	366 D	30.4%	40.2%	28.9%
5,776	FREEPORT	4,291	1,359	1,753	1,154	25	394 D	31.7%	40.9%	26.9%
5,050	GARDINER	3,572	1,054	1,391	1,115	12	276 D	29.5%	38.9%	31.2%
9,325	GORHAM	6,972	2,422	2,516	2,015	19	94 D	34.7%	36.1%	28.9%
4,730	GRAY	3,549	1,248	1,207	1,082	12	41 R	35.2%	34.0%	30.5%
5,421	HAMPDEN	3,782	1,282	1,206	1,282	12		33.9%	31.9%	33.9%
4,224	HARPSWELL	3,360	1,098	1,296	953	13	198 D	32.7%	38.6%	28.4%
4,029	HOULTON	3,006	1,403	849	746	8	554 R	46.7%	28.2%	24.8%
4,125	JAY	2,917	550	1,644	716	7	928 D	18.9%	56.4%	24.5%
8,192	KENNEBUNK	5,478	2,575	1,797	1,084	22	778 R	47.0%	32.8%	19.8%
6,769	KITTERY	5,070	1,794	2,100	1,143	33	306 D	35.4%	41.4%	22.5%
31,747	LEWISTON	19,886	4,372	9,265	6,180	69	3,085 D	22.0%	46.6%	31.1%
1,855	LIMESTONE	1,129	342	445	336	6	103 D	30.3%	39.4%	29.8%
4,095	LINCOLN TOWN	2,827	975	903	932	17	43 R	34.5%	31.9%	33.0%
7,196	LISBON	4,880	1,381	1,629	1,853	17	224 P	28.3%	33.4%	38.0%
5,309	MILLINOCKET	3,874	889	1,568	1,412	5	156 D	22.9%	40.5%	36.4%
5,013	OAKLAND	2,933	803	1,064	1,058	8	6 D	27.4%	36.3%	36.1%
7,811	OLD ORCHARD BEACH	5,047	1,503	2,162	1,365	17	659 D	29.8%	42.8%	27.0%
6,519	OLD TOWN	4,766	1,173	2,272	1,302	19	970 D	24.6%	47.7%	27.3%
8,842	ORONO	5,671	1,336	2,813	1,502	20	1,311 D	23.6%	49.6%	26.5%
59,111	PORTLAND	35,274	8,660	19,510	6,910	194	10,850 D	24.6%	55.3%	19.6%
8,732	PRESQUE ISLE	4,783	1,709	1,750	1,318	6	41 D	35.7%	36.6%	27.6%
6,539	ROCKLAND	3,355	1,081	1,192	1,059	23	111 D	32.2%	35.5%	31.6%
5,473	RUMFORD	3,947	736	1,896	1,301	14	595 D	18.6%	48.0%	33.0%
12,479	SACO	9,095	2,769	4,000	2,303	23	1,231 D	30.4%	44.0%	25.3%
12,848	SANFORD	10,149	3,030	3,854	3,215	50	639 D	29.9%	38.0%	31.7%
11,785	SCARBOROUGH	8,228	3,235	2,941	2,033	19	294 R	39.3%	35.7%	24.7%
7,000	SKOWHEGAN	4,260	1,078	1,717	1,458	7	259 D	25.3%	40.3%	34.2%
4,890	SOUTH BERWICK	3,148	1,211	1,058	866	13	153 R	38.5%	33.6%	27.5%
17,791	SOUTH PORTLAND	12,712	3,999	5,933	2,734	46	1,934 D	31.5%	46.7%	21.5%
5,773	STANDISH	4,181	1,416	1,440	1,307	18	24 D	33.9%	34.4%	31.3%
5,980	TOPSHAM	4,485	1,473	1,645	1,358	9	172 D	32.8%	36.7%	30.3%
10,355	WATERVILLE	7,977	1,832	3,868	2,257	20	1,611 D	23.0%	48.5%	28.3%
6,012	WELLS	4,783	1,884	1,549	1,336	14	335 R	39.4%	32.4%	27.9%
12,764	WESTBROOK	9,109	2,904	3,665	2,512	28	761 D	31.9%	40.2%	27.6%
9,884	WINDHAM	7,315	2,603	2,444	2,250	18	159 R	35.6%	33.4%	30.8%
7,570	WINSLOW	4,450	1,019	1,724	1,696	11	28 D	22.9%	38.7%	38.1%
5,289	WINTHROP	3,620	1,096	1,341	1,159	24	182 D	30.3%	37.0%	32.0%
7,661	YARMOUTH	5,321	2,027	2,078	1,191	25	51 D	38.1%	39.1%	22.4%
9,719	YORK TOWN	6,859	2,740	2,445	1,648	26	295 R	39.9%	35.6%	24.0%

MAINE

CONGRESS

CD	Year	Total Vote	Republican		Democratic		Other Vote	Rep.-Dem. Plurality	Percentage			
			Vote	Candidate	Vote	Candidate			Total Vote		Major Vote	
									Rep.	Dem.	Rep.	Dem.
1	1992	358,148	125,236	BEAN, LINDA	232,696	ANDREWS, THOMAS H.	216	107,460 D	35.0%	65.0%	35.0%	65.0%
1	1990	278,872	110,836	EMERY, DAVID F.	167,623	ANDREWS, THOMAS H.	413	56,787 D	39.7%	60.1%	39.8%	60.2%
1	1988	302,163	111,125	O'MEARA, EDWARD S.	190,989	BRENNAN, JOSEPH E.	49	79,864 D	36.8%	63.2%	36.8%	63.2%
1	1986	229,233	100,260	IVES, H. ROLLIN	121,848	BRENNAN, JOSEPH E.	7,125	21,588 D	43.7%	53.2%	45.1%	54.9%
1	1984	287,765	182,785	MCKERNAN, JOHN R.	104,972	HOBBINS, BARRY J.	8	77,813 R	63.5%	36.5%	63.5%	36.5%
2	1992	311,433	153,022	SNOWE, OLYMPIA J.	130,824	MCGOWAN, PATRICK K.	27,587	22,198 R	49.1%	42.0%	53.9%	46.1%
2	1990	238,522	121,704	SNOWE, OLYMPIA J.	116,798	MCGOWAN, PATRICK K.	20	4,906 R	51.0%	49.0%	51.0%	49.0%
2	1988	252,721	167,226	SNOWE, OLYMPIA J.	85,346	HAYES, KENNETH P.	149	81,880 R	66.2%	33.8%	66.2%	33.8%
2	1986	192,397	148,770	SNOWE, OLYMPIA J.	43,614	CHARETTE, RICHARD R.	13	105,156 R	77.3%	22.7%	77.3%	22.7%
2	1984	253,773	192,166	SNOWE, OLYMPIA J.	57,347	BULL, CHIPMAN C.	4,260	134,819 R	75.7%	22.6%	77.0%	23.0%

MAINE

1992 GENERAL ELECTION

In addition to the county-by-county figures, data are presented for selected Maine communities. Since not all jurisdictions of the state are listed in this special tabulation, state-wide totals are shown only with the county-by-county statistics.

President   Other vote was 1,681 Libertarian (Marrou); 519 New Alliance (Fulani); 464 Taxpayers (Phillips); 91 scattered write-in.

Congress   Maine did not redistrict prior to the 1992 elections. Other vote was scattered write-in in CD 1; 27,526 Green (Carter) and 61 scattered write-in in CD 2.

1992 PRIMARIES

JUNE 9 REPUBLICAN

Congress   Unopposed in CD 2. Contested as follows:

CD   1   21,806 Linda Bean; 15,673 Anthony M. Payne; 9,820 John E. Purcell; 26 scattered write-in.

JUNE 9 DEMOCRATIC

Congress   Unopposed in both CD's.

MARYLAND

GOVERNOR
William D. Schaefer (D). Re-elected 1990 to a four-year term. Previously elected 1986.

SENATORS
Barbara A. Mikulski (D). Re-elected 1992 to a six-year term. Previously elected 1986.

Paul S. Sarbanes (D). Re-elected 1988 to a six-year term. Previously elected 1982, 1976.

REPRESENTATIVES
1. Wayne T. Gilchrest (R)
2. Helen D. Bentley (R)
3. Benjamin L. Cardin (D)
4. Albert R. Wynn (D)
5. Steny H. Hoyer (D)
6. Roscoe Bartlett (R)
7. Kweisi Mfume (D)
8. Constance A. Morella (R)

POSTWAR VOTE FOR PRESIDENT

Year	Total Vote	Republican Vote	Candidate	Democratic Vote	Candidate	Other Vote	Plurality	Total Vote Rep.	Dem.	Major Vote Rep.	Dem.
1992 **	1,985,046	707,094	Bush, George	988,571	Clinton, Bill	289,381	281,477 D	35.6%	49.8%	41.7%	58.3%
1988	1,714,358	876,167	Bush, George	826,304	Dukakis, Michael S.	11,887	49,863 R	51.1%	48.2%	51.5%	48.5%
1984	1,675,873	879,918	Reagan, Ronald	787,935	Mondale, Walter F.	8,020	91,983 R	52.5%	47.0%	52.8%	47.2%
1980	1,540,496	680,606	Reagan, Ronald	726,161	Carter, Jimmy	133,729	45,555 D	44.2%	47.1%	48.4%	51.6%
1976	1,439,897	672,661	Ford, Gerald R.	759,612	Carter, Jimmy	7,624	86,951 D	46.7%	52.8%	47.0%	53.0%
1972	1,353,812	829,305	Nixon, Richard M.	505,781	McGovern, George S.	18,726	323,524 R	61.3%	37.4%	62.1%	37.9%
1968	1,235,039	517,995	Nixon, Richard M.	538,310	Humphrey, Hubert H.	178,734	20,315 D	41.9%	43.6%	49.0%	51.0%
1964	1,116,457	385,495	Goldwater, Barry M.	730,912	Johnson, Lyndon B.	50	345,417 D	34.5%	65.5%	34.5%	65.5%
1960	1,055,349	489,538	Nixon, Richard M.	565,808	Kennedy, John F.	3	76,270 D	46.4%	53.6%	46.4%	53.6%
1956	932,827	559,738	Eisenhower, Dwight D.	372,613	Stevenson, Adlai E.	476	187,125 R	60.0%	39.9%	60.0%	40.0%
1952	902,074	499,424	Eisenhower, Dwight D.	395,337	Stevenson, Adlai E.	7,313	104,087 R	55.4%	43.8%	55.8%	44.2%
1948	596,748	294,814	Dewey, Thomas E.	286,521	Truman, Harry S.	15,413	8,293 R	49.4%	48.0%	50.7%	49.3%

In 1992 the other vote column includes 281,414 votes cast for Perot.

POSTWAR VOTE FOR GOVERNOR

Year	Total Vote	Republican Vote	Candidate	Democratic Vote	Candidate	Other Vote	Rep.-Dem. Plurality	Total Vote Rep.	Dem.	Major Vote Rep.	Dem.
1990	1,111,088	446,980	Shepard, William S.	664,015	Schaefer, William D.	93	217,035 D	40.2%	59.8%	40.2%	59.8%
1986	1,101,476	194,185	Mooney, Thomas J.	907,291	Schaefer, William D.		713,106 D	17.6%	82.4%	17.6%	82.4%
1982	1,139,149	432,826	Pascal, Robert A.	705,910	Hughes, Harry	413	273,084 D	38.0%	62.0%	38.0%	62.0%
1978	1,011,963	293,635	Beall, J. Glenn, Jr.	718,328	Hughes, Harry		424,693 D	29.0%	71.0%	29.0%	71.0%
1974	949,097	346,449	Gore, Louise	602,648	Mandel, Marvin		256,199 D	36.5%	63.5%	36.5%	63.5%
1970	973,099	314,336	Blain, C. Stanley	639,579	Mandel, Marvin	19,184	325,243 D	32.3%	65.7%	33.0%	67.0%
1966	918,761	455,318	Agnew, Spiro T.	373,543	Mahoney, George P.	89,900	81,775 R	49.6%	40.7%	54.9%	45.1%
1962	775,101	343,051	Small, Frank	432,045	Tawes, J. Millard	5	88,994 D	44.3%	55.7%	44.3%	55.7%
1958	763,234	278,173	Devereux, James	485,061	Tawes, J. Millard		206,888 D	36.4%	63.6%	36.4%	63.6%
1954	700,484	381,451	McKeldin, Theodore	319,033	Byrd, Harry C.		62,418 R	54.5%	45.5%	54.5%	45.5%
1950	645,631	369,807	McKeldin, Theodore	275,824	Lane, William P.		93,983 R	57.3%	42.7%	57.3%	42.7%
1946	489,836	221,752	McKeldin, Theodore	268,084	Lane, William P.		46,332 D	45.3%	54.7%	45.3%	54.7%

MARYLAND

POSTWAR VOTE FOR SENATOR

Year	Total Vote	Republican		Democratic		Other Vote	Rep.-Dem. Plurality	Percentage			
		Vote	Candidate	Vote	Candidate			Total Vote		Major Vote	
								Rep.	Dem.	Rep.	Dem.
1992	1,841,735	533,688	Keyes, Alan L.	1,307,610	Mikulski, Barbara A.	437	773,922 D	29.0%	71.0%	29.0%	71.0%
1988	1,617,065	617,537	Keyes, Alan L.	999,166	Sarbanes, Paul S.	362	381,629 D	38.2%	61.8%	38.2%	61.8%
1986	1,112,637	437,411	Chavez, Linda	675,225	Mikulski, Barbara A.	1	237,814 D	39.3%	60.7%	39.3%	60.7%
1982	1,114,690	407,334	Hogan, Lawrence J.	707,356	Sarbanes, Paul S.		300,022 D	36.5%	63.5%	36.5%	63.5%
1980	1,286,088	850,970	Mathias, Charles	435,118	Conroy, Edward T.		415,852 R	66.2%	33.8%	66.2%	33.8%
1976	1,365,568	530,439	Beall, J. Glenn, Jr.	772,101	Sarbanes, Paul S.	63,028	241,662 D	38.8%	56.5%	40.7%	59.3%
1974	877,786	503,223	Mathias, Charles	374,563	Mikulski, Barbara A.		128,660 R	57.3%	42.7%	57.3%	42.7%
1970	956,370	484,960	Beall, J. Glenn, Jr.	460,422	Tydings, Joseph D.	10,988	24,538 R	50.7%	48.1%	51.3%	48.7%
1968	1,133,727	541,893	Mathias, Charles	443,367	Brewster, Daniel B.	148,467	98,526 R	47.8%	39.1%	55.0%	45.0%
1964	1,081,049	402,393	Beall, J. Glenn	678,649	Tydings, Joseph D.	7	276,256 D	37.2%	62.8%	37.2%	62.8%
1962	714,248	270,312	Miller, Edward T.	443,935	Brewster, Daniel B.	1	173,623 D	37.8%	62.2%	37.8%	62.2%
1958	749,291	382,021	Beall, J. Glenn	367,270	D'Alesandro, Thomas		14,751 R	51.0%	49.0%	51.0%	49.0%
1956	892,167	473,059	Butler, John Marshall	419,108	Mahoney, George P.		53,951 R	53.0%	47.0%	53.0%	47.0%
1952	856,193	449,823	Beall, J. Glenn	406,370	Mahoney, George P.		43,453 R	52.5%	47.5%	52.5%	47.5%
1950	615,614	326,291	Butler, John Marshall	283,180	Tydings, Millard E.	6,143	43,111 R	53.0%	46.0%	53.5%	46.5%
1946	472,232	235,000	Markey, David John	237,232	O'Conor, Herbert R.		2,232 D	49.8%	50.2%	49.8%	50.2%

MARYLAND

Districts Established October 23, 1991

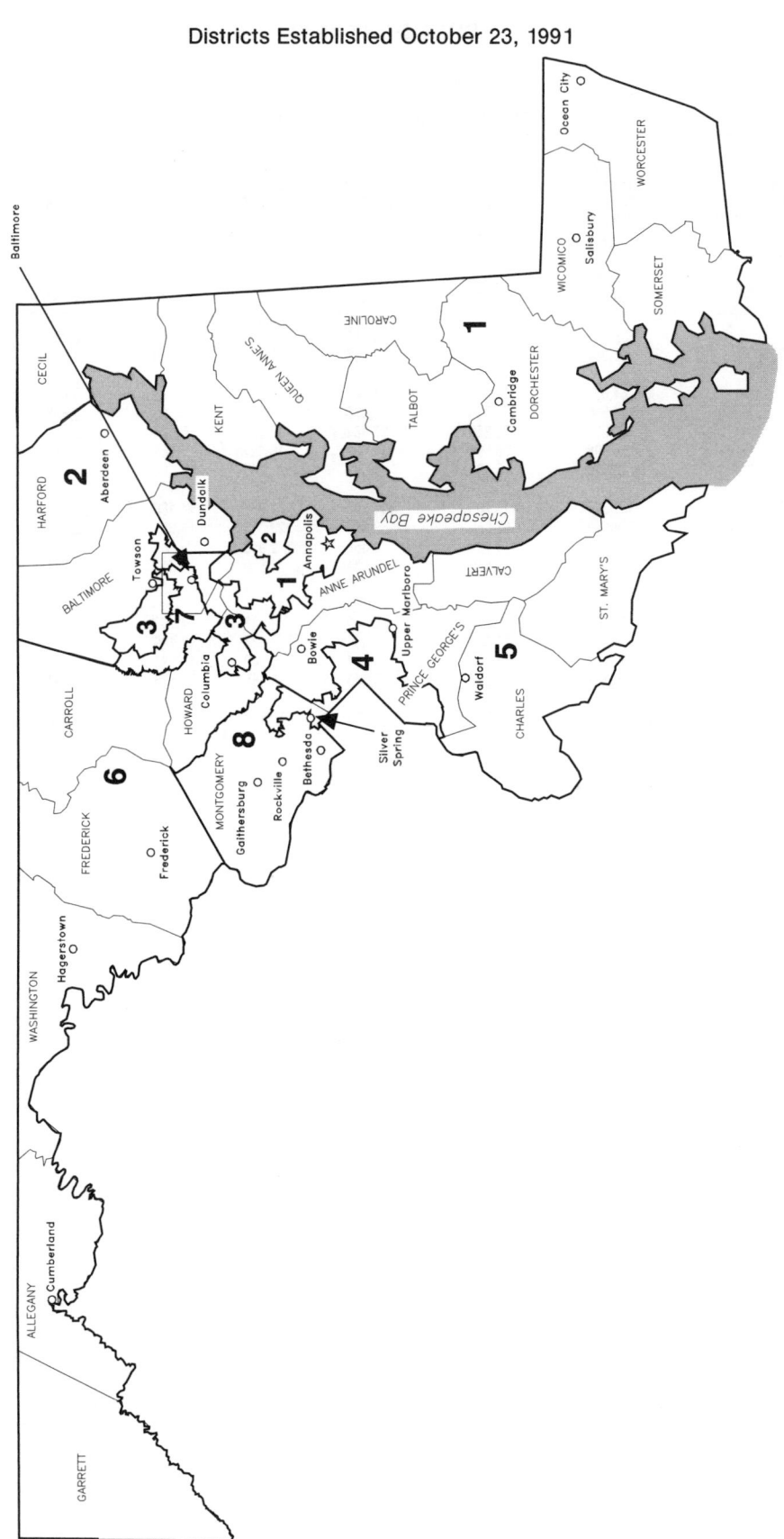

MARYLAND

PRESIDENT 1992

Registration	County	Total Vote	Republican	Democratic	Perot	Other	Plurality	Percentage Total Vote		
								Rep.	Dem.	Perot
38,870	ALLEGANY	30,595	13,862	11,501	5,081	151	2,361 R	45.3%	37.6%	16.6%
214,050	ANNE ARUNDEL	185,634	81,467	68,629	35,191	347	12,838 R	43.9%	37.0%	19.0%
360,405	BALTIMORE CITY	245,091	40,725	185,753	17,381	1,232	145,028 D	16.6%	75.8%	7.1%
401,278	BALTIMORE COUNTY	323,220	126,728	143,498	51,757	1,237	16,770 D	39.2%	44.4%	16.0%
28,562	CALVERT	23,249	10,026	8,619	4,499	105	1,407 R	43.1%	37.1%	19.4%
10,642	CAROLINE	8,459	3,856	2,822	1,729	52	1,034 R	45.6%	33.4%	20.4%
65,337	CARROLL	54,930	28,405	15,447	10,965	113	12,958 R	51.7%	28.1%	20.0%
33,819	CECIL	27,319	10,784	10,232	6,115	188	552 R	39.5%	37.5%	22.4%
49,058	CHARLES	38,454	17,293	14,498	6,501	162	2,795 R	45.0%	37.7%	16.9%
14,032	DORCHESTER	10,957	4,934	3,933	2,010	80	1,001 R	45.0%	35.9%	18.3%
77,498	FREDERICK	64,691	31,290	21,848	11,373	180	9,442 R	48.4%	33.8%	17.6%
12,918	GARRETT	10,580	5,714	2,856	1,987	23	2,858 R	54.0%	27.0%	18.8%
96,392	HARFORD	80,687	36,350	27,164	17,002	171	9,186 R	45.1%	33.7%	21.1%
113,764	HOWARD	99,798	38,594	44,763	16,182	259	6,169 D	38.7%	44.9%	16.2%
9,357	KENT	7,628	3,094	3,093	1,411	30	1 R	40.6%	40.5%	18.5%
428,740	MONTGOMERY	362,613	119,705	199,757	41,971	1,180	80,052 D	33.0%	55.1%	11.6%
318,524	PRINCE GEORGES	256,859	62,955	168,691	23,355	1,858	105,736 D	24.5%	65.7%	9.1%
17,180	QUEEN ANNES	14,514	6,829	4,668	2,958	59	2,161 R	47.1%	32.2%	20.4%
31,782	ST. MARYS	25,085	11,485	8,931	4,550	119	2,554 R	45.8%	35.6%	18.1%
10,034	SOMERSET	7,936	3,450	3,210	1,230	46	240 R	43.5%	40.4%	15.5%
16,723	TALBOT	13,708	6,774	4,642	2,233	59	2,132 R	49.4%	33.9%	16.3%
54,947	WASHINGTON	46,208	21,977	16,495	7,537	199	5,482 R	47.6%	35.7%	16.3%
37,617	WICOMICO	30,272	13,560	11,481	5,140	91	2,079 R	44.8%	37.9%	17.0%
21,481	WORCESTER	16,559	7,237	6,040	3,256	26	1,197 R	43.7%	36.5%	19.7%
2,463,010	TOTAL	1,985,046	707,094	988,571	281,414	7,967	281,477 D	35.6%	49.8%	14.2%

MARYLAND

SENATOR 1992

Registration	County	Total Vote	Republican	Democratic	Other	Rep.-Dem. Plurality	Percentage			
							Total Vote		Major Vote	
							Rep.	Dem.	Rep.	Dem.
38,870	ALLEGANY	26,072	9,199	16,872	1	7,673 D	35.3%	64.7%	35.3%	64.7%
214,050	ANNE ARUNDEL	180,997	59,512	121,290	195	61,778 D	32.9%	67.0%	32.9%	67.1%
360,405	BALTIMORE CITY	225,943	29,834	196,086	23	166,252 D	13.2%	86.8%	13.2%	86.8%
401,278	BALTIMORE COUNTY	293,539	85,374	208,164	1	122,790 D	29.1%	70.9%	29.1%	70.9%
28,562	CALVERT	19,761	7,781	11,980		4,199 D	39.4%	60.6%	39.4%	60.6%
10,642	CAROLINE	7,154	2,531	4,622	1	2,091 D	35.4%	64.6%	35.4%	64.6%
65,337	CARROLL	53,799	23,293	30,495	11	7,202 D	43.3%	56.7%	43.3%	56.7%
33,819	CECIL	23,120	8,374	14,744	2	6,370 D	36.2%	63.8%	36.2%	63.8%
49,058	CHARLES	32,494	12,439	20,053	2	7,614 D	38.3%	61.7%	38.3%	61.7%
14,032	DORCHESTER	9,111	2,765	6,346		3,581 D	30.3%	69.7%	30.3%	69.7%
77,498	FREDERICK	62,854	26,055	36,788	11	10,733 D	41.5%	58.5%	41.5%	58.5%
12,918	GARRETT	8,501	5,028	3,473		1,555 R	59.1%	40.9%	59.1%	40.9%
96,392	HARFORD	79,066	27,966	51,096	4	23,130 D	35.4%	64.6%	35.4%	64.6%
113,764	HOWARD	97,354	31,664	65,681	9	34,017 D	32.5%	67.5%	32.5%	67.5%
9,357	KENT	6,282	1,732	4,550		2,818 D	27.6%	72.4%	27.6%	72.4%
428,740	MONTGOMERY	353,628	105,997	247,505	126	141,508 D	30.0%	70.0%	30.0%	70.0%
318,524	PRINCE GEORGES	228,249	48,093	180,129	27	132,036 D	21.1%	78.9%	21.1%	78.9%
17,180	QUEEN ANNES	12,493	4,414	8,079		3,665 D	35.3%	64.7%	35.3%	64.7%
31,782	ST. MARYS	21,493	7,541	13,943	9	6,402 D	35.1%	64.9%	35.1%	64.9%
10,034	SOMERSET	6,535	1,970	4,565		2,595 D	30.1%	69.9%	30.1%	69.9%
16,723	TALBOT	11,407	3,966	7,437	4	3,471 D	34.8%	65.2%	34.8%	65.2%
54,947	WASHINGTON	39,750	15,240	24,499	11	9,259 D	38.3%	61.6%	38.4%	61.6%
37,617	WICOMICO	26,364	8,651	17,713		9,062 D	32.8%	67.2%	32.8%	67.2%
21,481	WORCESTER	15,769	4,269	11,500		7,231 D	27.1%	72.9%	27.1%	72.9%
2,463,010	TOTAL	1,841,735	533,688	1,307,610	437	773,922 D	29.0%	71.0%	29.0%	71.0%

MARYLAND

CONGRESS

CD	Year	Total Vote	Republican		Democratic		Other Vote	Rep.-Dem. Plurality	Percentage			
			Vote	Candidate	Vote	Candidate			Total Vote		Major Vote	
									Rep.	Dem.	Rep.	Dem.
1	1992	234,203	120,084	GILCHREST, WAYNE T.	112,771	MCMILLEN, THOMAS	1,348	7,313 R	51.3%	48.2%	51.6%	48.4%
2	1992	254,106	165,443	BENTLEY, HELEN D.	88,658	HICKEY, MICHAEL C.	5	76,785 R	65.1%	34.9%	65.1%	34.9%
3	1992	222,255	58,869	BRICKER, WILLIAM T. S.	163,354	CARDIN, BENJAMIN L.	32	104,485 D	26.5%	73.5%	26.5%	73.5%
4	1992	182,185	45,166	DYSON, MICHELE	136,902	WYNN, ALBERT R.	117	91,736 D	24.8%	75.1%	24.8%	75.2%
5	1992	223,326	97,982	HOGAN, LAWRENCE J., JR.	118,312	HOYER, STENY H.	7,032	20,330 D	43.9%	53.0%	45.3%	54.7%
6	1992	231,959	125,564	BARTLETT, ROSCOE	106,224	HATTERY, THOMAS H.	171	19,340 R	54.1%	45.8%	54.2%	45.8%
7	1992	178,998	26,304	KONDNER, KENNETH	152,689	MFUME, KWEISI	5	126,385 D	14.7%	85.3%	14.7%	85.3%
8	1992	280,475	203,377	MORELLA, CONSTANCE A.	77,042	HEFFERNAN, EDWARD J.	56	126,335 R	72.5%	27.5%	72.5%	27.5%

MARYLAND

1992 GENERAL ELECTION

President   Other vote was 4,715 Libertarian (Marrou); 2,786 New Alliance (Fulani); 191 Hagelin (write-in); 167 Daniels (write-in); 41 Gritz (write-in); 25 Warren (write-in); 22 Phillips (write-in); 18 LaRouche (write-in); 2 scattered write-in.

Senator   Other vote was write-in as follows: 196 Estrada-Palma, 84 Gaige, 72 Zarwell, 63 Clapp, 20 Bowman, 2 Thompson.

Congress   Other vote was 1,320 Gies (write-in), 24 Beauregard (write-in) and 4 Stephens (write-in) in CD 1; Godfrey (write-in) in CD 2; 29 Fitzgerald (write-in) and 3 Eric Ashelman (write-in) in CD 3; 68 Turner (write-in), 47 Haney (write-in) and 2 Kramer (write-in) in CD 4; 6,990 Independent (Johnston), 40 McLaughlin (write-in) and 2 Lisa Ashelman (write-in) in CD 5; 102 Miller (write-in), 60 Dougherty (write-in) and 9 Condon (write-in) in CD 6; 4 Scott (write-in) and 1 Margaret Ashelman (write-in) in CD 7; 56 Lonsdorf (write-in) in CD 8.

1992 PRIMARIES

MARCH 3 REPUBLICAN

Senator   95,831 Alan L. Keyes; 20,758 Martha S. Klima; 16,091 Joseph I. Cassilly; 12,658 Ross Z. Pierpont; 12,423 S. Rob Sobhani; 9,451 John J. Bishop; 6,535 Eugene R. Zarwell; 6,282 James H. Berry; 6,030 Romie A. Songer; 5,835 Joyce Friend-Nalepka; 4,578 Edward R. Shannon; 4,372 Scott L. Meredith; 3,717 Stuart Hopkins; 2,771 Herman J. Hannan; 1,258 William H. Krehnbrink.

Congress   Unopposed in two CD's. Contested as follows:

CD 1   17,469 Wayne T. Gilchrest; 10,933 Lisa G. Renshaw; 6,915 Robert P. Duckworth; 1,261 Edward F. Taylor; 482 Michael P. Jackson.
CD 2   29,814 Helen D. Bentley; 4,435 Robert T. Petr.
CD 3   3,667 William T. S. Bricker; 3,307 Mark K. White; 2,659 Christopher E. Bouchat; 1,885 Fredric M. Parker; 1,714 Wyatt A. Rogers; 1,013 Joseph M. Werner; 890 Edward Lerp.
CD 4   5,278 Michele Dyson; 1,542 Herbert S. Rosenberg; 1,541 John M. Brown; 945 Roy L. Chambers; 874 Andrew Arnold; 469 Claude W. Roxborough; 457 William R. Diamond.
CD 5   12,661 Lawrence J. Hogan, Jr.; 4,967 Gerald Schuster; 4,020 John D. Parran; 2,275 Theodore Henderson; 1,495 Michael Swetnam; 633 John M. Fleig.
CD 6   15,374 Roscoe Bartlett; 14,728 Michael Downey; 6,201 Frank K. Nethken.

MARCH 3 DEMOCRATIC

Senator   376,444 Barbara A. Mikulski; 31,214 Thomas M. Wheatley; 26,467 Walter Boyd; 19,731 Don Allensworth; 13,001 Scott D. Britt; 12,470 James L. White; 11,150 Emerson Sweatt.

Congress   Contested as follows:

CD 1   33,627 Thomas McMillen; 14,964 Samuel Q. Johnson; 8,586 John C. Astle; 2,645 James Brown; 1,428 Herbert A. Mamet.
CD 2   16,969 Michael C. Hickey; 11,368 James E. DeLoach; 8,813 Joseph J. Bish; 7,838 Cornelius U. Morgan; 7,122 Paul D. Raschke.
CD 3   63,793 Benjamin L. Cardin; 11,707 Carl A. Mueller.
CD 4   18,353 Albert R. Wynn; 17,067 Alexander Williams; 9,928 Dana L. Dembrow; 8,480 Hilda R. Pemberton; 3,774 Francis J. Aluisi; 2,564 Tommie Broadwater; 1,448 Linda A. Kelly; 1,325 Maria Turner; 908 Robert Bates; 686 Michael B. Dupuy; 475 E. George Post; 439 Claudio B. Pedery; 184 Horace J. Hillsman.
CD 5   46,400 Steny H. Hoyer; 8,802 Ricardo V. Johnson.
CD 6   29,959 Thomas H. Hattery; 23,434 Beverly B. Byron.

MARYLAND

CD 7   55,842 Kweisi Mfume; 10,310 Michael V. Dobson.

CD 8   10,927 Edward J. Heffernan; 10,383 Anthony P. Puca; 8,217 Sidney Altman; 6,878 Shelton Skolnick; 6,506 Dennis Ketterer; 6,394 James Walker; 3,582 Joseph S. Incarnato; 2,665 John E. Boehm.

MASSACHUSETTS

GOVERNOR
William F. Weld (R). Elected 1990 to a four year term.

SENATORS
Edward M. Kennedy (D). Re-elected 1988 to a six-year term. Previously elected 1982, 1976, 1970, 1964 and in 1962 to fill out term vacated by the December 1960 resignation of Senator John F. Kennedy who was elected President November 1960.

John F. Kerry (D). Re-elected 1990 to a six-year term. Previously elected 1984.

REPRESENTATIVES
1. John Olver (D)
2. Richard E. Neal (D)
3. Peter Blute (R)
4. Barney Frank (D)
5. Martin T. Meehan (D)
6. Peter Torkildsen (R)
7. Edward J. Markey (D)
8. Joseph P. Kennedy (D)
9. John J. Moakley (D)
10. Gerry E. Studds (D)

POSTWAR VOTE FOR PRESIDENT

Year	Total Vote	Republican		Democratic		Other Vote	Plurality	Percentage			
								Total Vote		Major Vote	
		Vote	Candidate	Vote	Candidate			Rep.	Dem.	Rep.	Dem.
1992 **	2,773,700	805,049	Bush, George	1,318,662	Clinton, Bill	649,989	513,613 D	29.0%	47.5%	37.9%	62.1%
1988	2,632,805	1,194,635	Bush, George	1,401,415	Dukakis, Michael S.	36,755	206,780 D	45.4%	53.2%	46.0%	54.0%
1984	2,559,453	1,310,936	Reagan, Ronald	1,239,606	Mondale, Walter F.	8,911	71,330 R	51.2%	48.4%	51.4%	48.6%
1980	2,524,298	1,057,631	Reagan, Ronald	1,053,802	Carter, Jimmy	412,865	3,829 R	41.9%	41.7%	50.1%	49.9%
1976	2,547,558	1,030,276	Ford, Gerald R.	1,429,475	Carter, Jimmy	87,807	399,199 D	40.4%	56.1%	41.9%	58.1%
1972	2,458,756	1,112,078	Nixon, Richard M.	1,332,540	McGovern, George S.	14,138	220,462 D	45.2%	54.2%	45.5%	54.5%
1968	2,331,752	766,844	Nixon, Richard M.	1,469,218	Humphrey, Hubert H.	95,690	702,374 D	32.9%	63.0%	34.3%	65.7%
1964	2,344,798	549,727	Goldwater, Barry M.	1,786,422	Johnson, Lyndon B.	8,649	1,236,695 D	23.4%	76.2%	23.5%	76.5%
1960	2,469,480	976,750	Nixon, Richard M.	1,487,174	Kennedy, John F.	5,556	510,424 D	39.6%	60.2%	39.6%	60.4%
1956	2,348,506	1,393,197	Eisenhower, Dwight D.	948,190	Stevenson, Adlai E.	7,119	445,007 R	59.3%	40.4%	59.5%	40.5%
1952	2,383,398	1,292,325	Eisenhower, Dwight D.	1,083,525	Stevenson, Adlai E.	7,548	208,800 R	54.2%	45.5%	54.4%	45.6%
1948	2,107,146	909,370	Dewey, Thomas E.	1,151,788	Truman, Harry S.	45,988	242,418 D	43.2%	54.7%	44.1%	55.9%

In 1992 the other vote column includes 630,731 votes cast for Perot.

MASSACHUSETTS

POSTWAR VOTE FOR GOVERNOR

Year	Total Vote	Republican		Democratic		Other Vote	Rep.-Dem. Plurality	Percentage			
								Total Vote		Major Vote	
		Vote	Candidate	Vote	Candidate			Rep.	Dem.	Rep.	Dem.
1990	2,342,927	1,175,817	Weld, William F.	1,099,878	Silber, John	67,232	75,939 R	50.2%	46.9%	51.7%	48.3%
1986	1,684,079	525,364	Kariotis, George	1,157,786	Dukakis, Michael S.	929	632,422 D	31.2%	68.7%	31.2%	68.8%
1982	2,050,254	749,679	Sears, John W.	1,219,109	Dukakis, Michael S.	81,466	469,430 D	36.6%	59.5%	38.1%	61.9%
1978	1,962,251	926,072	Hatch, Francis W.	1,030,294	King, Edward J.	5,885	104,222 D	47.2%	52.5%	47.3%	52.7%
1974	1,854,798	784,353	Sargent, Francis W.	992,284	Dukakis, Michael S.	78,161	207,931 D	42.3%	53.5%	44.1%	55.9%
1970	1,867,906	1,058,623	Sargent, Francis W.	799,269	White, Kevin H.	10,014	259,354 R	56.7%	42.8%	57.0%	43.0%
1966 **	2,041,177	1,277,358	Volpe, John A.	752,720	McCormack, Edward J.	11,099	524,638 R	62.6%	36.9%	62.9%	37.1%
1964	2,340,130	1,176,462	Volpe, John A.	1,153,416	Bellotti, Francis X.	10,252	23,046 R	50.3%	49.3%	50.5%	49.5%
1962	2,109,089	1,047,891	Volpe, John A.	1,053,322	Peabody, Endicott	7,876	5,431 D	49.7%	49.9%	49.9%	50.1%
1960	2,417,133	1,269,295	Volpe, John A.	1,130,810	Ward, Joseph D.	17,028	138,485 R	52.5%	46.8%	52.9%	47.1%
1958	1,899,117	818,463	Gibbons, Charles	1,067,020	Furcolo, Foster	13,634	248,557 D	43.1%	56.2%	43.4%	56.6%
1956	2,339,884	1,096,759	Whittier, Sumner G.	1,234,618	Furcolo, Foster	8,507	137,859 D	46.9%	52.8%	47.0%	53.0%
1954	1,903,774	985,339	Herter, Christian A.	910,087	Murphy, Robert F.	8,348	75,252 R	51.8%	47.8%	52.0%	48.0%
1952	2,356,298	1,175,955	Herter, Christian A.	1,161,499	Dever, Paul A.	18,844	14,456 R	49.9%	49.3%	50.3%	49.7%
1950	1,910,180	824,069	Coolidge, Arthur W.	1,074,570	Dever, Paul A.	11,541	250,501 D	43.1%	56.3%	43.4%	56.6%
1948	2,099,250	849,895	Bradford, Robert F.	1,239,247	Dever, Paul A.	10,108	389,352 D	40.5%	59.0%	40.7%	59.3%
1946	1,683,452	911,152	Bradford, Robert F.	762,743	Tobin, Maurice	9,557	148,409 R	54.1%	45.3%	54.4%	45.6%

The term of office of Massachusetts' Governor was increased from two to four years effective with the 1966 election.

POSTWAR VOTE FOR SENATOR

Year	Total Vote	Republican		Democratic		Other Vote	Rep.-Dem. Plurality	Percentage			
								Total Vote		Major Vote	
		Vote	Candidate	Vote	Candidate			Rep.	Dem.	Rep.	Dem.
1990	2,316,212	992,917	Rappaport, Jim	1,321,712	Kerry, John F.	1,583	328,795 D	42.9%	57.1%	42.9%	57.1%
1988	2,606,225	884,267	Malone, Joseph	1,693,344	Kennedy, Edward M.	28,614	809,077 D	33.9%	65.0%	34.3%	65.7%
1984	2,530,195	1,136,806	Shamie, Raymond	1,392,981	Kerry, John F.	408	256,175 D	44.9%	55.1%	44.9%	55.1%
1982	2,050,769	784,602	Shamie, Raymond	1,247,084	Kennedy, Edward M.	19,083	462,482 D	38.3%	60.8%	38.6%	61.4%
1978	1,985,700	890,584	Brooke, Edward W.	1,093,283	Tsongas, Paul E.	1,833	202,699 D	44.8%	55.1%	44.9%	55.1%
1976	2,491,255	722,641	Robertson, Michael	1,726,657	Kennedy, Edward M.	41,957	1,004,016 D	29.0%	69.3%	29.5%	70.5%
1972	2,370,676	1,505,932	Brooke, Edward W.	823,278	Droney, John J.	41,466	682,654 R	63.5%	34.7%	64.7%	35.3%
1970	1,935,607	715,978	Spaulding, Josiah A.	1,202,856	Kennedy, Edward M.	16,773	486,878 D	37.0%	62.1%	37.3%	62.7%
1966	1,999,949	1,213,473	Brooke, Edward W.	774,761	Peabody, Endicott	11,715	438,712 R	60.7%	38.7%	61.0%	39.0%
1964	2,312,028	587,663	Whitmore, Howard	1,716,907	Kennedy, Edward M.	7,458	1,129,244 D	25.4%	74.3%	25.5%	74.5%
1962 S	2,097,085	877,669	Lodge, George C.	1,162,611	Kennedy, Edward M.	56,805	284,942 D	41.9%	55.4%	43.0%	57.0%
1960	2,417,813	1,358,556	Saltonstall, Leverett	1,050,725	O'Connor, Thomas J.	8,532	307,831 R	56.2%	43.5%	56.4%	43.6%
1958	1,862,041	488,318	Celeste, Vincent J.	1,362,926	Kennedy, John F.	10,797	874,608 D	26.2%	73.2%	26.4%	73.6%
1954	1,892,710	956,605	Saltonstall, Leverett	927,899	Furcolo, Foster	8,206	28,706 R	50.5%	49.0%	50.8%	49.2%
1952	2,360,425	1,141,247	Lodge, Henry Cabot	1,211,984	Kennedy, John F.	7,194	70,737 D	48.3%	51.3%	48.5%	51.5%
1948	2,055,798	1,088,475	Saltonstall, Leverett	954,398	Fitzgerald, John I.	12,925	134,077 R	52.9%	46.4%	53.3%	46.7%
1946	1,662,063	989,736	Lodge, Henry Cabot	660,200	Walsh, David I.	12,127	329,536 R	59.5%	39.7%	60.0%	40.0%

The 1962 election was for a short term to fill a vacancy.

MASSACHUSETTS

Districts Established July 9, 1992

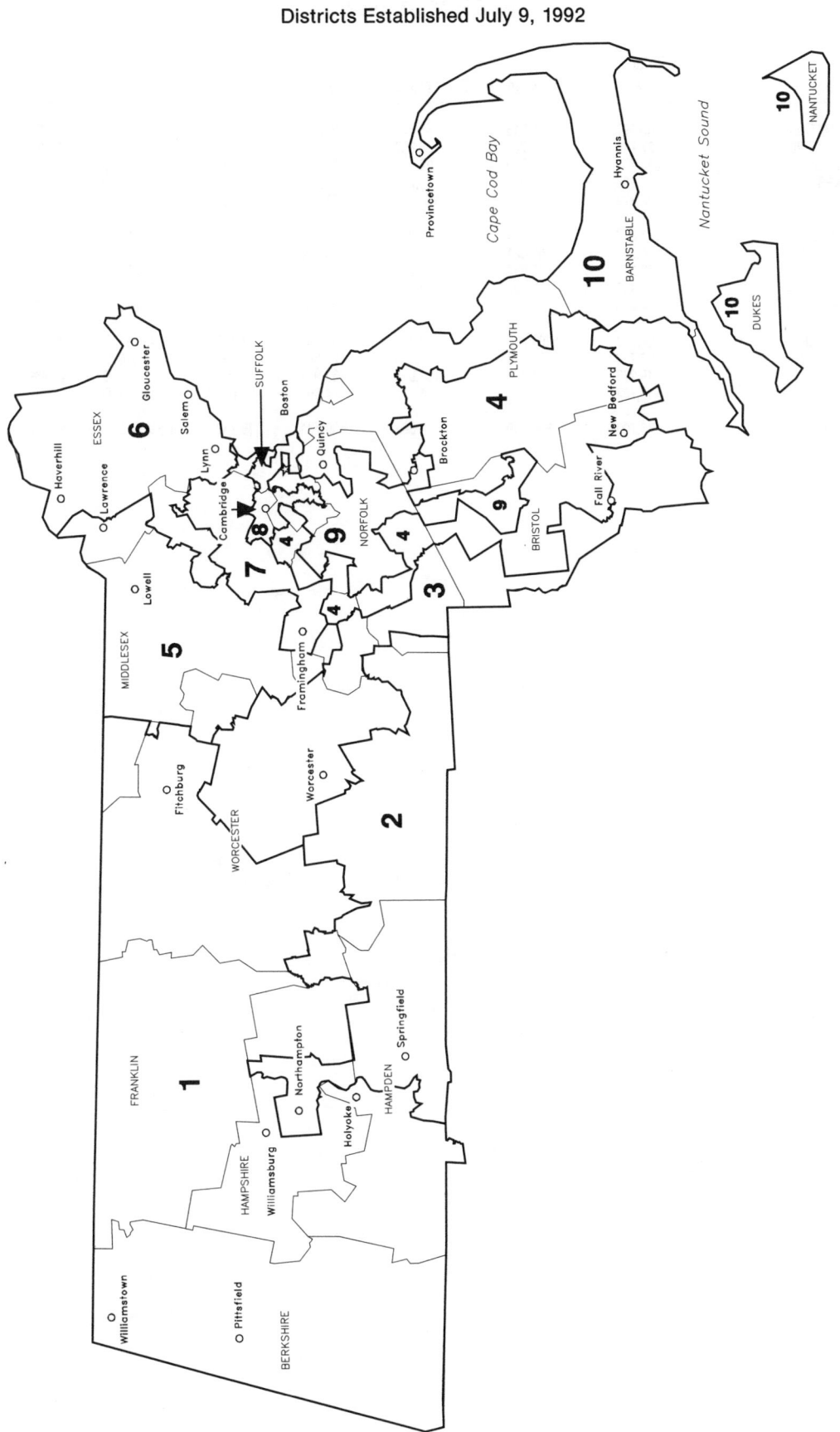

MASSACHUSETTS

PRESIDENT 1992

Registration	County	Total Vote	Republican	Democratic	Perot	Other	Plurality	Percentage Total Vote		
								Rep.	Dem.	Perot
129,036	BARNSTABLE	108,997	33,916	46,641	27,727	713	12,725 D	31.1%	42.8%	25.4%
80,700	BERKSHIRE	67,746	14,726	36,857	15,799	364	21,058 D	21.7%	54.4%	23.3%
255,380	BRISTOL	211,754	52,370	102,406	55,845	1,133	46,561 D	24.7%	48.4%	26.4%
9,048	DUKES	7,888	1,827	4,292	1,714	55	2,465 D	23.2%	54.4%	21.7%
384,383	ESSEX	322,328	102,212	140,593	77,459	2,064	38,381 D	31.7%	43.6%	24.0%
42,570	FRANKLIN	35,827	8,691	17,246	9,596	294	7,650 D	24.3%	48.1%	26.8%
225,086	HAMPDEN	188,265	54,621	86,026	46,678	940	31,405 D	29.0%	45.7%	24.8%
80,899	HAMPSHIRE	70,071	15,694	37,879	15,705	793	22,174 D	22.4%	54.1%	22.4%
815,979	MIDDLESEX	689,453	193,703	343,994	146,831	4,925	150,291 D	28.1%	49.9%	21.3%
5,164	NANTUCKET	4,216	1,158	2,037	989	32	879 D	27.5%	48.3%	23.5%
382,485	NORFOLK	324,390	103,255	150,488	67,537	3,110	47,233 D	31.8%	46.4%	20.8%
262,907	PLYMOUTH	207,710	69,514	79,160	57,886	1,150	9,646 D	33.5%	38.1%	27.9%
303,727	SUFFOLK	219,273	51,378	132,921	32,914	2,060	81,543 D	23.4%	60.6%	15.0%
374,554	WORCESTER	315,782	101,984	138,122	74,051	1,625	36,138 D	32.3%	43.7%	23.5%
3,351,918	TOTAL	2,773,700	805,049	1,318,662	630,731	19,258	513,613 D	29.0%	47.5%	22.7%

MASSACHUSETTS

PRESIDENT 1992

Registration	City/Town	Total Vote	Republican	Democratic	Perot	Other	Plurality	Percentage Total Vote		
								Rep.	Dem.	Perot
15,692	AGAWAM	13,498	4,239	5,479	3,742	38	1,240 D	31.4%	40.6%	27.7%
13,215	AMHERST	11,775	1,646	8,563	1,436	130	6,917 D	14.0%	72.7%	12.2%
19,129	ANDOVER	16,836	6,487	6,649	3,590	110	162 D	38.5%	39.5%	21.3%
29,625	ARLINGTON	25,685	6,646	14,453	4,384	202	7,807 D	25.9%	56.3%	17.1%
18,379	ATTLEBORO	15,114	4,779	5,831	4,413	91	1,052 D	31.6%	38.6%	29.2%
25,902	BARNSTABLE TOWN	21,584	6,558	8,972	5,920	134	2,414 D	30.4%	41.6%	27.4%
17,055	BELMONT	14,656	4,684	7,588	2,294	90	2,904 D	32.0%	51.8%	15.7%
23,320	BEVERLY	19,791	6,174	8,507	4,979	131	2,333 D	31.2%	43.0%	25.2%
20,443	BILLERICA	17,042	4,958	6,501	5,429	154	1,072 D	29.1%	38.1%	31.9%
255,876	BOSTON	183,131	41,868	114,260	25,189	1,814	72,392 D	22.9%	62.4%	13.8%
21,172	BRAINTREE	18,730	6,598	7,702	4,350	80	1,104 D	35.2%	41.1%	23.2%
10,701	BRIDGEWATER	8,221	2,757	2,950	2,427	87	193 D	33.5%	35.9%	29.5%
42,538	BROCKTON	29,799	8,863	13,209	7,579	148	4,346 D	29.7%	44.3%	25.4%
35,234	BROOKLINE	27,547	4,892	19,848	2,629	178	14,956 D	17.8%	72.1%	9.5%
14,596	BURLINGTON	12,697	4,192	5,145	3,278	82	953 D	33.0%	40.5%	25.8%
50,310	CAMBRIDGE	41,103	5,847	30,737	4,106	413	24,890 D	14.2%	74.8%	10.0%
20,392	CHELMSFORD	18,302	6,151	6,832	5,175	144	681 D	33.6%	37.3%	28.3%
10,920	CHELSEA	7,847	1,957	4,408	1,441	41	2,451 D	24.9%	56.2%	18.4%
28,469	CHICOPEE	24,129	6,138	11,433	6,452	106	4,981 D	25.4%	47.4%	26.7%
15,453	DANVERS	13,088	4,640	4,947	3,440	61	307 D	35.5%	37.8%	26.3%
14,664	DARTMOUTH	12,934	2,846	6,571	3,437	80	3,134 D	22.0%	50.8%	26.6%
14,550	DEDHAM	13,056	4,409	5,675	2,907	65	1,266 D	33.8%	43.5%	22.3%
15,884	DRACUT	12,588	3,667	4,509	4,360	52	149 D	29.1%	35.8%	34.6%
18,369	EVERETT	15,250	4,063	8,037	3,051	99	3,974 D	26.6%	52.7%	20.0%
39,921	FALL RIVER	31,210	5,456	18,652	6,922	180	11,730 D	17.5%	59.8%	22.2%
20,151	FALMOUTH	15,996	4,514	7,622	3,771	89	3,108 D	28.2%	47.6%	23.6%
18,101	FITCHBURG	13,731	3,812	6,713	3,108	98	2,901 D	27.8%	48.9%	22.6%
35,167	FRAMINGHAM	29,542	8,114	15,165	6,089	174	7,051 D	27.5%	51.3%	20.6%
13,414	FRANKLIN	11,487	3,698	4,844	2,864	81	1,146 D	32.2%	42.2%	24.9%
9,763	GARDNER	8,157	2,231	3,973	1,920	33	1,742 D	27.4%	48.7%	23.5%
17,739	GLOUCESTER	14,099	3,982	6,808	3,232	77	2,826 D	28.2%	48.3%	22.9%
27,019	HAVERHILL	22,678	6,854	10,216	5,450	158	3,362 D	30.2%	45.0%	24.0%
21,822	HOLYOKE	15,582	4,476	7,812	3,207	87	3,336 D	28.7%	50.1%	20.6%
22,237	LAWRENCE	16,139	5,079	7,698	3,245	117	2,619 D	31.5%	47.7%	20.1%
20,084	LEOMINSTER	16,832	5,293	7,302	4,157	80	2,009 D	31.4%	43.4%	24.7%
21,172	LEXINGTON	17,960	5,001	10,015	2,796	148	5,014 D	27.8%	55.8%	15.6%
42,129	LOWELL	32,123	8,467	14,492	8,893	271	5,599 D	26.4%	45.1%	27.7%
38,578	LYNN	30,477	7,350	15,275	7,665	187	7,610 D	24.1%	50.1%	25.2%
27,934	MALDEN	23,192	5,725	12,653	4,673	141	6,928 D	24.7%	54.6%	20.1%
17,941	MARLBOROUGH	14,796	4,525	6,213	3,962	96	1,688 D	30.6%	42.0%	26.8%
14,617	MARSHFIELD	12,239	4,153	4,682	3,342	62	529 D	33.9%	38.3%	27.3%
32,709	MEDFORD	27,987	7,690	14,690	5,480	127	7,000 D	27.5%	52.5%	19.6%
18,586	MELROSE	16,232	5,108	7,464	3,582	78	2,356 D	31.5%	46.0%	22.1%
23,586	METHUEN	19,677	6,954	7,727	4,905	91	773 D	35.3%	39.3%	24.9%
13,318	MILFORD	11,561	3,306	5,583	2,632	40	2,277 D	28.6%	48.3%	22.8%
17,589	MILTON	14,999	5,409	6,634	2,900	56	1,225 D	36.1%	44.2%	19.3%
21,370	NATICK	17,296	5,220	8,529	3,446	101	3,309 D	30.2%	49.3%	19.9%
19,516	NEEDHAM	17,101	5,880	8,287	2,816	118	2,407 D	34.4%	48.5%	16.5%
39,945	NEW BEDFORD	33,322	5,255	20,880	6,965	222	13,915 D	15.8%	62.7%	20.9%
50,964	NEWTON	44,705	9,623	29,136	5,685	261	19,513 D	21.5%	65.2%	12.7%
17,378	NORTHAMPTON	15,296	2,741	9,750	2,513	292	7,009 D	17.9%	63.7%	16.4%
14,660	NORTH ANDOVER	12,569	4,937	4,652	2,891	89	285 R	39.3%	37.0%	23.0%
13,102	NORTH ATTLEBOROUGH	10,654	3,683	3,699	3,227	45	16 D	34.6%	34.7%	30.3%
17,575	NORWOOD	15,001	4,882	6,803	3,224	92	1,921 D	32.5%	45.4%	21.5%
28,621	PEABODY	24,704	6,709	11,694	6,155	146	4,985 D	27.2%	47.3%	24.9%
27,510	PITTSFIELD	22,882	4,541	13,012	5,189	140	7,823 D	19.8%	56.9%	22.7%
33,734	PLYMOUTH TOWN	21,614	6,620	8,360	6,521	113	1,740 D	30.6%	38.7%	30.2%
48,204	QUINCY	40,495	12,306	18,891	9,068	230	6,585 D	30.4%	46.7%	22.4%
16,594	RANDOLPH	14,245	3,443	7,817	2,915	70	4,374 D	24.2%	54.9%	20.5%
14,920	READING	13,446	4,516	5,753	3,083	94	1,237 D	33.6%	42.8%	22.9%

MASSACHUSETTS

PRESIDENT 1992

Registration	City/Town	Total Vote	Republican	Democratic	Perot	Other	Plurality	Percentage Total Vote		
								Rep.	Dem.	Perot
24,039	REVERE	18,826	4,896	9,628	4,175	127	4,732 D	26.0%	51.1%	22.2%
21,307	SALEM	17,985	4,471	9,385	4,025	104	4,914 D	24.9%	52.2%	22.4%
15,999	SAUGUS	13,405	3,938	5,764	3,637	66	1,826 D	29.4%	43.0%	27.1%
15,428	SHREWSBURY	13,494	5,044	5,670	2,708	72	626 D	37.4%	42.0%	20.1%
42,804	SOMERVILLE	30,399	5,883	19,792	4,416	308	13,909 D	19.4%	65.1%	14.5%
59,850	SPRINGFIELD	50,111	12,200	27,302	10,361	248	15,102 D	24.3%	54.5%	20.7%
13,329	STONEHAM	11,629	3,689	5,135	2,743	62	1,446 D	31.7%	44.2%	23.6%
15,531	STOUGHTON	13,065	3,749	6,274	2,986	56	2,525 D	28.7%	48.0%	22.9%
25,681	TAUNTON	19,483	5,049	8,683	5,673	78	3,010 D	25.9%	44.6%	29.1%
15,277	TEWKSBURY	14,038	4,340	5,328	4,276	94	988 D	30.9%	38.0%	30.5%
14,871	WAKEFIELD	13,776	4,300	5,922	3,465	89	1,622 D	31.2%	43.0%	25.2%
13,058	WALPOLE	11,257	4,288	4,317	2,592	60	29 D	38.1%	38.3%	23.0%
29,716	WALTHAM	23,975	7,365	11,333	5,092	185	3,968 D	30.7%	47.3%	21.2%
19,876	WATERTOWN	17,239	4,293	9,977	2,824	145	5,684 D	24.9%	57.9%	16.4%
16,203	WELLESLEY	14,691	5,507	6,990	2,112	82	1,483 D	37.5%	47.6%	14.4%
14,590	WEST SPRINGFIELD	12,649	4,190	5,122	3,274	63	932 D	33.1%	40.5%	25.9%
20,716	WESTFIELD	17,170	5,206	7,023	4,854	87	1,817 D	30.3%	40.9%	28.3%
34,017	WEYMOUTH	25,295	7,849	10,762	6,552	132	2,913 D	31.0%	42.5%	25.9%
14,296	WINCHESTER	12,668	4,506	5,717	2,378	67	1,211 D	35.6%	45.1%	18.8%
22,383	WOBURN	18,466	5,743	7,983	4,581	159	2,240 D	31.1%	43.2%	24.8%
75,979	WORCESTER CITY	60,307	17,228	32,326	10,488	265	15,098 D	28.6%	53.6%	17.4%
14,909	YARMOUTH	12,421	4,283	5,168	2,890	80	885 D	34.5%	41.6%	23.3%

MASSACHUSETTS

CONGRESS

CD	Year	Total Vote	Republican		Democratic		Other Vote	Rep.-Dem. Plurality	Percentage			
									Total Vote		Major Vote	
			Vote	Candidate	Vote	Candidate			Rep.	Dem.	Rep.	Dem.
1	1992	262,120	113,828	LARKIN, PATRICK	135,049	OLVER, JOHN	13,243	21,221 D	43.4%	51.5%	45.7%	54.3%
2	1992	247,151	76,795	RAVOSA, ANTHONY W.	131,215	NEAL, RICHARD E.	39,141	54,420 D	31.1%	53.1%	36.9%	63.1%
3	1992	260,941	131,476	BLUTE, PETER	115,592	EARLY, JOSEPH D.	13,873	15,884 R	50.4%	44.3%	53.2%	46.8%
4	1992	269,814	70,666	MCCORMICK, EDWARD J., III	182,633	FRANK, BARNEY	16,515	111,967 D	26.2%	67.7%	27.9%	72.1%
5	1992	256,564	96,206	CRONIN, PAUL W.	133,844	MEEHAN, MARTIN T.	26,514	37,638 D	37.5%	52.2%	41.8%	58.2%
6	1992	290,312	159,165	TORKILDSEN, PETER	130,248	MAVROULES, NICHOLAS	899	28,917 R	54.8%	44.9%	55.0%	45.0%
7	1992	281,558	78,262	SOHN, STEPHEN A.	174,837	MARKEY, EDWARD J.	28,459	96,575 D	27.8%	62.1%	30.9%	69.1%
8	1992	180,492			149,907	KENNEDY, JOSEPH P.	30,585	149,907 D		83.1%		100.0%
9	1992	253,634	54,291	CONBOY, MARTIN D.	175,550	MOAKLEY, JOHN J.	23,793	121,259 D	21.4%	69.2%	23.6%	76.4%
10	1992	311,651	75,887	DALY, DANIEL W.	189,343	STUDDS, GERRY E.	46,421	113,456 D	24.3%	60.8%	28.6%	71.4%

MASSACHUSETTS

1992 GENERAL ELECTION

In addition to the county-by-county figures, data are presented for selected Massachusetts communities. Since not all jurisdictions of the state are listed in this special tabulation, state-wide totals are shown only with the county-by-county statistics.

The data presented are from Public Document 43, "Massachusetts Elections 1992"which vary slightly from earlier returns.

President   Other vote was 9,024 Libertarian (Marrou); 3,172 New Alliance (Fulani); 2,218 Independent Voters (Phillips); 1,812 Natural Law (Hagelin); 1,027 LaRouche for President (LaRouche); 13 Brisben (write-in); 2 Dodge (write-in); 1,990 scattered write-in.

Congress   Other vote was 7,162 Peace Jobs Justice (Godena), 4,355 Pro-Democracy Reform (Kelly), 1,598 Freedom for LaRouche (Rebello) and 128 scattered write-in in CD 1; 38,963 For the People (Sheehan) and 178 scattered write-in in CD 2; 9,692 Independent Voters (Leonard Umina), 4,130 Natural Law (Moore) and 51 scattered write-in in CD 3; 13,671 Independent Voters (Lumina), 2,797 Freedom for LaRouche (Ingalls) and 47 scattered write-in in CD 4; 19,077 Independent (Farinelli), 7,214 Independent (Coleman) and 223 scattered write-in in CD 5; scattered write-in in CD 6; 28,421 Independent (Antonelli) and 38 scattered in CD 7; 30,406 Independent (Nakash) and 179 scattered write-in in CD 8; 15,637 Independent (Mackin), 8,084 Independent (Horan) and 72 scattered write-in in CD 9; 39,265 Independent (Bryan), 6,020 Independent Voters (Michael Umina), 1,106 Freedom for LaRouche (Knapp) and 30 scattered write-in in CD 10.

1992 PRIMARIES

SEPTEMBER 15 REPUBLICAN

Congress   Unopposed in three CD's. No candidate in CD 8. Contested as follows:

CD 3   11,989 Peter Blute; 8,984 David Lionett; 3,558 Michelle Flaherty; 16 scattered write-in.
CD 5   11,545 Paul W. Cronin; 10,249 Michael G. Conway; 57 scattered write-in.
CD 6   16,556 Peter Torkildsen; 13,043 Alexander T. Tennant; 124 scattered write-in.
CD 7   8,694 Stephen A. Sohn; 7,455 Frank Vallarelli; 83 scattered write-in.
CD 9   6,938 Martin D. Conboy; 6,023 Patrick J. Walsh; 24 scattered write-in.
CD 10   11,679 Daniel W. Daly; 9,704 Michael K. Crossen; 2,985 Robert E. King; 154 scattered write-in.

SEPTEMBER 15 DEMOCRATIC

Congress   Unopposed in four CD's. Contested as follows:

CD 2   30,370 Richard E. Neal; 21,709 Kateri Walsh; 11,513 Charles A. Platten; 49 scattered write-in.
CD 3   24,927 Joseph D. Early; 13,291 Gerard D'Amico; 12,185 John Walsh; 9,629 Martin F. Healey; 7,948 Brian A. O'Connell; 48 scattered write-in.
CD 5   50,300 Martin T. Meehan; 26,855 Chester G. Atkins; 53 scattered write-in.
CD 6   45,516 Nicholas Mavroules; 44,847 Barbara Hildt; 6,823 Eric Elbot; 136 scattered write-in.
CD 8   45,993 Joseph P. Kennedy; 11,005 Charles C. Yancey; 49 scattered write-ins.
CD 10   57,640 Gerry E. Studds; 34,280 Paul D. Harold; 3,175 William G. Zissulis; 145 scattered write-in.

MICHIGAN

GOVERNOR
John Engler (R). Elected 1990 to a four-year term.

SENATORS
Carl Levin (D). Re-elected 1990 to a six-year term. Previously elected 1984, 1978.

Donald W. Riegle (D). Re-elected 1988 to a six-year term. Previously elected 1982, 1976.

REPRESENTATIVES
1. Bart Stupak (D)
2. Peter Hoekstra (R)
3. Paul Henry (R) (see page 1)
4. Dave Camp (R)
5. James A. Barcia (D)
6. Frederick Upton (R)
7. Nick Smith (R)
8. M. Robert Carr (D)
9. Dale E. Kildee (D)
10. David E. Bonior (D)
11. Joseph K. Knollenberg (R)
12. Sander Levin (D)
13. William D. Ford (D)
14. John Conyers (D)
15. Barbara-Rose Collins (D)
16. John D. Dingell, Jr.(D)

POSTWAR VOTE FOR PRESIDENT

Year	Total Vote	Republican		Democratic		Other Vote	Plurality	Percentage			
								Total Vote		Major Vote	
		Vote	Candidate	Vote	Candidate			Rep.	Dem.	Rep.	Dem.
1992 **	4,274,673	1,554,940	Bush, George	1,871,182	Clinton, Bill	848,551	316,242 D	36.4%	43.8%	45.4%	54.6%
1988	3,669,163	1,965,486	Bush, George	1,675,783	Dukakis, Michael S.	27,894	289,703 R	53.6%	45.7%	54.0%	46.0%
1984	3,801,658	2,251,571	Reagan, Ronald	1,529,638	Mondale, Walter F.	20,449	721,933 R	59.2%	40.2%	59.5%	40.5%
1980	3,909,725	1,915,225	Reagan, Ronald	1,661,532	Carter, Jimmy	332,968	253,693 R	49.0%	42.5%	53.5%	46.5%
1976	3,653,749	1,893,742	Ford, Gerald R.	1,696,714	Carter, Jimmy	63,293	197,028 R	51.8%	46.4%	52.7%	47.3%
1972	3,489,727	1,961,721	Nixon, Richard M.	1,459,435	McGovern, George S.	68,571	502,286 R	56.2%	41.8%	57.3%	42.7%
1968	3,306,250	1,370,665	Nixon, Richard M.	1,593,082	Humphrey, Hubert H.	342,503	222,417 D	41.5%	48.2%	46.2%	53.8%
1964	3,203,102	1,060,152	Goldwater, Barry M.	2,136,615	Johnson, Lyndon B.	6,335	1,076,463 D	33.1%	66.7%	33.2%	66.8%
1960	3,318,097	1,620,428	Nixon, Richard M.	1,687,269	Kennedy, John F.	10,400	66,841 D	48.8%	50.9%	49.0%	51.0%
1956	3,080,468	1,713,647	Eisenhower, Dwight D.	1,359,898	Stevenson, Adlai E.	6,923	353,749 R	55.6%	44.1%	55.8%	44.2%
1952	2,798,592	1,551,529	Eisenhower, Dwight D.	1,230,657	Stevenson, Adlai E.	16,406	320,872 R	55.4%	44.0%	55.8%	44.2%
1948	2,109,609	1,038,595	Dewey, Thomas E.	1,003,448	Truman, Harry S.	67,566	35,147 R	49.2%	47.6%	50.9%	49.1%

In 1992 the other vote column includes 824,813 votes cast for Perot.

MICHIGAN

POSTWAR VOTE FOR GOVERNOR

Year	Total Vote	Republican Vote	Republican Candidate	Democratic Vote	Democratic Candidate	Other Vote	Rep.-Dem. Plurality	Total Vote Rep.	Total Vote Dem.	Major Vote Rep.	Major Vote Dem.
1990	2,564,563	1,276,134	Engler, John	1,258,539	Blanchard, James J.	29,890	17,595 R	49.8%	49.1%	50.3%	49.7%
1986	2,396,564	753,647	Lucas, William	1,632,138	Blanchard, James J.	10,779	878,491 D	31.4%	68.1%	31.6%	68.4%
1982	3,040,008	1,369,582	Headlee, Richard H.	1,561,291	Blanchard, James J.	109,135	191,709 D	45.1%	51.4%	46.7%	53.3%
1978	2,867,212	1,628,485	Milliken, William G.	1,237,256	Fitzgerald, William	1,471	391,229 R	56.8%	43.2%	56.8%	43.2%
1974	2,657,017	1,356,865	Milliken, William G.	1,242,247	Levin, Sander	57,905	114,618 R	51.1%	46.8%	52.2%	47.8%
1970	2,656,162	1,339,047	Milliken, William G.	1,294,638	Levin, Sander	22,477	44,409 R	50.4%	48.7%	50.8%	49.2%
1966 * *	2,461,909	1,490,430	Romney, George W.	963,383	Ferency, Zolton A.	8,096	527,047 R	60.5%	39.1%	60.7%	39.3%
1964	3,158,102	1,764,355	Romney, George W.	1,381,442	Staebler, Neil	12,305	382,913 R	55.9%	43.7%	56.1%	43.9%
1962	2,764,839	1,420,086	Romney, George W.	1,339,513	Swainson, John B.	5,240	80,573 R	51.4%	48.4%	51.5%	48.5%
1960	3,255,991	1,602,022	Bagwell, Paul D.	1,643,634	Swainson, John B.	10,335	41,612 D	49.2%	50.5%	49.4%	50.6%
1958	2,312,184	1,078,089	Bagwell, Paul D.	1,225,533	Williams, G. Mennen	8,562	147,444 D	46.6%	53.0%	46.8%	53.2%
1956	3,049,651	1,376,376	Cobo, Albert E.	1,666,689	Williams, G. Mennen	6,586	290,313 D	45.1%	54.7%	45.2%	54.8%
1954	2,187,027	963,300	Leonard, Donald S.	1,216,308	Williams, G. Mennen	7,419	253,008 D	44.0%	55.6%	44.2%	55.8%
1952	2,865,980	1,423,275	Alger, Fred M.	1,431,893	Williams, G. Mennen	10,812	8,618 D	49.7%	50.0%	49.8%	50.2%
1950	1,879,382	933,998	Kelly, Harry F.	935,152	Williams, G. Mennen	10,232	1,154 D	49.7%	49.8%	50.0%	50.0%
1948	2,113,122	964,810	Sigler, Kim	1,128,664	Williams, G. Mennen	19,648	163,854 D	45.7%	53.4%	46.1%	53.9%
1946	1,665,475	1,003,878	Sigler, Kim	644,540	Van Wagoner, Murray	17,057	359,338 R	60.3%	38.7%	60.9%	39.1%

The term of office of Michigan's Governor was increased from two to four years effective with the 1966 election.

POSTWAR VOTE FOR SENATOR

Year	Total Vote	Republican Vote	Republican Candidate	Democratic Vote	Democratic Candidate	Other Vote	Rep.-Dem. Plurality	Total Vote Rep.	Total Vote Dem.	Major Vote Rep.	Major Vote Dem.
1990	2,560,494	1,055,695	Schuette, Bill	1,471,753	Levin, Carl	33,046	416,058 D	41.2%	57.5%	41.8%	58.2%
1988	3,505,985	1,348,219	Dunn, Jim	2,116,865	Riegle, Donald W.	40,901	768,646 D	38.5%	60.4%	38.9%	61.1%
1984	3,700,938	1,745,302	Lousma, Jack	1,915,831	Levin, Carl	39,805	170,529 D	47.2%	51.8%	47.7%	52.3%
1982	2,994,334	1,223,288	Ruppe, Philip E.	1,728,793	Riegle, Donald W.	42,253	505,505 D	40.9%	57.7%	41.4%	58.6%
1978	2,846,630	1,362,165	Griffin, Robert P.	1,484,193	Levin, Carl	272	122,028 D	47.9%	52.1%	47.9%	52.1%
1976	3,490,664	1,635,087	Esch, Marvin L.	1,831,031	Riegle, Donald W.	24,546	195,944 D	46.8%	52.5%	47.2%	52.8%
1972	3,406,906	1,781,065	Griffin, Robert P.	1,577,178	Kelley, Frank J.	48,663	203,887 R	52.3%	46.3%	53.0%	47.0%
1970	2,610,839	858,470	Romney, Lenore	1,744,716	Hart, Philip A.	7,653	886,246 D	32.9%	66.8%	33.0%	67.0%
1966	2,439,365	1,363,530	Griffin, Robert P.	1,069,484	Williams, G. Mennen	6,351	294,046 R	55.9%	43.8%	56.0%	44.0%
1964	3,101,667	1,096,272	Peterson, Elly M.	1,996,912	Hart, Philip A.	8,483	900,640 D	35.3%	64.4%	35.4%	64.6%
1960	3,226,647	1,548,873	Bentley, Alvin M.	1,669,179	McNamara, Patrick V.	8,595	120,306 D	48.0%	51.7%	48.1%	51.9%
1958	2,271,644	1,046,963	Potter, Charles E.	1,216,966	Hart, Philip A.	7,715	170,003 D	46.1%	53.6%	46.2%	53.8%
1954	2,144,840	1,049,420	Ferguson, Homer	1,088,550	McNamara, Patrick V.	6,870	39,130 D	48.9%	50.8%	49.1%	50.9%
1952	2,821,133	1,428,352	Potter, Charles E.	1,383,416	Moody, Blair	9,365	44,936 R	50.6%	49.0%	50.8%	49.2%
1948	2,062,097	1,045,156	Ferguson, Homer	1,000,329	Hook, Frank E.	16,612	44,827 R	50.7%	48.5%	51.1%	48.9%
1946	1,618,720	1,085,570	Vandenberg, Arthur	517,923	Lee, James H.	15,227	567,647 R	67.1%	32.0%	67.7%	32.3%

MICHIGAN

Districts Established April 6, 1992

Districts 13, 14, 15 and 16 Wayne County, including city of Detroit

DETROIT AREA

CONGRESSIONAL DISTRICTS

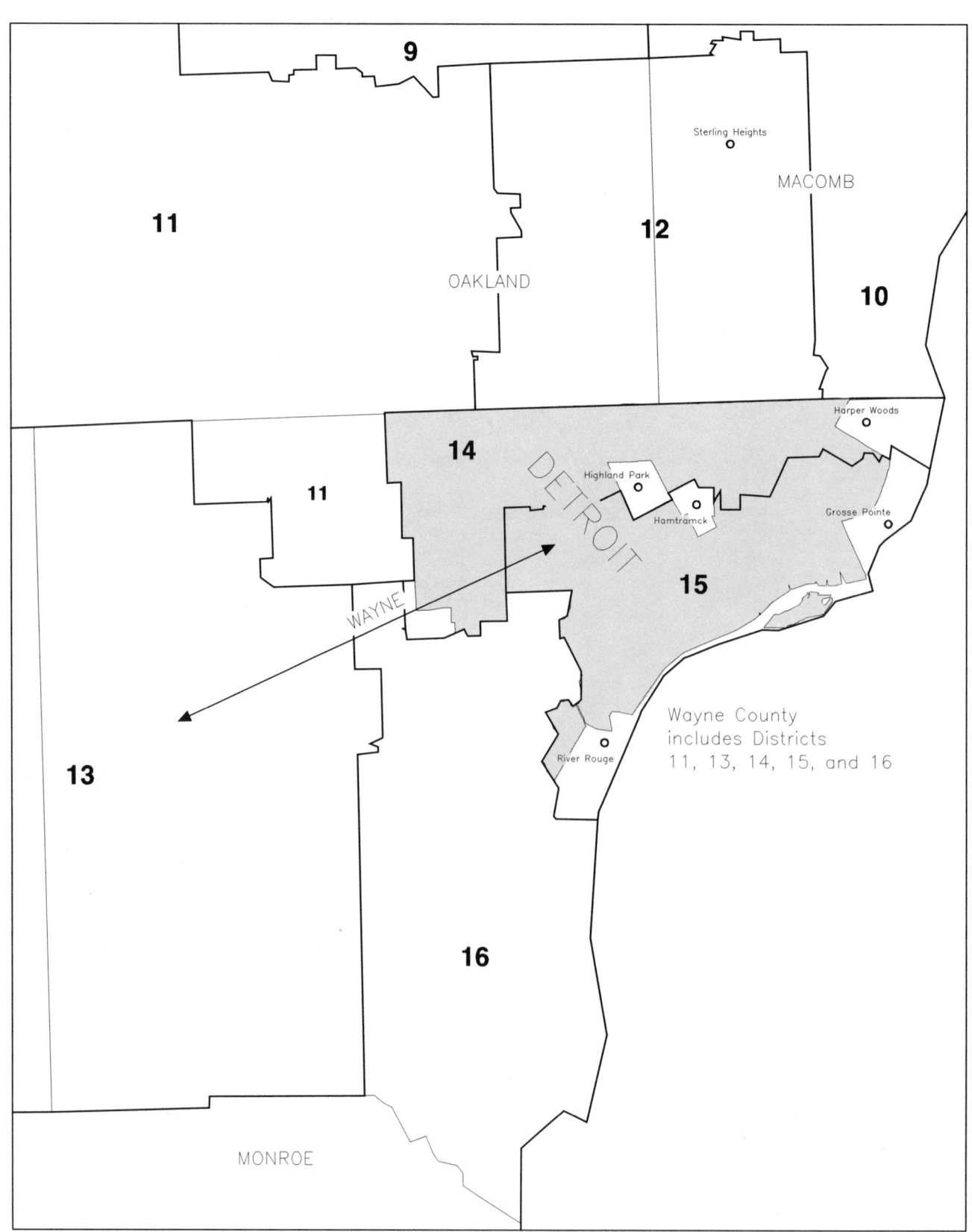

9

Sterling Heights

MACOMB

11

OAKLAND

12

10

14

DETROIT

Harper Woods

Highland Park

Hamtramck

Grosse Pointe

11

WAYNE

15

13

River Rouge

Wayne County includes Districts 11, 13, 14, 15, and 16

16

MONROE

MICHIGAN

PRESIDENT 1992

Registration	County	Total Vote	Republican	Democratic	Perot	Other	Plurality	Percentage Total Vote		
								Rep.	Dem.	Perot
8,752	ALCONA	5,779	2,247	2,383	1,117	32	136 D	38.9%	41.2%	19.3%
5,855	ALGER	4,570	1,471	2,144	941	14	673 D	32.2%	46.9%	20.6%
54,161	ALLEGAN	40,835	19,077	12,823	8,742	193	6,254 R	46.7%	31.4%	21.4%
21,604	ALPENA	15,069	4,878	6,894	3,236	61	2,016 D	32.4%	45.7%	21.5%
14,113	ANTRIM	9,991	3,984	3,431	2,528	48	553 R	39.9%	34.3%	25.3%
10,701	ARENAC	7,206	2,330	3,244	1,608	24	914 D	32.3%	45.0%	22.3%
5,788	BARAGA	3,630	1,160	1,695	754	21	535 D	32.0%	46.7%	20.8%
32,824	BARRY	24,599	9,489	8,652	6,303	155	837 R	38.6%	35.2%	25.6%
72,285	BAY	54,355	16,383	26,492	11,258	222	10,109 D	30.1%	48.7%	20.7%
9,181	BENZIE	6,852	2,438	2,715	1,657	42	277 D	35.6%	39.6%	24.2%
102,741	BERRIEN	69,615	29,252	25,840	14,056	467	3,412 R	42.0%	37.1%	20.2%
24,707	BRANCH	16,593	5,976	5,850	4,683	84	126 R	36.0%	35.3%	28.2%
85,426	CALHOUN	58,702	19,791	25,542	13,058	311	5,751 D	33.7%	43.5%	22.2%
29,929	CASS	20,283	7,391	8,047	4,756	89	656 D	36.4%	39.7%	23.4%
16,399	CHARLEVOIX	11,525	4,017	4,063	3,360	85	46 D	34.9%	35.3%	29.2%
15,414	CHEBOYGAN	10,864	3,864	4,459	2,495	46	595 D	35.6%	41.0%	23.0%
19,942	CHIPPEWA	13,647	5,462	5,434	2,706	45	28 R	40.0%	39.8%	19.8%
18,916	CLARE	12,163	3,916	5,346	2,812	89	1,430 D	32.2%	44.0%	23.1%
38,609	CLINTON	30,339	12,216	10,116	7,877	130	2,100 R	40.3%	33.3%	26.0%
8,765	CRAWFORD	5,925	2,193	2,252	1,442	38	59 D	37.0%	38.0%	24.3%
23,970	DELTA	17,962	6,027	8,387	3,485	63	2,360 D	33.6%	46.7%	19.4%
19,634	DICKINSON	13,031	4,273	5,689	3,022	47	1,416 D	32.8%	43.7%	23.2%
63,444	EATON	47,883	18,669	16,752	12,208	254	1,917 R	39.0%	35.0%	25.5%
17,861	EMMET	13,232	5,312	4,245	3,576	99	1,067 R	40.1%	32.1%	27.0%
314,202	GENESEE	199,998	47,834	105,156	46,259	749	57,322 D	23.9%	52.6%	23.1%
14,890	GLADWIN	10,776	3,616	4,457	2,649	54	841 D	33.6%	41.4%	24.6%
13,192	GOGEBIC	9,225	2,838	4,792	1,543	52	1,954 D	30.8%	51.9%	16.7%
44,988	GRAND TRAVERSE	34,461	13,629	11,148	9,495	189	2,481 R	39.5%	32.3%	27.6%
22,482	GRATIOT	15,879	6,280	5,678	3,866	55	602 R	39.5%	35.8%	24.3%
25,651	HILLSDALE	17,891	7,579	5,244	4,968	100	2,335 R	42.4%	29.3%	27.8%
23,202	HOUGHTON	15,173	5,575	6,558	2,945	95	983 D	36.7%	43.2%	19.4%
24,834	HURON	16,632	6,491	6,023	4,064	54	468 R	39.0%	36.2%	24.4%
196,257	INGHAM	133,792	43,926	61,596	27,683	587	17,670 D	32.8%	46.0%	20.7%
33,986	IONIA	23,822	9,135	8,370	6,211	106	765 R	38.3%	35.1%	26.1%
21,223	IOSCO	13,492	4,912	5,369	3,131	80	457 D	36.4%	39.8%	23.2%
9,430	IRON	7,000	1,971	3,648	1,344	37	1,677 D	28.2%	52.1%	19.2%
33,846	ISABELLA	22,037	7,706	8,784	5,434	113	1,078 D	35.0%	39.9%	24.7%
94,851	JACKSON	64,644	25,424	23,686	15,194	340	1,738 R	39.3%	36.6%	23.5%
142,551	KALAMAZOO	103,858	38,035	43,568	21,666	589	5,533 D	36.6%	41.9%	20.9%
9,920	KALKASKA	6,426	2,173	2,297	1,915	41	124 D	33.8%	35.7%	29.8%
333,333	KENT	242,553	115,285	82,305	43,707	1,256	32,980 R	47.5%	33.9%	18.0%
1,458	KEWEENAW	1,173	378	582	212	1	204 D	32.2%	49.6%	18.1%
6,632	LAKE	4,546	1,194	2,351	981	20	1,157 D	26.3%	51.7%	21.6%
47,942	LAPEER	35,084	12,326	11,982	10,541	235	344 R	35.1%	34.2%	30.0%
13,518	LEELANAU	10,187	3,993	3,445	2,685	64	548 R	39.2%	33.8%	26.4%
57,199	LENAWEE	39,365	14,297	15,399	9,517	152	1,102 D	36.3%	39.1%	24.2%
84,909	LIVINGSTON	61,735	27,539	17,851	15,971	374	9,688 R	44.6%	28.9%	25.9%
4,210	LUCE	2,603	958	972	660	13	14 D	36.8%	37.3%	25.4%
8,046	MACKINAC	5,977	2,278	2,293	1,379	27	15 D	38.1%	38.4%	23.1%
481,886	MACOMB	349,238	147,795	130,732	67,954	2,757	17,063 R	42.3%	37.4%	19.5%
16,360	MANISTEE	11,651	3,491	5,193	2,923	44	1,702 D	30.0%	44.6%	25.1%
44,635	MARQUETTE	31,629	9,665	16,038	5,768	158	6,373 D	30.6%	50.7%	18.2%
17,995	MASON	13,082	5,102	4,829	3,096	55	273 R	39.0%	36.9%	23.7%
22,712	MECOSTA	15,835	6,047	6,097	3,612	79	50 D	38.2%	38.5%	22.8%
15,912	MENOMINEE	11,082	3,995	4,559	2,487	41	564 D	36.0%	41.1%	22.4%
50,750	MIDLAND	38,624	16,149	13,382	8,945	148	2,767 R	41.8%	34.6%	23.2%
8,781	MISSAUKEE	6,058	2,829	1,893	1,306	30	936 R	46.7%	31.2%	21.6%
83,455	MONROE	59,031	20,250	24,957	13,551	273	4,707 D	34.3%	42.3%	23.0%
33,600	MONTCALM	22,780	8,420	8,730	5,504	126	310 D	37.0%	38.3%	24.2%
6,716	MONTMORENCY	4,791	1,794	1,903	1,077	17	109 D	37.4%	39.7%	22.5%

MICHIGAN

PRESIDENT 1992

Registration	County	Total Vote	Republican	Democratic	Perot	Other	Plurality	Percentage Total Vote		
								Rep.	Dem.	Perot
107,255	MUSKEGON	71,948	23,769	32,515	15,268	396	8,746 D	33.0%	45.2%	21.2%
25,887	NEWAYGO	17,916	7,333	6,455	4,056	72	878 R	40.9%	36.0%	22.6%
761,611	OAKLAND	555,760	242,160	214,733	94,911	3,956	27,427 R	43.6%	38.6%	17.1%
14,540	OCEANA	10,557	3,944	3,846	2,713	54	98 R	37.4%	36.4%	25.7%
14,072	OGEMAW	9,126	2,936	4,016	2,122	52	1,080 D	32.2%	44.0%	23.3%
6,164	ONTONAGON	4,745	1,463	2,451	805	26	988 D	30.8%	51.7%	17.0%
13,767	OSCEOLA	9,376	3,606	3,529	2,199	42	77 R	38.5%	37.6%	23.5%
5,498	OSCODA	3,831	1,583	1,471	755	22	112 R	41.3%	38.4%	19.7%
13,362	OTSEGO	9,207	3,393	3,129	2,635	50	264 R	36.9%	34.0%	28.6%
124,983	OTTAWA	96,211	56,862	22,180	16,855	314	34,682 R	59.1%	23.1%	17.5%
9,899	PRESQUE ISLE	7,345	2,398	3,308	1,612	27	910 D	32.6%	45.0%	21.9%
17,452	ROSCOMMON	12,007	4,170	5,243	2,551	43	1,073 D	34.7%	43.7%	21.2%
145,372	SAGINAW	96,905	32,103	43,819	20,523	460	11,716 D	33.1%	45.2%	21.2%
96,971	ST. CLAIR	66,832	24,508	23,385	18,523	416	1,123 R	36.7%	35.0%	27.7%
36,974	ST. JOSEPH	23,971	9,836	7,817	6,209	109	2,019 R	41.0%	32.6%	25.9%
26,212	SANILAC	18,758	7,891	5,868	4,894	105	2,023 R	42.1%	31.3%	26.1%
6,277	SCHOOLCRAFT	4,129	1,253	2,139	721	16	886 D	30.3%	51.8%	17.5%
46,013	SHIAWASSEE	32,360	10,930	12,629	8,632	169	1,699 D	33.8%	39.0%	26.7%
31,578	TUSCOLA	24,666	8,636	9,138	6,765	127	502 D	35.0%	37.0%	27.4%
45,982	VAN BUREN	30,237	10,357	12,466	7,255	159	2,109 D	34.3%	41.2%	24.0%
196,243	WASHTENAW	137,466	41,386	73,325	21,889	866	31,939 D	30.1%	53.3%	15.9%
1,296,934	WAYNE	841,965	227,002	508,464	102,074	4,425	281,462 D	27.0%	60.4%	12.1%
17,462	WEXFORD	12,575	4,696	4,894	2,923	62	198 D	37.3%	38.9%	23.2%
6,147,083	TOTAL	4,274,673	1,554,940	1,871,182	824,813	23,738	316,242 D	36.4%	43.8%	19.3%

DETROIT

PRESIDENT 1992

Registration	District	Total Vote	Republican	Democratic	Perot	Other	Plurality	Percentage Total Vote		
								Rep.	Dem.	Perot
13,317	DISTRICT 3	5,994	224	5,577	171	22	5,353 D	3.7%	93.0%	2.9%
29,097	DISTRICT 4	13,007	1,258	10,739	947	63	9,481 D	9.7%	82.6%	7.3%
28,804	DISTRICT 5	14,218	1,545	11,761	865	47	10,216 D	10.9%	82.7%	6.1%
28,126	DISTRICT 6	14,444	2,256	10,920	1,193	75	8,664 D	15.6%	75.6%	8.3%
21,092	DISTRICT 7	9,392	590	8,372	390	40	7,782 D	6.3%	89.1%	4.2%
19,362	DISTRICT 8	8,856	147	8,560	123	26	8,413 D	1.7%	96.7%	1.4%
19,802	DISTRICT 9	8,857	611	7,904	322	20	7,293 D	6.9%	89.2%	3.6%
8,807	DISTRICT 10	3,289	117	3,091	68	13	2,974 D	3.6%	94.0%	2.1%
15,674	DISTRICT 11	5,714	419	4,970	279	46	4,551 D	7.3%	87.0%	4.9%
17,511	DISTRICT 12	7,223	241	6,733	213	36	6,492 D	3.3%	93.2%	2.9%
31,117	DISTRICT 13	14,995	542	14,018	387	48	13,476 D	3.6%	93.5%	2.6%
27,357	DISTRICT 14	13,602	620	12,516	414	52	11,896 D	4.6%	92.0%	3.0%
44,132	DISTRICT 15	24,252	603	23,078	511	60	22,475 D	2.5%	95.2%	2.1%
38,180	DISTRICT 16	20,460	1,148	18,582	662	68	17,434 D	5.6%	90.8%	3.2%
36,917	DISTRICT 17	19,678	1,685	16,908	1,008	77	15,223 D	8.6%	85.9%	5.1%
31,342	DISTRICT 18	14,736	2,883	10,247	1,515	91	7,364 D	19.6%	69.5%	10.3%
31,458	DISTRICT 19	15,772	938	14,134	650	50	13,196 D	5.9%	89.6%	4.1%
32,266	DISTRICT 20	16,256	344	15,559	317	36	15,215 D	2.1%	95.7%	2.0%
29,751	DISTRICT 21	14,362	650	13,240	429	43	12,590 D	4.5%	92.2%	3.0%
22,380	DISTRICT 22	9,934	176	9,554	172	32	9,378 D	1.8%	96.2%	1.7%
18,775	DISTRICT 23	8,442	163	8,118	140	21	7,955 D	1.9%	96.2%	1.7%
10,890	DISTRICT 24	4,495	331	3,959	167	38	3,628 D	7.4%	88.1%	3.7%
19,118	DISTRICT 25	7,194	1,504	4,835	808	47	3,331 D	20.9%	67.2%	11.2%
11,768	DISTRICT 26	5,273	414	4,572	260	27	4,158 D	7.9%	86.7%	4.9%
	ABSENTEE	57,025	7,857	47,380	1,623	165	39,523 D	13.8%	83.1%	2.8%
587,043	TOTAL	337,470	27,266	295,327	13,634	1,243	268,061 D	8.1%	87.5%	4.0%

MICHIGAN

CONGRESS

CD	Year	Total Vote	Republican Vote	Republican Candidate	Democratic Vote	Democratic Candidate	Other Vote	Rep.-Dem. Plurality	Total Vote Rep.	Total Vote Dem.	Major Vote Rep.	Major Vote Dem.
1	1992	268,619	117,056	RUPPE, PHILIP E.	144,857	STUPAK, BART	6,706	27,801 D	43.6%	53.9%	44.7%	55.3%
2	1992	246,761	155,577	HOEKSTRA, PETER	86,265	MILTNER, JOHN H.	4,919	69,312 R	63.0%	35.0%	64.3%	35.7%
3	1992	264,948	162,451	HENRY, PAUL	95,927	KOOISTRA, CAROL S.	6,570	66,524 R	61.3%	36.2%	62.9%	37.1%
4	1992	251,539	157,337	CAMP, DAVE	87,573	DONALDSON, LISA	6,629	69,764 R	62.5%	34.8%	64.2%	35.8%
5	1992	244,992	93,098	MUXLOW, KEITH	147,618	BARCIA, JAMES A.	4,276	54,520 D	38.0%	60.3%	38.7%	61.3%
6	1992	233,112	144,083	UPTON, FREDERICK	89,020	DAVIS, ANDY	9	55,063 R	61.8%	38.2%	61.8%	38.2%
7	1992	152,868	133,972	SMITH, NICK			18,896	133,972 R	87.6%		100.0%	
8	1992	284,707	131,906	CHRYSLER, DICK	135,517	CARR, M. ROBERT	17,284	3,611 D	46.3%	47.6%	49.3%	50.7%
9	1992	249,530	111,798	O'NEILL, MEGAN	133,956	KILDEE, DALE E.	3,776	22,158 D	44.8%	53.7%	45.5%	54.5%
10	1992	260,213	114,918	CARL, DOUGLAS	138,193	BONIOR, DAVID E.	7,102	23,275 D	44.2%	53.1%	45.4%	54.6%
11	1992	293,098	168,940	KNOLLENBERG, JOSEPH K.	117,725	BRIGGS, WALTER	6,433	51,215 R	57.6%	40.2%	58.9%	41.1%
12	1992	261,349	119,357	PAPPAGEORGE, JOHN	137,514	LEVIN, SANDER	4,478	18,157 D	45.7%	52.6%	46.5%	53.5%
13	1992	245,888	105,169	GEAKE, R. ROBERT	127,642	FORD, WILLIAM D.	13,077	22,473 D	42.8%	51.9%	45.2%	54.8%
14	1992	200,879	32,036	GORDON, JOHN W.	165,496	CONYERS, JOHN	3,347	133,460 D	15.9%	82.4%	16.2%	83.8%
15	1992	184,964	31,849	VINCENT, CHARLES C.	148,908	COLLINS, BARBARA-ROSE	4,207	117,059 D	17.2%	80.5%	17.6%	82.4%
16	1992	240,936	75,694	BEAUMONT, FRANK	156,964	DINGELL, JOHN D., JR.	8,278	81,270 D	31.4%	65.1%	32.5%	67.5%

MICHIGAN

1992 GENERAL ELECTION

President   Other vote was 10,175 Libertarian (Marrou); 8,263 Tisch Independent Citizens (Phillips); 2,954 Natural Law (Hagelin); 1,432 Workers League (Halyard); 168 Gritz (write-in); 21 Fulani (write-in); 14 LaRouche (write-in); 711 scattered write-in.

Congress   Other vote was 4,094 Libertarian (Aydlott), 2,570 Natural Law (Clark) and 42 scattered write-in in CD 1; 4,840 Libertarian (Jacobs) and 79 scattered write-in in CD 2; 3,232 Libertarian (Whitelock), 3,228 Natural Law (Normandin) and 110 scattered write-in in CD 3; 3,344 Tisch Independent Citizens (Dennison), 2,027 Libertarian (Bradley), 1,247 Natural Law (List) and 11 scattered write-in in CD 4; 4,270 Workers World (Clarke) and 6 scattered in CD 5; scattered write-in in CD 6; 18,751 Libertarian (Proctor) and 145 scattered in CD 7; 12,155 Independent (McAlpine), 5,115 Libertarian (Marotta) and 14 scattered write-in in CD 8; 1,891 Natural Law (Halverson), 1,872 Workers League (White) and 13 scattered in CD 9; 7,098 Libertarian (Weidner) and 4 scattered write-in in CD 10; 4,144 Libertarian (Wright), 2,269 Natural Law (Clark) and 20 scattered in CD 11; 2,751 Libertarian (Hahn), 1,724 Natural Law (Montgomery) and 3 scattered write-in in CD 12; 8,626 Independent (Roe), 3,314 Tisch Independent Citizens (Jensen), 1,127 Workers League (Roberts) and 10 scattered write-in in CD 13; 2,043 Natural Law (Miller), 1,296 Workers League (Collier) and 8 scattered write-in in CD 14; 2,704 Independent (Harris), 1,496 Natural Law (Meade) and 7 scattered in CD 15; 4,048 Tisch Independent Citizens (Siegle), 2,387 Libertarian (Hampton), 1,842 Workers League (McLaughlin) and 1 scattered write-in in CD 16.

DETROIT

An election district map of Detroit was not available at publication date.

President   Other vote was 528 Libertarian (Marrou); 387 Tisch Independent Citizens (Phillips); 184 Workers League (Halyard); 144 Natural Law (Hagelin).

1992 PRIMARIES

AUGUST 4 REPUBLICAN

Congress   Unopposed in five CD's. Contested as follows:

CD 1   28,279 Philip E. Ruppe; 20,626 Bill Kurtz; 12,443 Stephen P. Dresch.
CD 2   34,470 Peter Hoekstra; 30,376 Guy Vander Jagt; 10,112 Melvin J. DeStigter.
CD 5   20,659 Keith Muxlow; 8,535 G. Stewart Francke; 8,332 Joseph E. Mellendorf.
CD 7   26,029 Nick Smith; 21,840 John Schwarz; 7,036 Thomas D. Wilson; 5,626 Brad Haskins.
CD 8   14,683 Dick Chrysler; 12,209 Margaret O'Connor; 11,408 Sandy Pensler; 1,824 John Mangopoulos.
CD 9   13,666 Megan O'Neill; 10,345 Michael J. Balian; 9,875 Chuck Forrest; 5,669 D. Todd Tindall.
CD 10   20,545 Douglas Carl; 10,845 Robert Huth.
CD 11   29,922 Joseph K. Knollenberg; 20 458 Dave Honigman; 18,870 Alice L. Gilbert.
CD 12   14,545 John Pappageorge; 10,519 Ron Chapman.
CD 13   10,777 R. Robert Geake; 4,711 Raymond Tanter; 3,600 Burl C. Adkins; 1,625 William H. Steele; 1,002 Glen Kassel; 973 Herbert A. Scott.
CD 15   2,919 Charles C. Vincent; 777 Timothy Theodore; 702 John Savage.

AUGUST 4 DEMOCRATIC

Congress   Unopposed in nine CD's. No candidate in CD 7. Contested as follows:

CD 1   24,058 Bart Stupak; 21,899 Mike McElroy; 4,105 Daniel F. Herringa.
CD 2   9,511 John H. Miltner; 7,961 Fred Strand.
CD 5   27,130 James A. Barcia; 16,919 John D. Cherry; 14,665 Don Hare.
CD 11   14,615 Walter Briggs; 9,936 Michael M. Meyer.
CD 14   39,311 John Conyers; 15,775 John Kelly; 5,275 Martha G. Scott; 1,040 Frederick H. Strickland.
CD 15   37,472 Barbara-Rose Collins; 17,774 Tom Barrow.

MICHIGAN

AUGUST 4 TISCH INDEPENDENT CITIZENS

Congress   Unopposed in CD's 4 and 6. Contested as follows:

   CD 16   267 Max Siegle; 214 Robert Bush.

MINNESOTA

GOVERNOR
Arne Carlson (R). Elected 1990 to a four-year term.

SENATORS
David Durenberger (R). Re-elected 1988 to a six-year term. Previously elected 1982 and in 1978 to fill out the remaining four years of the term vacated by the death of Senator Hubert H. Humphrey.

Paul D. Wellstone (D). Elected 1990 to a six-year term.

REPRESENTATIVES
1. Timothy J. Penny (D)
2. David Minge (D)
3. Jim Ramstad (R)
4. Bruce F. Vento (D)
5. Martin O. Sabo (D)
6. Rod Grams (R)
7. Collin C. Peterson (D)
8. James L. Oberstar (D)

POSTWAR VOTE FOR PRESIDENT

Year	Total Vote	Republican Vote	Candidate	Democratic Vote	Candidate	Other Vote	Plurality	Total Vote Rep.	Total Vote Dem.	Major Vote Rep.	Major Vote Dem.
1992 **	2,347,948	747,841	Bush, George	1,020,997	Clinton, Bill	579,110	273,156 D	31.9%	43.5%	42.3%	57.7%
1988	2,096,790	962,337	Bush, George	1,109,471	Dukakis, Michael S.	24,982	147,134 D	45.9%	52.9%	46.4%	53.6%
1984	2,084,449	1,032,603	Reagan, Ronald	1,036,364	Mondale, Walter F.	15,482	3,761 D	49.5%	49.7%	49.9%	50.1%
1980	2,051,980	873,268	Reagan, Ronald	954,174	Carter, Jimmy	224,538	80,906 D	42.6%	46.5%	47.8%	52.2%
1976	1,949,931	819,395	Ford, Gerald R.	1,070,440	Carter, Jimmy	60,096	251,045 D	42.0%	54.9%	43.4%	56.6%
1972	1,741,652	898,269	Nixon, Richard M.	802,346	McGovern, George S.	41,037	95,923 R	51.6%	46.1%	52.8%	47.2%
1968	1,588,506	658,643	Nixon, Richard M.	857,738	Humphrey, Hubert H.	72,125	199,095 D	41.5%	54.0%	43.4%	56.6%
1964	1,554,462	559,624	Goldwater, Barry M.	991,117	Johnson, Lyndon B.	3,721	431,493 D	36.0%	63.8%	36.1%	63.9%
1960	1,541,887	757,915	Nixon, Richard M.	779,933	Kennedy, John F.	4,039	22,018 D	49.2%	50.6%	49.3%	50.7%
1956	1,340,005	719,302	Eisenhower, Dwight D.	617,525	Stevenson, Adlai E.	3,178	101,777 R	53.7%	46.1%	53.8%	46.2%
1952	1,379,483	763,211	Eisenhower, Dwight D.	608,458	Stevenson, Adlai E.	7,814	154,753 R	55.3%	44.1%	55.6%	44.4%
1948	1,212,226	483,617	Dewey, Thomas E.	692,966	Truman, Harry S.	35,643	209,349 D	39.9%	57.2%	41.1%	58.9%

In 1992 the other vote column includes 562,506 votes cast for Perot.

MINNESOTA

POSTWAR VOTE FOR GOVERNOR

Year	Total Vote	Republican Vote	Republican Candidate	Democratic Vote	Democratic Candidate	Other Vote	Rep.-Dem. Plurality	Percentage Total Vote Rep.	Percentage Total Vote Dem.	Percentage Major Vote Rep.	Percentage Major Vote Dem.
1990	1,806,777	895,988	Carlson, Arne	836,218	Perpich, Rudy	74,571	59,770 R	49.6%	46.3%	51.7%	48.3%
1986	1,415,989	606,755	Ludeman, Cal R.	790,138	Perpich, Rudy	19,096	183,383 D	42.9%	55.8%	43.4%	56.6%
1982	1,789,539	715,796	Whitney, Wheelock	1,049,104	Perpich, Rudy	24,639	333,308 D	40.0%	58.6%	40.6%	59.4%
1978	1,585,702	830,019	Quie, Albert H.	718,244	Perpich, Rudy	37,439	111,775 R	52.3%	45.3%	53.6%	46.4%
1974	1,252,898	367,722	Johnson, John W.	786,787	Anderson, Wendell R.	98,389	419,065 D	29.3%	62.8%	31.9%	68.1%
1970	1,365,443	621,780	Head, Douglas M.	737,921	Anderson, Wendell R.	5,742	116,141 D	45.5%	54.0%	45.7%	54.3%
1966	1,295,058	680,593	LeVander, Harold	607,943	Rolvaag, Karl F.	6,522	72,650 R	52.6%	46.9%	52.8%	47.2%
1962 **	1,246,904	619,751	Andersen, Elmer L.	619,842	Rolvaag, Karl F.	7,311	91 D	49.7%	49.7%	50.0%	50.0%
1960	1,550,265	783,813	Andersen, Elmer L.	760,934	Freeman, Orville L.	5,518	22,879 R	50.6%	49.1%	50.7%	49.3%
1958	1,159,915	490,731	MacKinnon, George	658,326	Freeman, Orville L.	10,858	167,595 D	42.3%	56.8%	42.7%	57.3%
1956	1,422,161	685,196	Nelsen, Ancher	731,180	Freeman, Orville L.	5,785	45,984 D	48.2%	51.4%	48.4%	51.6%
1954	1,151,417	538,865	Anderson, C. Elmer	607,099	Freeman, Orville L.	5,453	68,234 D	46.8%	52.7%	47.0%	53.0%
1952	1,418,869	785,125	Anderson, C. Elmer	624,480	Freeman, Orville L.	9,264	160,645 R	55.3%	44.0%	55.7%	44.3%
1950	1,046,632	635,800	Youngdahl, Luther	400,637	Peterson, Harry H.	10,195	235,163 R	60.7%	38.3%	61.3%	38.7%
1948	1,210,894	643,572	Youngdahl, Luther	545,766	Halsted, Charles L.	21,556	97,806 R	53.1%	45.1%	54.1%	45.9%
1946	880,348	519,067	Youngdahl, Luther	349,565	Barker, Harold H.	11,716	169,502 R	59.0%	39.7%	59.8%	40.2%

The term of office of Minnesota's Governor was increased from two to four years effective with the 1962 election.

POSTWAR VOTE FOR SENATOR

Year	Total Vote	Republican Vote	Republican Candidate	Democratic Vote	Democratic Candidate	Other Vote	Rep.-Dem. Plurality	Percentage Total Vote Rep.	Percentage Total Vote Dem.	Percentage Major Vote Rep.	Percentage Major Vote Dem.
1990	1,808,045	864,375	Boschwitz, Rudy	911,999	Wellstone, Paul D.	31,671	47,624 D	47.8%	50.4%	48.7%	51.3%
1988	2,093,953	1,176,210	Durenberger, David	856,694	Humphrey, Hubert H.,III	61,049	319,516 R	56.2%	40.9%	57.9%	42.1%
1984	2,066,143	1,199,926	Boschwitz, Rudy	852,844	Growe, Joan Anderson	13,373	347,082 R	58.1%	41.3%	58.5%	41.5%
1982	1,804,675	949,207	Durenberger, David	840,401	Dayton, Mark	15,067	108,806 R	52.6%	46.6%	53.0%	47.0%
1978	1,580,778	894,092	Boschwitz, Rudy	638,375	Anderson, Wendell R.	48,311	255,717 R	56.6%	40.4%	58.3%	41.7%
1978 S	1,560,724	957,908	Durenberger, David	538,675	Short, Robert E.	64,141	419,233 R	61.4%	34.5%	64.0%	36.0%
1976	1,912,068	478,611	Brekke, Gerald W.	1,290,736	Humphrey, Hubert H.	142,721	812,125 D	25.0%	67.5%	27.1%	72.9%
1972	1,731,653	742,121	Hansen, Philip	981,340	Mondale, Walter F.	8,192	239,219 D	42.9%	56.7%	43.1%	56.9%
1970	1,364,887	568,025	MacGregor, Clark	788,256	Humphrey, Hubert H.	8,606	220,231 D	41.6%	57.8%	41.9%	58.1%
1966	1,271,426	574,868	Forsythe, Robert A.	685,840	Mondale, Walter F.	10,718	110,972 D	45.2%	53.9%	45.6%	54.4%
1964	1,543,590	605,933	Whitney, Wheelock	931,353	McCarthy, Eugene J.	6,304	325,420 D	39.3%	60.3%	39.4%	60.6%
1960	1,536,839	648,586	Peterson, P. K.	884,168	Humphrey, Hubert H.	4,085	235,582 D	42.2%	57.5%	42.3%	57.7%
1958	1,150,883	536,629	Thye, Edward J.	608,847	McCarthy, Eugene J.	5,407	72,218 D	46.6%	52.9%	46.8%	53.2%
1954	1,138,952	479,619	Bjornson, Val	642,193	Humphrey, Hubert H.	17,140	162,574 D	42.1%	56.4%	42.8%	57.2%
1952	1,387,419	785,649	Thye, Edward J.	590,011	Carlson, William E.	11,759	195,638 R	56.6%	42.5%	57.1%	42.9%
1948	1,220,250	485,801	Ball, Joseph H.	729,494	Humphrey, Hubert H.	4,955	243,693 D	39.8%	59.8%	40.0%	60.0%
1946	878,731	517,775	Thye, Edward J.	349,520	Jorgenson, Theodore	11,436	168,255 R	58.9%	39.8%	59.7%	40.3%

One of the 1978 elections was for a short term to fill a vacancy.

MINNESOTA

Districts Established February 19, 1992

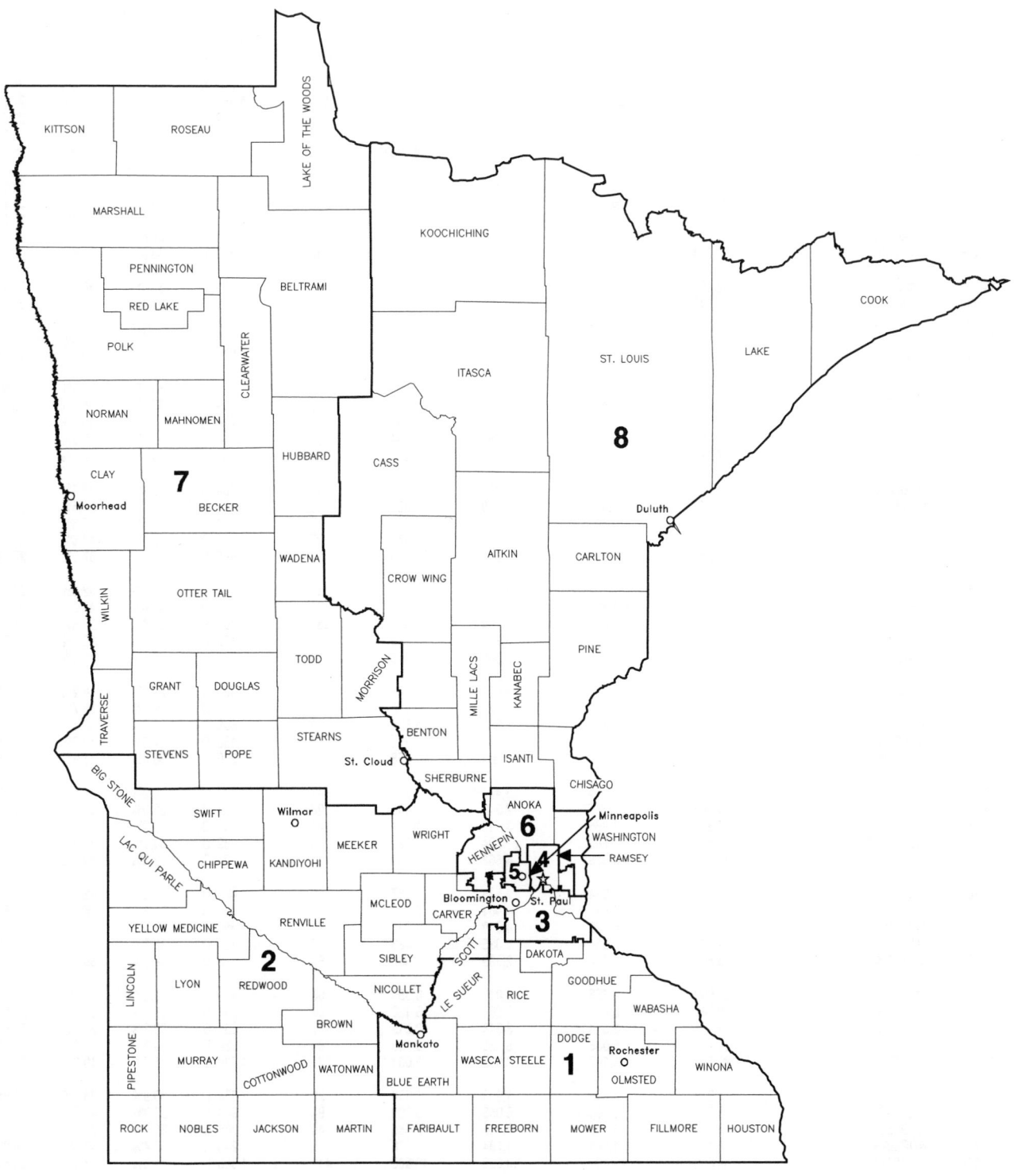

MINNESOTA

PRESIDENT 1992

Registration	County	Total Vote	Republican	Democratic	Perot	Other	Plurality	Percentage Total Vote Rep.	Dem.	Perot
10,590	AITKIN	7,559	2,151	3,400	1,951	57	1,249 D	28.5%	45.0%	25.8%
166,637	ANOKA	130,020	39,458	54,621	35,140	801	15,163 D	30.3%	42.0%	27.0%
18,367	BECKER	13,702	5,430	4,958	3,238	76	472 D	39.6%	36.2%	23.6%
22,205	BELTRAMI	15,987	5,204	7,210	3,473	100	2,006 D	32.6%	45.1%	21.7%
20,106	BENTON	14,371	5,053	5,156	4,048	114	103 D	35.2%	35.9%	28.2%
4,100	BIG STONE	3,420	1,052	1,610	740	18	558 D	30.8%	47.1%	21.6%
41,470	BLUE EARTH	27,847	8,813	11,531	7,299	204	2,718 D	31.6%	41.4%	26.2%
19,087	BROWN	13,621	5,390	4,278	3,845	108	1,112 R	39.6%	31.4%	28.2%
19,857	CARLTON	14,747	3,922	7,736	3,005	84	3,814 D	26.6%	52.5%	20.4%
35,476	CARVER	26,604	10,201	8,349	7,942	112	1,852 R	38.3%	31.4%	29.9%
16,549	CASS	12,197	4,276	4,901	2,939	81	625 D	35.1%	40.2%	24.1%
8,900	CHIPPEWA	6,617	2,143	2,929	1,505	40	786 D	32.4%	44.3%	22.7%
22,756	CHISAGO	17,119	4,813	7,077	5,098	131	1,979 D	28.1%	41.3%	29.8%
33,938	CLAY	23,478	9,666	9,845	3,835	132	179 D	41.2%	41.9%	16.3%
5,068	CLEARWATER	3,758	1,315	1,587	841	15	272 D	35.0%	42.2%	22.4%
3,482	COOK	2,618	878	1,005	704	31	127 D	33.5%	38.4%	26.9%
9,344	COTTONWOOD	6,651	2,481	2,382	1,749	39	99 R	37.3%	35.8%	26.3%
32,581	CROW WING	24,539	9,112	8,896	6,367	164	216 D	37.1%	36.3%	25.9%
206,967	DAKOTA	157,080	52,312	63,660	40,244	864	11,348 D	33.3%	40.5%	25.6%
10,746	DODGE	7,972	3,049	2,620	2,231	72	429 R	38.2%	32.9%	28.0%
20,196	DOUGLAS	15,859	6,356	5,252	4,138	113	1,104 R	40.1%	33.1%	26.1%
11,432	FARIBAULT	9,146	3,439	3,339	2,322	46	100 R	37.6%	36.5%	25.4%
13,953	FILLMORE	10,658	3,583	3,977	3,011	87	394 D	33.6%	37.3%	28.3%
23,012	FREEBORN	17,813	5,089	7,759	4,878	87	2,670 D	28.6%	43.6%	27.4%
26,540	GOODHUE	21,250	7,321	7,916	5,790	223	595 D	34.5%	37.3%	27.2%
5,257	GRANT	3,666	1,201	1,561	885	19	360 D	32.8%	42.6%	24.1%
790,678	HENNEPIN	586,619	179,581	278,648	123,659	4,731	99,067 D	30.6%	47.5%	21.1%
13,125	HOUSTON	10,451	3,853	3,744	2,697	157	109 R	36.9%	35.8%	25.8%
11,397	HUBBARD	8,589	3,227	3,362	1,949	51	135 D	37.6%	39.1%	22.7%
17,677	ISANTI	13,366	3,988	5,386	3,898	94	1,398 D	29.8%	40.3%	29.2%
27,100	ITASCA	20,838	5,952	9,621	5,147	118	3,669 D	28.6%	46.2%	24.7%
8,027	JACKSON	6,252	1,824	2,481	1,918	29	563 D	29.2%	39.7%	30.7%
8,413	KANABEC	6,288	1,876	2,532	1,836	44	656 D	29.8%	40.3%	29.2%
25,637	KANDIYOHI	19,656	6,784	7,914	4,869	89	1,130 D	34.5%	40.3%	24.8%
4,407	KITTSON	2,984	1,098	1,307	558	21	209 D	36.8%	43.8%	18.7%
9,995	KOOCHICHING	7,465	1,954	3,474	1,993	44	1,481 D	26.2%	46.5%	26.7%
6,480	LAC QUI PARLE	4,968	1,435	2,342	1,163	28	907 D	28.9%	47.1%	23.4%
7,957	LAKE	6,357	1,465	3,415	1,437	40	1,950 D	23.0%	53.7%	22.6%
2,623	LAKE OF THE WOODS	2,198	762	794	629	13	32 D	34.7%	36.1%	28.6%
16,923	LE SUEUR	11,954	3,858	4,662	3,363	71	804 D	32.3%	39.0%	28.1%
4,963	LINCOLN	3,636	1,084	1,555	967	30	471 D	29.8%	42.8%	26.6%
17,791	LYON	12,324	4,591	4,481	3,180	72	110 R	37.3%	36.4%	25.8%
20,972	MCLEOD	15,347	5,422	4,919	4,933	73	489 R	35.3%	32.1%	32.1%
3,566	MAHNOMEN	2,389	854	1,035	483	17	181 D	35.7%	43.3%	20.2%
6,855	MARSHALL	5,803	2,136	2,309	1,306	52	173 D	36.8%	39.8%	22.5%
14,656	MARTIN	11,609	4,438	4,019	3,089	63	419 R	38.2%	34.6%	26.6%
14,771	MEEKER	10,540	3,497	3,861	3,120	62	364 D	33.2%	36.6%	29.6%
13,038	MILLE LACS	9,154	2,814	3,648	2,615	77	834 D	30.7%	39.9%	28.6%
19,441	MORRISON	14,442	5,038	5,588	3,710	106	550 D	34.9%	38.7%	25.7%
26,270	MOWER	20,210	5,147	9,935	5,001	127	4,788 D	25.5%	49.2%	24.7%
6,500	MURRAY	5,213	1,609	1,993	1,588	23	384 D	30.9%	38.2%	30.5%
20,614	NICOLLET	15,039	5,091	6,055	3,799	94	964 D	33.9%	40.3%	25.3%
12,973	NOBLES	9,930	3,548	3,756	2,586	40	208 D	35.7%	37.8%	26.0%
5,476	NORMAN	4,121	1,541	1,784	776	20	243 D	37.4%	43.3%	18.8%
76,665	OLMSTED	56,662	23,404	19,039	13,806	413	4,365 R	41.3%	33.6%	24.4%
35,310	OTTER TAIL	26,670	11,074	9,176	6,274	146	1,898 R	41.5%	34.4%	23.5%
8,591	PENNINGTON	6,359	2,155	2,578	1,598	28	423 D	33.9%	40.5%	25.1%
15,377	PINE	10,813	2,841	4,929	2,952	91	1,977 D	26.3%	45.6%	27.3%
6,466	PIPESTONE	5,170	1,953	1,773	1,429	15	180 R	37.8%	34.3%	27.6%
20,207	POLK	14,934	5,817	5,850	3,176	91	33 D	39.0%	39.2%	21.3%

MINNESOTA

PRESIDENT 1992

Registration	County	Total Vote	Republican	Democratic	Perot	Other	Plurality	Percentage Total Vote		
								Rep.	Dem.	Perot
7,931	POPE	5,970	1,886	2,619	1,390	75	733 D	31.6%	43.9%	23.3%
333,718	RAMSEY	251,915	68,206	130,932	50,757	2,020	62,726 D	27.1%	52.0%	20.1%
3,212	RED LAKE	2,201	691	1,020	472	18	329 D	31.4%	46.3%	21.4%
11,111	REDWOOD	8,913	3,408	2,740	2,710	55	668 R	38.2%	30.7%	30.4%
11,584	RENVILLE	8,920	2,852	3,414	2,598	56	562 D	32.0%	38.3%	29.1%
32,496	RICE	24,113	7,015	10,908	6,057	133	3,893 D	29.1%	45.2%	25.1%
7,110	ROCK	5,338	2,065	2,006	1,244	23	59 R	38.7%	37.6%	23.3%
9,813	ROSEAU	7,269	2,785	2,346	2,099	39	439 R	38.3%	32.3%	28.9%
146,833	ST. LOUIS	108,815	24,579	61,813	21,714	709	37,234 D	22.6%	56.8%	20.0%
41,569	SCOTT	32,216	10,936	11,225	9,881	174	289 D	33.9%	34.8%	30.7%
28,513	SHERBURNE	21,841	7,339	7,843	6,534	125	504 D	33.6%	35.9%	29.9%
9,483	SIBLEY	7,185	2,315	2,421	2,407	42	14 D	32.2%	33.7%	33.5%
82,454	STEARNS	59,340	22,502	21,451	14,834	553	1,051 R	37.9%	36.1%	25.0%
20,550	STEELE	15,789	5,964	5,152	4,542	131	812 R	37.8%	32.6%	28.8%
6,820	STEVENS	5,816	2,229	2,466	1,086	35	237 D	38.3%	42.4%	18.7%
7,637	SWIFT	5,991	1,603	2,980	1,359	49	1,377 D	26.8%	49.7%	22.7%
15,411	TODD	11,104	3,990	4,059	2,976	79	69 D	35.9%	36.6%	26.8%
3,208	TRAVERSE	2,484	841	1,053	582	8	212 D	33.9%	42.4%	23.4%
13,420	WABASHA	10,217	3,397	3,736	3,012	72	339 D	33.2%	36.6%	29.5%
9,908	WADENA	6,398	2,492	2,340	1,535	31	152 R	38.9%	36.6%	24.0%
12,908	WASECA	9,006	3,118	3,146	2,621	121	28 D	34.6%	34.9%	29.1%
109,158	WASHINGTON	85,499	26,568	35,820	22,585	526	9,252 D	31.1%	41.9%	26.4%
7,584	WATONWAN	5,578	1,871	2,100	1,574	33	229 D	33.5%	37.6%	28.2%
4,737	WILKIN	3,510	1,626	1,122	748	14	504 R	46.3%	32.0%	21.3%
38,307	WINONA	24,518	8,585	9,707	5,993	233	1,122 D	35.0%	39.6%	24.4%
45,874	WRIGHT	35,160	11,650	12,465	10,829	216	815 D	33.1%	35.5%	30.8%
7,995	YELLOW MEDICINE	6,193	1,909	2,593	1,645	46	684 D	30.8%	41.9%	26.6%
3,138,901	TOTAL	2,347,948	747,841	1,020,997	562,506	16,604	273,156 D	31.9%	43.5%	24.0%

MINNESOTA

CONGRESS

CD	Year	Total Vote	Republican		Democratic		Other Vote	Rep.-Dem. Plurality	Percentage			
			Vote	Candidate	Vote	Candidate			Total Vote		Major Vote	
									Rep.	Dem.	Rep.	Dem.
1	1992	279,430	72,367	DROOGSMA, TIMOTHY R.	206,369	PENNY, TIMOTHY J.	694	134,002 D	25.9%	73.9%	26.0%	74.0%
2	1992	276,303	131,587	LUDEMAN, CAL R.	132,156	MINGE, DAVID	12,560	569 D	47.6%	47.8%	49.9%	50.1%
3	1992	314,731	200,240	RAMSTAD, JIM	104,606	MANDELL, PAUL	9,885	95,634 R	63.6%	33.2%	65.7%	34.3%
4	1992	277,956	101,744	MAITLAND, IAN	159,796	VENTO, BRUCE F.	16,416	58,052 D	36.6%	57.5%	38.9%	61.1%
5	1992	277,094	77,093	MORIARTY, STEPHEN A.	174,139	SABO, MARTIN O.	25,862	97,046 D	27.8%	62.8%	30.7%	69.3%
6	1992	301,023	133,564	GRAMS, ROD	100,016	SIKORSKI, GERRY	67,443	33,548 R	44.4%	33.2%	57.2%	42.8%
7	1992	265,524	130,396	OMANN, BERNIE	133,886	PETERSON, COLLIN C.	1,242	3,490 D	49.1%	50.4%	49.3%	50.7%
8	1992	283,031	83,823	HERWIG, PHIL	167,104	OBERSTAR, JAMES L.	32,104	83,281 D	29.6%	59.0%	33.4%	66.6%

MINNESOTA

1992 GENERAL ELECTION

In Minnesota the Democratic party is known as the Democratic-Farmer-Labor party an the Republican party as the Independent-Republican party; candidates appear on the ballot with these designations.

President   Other vote was 3,374 Libertarian (Marrou); 3,363 Constitution (Gritz); 2,659 Grassroots (Herer); 1,406 Natural Law (Hagelin); 990 Socialist Workers (Warren); 958 New Alliance (Fulani); 733 Taxpayers (Phillips); 622 Independents Economic Recovery (LaRouche); 2,499 scattered write-in.

Congress   Other vote was scattered write-in in CD 1; 12,146 Independent (Bentz) and 414 scattered write-in in CD 2; 9,164 Grassroots (Fellman) and 721 scattered write-in in CD 3; 6,732 Independent (Willess), 4,418 Grassroots (Vacek), 3,602 Natural Law (Johnson), 1,236 Socialist Workers (Rothenberg) and 428 scattered write-in in CD 4; 6,786 Grassroots (Bentley), 5,927 New Alliance (Coleman), 5,499 Natural Law (Mellen), 4,809 Independent (Mesaros), 2,062 Socialist Workers (Nisan) and 779 scattered write-in in CD 5; 48,329 Independent (Barkley), 16,411 Independents for Perot (Peterson); 2,400 Natural Law (Firnstahl) and 303 scattered write-in in CD 6; scattered write-in in CD 7; 22,619 Perot Choice (Welty), 8,602 Term Limits Candidate (Henspeter) and 883 scattered write-in in CD 8.

1992 PRIMARIES

SEPTEMBER 15 REPUBLICAN

Congress   Unopposed in three CD's. Contested as follows:

CD 1   14,380 Timothy R. Droogsma; 6,110 Elaine Prom; 4,500 E. B. Henderson.
CD 4   13,537 Ian Maitland; 4,720 Kevin Berglund; 3,857 Mary Jane Rachner.
CD 5   8,485 Stephen A. Moriarty; 4,149 Raymond Gilbertson.
CD 6   11,818 Rod Grams; 5,404 James C. Hillegass.
CD 7   15,345 Bernie Omann; 8,056 Phyllis Onsgard.

SEPTEMBER 15 DEMOCRATIC

Congress   Unopposed in CD 4. Contested as follows:

CD 1   29,816 Timothy J. Penny; 1,618 E. Douglas Anderson; 1,131 Joseph B. Campbell.
CD 2   13,468 David Minge; 7,465 Pat O'Reilly; 4,282 Andrew Olson.
CD 3   9,204 Paul Mandell; 8,526 Richard Franson; 3,586 Kent S. Herschbach.
CD 5   35,168 Martin O. Sabo; 14,519 Lisa Niebauer-Stall; 2,456 James W. Therkelsen.
CD 6   34,932 Gerry Sikorski; 32,881 Tad Jude; 1,747 Richard T. Van Bergen; 1,299 Lester Betts.
CD 7   30,917 Collin C. Peterson; 12,464 Lorelei Kraft.
CD 8   52,392 James L. Oberstar; 14,535 Leonard J. Richards.

MISSISSIPPI

GOVERNOR
Kirk Fordice (R). Elected 1991 to a four-year term.

SENATORS
Thad Cochran (R). Re-elected 1990 to a six-year term. Previously elected 1984, 1978.

Trent Lott (R). Elected 1988 to a six-year term.

REPRESENTATIVES
1. Jamie L. Whitten (D)
2. Mike Espy (D) (see page 1)
3. G. V. Montgomery (D)
4. Mike Parker (D)
5. Gene Taylor (D)

POSTWAR VOTE FOR PRESIDENT

| | | Republican | | Democratic | | Other | | Percentage | | | |
| | Total | | | | | | | Total Vote | | Major Vote | |
Year	Vote	Vote	Candidate	Vote	Candidate	Vote	Plurality	Rep.	Dem.	Rep.	Dem.
1992 **	981,793	487,793	Bush, George	400,258	Clinton, Bill	93,742	87,535 R	49.7%	40.8%	54.9%	45.1%
1988	931,527	557,890	Bush, George	363,921	Dukakis, Michael S.	9,716	193,969 R	59.9%	39.1%	60.5%	39.5%
1984	941,104	582,377	Reagan, Ronald	352,192	Mondale, Walter F.	6,535	230,185 R	61.9%	37.4%	62.3%	37.7%
1980	892,620	441,089	Reagan, Ronald	429,281	Carter, Jimmy	22,250	11,808 R	49.4%	48.1%	50.7%	49.3%
1976	769,361	366,846	Ford, Gerald R.	381,309	Carter, Jimmy	21,206	14,463 D	47.7%	49.6%	49.0%	51.0%
1972	645,963	505,125	Nixon, Richard M.	126,782	McGovern, George S.	14,056	378,343 R	78.2%	19.6%	79.9%	20.1%
1968 **	654,509	88,516	Nixon, Richard M.	150,644	Humphrey, Hubert H.	415,349	264,705 A	13.5%	23.0%	37.0%	63.0%
1964	409,146	356,528	Goldwater, Barry M.	52,618	Johnson, Lyndon B.		303,910 R	87.1%	12.9%	87.1%	12.9%
1960 **	298,171	73,561	Nixon, Richard M.	108,362	Kennedy, John F.	116,248	7,886 U	24.7%	36.3%	40.4%	59.6%
1956	248,104	60,685	Eisenhower, Dwight D.	144,453	Stevenson, Adlai E.	42,966	83,768 D	24.5%	58.2%	29.6%	70.4%
1952	285,532	112,966	Eisenhower, Dwight D.	172,566	Stevenson, Adlai E.		59,600 D	39.6%	60.4%	39.6%	60.4%
1948 **	192,190	5,043	Dewey, Thomas E.	19,384	Truman, Harry S.	167,763	148,154 SR	2.6%	10.1%	20.6%	79.4%

In 1992 the other vote column includes 85,626 votes cast for Perot. In 1968 other vote was Independent (Wallace). In 1960 other vote was Unpledged Independent Democratic. In 1948 other vote was 167,538 States Rights and 225 Progressive.

POSTWAR VOTE FOR GOVERNOR

| | | Republican | | Democratic | | Other | Rep.-Dem. | Percentage | | | |
| | Total | | | | | | | Total Vote | | Major Vote | |
Year	Vote	Vote	Candidate	Vote	Candidate	Vote	Plurality	Rep.	Dem.	Rep.	Dem.
1991	711,188	361,500	Fordice, Kirk	338,435	Mabus, Ray	11,253	23,065 R	50.8%	47.6%	51.6%	48.4%
1987	721,695	336,006	Reed, Jack	385,689	Mabus, Ray		49,683 D	46.6%	53.4%	46.6%	53.4%
1983	742,737	288,764	Bramlett, Leon	409,209	Allain, William A.	44,764	120,445 D	38.9%	55.1%	41.4%	58.6%
1979	677,322	263,702	Carmichael, Gil	413,620	Winter, William F.		149,918 D	38.9%	61.1%	38.9%	61.1%
1975	708,033	319,632	Carmichael, Gil	369,568	Finch, Cliff	18,833	49,936 D	45.1%	52.2%	46.4%	53.6%
1971	780,537		—	601,122	Waller, William L.	179,415	601,122 D		77.0%		100.0%
1967	448,697	133,379	Phillips, Rubel L.	315,318	Williams, John Bell		181,939 D	29.7%	70.3%	29.7%	70.3%
1963	363,971	138,515	Phillips, Rubel L.	225,456	Johnson, Paul B.		86,941 D	38.1%	61.9%	38.1%	61.9%
1959	57,671		—	57,671	Barnett, Ross R.		57,671 D		100.0%		100.0%
1955	40,707		—	40,707	Coleman, James P.		40,707 D		100.0%		100.0%
1951	43,422		—	43,422	White, Hugh		43,422 D		100.0%		100.0%
1947	166,095		—	161,993	Wright, Fielding L.	4,102	161,993 D		97.5%		100.0%

MISSISSIPPI

POSTWAR VOTE FOR SENATOR

Year	Total Vote	Republican Vote	Republican Candidate	Democratic Vote	Democratic Candidate	Other Vote	Rep.-Dem. Plurality	Percentage Total Vote Rep.	Percentage Total Vote Dem.	Percentage Major Vote Rep.	Percentage Major Vote Dem.
1990	274,244	274,244	Cochran, Thad		—		274,244 R	100.0%		100.0%	
1988	946,719	510,380	Lott, Trent	436,339	Dowdy, Wayne		74,041 R	53.9%	46.1%	53.9%	46.1%
1984	952,240	580,314	Cochran, Thad	371,926	Winter, William F.		208,388 R	60.9%	39.1%	60.9%	39.1%
1982	645,026	230,927	Barbour, Haley	414,099	Stennis, John		183,172 D	35.8%	64.2%	35.8%	64.2%
1978	583,936	263,089	Cochran, Thad	185,454	Dantin, Maurice	135,393	77,635 R	45.1%	31.8%	58.7%	41.3%
1976	554,433		—	554,433	Stennis, John		554,433 D		100.0%		100.0%
1972	645,746	249,779	Carmichael, Gil	375,102	Eastland, James O.	20,865	125,323 D	38.7%	58.1%	40.0%	60.0%
1970	324,215		—	286,622	Stennis, John	37,593	286,622 D		88.4%		100.0%
1966	393,900	105,150	Walker, Prentiss	258,248	Eastland, James O.	30,502	153,098 D	26.7%	65.6%	28.9%	71.1%
1964	343,364		—	343,364	Stennis, John		343,364 D		100.0%		100.0%
1960	266,148	21,807	Moore, Joe A.	244,341	Eastland, James O.		222,534 D	8.2%	91.8%	8.2%	91.8%
1958	61,039		—	61,039	Stennis, John		61,039 D		100.0%		100.0%
1954	105,526	4,678	White, James A.	100,848	Eastland, James O.		96,170 D	4.4%	95.6%	4.4%	95.6%
1952	233,919		—	233,919	Stennis, John		233,919 D		100.0%		100.0%
1948	151,478		—	151,478	Eastland, James O.		151,478 D		100.0%		100.0%
1947 S	193,709		[See note below]								
1946	46,747		—	46,747	Bilbo, Theodore		46,747 D		100.0%		100.0%

The 1947 election was for a short term to fill a vacancy and was held without party designation or nomination; John Stennis polled 52,068 votes (26.9% of the total vote) and won the election with a 6,343 plurality. Other candidate votes in this election were 45,725 W. M. Colmer; 43,642 Forrest B. Jackson; 27,159 Paul B. Johnson; 24,492 John E. Rankin and 623 R. L. Collins.

MISSISSIPPI

Districts Established February 21, 1992

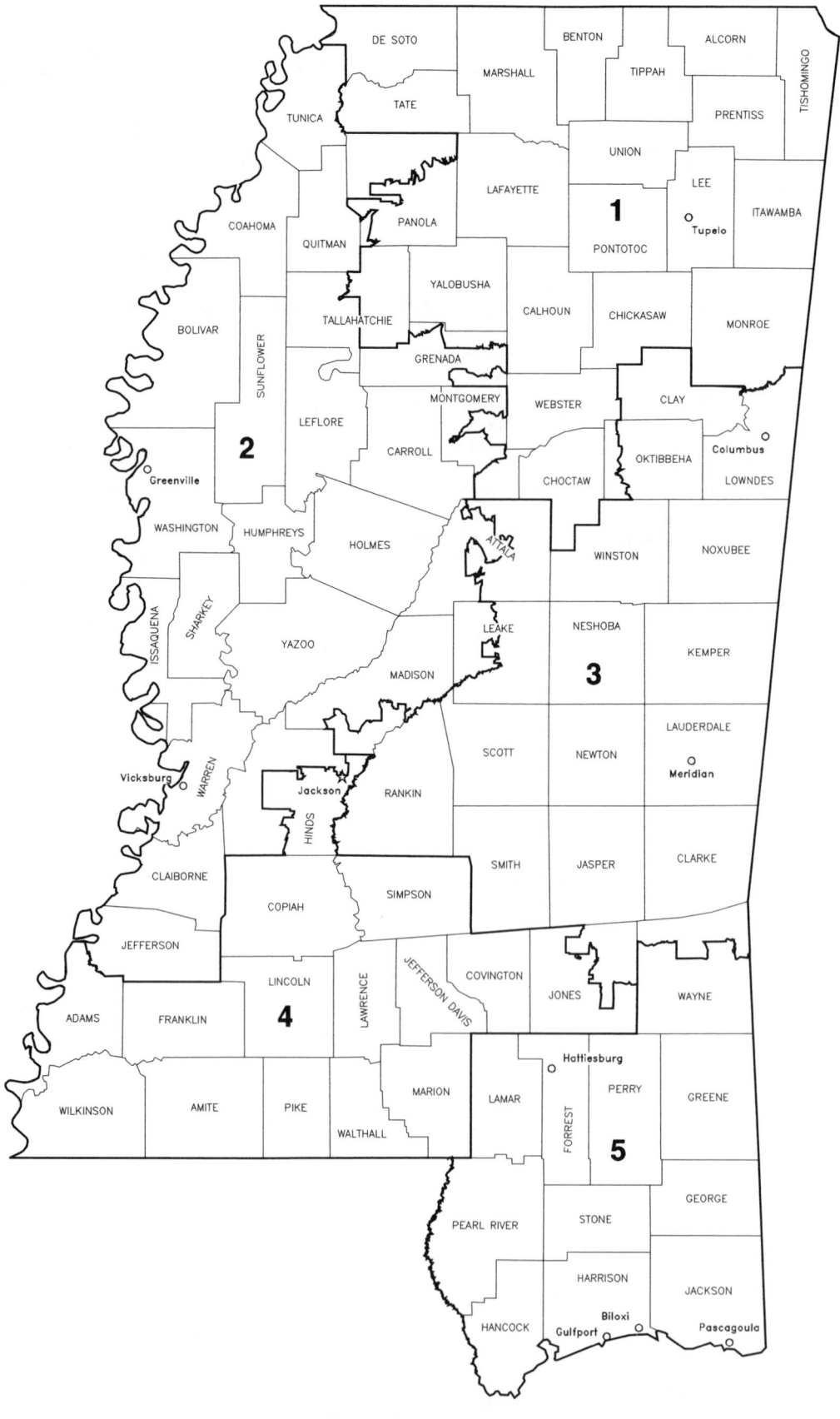

MISSISSIPPI

PRESIDENT 1992

Registration	County	Total Vote	Republican	Democratic	Perot	Other	Plurality	Percentage Total Vote		
								Rep.	Dem.	Perot
25,336	ADAMS	15,877	5,831	8,255	1,753	38	2,424 D	36.7%	52.0%	11.0%
22,004	ALCORN	14,136	6,249	6,373	1,349	165	124 D	44.2%	45.1%	9.5%
9,442	AMITE	5,681	2,561	2,608	498	14	47 D	45.1%	45.9%	8.8%
12,364	ATTALA	7,087	3,520	3,015	529	23	505 R	49.7%	42.5%	7.5%
6,305	BENTON	3,955	1,253	2,402	293	7	1,149 D	31.7%	60.7%	7.4%
23,835	BOLIVAR	14,226	4,752	8,801	593	80	4,049 D	33.4%	61.9%	4.2%
10,271	CALHOUN	6,273	3,191	2,462	607	13	729 R	50.9%	39.2%	9.7%
5,887	CARROLL	3,084	1,695	1,182	200	7	513 R	55.0%	38.3%	6.5%
12,041	CHICKASAW	7,007	3,150	3,220	629	8	70 D	45.0%	46.0%	9.0%
5,861	CHOCTAW	3,768	2,026	1,435	298	9	591 R	53.8%	38.1%	7.9%
7,923	CLAIBORNE	4,412	935	3,302	161	14	2,367 D	21.2%	74.8%	3.6%
10,547	CLARKE	6,934	4,207	2,259	450	18	1,948 R	60.7%	32.6%	6.5%
11,274	CLAY	8,563	3,297	4,620	626	20	1,323 D	38.5%	54.0%	7.3%
17,092	COAHOMA	11,180	4,120	6,409	518	133	2,289 D	36.9%	57.3%	4.6%
16,649	COPIAH	9,449	4,600	4,397	409	43	203 R	48.7%	46.5%	4.3%
13,678	COVINGTON	6,996	3,525	2,775	654	42	750 R	50.4%	39.7%	9.3%
40,300	DE SOTO	27,575	16,104	8,833	2,569	69	7,271 R	58.4%	32.0%	9.3%
31,505	FORREST	22,753	12,432	8,333	1,909	79	4,099 R	54.6%	36.6%	8.4%
5,781	FRANKLIN	3,938	1,942	1,587	393	16	355 R	49.3%	40.3%	10.0%
13,268	GEORGE	9,509	4,141	2,650	1,335	1,383	1,491 R	43.5%	27.9%	14.0%
9,078	GREENE	4,636	2,406	1,664	559	7	742 R	51.9%	35.9%	12.1%
15,740	GRENADA	9,568	4,721	4,203	609	35	518 R	49.3%	43.9%	6.4%
25,509	HANCOCK	13,440	6,422	4,651	2,302	65	1,771 R	47.8%	34.6%	17.1%
72,155	HARRISON	47,407	25,049	15,268	6,855	235	9,781 R	52.8%	32.2%	14.5%
149,538	HINDS	96,024	45,031	43,434	5,341	2,218	1,597 R	46.9%	45.2%	5.6%
14,582	HOLMES	6,014	1,694	4,092	203	25	2,398 D	28.2%	68.0%	3.4%
9,338	HUMPHREYS	4,683	1,721	2,696	258	8	975 D	36.7%	57.6%	5.5%
1,327	ISSAQUENA	990	298	550	79	63	252 D	30.1%	55.6%	8.0%
13,295	ITAWAMBA	8,713	4,142	3,635	918	18	507 R	47.5%	41.7%	10.5%
75,300	JACKSON	44,930	25,321	13,017	6,484	108	12,304 R	56.4%	29.0%	14.4%
11,979	JASPER	6,428	2,789	3,059	568	12	270 D	43.4%	47.6%	8.8%
6,274	JEFFERSON	3,522	562	2,796	156	8	2,234 D	16.0%	79.4%	4.4%
10,181	JEFFERSON DAVIS	5,633	2,228	2,991	382	32	763 D	39.6%	53.1%	6.8%
51,115	JONES	24,430	13,824	8,035	2,523	48	5,789 R	56.6%	32.9%	10.3%
6,947	KEMPER	4,361	1,830	2,243	278	10	413 D	42.0%	51.4%	6.4%
22,479	LAFAYETTE	11,397	5,251	5,224	861	61	27 R	46.1%	45.8%	7.6%
19,385	LAMAR	13,032	8,259	3,208	1,543	22	5,051 R	63.4%	24.6%	11.8%
45,934	LAUDERDALE	27,466	17,098	8,489	1,659	220	8,609 R	62.3%	30.9%	6.0%
10,007	LAWRENCE	6,095	2,689	2,582	765	59	107 R	44.1%	42.4%	12.6%
11,995	LEAKE	7,786	3,943	3,333	497	13	610 R	50.6%	42.8%	6.4%
36,380	LEE	22,501	12,231	7,710	2,041	519	4,521 R	54.4%	34.3%	9.1%
30,261	LEFLORE	12,498	5,298	6,374	611	215	1,076 D	42.4%	51.0%	4.9%
20,057	LINCOLN	13,091	7,040	4,744	1,281	26	2,296 R	53.8%	36.2%	9.8%
31,341	LOWNDES	18,835	10,509	6,552	1,716	58	3,957 R	55.8%	34.8%	9.1%
34,453	MADISON	23,721	12,810	9,386	1,478	47	3,424 R	54.0%	39.6%	6.2%
21,994	MARION	11,613	5,776	4,654	1,162	21	1,122 R	49.7%	40.1%	10.0%
19,686	MARSHALL	12,512	3,847	7,913	689	63	4,066 D	30.7%	63.2%	5.5%
22,418	MONROE	12,224	5,994	4,933	1,255	42	1,061 R	49.0%	40.4%	10.3%
9,704	MONTGOMERY	4,776	2,324	2,076	370	6	248 R	48.7%	43.5%	7.7%
19,268	NESHOBA	10,042	6,135	3,090	794	23	3,045 R	61.1%	30.8%	7.9%
14,238	NEWTON	7,806	5,128	2,146	494	38	2,982 R	65.7%	27.5%	6.3%
8,870	NOXUBEE	5,037	1,623	3,188	203	23	1,565 D	32.2%	63.3%	4.0%
18,576	OKTIBBEHA	13,156	6,381	5,726	984	65	655 R	48.5%	43.5%	7.5%
22,192	PANOLA	11,460	4,644	6,066	729	21	1,422 D	40.5%	52.9%	6.4%
21,887	PEARL RIVER	14,797	7,726	4,683	2,352	36	3,043 R	52.2%	31.6%	15.9%
8,398	PERRY	4,501	2,538	1,490	462	11	1,048 R	56.4%	33.1%	10.3%
18,955	PIKE	13,679	6,005	6,279	1,380	15	274 D	43.9%	45.9%	10.1%
12,028	PONTOTOC	8,366	4,595	2,965	777	29	1,630 R	54.9%	35.4%	9.3%
14,753	PRENTISS	8,526	4,317	3,385	781	43	932 R	50.6%	39.7%	9.2%
7,889	QUITMAN	4,093	1,451	2,422	210	10	971 D	35.5%	59.2%	5.1%

MISSISSIPPI

PRESIDENT 1992

Registration	County	Total Vote	Republican	Democratic	Perot	Other	Plurality	Percentage Total Vote		
								Rep.	Dem.	Perot
50,130	RANKIN	36,210	24,537	8,155	3,454	64	16,382 R	67.8%	22.5%	9.5%
18,965	SCOTT	9,329	5,268	3,349	691	21	1,919 R	56.5%	35.9%	7.4%
3,121	SHARKEY	2,752	1,008	1,526	145	73	518 D	36.6%	55.5%	5.3%
13,058	SIMPSON	9,326	5,358	3,213	726	29	2,145 R	57.5%	34.5%	7.8%
9,186	SMITH	6,788	4,106	1,968	680	34	2,138 R	60.5%	29.0%	10.0%
8,551	STONE	4,209	2,295	1,447	447	20	848 R	54.5%	34.4%	10.6%
22,165	SUNFLOWER	9,391	3,726	5,050	600	15	1,324 D	39.7%	53.8%	6.4%
11,747	TALLAHATCHIE	5,518	2,213	2,902	380	23	689 D	40.1%	52.6%	6.9%
17,586	TATE	8,371	4,196	3,519	634	22	677 R	50.1%	42.0%	7.6%
18,343	TIPPAH	8,739	4,444	3,475	802	18	969 R	50.9%	39.8%	9.2%
13,939	TISHOMINGO	8,072	3,393	3,910	751	18	517 D	42.0%	48.4%	9.3%
6,228	TUNICA	2,243	693	1,451	96	3	758 D	30.9%	64.7%	4.3%
16,435	UNION	9,742	5,173	3,714	816	39	1,459 R	53.1%	38.1%	8.4%
10,890	WALTHALL	5,967	2,728	2,476	711	52	252 R	45.7%	41.5%	11.9%
38,231	WARREN	20,578	10,209	8,175	2,146	48	2,034 R	49.6%	39.7%	10.4%
30,960	WASHINGTON	19,689	7,598	10,588	795	708	2,990 D	38.6%	53.8%	4.0%
12,500	WAYNE	7,783	3,874	3,064	824	21	810 R	49.8%	39.4%	10.6%
8,453	WEBSTER	4,988	2,791	1,746	444	7	1,045 R	56.0%	35.0%	8.9%
7,883	WILKINSON	4,945	1,399	3,210	307	29	1,811 D	28.3%	64.9%	6.2%
14,604	WINSTON	8,968	4,311	3,953	688	16	358 R	48.1%	44.1%	7.7%
10,219	YALOBUSHA	5,248	2,179	2,617	438	14	438 D	41.5%	49.9%	8.3%
20,087	YAZOO	10,745	5,113	4,880	669	83	233 R	47.6%	45.4%	6.2%
1,640,150	TOTAL	981,793	487,793	400,258	85,626	8,116	87,535 R	49.7%	40.8%	8.7%

MISSISSIPPI

GOVERNOR 1991

Registration	County	Total Vote	Republican	Democratic	Other	Rep.-Dem. Plurality	Total Vote Rep.	Total Vote Dem.	Major Vote Rep.	Major Vote Dem.
25,110	ADAMS	11,293	4,554	6,631	108	2,077 D	40.3%	58.7%	40.7%	59.3%
20,917	ALCORN	6,455	3,216	3,070	169	146 R	49.8%	47.6%	51.2%	48.8%
9,355	AMITE	4,704	2,552	2,097	55	455 R	54.3%	44.6%	54.9%	45.1%
12,282	ATTALA	5,703	3,269	2,384	50	885 R	57.3%	41.8%	57.8%	42.2%
6,274	BENTON	2,661	861	1,755	45	894 D	32.4%	66.0%	32.9%	67.1%
23,164	BOLIVAR	8,350	3,062	5,146	142	2,084 D	36.7%	61.6%	37.3%	62.7%
10,480	CALHOUN	5,920	3,208	2,612	100	596 R	54.2%	44.1%	55.1%	44.9%
5,570	CARROLL	3,108	1,789	1,295	24	494 R	57.6%	41.7%	58.0%	42.0%
11,966	CHICKASAW	5,439	2,691	2,657	91	34 R	49.5%	48.9%	50.3%	49.7%
5,996	CHOCTAW	2,999	1,354	1,611	34	257 D	45.1%	53.7%	45.7%	54.3%
8,078	CLAIBORNE	4,150	1,057	3,045	48	1,988 D	25.5%	73.4%	25.8%	74.2%
9,865	CLARKE	5,896	3,967	1,755	174	2,212 R	67.3%	29.8%	69.3%	30.7%
13,024	CLAY	5,383	2,192	3,131	60	939 D	40.7%	58.2%	41.2%	58.8%
17,829	COAHOMA	8,245	2,704	5,452	89	2,748 D	32.8%	66.1%	33.2%	66.8%
16,260	COPIAH	7,993	4,212	3,703	78	509 R	52.7%	46.3%	53.2%	46.8%
13,197	COVINGTON	6,347	3,948	2,270	129	1,678 R	62.2%	35.8%	63.5%	36.5%
34,554	DE SOTO	15,727	5,486	9,993	248	4,507 D	34.9%	63.5%	35.4%	64.6%
29,829	FORREST	17,732	10,072	7,371	289	2,701 R	56.8%	41.6%	57.7%	42.3%
5,864	FRANKLIN	3,159	1,933	1,187	39	746 R	61.2%	37.6%	62.0%	38.0%
13,119	GEORGE	4,548	2,352	2,119	77	233 R	51.7%	46.6%	52.6%	47.4%
9,079	GREENE	3,314	1,884	1,372	58	512 R	56.8%	41.4%	57.9%	42.1%
15,611	GRENADA	5,531	2,758	2,728	45	30 R	49.9%	49.3%	50.3%	49.7%
22,268	HANCOCK	9,888	3,437	6,278	173	2,841 D	34.8%	63.5%	35.4%	64.6%
69,203	HARRISON	35,507	13,629	21,520	358	7,891 D	38.4%	60.6%	38.8%	61.2%
149,112	HINDS	68,939	32,399	34,574	1,966	2,175 D	47.0%	50.2%	48.4%	51.6%
16,055	HOLMES	6,084	1,873	4,179	32	2,306 D	30.8%	68.7%	30.9%	69.1%
9,502	HUMPHREYS	3,344	1,482	1,838	24	356 D	44.3%	55.0%	44.6%	55.4%
1,349	ISSAQUENA	773	338	421	14	83 D	43.7%	54.5%	44.5%	55.5%
13,186	ITAWAMBA	5,081	2,598	2,421	62	177 R	51.1%	47.6%	51.8%	48.2%
81,577	JACKSON	29,357	13,986	14,955	416	969 D	47.6%	50.9%	48.3%	51.7%
11,596	JASPER	5,819	3,409	2,234	176	1,175 R	58.6%	38.4%	60.4%	39.6%
6,275	JEFFERSON	3,549	716	2,799	34	2,083 D	20.2%	78.9%	20.4%	79.6%
10,108	JEFFERSON DAVIS	4,690	2,324	2,313	53	11 R	49.6%	49.3%	50.1%	49.9%
51,837	JONES	18,635	12,568	5,760	307	6,808 R	67.4%	30.9%	68.6%	31.4%
6,250	KEMPER	4,042	2,272	1,628	142	644 R	56.2%	40.3%	58.3%	41.7%
21,535	LAFAYETTE	6,939	3,594	3,233	112	361 R	51.8%	46.6%	52.6%	47.4%
19,236	LAMAR	9,774	6,706	2,892	176	3,814 R	68.6%	29.6%	69.9%	30.1%
44,703	LAUDERDALE	19,852	12,395	6,936	521	5,459 R	62.4%	34.9%	64.1%	35.9%
9,710	LAWRENCE	5,967	3,149	2,745	73	404 R	52.8%	46.0%	53.4%	46.6%
11,858	LEAKE	6,936	3,760	3,119	57	641 R	54.2%	45.0%	54.7%	45.3%
32,305	LEE	15,607	8,028	7,146	433	882 R	51.4%	45.8%	52.9%	47.1%
29,823	LEFLORE	9,774	3,932	5,554	288	1,622 D	40.2%	56.8%	41.5%	58.5%
19,808	LINCOLN	9,992	6,423	3,488	81	2,935 R	64.3%	34.9%	64.8%	35.2%
31,204	LOWNDES	13,857	6,518	7,182	157	664 D	47.0%	51.8%	47.6%	52.4%
32,098	MADISON	15,712	8,216	7,414	82	802 R	52.3%	47.2%	52.6%	47.4%
21,606	MARION	8,564	5,170	3,278	116	1,892 R	60.4%	38.3%	61.2%	38.8%
19,275	MARSHALL	6,825	1,835	4,871	119	3,036 D	26.9%	71.4%	27.4%	72.6%
22,607	MONROE	7,722	3,665	3,962	95	297 D	47.5%	51.3%	48.1%	51.9%
9,889	MONTGOMERY	3,509	1,749	1,741	19	8 R	49.8%	49.6%	50.1%	49.9%
19,140	NESHOBA	7,559	5,105	2,324	130	2,781 R	67.5%	30.7%	68.7%	31.3%
13,454	NEWTON	7,346	4,828	2,366	152	2,462 R	65.7%	32.2%	67.1%	32.9%
8,870	NOXUBEE	4,861	1,608	3,192	61	1,584 D	33.1%	65.7%	33.5%	66.5%
18,115	OKTIBBEHA	9,576	4,333	5,103	140	770 D	45.2%	53.3%	45.9%	54.1%
21,540	PANOLA	7,213	2,955	4,173	85	1,218 D	41.0%	57.9%	41.5%	58.5%
21,800	PEARL RIVER	11,510	5,895	5,386	229	509 R	51.2%	46.8%	52.3%	47.7%
8,065	PERRY	3,710	2,502	1,086	122	1,416 R	67.4%	29.3%	69.7%	30.3%
18,382	PIKE	9,407	5,161	4,168	78	993 R	54.9%	44.3%	55.3%	44.7%
11,636	PONTOTOC	6,289	3,968	2,195	126	1,773 R	63.1%	34.9%	64.4%	35.6%
14,627	PRENTISS	4,511	2,272	2,159	80	113 R	50.4%	47.9%	51.3%	48.7%
8,031	QUITMAN	3,275	1,187	2,041	47	854 D	36.2%	62.3%	36.8%	63.2%

MISSISSIPPI

GOVERNOR 1991

Registration	County	Total Vote	Republican	Democratic	Other	Rep.-Dem. Plurality	Percentage			
							Total Vote		Major Vote	
							Rep.	Dem.	Rep.	Dem.
46,901	RANKIN	28,000	18,775	9,042	183	9,733 R	67.1%	32.3%	67.5%	32.5%
18,624	SCOTT	6,908	4,285	2,555	68	1,730 R	62.0%	37.0%	62.6%	37.4%
5,948	SHARKEY	2,401	1,164	1,202	35	38 D	48.5%	50.1%	49.2%	50.8%
12,243	SIMPSON	8,024	5,052	2,904	68	2,148 R	63.0%	36.2%	63.5%	36.5%
11,759	SMITH	6,052	4,321	1,652	79	2,669 R	71.4%	27.3%	72.3%	27.7%
7,874	STONE	4,118	2,234	1,809	75	425 R	54.2%	43.9%	55.3%	44.7%
21,887	SUNFLOWER	6,997	3,068	3,871	58	803 D	43.8%	55.3%	44.2%	55.8%
11,747	TALLAHATCHIE	5,167	2,230	2,861	76	631 D	43.2%	55.4%	43.8%	56.2%
17,141	TATE	7,335	3,495	3,752	88	257 D	47.6%	51.2%	48.2%	51.8%
18,071	TIPPAH	4,883	2,512	2,265	106	247 R	51.4%	46.4%	52.6%	47.4%
13,939	TISHOMINGO	4,066	1,775	2,228	63	453 D	43.7%	54.8%	44.3%	55.7%
6,212	TUNICA	1,912	452	1,427	33	975 D	23.6%	74.6%	24.1%	75.9%
16,630	UNION	5,889	3,366	2,408	115	958 R	57.2%	40.9%	58.3%	41.7%
10,438	WALTHALL	3,664	2,066	1,556	42	510 R	56.4%	42.5%	57.0%	43.0%
38,092	WARREN	15,120	8,925	6,090	105	2,835 R	59.0%	40.3%	59.4%	40.6%
29,650	WASHINGTON	11,327	5,357	5,889	81	532 D	47.3%	52.0%	47.6%	52.4%
13,466	WAYNE	7,108	4,505	2,366	237	2,139 R	63.4%	33.3%	65.6%	34.4%
8,442	WEBSTER	4,026	2,508	1,461	57	1,047 R	62.3%	36.3%	63.2%	36.8%
7,964	WILKINSON	3,044	1,069	1,944	31	875 D	35.1%	63.9%	35.5%	64.5%
15,453	WINSTON	6,149	3,341	2,748	60	593 R	54.3%	44.7%	54.9%	45.1%
10,105	YALOBUSHA	4,200	1,651	2,489	60	838 D	39.3%	59.3%	39.9%	60.1%
20,024	YAZOO	8,146	4,243	3,858	45	385 R	52.1%	47.4%	52.4%	47.6%
1,617,668	TOTAL	711,188	361,500	338,435	11,253	23,065 R	50.8%	47.6%	51.6%	48.4%

MISSISSIPPI

CONGRESS

CD	Year	Total Vote	Republican		Democratic		Other Vote	Rep.-Dem. Plurality	Percentage			
									Total Vote		Major Vote	
			Vote	Candidate	Vote	Candidate			Rep.	Dem.	Rep.	Dem.
1	1992	204,616	82,952	WHITAKER, CLYDE E.	121,664	WHITTEN, JAMIE L.		38,712 D	40.5%	59.5%	40.5%	59.5%
2	1992	174,609	41,248	BENFORD, DOROTHY	133,361	EPSY, MIKE		92,113 D	23.6%	76.4%	23.6%	76.4%
3	1992	200,574	37,710	WILLIAMS, MICHAEL E.	162,864	MONTGOMERY, G. V.		125,154 D	18.8%	81.2%	18.8%	81.2%
4	1992	194,544	43,705	MCMILLAN, JACK L.	130,927	PARKER, MIKE	19,912	87,222 D	22.5%	67.3%	25.0%	75.0%
5	1992	191,058	67,619	HARVEY, PAUL A.	120,766	TAYLOR, GENE	2,673	53,147 D	35.4%	63.2%	35.9%	64.1%

MISSISSIPPI

1991 GENERAL ELECTION

Governor   Other vote was Independent (O'Hara).

1992 GENERAL ELECTION

President   Other vote was 2,625 Independent (Fulani); 2,154 Libertarian (Marrou); 1,652 Taxpayers (Phillips); 1,140 Independent (Hagelin); 545 Independent (Gritz).

Congress   Other vote was 10,523 Independent (Gilchrist) and 9,389 Independent (Meredith) in CD 4; Independent (O'Hara) in CD 5.

1991 PRIMARIES

SEPTEMBER 17 REPUBLICAN

Governor   28,411 Kirk Fordice; 27,561 Pete Johnson; 7,589 Bobby Clanton.

SEPTEMBER 17 DEMOCRATIC

Governor   368,679 Ray Mabus; 299,172 Wayne Dowdy; 58,614 George Blair.

OCTOBER 8 REPUBLICAN RUN-OFF

Governor   31,753 Kirk Fordice; 20,622 Pete Johnson.

1992 PRIMARIES

MARCH 10 REPUBLICAN

Congress   Unopposed in four CD's. Contested as follows:

   CD   5   17,469 Paul A. Harvey; 13,893 Billy Hewes; 8,932 W. T. Bramlett; 8,164 Chris Roosa.

MARCH 10 DEMOCRATIC

Congress   Unopposed in three CD's. Contested as follows:

   CD   1   36,817 Jamie L. Whitten; 8,114 Rex N. Weathers.
   CD   3   26,468 G. V. Montgomery; 4,563 Henry P. Clanton.

MARCH 31 REPUBLICAN RUN-OFF

Congress   Contested as follows:

   CD   5   12,146 Paul A. Harvey; 8,377 Billy Hewes.

MISSOURI

GOVERNOR
Mel Carnahan (D). Elected 1992 to a four-year term.

SENATORS
Christopher Bond (R). Re-elected 1992 to a six-year term. Previously elected 1986.

John C. Danforth (R). Re-elected 1988 to a six-year term. Previously elected 1982, 1976.

REPRESENTATIVES
1. William Clay (D)
2. James M. Talent (R)
3. Richard A. Gephardt (D)
4. Ike Skelton (D)
5. Alan Wheat (D)
6. Pat Danner (D)
7. Melton D. Hancock (R)
8. Bill Emerson (R)
9. Harold Volkmer (D)

POSTWAR VOTE FOR PRESIDENT

| | | Republican | | Democratic | | | | Percentage | | | |
| | | | | | | | | Total Vote | | Major Vote | |
Year	Total Vote	Vote	Candidate	Vote	Candidate	Other Vote	Plurality	Rep.	Dem.	Rep.	Dem.
1992 **	2,391,565	811,159	Bush, George	1,053,873	Clinton, Bill	526,533	242,714 D	33.9%	44.1%	43.5%	56.5%
1988	2,093,713	1,084,953	Bush, George	1,001,619	Dukakis, Michael S.	7,141	83,334 R	51.8%	47.8%	52.0%	48.0%
1984	2,122,783	1,274,188	Reagan, Ronald	848,583	Mondale, Walter F.	12	425,605 R	60.0%	40.0%	60.0%	40.0%
1980	2,099,824	1,074,181	Reagan, Ronald	931,182	Carter, Jimmy	94,461	142,999 R	51.2%	44.3%	53.6%	46.4%
1976	1,953,600	927,443	Ford, Gerald R.	998,387	Carter, Jimmy	27,770	70,944 D	47.5%	51.1%	48.2%	51.8%
1972	1,855,803	1,153,852	Nixon, Richard M.	697,147	McGovern, George S.	4,804	456,705 R	62.2%	37.6%	62.3%	37.7%
1968	1,809,502	811,932	Nixon, Richard M.	791,444	Humphrey, Hubert H.	206,126	20,488 R	44.9%	43.7%	50.6%	49.4%
1964	1,817,879	653,535	Goldwater, Barry M.	1,164,344	Johnson, Lyndon B.		510,809 D	36.0%	64.0%	36.0%	64.0%
1960	1,934,422	962,221	Nixon, Richard M.	972,201	Kennedy, John F.		9,980 D	49.7%	50.3%	49.7%	50.3%
1956	1,832,562	914,289	Eisenhower, Dwight D.	918,273	Stevenson, Adlai E.		3,984 D	49.9%	50.1%	49.9%	50.1%
1952	1,892,062	959,429	Eisenhower, Dwight D.	929,830	Stevenson, Adlai E.	2,803	29,599 R	50.7%	49.1%	50.8%	49.2%
1948	1,578,628	655,039	Dewey, Thomas E.	917,315	Truman, Harry S.	6,274	262,276 D	41.5%	58.1%	41.7%	58.3%

In 1992 the other vote column includes 518,741 votes cast for Perot.

POSTWAR VOTE FOR GOVERNOR

| | | Republican | | Democratic | | | | Percentage | | | |
| | | | | | | | | Total Vote | | Major Vote | |
Year	Total Vote	Vote	Candidate	Vote	Candidate	Other Vote	Rep.-Dem. Plurality	Rep.	Dem.	Rep.	Dem.
1992	2,344,121	968,574	Webster, William L.	1,375,425	Carnahan, Mel	122	406,851 D	41.3%	58.7%	41.3%	58.7%
1988	2,085,928	1,339,531	Ashcroft, John	724,919	Hearnes, Betty C.	21,478	614,612 R	64.2%	34.8%	64.9%	35.1%
1984	2,108,210	1,194,506	Ashcroft, John	913,700	Rothman, Kenneth J.	4	280,806 R	56.7%	43.3%	56.7%	43.3%
1980	2,088,028	1,098,950	Bond, Christopher	981,884	Teasdale, Joseph P.	7,194	117,066 R	52.6%	47.0%	52.8%	47.2%
1976	1,933,575	958,110	Bond, Christopher	971,184	Teasdale, Joseph P.	4,281	13,074 D	49.6%	50.2%	49.7%	50.3%
1972	1,865,683	1,029,451	Bond, Christopher	832,751	Dowd, Edward L.	3,481	196,700 R	55.2%	44.6%	55.3%	44.7%
1968	1,764,602	691,797	Roos, Lawrence K.	1,072,805	Hearnes, Warren E.		381,008 D	39.2%	60.8%	39.2%	60.8%
1964	1,789,600	678,949	Shepley, Ethan	1,110,651	Hearnes, Warren E.		431,702 D	37.9%	62.1%	37.9%	62.1%
1960	1,887,331	792,131	Farmer, Edward G.	1,095,200	Dalton, John M.		303,069 D	42.0%	58.0%	42.0%	58.0%
1956	1,808,338	866,810	Hocker, Lon	941,528	Blair, James T.		74,718 D	47.9%	52.1%	47.9%	52.1%
1952	1,871,095	886,370	Elliott, Howard	983,166	Donnelly, Phil M.	1,559	96,796 D	47.4%	52.5%	47.4%	52.6%
1948	1,567,338	670,064	Thompson, Murray	893,092	Smith, Forrest	4,182	223,028 D	42.8%	57.0%	42.9%	57.1%

MISSOURI

POSTWAR VOTE FOR SENATOR

Year	Total Vote	Republican		Democratic		Other Vote	Rep.-Dem. Plurality	Percentage			
		Vote	Candidate	Vote	Candidate			Total Vote		Major Vote	
								Rep.	Dem.	Rep.	Dem.
1992	2,354,925	1,221,901	Bond, Christopher	1,057,967	Rothman-Serot, Geri	75,057	163,934 R	51.9%	44.9%	53.6%	46.4%
1988	2,078,875	1,407,416	Danforth, John C.	660,045	Nixon, Jeremiah W.	11,414	747,371 R	67.7%	31.8%	68.1%	31.9%
1986	1,477,327	777,612	Bond, Christopher	699,624	Woods, Harriett	91	77,988 R	52.6%	47.4%	52.6%	47.4%
1982	1,543,521	784,876	Danforth, John C.	758,629	Woods, Harriett	16	26,247 R	50.8%	49.1%	50.9%	49.1%
1980	2,066,965	985,399	McNary, Gene	1,074,859	Eagleton, Thomas F.	6,707	89,460 D	47.7%	52.0%	47.8%	52.2%
1976	1,914,777	1,090,067	Danforth, John C.	813,571	Hearnes, Warren E.	11,139	276,496 R	56.9%	42.5%	57.3%	42.7%
1974	1,224,303	480,900	Curtis, Thomas B.	735,433	Eagleton, Thomas F.	7,970	254,533 D	39.3%	60.1%	39.5%	60.5%
1970	1,283,912	617,903	Danforth, John C.	655,431	Symington, Stuart	10,578	37,528 D	48.1%	51.0%	48.5%	51.5%
1968	1,737,958	850,544	Curtis, Thomas B.	887,414	Eagleton, Thomas F.		36,870 D	48.9%	51.1%	48.9%	51.1%
1964	1,783,043	596,377	Bradshaw, Jean P.	1,186,666	Symington, Stuart		590,289 D	33.4%	66.6%	33.4%	66.6%
1962	1,222,259	555,330	Kemper, Crosby	666,929	Long, Edward V.		111,599 D	45.4%	54.6%	45.4%	54.6%
1960 S	1,880,232	880,576	Hocker, Lon	999,656	Long, Edward V.		119,080 D	46.8%	53.2%	46.8%	53.2%
1958	1,173,903	393,847	Palmer, Hazel	780,056	Symington, Stuart		386,209 D	33.6%	66.4%	33.6%	66.4%
1956	1,800,984	785,048	Douglas, Herbert	1,015,936	Hennings, Thomas C.		230,888 D	43.6%	56.4%	43.6%	56.4%
1952	1,868,083	858,170	Kem, James P.	1,008,523	Symington, Stuart	1,390	150,353 D	45.9%	54.0%	46.0%	54.0%
1950	1,279,414	592,922	Donnell, Forrest C.	685,732	Hennings, Thomas C.	760	92,810 D	46.3%	53.6%	46.4%	53.6%
1946	1,084,100	572,556	Kem, James P.	511,544	Briggs, Frank P.		61,012 R	52.8%	47.2%	52.8%	47.2%

The 1960 election was for a short term to fill a vacancy.

MISSOURI

Districts Established July 8, 1991

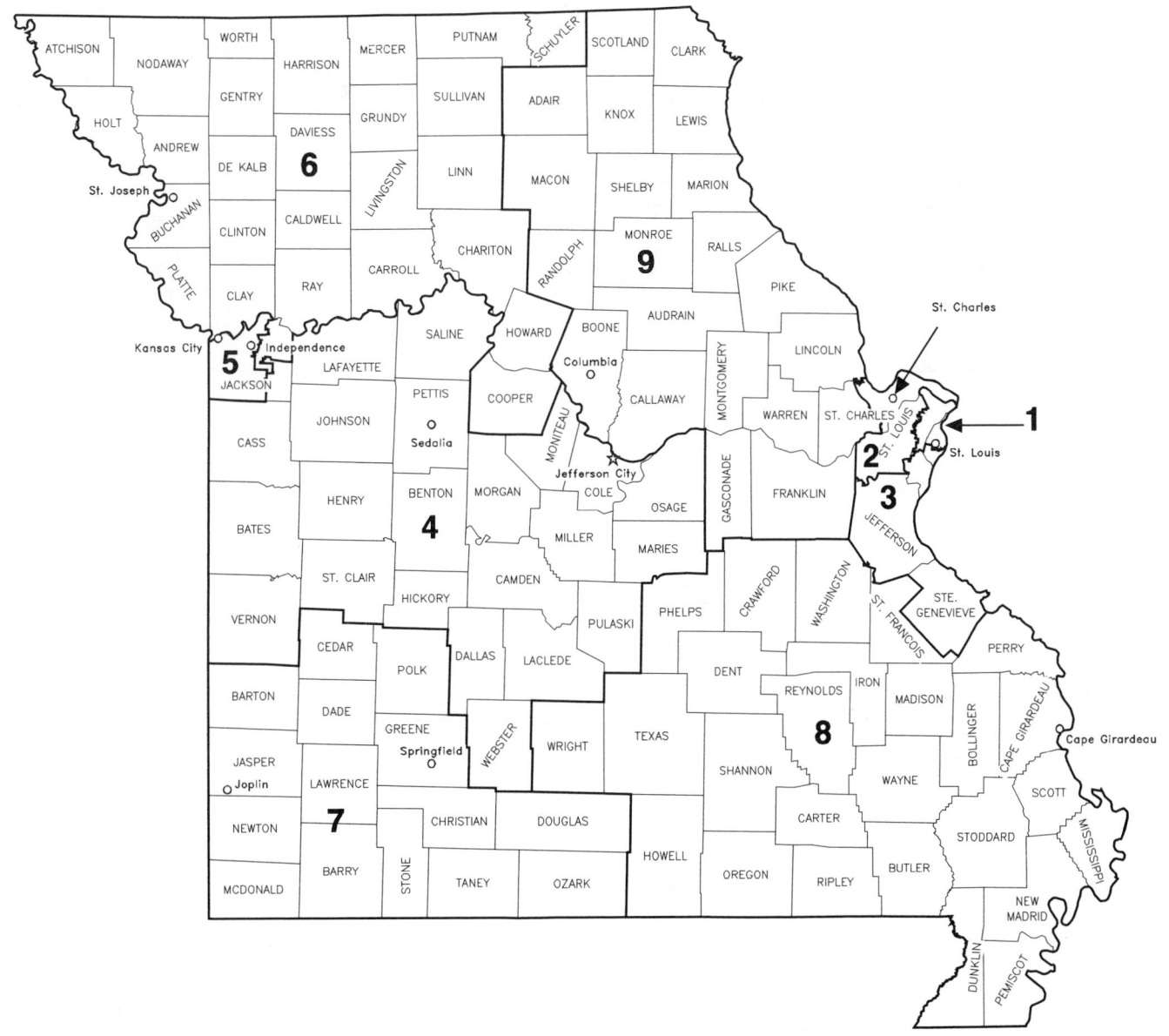

MISSOURI

PRESIDENT 1992

Registration	County	Total Vote	Republican	Democratic	Perot	Other	Plurality	Percentage Total Vote		
								Rep.	Dem.	Perot
13,000	ADAIR	10,640	4,141	4,232	2,224	43	91 D	38.9%	39.8%	20.9%
9,963	ANDREW	7,489	2,652	2,675	2,151	11	23 D	35.4%	35.7%	28.7%
4,229	ATCHISON	3,199	1,140	1,208	840	11	68 D	35.6%	37.8%	26.3%
13,446	AUDRAIN	10,654	3,798	4,731	2,099	26	933 D	35.6%	44.4%	19.7%
18,722	BARRY	12,757	5,565	4,791	2,381	20	774 R	43.6%	37.6%	18.7%
7,113	BARTON	5,194	2,775	1,433	971	15	1,342 R	53.4%	27.6%	18.7%
10,960	BATES	7,730	2,499	2,993	2,225	13	494 D	32.3%	38.7%	28.8%
9,081	BENTON	7,276	2,511	3,195	1,551	19	684 D	34.5%	43.9%	21.3%
7,428	BOLLINGER	5,363	2,289	2,150	909	15	139 R	42.7%	40.1%	16.9%
76,011	BOONE	57,890	19,405	26,176	12,040	269	6,771 D	33.5%	45.2%	20.8%
47,879	BUCHANAN	37,365	11,275	16,570	9,404	116	5,295 D	30.2%	44.3%	25.2%
25,200	BUTLER	15,272	6,450	6,602	2,189	31	152 D	42.2%	43.2%	14.3%
6,020	CALDWELL	4,055	1,295	1,456	1,283	21	161 D	31.9%	35.9%	31.6%
17,780	CALLAWAY	13,981	4,880	5,799	3,266	36	919 D	34.9%	41.5%	23.4%
18,875	CAMDEN	14,627	5,554	5,140	3,891	42	414 R	38.0%	35.1%	26.6%
34,000	CAPE GIRARDEAU	28,355	13,464	9,605	5,199	87	3,859 R	47.5%	33.9%	18.3%
7,500	CARROLL	5,378	1,774	2,100	1,495	9	326 D	33.0%	39.0%	27.8%
3,800	CARTER	2,686	1,101	1,169	405	11	68 D	41.0%	43.5%	15.1%
34,000	CASS	29,905	10,349	10,246	9,216	94	103 R	34.6%	34.3%	30.8%
8,100	CEDAR	5,339	2,085	2,064	1,173	17	21 R	39.1%	38.7%	22.0%
6,950	CHARITON	4,601	1,378	2,141	1,067	15	763 D	30.0%	46.5%	23.2%
23,000	CHRISTIAN	17,145	7,422	6,242	3,422	59	1,180 R	43.3%	36.4%	20.0%
5,400	CLARK	3,584	1,039	1,815	725	5	776 D	29.0%	50.6%	20.2%
88,585	CLAY	75,778	23,798	30,565	20,951	464	6,767 D	31.4%	40.3%	27.6%
10,000	CLINTON	8,228	2,391	3,400	2,423	14	977 D	29.1%	41.3%	29.4%
37,000	COLE	31,304	15,270	10,201	5,770	63	5,069 R	48.8%	32.6%	18.4%
8,978	COOPER	7,339	2,867	2,709	1,735	28	158 R	39.1%	36.9%	23.6%
12,419	CRAWFORD	8,385	2,831	3,515	2,002	37	684 D	33.8%	41.9%	23.9%
5,000	DADE	3,751	1,577	1,332	834	8	245 R	42.0%	35.5%	22.2%
8,300	DALLAS	6,051	2,116	2,533	1,392	10	417 D	35.0%	41.9%	23.0%
5,200	DAVIESS	3,732	1,107	1,477	1,143	5	334 D	29.7%	39.6%	30.6%
5,500	DE KALB	4,171	1,318	1,630	1,207	16	312 D	31.6%	39.1%	28.9%
11,000	DENT	5,877	2,125	2,689	1,049	14	564 D	36.2%	45.8%	17.8%
8,700	DOUGLAS	5,792	2,569	2,126	1,081	16	443 R	44.4%	36.7%	18.7%
17,300	DUNKLIN	11,479	4,024	6,277	1,166	12	2,253 D	35.1%	54.7%	10.2%
44,000	FRANKLIN	36,064	11,477	13,431	11,043	113	1,954 D	31.8%	37.2%	30.6%
9,057	GASCONADE	6,334	2,690	1,952	1,672	20	738 R	42.5%	30.8%	26.4%
4,825	GENTRY	3,724	1,272	1,519	921	12	247 D	34.2%	40.8%	24.7%
133,033	GREENE	105,713	46,457	41,137	17,770	349	5,320 R	43.9%	38.9%	16.8%
6,800	GRUNDY	5,105	1,749	1,968	1,372	16	219 D	34.3%	38.6%	26.9%
5,850	HARRISON	4,222	1,563	1,590	1,059	10	27 D	37.0%	37.7%	25.1%
12,600	HENRY	9,740	2,681	4,232	2,807	20	1,425 D	27.5%	43.4%	28.8%
5,183	HICKORY	4,058	1,259	1,929	864	6	670 D	31.0%	47.5%	21.3%
3,977	HOLT	3,044	1,202	1,050	781	11	152 R	39.5%	34.5%	25.7%
6,348	HOWARD	4,443	1,253	2,085	1,090	15	832 D	28.2%	46.9%	24.5%
18,400	HOWELL	13,537	5,360	5,492	2,650	35	132 D	39.6%	40.6%	19.6%
6,425	IRON	4,634	1,276	2,507	841	10	1,231 D	27.5%	54.1%	18.1%
374,000	JACKSON	291,595	78,611	145,999	66,142	843	67,388 D	27.0%	50.1%	22.7%
48,500	JASPER	35,872	17,592	11,727	6,440	113	5,865 R	49.0%	32.7%	18.0%
90,000	JEFFERSON	73,501	20,637	32,569	20,057	238	11,932 D	28.1%	44.3%	27.3%
19,193	JOHNSON	15,203	5,032	5,546	4,578	47	514 D	33.1%	36.5%	30.1%
3,124	KNOX	2,262	724	1,010	523	5	286 D	32.0%	44.7%	23.1%
15,200	LACLEDE	12,222	5,176	4,179	2,852	15	997 R	42.3%	34.2%	23.3%
18,603	LAFAYETTE	13,467	4,651	5,213	3,561	42	562 D	34.5%	38.7%	26.4%
16,500	LAWRENCE	12,891	5,608	4,666	2,570	47	942 R	43.5%	36.2%	19.9%
5,809	LEWIS	4,562	1,461	2,196	892	13	735 D	32.0%	48.1%	19.6%
15,424	LINCOLN	12,765	3,718	5,453	3,572	22	1,735 D	29.1%	42.7%	28.0%
9,465	LINN	6,436	1,967	2,916	1,524	29	949 D	30.6%	45.3%	23.7%
8,614	LIVINGSTON	6,863	2,370	2,505	1,976	12	135 D	34.5%	36.5%	28.8%
11,434	MCDONALD	6,875	3,010	2,281	1,551	33	729 R	43.8%	33.2%	22.6%

MISSOURI

PRESIDENT 1992

Registration	County	Total Vote	Republican	Democratic	Perot	Other	Plurality	Percentage Total Vote		
								Rep.	Dem.	Perot
9,898	MACON	7,164	2,256	3,194	1,697	17	938 D	31.5%	44.6%	23.7%
7,354	MADISON	5,082	1,673	2,501	899	9	828 D	32.9%	49.2%	17.7%
5,335	MARIES	4,015	1,356	1,732	915	12	376 D	33.8%	43.1%	22.8%
14,429	MARION	11,783	4,762	5,156	1,841	24	394 D	40.4%	43.8%	15.6%
2,600	MERCER	1,849	626	843	378	2	217 D	33.9%	45.6%	20.4%
11,767	MILLER	9,487	4,175	2,905	2,391	16	1,270 R	44.0%	30.6%	25.2%
8,098	MISSISSIPPI	5,687	1,675	3,226	776	10	1,551 D	29.5%	56.7%	13.6%
7,677	MONITEAU	6,088	2,566	2,018	1,499	5	548 R	42.1%	33.1%	24.6%
6,005	MONROE	4,187	1,153	2,060	969	5	907 D	27.5%	49.2%	23.1%
7,038	MONTGOMERY	5,319	1,974	2,063	1,266	16	89 D	37.1%	38.8%	23.8%
9,400	MORGAN	7,770	2,819	2,906	2,028	17	87 D	36.3%	37.4%	26.1%
12,250	NEW MADRID	8,289	2,431	4,883	962	13	2,452 D	29.3%	58.9%	11.6%
26,688	NEWTON	18,479	8,804	5,987	3,567	121	2,817 R	47.6%	32.4%	19.3%
11,800	NODAWAY	9,388	3,147	3,723	2,484	34	576 D	33.5%	39.7%	26.5%
5,925	OREGON	4,236	1,402	2,258	564	12	856 D	33.1%	53.3%	13.3%
7,400	OSAGE	6,073	2,784	1,860	1,423	6	924 R	45.8%	30.6%	23.4%
6,646	OZARK	4,271	1,772	1,581	906	12	191 R	41.5%	37.0%	21.2%
13,055	PEMISCOT	6,768	2,161	3,924	670	13	1,763 D	31.9%	58.0%	9.9%
9,250	PERRY	7,252	3,205	2,525	1,498	24	680 R	44.2%	34.8%	20.7%
23,200	PETTIS	16,470	6,823	5,314	4,278	55	1,509 R	41.4%	32.3%	26.0%
20,450	PHELPS	16,739	6,040	6,852	3,774	73	812 D	36.1%	40.9%	22.5%
12,165	PIKE	7,336	2,255	3,609	1,464	8	1,354 D	30.7%	49.2%	20.0%
33,000	PLATTE	29,478	9,380	10,920	9,062	116	1,540 D	31.8%	37.0%	30.7%
12,993	POLK	8,675	3,465	3,316	1,879	15	149 R	39.9%	38.2%	21.7%
13,301	PULASKI	9,988	3,793	4,113	2,057	25	320 D	38.0%	41.2%	20.6%
3,498	PUTNAM	2,503	1,143	838	522		305 R	45.7%	33.5%	20.9%
6,000	RALLS	4,393	1,349	2,158	880	6	809 D	30.7%	49.1%	20.0%
16,000	RANDOLPH	10,210	3,025	4,951	2,212	22	1,926 D	29.6%	48.5%	21.7%
13,800	RAY	9,620	2,563	4,457	2,567	33	1,890 D	26.6%	46.3%	26.7%
5,300	REYNOLDS	3,325	776	2,014	532	3	1,238 D	23.3%	60.6%	16.0%
7,730	RIPLEY	4,860	1,814	2,300	739	7	486 D	37.3%	47.3%	15.2%
123,602	ST. CHARLES	106,563	38,673	37,263	30,351	276	1,410 R	36.3%	35.0%	28.5%
5,650	ST. CLAIR	4,611	1,555	1,965	1,083	8	410 D	33.7%	42.6%	23.5%
27,000	ST. FRANCOIS	18,947	5,889	9,367	3,635	56	3,478 D	31.1%	49.4%	19.2%
206,000	ST. LOUIS CITY	147,404	25,441	102,356	18,864	743	76,915 D	17.3%	69.4%	12.8%
637,685	ST. LOUIS COUNTY	534,763	188,285	235,760	109,099	1,619	47,475 D	35.2%	44.1%	20.4%
9,725	STE. GENEVIEVE	7,137	1,780	3,795	1,547	15	2,015 D	24.9%	53.2%	21.7%
15,174	SALINE	10,166	2,688	4,643	2,815	20	1,828 D	26.4%	45.7%	27.7%
3,347	SCHUYLER	2,170	742	936	487	5	194 D	34.2%	43.1%	22.4%
3,616	SCOTLAND	2,494	798	1,070	617	9	272 D	32.0%	42.9%	24.7%
23,850	SCOTT	16,507	6,265	7,452	2,763	27	1,187 D	38.0%	45.1%	16.7%
5,490	SHANNON	3,952	1,224	2,135	579	14	911 D	31.0%	54.0%	14.7%
4,583	SHELBY	3,394	1,169	1,435	786	4	266 D	34.4%	42.3%	23.2%
15,500	STODDARD	12,308	4,608	5,720	1,977	3	1,112 D	37.4%	46.5%	16.1%
13,400	STONE	9,196	4,035	3,256	1,884	21	779 R	43.9%	35.4%	20.5%
5,000	SULLIVAN	3,436	1,326	1,510	596	4	184 D	38.6%	43.9%	17.3%
16,500	TANEY	13,205	6,081	4,682	2,395	47	1,399 R	46.1%	35.5%	18.1%
13,282	TEXAS	10,001	3,470	4,597	1,900	34	1,127 D	34.7%	46.0%	19.0%
10,400	VERNON	8,303	2,851	3,546	1,890	16	695 D	34.3%	42.7%	22.8%
12,000	WARREN	8,659	2,953	3,213	2,471	22	260 D	34.1%	37.1%	28.5%
12,308	WASHINGTON	8,010	2,157	4,211	1,618	24	2,054 D	26.9%	52.6%	20.2%
8,500	WAYNE	6,019	2,101	3,073	837	8	972 D	34.9%	51.1%	13.9%
14,388	WEBSTER	10,640	4,361	4,149	2,108	22	212 R	41.0%	39.0%	19.8%
1,850	WORTH	1,413	483	599	328	3	116 D	34.2%	42.4%	23.2%
10,250	WRIGHT	7,684	3,427	2,814	1,425	18	613 R	44.6%	36.6%	18.5%
3,067,955	TOTAL	2,391,565	811,159	1,053,873	518,741	7,792	242,714 D	33.9%	44.1%	21.7%

MISSOURI

GOVERNOR 1992

Registration	County	Total Vote	Republican	Democratic	Other	Rep.-Dem. Plurality	Percentage			
							Total Vote		Major Vote	
							Rep.	Dem.	Rep.	Dem.
13,000	ADAIR	10,420	4,931	5,489		558 D	47.3%	52.7%	47.3%	52.7%
9,963	ANDREW	7,314	3,657	3,657			50.0%	50.0%	50.0%	50.0%
4,229	ATCHISON	3,164	1,604	1,560		44 R	50.7%	49.3%	50.7%	49.3%
13,446	AUDRAIN	10,431	4,504	5,927		1,423 D	43.2%	56.8%	43.2%	56.8%
18,722	BARRY	12,422	6,529	5,893		636 R	52.6%	47.4%	52.6%	47.4%
7,113	BARTON	5,141	3,330	1,811		1,519 R	64.8%	35.2%	64.8%	35.2%
10,960	BATES	7,618	3,204	4,414		1,210 D	42.1%	57.9%	42.1%	57.9%
9,081	BENTON	7,104	3,245	3,859		614 D	45.7%	54.3%	45.7%	54.3%
7,428	BOLLINGER	5,212	2,867	2,345		522 R	55.0%	45.0%	55.0%	45.0%
76,011	BOONE	56,975	21,834	35,141		13,307 D	38.3%	61.7%	38.3%	61.7%
47,879	BUCHANAN	36,813	15,674	21,139		5,465 D	42.6%	57.4%	42.6%	57.4%
25,200	BUTLER	14,916	7,335	7,581		246 D	49.2%	50.8%	49.2%	50.8%
6,020	CALDWELL	3,931	1,804	2,127		323 D	45.9%	54.1%	45.9%	54.1%
17,780	CALLAWAY	13,842	5,453	8,389		2,936 D	39.4%	60.6%	39.4%	60.6%
18,875	CAMDEN	14,334	6,918	7,416		498 D	48.3%	51.7%	48.3%	51.7%
34,000	CAPE GIRARDEAU	27,716	15,080	12,636		2,444 R	54.4%	45.6%	54.4%	45.6%
7,500	CARROLL	5,238	2,489	2,749		260 D	47.5%	52.5%	47.5%	52.5%
3,800	CARTER	2,614	1,144	1,470		326 D	43.8%	56.2%	43.8%	56.2%
34,000	CASS	29,258	13,129	16,129		3,000 D	44.9%	55.1%	44.9%	55.1%
8,100	CEDAR	5,231	2,713	2,518		195 R	51.9%	48.1%	51.9%	48.1%
6,950	CHARITON	4,391	1,734	2,657		923 D	39.5%	60.5%	39.5%	60.5%
23,000	CHRISTIAN	16,936	8,939	7,997		942 R	52.8%	47.2%	52.8%	47.2%
5,400	CLARK	3,460	1,518	1,942		424 D	43.9%	56.1%	43.9%	56.1%
88,585	CLAY	72,415	29,360	43,055		13,695 D	40.5%	59.5%	40.5%	59.5%
10,000	CLINTON	8,132	3,296	4,836		1,540 D	40.5%	59.5%	40.5%	59.5%
37,000	COLE	31,010	14,200	16,810		2,610 D	45.8%	54.2%	45.8%	54.2%
8,978	COOPER	7,267	3,494	3,773		279 D	48.1%	51.9%	48.1%	51.9%
12,419	CRAWFORD	8,228	3,470	4,758		1,288 D	42.2%	57.8%	42.2%	57.8%
5,000	DADE	3,644	1,944	1,700		244 R	53.3%	46.7%	53.3%	46.7%
8,300	DALLAS	5,859	2,871	2,988		117 D	49.0%	51.0%	49.0%	51.0%
5,200	DAVIESS	3,688	1,596	2,092		496 D	43.3%	56.7%	43.3%	56.7%
5,500	DE KALB	4,119	1,853	2,266		413 D	45.0%	55.0%	45.0%	55.0%
11,000	DENT	5,824	2,582	3,242		660 D	44.3%	55.7%	44.3%	55.7%
8,700	DOUGLAS	5,606	3,203	2,403		800 R	57.1%	42.9%	57.1%	42.9%
17,300	DUNKLIN	10,949	4,309	6,640		2,331 D	39.4%	60.6%	39.4%	60.6%
44,000	FRANKLIN	35,103	14,912	20,191		5,279 D	42.5%	57.5%	42.5%	57.5%
9,057	GASCONADE	6,227	3,282	2,945		337 R	52.7%	47.3%	52.7%	47.3%
4,825	GENTRY	3,626	1,609	2,017		408 D	44.4%	55.6%	44.4%	55.6%
133,033	GREENE	104,107	51,291	52,816		1,525 D	49.3%	50.7%	49.3%	50.7%
6,800	GRUNDY	4,958	2,277	2,681		404 D	45.9%	54.1%	45.9%	54.1%
5,850	HARRISON	4,009	1,931	2,078		147 D	48.2%	51.8%	48.2%	51.8%
12,600	HENRY	9,470	3,385	6,085		2,700 D	35.7%	64.3%	35.7%	64.3%
5,183	HICKORY	3,959	1,615	2,344		729 D	40.8%	59.2%	40.8%	59.2%
3,977	HOLT	2,927	1,603	1,324		279 R	54.8%	45.2%	54.8%	45.2%
6,348	HOWARD	4,385	1,740	2,645		905 D	39.7%	60.3%	39.7%	60.3%
18,400	HOWELL	13,263	6,401	6,862		461 D	48.3%	51.7%	48.3%	51.7%
6,425	IRON	4,459	1,653	2,806		1,153 D	37.1%	62.9%	37.1%	62.9%
374,000	JACKSON	286,241	99,917	186,324		86,407 D	34.9%	65.1%	34.9%	65.1%
48,500	JASPER	35,484	23,084	12,400		10,684 R	65.1%	34.9%	65.1%	34.9%
90,000	JEFFERSON	72,209	26,542	45,667		19,125 D	36.8%	63.2%	36.8%	63.2%
19,193	JOHNSON	14,953	6,395	8,558		2,163 D	42.8%	57.2%	42.8%	57.2%
3,124	KNOX	2,202	965	1,237		272 D	43.8%	56.2%	43.8%	56.2%
15,200	LACLEDE	12,089	6,402	5,687		715 R	53.0%	47.0%	53.0%	47.0%
18,603	LAFAYETTE	13,213	5,961	7,252		1,291 D	45.1%	54.9%	45.1%	54.9%
16,500	LAWRENCE	12,589	6,484	6,105		379 R	51.5%	48.5%	51.5%	48.5%
5,809	LEWIS	4,364	1,891	2,473		582 D	43.3%	56.7%	43.3%	56.7%
15,424	LINCOLN	12,574	5,019	7,555		2,536 D	39.9%	60.1%	39.9%	60.1%
9,465	LINN	6,266	2,565	3,701		1,136 D	40.9%	59.1%	40.9%	59.1%
8,614	LIVINGSTON	6,645	2,921	3,724		803 D	44.0%	56.0%	44.0%	56.0%
11,434	MCDONALD	6,702	3,881	2,821		1,060 R	57.9%	42.1%	57.9%	42.1%

MISSOURI

GOVERNOR 1992

Registration	County	Total Vote	Republican	Democratic	Other	Rep.-Dem. Plurality	Total Vote Rep.	Total Vote Dem.	Major Vote Rep.	Major Vote Dem.
9,898	MACON	6,966	2,813	4,153		1,340 D	40.4%	59.6%	40.4%	59.6%
7,354	MADISON	5,017	2,289	2,728		439 D	45.6%	54.4%	45.6%	54.4%
5,335	MARIES	3,967	1,579	2,388		809 D	39.8%	60.2%	39.8%	60.2%
14,429	MARION	11,562	5,183	6,379		1,196 D	44.8%	55.2%	44.8%	55.2%
2,600	MERCER	1,753	780	973		193 D	44.5%	55.5%	44.5%	55.5%
11,767	MILLER	9,392	4,933	4,459		474 R	52.5%	47.5%	52.5%	47.5%
8,098	MISSISSIPPI	5,519	2,315	3,204		889 D	41.9%	58.1%	41.9%	58.1%
7,677	MONITEAU	6,009	2,900	3,109		209 D	48.3%	51.7%	48.3%	51.7%
6,005	MONROE	4,130	1,510	2,620		1,110 D	36.6%	63.4%	36.6%	63.4%
7,038	MONTGOMERY	5,165	2,427	2,738		311 D	47.0%	53.0%	47.0%	53.0%
9,400	MORGAN	7,647	3,775	3,872		97 D	49.4%	50.6%	49.4%	50.6%
12,250	NEW MADRID	7,917	3,087	4,830		1,743 D	39.0%	61.0%	39.0%	61.0%
26,688	NEWTON	17,342	10,586	6,756		3,830 R	61.0%	39.0%	61.0%	39.0%
11,800	NODAWAY	9,219	4,218	5,001		783 D	45.8%	54.2%	45.8%	54.2%
5,925	OREGON	4,164	1,635	2,529		894 D	39.3%	60.7%	39.3%	60.7%
7,400	OSAGE	5,979	2,790	3,189		399 D	46.7%	53.3%	46.7%	53.3%
6,646	OZARK	4,176	2,222	1,954		268 R	53.2%	46.8%	53.2%	46.8%
13,055	PEMISCOT	6,542	2,275	4,267		1,992 D	34.8%	65.2%	34.8%	65.2%
9,250	PERRY	7,096	4,020	3,076		944 R	56.7%	43.3%	56.7%	43.3%
23,200	PETTIS	16,159	7,650	8,509		859 D	47.3%	52.7%	47.3%	52.7%
20,450	PHELPS	16,547	6,687	9,860		3,173 D	40.4%	59.6%	40.4%	59.6%
12,165	PIKE	7,182	2,762	4,420		1,658 D	38.5%	61.5%	38.5%	61.5%
33,000	PLATTE	29,309	12,530	16,779		4,249 D	42.8%	57.2%	42.8%	57.2%
12,993	POLK	8,562	4,289	4,273		16 R	50.1%	49.9%	50.1%	49.9%
13,301	PULASKI	9,848	4,540	5,308		768 D	46.1%	53.9%	46.1%	53.9%
3,498	PUTNAM	2,371	1,352	1,019		333 R	57.0%	43.0%	57.0%	43.0%
6,000	RALLS	4,364	1,670	2,694		1,024 D	38.3%	61.7%	38.3%	61.7%
16,000	RANDOLPH	10,049	3,874	6,175		2,301 D	38.6%	61.4%	38.6%	61.4%
13,800	RAY	9,515	3,578	5,937		2,359 D	37.6%	62.4%	37.6%	62.4%
5,300	REYNOLDS	3,192	1,034	2,158		1,124 D	32.4%	67.6%	32.4%	67.6%
7,730	RIPLEY	4,739	2,155	2,584		429 D	45.5%	54.5%	45.5%	54.5%
123,602	ST. CHARLES	104,597	46,585	58,012		11,427 D	44.5%	55.5%	44.5%	55.5%
5,650	ST. CLAIR	4,500	1,953	2,547		594 D	43.4%	56.6%	43.4%	56.6%
27,000	ST. FRANCOIS	18,637	7,350	11,287		3,937 D	39.4%	60.6%	39.4%	60.6%
206,000	ST. LOUIS CITY	144,240	32,878	111,362		78,484 D	22.8%	77.2%	22.8%	77.2%
637,685	ST. LOUIS COUNTY	526,368	206,155	320,213		114,058 D	39.2%	60.8%	39.2%	60.8%
9,725	STE. GENEVIEVE	6,982	2,372	4,610		2,238 D	34.0%	66.0%	34.0%	66.0%
15,174	SALINE	10,031	3,603	6,428		2,825 D	35.9%	64.1%	35.9%	64.1%
3,347	SCHUYLER	2,093	929	1,164		235 D	44.4%	55.6%	44.4%	55.6%
3,616	SCOTLAND	2,344	1,037	1,307		270 D	44.2%	55.8%	44.2%	55.8%
23,850	SCOTT	15,986	7,564	8,422		858 D	47.3%	52.7%	47.3%	52.7%
5,490	SHANNON	3,791	1,453	2,338		885 D	38.3%	61.7%	38.3%	61.7%
4,583	SHELBY	3,385	1,494	1,891		397 D	44.1%	55.9%	44.1%	55.9%
15,500	STODDARD	11,752	5,487	6,265		778 D	46.7%	53.3%	46.7%	53.3%
13,400	STONE	8,985	4,615	4,370		245 R	51.4%	48.6%	51.4%	48.6%
5,000	SULLIVAN	3,329	1,588	1,741		153 D	47.7%	52.3%	47.7%	52.3%
16,500	TANEY	12,974	6,978	5,996		982 R	53.8%	46.2%	53.8%	46.2%
13,282	TEXAS	9,887	4,544	5,343		799 D	46.0%	54.0%	46.0%	54.0%
10,400	VERNON	8,087	3,529	4,558		1,029 D	43.6%	56.4%	43.6%	56.4%
12,000	WARREN	8,503	3,901	4,602		701 D	45.9%	54.1%	45.9%	54.1%
12,308	WASHINGTON	7,700	3,049	4,651		1,602 D	39.6%	60.4%	39.6%	60.4%
8,500	WAYNE	5,845	2,493	3,352		859 D	42.7%	57.3%	42.7%	57.3%
14,388	WEBSTER	10,376	5,102	5,274		172 D	49.2%	50.8%	49.2%	50.8%
1,850	WORTH	1,368	638	730		92 D	46.6%	53.4%	46.6%	53.4%
10,250	WRIGHT	7,594	4,280	3,314		966 R	56.4%	43.6%	56.4%	43.6%
3,067,955	TOTAL	2,344,121	968,574	1,375,425	122	406,851 D	41.3%	58.7%	41.3%	58.7%

MISSOURI

SENATOR 1992

Registration	County	Total Vote	Republican	Democratic	Other	Rep.-Dem. Plurality	Percentage Total Vote Rep.	Dem.	Major Vote Rep.	Dem.
13,000	ADAIR	10,414	6,329	3,759	326	2,570 R	60.8%	36.1%	62.7%	37.3%
9,963	ANDREW	7,316	4,198	2,912	206	1,286 R	57.4%	39.8%	59.0%	41.0%
4,229	ATCHISON	3,183	1,935	1,143	105	792 R	60.8%	35.9%	62.9%	37.1%
13,446	AUDRAIN	10,506	6,092	4,080	334	2,012 R	58.0%	38.8%	59.9%	40.1%
18,722	BARRY	12,345	7,334	4,676	335	2,658 R	59.4%	37.9%	61.1%	38.9%
7,113	BARTON	5,170	3,676	1,307	187	2,369 R	71.1%	25.3%	73.8%	26.2%
10,960	BATES	7,657	4,144	3,264	249	880 R	54.1%	42.6%	55.9%	44.1%
9,081	BENTON	7,129	3,643	3,215	271	428 R	51.1%	45.1%	53.1%	46.9%
7,428	BOLLINGER	5,152	3,179	1,898	75	1,281 R	61.7%	36.8%	62.6%	37.4%
76,011	BOONE	57,604	28,466	26,655	2,483	1,811 R	49.4%	46.3%	51.6%	48.4%
47,879	BUCHANAN	37,072	19,139	16,435	1,498	2,704 R	51.6%	44.3%	53.8%	46.2%
25,200	BUTLER	14,936	9,162	5,476	298	3,686 R	61.3%	36.7%	62.6%	37.4%
6,020	CALDWELL	3,978	2,163	1,622	193	541 R	54.4%	40.8%	57.1%	42.9%
17,780	CALLAWAY	13,874	6,911	6,410	553	501 R	49.8%	46.2%	51.9%	48.1%
18,875	CAMDEN	14,398	8,127	5,706	565	2,421 R	56.4%	39.6%	58.8%	41.2%
34,000	CAPE GIRARDEAU	27,948	18,325	8,948	675	9,377 R	65.6%	32.0%	67.2%	32.8%
7,500	CARROLL	5,237	2,951	2,178	108	773 R	56.3%	41.6%	57.5%	42.5%
3,800	CARTER	2,569	1,603	917	49	686 R	62.4%	35.7%	63.6%	36.4%
34,000	CASS	29,529	16,254	11,800	1,475	4,454 R	55.0%	40.0%	57.9%	42.1%
8,100	CEDAR	5,261	2,901	2,140	220	761 R	55.1%	40.7%	57.5%	42.5%
6,950	CHARITON	4,378	2,099	2,181	98	82 D	47.9%	49.8%	49.0%	51.0%
23,000	CHRISTIAN	17,034	9,932	6,557	545	3,375 R	58.3%	38.5%	60.2%	39.8%
5,400	CLARK	3,452	1,621	1,738	93	117 D	47.0%	50.3%	48.3%	51.7%
88,585	CLAY	71,689	37,057	31,630	3,002	5,427 R	51.7%	44.1%	54.0%	46.0%
10,000	CLINTON	8,180	4,194	3,657	329	537 R	51.3%	44.7%	53.4%	46.6%
37,000	COLE	31,171	20,061	10,275	835	9,786 R	64.4%	33.0%	66.1%	33.9%
8,978	COOPER	7,300	4,161	2,875	264	1,286 R	57.0%	39.4%	59.1%	40.9%
12,419	CRAWFORD	8,298	4,246	3,757	295	489 R	51.2%	45.3%	53.1%	46.9%
5,000	DADE	3,646	2,160	1,375	111	785 R	59.2%	37.7%	61.1%	38.9%
8,300	DALLAS	5,808	3,107	2,535	166	572 R	53.5%	43.6%	55.1%	44.9%
5,200	DAVIESS	3,717	2,024	1,563	130	461 R	54.5%	42.1%	56.4%	43.6%
5,500	DE KALB	4,140	2,249	1,729	162	520 R	54.3%	41.8%	56.5%	43.5%
11,000	DENT	5,847	2,990	2,670	187	320 R	51.1%	45.7%	52.8%	47.2%
8,700	DOUGLAS	5,556	3,434	1,984	138	1,450 R	61.8%	35.7%	63.4%	36.6%
17,300	DUNKLIN	10,715	5,723	4,820	172	903 R	53.4%	45.0%	54.3%	45.7%
44,000	FRANKLIN	35,498	19,402	14,685	1,411	4,717 R	54.7%	41.4%	56.9%	43.1%
9,057	GASCONADE	6,281	3,928	2,130	223	1,798 R	62.5%	33.9%	64.8%	35.2%
4,825	GENTRY	3,612	2,028	1,506	78	522 R	56.1%	41.7%	57.4%	42.6%
133,033	GREENE	104,655	59,685	42,060	2,910	17,625 R	57.0%	40.2%	58.7%	41.3%
6,800	GRUNDY	4,961	3,090	1,780	91	1,310 R	62.3%	35.9%	63.4%	36.6%
5,850	HARRISON	4,049	2,491	1,477	81	1,014 R	61.5%	36.5%	62.8%	37.2%
12,600	HENRY	9,537	4,513	4,596	428	83 D	47.3%	48.2%	49.5%	50.5%
5,183	HICKORY	3,916	1,888	1,938	90	50 D	48.2%	49.5%	49.3%	50.7%
3,977	HOLT	2,950	1,832	1,022	96	810 R	62.1%	34.6%	64.2%	35.8%
6,348	HOWARD	4,413	2,170	2,111	132	59 R	49.2%	47.8%	50.7%	49.3%
18,400	HOWELL	13,403	7,967	4,971	465	2,996 R	59.4%	37.1%	61.6%	38.4%
6,425	IRON	4,432	2,018	2,307	107	289 D	45.5%	52.1%	46.7%	53.3%
374,000	JACKSON	287,173	129,016	146,449	11,708	17,433 D	44.9%	51.0%	46.8%	53.2%
48,500	JASPER	35,319	23,414	10,578	1,327	12,836 R	66.3%	29.9%	68.9%	31.1%
90,000	JEFFERSON	72,787	35,411	34,443	2,933	968 R	48.7%	47.3%	50.7%	49.3%
19,193	JOHNSON	15,097	8,426	5,957	714	2,469 R	55.8%	39.5%	58.6%	41.4%
3,124	KNOX	2,186	1,115	1,029	42	86 R	51.0%	47.1%	52.0%	48.0%
15,200	LACLEDE	12,137	7,464	4,300	373	3,164 R	61.5%	35.4%	63.4%	36.6%
18,603	LAFAYETTE	13,276	7,241	5,507	528	1,734 R	54.5%	41.5%	56.8%	43.2%
16,500	LAWRENCE	12,638	7,371	4,807	460	2,564 R	58.3%	38.0%	60.5%	39.5%
5,809	LEWIS	4,372	1,933	2,335	104	402 D	44.2%	53.4%	45.3%	54.7%
15,424	LINCOLN	12,680	6,638	5,622	420	1,016 R	52.4%	44.3%	54.1%	45.9%
9,465	LINN	6,304	3,208	2,886	210	322 R	50.9%	45.8%	52.6%	47.4%
8,614	LIVINGSTON	6,632	3,900	2,571	161	1,329 R	58.8%	38.8%	60.3%	39.7%
11,434	MCDONALD	6,732	4,192	2,244	296	1,948 R	62.3%	33.3%	65.1%	34.9%

MISSOURI

SENATOR 1992

Registration	County	Total Vote	Republican	Democratic	Other	Rep.-Dem. Plurality	Percentage Total Vote Rep.	Dem.	Major Vote Rep.	Dem.
9,898	MACON	6,994	3,897	2,860	237	1,037 R	55.7%	40.9%	57.7%	42.3%
7,354	MADISON	5,037	2,732	2,179	126	553 R	54.2%	43.3%	55.6%	44.4%
5,335	MARIES	3,965	2,033	1,767	165	266 R	51.3%	44.6%	53.5%	46.5%
14,429	MARION	11,639	5,937	5,442	260	495 R	51.0%	46.8%	52.2%	47.8%
2,600	MERCER	1,751	1,088	634	29	454 R	62.1%	36.2%	63.2%	36.8%
11,767	MILLER	9,422	5,848	3,266	308	2,582 R	62.1%	34.7%	64.2%	35.8%
8,098	MISSISSIPPI	5,532	2,819	2,565	148	254 R	51.0%	46.4%	52.4%	47.6%
7,677	MONITEAU	6,052	3,843	1,993	216	1,850 R	63.5%	32.9%	65.8%	34.2%
6,005	MONROE	4,151	2,002	2,028	121	26 D	48.2%	48.9%	49.7%	50.3%
7,038	MONTGOMERY	5,170	2,949	2,094	127	855 R	57.0%	40.5%	58.5%	41.5%
9,400	MORGAN	7,696	4,330	3,078	288	1,252 R	56.3%	40.0%	58.5%	41.5%
12,250	NEW MADRID	7,874	3,899	3,863	112	36 R	49.5%	49.1%	50.2%	49.8%
26,688	NEWTON	17,150	11,179	5,548	423	5,631 R	65.2%	32.3%	66.8%	33.2%
11,800	NODAWAY	9,270	5,376	3,557	337	1,819 R	58.0%	38.4%	60.2%	39.8%
5,925	OREGON	4,178	2,068	2,008	102	60 R	49.5%	48.1%	50.7%	49.3%
7,400	OSAGE	5,972	3,863	1,939	170	1,924 R	64.7%	32.5%	66.6%	33.4%
6,646	OZARK	4,176	2,491	1,544	141	947 R	59.7%	37.0%	61.7%	38.3%
13,055	PEMISCOT	6,555	3,118	3,311	126	193 D	47.6%	50.5%	48.5%	51.5%
9,250	PERRY	7,179	4,774	2,211	194	2,563 R	66.5%	30.8%	68.3%	31.7%
23,200	PETTIS	16,266	9,758	5,886	622	3,872 R	60.0%	36.2%	62.4%	37.6%
20,450	PHELPS	16,526	8,747	7,131	648	1,616 R	52.9%	43.2%	55.1%	44.9%
12,165	PIKE	7,248	3,669	3,393	186	276 R	50.6%	46.8%	52.0%	48.0%
33,000	PLATTE	29,411	15,452	12,516	1,443	2,936 R	52.5%	42.6%	55.2%	44.8%
12,993	POLK	8,585	4,901	3,436	248	1,465 R	57.1%	40.0%	58.8%	41.2%
13,301	PULASKI	9,894	5,325	4,238	331	1,087 R	53.8%	42.8%	55.7%	44.3%
3,498	PUTNAM	2,372	1,674	659	39	1,015 R	70.6%	27.8%	71.8%	28.2%
6,000	RALLS	4,357	1,891	2,361	105	470 D	43.4%	54.2%	44.5%	55.5%
16,000	RANDOLPH	10,112	4,827	4,922	363	95 D	47.7%	48.7%	49.5%	50.5%
13,800	RAY	9,488	4,443	4,646	399	203 D	46.8%	49.0%	48.9%	51.1%
5,300	REYNOLDS	3,151	1,363	1,719	69	356 D	43.3%	54.6%	44.2%	55.8%
7,730	RIPLEY	4,756	2,834	1,812	110	1,022 R	59.6%	38.1%	61.0%	39.0%
123,602	ST. CHARLES	105,609	61,322	40,887	3,400	20,435 R	58.1%	38.7%	60.0%	40.0%
5,650	ST. CLAIR	4,505	2,296	2,068	141	228 R	51.0%	45.9%	52.6%	47.4%
27,000	ST. FRANCOIS	18,715	9,068	9,084	563	16 D	48.5%	48.5%	50.0%	50.0%
206,000	ST. LOUIS CITY	145,054	43,869	97,257	3,928	53,388 D	30.2%	67.0%	31.1%	68.9%
637,685	ST. LOUIS COUNTY	530,931	276,715	241,350	12,866	35,365 R	52.1%	45.5%	53.4%	46.6%
9,725	STE. GENEVIEVE	7,053	3,258	3,534	261	276 D	46.2%	50.1%	48.0%	52.0%
15,174	SALINE	10,073	5,168	4,572	333	596 R	51.3%	45.4%	53.1%	46.9%
3,347	SCHUYLER	2,085	1,109	925	51	184 R	53.2%	44.4%	54.5%	45.5%
3,616	SCOTLAND	2,309	1,173	1,070	66	103 R	50.8%	46.3%	52.3%	47.7%
23,850	SCOTT	15,823	9,001	6,563	259	2,438 R	56.9%	41.5%	57.8%	42.2%
5,490	SHANNON	3,716	1,829	1,796	91	33 R	49.2%	48.3%	50.5%	49.5%
4,583	SHELBY	3,384	1,782	1,527	75	255 R	52.7%	45.1%	53.9%	46.1%
15,500	STODDARD	11,731	6,958	4,632	141	2,326 R	59.3%	39.5%	60.0%	40.0%
13,400	STONE	9,054	5,185	3,560	309	1,625 R	57.3%	39.3%	59.3%	40.7%
5,000	SULLIVAN	3,332	1,895	1,395	42	500 R	56.9%	41.9%	57.6%	42.4%
16,500	TANEY	12,962	7,795	4,740	427	3,055 R	60.1%	36.6%	62.2%	37.8%
13,282	TEXAS	9,944	5,178	4,425	341	753 R	52.1%	44.5%	53.9%	46.1%
10,400	VERNON	8,030	4,334	3,457	239	877 R	54.0%	43.1%	55.6%	44.4%
12,000	WARREN	8,555	4,790	3,496	269	1,294 R	56.0%	40.9%	57.8%	42.2%
12,308	WASHINGTON	7,729	3,685	3,771	273	86 D	47.7%	48.8%	49.4%	50.6%
8,500	WAYNE	5,784	3,111	2,585	88	526 R	53.8%	44.7%	54.6%	45.4%
14,388	WEBSTER	10,390	5,817	4,254	319	1,563 R	56.0%	40.9%	57.8%	42.2%
1,850	WORTH	1,365	791	544	30	247 R	57.9%	39.9%	59.3%	40.7%
10,250	WRIGHT	7,605	4,711	2,671	223	2,040 R	61.9%	35.1%	63.8%	36.2%
3,067,955	TOTAL	2,354,925	1,221,901	1,057,967	75,057	163,934 R	51.9%	44.9%	53.6%	46.4%

MISSOURI
CONGRESS

CD	Year	Total Vote	Republican		Democratic		Other Vote	Rep.-Dem. Plurality	Percentage			
									Total Vote		Major Vote	
			Vote	Candidate	Vote	Candidate			Rep.	Dem.	Rep.	Dem.
1	1992	233,175	74,482	MONTGOMERY, ARTHUR S.	158,693	CLAY, WILLIAM		84,211 D	31.9%	68.1%	31.9%	68.1%
2	1992	312,445	157,594	TALENT, JAMES M.	148,729	HORN, JOAN KELLY	6,122	8,865 R	50.4%	47.6%	51.4%	48.6%
3	1992	271,834	90,006	HOLEKAMP, MALCOLM L.	174,000	GEPHARDT, RICHARD A.	7,828	83,994 D	33.1%	64.0%	34.1%	65.9%
4	1992	251,452	74,475	CARLEY, JOHN	176,977	SKELTON, IKE		102,502 D	29.6%	70.4%	29.6%	70.4%
5	1992	255,312	93,562	MOODY, EDWARD	151,014	WHEAT, ALAN	10,736	57,452 D	36.6%	59.1%	38.3%	61.7%
6	1992	268,524	119,637	COLEMAN, E. THOMAS	148,887	DANNER, PAT		29,250 D	44.6%	55.4%	44.6%	55.4%
7	1992	260,065	160,303	HANCOCK, MELTON D.	99,762	DEATON, THOMAS P.		60,541 R	61.6%	38.4%	61.6%	38.4%
8	1992	234,418	147,398	EMERSON, BILL	86,730	BULLOCK, THAD	290	60,668 R	62.9%	37.0%	63.0%	37.0%
9	1992	261,335	118,811	HARDY, RICK	124,694	VOLKMER, HAROLD	17,830	5,883 D	45.5%	47.7%	48.8%	51.2%

MISSOURI

1992 GENERAL ELECTION

Registration data provided by the Missouri Secretary of State includes estimated figures in a number of counties.

President   Other vote was 7,497 Libertarian (Marrou); 180 Gritz (write-in); 64 Hagelin (write-in); 17 Fulani (write-in); 13 LaRouche (write-in); 12 Daniels (write-in); 6 Warren (write-in); 3 scattered write-in. The total of the other vote column includes the write-ins not available by county.

Governor   The total in the other vote column represents 122 scattered write-in votes not available by county.

Senator   Other vote was 75,048 Libertarian (Bojarski) and 9 scattered write-in. The total of the other vote column includes the write-ins not available by county.

Congress   Other vote was 6,119 Libertarian (Higgins) and 3 scattered write-in in CD 2; Libertarian (Stockhausen) in CD 3; 6,107 Green (Danaher) and 4,629 Libertarian (Stauffer) in CD 5; 282 Reed (write-in) and 8 scattered write-in in CD 8; 10,565 Green (Barrow) and 7,265 Independent (Burghard) in CD 9.

1992 PRIMARIES

AUGUST 4 REPUBLICAN

Governor   183,968 William L. Webster; 163,719 Roy D. Blunt; 63,481 Wendell Bailey; 5,019 Dwight Watts; 3,958 Fred Salmons.

Senator   337,795 Christopher Bond; 70,626 Wes Hummel.

Congress   Unopposed in CD 6. Contested as follows:

CD 1   5,501 Arthur S. Montgomery; 4,052 Jim Rapp; 3,852 Joseph A. Schwan; 3,522 Bevis Schock.
CD 2   35,791 James M. Talent; 19,555 George H. Walker; 4,322 Tom McCoy; 1,915 Hugh V. Murray.
CD 3   22,118 Malcolm L. Holekamp; 5,300 Gary Carter; 3,493 Wallace Anderson; 3,312 Gerald Bollinger; 1,263 Joe Carron; 1,217 Bernard L. Mazurkiewicz.
CD 4   27,369 John Carley; 16,308 Damon Eyerly.
CD 5   11,584 Edward Moody; 9,169 Ron Freeman; 3,265 Joyce Lea; 2,535 Joseph A. Privitera.
CD 7   66,667 Melton D. Hancock; 13,469 Ronald Houseman; 6,304 Stephen K. Pennington.
CD 8   28,973 Bill Emerson; 12,807 E. Earl Durnell.
CD 9   25,477 Rick Hardy; 7,191 Joseph Brajdich.

AUGUST 4 DEMOCRATIC

Governor   388,098 Mel Carnahan; 235,652 Vince Schoemehl; 35,104 Sharon Rogers; 22,273 Mary J. Johnson; 11,514 Anthony B. Cox; 4,328 Elmer Dapron; 4,019 Cedric N. Hawkins.

Senator   224,984 Geri Rothman-Serot; 67,723 Bill Peacock; 59,290 Mert Bernstein; 57,254 George D. Weber; 50,091 Barbara M. Manson; 48,634 Carol A. Coe; 38,509 David Westfall; 18,312 Dan Dodson; 16,313 Ned Sutherland; 15,253 Ken Dudley; 10,334 Jim Krueger; 9,588 Earl Carey; 8,152 Richard C. Tolbert; 7,830 Nicholas Clement.

Congress   Contested as follows:

CD 1   57,242 William Clay; 26,677 Donald Cross.
CD 2   50,882 Joan Kelly Horn; 12,760 Susan Johnson.
CD 3   71,773 Richard A. Gephardt; 13,433 Leif Johnson; 8,957 Ned L. Abernathy.
CD 4   60,347 Ike Skelton; 11,540 Ron Beller; 4,638 Lewis E. Seay.
CD 5   50,873 Alan Wheat; 32,773 Fred Arbanas; 1,972 Michael Boatright; 1,682 Lou Ferro.

MISSOURI

CD 6   43,821 Pat Danner; 20,842 Sandra L. Reeves; 6,795 John J. Kauffman; 4,671 John Gallagher; 3,327 Jeff Bailey; 2,045 Gene Simmons; 1,245 Don Pine; 1,099 Ed O'Herin.

CD 7   20,428 Thomas P. Deaton; 15,629 Doug Harpool; 1,764 Gary Hamlin; 1,211 William Jacobs; 1,073 Bill Rosen; 896 Rodney J. Roberson.

CD 8   17,981 Thad Bullock; 17,777 James L. Thompson; 11,474 Shannon Russell; 10,920 Jon A. Kiser; 8,608 Dean Burk; 7,982 Johnny Dover.

CD 9   45,899 Harold Volkmer; 16,785 Justus D. Griffin; 9,124 Joseph P. Caulfield; 3,567 Anthony DeFranco; 2,630 Duane Messick; 2,340 Rob Shiverdecker.

MONTANA

GOVERNOR
Marc Racicot (R). Elected 1992 to a four-year term.

SENATORS
Max S. Baucus (D). Re-elected 1990 to a six-year term. Previously elected 1984, 1978.

Conrad Burns (R). Elected 1988 to a six-year term.

REPRESENTATIVE
At-Large. Pat Williams (D)

POSTWAR VOTE FOR PRESIDENT

| Year | Total Vote | Republican | | Democratic | | Other Vote | Plurality | Percentage | | | |
| | | Vote | Candidate | Vote | Candidate | | | Total Vote | | Major Vote | |
								Rep.	Dem.	Rep.	Dem.
1992 **	410,611	144,207	Bush, George	154,507	Clinton, Bill	111,897	10,300 D	35.1%	37.6%	48.3%	51.7%
1988	365,674	190,412	Bush, George	168,936	Dukakis, Michael S.	6,326	21,476 R	52.1%	46.2%	53.0%	47.0%
1984	384,377	232,450	Reagan, Ronald	146,742	Mondale, Walter F.	5,185	85,708 R	60.5%	38.2%	61.3%	38.7%
1980	363,952	206,814	Reagan, Ronald	118,032	Carter, Jimmy	39,106	88,782 R	56.8%	32.4%	63.7%	36.3%
1976	328,734	173,703	Ford, Gerald R.	149,259	Carter, Jimmy	5,772	24,444 R	52.8%	45.4%	53.8%	46.2%
1972	317,603	183,976	Nixon, Richard M.	120,197	McGovern, George S.	13,430	63,779 R	57.9%	37.8%	60.5%	39.5%
1968	274,404	138,835	Nixon, Richard M.	114,117	Humphrey, Hubert H.	21,452	24,718 R	50.6%	41.6%	54.9%	45.1%
1964	278,628	113,032	Goldwater, Barry M.	164,246	Johnson, Lyndon B.	1,350	51,214 D	40.6%	58.9%	40.8%	59.2%
1960	277,579	141,841	Nixon, Richard M.	134,891	Kennedy, John F.	847	6,950 R	51.1%	48.6%	51.3%	48.7%
1956	271,171	154,933	Eisenhower, Dwight D.	116,238	Stevenson, Adlai E.		38,695 R	57.1%	42.9%	57.1%	42.9%
1952	265,037	157,394	Eisenhower, Dwight D.	106,213	Stevenson, Adlai E.	1,430	51,181 R	59.4%	40.1%	59.7%	40.3%
1948	224,278	96,770	Dewey, Thomas E.	119,071	Truman, Harry S.	8,437	22,301 D	43.1%	53.1%	44.8%	55.2%

In 1992 the other vote column includes 107,225 votes cast for Perot.

POSTWAR VOTE FOR GOVERNOR

| Year | Total Vote | Republican | | Democratic | | Other Vote | Rep.-Dem. Plurality | Percentage | | | |
| | | Vote | Candidate | Vote | Candidate | | | Total Vote | | Major Vote | |
								Rep.	Dem.	Rep.	Dem.
1992	407,842	209,401	Racicot, Marc	198,421	Bradley, Dorothy	20	10,980 R	51.3%	48.7%	51.3%	48.7%
1988	367,021	190,604	Stephens, Stan	169,313	Judge, Thomas L.	7,104	21,291 R	51.9%	46.1%	53.0%	47.0%
1984	378,970	100,070	Goodover, Pat M.	266,578	Schwinden, Ted	12,322	166,508 D	26.4%	70.3%	27.3%	72.7%
1980	360,466	160,892	Ramirez, Jack	199,574	Schwinden, Ted		38,682 D	44.6%	55.4%	44.6%	55.4%
1976	316,720	115,848	Woodahl, Robert	195,420	Judge, Thomas L.	5,452	79,572 D	36.6%	61.7%	37.2%	62.8%
1972	318,754	146,231	Smith, Ed	172,523	Judge, Thomas L.		26,292 D	45.9%	54.1%	45.9%	54.1%
1968	278,112	116,432	Babcock, Tim M.	150,481	Anderson, Forrest H.	11,199	34,049 D	41.9%	54.1%	43.6%	56.4%
1964	280,975	144,113	Babcock, Tim M.	136,862	Renne, Roland		7,251 R	51.3%	48.7%	51.3%	48.7%
1960	279,881	154,230	Nutter, Donald G.	125,651	Cannon, Paul		28,579 R	55.1%	44.9%	55.1%	44.9%
1956	270,366	138,878	Aronson, J. Hugo	131,488	Olsen, Arnold H.		7,390 R	51.4%	48.6%	51.4%	48.6%
1952	263,792	134,423	Aronson, J. Hugo	129,369	Bonner, John W.		5,054 R	51.0%	49.0%	51.0%	49.0%
1948	222,964	97,792	Ford, Sam C.	124,267	Bonner, John W.	905	26,475 D	43.9%	55.7%	44.0%	56.0%

MONTANA

POSTWAR VOTE FOR SENATOR

Year	Total Vote	Republican Vote	Republican Candidate	Democratic Vote	Democratic Candidate	Other Vote	Rep.-Dem. Plurality	Percentage Total Vote Rep.	Percentage Total Vote Dem.	Percentage Major Vote Rep.	Percentage Major Vote Dem.
1990	319,336	93,836	Kolstad, Allen C.	217,563	Baucus, Max S.	7,937	123,727 D	29.4%	68.1%	30.1%	69.9%
1988	365,254	189,445	Burns, Conrad	175,809	Melcher, John		13,636 R	51.9%	48.1%	51.9%	48.1%
1984	379,155	154,308	Cozzens, Chuck	215,704	Baucus, Max S.	9,143	61,396 D	40.7%	56.9%	41.7%	58.3%
1982	321,062	133,789	Williams, Larry	174,861	Melcher, John	12,412	41,072 D	41.7%	54.5%	43.3%	56.7%
1978	287,942	127,589	Williams, Larry	160,353	Baucus, Max S.		32,764 D	44.3%	55.7%	44.3%	55.7%
1976	321,445	115,213	Burger, Stanley C.	206,232	Melcher, John		91,019 D	35.8%	64.2%	35.8%	64.2%
1972	314,925	151,316	Hibbard, Henry S.	163,609	Metcalf, Lee		12,293 D	48.0%	52.0%	48.0%	52.0%
1970	247,869	97,809	Wallace, Harold E.	150,060	Mansfield, Mike		52,251 D	39.5%	60.5%	39.5%	60.5%
1966	259,863	121,697	Babcock, Tim M.	138,166	Metcalf, Lee		16,469 D	46.8%	53.2%	46.8%	53.2%
1964	280,010	99,367	Blewett, Alex	180,643	Mansfield, Mike		81,276 D	35.5%	64.5%	35.5%	64.5%
1960	276,612	136,281	Fjare, Orvin B.	140,331	Metcalf, Lee		4,050 D	49.3%	50.7%	49.3%	50.7%
1958	229,483	54,573	Welch. Lou W.	174,910	Mansfield, Mike		120,337 D	23.8%	76.2%	23.8%	76.2%
1954	227,454	112,863	D'Ewart, Wesley A.	114,591	Murray, James E.		1,728 D	49.6%	50.4%	49.6%	50.4%
1952	262,297	127,360	Ecton, Zales N.	133,109	Mansfield, Mike	1,828	5,749 D	48.6%	50.7%	48.9%	51.1%
1948	221,003	94,458	David, Tom J.	125,193	Murray, James E.	1,352	30,735 D	42.7%	56.6%	43.0%	57.0%
1946	190,566	101,901	Ecton, Zales N.	86,476	Erickson, Leif	2,189	15,425 R	53.5%	45.4%	54.1%	45.9%

MONTANA

One At Large

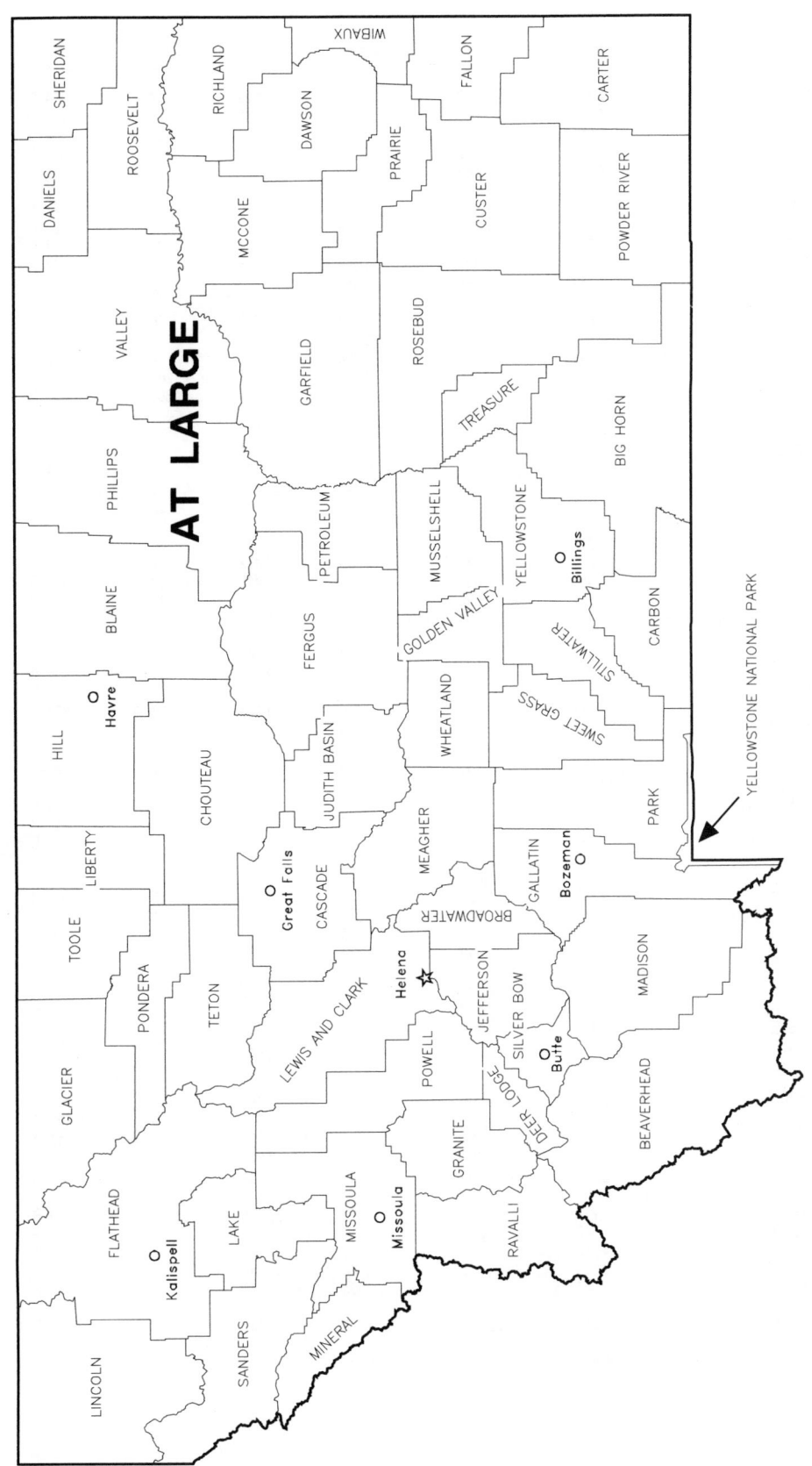

MONTANA

PRESIDENT 1992

Registration	County	Total Vote	Republican	Democratic	Perot	Other	Plurality	Percentage Total Vote		
								Rep.	Dem.	Perot
5,286	BEAVERHEAD	4,160	1,746	1,098	1,202	114	544 R	42.0%	26.4%	28.9%
6,268	BIG HORN	4,394	1,377	2,154	840	23	777 D	31.3%	49.0%	19.1%
4,297	BLAINE	3,046	971	1,355	699	21	384 D	31.9%	44.5%	22.9%
2,388	BROADWATER	1,842	830	491	505	16	325 R	45.1%	26.7%	27.4%
6,013	CARBON	4,620	1,562	1,549	1,482	27	13 R	33.8%	33.5%	32.1%
1,126	CARTER	874	497	154	220	3	277 R	56.9%	17.6%	25.2%
46,129	CASCADE	36,580	12,494	14,719	9,151	216	2,225 D	34.2%	40.2%	25.0%
3,814	CHOUTEAU	3,236	1,380	959	870	27	421 R	42.6%	29.6%	26.9%
7,170	CUSTER	5,611	2,105	1,968	1,505	33	137 R	37.5%	35.1%	26.8%
1,622	DANIELS	1,363	496	457	402	8	39 R	36.4%	33.5%	29.5%
6,400	DAWSON	4,850	1,679	1,785	1,370	16	106 D	34.6%	36.8%	28.2%
6,519	DEER LODGE	5,269	832	3,174	1,207	56	1,967 D	15.8%	60.2%	22.9%
2,011	FALLON	1,608	731	446	427	4	285 R	45.5%	27.7%	26.6%
8,130	FERGUS	6,491	2,736	1,615	1,934	206	802 R	42.2%	24.9%	29.8%
39,749	FLATHEAD	31,417	11,699	9,746	9,109	863	1,953 R	37.2%	31.0%	29.0%
37,750	GALLATIN	28,787	11,109	9,535	7,711	432	1,574 R	38.6%	33.1%	26.8%
1,049	GARFIELD	819	403	125	281	10	122 R	49.2%	15.3%	34.3%
6,559	GLACIER	4,323	1,222	2,076	997	28	854 D	28.3%	48.0%	23.1%
631	GOLDEN VALLEY	496	192	142	157	5	35 R	38.7%	28.6%	31.7%
1,726	GRANITE	1,323	556	358	386	23	170 R	42.0%	27.1%	29.2%
10,657	HILL	8,082	2,408	3,618	2,017	39	1,210 D	29.8%	44.8%	25.0%
5,542	JEFFERSON	4,225	1,541	1,415	1,172	97	126 R	36.5%	33.5%	27.7%
1,819	JUDITH BASIN	1,447	610	409	415	13	195 R	42.2%	28.3%	28.7%
13,180	LAKE	10,553	3,596	3,938	2,878	141	342 D	34.1%	37.3%	27.3%
33,003	LEWIS AND CLARK	26,181	9,351	11,117	5,560	153	1,766 D	35.7%	42.5%	21.2%
1,439	LIBERTY	1,211	512	321	363	15	149 R	42.3%	26.5%	30.0%
11,482	LINCOLN	8,378	2,799	2,765	2,637	177	34 R	33.4%	33.0%	31.5%
1,622	MCCONE	1,354	528	424	395	7	104 R	39.0%	31.3%	29.2%
4,133	MADISON	3,299	1,415	779	1,043	62	372 R	42.9%	23.6%	31.6%
1,287	MEAGHER	1,002	422	260	310	10	112 R	42.1%	25.9%	30.9%
2,175	MINERAL	1,635	403	664	543	25	121 D	24.6%	40.6%	33.2%
57,490	MISSOULA	43,307	12,898	20,347	9,735	327	7,449 D	29.8%	47.0%	22.5%
2,882	MUSSELSHELL	2,228	876	648	691	13	185 R	39.3%	29.1%	31.0%
9,808	PARK	7,483	2,846	2,258	2,182	197	588 R	38.0%	30.2%	29.2%
367	PETROLEUM	296	135	61	95	5	40 R	45.6%	20.6%	32.1%
3,258	PHILLIPS	2,625	1,026	634	949	16	77 R	39.1%	24.2%	36.2%
3,955	PONDERA	3,165	1,252	1,046	855	12	206 R	39.6%	33.0%	27.0%
1,482	POWDER RIVER	1,156	547	258	340	11	207 R	47.3%	22.3%	29.4%
3,675	POWELL	2,938	1,058	989	872	19	69 R	36.0%	33.7%	29.7%
1,040	PRAIRIE	856	412	260	179	5	152 R	48.1%	30.4%	20.9%
19,134	RAVALLI	15,020	5,392	4,644	4,573	411	748 R	35.9%	30.9%	30.4%
6,100	RICHLAND	4,748	1,760	1,440	1,525	23	235 R	37.1%	30.3%	32.1%
6,249	ROOSEVELT	4,193	1,212	1,827	1,089	65	615 D	28.9%	43.6%	26.0%
5,533	ROSEBUD	3,918	1,130	1,669	1,099	20	539 D	28.8%	42.6%	28.1%
5,961	SANDERS	4,506	1,361	1,689	1,378	78	311 D	30.2%	37.5%	30.6%
3,206	SHERIDAN	2,663	795	1,077	782	9	282 D	29.9%	40.4%	29.4%
22,827	SILVER BOW	18,146	3,491	9,960	4,570	125	5,390 D	19.2%	54.9%	25.2%
4,597	STILLWATER	3,640	1,390	1,178	1,056	16	212 R	38.2%	32.4%	29.0%
2,169	SWEET GRASS	1,802	880	395	507	20	373 R	48.8%	21.9%	28.1%
4,105	TETON	3,405	1,364	1,043	969	29	321 R	40.1%	30.6%	28.5%
3,273	TOOLE	2,717	943	854	903	17	40 R	34.7%	31.4%	33.2%
664	TREASURE	547	206	157	178	6	28 R	37.7%	28.7%	32.5%
5,707	VALLEY	4,568	1,497	1,715	1,320	36	218 D	32.8%	37.5%	28.9%
1,503	WHEATLAND	1,150	478	384	284	4	94 R	41.6%	33.4%	24.7%
837	WIBAUX	607	234	195	173	5	39 R	38.6%	32.1%	28.5%
73,024	YELLOWSTONE	56,451	22,822	20,163	13,133	333	2,659 R	40.4%	35.7%	23.3%
529,822	TOTAL	410,611	144,207	154,507	107,225	4,672	10,300 D	35.1%	37.6%	26.1%

MONTANA

GOVERNOR 1992

							Percentage			
							Total Vote		Major Vote	
Registration	County	Total Vote	Republican	Democratic	Other	Rep.-Dem. Plurality	Rep.	Dem.	Rep.	Dem.
5,286	BEAVERHEAD	4,122	2,553	1,569		984 R	61.9%	38.1%	61.9%	38.1%
6,268	BIG HORN	4,358	1,827	2,531		704 D	41.9%	58.1%	41.9%	58.1%
4,297	BLAINE	3,001	1,319	1,682		363 D	44.0%	56.0%	44.0%	56.0%
2,388	BROADWATER	1,812	1,155	657		498 R	63.7%	36.3%	63.7%	36.3%
6,013	CARBON	4,681	2,566	2,115		451 R	54.8%	45.2%	54.8%	45.2%
1,126	CARTER	852	637	215		422 R	74.8%	25.2%	74.8%	25.2%
46,129	CASCADE	36,226	16,819	19,405	2	2,586 D	46.4%	53.6%	46.4%	53.6%
3,814	CHOUTEAU	3,194	1,818	1,376		442 R	56.9%	43.1%	56.9%	43.1%
7,170	CUSTER	5,594	2,936	2,658		278 R	52.5%	47.5%	52.5%	47.5%
1,622	DANIELS	1,351	820	531		289 R	60.7%	39.3%	60.7%	39.3%
6,400	DAWSON	4,845	2,607	2,238		369 R	53.8%	46.2%	53.8%	46.2%
6,519	DEER LODGE	5,188	1,510	3,677	1	2,167 D	29.1%	70.9%	29.1%	70.9%
2,011	FALLON	1,572	980	592		388 R	62.3%	37.7%	62.3%	37.7%
8,130	FERGUS	6,486	3,973	2,512	1	1,461 R	61.3%	38.7%	61.3%	38.7%
39,749	FLATHEAD	31,190	17,538	13,652		3,886 R	56.2%	43.8%	56.2%	43.8%
37,750	GALLATIN	28,629	15,654	12,969	6	2,685 R	54.7%	45.3%	54.7%	45.3%
1,049	GARFIELD	806	607	199		408 R	75.3%	24.7%	75.3%	24.7%
6,559	GLACIER	4,343	1,701	2,642		941 D	39.2%	60.8%	39.2%	60.8%
631	GOLDEN VALLEY	490	308	182		126 R	62.9%	37.1%	62.9%	37.1%
1,726	GRANITE	1,310	821	488	1	333 R	62.7%	37.3%	62.7%	37.3%
10,657	HILL	8,029	3,447	4,582		1,135 D	42.9%	57.1%	42.9%	57.1%
5,542	JEFFERSON	4,221	2,231	1,990		241 R	52.9%	47.1%	52.9%	47.1%
1,819	JUDITH BASIN	1,432	896	536		360 R	62.6%	37.4%	62.6%	37.4%
13,180	LAKE	10,474	5,475	4,998	1	477 R	52.3%	47.7%	52.3%	47.7%
33,003	LEWIS AND CLARK	26,103	13,115	12,988		127 R	50.2%	49.8%	50.2%	49.8%
1,439	LIBERTY	1,212	755	457		298 R	62.3%	37.7%	62.3%	37.7%
11,482	LINCOLN	8,236	4,588	3,648		940 R	55.7%	44.3%	55.7%	44.3%
1,622	MCCONE	1,347	808	539		269 R	60.0%	40.0%	60.0%	40.0%
4,133	MADISON	3,259	2,148	1,111		1,037 R	65.9%	34.1%	65.9%	34.1%
1,287	MEAGHER	985	579	406		173 R	58.8%	41.2%	58.8%	41.2%
2,175	MINERAL	1,615	682	933		251 D	42.2%	57.8%	42.2%	57.8%
57,490	MISSOULA	42,988	18,531	24,453	4	5,922 D	43.1%	56.9%	43.1%	56.9%
2,882	MUSSELSHELL	2,204	1,483	721		762 R	67.3%	32.7%	67.3%	32.7%
9,808	PARK	7,445	4,288	3,156	1	1,132 R	57.6%	42.4%	57.6%	42.4%
367	PETROLEUM	296	204	92		112 R	68.9%	31.1%	68.9%	31.1%
3,258	PHILLIPS	2,604	1,720	884		836 R	66.1%	33.9%	66.1%	33.9%
3,955	PONDERA	3,175	1,892	1,283		609 R	59.6%	40.4%	59.6%	40.4%
1,482	POWDER RIVER	1,029	646	382	1	264 R	62.8%	37.1%	62.8%	37.2%
3,675	POWELL	2,948	1,562	1,386		176 R	53.0%	47.0%	53.0%	47.0%
1,040	PRAIRIE	844	539	305		234 R	63.9%	36.1%	63.9%	36.1%
19,134	RAVALLI	14,854	8,814	6,040		2,774 R	59.3%	40.7%	59.3%	40.7%
6,100	RICHLAND	4,730	2,722	2,008		714 R	57.5%	42.5%	57.5%	42.5%
6,249	ROOSEVELT	4,156	1,765	2,391		626 D	42.5%	57.5%	42.5%	57.5%
5,533	ROSEBUD	3,940	1,716	2,224		508 D	43.6%	56.4%	43.6%	56.4%
5,961	SANDERS	4,432	2,352	2,080		272 R	53.1%	46.9%	53.1%	46.9%
3,206	SHERIDAN	2,623	1,161	1,462		301 D	44.3%	55.7%	44.3%	55.7%
22,827	SILVER BOW	17,998	6,528	11,470		4,942 D	36.3%	63.7%	36.3%	63.7%
4,597	STILLWATER	3,626	2,113	1,513		600 R	58.3%	41.7%	58.3%	41.7%
2,169	SWEET GRASS	1,775	1,233	541	1	692 R	69.5%	30.5%	69.5%	30.5%
4,105	TETON	3,359	2,018	1,341		677 R	60.1%	39.9%	60.1%	39.9%
3,273	TOOLE	2,699	1,539	1,160		379 R	57.0%	43.0%	57.0%	43.0%
664	TREASURE	544	344	200		144 R	63.2%	36.8%	63.2%	36.8%
5,707	VALLEY	4,335	2,278	2,057		221 R	52.5%	47.5%	52.5%	47.5%
1,503	WHEATLAND	1,138	672	466		206 R	59.1%	40.9%	59.1%	40.9%
837	WIBAUX	598	383	215		168 R	64.0%	36.0%	64.0%	36.0%
73,024	YELLOWSTONE	56,539	30,025	26,513	1	3,512 R	53.1%	46.9%	53.1%	46.9%
529,822	TOTAL	407,842	209,401	198,421	20	10,980 R	51.3%	48.7%	51.3%	48.7%

MONTANA

CONGRESS

CD	Year	Total Vote	Republican		Democratic		Other Vote	Rep.-Dem. Plurality	Percentage			
			Vote	Candidate	Vote	Candidate			Total Vote		Major Vote	
									Rep.	Dem.	Rep.	Dem.
AL	1992	403,735	189,570	MARLENEE, RON	203,711	WILLIAMS, PAT	10,454	14,141 D	47.0%	50.5%	48.2%	51.8%

MONTANA

1992 GENERAL ELECTION

President   Other vote was 3,658 Independent (Gritz); 986 Libertarian (Marrou); 20 Hagelin (write-in); 8 Fulani (write-in).

Governor   Other vote was scattered write-in.

Congress   Other vote at-large was Libertarian (Wilverding).

1992 PRIMARIES

JUNE 2 REPUBLICAN

Governor   68,013 Marc Racicot; 31,038 Andrea Bennett.

Congress   Unopposed at-large.

JUNE 2 DEMOCRATIC

Governor   54,453 Dorothy Bradley; 44,323 Mike McGrath; 23,883 Frank Morrison; 4,216 Bob Kelleher; 2,773 Martin J. Beckman; 2,628 Curly Thornton.

Congress   Unopposed at-large.

NEBRASKA

GOVERNOR
Ben Nelson (D). Elected 1990 to a four-year term.

SENATORS
J. J. Exon (D). Re-elected 1990 to a six-year term. Previously elected 1984, 1978.

Bob Kerrey (D). Elected 1988 to a six-year term.

REPRESENTATIVES
1. Douglas K. Bereuter (R)   2. Peter Hoagland (D)   3. Bill Barrett (R)

POSTWAR VOTE FOR PRESIDENT

Year	Total Vote	Republican Vote	Republican Candidate	Democratic Vote	Democratic Candidate	Other Vote	Plurality	Total Vote Rep.	Total Vote Dem.	Major Vote Rep.	Major Vote Dem.
1992 **	737,546	343,678	Bush, George	216,864	Clinton, Bill	177,004	126,814 R	46.6%	29.4%	61.3%	38.7%
1988	661,465	397,956	Bush, George	259,235	Dukakis, Michael S.	4,274	138,721 R	60.2%	39.2%	60.6%	39.4%
1984	652,090	460,054	Reagan, Ronald	187,866	Mondale, Walter F.	4,170	272,188 R	70.6%	28.8%	71.0%	29.0%
1980	640,854	419,937	Reagan, Ronald	166,851	Carter, Jimmy	54,066	253,086 R	65.5%	26.0%	71.6%	28.4%
1976	607,668	359,705	Ford, Gerald R.	233,692	Carter, Jimmy	14,271	126,013 R	59.2%	38.5%	60.6%	39.4%
1972	576,289	406,298	Nixon, Richard M.	169,991	McGovern, George S.		236,307 R	70.5%	29.5%	70.5%	29.5%
1968	536,851	321,163	Nixon, Richard M.	170,784	Humphrey, Hubert H.	44,904	150,379 R	59.8%	31.8%	65.3%	34.7%
1964	584,154	276,847	Goldwater, Barry M.	307,307	Johnson, Lyndon B.		30,460 D	47.4%	52.6%	47.4%	52.6%
1960	613,095	380,553	Nixon, Richard M.	232,542	Kennedy, John F.		148,011 R	62.1%	37.9%	62.1%	37.9%
1956	577,137	378,108	Eisenhower, Dwight D.	199,029	Stevenson, Adlai E.		179,079 R	65.5%	34.5%	65.5%	34.5%
1952	609,660	421,603	Eisenhower, Dwight D.	188,057	Stevenson, Adlai E.		233,546 R	69.2%	30.8%	69.2%	30.8%
1948	488,940	264,774	Dewey, Thomas E.	224,165	Truman, Harry S.	1	40,609 R	54.2%	45.8%	54.2%	45.8%

In 1992 the other vote column includes 174,104 votes cast for Perot.

POSTWAR VOTE FOR GOVERNOR

Year	Total Vote	Republican Vote	Republican Candidate	Democratic Vote	Democratic Candidate	Other Vote	Rep.-Dem. Plurality	Total Vote Rep.	Total Vote Dem.	Major Vote Rep.	Major Vote Dem.
1990	586,542	288,741	Orr, Kay	292,771	Nelson, Ben	5,030	4,030 D	49.2%	49.9%	49.7%	50.3%
1986	564,422	298,325	Orr, Kay	265,156	Boosalis, Helen	941	33,169 R	52.9%	47.0%	52.9%	47.1%
1982	547,902	270,203	Thone, Charles	277,436	Kerrey, Bob	263	7,233 D	49.3%	50.6%	49.3%	50.7%
1978	492,423	275,473	Thone, Charles	216,754	Whelan, Gerald T.	196	58,719 R	55.9%	44.0%	56.0%	44.0%
1974	451,306	159,780	Marvel, Richard D.	267,012	Exon, J. J.	24,514	107,232 D	35.4%	59.2%	37.4%	62.6%
1970	461,619	201,994	Tiemann, Norbert T.	248,552	Exon, J. J.	11,073	46,558 D	43.8%	53.8%	44.8%	55.2%
1966 **	486,396	299,245	Tiemann, Norbert T.	186,985	Sorensen, Philip C.	166	112,260 R	61.5%	38.4%	61.5%	38.5%
1964	578,090	231,029	Burney, Dwight W.	347,026	Morrison, Frank B.	35	115,997 D	40.0%	60.0%	40.0%	60.0%
1962	464,585	221,885	Seaton, Fred A.	242,669	Morrison, Frank B.	31	20,784 D	47.8%	52.2%	47.8%	52.2%
1960	598,971	287,302	Cooper, John R.	311,344	Morrison, Frank B.	325	24,042 D	48.0%	52.0%	48.0%	52.0%
1958	421,067	209,705	Anderson, Victor E.	211,345	Brooks, Ralph G.	17	1,640 D	49.8%	50.2%	49.8%	50.2%
1956	567,933	308,293	Anderson, Victor E.	228,048	Sorrell, Frank	31,592	80,245 R	54.3%	40.2%	57.5%	42.5%
1954	414,841	250,080	Anderson, Victor E.	164,753	Ritchie, William	8	85,327 R	60.3%	39.7%	60.3%	39.7%
1952	595,714	366,009	Crosby, Robert B.	229,700	Raecke, Walter R.	5	136,309 R	61.4%	38.6%	61.4%	38.6%
1950	449,720	247,081	Peterson, Val	202,638	Raecke, Walter R.	1	44,443 R	54.9%	45.1%	54.9%	45.1%
1948	476,352	286,119	Peterson, Val	190,214	Sorrell, Frank	19	95,905 R	60.1%	39.9%	60.1%	39.9%
1946	380,835	249,468	Peterson, Val	131,367	Sorrell, Frank		118,101 R	65.5%	34.5%	65.5%	34.5%

The term of office of Nebraska's Governor was increased from two to four years effective with the 1966 election.

NEBRASKA

POSTWAR VOTE FOR SENATOR

Year	Total Vote	Republican		Democratic		Other Vote	Rep.-Dem. Plurality	Percentage			
								Total Vote		Major Vote	
		Vote	Candidate	Vote	Candidate			Rep.	Dem.	Rep.	Dem.
1990	593,828	243,013	Daub, Harold J.	349,779	Exon, J. J.	1,036	106,766 D	40.9%	58.9%	41.0%	59.0%
1988	667,860	278,250	Karnes, David	378,717	Kerrey, Bob	10,893	100,467 D	41.7%	56.7%	42.4%	57.6%
1984	639,668	307,147	Hoch, Nancy	332,217	Exon, J. J.	304	25,070 D	48.0%	51.9%	48.0%	52.0%
1982	545,647	155,760	Keck, Jim	363,350	Zorinsky, Edward	26,537	207,590 D	28.5%	66.6%	30.0%	70.0%
1978	494,368	159,806	Shasteen, Donald	334,276	Exon, J. J.	286	174,470 D	32.3%	67.6%	32.3%	67.7%
1976	598,314	284,284	McCollister, John Y.	313,809	Zorinsky, Edward	221	29,525 D	47.5%	52.4%	47.5%	52.5%
1972	568,580	301,841	Curtis, Carl T.	265,922	Carpenter, Terry	817	35,919 R	53.1%	46.8%	53.2%	46.8%
1970	458,966	240,894	Hruska, Roman L.	217,681	Morrison, Frank B.	391	23,213 R	52.5%	47.4%	52.5%	47.5%
1966	485,101	296,116	Curtis, Carl T.	187,950	Morrison, Frank B.	1,035	108,166 R	61.0%	38.7%	61.2%	38.8%
1964	563,401	345,772	Hruska, Roman L.	217,605	Arndt, Raymond W.	24	128,167 R	61.4%	38.6%	61.4%	38.6%
1960	598,743	352,748	Curtis, Carl T.	245,837	Conrad, Robert	158	106,911 R	58.9%	41.1%	58.9%	41.1%
1958	417,385	232,227	Hruska, Roman L.	185,152	Morrison, Frank B.	6	47,075 R	55.6%	44.4%	55.6%	44.4%
1954	418,691	255,695	Curtis, Carl T.	162,990	Neville, Keith	6	92,705 R	61.1%	38.9%	61.1%	38.9%
1954 S	411,225	250,341	Hruska, Roman L.	160,881	Green, James F.	3	89,460 R	60.9%	39.1%	60.9%	39.1%
1952	591,749	408,971	Butler, Hugh	164,660	Long, Stanley D.	18,118	244,311 R	69.1%	27.8%	71.3%	28.7%
1952 S	581,750	369,841	Griswold, Dwight	211,898	Ritchie, William	11	157,943 R	63.6%	36.4%	63.6%	36.4%
1948	471,895	267,575	Wherry, Kenneth S.	204,320	Carpenter, Terry		63,255 R	56.7%	43.3%	56.7%	43.3%
1946	382,958	271,208	Butler, Hugh	111,750	Mekota, John E.		159,458 R	70.8%	29.2%	70.8%	29.2%

One each of the 1954 and 1952 elections was for a short term to fill a vacancy.

316

NEBRASKA

Districts Established June 10, 1991

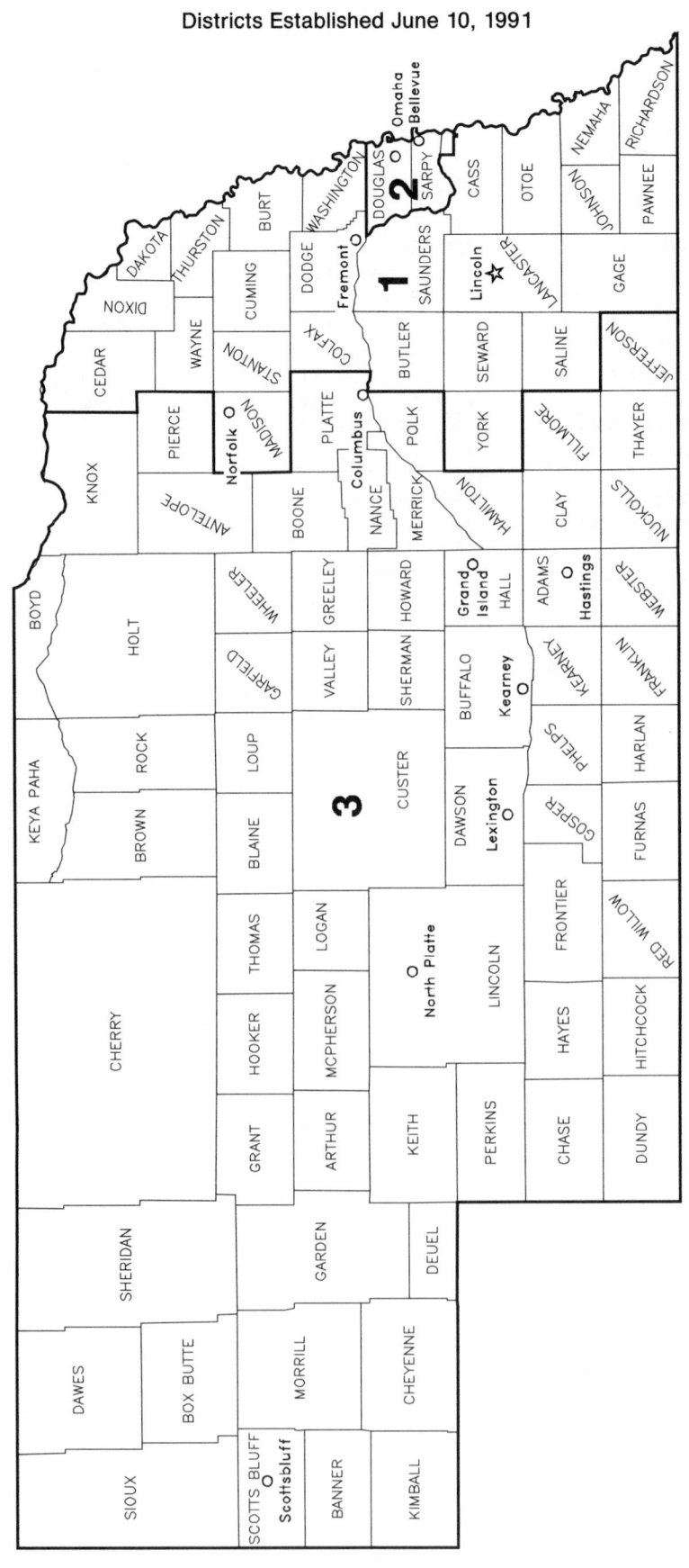

NEBRASKA

PRESIDENT 1992

Registration	County	Total Vote	Republican	Democratic	Perot	Other	Plurality	Percentage Total Vote		
								Rep.	Dem.	Perot
16,619	ADAMS	13,110	6,346	3,445	3,273	46	2,901 R	48.4%	26.3%	25.0%
5,121	ANTELOPE	3,776	1,979	650	1,134	13	845 R	52.4%	17.2%	30.0%
325	ARTHUR	263	148	18	97		51 R	56.3%	6.8%	36.9%
578	BANNER	480	284	68	128		156 R	59.2%	14.2%	26.7%
506	BLAINE	453	256	64	130	3	126 R	56.5%	14.1%	28.7%
4,183	BOONE	3,162	1,588	604	956	14	632 R	50.2%	19.1%	30.2%
8,336	BOX BUTTE	5,670	2,198	1,935	1,508	29	263 R	38.8%	34.1%	26.6%
2,077	BOYD	1,571	744	353	468	6	276 R	47.4%	22.5%	29.8%
2,383	BROWN	1,846	999	311	525	11	474 R	54.1%	16.8%	28.4%
21,808	BUFFALO	17,617	9,708	3,742	4,083	84	5,625 R	55.1%	21.2%	23.2%
5,203	BURT	3,912	1,667	1,224	1,009	12	443 R	42.6%	31.3%	25.8%
5,767	BUTLER	4,147	1,881	1,087	1,157	22	724 R	45.4%	26.2%	27.9%
13,505	CASS	9,979	4,314	2,949	2,657	59	1,365 R	43.2%	29.6%	26.6%
6,161	CEDAR	4,518	1,981	1,007	1,507	23	474 R	43.8%	22.3%	33.4%
2,791	CHASE	2,082	1,000	398	674	10	326 R	48.0%	19.1%	32.4%
4,243	CHERRY	3,008	1,707	563	730	8	977 R	56.7%	18.7%	24.3%
5,757	CHEYENNE	4,241	2,197	967	1,061	16	1,136 R	51.8%	22.8%	25.0%
4,838	CLAY	3,581	1,818	802	952	9	866 R	50.8%	22.4%	26.6%
5,452	COLFAX	4,144	1,915	1,011	1,197	21	718 R	46.2%	24.4%	28.9%
6,617	CUMING	4,746	2,711	835	1,192	8	1,519 R	57.1%	17.6%	25.1%
8,612	CUSTER	5,820	3,180	1,126	1,492	22	1,688 R	54.6%	19.3%	25.6%
8,635	DAKOTA	6,414	2,771	2,322	1,307	14	449 R	43.2%	36.2%	20.4%
5,153	DAWES	4,068	1,961	987	1,103	17	858 R	48.2%	24.3%	27.1%
11,212	DAWSON	8,781	4,710	1,739	2,305	27	2,405 R	53.6%	19.8%	26.2%
1,498	DEUEL	1,120	558	232	327	3	231 R	49.8%	20.7%	29.2%
4,001	DIXON	3,054	1,484	830	726	14	654 R	48.6%	27.2%	23.8%
20,223	DODGE	16,408	7,269	4,665	4,432	42	2,604 R	44.3%	28.4%	27.0%
252,367	DOUGLAS	199,880	93,421	67,003	38,641	815	26,418 R	46.7%	33.5%	19.3%
1,575	DUNDY	1,252	664	244	332	12	332 R	53.0%	19.5%	26.5%
4,438	FILLMORE	3,483	1,495	988	993	7	502 R	42.9%	28.4%	28.5%
2,823	FRANKLIN	1,980	967	477	527	9	440 R	48.8%	24.1%	26.6%
2,074	FRONTIER	1,571	785	302	479	5	306 R	50.0%	19.2%	30.5%
3,664	FURNAS	2,801	1,365	624	804	8	561 R	48.7%	22.3%	28.7%
13,950	GAGE	10,073	3,995	3,309	2,726	43	686 R	39.7%	32.9%	27.1%
1,888	GARDEN	1,303	697	212	385	9	312 R	53.5%	16.3%	29.5%
1,544	GARFIELD	1,087	595	221	270	1	325 R	54.7%	20.3%	24.8%
1,302	GOSPER	1,048	492	254	297	5	195 R	46.9%	24.2%	28.3%
548	GRANT	449	247	75	124	3	123 R	55.0%	16.7%	27.6%
1,891	GREELEY	1,418	587	435	395	1	152 R	41.4%	30.7%	27.9%
26,303	HALL	20,692	9,264	5,519	5,822	87	3,442 R	44.8%	26.7%	28.1%
5,801	HAMILTON	4,599	2,379	992	1,213	15	1,166 R	51.7%	21.6%	26.4%
2,916	HARLAN	2,112	991	488	623	10	368 R	46.9%	23.1%	29.5%
798	HAYES	654	362	85	207		155 R	55.4%	13.0%	31.7%
2,222	HITCHCOCK	1,731	824	359	540	8	284 R	47.6%	20.7%	31.2%
7,944	HOLT	5,703	3,131	835	1,714	23	1,417 R	54.9%	14.6%	30.1%
650	HOOKER	455	283	70	102		181 R	62.2%	15.4%	22.4%
4,024	HOWARD	2,868	1,138	778	940	12	198 R	39.7%	27.1%	32.8%
5,972	JEFFERSON	4,491	1,783	1,506	1,177	25	277 R	39.7%	33.5%	26.2%
3,441	JOHNSON	2,360	885	822	642	11	63 R	37.5%	34.8%	27.2%
4,226	KEARNEY	3,254	1,751	644	844	15	907 R	53.8%	19.8%	25.9%
5,348	KEITH	3,897	2,019	731	1,130	17	889 R	51.8%	18.8%	29.0%
834	KEYA PAHA	631	368	105	158		210 R	58.3%	16.6%	25.0%
2,723	KIMBALL	1,788	931	408	440	9	491 R	52.1%	22.8%	24.6%
6,256	KNOX	4,263	2,112	968	1,166	17	946 R	49.5%	22.7%	27.4%
128,428	LANCASTER	104,843	41,400	41,207	21,783	453	193 R	39.5%	39.3%	20.8%
20,304	LINCOLN	15,593	7,025	5,142	3,384	42	1,883 R	45.1%	33.0%	21.7%
589	LOGAN	451	271	80	98	2	173 R	60.1%	17.7%	21.7%
525	LOUP	389	233	58	96	2	137 R	59.9%	14.9%	24.7%
395	MCPHERSON	329	217	49	62	1	155 R	66.0%	14.9%	18.8%
18,846	MADISON	13,736	7,851	2,352	3,486	47	4,365 R	57.2%	17.1%	25.4%

NEBRASKA

PRESIDENT 1992

Registration	County	Total Vote	Republican	Democratic	Perot	Other	Plurality	Percentage Total Vote		
								Rep.	Dem.	Perot
5,127	MERRICK	3,811	1,854	864	1,072	21	782 R	48.6%	22.7%	28.1%
3,492	MORRILL	2,525	1,184	577	752	12	432 R	46.9%	22.9%	29.8%
2,663	NANCE	1,987	851	559	569	8	282 R	42.8%	28.1%	28.6%
4,905	NEMAHA	3,854	1,696	1,110	1,020	28	586 R	44.0%	28.8%	26.5%
3,957	NUCKOLLS	2,956	1,277	834	825	20	443 R	43.2%	28.2%	27.9%
9,135	OTOE	6,838	2,960	2,038	1,800	40	922 R	43.3%	29.8%	26.3%
2,294	PAWNEE	1,808	670	566	565	7	104 R	37.1%	31.3%	31.3%
2,075	PERKINS	1,666	842	300	522	2	320 R	50.5%	18.0%	31.3%
6,429	PHELPS	4,894	2,748	829	1,298	19	1,450 R	56.2%	16.9%	26.5%
4,856	PIERCE	3,562	1,853	611	1,084	14	769 R	52.0%	17.2%	30.4%
17,897	PLATTE	13,823	7,712	2,409	3,656	46	4,056 R	55.8%	17.4%	26.4%
3,652	POLK	2,916	1,435	661	812	8	623 R	49.2%	22.7%	27.8%
7,626	RED WILLOW	5,323	2,488	1,164	1,660	11	828 R	46.7%	21.9%	31.2%
7,084	RICHARDSON	4,940	2,050	1,513	1,356	21	537 R	41.5%	30.6%	27.4%
1,274	ROCK	987	588	162	233	4	355 R	59.6%	16.4%	23.6%
8,329	SALINE	5,765	1,740	2,425	1,576	24	685 D	30.2%	42.1%	27.3%
52,312	SARPY	40,604	20,482	10,720	9,270	132	9,762 R	50.4%	26.4%	22.8%
12,097	SAUNDERS	9,152	4,037	2,509	2,567	39	1,470 R	44.1%	27.4%	28.0%
17,894	SCOTTS BLUFF	14,947	7,213	4,173	3,514	47	3,040 R	48.3%	27.9%	23.5%
8,534	SEWARD	6,908	3,044	2,118	1,722	24	926 R	44.1%	30.7%	24.9%
3,945	SHERIDAN	2,996	1,698	535	751	12	947 R	56.7%	17.9%	25.1%
2,367	SHERMAN	1,899	736	568	582	13	154 R	38.8%	29.9%	30.6%
1,135	SIOUX	802	445	148	206	3	239 R	55.5%	18.5%	25.7%
3,551	STANTON	2,563	1,274	496	786	7	488 R	49.7%	19.4%	30.7%
4,244	THAYER	3,403	1,387	923	1,077	16	310 R	40.8%	27.1%	31.6%
599	THOMAS	468	283	69	115	1	168 R	60.5%	14.7%	24.6%
3,800	THURSTON	2,257	898	865	487	7	33 R	39.8%	38.3%	21.6%
3,422	VALLEY	2,590	1,173	716	693	8	457 R	45.3%	27.6%	26.8%
9,936	WASHINGTON	8,307	4,035	2,108	2,148	16	1,887 R	48.6%	25.4%	25.9%
5,652	WAYNE	4,102	2,122	921	1,047	12	1,075 R	51.7%	22.5%	25.5%
2,960	WEBSTER	2,262	972	624	657	9	315 R	43.0%	27.6%	29.0%
598	WHEELER	464	246	88	127	3	119 R	53.0%	19.0%	27.4%
9,341	YORK	7,012	3,783	1,385	1,825	19	1,958 R	54.0%	19.8%	26.0%
951,395	TOTAL	737,546	343,678	216,864	174,104	2,900	126,814 R	46.6%	29.4%	23.6%

NEBRASKA

CONGRESS

CD	Year	Total Vote	Republican		Democratic		Other Vote	Rep.-Dem. Plurality	Percentage			
			Vote	Candidate	Vote	Candidate			Total Vote		Major Vote	
									Rep.	Dem.	Rep.	Dem.
1	1992	239,108	142,713	BEREUTER, DOUGLAS K.	96,309	FINNEGAN, GERRY	86	46,404 R	59.7%	40.3%	59.7%	40.3%
2	1992	233,372	113,828	STASKIEWICZ, RONALD L.	119,512	HOAGLAND, PETER	32	5,684 D	48.8%	51.2%	48.8%	51.2%
3	1992	238,355	170,857	BARRETT, BILL	67,457	FISHER, LOWELL	41	103,400 R	71.7%	28.3%	71.7%	28.3%

NEBRASKA

1992 GENERAL ELECTION

President   Other vote was 1,340 Libertarian (Marrou); 846 Independent (Fulani); 714 Independent (Hagelin).

Congress   Other vote was scattered write-in in all three CD's.

1992 PRIMARIES

MAY 12 REPUBLICAN

Congress   Unopposed in all three CD's.

MAY 12 DEMOCRATIC

Congress   Unopposed in CD 3. Contested as follows:

CD   1   20,366 Gerry Finnegan; 16,726 Ken L. Michaelis; 6,310 Marlin R. Pals; 393 scattered write-in.
CD   2   42,825 Peter Hoagland; 7,501 Jess M. Pritchett; 246 scattered write-in.

NEVADA

GOVERNOR
Robert J. Miller (D). Elected 1990 to a four-year term. Had been elected Lieutenant-Governor 1986 and became Governor January 1989 on the resignation of Governor Richard H. Bryan (D) following his election November 1988 to the U. S. Senate.

SENATORS
Richard H. Bryan (D). Elected 1988 to a six-year term.

Harry Reid (D). Re-elected 1992 to a six-year term. Previously elected 1986.

REPRESENTATIVES
1. James Bilbray (D)   2. Barbara Vucanovich (R)

POSTWAR VOTE FOR PRESIDENT

| | | | | | | | | Percentage | | | |
| | | Republican | | Democratic | | | | Total Vote | | Major Vote | |
Year	Total Vote	Vote	Candidate	Vote	Candidate	Other Vote	Plurality	Rep.	Dem.	Rep.	Dem.
1992 **	506,318	175,828	Bush, George	189,148	Clinton, Bill	141,342	13,320 D	34.7%	37.4%	48.2%	51.8%
1988	350,067	206,040	Bush, George	132,738	Dukakis, Michael S.	11,289	73,302 R	58.9%	37.9%	60.8%	39.2%
1984	286,667	188,770	Reagan, Ronald	91,655	Mondale, Walter F.	6,242	97,115 R	65.8%	32.0%	67.3%	32.7%
1980	247,885	155,017	Reagan, Ronald	66,666	Carter, Jimmy	26,202	88,351 R	62.5%	26.9%	69.9%	30.1%
1976	201,876	101,273	Ford, Gerald R.	92,479	Carter, Jimmy	8,124	8,794 R	50.2%	45.8%	52.3%	47.7%
1972	181,766	115,750	Nixon, Richard M.	66,016	McGovern, George S.		49,734 R	63.7%	36.3%	63.7%	36.3%
1968	154,218	73,188	Nixon, Richard M.	60,598	Humphrey, Hubert H.	20,432	12,590 R	47.5%	39.3%	54.7%	45.3%
1964	135,433	56,094	Goldwater, Barry M.	79,339	Johnson, Lyndon B.		23,245 D	41.4%	58.6%	41.4%	58.6%
1960	107,267	52,387	Nixon, Richard M.	54,880	Kennedy, John F.		2,493 D	48.8%	51.2%	48.8%	51.2%
1956	96,689	56,049	Eisenhower, Dwight D.	40,640	Stevenson, Adlai E.		15,409 R	58.0%	42.0%	58.0%	42.0%
1952	82,190	50,502	Eisenhower, Dwight D.	31,688	Stevenson, Adlai E.		18,814 R	61.4%	38.6%	61.4%	38.6%
1948	62,117	29,357	Dewey, Thomas E.	31,291	Truman, Harry S.	1,469	1,934 D	47.3%	50.4%	48.4%	51.6%

In 1992 the other vote column includes 132,580 votes cast for Perot.

POSTWAR VOTE FOR GOVERNOR

| | | | | | | | | Percentage | | | |
| | | Republican | | Democratic | | | | Total Vote | | Major Vote | |
Year	Total Vote	Vote	Candidate	Vote	Candidate	Other Vote	Rep.-Dem. Plurality	Rep.	Dem.	Rep.	Dem.
1990	320,743	95,789	Gallaway, Jim	207,878	Miller, Robert J.	17,076	112,089 D	29.9%	64.8%	31.5%	68.5%
1986	260,375	65,081	Cafferata, Patty	187,268	Bryan, Richard H.	8,026	122,187 D	25.0%	71.9%	25.8%	74.2%
1982	239,751	100,104	List, Robert F.	128,132	Bryan, Richard H.	11,515	28,028 D	41.8%	53.4%	43.9%	56.1%
1978	192,445	108,097	List, Robert F.	76,361	Rose, Robert E.	7,987	31,736 R	56.2%	39.7%	58.6%	41.4%
1974	169,358	28,959	Crumpler, Shirley	114,114	O'Callaghan, Mike	26,285	85,155 D	17.1%	67.4%	20.2%	79.8%
1970	146,991	64,400	Fike, Ed	70,697	O'Callaghan, Mike	11,894	6,297 D	43.8%	48.1%	47.7%	52.3%
1966	137,677	71,807	Laxalt, Paul	65,870	Sawyer, Grant		5,937 R	52.2%	47.8%	52.2%	47.8%
1962	96,929	32,145	Gragson, Oran K.	64,784	Sawyer, Grant		32,639 D	33.2%	66.8%	33.2%	66.8%
1958	84,889	34,025	Russell, Charles H.	50,864	Sawyer, Grant		16,839 D	40.1%	59.9%	40.1%	59.9%
1954	78,462	41,665	Russell, Charles H.	36,797	Pittman, Vail		4,868 R	53.1%	46.9%	53.1%	46.9%
1950	61,773	35,609	Russell, Charles H.	26,164	Pittman, Vail		9,445 R	57.6%	42.4%	57.6%	42.4%
1946	49,902	21,247	Jepson, Melvin E.	28,655	Pittman, Vail		7,408 D	42.6%	57.4%	42.6%	57.4%

NEVADA

POSTWAR VOTE FOR SENATOR

Year	Total Vote	Republican		Democratic		Other Vote	Rep.-Dem. Plurality	Percentage			
		Vote	Candidate	Vote	Candidate			Total Vote		Major Vote	
								Rep.	Dem.	Rep.	Dem.
1992	495,887	199,413	Dahl, Demar	253,150	Reid, Harry	43,324	53,737 D	40.2%	51.0%	44.1%	55.9%
1988	349,649	161,336	Hecht, Chic	175,548	Bryan, Richard H.	12,765	14,212 D	46.1%	50.2%	47.9%	52.1%
1986	261,932	116,606	Santini, James	130,955	Reid, Harry	14,371	14,349 D	44.5%	50.0%	47.1%	52.9%
1982	240,394	120,377	Hecht, Chic	114,720	Cannon, Howard W.	5,297	5,657 R	50.1%	47.7%	51.2%	48.8%
1980	246,436	144,224	Laxalt, Paul	92,129	Gojack, Mary	10,083	52,095 R	58.5%	37.4%	61.0%	39.0%
1976	201,980	63,471	Towell, David	127,295	Cannon, Howard W.	11,214	63,824 D	31.4%	63.0%	33.3%	66.7%
1974	169,473	79,605	Laxalt, Paul	78,981	Reid, Harry	10,887	624 R	47.0%	46.6%	50.2%	49.8%
1970	147,768	60,838	Raggio, William J.	85,187	Cannon, Howard W.	1,743	24,349 D	41.2%	57.6%	41.7%	58.3%
1968	152,690	69,068	Fike, Ed	83,622	Bible, Alan		14,554 D	45.2%	54.8%	45.2%	54.8%
1964	134,624	67,288	Laxalt, Paul	67,336	Cannon, Howard W.		48 D	50.0%	50.0%	50.0%	50.0%
1962	97,192	33,749	Wright, William B.	63,443	Bible, Alan		29,694 D	34.7%	65.3%	34.7%	65.3%
1958	84,492	35,760	Malone, George W.	48,732	Cannon, Howard W.		12,972 D	42.3%	57.7%	42.3%	57.7%
1956	96,389	45,712	Young, Clifton	50,677	Bible, Alan		4,965 D	47.4%	52.6%	47.4%	52.6%
1954 S	77,513	32,470	Brown, Ernest S.	45,043	Bible, Alan		12,573 D	41.9%	58.1%	41.9%	58.1%
1952	81,090	41,906	Malone, George W.	39,184	Mechling, Thomas B.		2,722 R	51.7%	48.3%	51.7%	48.3%
1950	61,762	25,933	Marshall, George E.	35,829	McCarran, Pat		9,896 D	42.0%	58.0%	42.0%	58.0%
1946	50,354	27,801	Malone, George W.	22,553	Bunker, Berkeley		5,248 R	55.2%	44.8%	55.2%	44.8%

The 1954 election was for a short term to fill a vacancy.

NEVADA

Districts Established June 20, 1991

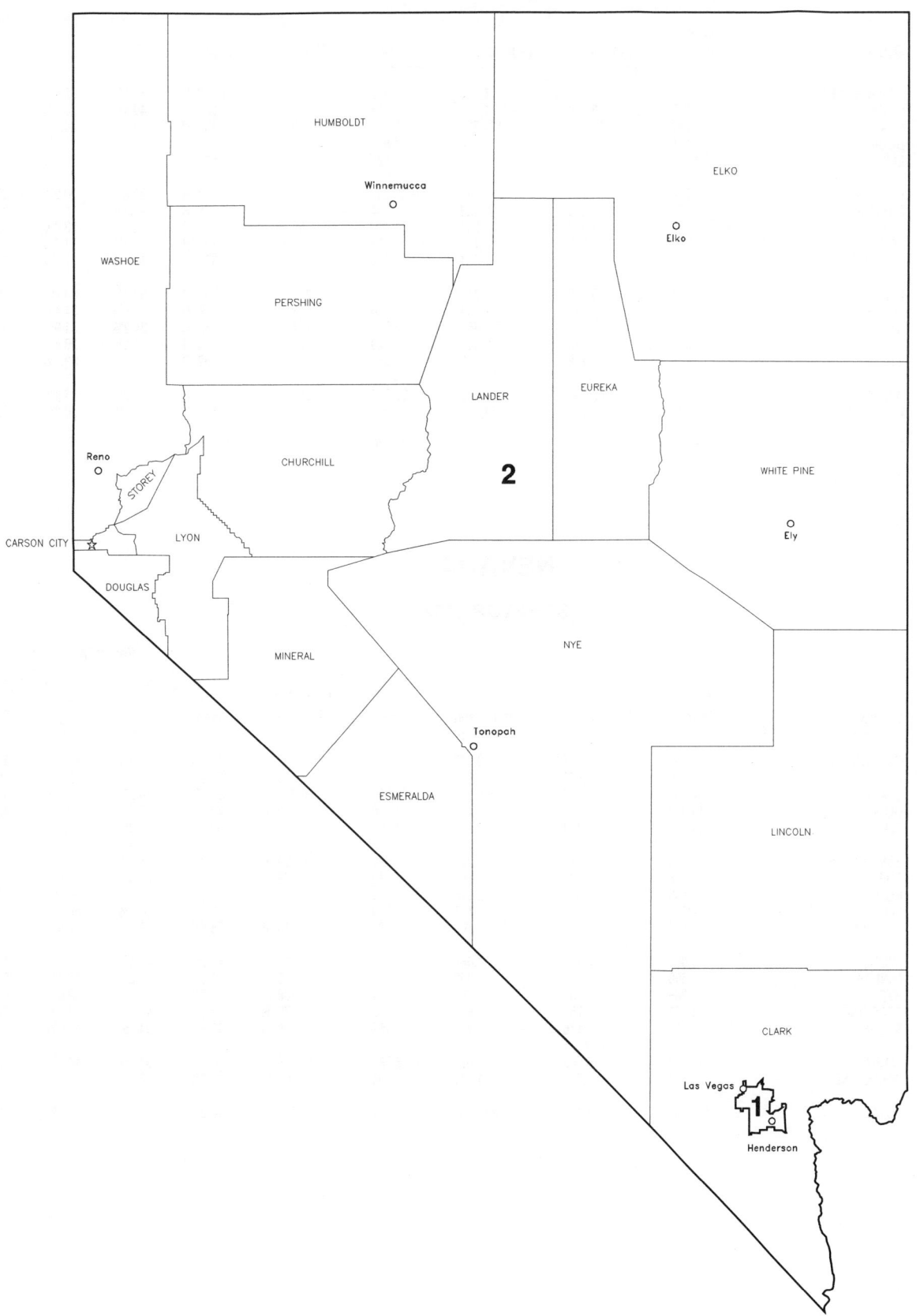

NEVADA

PRESIDENT 1992

Registration	County	Total Vote	Republican	Democratic	Perot	Other	Plurality	Percentage Total Vote		
								Rep.	Dem.	Perot
23,035	CARSON CITY	18,803	7,302	6,035	5,195	271	1,267 R	38.8%	32.1%	27.6%
9,469	CHURCHILL	7,663	3,789	1,770	1,964	140	1,825 R	49.4%	23.1%	25.6%
396,628	CLARK	302,782	97,403	124,586	75,364	5,429	27,183 D	32.2%	41.1%	24.9%
18,470	DOUGLAS	15,145	6,182	3,928	4,814	221	1,368 R	40.8%	25.9%	31.8%
15,557	ELKO	11,926	5,208	2,782	3,628	308	1,580 R	43.7%	23.3%	30.4%
716	ESMERALDA	584	221	118	220	25	1 R	37.8%	20.2%	37.7%
832	EUREKA	690	330	129	214	17	116 R	47.8%	18.7%	31.0%
5,546	HUMBOLDT	3,523	1,505	810	1,149	59	356 R	42.7%	23.0%	32.6%
2,718	LANDER	1,992	885	423	652	32	233 R	44.4%	21.2%	32.7%
2,182	LINCOLN	1,857	890	511	394	62	379 R	47.9%	27.5%	21.2%
11,487	LYON	9,204	3,509	2,777	2,716	202	732 R	38.1%	30.2%	29.5%
3,455	MINERAL	2,641	918	909	746	68	9 R	34.8%	34.4%	28.2%
10,778	NYE	8,022	2,743	2,561	2,501	217	182 R	34.2%	31.9%	31.2%
1,844	PERSHING	1,566	643	467	429	27	176 R	41.1%	29.8%	27.4%
1,888	STOREY	1,519	458	488	550	23	62 P	30.2%	32.1%	36.2%
140,701	WASHOE	114,671	42,636	39,500	30,974	1,561	3,136 R	37.2%	34.4%	27.0%
4,607	WHITE PINE	3,730	1,206	1,354	1,070	100	148 D	32.3%	36.3%	28.7%
649,913	TOTAL	506,318	175,828	189,148	132,580	8,762	13,320 D	34.7%	37.4%	26.2%

NEVADA

SENATOR 1992

Registration	County	Total Vote	Republican	Democratic	Other	Rep.-Dem. Plurality	Percentage			
							Total Vote		Major Vote	
							Rep.	Dem.	Rep.	Dem.
23,035	CARSON CITY	18,691	8,165	9,057	1,469	892 D	43.7%	48.5%	47.4%	52.6%
9,469	CHURCHILL	7,546	4,968	1,812	766	3,156 R	65.8%	24.0%	73.3%	26.7%
396,628	CLARK	294,737	109,510	159,721	25,506	50,211 D	37.2%	54.2%	40.7%	59.3%
18,470	DOUGLAS	14,909	7,198	6,423	1,288	775 R	48.3%	43.1%	52.8%	47.2%
15,557	ELKO	11,782	7,404	3,227	1,151	4,177 R	62.8%	27.4%	69.6%	30.4%
716	ESMERALDA	578	277	223	78	54 R	47.9%	38.6%	55.4%	44.6%
832	EUREKA	686	433	181	72	252 R	63.1%	26.4%	70.5%	29.5%
5,546	HUMBOLDT	4,586	2,085	2,076	425	9 R	45.5%	45.3%	50.1%	49.9%
2,718	LANDER	2,225	1,333	678	214	655 R	59.9%	30.5%	66.3%	33.7%
2,182	LINCOLN	1,857	1,089	601	167	488 R	58.6%	32.4%	64.4%	35.6%
11,487	LYON	9,061	4,105	4,089	867	16 R	45.3%	45.1%	50.1%	49.9%
3,455	MINERAL	2,608	1,016	1,309	283	293 D	39.0%	50.2%	43.7%	56.3%
10,778	NYE	7,886	3,550	3,162	1,174	388 R	45.0%	40.1%	52.9%	47.1%
1,844	PERSHING	1,557	751	681	125	70 R	48.2%	43.7%	52.4%	47.6%
1,888	STOREY	1,492	576	762	154	186 D	38.6%	51.1%	43.0%	57.0%
140,701	WASHOE	111,999	45,440	57,578	8,981	12,138 D	40.6%	51.4%	44.1%	55.9%
4,607	WHITE PINE	3,687	1,513	1,570	604	57 D	41.0%	42.6%	49.1%	50.9%
649,913	TOTAL	495,887	199,413	253,150	43,324	53,737 D	40.2%	51.0%	44.1%	55.9%

NEVADA

CONGRESS

CD	Year	Total Vote	Republican		Democratic		Other Vote	Rep.-Dem. Plurality	Percentage			
			Vote	Candidate	Vote	Candidate			Total Vote		Major Vote	
									Rep.	Dem.	Rep.	Dem.
1	1992	221,488	84,217	PETTYJOHN, J. COY	128,278	BILBRAY, JAMES	8,993	44,061 D	38.0%	57.9%	39.6%	60.4%
2	1992	270,461	129,575	VUCANOVICH, BARBARA	117,199	SFERRAZZA, PETE	23,687	12,376 R	47.9%	43.3%	52.5%	47.5%

NEVADA

1992 GENERAL ELECTION

President   Other vote was 2,892 Populist (Gritz); 1,835 Libertarian (Marrou); 677 Independent American (Phillips); 483 Independent (Fulani); 338 Natural Law (Hagelin); 2,537 "None of these Candidates".

Senator   Other vote was 11,240 Independent American (Garcia); 7,279 Natural Law (Avery); 7,222 Libertarian (Cromwell); 4,429 Populist (Tootle); 13,154 "None of these Candidates".

Congress   Other vote was Libertarian (Kjar) in CD 1; 13,285 Independent American (Hansen), 7,552 Libertarian (Becan) and 2,850 Populist (Golden) in CD 2.

1992 PRIMARIES

SEPTEMBER 1 REPUBLICAN

Senator   37,667 Demar Dahl; 31,963 Bob Gore; 8,351 Andy Anderson; 4,772 Patrick M. Fitzpatrick; 4,243 Sam Cavnar; 1,542 Kirby Vanburch; 13,523 "None of these Candidates".

Congress   Unopposed in CD 1. Contested as follows:

CD   2   45,792 Barbara Vucanovich; 9,843 Don Hensley; 5,697 Dick Baker; 4,583 Terry L. Flower.

SEPTEMBER 1 DEMOCRATIC

Senator   64,828 Harry Reid; 48,364 Charles Wood; 3,253 Norman Hollingsworth; 1,869 God Almighty; 4,429 "None of these Candidates".

Congress   Unopposed in CD 1. Contested as follows:

CD   2   34,035 Pete Sferrazza; 25,117 Jerry Maldonado.

NEW HAMPSHIRE

GOVERNOR
Steve Merrill (R). Elected 1992 to a two-year term.

SENATORS
Judd Gregg (R). Elected 1992 to a six-year term.

Robert C. Smith (R). Elected 1990 to a six-year term; was appointed December 1990 to fill the last few weeks of the term vacated when Senator Gordon J. Humphrey resigned to be sworn in as a state senator in New Hampshire.

REPRESENTATIVES
1. Bill Zeliff (R)
2. Dick Swett (D)

POSTWAR VOTE FOR PRESIDENT

| | | Republican | | Democratic | | | | Percentage | | | |
| | | | | | | Other | | Total Vote | | Major Vote | |
Year	Total Vote	Vote	Candidate	Vote	Candidate	Vote	Plurality	Rep.	Dem.	Rep.	Dem.
1992 **	537,943	202,484	Bush, George	209,040	Clinton, Bill	126,419	6,556 D	37.6%	38.9%	49.2%	50.8%
1988	451,074	281,537	Bush, George	163,696	Dukakis, Michael S.	5,841	117,841 R	62.4%	36.3%	63.2%	36.8%
1984	389,066	267,051	Reagan, Ronald	120,395	Mondale, Walter F.	1,620	146,656 R	68.6%	30.9%	68.9%	31.1%
1980	383,990	221,705	Reagan, Ronald	108,864	Carter, Jimmy	53,421	112,841 R	57.7%	28.4%	67.1%	32.9%
1976	339,618	185,935	Ford, Gerald R.	147,635	Carter, Jimmy	6,048	38,300 R	54.7%	43.5%	55.7%	44.3%
1972	334,055	213,724	Nixon, Richard M.	116,435	McGovern, George S.	3,896	97,289 R	64.0%	34.9%	64.7%	35.3%
1968	297,298	154,903	Nixon, Richard M.	130,589	Humphrey, Hubert H.	11,806	24,314 R	52.1%	43.9%	54.3%	45.7%
1964	288,093	104,029	Goldwater, Barry M.	184,064	Johnson, Lyndon B.		80,035 D	36.1%	63.9%	36.1%	63.9%
1960	295,761	157,989	Nixon, Richard M.	137,772	Kennedy, John F.		20,217 R	53.4%	46.6%	53.4%	46.6%
1956	266,994	176,519	Eisenhower, Dwight D.	90,364	Stevenson, Adlai E.	111	86,155 R	66.1%	33.8%	66.1%	33.9%
1952	272,950	166,287	Eisenhower, Dwight D.	106,663	Stevenson, Adlai E.		59,624 R	60.9%	39.1%	60.9%	39.1%
1948	231,440	121,299	Dewey, Thomas E.	107,995	Truman, Harry S.	2,146	13,304 R	52.4%	46.7%	52.9%	47.1%

In 1992 the other vote column includes 121,337 votes cast for Perot.

NEW HAMPSHIRE

POSTWAR VOTE FOR GOVERNOR

Year	Total Vote	Republican Vote	Republican Candidate	Democratic Vote	Democratic Candidate	Other Vote	Rep.-Dem. Plurality	Total Vote Rep.	Total Vote Dem.	Major Vote Rep.	Major Vote Dem.
1992	516,170	289,170	Merrill, Steve	206,232	Arnesen, Deborah A.	20,768	82,938 R	56.0%	40.0%	58.4%	41.6%
1990	295,018	177,773	Gregg, Judd	101,923	Grandmaison, J. Joseph	15,322	75,850 R	60.3%	34.5%	63.6%	36.4%
1988	441,923	267,064	Gregg, Judd	172,543	McEachern, Paul	2,316	94,521 R	60.4%	39.0%	60.8%	39.2%
1986	251,107	134,824	Sununu, John H.	116,142	McEachern, Paul	141	18,682 R	53.7%	46.3%	53.7%	46.3%
1984	383,910	256,574	Sununu, John H.	127,156	Spirou, Chris	180	129,418 R	66.8%	33.1%	66.9%	33.1%
1982	282,588	145,389	Sununu, John H.	132,317	Gallen, Hugh J.	4,882	13,072 R	51.4%	46.8%	52.4%	47.6%
1980	384,031	156,178	Thomson, Meldrim	226,436	Gallen, Hugh J.	1,417	70,258 D	40.7%	59.0%	40.8%	59.2%
1978	269,587	122,464	Thomson, Meldrim	133,133	Gallen, Hugh J.	13,990	10,669 D	45.4%	49.4%	47.9%	52.1%
1976	342,669	197,589	Thomson, Meldrim	145,015	Spanos, Harry V.	65	52,574 R	57.7%	42.3%	57.7%	42.3%
1974	226,665	115,933	Thomson, Meldrim	110,591	Leonard, Richard W.	141	5,342 R	51.1%	48.8%	51.2%	48.8%
1972	323,102	133,702	Thomson, Meldrim	126,107	Crowley, Roger J.	63,293	7,595 R	41.4%	39.0%	51.5%	48.5%
1970	222,441	102,298	Peterson, Walter R.	98,098	Crowley, Roger J.	22,045	4,200 R	46.0%	44.1%	51.0%	49.0%
1968	285,342	149,902	Peterson, Walter R.	135,378	Bussiere, Emile R.	62	14,524 R	52.5%	47.4%	52.5%	47.5%
1966	233,642	107,259	Gregg, Hugh	125,882	King, John W.	501	18,623 D	45.9%	53.9%	46.0%	54.0%
1964	285,863	94,824	Pillsbury, John	190,863	King, John W.	176	96,039 D	33.2%	66.8%	33.2%	66.8%
1962	230,048	94,567	Pillsbury, John	135,481	King, John W.		40,914 D	41.1%	58.9%	41.1%	58.9%
1960	290,527	161,123	Powell, Wesley	129,404	Boutin, Bernard L.		31,719 R	55.5%	44.5%	55.5%	44.5%
1958	206,745	106,790	Powell, Wesley	99,955	Boutin, Bernard L.		6,835 R	51.7%	48.3%	51.7%	48.3%
1956	258,695	141,578	Dwinell, Lane	117,117	Shaw, John		24,461 R	54.7%	45.3%	54.7%	45.3%
1954	194,631	107,287	Dwinell, Lane	87,344	Shaw, John		19,943 R	55.1%	44.9%	55.1%	44.9%
1952	265,715	167,791	Gregg, Hugh	97,924	Craig, William H.		69,867 R	63.1%	36.9%	63.1%	36.9%
1950	191,239	108,907	Adams, Sherman	82,258	Bingham, Robert P.	74	26,649 R	56.9%	43.0%	57.0%	43.0%
1948	222,571	116,212	Adams, Sherman	105,207	Hill, Herbert W.	1,152	11,005 R	52.2%	47.3%	52.5%	47.5%
1946	163,451	103,204	Dale, Charles M.	60,247	Keefe, F. Clyde		42,957 R	63.1%	36.9%	63.1%	36.9%

POSTWAR VOTE FOR SENATOR

Year	Total Vote	Republican Vote	Republican Candidate	Democratic Vote	Democratic Candidate	Other Vote	Rep.-Dem. Plurality	Total Vote Rep.	Total Vote Dem.	Major Vote Rep.	Major Vote Dem.
1992	518,416	249,591	Gregg, Judd	234,982	Rauh, John	33,843	14,609 R	48.1%	45.3%	51.5%	48.5%
1990	291,393	189,792	Smith, Robert C.	91,299	Durkin, John A.	10,302	98,493 R	65.1%	31.3%	67.5%	32.5%
1986	244,797	154,090	Rudman, Warren	79,225	Peabody, Endicott	11,482	74,865 R	62.9%	32.4%	66.0%	34.0%
1984	384,406	225,828	Humphrey, Gordon J.	157,447	D'Amours, Norman E.	1,131	68,381 R	58.7%	41.0%	58.9%	41.1%
1980	375,064	195,563	Rudman, Warren	179,455	Durkin, John A.	46	16,108 R	52.1%	47.8%	52.1%	47.9%
1978	263,779	133,745	Humphrey, Gordon J.	127,945	McIntyre, Thomas J.	2,089	5,800 R	50.7%	48.5%	51.1%	48.9%
1975 S	262,682	113,007	Wyman, Louis C.	140,778	Durkin, John A.	8,897	27,771 D	43.0%	53.6%	44.5%	55.5%
1974 **	223,363	110,926	Wyman, Louis C.	110,924	Durkin, John A.	1,513	2 R	49.7%	49.7%	50.0%	50.0%
1972	324,354	139,852	Powell, Wesley	184,495	McIntyre, Thomas J.	7	44,643 D	43.1%	56.9%	43.1%	56.9%
1968	286,989	170,163	Cotton, Norris	116,816	King, John W.	10	53,347 R	59.3%	40.7%	59.3%	40.7%
1966	229,305	105,241	Thyng, Harrison R.	123,888	McIntyre, Thomas J.	176	18,647 D	45.9%	54.0%	45.9%	54.1%
1962	224,479	134,035	Cotton, Norris	90,444	Catalfo, Alfred		43,591 R	59.7%	40.3%	59.7%	40.3%
1962 S	224,811	107,199	Bass, Perkins	117,612	McIntyre, Thomas J.		10,413 D	47.7%	52.3%	47.7%	52.3%
1960	287,545	173,521	Bridges, Styles	114,024	Hill, Herbert W.		59,497 R	60.3%	39.7%	60.3%	39.7%
1956	251,943	161,424	Cotton, Norris	90,519	Pickett, Laurence M.		70,905 R	64.1%	35.9%	64.1%	35.9%
1954	194,536	117,150	Bridges, Styles	77,386	Morin, Gerard L.		39,764 R	60.2%	39.8%	60.2%	39.8%
1954 S	189,558	114,068	Cotton, Norris	75,490	Bentley, Stanley J.		38,578 R	60.2%	39.8%	60.2%	39.8%
1950	190,573	106,142	Tobey, Charles W.	72,473	Kelley, Emmet J.	11,958	33,669 R	55.7%	38.0%	59.4%	40.6%
1948	222,898	129,600	Bridges, Styles	91,760	Fortin, Alfred E.	1,538	37,840 R	58.1%	41.2%	58.5%	41.5%

One each of the 1962 and 1954 elections were for short terms to fill vacancies. Following the 1974 election, neither candidate was seated and the 1975 special election was held for the remaining years of this term.

NEW HAMPSHIRE

Districts Established March 27, 1992

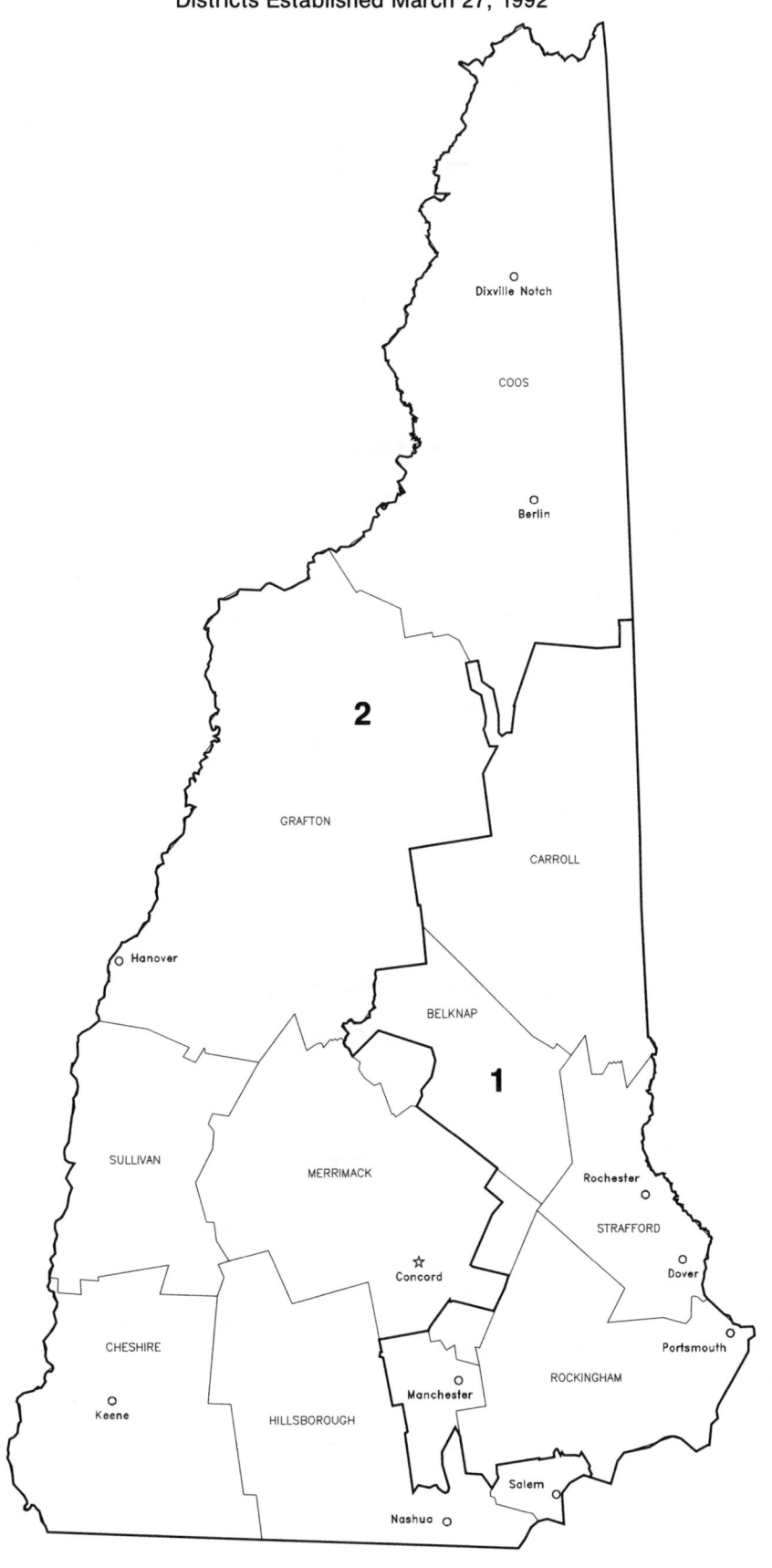

NEW HAMPSHIRE

PRESIDENT 1992

Registration	County	Total Vote	Republican	Democratic	Perot	Other	Plurality	Percentage Total Vote		
								Rep.	Dem.	Perot
30,312	BELKNAP	25,121	10,578	8,405	5,970	168	2,173 R	42.1%	33.5%	23.8%
27,077	CARROLL	21,715	8,715	7,258	5,546	196	1,457 R	40.1%	33.4%	25.5%
39,550	CHESHIRE	32,505	11,037	15,037	6,195	236	4,000 D	34.0%	46.3%	19.1%
19,810	COOS	15,817	5,271	6,559	3,868	119	1,288 D	33.3%	41.5%	24.5%
45,223	GRAFTON	36,429	13,450	15,389	7,296	294	1,939 D	36.9%	42.2%	20.0%
193,170	HILLSBOROUGH	158,056	61,620	58,470	36,067	1,899	3,150 R	39.0%	37.0%	22.8%
71,334	MERRIMACK	58,904	22,114	24,437	11,860	493	2,323 D	37.5%	41.5%	20.1%
154,117	ROCKINGHAM	123,965	47,353	44,317	31,192	1,103	3,036 R	38.2%	35.7%	25.2%
58,612	STRAFFORD	47,595	16,028	21,247	9,920	400	5,219 D	33.7%	44.6%	20.8%
21,780	SULLIVAN	17,836	6,318	7,921	3,423	174	1,603 D	35.4%	44.4%	19.2%
660,985	TOTAL	537,943	202,484	209,040	121,337	5,082	6,556 D	37.6%	38.9%	22.6%

NEW HAMPSHIRE

GOVERNOR 1992

Registration	County	Total Vote	Republican	Democratic	Other	Rep.-Dem. Plurality	Percentage			
							Total Vote		Major Vote	
							Rep.	Dem.	Rep.	Dem.
30,312	BELKNAP	24,626	14,795	8,705	1,126	6,090 R	60.1%	35.3%	63.0%	37.0%
27,077	CARROLL	20,862	12,797	7,226	839	5,571 R	61.3%	34.6%	63.9%	36.1%
39,550	CHESHIRE	31,352	14,399	16,005	948	1,606 D	45.9%	51.0%	47.4%	52.6%
19,810	COOS	14,923	8,287	6,301	335	1,986 R	55.5%	42.2%	56.8%	43.2%
45,223	GRAFTON	35,136	18,121	16,096	919	2,025 R	51.6%	45.8%	53.0%	47.0%
193,170	HILLSBOROUGH	149,371	90,441	52,260	6,670	38,181 R	60.5%	35.0%	63.4%	36.6%
71,334	MERRIMACK	57,608	29,617	25,697	2,294	3,920 R	51.4%	44.6%	53.5%	46.5%
154,117	ROCKINGHAM	119,748	69,135	45,173	5,440	23,962 R	57.7%	37.7%	60.5%	39.5%
58,612	STRAFFORD	45,397	23,475	20,246	1,676	3,229 R	51.7%	44.6%	53.7%	46.3%
21,780	SULLIVAN	17,147	8,103	8,523	521	420 D	47.3%	49.7%	48.7%	51.3%
660,985	TOTAL	516,170	289,170	206,232	20,768	82,938 R	56.0%	40.0%	58.4%	41.6%

NEW HAMPSHIRE

SENATOR 1992

Registration	County	Total Vote	Republican	Democratic	Other	Rep.-Dem. Plurality	Percentage			
							Total Vote		Major Vote	
							Rep.	Dem.	Rep.	Dem.
30,312	BELKNAP	24,628	12,316	10,390	1,922	1,926 R	50.0%	42.2%	54.2%	45.8%
27,077	CARROLL	20,793	11,250	7,898	1,645	3,352 R	54.1%	38.0%	58.8%	41.2%
39,550	CHESHIRE	31,258	12,219	17,422	1,617	5,203 D	39.1%	55.7%	41.2%	58.8%
19,810	COOS	15,033	7,724	6,188	1,121	1,536 R	51.4%	41.2%	55.5%	44.5%
45,223	GRAFTON	34,830	16,373	16,461	1,996	88 D	47.0%	47.3%	49.9%	50.1%
193,170	HILLSBOROUGH	152,152	78,430	63,890	9,832	14,540 R	51.5%	42.0%	55.1%	44.9%
71,334	MERRIMACK	57,472	23,390	30,489	3,593	7,099 D	40.7%	53.1%	43.4%	56.6%
154,117	ROCKINGHAM	119,739	60,374	50,773	8,592	9,601 R	50.4%	42.4%	54.3%	45.7%
58,612	STRAFFORD	45,327	19,956	22,614	2,757	2,658 D	44.0%	49.9%	46.9%	53.1%
21,780	SULLIVAN	17,184	7,559	8,857	768	1,298 D	44.0%	51.5%	46.0%	54.0%
660,985	TOTAL	518,416	249,591	234,982	33,843	14,609 R	48.1%	45.3%	51.5%	48.5%

NEW HAMPSHIRE

PRESIDENT 1992

Registration	City/Town	Total Vote	Republican	Democratic	Perot	Other	Plurality	Percentage Total Vote		
								Rep.	Dem.	Perot
6,012	AMHERST	5,260	2,319	1,687	1,217	37	632 R	44.1%	32.1%	23.1%
3,618	ATKINSON	3,128	1,378	908	820	22	470 R	44.1%	29.0%	26.2%
3,644	BARRINGTON	2,904	977	1,180	720	27	203 D	33.6%	40.6%	24.8%
9,727	BEDFORD	8,085	4,145	2,251	1,652	37	1,894 R	51.3%	27.8%	20.4%
2,849	BELMONT	2,461	982	774	688	17	208 R	39.9%	31.5%	28.0%
6,175	BERLIN	5,140	1,272	2,680	1,162	26	1,408 D	24.7%	52.1%	22.6%
3,748	BOW	3,298	1,532	1,175	575	16	357 R	46.5%	35.6%	17.4%
6,839	CLAREMONT	5,411	1,822	2,650	904	35	828 D	33.7%	49.0%	16.7%
20,951	CONCORD	16,923	5,651	8,325	2,843	104	2,674 D	33.4%	49.2%	16.8%
5,249	CONWAY	4,112	1,510	1,509	1,033	60	1 R	36.7%	36.7%	25.1%
15,543	DERRY	12,166	4,750	3,962	3,363	91	788 R	39.0%	32.6%	27.6%
15,513	DOVER	11,988	4,197	5,449	2,246	96	1,252 D	35.0%	45.5%	18.7%
7,162	DURHAM	5,741	1,486	3,349	889	17	1,863 D	25.9%	58.3%	15.5%
2,963	EPPING	2,348	794	915	625	14	121 D	33.8%	39.0%	26.6%
8,545	EXETER	6,576	2,465	2,654	1,384	73	189 D	37.5%	40.4%	21.0%
2,752	FARMINGTON	2,160	819	805	519	17	14 R	37.9%	37.3%	24.0%
4,000	FRANKLIN	3,097	1,139	1,252	691	15	113 D	36.8%	40.4%	22.3%
4,682	GILFORD	3,608	1,611	1,166	813	18	445 R	44.7%	32.3%	22.5%
8,723	GOFFSTOWN	6,960	3,041	2,313	1,557	49	728 R	43.7%	33.2%	22.4%
4,658	HAMPSTEAD	3,809	1,586	1,160	1,045	18	426 R	41.6%	30.5%	27.4%
9,170	HAMPTON	7,729	2,822	3,072	1,790	45	250 D	36.5%	39.7%	23.2%
5,987	HANOVER	4,635	1,201	2,906	505	23	1,705 D	25.9%	62.7%	10.9%
4,047	HOLLIS	3,657	1,465	1,315	755	122	150 R	40.1%	36.0%	20.6%
5,739	HOOKSETT	4,757	2,161	1,524	1,046	26	637 R	45.4%	32.0%	22.0%
11,307	HUDSON	9,199	3,315	3,053	2,774	57	262 R	36.0%	33.2%	30.2%
2,799	JAFFREY	2,372	857	984	517	14	127 D	36.1%	41.5%	21.8%
12,817	KEENE	10,246	3,257	5,210	1,736	43	1,953 D	31.8%	50.8%	16.9%
3,262	KINGSTON	2,821	1,070	903	818	30	167 R	37.9%	32.0%	29.0%
8,145	LACONIA	6,943	3,033	2,390	1,496	24	643 R	43.7%	34.4%	21.5%
6,508	LEBANON	5,293	1,849	2,579	827	38	730 D	34.9%	48.7%	15.6%
3,192	LITCHFIELD	2,685	1,005	854	810	16	151 R	37.4%	31.8%	30.2%
3,111	LITTLETON	2,490	1,095	832	554	9	263 R	44.0%	33.4%	22.2%
11,103	LONDONDERRY	9,467	3,960	2,915	2,532	60	1,045 R	41.8%	30.8%	26.7%
50,889	MANCHESTER	40,643	16,298	16,627	7,441	277	329 D	40.1%	40.9%	18.3%
13,196	MERRIMACK TOWN	11,054	4,410	3,764	2,787	93	646 R	39.9%	34.1%	25.2%
7,515	MILFORD	5,683	2,230	1,903	1,498	52	327 R	39.2%	33.5%	26.4%
44,674	NASHUA	36,261	12,514	14,777	8,306	664	2,263 D	34.5%	40.8%	22.9%
4,451	NEWMARKET	3,425	954	1,713	731	27	759 D	27.9%	50.0%	21.3%
2,915	NEWPORT	2,401	882	1,044	455	20	162 D	36.7%	43.5%	19.0%
5,771	PELHAM	4,824	1,827	1,380	1,597	20	230 R	37.9%	28.6%	33.1%
3,767	PEMBROKE	3,136	1,220	1,228	667	21	8 D	38.9%	39.2%	21.3%
3,621	PETERBOROUGH	2,985	1,138	1,295	504	48	157 D	38.1%	43.4%	16.9%
4,143	PLAISTOW	3,474	1,334	1,128	994	18	206 R	38.4%	32.5%	28.6%
3,158	PLYMOUTH	2,439	768	1,133	524	14	365 D	31.5%	46.5%	21.5%
15,585	PORTSMOUTH	11,858	3,563	6,132	2,088	75	2,569 D	30.0%	51.7%	17.6%
4,032	RAYMOND	3,468	1,319	1,108	1,001	40	211 R	38.0%	31.9%	28.9%
13,218	ROCHESTER	11,461	4,272	4,588	2,541	60	316 D	37.3%	40.0%	22.2%
14,905	SALEM	12,495	4,864	4,184	3,382	65	680 R	38.9%	33.5%	27.1%
4,898	SEABROOK	3,582	1,321	1,259	973	29	62 R	36.9%	35.1%	27.2%
5,746	SOMERSWORTH	4,711	1,450	2,249	974	38	799 D	30.8%	47.7%	20.7%
3,221	SWANZEY	2,849	1,045	1,231	561	12	186 D	36.7%	43.2%	19.7%
3,598	WEARE	2,987	1,241	973	736	37	268 R	41.5%	32.6%	24.6%
5,493	WINDHAM	4,714	2,018	1,300	1,372	24	646 R	42.8%	27.6%	29.1%

NEW HAMPSHIRE

GOVERNOR 1992

Registration	City/Town	Total Vote	Republican	Democratic	Other	Rep.-Dem. Plurality	Percentage Total Vote Rep.	Dem.	Major Vote Rep.	Dem.
6,012	AMHERST	5,102	3,213	1,691	198	1,522 R	63.0%	33.1%	65.5%	34.5%
3,618	ATKINSON	2,968	1,892	991	85	901 R	63.7%	33.4%	65.6%	34.4%
3,644	BARRINGTON	2,830	1,439	1,255	136	184 R	50.8%	44.3%	53.4%	46.6%
9,727	BEDFORD	7,912	5,619	1,973	320	3,646 R	71.0%	24.9%	74.0%	26.0%
2,849	BELMONT	2,430	1,488	800	142	688 R	61.2%	32.9%	65.0%	35.0%
6,175	BERLIN	4,866	2,519	2,269	78	250 R	51.8%	46.6%	52.6%	47.4%
3,748	BOW	3,264	1,969	1,203	92	766 R	60.3%	36.9%	62.1%	37.9%
6,839	CLAREMONT	5,178	2,351	2,700	127	349 D	45.4%	52.1%	46.5%	53.5%
20,951	CONCORD	16,675	7,115	8,943	617	1,828 D	42.7%	53.6%	44.3%	55.7%
5,249	CONWAY	4,008	2,357	1,444	207	913 R	58.8%	36.0%	62.0%	38.0%
15,543	DERRY	11,918	7,286	4,049	583	3,237 R	61.1%	34.0%	64.3%	35.7%
15,513	DOVER	11,582	5,981	5,189	412	792 R	51.6%	44.8%	53.5%	46.5%
7,162	DURHAM	5,419	1,809	3,511	99	1,702 D	33.4%	64.8%	34.0%	66.0%
2,963	EPPING	2,259	1,277	895	87	382 R	56.5%	39.6%	58.8%	41.2%
8,545	EXETER	6,165	3,157	2,737	271	420 R	51.2%	44.4%	53.6%	46.4%
2,752	FARMINGTON	1,896	1,044	772	80	272 R	55.1%	40.7%	57.5%	42.5%
4,000	FRANKLIN	2,967	1,758	1,124	85	634 R	59.3%	37.9%	61.0%	39.0%
4,682	GILFORD	3,540	2,174	1,256	110	918 R	61.4%	35.5%	63.4%	36.6%
8,723	GOFFSTOWN	6,844	4,563	1,957	324	2,606 R	66.7%	28.6%	70.0%	30.0%
4,658	HAMPSTEAD	3,724	2,300	1,279	145	1,021 R	61.8%	34.3%	64.3%	35.7%
9,170	HAMPTON	7,409	4,160	2,976	273	1,184 R	56.1%	40.2%	58.3%	41.7%
5,987	HANOVER	4,476	1,510	2,875	91	1,365 D	33.7%	64.2%	34.4%	65.6%
4,047	HOLLIS	3,531	2,045	1,347	139	698 R	57.9%	38.1%	60.3%	39.7%
5,739	HOOKSETT	4,633	3,180	1,243	210	1,937 R	68.6%	26.8%	71.9%	28.1%
11,307	HUDSON	8,910	5,357	3,058	495	2,299 R	60.1%	34.3%	63.7%	36.3%
2,799	JAFFREY	2,281	1,169	1,045	67	124 R	51.2%	45.8%	52.8%	47.2%
12,817	KEENE	9,965	4,145	5,547	273	1,402 D	41.6%	55.7%	42.8%	57.2%
3,262	KINGSTON	2,670	1,580	969	121	8 R	59.2%	36.3%	62.0%	38.0%
8,145	LACONIA	6,838	4,058	2,530	250	1,528 R	59.3%	37.0%	61.6%	38.4%
6,508	LEBANON	5,126	2,555	2,461	110	94 R	49.8%	48.0%	50.9%	49.1%
3,192	LITCHFIELD	2,611	1,713	770	128	943 R	65.6%	29.5%	69.0%	31.0%
3,111	LITTLETON	2,381	1,421	911	49	510 R	59.7%	38.3%	60.9%	39.1%
11,103	LONDONDERRY	9,282	5,915	2,946	421	2,969 R	63.7%	31.7%	66.8%	33.2%
50,889	MANCHESTER	38,277	23,978	12,813	1,486	11,165 R	62.6%	33.5%	65.2%	34.8%
13,196	MERRIMACK TOWN	10,848	7,158	3,165	525	3,993 R	66.0%	29.2%	69.3%	30.7%
7,515	MILFORD	5,465	3,364	1,864	237	1,500 R	61.6%	34.1%	64.3%	35.7%
44,674	NASHUA	32,399	17,937	13,007	1,455	4,930 R	55.4%	40.1%	58.0%	42.0%
4,451	NEWMARKET	3,327	1,517	1,665	145	148 D	45.6%	50.0%	47.7%	52.3%
2,915	NEWPORT	2,332	1,086	1,164	82	78 D	46.6%	49.9%	48.3%	51.7%
5,771	PELHAM	4,672	2,728	1,749	195	979 R	58.4%	37.4%	60.9%	39.1%
3,767	PEMBROKE	3,061	1,698	1,241	122	457 R	55.5%	40.5%	57.8%	42.2%
3,621	PETERBOROUGH	2,913	1,393	1,433	87	40 D	47.8%	49.2%	49.3%	50.7%
4,143	PLAISTOW	3,256	1,935	1,221	100	714 R	59.4%	37.5%	61.3%	38.7%
3,158	PLYMOUTH	2,331	1,120	1,165	46	45 D	48.0%	50.0%	49.0%	51.0%
15,585	PORTSMOUTH	11,610	4,895	6,195	520	1,300 D	42.2%	53.4%	44.1%	55.9%
4,032	RAYMOND	3,359	2,153	991	215	1,162 R	64.1%	29.5%	68.5%	31.5%
13,218	ROCHESTER	10,898	6,545	3,991	362	2,554 R	60.1%	36.6%	62.1%	37.9%
14,905	SALEM	12,248	7,481	4,309	458	3,172 R	61.1%	35.2%	63.5%	36.5%
4,898	SEABROOK	3,168	1,924	1,135	109	789 R	60.7%	35.8%	62.9%	37.1%
5,746	SOMERSWORTH	4,455	2,361	1,913	181	448 R	53.0%	42.9%	55.2%	44.8%
3,221	SWANZEY	2,760	1,373	1,294	93	79 R	49.7%	46.9%	51.5%	48.5%
3,598	WEARE	2,932	1,844	899	189	945 R	62.9%	30.7%	67.2%	32.8%
5,493	WINDHAM	4,583	2,956	1,424	203	1,532 R	64.5%	31.1%	67.5%	32.5%

NEW HAMPSHIRE

SENATOR 1992

Registration	City/Town	Total Vote	Republican	Democratic	Other	Rep.-Dem. Plurality	Percentage Total Vote Rep.	Dem.	Major Vote Rep.	Dem.
6,012	AMHERST	5,126	2,829	2,047	250	782 R	55.2%	39.9%	58.0%	42.0%
3,618	ATKINSON	2,965	1,764	1,020	181	744 R	59.5%	34.4%	63.4%	36.6%
3,644	BARRINGTON	2,830	1,228	1,358	244	130 D	43.4%	48.0%	47.5%	52.5%
9,727	BEDFORD	7,943	4,795	2,656	492	2,139 R	60.4%	33.4%	64.4%	35.6%
2,849	BELMONT	2,426	1,156	1,037	233	119 R	47.7%	42.7%	52.7%	47.3%
6,175	BERLIN	4,894	2,295	2,327	272	32 D	46.9%	47.5%	49.7%	50.3%
3,748	BOW	3,256	1,489	1,580	187	91 D	45.7%	48.5%	48.5%	51.5%
6,839	CLAREMONT	5,168	2,208	2,777	183	569 D	42.7%	53.7%	44.3%	55.7%
20,951	CONCORD	16,691	5,520	10,251	920	4,731 D	33.1%	61.4%	35.0%	65.0%
5,249	CONWAY	3,992	1,964	1,605	423	359 R	49.2%	40.2%	55.0%	45.0%
15,543	DERRY	11,897	6,414	4,533	950	1,881 R	53.9%	38.1%	58.6%	41.4%
15,513	DOVER	11,596	5,117	5,865	614	748 D	44.1%	50.6%	46.6%	53.4%
7,162	DURHAM	5,204	1,574	3,390	240	1,816 D	30.2%	65.1%	31.7%	68.3%
2,963	EPPING	2,269	1,036	1,040	193	4 D	45.7%	45.8%	49.9%	50.1%
8,545	EXETER	6,144	2,810	2,929	405	119 D	45.7%	47.7%	49.0%	51.0%
2,752	FARMINGTON	2,043	996	892	155	104 R	48.8%	43.7%	52.8%	47.2%
4,000	FRANKLIN	2,919	1,379	1,412	128	33 D	47.2%	48.4%	49.4%	50.6%
4,682	GILFORD	3,533	1,884	1,417	232	467 R	53.3%	40.1%	57.1%	42.9%
8,723	GOFFSTOWN	6,848	3,816	2,499	533	1,317 R	55.7%	36.5%	60.4%	39.6%
4,658	HAMPSTEAD	3,706	2,072	1,371	263	701 R	55.9%	37.0%	60.2%	39.8%
9,170	HAMPTON	7,275	3,241	3,618	416	377 D	44.5%	49.7%	47.3%	52.7%
5,987	HANOVER	4,508	1,380	2,979	149	1,599 D	30.6%	66.1%	31.7%	68.3%
4,047	HOLLIS	3,562	1,815	1,580	167	235 R	51.0%	44.4%	53.5%	46.5%
5,739	HOOKSETT	4,641	2,506	1,789	346	717 R	54.0%	38.5%	58.3%	41.7%
11,307	HUDSON	8,958	4,660	3,624	674	1,036 R	52.0%	40.5%	56.3%	43.7%
2,799	JAFFREY	2,301	1,017	1,135	149	118 D	44.2%	49.3%	47.3%	52.7%
12,817	KEENE	9,792	3,297	6,038	457	2,741 D	33.7%	61.7%	35.3%	64.7%
3,262	KINGSTON	2,667	1,391	1,042	234	8 R	52.2%	39.1%	57.2%	42.8%
8,145	LACONIA	6,841	3,348	3,022	471	326 R	48.9%	44.2%	52.6%	47.4%
6,508	LEBANON	5,123	2,254	2,691	178	437 D	44.0%	52.5%	45.6%	54.4%
3,192	LITCHFIELD	2,603	1,389	1,016	198	373 R	53.4%	39.0%	57.8%	42.2%
3,111	LITTLETON	2,351	1,325	883	143	442 R	56.4%	37.6%	60.0%	40.0%
11,103	LONDONDERRY	9,278	5,172	3,419	687	1,753 R	55.7%	36.9%	60.2%	39.8%
50,889	MANCHESTER	39,439	20,022	16,936	2,481	3,086 R	50.8%	42.9%	54.2%	45.8%
13,196	MERRIMACK TOWN	10,832	5,844	4,219	769	1,625 R	54.0%	38.9%	58.1%	41.9%
7,515	MILFORD	5,485	2,948	2,164	373	784 R	53.7%	39.5%	57.7%	42.3%
44,674	NASHUA	33,758	16,436	15,400	1,922	1,036 R	48.7%	45.6%	51.6%	48.4%
4,451	NEWMARKET	3,288	1,202	1,865	221	663 D	36.6%	56.7%	39.2%	60.8%
2,915	NEWPORT	2,325	1,011	1,191	123	180 D	43.5%	51.2%	45.9%	54.1%
5,771	PELHAM	4,690	2,621	1,700	369	921 R	55.9%	36.2%	60.7%	39.3%
3,767	PEMBROKE	3,045	1,296	1,550	199	254 D	42.6%	50.9%	45.5%	54.5%
3,621	PETERBOROUGH	2,952	1,349	1,483	120	134 D	45.7%	50.2%	47.6%	52.4%
4,143	PLAISTOW	3,254	1,796	1,244	214	552 R	55.2%	38.2%	59.1%	40.9%
3,158	PLYMOUTH	2,290	1,012	1,098	180	86 D	44.2%	47.9%	48.0%	52.0%
15,585	PORTSMOUTH	11,629	4,114	6,759	756	2,645 D	35.4%	58.1%	37.8%	62.2%
4,032	RAYMOND	3,373	1,786	1,278	309	508 R	52.9%	37.9%	58.3%	41.7%
13,218	ROCHESTER	10,983	5,430	4,964	589	466 R	49.4%	45.2%	52.2%	47.8%
14,905	SALEM	12,173	6,589	4,764	820	1,825 R	54.1%	39.1%	58.0%	42.0%
4,898	SEABROOK	3,598	2,039	1,345	214	694 R	56.7%	37.4%	60.3%	39.7%
5,746	SOMERSWORTH	4,473	1,957	2,264	252	307 D	43.8%	50.6%	46.4%	53.6%
3,221	SWANZEY	2,759	1,146	1,488	125	342 D	41.5%	53.9%	43.5%	56.5%
3,598	WEARE	2,939	1,561	1,147	231	414 R	53.1%	39.0%	57.6%	42.4%
5,493	WINDHAM	4,576	2,743	1,510	323	1,233 R	59.9%	33.0%	64.5%	35.5%

NEW HAMPSHIRE

CONGRESS

CD	Year	Total Vote	Republican Vote	Republican Candidate	Democratic Vote	Democratic Candidate	Other Vote	Rep.-Dem. Plurality	Percentage Total Vote Rep.	Dem.	Major Vote Rep.	Dem.
1	1992	255,853	135,936	ZELIFF, BILL	108,578	PRESTON, ROBERT T.	11,339	27,358 R	53.1%	42.4%	55.6%	44.4%
2	1992	255,185	91,126	HATCH, BILL	157,328	SWETT, DICK	6,731	66,202 D	35.7%	61.7%	36.7%	63.3%

NEW HAMPSHIRE

1992 GENERAL ELECTION

In addition to the county-by-county figures, data are presented for selected New Hampshire communities. Since not all jurisdictions of the state are listed in this special tabulation, state-wide totals are shown only with the county-by-county statistics.

President Other vote was 3,548 Libertarian (Marrou); 512 New Alliance (Fulani); 292 Natural Law (Hagelin); 730 scattered write-in.

Governor Other vote was 20,663 Libertarian (Luce); 105 scattered write-in.

Senator Other vote was 18,214 Libertarian (Alexander); 9,340 Independent (Brady); 4,752 Independent (Blevens); 1,284 Natural Law (Haight); 21 Sullivan (write-in) and 232 scattered write-in.

Congress Other vote was 5,633 Libertarian (Bickford), 3,537 Independent (Bosa), 1,997 Natural Law (Spitzfaden) and 172 scattered write-in in CD 1; 5,977 Libertarian (Lewicke), 657 Natural Law (Bingham) and 97 scattered write-in in CD 2.

1992 PRIMARIES

SEPTEMBER 8 REPUBLICAN

Governor 60,809 Steve Merrill; 25,530 Edward C. duPont; 24,433 Elizabeth Hager; 1,776 Melvin D. Newton; 815 Livius V. Fisteag; 1,949 scattered write-in.

Senator 57,141 Judd Gregg; 43,264 Harold Eckman; 10,642 Jean T. White; 2,295 Mark W. Farnham; 1,395 scattered write-in.

Congress Contested as follows:

CD 1 28,877 Bill Zeliff; 20,493 Ovide Lamontagne; 8,447 Maureen E. Barrows; 173 scattered write-in.
CD 2 17,176 Bill Hatch; 15,818 Stephen M. Duprey; 13,194 Peter J. Spaulding; 2,909 Ted deWinter; 2,073 Arthur C. Godjikian; 24 scattered write-in.

SEPTEMBER 8 DEMOCRATIC

Governor 41,770 Deborah A. Arnesen; 23,919 Norman E. D'Amours; 19,792 Ned Helms; 2,110 scattered write-in.

Senator 41,923 John Rauh; 15,943 Brenda J. Elias; 11,699 Terry Bennett; 7,804 Jeanne Stapleton; 3,836 Lynn R. Chong; 1,796 scattered write-in.

Congress Contested as follows:

CD 1 24,170 Robert F. Preston; 13,569 Bill Verge; 856 scattered write-in.
CD 2 27,552 Dick Swett; 14,543 Emily Northrop; 425 scattered write-in.

NEW JERSEY

GOVERNOR
James J. Florio (D). Elected 1989 to a four-year term.

SENATORS
Bill Bradley (D). Re-elected 1990 to a six-year term. Previously elected 1984, 1978.

Frank R. Lautenberg (D). Re-elected 1988 to a six-year term. Previously elected 1982.

REPRESENTATIVES
1. Robert E. Andrews (D)
2. William J. Hughes (D)
3. H. James Saxton (R)
4. Christopher H. Smith (R)
5. Margaret S. Roukema (R)
6. Frank Pallone (D)
7. Bob Franks (R)
8. Herbert C. Klein (D)
9. Robert G. Torricelli (D)
10. Donald M. Payne (D)
11. Dean A. Gallo (R)
12. Dick Zimmer (R)
13. Robert Menendez (D)

POSTWAR VOTE FOR PRESIDENT

| | | Republican | | Democratic | | Other | | Percentage | | | |
| | | | | | | | | Total Vote | | Major Vote | |
Year	Total Vote	Vote	Candidate	Vote	Candidate	Vote	Plurality	Rep.	Dem.	Rep.	Dem.
1992 **	3,343,594	1,356,865	Bush, George	1,436,206	Clinton, Bill	550,523	79,341 D	40.6%	43.0%	48.6%	51.4%
1988	3,099,553	1,743,192	Bush, George	1,320,352	Dukakis, Michael S.	36,009	422,840 R	56.2%	42.6%	56.9%	43.1%
1984	3,217,862	1,933,630	Reagan, Ronald	1,261,323	Mondale, Walter F.	22,909	672,307 R	60.1%	39.2%	60.5%	39.5%
1980	2,975,684	1,546,557	Reagan, Ronald	1,147,364	Carter, Jimmy	281,763	399,193 R	52.0%	38.6%	57.4%	42.6%
1976	3,014,472	1,509,688	Ford, Gerald R.	1,444,653	Carter, Jimmy	60,131	65,035 R	50.1%	47.9%	51.1%	48.9%
1972	2,997,229	1,845,502	Nixon, Richard M.	1,102,211	McGovern, George S.	49,516	743,291 R	61.6%	36.8%	62.6%	37.4%
1968	2,875,395	1,325,467	Nixon, Richard M.	1,264,206	Humphrey, Hubert H.	285,722	61,261 R	46.1%	44.0%	51.2%	48.8%
1964	2,847,663	964,174	Goldwater, Barry M.	1,868,231	Johnson, Lyndon B.	15,258	904,057 D	33.9%	65.6%	34.0%	66.0%
1960	2,773,111	1,363,324	Nixon, Richard M.	1,385,415	Kennedy, John F.	24,372	22,091 D	49.2%	50.0%	49.6%	50.4%
1956	2,484,312	1,606,942	Eisenhower, Dwight D.	850,337	Stevenson, Adlai E.	27,033	756,605 R	64.7%	34.2%	65.4%	34.6%
1952	2,418,554	1,373,613	Eisenhower, Dwight D.	1,015,902	Stevenson, Adlai E.	29,039	357,711 R	56.8%	42.0%	57.5%	42.5%
1948	1,949,555	981,124	Dewey, Thomas E.	895,455	Truman, Harry S.	72,976	85,669 R	50.3%	45.9%	52.3%	47.7%

In 1992 the other vote column includes 521,829 votes cast for Perot.

POSTWAR VOTE FOR GOVERNOR

| | | Republican | | Democratic | | Other | Rep.-Dem. | Percentage | | | |
| | | | | | | | | Total Vote | | Major Vote | |
Year	Total Vote	Vote	Candidate	Vote	Candidate	Vote	Plurality	Rep.	Dem.	Rep.	Dem.
1989	2,253,764	838,553	Courter, James A.	1,379,937	Florio, James J.	35,274	541,384 D	37.2%	61.2%	37.8%	62.2%
1985	1,972,624	1,372,631	Kean, Thomas H.	578,402	Shapiro, Peter	21,591	794,229 R	69.6%	29.3%	70.4%	29.6%
1981	2,317,239	1,145,999	Kean, Thomas H.	1,144,202	Florio, James J.	27,038	1,797 R	49.5%	49.4%	50.0%	50.0%
1977	2,126,264	888,880	Bateman, Raymond H.	1,184,564	Byrne, Brendan T.	52,820	295,684 D	41.8%	55.7%	42.9%	57.1%
1973	2,122,009	676,235	Sandman, Charles W.	1,414,613	Byrne, Brendan T.	31,161	738,378 D	31.9%	66.7%	32.3%	67.7%
1969	2,366,606	1,411,905	Cahill, William T.	911,003	Meyner, Robert B.	43,698	500,902 R	59.7%	38.5%	60.8%	39.2%
1965	2,229,583	915,996	Dumont, Wayne	1,279,568	Hughes, Richard J.	34,019	363,572 D	41.1%	57.4%	41.7%	58.3%
1961	2,152,662	1,049,274	Mitchell, James P.	1,084,194	Hughes, Richard J.	19,194	34,920 D	48.7%	50.4%	49.2%	50.8%
1957	2,018,488	897,321	Forbes, Malcolm S.	1,101,130	Meyner, Robert B.	20,037	203,809 D	44.5%	54.6%	44.9%	55.1%
1953	1,810,812	809,068	Troast, Paul L.	962,710	Meyner, Robert B.	39,034	153,642 D	44.7%	53.2%	45.7%	54.3%
1949 **	1,718,788	885,882	Driscoll, Alfred	810,022	Wene, Elmer H.	22,884	75,860 R	51.5%	47.1%	52.2%	47.8%
1946	1,414,527	807,378	Driscoll, Alfred	585,960	Hansen, Lewis G.	21,189	221,418 R	57.1%	41.4%	57.9%	42.1%

The term of office of New Jersey's Governor was increased from three to four years effective with the 1949 election.

NEW JERSEY

POSTWAR VOTE FOR SENATOR

Year	Total Vote	Republican		Democratic		Other Vote	Rep.-Dem. Plurality	Percentage			
								Total Vote		Major Vote	
		Vote	Candidate	Vote	Candidate			Rep.	Dem.	Rep.	Dem.
1990	1,938,454	918,874	Whitman, Christine T.	977,810	Bradley, Bill	41,770	58,936 D	47.4%	50.4%	48.4%	51.6%
1988	2,987,634	1,349,937	Dawkins, Peter M.	1,599,905	Lautenberg, Frank R.	37,792	249,968 D	45.2%	53.6%	45.8%	54.2%
1984	3,096,456	1,080,100	Mochary, Mary V.	1,986,644	Bradley, Bill	29,712	906,544 D	34.9%	64.2%	35.2%	64.8%
1982	2,193,945	1,047,626	Fenwick, Millicent	1,117,549	Lautenberg, Frank R.	28,770	69,923 D	47.8%	50.9%	48.4%	51.6%
1978	1,957,515	844,200	Bell, Jeffrey	1,082,960	Bradley, Bill	30,355	238,760 D	43.1%	55.3%	43.8%	56.2%
1976	2,771,390	1,054,508	Norcross, David F.	1,681,140	Williams, Harrison	35,742	626,632 D	38.0%	60.7%	38.5%	61.5%
1972	2,791,907	1,743,854	Case, Clifford P.	963,573	Krebs, Paul J.	84,480	780,281 R	62.5%	34.5%	64.4%	35.6%
1970	2,142,105	903,026	Gross, Nelson G.	1,157,074	Williams, Harrison	82,005	254,048 D	42.2%	54.0%	43.8%	56.2%
1966	2,131,188	1,279,343	Case, Clifford P.	788,021	Wilentz, Warren W.	63,824	491,322 R	60.0%	37.0%	61.9%	38.1%
1964	2,710,441	1,011,610	Shanley, Bernard M.	1,678,051	Williams, Harrison	20,780	666,441 D	37.3%	61.9%	37.6%	62.4%
1960	2,664,556	1,483,832	Case, Clifford P.	1,151,385	Lord, Thorn	29,339	332,447 R	55.7%	43.2%	56.3%	43.7%
1958	1,881,329	882,287	Kean, Robert W.	966,832	Williams, Harrison	32,210	84,545 D	46.9%	51.4%	47.7%	52.3%
1954	1,770,557	861,528	Case, Clifford P.	858,158	Howell, Charles R.	50,871	3,370 R	48.7%	48.5%	50.1%	49.9%
1952	2,318,232	1,286,782	Smith, H. Alexander	1,011,187	Alexander, Archibald	20,263	275,595 R	55.5%	43.6%	56.0%	44.0%
1948	1,869,882	934,720	Hendrickson, Robert	884,414	Alexander, Archibald	50,748	50,306 R	50.0%	47.3%	51.4%	48.6%
1946	1,367,155	799,808	Smith, H. Alexander	548,458	Brunner, George E.	18,889	251,350 R	58.5%	40.1%	59.3%	40.7%

NEW JERSEY

Districts Established March 20, 1992

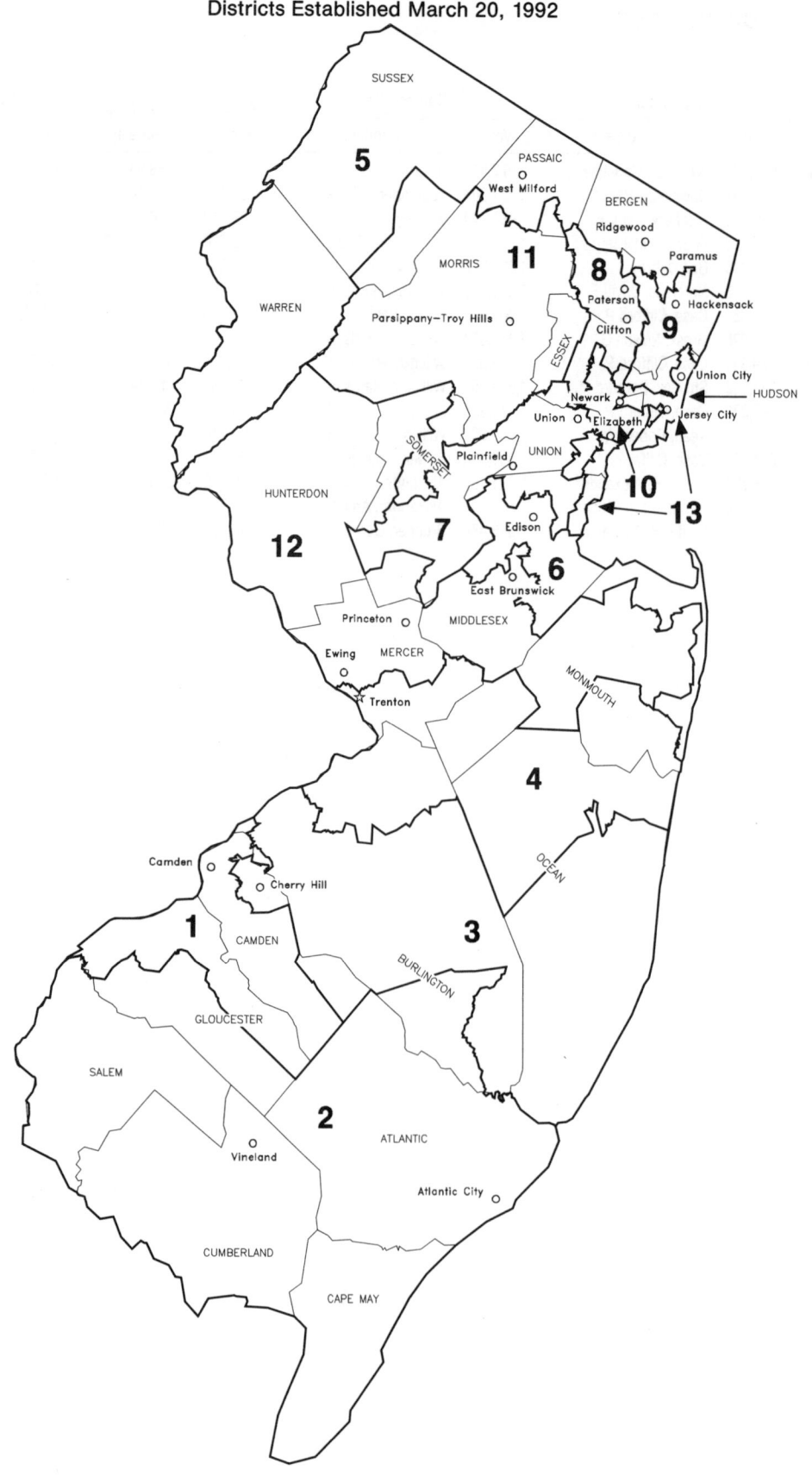

NEW JERSEY

PRESIDENT 1992

Registration	County	Total Vote	Republican	Democratic	Perot	Other	Plurality	Percentage Total Vote		
								Rep.	Dem.	Perot
113,854	ATLANTIC	90,298	34,279	39,633	15,890	496	5,354 D	38.0%	43.9%	17.6%
475,151	BERGEN	403,137	178,223	171,104	52,082	1,728	7,119 R	44.2%	42.4%	12.9%
204,525	BURLINGTON	173,357	63,709	72,845	35,322	1,481	9,136 D	36.8%	42.0%	20.4%
258,320	CAMDEN	210,886	67,205	104,915	37,144	1,622	37,710 D	31.9%	49.7%	17.6%
59,232	CAPE MAY	48,856	21,502	17,324	9,798	232	4,178 R	44.0%	35.5%	20.1%
66,776	CUMBERLAND	52,116	19,253	22,220	9,901	742	2,967 D	36.9%	42.6%	19.0%
355,973	ESSEX	276,858	89,146	158,130	26,961	2,621	68,984 D	32.2%	57.1%	9.7%
126,146	GLOUCESTER	104,619	37,335	42,425	24,132	727	5,090 D	35.7%	40.6%	23.1%
237,996	HUDSON	185,057	66,505	99,799	14,569	4,184	33,294 D	35.9%	53.9%	7.9%
62,089	HUNTERDON	53,974	25,130	15,423	12,736	685	9,707 R	46.6%	28.6%	23.6%
177,889	MERCER	145,260	50,473	71,383	22,503	901	20,910 D	34.7%	49.1%	15.5%
360,115	MIDDLESEX	285,271	108,701	128,824	45,055	2,691	20,123 D	38.1%	45.2%	15.8%
313,740	MONMOUTH	266,116	117,715	101,750	45,445	1,206	15,965 R	44.2%	38.2%	17.1%
241,313	MORRIS	209,232	108,431	67,593	32,447	761	40,838 R	51.8%	32.3%	15.5%
251,518	OCEAN	216,243	95,984	75,431	41,668	3,160	20,553 R	44.4%	34.9%	19.3%
210,432	PASSAIC	164,888	71,147	70,030	21,494	2,217	1,117 R	43.1%	42.5%	13.0%
34,013	SALEM	27,935	10,363	10,062	7,274	236	301 R	37.1%	36.0%	26.0%
144,947	SOMERSET	120,813	56,044	42,867	21,014	888	13,177 R	46.4%	35.5%	17.4%
66,268	SUSSEX	57,064	29,510	14,775	12,537	242	14,735 R	51.7%	25.9%	22.0%
252,399	UNION	210,112	87,742	96,671	23,991	1,708	8,929 D	41.8%	46.0%	11.4%
46,776	WARREN	41,502	18,468	13,002	9,866	166	5,466 R	44.5%	31.3%	23.8%
4,059,472	TOTAL	3,343,594	1,356,865	1,436,206	521,829	28,694	79,341 D	40.6%	43.0%	15.6%

NEW JERSEY

CONGRESS

CD	Year	Total Vote	Republican		Democratic		Other Vote	Rep.-Dem. Plurality	Percentage			
									Total Vote		Major Vote	
			Vote	Candidate	Vote	Candidate			Rep.	Dem.	Rep.	Dem.
1	1992	228,072	65,123	SOLOMON, LEE A.	153,525	ANDREWS, ROBERT E.	9,424	88,402 D	28.6%	67.3%	29.8%	70.2%
2	1992	237,027	98,315	LOBIONDO, FRANK A.	132,465	HUGHES, WILLIAM J.	6,247	34,150 D	41.5%	55.9%	42.6%	57.4%
3	1992	255,798	151,368	SAXTON, H. JAMES	94,012	RYAN, TIMOTHY E.	10,418	57,356 R	59.2%	36.8%	61.7%	38.3%
4	1992	241,225	149,095	SMITH, CHRISTOPHER H.	84,514	HUGHES, BRIAN M.	7,616	64,581 R	61.8%	35.0%	63.8%	36.2%
5	1992	274,371	196,198	ROUKEMA, MARGARET S.	67,579	LUCAS, FRANK R.	10,594	128,619 R	71.5%	24.6%	74.4%	25.6%
6	1992	226,093	100,949	KYRILLOS, JOSEPH M.	118,266	PALLONE, FRANK	6,878	17,317 D	44.6%	52.3%	46.1%	53.9%
7	1992	248,082	132,174	FRANKS, BOB	105,761	SENDELSKY, LEONARD R.	10,147	26,413 R	53.3%	42.6%	55.6%	44.4%
8	1992	205,828	84,674	BUBBA, JOSEPH L.	96,742	KLEIN, HERBERT C.	24,412	12,068 D	41.1%	47.0%	46.7%	53.3%
9	1992	238,704	88,179	ROMA, PATRICK J.	139,188	TORRICELLI, ROBERT G.	11,337	51,009 D	36.9%	58.3%	38.8%	61.2%
10	1992	149,632	30,160	PALERMO, ALFRED D.	117,287	PAYNE, DONALD M.	2,185	87,127 D	20.2%	78.4%	20.5%	79.5%
11	1992	268,436	188,165	GALLO, DEAN A.	68,871	SPIRIDELLIS, ONA	11,400	119,294 R	70.1%	25.7%	73.2%	26.8%
12	1992	272,757	174,216	ZIMMER, DICK	83,035	ABATE, FRANK G.	15,506	91,181 R	63.9%	30.4%	67.7%	32.3%
13	1992	145,714	44,529	THEEMLING, FRED J.	93,670	MENENDEZ, ROBERT	7,515	49,141 D	30.6%	64.3%	32.2%	67.8%

NEW JERSEY

1992 GENERAL ELECTION

President   Other vote was 6,822 Libertarian (Marrou); 4,749 Independent (Bradford); 3,513 New Alliance (Fulani); 2,670 Taxpayers (Phillips); 2,095 Six Million Jobs (LaRouche); 2,011 Socialist Workers (Warren); 1,996 Independent (Daniels); 1,867 Populist (Gritz); 1,618 Workers League (Halyard); 1,353 Natural Law (Hagelin).

Congress   Other vote was 3,761 Pro-Life Pro-Family Veteran (Smith), 2,641 Libertarian (Zeldin), 2,163 Pro-Life Independent Conservative (Lowndes) and 859 America First Populist (Pastuch) in CD 1; 2,575 Libertarian (Bacon), 2,067 Anti-Tax (Ponczek) and 1,605 Freedom Equality Prosperity (Lippi) in CD 2; 2,711 Libertarian (Radder), 2,309 America First Populist (Plonski), 1,728 New Jersey Conservative (Permuko), 915 Independent (Reilly), 901 "Donald of Moorestown"(McMahon), 749 Independent Party (Verderse), 593 Independent (King) and 512 Basic Reformed Government (Burke) in CD 3; 2,984 Libertarian (Grindlinger), 2,137 Independent (Pasculli), 1,630 New Jersey Conservative (James) and 865 America First Populist (Notaragelo) in CD 4; 6,182 Independent (Leonard), 2,636 Libertarian (Pierone), 994 Equality Brotherhood Justice (Lahood) and 782 America First Independent (Bacha) in CD 5; 2,153 The People's Candidate (Spalletta), 1,404 Libertarian (Stewart), 1,073 Independent for Freedom (Cerrato), 951 "You Gotta Believe"(Predham), 613 Socialist Workers (Berg), 411 America First Populist (Matto) and 273 Capitalist (Dickson) in CD 6; 4,043 Independent (Gillespie), 2,612 No Nonsense Government (Campbell), 1,964 Libertarian (Layman), 844 America First Populist (Kucek) and 684 People's Congressional Preference (Criss) in CD 7; 16,170 Independent for Change (Kolodziej), 2,916 Independents for Change (Caslander), 2,135 Independent People's Network (Pellosie), 1,109 Libertarian (Stefanelli), 1,099 Restore Public Trust (Dominianni), 392 Socialist Workers (Redrup), 316 America First Populist (Dzula) and 275 New Jersey Independents (Gorfinkle) in CD 8; 4,491 Clean Up Congress (Russo), 2,257 New Jersey Independents (Novosielski), 1,606 America First Populist (D'Alessio), 1,369 Politicians are Crooks (Shaw), 1,099 Libertarian (Karlan) and 515 An Independent Voice (Haas) in CD 9; 1,272 Libertarian (Caraballo) and 913 Socialist Workers (Leonard) in CD 10; 3,538 Libertarian (Roth), 3,127 Time For Change (Fitzpatrick), 1,882 Independent (Karlen), 1,711 Independent (Safier) and 1,142 America First Populist (Hrazanek) in CD 11; 11,051 Independent (Mayer), 1,906 Libertarian (Peters), 1,804 Independent (Eggert) and 745 America First Populist (Pakenham) in CD 12; 2,363 Stop Tax Increases (Bonacci), 1,539 Libertarian (Flynn), 1,525 Communist (Rummel), 1,406 Socialist Workers (Harris) and 682 America First Populist (Stovenken) in CD 13.

1992 PRIMARIES

JUNE 2 REPUBLICAN

Congress   Unopposed in eight CD's. In CD 7, unopposed candidate Matthew J. Rinaldo withdrew after the primary and Bob Franks was substituted by the local party committee. Contested as follows:

CD   2   18,927 Frank A. LoBiondo; 4,833 Joseph L. Breeden.
CD   3   25,388 H. James Saxton; 3,044 Frank W. Drake.
CD   5   27,030 Margaret S. Roukema; 10,243 Lou Sette; 4,839 Ira M. Marlowe; 1,372 C. Larry Fisher.
CD   6   8,179 Joseph M. Kyrillos; 4,397 Grace C. Applegate; 3,986 Paul Danielczyk; 670 James R. Sheldon.
CD   8   10,584 Joseph L. Bubba; 4,184 Norman M. Robertson; 1,690 Bob Davis; 278 Bernard George.

JUNE 2 DEMOCRATIC

Congress   Unopposed in three CD's. Contested as follows:

CD   3   15,407 Timothy E. Ryan; 2,626 Howard S. Pearlman.
CD   4   12,666 Brian M. Hughes; 2,907 Michael DiMarco.
CD   5   13,185 Frank R. Lucas; 5,081 John Scully.
CD   6   19,087 Frank Pallone; 12,769 Bob Smith; 1,784 Barbara Jensen; 1,286 Jeffrey R. Gorman.
CD   7   9,992 Leonard R. Sendelsky; 7,615 Karen Carroll.

NEW JERSEY

CD 8   9,456 Herbert C. Klein; 6,786 Harry A. McEnroe; 6,510 Clare I. Lagermasini; 1,127 Joseph C. Iozia; 502 Roger P. Ham.

CD 9   24,010 Robert G. Torricelli; 4,733 Nancy Harrigan; 1,429 Matthew C. Guice.

CD 10   31,846 Donald M. Payne; 4,167 Willie L. Flood; 3,601 Brian Connors; 3,502 Stanley J. Moskal.

CD 11   7,237 Ona Spiridellis; 4,767 Mary Frueholz.

CD 13   24,245 Robert Menendez; 11,409 Robert P. Haney.

NEW MEXICO

GOVERNOR
Bruce King (D). Elected 1990 to a four-year term. Previously elected 1978, 1970.

SENATORS
Jeff Bingaman (D). Re-elected 1988 to a six-year term. Previously elected 1982.

Peter V. Domenici (R). Re-elected 1990 to a six-year term. Previously elected 1984, 1978, 1972.

REPRESENTATIVES
1. Steven H. Schiff (R)   2. Joseph R. Skeen (R)   3. Bill Richardson (D)

POSTWAR VOTE FOR PRESIDENT

		Republican		Democratic		Other		Total Vote		Major Vote	
Year	Total Vote	Vote	Candidate	Vote	Candidate	Vote	Plurality	Rep.	Dem.	Rep.	Dem.
1992 **	569,986	212,824	Bush, George	261,617	Clinton, Bill	95,545	48,793 D	37.3%	45.9%	44.9%	55.1%
1988	521,287	270,341	Bush, George	244,497	Dukakis, Michael S.	6,449	25,844 R	51.9%	46.9%	52.5%	47.5%
1984	514,370	307,101	Reagan, Ronald	201,769	Mondale, Walter F.	5,500	105,332 R	59.7%	39.2%	60.3%	39.7%
1980	456,971	250,779	Reagan, Ronald	167,826	Carter, Jimmy	38,366	82,953 R	54.9%	36.7%	59.9%	40.1%
1976	418,409	211,419	Ford, Gerald R.	201,148	Carter, Jimmy	5,842	10,271 R	50.5%	48.1%	51.2%	48.8%
1972	386,241	235,606	Nixon, Richard M.	141,084	McGovern, George S.	9,551	94,522 R	61.0%	36.5%	62.5%	37.5%
1968	327,350	169,692	Nixon, Richard M.	130,081	Humphrey, Hubert H.	27,577	39,611 R	51.8%	39.7%	56.6%	43.4%
1964	328,645	132,838	Goldwater, Barry M.	194,015	Johnson, Lyndon B.	1,792	61,177 D	40.4%	59.0%	40.6%	59.4%
1960	311,107	153,733	Nixon, Richard M.	156,027	Kennedy, John F.	1,347	2,294 D	49.4%	50.2%	49.6%	50.4%
1956	253,926	146,788	Eisenhower, Dwight D.	106,098	Stevenson, Adlai E.	1,040	40,690 R	57.8%	41.8%	58.0%	42.0%
1952	238,608	132,170	Eisenhower, Dwight D.	105,661	Stevenson, Adlai E.	777	26,509 R	55.4%	44.3%	55.6%	44.4%
1948	187,063	80,303	Dewey, Thomas E.	105,464	Truman, Harry S.	1,296	25,161 D	42.9%	56.4%	43.2%	56.8%

In 1992 the other vote column includes 91,895 votes cast for Perot.

POSTWAR VOTE FOR GOVERNOR

		Republican		Democratic		Other	Rep.-Dem.	Total Vote		Major Vote	
Year	Total Vote	Vote	Candidate	Vote	Candidate	Vote	Plurality	Rep.	Dem.	Rep.	Dem.
1990	411,236	185,692	Bond, Frank M.	224,564	King, Bruce	980	38,872 D	45.2%	54.6%	45.3%	54.7%
1986	394,833	209,455	Carruthers, Garrey E.	185,378	Powell. Ray B.		24,077 R	53.0%	47.0%	53.0%	47.0%
1982	407,466	191,626	Irick, John B.	215,840	Anaya, Toney		24,214 D	47.0%	53.0%	47.0%	53.0%
1978	345,577	170,848	Skeen, Joseph R.	174,631	King, Bruce	98	3,783 D	49.4%	50.5%	49.5%	50.5%
1974	328,742	160,430	Skeen, Joseph R.	164,172	Apodaca, Jerry	4,140	3,742 D	48.8%	49.9%	49.4%	50.6%
1970 **	290,375	134,640	Domenici, Peter V.	148,835	King, Bruce	6,900	14,195 D	46.4%	51.3%	47.5%	52.5%
1968	318,975	160,140	Cargo, David F.	157,230	Chavez, Fabian	1,605	2,910 R	50.2%	49.3%	50.5%	49.5%
1966	260,232	134,625	Cargo, David F.	125,587	Lusk, Thomas E.	20	9,038 R	51.7%	48.3%	51.7%	48.3%
1964	318,042	126,540	Tucker, Merle H.	191,497	Campbell, Jack M.	5	64,957 D	39.8%	60.2%	39.8%	60.2%
1962	247,135	116,184	Mechem, Edwin L.	130,933	Campbell, Jack M.	18	14,749 D	47.0%	53.0%	47.0%	53.0%
1960	305,542	153,765	Mechem, Edwin L.	151,777	Burroughs, John		1,988 R	50.3%	49.7%	50.3%	49.7%
1958	205,048	101,567	Mechem, Edwin L.	103,481	Burroughs, John		1,914 D	49.5%	50.5%	49.5%	50.5%
1956	251,751	131,488	Mechem, Edwin L.	120,263	Simms, John F.		11,225 R	52.2%	47.8%	52.2%	47.8%
1954	193,956	83,373	Stockton, Alvin	110,583	Simms, John F.		27,210 D	43.0%	57.0%	43.0%	57.0%
1952	240,150	129,116	Mechem, Edwin L.	111,034	Grantham, Everett		18,082 R	53.8%	46.2%	53.8%	46.2%
1950	180,205	96,846	Mechem, Edwin L.	83,359	Miles, John E.		13,487 R	53.7%	46.3%	53.7%	46.3%
1948	189,992	86,023	Lujan, Manuel	103,969	Mabry, Thomas J.		17,946 D	45.3%	54.7%	45.3%	54.7%
1946	132,930	62,875	Safford, Edward L.	70,055	Mabry, Thomas J.		7,180 D	47.3%	52.7%	47.3%	52.7%

The term of New Mexico's Governor was increased from two to four years effective with the 1970 election.

NEW MEXICO

POSTWAR VOTE FOR SENATOR

Year	Total Vote	Republican Vote	Republican Candidate	Democratic Vote	Democratic Candidate	Other Vote	Rep.-Dem. Plurality	Percentage Total Vote Rep.	Total Vote Dem.	Major Vote Rep.	Major Vote Dem.
1990	406,938	296,712	Domenici, Peter V.	110,033	Benavides, Tom R.	193	186,679 R	72.9%	27.0%	72.9%	27.1%
1988	508,598	186,579	Valentine, William	321,983	Bingaman, Jeff	36	135,404 D	36.7%	63.3%	36.7%	63.3%
1984	502,634	361,371	Domenici, Peter V.	141,253	Pratt, Judith A.	10	220,118 R	71.9%	28.1%	71.9%	28.1%
1982	404,810	187,128	Schmitt, Harrison	217,682	Bingaman, Jeff		30,554 D	46.2%	53.8%	46.2%	53.8%
1978	343,554	183,442	Domenici, Peter V.	160,045	Anaya, Toney	67	23,397 R	53.4%	46.6%	53.4%	46.6%
1976	413,141	234,681	Schmitt, Harrison	176,382	Montoya, Joseph M.	2,078	58,299 R	56.8%	42.7%	57.1%	42.9%
1972	378,330	204,253	Domenici, Peter V.	173,815	Daniels, Jack	262	30,438 R	54.0%	45.9%	54.0%	46.0%
1970	289,906	135,004	Carter, Anderson	151,486	Montoya, Joseph M.	3,416	16,482 D	46.6%	52.3%	47.1%	52.9%
1966	258,203	120,988	Carter, Anderson	137,205	Anderson, Clinton P.	10	16,217 D	46.9%	53.1%	46.9%	53.1%
1964	325,774	147,562	Mechem, Edwin L.	178,209	Montoya, Joseph M.	3	30,647 D	45.3%	54.7%	45.3%	54.7%
1960	300,551	109,897	Colwes, William F.	190,654	Anderson, Clinton P.		80,757 D	36.6%	63.4%	36.6%	63.4%
1958	203,323	75,827	Atchley, Forrest S.	127,496	Chavez, Dennis		51,669 D	37.3%	62.7%	37.3%	62.7%
1954	194,422	83,071	Mechem, Edwin L.	111,351	Anderson, Clinton P.		28,280 D	42.7%	57.3%	42.7%	57.3%
1952	239,711	117,168	Hurley, Patrick J.	122,543	Chavez, Dennis		5,375 D	48.9%	51.1%	48.9%	51.1%
1948	188,495	80,226	Hurley, Patrick J.	108,269	Anderson, Clinton P.		28,043 D	42.6%	57.4%	42.6%	57.4%
1946	133,282	64,632	Hurley, Patrick J.	68,650	Chavez, Dennis		4,018 D	48.5%	51.5%	48.5%	51.5%

NEW MEXICO

Districts Established December 18, 1991

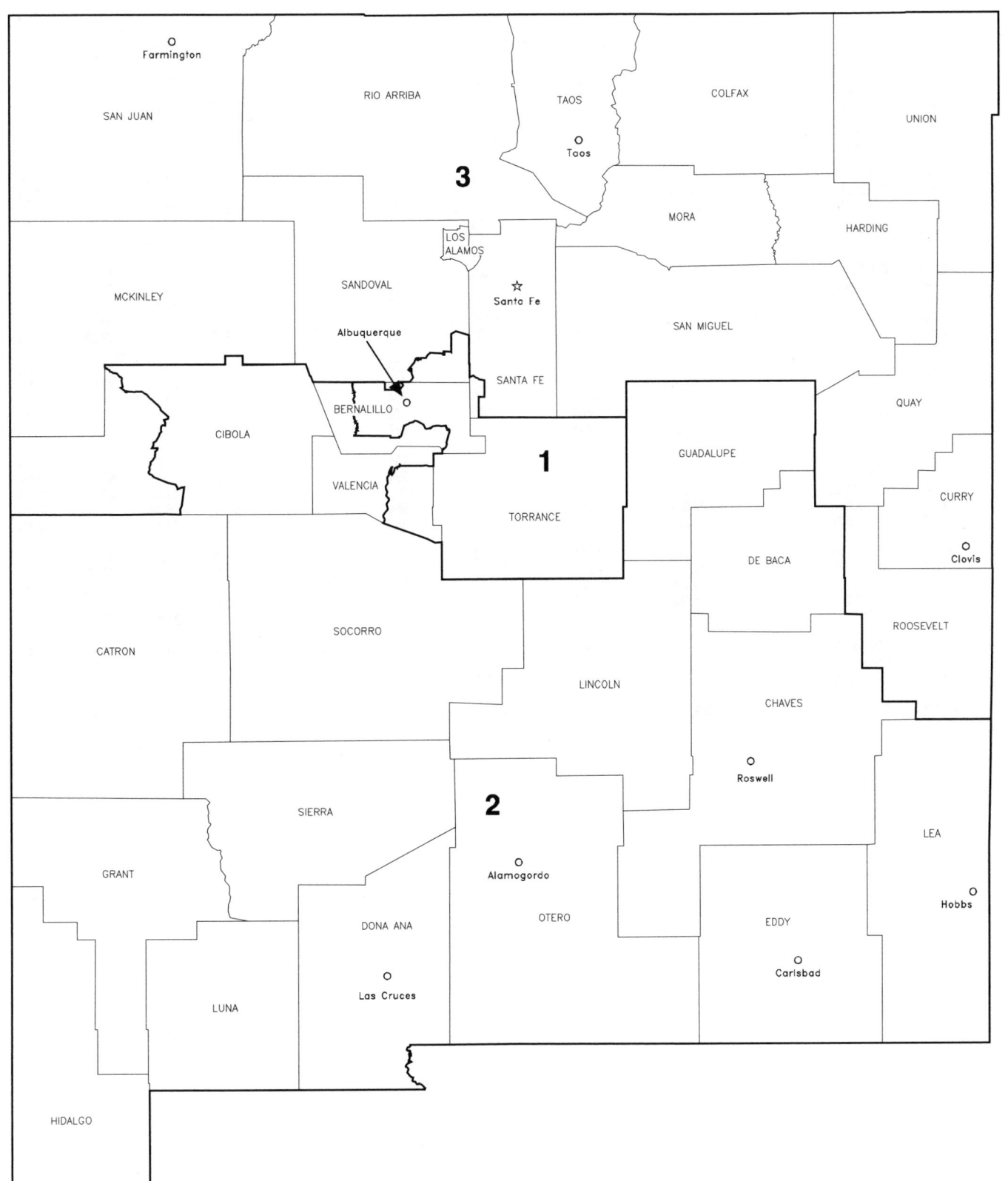

NEW MEXICO

PRESIDENT 1992

Registration	County	Total Vote	Republican	Democratic	Perot	Other	Plurality	Percentage Total Vote		
								Rep.	Dem.	Perot
240,661	BERNALILLO	200,698	77,304	90,863	31,241	1,290	13,559 D	38.5%	45.3%	15.6%
1,938	CATRON	1,553	771	465	289	28	306 R	49.6%	29.9%	18.6%
23,735	CHAVES	18,898	8,872	6,360	3,590	76	2,512 R	46.9%	33.7%	19.0%
7,655	CIBOLA	6,284	2,051	3,334	847	52	1,283 D	32.6%	53.1%	13.5%
6,323	COLFAX	5,228	1,730	2,607	871	20	877 D	33.1%	49.9%	16.7%
15,390	CURRY	12,633	6,831	3,699	2,056	47	3,132 R	54.1%	29.3%	16.3%
1,424	DE BACA	1,185	526	451	204	4	75 R	44.4%	38.1%	17.2%
59,666	DONA ANA	44,217	16,308	19,894	7,682	333	3,586 D	36.9%	45.0%	17.4%
21,932	EDDY	18,202	7,313	7,409	3,430	50	96 D	40.2%	40.7%	18.8%
13,315	GRANT	10,277	2,917	5,603	1,685	72	2,686 D	28.4%	54.5%	16.4%
2,850	GUADALUPE	2,102	691	1,225	173	13	534 D	32.9%	58.3%	8.2%
797	HARDING	678	312	268	98		44 R	46.0%	39.5%	14.5%
2,906	HIDALGO	2,315	871	995	442	7	124 D	37.6%	43.0%	19.1%
20,768	LEA	16,311	7,921	5,047	3,233	110	2,874 R	48.6%	30.9%	19.8%
6,618	LINCOLN	5,857	2,669	1,730	1,431	27	939 R	45.6%	29.5%	24.4%
11,597	LOS ALAMOS	10,642	4,320	3,897	2,339	86	423 R	40.6%	36.6%	22.0%
7,653	LUNA	6,272	2,166	2,637	1,445	24	471 D	34.5%	42.0%	23.0%
21,236	MCKINLEY	15,531	4,720	9,405	1,304	102	4,685 D	30.4%	60.6%	8.4%
3,285	MORA	2,421	668	1,555	188	10	887 D	27.6%	64.2%	7.8%
19,857	OTERO	16,203	7,481	5,377	3,257	88	2,104 R	46.2%	33.2%	20.1%
5,094	QUAY	4,289	1,759	1,758	755	17	1 R	41.0%	41.0%	17.6%
15,972	RIO ARRIBA	11,542	2,680	7,832	984	46	5,152 D	23.2%	67.9%	8.5%
7,994	ROOSEVELT	6,513	3,215	2,172	1,085	41	1,043 R	49.4%	33.3%	16.7%
29,886	SANDOVAL	23,574	8,491	10,951	3,954	178	2,460 D	36.0%	46.5%	16.8%
36,770	SAN JUAN	30,281	13,415	11,302	5,351	213	2,113 R	44.3%	37.3%	17.7%
12,777	SAN MIGUEL	9,387	2,183	6,186	965	53	4,003 D	23.3%	65.9%	10.3%
53,550	SANTA FE	42,917	9,684	27,189	5,656	388	17,505 D	22.6%	63.4%	13.2%
5,648	SIERRA	4,418	1,562	1,771	1,055	30	209 D	35.4%	40.1%	23.9%
7,987	SOCORRO	6,088	2,186	2,908	918	76	722 D	35.9%	47.8%	15.1%
13,391	TAOS	10,681	2,260	7,051	1,300	70	4,791 D	21.2%	66.0%	12.2%
5,618	TORRANCE	4,167	1,667	1,662	810	28	5 R	40.0%	39.9%	19.4%
2,271	UNION	1,854	975	519	355	5	456 R	52.6%	28.0%	19.1%
20,402	VALENCIA	16,768	6,305	7,495	2,902	66	1,190 D	37.6%	44.7%	17.3%
706,966	TOTAL	569,986	212,824	261,617	91,895	3,650	48,793 D	37.3%	45.9%	16.1%

NEW MEXICO

CONGRESS

CD	Year	Total Vote	Republican		Democratic		Other Vote	Rep.-Dem. Plurality	Percentage			
			Vote	Candidate	Vote	Candidate			Total Vote		Major Vote	
									Rep.	Dem.	Rep.	Dem.
1	1992	205,214	128,426	SCHIFF, STEVEN H.	76,600	ARAGON, ROBERT J.	188	51,826 R	62.6%	37.3%	62.6%	37.4%
2	1992	168,170	94,838	SKEEN, JOSEPH R.	73,157	SOSA, DAN	175	21,681 R	56.4%	43.5%	56.5%	43.5%
3	1992	182,217	54,569	BEMIS, F. GREGG	122,850	RICHARDSON, BILL	4,798	68,281 D	29.9%	67.4%	30.8%	69.2%

NEW MEXICO

1992 GENERAL ELECTION

President   Other vote was 1,615 Libertarian (Marrou); 620 Taxpayers (Phillips); 369 New Alliance (Fulani); 183 Socialist Workers (Warren); 181 Workers World (LaRiva); 120 Prohibition (Dodge); 562 scattered write-in.

Congress   Other vote was Cole (write-in) in CD 1; Pilley (write-in) in CD 2; Libertarian (Nagel) in CD 3.

1992 PRIMARIES

JUNE 2 REPUBLICAN

Congress   Unopposed in all three CD's.

JUNE 2 DEMOCRATIC

Congress   Unopposed in CD 3. Contested as follows:

CD   1   22,257 Robert J. Aragon; 14,903 James A Nance; 7,257 Alan Merson; 5,307 Stephen M. Petty; 291 Robert R. Sims (write-in).

CD   2   23,302 Dan Sosa; 15,736 Donald B. Wilson; 12,606 Patsy D. Reinard.

NEW YORK

GOVERNOR
Mario M. Cuomo (D). Re-elected 1990 to a four-year term. Previously elected 1986, 1982.

SENATORS
Alfonse M. D'Amato (R). Re-elected 1992 to a six-year term. Previously elected 1986, 1980.

Daniel P. Moynihan (D). Re-elected 1988 to a six-year term. Previously elected 1982, 1976.

REPRESENTATIVES

1. George J. Hochbrueckner (D)
2. Rick A. Lazio (R)
3. Peter T. King (R)
4. David A. Levy (R)
5. Gary L. Ackerman (D)
6. Floyd H. Flake (D)
7. Thomas J. Manton (D)
8. Jerrold Nadler (D)
9. Charles E. Schumer (D)
10. Edolphus Towns (D)
11. Major R. Owens (D)
12. Nydia M. Velazquez (D)
13. Susan Molinari (R)
14. Carolyn B. Maloney (D)
15. Charles B. Rangel (D)
16. Jose E. Serrano (D)
17. Eliot L. Engel (D)
18. Nita M. Lowey (D)
19. Hamilton Fish (R)
20. Benjamin A. Gilman (R)
21. Michael R. McNulty (D)
22. Gerald B. Solomon (R)
23. Sherwood L. Boehlert (R)
24. John M. McHugh (R)
25. James T. Walsh (R)
26. Maruice D. Hinchey (D)
27. L. William Paxon (R)
28. Louise M. Slaughter (D)
29. John J. LaFalce (D)
30. Jack Quinn (R)
31. Amory Houghton (R)

POSTWAR VOTE FOR PRESIDENT

| | | Republican | | Democratic | | | | Percentage | | | |
| | | | | | | | | Total Vote | | Major Vote | |
Year	Total Vote	Vote	Candidate	Vote	Candidate	Other Vote	Plurality	Rep.	Dem.	Rep.	Dem.
1992 **	6,926,925	2,346,649	Bush, George	3,444,450	Clinton, Bill	1,135,826	1,097,801 D	33.9%	49.7%	40.5%	59.5%
1988	6,485,683	3,081,871	Bush, George	3,347,882	Dukakis, Michael S.	55,930	266,011 D	47.5%	51.6%	47.9%	52.1%
1984	6,806,810	3,664,763	Reagan, Ronald	3,119,609	Mondale, Walter F.	22,438	545,154 R	53.8%	45.8%	54.0%	46.0%
1980	6,201,959	2,893,831	Reagan, Ronald	2,728,372	Carter, Jimmy	579,756	165,459 R	46.7%	44.0%	51.5%	48.5%
1976	6,534,170	3,100,791	Ford, Gerald R.	3,389,558	Carter, Jimmy	43,821	288,767 D	47.5%	51.9%	47.8%	52.2%
1972	7,165,919	4,192,778	Nixon, Richard M.	2,951,084	McGovern, George S.	22,057	1,241,694 R	58.5%	41.2%	58.7%	41.3%
1968	6,791,688	3,007,932	Nixon, Richard M.	3,378,470	Humphrey, Hubert H.	405,286	370,538 D	44.3%	49.7%	47.1%	52.9%
1964	7,166,275	2,243,559	Goldwater, Barry M.	4,913,102	Johnson, Lyndon B.	9,614	2,669,543 D	31.3%	68.6%	31.3%	68.7%
1960	7,291,079	3,446,419	Nixon, Richard M.	3,830,085	Kennedy, John F.	14,575	383,666 D	47.3%	52.5%	47.4%	52.6%
1956	7,095,971	4,345,506	Eisenhower, Dwight D.	2,747,944	Stevenson, Adlai E.	2,521	1,597,562 R	61.2%	38.7%	61.3%	38.7%
1952	7,128,239	3,952,813	Eisenhower, Dwight D.	3,104,601	Stevenson, Adlai E.	70,825	848,212 R	55.5%	43.6%	56.0%	44.0%
1948	6,177,337	2,841,163	Dewey, Thomas E.	2,780,204	Truman, Harry S.	555,970	60,959 R	46.0%	45.0%	50.5%	49.5%

In 1992 the other vote column includes 1,090,721 votes cast for Perot.

NEW YORK

POSTWAR VOTE FOR GOVERNOR

Year	Total Vote	Republican		Democratic		Other Vote	Rep.-Dem. Plurality	Percentage			
								Total Vote		Major Vote	
		Vote	Candidate	Vote	Candidate			Rep.	Dem.	Rep.	Dem.
1990 * *	4,056,896	865,948	Rinfret, Pierre A.	2,157,087	Cuomo, Mario M.	1,033,861	1,291,139 D	21.3%	53.2%	28.6%	71.4%
1986	4,294,124	1,363,810	O'Rourke, Andrew P.	2,775,229	Cuomo, Mario M.	155,085	1,411,419 D	31.8%	64.6%	32.9%	67.1%
1982	5,254,891	2,494,827	Lehrman, Lew	2,675,213	Cuomo, Mario M.	84,851	180,386 D	47.5%	50.9%	48.3%	51.7%
1978	4,768,820	2,156,404	Duryea, Perry B.	2,429,272	Carey, Hugh L.	183,144	272,868 D	45.2%	50.9%	47.0%	53.0%
1974	5,293,176	2,219,667	Wilson, Malcolm	3,028,503	Carey, Hugh L.	45,006	808,836 D	41.9%	57.2%	42.3%	57.7%
1970	6,013,064	3,151,432	Rockefeller, Nelson A.	2,421,426	Goldberg, Arthur	440,206	730,006 R	52.4%	40.3%	56.5%	43.5%
1966 * *	6,031,585	2,690,626	Rockefeller, Nelson A.	2,298,363	O'Connor, Frank D.	1,042,596	392,263 R	44.6%	38.1%	53.9%	46.1%
1962	5,805,631	3,081,587	Rockefeller, Nelson A.	2,552,418	Morgenthau, Robert M.	171,626	529,169 R	53.1%	44.0%	54.7%	45.3%
1958	5,712,665	3,126,929	Rockefeller, Nelson A.	2,553,895	Harriman, Averell	31,841	573,034 R	54.7%	44.7%	55.0%	45.0%
1954	5,161,942	2,549,613	Ives, Irving M.	2,560,738	Harriman, Averell	51,591	11,125 D	49.4%	49.6%	49.9%	50.1%
1950	5,308,889	2,819,523	Dewey, Thomas E.	2,246,855	Lynch, Walter A.	242,511	572,668 R	53.1%	42.3%	55.7%	44.3%
1946	4,964,552	2,825,633	Dewey, Thomas E.	2,138,482	Mead, James M.	437	687,151 R	56.9%	43.1%	56.9%	43.1%

In 1966 other vote was 510,023 Conservative (Adams); 507,234 Liberal (F. D. Roosevelt, Jr.); 12,730 Socialist Labor (Herder); 12,506 Socialist Workers (White) and 103 scattered. In 1990 other vote was 827,614 Conservative (London); 137,804 Right to Life (Wein); 31,089 New Alliance (Fulani); 24,611 Libertarian (Johnson) and 12,743 Socialist Workers (Gannon).

POSTWAR VOTE FOR SENATOR

Year	Total Vote	Republican		Democratic		Other Vote	Rep.-Dem. Plurality	Percentage			
								Total Vote		Major Vote	
		Vote	Candidate	Vote	Candidate			Rep.	Dem.	Rep.	Dem.
1992	6,458,826	3,166,994	D'Amato, Alfonse M.	3,086,200	Abrams, Robert	205,632	80,794 R	49.0%	47.8%	50.6%	49.4%
1988	6,040,980	1,875,784	McMillan, Robert	4,048,649	Moynihan, Daniel P.	116,547	2,172,865 D	31.1%	67.0%	31.7%	68.3%
1986	4,179,447	2,378,197	D'Amato, Alfonse M.	1,723,216	Green, Mark	78,034	654,981 R	56.9%	41.2%	58.0%	42.0%
1982	4,967,729	1,696,766	Sullivan, Florence M.	3,232,146	Moynihan, Daniel P.	38,817	1,535,380 D	34.2%	65.1%	34.4%	65.6%
1980	6,014,914	2,699,652	D'Amato, Alfonse M.	2,618,661	Holtzman, Elizabeth	696,601	80,991 R	44.9%	43.5%	50.8%	49.2%
1976	6,319,755	2,836,633	Buckley, James L.	3,422,594	Moynihan, Daniel P.	60,528	585,961 D	44.9%	54.2%	45.3%	54.7%
1974	5,163,600	2,340,188	Javits, Jacob K.	1,973,781	Clark, Ramsey	849,631	366,407 R	45.3%	38.2%	54.2%	45.8%
1970 * *	5,904,782	1,434,472	Goodell, Charles	2,171,232	Ottinger, Richard L.	2,299,078	736,760 D	24.3%	36.8%	39.8%	60.2%
1968 * *	6,581,587	3,269,772	Javits, Jacob K.	2,150,695	O'Dwyer, Paul	1,161,120	1,119,077 R	49.7%	32.7%	60.3%	39.7%
1964	7,151,686	3,104,056	Keating, Kenneth B.	3,823,749	Kennedy, Robert F.	223,881	719,693 D	43.4%	53.5%	44.8%	55.2%
1962	5,700,186	3,269,417	Javits, Jacob K.	2,289,341	Donovan, James B.	141,428	980,076 R	57.4%	40.2%	58.8%	41.2%
1958	5,602,088	2,842,942	Keating, Kenneth B.	2,709,950	Hogan, Frank S.	49,196	132,992 R	50.7%	48.4%	51.2%	48.8%
1956	6,991,136	3,723,933	Javits, Jacob K.	3,265,159	Wagner, Robert F.	2,044	458,774 R	53.3%	46.7%	53.3%	46.7%
1952	6,980,259	3,853,934	Ives, Irving M.	2,521,736	Cashmore, John	604,589	1,332,198 R	55.2%	36.1%	60.4%	39.6%
1950	5,228,403	2,367,353	Hanley, Joe R.	2,632,313	Lehman, Herbert H.	228,737	264,960 D	45.3%	50.3%	47.4%	52.6%
1949 S	4,966,878	2,384,381	Dulles, John Foster	2,582,438	Lehman, Herbert H.	59	198,057 D	48.0%	52.0%	48.0%	52.0%
1946	4,867,564	2,559,365	Ives, Irving M.	2,308,112	Lehman, Herbert H.	87	251,253 R	52.6%	47.4%	52.6%	47.4%

The 1949 election was for a short term to fill a vacancy. In 1968 other vote was 1,139,402 Conservative (Buckley); 8,775 Freedom and Peace (Ferguson); 7,964 Socialist Labor (Emanuel); 4,979 Socialist Workers (Garza). In 1970 James L. Buckley, the Conservative candidate, polled 2,288,190 votes (38.8% of the total vote) and won the election with a 116,958 plurality.

NEW YORK

Districts Established June 9, 1992

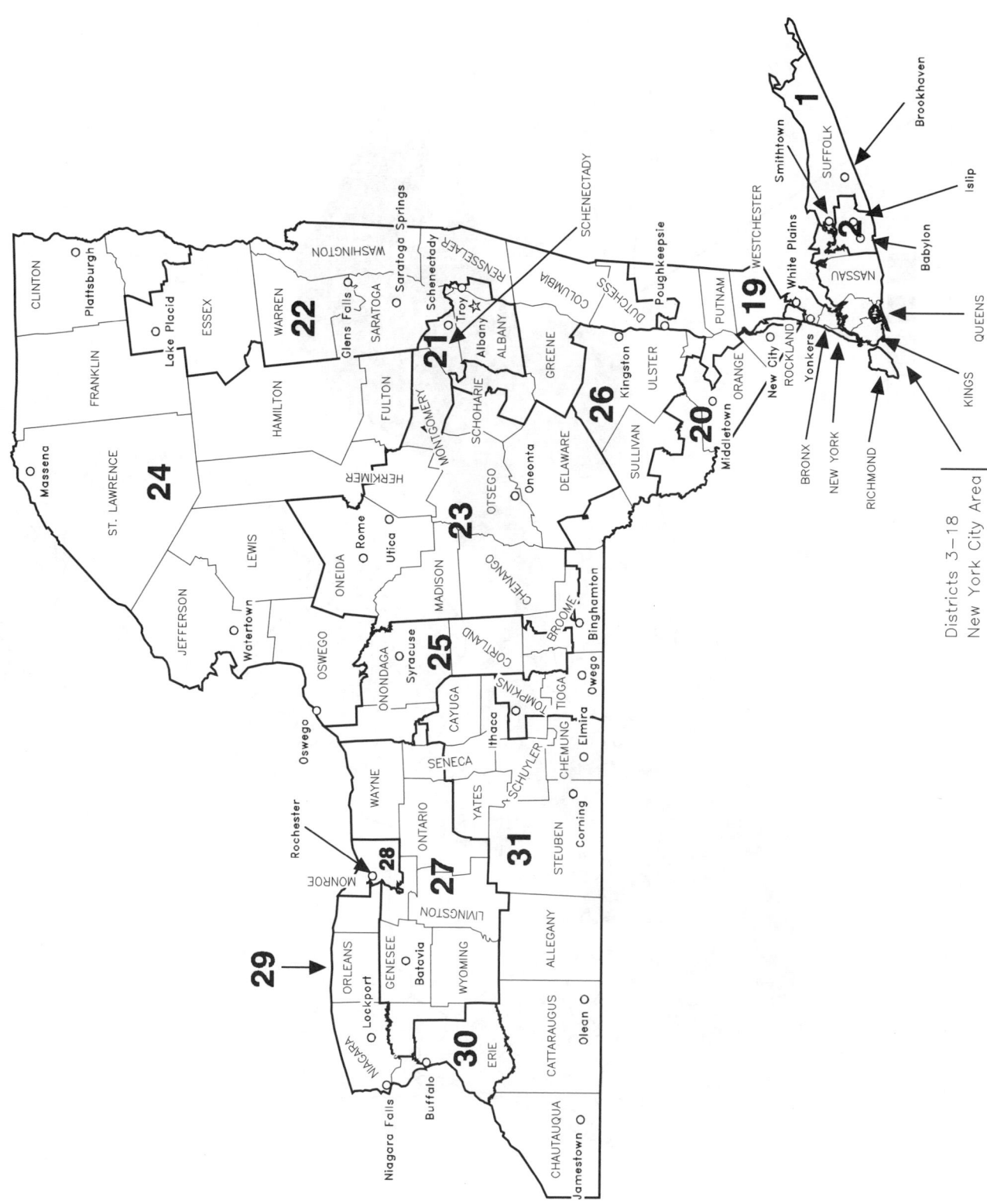

Districts 3–18
New York City Area

NEW YORK CITY AREA

CONGRESSIONAL DISTRICTS

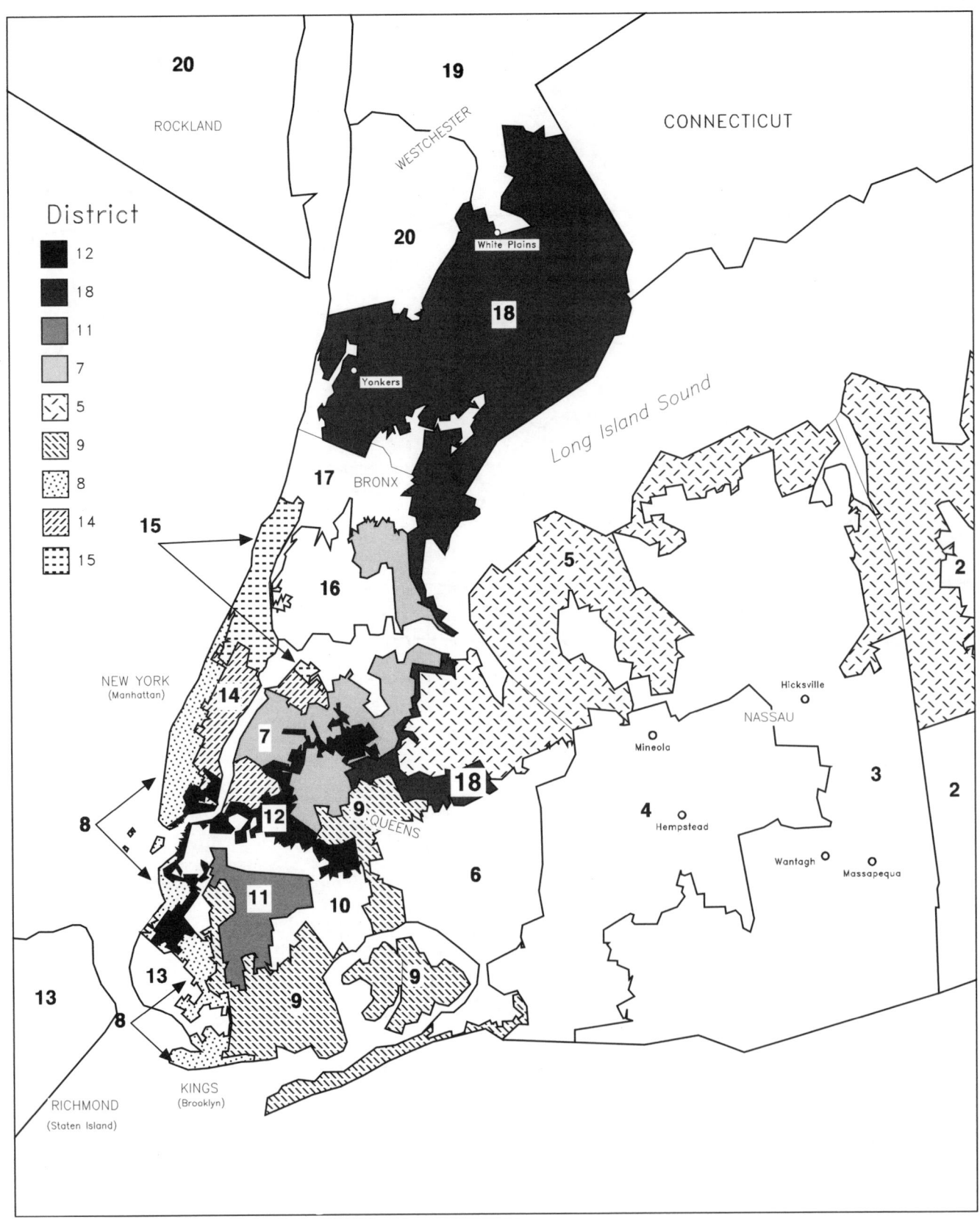

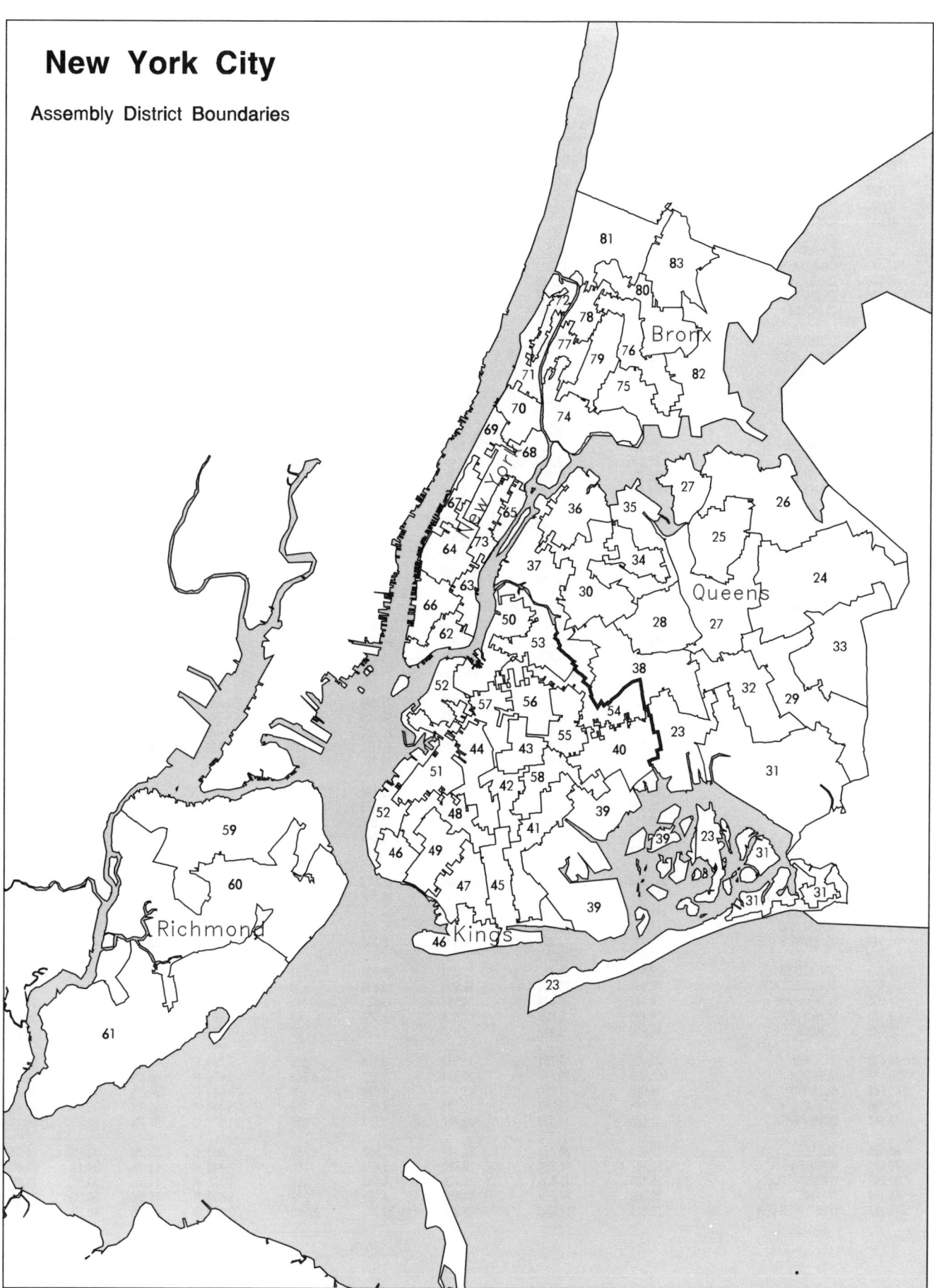

New York City

Assembly District Boundaries

NEW YORK

PRESIDENT 1992

Registration	County	Total Vote	Republican	Democratic	Perot	Other	Plurality	Percentage Total Vote Rep.	Dem.	Perot
192,816	ALBANY	155,357	49,452	80,641	24,064	1,200	31,189 D	31.8%	51.9%	15.5%
22,120	ALLEGANY	18,719	8,976	4,848	4,703	192	4,128 R	48.0%	25.9%	25.1%
521,102	BRONX	305,460	63,310	225,038	15,115	1,997	161,728 D	20.7%	73.7%	4.9%
115,123	BROOME	99,846	34,653	43,444	21,280	469	8,791 D	34.7%	43.5%	21.3%
41,851	CATTARAUGUS	35,092	13,944	10,150	10,662	336	3,282 R	39.7%	28.9%	30.4%
41,246	CAYUGA	35,671	12,065	13,088	10,279	239	1,023 D	33.8%	36.7%	28.8%
77,513	CHAUTAUQUA	62,785	21,222	22,645	18,455	463	1,423 D	33.8%	36.1%	29.4%
45,860	CHEMUNG	39,135	16,088	15,099	7,493	455	989 R	41.1%	38.6%	19.1%
25,410	CHENANGO	21,787	8,114	8,017	5,356	300	97 R	37.2%	36.8%	24.6%
39,363	CLINTON	31,987	13,455	12,881	5,389	262	574 R	42.1%	40.3%	16.8%
33,800	COLUMBIA	29,056	11,568	11,368	5,829	291	200 R	39.8%	39.1%	20.1%
24,429	CORTLAND	20,851	7,782	7,815	5,098	156	33 D	37.3%	37.5%	24.4%
23,313	DELAWARE	20,530	8,829	7,152	4,404	145	1,677 R	43.0%	34.8%	21.5%
137,918	DUTCHESS	115,328	46,709	41,655	26,320	644	5,054 R	40.5%	36.1%	22.8%
540,215	ERIE	451,496	129,444	196,233	123,358	2,461	66,789 D	28.7%	43.5%	27.3%
22,911	ESSEX	18,973	8,278	6,717	3,784	194	1,561 R	43.6%	35.4%	19.9%
23,403	FRANKLIN	18,365	6,635	7,654	3,857	219	1,019 D	36.1%	41.7%	21.0%
26,635	FULTON	22,845	9,137	8,400	5,120	188	737 R	40.0%	36.8%	22.4%
30,316	GENESEE	26,222	11,663	8,071	6,192	296	3,592 R	44.5%	30.8%	23.6%
25,042	GREENE	21,190	9,390	6,924	4,689	187	2,466 R	44.3%	32.7%	22.1%
4,569	HAMILTON	3,817	2,038	963	793	23	1,075 R	53.4%	25.2%	20.8%
35,710	HERKIMER	29,939	12,052	10,880	6,866	141	1,172 R	40.3%	36.3%	22.9%
45,696	JEFFERSON	37,426	14,227	13,380	9,461	358	847 R	38.0%	35.8%	25.3%
967,539	KINGS	581,594	133,344	411,183	33,014	4,053	277,839 D	22.9%	70.7%	5.7%
13,816	LEWIS	11,032	4,101	3,676	3,164	91	425 R	37.2%	33.3%	28.7%
30,531	LIVINGSTON	26,813	12,122	8,648	5,775	268	3,474 R	45.2%	32.3%	21.5%
33,730	MADISON	29,033	11,293	10,099	7,391	250	1,194 R	38.9%	34.8%	25.5%
386,876	MONROE	340,369	134,021	141,502	63,229	1,617	7,481 D	39.4%	41.6%	18.6%
27,458	MONTGOMERY	23,443	8,802	9,509	5,020	112	707 D	37.5%	40.6%	21.4%
760,028	NASSAU	609,326	246,881	282,593	77,097	2,755	35,712 D	40.5%	46.4%	12.7%
859,861	NEW YORK	531,753	84,501	416,142	27,689	3,421	331,641 D	15.9%	78.3%	5.2%
113,550	NIAGRA	96,584	30,401	35,649	30,126	408	5,248 D	31.5%	36.9%	31.2%
136,626	ONEIDA	108,342	43,806	40,966	22,717	853	2,840 R	40.4%	37.8%	21.0%
250,388	ONONDAGA	214,886	77,642	90,645	45,175	1,424	13,003 D	36.1%	42.2%	21.0%
51,775	ONTARIO	44,889	18,995	16,064	9,571	259	2,931 R	42.3%	35.8%	21.3%
149,018	ORANGE	122,520	53,493	45,946	22,499	582	7,547 R	43.7%	37.5%	18.4%
20,040	ORLEANS	16,749	7,468	4,927	4,275	79	2,541 R	44.6%	29.4%	25.5%
64,541	OSWEGO	50,931	18,530	16,990	14,853	558	1,540 R	36.4%	33.4%	29.2%
31,214	OTSEGO	26,606	10,141	10,471	5,841	153	330 D	38.1%	39.4%	22.0%
49,444	PUTNAM	41,263	18,934	14,048	8,011	270	4,886 R	45.9%	34.0%	19.4%
821,019	QUEENS	555,956	157,561	349,520	46,014	2,861	191,959 D	28.3%	62.9%	8.3%
87,283	RENSSELAER	74,579	28,937	29,793	15,198	651	856 D	38.8%	39.9%	20.4%
196,811	RICHMOND	147,760	70,707	56,901	19,678	474	13,806 R	47.9%	38.5%	13.3%
143,691	ROCKLAND	121,831	49,608	56,759	15,026	438	7,151 D	40.7%	46.6%	12.3%
51,511	ST. LAWRENCE	42,317	13,901	18,197	9,758	461	4,296 D	32.8%	43.0%	23.1%
110,227	SARATOGA	89,810	36,917	33,011	19,091	791	3,906 R	41.1%	36.8%	21.3%
89,553	SCHENECTADY	73,869	26,258	32,335	14,838	438	6,077 D	35.5%	43.8%	20.1%
17,065	SCHOHARIE	14,147	5,678	4,997	3,327	145	681 R	40.1%	35.3%	23.5%
9,125	SCHUYLER	8,199	3,226	2,859	2,051	63	367 R	39.3%	34.9%	25.0%
17,039	SENECA	14,974	5,432	5,810	3,660	72	378 D	36.3%	38.8%	24.4%
48,498	STEUBEN	41,408	19,761	12,043	9,378	226	7,718 R	47.7%	29.1%	22.6%
730,094	SUFFOLK	567,953	229,467	220,811	112,973	4,702	8,656 R	40.4%	38.9%	19.9%
40,968	SULLIVAN	31,635	11,396	13,717	6,336	186	2,321 D	36.0%	43.4%	20.0%
26,790	TIOGA	23,065	9,287	7,791	5,867	120	1,496 R	40.3%	33.8%	25.4%
47,557	TOMPKINS	41,658	11,520	23,197	6,704	237	11,677 D	27.7%	55.7%	16.1%
93,435	ULSTER	80,821	29,223	32,886	17,952	760	3,663 D	36.2%	40.7%	22.2%
33,621	WARREN	28,767	12,260	9,820	6,401	286	2,440 R	42.6%	34.1%	22.3%
30,299	WASHINGTON	25,135	10,305	8,429	6,143	258	1,876 R	41.0%	33.5%	24.4%
45,494	WAYNE	39,306	18,019	11,866	9,188	233	6,153 R	45.8%	30.2%	23.4%
479,127	WESTCHESTER	378,815	151,990	184,300	39,933	2,592	32,310 D	40.1%	48.7%	10.5%

NEW YORK

PRESIDENT 1992

Registration	County	Total Vote	Republican	Democratic	Perot	Other	Plurality	Percentage Total Vote		
								Rep.	Dem.	Perot
19,391	WYOMING	16,374	7,324	4,045	4,837	168	2,487 R	44.7%	24.7%	29.5%
11,997	YATES	10,092	4,366	3,242	2,354	130	1,124 R	43.3%	32.1%	23.3%
9,193,391	TOTAL	6,926,925	2,346,649	3,444,450	1,090,721	45,105	1,097,801 D	33.9%	49.7%	15.7%

NEW YORK

SENATOR 1992

Registration	County	Total Vote	Republican	Democratic	Other	Rep.-Dem. Plurality	Total Vote Rep.	Total Vote Dem.	Major Vote Rep.	Major Vote Dem.
192,816	ALBANY	147,922	64,073	78,275	5,574	14,202 D	43.3%	52.9%	45.0%	55.0%
22,120	ALLEGANY	17,177	10,229	6,005	943	4,224 R	59.6%	35.0%	63.0%	37.0%
521,102	BRONX	276,922	87,215	184,619	5,088	97,404 D	31.5%	66.7%	32.1%	67.9%
115,123	BROOME	92,888	51,049	39,163	2,676	11,886 R	55.0%	42.2%	56.6%	43.4%
41,851	CATTARAUGUS	32,094	17,011	12,641	2,442	4,370 R	53.0%	39.4%	57.4%	42.6%
41,246	CAYUGA	31,909	17,743	12,066	2,100	5,677 R	55.6%	37.8%	59.5%	40.5%
77,513	CHAUTAUQUA	57,346	28,465	25,596	3,285	2,869 R	49.6%	44.6%	52.7%	47.3%
45,860	CHEMUNG	36,450	23,243	12,092	1,115	11,151 R	63.8%	33.2%	65.8%	34.2%
25,410	CHENANGO	19,870	11,553	7,172	1,145	4,381 R	58.1%	36.1%	61.7%	38.3%
39,363	CLINTON	29,172	16,066	11,824	1,282	4,242 R	55.1%	40.5%	57.6%	42.4%
33,800	COLUMBIA	27,183	15,042	10,925	1,216	4,117 R	55.3%	40.2%	57.9%	42.1%
24,429	CORTLAND	19,018	10,938	7,043	1,037	3,895 R	57.5%	37.0%	60.8%	39.2%
23,313	DELAWARE	18,707	10,590	7,367	750	3,223 R	56.6%	39.4%	59.0%	41.0%
137,918	DUTCHESS	108,648	61,406	43,477	3,765	17,929 R	56.5%	40.0%	58.5%	41.5%
540,215	ERIE	409,036	186,314	200,284	22,438	13,970 D	45.5%	49.0%	48.2%	51.8%
22,911	ESSEX	16,748	9,283	6,637	828	2,646 R	55.4%	39.6%	58.3%	41.7%
23,403	FRANKLIN	16,518	8,791	6,949	778	1,842 R	53.2%	42.1%	55.9%	44.1%
26,635	FULTON	21,330	12,328	8,115	887	4,213 R	57.8%	38.0%	60.3%	39.7%
30,316	GENESEE	23,747	13,715	8,830	1,202	4,885 R	57.8%	37.2%	60.8%	39.2%
25,042	GREENE	19,945	12,222	6,827	896	5,395 R	61.3%	34.2%	64.2%	35.8%
4,569	HAMILTON	3,495	2,206	1,149	140	1,057 R	63.1%	32.9%	65.8%	34.2%
35,710	HERKIMER	26,874	15,849	9,917	1,108	5,932 R	59.0%	36.9%	61.5%	38.5%
45,696	JEFFERSON	34,300	20,199	12,196	1,905	8,003 R	58.9%	35.6%	62.4%	37.6%
967,539	KINGS	536,460	210,643	315,709	10,108	105,066 D	39.3%	58.9%	40.0%	60.0%
13,816	LEWIS	10,106	5,990	3,573	543	2,417 R	59.3%	35.4%	62.6%	37.4%
30,531	LIVINGSTON	23,926	13,813	8,976	1,137	4,837 R	57.7%	37.5%	60.6%	39.4%
33,730	MADISON	26,204	14,596	9,882	1,726	4,714 R	55.7%	37.7%	59.6%	40.4%
386,876	MONROE	309,744	158,382	139,163	12,199	19,219 R	51.1%	44.9%	53.2%	46.8%
27,458	MONTGOMERY	21,646	11,634	9,255	757	2,379 R	53.7%	42.8%	55.7%	44.3%
760,028	NASSAU	586,959	337,715	237,692	11,552	100,023 R	57.5%	40.5%	58.7%	41.3%
859,861	NEW YORK	501,926	110,023	382,877	9,026	272,854 D	21.9%	76.3%	22.3%	77.7%
113,550	NIAGARA	87,512	42,386	40,232	4,894	2,154 R	48.4%	46.0%	51.3%	48.7%
136,626	ONEIDA	99,961	58,671	37,411	3,879	21,260 R	58.7%	37.4%	61.1%	38.9%
250,388	ONONDAGA	198,537	106,654	79,954	11,929	26,700 R	53.7%	40.3%	57.2%	42.8%
51,775	ONTARIO	40,715	22,605	16,167	1,943	6,438 R	55.5%	39.7%	58.3%	41.7%
149,018	ORANGE	113,765	67,921	42,568	3,276	25,353 R	59.7%	37.4%	61.5%	38.5%
20,040	ORLEANS	14,798	8,716	5,298	784	3,418 R	58.9%	35.8%	62.2%	37.8%
64,541	OSWEGO	46,375	26,242	16,310	3,823	9,932 R	56.6%	35.2%	61.7%	38.3%
31,214	OTSEGO	24,418	12,576	10,766	1,076	1,810 R	51.5%	44.1%	53.9%	46.1%
49,444	PUTNAM	39,303	24,616	13,560	1,127	11,056 R	62.6%	34.5%	64.5%	35.5%
821,019	QUEENS	523,149	238,407	275,737	9,005	37,330 D	45.6%	52.7%	46.4%	53.6%
87,283	RENSSELAER	70,603	37,288	30,104	3,211	7,184 R	52.8%	42.6%	55.3%	44.7%
196,811	RICHMOND	140,780	94,825	43,783	2,172	51,042 R	67.4%	31.1%	68.4%	31.6%
143,691	ROCKLAND	116,287	67,829	46,265	2,193	21,564 R	58.3%	39.8%	59.5%	40.5%
51,511	ST. LAWRENCE	38,085	18,916	16,786	2,383	2,130 R	49.7%	44.1%	53.0%	47.0%
110,227	SARATOGA	84,041	46,375	33,988	3,678	12,387 R	55.2%	40.4%	57.7%	42.3%
89,553	SCHENECTADY	69,500	34,790	31,840	2,870	2,950 R	50.1%	45.8%	52.2%	47.8%
17,065	SCHOHARIE	13,358	7,590	5,132	636	2,458 R	56.8%	38.4%	59.7%	40.3%
9,125	SCHUYLER	7,382	4,433	2,596	353	1,837 R	60.1%	35.2%	63.1%	36.9%
17,039	SENECA	13,496	8,067	4,791	638	3,276 R	59.8%	35.5%	62.7%	37.3%
48,498	STEUBEN	37,532	24,350	11,472	1,710	12,878 R	64.9%	30.6%	68.0%	32.0%
730,094	SUFFOLK	541,191	313,515	212,688	14,988	100,827 R	57.9%	39.3%	59.6%	40.4%
40,968	SULLIVAN	29,464	15,665	12,886	913	2,779 R	53.2%	43.7%	54.9%	45.1%
26,790	TIOGA	21,021	12,492	7,689	840	4,803 R	59.4%	36.6%	61.9%	38.1%
47,557	TOMPKINS	37,852	14,536	22,094	1,222	7,558 D	38.4%	58.4%	39.7%	60.3%
93,435	ULSTER	74,835	39,830	31,912	3,093	7,918 R	53.2%	42.6%	55.5%	44.5%
33,621	WARREN	26,337	14,453	10,755	1,129	3,698 R	54.9%	40.8%	57.3%	42.7%
30,299	WASHINGTON	22,933	12,959	8,815	1,159	4,144 R	56.5%	38.4%	59.5%	40.5%
45,494	WAYNE	35,280	21,044	12,392	1,844	8,652 R	59.6%	35.1%	62.9%	37.1%
479,127	WESTCHESTER	362,127	186,675	167,719	7,733	18,956 R	51.5%	46.3%	52.7%	47.3%

NEW YORK

SENATOR 1992

Registration	County	Total Vote	Republican	Democratic	Other	Rep.-Dem. Plurality	Percentage			
							Total Vote		Major Vote	
							Rep.	Dem.	Rep.	Dem.
19,391	WYOMING	14,759	8,870	4,962	927	3,908 R	60.1%	33.6%	64.1%	35.9%
11,997	YATES	9,160	5,372	3,232	556	2,140 R	58.6%	35.3%	62.4%	37.6%
9,193,391	TOTAL	6,458,826	3,166,994	3,086,200	205,632	80,794 R	49.0%	47.8%	50.6%	49.4%

NEW YORK CITY

BRONX COUNTY
PRESIDENT 1992

Registration	Assembly District	Total Vote	Republican	Democratic	Perot	Other	Plurality	Percentage Total Vote Rep.	Dem.	Perot
55,332	DISTRICT 74	26,781	4,014	21,830	762	175	17,816 D	15.0%	81.5%	2.8%
48,670	DISTRICT 75	26,239	3,859	21,356	863	161	17,497 D	14.7%	81.4%	3.3%
51,427	DISTRICT 76	29,272	5,721	22,068	1,286	197	16,347 D	19.5%	75.4%	4.4%
46,408	DISTRICT 77	23,432	2,531	20,044	627	230	17,513 D	10.8%	85.5%	2.7%
41,109	DISTRICT 78	20,929	3,352	16,687	757	133	13,335 D	16.0%	79.7%	3.6%
54,952	DISTRICT 79	27,235	3,647	22,614	766	208	18,967 D	13.4%	83.0%	2.8%
51,986	DISTRICT 80	35,077	10,668	21,725	2,525	159	11,057 D	30.4%	61.9%	7.2%
57,768	DISTRICT 81	41,020	10,481	27,741	2,606	192	17,260 D	25.6%	67.6%	6.4%
63,712	DISTRICT 82	44,478	14,532	25,971	3,733	242	11,439 D	32.7%	58.4%	8.4%
49,386	DISTRICT 83	30,997	4,505	25,002	1190	300	20,497 D	14.5%	80.7%	3.8%
520,750	TOTAL	305,460	63,310	225,038	15,115	1,997	161,728 D	20.7%	73.7%	4.9%

NEW YORK CITY

KINGS COUNTY
PRESIDENT 1992

Registration	Assembly District	Total Vote	Republican	Democratic	Perot	Other	Plurality	Percentage Total Vote Rep.	Dem.	Perot
58,973	DISTRICT 39	42,018	14,377	23,873	3,637	131	9,496 D	34.2%	56.8%	8.7%
49,328	DISTRICT 40	25,115	1,916	22,230	709	260	20,314 D	7.6%	88.5%	2.8%
53,075	DISTRICT 41	37,384	8,288	26,765	2,190	141	18,477 D	22.2%	71.6%	5.9%
31,542	DISTRICT 42	18,515	1,881	15,881	584	169	14,000 D	10.2%	85.8%	3.2%
38,804	DISTRICT 43	22,081	1,290	19,897	613	281	18,607 D	5.8%	90.1%	2.8%
54,432	DISTRICT 44	38,456	8,115	27,707	2,385	249	19,592 D	21.1%	72.0%	6.2%
49,658	DISTRICT 45	34,545	9,716	22,328	2,393	108	12,612 D	28.1%	64.6%	6.9%
49,773	DISTRICT 46	32,319	9,004	20,980	2,201	134	11,976 D	27.9%	64.9%	6.8%
44,385	DISTRICT 47	30,364	11,563	16,082	2,637	82	4,519 D	38.1%	53.0%	8.7%
41,227	DISTRICT 48	28,118	10,590	15,573	1,888	67	4,983 D	37.7%	55.4%	6.7%
42,966	DISTRICT 49	29,743	13,068	13,954	2,617	104	886 D	43.9%	46.9%	8.8%
44,961	DISTRICT 50	26,108	8,566	15,839	1,526	177	7,273 D	32.8%	60.7%	5.8%
45,949	DISTRICT 51	24,405	6,075	16,750	1,433	147	10,675 D	24.9%	68.6%	5.9%
66,228	DISTRICT 52	46,450	13,729	28,692	3,778	251	14,963 D	29.6%	61.8%	8.1%
47,752	DISTRICT 53	20,997	4,826	15,166	910	95	10,340 D	23.0%	72.2%	4.3%
46,140	DISTRICT 54	20,050	4,073	15,100	767	110	11,027 D	20.3%	75.3%	3.8%
53,214	DISTRICT 55	25,448	1,388	23,199	552	309	21,811 D	5.5%	91.2%	2.2%
57,368	DISTRICT 56	27,549	1,324	25,154	675	396	23,830 D	4.8%	91.3%	2.5%
53,477	DISTRICT 57	29,813	1,681	26,576	919	637	24,895 D	5.6%	89.1%	3.1%
37,822	DISTRICT 58	22,116	1,874	19,437	600	205	17,563 D	8.5%	87.9%	2.7%
967,074	TOTAL	581,594	133,344	411,183	33,014	4,053	277,839 D	22.9%	70.7%	5.7%

NEW YORK CITY

NEW YORK COUNTY
PRESIDENT 1992

Registration	Assembly District	Total Vote	Republican	Democratic	Perot	Other	Plurality	Percentage Total Vote		
								Rep.	Dem.	Perot
51,498	DISTRICT 62	30,258	7,391	21,097	1,598	172	13,706 D	24.4%	69.7%	5.3%
77,581	DISTRICT 63	50,027	9,117	37,835	2,789	286	28,718 D	18.2%	75.6%	5.6%
78,637	DISTRICT 64	51,056	7,916	39,534	3,318	288	31,618 D	15.5%	77.4%	6.5%
75,689	DISTRICT 65	54,970	12,669	38,010	4,065	226	25,341 D	23.0%	69.1%	7.4%
87,462	DISTRICT 66	60,075	6,119	50,477	3,085	394	44,358 D	10.2%	84.0%	5.1%
85,648	DISTRICT 67	60,632	7,814	49,172	3,313	333	41,358 D	12.9%	81.1%	5.5%
75,559	DISTRICT 68	34,740	4,395	28,971	1,082	292	24,576 D	12.7%	83.4%	3.1%
79,160	DISTRICT 69	49,571	4,658	42,460	2,071	382	37,802 D	9.4%	85.7%	4.2%
72,403	DISTRICT 70	32,813	1,707	29,868	802	436	28,161 D	5.2%	91.0%	2.4%
58,928	DISTRICT 71	33,470	4,056	27,891	1,224	299	23,835 D	12.1%	83.3%	3.7%
35,673	DISTRICT 72	19,512	3,746	14,918	742	106	11,172 D	19.2%	76.5%	3.8%
78,307	DISTRICT 73	54,629	14,913	35,909	3600	207	20,996 D	27.3%	65.7%	6.6%
856,545	TOTAL	531,753	84,501	416,142	27,689	3,421	331,641 D	15.9%	78.3%	5.2%

NEW YORK CITY

QUEENS COUNTY
PRESIDENT 1992

Registration	Assembly District	Total Vote	Republican	Democratic	Perot	Other	Plurality	Percentage Total Vote		
								Rep.	Dem.	Perot
59,262	DISTRICT 23	41,024	16,111	20,453	4,345	115	4,342 D	39.3%	49.9%	10.6%
66,294	DISTRICT 24	49,792	14,827	30,453	4,368	144	15,626 D	29.8%	61.2%	8.8%
39,551	DISTRICT 25	27,014	9,147	15,143	2,606	118	5,996 D	33.9%	56.1%	9.6%
65,849	DISTRICT 26	50,160	17,326	27,570	5,151	113	10,244 D	34.5%	55.0%	10.3%
55,875	DISTRICT 27	40,597	10,350	26,506	3,571	170	16,156 D	25.5%	65.3%	8.8%
62,226	DISTRICT 28	45,959	13,013	29,380	3,412	154	16,367 D	28.3%	63.9%	7.4%
52,178	DISTRICT 29	31,999	4,007	26,171	1,502	319	22,164 D	12.5%	81.8%	4.7%
49,208	DISTRICT 30	34,387	13,582	17,137	3,565	103	3,555 D	39.5%	49.8%	10.4%
49,775	DISTRICT 31	28,552	3,808	23,111	1,341	292	19,303 D	13.3%	80.9%	4.7%
52,263	DISTRICT 32	31,021	3,607	25,733	1,313	368	22,126 D	11.6%	83.0%	4.2%
60,153	DISTRICT 33	39,428	6,582	30,271	2,200	375	23,689 D	16.7%	76.8%	5.6%
30,653	DISTRICT 34	19,684	6,262	11,936	1,414	72	5,674 D	31.8%	60.6%	7.2%
35,061	DISTRICT 35	21,974	4,836	15,765	1,217	156	10,929 D	22.0%	71.7%	5.5%
48,197	DISTRICT 36	32,518	9,874	19,404	3,115	125	9,530 D	30.4%	59.7%	9.6%
41,295	DISTRICT 37	25,346	7,552	15,485	2,181	128	7,933 D	29.8%	61.1%	8.6%
51,891	DISTRICT 38	36,501	16,677	15,002	4,713	109	1,675 R	45.7%	41.1%	12.9%
819,731	TOTAL	555,956	157,561	349,520	46,014	2,861	191,959 D	28.3%	62.9%	8.3%

NEW YORK CITY

RICHMOND COUNTY
PRESIDENT 1992

Registration	Assembly District	Total Vote	Republican	Democratic	Perot	Other	Plurality	Percentage Total Vote		
								Rep.	Dem.	Perot
63,078	DISTRICT 59	44,736	17,688	21,347	5,468	233	3,659 D	39.5%	47.7%	12.2%
64,222	DISTRICT 60	49,091	22,961	19,701	6,289	140	3,260 R	46.8%	40.1%	12.8%
69,127	DISTRICT 61	53,933	30,058	15,853	7,921	101	14,205 R	55.7%	29.4%	14.7%
196,427	TOTAL	147,760	70,707	56,901	19,678	474	13,806 R	47.9%	38.5%	13.3%

NEW YORK CITY

PRESIDENT 1992

Registration	County	Total Vote	Republican	Democratic	Perot	Other	Plurality	Percentage Total Vote		
								Rep.	Dem.	Perot
520,750	BRONX	305,460	63,310	225,038	15,115	1,997	161,728 D	20.7%	73.7%	4.9%
967,074	KINGS	581,594	133,344	411,183	33,014	4,053	277,839 D	22.9%	70.7%	5.7%
856,545	NEW YORK	531,753	84,501	416,142	27,689	3,421	331,641 D	15.9%	78.3%	5.2%
819,731	QUEENS	555,956	157,561	349,520	46,014	2,861	191,959 D	28.3%	62.9%	8.3%
196,427	RICHMOND	147,760	70,707	56,901	19,678	474	13,806 R	47.9%	38.5%	13.3%
3,360,527	TOTAL	2,122,523	509,423	1,458,784	141,510	12,806	949,361 D	24.0%	68.7%	6.7%

NEW YORK CITY

BRONX COUNTY
SENATOR 1992

Registration	Assembly District	Total Vote	Republican	Democratic	Other	Rep.-Dem. Plurality	Percentage Total Vote Rep.	Dem.	Major Vote Rep.	Dem.
55,332	DISTRICT 74	22,313	4,147	17,743	423	13,596 D	18.6%	79.5%	18.9%	81.1%
48,670	DISTRICT 75	22,559	4,436	17,669	454	13,233 D	19.7%	78.3%	20.1%	79.9%
51,427	DISTRICT 76	26,508	7,232	18,786	490	11,554 D	27.3%	70.9%	27.8%	72.2%
46,408	DISTRICT 77	20,411	3,366	16,545	500	13,179 D	16.5%	81.1%	16.9%	83.1%
41,109	DISTRICT 78	18,255	4,005	13,885	365	9,880 D	21.9%	76.1%	22.4%	77.6%
54,952	DISTRICT 79	23,500	4,595	18,441	464	13,846 D	19.6%	78.5%	19.9%	80.1%
51,986	DISTRICT 80	33,290	16,094	16,775	421	681 D	48.3%	50.4%	49.0%	51.0%
57,768	DISTRICT 81	39,249	15,441	23,220	588	7,779 D	39.3%	59.2%	39.9%	60.1%
63,712	DISTRICT 82	42,168	21,102	20,374	692	728 R	50.0%	48.3%	50.9%	49.1%
49,386	DISTRICT 83	28,669	6,797	21,181	691	14,384 D	23.7%	73.9%	24.3%	75.7%
520,750	TOTAL	276,922	87,215	184,619	5,088	97,404 D	31.5%	66.7%	32.1%	67.9%

NEW YORK CITY

KINGS COUNTY
SENATOR 1992

Registration	Assembly District	Total Vote	Republican	Democratic	Other	Rep.-Dem. Plurality	Percentage Total Vote Rep.	Dem.	Major Vote Rep.	Dem.
58,973	DISTRICT 39	40,601	23,522	16,670	409	6,852 R	57.9%	41.1%	58.5%	41.5%
49,328	DISTRICT 40	22,174	3,317	18,215	642	14,898 D	15.0%	82.1%	15.4%	84.6%
53,075	DISTRICT 41	35,654	15,397	19,772	485	4,375 D	43.2%	55.5%	43.8%	56.2%
31,542	DISTRICT 42	16,789	3,673	12,694	422	9,021 D	21.9%	75.6%	22.4%	77.6%
38,804	DISTRICT 43	19,916	3,838	15,483	595	11,645 D	19.3%	77.7%	19.9%	80.1%
54,432	DISTRICT 44	36,815	12,628	23,526	661	10,898 D	34.3%	63.9%	34.9%	65.1%
49,658	DISTRICT 45	33,512	18,209	14,989	314	3,220 R	54.3%	44.7%	54.8%	45.2%
49,773	DISTRICT 46	30,112	13,573	16,124	415	2,551 D	45.1%	53.5%	45.7%	54.3%
44,385	DISTRICT 47	29,441	18,226	10,933	282	7,293 R	61.9%	37.1%	62.5%	37.5%
41,227	DISTRICT 48	26,719	19,340	7,160	219	12,180 R	72.4%	26.8%	73.0%	27.0%
42,966	DISTRICT 49	27,666	20,062	7,342	262	12,720 R	72.5%	26.5%	73.2%	26.8%
44,961	DISTRICT 50	23,852	11,003	12,390	459	1,387 D	46.1%	51.9%	47.0%	53.0%
45,949	DISTRICT 51	21,556	7,460	13,689	407	6,229 D	34.6%	63.5%	35.3%	64.7%
66,228	DISTRICT 52	44,540	18,144	25,560	836	7,416 D	40.7%	57.4%	41.5%	58.5%
47,752	DISTRICT 53	17,387	5,432	11,675	280	6,243 D	31.2%	67.1%	31.8%	68.2%
46,140	DISTRICT 54	16,886	4,661	11,787	438	7,126 D	27.6%	69.8%	28.3%	71.7%
53,214	DISTRICT 55	21,833	2,611	18,635	587	16,024 D	12.0%	85.4%	12.3%	87.7%
57,368	DISTRICT 56	23,899	2,792	20,278	829	17,486 D	11.7%	84.8%	12.1%	87.9%
53,477	DISTRICT 57	26,623	3,269	22,287	1,067	19,018 D	12.3%	83.7%	12.8%	87.2%
37,822	DISTRICT 58	20,485	3,486	16,500	499	13,014 D	17.0%	80.5%	17.4%	82.6%
967,074	TOTAL	536,460	210,643	315,709	10,108	105,066 D	39.3%	58.9%	40.0%	60.0%

NEW YORK CITY

NEW YORK COUNTY
SENATOR 1992

Registration	Assembly District	Total Vote	Republican	Democratic	Other	Rep.-Dem. Plurality	Percentage			
							Total Vote		Major Vote	
							Rep.	Dem.	Rep.	Dem.
51,498	DISTRICT 62	27,958	9,542	17,979	437	8,437 D	34.1%	64.3%	34.7%	65.3%
77,581	DISTRICT 63	47,425	11,531	35,063	831	23,532 D	24.3%	73.9%	24.7%	75.3%
78,637	DISTRICT 64	48,936	10,420	37,640	876	27,220 D	21.3%	76.9%	21.7%	78.3%
75,689	DISTRICT 65	53,056	15,685	36,603	768	20,918 D	29.6%	69.0%	30.0%	70.0%
87,462	DISTRICT 66	58,170	8,604	48,591	975	39,987 D	14.8%	83.5%	15.0%	85.0%
85,648	DISTRICT 67	58,540	10,957	46,679	904	35,722 D	18.7%	79.7%	19.0%	81.0%
75,559	DISTRICT 68	30,910	5,443	24,755	712	19,312 D	17.6%	80.1%	18.0%	82.0%
79,160	DISTRICT 69	46,947	6,598	39,425	924	32,827 D	14.1%	84.0%	14.3%	85.7%
72,403	DISTRICT 70	29,320	3,154	25,230	936	22,076 D	10.8%	86.1%	11.1%	88.9%
58,928	DISTRICT 71	30,776	6,523	23,509	744	16,986 D	21.2%	76.4%	21.7%	78.3%
35,673	DISTRICT 72	17,362	4,912	12,148	302	7,236 D	28.3%	70.0%	28.8%	71.2%
78,307	DISTRICT 73	52,526	16,654	35,255	617	18,601 D	31.7%	67.1%	32.1%	67.9%
856,545	TOTAL	501,926	110,023	382,877	9,026	272,854 D	21.9%	76.3%	22.3%	77.7%

NEW YORK CITY

QUEENS COUNTY
SENATOR 1992

Registration	Assembly District	Total Vote	Republican	Democratic	Other	Rep.-Dem. Plurality	Percentage			
							Total Vote		Major Vote	
							Rep.	Dem.	Rep.	Dem.
59,262	DISTRICT 23	39,355	24,507	14,378	470	10,129 R	62.3%	36.5%	63.0%	37.0%
66,294	DISTRICT 24	48,231	23,171	24,469	591	1,298 D	48.0%	50.7%	48.6%	51.4%
39,551	DISTRICT 25	25,148	12,364	12,367	417	3 D	49.2%	49.2%	50.0%	50.0%
65,849	DISTRICT 26	48,323	25,841	21,926	556	3,915 R	53.5%	45.4%	54.1%	45.9%
55,875	DISTRICT 27	38,792	18,669	19,557	566	888 D	48.1%	50.4%	48.8%	51.2%
62,226	DISTRICT 28	44,383	20,406	23,450	527	3,044 D	46.0%	52.8%	46.5%	53.5%
52,178	DISTRICT 29	29,425	6,849	21,805	771	14,956 D	23.3%	74.1%	23.9%	76.1%
49,208	DISTRICT 30	32,405	18,740	13,179	486	5,561 R	57.8%	40.7%	58.7%	41.3%
49,775	DISTRICT 31	25,571	6,620	18,262	689	11,642 D	25.9%	71.4%	26.6%	73.4%
52,263	DISTRICT 32	28,081	6,365	20,933	783	14,568 D	22.7%	74.5%	23.3%	76.7%
60,153	DISTRICT 33	36,440	10,556	24,994	890	14,438 D	29.0%	68.6%	29.7%	70.3%
30,653	DISTRICT 34	18,097	8,365	9,406	326	1,041 D	46.2%	52.0%	47.1%	52.9%
35,061	DISTRICT 35	20,307	6,449	13,374	484	6,925 D	31.8%	65.9%	32.5%	67.5%
48,197	DISTRICT 36	30,415	15,455	14,472	488	983 R	50.8%	47.6%	51.6%	48.4%
41,295	DISTRICT 37	23,587	10,796	12,341	450	1,545 D	45.8%	52.3%	46.7%	53.3%
51,891	DISTRICT 38	34,589	23,254	10,824	511	12,430 R	67.2%	31.3%	68.2%	31.8%
819,731	TOTAL	523,149	238,407	275,737	9,005	37,330 D	45.6%	52.7%	46.4%	53.6%

NEW YORK CITY

RICHMOND COUNTY
SENATOR 1992

| | | | | | | | | Percentage | | | |
| | | | | | | | | Total Vote | | Major Vote | |
Registration	Assembly District	Total Vote	Republican	Democratic	Other	Rep.-Dem. Plurality		Rep.	Dem.	Rep.	Dem.
63,078	DISTRICT 59	42,222	24,107	17,285	830	6,822	R	57.1%	40.9%	58.2%	41.8%
64,222	DISTRICT 60	46,910	31,761	14,457	692	17,304	R	67.7%	30.8%	68.7%	31.3%
69,127	DISTRICT 61	51,648	38,957	12,041	650	26,916	R	75.4%	23.3%	76.4%	23.6%
196,427	TOTAL	140,780	94,825	43,783	2,172	51,042	R	67.4%	31.1%	68.4%	31.6%

NEW YORK CITY

SENATOR 1992

| | | | | | | | | Percentage | | | |
| | | | | | | | | Total Vote | | Major Vote | |
Registration	County	Total Vote	Republican	Democratic	Other	Rep.-Dem. Plurality		Rep.	Dem.	Rep.	Dem.
520,750	BRONX	276,922	87,215	184,619	5,088	97,404	D	31.5%	66.7%	32.1%	67.9%
967,074	KINGS	536,460	210,643	315,709	10,108	105,066	D	39.3%	58.9%	40.0%	60.0%
856,545	NEW YORK	501,926	110,023	382,877	9,026	272,854	D	21.9%	76.3%	22.3%	77.7%
819,731	QUEENS	523,149	238,407	275,737	9,005	37,330	D	45.6%	52.7%	46.4%	53.6%
196,427	RICHMOND	140,780	94,825	43,783	2,172	51,042	R	67.4%	31.1%	68.4%	31.6%
3,360,527	TOTAL	1,979,237	741,113	1,202,725	35,399	461,612	D	37.4%	60.8%	38.1%	61.9%

NEW YORK

CONGRESS

CD	Year	Total Vote	Republican Vote	Republican Candidate	Democratic Vote	Democratic Candidate	Other Vote	Rep.-Dem. Plurality	Total Vote Rep.	Total Vote Dem.	Major Vote Rep.	Major Vote Dem.
1	1992	227,983	110,043 *	ROMAINE, EDWARD P.	117,940 *	HOCHBRUECKNER, GEORGE J.		7,897 D	48.3%	51.7%	48.3%	51.7%
2	1992	205,714	109,386 *	LAZIO, RICK A.	96,328 *	DOWNEY, THOMAS J.		13,058 R	53.2%	46.8%	53.2%	46.8%
3	1992	251,622	124,727 *	KING, PETER T.	116,915	ORLINS, STEVE A.	9,980	7,812 R	49.6%	46.5%	51.6%	48.4%
4	1992	220,644	110,710 *	LEVY, DAVID A.	100,386 *	SCHILIRO, PHILIP	9,548	10,324 R	50.2%	45.5%	52.4%	47.6%
5	1992	210,831	94,907 *	BINDER, ALLAN E.	110,476 *	ACKERMAN, GARY L.	5,448	15,569 D	45.0%	52.4%	46.2%	53.8%
6	1992	119,659	22,687 *	BHAGWANDIN, DIANAND D.	96,972	FLAKE, FLOYD H.		74,285 D	19.0%	81.0%	19.0%	81.0%
7	1992	126,919	54,639 *	SHEA, DENNIS C.	72,280	MANTON, THOMAS J.		17,641 D	43.1%	56.9%	43.1%	56.9%
8	1992	170,248	25,548	ASKREN, DAVID L.	138,296 *	NADLER, JERROLD	6,404	112,748 D	15.0%	81.2%	15.6%	84.4%
9	1992	131,530			116,545 *	SCHUMER, CHARLES E.	14,985	116,545 D		88.6%		100.0%
10	1992	101,824			97,509 *	TOWNS, EDOLPHUS	4,315	97,509 D		95.8%		100.0%
11	1992	85,494			80,028 *	OWENS, MAJOR R.	5,466	80,028 D		93.6%		100.0%
12	1992	73,067	14,976 *	DIAZ, ANGEL	55,926	VELAZQUEZ, NYDIA M.	2,165	40,950 D	20.5%	76.5%	21.1%	78.9%
13	1992	192,248	107,903 *	MOLINARI, SUSAN	73,520 *	ALBANESE, SAL F.	10,825	34,383 R	56.1%	38.2%	59.5%	40.5%
14	1992	201,837	97,215 *	GREEN, S. WILLIAM	101,652 *	MALONEY, CAROLYN B.	2,970	4,437 D	48.2%	50.4%	48.9%	51.1%
15	1992	110,693			105,011 *	RANGEL, CHARLES B.	5,682	105,011 D		94.9%		100.0%
16	1992	93,197	7,975 *	WALTERS, MICHAEL	85,222 *	SERRANO, JOSE E.		77,247 D	8.6%	91.4%	8.6%	91.4%
17	1992	122,381	16,511	RICHMAN, MARTIN	98,068 *	ENGEL, ELIOT L.	7,802	81,557 D	13.5%	80.1%	14.4%	85.6%
18	1992	208,528	92,687 *	DIOGUARDI, JOSEPH J.	115,841	LOWEY, NITA M.		23,154 D	44.4%	55.6%	44.4%	55.6%
19	1992	232,464	139,610 *	FISH, HAMILTON	92,854	MCCARTHY, CORNELIUS P.		46,756 R	60.1%	39.9%	60.1%	39.9%
20	1992	227,331	150,301	GILMAN, BENJAMIN A.	66,826	LEVINE, JOHATHAN L.	10,204	83,475 R	66.1%	29.4%	69.2%	30.8%
21	1992	265,278	91,184 *	NORMAN, NANCY	166,371 *	MCNULTY, MICHAEL R.	7,723	75,187 D	34.4%	62.7%	35.4%	64.6%
22	1992	251,332	164,436 *	SOLOMON, GERALD B.	86,896	ROBERTS, DAVID		77,540 R	65.4%	34.6%	65.4%	34.6%
23	1992	219,662	139,774	BOEHLERT, SHERWOOD L.	61,835	DIPERNA, PAULA	18,053	77,939 R	63.6%	28.2%	69.3%	30.7%
24	1992	201,069	122,257 *	MCHUGH, JOHN M.	47,675	RAVENSCROFT, MARGARET M.	31,137	74,582 R	60.8%	23.7%	71.9%	28.1%
25	1992	242,386	135,076 *	WALSH, JAMES T.	107,310 *	JEZER, RHEA		27,766 R	55.7%	44.3%	55.7%	44.3%
26	1992	237,116	110,738 *	MOPPERT, BOB	119,557 *	HINCHEY, MAURICE D.	6,821	8,819 D	46.7%	50.4%	48.1%	51.9%
27	1992	246,502	156,596 *	PAXON, L. WILLIAM	89,906	CALL, W. DOUGLAS		66,690 R	63.5%	36.5%	63.5%	36.5%
28	1992	255,078	112,273 *	POLITO, WILLIAM P.	140,908	SLAUGHTER, LOUISE M.	1,897	28,635 D	44.0%	55.2%	44.3%	55.7%
29	1992	235,458	98,031 *	MILLER, WILLIAM E., JR.	128,230 *	LAFALCE, JOHN J.	9,197	30,199 D	41.6%	54.5%	43.3%	56.7%
30	1992	243,204	125,734 *	QUINN, JACK	111,445 *	GORSKI, DENNIS T.	6,025	14,289 R	51.7%	45.8%	53.0%	47.0%
31	1992	213,554	150,696 *	HOUGHTON, AMORY	52,010	LEAHEY, JOSEPH P.	10,848	98,686 R	70.6%	24.4%	74.3%	25.7%

NEW YORK

1992 GENERAL ELECTION

President Other vote was 15,472 Socialist Workers (Warren); 13,451 Libertarian (Marrou); 11,318 New Alliance (Fulani); 4,420 Natural Law (Hagelin); 385 Daniels (write-in); 23 Gritz (write-in); 20 LaRouche (write-in); 16 Brisben (write-in). The total of the other vote column includes the 444 write-in votes not available by county. The Republican candidate was also the Conservative and Right to Life nominee; 177,000 of his votes were received as the Conservative candidate and 127,959 as the Right to Life candidate. The Democratic candidate was also the Liberal nominee and 97,556 of his votes were received as the Liberal candidate.

Senator Other vote was 108,530 Libertarian (Segal); 56,631 New Alliance (Mehdi); 23,747 Natural Law (Nelson); 16,724 Socialist Workers (Warren). The Republican candidate was also the Conservative and Right to Life nominee; 289,258 of his votes were received as the Conservative candidate and 224,914 as the Right to Life candidate. The Democratic candidate was also the Liberal nominee and 143,199 of his votes were received as the Liberal candidate.

Congress An asterisk in the Congressional vote table indicates a candidate received votes as the nominee of an additional party/parties. Other vote was 6,888 Right to Life (Roccanova) and 3,092 Liberal (Heyman) in CD 3; Right to Life (Garbitelli) in CD 4; Right to Life (Duff) in CD 5; 5,180 Conservative (Byrnes) and 1,224 New Alliance (Block) in CD 8; Conservative (Alice Gaffney) in CD 9; Conservative (Augustin) in CD 10; 4,287 Conservative (Michael Gaffney) and 1,179 New Alliance (Foster) in CD 11; 1,556 Liberal (Franco) and 609 New Alliance (Mendez) in CD 12; Right to Life (Murphy) in CD 13; Better East Side (Hirschfeld) in CD 14; 4,345 Conservative & Independent Fusion (Suero) and 1,337 New Alliance (Fields) in CD 15; 3,143 Conservative (Brawley), 3,067 Right to Life (O'Grady) and 1,592 Natural Law (LaLuz) in CD 17; Right to Life (Garrison) in CD 20; Right to Life (Donnelly) in CD 21; 8,688 Right to Life (Terry), 8,011 Conservative (Grace) and 1,354 Natural Law (Janowski) in CD 23; 26,763 Conservative & Right to Life (Hosley) and 4,374 Liberal (Burke) in CD 24; Right to Life (Dixon) in CD 26; Economic Justice (Perez) in CD 28; 7,367 Right to Life (Kowalski) and 1,830 Economic Justice (Basar) in CD 29; Right to Life (Refermat) in CD 30; Right to Life (McManus) in CD 31.

NEW YORK CITY

The City is composed of five counties, each of which, for municipal government purposes, is known as a borough. For Bronx county and Queens county, the name of the county and borough is the same. New York county is Manhattan borough; Kings county is Brooklyn borough and Richmond county is Staten Island borough.

President The Republican vote includes 40,875 votes cast for George Bush as the Conservative candidate and 23,572 votes as the Right to Life candidate. The Democratic vote includes 44,680 votes cast for Bill Clinton as the Liberal candidate. Other vote was 6,748 New Alliance (Fulani); 3,817 Libertarian (Marrou); 1,396 Socialist Workers (Warren); 845 Natural Law (Hagelin).

Senator The Republican vote includes 65,393 votes cast for Alfonse M. D'Amato as the Conservative candidate and 43,010 as the Right to Life candidate. The Democratic vote includes 47,518 votes cast for Robert Abrams as the Liberal candidate. Other vote was 14,800 New Alliance (Mehdi); 13,450 Libertarian (Segal); 4,670 Socialist Workers (Warren); 2,479 Natural Law (Nelson).

1992 PRIMARIES

SEPTEMBER 15 REPUBLICAN

Senator Alfonse M. D'Amato, unopposed.

Congress Unopposed in twenty CD's. No candidate in CD's 9, 10, 11 and 15. Contested as follows:

CD 3 8,346 Peter T. King; 3,853 Robert Previdi.
CD 4 12,646 David A. Levy; 9,890 Daniel Frisa; 1,410 Francis A. Lees.
CD 7 3,412 Dennis C. Shea; 706 Ann P. Darby.

NEW YORK

CD 13 10,136 Susan Molinari; 3,439 Kathleen M. Murphy.
CD 24 21,452 John M. McHugh; 9,320 Morrison J. Hosley.
CD 26 18,301 Bob Moppert; 8,010 Robert R. Rossi.
CD 28 10,241 William P. Polito; 3,496 Edward T. Zonnevylle.

SEPTEMBER 15 DEMOCRATIC

Senator   426,904 Robert Abrams; 415,650 Geraldine A. Ferraro; 166,665 Al Sharpton; 144,026 Elizabeth Holtzman.

Congress   Unopposed in eighteen CD's. Contested as follows:

CD 4 11,764 Philip Schiliro; 11,243 Joan F. Axinn.
CD 5 25,328 Gary L. Ackerman; 15,656 Rita Louise Morris.
CD 6 36,343 Floyd H. Flake; 11,036 Simeon Golar.
CD 8 58,115 Theodore S. Weiss; 7,026 Arthur R. Block. Mr. Weiss died September 14 (one day before the primary); Jerrold Nadler was substituted after the primary by the local party committee.
CD 10 34,734 Edolphus Towns; 15,407 Susan D. Alter; 5,042 Frank R. Seddio.
CD 12 11,508 Nydia M. Velazquez; 9,581 Stephen J. Solarz; 8,839 Elizabeth Colon; 2,499 Ruben Franco; 1,087 Rafael Mendez; 614 Eric R. Melendez.
CD 14 37,415 Carolyn B. Maloney; 12,864 Abraham J. Hirschfeld; 3,521 Charles W. Juntikka; 2,534 Frederick D. Newman.
CD 15 41,391 Charles B. Rangel; 4,984 Jessie Fields; 4,219 Harry C. Fotopoulos.
CD 17 35,859 Eliot L. Engel; 12,680 Mario Biaggi.
CD 19 9,295 Cornelius P. McCarthy; 5,733 Catherine Portman-Laux.
CD 24 4,560 Margaret M. Ravenscroft; 3,683 Stephen Burke; 2,711 Danny M. Francis.
CD 26 19,426 Maurice D. Hinchey; 14,226 Juanita M. Crabb; 2,002 Barbara A. Wolfson.
CD 30 35,263 Dennis T. Gorski; 20,882 Thomas F. Higgins.

SEPTEMBER 15 CONSERVATIVE

Senator   Alfonse M. D'Amato, unopposed.

Congress   Other party candidates endorsed or nominees unopposed in all CD's in which a candidate was named.

SEPTEMBER 15 LIBERAL

Senator   Robert Abrams, unopposed.

Congress   Other party candidates endorsed or nominees unopposed in all CD's in which a candidate was named.

SEPTEMBER 15 RIGHT TO LIFE

Senator   Alfonse M. D'Amato, unopposed.

Congress   Other party candidates endorsed or nominees unopposed in all CD's in which a candidate was named.

NORTH CAROLINA

GOVERNOR
James B. Hunt (D). Re-elected 1992 to a four-year term. Previously elected 1980, 1976.

SENATORS
Lauch Faircloth (R). Elected 1992 to a six-year term.

Jesse Helms (R). Re-elected 1990 to a six-year term. Previously elected 1984, 1978, 1972.

REPRESENTATIVES
1. Eva Clayton (D)
2. I. T. Valentine (D)
3. Martin Lancaster (D)
4. David E. Price (D)
5. Stephen L. Neal (D)
6. Howard Coble (R)
7. Charles G. Rose (D)
8. W. G. Hefner (D)
9. J. Alex McMillan (R)
10. Cass Ballenger (R)
11. Charles H. Taylor (R)
12. Melvin Watt (D)

POSTWAR VOTE FOR PRESIDENT

| | | Republican | | Democratic | | Other | | Percentage | | | |
| | Total | | | | | | | Total Vote | | Major Vote | |
Year	Vote	Vote	Candidate	Vote	Candidate	Vote	Plurality	Rep.	Dem.	Rep.	Dem.
1992 **	2,611,850	1,134,661	Bush, George	1,114,042	Clinton, Bill	363,147	20,619 R	43.4%	42.7%	50.5%	49.5%
1988	2,134,370	1,237,258	Bush, George	890,167	Dukakis, Michael S.	6,945	347,091 R	58.0%	41.7%	58.2%	41.8%
1984	2,175,361	1,346,481	Reagan, Ronald	824,287	Mondale, Walter F.	4,593	522,194 R	61.9%	37.9%	62.0%	38.0%
1980	1,855,833	915,018	Reagan, Ronald	875,635	Carter, Jimmy	65,180	39,383 R	49.3%	47.2%	51.1%	48.9%
1976	1,678,914	741,960	Ford, Gerald R.	927,365	Carter, Jimmy	9,589	185,405 D	44.2%	55.2%	44.4%	55.6%
1972	1,518,612	1,054,889	Nixon, Richard M.	438,705	McGovern, George S.	25,018	616,184 R	69.5%	28.9%	70.6%	29.4%
1968 **	1,587,493	627,192	Nixon, Richard M.	464,113	Humphrey, Hubert H.	496,188	131,004 R	39.5%	29.2%	57.5%	42.5%
1964	1,424,983	624,844	Goldwater, Barry M.	800,139	Johnson, Lyndon B.		175,295 D	43.8%	56.2%	43.8%	56.2%
1960	1,368,556	655,420	Nixon, Richard M.	713,136	Kennedy, John F.		57,716 D	47.9%	52.1%	47.9%	52.1%
1956	1,165,592	575,062	Eisenhower, Dwight D.	590,530	Stevenson, Adlai E.		15,468 D	49.3%	50.7%	49.3%	50.7%
1952	1,210,910	558,107	Eisenhower, Dwight D.	652,803	Stevenson, Adlai E.		94,696 D	46.1%	53.9%	46.1%	53.9%
1948	791,209	258,572	Dewey, Thomas E.	459,070	Truman, Harry S.	73,567	200,498 D	32.7%	58.0%	36.0%	64.0%

In 1992 the other vote column includes 357,864 votes cast for Perot. In 1968 other vote was American (Wallace).

POSTWAR VOTE FOR GOVERNOR

| | | Republican | | Democratic | | Other | Rep.-Dem. | Percentage | | | |
| | Total | | | | | | | Total Vote | | Major Vote | |
Year	Vote	Vote	Candidate	Vote	Candidate	Vote	Plurality	Rep.	Dem.	Rep.	Dem.
1992	2,595,184	1,121,955	Gardner, James C.	1,368,246	Hunt, James B.	104,983	246,291 D	43.2%	52.7%	45.1%	54.9%
1988	2,180,025	1,222,338	Martin, James G.	957,687	Jordan, Robert B.		264,651 R	56.1%	43.9%	56.1%	43.9%
1984	2,226,727	1,208,167	Martin, James G.	1,011,209	Edmisten, Rufus	7,351	196,958 R	54.3%	45.4%	54.4%	45.6%
1980	1,847,432	691,449	Lake, Beverly	1,143,145	Hunt, James B.	12,838	451,696 D	37.4%	61.9%	37.7%	62.3%
1976	1,663,824	564,102	Flaherty, David T.	1,081,293	Hunt, James B.	18,429	517,191 D	33.9%	65.0%	34.3%	65.7%
1972	1,504,785	767,470	Holshouser, James E.	729,104	Bowles, Hargrove	8,211	38,366 R	51.0%	48.5%	51.3%	48.7%
1968	1,558,308	737,075	Gardner, James C.	821,233	Scott, Robert W.		84,158 D	47.3%	52.7%	47.3%	52.7%
1964	1,396,508	606,165	Gavin, Robert L.	790,343	Moore, Dan K.		184,178 D	43.4%	56.6%	43.4%	56.6%
1960	1,350,360	613,975	Gavin, Robert L.	735,248	Sanford, Terry	1,137	121,273 D	45.5%	54.4%	45.5%	54.5%
1956	1,135,859	375,379	Hayes, Kyle	760,480	Hodges, Luther H.		385,101 D	33.0%	67.0%	33.0%	67.0%
1952	1,179,635	383,329	Seawell, H. F.	796,306	Umstead, William B.		412,977 D	32.5%	67.5%	32.5%	67.5%
1948	780,525	206,166	Pritchard, George	570,995	Scott, William Kerr	3,364	364,829 D	26.4%	73.2%	26.5%	73.5%

NORTH CAROLINA

POSTWAR VOTE FOR SENATOR

Year	Total Vote	Republican		Democratic		Other Vote	Rep.-Dem. Plurality	Percentage			
								Total Vote		Major Vote	
		Vote	Candidate	Vote	Candidate			Rep.	Dem.	Rep.	Dem.
1992	2,577,891	1,297,892	Faircloth, Lauch	1,194,015	Sanford, Terry	85,984	103,877 R	50.3%	46.3%	52.1%	47.9%
1990	2,069,585	1,087,331	Helms, Jesse	981,573	Gantt, Harvy B.	681	105,758 R	52.5%	47.4%	52.6%	47.4%
1986	1,591,330	767,668	Broyhill, James T.	823,662	Sanford, Terry		55,994 D	48.2%	51.8%	48.2%	51.8%
1984	2,239,051	1,156,768	Helms, Jesse	1,070,488	Hunt, James B.	11,795	86,280 R	51.7%	47.8%	51.9%	48.1%
1980	1,797,665	898,064	East, John P.	887,653	Morgan, Robert	11,948	10,411 R	50.0%	49.4%	50.3%	49.7%
1978	1,135,814	619,151	Helms, Jesse	516,663	Ingram, John		102,488 R	54.5%	45.5%	54.5%	45.5%
1974	1,020,367	377,618	Stevens, William E.	633,775	Morgan, Robert	8,974	256,157 D	37.0%	62.1%	37.3%	62.7%
1972	1,472,541	795,248	Helms, Jesse	677,293	Galifianakis, Nick		117,955 R	54.0%	46.0%	54.0%	46.0%
1968	1,437,340	566,934	Somers, Robert V.	870,406	Ervin, Sam J.		303,472 D	39.4%	60.6%	39.4%	60.6%
1966	901,978	400,502	Shallcross, John S.	501,440	Jordan, B. Everett	36	100,938 D	44.4%	55.6%	44.4%	55.6%
1962	813,155	321,635	Greene, Claude L.	491,520	Ervin, Sam J.		169,885 D	39.6%	60.4%	39.6%	60.4%
1960	1,291,485	497,964	Hayes, Kyle	793,521	Jordan, B. Everett		295,557 D	38.6%	61.4%	38.6%	61.4%
1958 S	616,469	184,977	Clarke, Richard C.	431,492	Jordan, B. Everett		246,515 D	30.0%	70.0%	30.0%	70.0%
1956	1,098,828	367,475	Johnson, Joel A.	731,353	Ervin, Sam J.		363,878 D	33.4%	66.6%	33.4%	66.6%
1954	619,634	211,322	West, Paul C.	408,312	Scott, William Kerr		196,990 D	34.1%	65.9%	34.1%	65.9%
1954 S	410,574		—	410,574	Ervin, Sam J.		410,574 D		100.0%		100.0%
1950	548,276	171,804	Leavitt, Halsey B.	376,472	Hoey, Clyde R.		204,668 D	31.3%	68.7%	31.3%	68.7%
1950 S	544,924	177,753	Gavin, E. L.	364,912	Smith, Willis	2,259	187,159 D	32.6%	67.0%	32.8%	67.2%
1948	764,559	220,307	Wilkinson, John A.	540,762	Broughton, J. M.	3,490	320,455 D	28.8%	70.7%	28.9%	71.1%

The 1958 election and one each of the 1954 and 1950 elections were for short terms to fill vacancies.

NORTH CAROLINA

Districts Established February 6, 1992

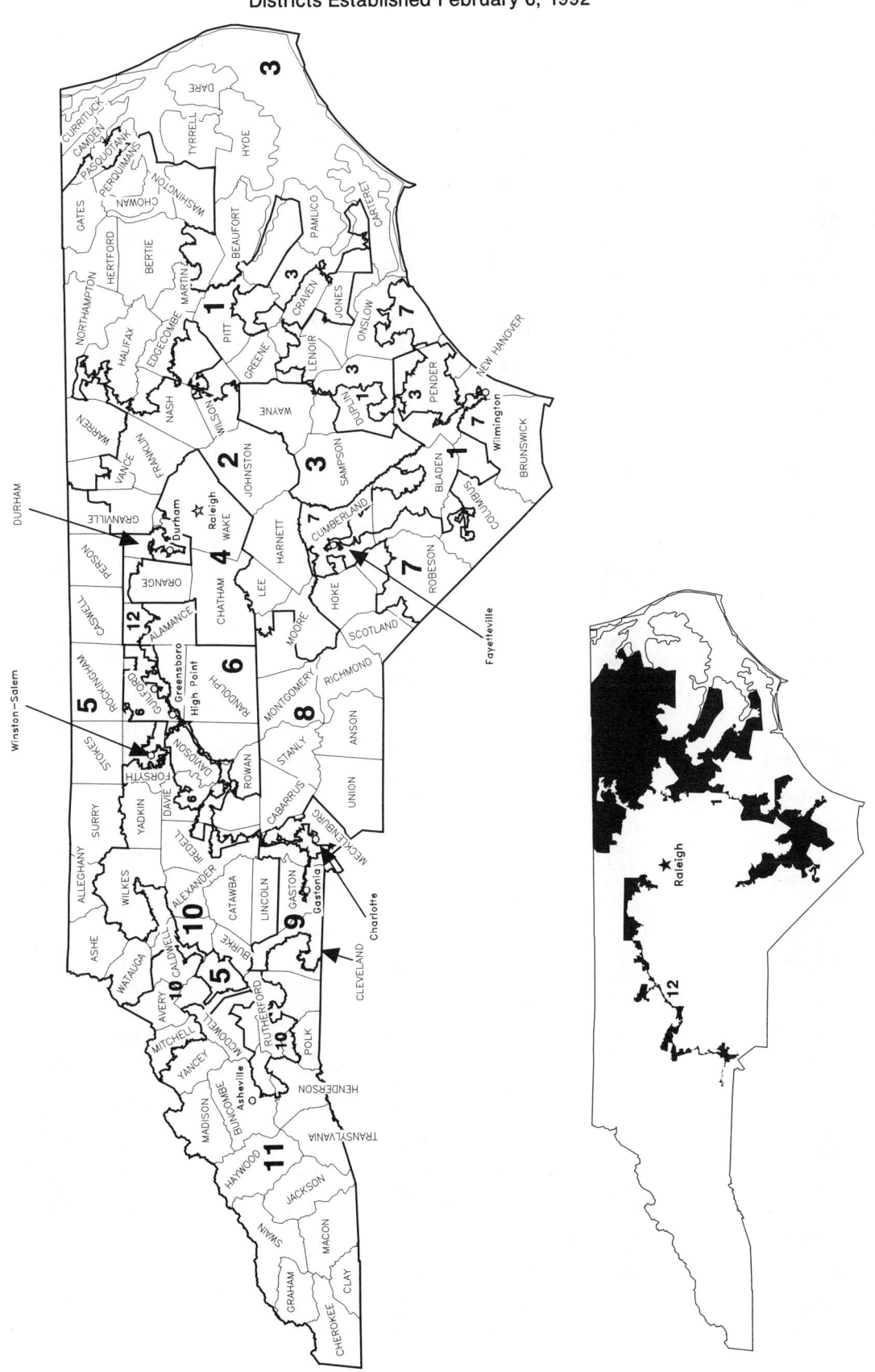

NORTH CAROLINA

PRESIDENT 1992

Registration	County	Total Vote	Republican	Democratic	Perot	Other	Plurality	Percentage Total Vote		
								Rep.	Dem.	Perot
63,270	ALAMANCE	42,701	20,637	15,521	6,444	99	5,116 R	48.3%	36.3%	15.1%
19,233	ALEXANDER	13,626	6,764	4,849	2,002	11	1,915 R	49.6%	35.6%	14.7%
6,480	ALLEGHANY	4,730	1,853	2,271	600	6	418 D	39.2%	48.0%	12.7%
12,030	ANSON	8,539	2,334	5,269	921	15	2,935 D	27.3%	61.7%	10.8%
15,421	ASHE	11,070	5,200	4,624	1,220	26	576 R	47.0%	41.8%	11.0%
9,794	AVERY	6,787	3,895	1,755	1,123	14	2,140 R	57.4%	25.9%	16.5%
22,712	BEAUFORT	15,980	7,337	6,445	2,174	24	892 R	45.9%	40.3%	13.6%
11,716	BERTIE	6,743	1,756	4,382	600	5	2,626 D	26.0%	65.0%	8.9%
16,465	BLADEN	10,177	3,214	5,700	1,248	15	2,486 D	31.6%	56.0%	12.3%
32,769	BRUNSWICK	22,400	8,833	10,177	3,349	41	1,344 D	39.4%	45.4%	15.0%
109,805	BUNCOMBE	75,492	30,892	32,955	11,481	164	2,063 D	40.9%	43.7%	15.2%
41,850	BURKE	30,122	13,397	12,565	4,124	36	832 R	44.5%	41.7%	13.7%
60,252	CABARRUS	41,123	21,281	13,513	6,251	78	7,768 R	51.7%	32.9%	15.2%
38,196	CALDWELL	25,576	12,543	9,033	3,965	35	3,510 R	49.0%	35.3%	15.5%
3,829	CAMDEN	2,675	1,039	1,153	479	4	114 D	38.8%	43.1%	17.9%
30,526	CARTERET	21,819	10,334	8,028	3,401	56	2,306 R	47.4%	36.8%	15.6%
11,900	CASWELL	8,363	2,793	4,725	827	18	1,932 D	33.4%	56.5%	9.9%
68,487	CATAWBA	49,409	25,466	16,334	7,523	86	9,132 R	51.5%	33.1%	15.2%
24,907	CHATHAM	18,577	6,568	9,520	2,425	64	2,952 D	35.4%	51.2%	13.1%
14,394	CHEROKEE	8,758	4,021	3,686	1,040	11	335 R	45.9%	42.1%	11.9%
7,412	CHOWAN	4,506	1,661	2,136	700	9	475 D	36.9%	47.4%	15.5%
5,715	CLAY	3,960	1,890	1,600	465	5	290 R	47.7%	40.4%	11.7%
43,359	CLEVELAND	30,522	13,650	13,037	3,784	51	613 R	44.7%	42.7%	12.4%
31,344	COLUMBUS	18,916	5,462	11,469	1,963	22	6,007 D	28.9%	60.6%	10.4%
39,362	CRAVEN	25,287	11,575	9,998	3,679	35	1,577 R	45.8%	39.5%	14.5%
104,468	CUMBERLAND	64,470	27,139	30,291	6,792	248	3,152 D	42.1%	47.0%	10.5%
7,311	CURRITUCK	5,297	2,188	1,935	1,163	11	253 R	41.3%	36.5%	22.0%
14,941	DARE	10,696	4,357	3,925	2,388	26	432 R	40.7%	36.7%	22.3%
69,608	DAVIDSON	49,725	24,869	16,462	8,324	70	8,407 R	50.0%	33.1%	16.7%
16,369	DAVIE	12,387	6,796	3,675	1,903	13	3,121 R	54.9%	29.7%	15.4%
21,182	DUPLIN	13,747	5,286	6,816	1,636	9	1,530 D	38.5%	49.6%	11.9%
117,678	DURHAM	82,682	27,581	47,331	7,504	266	19,750 D	33.4%	57.2%	9.1%
31,927	EDGECOMBE	19,657	6,275	11,174	2,175	33	4,899 D	31.9%	56.8%	11.1%
161,423	FORSYTH	116,274	52,787	49,006	14,262	219	3,781 R	45.4%	42.1%	12.3%
19,860	FRANKLIN	13,266	4,669	6,517	2,062	18	1,848 D	35.2%	49.1%	15.5%
87,728	GASTON	61,435	34,714	19,121	7,490	110	15,593 R	56.5%	31.1%	12.2%
5,546	GATES	3,834	1,158	2,206	466	4	1,048 D	30.2%	57.5%	12.2%
5,730	GRAHAM	3,876	1,919	1,551	403	3	368 R	49.5%	40.0%	10.4%
18,327	GRANVILLE	12,128	4,538	6,178	1,321	91	1,640 D	37.4%	50.9%	10.9%
8,136	GREENE	5,732	2,180	2,768	780	4	588 D	38.0%	48.3%	13.6%
229,000	GUILFORD	146,399	60,140	66,319	19,601	339	6,179 D	41.1%	45.3%	13.4%
27,839	HALIFAX	17,804	5,769	9,960	2,047	28	4,191 D	32.4%	55.9%	11.5%
29,552	HARNETT	20,932	9,751	8,473	2,684	24	1,278 R	46.6%	40.5%	12.8%
30,910	HAYWOOD	21,009	7,292	10,385	3,303	29	3,093 D	34.7%	49.4%	15.7%
45,893	HENDERSON	33,072	17,010	10,747	5,260	55	6,263 R	51.4%	32.5%	15.9%
14,019	HERTFORD	7,672	2,208	4,609	846	9	2,401 D	28.8%	60.1%	11.0%
9,741	HOKE	6,337	1,711	3,730	887	9	2,019 D	27.0%	58.9%	14.0%
3,388	HYDE	2,288	740	1,206	340	2	466 D	32.3%	52.7%	14.9%
55,014	IREDELL	38,980	19,411	13,263	6,204	102	6,148 R	49.8%	34.0%	15.9%
17,529	JACKSON	11,558	4,275	5,753	1,516	14	1,478 D	37.0%	49.8%	13.1%
44,429	JOHNSTON	31,679	15,418	11,284	4,939	38	4,134 R	48.7%	35.6%	15.6%
5,467	JONES	3,846	1,438	1,962	444	2	524 D	37.4%	51.0%	11.5%
21,035	LEE	14,659	6,658	5,852	2,125	24	806 R	45.4%	39.9%	14.5%
28,335	LENOIR	19,842	8,932	8,793	2,107	10	139 R	45.0%	44.3%	10.6%
30,871	LINCOLN	22,355	11,018	8,150	3,142	45	2,868 R	49.3%	36.5%	14.1%
19,608	MCDOWELL	13,295	6,090	5,309	1,881	15	781 R	45.8%	39.9%	14.1%
16,417	MACON	11,279	4,797	4,624	1,829	29	173 R	42.5%	41.0%	16.2%
12,435	MADISON	7,989	3,121	3,980	857	31	859 D	39.1%	49.8%	10.7%
13,282	MARTIN	8,016	2,958	4,069	981	8	1,111 D	36.9%	50.8%	12.2%
326,005	MECKLENBURG	228,375	99,496	97,065	31,283	531	2,431 R	43.6%	42.5%	13.7%

NORTH CAROLINA

PRESIDENT 1992

Registration	County	Total Vote	Republican	Democratic	Perot	Other	Plurality	Percentage Total Vote		
								Rep.	Dem.	Perot
10,782	MITCHELL	7,015	4,405	1,727	877	6	2,678 R	62.8%	24.6%	12.5%
13,153	MONTGOMERY	9,161	3,543	4,422	1,185	11	879 D	38.7%	48.3%	12.9%
37,001	MOORE	26,591	12,448	9,649	4,448	46	2,799 R	46.8%	36.3%	16.7%
42,600	NASH	29,886	14,446	10,809	4,544	87	3,637 R	48.3%	36.2%	15.2%
77,169	NEW HANOVER	52,154	24,338	20,291	7,401	124	4,047 R	46.7%	38.9%	14.2%
12,951	NORTHAMPTON	7,967	1,845	5,195	916	11	3,350 D	23.2%	65.2%	11.5%
36,947	ONSLOW	24,318	11,842	8,045	4,387	44	3,797 R	48.7%	33.1%	18.0%
68,606	ORANGE	47,300	13,009	28,595	5,535	161	15,586 D	27.5%	60.5%	11.7%
7,000	PAMLICO	4,975	1,929	2,229	809	8	300 D	38.8%	44.8%	16.3%
15,609	PASQUOTANK	9,581	3,419	4,709	1,434	19	1,290 D	35.7%	49.1%	15.0%
17,757	PENDER	12,430	4,857	5,825	1,725	23	968 D	39.1%	46.9%	13.9%
5,948	PERQUIMANS	3,878	1,429	1,818	624	7	389 D	36.8%	46.9%	16.1%
15,235	PERSON	10,230	4,460	4,323	1,431	16	137 R	43.6%	42.3%	14.0%
59,372	PITT	39,895	16,609	17,959	5,262	65	1,350 D	41.6%	45.0%	13.2%
11,040	POLK	7,533	3,448	2,939	1,134	12	509 R	45.8%	39.0%	15.1%
56,783	RANDOLPH	38,902	20,697	11,274	6,870	61	9,423 R	53.2%	29.0%	17.7%
24,316	RICHMOND	15,553	4,356	9,163	2,015	19	4,807 D	28.0%	58.9%	13.0%
56,869	ROBESON	30,474	7,777	19,378	3,277	42	11,601 D	25.5%	63.6%	10.8%
44,424	ROCKINGHAM	31,269	12,678	13,880	4,671	40	1,202 D	40.5%	44.4%	14.9%
61,716	ROWAN	42,732	21,297	14,308	7,053	74	6,989 R	49.8%	33.5%	16.5%
29,280	RUTHERFORD	20,329	9,748	7,855	2,695	31	1,893 R	48.0%	38.6%	13.3%
28,074	SAMPSON	18,568	8,007	8,698	1,852	11	691 D	43.1%	46.8%	10.0%
17,997	SCOTLAND	9,360	2,980	5,175	1,196	9	2,195 D	31.8%	55.3%	12.8%
29,884	STANLY	21,664	11,030	7,735	2,855	44	3,295 R	50.9%	35.7%	13.2%
23,012	STOKES	16,657	7,979	6,463	2,183	32	1,516 R	47.9%	38.8%	13.1%
34,164	SURRY	23,453	10,866	9,392	3,164	31	1,474 R	46.3%	40.0%	13.5%
8,568	SWAIN	4,330	1,640	2,117	568	5	477 D	37.9%	48.9%	13.1%
17,868	TRANSYLVANIA	13,137	5,984	5,120	2,006	27	864 R	45.6%	39.0%	15.3%
2,213	TYRRELL	1,674	553	928	189	4	375 D	33.0%	55.4%	11.3%
48,511	UNION	31,992	16,542	10,789	4,601	60	5,753 R	51.7%	33.7%	14.4%
19,862	VANCE	12,800	4,747	6,598	1,444	11	1,851 D	37.1%	51.5%	11.3%
278,030	WAKE	207,467	86,798	88,979	31,140	550	2,181 D	41.8%	42.9%	15.0%
10,987	WARREN	7,125	1,767	4,656	693	9	2,889 D	24.8%	65.3%	9.7%
7,882	WASHINGTON	5,253	1,780	2,902	563	8	1,122 D	33.9%	55.2%	10.7%
27,705	WATAUGA	19,225	7,899	8,262	3,007	57	363 D	41.1%	43.0%	15.6%
42,720	WAYNE	27,532	14,397	10,307	2,798	30	4,090 R	52.3%	37.4%	10.2%
37,484	WILKES	23,868	12,547	7,991	3,307	23	4,556 R	52.6%	33.5%	13.9%
36,212	WILSON	22,937	10,176	10,105	2,630	26	71 R	44.4%	44.1%	11.5%
17,144	YADKIN	12,977	7,311	3,913	1,725	28	3,398 R	56.3%	30.2%	13.3%
12,274	YANCEY	9,208	3,994	4,285	917	12	291 D	43.4%	46.5%	10.0%
3,817,380	TOTAL	2,611,850	1,134,661	1,114,042	357,864	5,283	20,619 R	43.4%	42.7%	13.7%

NORTH CAROLINA

GOVERNOR 1992

| | | | | | | | Percentage | | | |
| | | | | | | | Total Vote | | Major Vote | |
Registration	County	Total Vote	Republican	Democratic	Other	Rep.-Dem. Plurality	Rep.	Dem.	Rep.	Dem.
63,270	ALAMANCE	43,140	20,711	20,599	1,830	112 R	48.0%	47.7%	50.1%	49.9%
19,233	ALEXANDER	13,843	7,262	6,144	437	1,118 R	52.5%	44.4%	54.2%	45.8%
6,480	ALLEGHANY	4,559	2,019	2,404	136	385 D	44.3%	52.7%	45.6%	54.4%
12,030	ANSON	8,304	2,316	5,850	138	3,534 D	27.9%	70.4%	28.4%	71.6%
15,421	ASHE	10,975	5,363	5,376	236	13 D	48.9%	49.0%	49.9%	50.1%
9,794	AVERY	6,597	4,054	2,322	221	1,732 R	61.5%	35.2%	63.6%	36.4%
22,712	BEAUFORT	15,955	7,379	8,093	483	714 D	46.2%	50.7%	47.7%	52.3%
11,716	BERTIE	6,304	1,966	4,251	87	2,285 D	31.2%	67.4%	31.6%	68.4%
16,465	BLADEN	9,860	3,275	6,424	161	3,149 D	33.2%	65.2%	33.8%	66.2%
32,769	BRUNSWICK	22,207	9,442	11,520	1,245	2,078 D	42.5%	51.9%	45.0%	55.0%
109,805	BUNCOMBE	74,243	33,659	38,748	1,836	5,089 D	45.3%	52.2%	46.5%	53.5%
41,850	BURKE	30,632	14,104	15,356	1,172	1,252 D	46.0%	50.1%	47.9%	52.1%
60,252	CABARRUS	41,534	20,305	18,841	2,388	1,464 R	48.9%	45.4%	51.9%	48.1%
38,196	CALDWELL	26,185	13,333	11,593	1,259	1,740 R	50.9%	44.3%	53.5%	46.5%
3,829	CAMDEN	2,627	1,077	1,483	67	406 D	41.0%	56.5%	42.1%	57.9%
30,526	CARTERET	21,986	10,187	10,806	993	619 D	46.3%	49.1%	48.5%	51.5%
11,900	CASWELL	8,014	2,579	5,311	124	2,732 D	32.2%	66.3%	32.7%	67.3%
68,487	CATAWBA	49,338	26,121	20,760	2,457	5,361 R	52.9%	42.1%	55.7%	44.3%
24,907	CHATHAM	18,412	6,690	10,912	810	4,222 D	36.3%	59.3%	38.0%	62.0%
14,394	CHEROKEE	8,783	4,412	4,306	65	106 R	50.2%	49.0%	50.6%	49.4%
7,412	CHOWAN	4,610	1,666	2,851	93	1,185 D	36.1%	61.8%	36.9%	63.1%
5,715	CLAY	3,918	2,004	1,871	43	133 R	51.1%	47.8%	51.7%	48.3%
43,359	CLEVELAND	30,396	12,824	16,333	1,239	3,509 D	42.2%	53.7%	44.0%	56.0%
31,344	COLUMBUS	19,377	5,654	13,240	483	7,586 D	29.2%	68.3%	29.9%	70.1%
39,362	CRAVEN	25,114	12,550	11,955	609	595 R	50.0%	47.6%	51.2%	48.8%
104,468	CUMBERLAND	66,683	25,645	38,327	2,711	12,682 D	38.5%	57.5%	40.1%	59.9%
7,311	CURRITUCK	5,237	2,287	2,805	145	518 D	43.7%	53.6%	44.9%	55.1%
14,941	DARE	10,681	4,434	5,927	320	1,493 D	41.5%	55.5%	42.8%	57.2%
69,608	DAVIDSON	49,658	25,901	20,964	2,793	4,937 R	52.2%	42.2%	55.3%	44.7%
16,369	DAVIE	12,309	7,188	4,630	491	2,558 R	58.4%	37.6%	60.8%	39.2%
21,182	DUPLIN	14,138	5,698	8,146	294	2,448 D	40.3%	57.6%	41.2%	58.8%
117,678	DURHAM	83,127	25,817	54,278	3,032	28,461 D	31.1%	65.3%	32.2%	67.8%
31,927	EDGECOMBE	19,550	6,571	12,519	460	5,948 D	33.6%	64.0%	34.4%	65.6%
161,423	FORSYTH	115,823	51,448	58,904	5,471	7,456 D	44.4%	50.9%	46.6%	53.4%
19,860	FRANKLIN	13,481	5,232	7,662	587	2,430 D	38.8%	56.8%	40.6%	59.4%
87,728	GASTON	61,532	32,627	25,382	3,523	7,245 R	53.0%	41.3%	56.2%	43.8%
5,546	GATES	3,698	907	2,762	29	1,855 D	24.5%	74.7%	24.7%	75.3%
5,730	GRAHAM	3,812	1,911	1,866	35	45 R	50.1%	49.0%	50.6%	49.4%
18,327	GRANVILLE	12,609	4,524	7,527	558	3,003 D	35.9%	59.7%	37.5%	62.5%
8,136	GREENE	5,632	2,209	3,347	76	1,138 D	39.2%	59.4%	39.8%	60.2%
229,000	GUILFORD	147,043	55,422	83,458	8,163	28,036 D	37.7%	56.8%	39.9%	60.1%
27,839	HALIFAX	17,710	6,128	11,070	512	4,942 D	34.6%	62.5%	35.6%	64.4%
29,552	HARNETT	20,670	9,549	10,399	722	850 D	46.2%	50.3%	47.9%	52.1%
30,910	HAYWOOD	21,258	8,764	11,831	663	3,067 D	41.2%	55.7%	42.6%	57.4%
45,893	HENDERSON	32,784	18,617	13,414	753	5,203 R	56.8%	40.9%	58.1%	41.9%
14,019	HERTFORD	7,464	2,096	5,302	66	3,206 D	28.1%	71.0%	28.3%	71.7%
9,741	HOKE	6,173	1,737	4,296	140	2,559 D	28.1%	69.6%	28.8%	71.2%
3,388	HYDE	2,228	746	1,433	49	687 D	33.5%	64.3%	34.2%	65.8%
55,014	IREDELL	38,746	20,035	16,667	2,044	3,368 R	51.7%	43.0%	54.6%	45.4%
17,529	JACKSON	11,633	4,722	6,687	224	1,965 D	40.6%	57.5%	41.4%	58.6%
44,429	JOHNSTON	31,283	15,171	14,782	1,330	389 R	48.5%	47.3%	50.6%	49.4%
5,467	JONES	3,823	1,468	2,263	92	795 D	38.4%	59.2%	39.3%	60.7%
21,035	LEE	14,528	6,216	7,736	576	1,520 D	42.8%	53.2%	44.6%	55.4%
28,335	LENOIR	19,388	8,129	10,931	328	2,802 D	41.9%	56.4%	42.6%	57.4%
30,871	LINCOLN	22,187	11,160	9,929	1,098	1,231 R	50.3%	44.8%	52.9%	47.1%
19,608	MCDOWELL	13,402	6,320	6,654	428	334 D	47.2%	49.6%	48.7%	51.3%
16,417	MACON	11,282	5,577	5,490	215	87 R	49.4%	48.7%	50.4%	49.6%
12,435	MADISON	7,457	3,185	4,170	102	985 D	42.7%	55.9%	43.3%	56.7%
13,282	MARTIN	8,073	3,058	4,916	99	1,858 D	37.9%	60.9%	38.3%	61.7%
326,005	MECKLENBURG	215,036	89,277	114,568	11,191	25,291 D	41.5%	53.3%	43.8%	56.2%

NORTH CAROLINA

GOVERNOR 1992

Registration	County	Total Vote	Republican	Democratic	Other	Rep.-Dem. Plurality	Percentage			
							Total Vote		Major Vote	
							Rep.	Dem.	Rep.	Dem.
10,782	MITCHELL	6,904	4,536	2,196	172	2,340 R	65.7%	31.8%	67.4%	32.6%
13,153	MONTGOMERY	8,964	3,576	5,137	251	1,561 D	39.9%	57.3%	41.0%	59.0%
37,001	MOORE	26,376	13,235	12,415	726	820 R	50.2%	47.1%	51.6%	48.4%
42,600	NASH	29,635	15,839	12,848	948	2,991 R	53.4%	43.4%	55.2%	44.8%
77,169	NEW HANOVER	51,517	22,344	25,394	3,779	3,050 D	43.4%	49.3%	46.8%	53.2%
12,951	NORTHAMPTON	7,758	2,066	5,585	107	3,519 D	26.6%	72.0%	27.0%	73.0%
36,947	ONSLOW	24,102	11,862	11,069	1,171	793 R	49.2%	45.9%	51.7%	48.3%
68,606	ORANGE	46,318	12,476	31,999	1,843	19,523 D	26.9%	69.1%	28.1%	71.9%
7,000	PAMLICO	4,900	1,958	2,753	189	795 D	40.0%	56.2%	41.6%	58.4%
15,609	PASQUOTANK	9,581	3,416	6,058	107	2,642 D	35.7%	63.2%	36.1%	63.9%
17,757	PENDER	12,546	5,237	6,578	731	1,341 D	41.7%	52.4%	44.3%	55.7%
5,948	PERQUIMANS	3,786	1,359	2,372	55	1,013 D	35.9%	62.7%	36.4%	63.6%
15,235	PERSON	9,992	4,703	4,870	419	167 D	47.1%	48.7%	49.1%	50.9%
59,372	PITT	39,422	16,572	22,021	829	5,449 D	42.0%	55.9%	42.9%	57.1%
11,040	POLK	7,239	3,537	3,555	147	18 D	48.9%	49.1%	49.9%	50.1%
56,783	RANDOLPH	39,101	21,678	15,552	1,871	6,126 R	55.4%	39.8%	58.2%	41.8%
24,316	RICHMOND	15,017	4,368	10,119	530	5,751 D	29.1%	67.4%	30.2%	69.8%
56,869	ROBESON	31,295	8,194	22,431	670	14,237 D	26.2%	71.7%	26.8%	73.2%
44,424	ROCKINGHAM	31,156	12,561	17,043	1,552	4,482 D	40.3%	54.7%	42.4%	57.6%
61,716	ROWAN	42,625	21,584	18,618	2,423	2,966 R	50.6%	43.7%	53.7%	46.3%
29,280	RUTHERFORD	20,390	9,693	9,882	815	189 D	47.5%	48.5%	49.5%	50.5%
28,074	SAMPSON	18,900	8,333	10,216	351	1,883 D	44.1%	54.1%	44.9%	55.1%
17,997	SCOTLAND	8,844	2,531	6,174	139	3,643 D	28.6%	69.8%	29.1%	70.9%
29,884	STANLY	21,703	11,075	9,838	790	1,237 R	51.0%	45.3%	53.0%	47.0%
23,012	STOKES	16,775	8,217	7,997	561	220 R	49.0%	47.7%	50.7%	49.3%
34,164	SURRY	23,834	11,352	11,967	515	615 D	47.6%	50.2%	48.7%	51.3%
8,568	SWAIN	4,341	1,897	2,392	52	495 D	43.7%	55.1%	44.2%	55.8%
17,868	TRANSYLVANIA	12,885	6,269	6,195	421	74 R	48.7%	48.1%	50.3%	49.7%
2,213	TYRRELL	1,607	540	1,036	31	496 D	33.6%	64.5%	34.3%	65.7%
48,511	UNION	31,299	15,462	14,354	1,483	1,108 R	49.4%	45.9%	51.9%	48.1%
19,862	VANCE	12,978	4,636	8,009	333	3,373 D	35.7%	61.7%	36.7%	63.3%
278,030	WAKE	207,893	79,808	118,345	9,740	38,537 D	38.4%	56.9%	40.3%	59.7%
10,987	WARREN	7,150	2,308	4,638	204	2,330 D	32.3%	64.9%	33.2%	66.8%
7,882	WASHINGTON	5,277	1,824	3,371	82	1,547 D	34.6%	63.9%	35.1%	64.9%
27,705	WATAUGA	18,949	8,361	9,702	886	1,341 D	44.1%	51.2%	46.3%	53.7%
42,720	WAYNE	26,936	13,267	13,104	565	163 R	49.3%	48.6%	50.3%	49.7%
37,484	WILKES	25,232	14,077	10,369	786	3,708 R	55.8%	41.1%	57.6%	42.4%
36,212	WILSON	23,030	8,508	14,205	317	5,697 D	36.9%	61.7%	37.5%	62.5%
17,144	YADKIN	12,780	7,749	4,659	372	3,090 R	60.6%	36.5%	62.5%	37.5%
12,274	YANCEY	9,096	4,219	4,789	88	570 D	46.4%	52.6%	46.8%	53.2%
3,817,380	TOTAL	2,595,184	1,121,955	1,368,246	104,983	246,291 D	43.2%	52.7%	45.1%	54.9%

NORTH CAROLINA

SENATOR 1992

| | | | | | | | Percentage | | | |
| | | | | | | | Total Vote | | Major Vote | |
Registration	County	Total Vote	Republican	Democratic	Other	Rep.-Dem. Plurality	Rep.	Dem.	Rep.	Dem.
63,270	ALAMANCE	42,214	23,299	17,573	1,342	5,726 R	55.2%	41.6%	57.0%	43.0%
19,233	ALEXANDER	13,700	7,885	5,392	423	2,493 R	57.6%	39.4%	59.4%	40.6%
6,480	ALLEGHANY	4,597	2,259	2,198	140	61 R	49.1%	47.8%	50.7%	49.3%
12,030	ANSON	8,131	2,532	5,473	126	2,941 D	31.1%	67.3%	31.6%	68.4%
15,421	ASHE	10,926	6,077	4,580	269	1,497 R	55.6%	41.9%	57.0%	43.0%
9,794	AVERY	6,612	4,507	1,879	226	2,628 R	68.2%	28.4%	70.6%	29.4%
22,712	BEAUFORT	15,677	8,717	6,564	396	2,153 R	55.6%	41.9%	57.0%	43.0%
11,716	BERTIE	6,319	2,083	4,165	71	2,082 D	33.0%	65.9%	33.3%	66.7%
16,465	BLADEN	9,643	3,436	6,064	143	2,628 D	35.6%	62.9%	36.2%	63.8%
32,769	BRUNSWICK	21,750	10,617	10,015	1,118	602 R	48.8%	46.0%	51.5%	48.5%
109,805	BUNCOMBE	73,295	37,250	34,458	1,587	2,792 R	50.8%	47.0%	51.9%	48.1%
41,850	BURKE	30,105	15,833	13,080	1,192	2,753 R	52.6%	43.4%	54.8%	45.2%
60,252	CABARRUS	41,210	24,051	15,115	2,044	8,936 R	58.4%	36.7%	61.4%	38.6%
38,196	CALDWELL	26,029	15,341	9,517	1,171	5,824 R	58.9%	36.6%	61.7%	38.3%
3,829	CAMDEN	2,613	1,159	1,405	49	246 D	44.4%	53.8%	45.2%	54.8%
30,526	CARTERET	21,848	11,934	9,041	873	2,893 R	54.6%	41.4%	56.9%	43.1%
11,900	CASWELL	7,794	2,732	4,950	112	2,218 D	35.1%	63.5%	35.6%	64.4%
68,487	CATAWBA	49,190	29,829	16,754	2,607	13,075 R	60.6%	34.1%	64.0%	36.0%
24,907	CHATHAM	18,024	7,599	9,830	595	2,231 D	42.2%	54.5%	43.6%	56.4%
14,394	CHEROKEE	8,597	4,533	4,000	64	533 R	52.7%	46.5%	53.1%	46.9%
7,412	CHOWAN	4,397	1,867	2,440	90	573 D	42.5%	55.5%	43.3%	56.7%
5,715	CLAY	3,854	2,064	1,749	41	315 R	53.6%	45.4%	54.1%	45.9%
43,359	CLEVELAND	30,125	15,575	13,353	1,197	2,222 R	51.7%	44.3%	53.8%	46.2%
31,344	COLUMBUS	19,252	6,610	12,163	479	5,553 D	34.3%	63.2%	35.2%	64.8%
39,362	CRAVEN	24,702	13,901	10,257	544	3,644 R	56.3%	41.5%	57.5%	42.5%
104,468	CUMBERLAND	66,338	29,654	34,076	2,608	4,422 D	44.7%	51.4%	46.5%	53.5%
7,311	CURRITUCK	5,136	2,457	2,546	133	89 D	47.8%	49.6%	49.1%	50.9%
14,941	DARE	10,540	5,121	5,121	298		48.6%	48.6%	50.0%	50.0%
69,608	DAVIDSON	49,496	29,413	18,053	2,030	11,360 R	59.4%	36.5%	62.0%	38.0%
16,369	DAVIE	12,065	7,812	3,841	412	3,971 R	64.7%	31.8%	67.0%	33.0%
21,182	DUPLIN	14,032	6,589	7,120	323	531 D	47.0%	50.7%	48.1%	51.9%
117,678	DURHAM	83,257	29,970	51,016	2,271	21,046 D	36.0%	61.3%	37.0%	63.0%
31,927	EDGECOMBE	19,525	7,264	11,856	405	4,592 D	37.2%	60.7%	38.0%	62.0%
161,423	FORSYTH	115,393	59,574	52,080	3,739	7,494 R	51.6%	45.1%	53.4%	46.6%
19,860	FRANKLIN	13,392	6,117	6,810	465	693 D	45.7%	50.9%	47.3%	52.7%
87,728	GASTON	61,233	38,774	19,133	3,326	19,641 R	63.3%	31.2%	67.0%	33.0%
5,546	GATES	3,598	1,014	2,530	54	1,516 D	28.2%	70.3%	28.6%	71.4%
5,730	GRAHAM	3,734	2,081	1,618	35	463 R	55.7%	43.3%	56.3%	43.7%
18,327	GRANVILLE	12,493	5,336	6,712	445	1,376 D	42.7%	53.7%	44.3%	55.7%
8,136	GREENE	5,417	2,653	2,683	81	30 D	49.0%	49.5%	49.7%	50.3%
229,000	GUILFORD	145,964	69,752	71,511	4,701	1,759 D	47.8%	49.0%	49.4%	50.6%
27,839	HALIFAX	18,556	7,173	10,919	464	3,746 D	38.7%	58.8%	39.6%	60.4%
29,552	HARNETT	20,633	10,785	9,088	760	1,697 R	52.3%	44.0%	54.3%	45.7%
30,910	HAYWOOD	20,952	9,530	10,871	551	1,341 D	45.5%	51.9%	46.7%	53.3%
45,893	HENDERSON	32,158	20,073	11,202	883	8,871 R	62.4%	34.8%	64.2%	35.8%
14,019	HERTFORD	7,271	2,350	4,860	61	2,510 D	32.3%	66.8%	32.6%	67.4%
9,741	HOKE	6,101	2,000	3,961	140	1,961 D	32.8%	64.9%	33.6%	66.4%
3,388	HYDE	2,137	834	1,260	43	426 D	39.0%	59.0%	39.8%	60.2%
55,014	IREDELL	38,799	22,514	14,266	2,019	8,248 R	58.0%	36.8%	61.2%	38.8%
17,529	JACKSON	11,495	5,093	6,236	166	1,143 D	44.3%	54.2%	45.0%	55.0%
44,429	JOHNSTON	30,948	17,755	12,003	1,190	5,752 R	57.4%	38.8%	59.7%	40.3%
5,467	JONES	3,784	1,677	2,017	90	340 D	44.3%	53.3%	45.4%	54.6%
21,035	LEE	14,471	7,578	6,361	532	1,217 R	52.4%	44.0%	54.4%	45.6%
28,335	LENOIR	18,793	9,477	9,048	268	429 R	50.4%	48.1%	51.2%	48.8%
30,871	LINCOLN	22,099	12,669	8,332	1,098	4,337 R	57.3%	37.7%	60.3%	39.7%
19,608	MCDOWELL	13,267	6,977	5,950	340	1,027 R	52.6%	44.8%	54.0%	46.0%
16,417	MACON	11,244	5,940	5,030	274	910 R	52.8%	44.7%	54.1%	45.9%
12,435	MADISON	7,312	3,364	3,857	91	493 D	46.0%	52.7%	46.6%	53.4%
13,282	MARTIN	7,797	3,450	4,249	98	799 D	44.2%	54.5%	44.8%	55.2%
326,005	MECKLENBURG	218,643	105,867	104,373	8,403	1,494 R	48.4%	47.7%	50.4%	49.6%

NORTH CAROLINA

SENATOR 1992

Registration	County	Total Vote	Republican	Democratic	Other	Rep.-Dem. Plurality	Percentage			
							Total Vote		Major Vote	
							Rep.	Dem.	Rep.	Dem.
10,782	MITCHELL	6,784	4,784	1,811	189	2,973 R	70.5%	26.7%	72.5%	27.5%
13,153	MONTGOMERY	8,772	4,065	4,486	221	421 D	46.3%	51.1%	47.5%	52.5%
37,001	MOORE	26,320	15,004	10,674	642	4,330 R	57.0%	40.6%	58.4%	41.6%
42,600	NASH	29,597	16,826	11,971	800	4,855 R	56.9%	40.4%	58.4%	41.6%
77,169	NEW HANOVER	51,100	27,540	20,976	2,584	6,564 R	53.9%	41.0%	56.8%	43.2%
12,951	NORTHAMPTON	7,378	2,076	5,211	91	3,135 D	28.1%	70.6%	28.5%	71.5%
36,947	ONSLOW	23,861	13,878	8,873	1,110	5,005 R	58.2%	37.2%	61.0%	39.0%
68,606	ORANGE	46,655	14,805	30,320	1,530	15,515 D	31.7%	65.0%	32.8%	67.2%
7,000	PAMLICO	4,860	2,262	2,414	184	152 D	46.5%	49.7%	48.4%	51.6%
15,609	PASQUOTANK	9,305	3,832	5,387	86	1,555 D	41.2%	57.9%	41.6%	58.4%
17,757	PENDER	12,474	6,177	5,729	568	448 R	49.5%	45.9%	51.9%	48.1%
5,948	PERQUIMANS	3,675	1,666	1,947	62	281 D	45.3%	53.0%	46.1%	53.9%
15,235	PERSON	9,698	4,926	4,417	355	509 R	50.8%	45.5%	52.7%	47.3%
59,372	PITT	38,810	18,827	19,299	684	472 D	48.5%	49.7%	49.4%	50.6%
11,040	POLK	7,067	3,835	3,100	132	735 R	54.3%	43.9%	55.3%	44.7%
56,783	RANDOLPH	38,213	24,467	12,454	1,292	12,013 R	64.0%	32.6%	66.3%	33.7%
24,316	RICHMOND	15,195	5,310	9,177	708	3,867 D	34.9%	60.4%	36.7%	63.3%
56,869	ROBESON	31,070	9,098	21,308	664	12,210 D	29.3%	68.6%	29.9%	70.1%
44,424	ROCKINGHAM	30,838	14,885	14,800	1,153	85 R	48.3%	48.0%	50.1%	49.9%
61,716	ROWAN	42,431	24,344	15,847	2,240	8,497 R	57.4%	37.3%	60.6%	39.4%
29,280	RUTHERFORD	20,168	10,830	8,628	710	2,202 R	53.7%	42.8%	55.7%	44.3%
28,074	SAMPSON	18,925	9,945	8,740	240	1,205 R	52.5%	46.2%	53.2%	46.8%
17,997	SCOTLAND	8,753	2,924	5,690	139	2,766 D	33.4%	65.0%	33.9%	66.1%
29,884	STANLY	21,614	12,297	8,529	788	3,768 R	56.9%	39.5%	59.0%	41.0%
23,012	STOKES	16,596	9,133	6,983	480	2,150 R	55.0%	42.1%	56.7%	43.3%
34,164	SURRY	23,396	12,566	10,387	443	2,179 R	53.7%	44.4%	54.7%	45.3%
8,568	SWAIN	4,275	1,984	2,237	54	253 D	46.4%	52.3%	47.0%	53.0%
17,868	TRANSYLVANIA	12,848	6,940	5,483	425	1,457 R	54.0%	42.7%	55.9%	44.1%
2,213	TYRRELL	1,541	605	911	25	306 D	39.3%	59.1%	39.9%	60.1%
48,511	UNION	31,086	18,165	11,716	1,205	6,449 R	58.4%	37.7%	60.8%	39.2%
19,862	VANCE	12,941	5,407	7,281	253	1,874 D	41.8%	56.3%	42.6%	57.4%
278,030	WAKE	206,897	100,311	99,315	7,271	996 R	48.5%	48.0%	50.2%	49.8%
10,987	WARREN	7,038	2,152	4,762	124	2,610 D	30.6%	67.7%	31.1%	68.9%
7,882	WASHINGTON	5,101	2,138	2,908	55	770 D	41.9%	57.0%	42.4%	57.6%
27,705	WATAUGA	18,743	9,372	8,577	794	795 R	50.0%	45.8%	52.2%	47.8%
42,720	WAYNE	26,452	14,899	11,082	471	3,817 R	56.3%	41.9%	57.3%	42.7%
37,484	WILKES	25,026	15,515	8,717	794	6,798 R	62.0%	34.8%	64.0%	36.0%
36,212	WILSON	22,048	10,797	10,941	310	144 D	49.0%	49.6%	49.7%	50.3%
17,144	YADKIN	12,635	8,431	3,871	333	4,560 R	66.7%	30.6%	68.5%	31.5%
12,274	YANCEY	9,028	4,497	4,452	79	45 R	49.8%	49.3%	50.3%	49.7%
3,817,380	TOTAL	2,577,891	1,297,892	1,194,015	85,984	103,877 R	50.3%	46.3%	52.1%	47.9%

NORTH CAROLINA

CONGRESS

CD	Year	Total Vote	Republican Vote	Republican Candidate	Democratic Vote	Democratic Candidate	Other Vote	Rep.-Dem. Plurality	Total Vote Rep.	Total Vote Dem.	Major Vote Rep.	Major Vote Dem.
1	1992	173,262	54,457	TYLER, TED	116,078	CLAYTON, EVA	2,727	61,621 D	31.4%	67.0%	31.9%	68.1%
2	1992	211,569	93,893	DAVIS, DON	113,693	VALENTINE, I. T.	3,983	19,800 D	44.4%	53.7%	45.2%	54.8%
3	1992	187,050	80,759	POLLARD, TOMMY	101,739	LANCASTER, MARTIN	4,552	20,980 D	43.2%	54.4%	44.3%	55.7%
4	1992	265,060	89,345	GOUDIE, VICKY	171,299	PRICE, DAVID E.	4,416	81,954 D	33.7%	64.6%	34.3%	65.7%
5	1992	223,683	102,086	BURR, RICHARD M.	117,835	NEAL, STEPHEN L.	3,762	15,749 D	45.6%	52.7%	46.4%	53.6%
6	1992	230,022	162,822	COBLE, HOWARD	67,200	HOOD, ROBIN		95,622 R	70.8%	29.2%	70.8%	29.2%
7	1992	163,101	66,536	ANDERSON, ROBERT C.	92,414	ROSE, CHARLES G.	4,151	25,878 D	40.8%	56.7%	41.9%	58.1%
8	1992	190,951	71,842	PRIVETTE, COY C.	113,162	HEFNER, W. G.	5,947	41,320 D	37.6%	59.3%	38.8%	61.2%
9	1992	228,245	153,650	MCMILLAN, J. ALEX	74,583	BLAKE, RORY	12	79,067 R	67.3%	32.7%	67.3%	32.7%
10	1992	235,127	149,033	BALLENGER, CASS	79,206	NEILL, BEN	6,888	69,827 R	63.4%	33.7%	65.3%	34.7%
11	1992	238,161	130,158	TAYLOR, CHARLES H.	108,003	STEVENS, JOHN S.		22,155 R	54.7%	45.3%	54.7%	45.3%
12	1992	180,824	49,402	WASHINGTON, BARBARA G.	127,262	WATT, MELVIN	4,160	77,860 D	27.3%	70.4%	28.0%	72.0%

NORTH CAROLINA

1992 GENERAL ELECTION

President   Other vote was 5,171 Libertarian (Marrou); 59 Fulani (write-in); 41 Hagelin (write-in); 12 Warren (write-in).

Governor   Other vote was Libertarian (McLaughlin).

Senator   Other vote was 85,948 Libertarian (Emory); 23 Kimball (write-in); 13 Zakutney (write-in).

Congress   Other vote was Libertarian (Williams) in CD 1; Libertarian (Lubahn) in CD 2; Libertarian (Jackson) in CD 3; Libertarian (Paczelt) in CD 4; 3,758 Libertarian (Albrecht) and 4 Weathers (write-in) in CD 5; Libertarian (Kelley) in CD 7; Libertarian (Drye) in CD 8; Russell (write-in) in CD 9; Libertarian (Brown) in CD 10; Libertarian (Krumel) in CD 12. In CD 8, the Richmond county vote was corrected from 4,996 to 496 and the total Libertarian vote revised from 10,447 to 5,947.

1992 PRIMARIES

MAY 5 REPUBLICAN

Governor   215,528 James C. Gardner; 26,179 Ruby T. Hooper; 21,256 Gary M. Dunn.

Senator   129,159 Lauch Faircloth; 81,801 Sue Myrick; 46,112 Eugene Johnston; 13,496 Larry E. Harrington.

Congress   Unopposed in seven CD's. Contested as follows:

CD 2   4,848 Don Davis; 4,825 William L. Israel; 4,076 Ted G. Stone; 3,881 Hal C. Sharpe; 2,206 James P. Gunter.
CD 5   11,135 Richard M. Burr; 6,839 Reginald Bowman.
CD 7   8,815 Robert C. Anderson; 4,742 Scott C. Dorman.
CD 8   11,748 Coy C. Privette; 5,958 George E. Crump.
CD 12   2,938 Barbara G. Washington; 1,917 George Jones; 1,758 O. C. Stafford; 1,531 Max Kent; 543 E. A. Dreano.

MAY 5 DEMOCRATIC

Governor   459,300 James B. Hunt; 188,806 Lacy H. Thornburg; 25,660 Marcus W. Williams; 18,807 Jim Hatcher; 9,033 M. Wendell Briggs.

Senator   Terry Sanford, unopposed.

Congress   Unopposed in nine CD's. Contested as follows:

CD 1   33,634 Walter B. Jones, Jr.; 27,477 Eva Clayton; 9,112 Willie D. Riddick; 5,893 Staccato Powell; 5,771 Thomas C. Hardaway; 5,085 Thomas B. Brandon; 1,227 Don Smith.
CD 8   32,790 W. G. Hefner; 16,373 Don Dawkins.
CD 12   26,495 Melvin Watt; 16,187 Mickey Michaux; 8,298 Larry D. Little; 5,338 Earl Jones.

JUNE 2 REPUBLICAN RUN-OFF

Congress   Contested as follows:

CD 2   5,005 Don Davis; 2,311 William L. Israel.
CD 12   1,071 Barbara G. Washington; 861 George Jones.

JUNE 2 DEMOCRATIC RUN-OFF

Congress   Contested as follows:

CD 1   43,210 Eva Clayton; 35,729 Walter B. Jones, Jr.

NORTH DAKOTA

GOVERNOR
Edward T. Schafer (R). Elected 1992 to a four-year term.

SENATORS
Kent Conrad (D). Elected in a special election December 1992 to fill out the remaining two years of the term vacated by the death of Senator Quentin N. Burdick (D) who died in September 1992. Previously elected 1986 to a six-year term.

Byron L. Dorgan (D). Elected 1992 to a six year term.

REPRESENTATIVE
At-large. Earl Pomeroy (D)

POSTWAR VOTE FOR PRESIDENT

Year	Total Vote	Republican Vote	Republican Candidate	Democratic Vote	Democratic Candidate	Other Vote	Plurality	Percentage Total Vote Rep.	Total Vote Dem.	Major Vote Rep.	Major Vote Dem.
1992 **	308,133	136,244	Bush, George	99,168	Clinton, Bill	72,721	37,076 R	44.2%	32.2%	57.9%	42.1%
1988	297,261	166,559	Bush, George	127,739	Dukakis, Michael S.	2,963	38,820 R	56.0%	43.0%	56.6%	43.4%
1984	308,971	200,336	Reagan, Ronald	104,429	Mondale, Walter F.	4,206	95,907 R	64.8%	33.8%	65.7%	34.3%
1980	301,545	193,695	Reagan, Ronald	79,189	Carter, Jimmy	28,661	114,506 R	64.2%	26.3%	71.0%	29.0%
1976	297,188	153,470	Ford, Gerald R.	136,078	Carter, Jimmy	7,640	17,392 R	51.6%	45.8%	53.0%	47.0%
1972	280,514	174,109	Nixon, Richard M.	100,384	McGovern, George S.	6,021	73,725 R	62.1%	35.8%	63.4%	36.6%
1968	247,882	138,669	Nixon, Richard M.	94,769	Humphrey, Hubert H.	14,444	43,900 R	55.9%	38.2%	59.4%	40.6%
1964	258,389	108,207	Goldwater, Barry M.	149,784	Johnson, Lyndon B.	398	41,577 D	41.9%	58.0%	41.9%	58.1%
1960	278,431	154,310	Nixon, Richard M.	123,963	Kennedy, John F.	158	30,347 R	55.4%	44.5%	55.5%	44.5%
1956	253,991	156,766	Eisenhower, Dwight D.	96,742	Stevenson, Adlai E.	483	60,024 R	61.7%	38.1%	61.8%	38.2%
1952	270,127	191,712	Eisenhower, Dwight D.	76,694	Stevenson, Adlai E.	1,721	115,018 R	71.0%	28.4%	71.4%	28.6%
1948	220,716	115,139	Dewey, Thomas E.	95,812	Truman, Harry S.	9,765	19,327 R	52.2%	43.4%	54.6%	45.4%

In 1992 the other vote column includes 71,084 votes cast for Perot.

NORTH DAKOTA

POSTWAR VOTE FOR GOVERNOR

Year	Total Vote	Republican Vote	Republican Candidate	Democratic Vote	Democratic Candidate	Other Vote	Rep.-Dem. Plurality	Percentage Total Vote Rep.	Percentage Total Vote Dem.	Percentage Major Vote Rep.	Percentage Major Vote Dem.
1992	304,861	176,398	Schafer, Edward T.	123,845	Spaeth, Nicholas	4,618	52,553 R	57.9%	40.6%	58.8%	41.2%
1988	299,080	119,986	Mallberg, Leon L.	179,094	Sinner, George		59,108 D	40.1%	59.9%	40.1%	59.9%
1984	314,382	140,460	Olson, Allen I.	173,922	Sinner, George		33,462 D	44.7%	55.3%	44.7%	55.3%
1980	302,621	162,230	Olson, Allen I.	140,391	Link, Arthur A.		21,839 R	53.6%	46.4%	53.6%	46.4%
1976	297,249	138,321	Elkin, Richard	153,309	Link, Arthur A.	5,619	14,988 D	46.5%	51.6%	47.4%	52.6%
1972	281,931	138,032	Larsen, Richard	143,899	Link, Arthur A.		5,867 D	49.0%	51.0%	49.0%	51.0%
1968	248,000	108,382	McCarney, Robert P.	135,955	Guy, William L.	3,663	27,573 D	43.7%	54.8%	44.4%	55.6%
1964 **	262,661	116,247	Halcrow, Donald M.	146,414	Guy, William L.		30,167 D	44.3%	55.7%	44.3%	55.7%
1962	228,509	113,251	Andrews, Mark	115,258	Guy, William L.		2,007 D	49.6%	50.4%	49.6%	50.4%
1960	275,375	122,486	Dahl, C. P.	136,148	Guy, William L.	16,741	13,662 D	44.5%	49.4%	47.4%	52.6%
1958	210,599	111,836	Davis, John E.	98,763	Lord, John F.		13,073 R	53.1%	46.9%	53.1%	46.9%
1956	252,435	147,566	Davis, John E.	104,869	Warner, Wallace E.		42,697 R	58.5%	41.5%	58.5%	41.5%
1954	193,501	124,253	Brunsdale, C. Norman	69,248	Bymers, Cornelius		55,005 R	64.2%	35.8%	64.2%	35.8%
1952	253,934	199,944	Brunsdale, C. Norman	53,990	Johnson, Ole C.		145,954 R	78.7%	21.3%	78.7%	21.3%
1950	183,772	121,822	Brunsdale, C. Norman	61,950	Byerly, Clyde G.		59,872 R	66.3%	33.7%	66.3%	33.7%
1948	214,858	131,764	Aandahl, Fred G.	80,555	Henry, Howard	2,539	51,209 R	61.3%	37.5%	62.1%	37.9%
1946	169,391	116,672	Aandahl, Fred G.	52,719	Burdick, Quentin N.		63,953 R	68.9%	31.1%	68.9%	31.1%

The term of office of North Dakota's Governor was increased from two to four years effective with the 1964 election.

POSTWAR VOTE FOR SENATOR

Year	Total Vote	Republican Vote	Republican Candidate	Democratic Vote	Democratic Candidate	Other Vote	Rep.-Dem. Plurality	Percentage Total Vote Rep.	Percentage Total Vote Dem.	Percentage Major Vote Rep.	Percentage Major Vote Dem.
1992	303,957	118,162	Sydness, Steve	179,347	Dorgan, Byron L.	6,448	61,185 D	38.9%	59.0%	39.7%	60.3%
1992 S	163,311	55,194	Dalrymple, Jack	103,246	Conrad, Kent	4,871	48,052 D	33.8%	63.2%	34.8%	65.2%
1988	289,170	112,937	Striden, Earl	171,899	Burdick, Quentin N.	4,334	58,962 D	39.1%	59.4%	39.6%	60.4%
1986	288,998	141,797	Andrews, Mark	143,932	Conrad, Kent	3,269	2,135 D	49.1%	49.8%	49.6%	50.4%
1982	262,465	89,304	Knorr, Gene	164,873	Burdick, Quentin N.	8,288	75,569 D	34.0%	62.8%	35.1%	64.9%
1980	299,272	210,347	Andrews, Mark	86,658	Johanneson, Kent	2,267	123,689 R	70.3%	29.0%	70.8%	29.2%
1976	283,062	103,466	Stroup, Richard	175,772	Burdick, Quentin N.	3,824	72,306 D	36.6%	62.1%	37.1%	62.9%
1974	235,661	114,117	Young, Milton R.	113,931	Guy, William L.	7,613	186 R	48.4%	48.3%	50.0%	50.0%
1970	219,560	82,996	Kleppe, Tom	134,519	Burdick, Quentin N.	2,045	51,523 D	37.8%	61.3%	38.2%	61.8%
1968	239,776	154,968	Young, Milton R.	80,815	Lashkowitz, Herschel	3,993	74,153 R	64.6%	33.7%	65.7%	34.3%
1964	258,945	109,681	Kleppe, Tom	149,264	Burdick, Quentin N.		39,583 D	42.4%	57.6%	42.4%	57.6%
1962	223,737	135,705	Young, Milton R.	88,032	Lanier, William		47,673 R	60.7%	39.3%	60.7%	39.3%
1960 S	210,349	103,475	Davis, John E.	104,593	Burdick, Quentin N.	2,281	1,118 D	49.2%	49.7%	49.7%	50.3%
1958	204,635	117,070	Langer, William	84,892	Vendsel, Raymond	2,673	32,178 R	57.2%	41.5%	58.0%	42.0%
1956	244,161	155,305	Young, Milton R.	87,919	Burdick, Quentin N.	937	67,386 R	63.6%	36.0%	63.9%	36.1%
1952	237,995	157,907	Langer, William	55,347	Morrison, Harold A.	24,741	102,560 R	66.3%	23.3%	74.0%	26.0%
1950	186,716	126,209	Young, Milton R.	60,507	O'Brien, Harry		65,702 R	67.6%	32.4%	67.6%	32.4%
1946 **	165,382	88,210	Langer, William	38,368	Larson, Abner B.	38,804	49,842 R	53.3%	23.2%	69.7%	30.3%
1946 S	136,852	75,998	Young, Milton R.	37,507	Lanier, William	23,347	38,491 R	55.5%	27.4%	67.0%	33.0%

One of the 1992 elections was for a short term to fill a vacancy and the special election was held in December. The 1960 and 1946 special elections were held in June for short terms to fill vacancies. In 1946 other vote was Arthur Thompson (Independent) who received 23.5% of the total vote and ran second.

NORTH DAKOTA

One At Large

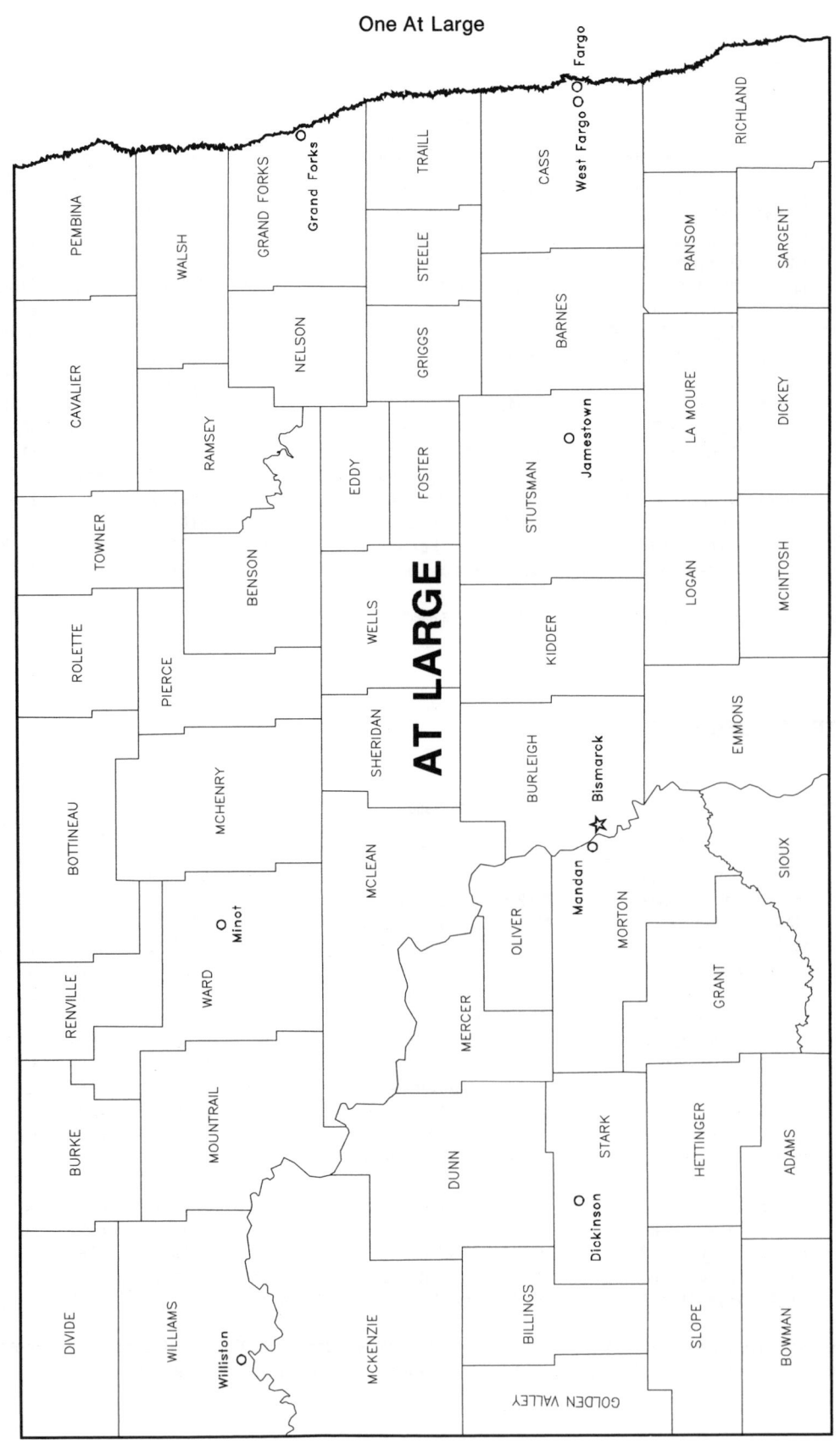

NORTH DAKOTA

PRESIDENT 1992

1990 Voting Age Population	County	Total Vote	Republican	Democratic	Perot	Other	Plurality	Percentage Total Vote		
								Rep.	Dem.	Perot
2,347	ADAMS	1,626	647	469	499	11	148 R	39.8%	28.8%	30.7%
9,453	BARNES	6,449	2,728	2,124	1,568	29	604 R	42.3%	32.9%	24.3%
4,696	BENSON	2,625	874	1,126	610	15	252 D	33.3%	42.9%	23.2%
744	BILLINGS	678	279	123	270	6	9 R	41.2%	18.1%	39.8%
5,948	BOTTINEAU	4,104	1,787	1,266	1,036	15	521 R	43.5%	30.8%	25.2%
2,587	BOWMAN	1,907	712	506	678	11	34 R	37.3%	26.5%	35.6%
2,260	BURKE	1,524	551	458	506	9	45 R	36.2%	30.1%	33.2%
43,387	BURLEIGH	32,384	16,484	8,940	6,780	180	7,544 R	50.9%	27.6%	20.9%
77,184	CASS	53,116	25,312	18,077	9,513	214	7,235 R	47.7%	34.0%	17.9%
4,431	CAVALIER	3,126	1,527	866	723	10	661 R	48.8%	27.7%	23.1%
4,580	DICKEY	3,060	1,514	918	616	12	596 R	49.5%	30.0%	20.1%
2,207	DIVIDE	1,620	515	634	456	15	119 D	31.8%	39.1%	28.1%
2,768	DUNN	2,105	784	667	637	17	117 R	37.2%	31.7%	30.3%
2,213	EDDY	1,615	591	575	432	17	16 R	36.6%	35.6%	26.7%
3,587	EMMONS	2,430	1,047	595	774	14	273 R	43.1%	24.5%	31.9%
2,889	FOSTER	1,940	803	565	556	16	238 R	41.4%	29.1%	28.7%
1,457	GOLDEN VALLEY	1,114	503	255	352	4	151 R	45.2%	22.9%	31.6%
52,306	GRAND FORKS	31,104	13,705	10,930	6,349	120	2,775 R	44.1%	35.1%	20.4%
2,607	GRANT	1,959	900	415	629	15	271 R	45.9%	21.2%	32.1%
2,446	GRIGGS	1,756	773	647	330	6	126 R	44.0%	36.8%	18.8%
2,545	HETTINGER	1,838	854	465	500	19	354 R	46.5%	25.3%	27.2%
2,416	KIDDER	1,711	739	468	489	15	250 R	43.2%	27.4%	28.6%
3,918	LA MOURE	2,763	1,270	797	679	17	473 R	46.0%	28.8%	24.6%
2,141	LOGAN	1,486	703	383	390	10	313 R	47.3%	25.8%	26.2%
4,758	MCHENRY	3,396	1,321	1,173	886	16	148 R	38.9%	34.5%	26.1%
3,148	MCINTOSH	2,054	1,134	450	454	16	680 R	55.2%	21.9%	22.1%
4,272	MCKENZIE	3,090	1,324	787	969	10	355 R	42.8%	25.5%	31.4%
7,404	MCLEAN	5,303	2,124	1,808	1,330	41	316 R	40.1%	34.1%	25.1%
6,629	MERCER	5,017	2,274	1,323	1,378	42	896 R	45.3%	26.4%	27.5%
16,539	MORTON	11,522	5,042	3,594	2,787	99	1,448 R	43.8%	31.2%	24.2%
4,913	MOUNTRAIL	3,289	1,017	1,393	861	18	376 D	30.9%	42.4%	26.2%
3,383	NELSON	2,206	864	841	486	15	23 R	39.2%	38.1%	22.0%
1,581	OLIVER	1,228	503	306	407	12	96 R	41.0%	24.9%	33.1%
6,647	PEMBINA	4,127	1,917	1,186	991	33	731 R	46.5%	28.7%	24.0%
3,765	PIERCE	2,431	1,099	761	554	17	338 R	45.2%	31.3%	22.8%
9,336	RAMSEY	6,054	2,516	2,008	1,507	23	508 R	41.6%	33.2%	24.9%
4,390	RANSOM	2,903	1,102	1,166	625	10	64 D	38.0%	40.2%	21.5%
2,287	RENVILLE	1,670	655	580	429	6	75 R	39.2%	34.7%	25.7%
13,231	RICHLAND	8,301	3,873	2,688	1,698	42	1,185 R	46.7%	32.4%	20.5%
7,895	ROLETTE	3,606	895	2,002	660	49	1,107 D	24.8%	55.5%	18.3%
3,325	SARGENT	2,254	816	961	463	14	145 D	36.2%	42.6%	20.5%
1,632	SHERIDAN	1,175	589	276	304	6	285 R	50.1%	23.5%	25.9%
2,140	SIOUX	984	264	463	244	13	199 D	26.8%	47.1%	24.8%
635	SLOPE	535	226	145	162	2	64 R	42.2%	27.1%	30.3%
16,059	STARK	10,678	4,491	3,003	3,123	61	1,368 R	42.1%	28.1%	29.2%
1,788	STEELE	1,370	503	598	267	2	95 D	36.7%	43.6%	19.5%
16,456	STUTSMAN	10,001	4,039	3,313	2,580	69	726 R	40.4%	33.1%	25.8%
2,652	TOWNER	1,757	600	748	402	7	148 D	34.1%	42.6%	22.9%
6,508	TRAILL	4,553	2,019	1,638	875	21	381 R	44.3%	36.0%	19.2%
10,023	WALSH	5,904	2,544	1,936	1,384	40	608 R	43.1%	32.8%	23.4%
41,669	WARD	25,852	12,056	7,856	5,856	84	4,200 R	46.6%	30.4%	22.7%
4,430	WELLS	2,916	1,171	888	850	7	283 R	40.2%	30.5%	29.1%
14,803	WILLIAMS	9,917	3,664	3,008	3,180	65	484 R	36.9%	30.3%	32.1%
463,415	TOTAL	308,133	136,244	99,168	71,084	1,637	37,076 R	44.2%	32.2%	23.1%

NORTH DAKOTA

GOVERNOR 1992

1990 Voting Age Population	County	Total Vote	Republican	Democratic	Other	Rep.-Dem. Plurality	Percentage Total Vote Rep.	Percentage Total Vote Dem.	Percentage Major Vote Rep.	Percentage Major Vote Dem.
2,347	ADAMS	1,608	948	638	22	310 R	59.0%	39.7%	59.8%	40.2%
9,453	BARNES	6,442	3,453	2,795	194	658 R	53.6%	43.4%	55.3%	44.7%
4,696	BENSON	2,603	1,328	1,225	50	103 R	51.0%	47.1%	52.0%	48.0%
744	BILLINGS	677	364	295	18	69 R	53.8%	43.6%	55.2%	44.8%
5,948	BOTTINEAU	4,070	2,242	1,769	59	473 R	55.1%	43.5%	55.9%	44.1%
2,587	BOWMAN	1,887	1,082	769	36	313 R	57.3%	40.8%	58.5%	41.5%
2,260	BURKE	1,512	781	704	27	77 R	51.7%	46.6%	52.6%	47.4%
43,387	BURLEIGH	30,977	21,144	9,452	381	11,692 R	68.3%	30.5%	69.1%	30.9%
77,184	CASS	52,843	29,948	22,338	557	7,610 R	56.7%	42.3%	57.3%	42.7%
4,431	CAVALIER	3,056	1,985	1,013	58	972 R	65.0%	33.1%	66.2%	33.8%
4,580	DICKEY	2,994	1,727	1,223	44	504 R	57.7%	40.8%	58.5%	41.5%
2,207	DIVIDE	1,603	756	826	21	70 D	47.2%	51.5%	47.8%	52.2%
2,768	DUNN	2,105	1,212	861	32	351 R	57.6%	40.9%	58.5%	41.5%
2,213	EDDY	1,602	887	696	19	191 R	55.4%	43.4%	56.0%	44.0%
3,587	EMMONS	2,415	1,470	912	33	558 R	60.9%	37.8%	61.7%	38.3%
2,889	FOSTER	1,922	1,158	733	31	425 R	60.2%	38.1%	61.2%	38.8%
1,457	GOLDEN VALLEY	1,102	638	447	17	191 R	57.9%	40.6%	58.8%	41.2%
52,306	GRAND FORKS	30,525	18,279	11,790	456	6,489 R	59.9%	38.6%	60.8%	39.2%
2,607	GRANT	1,940	1,289	617	34	672 R	66.4%	31.8%	67.6%	32.4%
2,446	GRIGGS	1,766	923	822	21	101 R	52.3%	46.5%	52.9%	47.1%
2,545	HETTINGER	1,853	1,072	765	16	307 R	57.9%	41.3%	58.4%	41.6%
2,416	KIDDER	1,694	1,104	564	26	540 R	65.2%	33.3%	66.2%	33.8%
3,918	LA MOURE	2,750	1,569	1,140	41	429 R	57.1%	41.5%	57.9%	42.1%
2,141	LOGAN	1,475	983	476	16	507 R	66.6%	32.3%	67.4%	32.6%
4,758	MCHENRY	3,401	1,678	1,663	60	15 R	49.3%	48.9%	50.2%	49.8%
3,148	MCINTOSH	2,046	1,397	633	16	764 R	68.3%	30.9%	68.8%	31.2%
4,272	MCKENZIE	3,072	1,751	1,288	33	463 R	57.0%	41.9%	57.6%	42.4%
7,404	MCLEAN	5,323	2,942	2,291	90	651 R	55.3%	43.0%	56.2%	43.8%
6,629	MERCER	4,974	3,177	1,719	78	1,458 R	63.9%	34.6%	64.9%	35.1%
16,539	MORTON	11,580	7,351	4,074	155	3,277 R	63.5%	35.2%	64.3%	35.7%
4,913	MOUNTRAIL	3,273	1,473	1,734	66	261 D	45.0%	53.0%	45.9%	54.1%
3,383	NELSON	2,202	1,172	1,001	29	171 R	53.2%	45.5%	53.9%	46.1%
1,581	OLIVER	1,238	803	412	23	391 R	64.9%	33.3%	66.1%	33.9%
6,647	PEMBINA	4,122	2,747	1,324	51	1,423 R	66.6%	32.1%	67.5%	32.5%
3,765	PIERCE	2,410	1,330	1,047	33	283 R	55.2%	43.4%	56.0%	44.0%
9,336	RAMSEY	6,029	3,418	2,519	92	899 R	56.7%	41.8%	57.6%	42.4%
4,390	RANSOM	2,893	1,410	1,444	39	34 D	48.7%	49.9%	49.4%	50.6%
2,287	RENVILLE	1,648	850	765	33	85 R	51.6%	46.4%	52.6%	47.4%
13,231	RICHLAND	8,193	4,413	3,653	127	760 R	53.9%	44.6%	54.7%	45.3%
7,895	ROLETTE	3,557	1,206	2,243	108	1,037 D	33.9%	63.1%	35.0%	65.0%
3,325	SARGENT	2,243	1,012	1,197	34	185 D	45.1%	53.4%	45.8%	54.2%
1,632	SHERIDAN	1,159	808	337	14	471 R	69.7%	29.1%	70.6%	29.4%
2,140	SIOUX	980	394	569	17	175 D	40.2%	58.1%	40.9%	59.1%
635	SLOPE	534	290	234	10	56 R	54.3%	43.8%	55.3%	44.7%
16,059	STARK	10,592	5,999	4,413	180	1,586 R	56.6%	41.7%	57.6%	42.4%
1,788	STEELE	1,383	638	726	19	88 D	46.1%	52.5%	46.8%	53.2%
16,456	STUTSMAN	9,936	5,755	3,959	222	1,796 R	57.9%	39.8%	59.2%	40.8%
2,652	TOWNER	1,728	877	825	26	52 R	50.8%	47.7%	51.5%	48.5%
6,508	TRAILL	4,558	2,442	2,040	76	402 R	53.6%	44.8%	54.5%	45.5%
10,023	WALSH	5,904	3,627	2,217	60	1,410 R	61.4%	37.6%	62.1%	37.9%
41,669	WARD	25,652	14,111	11,053	488	3,058 R	55.0%	43.1%	56.1%	43.9%
4,430	WELLS	2,913	1,763	1,099	51	664 R	60.5%	37.7%	61.6%	38.4%
14,803	WILLIAMS	9,897	5,222	4,496	179	726 R	52.8%	45.4%	53.7%	46.3%
463,415	TOTAL	304,861	176,398	123,845	4,618	52,553 R	57.9%	40.6%	58.8%	41.2%

NORTH DAKOTA

SENATOR 1992
(FULL TERM)

1990 Voting Age Population	County	Total Vote	Republican	Democratic	Other	Rep.-Dem. Plurality	Percentage			
							Total Vote		Major Vote	
							Rep.	Dem.	Rep.	Dem.
2,347	ADAMS	1,578	594	928	56	334 D	37.6%	58.8%	39.0%	61.0%
9,453	BARNES	6,518	2,452	3,957	109	1,505 D	37.6%	60.7%	38.3%	61.7%
4,696	BENSON	2,585	792	1,756	37	964 D	30.6%	67.9%	31.1%	68.9%
744	BILLINGS	676	280	363	33	83 D	41.4%	53.7%	43.5%	56.5%
5,948	BOTTINEAU	4,049	1,511	2,473	65	962 D	37.3%	61.1%	37.9%	62.1%
2,587	BOWMAN	1,885	716	1,098	71	382 D	38.0%	58.2%	39.5%	60.5%
2,260	BURKE	1,497	486	986	25	500 D	32.5%	65.9%	33.0%	67.0%
43,387	BURLEIGH	31,065	13,277	16,916	872	3,639 D	42.7%	54.5%	44.0%	56.0%
77,184	CASS	52,414	20,420	31,179	815	10,759 D	39.0%	59.5%	39.6%	60.4%
4,431	CAVALIER	3,100	1,197	1,845	58	648 D	38.6%	59.5%	39.3%	60.7%
4,580	DICKEY	2,975	1,332	1,600	43	268 D	44.8%	53.8%	45.4%	54.6%
2,207	DIVIDE	1,618	460	1,127	31	667 D	28.4%	69.7%	29.0%	71.0%
2,768	DUNN	2,108	813	1,247	48	434 D	38.6%	59.2%	39.5%	60.5%
2,213	EDDY	1,618	628	939	51	311 D	38.8%	58.0%	40.1%	59.9%
3,587	EMMONS	2,441	1,099	1,258	84	159 D	45.0%	51.5%	46.6%	53.4%
2,889	FOSTER	1,892	762	1,091	39	329 D	40.3%	57.7%	41.1%	58.9%
1,457	GOLDEN VALLEY	1,096	458	612	26	154 D	41.8%	55.8%	42.8%	57.2%
52,306	GRAND FORKS	30,305	12,201	17,506	598	5,305 D	40.3%	57.8%	41.1%	58.9%
2,607	GRANT	1,948	813	1,002	133	189 D	41.7%	51.4%	44.8%	55.2%
2,446	GRIGGS	1,738	647	1,069	22	422 D	37.2%	61.5%	37.7%	62.3%
2,545	HETTINGER	1,832	725	1,068	39	343 D	39.6%	58.3%	40.4%	59.6%
2,416	KIDDER	1,719	710	926	83	216 D	41.3%	53.9%	43.4%	56.6%
3,918	LA MOURE	2,740	1,141	1,555	44	414 D	41.6%	56.8%	42.3%	57.7%
2,141	LOGAN	1,497	676	776	45	100 D	45.2%	51.8%	46.6%	53.4%
4,758	MCHENRY	3,332	1,161	2,121	50	960 D	34.8%	63.7%	35.4%	64.6%
3,148	MCINTOSH	2,034	1,123	868	43	255 R	55.2%	42.7%	56.4%	43.6%
4,272	MCKENZIE	3,033	1,218	1,746	69	528 D	40.2%	57.6%	41.1%	58.9%
7,404	MCLEAN	5,370	2,041	3,202	127	1,161 D	38.0%	59.6%	38.9%	61.1%
6,629	MERCER	4,949	1,998	2,835	116	837 D	40.4%	57.3%	41.3%	58.7%
16,539	MORTON	11,670	4,389	6,930	351	2,541 D	37.6%	59.4%	38.8%	61.2%
4,913	MOUNTRAIL	3,259	914	2,273	72	1,359 D	28.0%	69.7%	28.7%	71.3%
3,383	NELSON	2,223	684	1,508	31	824 D	30.8%	67.8%	31.2%	68.8%
1,581	OLIVER	1,245	464	743	38	279 D	37.3%	59.7%	38.4%	61.6%
6,647	PEMBINA	4,146	1,667	2,390	89	723 D	40.2%	57.6%	41.1%	58.9%
3,765	PIERCE	2,394	1,022	1,334	38	312 D	42.7%	55.7%	43.4%	56.6%
9,336	RAMSEY	5,989	2,220	3,675	94	1,455 D	37.1%	61.4%	37.7%	62.3%
4,390	RANSOM	2,876	876	1,952	48	1,076 D	30.5%	67.9%	31.0%	69.0%
2,287	RENVILLE	1,646	516	1,104	26	588 D	31.3%	67.1%	31.9%	68.1%
13,231	RICHLAND	8,116	3,144	4,838	134	1,694 D	38.7%	59.6%	39.4%	60.6%
7,895	ROLETTE	3,643	789	2,789	65	2,000 D	21.7%	76.6%	22.1%	77.9%
3,325	SARGENT	2,226	718	1,470	38	752 D	32.3%	66.0%	32.8%	67.2%
1,632	SHERIDAN	1,158	612	527	19	85 R	52.8%	45.5%	53.7%	46.3%
2,140	SIOUX	987	239	708	40	469 D	24.2%	71.7%	25.2%	74.8%
635	SLOPE	543	215	306	22	91 D	39.6%	56.4%	41.3%	58.7%
16,059	STARK	10,649	4,186	6,199	264	2,013 D	39.3%	58.2%	40.3%	59.7%
1,788	STEELE	1,358	385	955	18	570 D	28.4%	70.3%	28.7%	71.3%
16,456	STUTSMAN	9,960	4,127	5,594	239	1,467 D	41.4%	56.2%	42.5%	57.5%
2,652	TOWNER	1,722	490	1,211	21	721 D	28.5%	70.3%	28.8%	71.2%
6,508	TRAILL	4,530	1,595	2,883	52	1,288 D	35.2%	63.6%	35.6%	64.4%
10,023	WALSH	5,937	2,325	3,520	92	1,195 D	39.2%	59.3%	39.8%	60.2%
41,669	WARD	25,243	9,676	15,040	527	5,364 D	38.3%	59.6%	39.1%	60.9%
4,430	WELLS	2,879	1,199	1,612	68	413 D	41.6%	56.0%	42.7%	57.3%
14,803	WILLIAMS	9,946	3,979	5,737	230	1,758 D	40.0%	57.7%	41.0%	59.0%
463,415	TOTAL	303,957	118,162	179,347	6,448	61,185 D	38.9%	59.0%	39.7%	60.3%

NORTH DAKOTA

SENATOR DECEMBER 1992
(SHORT TERM)

1990 Voting Age Population	County	Total Vote	Republican	Democratic	Other	Rep.-Dem. Plurality	Percentage			
							Total Vote		Major Vote	
							Rep.	Dem.	Rep.	Dem.
2,347	ADAMS	787	281	503	3	222 D	35.7%	63.9%	35.8%	64.2%
9,453	BARNES	3,742	1,206	2,402	134	1,196 D	32.2%	64.2%	33.4%	66.6%
4,696	BENSON	1,666	411	1,192	63	781 D	24.7%	71.5%	25.6%	74.4%
744	BILLINGS	381	184	182	15	2 R	48.3%	47.8%	50.3%	49.7%
5,948	BOTTINEAU	2,336	770	1,500	66	730 D	33.0%	64.2%	33.9%	66.1%
2,587	BOWMAN	989	339	627	23	288 D	34.3%	63.4%	35.1%	64.9%
2,260	BURKE	916	287	620	9	333 D	31.3%	67.7%	31.6%	68.4%
43,387	BURLEIGH	17,318	7,364	9,587	367	2,223 D	42.5%	55.4%	43.4%	56.6%
77,184	CASS	26,502	9,600	16,053	849	6,453 D	36.2%	60.6%	37.4%	62.6%
4,431	CAVALIER	2,133	681	1,276	176	595 D	31.9%	59.8%	34.8%	65.2%
4,580	DICKEY	1,674	641	968	65	327 D	38.3%	57.8%	39.8%	60.2%
2,207	DIVIDE	1,016	252	741	23	489 D	24.8%	72.9%	25.4%	74.6%
2,768	DUNN	1,249	467	759	23	292 D	37.4%	60.8%	38.1%	61.9%
2,213	EDDY	1,024	311	653	60	342 D	30.4%	63.8%	32.3%	67.7%
3,587	EMMONS	1,422	596	790	36	194 D	41.9%	55.6%	43.0%	57.0%
2,889	FOSTER	1,273	552	698	23	146 D	43.4%	54.8%	44.2%	55.8%
1,457	GOLDEN VALLEY	609	217	378	14	161 D	35.6%	62.1%	36.5%	63.5%
52,306	GRAND FORKS	15,692	4,480	10,737	475	6,257 D	28.5%	68.4%	29.4%	70.6%
2,607	GRANT	1,197	532	631	34	99 D	44.4%	52.7%	45.7%	54.3%
2,446	GRIGGS	1,216	407	761	48	354 D	33.5%	62.6%	34.8%	65.2%
2,545	HETTINGER	1,069	417	629	23	212 D	39.0%	58.8%	39.9%	60.1%
2,416	KIDDER	1,054	447	575	32	128 D	42.4%	54.6%	43.7%	56.3%
3,918	LA MOURE	1,784	659	1,068	57	409 D	36.9%	59.9%	38.2%	61.8%
2,141	LOGAN	964	437	505	22	68 D	45.3%	52.4%	46.4%	53.6%
4,758	MCHENRY	2,155	553	1,537	65	984 D	25.7%	71.3%	26.5%	73.5%
3,148	MCINTOSH	1,195	640	530	25	110 R	53.6%	44.4%	54.7%	45.3%
4,272	MCKENZIE	1,675	597	1,050	28	453 D	35.6%	62.7%	36.2%	63.8%
7,404	MCLEAN	3,468	1,245	2,133	90	888 D	35.9%	61.5%	36.9%	63.1%
6,629	MERCER	2,610	997	1,556	57	559 D	38.2%	59.6%	39.1%	60.9%
16,539	MORTON	5,510	1,979	3,397	134	1,418 D	35.9%	61.7%	36.8%	63.2%
4,913	MOUNTRAIL	1,845	399	1,394	52	995 D	21.6%	75.6%	22.3%	77.7%
3,383	NELSON	1,590	417	1,124	49	707 D	26.2%	70.7%	27.1%	72.9%
1,581	OLIVER	709	287	410	12	123 D	40.5%	57.8%	41.2%	58.8%
6,647	PEMBINA	2,275	760	1,413	102	653 D	33.4%	62.1%	35.0%	65.0%
3,765	PIERCE	1,396	411	920	65	509 D	29.4%	65.9%	30.9%	69.1%
9,336	RAMSEY	3,131	857	2,128	146	1,271 D	27.4%	68.0%	28.7%	71.3%
4,390	RANSOM	1,769	472	1,258	39	786 D	26.7%	71.1%	27.3%	72.7%
2,287	RENVILLE	1,092	267	792	33	525 D	24.5%	72.5%	25.2%	74.8%
13,231	RICHLAND	4,268	1,442	2,608	218	1,166 D	33.8%	61.1%	35.6%	64.4%
7,895	ROLETTE	1,709	336	1,321	52	985 D	19.7%	77.3%	20.3%	79.7%
3,325	SARGENT	1,490	465	1,001	24	536 D	31.2%	67.2%	31.7%	68.3%
1,632	SHERIDAN	828	448	359	21	89 R	54.1%	43.4%	55.5%	44.5%
2,140	SIOUX	374	113	256	5	143 D	30.2%	68.4%	30.6%	69.4%
635	SLOPE	344	119	216	9	97 D	34.6%	62.8%	35.5%	64.5%
16,059	STARK	4,822	1,747	2,979	96	1,232 D	36.2%	61.8%	37.0%	63.0%
1,788	STEELE	1,021	275	729	17	454 D	26.9%	71.4%	27.4%	72.6%
16,456	STUTSMAN	5,330	1,678	3,511	141	1,833 D	31.5%	65.9%	32.3%	67.7%
2,652	TOWNER	1,110	279	783	48	504 D	25.1%	70.5%	26.3%	73.7%
6,508	TRAILL	2,824	927	1,827	70	900 D	32.8%	64.7%	33.7%	66.3%
10,023	WALSH	3,098	923	2,022	153	1,099 D	29.8%	65.3%	31.3%	68.7%
41,669	WARD	11,399	2,922	8,128	349	5,206 D	25.6%	71.3%	26.4%	73.6%
4,430	WELLS	1,814	733	1,032	49	299 D	40.4%	56.9%	41.5%	58.5%
14,803	WILLIAMS	4,447	1,368	2,997	82	1,629 D	30.8%	67.4%	31.3%	68.7%
463,415	TOTAL	163,311	55,194	103,246	4,871	48,052 D	33.8%	63.2%	34.8%	65.2%

NORTH DAKOTA

CONGRESS

CD	Year	Total Vote	Republican		Democratic		Other Vote	Rep.-Dem. Plurality	Percentage			
			Vote	Candidate	Vote	Candidate			Total Vote		Major Vote	
									Rep.	Dem.	Rep.	Dem.
AL	1992	297,898	117,442	KORSMO, JOHN T.	169,273	POMEROY, EARL	11,183	51,831 D	39.4%	56.8%	41.0%	59.0%
AL	1990	233,979	81,443	SCHAFER, EDWARD T.	152,530	DORGAN, BYRON L.	6	71,087 D	34.8%	65.2%	34.8%	65.2%
AL	1988	299,982	84,475	SYDNESS, STEVE	212,583	DORGAN, BYRON L.	2,924	128,108 D	28.2%	70.9%	28.4%	71.6%
AL	1986	286,361	66,989	VINJE, SYVER	216,258	DORGAN, BYRON L.	3,114	149,269 D	23.4%	75.5%	23.7%	76.3%
AL	1984	308,729	65,761	ALTENBURG, LOIS I.	242,968	DORGAN, BYRON L.		177,207 D	21.3%	78.7%	21.3%	78.7%
AL	1982	260,499	72,241	JONES, KENT	186,534	DORGAN, BYRON L.	1,724	114,293 D	27.7%	71.6%	27.9%	72.1%
AL	1980	293,076	124,707	SMYKOWSKI, JIM	166,437	DORGAN, BYRON L.	1,932	41,730 D	42.6%	56.8%	42.8%	57.2%
AL	1978	220,348	147,746	ANDREWS, MARK	68,016	HAGEN, BRUCE	4,586	79,730 R	67.1%	30.9%	68.5%	31.5%
AL	1976	289,881	181,018	ANDREWS, MARK	104,263	OMDAHL, LLOYD B.	4,600	76,755 R	62.4%	36.0%	63.5%	36.5%
AL	1974	233,688	130,184	ANDREWS, MARK	103,504	DORGAN, BYRON L.		26,680 R	55.7%	44.3%	55.7%	44.3%
AL	1972	268,721	195,360	ANDREWS, MARK	72,850	ISTA, RICHARD	511	122,510 R	72.7%	27.1%	72.8%	27.2%

NORTH DAKOTA

1992 GENERAL ELECTION

North Dakota has no formal registration system; the data presented in the registration column in the tables are the 1990 Voting Age Population.

President   Other vote was 642 Independent (LaRouche); 416 Independent (Marrou); 240 Independent (Hagelin); 193 Independent (Warren); 143 Independent (Fulani); 3 Dodge (write-in).

Governor   Other vote was 2,614 Independent (McLain); 2,004 Independent (DuPaul).

Senator   Other vote was Independent (Asbridge).
Full Term

Senator   A special election was held December 4, 1992 to fill the vacancy created by the death of Senator
Short Term   Quentin N. Burdick. Both major-party candidates were nominated by the state party committees and no primaries were held. Other vote was Independent (Larson).

Congress   Other vote at-large was 7,394 Independent (Bourgois) and 3,789 Independent (Blount).

1992 PRIMARIES

JUNE 9 REPUBLICAN

Governor   Edward T. Schafer, unopposed

Senator   Steve Sydness, unopposed.

Congress   Unopposed at-large.

JUNE 9 DEMOCRATIC

Governor   50,607 Nicholas Spaeth; 27,161 Bill Heigaard.

Senator   Byron L. Dorgan, unopposed.

Congress   Unopposed at-large.

OHIO

GOVERNOR
George Voinovich (R). Elected 1990 to a four-year term.

SENATORS
John H. Glenn (D). Re-elected 1992 to a six-year term. Previously elected 1986, 1980, 1974.

Howard Metzenbaum (D). Re-elected 1988 to a six-year term. Previously elected 1982, 1976.

REPRESENTATIVES
1. David Mann (D)
2. Willis D. Gradison (R) (see page 1)
3. Tony P. Hall (D)
4. Michael G. Oxley (R)
5. Paul E. Gillmor (R)
6. Ted Strickland (D)
7. David L. Hobson (R)
8. John A. Boehner (R)
9. Marcy Kaptur (D)
10. Martin R. Hoke (R)
11. Louis Stokes (D)
12. John R. Kasich (R)
13. Sherrod Brown (D)
14. Thomas C. Sawyer (D)
15. Deborah Pryce (R)
16. Ralph S. Regula (R)
17. James A. Traficant (D)
18. Douglas Applegate (D)
19. Eric D. Fingerhut (D)

POSTWAR VOTE FOR PRESIDENT

Year	Total Vote	Republican Vote	Republican Candidate	Democratic Vote	Democratic Candidate	Other Vote	Plurality	Total Vote Rep.	Total Vote Dem.	Major Vote Rep.	Major Vote Dem.
1992 **	4,939,967	1,894,310	Bush, George	1,984,942	Clinton, Bill	1,060,715	90,632 D	38.3%	40.2%	48.8%	51.2%
1988	4,393,699	2,416,549	Bush, George	1,939,629	Dukakis, Michael S.	37,521	476,920 R	55.0%	44.1%	55.5%	44.5%
1984	4,547,619	2,678,560	Reagan, Ronald	1,825,440	Mondale, Walter F.	43,619	853,120 R	58.9%	40.1%	59.5%	40.5%
1980	4,283,603	2,206,545	Reagan, Ronald	1,752,414	Carter, Jimmy	324,644	454,131 R	51.5%	40.9%	55.7%	44.3%
1976	4,111,873	2,000,505	Ford, Gerald R.	2,011,621	Carter, Jimmy	99,747	11,116 D	48.7%	48.9%	49.9%	50.1%
1972	4,094,787	2,441,827	Nixon, Richard M.	1,558,889	McGovern, George S.	94,071	882,938 R	59.6%	38.1%	61.0%	39.0%
1968	3,959,698	1,791,014	Nixon, Richard M.	1,700,586	Humphrey, Hubert H.	468,098	90,428 R	45.2%	42.9%	51.3%	48.7%
1964	3,969,196	1,470,865	Goldwater, Barry M.	2,498,331	Johnson, Lyndon B.		1,027,466 D	37.1%	62.9%	37.1%	62.9%
1960	4,161,859	2,217,611	Nixon, Richard M.	1,944,248	Kennedy, John F.		273,363 R	53.3%	46.7%	53.3%	46.7%
1956	3,702,265	2,262,610	Eisenhower, Dwight D.	1,439,655	Stevenson, Adlai E.		822,955 R	61.1%	38.9%	61.1%	38.9%
1952	3,700,758	2,100,391	Eisenhower, Dwight D.	1,600,367	Stevenson, Adlai E.		500,024 R	56.8%	43.2%	56.8%	43.2%
1948	2,936,071	1,445,684	Dewey, Thomas E.	1,452,791	Truman, Harry S.	37,596	7,107 D	49.2%	49.5%	49.9%	50.1%

In 1992 the other vote column includes 1,036,426 votes cast for Perot.

OHIO

POSTWAR VOTE FOR GOVERNOR

Year	Total Vote	Republican		Democratic		Other Vote	Rep.-Dem. Plurality	Percentage			
								Total Vote		Major Vote	
		Vote	Candidate	Vote	Candidate			Rep.	Dem.	Rep.	Dem.
1990	3,477,650	1,938,103	Voinovich, George	1,539,416	Celebrezze, Anthony J.	131	398,687 R	55.7%	44.3%	55.7%	44.3%
1986	3,066,611	1,207,264	Rhodes, James A.	1,858,372	Celeste, Richard F.	975	651,108 D	39.4%	60.6%	39.4%	60.6%
1982	3,356,721	1,303,962	Brown, Clarence, Jr.	1,981,882	Celeste, Richard F.	70,877	677,920 D	38.8%	59.0%	39.7%	60.3%
1978	2,843,351	1,402,167	Rhodes, James A.	1,354,631	Celeste, Richard F.	86,553	47,536 R	49.3%	47.6%	50.9%	49.1%
1974	3,072,010	1,493,679	Rhodes, James A.	1,482,191	Gilligan, John J.	96,140	11,488 R	48.6%	48.2%	50.2%	49.8%
1970	3,184,133	1,382,659	Cloud, Roger	1,725,560	Gilligan, John J.	75,914	342,901 D	43.4%	54.2%	44.5%	55.5%
1966	2,887,331	1,795,277	Rhodes, James A.	1,092,054	Reams, Frazier, Jr.		703,223 R	62.2%	37.8%	62.2%	37.8%
1962	3,116,711	1,836,190	Rhodes, James A.	1,280,521	DiSalle, Michael V.		555,669 R	58.9%	41.1%	58.9%	41.1%
1958 **	3,284,134	1,414,874	O'Neill, C. William	1,869,260	DiSalle, Michael V.		454,386 D	43.1%	56.9%	43.1%	56.9%
1956	3,542,091	1,984,988	O'Neill, C. William	1,557,103	DiSalle, Michael V.		427,885 R	56.0%	44.0%	56.0%	44.0%
1954	2,597,790	1,192,528	Rhodes, James A.	1,405,262	Lausche, Frank J.		212,734 D	45.9%	54.1%	45.9%	54.1%
1952	3,605,168	1,590,058	Taft, Charles P.	2,015,110	Lausche, Frank J.		425,052 D	44.1%	55.9%	44.1%	55.9%
1950	2,892,819	1,370,570	Ebright, Don H.	1,522,249	Lausche, Frank J.		151,679 D	47.4%	52.6%	47.4%	52.6%
1948	3,018,289	1,398,514	Herbert, Thomas J.	1,619,775	Lausche, Frank J.		221,261 D	46.3%	53.7%	46.3%	53.7%
1946	2,303,750	1,166,550	Herbert, Thomas J.	1,125,997	Lausche, Frank J.	11,203	40,553 R	50.6%	48.9%	50.9%	49.1%

The term of office of Ohio's Governor was increased from two to four years effective with the 1958 election.

POSTWAR VOTE FOR SENATOR

Year	Total Vote	Republican		Democratic		Other Vote	Rep.-Dem. Plurality	Percentage			
								Total Vote		Major Vote	
		Vote	Candidate	Vote	Candidate			Rep.	Dem.	Rep.	Dem.
1992	4,793,953	2,028,300	DeWine, Mike	2,444,419	Glenn, John H.	321,234	416,119 D	42.3%	51.0%	45.3%	54.7%
1988	4,352,905	1,872,716	Voinovich, George	2,480,038	Metzenbaum, Howard	151	607,322 D	43.0%	57.0%	43.0%	57.0%
1986	3,121,189	1,171,893	Kindness, Thomas N.	1,949,208	Glenn, John H.	88	777,315 D	37.5%	62.5%	37.5%	62.5%
1982	3,395,463	1,396,790	Pfeifer, Paul E.	1,923,767	Metzenbaum, Howard	74,906	526,977 D	41.1%	56.7%	42.1%	57.9%
1980	4,027,303	1,137,695	Betts, James E.	2,770,786	Glenn, John H.	118,822	1,633,091 D	28.2%	68.8%	29.1%	70.9%
1976	3,920,613	1,823,774	Taft, Robert A.,Jr.	1,941,113	Metzenbaum, Howard	155,726	117,339 D	46.5%	49.5%	48.4%	51.6%
1974	2,987,951	918,133	Perk, Ralph J.	1,930,670	Glenn, John H.	139,148	1,012,537 D	30.7%	64.6%	32.2%	67.8%
1970	3,151,274	1,565,682	Taft, Robert A.,Jr.	1,495,262	Metzenbaum, Howard	90,330	70,420 R	49.7%	47.4%	51.2%	48.8%
1968	3,743,121	1,928,964	Saxbe, William B.	1,814,152	Gilligan, John J.	5	114,812 R	51.5%	48.5%	51.5%	48.5%
1964	3,830,389	1,906,781	Taft, Robert A.,Jr.	1,923,608	Young, Stephen M.		16,827 D	49.8%	50.2%	49.8%	50.2%
1962	2,994,986	1,151,173	Briley, John M.	1,843,813	Lausche, Frank J.		692,640 D	38.4%	61.6%	38.4%	61.6%
1958	3,149,410	1,497,199	Bricker, John W.	1,652,211	Young, Stephen M.		155,012 D	47.5%	52.5%	47.5%	52.5%
1956	3,525,499	1,660,910	Bender, George H.	1,864,589	Lausche, Frank J.		203,679 D	47.1%	52.9%	47.1%	52.9%
1954 S	2,512,778	1,257,874	Bender, George H.	1,254,904	Burke, Thomas A.		2,970 R	50.1%	49.9%	50.1%	49.9%
1952	3,442,291	1,878,961	Bricker, John W.	1,563,330	DiSalle, Michael V.		315,631 R	54.6%	45.4%	54.6%	45.4%
1950	2,860,102	1,645,643	Taft, Robert A.	1,214,459	Ferguson, Joseph T.		431,184 R	57.5%	42.5%	57.5%	42.5%
1946	2,237,269	1,275,774	Bricker, John W.	947,610	Huffman, James W.	13,885	328,164 R	57.0%	42.4%	57.4%	42.6%

The 1954 election was for a short term to fill a vacancy.

OHIO

Districts Established March 27, 1992

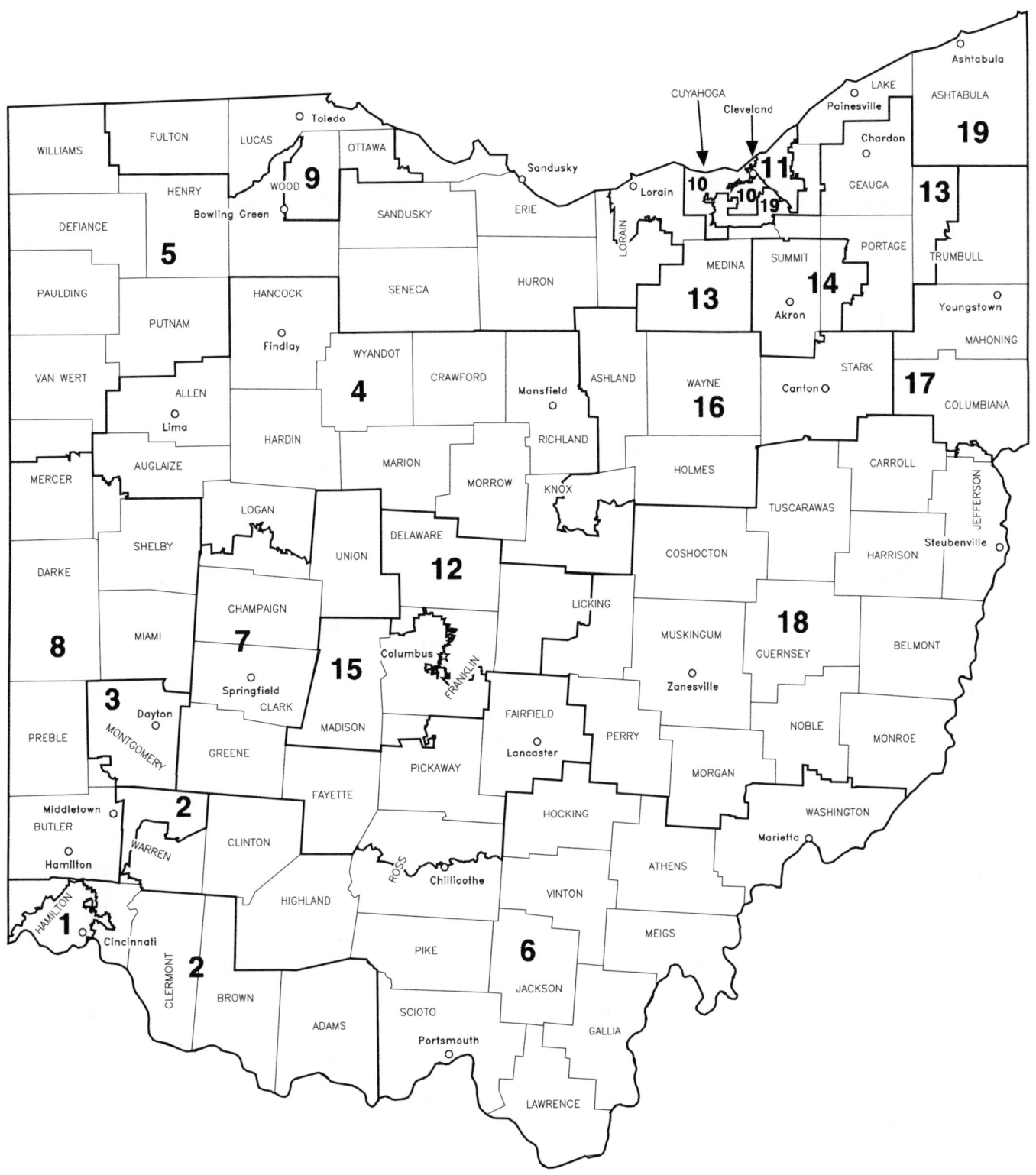

OHIO

PRESIDENT 1992

Registration	County	Total Vote	Republican	Democratic	Perot	Other	Plurality	Percentage Total Vote		
								Rep.	Dem.	Perot
14,904	ADAMS	10,758	4,722	3,998	1,993	45	724 R	43.9%	37.2%	18.5%
60,797	ALLEN	47,350	25,322	13,777	8,131	120	11,545 R	53.5%	29.1%	17.2%
25,906	ASHLAND	20,855	9,864	5,985	4,950	56	3,879 R	47.3%	28.7%	23.7%
57,224	ASHTABULA	43,028	13,254	18,843	10,765	166	5,589 D	30.8%	43.8%	25.0%
39,542	ATHENS	25,793	7,184	13,423	5,074	112	6,239 D	27.9%	52.0%	19.7%
26,031	AUGLAIZE	20,306	10,455	4,960	4,840	51	5,495 R	51.5%	24.4%	23.8%
45,824	BELMONT	33,421	8,614	18,527	6,142	138	9,913 D	25.8%	55.4%	18.4%
19,984	BROWN	15,186	5,912	5,540	3,676	58	372 R	38.9%	36.5%	24.2%
173,780	BUTLER	131,112	63,375	39,682	27,527	528	23,693 R	48.3%	30.3%	21.0%
16,328	CARROLL	12,463	4,224	4,731	3,434	74	507 D	33.9%	38.0%	27.6%
21,337	CHAMPAIGN	16,252	7,004	5,201	3,992	55	1,803 R	43.1%	32.0%	24.6%
83,007	CLARK	63,538	24,011	26,692	12,571	264	2,681 D	37.8%	42.0%	19.8%
81,930	CLERMONT	64,142	32,065	17,558	14,279	240	14,507 R	50.0%	27.4%	22.3%
20,048	CLINTON	15,391	7,290	4,638	3,402	61	2,652 R	47.4%	30.1%	22.1%
63,496	COLUMBIANA	47,554	15,016	19,765	12,611	162	4,749 D	31.6%	41.6%	26.5%
20,638	COSHOCTON	16,173	5,705	6,212	4,081	175	507 D	35.3%	38.4%	25.2%
27,506	CRAWFORD	20,835	8,618	6,351	5,764	102	2,267 R	41.4%	30.5%	27.7%
932,611	CUYAHOGA	640,241	187,186	337,548	112,352	3,155	150,362 D	29.2%	52.7%	17.5%
31,057	DARKE	24,426	11,098	7,016	6,217	95	4,082 R	45.4%	28.7%	25.5%
21,940	DEFIANCE	17,211	7,195	5,735	4,187	94	1,460 R	41.8%	33.3%	24.3%
46,760	DELAWARE	36,873	18,225	9,263	9,244	141	8,962 R	49.4%	25.1%	25.1%
46,549	ERIE	35,828	12,459	14,531	8,720	118	2,072 D	34.8%	40.6%	24.3%
63,661	FAIRFIELD	50,789	24,125	14,249	12,246	169	9,876 R	47.5%	28.1%	24.1%
13,274	FAYETTE	10,086	4,916	2,976	2,162	32	1,940 R	48.7%	29.5%	21.4%
582,202	FRANKLIN	444,801	186,324	176,656	79,049	2,772	9,668 R	41.9%	39.7%	17.8%
23,613	FULTON	18,804	8,358	5,576	4,798	72	2,782 R	44.4%	29.7%	25.5%
19,657	GALLIA	13,738	5,776	5,350	2,549	63	426 R	42.0%	38.9%	18.6%
50,445	GEAUGA	40,518	18,200	11,466	10,577	275	6,734 R	44.9%	28.3%	26.1%
82,837	GREENE	59,502	27,651	20,139	11,459	253	7,512 R	46.5%	33.8%	19.3%
22,317	GUERNSEY	16,348	5,749	6,428	4,103	68	679 D	35.2%	39.3%	25.1%
536,386	HAMILTON	403,420	192,447	148,409	60,145	2,419	44,038 R	47.7%	36.8%	14.9%
39,692	HANCOCK	31,963	16,821	7,944	7,002	196	8,877 R	52.6%	24.9%	21.9%
16,812	HARDIN	13,215	5,851	4,364	2,867	133	1,487 R	44.3%	33.0%	21.7%
10,000	HARRISON	7,827	2,289	3,830	1,679	29	1,541 D	29.2%	48.9%	21.5%
16,932	HENRY	13,359	6,196	3,933	3,178	52	2,263 R	46.4%	29.4%	23.8%
20,426	HIGHLAND	15,242	7,020	4,866	3,315	41	2,154 R	46.1%	31.9%	21.7%
14,406	HOCKING	10,574	3,761	3,935	2,831	47	174 D	35.6%	37.2%	26.8%
13,588	HOLMES	9,056	5,079	1,969	1,945	63	3,110 R	56.1%	21.7%	21.5%
31,666	HURON	24,471	9,480	7,930	6,751	310	1,550 R	38.7%	32.4%	27.6%
20,210	JACKSON	12,883	5,422	5,016	2,389	56	406 R	42.1%	38.9%	18.5%
50,591	JEFFERSON	38,798	10,764	20,978	6,910	146	10,214 D	27.7%	54.1%	17.8%
26,996	KNOX	21,745	9,044	7,259	5,282	160	1,785 R	41.6%	33.4%	24.3%
135,000	LAKE	105,990	40,766	37,682	26,878	664	3,084 R	38.5%	35.6%	25.4%
38,530	LAWRENCE	27,021	10,044	12,325	4,536	116	2,281 D	37.2%	45.6%	16.8%
78,024	LICKING	60,434	26,918	18,898	13,806	812	8,020 R	44.5%	31.3%	22.8%
26,424	LOGAN	18,787	9,364	4,889	4,472	62	4,475 R	49.8%	26.0%	23.8%
161,238	LORAIN	118,605	36,803	50,962	30,425	415	14,159 D	31.0%	43.0%	25.7%
262,219	LUCAS	203,019	63,297	99,989	38,108	1,625	36,692 D	31.2%	49.3%	18.8%
17,925	MADISON	14,071	6,865	3,998	3,170	38	2,867 R	48.8%	28.4%	22.5%
165,241	MAHONING	125,650	31,191	64,731	29,417	311	33,540 D	24.8%	51.5%	23.4%
35,444	MARION	27,715	11,675	9,444	6,471	125	2,231 R	42.1%	34.1%	23.3%
75,769	MEDINA	60,601	24,090	18,995	17,290	226	5,095 R	39.8%	31.3%	28.5%
14,419	MEIGS	10,286	3,916	4,226	2,098	46	310 D	38.1%	41.1%	20.4%
23,199	MERCER	18,548	8,683	4,883	4,913	69	3,770 R	46.8%	26.3%	26.5%
53,070	MIAMI	43,006	19,741	12,547	10,544	174	7,194 R	45.9%	29.2%	24.5%
10,034	MONROE	7,591	1,823	4,235	1,505	28	2,412 D	24.0%	55.8%	19.8%
343,172	MONTGOMERY	261,720	104,751	108,017	47,854	1,098	3,266 D	40.0%	41.3%	18.3%
8,672	MORGAN	6,707	2,719	2,402	1,551	35	317 R	40.5%	35.8%	23.1%
17,300	MORROW	12,791	5,208	3,907	3,623	53	1,301 R	40.7%	30.5%	28.3%
45,354	MUSKINGUM	34,720	14,168	11,670	8,731	151	2,498 R	40.8%	33.6%	25.1%

OHIO

PRESIDENT 1992

Registration	County	Total Vote	Republican	Democratic	Perot	Other	Plurality	Percentage Total Vote		
								Rep.	Dem.	Perot
7,667	NOBLE	5,883	2,223	2,201	1,429	30	22 R	37.8%	37.4%	24.3%
24,766	OTTAWA	19,795	6,782	8,128	4,832	53	1,346 D	34.3%	41.1%	24.4%
12,114	PAULDING	9,510	3,652	3,293	2,510	55	359 R	38.4%	34.6%	26.4%
18,454	PERRY	13,547	4,712	4,972	3,810	53	260 D	34.8%	36.7%	28.1%
24,657	PICKAWAY	18,930	8,690	5,765	4,319	156	2,925 R	45.9%	30.5%	22.8%
17,163	PIKE	11,393	4,094	5,057	2,192	50	963 D	35.9%	44.4%	19.2%
82,388	PORTAGE	62,135	18,447	26,325	17,065	298	7,878 D	29.7%	42.4%	27.5%
22,969	PREBLE	18,098	8,023	5,557	4,460	58	2,466 R	44.3%	30.7%	24.6%
20,236	PUTNAM	17,004	9,338	3,962	3,648	56	5,376 R	54.9%	23.3%	21.5%
70,300	RICHLAND	56,697	23,532	19,606	13,370	189	3,926 R	41.5%	34.6%	23.6%
34,759	ROSS	27,173	10,825	10,452	5,616	280	373 R	39.8%	38.5%	20.7%
32,704	SANDUSKY	27,472	10,772	9,878	6,682	140	894 R	39.2%	36.0%	24.3%
45,756	SCIOTO	33,624	11,931	14,715	6,860	118	2,784 D	35.5%	43.8%	20.4%
33,397	SENECA	26,150	9,763	9,280	6,967	140	483 R	37.3%	35.5%	26.6%
24,847	SHELBY	20,011	8,854	5,262	5,835	60	3,019 R	44.2%	26.3%	29.2%
220,522	STARK	175,092	61,863	70,064	42,413	752	8,201 D	35.3%	40.0%	24.2%
313,004	SUMMIT	241,492	77,530	107,881	55,151	930	30,351 D	32.1%	44.7%	22.8%
138,776	TRUMBULL	107,606	25,831	54,591	26,791	393	27,800 D	24.0%	50.7%	24.9%
48,419	TUSCARAWAS	36,894	13,179	14,787	8,785	143	1,608 D	35.7%	40.1%	23.8%
18,542	UNION	14,777	7,818	3,465	3,433	61	4,353 R	52.9%	23.4%	23.2%
18,185	VAN WERT	14,217	7,227	3,822	3,102	66	3,405 R	50.8%	26.9%	21.8%
7,586	VINTON	5,363	1,975	2,308	1,050	30	333 D	36.8%	43.0%	19.6%
67,574	WARREN	52,802	27,998	13,542	11,115	147	14,456 R	53.0%	25.6%	21.1%
35,218	WASHINGTON	28,073	12,204	10,380	5,415	74	1,824 R	43.5%	37.0%	19.3%
52,549	WAYNE	41,982	18,350	13,953	9,482	197	4,397 R	43.7%	33.2%	22.6%
22,391	WILLIAMS	17,464	7,614	4,862	4,902	86	2,712 R	43.6%	27.8%	28.1%
71,030	WOOD	53,203	20,579	20,754	11,682	188	175 D	38.7%	39.0%	22.0%
13,014	WYANDOT	10,443	4,411	3,031	2,929	72	1,380 R	42.2%	29.0%	28.0%
6,542,931	TOTAL	4,939,967	1,894,310	1,984,942	1,036,426	24,289	90,632 D	38.3%	40.2%	21.0%

OHIO

SENATOR 1992

Registration	County	Total Vote	Republican	Democratic	Other	Rep.-Dem. Plurality	Percentage Total Vote Rep.	Dem.	Major Vote Rep.	Dem.
14,904	ADAMS	10,507	5,152	4,792	563	360 R	49.0%	45.6%	51.8%	48.2%
60,797	ALLEN	46,744	28,464	15,580	2,700	12,884 R	60.9%	33.3%	64.6%	35.4%
25,906	ASHLAND	20,595	11,433	7,684	1,478	3,749 R	55.5%	37.3%	59.8%	40.2%
57,224	ASHTABULA	42,032	16,751	21,958	3,323	5,207 D	39.9%	52.2%	43.3%	56.7%
39,542	ATHENS	25,320	8,870	14,967	1,483	6,097 D	35.0%	59.1%	37.2%	62.8%
26,031	AUGLAIZE	20,042	12,362	6,337	1,343	6,025 R	61.7%	31.6%	66.1%	33.9%
45,824	BELMONT	32,834	8,166	21,977	2,691	13,811 D	24.9%	66.9%	27.1%	72.9%
19,984	BROWN	14,795	6,497	7,041	1,257	544 D	43.9%	47.6%	48.0%	52.0%
173,780	BUTLER	128,022	63,798	54,848	9,376	8,950 R	49.8%	42.8%	53.8%	46.2%
16,328	CARROLL	12,224	4,939	6,225	1,060	1,286 D	40.4%	50.9%	44.2%	55.8%
21,337	CHAMPAIGN	16,033	8,687	6,550	796	2,137 R	54.2%	40.9%	57.0%	43.0%
83,007	CLARK	62,952	29,431	30,871	2,650	1,440 D	46.8%	49.0%	48.8%	51.2%
81,930	CLERMONT	63,357	32,350	25,744	5,263	6,606 R	51.1%	40.6%	55.7%	44.3%
20,048	CLINTON	15,096	7,983	6,166	947	1,817 R	52.9%	40.8%	56.4%	43.6%
63,496	COLUMBIANA	46,740	17,454	25,353	3,933	7,899 D	37.3%	54.2%	40.8%	59.2%
20,638	COSHOCTON	15,747	7,271	7,151	1,325	120 R	46.2%	45.4%	50.4%	49.6%
27,506	CRAWFORD	20,446	10,121	8,180	2,145	1,941 R	49.5%	40.0%	55.3%	44.7%
932,611	CUYAHOGA	620,903	197,776	390,743	32,384	192,967 D	31.9%	62.9%	33.6%	66.4%
31,057	DARKE	23,997	12,102	10,074	1,821	2,028 R	50.4%	42.0%	54.6%	45.4%
21,940	DEFIANCE	16,876	8,280	7,036	1,560	1,244 R	49.1%	41.7%	54.1%	45.9%
46,760	DELAWARE	36,254	19,407	13,697	3,150	5,710 R	53.5%	37.8%	58.6%	41.4%
46,549	ERIE	35,272	14,716	18,091	2,465	3,375 D	41.7%	51.3%	44.9%	55.1%
63,661	FAIRFIELD	50,226	25,925	20,537	3,764	5,388 R	51.6%	40.9%	55.8%	44.2%
13,274	FAYETTE	10,013	5,878	3,649	486	2,229 R	58.7%	36.4%	61.7%	38.3%
582,202	FRANKLIN	418,009	186,979	201,716	29,314	14,737 D	44.7%	48.3%	48.1%	51.9%
23,613	FULTON	18,368	7,890	8,863	1,615	973 D	43.0%	48.3%	47.1%	52.9%
19,657	GALLIA	13,403	6,231	6,391	781	160 D	46.5%	47.7%	49.4%	50.6%
50,445	GEAUGA	37,069	19,236	15,767	2,066	3,469 R	51.9%	42.5%	55.0%	45.0%
82,837	GREENE	59,708	31,231	25,643	2,834	5,588 R	52.3%	42.9%	54.9%	45.1%
22,317	GUERNSEY	16,106	7,201	7,399	1,506	198 D	44.7%	45.9%	49.3%	50.7%
536,386	HAMILTON	394,049	180,880	185,201	27,968	4,321 D	45.9%	47.0%	49.4%	50.6%
39,692	HANCOCK	30,647	16,312	12,037	2,298	4,275 R	53.2%	39.3%	57.5%	42.5%
16,812	HARDIN	12,947	6,625	5,309	1,013	1,316 R	51.2%	41.0%	55.5%	44.5%
10,000	HARRISON	7,675	2,224	4,814	637	2,590 D	29.0%	62.7%	31.6%	68.4%
16,932	HENRY	13,129	5,994	6,036	1,099	42 D	45.7%	46.0%	49.8%	50.2%
20,426	HIGHLAND	15,095	7,819	6,470	806	1,349 R	51.8%	42.9%	54.7%	45.3%
14,406	HOCKING	10,410	4,674	4,890	846	216 D	44.9%	47.0%	48.9%	51.1%
13,588	HOLMES	8,580	5,070	2,972	538	2,098 R	59.1%	34.6%	63.0%	37.0%
31,666	HURON	23,785	10,921	11,029	1,835	108 D	45.9%	46.4%	49.8%	50.2%
20,210	JACKSON	12,550	6,253	5,558	739	695 R	49.8%	44.3%	52.9%	47.1%
50,591	JEFFERSON	37,932	9,712	24,839	3,381	15,127 D	25.6%	65.5%	28.1%	71.9%
26,996	KNOX	20,673	10,220	8,512	1,941	1,708 R	49.4%	41.2%	54.6%	45.4%
135,000	LAKE	98,148	46,213	46,441	5,494	228 D	47.1%	47.3%	49.9%	50.1%
38,530	LAWRENCE	26,347	10,995	13,668	1,684	2,673 D	41.7%	51.9%	44.6%	55.4%
78,024	LICKING	60,079	29,170	25,259	5,650	3,911 R	48.6%	42.0%	53.6%	46.4%
26,424	LOGAN	18,617	10,924	6,400	1,293	4,524 R	58.7%	34.4%	63.1%	36.9%
161,238	LORAIN	116,990	43,928	64,362	8,700	20,434 D	37.5%	55.0%	40.6%	59.4%
262,219	LUCAS	182,686	55,274	124,867	2,545	69,593 D	30.3%	68.4%	30.7%	69.3%
17,925	MADISON	13,887	7,548	5,271	1,068	2,277 R	54.4%	38.0%	58.9%	41.1%
165,241	MAHONING	125,058	37,178	79,530	8,350	42,352 D	29.7%	63.6%	31.9%	68.1%
35,444	MARION	27,475	14,527	10,857	2,091	3,670 R	52.9%	39.5%	57.2%	42.8%
75,769	MEDINA	59,456	27,247	27,410	4,799	163 D	45.8%	46.1%	49.9%	50.1%
14,419	MEIGS	10,056	4,783	4,596	677	187 R	47.6%	45.7%	51.0%	49.0%
23,199	MERCER	18,298	11,161	6,015	1,122	5,146 R	61.0%	32.9%	65.0%	35.0%
53,070	MIAMI	42,461	20,694	18,267	3,500	2,427 R	48.7%	43.0%	53.1%	46.9%
10,034	MONROE	7,375	2,123	4,676	576	2,553 D	28.8%	63.4%	31.2%	68.8%
343,172	MONTGOMERY	257,265	105,444	139,234	12,587	33,790 D	41.0%	54.1%	43.1%	56.9%
8,672	MORGAN	6,572	3,487	2,642	443	845 R	53.1%	40.2%	56.9%	43.1%
17,300	MORROW	12,595	6,082	5,218	1,295	864 R	48.3%	41.4%	53.8%	46.2%
45,354	MUSKINGUM	34,251	18,072	13,688	2,491	4,384 R	52.8%	40.0%	56.9%	43.1%

OHIO

SENATOR 1992

Registration	County	Total Vote	Republican	Democratic	Other	Rep.-Dem. Plurality	Percentage Total Vote Rep.	Dem.	Major Vote Rep.	Dem.
7,667	NOBLE	5,699	2,667	2,549	483	118 R	46.8%	44.7%	51.1%	48.9%
24,766	OTTAWA	19,634	6,729	11,230	1,675	4,501 D	34.3%	57.2%	37.5%	62.5%
12,114	PAULDING	9,301	4,897	3,705	699	1,192 R	52.7%	39.8%	56.9%	43.1%
18,454	PERRY	13,374	5,805	6,484	1,085	679 D	43.4%	48.5%	47.2%	52.8%
24,657	PICKAWAY	18,447	10,201	7,062	1,184	3,139 R	55.3%	38.3%	59.1%	40.9%
17,163	PIKE	11,068	4,512	6,025	531	1,513 D	40.8%	54.4%	42.8%	57.2%
82,388	PORTAGE	61,277	23,150	32,328	5,799	9,178 D	37.8%	52.8%	41.7%	58.3%
22,969	PREBLE	17,848	8,248	8,113	1,487	135 R	46.2%	45.5%	50.4%	49.6%
20,236	PUTNAM	16,789	10,228	5,326	1,235	4,902 R	60.9%	31.7%	65.8%	34.2%
70,300	RICHLAND	55,889	27,265	24,666	3,958	2,599 R	48.8%	44.1%	52.5%	47.5%
34,759	ROSS	24,557	11,975	11,043	1,539	932 R	48.8%	45.0%	52.0%	48.0%
32,704	SANDUSKY	26,776	10,365	13,422	2,989	3,057 D	38.7%	50.1%	43.6%	56.4%
45,756	SCIOTO	33,091	13,796	17,517	1,778	3,721 D	41.7%	52.9%	44.1%	55.9%
33,397	SENECA	25,753	11,020	12,165	2,568	1,145 D	42.8%	47.2%	47.5%	52.5%
24,847	SHELBY	16,614	8,835	6,301	1,478	2,534 R	53.2%	37.9%	58.4%	41.6%
220,522	STARK	173,359	75,847	84,543	12,969	8,696 D	43.8%	48.8%	47.3%	52.7%
313,004	SUMMIT	235,740	89,168	128,438	18,134	39,270 D	37.8%	54.5%	41.0%	59.0%
138,776	TRUMBULL	105,648	32,316	65,970	7,362	33,654 D	30.6%	62.4%	32.9%	67.1%
48,419	TUSCARAWAS	35,163	13,237	18,824	3,102	5,587 D	37.6%	53.5%	41.3%	58.7%
18,542	UNION	14,611	8,871	4,655	1,085	4,216 R	60.7%	31.9%	65.6%	34.4%
18,185	VAN WERT	14,041	9,007	4,211	823	4,796 R	64.1%	30.0%	68.1%	31.9%
7,586	VINTON	5,168	2,347	2,538	283	191 D	45.4%	49.1%	48.0%	52.0%
67,574	WARREN	52,112	27,862	20,184	4,066	7,678 R	53.5%	38.7%	58.0%	42.0%
35,218	WASHINGTON	26,910	13,765	11,643	1,502	2,122 R	51.2%	43.3%	54.2%	45.8%
52,549	WAYNE	41,111	20,400	17,576	3,135	2,824 R	49.6%	42.8%	53.7%	46.3%
22,391	WILLIAMS	16,998	8,263	7,068	1,667	1,195 R	48.6%	41.6%	53.9%	46.1%
71,030	WOOD	51,934	18,517	29,435	3,982	10,918 D	35.7%	56.7%	38.6%	61.4%
13,014	WYANDOT	10,263	4,872	4,300	1,091	572 R	47.5%	41.9%	53.1%	46.9%
6,542,931	TOTAL	4,793,953	2,028,300	2,444,419	321,234	416,119 D	42.3%	51.0%	45.3%	54.7%

OHIO

CONGRESS

CD	Year	Total Vote	Republican Vote	Republican Candidate	Democratic Vote	Democratic Candidate	Other Vote	Rep.-Dem. Plurality	Total Vote Rep.	Total Vote Dem.	Major Vote Rep.	Major Vote Dem.
1	1992	234,433			120,190	MANN, DAVID	114,243	120,190 D		51.3%		100.0%
2	1992	253,651	177,720	GRADISON, WILLIS D.	75,924	CHANDLER, THOMAS R.	7	101,796 R	70.1%	29.9%	70.1%	29.9%
3	1992	244,811	98,733	DAVIS, PETER W.	146,072	HALL, TONY P.	6	47,339 D	40.3%	59.7%	40.3%	59.7%
4	1992	240,440	147,346	OXLEY, MICHAEL G.	92,608	BALL, RAYMOND M.	486	54,738 R	61.3%	38.5%	61.4%	38.6%
5	1992	187,860	187,860	GILLMOR, PAUL E.				187,860 R	100.0%		100.0%	
6	1992	241,972	119,252	MCEWEN, BOB	122,720	STRICKLAND, TED		3,468 D	49.3%	50.7%	49.3%	50.7%
7	1992	230,432	164,195	HOBSON, DAVID L.	66,237	HESKETT, CLIFFORD S.		97,958 R	71.3%	28.7%	71.3%	28.7%
8	1992	238,395	176,362	BOEHNER, JOHN A.	62,033	STENNET, FRED		114,329 R	74.0%	26.0%	74.0%	26.0%
9	1992	243,102	53,011	BROWN, KEN D.	178,879	KAPTUR, MARCY	11,212	125,868 D	21.8%	73.6%	22.9%	77.1%
10	1992	240,239	136,433	HOKE, MARTIN R.	103,788	OAKAR, MARY ROSE	18	32,645 R	56.8%	43.2%	56.8%	43.2%
11	1992	223,624	43,866	ROTHSCHILD, BERYL E.	154,718	STOKES, LOUIS	25,040	110,852 D	19.6%	69.2%	22.1%	77.9%
12	1992	239,058	170,297	KASICH, JOHN R.	68,761	FITRAKIS, BOB		101,536 R	71.2%	28.8%	71.2%	28.8%
13	1992	252,258	88,889	MUELLER, MARGARET R.	134,486	BROWN, SHERROD	28,883	45,597 D	35.2%	53.3%	39.8%	60.2%
14	1992	243,994	78,659	MORGAN, ROBERT	165,335	SAWYER, THOMAS C.		86,676 D	32.2%	67.8%	32.2%	67.8%
15	1992	250,205	110,390	PRYCE, DEBORAH	94,907	CORDRAY, RICHARD	44,908	15,483 R	44.1%	37.9%	53.8%	46.2%
16	1992	248,713	158,489	REGULA, RALPH S.	90,224	MENDENHALL, WARNER D.		68,265 R	63.7%	36.3%	63.7%	36.3%
17	1992	257,246	40,743	PANSINO, SALVATORE	216,503	TRAFICANT, JAMES A.		175,760 D	15.8%	84.2%	15.8%	84.2%
18	1992	243,418	77,229	RESS, BILL	166,189	APPLEGATE, DOUGLAS		88,960 D	31.7%	68.3%	31.7%	68.3%
19	1992	263,083	124,606	GARDNER, ROBERT A.	138,465	FINGERHUT, ERIC D.	12	13,859 D	47.4%	52.6%	47.4%	52.6%

OHIO

1992 GENERAL ELECTION

President   Other vote was 7,252 Independent (Marrou); 6,413 Independent (Fulani); 4,699 Independent (Gritz); 3,437 Independent (Hagelin); 2,446 Independent (LaRouche); 32 Warren (write-in); 10 scattered write-in. The vote from Clermont county was amended by the Ohio Secretary of State before the final, official returns were printed. This minor adjustment changed the statewide vote for the three major candidates.

Senator   Other vote was Independent (Grevatt). The vote from Clermont county was amended by the Ohio Secretary of State before the final, official returns were printed. This minor adjustment changed the statewide vote for all candidates.

Congress   Other vote was 101,498 Independent (Grote), 12,734 Independent (Berns), 6 Mayberry (write-in) and 5 Taylor (write-in) in CD 1; Wood (write-in) in CD 2; McDonald (write-in) in CD 3; Stahl (write-in) in CD 4; 11,162 Independent (Howard) and 50 Haupricht (write-in) in CD 9; 12 Thierjung (write-in) and 6 Black (write-in) in CD 10; 19,773 Independent (Gudenas) and 5,267 Independent (Henley) in CD 11; 20,320 Independent (Miller), 4,719 Independent (Lawson) and 3,844 Independent (Lange) in CD 13; 44,906 Independent (Reidelbach) and 2 Oliver (write-in) in CD 15; 7 Mononen (write-in) and 5 Mackle (write-in) in CD 19.

1992 PRIMARIES

JUNE 2 REPUBLICAN

Senator   583,805 Mike DeWine; 246,625 George H. Rhodes.

Congress   Unopposed in eleven CD's. No candidate in CD 1. Contested as follows:

CD 3   24,898 Peter W. Davis; 10,609 Tom Rudwall.
CD 6   33,219 Bob McEwen; 32,922 Clarence E. Miller.
CD 10   13,119 Martin R. Hoke; 11,016 Earl Martin; 9,744 Sally C. Kilbane; 3,621 Carol Fedor; 1,704 Bill Smith.
CD 11   6,837 Beryl E. Rothschild; 3,294 Kenneth I. MacPherson; 2,628 Franklin H. Roski; 2,375 Robert Woodall.
CD 13   18,644 Margaret R. Mueller; 13,722 Jeffrey P. Jacobs; 6,492 William D. Nielson; 5,328 Neil P. Yingling; 4,062 John R. Groselle; 1,990 Kirk A. Mason.
CD 18   25,703 Bill Ress; 13,995 Charles L. Graber.
CD 19   16,366 Robert A. Gardner; 14,105 Tucker Marston; 12,808 Matthew J. Hatchadorian; 2,463 Lyle Williams; 2,426 Ceatta Mickey.

JUNE 2 DEMOCRATIC

Senator   John H. Glenn, unopposed.

Congress   Unopposed in ten CD's. In CD 1, unopposed candidate Charles Luken withdrew after the primary and a special primary was held August 4th as follows: 14,794 David Mann; 14,378 William F. Bowen; 6,387 Virginia Rhodes; 3,638 Mary Anne Boyd; 1,929 Steven Reece; 1,011 Earladeen Badger; 651 Raymond Ellis; 395 Ray Mitchell. No candidate in CD 5. Contested as follows:

CD 6   23,339 Ted Strickland; 11,015 Joseph P. Sulzer; 8,427 Bob Smith.
CD 10   40,230 Mary Rose Oakar; 30,810 Timothy F. Hagan; 10,866 Doug Bugie; 8,059 Thomas J. Coyne; 5,492 William Green; 5,446 Eileen M. Gallagher; 1,126 David Perry.
CD 12   15,807 Bob Fitrakis; 11,767 Ralph A. Applegate.
CD 13   30,820 Sherrod Brown; 15,234 Margaret R. Mathna; 4,825 Christopher R. Rothgery; 4,237 Thomas A. Muzilla; 3,968 Ed Boyle; 3,347 Bernice E. Kammiller; 3,064 William VanderWyden; 2,317 F. James Hammar.
CD 14   54,933 Thomas C. Sawyer; 13,109 Jack Resnick; 4,786 Dennis S. Chrobak.
CD 15   18,859 Richard Cordray; 5,256 Bill Buckel.
CD 17   108,658 James A. Traficant; 10,054 M. Ross Norris.
CD 19   20,929 Eric D. Fingerhut; 16,053 Tim McCormack; 15,453 Dennis J. Kucinich; 14,254 Frank J. Valenta; 11,258 Thomas J. Coyne; 4,407 Kathleen M. Cotter; 1,974 Tom Milkovich; 1,011 Jackie Hrnyak; 957 Joan C. Durbak.

OKLAHOMA

GOVERNOR
David Walters (D). Elected 1990 to a four-year term.

SENATORS
David L. Boren (D). Re-elected 1990 to a six-year term. Previously elected 1984, 1978.

Don Nickles (R). Re-elected 1992 to a six-year term. Previously elected 1986, 1980.

REPRESENTATIVES
1. James M. Inhofe (R)
2. Mike Synar (D)
3. Bill Brewster (D)
4. Dave McCurdy (D)
5. Ernest J. Istook (R)
6. Glenn English (D)

POSTWAR VOTE FOR PRESIDENT

Year	Total Vote	Republican Vote	Republican Candidate	Democratic Vote	Democratic Candidate	Other Vote	Plurality	Total Vote Rep.	Total Vote Dem.	Major Vote Rep.	Major Vote Dem.
1992 **	1,390,359	592,929	Bush, George	473,066	Clinton, Bill	324,364	119,863 R	42.6%	34.0%	55.6%	44.4%
1988	1,171,036	678,367	Bush, George	483,423	Dukakis, Michael S.	9,246	194,944 R	57.9%	41.3%	58.4%	41.6%
1984	1,255,676	861,530	Reagan, Ronald	385,080	Mondale, Walter F.	9,066	476,450 R	68.6%	30.7%	69.1%	30.9%
1980	1,149,708	695,570	Reagan, Ronald	402,026	Carter, Jimmy	52,112	293,544 R	60.5%	35.0%	63.4%	36.6%
1976	1,092,251	545,708	Ford, Gerald R.	532,442	Carter, Jimmy	14,101	13,266 R	50.0%	48.7%	50.6%	49.4%
1972	1,029,900	759,025	Nixon, Richard M.	247,147	McGovern, George S.	23,728	511,878 R	73.7%	24.0%	75.4%	24.6%
1968	943,086	449,697	Nixon, Richard M.	301,658	Humphrey, Hubert H.	191,731	148,039 R	47.7%	32.0%	59.9%	40.1%
1964	932,499	412,665	Goldwater, Barry M.	519,834	Johnson, Lyndon B.		107,169 D	44.3%	55.7%	44.3%	55.7%
1960	903,150	533,039	Nixon, Richard M.	370,111	Kennedy, John F.		162,928 R	59.0%	41.0%	59.0%	41.0%
1956	859,350	473,769	Eisenhower, Dwight D.	385,581	Stevenson, Adlai E.		88,188 R	55.1%	44.9%	55.1%	44.9%
1952	948,984	518,045	Eisenhower, Dwight D.	430,939	Stevenson, Adlai E.		87,106 R	54.6%	45.4%	54.6%	45.4%
1948	721,599	268,817	Dewey, Thomas E.	452,782	Truman, Harry S.		183,965 D	37.3%	62.7%	37.3%	62.7%

In 1992 the other vote column includes 319,878 votes cast for Perot.

POSTWAR VOTE FOR GOVERNOR

Year	Total Vote	Republican Vote	Republican Candidate	Democratic Vote	Democratic Candidate	Other Vote	Rep.-Dem. Plurality	Total Vote Rep.	Total Vote Dem.	Major Vote Rep.	Major Vote Dem.
1990	911,314	297,584	Price, Bill	523,196	Walters, David	90,534	225,612 D	32.7%	57.4%	36.3%	63.7%
1986	909,925	431,762	Bellmon, Henry	405,295	Walters, David	72,868	26,467 R	47.5%	44.5%	51.6%	48.4%
1982	883,130	332,207	Daxon, Tom	548,159	Nigh, George	2,764	215,952 D	37.6%	62.1%	37.7%	62.3%
1978	777,414	367,055	Shotts, Ron	402,240	Nigh, George	8,119	35,185 D	47.2%	51.7%	47.7%	52.3%
1974	804,848	290,459	Inhofe, James M.	514,389	Boren, David L.		223,930 D	36.1%	63.9%	36.1%	63.9%
1970	698,790	336,157	Bartlett, Dewey F.	338,338	Hall, David	24,295	2,181 D	48.1%	48.4%	49.8%	50.2%
1966	677,258	377,078	Bartlett, Dewey F.	296,328	Moore, Preston J.	3,852	80,750 R	55.7%	43.8%	56.0%	44.0%
1962	709,763	392,316	Bellmon, Henry	315,357	Atkinson, W. P.	2,090	76,959 R	55.3%	44.4%	55.4%	44.6%
1958	538,839	107,495	Ferguson, Phil	399,504	Edmondson, J. Howard	31,840	292,009 D	19.9%	74.1%	21.2%	78.8%
1954	609,194	251,808	Sparks, Reuben K.	357,386	Gary, Raymond		105,578 D	41.3%	58.7%	41.3%	58.7%
1950	644,276	313,205	Ferguson, Jo O.	329,308	Murray, Johnston	1,763	16,103 D	48.6%	51.1%	48.7%	51.3%
1946	494,599	227,426	Flynn, Olney F.	259,491	Turner, Roy J.	7,682	32,065 D	46.0%	52.5%	46.7%	53.3%

OKLAHOMA

POSTWAR VOTE FOR SENATOR

Year	Total Vote	Republican		Democratic		Other Vote	Rep.-Dem. Plurality	Percentage			
								Total Vote		Major Vote	
		Vote	Candidate	Vote	Candidate			Rep.	Dem.	Rep.	Dem.
1992	1,294,423	757,876	Nickles, Don	494,350	Lewis, Steve	42,197	263,526 R	58.5%	38.2%	60.5%	39.5%
1990	884,498	148,814	Jones, Stephen	735,684	Boren, David L.		586,870 D	16.8%	83.2%	16.8%	83.2%
1986	893,666	493,436	Nickles, Don	400,230	Jones, James R.		93,206 R	55.2%	44.8%	55.2%	44.8%
1984	1,197,937	280,638	Crozier, Will E.	906,131	Boren, David L.	11,168	625,493 D	23.4%	75.6%	23.6%	76.4%
1980	1,098,294	587,252	Nickles, Don	478,283	Coats, Andrew	32,759	108,969 R	53.5%	43.5%	55.1%	44.9%
1978	754,264	247,857	Kamm, Robert B.	493,953	Boren, David L.	12,454	246,096 D	32.9%	65.5%	33.4%	66.6%
1974	791,809	390,997	Bellmon, Henry	387,162	Edmondson, Ed	13,650	3,835 R	49.4%	48.9%	50.2%	49.8%
1972	1,005,148	516,934	Bartlett, Dewey F.	478,212	Edmondson, Ed	10,002	38,722 R	51.4%	47.6%	51.9%	48.1%
1968	909,119	470,120	Bellmon, Henry	419,658	Monroney, A. S. Mike	19,341	50,462 R	51.7%	46.2%	52.8%	47.2%
1966	638,742	295,585	Patterson, Pat J.	343,157	Harris, Fred R.		47,572 D	46.3%	53.7%	46.3%	53.7%
1964 S	912,174	445,392	Wilkinson, Bud	466,782	Harris, Fred R.		21,390 D	48.8%	51.2%	48.8%	51.2%
1962	664,712	307,966	Crawford, B. Hayden	353,890	Monroney, A. S. Mike	2,856	45,924 D	46.3%	53.2%	46.5%	53.5%
1960	864,475	385,646	Crawford, B. Hayden	474,116	Kerr, Robert S.	4,713	88,470 D	44.6%	54.8%	44.9%	55.1%
1956	831,142	371,146	McKeever, Douglas	459,996	Monroney, A. S. Mike		88,850 D	44.7%	55.3%	44.7%	55.3%
1954	600,120	262,013	Mock, Fred M.	335,127	Kerr, Robert S.	2,980	73,114 D	43.7%	55.8%	43.9%	56.1%
1950	631,177	285,224	Alexander, W. H.	345,953	Monroney, A. S. Mike		60,729 D	45.2%	54.8%	45.2%	54.8%
1948	708,931	265,169	Rizley, Ross	441,654	Kerr, Robert S.	2,108	176,485 D	37.4%	62.3%	37.5%	62.5%

The 1964 election was for a short term to fill a vacancy.

OKLAHOMA

Districts Established May 27, 1991

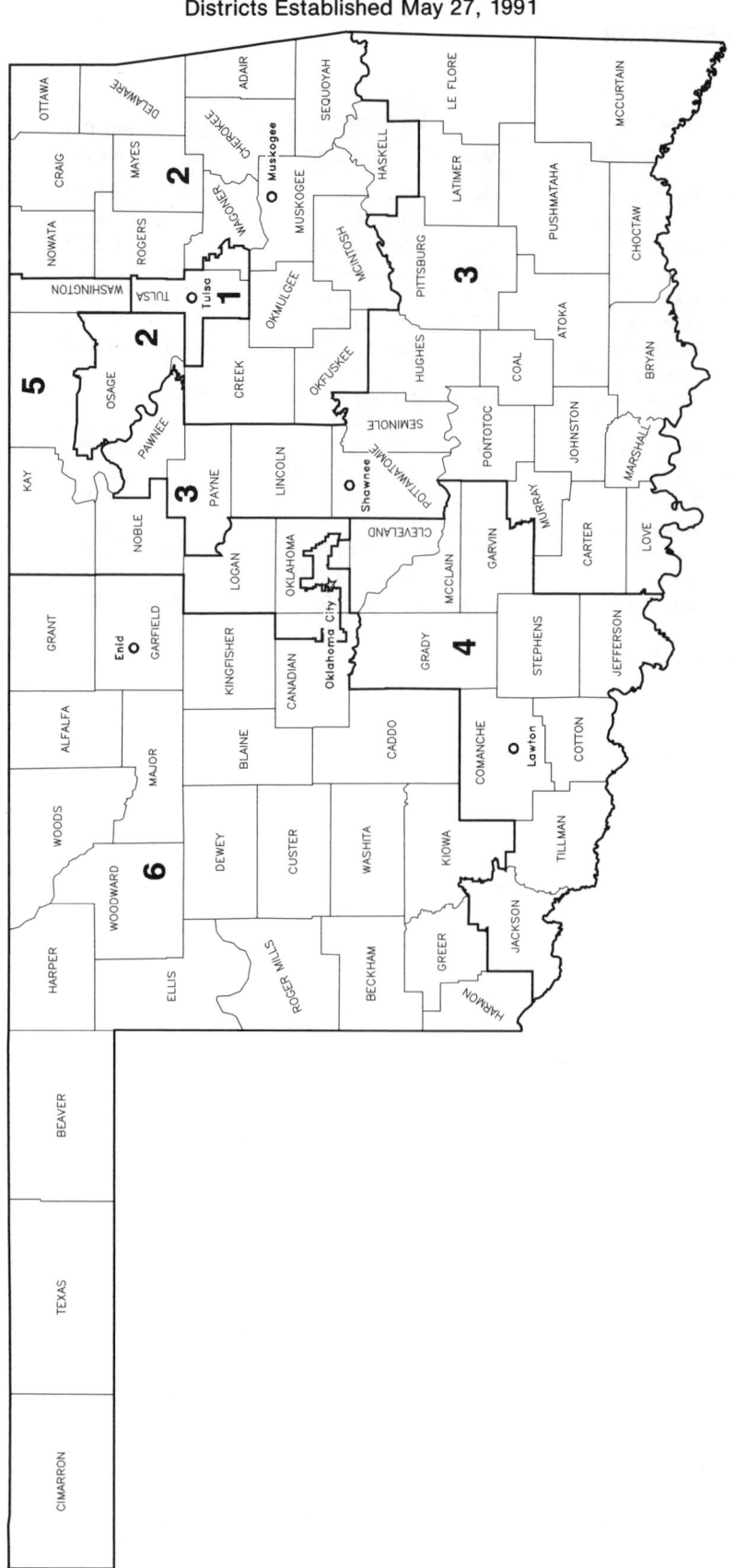

OKLAHOMA

PRESIDENT 1992

Registration	County	Total Vote	Republican	Democratic	Perot	Other	Plurality	Percentage Total Vote		
								Rep.	Dem.	Perot
12,679	ADAIR	6,583	2,994	2,645	914	30	349 R	45.5%	40.2%	13.9%
4,591	ALFALFA	3,045	1,567	741	722	15	826 R	51.5%	24.3%	23.7%
8,727	ATOKA	5,167	1,561	2,336	1,255	15	775 D	30.2%	45.2%	24.3%
4,283	BEAVER	2,850	1,699	580	565	6	1,119 R	59.6%	20.4%	19.8%
13,067	BECKHAM	7,820	2,913	2,947	1,929	31	34 D	37.3%	37.7%	24.7%
7,892	BLAINE	5,052	2,209	1,564	1,258	21	645 R	43.7%	31.0%	24.9%
23,269	BRYAN	13,468	3,452	6,259	3,713	44	2,546 D	25.6%	46.5%	27.6%
18,741	CADDO	11,488	3,664	4,861	2,911	52	1,197 D	31.9%	42.3%	25.3%
49,438	CANADIAN	33,050	16,756	7,215	8,985	94	7,771 R	50.7%	21.8%	27.2%
30,343	CARTER	18,368	5,947	7,171	5,188	62	1,224 D	32.4%	39.0%	28.2%
25,506	CHEROKEE	15,111	4,977	6,794	3,297	43	1,817 D	32.9%	45.0%	21.8%
12,074	CHOCTAW	6,377	1,641	3,413	1,298	25	1,772 D	25.7%	53.5%	20.4%
2,454	CIMARRON	1,624	965	395	254	10	570 R	59.4%	24.3%	15.6%
126,852	CLEVELAND	80,629	35,561	24,404	20,352	312	11,157 R	44.1%	30.3%	25.2%
4,842	COAL	2,800	714	1,448	618	20	734 D	25.5%	51.7%	22.1%
56,827	COMANCHE	35,520	15,704	12,237	7,463	116	3,467 R	44.2%	34.5%	21.0%
4,837	COTTON	3,091	910	1,314	853	14	404 D	29.4%	42.5%	27.6%
10,256	CRAIG	6,219	2,106	2,780	1,316	17	674 D	33.9%	44.7%	21.2%
39,753	CREEK	25,238	10,055	9,118	5,984	81	937 R	39.8%	36.1%	23.7%
20,418	CUSTER	11,694	5,362	3,540	2,741	51	1,822 R	45.9%	30.3%	23.4%
21,856	DELAWARE	12,426	4,840	4,842	2,689	55	2 D	39.0%	39.0%	21.6%
4,268	DEWEY	2,782	1,244	845	684	9	399 R	44.7%	30.4%	24.6%
3,437	ELLIS	2,307	1,072	594	632	9	440 R	46.5%	25.7%	27.4%
38,067	GARFIELD	25,485	13,095	6,720	5,559	111	6,375 R	51.4%	26.4%	21.8%
18,971	GARVIN	11,863	3,983	4,811	3,014	55	828 D	33.6%	40.6%	25.4%
28,869	GRADY	17,757	6,997	6,177	4,528	55	820 R	39.4%	34.8%	25.5%
4,575	GRANT	3,056	1,311	864	871	10	440 R	42.9%	28.3%	28.5%
4,903	GREER	2,779	964	1,162	640	13	198 D	34.7%	41.8%	23.0%
2,707	HARMON	1,611	496	783	326	6	287 D	30.8%	48.6%	20.2%
3,039	HARPER	2,035	1,038	486	501	10	537 R	51.0%	23.9%	24.6%
10,570	HASKELL	5,546	1,461	3,069	995	21	1,608 D	26.3%	55.3%	17.9%
9,736	HUGHES	5,554	1,522	2,850	1,158	24	1,328 D	27.4%	51.3%	20.8%
16,045	JACKSON	9,420	3,893	3,273	2,227	27	620 R	41.3%	34.7%	23.6%
5,227	JEFFERSON	3,019	671	1,580	758	10	822 D	22.2%	52.3%	25.1%
8,213	JOHNSTON	4,339	1,191	2,096	1,040	12	905 D	27.4%	48.3%	24.0%
35,856	KAY	22,828	9,115	6,643	6,984	86	2,131 R	39.9%	29.1%	30.6%
9,490	KINGFISHER	6,411	3,479	1,379	1,534	19	1,945 R	54.3%	21.5%	23.9%
8,077	KIOWA	4,910	1,635	2,143	1,114	18	508 D	33.3%	43.6%	22.7%
8,536	LATIMER	4,885	1,212	2,606	1,049	18	1,394 D	24.8%	53.3%	21.5%
29,211	LE FLORE	16,763	5,850	7,843	3,021	49	1,993 D	34.9%	46.8%	18.0%
19,354	LINCOLN	12,423	5,315	3,904	3,160	44	1,411 R	42.8%	31.4%	25.4%
24,538	LOGAN	13,806	6,071	4,453	3,239	43	1,618 R	44.0%	32.3%	23.5%
6,341	LOVE	3,679	922	1,708	1,033	16	675 D	25.1%	46.4%	28.1%
16,368	MCCLAIN	10,776	4,377	3,378	2,996	25	999 R	40.6%	31.3%	27.8%
25,098	MCCURTAIN	11,494	3,519	5,082	2,852	41	1,563 D	30.6%	44.2%	24.8%
13,410	MCINTOSH	7,893	2,225	4,184	1,469	15	1,959 D	28.2%	53.0%	18.6%
5,578	MAJOR	3,755	2,154	731	857	13	1,297 R	57.4%	19.5%	22.8%
8,811	MARSHALL	5,498	1,478	2,519	1,486	15	1,033 D	26.9%	45.8%	27.0%
23,556	MAYES	15,171	5,445	6,432	3,235	59	987 D	35.9%	42.4%	21.3%
9,083	MURRAY	5,588	1,536	2,594	1,447	11	1,058 D	27.5%	46.4%	25.9%
45,619	MUSKOGEE	27,932	8,782	13,619	5,454	77	4,837 D	31.4%	48.8%	19.5%
8,072	NOBLE	5,283	2,474	1,333	1,449	27	1,025 R	46.8%	25.2%	27.4%
7,503	NOWATA	4,524	1,531	1,912	1,063	18	381 D	33.8%	42.3%	23.5%
7,887	OKFUSKEE	4,630	1,580	2,141	889	20	561 D	34.1%	46.2%	19.2%
481,012	OKLAHOMA	259,923	126,788	76,271	56,139	725	50,517 R	48.8%	29.3%	21.6%
26,772	OKMULGEE	15,421	4,586	7,767	3,013	55	3,181 D	29.7%	50.4%	19.5%
27,511	OSAGE	17,322	5,891	6,894	4,477	60	1,003 D	34.0%	39.8%	25.8%
21,342	OTTAWA	13,209	4,141	6,304	2,721	43	2,163 D	31.3%	47.7%	20.6%
11,640	PAWNEE	6,973	2,675	2,612	1,656	30	63 R	38.4%	37.5%	23.7%
58,235	PAYNE	30,880	13,032	9,886	7,852	110	3,146 R	42.2%	32.0%	25.4%

OKLAHOMA

PRESIDENT 1992

Registration	County	Total Vote	Republican	Democratic	Perot	Other	Plurality	Percentage Total Vote		
								Rep.	Dem.	Perot
32,043	PITTSBURG	18,827	5,659	8,523	4,594	51	2,864 D	30.1%	45.3%	24.4%
24,130	PONTOTOC	15,521	5,206	6,350	3,916	49	1,144 D	33.5%	40.9%	25.2%
40,424	POTTAWATOMIE	25,572	10,350	8,616	6,520	86	1,734 R	40.5%	33.7%	25.5%
8,890	PUSHMATAHA	4,897	1,319	2,553	1,000	25	1,234 D	26.9%	52.1%	20.4%
3,389	ROGER MILLS	2,173	890	767	505	11	123 R	41.0%	35.3%	23.2%
41,613	ROGERS	27,892	12,455	8,257	7,101	79	4,198 R	44.7%	29.6%	25.5%
17,853	SEMINOLE	10,240	3,253	4,624	2,330	33	1,371 D	31.8%	45.2%	22.8%
23,995	SEQUOYAH	13,556	4,925	6,092	2,486	53	1,167 D	36.3%	44.9%	18.3%
31,667	STEPHENS	20,471	7,085	7,644	5,692	50	559 D	34.6%	37.3%	27.8%
11,147	TEXAS	6,980	4,059	1,487	1,417	17	2,572 R	58.2%	21.3%	20.3%
7,275	TILLMAN	4,178	1,377	1,749	1,039	13	372 D	33.0%	41.9%	24.9%
366,145	TULSA	239,068	117,465	71,165	49,760	678	46,300 R	49.1%	29.8%	20.8%
33,605	WAGONER	21,529	9,053	7,041	5,381	54	2,012 R	42.1%	32.7%	25.0%
35,059	WASHINGTON	23,663	11,342	6,593	5,664	64	4,749 R	47.9%	27.9%	23.9%
8,041	WASHITA	5,339	1,912	1,929	1,468	30	17 D	35.8%	36.1%	27.5%
7,563	WOODS	4,777	2,225	1,361	1,167	24	864 R	46.6%	28.5%	24.4%
13,208	WOODWARD	8,526	4,006	2,063	2,411	46	1,595 R	47.0%	24.2%	28.3%
2,302,279	TOTAL	1,390,359	592,929	473,066	319,878	4,486	119,863 R	42.6%	34.0%	23.0%

OKLAHOMA

SENATOR 1992

							Percentage			
						Rep.-Dem.	Total Vote		Major Vote	
Registration	County	Total Vote	Republican	Democratic	Other	Plurality	Rep.	Dem.	Rep.	Dem.
12,679	ADAIR	6,054	3,526	2,377	151	1,149 R	58.2%	39.3%	59.7%	40.3%
4,591	ALFALFA	2,890	1,986	819	85	1,167 R	68.7%	28.3%	70.8%	29.2%
8,727	ATOKA	4,916	2,311	2,476	129	165 D	47.0%	50.4%	48.3%	51.7%
4,283	BEAVER	2,637	1,945	614	78	1,331 R	73.8%	23.3%	76.0%	24.0%
13,067	BECKHAM	7,435	4,194	3,003	238	1,191 R	56.4%	40.4%	58.3%	41.7%
7,892	BLAINE	4,799	3,189	1,453	157	1,736 R	66.5%	30.3%	68.7%	31.3%
23,269	BRYAN	12,438	5,388	6,720	330	1,332 D	43.3%	54.0%	44.5%	55.5%
18,741	CADDO	10,813	5,707	4,774	332	933 R	52.8%	44.2%	54.5%	45.5%
49,438	CANADIAN	31,132	21,231	8,660	1,241	12,571 R	68.2%	27.8%	71.0%	29.0%
30,343	CARTER	17,237	8,659	7,962	616	697 R	50.2%	46.2%	52.1%	47.9%
25,506	CHEROKEE	14,385	6,716	7,196	473	480 D	46.7%	50.0%	48.3%	51.7%
12,074	CHOCTAW	5,899	2,323	3,447	129	1,124 D	39.4%	58.4%	40.3%	59.7%
2,454	CIMARRON	1,493	1,032	434	27	598 R	69.1%	29.1%	70.4%	29.6%
126,852	CLEVELAND	74,967	44,271	26,998	3,698	17,273 R	59.1%	36.0%	62.1%	37.9%
4,842	COAL	2,565	1,081	1,415	69	334 D	42.1%	55.2%	43.3%	56.7%
56,827	COMANCHE	33,401	21,574	10,948	879	10,626 R	64.6%	32.8%	66.3%	33.7%
4,837	COTTON	2,892	1,504	1,303	85	201 R	52.0%	45.1%	53.6%	46.4%
10,256	CRAIG	5,843	2,865	2,819	159	46 R	49.0%	48.2%	50.4%	49.6%
39,753	CREEK	23,783	13,296	9,704	783	3,592 R	55.9%	40.8%	57.8%	42.2%
20,418	CUSTER	11,216	7,193	3,695	328	3,498 R	64.1%	32.9%	66.1%	33.9%
21,856	DELAWARE	11,529	6,263	4,885	381	1,378 R	54.3%	42.4%	56.2%	43.8%
4,268	DEWEY	2,639	1,739	836	64	903 R	65.9%	31.7%	67.5%	32.5%
3,437	ELLIS	2,181	1,423	705	53	718 R	65.2%	32.3%	66.9%	33.1%
38,067	GARFIELD	24,126	16,004	7,238	884	8,766 R	66.3%	30.0%	68.9%	31.1%
18,971	GARVIN	11,087	5,830	4,839	418	991 R	52.6%	43.6%	54.6%	45.4%
28,869	GRADY	16,505	9,341	6,479	685	2,862 R	56.6%	39.3%	59.0%	41.0%
4,575	GRANT	2,894	1,898	885	111	1,013 R	65.6%	30.6%	68.2%	31.8%
4,903	GREER	2,582	1,449	1,062	71	387 R	56.1%	41.1%	57.7%	42.3%
2,707	HARMON	1,467	778	668	21	110 R	53.0%	45.5%	53.8%	46.2%
3,039	HARPER	1,915	1,304	556	55	748 R	68.1%	29.0%	70.1%	29.9%
10,570	HASKELL	5,190	2,089	2,953	148	864 D	40.3%	56.9%	41.4%	58.6%
9,736	HUGHES	5,151	2,401	2,615	135	214 D	46.6%	50.8%	47.9%	52.1%
16,045	JACKSON	8,865	5,653	2,984	228	2,669 R	63.8%	33.7%	65.5%	34.5%
5,227	JEFFERSON	2,774	1,204	1,495	75	291 D	43.4%	53.9%	44.6%	55.4%
8,213	JOHNSTON	4,115	1,874	2,126	115	252 D	45.5%	51.7%	46.9%	53.2%
35,856	KAY	21,499	13,500	7,350	649	6,150 R	62.8%	34.2%	64.7%	35.3%
9,490	KINGFISHER	6,118	4,517	1,439	162	3,078 R	73.8%	23.5%	75.8%	24.2%
8,077	KIOWA	4,577	2,576	1,897	104	679 R	56.3%	41.4%	57.6%	42.4%
8,536	LATIMER	4,610	1,886	2,569	155	683 D	40.9%	55.7%	42.3%	57.7%
29,211	LE FLORE	15,428	7,196	7,815	417	619 D	46.6%	50.7%	47.9%	52.1%
19,354	LINCOLN	11,716	7,237	4,001	478	3,236 R	61.8%	34.1%	64.4%	35.6%
24,538	LOGAN	13,039	7,894	4,639	506	3,255 R	60.5%	35.6%	63.0%	37.0%
6,341	LOVE	3,435	1,453	1,885	97	432 D	42.3%	54.9%	43.5%	56.5%
16,368	MCCLAIN	10,056	5,893	3,720	443	2,173 R	58.6%	37.0%	61.3%	38.7%
25,098	MCCURTAIN	10,741	5,001	5,497	243	496 D	46.6%	51.2%	47.6%	52.4%
13,410	MCINTOSH	7,471	3,376	3,891	204	515 D	45.2%	52.1%	46.5%	53.5%
5,578	MAJOR	3,581	2,653	815	113	1,838 R	74.1%	22.8%	76.5%	23.5%
8,811	MARSHALL	5,166	2,396	2,612	158	216 D	46.4%	50.6%	47.8%	52.2%
23,556	MAYES	14,211	7,211	6,568	432	643 R	50.7%	46.2%	52.3%	47.7%
9,083	MURRAY	5,226	2,445	2,607	174	162 D	46.8%	49.9%	48.4%	51.6%
45,619	MUSKOGEE	26,494	12,742	13,082	670	340 D	48.1%	49.4%	49.3%	50.7%
8,072	NOBLE	5,030	3,373	1,473	184	1,900 R	67.1%	29.3%	69.6%	30.4%
7,503	NOWATA	4,226	2,185	1,906	135	279 R	51.7%	45.1%	53.4%	46.6%
7,887	OKFUSKEE	4,287	2,192	1,976	119	216 R	51.1%	46.1%	52.6%	47.4%
481,012	OKLAHOMA	240,062	152,261	78,643	9,158	73,618 R	63.4%	32.8%	65.9%	34.1%
26,772	OKMULGEE	14,506	6,377	7,740	389	1,363 D	44.0%	53.4%	45.2%	54.8%
27,511	OSAGE	16,165	8,273	7,395	497	878 R	51.2%	45.7%	52.8%	47.2%
21,342	OTTAWA	11,969	5,170	6,409	390	1,239 D	43.2%	53.5%	44.6%	55.4%
11,640	PAWNEE	6,582	3,670	2,704	208	966 R	55.8%	41.1%	57.6%	42.4%
58,235	PAYNE	29,120	17,282	10,786	1,052	6,496 R	59.3%	37.0%	61.6%	38.4%

OKLAHOMA

SENATOR 1992

Registration	County	Total Vote	Republican	Democratic	Other	Rep.-Dem. Plurality	Percentage			
							Total Vote		Major Vote	
							Rep.	Dem.	Rep.	Dem.
32,043	PITTSBURG	17,718	7,803	9,317	598	1,514 D	44.0%	52.6%	45.6%	54.4%
24,130	PONTOTOC	14,625	7,511	6,689	425	822 R	51.4%	45.7%	52.9%	47.1%
40,424	POTTAWATOMIE	24,089	13,656	9,474	959	4,182 R	56.7%	39.3%	59.0%	41.0%
8,890	PUSHMATAHA	4,535	2,061	2,377	97	316 D	45.4%	52.4%	46.4%	53.6%
3,389	ROGER MILLS	2,061	1,169	813	79	356 R	56.7%	39.4%	59.0%	41.0%
41,613	ROGERS	26,340	15,643	9,862	835	5,781 R	59.4%	37.4%	61.3%	38.7%
17,853	SEMINOLE	9,539	4,514	4,650	375	136 D	47.3%	48.7%	49.3%	50.7%
23,995	SEQUOYAH	12,387	5,895	6,123	369	228 D	47.6%	49.4%	49.1%	50.9%
31,667	STEPHENS	19,529	11,343	7,430	756	3,913 R	58.1%	38.0%	60.4%	39.6%
11,147	TEXAS	6,434	4,569	1,674	191	2,895 R	71.0%	26.0%	73.2%	26.8%
7,275	TILLMAN	3,890	2,226	1,583	81	643 R	57.2%	40.7%	58.4%	41.6%
366,145	TULSA	218,291	136,405	76,893	4,993	59,512 R	62.5%	35.2%	64.0%	36.0%
33,605	WAGONER	20,374	11,810	7,938	626	3,872 R	58.0%	39.0%	59.8%	40.2%
35,059	WASHINGTON	21,703	13,864	7,112	727	6,752 R	63.9%	32.8%	66.1%	33.9%
8,041	WASHITA	5,035	3,096	1,789	150	1,307 R	61.5%	35.5%	63.4%	36.6%
7,563	WOODS	4,506	2,875	1,499	132	1,376 R	63.8%	33.3%	65.7%	34.3%
13,208	WOODWARD	8,237	5,436	2,565	236	2,871 R	66.0%	31.1%	67.9%	32.1%
2,302,279	TOTAL	1,294,423	757,876	494,350	42,197	263,526 R	58.5%	38.2%	60.5%	39.5%

OKLAHOMA
CONGRESS

CD	Year	Total Vote	Republican Vote	Candidate	Democratic Vote	Candidate	Other Vote	Rep.-Dem. Plurality	Percentage Total Vote Rep.	Dem.	Major Vote Rep.	Dem.
1	1992	225,830	119,211	INHOFE, JAMES M.	106,619	SELPH, JOHN		12,592 R	52.8%	47.2%	52.8%	47.2%
2	1992	213,513	87,657	HILL, JERRY	118,542	SYNAR, MIKE	7,314	30,885 D	41.1%	55.5%	42.5%	57.5%
3	1992	207,659	51,725	STOKES, ROBERT W.	155,934	BREWSTER, BILL		104,209 D	24.9%	75.1%	24.9%	75.1%
4	1992	199,076	58,235	BELL, HOWARD	140,841	MCCURDY, DAVE		82,606 D	29.3%	70.7%	29.3%	70.7%
5	1992	230,816	123,237	ISTOOK, ERNEST J.	107,579	WILLIAMS, LAURIE		15,658 R	53.4%	46.6%	53.4%	46.6%
6	1992	198,802	64,068	ANTHONY, BOB	134,734	ENGLISH, GLENN		70,666 D	32.2%	67.8%	32.2%	67.8%

OKLAHOMA

1992 GENERAL ELECTION

President   Other vote was Libertarian (Marrou).

Senator   Other vote was 21,225 Independent (Edwards); 20,972 Independent (Ledgerwood).

Congress   Other vote was Independent (Vardeman) in CD 2.

1992 PRIMARIES

AUGUST 25 REPUBLICAN

Senator   Don Nickles, unopposed.

Congress   Unopposed in CD 6. Contested as follows:

CD 1   36,354 James M. Inhofe; 17,339 Richard L. Bunn.
CD 2   5,011 Terry M. Gorham; 4,812 Jerry Hill; 4,112 Ted Jones; 3,275 Brent Davis.
CD 3   7,332 Robert W. Stokes; 2,361 James O. Braly.
CD 4   8,225 Howard Bell; 5,873 Robert W. Best.
CD 5   20,485 Bill Price; 17,975 Ernest J. Istook; 14,519 M. H. Edwards; 2,294 John D. Hershberger; 659 Robert W. Schafer.

AUGUST 25 DEMOCRATIC

Senator   Steve Lewis, unopposed.

Congress   Unopposed in three CD's. Contested as follows:

CD 1   30,884 John Selph; 24,245 Dan Morrissey.
CD 2   47,562 Mike Synar; 42,080 Drew Edmondson; 15,446 Robert W. Blackstock; 5,059 Charles L. Kilgore.
CD 5   23,866 Laurie Williams; 8,279 John Barnett; 5,398 John Crawford; 5,048 Charles Lamb; 1,547 Willard M. Woods.

SEPTEMBER 15 REPUBLICAN RUN-OFF

Congress   Contested as follows:

CD 2   6,644 Jerry Hill; 5,255 Terry M. Gorham.
CD 5   26,659 Ernest J. Istook; 20,679 Bill Price.

SEPTEMBER 15 DEMOCRATIC RUN-OFF

Congress   Contested as follows:

CD 2   56,662 Mike Synar; 50,084 Drew Edmondson.

OREGON

GOVERNOR
Barbara Roberts (D). Elected 1990 to a four-year term.

SENATORS
Mark Hatfield (R). Re-elected 1990 to a six-year term. Previously elected 1984, 1978, 1972, 1966.

Robert W. Packwood (R). Re-elected 1992 to a six-year term. Previously elected 1986, 1980, 1974, 1968.

REPRESENTATIVES
1. Elizabeth Furse (D)
2. Robert F. Smith (R)
3. Ron Wyden (D)
4. Peter A. DeFazio (D)
5. Mike Kopetski (D)

POSTWAR VOTE FOR PRESIDENT

Year	Total Vote	Republican Vote	Candidate	Democratic Vote	Candidate	Other Vote	Plurality	Total Vote Rep.	Dem.	Major Vote Rep.	Dem.
1992 **	1,462,643	475,757	Bush, George	621,314	Clinton, Bill	365,572	145,557 D	32.5%	42.5%	43.4%	56.6%
1988	1,201,694	560,126	Bush, George	616,206	Dukakis, Michael S.	25,362	56,080 D	46.6%	51.3%	47.6%	52.4%
1984	1,226,527	685,700	Reagan, Ronald	536,479	Mondale, Walter F.	4,348	149,221 R	55.9%	43.7%	56.1%	43.9%
1980	1,181,516	571,044	Reagan, Ronald	456,890	Carter, Jimmy	153,582	114,154 R	48.3%	38.7%	55.6%	44.4%
1976	1,029,876	492,120	Ford, Gerald R.	490,407	Carter, Jimmy	47,349	1,713 R	47.8%	47.6%	50.1%	49.9%
1972	927,946	486,686	Nixon, Richard M.	392,760	McGovern, George S.	48,500	93,926 R	52.4%	42.3%	55.3%	44.7%
1968	819,622	408,433	Nixon, Richard M.	358,866	Humphrey, Hubert H.	52,323	49,567 R	49.8%	43.8%	53.2%	46.8%
1964	786,305	282,779	Goldwater, Barry M.	501,017	Johnson, Lyndon B.	2,509	218,238 D	36.0%	63.7%	36.1%	63.9%
1960	776,421	408,060	Nixon, Richard M.	367,402	Kennedy, John F.	959	40,658 R	52.6%	47.3%	52.6%	47.4%
1956	736,132	406,393	Eisenhower, Dwight D.	329,204	Stevenson, Adlai E.	535	77,189 R	55.2%	44.7%	55.2%	44.8%
1952	695,059	420,815	Eisenhower, Dwight D.	270,579	Stevenson, Adlai E.	3,665	150,236 R	60.5%	38.9%	60.9%	39.1%
1948	524,080	260,904	Dewey, Thomas E.	243,147	Truman, Harry S.	20,029	17,757 R	49.8%	46.4%	51.8%	48.2%

In 1992 the other vote column includes 354,091 votes cast for Perot.

POSTWAR VOTE FOR GOVERNOR

Year	Total Vote	Republican Vote	Candidate	Democratic Vote	Candidate	Other Vote	Rep.-Dem. Plurality	Total Vote Rep.	Dem.	Major Vote Rep.	Dem.
1990	1,112,847	444,646	Frohnmayer, Dave	508,749	Roberts, Barbara	159,452	64,103 D	40.0%	45.7%	46.6%	53.4%
1986	1,059,630	506,986	Paulus, Norma	549,456	Goldschmidt, Neil	3,188	42,470 D	47.8%	51.9%	48.0%	52.0%
1982	1,042,009	639,841	Atiyeh, Victor	374,316	Kulongoski, Ted	27,852	265,525 R	61.4%	35.9%	63.1%	36.9%
1978	911,143	498,452	Atiyeh, Victor	409,411	Straub, Robert W.	3,280	89,041 R	54.7%	44.9%	54.9%	45.1%
1974	770,574	324,751	Atiyeh, Victor	444,812	Straub, Robert W.	1,011	120,061 D	42.1%	57.7%	42.2%	57.8%
1970	666,394	369,964	McCall, Tom	293,892	Straub, Robert W.	2,538	76,072 R	55.5%	44.1%	55.7%	44.3%
1966	682,862	377,346	McCall, Tom	305,008	Straub, Robert W.	508	72,338 R	55.3%	44.7%	55.3%	44.7%
1962	637,407	345,497	Hatfield, Mark	265,359	Thornton, Robert Y.	26,551	80,138 R	54.2%	41.6%	56.6%	43.4%
1958	599,994	331,900	Hatfield, Mark	267,934	Holmes, Robert D.	160	63,966 R	55.3%	44.7%	55.3%	44.7%
1956 S	731,279	361,840	Smith, Elmo E.	369,439	Holmes, Robert D.		7,599 D	49.5%	50.5%	49.5%	50.5%
1954	566,701	322,522	Patterson, Paul	244,179	Carson, Joseph K.		78,343 R	56.9%	43.1%	56.9%	43.1%
1950	505,910	334,160	McKay, Douglas	171,750	Flegel, Austin F.		162,410 R	66.1%	33.9%	66.1%	33.9%
1948 S	509,633	271,295	McKay, Douglas	226,958	Wallace, Lew	11,380	44,337 R	53.2%	44.5%	54.4%	45.6%
1946	344,155	237,681	Snell, Earl	106,474	Donaugh, Carl C.		131,207 R	69.1%	30.9%	69.1%	30.9%

The 1956 and 1948 elections were for short terms to fill vacancies.

OREGON

POSTWAR VOTE FOR SENATOR

Year	Total Vote	Republican Vote	Republican Candidate	Democratic Vote	Democratic Candidate	Other Vote	Rep.-Dem. Plurality	Percentage Total Vote Rep.	Percentage Total Vote Dem.	Percentage Major Vote Rep.	Percentage Major Vote Dem.
1992	1,376,033	717,455	Packwood, Robert W.	639,851	AuCoin, Les	18,727	77,604 R	52.1%	46.5%	52.9%	47.1%
1990	1,099,255	590,095	Hatfield, Mark	507,743	Lonsdale, Harry	1,417	82,352 R	53.7%	46.2%	53.8%	46.2%
1986	1,042,555	656,317	Packwood, Robert W.	375,735	Bauman, Rick	10,503	280,582 R	63.0%	36.0%	63.6%	36.4%
1984	1,214,735	808,152	Hatfield, Mark	406,122	Hendriksen, Margie	461	402,030 R	66.5%	33.4%	66.6%	33.4%
1980	1,140,494	594,290	Packwood, Robert W.	501,963	Kulongoski, Ted	44,241	92,327 R	52.1%	44.0%	54.2%	45.8%
1978	892,518	550,165	Hatfield, Mark	341,616	Cook, Vernon	737	208,549 R	61.6%	38.3%	61.7%	38.3%
1974	766,414	420,984	Packwood, Robert W.	338,591	Roberts, Betty	6,839	82,393 R	54.9%	44.2%	55.4%	44.6%
1972	920,833	494,671	Hatfield, Mark	425,036	Morse, Wayne L.	1,126	69,635 R	53.7%	46.2%	53.8%	46.2%
1968	814,176	408,646	Packwood, Robert W.	405,353	Morse, Wayne L.	177	3,293 R	50.2%	49.8%	50.2%	49.8%
1966	685,067	354,391	Hatfield, Mark	330,374	Duncan, Robert B.	302	24,017 R	51.7%	48.2%	51.8%	48.2%
1962	636,558	291,587	Unander, Sig	344,716	Morse, Wayne L.	255	53,129 D	45.8%	54.2%	45.8%	54.2%
1960	755,875	343,009	Smith, Elmo E.	412,757	Neuberger, Maurine	109	69,748 D	45.4%	54.6%	45.4%	54.6%
1956	732,254	335,405	McKay, Douglas	396,849	Morse, Wayne L.		61,444 D	45.8%	54.2%	45.8%	54.2%
1954	569,088	283,313	Cordon, Guy	285,775	Neuberger, Richard L.		2,462 D	49.8%	50.2%	49.8%	50.2%
1950	503,455	376,510	Morse, Wayne L.	116,780	Latourette, Howard	10,165	259,730 R	74.8%	23.2%	76.3%	23.7%
1948	498,570	299,295	Cordon, Guy	199,275	Wilson, Manley J.		100,020 R	60.0%	40.0%	60.0%	40.0%

OREGON

Districts Established December 18, 1991

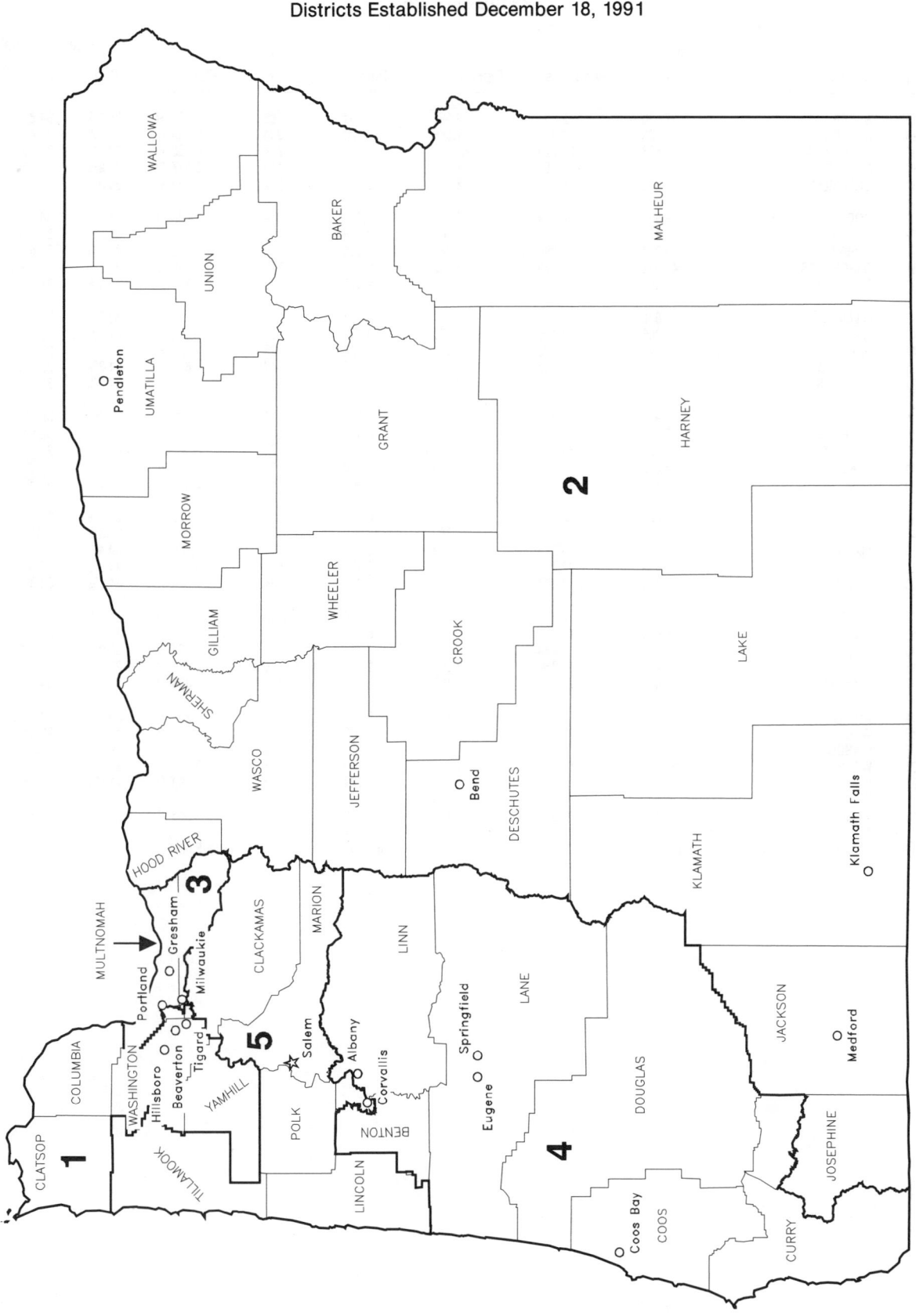

OREGON

PRESIDENT 1992

Registration	County	Total Vote	Republican	Democratic	Perot	Other	Plurality	Percentage Total Vote		
								Rep.	Dem.	Perot
10,116	BAKER	7,530	2,862	2,395	2,191	82	467 R	38.0%	31.8%	29.1%
45,598	BENTON	37,923	11,550	17,966	8,103	304	6,416 D	30.5%	47.4%	21.4%
183,386	CLACKAMAS	154,538	53,724	60,310	39,776	728	6,586 D	34.8%	39.0%	25.7%
19,989	CLATSOP	16,812	4,683	7,700	4,316	113	3,017 D	27.9%	45.8%	25.7%
22,652	COLUMBIA	19,402	5,227	8,298	5,670	207	2,628 D	26.9%	42.8%	29.2%
36,462	COOS	29,659	9,284	12,072	7,989	314	2,788 D	31.3%	40.7%	26.9%
8,672	CROOK	7,271	2,703	2,508	2,024	36	195 R	37.2%	34.5%	27.8%
13,592	CURRY	11,050	3,809	3,841	3,310	90	32 D	34.5%	34.8%	30.0%
52,837	DESCHUTES	43,918	15,655	15,693	12,293	277	38 D	35.6%	35.7%	28.0%
56,650	DOUGLAS	45,860	19,011	14,137	12,377	335	4,874 R	41.5%	30.8%	27.0%
1,199	GILLIAM	1,038	377	374	283	4	3 R	36.3%	36.0%	27.3%
4,910	GRANT	3,986	1,496	1,135	1,302	53	194 R	37.5%	28.5%	32.7%
4,047	HARNEY	3,372	1,350	973	1,024	25	326 R	40.0%	28.9%	30.4%
9,401	HOOD RIVER	7,841	2,453	3,106	2,235	47	653 D	31.3%	39.6%	28.5%
92,551	JACKSON	77,096	28,704	29,146	18,633	613	442 D	37.2%	37.8%	24.2%
7,174	JEFFERSON	5,906	1,962	2,161	1,741	42	199 D	33.2%	36.6%	29.5%
39,355	JOSEPHINE	33,559	13,003	11,007	8,426	1,123	1,996 R	38.7%	32.8%	25.1%
34,375	KLAMATH	26,593	11,864	7,918	6,636	175	3,946 R	44.6%	29.8%	25.0%
4,674	LAKE	3,802	1,791	1,019	980	12	772 R	47.1%	26.8%	25.8%
181,900	LANE	151,862	41,789	74,083	34,906	1,084	32,294 D	27.5%	48.8%	23.0%
25,880	LINCOLN	21,623	5,716	9,603	6,127	177	3,476 D	26.4%	44.4%	28.3%
54,747	LINN	45,287	16,461	15,399	13,256	171	1,062 R	36.3%	34.0%	29.3%
13,050	MALHEUR	10,663	5,374	2,539	2,654	96	2,720 R	50.4%	23.8%	24.9%
132,225	MARION	110,334	42,145	41,137	26,156	896	1,008 R	38.2%	37.3%	23.7%
4,529	MORROW	3,474	1,187	1,174	1,089	24	13 R	34.2%	33.8%	31.3%
374,471	MULTNOMAH	298,291	72,326	165,081	58,236	2,648	92,755 D	24.2%	55.3%	19.5%
31,666	POLK	25,614	10,082	9,551	5,818	163	531 D	39.4%	37.3%	22.7%
1,305	SHERMAN	1,116	424	362	326	4	62 R	38.0%	32.4%	29.2%
13,518	TILLAMOOK	11,484	3,359	5,040	2,997	88	1,681 D	29.2%	43.9%	26.1%
28,607	UMATILLA	19,643	7,095	6,787	5,581	180	308 R	36.1%	34.6%	28.4%
14,584	UNION	11,588	4,223	3,990	3,305	70	233 R	36.4%	34.4%	28.5%
4,738	WALLOWA	4,074	1,630	1,203	1,209	32	421 R	40.0%	29.5%	29.7%
12,157	WASCO	10,973	3,242	4,663	3,008	60	1,421 D	29.5%	42.5%	27.4%
195,431	WASHINGTON	167,195	57,146	67,528	41,575	946	10,382 D	34.2%	40.4%	24.9%
987	WHEELER	860	357	267	227	9	90 R	41.5%	31.0%	26.4%
37,014	YAMHILL	31,406	11,693	11,148	8,312	253	545 R	37.2%	35.5%	26.5%
1,774,449	TOTAL	1,462,643	475,757	621,314	354,091	11,481	145,557 D	32.5%	42.5%	24.2%

OREGON

SENATOR 1992

Registration	County	Total Vote	Republican	Democratic	Other	Rep.-Dem. Plurality	Total Vote Rep.	Dem.	Major Vote Rep.	Dem.
10,116	BAKER	7,249	4,847	2,283	119	2,564 R	66.9%	31.5%	68.0%	32.0%
45,598	BENTON	36,532	17,405	18,300	827	895 D	47.6%	50.1%	48.7%	51.3%
183,386	CLACKAMAS	142,305	77,210	63,998	1,097	13,212 R	54.3%	45.0%	54.7%	45.3%
19,989	CLATSOP	16,170	7,173	8,927	70	1,754 D	44.4%	55.2%	44.6%	55.4%
22,652	COLUMBIA	18,689	9,042	9,056	591	14 D	48.4%	48.5%	50.0%	50.0%
36,462	COOS	28,433	15,809	11,973	651	3,836 R	55.6%	42.1%	56.9%	43.1%
8,672	CROOK	6,942	4,658	2,165	119	2,493 R	67.1%	31.2%	68.3%	31.7%
13,592	CURRY	10,647	6,611	3,913	123	2,698 R	62.1%	36.8%	62.8%	37.2%
52,837	DESCHUTES	42,168	25,920	15,395	853	10,525 R	61.5%	36.5%	62.7%	37.3%
56,650	DOUGLAS	43,819	28,663	15,023	133	13,640 R	65.4%	34.3%	65.6%	34.4%
1,199	GILLIAM	977	591	374	12	217 R	60.5%	38.3%	61.2%	38.8%
4,910	GRANT	3,869	2,574	1,287	8	1,287 R	66.5%	33.3%	66.7%	33.3%
4,047	HARNEY	3,220	2,340	880		1,460 R	72.7%	27.3%	72.7%	27.3%
9,401	HOOD RIVER	7,547	4,334	3,179	34	1,155 R	57.4%	42.1%	57.7%	42.3%
92,551	JACKSON	58,836	33,046	25,470	320	7,576 R	56.2%	43.3%	56.5%	43.5%
7,174	JEFFERSON	5,785	3,502	2,148	135	1,354 R	60.5%	37.1%	62.0%	38.0%
39,355	JOSEPHINE	31,912	19,742	11,361	809	8,381 R	61.9%	35.6%	63.5%	36.5%
34,375	KLAMATH	26,055	18,283	7,585	187	10,698 R	70.2%	29.1%	70.7%	29.3%
4,674	LAKE	3,416	2,590	826		1,764 R	75.8%	24.2%	75.8%	24.2%
181,900	LANE	145,264	67,268	77,296	700	10,028 D	46.3%	53.2%	46.5%	53.5%
25,880	LINCOLN	20,563	9,746	10,692	125	946 D	47.4%	52.0%	47.7%	52.3%
54,747	LINN	39,326	23,823	15,101	402	8,722 R	60.6%	38.4%	61.2%	38.8%
13,050	MALHEUR	10,351	7,362	2,953	36	4,409 R	71.1%	28.5%	71.4%	28.6%
132,225	MARION	105,741	59,302	42,748	3,691	16,554 R	56.1%	40.4%	58.1%	41.9%
4,529	MORROW	3,366	2,078	1,281	7	797 R	61.7%	38.1%	61.9%	38.1%
374,471	MULTNOMAH	291,020	115,905	170,839	4,276	54,934 D	39.8%	58.7%	40.4%	59.6%
31,666	POLK	21,621	12,697	8,693	231	4,004 R	58.7%	40.2%	59.4%	40.6%
1,305	SHERMAN	1,070	669	393	8	276 R	62.5%	36.7%	63.0%	37.0%
13,518	TILLAMOOK	10,957	5,067	5,698	192	631 D	46.2%	52.0%	47.1%	52.9%
28,607	UMATILLA	21,759	13,921	7,677	161	6,244 R	64.0%	35.3%	64.5%	35.5%
14,584	UNION	11,045	7,317	3,671	57	3,646 R	66.2%	33.2%	66.6%	33.4%
4,738	WALLOWA	3,875	2,823	1,041	11	1,782 R	72.9%	26.9%	73.1%	26.9%
12,157	WASCO	10,525	5,547	4,811	167	736 R	52.7%	45.7%	53.6%	46.4%
195,431	WASHINGTON	154,143	82,392	70,299	1,452	12,093 R	53.5%	45.6%	54.0%	46.0%
987	WHEELER	815	542	263	10	279 R	66.5%	32.3%	67.3%	32.7%
37,014	YAMHILL	30,021	16,656	12,252	1,113	4,404 R	55.5%	40.8%	57.6%	42.4%
1,774,449	TOTAL	1,376,033	717,455	639,851	18,727	77,604 R	52.1%	46.5%	52.9%	47.1%

OREGON

CONGRESS

CD	Year	Total Vote	Republican		Democratic		Other Vote	Rep.-Dem. Plurality	Percentage			
			Vote	Candidate	Vote	Candidate			Total Vote		Major Vote	
									Rep.	Dem.	Rep.	Dem.
1	1992	294,154	140,986	MEEKER, ANTONY	152,917	FURSE, ELIZABETH	251	11,931 D	47.9%	52.0%	48.0%	52.0%
2	1992	274,478	184,163	SMITH, ROBERT F.	90,036	FERGUSON, DENZEL	279	94,127 R	67.1%	32.8%	67.2%	32.8%
3	1992	269,879	50,235	RITTER, AL	208,028	WYDEN, RON	11,616	157,793 D	18.6%	77.1%	19.5%	80.5%
4	1992	279,299	79,733	SCHULZ, RICHARD L.	199,372	DEFAZIO, PETER A.	194	119,639 D	28.5%	71.4%	28.6%	71.4%
5	1992	272,944	97,984	SEAGRAVES, JIM	174,443	KOPETSKI, MIKE	517	76,459 D	35.9%	63.9%	36.0%	64.0%

OREGON

1992 GENERAL ELECTION

President   Other vote was 4,277 Libertarian (Marrou); 3,030 New Alliance (Fulani); 1,470 Gritz (write-in); 91 Hagelin (write-in); 4 Brisben (write-in); 2,609 scattered write-in.

Senator   Other vote was 5,793 Lonsdale (write-in); 12,934 scattered write-in.

Congress   Other vote was scattered write-in in CD's 1, 2, 4 and 5; 11,413 Libertarian (Bobier) and 203 scattered write-in in CD 3.

1992 PRIMARIES

MAY 19 REPUBLICAN

Senator   176,939 Robert W. Packwood; 61,128 John DeZell; 27,088 Stephanie J. Salvey; 20,358 Randy Prince; 10,501 Valentine Christian; 3,397 scattered write-in.

Congress   Unopposed in two CD's. Contested as follows:

CD   1   41,522 Antony Meeker; 23,467 Rick Rolf; 188 scattered write-in.
CD   4   26,590 Richard L. Schulz; 18,697 John D. Newkirk; 525 scattered write-in.
CD   5   23,178 Jim Seagraves; 12,457 Dan Nordgren; 10,494 Irv Blake; 656 scattered write-in.

MAY 19 DEMOCRATIC

Senator   153,029 Les AuCoin; 152,699 Harry Lonsdale; 32,183 Joseph Wetzel; 23,700 Bob Bell; 1,194 scattered write-in. These figures are for the recount.

Congress   Unopposed in three CD's. Contested as follows:

CD   1   38,600 Elizabeth Furse; 25,684 Gary Conkling; 194 scattered write-in.
CD   2   29,334 Denzel Ferguson; 21,366 Jim Smiley; 884 scattered write-in.

PENNSYLVANIA

GOVERNOR
Robert Casey (D). Re-elected 1990 to a four-year term. Previously elected 1986.

SENATORS
Harris Wofford (D). Elected in a special election November 1991 for the remaining three years of the term vacated upon the death of Senator H. John Heinz (R) in April 1991. Had been appointed May 1991 to fill the vacancy until the special election.

Arlen Specter (R). Re-elected 1992 to a six-year term. Previously elected 1986, 1980.

REPRESENTATIVES
1. Thomas M. Foglietta (D)
2. Lucien E. Blackwell (D)
3. Robert A. Borski (D)
4. Ron Klink (D)
5. William F. Clinger (R)
6. Tim Holden (D)
7. Curt Weldon (R)
8. James C. Greenwood (R)
9. E. G. Shuster (R)
10. Joseph M. McDade (R)
11. Paul E. Kanjorski (D)
12. John P. Murtha (D)
13. Marjorie M. Mezvinsky (D)
14. William J. Coyne (D)
15. Paul McHale (D)
16. Robert S. Walker (R)
17. George W. Gekas (R)
18. Rick Santorum (R)
19. William F. Goodling (R)
20. Austin J. Murphy (D)
21. Thomas J. Ridge (R)

POSTWAR VOTE FOR PRESIDENT

		Republican		Democratic				Total Vote		Major Vote	
Year	Total Vote	Vote	Candidate	Vote	Candidate	Other Vote	Plurality	Rep.	Dem.	Rep.	Dem.
1992 **	4,959,810	1,791,841	Bush, George	2,239,164	Clinton, Bill	928,805	447,323 D	36.1%	45.1%	44.5%	55.5%
1988	4,536,251	2,300,087	Bush, George	2,194,944	Dukakis, Michael S.	41,220	105,143 R	50.7%	48.4%	51.2%	48.8%
1984	4,844,903	2,584,323	Reagan, Ronald	2,228,131	Mondale, Walter F.	32,449	356,192 R	53.3%	46.0%	53.7%	46.3%
1980	4,561,501	2,261,872	Reagan, Ronald	1,937,540	Carter, Jimmy	362,089	324,332 R	49.6%	42.5%	53.9%	46.1%
1976	4,620,787	2,205,604	Ford, Gerald R.	2,328,677	Carter, Jimmy	86,506	123,073 D	47.7%	50.4%	48.6%	51.4%
1972	4,592,106	2,714,521	Nixon, Richard M.	1,796,951	McGovern, George S.	80,634	917,570 R	59.1%	39.1%	60.2%	39.8%
1968	4,747,928	2,090,017	Nixon, Richard M.	2,259,405	Humphrey, Hubert H.	398,506	169,388 D	44.0%	47.6%	48.1%	51.9%
1964	4,822,690	1,673,657	Goldwater, Barry M.	3,130,954	Johnson, Lyndon B.	18,079	1,457,297 D	34.7%	64.9%	34.8%	65.2%
1960	5,006,541	2,439,956	Nixon, Richard M.	2,556,282	Kennedy, John F.	10,303	116,326 D	48.7%	51.1%	48.8%	51.2%
1956	4,576,503	2,585,252	Eisenhower, Dwight D.	1,981,769	Stevenson, Adlai E.	9,482	603,483 R	56.5%	43.3%	56.6%	43.4%
1952	4,580,969	2,415,789	Eisenhower, Dwight D.	2,146,269	Stevenson, Adlai E.	18,911	269,520 R	52.7%	46.9%	53.0%	47.0%
1948	3,735,348	1,902,197	Dewey, Thomas E.	1,752,426	Truman, Harry S.	80,725	149,771 R	50.9%	46.9%	52.0%	48.0%

In 1992 the other vote column includes 902,667 votes cast for Perot.

PENNSYLVANIA

POSTWAR VOTE FOR GOVERNOR

Year	Total Vote	Republican Vote	Republican Candidate	Democratic Vote	Democratic Candidate	Other Vote	Rep.-Dem. Plurality	Percentage Total Vote Rep.	Percentage Total Vote Dem.	Percentage Major Vote Rep.	Percentage Major Vote Dem.
1990	3,052,760	987,516	Hafer, Barbara	2,065,244	Casey, Robert		1,077,728 D	32.3%	67.7%	32.3%	67.7%
1986	3,388,275	1,638,268	Scranton, William W.,III	1,717,484	Casey, Robert	32,523	79,216 D	48.4%	50.7%	48.8%	51.2%
1982	3,683,985	1,872,784	Thornburgh, Richard L.	1,772,353	Ertel, Allen E.	38,848	100,431 R	50.8%	48.1%	51.4%	48.6%
1978	3,741,969	1,966,042	Thornburgh, Richard L.	1,737,888	Flaherty, Peter	38,039	228,154 R	52.5%	46.4%	53.1%	46.9%
1974	3,491,234	1,578,917	Lewis, Andrew L.	1,878,252	Shapp, Milton	34,065	299,335 D	45.2%	53.8%	45.7%	54.3%
1970	3,700,060	1,542,854	Broderick, Raymond	2,043,029	Shapp, Milton	114,177	500,175 D	41.7%	55.2%	43.0%	57.0%
1966	4,050,668	2,110,349	Shafer, Raymond P.	1,868,719	Shapp, Milton	71,600	241,630 R	52.1%	46.1%	53.0%	47.0%
1962	4,378,042	2,424,918	Scranton, William W.	1,938,627	Dilworth, Richardson	14,497	486,291 R	55.4%	44.3%	55.6%	44.4%
1958	3,986,918	1,948,769	McGonigle, A. T.	2,024,852	Lawrence, David	13,297	76,083 D	48.9%	50.8%	49.0%	51.0%
1954	3,720,457	1,717,070	Wood, Lloyd H.	1,996,266	Leader, George M.	7,121	279,196 D	46.2%	53.7%	46.2%	53.8%
1950	3,540,059	1,796,119	Fine, John S.	1,710,355	Dilworth, Richardson	33,585	85,764 R	50.7%	48.3%	51.2%	48.8%
1946	3,123,994	1,828,462	Duff, James H.	1,270,947	Rice, John S.	24,585	557,515 R	58.5%	40.7%	59.0%	41.0%

POSTWAR VOTE FOR SENATOR

Year	Total Vote	Republican Vote	Republican Candidate	Democratic Vote	Democratic Candidate	Other Vote	Rep.-Dem. Plurality	Percentage Total Vote Rep.	Percentage Total Vote Dem.	Percentage Major Vote Rep.	Percentage Major Vote Dem.
1992	4,802,410	2,358,125	Specter, Arlen	2,224,966	Yeakel, Lynn	219,319	133,159 R	49.1%	46.3%	51.5%	48.5%
1991 S	3,382,746	1,521,986	Thornburgh, Richard	1,860,760	Wofford, Harris		338,774 D	45.0%	55.0%	45.0%	55.0%
1988	4,366,598	2,901,715	Heinz, H. John	1,416,764	Vignola, Joseph C.	48,119	1,484,951 R	66.5%	32.4%	67.2%	32.8%
1986	3,378,226	1,906,537	Specter, Arlen	1,448,219	Edgar, Robert W.	23,470	458,318 R	56.4%	42.9%	56.8%	43.2%
1982	3,604,108	2,136,418	Heinz, H. John	1,412,965	Wecht, Cyril H.	54,725	723,453 R	59.3%	39.2%	60.2%	39.8%
1980	4,418,042	2,230,404	Specter, Arlen	2,122,391	Flaherty, Peter	65,247	108,013 R	50.5%	48.0%	51.2%	48.8%
1976	4,546,353	2,381,891	Heinz, H. John	2,126,977	Green, William J., III	37,485	254,914 R	52.4%	46.8%	52.8%	47.2%
1974	3,477,812	1,843,317	Schweiker, Richard S.	1,596,121	Flaherty, Peter	38,374	247,196 R	53.0%	45.9%	53.6%	46.4%
1970	3,644,305	1,874,106	Scott, Hugh	1,653,774	Sesler, William G.	116,425	220,332 R	51.4%	45.4%	53.1%	46.9%
1968	4,624,218	2,399,762	Schweiker, Richard S.	2,117,662	Clark, Joseph S.	106,794	282,100 R	51.9%	45.8%	53.1%	46.9%
1964	4,803,835	2,429,858	Scott, Hugh	2,359,223	Blatt, Genevieve	14,754	70,635 R	50.6%	49.1%	50.7%	49.3%
1962	4,383,475	2,134,649	Van Zandt, James E.	2,238,383	Clark, Joseph S.	10,443	103,734 D	48.7%	51.1%	48.8%	51.2%
1958	3,988,622	2,042,586	Scott, Hugh	1,929,821	Leader, George M.	16,215	112,765 R	51.2%	48.4%	51.4%	48.6%
1956	4,529,874	2,250,671	Duff, James H.	2,268,641	Clark, Joseph S.	10,562	17,970 D	49.7%	50.1%	49.8%	50.2%
1952	4,519,761	2,331,034	Martin, Edward	2,168,546	Bard, Guy Kurtz	20,181	162,488 R	51.6%	48.0%	51.8%	48.2%
1950	3,548,703	1,820,400	Duff, James H.	1,694,076	Myers, Francis J.	34,227	126,324 R	51.3%	47.7%	51.8%	48.2%
1946	3,127,860	1,853,458	Martin, Edward	1,245,338	Guffey, Joseph F.	29,064	608,120 R	59.3%	39.8%	59.8%	40.2%

The 1991 election was for a short term to fill a vacancy.

PENNSYLVANIA

Districts Established March 3, 1992

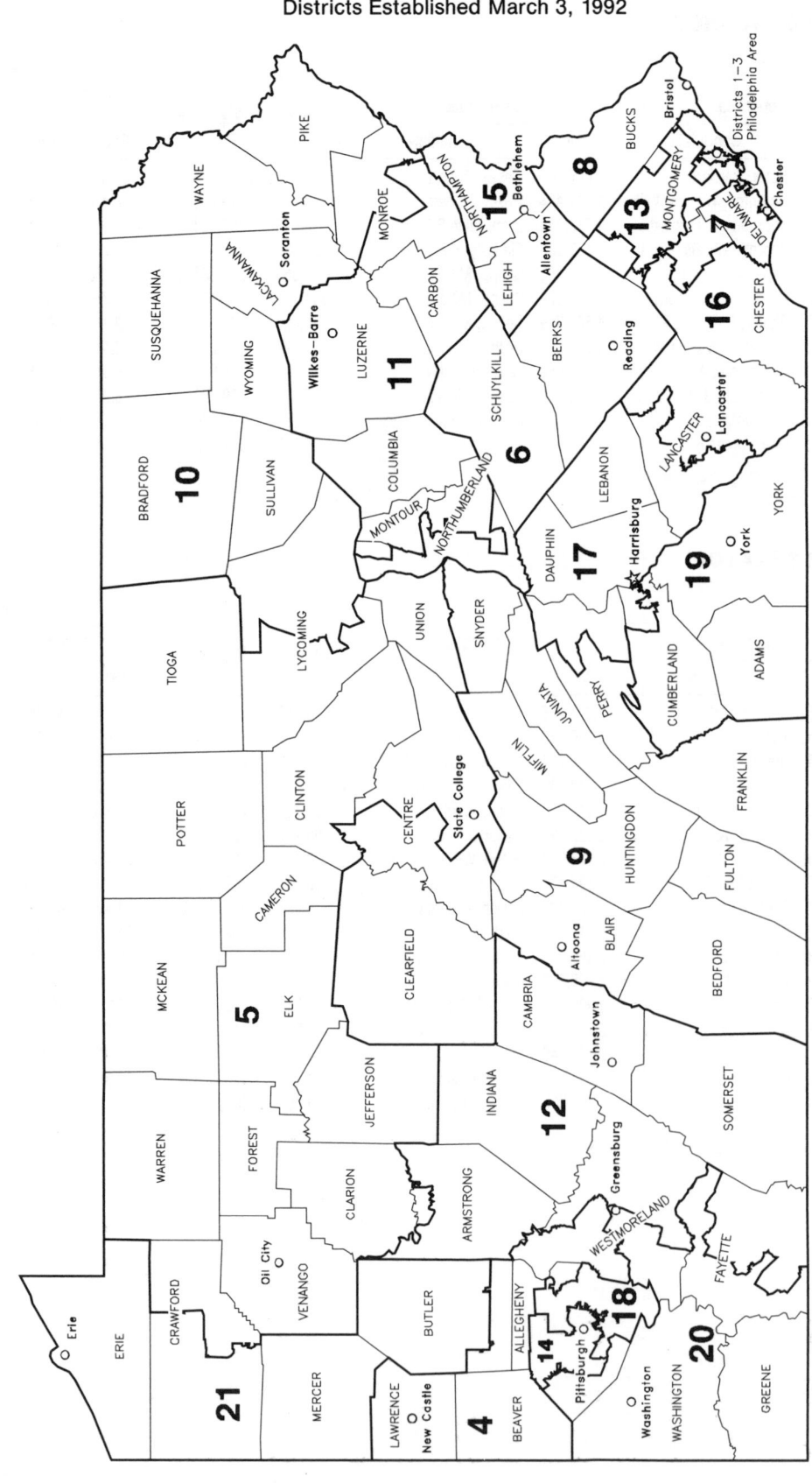

SOUTHEAST PENNSYLVANIA

CONGRESSIONAL DISTRICTS

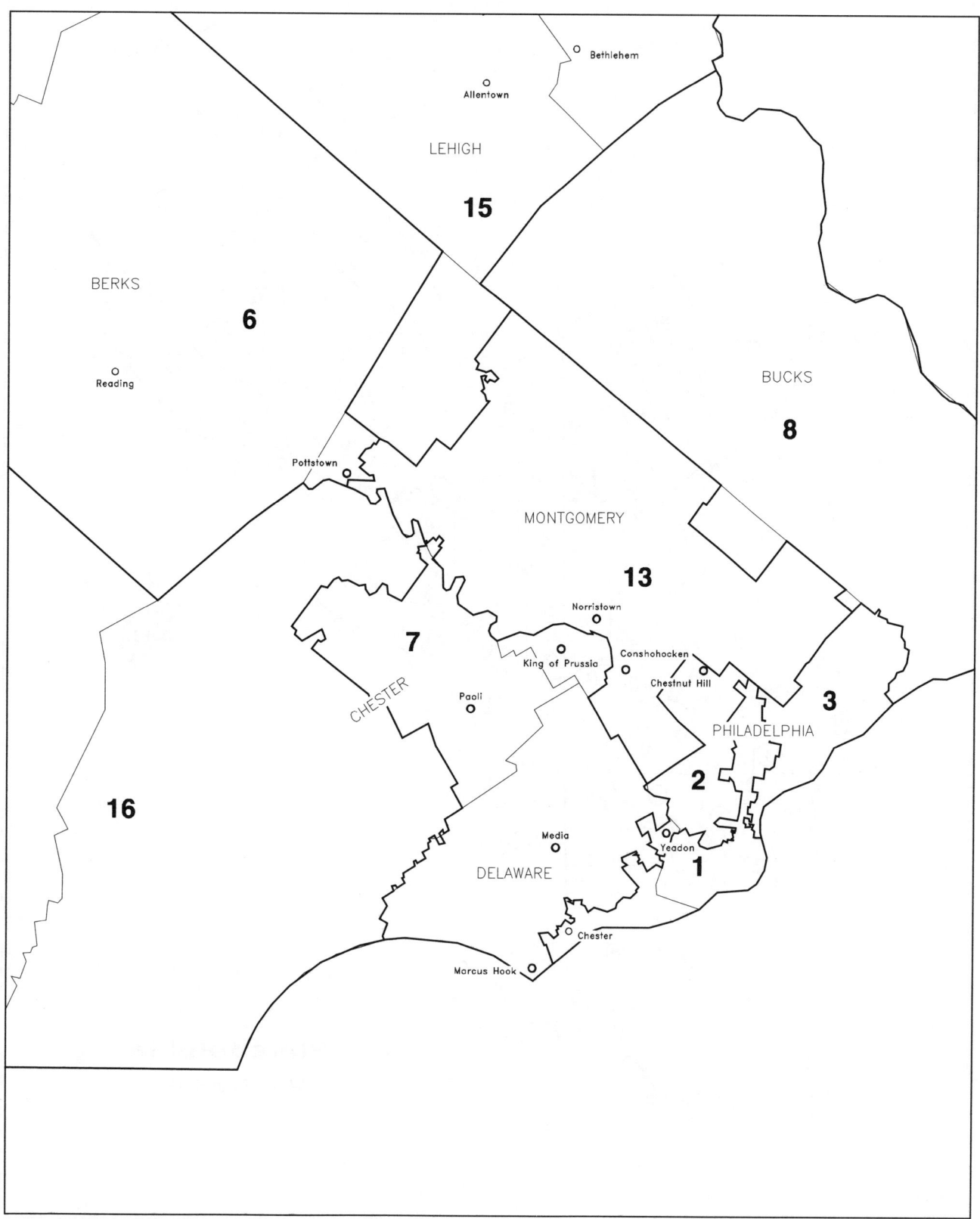

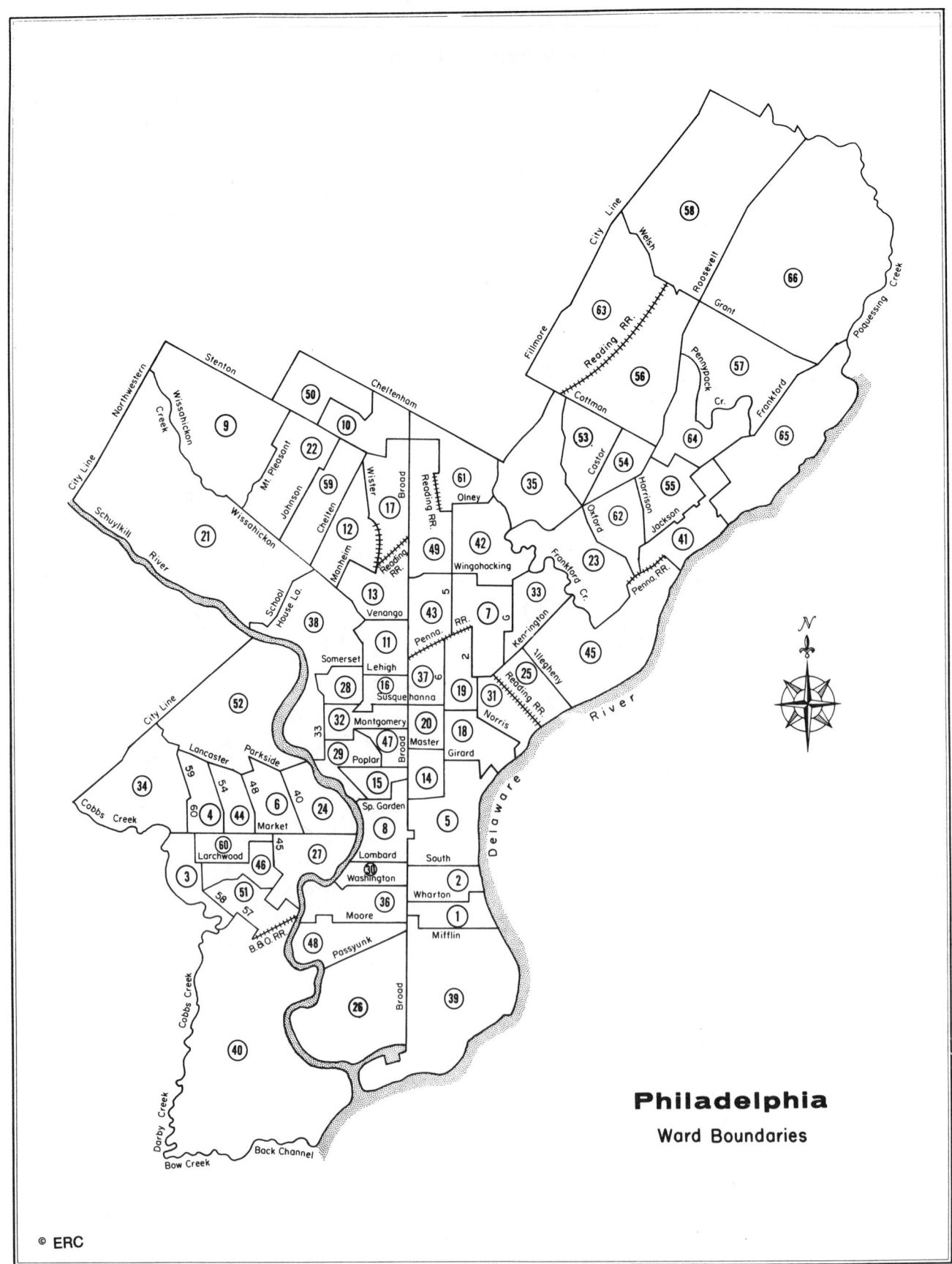

Philadelphia

Ward Boundaries

© ERC

PENNSYLVANIA

PRESIDENT 1992

Registration	County	Total Vote	Republican	Democratic	Perot	Other	Plurality	Percentage Total Vote		
								Rep.	Dem.	Perot
33,436	ADAMS	29,501	13,552	9,576	6,313	60	3,976 R	45.9%	32.5%	21.4%
730,613	ALLEGHENY	614,187	183,035	324,004	103,470	3,678	140,969 D	29.8%	52.8%	16.8%
33,272	ARMSTRONG	28,333	9,122	12,995	6,166	50	3,873 D	32.2%	45.9%	21.8%
95,851	BEAVER	82,340	21,361	44,877	15,954	148	23,516 D	25.9%	54.5%	19.4%
22,754	BEDFORD	18,817	9,216	5,840	3,731	30	3,376 R	49.0%	31.0%	19.8%
153,654	BERKS	131,407	52,939	46,031	31,663	774	6,908 R	40.3%	35.0%	24.1%
54,496	BLAIR	44,758	21,447	14,857	8,284	170	6,590 R	47.9%	33.2%	18.5%
26,909	BRADFORD	22,628	10,221	6,903	5,452	52	3,318 R	45.2%	30.5%	24.1%
290,841	BUCKS	248,507	94,584	97,902	53,931	2,090	3,318 D	38.1%	39.4%	21.7%
71,599	BUTLER	61,130	23,656	22,303	15,013	158	1,353 R	38.7%	36.5%	24.6%
78,652	CAMBRIA	66,349	20,770	34,334	11,070	175	13,564 D	31.3%	51.7%	16.7%
3,506	CAMERON	2,678	1,173	824	676	5	349 R	43.8%	30.8%	25.2%
25,552	CARBON	21,659	7,243	9,072	5,222	122	1,829 D	33.4%	41.9%	24.1%
60,414	CENTRE	51,225	20,478	21,177	9,356	214	699 D	40.0%	41.3%	18.3%
198,172	CHESTER	169,208	74,002	59,643	34,536	1,027	14,359 R	43.7%	35.2%	20.4%
18,543	CLARION	15,718	6,477	5,584	3,619	38	893 R	41.2%	35.5%	23.0%
36,004	CLEARFIELD	30,847	11,553	12,247	6,989	58	694 D	37.5%	39.7%	22.7%
15,103	CLINTON	12,569	4,471	5,397	2,654	47	926 D	35.6%	42.9%	21.1%
30,622	COLUMBIA	23,739	9,742	8,261	5,683	53	1,481 R	41.0%	34.8%	23.9%
41,738	CRAWFORD	34,628	14,112	12,813	7,392	311	1,299 R	40.8%	37.0%	21.3%
98,528	CUMBERLAND	84,573	43,447	26,635	14,344	147	16,812 R	51.4%	31.5%	17.0%
117,846	DAUPHIN	98,910	45,479	36,990	16,063	378	8,489 R	46.0%	37.4%	16.2%
324,241	DELAWARE	266,074	108,587	111,210	43,728	2,549	2,623 D	40.8%	41.8%	16.4%
16,469	ELK	13,832	4,908	5,016	3,885	23	108 D	35.5%	36.3%	28.1%
136,847	ERIE	117,804	39,283	56,381	21,510	630	17,098 D	33.3%	47.9%	18.3%
64,580	FAYETTE	53,861	12,820	30,577	10,162	302	17,757 D	23.8%	56.8%	18.9%
2,640	FOREST	2,144	801	890	448	5	89 D	37.4%	41.5%	20.9%
51,282	FRANKLIN	43,834	23,387	13,440	6,941	66	9,947 R	53.4%	30.7%	15.8%
6,042	FULTON	5,023	2,558	1,588	869	8	970 R	50.9%	31.6%	17.3%
17,533	GREENE	15,135	3,482	8,438	3,186	29	4,956 D	23.0%	55.8%	21.1%
18,926	HUNTINGDON	15,700	7,249	5,153	3,273	25	2,096 R	46.2%	32.8%	20.8%
39,090	INDIANA	33,314	10,966	15,194	7,089	65	4,228 D	32.9%	45.6%	21.3%
21,186	JEFFERSON	17,711	7,271	5,998	4,403	39	1,273 R	41.1%	33.9%	24.9%
9,704	JUNIATA	8,420	3,980	2,601	1,819	20	1,379 R	47.3%	30.9%	21.6%
124,822	LACKAWANNA	94,968	33,443	45,054	15,667	804	11,611 D	35.2%	47.4%	16.5%
186,386	LANCASTER	160,180	88,447	44,255	26,807	671	44,192 R	55.2%	27.6%	16.7%
48,794	LAWRENCE	41,203	12,359	20,830	7,950	64	8,471 D	30.0%	50.6%	19.3%
48,704	LEBANON	43,021	21,512	12,350	9,005	154	9,162 R	50.0%	28.7%	20.9%
137,326	LEHIGH	114,836	42,631	46,711	24,853	641	4,080 D	37.1%	40.7%	21.6%
151,277	LUZERNE	127,146	49,285	56,623	21,007	231	7,338 D	38.8%	44.5%	16.5%
50,739	LYCOMING	43,172	20,536	13,315	9,170	151	7,221 R	47.6%	30.8%	21.2%
19,591	MCKEAN	16,400	6,965	5,331	4,019	85	1,634 R	42.5%	32.5%	24.5%
57,945	MERCER	49,836	16,081	23,264	10,277	214	7,183 D	32.3%	46.7%	20.6%
17,490	MIFFLIN	14,688	6,300	4,946	3,382	60	1,354 R	42.9%	33.7%	23.0%
48,052	MONROE	37,500	14,557	13,468	9,257	218	1,089 R	38.8%	35.9%	24.7%
371,118	MONTGOMERY	318,576	125,704	136,572	53,738	2,562	10,868 D	39.5%	42.9%	16.9%
8,496	MONTOUR	6,646	3,096	2,150	1,373	27	946 R	46.6%	32.4%	20.7%
114,681	NORTHAMPTON	97,525	34,429	42,203	20,234	659	7,774 D	35.3%	43.3%	20.7%
41,795	NORTHUMBERLAND	35,792	15,057	12,814	7,782	139	2,243 R	42.1%	35.8%	21.7%
18,174	PERRY	15,327	7,871	4,086	3,334	36	3,785 R	51.4%	26.7%	21.8%
874,181	PHILADELPHIA	638,058	133,328	434,904	65,455	4,371	301,576 D	20.9%	68.2%	10.3%
15,713	PIKE	13,603	6,084	4,382	3,019	118	1,702 R	44.7%	32.2%	22.2%
8,509	POTTER	7,044	3,452	1,892	1,687	13	1,560 R	49.0%	26.9%	23.9%
71,492	SCHUYLKILL	63,029	25,780	23,679	13,398	172	2,101 R	40.9%	37.6%	21.3%
14,703	SNYDER	12,596	6,934	2,952	2,686	24	3,982 R	55.0%	23.4%	21.3%
38,978	SOMERSET	32,759	13,858	12,493	6,333	75	1,365 R	42.3%	38.1%	19.3%
3,723	SULLIVAN	3,113	1,340	1,030	731	12	310 R	43.0%	33.1%	23.5%
19,609	SUSQUEHANNA	16,709	7,356	5,368	3,946	39	1,988 R	44.0%	32.1%	23.6%
19,429	TIOGA	16,543	7,823	4,868	3,804	48	2,955 R	47.3%	29.4%	23.0%
14,238	UNION	12,265	6,362	3,623	2,255	25	2,739 R	51.9%	29.5%	18.4%

PENNSYLVANIA

PRESIDENT 1992

Registration	County	Total Vote	Republican	Democratic	Perot	Other	Plurality	Percentage Total Vote		
								Rep.	Dem.	Perot
25,903	VENANGO	21,554	8,545	8,230	4,695	84	315 R	39.6%	38.2%	21.8%
22,264	WARREN	18,426	6,585	6,972	4,795	74	387 D	35.7%	37.8%	26.0%
102,501	WASHINGTON	84,364	21,977	46,143	16,083	161	24,166 D	26.1%	54.7%	19.1%
19,316	WAYNE	16,822	8,184	4,817	3,727	94	3,367 R	48.7%	28.6%	22.2%
182,109	WESTMORELAND	154,451	47,315	69,817	37,036	283	22,502 D	30.6%	45.2%	24.0%
12,720	WYOMING	10,850	5,143	3,158	2,525	24	1,985 R	47.4%	29.1%	23.3%
155,579	YORK	134,245	60,130	46,113	27,743	259	14,017 R	44.8%	34.3%	20.7%
5,993,002	TOTAL	4,959,810	1,791,841	2,239,164	902,667	26,138	447,323 D	36.1%	45.1%	18.2%

PENNSYLVANIA

SENATOR 1992

Registration	County	Total Vote	Republican	Democratic	Other	Rep.-Dem. Plurality	Percentage Total Vote Rep.	Total Vote Dem.	Major Vote Rep.	Major Vote Dem.
33,436	ADAMS	29,057	14,925	12,141	1,991	2,784 R	51.4%	41.8%	55.1%	44.9%
730,613	ALLEGHENY	593,862	293,156	277,191	23,515	15,965 R	49.4%	46.7%	51.4%	48.6%
33,272	ARMSTRONG	28,101	13,979	12,206	1,916	1,773 R	49.7%	43.4%	53.4%	46.6%
95,851	BEAVER	81,568	32,418	43,716	5,434	11,298 D	39.7%	53.6%	42.6%	57.4%
22,754	BEDFORD	18,637	10,251	6,848	1,538	3,403 R	55.0%	36.7%	60.0%	40.0%
153,654	BERKS	127,759	64,062	56,993	6,704	7,069 R	50.1%	44.6%	52.9%	47.1%
54,496	BLAIR	44,714	24,337	16,960	3,417	7,377 R	54.4%	37.9%	58.9%	41.1%
26,909	BRADFORD	22,199	11,667	8,951	1,581	2,716 R	52.6%	40.3%	56.6%	43.4%
290,841	BUCKS	240,050	121,763	109,859	8,428	11,904 R	50.7%	45.8%	52.6%	47.4%
71,599	BUTLER	60,555	30,929	24,901	4,725	6,028 R	51.1%	41.1%	55.4%	44.6%
78,652	CAMBRIA	66,239	30,988	31,589	3,662	601 D	46.8%	47.7%	49.5%	50.5%
3,506	CAMERON	2,610	1,290	1,126	194	164 R	49.4%	43.1%	53.4%	46.6%
25,552	CARBON	20,705	9,500	10,571	634	1,071 D	45.9%	51.1%	47.3%	52.7%
60,414	CENTRE	50,595	23,626	23,863	3,106	237 D	46.7%	47.2%	49.8%	50.2%
198,172	CHESTER	167,121	86,581	70,948	9,592	15,633 R	51.8%	42.5%	55.0%	45.0%
18,543	CLARION	15,583	7,895	6,431	1,257	1,464 R	50.7%	41.3%	55.1%	44.9%
36,004	CLEARFIELD	30,609	13,756	14,248	2,605	492 D	44.9%	46.5%	49.1%	50.9%
15,103	CLINTON	12,278	5,151	6,025	1,102	874 D	42.0%	49.1%	46.1%	53.9%
30,622	COLUMBIA	23,558	11,512	10,814	1,232	698 R	48.9%	45.9%	51.6%	48.4%
41,738	CRAWFORD	32,956	16,580	13,972	2,404	2,608 R	50.3%	42.4%	54.3%	45.7%
98,528	CUMBERLAND	81,757	48,377	30,245	3,135	18,132 R	59.2%	37.0%	61.5%	38.5%
117,846	DAUPHIN	97,010	54,399	37,178	5,433	17,221 R	56.1%	38.3%	59.4%	40.6%
324,241	DELAWARE	256,229	136,228	111,242	8,759	24,986 R	53.2%	43.4%	55.0%	45.0%
16,469	ELK	13,750	6,135	6,607	1,008	472 D	44.6%	48.1%	48.1%	51.9%
136,847	ERIE	112,474	51,555	54,095	6,824	2,540 D	45.8%	48.1%	48.8%	51.2%
64,580	FAYETTE	51,439	21,812	27,261	2,366	5,449 D	42.4%	53.0%	44.4%	55.6%
2,640	FOREST	2,147	1,101	944	102	157 R	51.3%	44.0%	53.8%	46.2%
51,282	FRANKLIN	43,111	23,665	15,773	3,673	7,892 R	54.9%	36.6%	60.0%	40.0%
6,042	FULTON	4,937	2,786	1,888	263	898 R	56.4%	38.2%	59.6%	40.4%
17,533	GREENE	14,878	5,996	8,248	634	2,252 D	40.3%	55.4%	42.1%	57.9%
18,926	HUNTINGDON	15,432	8,181	5,990	1,261	2,191 R	53.0%	38.8%	57.7%	42.3%
39,090	INDIANA	33,011	15,976	14,998	2,037	978 R	48.4%	45.4%	51.6%	48.4%
21,186	JEFFERSON	17,646	8,923	7,107	1,616	1,816 R	50.6%	40.3%	55.7%	44.3%
9,704	JUNIATA	8,316	4,663	3,120	533	1,543 R	56.1%	37.5%	59.9%	40.1%
124,822	LACKAWANNA	92,189	44,009	45,349	2,831	1,340 D	47.7%	49.2%	49.3%	50.7%
186,386	LANCASTER	152,489	87,828	49,815	14,846	38,013 R	57.6%	32.7%	63.8%	36.2%
48,794	LAWRENCE	40,557	16,707	21,718	2,132	5,011 D	41.2%	53.5%	43.5%	56.5%
48,704	LEBANON	41,572	24,527	14,708	2,337	9,819 R	59.0%	35.4%	62.5%	37.5%
137,326	LEHIGH	110,647	53,763	53,125	3,759	638 R	48.6%	48.0%	50.3%	49.7%
151,277	LUZERNE	121,048	59,642	58,125	3,281	1,517 R	49.3%	48.0%	50.6%	49.4%
50,739	LYCOMING	41,989	21,986	17,285	2,718	4,701 R	52.4%	41.2%	56.0%	44.0%
19,591	MCKEAN	14,967	7,768	6,455	744	1,313 R	51.9%	43.1%	54.6%	45.4%
57,945	MERCER	45,717	19,749	24,113	1,855	4,364 D	43.2%	52.7%	45.0%	55.0%
17,490	MIFFLIN	14,122	7,280	6,077	765	1,203 R	51.6%	43.0%	54.5%	45.5%
48,052	MONROE	35,727	17,580	16,792	1,355	788 R	49.2%	47.0%	51.1%	48.9%
371,118	MONTGOMERY	309,423	168,323	128,961	12,139	39,362 R	54.4%	41.7%	56.6%	43.4%
8,496	MONTOUR	6,606	3,320	2,888	398	432 R	50.3%	43.7%	53.5%	46.5%
114,681	NORTHAMPTON	93,258	41,455	48,641	3,162	7,186 D	44.5%	52.2%	46.0%	54.0%
41,795	NORTHUMBERLAND	34,313	17,076	15,476	1,761	1,600 R	49.8%	45.1%	52.5%	47.5%
18,174	PERRY	15,178	9,044	4,747	1,387	4,297 R	59.6%	31.3%	65.6%	34.4%
874,181	PHILADELPHIA	611,965	240,440	361,993	9,532	121,553 D	39.3%	59.2%	39.9%	60.1%
15,713	PIKE	12,660	6,834	5,456	370	1,378 R	54.0%	43.1%	55.6%	44.4%
8,509	POTTER	6,805	3,734	2,426	645	1,308 R	54.9%	35.7%	60.6%	39.4%
71,492	SCHUYLKILL	62,401	32,493	27,188	2,720	5,305 R	52.1%	43.6%	54.4%	45.6%
14,703	SNYDER	12,422	7,248	4,101	1,073	3,147 R	58.3%	33.0%	63.9%	36.1%
38,978	SOMERSET	32,419	16,669	13,335	2,415	3,334 R	51.4%	41.1%	55.6%	44.4%
3,723	SULLIVAN	3,082	1,585	1,334	163	251 R	51.4%	43.3%	54.3%	45.7%
19,609	SUSQUEHANNA	16,412	8,396	6,914	1,102	1,482 R	51.2%	42.1%	54.8%	45.2%
19,429	TIOGA	15,889	8,853	5,831	1,205	3,022 R	55.7%	36.7%	60.3%	39.7%
14,238	UNION	12,154	6,653	4,631	870	2,022 R	54.7%	38.1%	59.0%	41.0%

PENNSYLVANIA

SENATOR 1992

Registration	County	Total Vote	Republican	Democratic	Other	Rep.-Dem. Plurality	Percentage			
							Total Vote		Major Vote	
							Rep.	Dem.	Rep.	Dem.
25,903	VENANGO	21,426	10,731	9,184	1,511	1,547 R	50.1%	42.9%	53.9%	46.1%
22,264	WARREN	17,448	8,471	8,211	766	260 R	48.5%	47.1%	50.8%	49.2%
102,501	WASHINGTON	83,457	36,739	42,842	3,876	6,103 D	44.0%	51.3%	46.2%	53.8%
19,316	WAYNE	16,028	8,806	6,437	785	2,369 R	54.9%	40.2%	57.8%	42.2%
182,109	WESTMORELAND	148,002	72,024	69,777	6,201	2,247 R	48.7%	47.1%	50.8%	49.2%
12,720	WYOMING	10,722	5,805	4,154	763	1,651 R	54.1%	38.7%	58.3%	41.7%
155,579	YORK	128,423	68,424	52,828	7,171	15,596 R	53.3%	41.1%	56.4%	43.6%
5,993,002	TOTAL	4,802,410	2,358,125	2,224,966	219,319	133,159 R	49.1%	46.3%	51.5%	48.5%

PENNSYLVANIA

SENATOR 1991
(SHORT TERM)

Registration	County	Total Vote	Republican	Democratic	Other	Rep.-Dem. Plurality	Percentage Total Vote Rep.	Dem.	Major Vote Rep.	Dem.
28,940	ADAMS	19,855	11,110	8,745		2,365 R	56.0%	44.0%	56.0%	44.0%
645,094	ALLEGHENY	425,363	167,881	257,482		89,601 D	39.5%	60.5%	39.5%	60.5%
30,886	ARMSTRONG	23,125	9,756	13,369		3,613 D	42.2%	57.8%	42.2%	57.8%
87,789	BEAVER	61,073	18,673	42,400		23,727 D	30.6%	69.4%	30.6%	69.4%
21,380	BEDFORD	15,054	9,189	5,865		3,324 R	61.0%	39.0%	61.0%	39.0%
133,835	BERKS	82,723	47,276	35,447		11,829 R	57.1%	42.9%	57.1%	42.9%
48,580	BLAIR	32,289	18,157	14,132		4,025 R	56.2%	43.8%	56.2%	43.8%
24,051	BRADFORD	16,035	9,602	6,433		3,169 R	59.9%	40.1%	59.9%	40.1%
246,753	BUCKS	148,353	72,509	75,844		3,335 D	48.9%	51.1%	48.9%	51.1%
62,413	BUTLER	42,463	22,409	20,054		2,355 R	52.8%	47.2%	52.8%	47.2%
73,570	CAMBRIA	52,503	21,061	31,442		10,381 D	40.1%	59.9%	40.1%	59.9%
3,421	CAMERON	2,398	1,451	947		504 R	60.5%	39.5%	60.5%	39.5%
23,038	CARBON	16,270	6,827	9,443		2,616 D	42.0%	58.0%	42.0%	58.0%
48,065	CENTRE	31,630	17,250	14,380		2,870 R	54.5%	45.5%	54.5%	45.5%
162,112	CHESTER	98,382	54,989	43,393		11,596 R	55.9%	44.1%	55.9%	44.1%
16,964	CLARION	11,991	6,366	5,625		741 R	53.1%	46.9%	53.1%	46.9%
32,851	CLEARFIELD	23,506	11,479	12,027		548 D	48.8%	51.2%	48.8%	51.2%
13,679	CLINTON	9,551	4,143	5,408		1,265 D	43.4%	56.6%	43.4%	56.6%
26,774	COLUMBIA	16,414	8,905	7,509		1,396 R	54.3%	45.7%	54.3%	45.7%
37,063	CRAWFORD	24,947	11,769	13,178		1,409 D	47.2%	52.8%	47.2%	52.8%
85,310	CUMBERLAND	56,404	35,303	21,101		14,202 R	62.6%	37.4%	62.6%	37.4%
103,069	DAUPHIN	67,111	36,798	30,313		6,485 R	54.8%	45.2%	54.8%	45.2%
290,775	DELAWARE	179,805	89,192	90,613		1,421 D	49.6%	50.4%	49.6%	50.4%
15,250	ELK	10,982	5,448	5,534		86 D	49.6%	50.4%	49.6%	50.4%
119,774	ERIE	81,190	36,939	44,251		7,312 D	45.5%	54.5%	45.5%	54.5%
59,641	FAYETTE	39,404	11,219	28,185		16,966 D	28.5%	71.5%	28.5%	71.5%
2,413	FOREST	1,713	906	807		99 R	52.9%	47.1%	52.9%	47.1%
45,899	FRANKLIN	28,400	17,559	10,841		6,718 R	61.8%	38.2%	61.8%	38.2%
5,634	FULTON	3,948	2,382	1,566		816 R	60.3%	39.7%	60.3%	39.7%
16,442	GREENE	12,071	3,729	8,342		4,613 D	30.9%	69.1%	30.9%	69.1%
17,040	HUNTINGDON	12,443	7,363	5,080		2,283 R	59.2%	40.8%	59.2%	40.8%
34,020	INDIANA	23,879	10,838	13,041		2,203 D	45.4%	54.6%	45.4%	54.6%
19,731	JEFFERSON	14,310	7,865	6,445		1,420 R	55.0%	45.0%	55.0%	45.0%
9,307	JUNIATA	6,738	3,973	2,765		1,208 R	59.0%	41.0%	59.0%	41.0%
117,048	LACKAWANNA	72,175	26,030	46,145		20,115 D	36.1%	63.9%	36.1%	63.9%
159,783	LANCASTER	96,343	66,564	29,779		36,785 R	69.1%	30.9%	69.1%	30.9%
44,630	LAWRENCE	30,674	11,373	19,301		7,928 D	37.1%	62.9%	37.1%	62.9%
42,529	LEBANON	28,895	18,209	10,686		7,523 R	63.0%	37.0%	63.0%	37.0%
117,584	LEHIGH	71,560	34,489	37,071		2,582 D	48.2%	51.8%	48.2%	51.8%
139,324	LUZERNE	96,699	36,708	59,991		23,283 D	38.0%	62.0%	38.0%	62.0%
44,907	LYCOMING	31,021	17,727	13,294		4,433 R	57.1%	42.9%	57.1%	42.9%
17,234	MCKEAN	10,936	6,464	4,472		1,992 R	59.1%	40.9%	59.1%	40.9%
51,736	MERCER	33,647	13,497	20,150		6,653 D	40.1%	59.9%	40.1%	59.9%
15,325	MIFFLIN	10,460	5,844	4,616		1,228 R	55.9%	44.1%	55.9%	44.1%
39,342	MONROE	22,976	11,470	11,506		36 D	49.9%	50.1%	49.9%	50.1%
312,147	MONTGOMERY	202,284	98,069	104,215		6,146 D	48.5%	51.5%	48.5%	51.5%
7,484	MONTOUR	4,686	2,508	2,178		330 R	53.5%	46.5%	53.5%	46.5%
97,411	NORTHAMPTON	60,205	27,744	32,461		4,717 D	46.1%	53.9%	46.1%	53.9%
38,934	NORTHUMBERLAND	27,686	13,380	14,306		926 D	48.3%	51.7%	48.3%	51.7%
16,357	PERRY	11,163	7,395	3,768		3,627 R	66.2%	33.8%	66.2%	33.8%
821,872	PHILADELPHIA	445,655	114,017	331,638		217,621 D	25.6%	74.4%	25.6%	74.4%
12,846	PIKE	7,851	4,365	3,486		879 R	55.6%	44.4%	55.6%	44.4%
7,901	POTTER	5,562	3,589	1,973		1,616 R	64.5%	35.5%	64.5%	35.5%
65,400	SCHUYLKILL	48,383	21,996	26,387		4,391 D	45.5%	54.5%	45.5%	54.5%
13,247	SNYDER	9,399	6,426	2,973		3,453 R	68.4%	31.6%	68.4%	31.6%
36,387	SOMERSET	25,568	13,152	12,416		736 R	51.4%	48.6%	51.4%	48.6%
3,504	SULLIVAN	2,802	1,569	1,233		336 R	56.0%	44.0%	56.0%	44.0%
17,988	SUSQUEHANNA	12,747	6,916	5,831		1,085 R	54.3%	45.7%	54.3%	45.7%
18,078	TIOGA	12,624	8,073	4,551		3,522 R	63.9%	36.1%	63.9%	36.1%
12,385	UNION	8,821	5,486	3,335		2,151 R	62.2%	37.8%	62.2%	37.8%

PENNSYLVANIA

SENATOR 1991
(SHORT TERM)

Registration	County	Total Vote	Republican	Democratic	Other	Rep.-Dem. Plurality	Percentage			
							Total Vote		Major Vote	
							Rep.	Dem.	Rep.	Dem.
23,263	VENANGO	15,066	7,562	7,504		58 R	50.2%	49.8%	50.2%	49.8%
19,867	WARREN	12,947	6,684	6,263		421 R	51.6%	48.4%	51.6%	48.4%
93,202	WASHINGTON	62,027	21,612	40,415		18,803 D	34.8%	65.2%	34.8%	65.2%
17,213	WAYNE	11,783	7,101	4,682		2,419 R	60.3%	39.7%	60.3%	39.7%
163,897	WESTMORELAND	108,501	44,628	63,873		19,245 D	41.1%	58.9%	41.1%	58.9%
11,302	WYOMING	7,388	4,298	3,090		1,208 R	58.2%	41.8%	58.2%	41.8%
131,366	YORK	81,889	46,725	35,164		11,561 R	57.1%	42.9%	57.1%	42.9%
5,323,056	TOTAL	3,382,746	1,521,986	1,860,760		338,774 D	45.0%	55.0%	45.0%	55.0%

PHILADELPHIA

PRESIDENT 1992

Registration	Ward	Total Vote	Republican	Democratic	Perot	Other	Plurality	Percentage Total Vote		
								Rep.	Dem.	Perot
10,867	WARD 1	7,907	2,375	4,501	997	34	2,126 D	30.0%	56.9%	12.6%
12,946	WARD 2	9,755	2,089	6,736	875	55	4,647 D	21.4%	69.1%	9.0%
12,453	WARD 3	9,295	340	8,622	264	69	8,282 D	3.7%	92.8%	2.8%
12,196	WARD 4	8,350	302	7,787	207	54	7,485 D	3.6%	93.3%	2.5%
16,406	WARD 5	11,801	2,164	8,575	977	85	6,411 D	18.3%	72.7%	8.3%
8,682	WARD 6	4,922	266	4,448	161	47	4,182 D	5.4%	90.4%	3.3%
10,972	WARD 7	5,360	1,560	3,179	594	27	1,619 D	29.1%	59.3%	11.1%
19,134	WARD 8	14,963	2,561	11,313	927	162	8,752 D	17.1%	75.6%	6.2%
10,467	WARD 9	8,475	2,027	5,819	590	39	3,792 D	23.9%	68.7%	7.0%
15,913	WARD 10	11,737	427	10,866	351	93	10,439 D	3.6%	92.6%	3.0%
9,610	WARD 11	6,134	290	5,619	176	49	5,329 D	4.7%	91.6%	2.9%
13,778	WARD 12	8,476	575	7,426	391	84	6,851 D	6.8%	87.6%	4.6%
12,143	WARD 13	8,433	567	7,475	308	83	6,908 D	6.7%	88.6%	3.7%
6,130	WARD 14	3,070	175	2,771	100	24	2,596 D	5.7%	90.3%	3.3%
11,001	WARD 15	7,812	1,463	5,639	655	55	4,176 D	18.7%	72.2%	8.4%
9,397	WARD 16	5,612	268	5,157	133	54	4,889 D	4.8%	91.9%	2.4%
14,258	WARD 17	10,638	490	9,694	391	63	9,204 D	4.6%	91.1%	3.7%
8,893	WARD 18	5,591	1,419	3,345	780	47	1,926 D	25.4%	59.8%	14.0%
10,235	WARD 19	4,398	1,030	3,155	186	27	2,125 D	23.4%	71.7%	4.2%
4,905	WARD 20	2,839	172	2,555	92	20	2,383 D	6.1%	90.0%	3.2%
25,565	WARD 21	21,333	7,710	10,272	3,208	143	2,562 D	36.1%	48.2%	15.0%
14,865	WARD 22	11,717	740	10,470	421	86	9,730 D	6.3%	89.4%	3.6%
11,413	WARD 23	8,162	2,286	4,509	1,308	59	2,223 D	28.0%	55.2%	16.0%
7,882	WARD 24	4,978	322	4,344	274	38	4,022 D	6.5%	87.3%	5.5%
11,401	WARD 25	8,208	2,462	4,108	1,583	55	1,646 D	30.0%	50.0%	19.3%
12,162	WARD 26	9,703	3,954	4,317	1,390	42	363 D	40.8%	44.5%	14.3%
9,730	WARD 27	7,002	1,112	5,284	551	55	4,172 D	15.9%	75.5%	7.9%
9,001	WARD 28	5,930	316	5,437	142	35	5,121 D	5.3%	91.7%	2.4%
8,431	WARD 29	5,091	271	4,657	132	31	4,386 D	5.3%	91.5%	2.6%
8,719	WARD 30	5,805	596	4,856	300	53	4,260 D	10.3%	83.7%	5.2%
9,750	WARD 31	6,490	1,898	3,227	1,319	46	1,329 D	29.2%	49.7%	20.3%
13,834	WARD 32	8,256	415	7,535	242	64	7,120 D	5.0%	91.3%	2.9%
12,094	WARD 33	9,014	2,723	4,448	1,795	48	1,725 D	30.2%	49.3%	19.9%
19,932	WARD 34	15,912	2,737	11,975	1,106	94	9,238 D	17.2%	75.3%	7.0%
16,324	WARD 35	13,101	5,043	5,665	2,253	140	622 D	38.5%	43.2%	17.2%
18,263	WARD 36	12,896	1,400	10,664	752	80	9,264 D	10.9%	82.7%	5.8%
11,458	WARD 37	5,674	499	5,004	144	27	4,505 D	8.8%	88.2%	2.5%
11,295	WARD 38	8,201	1,167	6,447	544	43	5,280 D	14.2%	78.6%	6.6%
25,135	WARD 39	18,812	6,249	9,778	2,713	72	3,529 D	33.2%	52.0%	14.4%
22,911	WARD 40	16,892	4,262	10,391	2,139	100	6,129 D	25.2%	61.5%	12.7%
13,434	WARD 41	10,216	3,143	4,949	2,063	61	1,806 D	30.8%	48.4%	20.2%
11,798	WARD 42	7,896	2,029	4,799	1,010	58	2,770 D	25.7%	60.8%	12.8%
13,149	WARD 43	7,224	971	5,926	285	42	4,955 D	13.4%	82.0%	3.9%
9,167	WARD 44	6,136	265	5,636	187	48	5,371 D	4.3%	91.9%	3.0%
13,347	WARD 45	10,072	3,099	4,811	2,091	71	1,712 D	30.8%	47.8%	20.8%
12,429	WARD 46	8,850	565	7,883	337	65	7,318 D	6.4%	89.1%	3.8%
5,852	WARD 47	3,101	178	2,795	91	37	2,617 D	5.7%	90.1%	2.9%
10,942	WARD 48	7,801	2,180	4,759	822	40	2,579 D	27.9%	61.0%	10.5%
13,432	WARD 49	8,976	739	7,758	411	68	7,019 D	8.2%	86.4%	4.6%
17,030	WARD 50	13,221	597	12,069	470	85	11,472 D	4.5%	91.3%	3.6%
13,387	WARD 51	8,961	347	8,287	261	66	7,940 D	3.9%	92.5%	2.9%
15,320	WARD 52	11,820	1,202	10,022	472	124	8,820 D	10.2%	84.8%	4.0%
13,072	WARD 53	10,690	2,755	6,342	1,524	69	3,587 D	25.8%	59.3%	14.3%
11,341	WARD 54	9,187	1,926	6,090	1,130	41	4,164 D	21.0%	66.3%	12.3%
15,658	WARD 55	13,180	4,625	6,097	2,389	69	1,472 D	35.1%	46.3%	18.1%
20,736	WARD 56	16,784	4,620	10,123	1,942	99	5,503 D	27.5%	60.3%	11.6%
14,672	WARD 57	12,215	4,113	6,021	2,008	73	1,908 D	33.7%	49.3%	16.4%
24,077	WARD 58	20,517	6,845	10,567	2,994	111	3,722 D	33.4%	51.5%	14.6%
12,962	WARD 59	9,056	560	8,087	335	74	7,527 D	6.2%	89.3%	3.7%
11,543	WARD 60	8,061	318	7,474	212	57	7,156 D	3.9%	92.7%	2.6%

PHILADELPHIA

PRESIDENT 1992

Registration	Ward	Total Vote	Republican	Democratic	Perot	Other	Plurality	Percentage Total Vote		
								Rep.	Dem.	Perot
11,926	WARD 61	9,126	2,610	5,376	1,068	72	2,766 D	28.6%	58.9%	11.7%
15,666	WARD 62	12,496	3,758	6,225	2,429	84	2,467 D	30.1%	49.8%	19.4%
13,660	WARD 63	11,317	4,142	5,469	1,630	76	1,327 D	36.6%	48.3%	14.4%
10,067	WARD 64	8,319	3,230	3,629	1,413	47	399 D	38.8%	43.6%	17.0%
14,356	WARD 65	10,978	3,272	5,689	1,952	65	2,417 D	29.8%	51.8%	17.8%
25,736	WARD 66	21,409	8,070	8,907	4,299	133	837 D	37.7%	41.6%	20.1%
874,181	TOTAL	638,058	133,328	434,904	65,455	4,371	301,576 D	20.9%	68.2%	10.3%

PHILIDELPHIA

SENATOR 1992

Registration	Ward	Total Vote	Republican	Democratic	Other	Rep.-Dem. Plurality	Total Vote Rep.	Total Vote Dem.	Major Vote Rep.	Major Vote Dem.
10,867	WARD 1	7,667	3,455	4,123	89	668 D	45.1%	53.8%	45.6%	54.4%
12,946	WARD 2	9,576	3,534	5,941	101	2,407 D	36.9%	62.0%	37.3%	62.7%
12,453	WARD 3	8,958	2,445	6,468	45	4,023 D	27.3%	72.2%	27.4%	72.6%
12,196	WARD 4	7,976	1,929	6,011	36	4,082 D	24.2%	75.4%	24.3%	75.7%
16,406	WARD 5	11,467	3,805	7,532	130	3,727 D	33.2%	65.7%	33.6%	66.4%
8,682	WARD 6	4,829	1,133	3,669	27	2,536 D	23.5%	76.0%	23.6%	76.4%
10,972	WARD 7	4,985	1,911	3,000	74	1,089 D	38.3%	60.2%	38.9%	61.1%
19,134	WARD 8	14,670	5,554	8,959	157	3,405 D	37.9%	61.1%	38.3%	61.7%
10,467	WARD 9	8,601	3,181	5,187	233	2,006 D	37.0%	60.3%	38.0%	62.0%
15,913	WARD 10	11,714	2,665	8,988	61	6,323 D	22.8%	76.7%	22.9%	77.1%
9,610	WARD 11	5,943	1,331	4,573	39	3,242 D	22.4%	76.9%	22.5%	77.5%
13,778	WARD 12	8,544	1,896	6,571	77	4,675 D	22.2%	76.9%	22.4%	77.6%
12,143	WARD 13	8,109	1,938	6,115	56	4,177 D	23.9%	75.4%	24.1%	75.9%
6,130	WARD 14	2,989	599	2,370	20	1,771 D	20.0%	79.3%	20.2%	79.8%
11,001	WARD 15	7,514	2,452	4,974	88	2,522 D	32.6%	66.2%	33.0%	67.0%
9,397	WARD 16	5,536	1,120	4,340	76	3,220 D	20.2%	78.4%	20.5%	79.5%
14,258	WARD 17	10,391	2,458	7,882	51	5,424 D	23.7%	75.9%	23.8%	76.2%
8,893	WARD 18	5,238	1,962	3,199	77	1,237 D	37.5%	61.1%	38.0%	62.0%
10,235	WARD 19	4,159	1,296	2,829	34	1,533 D	31.2%	68.0%	31.4%	68.6%
4,905	WARD 20	2,809	556	2,234	19	1,678 D	19.8%	79.5%	19.9%	80.1%
25,565	WARD 21	20,435	10,516	9,423	496	1,093 R	51.5%	46.1%	52.7%	47.3%
14,865	WARD 22	11,500	3,185	8,239	76	5,054 D	27.7%	71.6%	27.9%	72.1%
11,413	WARD 23	7,675	3,327	4,160	188	833 D	43.3%	54.2%	44.4%	55.6%
7,882	WARD 24	4,859	994	3,826	39	2,832 D	20.5%	78.7%	20.6%	79.4%
11,401	WARD 25	7,658	3,464	4,040	154	576 D	45.2%	52.8%	46.2%	53.8%
12,162	WARD 26	9,089	5,032	3,943	114	1,089 R	55.4%	43.4%	56.1%	43.9%
9,730	WARD 27	6,777	2,033	4,654	90	2,621 D	30.0%	68.7%	30.4%	69.6%
9,001	WARD 28	5,503	1,103	4,377	23	3,274 D	20.0%	79.5%	20.1%	79.9%
8,431	WARD 29	4,875	809	4,029	37	3,220 D	16.6%	82.6%	16.7%	83.3%
8,719	WARD 30	5,544	1,379	4,113	52	2,734 D	24.9%	74.2%	25.1%	74.9%
9,750	WARD 31	5,925	2,649	3,143	133	494 D	44.7%	53.0%	45.7%	54.3%
13,834	WARD 32	7,825	1,640	6,087	98	4,447 D	21.0%	77.8%	21.2%	78.8%
12,094	WARD 33	8,353	3,959	4,148	246	189 D	47.4%	49.7%	48.8%	51.2%
19,932	WARD 34	15,438	6,134	9,109	195	2,975 D	39.7%	59.0%	40.2%	59.8%
16,324	WARD 35	12,533	7,153	4,976	404	2,177 R	57.1%	39.7%	59.0%	41.0%
18,263	WARD 36	12,278	3,617	8,578	83	4,961 D	29.5%	69.9%	29.7%	70.3%
11,458	WARD 37	5,358	1,006	4,327	25	3,321 D	18.8%	80.8%	18.9%	81.1%
11,295	WARD 38	7,875	2,439	5,365	71	2,926 D	31.0%	68.1%	31.3%	68.7%
25,135	WARD 39	17,647	8,826	8,608	213	218 R	50.0%	48.8%	50.6%	49.4%
22,911	WARD 40	16,197	6,981	8,999	217	2,018 D	43.1%	55.6%	43.7%	56.3%
13,434	WARD 41	9,548	4,569	4,681	298	112 D	47.9%	49.0%	49.4%	50.6%
11,798	WARD 42	7,553	2,993	4,423	137	1,430 D	39.6%	58.6%	40.4%	59.6%
13,149	WARD 43	6,898	1,635	5,213	50	3,578 D	23.7%	75.6%	23.9%	76.1%
9,167	WARD 44	5,928	1,317	4,589	22	3,272 D	22.2%	77.4%	22.3%	77.7%
13,347	WARD 45	9,370	4,393	4,677	300	284 D	46.9%	49.9%	48.4%	51.6%
12,429	WARD 46	8,470	1,910	6,505	55	4,595 D	22.6%	76.8%	22.7%	77.3%
5,852	WARD 47	2,952	484	2,441	27	1,957 D	16.4%	82.7%	16.5%	83.5%
10,942	WARD 48	7,484	3,189	4,211	84	1,022 D	42.6%	56.3%	43.1%	56.9%
13,432	WARD 49	8,824	2,352	6,399	73	4,047 D	26.7%	72.5%	26.9%	73.1%
17,030	WARD 50	13,130	3,654	9,393	83	5,739 D	27.8%	71.5%	28.0%	72.0%
13,387	WARD 51	8,595	1,811	6,744	40	4,933 D	21.1%	78.5%	21.2%	78.8%
15,320	WARD 52	11,713	4,407	7,207	99	2,800 D	37.6%	61.5%	37.9%	62.1%
13,072	WARD 53	10,461	6,100	4,113	248	1,987 R	58.3%	39.3%	59.7%	40.3%
11,341	WARD 54	8,739	4,570	4,023	146	547 R	52.3%	46.0%	53.2%	46.8%
15,658	WARD 55	12,784	6,794	5,657	333	1,137 R	53.1%	44.3%	54.6%	45.4%
20,736	WARD 56	16,114	9,135	6,585	394	2,550 R	56.7%	40.9%	58.1%	41.9%
14,672	WARD 57	11,797	6,517	4,930	350	1,587 R	55.2%	41.8%	56.9%	43.1%
24,077	WARD 58	19,952	12,065	7,455	432	4,610 R	60.5%	37.4%	61.8%	38.2%
12,962	WARD 59	8,771	2,067	6,651	53	4,584 D	23.6%	75.8%	23.7%	76.3%
11,543	WARD 60	7,820	1,932	5,854	34	3,922 D	24.7%	74.9%	24.8%	75.2%

PHILIDELPHIA

SENATOR 1992

| | | | | | | | | Percentage | | | |
| | | | | | | | | Total Vote | | Major Vote | |
Registration	Ward	Total Vote	Republican	Democratic	Other	Rep.-Dem. Plurality		Rep.	Dem.	Rep.	Dem.
11,926	WARD 61	8,848	4,089	4,526	233	437	D	46.2%	51.2%	47.5%	52.5%
15,666	WARD 62	11,807	5,563	5,877	367	314	D	47.1%	49.8%	48.6%	51.4%
13,660	WARD 63	11,085	6,831	3,918	336	2,913	R	61.6%	35.3%	63.6%	36.4%
10,067	WARD 64	7,999	4,544	3,227	228	1,317	R	56.8%	40.3%	58.5%	41.5%
14,356	WARD 65	10,194	5,147	4,826	221	321	R	50.5%	47.3%	51.6%	48.4%
25,736	WARD 66	20,115	10,806	8,749	560	2,057	R	53.7%	43.5%	55.3%	44.7%
874,181	TOTAL	611,965	240,440	361,993	9,532	121,553	D	39.3%	59.2%	39.9%	60.1%

PHILIDELPHIA

SENATOR 1991

Registration	Ward	Total Vote	Republican	Democratic	Other	Rep.-Dem. Plurality	Percentage			
							Total Vote		Major Vote	
							Rep.	Dem.	Rep.	Dem.
10,352	WARD 1	5,866	1,964	3,902		1,938 D	33.5%	66.5%	33.5%	66.5%
12,216	WARD 2	7,032	2,003	5,029		3,026 D	28.5%	71.5%	28.5%	71.5%
11,564	WARD 3	6,419	377	6,042		5,665 D	5.9%	94.1%	5.9%	94.1%
11,179	WARD 4	5,275	313	4,962		4,649 D	5.9%	94.1%	5.9%	94.1%
12,912	WARD 5	7,063	1,401	5,662		4,261 D	19.8%	80.2%	19.8%	80.2%
7,550	WARD 6	2,975	241	2,734		2,493 D	8.1%	91.9%	8.1%	91.9%
9,509	WARD 7	3,215	1,077	2,138		1,061 D	33.5%	66.5%	33.5%	66.5%
14,668	WARD 8	9,711	1,864	7,847		5,983 D	19.2%	80.8%	19.2%	80.8%
8,961	WARD 9	6,547	1,630	4,917		3,287 D	24.9%	75.1%	24.9%	75.1%
14,189	WARD 10	8,214	413	7,801		7,388 D	5.0%	95.0%	5.0%	95.0%
8,601	WARD 11	3,858	256	3,602		3,346 D	6.6%	93.4%	6.6%	93.4%
11,681	WARD 12	5,414	446	4,968		4,522 D	8.2%	91.8%	8.2%	91.8%
10,663	WARD 13	5,219	455	4,764		4,309 D	8.7%	91.3%	8.7%	91.3%
5,456	WARD 14	1,771	169	1,602		1,433 D	9.5%	90.5%	9.5%	90.5%
9,369	WARD 15	5,367	1,035	4,332		3,297 D	19.3%	80.7%	19.3%	80.7%
8,706	WARD 16	3,631	311	3,320		3,009 D	8.6%	91.4%	8.6%	91.4%
12,534	WARD 17	6,806	419	6,387		5,968 D	6.2%	93.8%	6.2%	93.8%
7,703	WARD 18	3,425	966	2,459		1,493 D	28.2%	71.8%	28.2%	71.8%
9,073	WARD 19	2,336	443	1,893		1,450 D	19.0%	81.0%	19.0%	81.0%
4,298	WARD 20	1,773	149	1,624		1,475 D	8.4%	91.6%	8.4%	91.6%
23,755	WARD 21	14,659	5,746	8,913		3,167 D	39.2%	60.8%	39.2%	60.8%
12,744	WARD 22	7,999	513	7,486		6,973 D	6.4%	93.6%	6.4%	93.6%
10,963	WARD 23	5,818	2,106	3,712		1,606 D	36.2%	63.8%	36.2%	63.8%
6,405	WARD 24	3,075	317	2,758		2,441 D	10.3%	89.7%	10.3%	89.7%
10,802	WARD 25	6,111	2,312	3,799		1,487 D	37.8%	62.2%	37.8%	62.2%
11,559	WARD 26	7,102	2,965	4,137		1,172 D	41.7%	58.3%	41.7%	58.3%
5,943	WARD 27	2,704	410	2,294		1,884 D	15.2%	84.8%	15.2%	84.8%
8,038	WARD 28	3,853	197	3,656		3,459 D	5.1%	94.9%	5.1%	94.9%
7,803	WARD 29	3,360	274	3,086		2,812 D	8.2%	91.8%	8.2%	91.8%
7,272	WARD 30	3,577	387	3,190		2,803 D	10.8%	89.2%	10.8%	89.2%
9,220	WARD 31	4,782	1,774	3,008		1,234 D	37.1%	62.9%	37.1%	62.9%
12,526	WARD 32	5,096	561	4,535		3,974 D	11.0%	89.0%	11.0%	89.0%
11,875	WARD 33	6,673	2,568	4,105		1,537 D	38.5%	61.5%	38.5%	61.5%
19,413	WARD 34	11,906	2,600	9,306		6,706 D	21.8%	78.2%	21.8%	78.2%
15,699	WARD 35	10,614	5,011	5,603		592 D	47.2%	52.8%	47.2%	52.8%
16,895	WARD 36	9,055	1,248	7,807		6,559 D	13.8%	86.2%	13.8%	86.2%
9,646	WARD 37	3,292	270	3,022		2,752 D	8.2%	91.8%	8.2%	91.8%
9,616	WARD 38	5,325	1,007	4,318		3,311 D	18.9%	81.1%	18.9%	81.1%
23,696	WARD 39	13,835	4,884	8,951		4,067 D	35.3%	64.7%	35.3%	64.7%
21,474	WARD 40	11,682	3,283	8,399		5,116 D	28.1%	71.9%	28.1%	71.9%
12,456	WARD 41	7,423	2,865	4,558		1,693 D	38.6%	61.4%	38.6%	61.4%
10,673	WARD 42	5,301	1,612	3,689		2,077 D	30.4%	69.6%	30.4%	69.6%
11,136	WARD 43	4,237	618	3,619		3,001 D	14.6%	85.4%	14.6%	85.4%
8,196	WARD 44	4,152	316	3,836		3,520 D	7.6%	92.4%	7.6%	92.4%
12,822	WARD 45	7,555	2,959	4,596		1,637 D	39.2%	60.8%	39.2%	60.8%
10,664	WARD 46	5,755	413	5,342		4,929 D	7.2%	92.8%	7.2%	92.8%
5,774	WARD 47	1,902	170	1,732		1,562 D	8.9%	91.1%	8.9%	91.1%
10,442	WARD 48	5,592	1,690	3,902		2,212 D	30.2%	69.8%	30.2%	69.8%
11,350	WARD 49	5,332	666	4,666		4,000 D	12.5%	87.5%	12.5%	87.5%
15,472	WARD 50	9,017	557	8,460		7,903 D	6.2%	93.8%	6.2%	93.8%
11,868	WARD 51	5,520	328	5,192		4,864 D	5.9%	94.1%	5.9%	94.1%
14,172	WARD 52	7,714	879	6,835		5,956 D	11.4%	88.6%	11.4%	88.6%
12,962	WARD 53	9,082	2,865	6,217		3,352 D	31.5%	68.5%	31.5%	68.5%
11,120	WARD 54	7,606	1,743	5,863		4,120 D	22.9%	77.1%	22.9%	77.1%
15,081	WARD 55	10,075	3,980	6,095		2,115 D	39.5%	60.5%	39.5%	60.5%
20,051	WARD 56	13,510	4,192	9,318		5,126 D	31.0%	69.0%	31.0%	69.0%
13,783	WARD 57	9,537	3,659	5,878		2,219 D	38.4%	61.6%	38.4%	61.6%
23,420	WARD 58	15,871	6,366	9,505		3,139 D	40.1%	59.9%	40.1%	59.9%
11,482	WARD 59	6,033	492	5,541		5,049 D	8.2%	91.8%	8.2%	91.8%
10,445	WARD 60	5,583	316	5,267		4,951 D	5.7%	94.3%	5.7%	94.3%

428

PHILIDELPHIA

SENATOR 1991

Registration	Ward	Total Vote	Republican	Democratic	Other	Rep.-Dem. Plurality	Percentage			
							Total Vote		Major Vote	
							Rep.	Dem.	Rep.	Dem.
10,708	WARD 61	6,897	2,298	4,599		2,301 D	33.3%	66.7%	33.3%	66.7%
15,952	WARD 62	9,581	3,388	6,193		2,805 D	35.4%	64.6%	35.4%	64.6%
13,294	WARD 63	9,198	3,969	5,229		1,260 D	43.2%	56.8%	43.2%	56.8%
9,824	WARD 64	6,554	3,131	3,423		292 D	47.8%	52.2%	47.8%	52.2%
13,012	WARD 65	8,418	2,919	5,499		2,580 D	34.7%	65.3%	34.7%	65.3%
23,270	WARD 66	15,472	7,163	8,309		1,146 D	46.3%	53.7%	46.3%	53.7%
821,872	TOTAL	445,655	114,017	331,638		217,621 D	25.6%	74.4%	25.6%	74.4%

PENNSYLVANIA

CONGRESS

CD	Year	Total Vote	Republican		Democratic		Other Vote	Rep.-Dem. Plurality	Percentage			
			Vote	Candidate	Vote	Candidate			Total Vote		Major Vote	
									Rep.	Dem.	Rep.	Dem.
1	1992	185,591	35,419	SNYDER, CRAIG	150,172	FOGLIETTA, THOMAS M.		114,753 D	19.1%	80.9%	19.1%	80.9%
2	1992	213,927	47,906	HOLLIN, LARRY	164,355	BLACKWELL, LUCIEN E.	1,666	116,449 D	22.4%	76.8%	22.6%	77.4%
3	1992	221,971	86,787	DOUGHERTY, CHARLES F.	130,828	BORSKI, ROBERT A.	4,356	44,041 D	39.1%	58.9%	39.9%	60.1%
4	1992	237,922	48,484	JOHNSTON, GORDON R.	186,684	KLINK, RON	2,754	138,200 D	20.4%	78.5%	20.6%	79.4%
5	1992	188,911	188,911*	CLINGER, WILLIAM F.				188,911 R	100.0%		100.0%	
6	1992	208,006	99,694	JONES, JOHN E.	108,312	HOLDEN, TIM		8,618 D	47.9%	52.1%	47.9%	52.1%
7	1992	273,898	180,648	WELDON, CURT	91,623	DALY, FRANK	1,627	89,025 R	66.0%	33.5%	66.3%	33.7%
8	1992	249,538	129,593	GREENWOOD, JAMES C.	114,095	KOSTMAYER, PETER H.	5,850	15,498 R	51.9%	45.7%	53.2%	46.8%
9	1992	182,406	182,406*	SHUSTER, E. G.				182,406 R	100.0%		100.0%	
10	1992	209,548	189,414*	MCDADE, JOSEPH M.			20,134	189,414 R	90.4%		100.0%	
11	1992	206,987	68,112	FESCINA, MICHAEL A.	138,875	KANJORSKI, PAUL E.		70,763 D	32.9%	67.1%	32.9%	67.1%
12	1992	166,916			166,916	MURTHA, JOHN P.		166,916 D		100.0%		100.0%
13	1992	253,997	126,312	FOX, JON D.	127,685	MEZVINSKY, MARJORIE M.		1,373 D	49.7%	50.3%	49.7%	50.3%
14	1992	229,038	61,311	KING, BYRON W.	165,633	COYNE, WILLLIAM J.	2,094	104,322 D	26.8%	72.3%	27.0%	73.0%
15	1992	213,324	99,520	RITTER, DONALD L.	111,419	MCHALE, PAUL	2,385	11,899 D	46.7%	52.2%	47.2%	52.8%
16	1992	212,564	137,823	WALKER, ROBERT S.	74,741	PETERS, ROBERT		63,082 R	64.8%	35.2%	64.8%	35.2%
17	1992	216,039	150,158	GEKAS, GEORGE W.	65,881	STURGES, BILL		84,277 R	69.5%	30.5%	69.5%	30.5%
18	1992	254,329	154,024	SANTORUM, RICK	96,655	PECORA, FRANK A.	3,650	57,369 R	60.6%	38.0%	61.4%	38.6%
19	1992	217,587	98,599	GOODLING, WILLIAM F.	74,798	KILKER, PAUL V.	44,190	23,801 R	45.3%	34.4%	56.9%	43.1%
20	1992	226,489	111,591	TOWNSEND, BILL	114,898	MURPHY, AUSTIN J.		3,307 D	49.3%	50.7%	49.3%	50.7%
21	1992	221,531	150,729	RIDGE, THOMAS J.	70,802	HARKINS, JOHN C.		79,927 R	68.0%	32.0%	68.0%	32.0%

PENNSYLVANIA

1991 GENERAL ELECTION

Senator   A special election was held November 5, 1991 to fill the vacancy created by the death of Senator H. John Heinz. Candidates were nominated by the state party committees therefore no primaries were held.

1992 GENERAL ELECTION

President   Other vote was 21,477 Libertarian (Marrou); 4,661 New Alliance (Fulani). The Perot vote in Huntingdon county was amended from 7,273 to 3,273 thereby changing the total statewide vote from 906,667 to 902,667.

Senator   Other vote was Libertarian (Perry).

Congress   As asterisk in the Congressional table indicates a candidate received votes from another party. Other vote was Socialist Workers (Wyatt) in CD 2; Independent (Hughes) in CD 3; Independent (Ley) in CD 4; Natural Law (Hickman) in CD 7; Independent (Magerman) in CD 8; Libertarian (Smith) in CD 10; 1,300 Socialist Workers (Kuniansky) and 794 Workers League (Scherrer) in CD 14; Natural Law (Nau) in CD 15; New Independent (Edwards) in CD 18; Independent (Humbert) in CD 19.

PHILADELPHIA

Philadelphia city and county are coterminous. In the tables of the vote and registration by ward, there are small differences between the state certified totals and the addition of the vote and registration by wards. The state certified totals are used in the total line; the ward-by-ward figures are from the Philadelphia Registration Commission.

President   Other vote was 2,417 Libertarian (Marrou); 1,954 New Alliance (Fulani).

Senator   Other vote was Libertarian (Perry).

1992 PRIMARIES

APRIL 28 REPUBLICAN

Senator   683,118 Arlen Specter; 366,608 Stephen F. Freind.

Congress   Unopposed in fourteen CD's. No candidate in CD 12. Contested as follows:

CD 6   24,201 John E. Jones; 14,498 James J. Gallen; 10,947 James P. Troutman.
CD 7   73,304 Curt Weldon; 21,413 Fiorindo Vagnozzi.
CD 8   36,394 James C. Greenwood; 9,472 Joseph P. Schiaffino.
CD 11   19,411 Michael A. Fescina; 11,122 Jurij A. Podolak.
CD 13   39,144 Jon D. Fox; 19,902 William W. Evans; 15,725 Susan Boyer.
CD 20   15,810 Bill Townsend; 15,568 Suzanne Hayden.

APRIL 28 DEMOCRATIC

Senator   556,372 Lynn Yeakel; 403,656 Mark S. Singel; 172,845 Bob Colville; 62,149 Freddy M. Friedman; 47,314 Philip Valenti.

Congress   Unopposed in seven CD's. No candidate in CD's 5, 9 and 10. In CD 5 William F. Clinger, the Republican nominee, received write-in votes in the Democratic primary and became the nominee of both parties. In CD 9 E. G. Shuster, the Republican nominee, received write-in votes in the Democratic primary and became the nominee of both parties. In CD 10 Joseph M. McDade, the Republican nominee, received write-in votes in the Democratic primary and became the nominee of both parties.

PENNSYLVANIA

Contested as follows:

CD 2   48,299 Lucien E.Blackwell; 41,528 C. Delores Tucker.

CD 4   45,884 Ron Klink; 22,379 Mike Veon; 19,683 Joseph P. Kolter; 13,153 Frank LaGrotta.

CD 6   20,057 Tim Holden; 16,647 Warren H. Haggerty; 14,193 John A. Reusing.

CD 7   16,191 Frank Daly; 12,123 John Innelli; 2,716 Donald T. Hadley.

CD 8   29,442 Peter H. Kostmayer; 9,547 Joe Hayes.

CD 13   28,095 Marjorie M. Mezvinsky; 7,318 Bernard Tomkin.

CD 14   70,162 William J. Coyne; 21,607 Al Guttman.

CD 15   30,818 Paul McHale; 10,891 Dave Clark.

CD 18   19,839 Frank A. Pecora; 13,939 Mike Adams; 13,608 David Levdansky; 11,924 Jim West; 10,353 Jeff Pribanic; 7,421 Luke Kelly; 6,796 Marick Masters; 6,132 Richard Caligiuri; 5,601 Emil Mrkonic; 4,218 Susan A. Roach; 2,878 Constance B. Komm; 1,534 Jim Olson.

CD 20   36,585 Austin J. Murphy; 33,942 Frank R. Mascara; 14,422 Kenneth B. Burkley; 8,520 William A. Nicolella; 7,755 Eugene G. Saloom.

CD 21   23,438 John C. Harkins; 19,044 Mary McDanniels-Kulesa.

RHODE ISLAND

GOVERNOR
Bruce G. Sundlun (D). Elected 1992 to a two-year term. Previously elected 1990.

SENATORS
John H. Chafee (R). Re-elected 1988 to a six-year term. Previously elected 1982, 1976.

Claiborne Pell (D). Re-elected 1990 to a six-year term. Previously elected 1984, 1978, 1972, 1966, 1960.

REPRESENTATIVES
1. Ronald K. Machtley (R)   2. John F. Reed (D)

POSTWAR VOTE FOR PRESIDENT

Year	Total Vote	Republican Vote	Republican Candidate	Democratic Vote	Democratic Candidate	Other Vote	Plurality	Total Vote Rep.	Total Vote Dem.	Major Vote Rep.	Major Vote Dem.
1992 **	453,477	131,601	Bush, George	213,299	Clinton, Bill	108,577	81,698 D	29.0%	47.0%	38.2%	61.8%
1988	404,620	177,761	Bush, George	225,123	Dukakis, Michael S.	1,736	47,362 D	43.9%	55.6%	44.1%	55.9%
1984	410,492	212,080	Reagan, Ronald	197,106	Mondale, Walter F.	1,306	14,974 R	51.7%	48.0%	51.8%	48.2%
1980	416,072	154,793	Reagan, Ronald	198,342	Carter, Jimmy	62,937	43,549 D	37.2%	47.7%	43.8%	56.2%
1976	411,170	181,249	Ford, Gerald R.	227,636	Carter, Jimmy	2,285	46,387 D	44.1%	55.4%	44.3%	55.7%
1972	415,808	220,383	Nixon, Richard M.	194,645	McGovern, George S.	780	25,738 R	53.0%	46.8%	53.1%	46.9%
1968	385,000	122,359	Nixon, Richard M.	246,518	Humphrey, Hubert H.	16,123	124,159 D	31.8%	64.0%	33.2%	66.8%
1964	390,091	74,615	Goldwater, Barry M.	315,463	Johnson, Lyndon B.	13	240,848 D	19.1%	80.9%	19.1%	80.9%
1960	405,535	147,502	Nixon, Richard M.	258,032	Kennedy, John F.	1	110,530 D	36.4%	63.6%	36.4%	63.6%
1956	387,609	225,819	Eisenhower, Dwight D.	161,790	Stevenson, Adlai E.		64,029 R	58.3%	41.7%	58.3%	41.7%
1952	414,498	210,935	Eisenhower, Dwight D.	203,293	Stevenson, Adlai E.	270	7,642 R	50.9%	49.0%	50.9%	49.1%
1948	327,702	135,787	Dewey, Thomas E.	188,736	Truman, Harry S.	3,179	52,949 D	41.4%	57.6%	41.8%	58.2%

In 1992 the other vote column includes 105,045 votes cast for Perot.

RHODE ISLAND

POSTWAR VOTE FOR GOVERNOR

Year	Total Vote	Republican Vote	Republican Candidate	Democratic Vote	Democratic Candidate	Other Vote	Rep.-Dem. Plurality	Percentage Total Vote Rep.	Dem.	Major Vote Rep.	Dem.
1992	425,026	145,590	Leonard, Elizabeth Ann	261,484	Sundlun, Bruce G.	17,952	115,894 D	34.3%	61.5%	35.8%	64.2%
1990	356,672	92,177	DiPrete, Edward	264,411	Sundlun, Bruce G.	84	172,234 D	25.8%	74.1%	25.8%	74.2%
1988	400,516	203,550	DiPrete, Edward	196,936	Sundlun, Bruce G.	30	6,614 R	50.8%	49.2%	50.8%	49.2%
1986	322,724	208,822	DiPrete, Edward	104,508	Sundlun, Bruce G.	9,394	104,314 R	64.7%	32.4%	66.6%	33.4%
1984	408,375	245,059	DiPrete, Edward	163,311	Solomon, Anthony J.	5	81,748 R	60.0%	40.0%	60.0%	40.0%
1982	337,259	79,602	Marzullo, Vincent	247,208	Garrahy, J. Joseph	10,449	167,606 D	23.6%	73.3%	24.4%	75.6%
1980	405,916	106,729	Cianci, Vincent A.	299,174	Garrahy, J. Joseph	13	192,445 D	26.3%	73.7%	26.3%	73.7%
1978	314,363	96,596	Almond, Lincoln	197,386	Garrahy, J. Joseph	20,381	100,790 D	30.7%	62.8%	32.9%	67.1%
1976	398,683	178,254	Taft, James L.	218,561	Garrahy, J. Joseph	1,868	40,307 D	44.7%	54.8%	44.9%	55.1%
1974	321,660	69,224	Nugent, James W.	252,436	Noel, Philip W.		183,212 D	21.5%	78.5%	21.5%	78.5%
1972	412,866	194,315	DeSimone, Herbert F.	216,953	Noel, Philip W.	1,598	22,638 D	47.1%	52.5%	47.2%	52.8%
1970	346,342	171,549	DeSimone, Herbert F.	173,420	Licht, Frank	1,373	1,871 D	49.5%	50.1%	49.7%	50.3%
1968	383,725	187,958	Chafee, John H.	195,766	Licht, Frank	1	7,808 D	49.0%	51.0%	49.0%	51.0%
1966	332,064	210,202	Chafee, John H.	121,862	Hobbs, Horace E.		88,340 R	63.3%	36.7%	63.3%	36.7%
1964	391,668	239,501	Chafee, John H.	152,165	Gallogly, Edward P.	2	87,336 R	61.1%	38.9%	61.1%	38.9%
1962	327,506	163,952	Chafee, John H.	163,554	Notte, John A.		398 R	50.1%	49.9%	50.1%	49.9%
1960	401,362	174,044	Del Sesto, Christopher	227,318	Notte, John A.		53,274 D	43.4%	56.6%	43.4%	56.6%
1958	346,780	176,505	Del Sesto, Christopher	170,275	Roberts, Dennis J.		6,230 R	50.9%	49.1%	50.9%	49.1%
1956	383,919	191,604	Del Sesto, Christopher	192,315	Roberts, Dennis J.		711 D	49.9%	50.1%	49.9%	50.1%
1954	328,670	137,131	Lewis, Dean J.	189,595	Roberts, Dennis J.	1,944	52,464 D	41.7%	57.7%	42.0%	58.0%
1952	409,689	194,102	Archambault, Raoul	215,587	Roberts, Dennis J.		21,485 D	47.4%	52.6%	47.4%	52.6%
1950	296,809	120,684	Lachapelle, E. T.	176,125	Roberts, Dennis J.		55,441 D	40.7%	59.3%	40.7%	59.3%
1948	323,863	124,441	Ruerat, Albert P.	198,056	Pastore, John O.	1,366	73,615 D	38.4%	61.2%	38.6%	61.4%
1946	275,341	126,456	Murphy, John G.	148,885	Pastore, John O.		22,429 D	45.9%	54.1%	45.9%	54.1%

POSTWAR VOTE FOR SENATOR

Year	Total Vote	Republican Vote	Republican Candidate	Democratic Vote	Democratic Candidate	Other Vote	Rep.-Dem. Plurality	Percentage Total Vote Rep.	Dem.	Major Vote Rep.	Dem.
1990	364,062	138,947	Schneider, Claudine	225,105	Pell, Claiborne	10	86,158 D	38.2%	61.8%	38.2%	61.8%
1988	397,996	217,273	Chafee, John H.	180,717	Licht, Richard A.	6	36,556 R	54.6%	45.4%	54.6%	45.4%
1984	395,285	108,492	Leonard, Barbara	286,780	Pell, Claiborne	13	178,288 D	27.4%	72.6%	27.4%	72.6%
1982	342,779	175,495	Chafee, John H.	167,283	Michaelson, Julius C.	1	8,212 R	51.2%	48.8%	51.2%	48.8%
1978	305,618	76,061	Reynolds, James G.	229,557	Pell, Claiborne		153,496 D	24.9%	75.1%	24.9%	75.1%
1976	398,906	230,329	Chafee, John H.	167,665	Lorber, Richard P.	912	62,664 R	57.7%	42.0%	57.9%	42.1%
1972	413,432	188,990	Chafee, John H.	221,942	Pell, Claiborne	2,500	32,952 D	45.7%	53.7%	46.0%	54.0%
1970	341,222	107,351	McLaughlin, John	230,469	Pastore, John O.	3,402	123,118 D	31.5%	67.5%	31.8%	68.2%
1966	324,173	104,838	Briggs, Ruth M.	219,331	Pell, Claiborne	4	114,493 D	32.3%	67.7%	32.3%	67.7%
1964	386,322	66,715	Lagueux, Ronald R.	319,607	Pastore, John O.		252,892 D	17.3%	82.7%	17.3%	82.7%
1960	399,983	124,408	Archambault, Raoul	275,575	Pell, Claiborne		151,167 D	31.1%	68.9%	31.1%	68.9%
1958	344,519	122,353	Ewing, Bayard	222,166	Pastore, John O.		99,813 D	35.5%	64.5%	35.5%	64.5%
1954	326,624	132,970	Sundlun, Walter I.	193,654	Green, Theodore F.		60,684 D	40.7%	59.3%	40.7%	59.3%
1952	410,978	185,850	Ewing, Bayard	225,128	Pastore, John O.		39,278 D	45.2%	54.8%	45.2%	54.8%
1950 S	297,909	114,184	Levy, Austin T.	183,725	Pastore, John O.		69,541 D	38.3%	61.7%	38.3%	61.7%
1948	320,420	130,262	Hazard, Thomas P.	190,158	Green, Theodore F.		59,896 D	40.7%	59.3%	40.7%	59.3%
1946	273,528	122,780	Dyer, W. Gurnee	150,748	McGrath, J. Howard		27,968 D	44.9%	55.1%	44.9%	55.1%

The 1950 election was for a short term to fill a vacancy.

RHODE ISLAND

Districts Established May 22, 1992

Woonsocket

1

PROVIDENCE

Pawtucket

North Providence

Providence

Cranston

Warwick

BRISTOL

Bristol

2

KENT

NEWPORT (PT)

NEWPORT (PT)

NEWPORT (PART)

NEWPORT (PART)

WASHINGTON

Kingston

Newport

Westerly

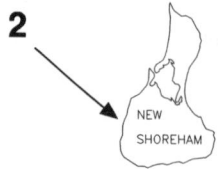

2

NEW SHOREHAM

RHODE ISLAND

PRESIDENT 1992

Registration	County	Total Vote	Republican	Democratic	Perot	Other	Plurality	Percentage Total Vote Rep.	Dem.	Perot
28,073	BRISTOL	24,911	8,208	11,414	5,132	157	3,206 D	32.9%	45.8%	20.6%
95,722	KENT	82,425	25,217	35,934	20,690	584	10,717 D	30.6%	43.6%	25.1%
46,397	NEWPORT	39,644	12,386	17,584	9,366	308	5,198 D	31.2%	44.4%	23.6%
321,253	PROVIDENCE	253,441	69,579	125,358	56,575	1,929	55,779 D	27.5%	49.5%	22.3%
63,219	WASHINGTON	52,944	16,211	23,009	13,282	442	6,798 D	30.6%	43.5%	25.1%
554,664	TOTAL	453,477	131,601	213,299	105,045	3,532	81,698 D	29.0%	47.0%	23.2%

RHODE ISLAND

GOVERNOR 1992

Registration	County	Total Vote	Republican	Democratic	Other	Rep.-Dem. Plurality	Percentage Total Vote Rep.	Dem.	Major Vote Rep.	Dem.
28,073	BRISTOL	23,230	8,410	14,223	597	5,813 D	36.2%	61.2%	37.2%	62.8%
95,722	KENT	78,566	27,145	47,746	3,675	20,601 D	34.6%	60.8%	36.2%	63.8%
46,397	NEWPORT	35,782	12,015	22,886	881	10,871 D	33.6%	64.0%	34.4%	65.6%
321,253	PROVIDENCE	237,449	81,276	145,250	10,923	63,974 D	34.2%	61.2%	35.9%	64.1%
63,219	WASHINGTON	49,791	16,744	31,379	1,668	14,635 D	33.6%	63.0%	34.8%	65.2%
554,664	TOTAL	425,026	145,590	261,484	17,952	115,894 D	34.3%	61.5%	35.8%	64.2%

RHODE ISLAND

PRESIDENT 1992

Registration	City/Town	Total Vote	Republican	Democratic	Perot	Other	Plurality	Percentage Total Vote		
								Rep.	Dem.	Perot
11,142	BARRINGTON	9,565	3,846	3,968	1,689	62	122 D	40.2%	41.5%	17.7%
11,166	BRISTOL TOWN	10,068	2,818	5,018	2,178	54	2,200 D	28.0%	49.8%	21.6%
7,697	BURRILLVILLE	6,423	1,880	2,454	2,018	71	436 D	29.3%	38.2%	31.4%
6,004	CENTRAL FALLS	4,086	955	2,269	831	31	1,314 D	23.4%	55.5%	20.3%
3,964	CHARLESTOWN	3,183	1,063	1,249	839	32	186 D	33.4%	39.2%	26.4%
17,311	COVENTRY	15,080	4,466	6,086	4,415	113	1,620 D	29.6%	40.4%	29.3%
52,176	CRANSTON	39,606	12,450	18,589	8,331	236	6,139 D	31.4%	46.9%	21.0%
17,213	CUMBERLAND	15,345	4,869	6,406	3,971	99	1,537 D	31.7%	41.7%	25.9%
7,944	EAST GREENWICH	6,762	2,838	2,400	1,489	35	438 R	42.0%	35.5%	22.0%
25,046	EAST PROVIDENCE	22,361	5,843	11,701	4,661	156	5,858 D	26.1%	52.3%	20.8%
3,133	EXETER	2,694	842	1,004	824	24	162 D	31.3%	37.3%	30.6%
2,395	FOSTER	2,138	627	848	648	15	200 D	29.3%	39.7%	30.3%
5,165	GLOCESTER	4,613	1,451	1,699	1,420	43	248 D	31.5%	36.8%	30.8%
4,036	HOPKINTON	3,285	1,000	1,186	1,055	44	131 D	30.4%	36.1%	32.1%
3,602	JAMESTOWN	2,997	900	1,432	635	30	532 D	30.0%	47.8%	21.2%
16,868	JOHNSTON	14,540	4,230	6,655	3,538	117	2,425 D	29.1%	45.8%	24.3%
11,835	LINCOLN	10,111	3,361	4,158	2,518	74	797 D	33.2%	41.1%	24.9%
2,379	LITTLE COMPTON	2,134	704	835	567	28	131 D	33.0%	39.1%	26.6%
7,819	MIDDLETOWN	7,327	2,452	3,147	1,672	56	695 D	33.5%	43.0%	22.8%
9,321	NARRAGANSETT	7,642	2,309	3,606	1,690	37	1,297 D	30.2%	47.2%	22.1%
13,772	NEWPORT CITY	11,118	3,412	5,363	2,278	65	1,951 D	30.7%	48.2%	20.5%
1,173	NEW SHOREHAM	815	186	414	210	5	204 D	22.8%	50.8%	25.8%
14,448	NORTH KINGSTOWN	12,303	4,199	5,070	2,929	105	871 D	34.1%	41.2%	23.8%
22,692	NORTH PROVIDENCE	18,657	5,108	9,111	4,310	128	4,003 D	27.4%	48.8%	23.1%
6,689	NORTH SMITHFIELD	5,747	1,886	2,187	1,626	48	301 D	32.8%	38.1%	28.3%
32,868	PAWTUCKET	26,962	6,322	14,177	6,244	219	7,855 D	23.4%	52.6%	23.2%
10,253	PORTSMOUTH	8,712	2,921	3,528	2,193	70	607 D	33.5%	40.5%	25.2%
79,093	PROVIDENCE CITY	52,288	11,519	32,536	7,816	417	21,017 D	22.0%	62.2%	14.9%
3,461	RICHMOND	2,915	737	1,199	952	27	247 D	25.3%	41.1%	32.7%
5,904	SCITUATE	5,316	1,996	1,759	1,493	68	237 R	37.5%	33.1%	28.1%
10,833	SMITHFIELD	9,773	3,086	4,155	2,460	72	1,069 D	31.6%	42.5%	25.2%
12,232	SOUTH KINGSTOWN	10,251	2,940	4,988	2,241	82	2,048 D	28.7%	48.7%	21.9%
8,572	TIVERTON	7,356	1,997	3,279	2,021	59	1,258 D	27.1%	44.6%	27.5%
5,765	WARREN	5,278	1,544	2,428	1,265	41	884 D	29.3%	46.0%	24.0%
51,821	WARWICK	44,692	13,348	20,504	10,526	314	7,156 D	29.9%	45.9%	23.6%
11,451	WESTERLY	9,856	2,935	4,293	2,542	86	1,358 D	29.8%	43.6%	25.8%
2,746	WEST GREENWICH	2,349	773	810	744	22	37 D	32.9%	34.5%	31.7%
15,900	WEST WARWICK	13,542	3,792	6,134	3,516	100	2,342 D	28.0%	45.3%	26.0%
18,775	WOONSOCKET	15,475	3,996	6,654	4,690	135	1,964 D	25.8%	43.0%	30.3%
554,664	TOTAL	453,477	131,601	213,299	105,045	3,532	81,698 D	29.0%	47.0%	23.2%

RHODE ISLAND

GOVERNOR 1992

Registration	City/Town	Total Vote	Republican	Democratic	Other	Rep.-Dem. Plurality	Total Vote Rep.	Total Vote Dem.	Major Vote Rep.	Major Vote Dem.
11,142	BARRINGTON	8,954	3,552	5,168	234	1,616 D	39.7%	57.7%	40.7%	59.3%
11,166	BRISTOL TOWN	9,384	3,103	6,058	223	2,955 D	33.1%	64.6%	33.9%	66.1%
7,697	BURRILLVILLE	5,941	2,026	3,641	274	1,615 D	34.1%	61.3%	35.8%	64.2%
6,004	CENTRAL FALLS	3,654	1,072	2,452	130	1,380 D	29.3%	67.1%	30.4%	69.6%
3,964	CHARLESTOWN	3,078	1,077	1,896	105	819 D	35.0%	61.6%	36.2%	63.8%
17,311	COVENTRY	14,173	4,931	8,611	631	3,680 D	34.8%	60.8%	36.4%	63.6%
52,176	CRANSTON	37,998	14,322	21,889	1,787	7,567 D	37.7%	57.6%	39.6%	60.4%
17,213	CUMBERLAND	14,517	4,799	9,185	533	4,386 D	33.1%	63.3%	34.3%	65.7%
7,944	EAST GREENWICH	6,448	2,221	4,016	211	1,795 D	34.4%	62.3%	35.6%	64.4%
25,046	EAST PROVIDENCE	21,070	8,275	11,909	886	3,634 D	39.3%	56.5%	41.0%	59.0%
3,133	EXETER	2,535	1,073	1,357	105	284 D	42.3%	53.5%	44.2%	55.8%
2,395	FOSTER	2,049	765	1,180	104	415 D	37.3%	57.6%	39.3%	60.7%
5,165	GLOCESTER	4,331	1,708	2,405	218	697 D	39.4%	55.5%	41.5%	58.5%
4,036	HOPKINTON	2,988	1,118	1,766	104	648 D	37.4%	59.1%	38.8%	61.2%
3,602	JAMESTOWN	2,795	909	1,796	90	887 D	32.5%	64.3%	33.6%	66.4%
16,868	JOHNSTON	13,744	5,557	7,366	821	1,809 D	40.4%	53.6%	43.0%	57.0%
11,835	LINCOLN	9,583	3,377	5,820	386	2,443 D	35.2%	60.7%	36.7%	63.3%
2,379	LITTLE COMPTON	1,793	693	1,057	43	364 D	38.7%	59.0%	39.6%	60.4%
7,819	MIDDLETOWN	6,460	2,205	4,136	119	1,931 D	34.1%	64.0%	34.8%	65.2%
9,321	NARRAGANSETT	7,080	2,277	4,537	266	2,260 D	32.2%	64.1%	33.4%	66.6%
13,772	NEWPORT CITY	9,926	3,001	6,649	276	3,648 D	30.2%	67.0%	31.1%	68.9%
1,173	NEW SHOREHAM	802	265	517	20	252 D	33.0%	64.5%	33.9%	66.1%
14,448	NORTH KINGSTOWN	12,068	4,385	7,208	475	2,823 D	36.3%	59.7%	37.8%	62.2%
22,692	NORTH PROVIDENCE	17,512	6,304	10,245	963	3,941 D	36.0%	58.5%	38.1%	61.9%
6,689	NORTH SMITHFIELD	5,406	1,754	3,449	203	1,695 D	32.4%	63.8%	33.7%	66.3%
32,868	PAWTUCKET	24,902	8,166	15,780	956	7,614 D	32.8%	63.4%	34.1%	65.9%
10,253	PORTSMOUTH	8,098	2,795	5,127	176	2,332 D	34.5%	63.3%	35.3%	64.7%
79,093	PROVIDENCE CITY	48,264	13,841	32,200	2,223	18,359 D	28.7%	66.7%	30.1%	69.9%
3,461	RICHMOND	2,680	921	1,654	105	733 D	34.4%	61.7%	35.8%	64.2%
5,904	SCITUATE	5,024	2,145	2,595	284	450 D	42.7%	51.7%	45.3%	54.7%
10,833	SMITHFIELD	9,244	3,179	5,472	593	2,293 D	34.4%	59.2%	36.7%	63.3%
12,232	SOUTH KINGSTOWN	9,689	2,990	6,414	285	3,424 D	30.9%	66.2%	31.8%	68.2%
8,572	TIVERTON	6,710	2,412	4,121	177	1,709 D	35.9%	61.4%	36.9%	63.1%
5,765	WARREN	4,892	1,755	2,997	140	1,242 D	35.9%	61.3%	36.9%	63.1%
51,821	WARWICK	43,054	15,195	25,794	2,065	10,599 D	35.3%	59.9%	37.1%	62.9%
11,451	WESTERLY	8,871	2,638	6,030	203	3,392 D	29.7%	68.0%	30.4%	69.6%
2,746	WEST GREENWICH	2,199	861	1,235	103	374 D	39.2%	56.2%	41.1%	58.9%
15,900	WEST WARWICK	12,692	3,937	8,090	665	4,153 D	31.0%	63.7%	32.7%	67.3%
18,775	WOONSOCKET	14,210	3,986	9,662	562	5,676 D	28.1%	68.0%	29.2%	70.8%
554,664	TOTAL	425,026	145,590	261,484	17,952	115,894 D	34.3%	61.5%	35.8%	64.2%

RHODE ISLAND

CONGRESS

CD	Year	Total Vote	Republican Vote	Republican Candidate	Democratic Vote	Democratic Candidate	Other Vote	Rep.-Dem. Plurality	Percentage Total Vote Rep.	Percentage Total Vote Dem.	Percentage Major Vote Rep.	Percentage Major Vote Dem.
1	1992	194,089	135,982	MACHTLEY, RONALD K.	48,092	CARLIN, DAVID R.	10,015	87,890 R	70.1%	24.8%	73.9%	26.1%
2	1992	204,413	49,998	BELL, JAMES W.	144,450	REED, JOHN F.	9,965	94,452 D	24.5%	70.7%	25.7%	74.3%

RHODE ISLAND

1992 GENERAL ELECTION

In addition to the county-by-county figures, data are presented by cities and towns.

President   Other vote was 1,878 New Alliance (Fulani); 571 Libertarian (Marrou); 494 Independent (LaRouche); 262 Natural Law (Hagelin); 215 Taxpayers (Phillips); 3 Gritz (write-in); 2 Brisben (write-in); 1 Daniels (write-in); 106 scattered write-in.

Governor   Other vote was 14,511 Reform '92 (Devine); 1,698 Populist (Potter); 1,535 Independent (Staradumsky); 208 scattered write-in.

Congress   Other vote was 6,012 Ross Perot Independent (Dick) and 4,003 Independent (Jacques) in CD 1; 6,715 Independent (Ricci) and 3,250 Independent Thinking (Turnbull) in CD 2.

1992 PRIMARIES

SEPTEMBER 15 REPUBLICAN

Governor   7,534 Elizabeth Ann Leonard; 6,926 J. Michael Levesque.

Congress   Unopposed in CD 1. Contested as follows:

  CD 2   4,978 James W. Bell; 1,883 Naomi D. Young.

SEPTEMBER 15 DEMOCRATIC

Governor   78,735 Bruce G. Sundlun; 72,011 Francis X. Flaherty.

Congress   Contested as follows:

  CD 1   20,198 David R. Carlin; 19,927 Suzette E. Gephard; 17,784 Robert A. Walsh.
  CD 2   50,518 John F. Reed; 15,592 Spencer E. Dickinson.

SOUTH CAROLINA

GOVERNOR
Carroll Campbell (R). Re-elected 1990 to a four-year term. Previously elected 1986.

SENATORS
Ernest F. Hollings (D). Re-elected 1992 to a six-year term. Previously elected 1986, 1980, 1974, 1968 and in 1966 to fill out term vacated by the death of Senator Olin D. Johnston (D).

Strom Thurmond (R). Re-elected 1990 to a six-year term. Previously elected 1984, 1978, 1972, 1966, 1960 and in 1956 to fill out term vacated by his own resignation in April 1956; had been elected to this term in 1954 as an Independent Democrat. Changed party affiliation from Democrat to Republican in September 1964.

REPRESENTATIVES
1. Arthur Ravenel (R)
2. Floyd Spence (R)
3. Butler Derrick (D)
4. Robert D. Inglis (R)
5. John Spratt (D)
6. James E. Clyburn (D)

POSTWAR VOTE FOR PRESIDENT

		Republican		Democratic		Other		Total Vote		Major Vote	
Year	Total Vote	Vote	Candidate	Vote	Candidate	Other Vote	Plurality	Rep.	Dem.	Rep.	Dem.
1992 **	1,202,527	577,507	Bush, George	479,514	Clinton, Bill	145,506	97,993 R	48.0%	39.9%	54.6%	45.4%
1988	986,009	606,443	Bush, George	370,554	Dukakis, Michael S.	9,012	235,889 R	61.5%	37.6%	62.1%	37.9%
1984	968,529	615,539	Reagan, Ronald	344,459	Mondale, Walter F.	8,531	271,080 R	63.6%	35.6%	64.1%	35.9%
1980	894,071	441,841	Reagan, Ronald	430,385	Carter, Jimmy	21,845	11,456 R	49.4%	48.1%	50.7%	49.3%
1976	802,583	346,149	Ford, Gerald R.	450,807	Carter, Jimmy	5,627	104,658 D	43.1%	56.2%	43.4%	56.6%
1972	673,960	477,044	Nixon, Richard M.	186,824	McGovern, George S.	10,092	290,220 R	70.8%	27.7%	71.9%	28.1%
1968 **	666,978	254,062	Nixon, Richard M.	197,486	Humphrey, Hubert H.	215,430	38,632 R	38.1%	29.6%	56.3%	43.7%
1964	524,779	309,048	Goldwater, Barry M.	215,723	Johnson, Lyndon B.	8	93,325 R	58.9%	41.1%	58.9%	41.1%
1960	386,688	188,558	Nixon, Richard M.	198,129	Kennedy, John F.	1	9,571 D	48.8%	51.2%	48.8%	51.2%
1956 **	300,583	75,700	Eisenhower, Dwight D.	136,372	Stevenson, Adlai E.	88,511	47,863 D	25.2%	45.4%	35.7%	64.3%
1952	341,087	168,082	Eisenhower, Dwight D.	173,004	Stevenson, Adlai E.	1	4,922 D	49.3%	50.7%	49.3%	50.7%
1948 **	142,571	5,386	Dewey, Thomas E.	34,423	Truman, Harry S.	102,762	68,184 SR	3.8%	24.1%	13.5%	86.5%

In 1992 the other vote column includes 138,872 votes cast for Perot. In 1968 other vote was Independent (Wallace). In 1956 other vote was 88,509 Independent (Uncommitted States Rights) and 2 scattered. In 1948 other vote was 102,607 States Rights; 154 Progressive and 1 Socialist.

POSTWAR VOTE FOR GOVERNOR

		Republican		Democratic		Other	Rep.-Dem.	Total Vote		Major Vote	
Year	Total Vote	Vote	Candidate	Vote	Candidate	Other Vote	Plurality	Rep.	Dem.	Rep.	Dem.
1990	760,965	528,831	Campbell, Carroll	212,034	Mitchell, Theo	20,100	316,797 R	69.5%	27.9%	71.4%	28.6%
1986	753,751	384,565	Campbell, Carroll	361,325	Daniel, Mike	7,861	23,240 R	51.0%	47.9%	51.6%	48.4%
1982	671,625	202,806	Workman, W. D.	468,819	Riley, Richard W.		266,013 D	30.2%	69.8%	30.2%	69.8%
1978	627,182	236,946	Young, Edward L.	384,898	Riley, Richard W.	5,338	147,952 D	37.8%	61.4%	38.1%	61.9%
1974	523,199	266,109	Edwards, James B.	248,938	Dorn, W. J. Bryan	8,152	17,171 R	50.9%	47.6%	51.7%	48.3%
1970	484,857	221,233	Watson, Albert W.	250,551	West, John C.	13,073	29,318 D	45.6%	51.7%	46.9%	53.1%
1966	439,942	184,088	Rogers, Joseph O.	255,854	McNair, Robert E.		71,766 D	41.8%	58.2%	41.8%	58.2%
1962	253,721		—	253,704	Russell, Donald S.	17	253,704 D		100.0%		100.0%
1958	77,740		—	77,714	Hollings, Ernest F.	26	77,714 D		100.0%		100.0%
1954	214,212		—	214,204	Timmerman, George B.	8	214,204 D		100.0%		100.0%
1950	50,642		—	50,633	Byrnes, James F.	9	50,633 D		100.0%		100.0%
1946	26,520		—	26,520	Thurmond, Strom		26,520 D		100.0%		100.0%

SOUTH CAROLINA

POSTWAR VOTE FOR SENATOR

Year	Total Vote	Republican Vote	Republican Candidate	Democratic Vote	Democratic Candidate	Other Vote	Rep.-Dem. Plurality	Percentage Total Vote Rep.	Percentage Total Vote Dem.	Percentage Major Vote Rep.	Percentage Major Vote Dem.
1992	1,180,438	554,175	Hartnett, Thomas F.	591,030	Hollings, Ernest F.	35,233	36,855 D	46.9%	50.1%	48.4%	51.6%
1990	750,716	482,032	Thurmond, Strom	244,112	Cunningham, Bob	24,572	237,920 R	64.2%	32.5%	66.4%	33.6%
1986	737,962	262,886	McMaster, Henry D.	465,500	Hollings, Ernest F.	9,576	202,614 D	35.6%	63.1%	36.1%	63.9%
1984	965,130	644,815	Thurmond, Strom	306,982	Purvis, Melvin	13,333	337,833 R	66.8%	31.8%	67.7%	32.3%
1980	870,594	257,946	Mays, Marshall T.	612,554	Hollings, Ernest F.	94	354,608 D	29.6%	70.4%	29.6%	70.4%
1978	632,852	351,733	Thurmond, Strom	281,119	Ravenel, Charles D.		70,614 R	55.6%	44.4%	55.6%	44.4%
1974	512,397	146,645	Bush, Gwenyfred	356,126	Hollings, Ernest F.	9,626	209,481 D	28.6%	69.5%	29.2%	70.8%
1972	672,246	426,601	Thurmond, Strom	245,457	Zeigler, Eugene N.	188	181,144 R	63.5%	36.5%	63.5%	36.5%
1968	652,855	248,780	Parker, Marshall	404,060	Hollings, Ernest F.	15	155,280 D	38.1%	61.9%	38.1%	61.9%
1966	436,252	271,297	Thurmond, Strom	164,955	Morrah, Bradley		106,342 R	62.2%	37.8%	62.2%	37.8%
1966 S	435,822	212,032	Parker, Marshall	223,790	Hollings, Ernest F.		11,758 D	48.7%	51.3%	48.7%	51.3%
1962	312,647	133,930	Workman, W. D.	178,712	Johnston, Olin D.	5	44,782 D	42.8%	57.2%	42.8%	57.2%
1960	330,266		—	330,164	Thurmond, Strom	102	330,164 D		100.0%		100.0%
1956	279,845	49,695	Crawford, Leon P.	230,150	Johnston, Olin D.		180,455 D	17.8%	82.2%	17.8%	82.2%
1956 S	251,907		—	251,907	Thurmond, Strom		251,907 D		100.0%		100.0%
1954 **	227,232		—	83,525	Brown, Edgar A.	143,707	83,525 D		36.8%		100.0%
1950	50,277		—	50,240	Johnston, Olin D.	37	50,240 D		99.9%		100.0%
1948	141,006	5,008	Gerald, J. Bates	135,998	Maybank, Burnet R.		130,990 D	3.6%	96.4%	3.6%	96.4%

One each of the 1966 and 1956 elections was for a short term to fill a vacancy. In 1954, Strom Thurmond polled 143,444 votes as an Independent Democratic write-in candidate (63.1% of the total vote) and won the election with a 59,919 pluarlity.

SOUTH CAROLINA

Districts Established May 1, 1992

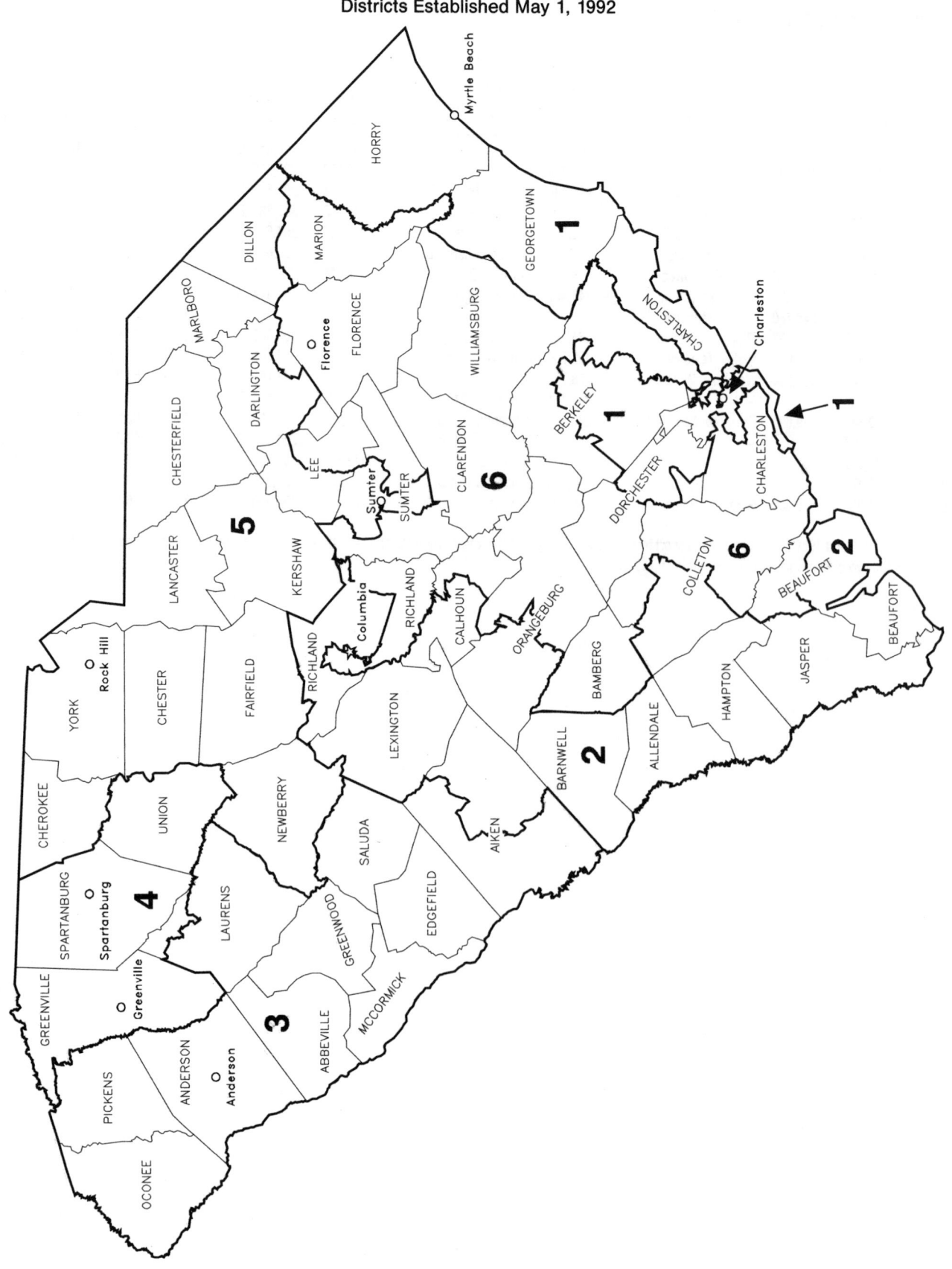

SOUTH CAROLINA

PRESIDENT 1992

Registration	County	Total Vote	Republican	Democratic	Perot	Other	Plurality	Percentage Total Vote Rep.	Dem.	Perot
10,665	ABBEVILLE	8,343	3,317	3,968	1,036	22	651 D	39.8%	47.6%	12.4%
58,458	AIKEN	46,778	25,731	14,802	6,056	189	10,929 R	55.0%	31.6%	12.9%
4,781	ALLENDALE	3,455	1,049	2,159	212	35	1,110 D	30.4%	62.5%	6.1%
58,978	ANDERSON	47,971	24,793	16,072	6,966	140	8,721 R	51.7%	33.5%	14.5%
7,684	BAMBERG	5,727	1,906	3,426	360	35	1,520 D	33.3%	59.8%	6.3%
10,085	BARNWELL	8,177	4,026	3,344	752	55	682 R	49.2%	40.9%	9.2%
41,238	BEAUFORT	31,287	14,735	11,466	4,966	120	3,269 R	47.1%	36.6%	15.9%
44,945	BERKELEY	35,479	18,048	12,533	4,632	266	5,515 R	50.9%	35.3%	13.1%
7,071	CALHOUN	5,778	2,418	2,770	564	26	352 D	41.8%	47.9%	9.8%
134,152	CHARLESTON	98,749	47,403	40,095	10,354	897	7,308 R	48.0%	40.6%	10.5%
18,910	CHEROKEE	14,557	6,887	5,453	2,186	31	1,434 R	47.3%	37.5%	15.0%
14,780	CHESTER	10,288	3,451	5,458	1,350	29	2,007 D	33.5%	53.1%	13.1%
14,758	CHESTERFIELD	11,212	4,183	5,691	1,315	23	1,508 D	37.3%	50.8%	11.7%
14,242	CLARENDON	10,945	4,147	6,033	744	21	1,886 D	37.9%	55.1%	6.8%
14,911	COLLETON	11,314	4,545	5,455	1,245	69	910 D	40.2%	48.2%	11.0%
24,786	DARLINGTON	20,253	8,912	9,090	1,863	388	178 D	44.0%	44.9%	9.2%
12,884	DILLON	9,390	3,575	4,953	831	31	1,378 D	38.1%	52.7%	8.8%
36,428	DORCHESTER	28,029	15,004	9,160	3,648	217	5,844 R	53.5%	32.7%	13.0%
9,449	EDGEFIELD	7,396	3,339	3,433	596	28	94 D	45.1%	46.4%	8.1%
10,345	FAIRFIELD	8,091	2,518	4,867	652	54	2,349 D	31.1%	60.2%	8.1%
50,192	FLORENCE	39,003	19,802	15,569	3,499	133	4,233 R	50.8%	39.9%	9.0%
21,788	GEORGETOWN	16,272	6,870	7,494	1,840	68	624 D	42.2%	46.1%	11.3%
140,040	GREENVILLE	113,907	65,066	34,651	13,699	491	30,415 R	57.1%	30.4%	12.0%
23,895	GREENWOOD	18,923	9,079	7,621	2,101	122	1,458 R	48.0%	40.3%	11.1%
9,793	HAMPTON	7,361	2,402	4,332	564	63	1,930 D	32.6%	58.9%	7.7%
66,616	HORRY	51,204	23,489	18,896	8,472	347	4,593 R	45.9%	36.9%	16.5%
7,568	JASPER	5,763	1,725	3,453	549	36	1,728 D	29.9%	59.9%	9.5%
21,620	KERSHAW	17,301	8,499	6,585	2,150	67	1,914 R	49.1%	38.1%	12.4%
22,225	LANCASTER	18,655	7,757	8,307	2,563	28	550 D	41.6%	44.5%	13.7%
22,050	LAURENS	17,200	8,347	6,638	2,157	58	1,709 R	48.5%	38.6%	12.5%
10,043	LEE	7,822	2,730	4,454	611	27	1,724 D	34.9%	56.9%	7.8%
84,399	LEXINGTON	69,022	41,759	18,312	8,652	299	23,447 R	60.5%	26.5%	12.5%
4,127	MCCORMICK	3,052	899	1,846	295	12	947 D	29.5%	60.5%	9.7%
14,552	MARION	10,376	3,647	5,843	822	64	2,196 D	35.1%	56.3%	7.9%
12,041	MARLBORO	8,570	2,526	5,111	895	38	2,585 D	29.5%	59.6%	10.4%
15,357	NEWBERRY	12,329	5,980	4,896	1,393	60	1,084 R	48.5%	39.7%	11.3%
25,709	OCONEE	20,479	10,379	6,617	3,405	78	3,762 R	50.7%	32.3%	16.6%
43,393	ORANGEBURG	32,234	11,328	18,440	2,383	83	7,112 D	35.1%	57.2%	7.4%
38,092	PICKENS	29,494	17,008	8,275	4,128	83	8,733 R	57.7%	28.1%	14.0%
132,980	RICHLAND	106,250	43,744	53,648	7,918	940	9,904 D	41.2%	50.5%	7.5%
7,833	SALUDA	6,209	2,968	2,393	833	15	575 R	47.8%	38.5%	13.4%
89,779	SPARTANBURG	72,635	37,707	25,488	8,900	540	12,219 R	51.9%	35.1%	12.3%
37,443	SUMTER	26,596	12,576	11,852	2,062	106	724 R	47.3%	44.6%	7.8%
13,656	UNION	10,680	4,647	4,644	1,371	18	3 R	43.5%	43.5%	12.8%
18,777	WILLIAMSBURG	14,277	5,289	8,077	864	47	2,788 D	37.0%	56.6%	6.1%
53,622	YORK	43,694	21,297	15,844	6,418	135	5,453 R	48.7%	36.3%	14.7%
1,537,140	TOTAL	1,202,527	577,507	479,514	138,872	6,634	97,993 R	48.0%	39.9%	11.5%

SOUTH CAROLINA

SENATOR 1992

Registration	County	Total Vote	Republican	Democratic	Other	Rep.-Dem. Plurality	Percentage Total Vote Rep.	Total Vote Dem.	Major Vote Rep.	Major Vote Dem.
10,665	ABBEVILLE	7,844	2,869	4,821	154	1,952 D	36.6%	61.5%	37.3%	62.7%
58,458	AIKEN	46,606	23,923	20,934	1,749	2,989 R	51.3%	44.9%	53.3%	46.7%
4,781	ALLENDALE	3,377	880	2,416	81	1,536 D	26.1%	71.5%	26.7%	73.3%
58,978	ANDERSON	47,737	24,864	21,485	1,388	3,379 R	52.1%	45.0%	53.6%	46.4%
7,684	BAMBERG	5,589	1,536	3,959	94	2,423 D	27.5%	70.8%	28.0%	72.0%
10,085	BARNWELL	7,931	3,252	4,457	222	1,205 D	41.0%	56.2%	42.2%	57.8%
41,238	BEAUFORT	31,133	16,681	13,479	973	3,202 R	53.6%	43.3%	55.3%	44.7%
44,945	BERKELEY	34,755	17,264	16,471	1,020	793 R	49.7%	47.4%	51.2%	48.8%
7,071	CALHOUN	5,492	2,049	3,305	138	1,256 D	37.3%	60.2%	38.3%	61.7%
134,152	CHARLESTON	95,772	42,400	50,923	2,449	8,523 D	44.3%	53.2%	45.4%	54.6%
18,910	CHEROKEE	14,674	6,698	7,563	413	865 D	45.6%	51.5%	47.0%	53.0%
14,780	CHESTER	10,239	3,713	6,184	342	2,471 D	36.3%	60.4%	37.5%	62.5%
14,758	CHESTERFIELD	11,254	4,500	6,510	244	2,010 D	40.0%	57.8%	40.9%	59.1%
14,242	CLARENDON	11,044	4,005	6,869	170	2,864 D	36.3%	62.2%	36.8%	63.2%
14,911	COLLETON	11,076	4,558	6,265	253	1,707 D	41.2%	56.6%	42.1%	57.9%
24,786	DARLINGTON	18,837	7,993	10,148	696	2,155 D	42.4%	53.9%	44.1%	55.9%
12,884	DILLON	9,073	3,108	5,838	127	2,730 D	34.3%	64.3%	34.7%	65.3%
36,428	DORCHESTER	26,804	13,958	12,158	688	1,800 R	52.1%	45.4%	53.4%	46.6%
9,449	EDGEFIELD	7,119	2,818	4,150	151	1,332 D	39.6%	58.3%	40.4%	59.6%
10,345	FAIRFIELD	7,812	2,178	5,410	224	3,232 D	27.9%	69.3%	28.7%	71.3%
50,192	FLORENCE	39,429	19,158	19,517	754	359 D	48.6%	49.5%	49.5%	50.5%
21,788	GEORGETOWN	16,656	7,086	9,184	386	2,098 D	42.5%	55.1%	43.6%	56.4%
140,040	GREENVILLE	114,664	65,508	45,761	3,395	19,747 R	57.1%	39.9%	58.9%	41.1%
23,895	GREENWOOD	18,280	8,852	8,894	534	42 D	48.4%	48.7%	49.9%	50.1%
9,793	HAMPTON	6,807	2,186	4,484	137	2,298 D	32.1%	65.9%	32.8%	67.2%
66,616	HORRY	48,011	24,133	22,058	1,820	2,075 R	50.3%	45.9%	52.2%	47.8%
7,568	JASPER	5,500	1,964	3,414	122	1,450 D	35.7%	62.1%	36.5%	63.5%
21,620	KERSHAW	17,535	8,238	8,635	662	397 D	47.0%	49.2%	48.8%	51.2%
22,225	LANCASTER	17,986	7,931	9,613	442	1,682 D	44.1%	53.4%	45.2%	54.8%
22,050	LAURENS	16,526	7,161	9,081	284	1,920 D	43.3%	54.9%	44.1%	55.9%
10,043	LEE	7,389	2,164	5,147	78	2,983 D	29.3%	69.7%	29.6%	70.4%
84,399	LEXINGTON	69,435	39,712	26,194	3,529	13,518 R	57.2%	37.7%	60.3%	39.7%
4,127	MCCORMICK	2,908	752	2,110	46	1,358 D	25.9%	72.6%	26.3%	73.7%
14,552	MARION	9,968	3,454	6,340	174	2,886 D	34.7%	63.6%	35.3%	64.7%
12,041	MARLBORO	7,987	2,021	5,786	180	3,765 D	25.3%	72.4%	25.9%	74.1%
15,357	NEWBERRY	11,981	5,362	6,202	417	840 D	44.8%	51.8%	46.4%	53.6%
25,709	OCONEE	20,752	11,123	8,840	789	2,283 R	53.6%	42.6%	55.7%	44.3%
43,393	ORANGEBURG	32,421	10,318	21,365	738	11,047 D	31.8%	65.9%	32.6%	67.4%
38,092	PICKENS	29,470	16,583	11,722	1,165	4,861 R	56.3%	39.8%	58.6%	41.4%
132,980	RICHLAND	101,085	39,118	58,841	3,126	19,723 D	38.7%	58.2%	39.9%	60.1%
7,833	SALUDA	6,180	2,693	3,265	222	572 D	43.6%	52.8%	45.2%	54.8%
89,779	SPARTANBURG	70,428	35,500	32,594	2,334	2,906 R	50.4%	46.3%	52.1%	47.9%
37,443	SUMTER	27,689	12,176	14,877	636	2,701 D	44.0%	53.7%	45.0%	55.0%
13,656	UNION	10,903	4,459	6,197	247	1,738 D	40.9%	56.8%	41.8%	58.2%
18,777	WILLIAMSBURG	13,238	4,492	8,593	153	4,101 D	33.9%	64.9%	34.3%	65.7%
53,622	YORK	43,042	22,784	18,971	1,287	3,813 R	52.9%	44.1%	54.6%	45.4%
1,537,140	TOTAL	1,180,438	554,175	591,030	35,233	36,855 D	46.9%	50.1%	48.4%	51.6%

SOUTH CAROLINA

CONGRESS

CD	Year	Total Vote	Republican Vote	Republican Candidate	Democratic Vote	Democratic Candidate	Other Vote	Rep.-Dem. Plurality	Percentage Total Vote Rep.	Dem.	Major Vote Rep.	Dem.
1	1992	184,549	121,938	RAVENEL, ARTHUR	59,908	OBERST, BILL	2,703	62,030 R	66.1%	32.5%	67.1%	32.9%
2	1992	169,670	148,667	SPENCE, FLOYD			21,003	148,667 R	87.6%		100.0%	
3	1992	194,864	75,660	BLAND, JAMES L.	119,119	DERRICK, BUTLER	85	43,459 D	38.8%	61.1%	38.8%	61.2%
4	1992	198,410	99,879	INGLIS, ROBERT D.	94,182	PATTERSON, ELIZABETH J.	4,349	5,697 R	50.3%	47.5%	51.5%	48.5%
5	1992	183,086	70,866	HORNE, WILLIAM T.	112,031	SPRATT, JOHN	189	41,165 D	38.7%	61.2%	38.7%	61.3%
6	1992	184,871	64,149	CHASE, JOHN R.	120,647	CLYBURN, JAMES E.	75	56,498 D	34.7%	65.3%	34.7%	65.3%

SOUTH CAROLINA

1992 GENERAL ELECTION

President   Other vote was 2,719 Libertarian (Marrou); 2,680 American (Phillips); 1,235 United Citizens (Fulani).

Senator   Other vote was 22,962 Libertarian (Johnson); 11,568 American (Clarkson); 703 scattered write-in.

Congress   Other vote was 2,608 American (Peeples) and 95 scattered write-in in CD 1; 20,816 Libertarian (Sommer) and 187 scattered write-in in CD 2; scattered write-in in CD 3; 4,286 Libertarian (Jorgensen) and 63 scattered write-in in CD 4; scattered write-in in CD's 5 and 6.

1992 PRIMARIES

AUGUST 25 REPUBLICAN

Senator   123,572 Thomas F. Hartnett; 37,352 Charlie E. Thompson.

Congress   Unopposed in three CD's. Contested as follows:

CD   4   21,301 Robert D. Inglis; 4,760 William G. McCuen; 4,029 Jerry L. Fowler.
CD   5   7,258 William T. Horne; 5,833 Earnest R. Archer.
CD   6   5,507 John R. Chase; 2,452 Delores P. DaCosta; 1,678 Toney Graham.

AUGUST 25 DEMOCRATIC

Senator   Ernest F. Hollings, unopposed.

Congress   Unopposed in four CD's. No candidate in CD 2. Contested as follows:

CD   6   41,415 James E. Clyburn; 11,089 Frank Gilbert; 9,494 Ken Mosely; 9,130 Herbert Fielding; 2,680 John R. Harper.

SOUTH DAKOTA

GOVERNOR
Walter D. Miller (R). Elected Lt. Governor 1990; became Governor April 1993 upon the death of Governor George S. Mickelson (R).

SENATORS
Thomas A. Daschle (D). Re-elected 1992 to a six-year term. Previously elected 1986.

Larry Pressler (R). Re-elected 1990 to a six-year term. Previously elected 1984, 1978.

REPRESENTATIVE
At-Large. Tim Johnson (D)

POSTWAR VOTE FOR PRESIDENT

Year	Total Vote	Republican		Democratic		Other Vote	Plurality	Percentage			
		Vote	Candidate	Vote	Candidate			Total Vote		Major Vote	
								Rep.	Dem.	Rep.	Dem.
1992 **	336,254	136,718	Bush, George	124,888	Clinton, Bill	74,648	11,830 R	40.7%	37.1%	52.3%	47.7%
1988	312,991	165,415	Bush, George	145,560	Dukakis, Michael S.	2,016	19,855 R	52.8%	46.5%	53.2%	46.8%
1984	317,867	200,267	Reagan, Ronald	116,113	Mondale, Walter F.	1,487	84,154 R	63.0%	36.5%	63.3%	36.7%
1980	327,703	198,343	Reagan, Ronald	103,855	Carter, Jimmy	25,505	94,488 R	60.5%	31.7%	65.6%	34.4%
1976	300,678	151,505	Ford, Gerald R.	147,068	Carter, Jimmy	2,105	4,437 R	50.4%	48.9%	50.7%	49.3%
1972	307,415	166,476	Nixon, Richard M.	139,945	McGovern, George S.	994	26,531 R	54.2%	45.5%	54.3%	45.7%
1968	281,264	149,841	Nixon, Richard M.	118,023	Humphrey, Hubert H.	13,400	31,818 R	53.3%	42.0%	55.9%	44.1%
1964	293,118	130,108	Goldwater, Barry M.	163,010	Johnson, Lyndon B.		32,902 D	44.4%	55.6%	44.4%	55.6%
1960	306,487	178,417	Nixon, Richard M.	128,070	Kennedy, John F.		50,347 R	58.2%	41.8%	58.2%	41.8%
1956	293,857	171,569	Eisenhower, Dwight D.	122,288	Stevenson, Adlai E.		49,281 R	58.4%	41.6%	58.4%	41.6%
1952	294,283	203,857	Eisenhower, Dwight D.	90,426	Stevenson, Adlai E.		113,431 R	69.3%	30.7%	69.3%	30.7%
1948	250,105	129,651	Dewey, Thomas E.	117,653	Truman, Harry S.	2,801	11,998 R	51.8%	47.0%	52.4%	47.6%

In 1992 the voter vote column includes 73,295 votes cast for Perot.

SOUTH DAKOTA

POSTWAR VOTE FOR GOVERNOR

Year	Total Vote	Republican		Democratic		Other Vote	Rep.-Dem. Plurality	Percentage			
								Total Vote		Major Vote	
		Vote	Candidate	Vote	Candidate			Rep.	Dem.	Rep.	Dem.
1990	256,723	151,198	Mickelson, George S.	105,525	Samuelson, Bob L.		45,673 R	58.9%	41.1%	58.9%	41.1%
1986	294,441	152,543	Mickelson, George S.	141,898	Herseth, R. Lars		10,645 R	51.8%	48.2%	51.8%	48.2%
1982	278,562	197,426	Janklow, William J.	81,136	O'Connor, Michael J.		116,290 R	70.9%	29.1%	70.9%	29.1%
1978	259,795	147,116	Janklow, William J.	112,679	McKellips, Roger		34,437 R	56.6%	43.4%	56.6%	43.4%
1974 **	278,228	129,077	Olson, John E.	149,151	Kneip, Richard F.		20,074 D	46.4%	53.6%	46.4%	53.6%
1972	308,177	123,165	Thompson, Carveth	185,012	Kneip, Richard F.		61,847 D	40.0%	60.0%	40.0%	60.0%
1970	239,963	108,347	Farrar, Frank	131,616	Kneip, Richard F.		23,269 D	45.2%	54.8%	45.2%	54.8%
1968	276,906	159,646	Farrar, Frank	117,260	Chamberlin, Robert		42,386 R	57.7%	42.3%	57.7%	42.3%
1966	228,214	131,710	Boe, Nils A.	96,504	Chamberlin, Robert		35,206 R	57.7%	42.3%	57.7%	42.3%
1964	290,570	150,151	Boe, Nils A.	140,419	Lindley, John F.		9,732 R	51.7%	48.3%	51.7%	48.3%
1962	256,120	143,682	Gubbrud, Archie M.	112,438	Herseth, Ralph		31,244 R	56.1%	43.9%	56.1%	43.9%
1960	304,625	154,530	Gubbrud, Archie M.	150,095	Herseth, Ralph		4,435 R	50.7%	49.3%	50.7%	49.3%
1958	258,281	125,520	Saunders, Phil	132,761	Herseth, Ralph		7,241 D	48.6%	51.4%	48.6%	51.4%
1956	292,017	158,819	Foss, Joe J.	133,198	Herseth, Ralph		25,621 R	54.4%	45.6%	54.4%	45.6%
1954	236,255	133,878	Foss, Joe J.	102,377	Martin, Ed C.		31,501 R	56.7%	43.3%	56.7%	43.3%
1952	289,515	203,102	Anderson, Sigurd	86,413	Iverson, Sherman A.		116,689 R	70.2%	29.8%	70.2%	29.8%
1950	253,316	154,254	Anderson, Sigurd	99,062	Robbie, Joseph		55,192 R	60.9%	39.1%	60.9%	39.1%
1948	245,372	149,883	Mickelson, George	95,489	Volz, Harold J.		54,394 R	61.1%	38.9%	61.1%	38.9%
1946	162,292	108,998	Mickelson, George	53,294	Haeder, Richard		55,704 R	67.2%	32.8%	67.2%	32.8%

The term of office of South Dakota's Governor was increased from two to four years effective with the 1974 election.

POSTWAR VOTE FOR SENATOR

Year	Total Vote	Republican		Democratic		Other Vote	Rep.-Dem. Plurality	Percentage			
								Total Vote		Major Vote	
		Vote	Candidate	Vote	Candidate			Rep.	Dem.	Rep.	Dem.
1992	334,495	108,733	Haar, Charlene	217,095	Daschle, Thomas A.	8,667	108,362 D	32.5%	64.9%	33.4%	66.6%
1990	258,976	135,682	Pressler, Larry	116,727	Muenster, Ted	6,567	18,955 R	52.4%	45.1%	53.8%	46.2%
1986	295,830	143,173	Abdnor, James	152,657	Daschle, Thomas A.		9,484 D	48.4%	51.6%	48.4%	51.6%
1984	315,713	235,176	Pressler, Larry	80,537	Cunningham, George V.		154,639 R	74.5%	25.5%	74.5%	25.5%
1980	327,478	190,594	Abdnor, James	129,018	McGovern, George S.	7,866	61,576 R	58.2%	39.4%	59.6%	40.4%
1978	255,599	170,832	Pressler, Larry	84,767	Barnett, Don		86,065 R	66.8%	33.2%	66.8%	33.2%
1974	278,884	130,955	Thorsness, Leo K.	147,929	McGovern, George S.		16,974 D	47.0%	53.0%	47.0%	53.0%
1972	306,386	131,613	Hirsch, Robert W.	174,773	Abourezk, James		43,160 D	43.0%	57.0%	43.0%	57.0%
1968	279,912	120,951	Gubbrud, Archie M.	158,961	McGovern, George S.		38,010 D	43.2%	56.8%	43.2%	56.8%
1966	227,080	150,517	Mundt, Karl E.	76,563	Wright, Donn H.		73,954 R	66.3%	33.7%	66.3%	33.7%
1962	254,319	126,861	Bottum, Joe H.	127,458	McGovern, George S.		597 D	49.9%	50.1%	49.9%	50.1%
1960	305,442	160,181	Mundt, Karl E.	145,261	McGovern, George S.		14,920 R	52.4%	47.6%	52.4%	47.6%
1956	290,622	147,621	Case, Francis	143,001	Holum, Kenneth		4,620 R	50.8%	49.2%	50.8%	49.2%
1954	235,745	135,071	Mundt, Karl E.	100,674	Holum, Kenneth		34,397 R	57.3%	42.7%	57.3%	42.7%
1950	251,362	160,670	Case, Francis	90,692	Engel, John A.		69,978 R	63.9%	36.1%	63.9%	36.1%
1948	242,833	144,084	Mundt, Karl E.	98,749	Engel, John A.		45,335 R	59.3%	40.7%	59.3%	40.7%

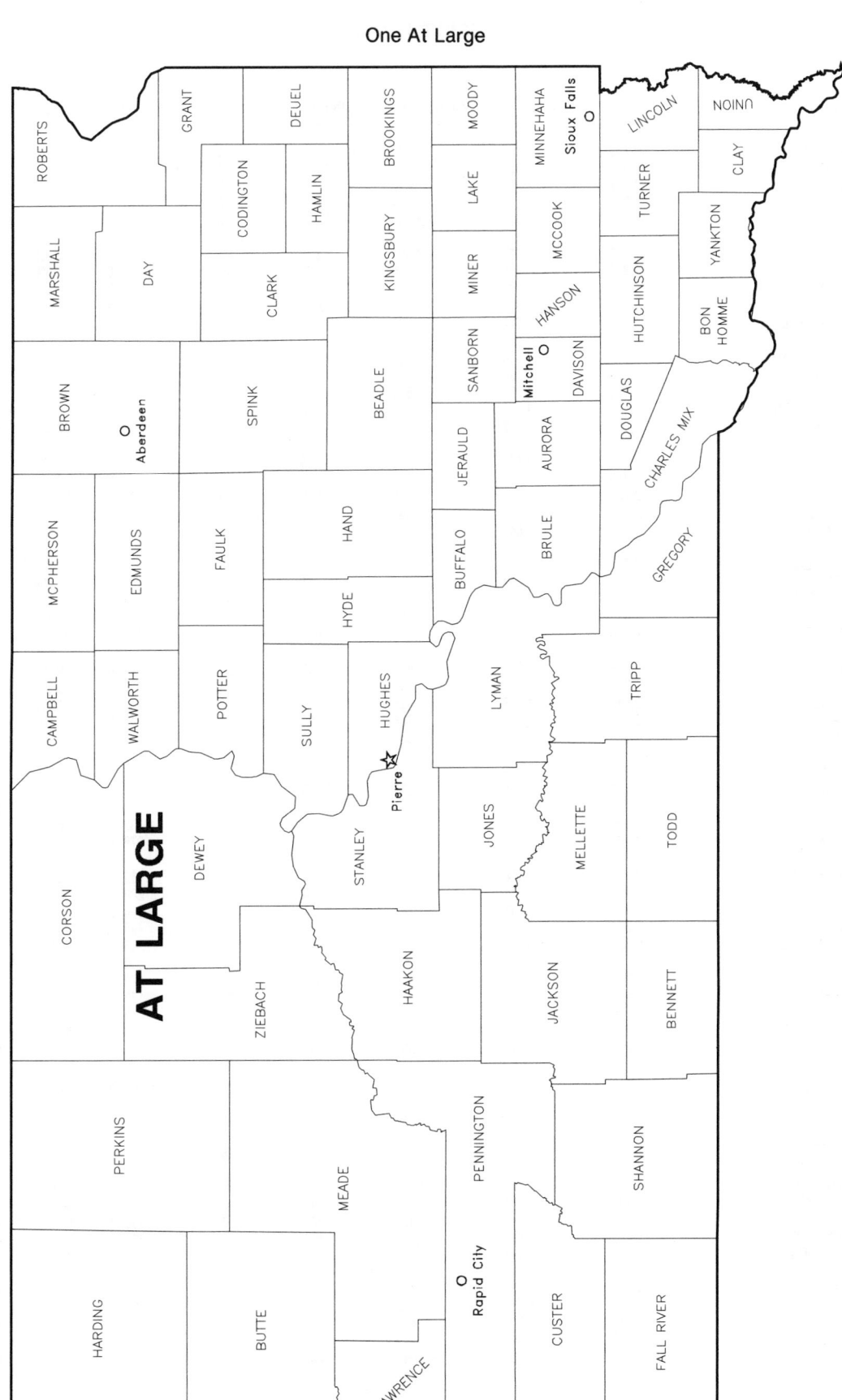

SOUTH DAKOTA

One At Large

449

SOUTH DAKOTA

PRESIDENT 1992

Registration	County	Total Vote	Republican	Democratic	Perot	Other	Plurality	Percentage Total Vote		
								Rep.	Dem.	Perot
2,232	AURORA	1,712	594	680	435	3	86 D	34.7%	39.7%	25.4%
12,063	BEADLE	9,136	3,363	3,925	1,819	29	562 D	36.8%	43.0%	19.9%
2,017	BENNETT	1,197	556	413	221	7	143 R	46.4%	34.5%	18.5%
4,810	BONHOMME	3,367	1,212	1,294	836	25	82 D	36.0%	38.4%	24.8%
15,933	BROOKINGS	12,002	4,698	4,645	2,614	45	53 R	39.1%	38.7%	21.8%
22,866	BROWN	18,047	6,665	7,521	3,812	49	856 D	36.9%	41.7%	21.1%
3,448	BRULE	2,676	908	1,060	687	21	152 D	33.9%	39.6%	25.7%
1,016	BUFFALO	496	137	282	72	5	145 D	27.6%	56.9%	14.5%
4,719	BUTTE	3,700	1,674	973	1,039	14	635 R	45.2%	26.3%	28.1%
1,469	CAMPBELL	1,053	574	222	252	5	322 R	54.5%	21.1%	23.9%
5,746	CHARLES MIX	4,099	1,570	1,639	886	4	69 D	38.3%	40.0%	21.6%
2,937	CLARK	2,375	803	799	761	12	4 R	33.8%	33.6%	32.0%
8,028	CLAY	6,036	1,869	2,826	1,303	38	957 D	31.0%	46.8%	21.6%
13,953	CODINGTON	10,943	3,943	3,701	3,262	37	242 R	36.0%	33.8%	29.8%
2,171	CORSON	1,251	483	444	321	3	39 R	38.6%	35.5%	25.7%
4,358	CUSTER	3,363	1,422	1,078	845	18	344 R	42.3%	32.1%	25.1%
10,646	DAVISON	8,146	3,111	3,285	1,706	44	174 D	38.2%	40.3%	20.9%
4,861	DAY	3,725	1,161	1,578	973	13	417 D	31.2%	42.4%	26.1%
3,092	DEUEL	2,423	778	880	761	4	102 D	32.1%	36.3%	31.4%
3,112	DEWEY	1,752	642	766	340	4	124 D	36.6%	43.7%	19.4%
2,563	DOUGLAS	2,067	1,175	481	403	8	694 R	56.8%	23.3%	19.5%
3,067	EDMUNDS	2,260	944	894	415	7	50 R	41.8%	39.6%	18.4%
5,250	FALL RIVER	3,754	1,533	1,416	792	13	117 R	40.8%	37.7%	21.1%
1,818	FAULK	1,434	658	488	281	7	170 R	45.9%	34.0%	19.6%
5,210	GRANT	4,110	1,595	1,484	1,018	13	111 R	38.8%	36.1%	24.8%
3,529	GREGORY	2,615	1,027	879	688	21	148 R	39.3%	33.6%	26.3%
1,604	HAAKON	1,318	860	209	245	4	615 R	65.3%	15.9%	18.6%
3,442	HAMLIN	2,740	1,133	826	774	7	307 R	41.4%	30.1%	28.2%
3,161	HAND	2,546	1,130	785	624	7	345 R	44.4%	30.8%	24.5%
2,032	HANSON	1,435	522	566	341	6	44 D	36.4%	39.4%	23.8%
1,109	HARDING	881	515	139	225	2	290 R	58.5%	15.8%	25.5%
10,313	HUGHES	8,121	4,325	2,578	1,160	58	1,747 R	53.3%	31.7%	14.3%
5,759	HUTCHINSON	4,156	2,002	1,211	920	23	791 R	48.2%	29.1%	22.1%
1,211	HYDE	955	440	301	211	3	139 R	46.1%	31.5%	22.1%
1,725	JACKSON	1,168	627	351	184	6	276 R	53.7%	30.1%	15.8%
1,770	JERAULD	1,467	518	600	346	3	82 D	35.3%	40.9%	23.6%
961	JONES	779	454	166	154	5	288 R	58.3%	21.3%	19.8%
3,986	KINGSBURY	3,143	1,113	1,267	744	19	154 D	35.4%	40.3%	23.7%
6,978	LAKE	5,590	1,890	2,388	1,299	13	498 D	33.8%	42.7%	23.2%
13,006	LAWRENCE	9,659	3,770	3,157	2,673	59	613 R	39.0%	32.7%	27.7%
10,045	LINCOLN	7,923	3,365	2,943	1,593	22	422 R	42.5%	37.1%	20.1%
1,979	LYMAN	1,480	669	486	311	14	183 R	45.2%	32.8%	21.0%
3,822	MCCOOK	2,984	1,177	1,167	617	23	10 R	39.4%	39.1%	20.7%
2,370	MCPHERSON	1,752	945	478	322	7	467 R	53.9%	27.3%	18.4%
3,046	MARSHALL	2,297	810	1,056	427	4	246 D	35.3%	46.0%	18.6%
13,948	MEADE	10,075	4,724	2,694	2,611	46	2,030 R	46.9%	26.7%	25.9%
1,237	MELLETTE	841	417	277	140	7	140 R	49.6%	32.9%	16.6%
2,093	MINER	1,584	543	698	332	11	155 D	34.3%	44.1%	21.0%
82,012	MINNEHAHA	63,786	25,081	27,016	11,496	193	1,935 D	39.3%	42.4%	18.0%
3,990	MOODY	3,104	898	1,473	715	18	575 D	28.9%	47.5%	23.0%
52,982	PENNINGTON	37,669	18,052	11,106	8,358	153	6,946 R	47.9%	29.5%	22.2%
2,801	PERKINS	1,991	872	566	541	12	306 R	43.8%	28.4%	27.2%
2,262	POTTER	1,778	901	493	375	9	408 R	50.7%	27.7%	21.1%
5,676	ROBERTS	4,121	1,437	1,716	954	14	279 D	34.9%	41.6%	23.1%
2,113	SANBORN	1,610	595	632	376	7	37 D	37.0%	39.3%	23.4%
4,404	SHANNON	1,651	225	1,267	137	22	1,042 D	13.6%	76.7%	8.3%
5,147	SPINK	4,112	1,527	1,732	839	14	205 D	37.1%	42.1%	20.4%
1,883	STANLEY	1,399	719	427	240	13	292 R	51.4%	30.5%	17.2%
1,271	SULLY	1,010	565	273	167	5	292 R	55.9%	27.0%	16.5%
3,411	TODD	1,630	456	915	246	13	459 D	28.0%	56.1%	15.1%

SOUTH DAKOTA

PRESIDENT 1992

Registration	County	Total Vote	Republican	Democratic	Perot	Other	Plurality	Percentage Total Vote		
								Rep.	Dem.	Perot
4,435	TRIPP	3,363	1,459	1,046	848	10	413 R	43.4%	31.1%	25.2%
5,883	TURNER	4,290	1,906	1,507	867	10	399 R	44.4%	35.1%	20.2%
6,516	UNION	5,097	1,784	2,210	1,085	18	426 D	35.0%	43.4%	21.3%
3,954	WALWORTH	2,908	1,439	829	628	12	610 R	49.5%	28.5%	21.6%
11,842	YANKTON	9,372	3,430	3,404	2,511	27	26 R	36.6%	36.3%	26.8%
1,199	ZIEBACH	730	328	280	117	5	48 R	44.9%	38.4%	16.0%
448,292	TOTAL	336,254	136,718	124,888	73,295	1,353	11,830 R	40.7%	37.1%	21.8%

SOUTH DAKOTA

SENATOR 1992

Registration	County	Total Vote	Republican	Democratic	Other	Rep.-Dem. Plurality	Percentage Total Vote Rep.	Percentage Total Vote Dem.	Percentage Major Vote Rep.	Percentage Major Vote Dem.
2,232	AURORA	1,717	540	1,147	30	607 D	31.5%	66.8%	32.0%	68.0%
12,063	BEADLE	9,170	2,953	6,014	203	3,061 D	32.2%	65.6%	32.9%	67.1%
2,017	BENNETT	1,198	384	782	32	398 D	32.1%	65.3%	32.9%	67.1%
4,810	BONHOMME	3,384	910	2,419	55	1,509 D	26.9%	71.5%	27.3%	72.7%
15,933	BROOKINGS	11,963	3,551	8,101	311	4,550 D	29.7%	67.7%	30.5%	69.5%
22,866	BROWN	18,056	4,317	12,867	872	8,550 D	23.9%	71.3%	25.1%	74.9%
3,448	BRULE	2,666	843	1,748	75	905 D	31.6%	65.6%	32.5%	67.5%
1,016	BUFFALO	495	134	352	9	218 D	27.1%	71.1%	27.6%	72.4%
4,719	BUTTE	3,621	1,632	1,911	78	279 D	45.1%	52.8%	46.1%	53.9%
1,469	CAMPBELL	1,032	429	581	22	152 D	41.6%	56.3%	42.5%	57.5%
5,746	CHARLES MIX	4,107	1,213	2,826	68	1,613 D	29.5%	68.8%	30.0%	70.0%
2,937	CLARK	2,355	738	1,547	70	809 D	31.3%	65.7%	32.3%	67.7%
8,028	CLAY	5,986	1,483	4,318	185	2,835 D	24.8%	72.1%	25.6%	74.4%
13,953	CODINGTON	10,926	3,752	6,908	266	3,156 D	34.3%	63.2%	35.2%	64.8%
2,171	CORSON	1,211	534	621	56	87 D	44.1%	51.3%	46.2%	53.8%
4,358	CUSTER	3,337	1,297	1,903	137	606 D	38.9%	57.0%	40.5%	59.5%
10,646	DAVISON	8,120	2,510	5,467	143	2,957 D	30.9%	67.3%	31.5%	68.5%
4,861	DAY	3,680	992	2,597	91	1,605 D	27.0%	70.6%	27.6%	72.4%
3,092	DEUEL	2,418	757	1,598	63	841 D	31.3%	66.1%	32.1%	67.9%
3,112	DEWEY	1,723	622	1,065	36	443 D	36.1%	61.8%	36.9%	63.1%
2,563	DOUGLAS	2,056	999	1,021	36	22 D	48.6%	49.7%	49.5%	50.5%
3,067	EDMUNDS	2,249	663	1,530	56	867 D	29.5%	68.0%	30.2%	69.8%
5,250	FALL RIVER	3,706	1,329	2,250	127	921 D	35.9%	60.7%	37.1%	62.9%
1,818	FAULK	1,426	450	950	26	500 D	31.6%	66.6%	32.1%	67.9%
5,210	GRANT	4,085	1,467	2,531	87	1,064 D	35.9%	62.0%	36.7%	63.3%
3,529	GREGORY	2,613	990	1,577	46	587 D	37.9%	60.4%	38.6%	61.4%
1,604	HAAKON	1,307	645	634	28	11 R	49.3%	48.5%	50.4%	49.6%
3,442	HAMLIN	2,742	1,008	1,648	86	640 D	36.8%	60.1%	38.0%	62.0%
3,161	HAND	2,548	813	1,695	40	882 D	31.9%	66.5%	32.4%	67.6%
2,032	HANSON	1,437	439	973	25	534 D	30.5%	67.7%	31.1%	68.9%
1,109	HARDING	862	394	452	16	58 D	45.7%	52.4%	46.6%	53.4%
10,313	HUGHES	8,001	3,042	4,751	208	1,709 D	38.0%	59.4%	39.0%	61.0%
5,759	HUTCHINSON	4,181	1,568	2,565	48	997 D	37.5%	61.3%	37.9%	62.1%
1,211	HYDE	942	373	549	20	176 D	39.6%	58.3%	40.5%	59.5%
1,725	JACKSON	1,155	529	597	29	68 D	45.8%	51.7%	47.0%	53.0%
1,770	JERAULD	1,474	435	1,018	21	583 D	29.5%	69.1%	29.9%	70.1%
961	JONES	777	359	400	18	41 D	46.2%	51.5%	47.3%	52.7%
3,986	KINGSBURY	3,150	957	2,117	76	1,160 D	30.4%	67.2%	31.1%	68.9%
6,978	LAKE	5,589	1,754	3,728	107	1,974 D	31.4%	66.7%	32.0%	68.0%
13,006	LAWRENCE	9,608	3,606	5,651	351	2,045 D	37.5%	58.8%	39.0%	61.0%
10,045	LINCOLN	7,850	2,346	5,360	144	3,014 D	29.9%	68.3%	30.4%	69.6%
1,979	LYMAN	1,488	614	836	38	222 D	41.3%	56.2%	42.3%	57.7%
3,822	MCCOOK	2,972	946	1,975	51	1,029 D	31.8%	66.5%	32.4%	67.6%
2,370	MCPHERSON	1,686	689	946	51	257 D	40.9%	56.1%	42.1%	57.9%
3,046	MARSHALL	2,276	597	1,634	45	1,037 D	26.2%	71.8%	26.8%	73.2%
13,948	MEADE	10,024	4,146	5,578	300	1,432 D	41.4%	55.6%	42.6%	57.4%
1,237	MELLETTE	856	269	579	8	310 D	31.4%	67.6%	31.7%	68.3%
2,093	MINER	1,582	456	1,093	33	637 D	28.8%	69.1%	29.4%	70.6%
82,012	MINNEHAHA	63,380	17,561	44,541	1,278	26,980 D	27.7%	70.3%	28.3%	71.7%
3,990	MOODY	3,110	789	2,255	66	1,466 D	25.4%	72.5%	25.9%	74.1%
52,982	PENNINGTON	37,659	14,560	21,679	1,420	7,119 D	38.7%	57.6%	40.2%	59.8%
2,801	PERKINS	1,978	848	1,074	56	226 D	42.9%	54.3%	44.1%	55.9%
2,262	POTTER	1,778	701	1,023	54	322 D	39.4%	57.5%	40.7%	59.3%
5,676	ROBERTS	3,910	1,296	2,545	69	1,249 D	33.1%	65.1%	33.7%	66.3%
2,113	SANBORN	1,604	486	1,080	38	594 D	30.3%	67.3%	31.0%	69.0%
4,404	SHANNON	1,633	165	1,416	52	1,251 D	10.1%	86.7%	10.4%	89.6%
5,147	SPINK	4,067	1,164	2,805	98	1,641 D	28.6%	69.0%	29.3%	70.7%
1,883	STANLEY	1,398	475	884	39	409 D	34.0%	63.2%	35.0%	65.0%
1,271	SULLY	1,010	422	566	22	144 D	41.8%	56.0%	42.7%	57.3%
3,411	TODD	1,626	394	1,197	35	803 D	24.2%	73.6%	24.8%	75.2%

SOUTH DAKOTA

SENATOR 1992

Registration	County	Total Vote	Republican	Democratic	Other	Rep.-Dem. Plurality	Percentage			
							Total Vote		Major Vote	
							Rep.	Dem.	Rep.	Dem.
4,435	TRIPP	3,363	1,308	1,994	61	686 D	38.9%	59.3%	39.6%	60.4%
5,883	TURNER	4,295	1,491	2,750	54	1,259 D	34.7%	64.0%	35.2%	64.8%
6,516	UNION	4,997	1,385	3,491	121	2,106 D	27.7%	69.9%	28.4%	71.6%
3,954	WALWORTH	2,873	1,195	1,607	71	412 D	41.6%	55.9%	42.6%	57.4%
11,842	YANKTON	9,309	2,729	6,396	184	3,667 D	29.3%	68.7%	29.9%	70.1%
1,199	ZIEBACH	698	290	382	26	92 D	41.5%	54.7%	43.2%	56.8%
448,292	TOTAL	334,495	108,733	217,095	8,667	108,362 D	32.5%	64.9%	33.4%	66.6%

SOUTH DAKOTA

CONGRESS

CD	Year	Total Vote	Republican Vote	Republican Candidate	Democratic Vote	Democratic Candidate	Other Vote	Rep.-Dem. Plurality	Percentage Total Vote Rep.	Percentage Total Vote Dem.	Percentage Major Vote Rep.	Percentage Major Vote Dem.
AL	1992	332,902	89,375	TIMMER, JOHN	230,070	JOHNSON, TIM	13,457	140,695 D	26.8%	69.1%	28.0%	72.0%
AL	1990	257,298	83,484	FRANKENFELD, DON	173,814	JOHNSON, TIM		90,330 D	32.4%	67.6%	32.4%	67.6%
AL	1988	311,916	88,157	VOLK, DAVID	223,759	JOHNSON, TIM		135,602 D	28.3%	71.7%	28.3%	71.7%
AL	1986	289,723	118,261	BELL, DALE	171,462	JOHNSON, TIM		53,201 D	40.8%	59.2%	40.8%	59.2%
AL	1984	316,222	134,821	BELL, DALE	181,401	DASCHLE, THOMAS A.		46,580 D	42.6%	57.4%	42.6%	57.4%
AL	1982	275,652	133,530	ROBERTS, CLINT	142,122	DASCHLE, THOMAS A.		8,592 D	48.4%	51.6%	48.4%	51.6%

SOUTH DAKOTA

1992 GENERAL ELECTION

President   Other vote was 814 Libertarian (Marrou); 429 Natural Law (Hagelin); 110 New Alliance (Fulani).

Senator   Other vote was 4,353 Libertarian (Hercules); 4,314 Natural Law (Hyde).

Congress   Other vote at-large was 6,746 Independent (Wieczorek); 3,931 Libertarian (Newland); 2,780 Independent (Balakier).

1992 PRIMARIES

JUNE 2 REPUBLICAN

Senator   Charlene Haar, unopposed

Congress   Unopposed at-large.

JUNE 2 DEMOCRATIC

Senator   Thomas A. Daschle, unopposed.

Congress   Unopposed at-large.

TENNESSEE

GOVERNOR
Ned McWherter (D). Re-elected 1990 to a four-year term. Previously elected 1986.

SENATORS
Harlan Mathews (D). Appointed January 1993 to fill the vacancy created when Senator Albert Gore, Jr. (D) resigned to become Vice-President. A special election will be held in 1994 to fill the remaining two years of this term.

James R. Sasser (D). Re-elected 1988 to a six-year term. Previously elected 1982, 1976.

REPRESENTATIVES
1. James H. Quillen (R)
2. John J. Duncan, Jr. (R)
3. Marilyn Lloyd (D)
4. Jim Cooper (D)
5. Bob Clement (D)
6. Bart Gordon (D)
7. Don Sundquist (R)
8. John Tanner (D)
9. Harold E. Ford (D)

POSTWAR VOTE FOR PRESIDENT

Year	Total Vote	Republican Vote	Candidate	Democratic Vote	Candidate	Other Vote	Plurality	Total Vote Rep.	Dem.	Major Vote Rep.	Dem.
1992 **	1,982,638	841,300	Bush, George	933,521	Clinton, Bill	207,817	92,221 D	42.4%	47.1%	47.4%	52.6%
1988	1,636,250	947,233	Bush, George	679,794	Dukakis, Michael S.	9,223	267,439 R	57.9%	41.5%	58.2%	41.8%
1984	1,711,994	990,212	Reagan, Ronald	711,714	Mondale, Walter F.	10,068	278,498 R	57.8%	41.6%	58.2%	41.8%
1980	1,617,616	787,761	Reagan, Ronald	783,051	Carter, Jimmy	46,804	4,710 R	48.7%	48.4%	50.1%	49.9%
1976	1,476,345	633,969	Ford, Gerald R.	825,879	Carter, Jimmy	16,497	191,910 D	42.9%	55.9%	43.4%	56.6%
1972	1,201,182	813,147	Nixon, Richard M.	357,293	McGovern, George S.	30,742	455,854 R	67.7%	29.7%	69.5%	30.5%
1968 **	1,248,617	472,592	Nixon, Richard M.	351,233	Humphrey, Hubert H.	424,792	47,800 R	37.8%	28.1%	57.4%	42.6%
1964	1,143,946	508,965	Goldwater, Barry M.	634,947	Johnson, Lyndon B.	34	125,982 D	44.5%	55.5%	44.5%	55.5%
1960	1,051,792	556,577	Nixon, Richard M.	481,453	Kennedy, John F.	13,762	75,124 R	52.9%	45.8%	53.6%	46.4%
1956	939,404	462,288	Eisenhower, Dwight D.	456,507	Stevenson, Adlai E.	20,609	5,781 R	49.2%	48.6%	50.3%	49.7%
1952	892,553	446,147	Eisenhower, Dwight D.	443,710	Stevenson, Adlai E.	2,696	2,437 R	50.0%	49.7%	50.1%	49.9%
1948	550,283	202,914	Dewey, Thomas E.	270,402	Truman, Harry S.	76,967	67,488 D	36.9%	49.1%	42.9%	57.1%

In 1992 the other vote column includes 199,968 votes cast for Perot. In 1968 other vote was American (Wallace).

TENNESSEE

POSTWAR VOTE FOR GOVERNOR

Year	Total Vote	Republican Vote	Republican Candidate	Democratic Vote	Democratic Candidate	Other Vote	Rep.-Dem. Plurality	Percentage Total Vote Rep.	Percentage Total Vote Dem.	Percentage Major Vote Rep.	Percentage Major Vote Dem.
1990	790,441	289,348	Henry, Dwight	480,885	McWherter, Ned	20,208	191,537 D	36.6%	60.8%	37.6%	62.4%
1986	1,210,339	553,449	Dunn, Winfield	656,602	McWherter, Ned	288	103,153 D	45.7%	54.2%	45.7%	54.3%
1982	1,238,927	737,963	Alexander, Lamar	500,937	Tyree, Randy	27	237,026 R	59.6%	40.4%	59.6%	40.4%
1978	1,189,695	661,959	Alexander, Lamar	523,495	Butcher, Jake	4,241	138,464 R	55.6%	44.0%	55.8%	44.2%
1974	1,040,714	455,467	Alexander, Lamar	576,833	Blanton, Ray	8,414	121,366 D	43.8%	55.4%	44.1%	55.9%
1970	1,108,247	575,777	Dunn, Winfield	509,521	Hooker, John J.	22,949	66,256 R	52.0%	46.0%	53.1%	46.9%
1966 **	656,566		—	532,998	Ellington, Buford	123,568	532,998 D		81.2%		100.0%
1962 **	621,064	100,190	Patty, Hubert D.	315,648	Clement, Frank G.	205,226	215,458 D	16.1%	50.8%	24.1%	75.9%
1958 **	432,545	35,938	Wall, Thomas P.	248,874	Ellington, Buford	147,733	212,936 D	8.3%	57.5%	12.6%	87.4%
1954 **	322,586		—	281,291	Clement, Frank G.	41,295	281,291 D		87.2%		100.0%
1952	806,771	166,377	Witt, R. Beecher	640,290	Clement, Frank G.	104	473,913 D	20.6%	79.4%	20.6%	79.4%
1950	236,194		—	184,437	Browning, Gordon	51,757	184,437 D		78.1%		100.0%
1948	543,881	179,957	Acuff, Roy	363,903	Browning, Gordon	21	183,946 D	33.1%	66.9%	33.1%	66.9%
1946	229,456	73,222	Lowe, W. O.	149,937	McCord, Jim Nance	6,297	76,715 D	31.9%	65.3%	32.8%	67.2%

The term of office of Tennessee's Governor was increased from two to four years effective with the 1954 election. In 1958 Jim Nance McCord (Independent) received 136,399 votes (31.5% of the total vote) and ran second. In 1962 other vote was 203,765 William R. Anderson (Independent) who ran second; 1,441 E. B. Bowles (Independent) and 20 scattered. In 1966 other vote was 64,602 H. L. Crawford (Independent); 50,221 Charles Moffett (Independent); 8,407 Charles G. Vick (Independent) and 338 scattered.

POSTWAR VOTE FOR SENATOR

Year	Total Vote	Republican Vote	Republican Candidate	Democratic Vote	Democratic Candidate	Other Vote	Rep.-Dem. Plurality	Percentage Total Vote Rep.	Percentage Total Vote Dem.	Percentage Major Vote Rep.	Percentage Major Vote Dem.
1990	783,922	233,703	Hawkins, William R.	530,898	Gore, Albert, Jr.	19,321	297,195 D	29.8%	67.7%	30.6%	69.4%
1988	1,567,181	541,033	Anderson, Bill	1,020,061	Sasser, James R.	6,087	479,028 D	34.5%	65.1%	34.7%	65.3%
1984	1,648,064	557,016	Ashe, Victor	1,000,607	Gore, Albert, Jr.	90,441	443,591 D	33.8%	60.7%	35.8%	64.2%
1982	1,259,785	479,642	Beard, Robin L.	780,113	Sasser, James R.	30	300,471 D	38.1%	61.9%	38.1%	61.9%
1978	1,157,094	642,644	Baker, Howard H., Jr.	466,228	Eskind, Jane	48,222	176,416 R	55.5%	40.3%	58.0%	42.0%
1976	1,432,046	673,231	Brock, William E.	751,180	Sasser, James R.	7,635	77,949 D	47.0%	52.5%	47.3%	52.7%
1972	1,164,195	716,539	Baker, Howard H., Jr.	440,599	Blanton, Ray	7,057	275,940 R	61.5%	37.8%	61.9%	38.1%
1970	1,097,041	562,645	Brock, William E.	519,858	Gore, Albert	14,538	42,787 R	51.3%	47.4%	52.0%	48.0%
1966	866,961	483,063	Baker, Howard H., Jr.	383,843	Clement, Frank G.	55	99,220 R	55.7%	44.3%	55.7%	44.3%
1964	1,064,018	493,475	Kuykendall, Daniel H.	570,542	Gore, Albert	1	77,067 D	46.4%	53.6%	46.4%	53.6%
1964 S	1,091,093	517,330	Baker, Howard H., Jr.	568,905	Bass, Ross	4,858	51,575 D	47.4%	52.1%	47.6%	52.4%
1960	828,519	234,053	Frazier, A. Bradley	594,460	Kefauver, Estes	6	360,407 D	28.2%	71.7%	28.2%	71.8%
1958	401,666	76,371	Atkins, Hobart F.	317,324	Gore, Albert	7,971	240,953 D	19.0%	79.0%	19.4%	80.6%
1954	356,094	106,971	Wall, Thomas P.	249,121	Kefauver, Estes	2	142,150 D	30.0%	70.0%	30.0%	70.0%
1952	735,219	153,479	Atkins, Hobart F.	545,432	Gore, Albert	36,308	391,953 D	20.9%	74.2%	22.0%	78.0%
1948	499,218	166,947	Reece, B. Carroll	326,142	Kefauver, Estes	6,129	159,195 D	33.4%	65.3%	33.9%	66.1%
1946	218,714	57,238	Ladd, William B.	145,654	McKellar, Kenneth	15,822	88,416 D	26.2%	66.6%	28.2%	71.8%

One of the 1964 elections was for a short term to fill a vacancy.

TENNESSEE

Districts Established May 7, 1992

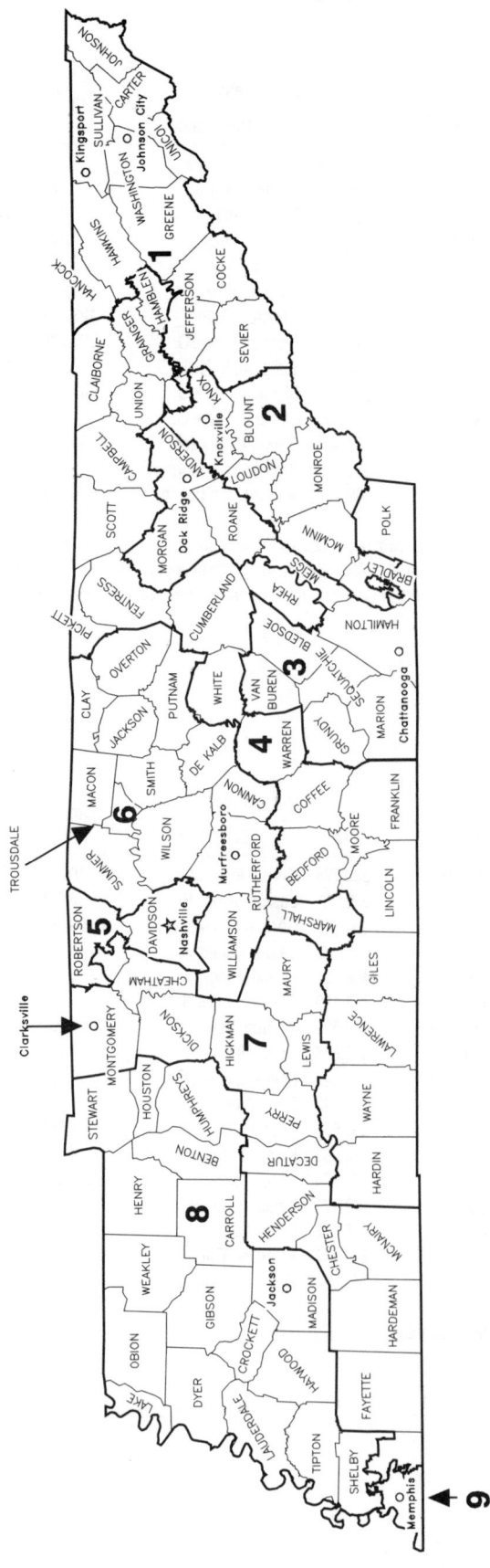

TENNESSEE

PRESIDENT 1992

Registration	County	Total Vote	Republican	Democratic	Perot	Other	Plurality	Percentage Total Vote Rep.	Dem.	Perot
36,402	ANDERSON	28,611	11,838	13,482	3,149	142	1,644 D	41.4%	47.1%	11.0%
15,324	BEDFORD	11,421	3,836	5,978	1,541	66	2,142 D	33.6%	52.3%	13.5%
9,290	BENTON	6,114	1,625	3,896	559	34	2,271 D	26.6%	63.7%	9.1%
6,357	BLEDSOE	4,018	1,776	1,884	352	6	108 D	44.2%	46.9%	8.8%
51,642	BLOUNT	37,651	18,415	14,655	4,468	113	3,760 R	48.9%	38.9%	11.9%
39,687	BRADLEY	29,696	16,528	9,889	3,212	67	6,639 R	55.7%	33.3%	10.8%
19,817	CAMPBELL	12,931	4,897	6,756	1,240	38	1,859 D	37.9%	52.2%	9.6%
5,783	CANNON	4,331	1,229	2,593	495	14	1,364 D	28.4%	59.9%	11.4%
16,080	CARROLL	11,799	4,842	5,741	1,139	77	899 D	41.0%	48.7%	9.7%
25,473	CARTER	19,190	10,712	6,502	1,898	78	4,210 R	55.8%	33.9%	9.9%
12,470	CHEATHAM	9,788	3,496	4,817	1,433	42	1,321 D	35.7%	49.2%	14.6%
7,806	CHESTER	5,596	2,834	2,317	439	6	517 R	50.6%	41.4%	7.8%
14,861	CLAIBORNE	9,485	4,065	4,509	860	51	444 D	42.9%	47.5%	9.1%
4,954	CLAY	3,226	1,072	1,922	223	9	850 D	33.2%	59.6%	6.9%
15,879	COCKE	10,000	5,298	3,495	1,124	83	1,803 R	53.0%	35.0%	11.2%
22,084	COFFEE	17,044	6,047	8,534	2,420	43	2,487 D	35.5%	50.1%	14.2%
8,230	CROCKETT	5,357	2,180	2,657	507	13	477 D	40.7%	49.6%	9.5%
21,120	CUMBERLAND	15,792	7,116	6,393	2,200	83	723 R	45.1%	40.5%	13.9%
278,359	DAVIDSON	203,807	76,567	106,355	20,184	701	29,788 D	37.6%	52.2%	9.9%
6,737	DECATUR	4,661	1,667	2,633	351	10	966 D	35.8%	56.5%	7.5%
9,730	DE KALB	6,722	1,714	4,382	608	18	2,668 D	25.5%	65.2%	9.0%
18,754	DICKSON	14,093	4,450	7,863	1,730	50	3,413 D	31.6%	55.8%	12.3%
19,550	DYER	12,787	5,668	5,845	1,241	33	177 D	44.3%	45.7%	9.7%
12,780	FAYETTE	8,609	3,713	4,211	657	28	498 D	43.1%	48.9%	7.6%
9,160	FENTRESS	5,759	2,391	2,730	606	32	339 D	41.5%	47.4%	10.5%
19,373	FRANKLIN	14,176	4,507	7,773	1,837	59	3,266 D	31.8%	54.8%	13.0%
24,231	GIBSON	18,332	7,161	9,555	1,536	80	2,394 D	39.1%	52.1%	8.4%
15,161	GILES	9,781	2,827	5,601	1,309	44	2,774 D	28.9%	57.3%	13.4%
8,767	GRAINGER	5,553	2,772	2,242	513	26	530 R	49.9%	40.4%	9.2%
27,845	GREENE	20,875	9,912	7,857	2,930	176	2,055 R	47.5%	37.6%	14.0%
6,187	GRUNDY	4,386	1,004	2,997	366	19	1,993 D	22.9%	68.3%	8.3%
26,190	HAMBLEN	17,854	8,898	7,114	1,760	82	1,784 R	49.8%	39.8%	9.9%
162,534	HAMILTON	115,085	53,476	46,770	14,400	439	6,706 R	46.5%	40.6%	12.5%
5,007	HANCOCK	2,449	1,274	1,000	151	24	274 R	52.0%	40.8%	6.2%
13,281	HARDEMAN	8,627	3,122	4,832	594	79	1,710 D	36.2%	56.0%	6.9%
12,206	HARDIN	8,592	3,875	3,922	734	61	47 D	45.1%	45.6%	8.5%
22,954	HAWKINS	16,285	7,758	6,623	1,847	57	1,135 R	47.6%	40.7%	11.3%
10,019	HAYWOOD	6,376	2,518	3,511	331	16	993 D	39.5%	55.1%	5.2%
13,473	HENDERSON	9,024	4,719	3,502	785	18	1,217 R	52.3%	38.8%	8.7%
15,352	HENRY	12,095	3,661	6,797	1,588	49	3,136 D	30.3%	56.2%	13.1%
9,626	HICKMAN	6,727	1,820	4,093	795	19	2,273 D	27.1%	60.8%	11.8%
3,892	HOUSTON	2,951	648	2,012	280	11	1,364 D	22.0%	68.2%	9.5%
9,454	HUMPHREYS	6,135	1,641	3,875	609	10	2,234 D	26.7%	63.2%	9.9%
6,422	JACKSON	4,258	708	3,208	332	10	2,500 D	16.6%	75.3%	7.8%
15,592	JEFFERSON	12,362	6,184	4,740	1,385	53	1,444 R	50.0%	38.3%	11.2%
7,633	JOHNSON	5,563	3,170	1,781	574	38	1,389 R	57.0%	32.0%	10.3%
187,762	KNOX	142,476	66,607	59,702	15,669	498	6,905 R	46.7%	41.9%	11.0%
3,517	LAKE	2,306	680	1,449	151	26	769 D	29.5%	62.8%	6.5%
13,308	LAUDERDALE	7,958	2,928	4,452	561	17	1,524 D	36.8%	55.9%	7.0%
18,367	LAWRENCE	13,864	5,608	6,816	1,403	37	1,208 D	40.5%	49.2%	10.1%
5,986	LEWIS	4,152	1,218	2,491	434	9	1,273 D	29.3%	60.0%	10.5%
13,554	LINCOLN	10,302	3,814	5,063	1,371	54	1,249 D	37.0%	49.1%	13.3%
18,787	LOUDON	13,510	6,444	5,414	1,602	50	1,030 R	47.7%	40.1%	11.9%
21,787	MCMINN	15,990	7,453	6,682	1,812	43	771 R	46.6%	41.8%	11.3%
12,879	MCNAIRY	9,595	4,093	4,691	774	37	598 D	42.7%	48.9%	8.1%
9,363	MACON	5,726	2,299	2,961	443	23	662 D	40.2%	51.7%	7.7%
43,129	MADISON	31,196	14,869	13,629	2,634	64	1,240 R	47.7%	43.7%	8.4%
20,116	MARION	10,068	3,262	5,589	1,186	31	2,327 D	32.4%	55.5%	11.8%
10,643	MARSHALL	8,098	2,516	4,491	1,050	41	1,975 D	31.1%	55.5%	13.0%
27,635	MAURY	20,459	7,440	9,997	2,821	201	2,557 D	36.4%	48.9%	13.8%

TENNESSEE

PRESIDENT 1992

Registration	County	Total Vote	Republican	Democratic	Perot	Other	Plurality	Percentage Total Vote		
								Rep.	Dem.	Perot
5,788	MEIGS	3,484	1,355	1,673	453	3	318 D	38.9%	48.0%	13.0%
19,044	MONROE	12,411	6,025	5,384	936	66	641 R	48.5%	43.4%	7.5%
39,461	MONTGOMERY	31,341	13,011	14,507	3,753	70	1,496 D	41.5%	46.3%	12.0%
2,934	MOORE	2,145	661	1,151	327	6	490 D	30.8%	53.7%	15.2%
8,872	MORGAN	6,184	2,306	3,190	658	30	884 D	37.3%	51.6%	10.6%
17,098	OBION	12,864	4,812	6,497	1,494	61	1,685 D	37.4%	50.5%	11.6%
9,551	OVERTON	6,651	1,657	4,489	468	37	2,832 D	24.9%	67.5%	7.0%
4,175	PERRY	2,919	708	1,889	317	5	1,181 D	24.3%	64.7%	10.9%
3,688	PICKETT	2,368	1,094	1,144	121	9	50 D	46.2%	48.3%	5.1%
8,300	POLK	4,610	1,584	2,583	419	24	999 D	34.4%	56.0%	9.1%
27,279	PUTNAM	21,482	7,998	10,858	2,473	153	2,860 D	37.2%	50.5%	11.5%
14,827	RHEA	10,348	4,860	4,289	1,163	36	571 D	47.0%	41.4%	11.2%
36,240	ROANE	20,999	8,719	9,812	2,396	72	1,093 D	41.5%	46.7%	11.4%
20,436	ROBERTSON	15,779	5,271	8,498	1,978	32	3,227 D	33.4%	53.9%	12.5%
62,389	RUTHERFORD	47,140	18,877	21,084	7,005	174	2,207 D	40.0%	44.7%	14.9%
10,852	SCOTT	6,418	3,011	2,730	643	34	281 R	46.9%	42.5%	10.0%
5,068	SEQUATCHIE	3,559	1,381	1,754	405	19	373 D	38.8%	49.3%	11.4%
28,772	SEVIER	21,266	11,714	6,719	2,760	73	4,995 R	55.1%	31.6%	13.0%
498,719	SHELBY	366,110	153,310	191,322	20,223	1,255	38,012 D	41.9%	52.3%	5.5%
9,797	SMITH	7,044	1,482	5,061	486	15	3,579 D	21.0%	71.8%	6.9%
5,764	STEWART	4,323	1,046	2,779	487	11	1,733 D	24.2%	64.3%	11.3%
72,494	SULLIVAN	56,980	28,801	20,935	6,730	514	7,866 R	50.5%	36.7%	11.8%
52,600	SUMNER	42,132	17,401	19,387	5,177	167	1,986 D	41.3%	46.0%	12.3%
19,403	TIPTON	13,717	6,757	5,652	1,279	29	1,105 R	49.3%	41.2%	9.3%
3,915	TROUSDALE	2,664	565	1,846	243	10	1,281 D	21.2%	69.3%	9.1%
8,973	UNICOI	6,447	3,344	2,375	709	19	969 R	51.9%	36.8%	11.0%
9,025	UNION	5,354	2,274	2,478	580	22	204 D	42.5%	46.3%	10.8%
3,420	VAN BUREN	2,080	555	1,329	191	5	774 D	26.7%	63.9%	9.2%
17,616	WARREN	12,355	3,704	7,189	1,415	47	3,485 D	30.0%	58.2%	11.5%
45,354	WASHINGTON	35,483	18,206	13,071	4,002	204	5,135 R	51.3%	36.8%	11.3%
8,147	WAYNE	5,266	2,955	1,868	424	19	1,087 R	56.1%	35.5%	8.1%
16,215	WEAKLEY	11,869	4,800	5,691	1,355	23	891 D	40.4%	47.9%	11.4%
11,229	WHITE	7,074	2,118	4,102	821	33	1,984 D	29.9%	58.0%	11.6%
51,756	WILLIAMSON	40,195	22,015	13,053	5,026	101	8,962 R	54.8%	32.5%	12.5%
36,887	WILSON	29,903	12,061	13,861	3,848	133	1,800 D	40.3%	46.4%	12.9%
2,726,449	TOTAL	1,982,638	841,300	933,521	199,968	7,849	92,221 D	42.4%	47.1%	10.1%

TENNESSEE

CONGRESS

CD	Year	Total Vote	Republican		Democratic		Other Vote	Rep.-Dem. Plurality	Percentage			
									Total Vote		Major Vote	
			Vote	Candidate	Vote	Candidate			Rep.	Dem.	Rep.	Dem.
1	1992	170,158	114,797	QUILLEN, JAMES H.	47,809	CHRISTIAN, J. CARR	7,552	66,988 R	67.5%	28.1%	70.6%	29.4%
2	1992	205,401	148,377	DUNCAN, JOHN J., JR.	52,887	GOODALE, TROY	4,137	95,490 R	72.2%	25.7%	73.7%	26.3%
3	1992	216,533	102,763	WAMP, ZACH	105,693	LLOYD, MARILYN	8,077	2,930 D	47.5%	48.8%	49.3%	50.7%
4	1992	154,511	50,340	JOHNSON, DALE	98,984	COOPER, JIM	5,187	48,644 D	32.6%	64.1%	33.7%	66.3%
5	1992	187,590	49,417	STONE, TOM	125,233	CLEMENT, BOB	12,940	75,816 D	26.3%	66.8%	28.3%	71.7%
6	1992	212,428	86,289	BLACKBURN, MARSHA	120,177	GORDON, BART	5,962	33,888 D	40.6%	56.6%	41.8%	58.2%
7	1992	202,866	125,101	SUNDQUIST, DON	72,062	DAVIS, DAVID R.	5,703	53,039 R	61.7%	35.5%	63.5%	36.5%
8	1992	163,432			136,852	TANNER, JOHN	26,580	136,852 D		83.7%		100.0%
9	1992	212,755	60,606	BLACK, CHARLES L.	123,276	FORD, HAROLD E.	28,873	62,670 D	28.5%	57.9%	33.0%	67.0%

TENNESSEE

1992 GENERAL ELECTION

President   Other vote was 1,847 Independent (Marrou); 1,356 Independent (Brisben); 756 Independent (Gritz); 727 Independent (Fulani); 599 Independent (Hagelin); 579 Independent (Phillips); 511 Independent (Daniels); 460 Independent (LaRouche); 343 Independent (Dodge); 277 Independent (Warren); 233 Independent (Yiamonyiannis); 161 scattered write-in.

Congress   Other vote was 4,126 Independent (Don Fox), 3,416 Independent (Hartley) and 10 scattered write-in in CD 1; 4,134 Independent (Krieg) and 3 scattered write-in in CD 2; 4,433 Independent (Hagan), 2,048 Independent (Melcher), 1,593 Independent (Martin) and 3 scattered write-in in CD 3; 3,970 Independent (Ginnia Fox), 1,210 Independent (Parks) and 7 scattered write-in in CD 4; 6,724 Independent (Edmondson), 3,507 Independent (Wyatt), 1,685 Independent (Haury), 1,002 Independent (Tomeo) and 22 scattered write-in in CD 5; 5,952 Independent (Benson) and 10 scattered write-in in CD 6; 2,290 Independent (Boyette), 1,831 Independent (Osburn), 1,573 Independent (Tapp) and 9 scattered write-in in CD 7; 9,605 Independent (Barnes), 6,930 Independent (Ward), 5,435 Independent (Vinson), 4,600 Independent (McKissack) and 10 scattered write-in in CD 8; 14,075 Independent (Liptock), 12,265 Independent (Vandergriff), 2,517 Independent (Rolen) and 16 scattered write-in in CD 9.

1992 PRIMARIES

AUGUST 6 REPUBLICAN

Congress   Unopposed in four CD's. No candidate in CD 8. Contested as follows:

   CD 3   18,506 Zach Wamp; 2,792 Todd Gardenhire; 2,665 Wayne Watson.
   CD 4   8,432 Dale Johnson; 5,711 Claiborne Sanders; 6 scattered write-in.
   CD 6   8,471 Marsha Blackburn; 3,964 Jeff Whitesides; 1,794 Robert Baker; 883 Porter Stark; 677 Gregory Cochran; 468 William B. Rainey; 460 David L. Schwab; 6 scattered write-in.
   CD 9   6,400 Charles L. Black; 6,240 Rod DeBerry; 2,478 Aaron C. Davis; 8 scattered write-in.

AUGUST 6 DEMOCRATIC

Congress   Unopposed in two CD's. Contested as follows:

   CD 1   8,408 J. Carr Christian; 3,703 Hal Dunning; 9 scattered write-in.
   CD 3   29,895 Marilyn Lloyd; 6,974 David R. Stacy.
   CD 4   52,281 Jim Cooper; 6,370 John Dooley; 3,025 J. Patrick Lyons; 3 scattered write-in.
   CD 5   42,794 Bob Clement; 15,724 Chip Forrester; 6,043 David Mills; 3 scattered write-in.
   CD 6   45,576 Bart Gordon; 4,912 Bob Ries; 4,371 Don Schneller; 7 scattered write-in.
   CD 7   19,538 David R. Davis; 16,004 Guthrie Castle; 5 scattered write-in.
   CD 9   74,145 Harold E.Ford; 36,321 Larry S. Patterson; 2,716 Mark F. Flanagan; 1,555 Terrance H. Endsley.

TEXAS

GOVERNOR
Ann Richards (D). Elected 1990 to a four-year term.

SENATORS
Kay Bailey Hutchison (R). Elected in a special election June 5, 1993 to fill out the remaining year and a half of the term vacated when Senator Lloyd Bentsen (D) resigned to become Secretary of the Tresury.

Phil Gramm (R). Re-elected 1990 to a six-year term. Previously elected 1984.

REPRESENTATIVES
1. James L. Chapman (D)
2. Charles Wilson (D)
3. Sam Johnson (R)
4. Ralph M. Hall (D)
5. John Bryant (D)
6. Joe L. Barton (R)
7. W. R. Archer (R)
8. Jack Fields (R)
9. Jack B. Brooks (D)
10. Jake Pickle (D)
11. Chet Edwards (D)
12. Pete Geren (D)
13. Bill Sarpalius (D)
14. Greg Laughlin (D)
15. Eligio de la Garza (D)
16. Ronald Coleman (D)
17. Charles W. Stenholm (D)
18. Craig A. Washington (D)
19. Larry Combest (R)
20. Henry B. Gonzalez (D)
21. Lamar Smith (R)
22. Thomas D. DeLay (R)
23. Henry Bonilla (R)
24. Martin Frost (D)
25. Mike Andrews (D)
26. Dick Armey (R)
27. Solomon P. Ortiz (D)
28. Frank M. Tejeda (D)
29. Gene Green (D)
30. Eddie B. Johnson (D)

POSTWAR VOTE FOR PRESIDENT

Year	Total Vote	Republican Vote	Republican Candidate	Democratic Vote	Democratic Candidate	Other Vote	Plurality	Total Vote Rep.	Total Vote Dem.	Major Vote Rep.	Major Vote Dem.
1992 * *	6,154,018	2,496,071	Bush, George	2,281,815	Clinton, Bill	1,376,132	214,256 R	40.6%	37.1%	52.2%	47.8%
1988	5,427,410	3,036,829	Bush, George	2,352,748	Dukakis, Michael S.	37,833	684,081 R	56.0%	43.3%	56.3%	43.7%
1984	5,397,571	3,433,428	Reagan, Ronald	1,949,276	Mondale, Walter F.	14,867	1,484,152 R	63.6%	36.1%	63.8%	36.2%
1980	4,541,636	2,510,705	Reagan, Ronald	1,881,147	Carter, Jimmy	149,784	629,558 R	55.3%	41.4%	57.2%	42.8%
1976	4,071,884	1,953,300	Ford, Gerald R.	2,082,319	Carter, Jimmy	36,265	129,019 D	48.0%	51.1%	48.4%	51.6%
1972	3,471,281	2,298,896	Nixon, Richard M.	1,154,289	McGovern, George S.	18,096	1,144,607 R	66.2%	33.3%	66.6%	33.4%
1968 * *	3,079,216	1,227,844	Nixon, Richard M.	1,266,804	Humphrey, Hubert H.	584,568	38,960 D	39.9%	41.1%	49.2%	50.8%
1964	2,626,811	958,566	Goldwater, Barry M.	1,663,185	Johnson, Lyndon B.	5,060	704,619 D	36.5%	63.3%	36.6%	63.4%
1960	2,311,084	1,121,310	Nixon, Richard M.	1,167,567	Kennedy, John F.	22,207	46,257 D	48.5%	50.5%	49.0%	51.0%
1956	1,955,168	1,080,619	Eisenhower, Dwight D.	859,958	Stevenson, Adlai E.	14,591	220,661 R	55.3%	44.0%	55.7%	44.3%
1952	2,075,946	1,102,878	Eisenhower, Dwight D.	969,228	Stevenson, Adlai E.	3,840	133,650 R	53.1%	46.7%	53.2%	46.8%
1948	1,249,577	303,467	Dewey, Thomas E.	824,235	Truman, Harry S.	121,875	520,768 D	24.3%	66.0%	26.9%	73.1%

In 1992 the other vote column includes 1,354,781 votes cast for Perot. In 1968 other vote was 584,269 American (Wallace) and 299 scattered.

TEXAS

POSTWAR VOTE FOR GOVERNOR

Year	Total Vote	Republican		Democratic		Other Vote	Rep.-Dem. Plurality	Percentage			
								Total Vote		Major Vote	
		Vote	Candidate	Vote	Candidate			Rep.	Dem.	Rep.	Dem.
1990	3,892,746	1,826,431	Williams, Clayton	1,925,670	Richards, Ann	140,645	99,239 D	46.9%	49.5%	48.7%	51.3%
1986	3,441,460	1,813,779	Clements, William P.	1,584,515	White, Mark	43,166	229,264 R	52.7%	46.0%	53.4%	46.6%
1982	3,191,091	1,465,937	Clements, William P.	1,697,870	White, Mark	27,284	231,933 D	45.9%	53.2%	46.3%	53.7%
1978	2,369,764	1,183,839	Clements, William P.	1,166,979	Hill, John	18,946	16,860 R	50.0%	49.2%	50.4%	49.6%
1974 **	1,654,984	514,725	Granberry, Jim	1,016,334	Briscoe, Dolph	123,925	501,609 D	31.1%	61.4%	33.6%	66.4%
1972	3,410,128	1,534,060	Grover, Henry C.	1,633,970	Briscoe, Dolph	242,098	99,910 D	45.0%	47.9%	48.4%	51.6%
1970	2,235,847	1,037,723	Eggers, Paul W.	1,197,726	Smith, Preston	398	160,003 D	46.4%	53.6%	46.4%	53.6%
1968	2,916,509	1,254,333	Eggers, Paul W.	1,662,019	Smith, Preston	157	407,686 D	43.0%	57.0%	43.0%	57.0%
1966	1,425,861	368,025	Kennerly, T. E.	1,037,517	Connally, John B.	20,319	669,492 D	25.8%	72.8%	26.2%	73.8%
1964	2,544,753	661,675	Crichton, Jack	1,877,793	Connally, John B.	5,285	1,216,118 D	26.0%	73.8%	26.1%	73.9%
1962	1,569,181	715,025	Cox, Jack	847,036	Connally, John B.	7,120	132,011 D	45.6%	54.0%	45.8%	54.2%
1960	2,250,718	612,963	Steger, William M.	1,637,755	Daniel, Price		1,024,792 D	27.2%	72.8%	27.2%	72.8%
1958	789,133	94,098	Mayer, Edwin S.	695,035	Daniel, Price		600,937 D	11.9%	88.1%	11.9%	88.1%
1956	1,828,161	271,088	Bryant, William R.	1,433,051	Daniel, Price	124,022	1,161,963 D	14.8%	78.4%	15.9%	84.1%
1954	636,892	66,154	Adams, Tod R.	569,533	Shivers, Allan	1,205	503,379 D	10.4%	89.4%	10.4%	89.6%
1952	1,881,202		—	1,844,530	Shivers, Allan	36,672	1,844,530 D		98.1%		100.0%
1950	394,747	39,737	Currie, Ralph W.	355,010	Shivers, Allan		315,273 D	10.1%	89.9%	10.1%	89.9%
1948	1,208,860	177,399	Lane, Alvin H.	1,024,160	Jester, Beauford	7,301	846,761 D	14.7%	84.7%	14.8%	85.2%
1946	378,744	33,231	Nolte, Eugene	345,513	Jester, Beauford		312,282 D	8.8%	91.2%	8.8%	91.2%

The term of office of Texas' Governor was increased from two to four years effective with the 1974 election.

POSTWAR VOTE FOR SENATOR

Year	Total Vote	Republican		Democratic		Other Vote	Rep.-Dem. Plurality	Percentage			
								Total Vote		Major Vote	
		Vote	Candidate	Vote	Candidate			Rep.	Dem.	Rep.	Dem.
1990	3,822,157	2,302,357	Gramm, Phil	1,429,986	Parmer, Hugh	89,814	872,371 R	60.2%	37.4%	61.7%	38.3%
1988	5,323,606	2,129,228	Boulter, Beau	3,149,806	Bentsen, Lloyd	44,572	1,020,578 D	40.0%	59.2%	40.3%	59.7%
1984	5,319,178	3,116,348	Gramm, Phil	2,202,557	Doggett, Lloyd	273	913,791 R	58.6%	41.4%	58.6%	41.4%
1982	3,103,167	1,256,759	Collins, James M.	1,818,223	Bentsen, Lloyd	28,185	561,464 D	40.5%	58.6%	40.9%	59.1%
1978	2,312,540	1,151,376	Tower, John G.	1,139,149	Krueger, Robert	22,015	12,227 R	49.8%	49.3%	50.3%	49.7%
1976	3,874,516	1,636,370	Steelman, Alan	2,199,956	Bentsen, Lloyd	38,190	563,586 D	42.2%	56.8%	42.7%	57.3%
1972	3,413,903	1,822,877	Tower, John G.	1,511,985	Sanders, Barefoot	79,041	310,892 R	53.4%	44.3%	54.7%	45.3%
1970	2,231,671	1,035,794	Bush, George	1,194,069	Bentsen, Lloyd	1,808	158,275 D	46.4%	53.5%	46.5%	53.5%
1966	1,493,182	842,501	Tower, John G.	643,855	Carr, Waggoner	6,826	198,646 R	56.4%	43.1%	56.7%	43.3%
1964	2,603,856	1,134,337	Bush, George	1,463,958	Yarborough, Ralph	5,561	329,621 D	43.6%	56.2%	43.7%	56.3%
1961 S	886,091	448,217	Tower, John G.	437,874	Blakley, William A.		10,343 R	50.6%	49.4%	50.6%	49.4%
1960	2,253,784	926,653	Tower, John G.	1,306,625	Johnson, Lyndon B.	20,506	379,972 D	41.1%	58.0%	41.5%	58.5%
1958	787,128	185,926	Whittenburg, Roy	587,030	Yarborough, Ralph	14,172	401,104 D	23.6%	74.6%	24.1%	75.9%
1957 S	957,298		[See note below]								
1954	636,475	94,131	Watson, Carlos G.	539,319	Johnson, Lyndon B.	3,025	445,188 D	14.8%	84.7%	14.9%	85.1%
1952	1,895,192		—	1,895,192	Daniel, Price		1,895,192 D		100.0%		100.0%
1948	1,061,563	349,665	Porter, Jack	702,985	Johnson, Lyndon B.	8,913	353,320 D	32.9%	66.2%	33.2%	66.8%
1946	380,681	43,750	Sells, Murray C.	336,931	Connally, Tom		293,181 D	11.5%	88.5%	11.5%	88.5%

The May 1961 and April 1957 elections were for short terms to fill vacancies. Though neither vote was held with official party designations, the 1961 vote above was a run-off contest between unofficial party candidates. In 1957 there was a single ballot without run-off and Ralph Yarborough polled 364,605 votes (38.1% of the total vote) and won the election with a 73,802 plurality.

TEXAS

Districts Established August 29, 1991

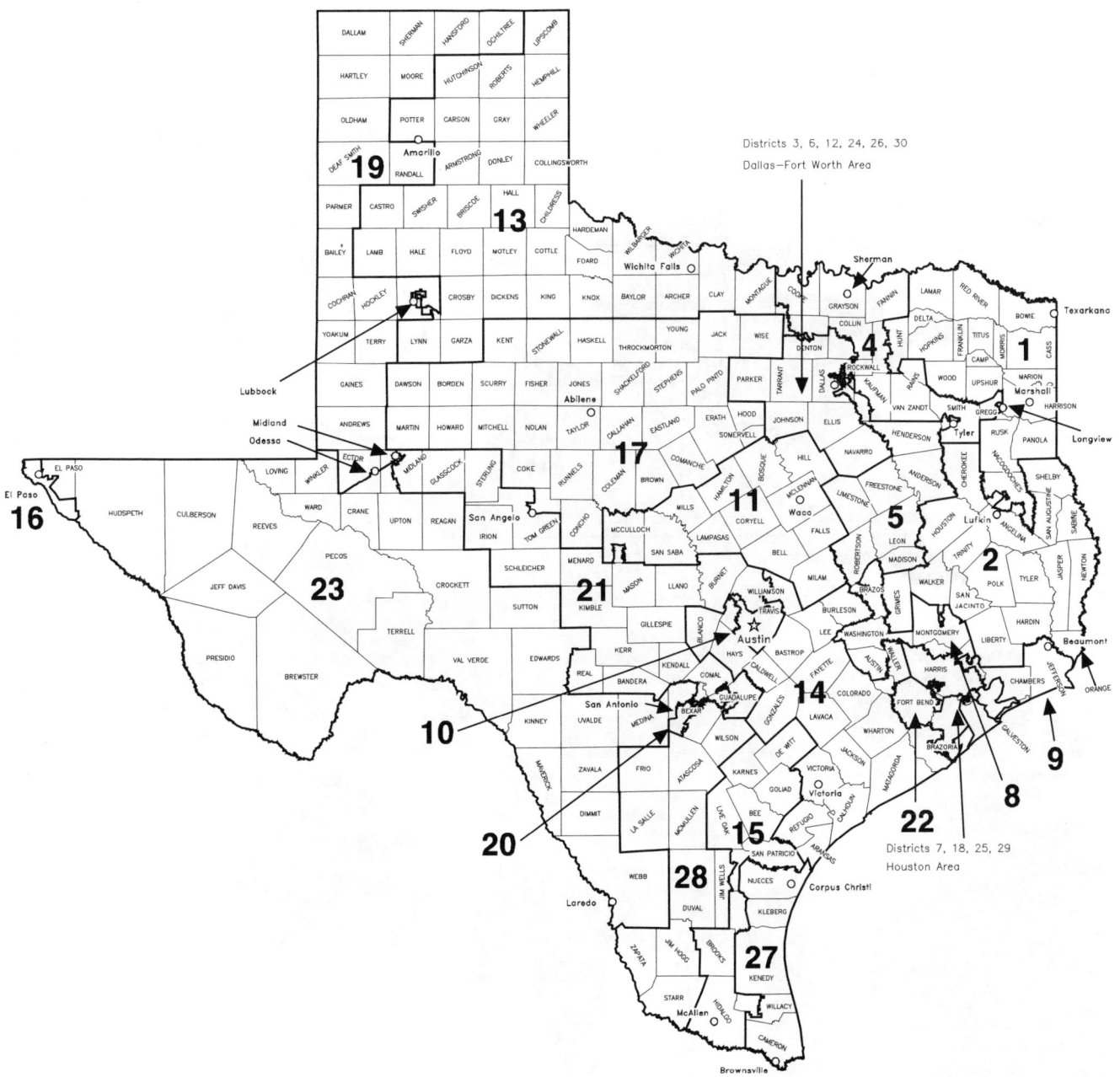

HOUSTON METROPOLITAN AREA

CONGRESSIONAL DISTRICTS

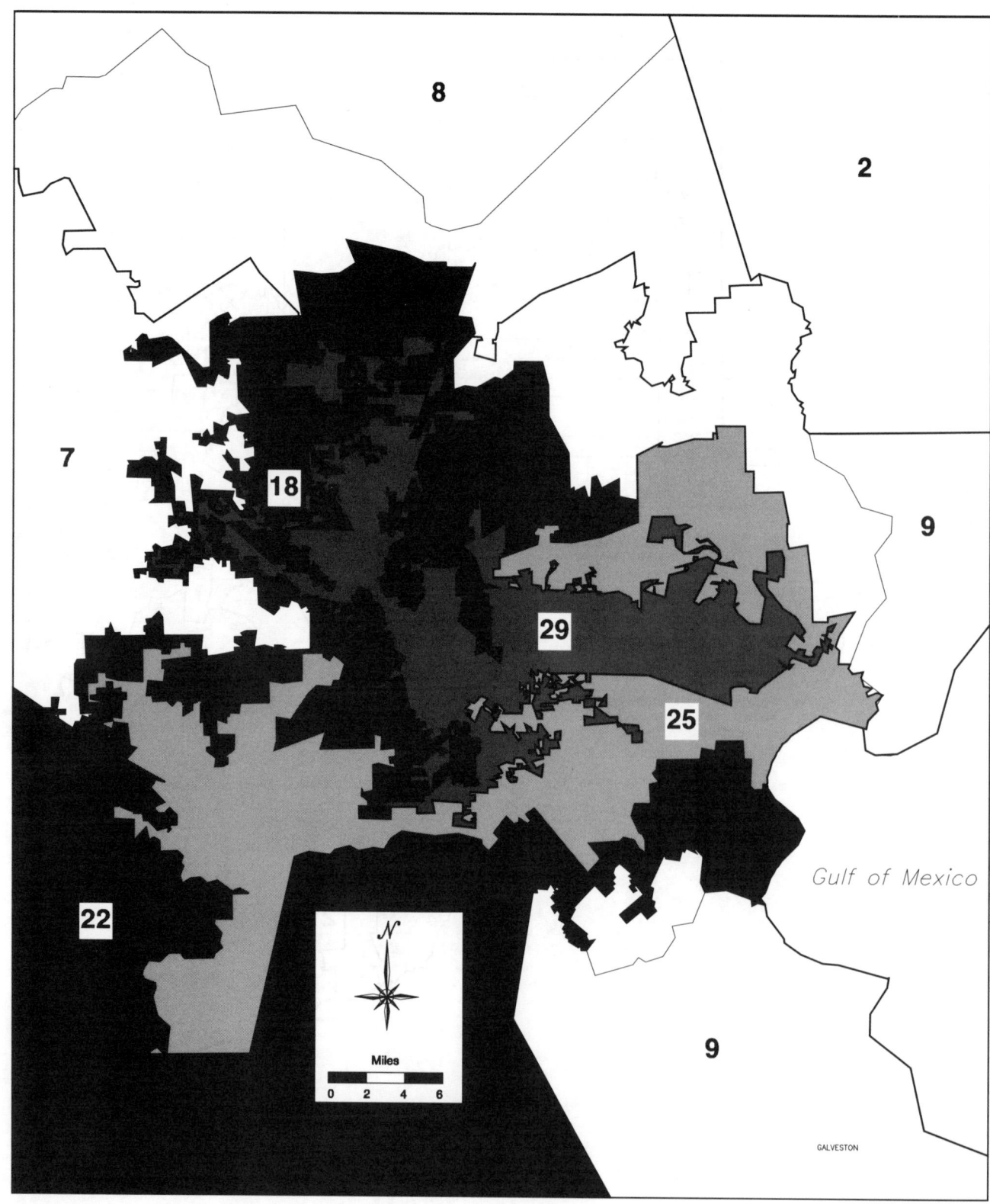

Harris County

Assembly District Boundaries

TEXAS

PRESIDENT 1992

Registration	County	Total Vote	Republican	Democratic	Perot	Other	Plurality	Percentage Total Vote Rep.	Dem.	Perot
20,747	ANDERSON	14,466	5,598	5,322	3,519	27	276 R	38.7%	36.8%	24.3%
6,057	ANDREWS	4,228	2,266	1,081	875	6	1,185 R	53.6%	25.6%	20.7%
35,811	ANGELINA	26,281	9,722	10,318	6,204	37	596 D	37.0%	39.3%	23.6%
8,814	ARANSAS	6,770	2,826	2,246	1,676	22	580 R	41.7%	33.2%	24.8%
5,128	ARCHER	3,967	1,560	1,284	1,106	17	276 R	39.3%	32.4%	27.9%
1,301	ARMSTRONG	1,028	561	278	187	2	283 R	54.6%	27.0%	18.2%
15,751	ATASCOSA	9,658	3,806	3,766	2,035	51	40 R	39.4%	39.0%	21.1%
10,633	AUSTIN	7,890	4,015	2,278	1,585	12	1,737 R	50.9%	28.9%	20.1%
3,437	BAILEY	2,365	1,308	677	376	4	631 R	55.3%	28.6%	15.9%
6,776	BANDERA	5,322	2,674	1,059	1,537	52	1,137 R	50.2%	19.9%	28.9%
20,624	BASTROP	14,474	4,980	6,252	3,240	2	1,272 D	34.4%	43.2%	22.4%
3,055	BAYLOR	2,132	611	990	529	2	379 D	28.7%	46.4%	24.8%
15,071	BEE	9,108	3,633	4,083	1,367	25	450 D	39.9%	44.8%	15.0%
73,966	BELL	55,077	24,936	18,684	11,026	431	6,252 R	45.3%	33.9%	20.0%
584,335	BEXAR	415,276	168,816	172,513	72,110	1,837	3,697 D	40.7%	41.5%	17.4%
3,831	BLANCO	3,109	1,370	891	830	18	479 R	44.1%	28.7%	26.7%
501	BORDEN	378	184	106	87	1	78 R	48.7%	28.0%	23.0%
8,710	BOSQUE	6,489	2,300	2,173	1,999	17	127 R	35.4%	33.5%	30.8%
43,047	BOWIE	30,365	11,776	11,825	6,659	105	49 D	38.8%	38.9%	21.9%
95,022	BRAZORIA	71,467	30,384	21,861	18,954	268	8,523 R	42.5%	30.6%	26.5%
60,915	BRAZOS	49,340	23,943	14,819	10,372	206	9,124 R	48.5%	30.0%	21.0%
5,117	BREWSTER	3,247	1,127	1,383	712	25	256 D	34.7%	42.6%	21.9%
1,328	BRISCOE	957	360	430	164	3	70 D	37.6%	44.9%	17.1%
6,236	BROOKS	3,765	585	2,856	318	6	2,271 D	15.5%	75.9%	8.4%
17,815	BROWN	12,630	5,313	4,264	3,034	19	1,049 R	42.1%	33.8%	24.0%
8,120	BURLESON	5,711	2,013	2,511	1,179	8	498 D	35.2%	44.0%	20.6%
13,844	BURNET	10,807	4,272	3,638	2,865	32	634 R	39.5%	33.7%	26.5%
12,299	CALDWELL	8,344	2,749	3,794	1,776	25	1,045 D	32.9%	45.5%	21.3%
10,126	CALHOUN	6,779	2,640	2,550	1,579	10	90 R	38.9%	37.6%	23.3%
7,037	CALLAHAN	5,285	2,134	1,694	1,452	5	440 R	40.4%	32.1%	27.5%
100,193	CAMERON	59,057	20,123	29,435	9,286	213	9,312 D	34.1%	49.8%	15.7%
5,786	CAMP	3,980	1,219	1,938	821	2	719 D	30.6%	48.7%	20.6%
3,986	CARSON	3,057	1,647	825	578	7	822 R	53.9%	27.0%	18.9%
17,352	CASS	11,660	3,999	5,476	2,168	17	1,477 D	34.3%	47.0%	18.6%
4,453	CASTRO	2,910	1,307	1,113	485	5	194 R	44.9%	38.2%	16.7%
11,575	CHAMBERS	8,366	3,398	2,832	2,122	14	566 R	40.6%	33.9%	25.4%
20,525	CHEROKEE	14,138	5,847	5,003	3,273	15	844 R	41.4%	35.4%	23.2%
3,306	CHILDRESS	2,338	1,033	881	421	3	152 R	44.2%	37.7%	18.0%
6,357	CLAY	4,910	1,586	1,919	1,397	8	333 D	32.3%	39.1%	28.5%
2,189	COCHRAN	1,461	750	454	255	2	296 R	51.3%	31.1%	17.5%
2,171	COKE	1,614	640	580	393	1	60 R	39.7%	35.9%	24.3%
6,001	COLEMAN	4,138	1,462	1,579	1,095	2	117 D	35.3%	38.2%	26.5%
153,736	COLLIN	128,833	60,514	24,508	43,287	524	17,227 R	47.0%	19.0%	33.6%
2,159	COLLINGSWORTH	1,600	697	635	265	3	62 R	43.6%	39.7%	16.6%
10,171	COLORADO	7,162	3,286	2,442	1,421	13	844 R	45.9%	34.1%	19.8%
31,616	COMAL	24,941	12,651	6,312	5,841	137	6,339 R	50.7%	25.3%	23.4%
7,204	COMANCHE	5,248	1,666	2,296	1,281	5	630 D	31.7%	43.8%	24.4%
1,732	CONCHO	1,236	414	489	329	4	75 D	33.5%	39.6%	26.6%
17,388	COOKE	13,084	5,299	3,105	4,658	22	641 R	40.5%	23.7%	35.6%
19,591	CORYELL	14,312	6,144	4,157	3,974	37	1,987 R	42.9%	29.0%	27.8%
1,562	COTTLE	1,025	245	542	235	3	297 D	23.9%	52.9%	22.9%
2,530	CRANE	1,845	918	514	412	1	404 R	49.8%	27.9%	22.3%
2,626	CROCKETT	1,645	623	653	368	1	30 D	37.9%	39.7%	22.4%
3,736	CROSBY	2,335	1,006	1,010	313	6	4 D	43.1%	43.3%	13.4%
1,730	CULBERSON	847	251	424	171	1	173 D	29.6%	50.1%	20.2%
2,328	DALLAM	1,683	922	434	325	2	488 R	54.8%	25.8%	19.3%
879,137	DALLAS	661,252	256,007	231,412	170,571	3,262	24,595 R	38.7%	35.0%	25.8%
7,427	DAWSON	4,855	2,691	1,639	518	7	1,052 R	55.4%	33.8%	10.7%
8,277	DEAF SMITH	5,559	3,137	1,642	772	8	1,495 R	56.4%	29.5%	13.9%
2,857	DELTA	2,015	599	864	551	1	265 D	29.7%	42.9%	27.3%

TEXAS

PRESIDENT 1992

Registration	County	Total Vote	Republican	Democratic	Perot	Other	Plurality	Percentage Total Vote		
								Rep.	Dem.	Perot
148,476	DENTON	116,576	48,492	27,891	39,653	540	8,839 R	41.6%	23.9%	34.0%
10,139	DE WITT	6,730	3,238	2,127	1,346	19	1,111 R	48.1%	31.6%	20.0%
1,687	DICKENS	1,160	373	536	250	1	163 D	32.2%	46.2%	21.6%
7,376	DIMMIT	4,380	844	3,172	361	3	2,328 D	19.3%	72.4%	8.2%
2,289	DONLEY	1,735	893	578	260	4	315 R	51.5%	33.3%	15.0%
9,178	DUVAL	5,035	698	4,006	326	5	3,308 D	13.9%	79.6%	6.5%
10,130	EASTLAND	7,281	2,830	2,738	1,698	15	92 R	38.9%	37.6%	23.3%
49,865	ECTOR	36,073	18,161	11,130	6,668	114	7,031 R	50.3%	30.9%	18.5%
1,333	EDWARDS	887	460	254	171	2	206 R	51.9%	28.6%	19.3%
44,756	ELLIS	33,495	13,564	9,537	10,303	91	3,261 R	40.5%	28.5%	30.8%
210,125	EL PASO	135,163	47,224	67,715	19,738	486	20,491 D	34.9%	50.1%	14.6%
13,128	ERATH	10,431	3,835	3,531	3,046	19	304 R	36.8%	33.9%	29.2%
9,075	FALLS	5,773	1,826	2,761	1,185	1	935 D	31.6%	47.8%	20.5%
13,338	FANNIN	9,615	2,510	4,164	2,919	22	1,245 D	26.1%	43.3%	30.4%
11,514	FAYETTE	8,823	3,789	2,923	2,088	23	866 R	42.9%	33.1%	23.7%
3,103	FISHER	2,225	539	1,242	442	2	703 D	24.2%	55.8%	19.9%
4,764	FLOYD	3,009	1,676	947	385	1	729 R	55.7%	31.5%	12.8%
1,178	FOARD	796	207	435	152	2	228 D	26.0%	54.6%	19.1%
101,368	FORT BEND	88,031	41,039	29,992	16,853	147	11,047 R	46.6%	34.1%	19.1%
4,468	FRANKLIN	3,342	1,058	1,338	942	4	280 D	31.7%	40.0%	28.2%
9,024	FREESTONE	6,365	2,316	2,445	1,596	8	129 D	36.4%	38.4%	25.1%
8,081	FRIO	4,319	1,275	2,377	654	13	1,102 D	29.5%	55.0%	15.1%
5,627	GAINES	3,933	2,138	1,095	696	4	1,043 R	54.4%	27.8%	17.7%
122,859	GALVESTON	90,242	31,303	38,623	20,103	213	7,320 D	34.7%	42.8%	22.3%
2,863	GARZA	1,888	982	558	345	3	424 R	52.0%	29.6%	18.3%
10,548	GILLESPIE	8,372	4,712	1,600	2,018	42	2,694 R	56.3%	19.1%	24.1%
729	GLASSCOCK	574	379	100	93	2	279 R	66.0%	17.4%	16.2%
3,776	GOLIAD	2,831	1,236	1,069	521	5	167 R	43.7%	37.8%	18.4%
9,757	GONZALES	5,557	2,502	2,006	1,018	31	496 R	45.0%	36.1%	18.3%
13,272	GRAY	10,372	6,105	2,426	1,810	31	3,679 R	58.9%	23.4%	17.5%
51,204	GRAYSON	38,332	12,322	12,547	13,327	136	780 P	32.1%	32.7%	34.8%
57,718	GREGG	41,829	20,542	12,797	8,437	53	7,745 R	49.1%	30.6%	20.2%
8,810	GRIMES	6,217	2,402	2,594	1,213	8	192 D	38.6%	41.7%	19.5%
32,208	GUADALUPE	23,120	10,818	6,567	5,618	117	4,251 R	46.8%	28.4%	24.3%
15,412	HALE	10,234	6,098	2,761	1,357	18	3,337 R	59.6%	27.0%	13.3%
2,783	HALL	1,714	631	819	263	1	188 D	36.8%	47.8%	15.3%
4,454	HAMILTON	3,259	1,232	1,100	921	6	132 R	37.8%	33.8%	28.3%
3,036	HANSFORD	2,403	1,660	345	398		1,262 R	69.1%	14.4%	16.6%
2,820	HARDEMAN	1,936	614	954	362	6	340 D	31.7%	49.3%	18.7%
26,140	HARDIN	16,793	5,885	6,753	4,129	26	868 D	35.0%	40.2%	24.6%
1,315,010	HARRIS	942,947	406,778	360,171	172,922	3,076	46,607 R	43.1%	38.2%	18.3%
31,776	HARRISON	22,683	8,733	9,538	4,371	41	805 D	38.5%	42.0%	19.3%
2,296	HARTLEY	1,797	1,081	406	308	2	675 R	60.2%	22.6%	17.1%
4,138	HASKELL	2,853	852	1,438	562	1	586 D	29.9%	50.4%	19.7%
36,020	HAYS	27,267	10,008	10,842	6,252	165	834 D	36.7%	39.8%	22.9%
2,103	HEMPHILL	1,700	989	479	232		510 R	58.2%	28.2%	13.6%
33,193	HENDERSON	24,261	8,368	9,105	6,746	42	737 D	34.5%	37.5%	27.8%
152,147	HIDALGO	88,160	26,976	51,205	9,757	222	24,229 D	30.6%	58.1%	11.1%
14,202	HILL	10,376	3,669	3,929	2,752	26	260 D	35.4%	37.9%	26.5%
11,497	HOCKLEY	7,868	4,261	2,301	1,291	15	1,960 R	54.2%	29.2%	16.4%
17,354	HOOD	14,162	5,313	4,359	4,457	33	856 R	37.5%	30.8%	31.5%
13,763	HOPKINS	10,643	3,398	4,085	3,147	13	687 D	31.9%	38.4%	29.6%
11,895	HOUSTON	8,020	3,067	3,250	1,690	13	183 D	38.2%	40.5%	21.1%
15,557	HOWARD	10,873	5,129	3,735	1,984	25	1,394 R	47.2%	34.4%	18.2%
1,367	HUDSPETH	869	325	364	178	2	39 D	37.4%	41.9%	20.5%
32,609	HUNT	24,650	9,739	7,452	7,387	72	2,287 R	39.5%	30.2%	30.0%
14,192	HUTCHINSON	10,888	6,034	2,833	1,993	28	3,201 R	55.4%	26.0%	18.3%
1,146	IRION	831	283	256	290	2	7 P	34.1%	30.8%	34.9%
4,332	JACK	3,347	1,041	1,254	1,045	7	209 D	31.1%	37.5%	31.2%
7,241	JACKSON	5,152	2,451	1,722	976	3	729 R	47.6%	33.4%	18.9%

TEXAS

PRESIDENT 1992

Registration	County	Total Vote	Republican	Democratic	Perot	Other	Plurality	Percentage Total Vote		
								Rep.	Dem.	Perot
20,259	JASPER	12,087	3,870	5,658	2,539	20	1,788 D	32.0%	46.8%	21.0%
1,210	JEFF DAVIS	876	360	321	187	8	39 R	41.1%	36.6%	21.3%
135,220	JEFFERSON	95,543	29,622	48,405	17,242	274	18,783 D	31.0%	50.7%	18.0%
3,735	JIM HOGG	2,110	478	1,520	107	5	1,042 D	22.7%	72.0%	5.1%
21,207	JIM WELLS	12,561	3,311	7,812	1,413	25	4,501 D	26.4%	62.2%	11.2%
49,801	JOHNSON	37,202	13,473	12,030	11,573	126	1,443 R	36.2%	32.3%	31.1%
8,043	JONES	5,932	2,088	2,400	1,436	8	312 D	35.2%	40.5%	24.2%
7,100	KARNES	4,700	1,990	1,897	802	11	93 R	42.3%	40.4%	17.1%
25,771	KAUFMAN	19,060	6,578	6,498	5,913	71	80 R	34.5%	34.1%	31.0%
9,248	KENDALL	7,354	4,162	1,374	1,773	45	2,389 R	56.6%	18.7%	24.1%
297	KENEDY	174	69	87	18		18 D	39.7%	50.0%	10.3%
801	KENT	610	175	271	163	1	96 D	28.7%	44.4%	26.7%
21,370	KERR	16,358	8,787	3,707	3,790	74	4,997 R	53.7%	22.7%	23.2%
2,264	KIMBLE	1,613	790	467	354	2	323 R	49.0%	29.0%	21.9%
223	KING	189	79	54	56		23 R	41.8%	28.6%	29.6%
1,930	KINNEY	1,539	634	598	299	8	36 R	41.2%	38.9%	19.4%
14,996	KLEBERG	10,564	3,897	5,109	1,470	88	1,212 D	36.9%	48.4%	13.9%
2,669	KNOX	1,815	521	854	438	2	333 D	28.7%	47.1%	24.1%
23,556	LAMAR	16,243	5,778	6,328	4,093	44	550 D	35.6%	39.0%	25.2%
8,340	LAMB	5,450	2,998	1,737	709	6	1,261 R	55.0%	31.9%	13.0%
7,101	LAMPASAS	5,185	2,233	1,508	1,432	12	725 R	43.1%	29.1%	27.6%
3,897	LA SALLE	2,319	586	1,522	211		936 D	25.3%	65.6%	9.1%
10,791	LAVACA	7,776	3,362	2,700	1,696	18	662 R	43.2%	34.7%	21.8%
6,708	LEE	5,058	2,108	1,847	1,088	15	261 R	41.7%	36.5%	21.5%
8,348	LEON	5,508	2,212	2,042	1,251	3	170 R	40.2%	37.1%	22.7%
26,497	LIBERTY	18,339	6,959	7,036	4,311	33	77 D	37.9%	38.4%	23.5%
10,712	LIMESTONE	7,060	2,358	3,188	1,505	9	830 D	33.4%	45.2%	21.3%
1,834	LIPSCOMB	1,453	839	338	270	6	501 R	57.7%	23.3%	18.6%
6,265	LIVE OAK	3,965	1,805	1,345	806	9	460 R	45.5%	33.9%	20.3%
8,723	LLANO	7,283	3,056	2,409	1,799	19	647 R	42.0%	33.1%	24.7%
116	LOVING	96	31	20	45		14 P	32.3%	20.8%	46.9%
109,552	LUBBOCK	82,858	48,847	22,240	11,618	153	26,607 R	59.0%	26.8%	14.0%
4,001	LYNN	2,428	1,233	902	291	2	331 R	50.8%	37.1%	12.0%
4,778	MCCULLOCH	3,491	1,108	1,393	986	4	285 D	31.7%	39.9%	28.2%
98,807	MCLENNAN	70,016	28,473	25,903	15,505	135	2,570 R	40.7%	37.0%	22.1%
631	MCMULLEN	443	274	78	89	2	185 R	61.9%	17.6%	20.1%
5,585	MADISON	3,883	1,544	1,553	778	8	9 D	39.8%	40.0%	20.0%
6,565	MARION	4,288	1,245	2,156	882	5	911 D	29.0%	50.3%	20.6%
2,744	MARTIN	1,988	986	641	356	5	345 R	49.6%	32.2%	17.9%
2,274	MASON	1,722	776	570	364	12	206 R	45.1%	33.1%	21.1%
18,513	MATAGORDA	13,165	5,328	4,759	3,045	33	569 R	40.5%	36.1%	23.1%
13,343	MAVERICK	7,339	2,002	4,540	771	26	2,538 D	27.3%	61.9%	10.5%
15,209	MEDINA	10,785	4,912	3,650	2,167	56	1,262 R	45.5%	33.8%	20.1%
1,643	MENARD	1,277	354	553	367	3	186 D	27.7%	43.3%	28.7%
51,714	MIDLAND	41,347	24,143	9,160	7,880	164	14,983 R	58.4%	22.2%	19.1%
11,919	MILAM	7,468	2,414	3,542	1,495	17	1,128 D	32.3%	47.4%	20.0%
2,569	MILLS	1,990	702	753	530	5	51 D	35.3%	37.8%	26.6%
4,542	MITCHELL	3,093	1,128	1,353	604	8	225 D	36.5%	43.7%	19.5%
10,227	MONTAGUE	7,526	2,304	2,885	2,330	7	555 D	30.6%	38.3%	31.0%
99,354	MONTGOMERY	77,958	39,976	18,551	19,203	228	20,773 R	51.3%	23.8%	24.6%
7,472	MOORE	5,498	3,147	1,361	976	14	1,786 R	57.2%	24.8%	17.8%
8,173	MORRIS	5,569	1,400	3,028	1,138	3	1,628 D	25.1%	54.4%	20.4%
1,099	MOTLEY	819	446	256	117		190 R	54.5%	31.3%	14.3%
30,727	NACOGDOCHES	21,643	9,864	6,937	4,803	39	2,927 R	45.6%	32.1%	22.2%
20,821	NAVARRO	14,721	4,897	6,006	3,800	18	1,109 D	33.3%	40.8%	25.8%
8,473	NEWTON	5,508	1,212	3,249	1,032	15	2,037 D	22.0%	59.0%	18.7%
8,222	NOLAN	5,952	1,993	2,490	1,455	14	497 D	33.5%	41.8%	24.4%
144,844	NUECES	100,791	36,781	46,317	17,374	319	9,536 D	36.5%	46.0%	17.2%
4,561	OCHILTREE	3,554	2,419	557	576	2	1,843 R	68.1%	15.7%	16.2%
1,290	OLDHAM	987	583	225	177	2	358 R	59.1%	22.8%	17.9%

TEXAS

PRESIDENT 1992

Registration	County	Total Vote	Republican	Democratic	Perot	Other	Plurality	Percentage Total Vote		
								Rep.	Dem.	Perot
43,821	ORANGE	32,490	9,793	15,305	7,321	71	5,512 D	30.1%	47.1%	22.5%
13,164	PALO PINTO	9,275	2,852	3,392	3,010	21	382 D	30.7%	36.6%	32.5%
12,926	PANOLA	9,332	3,473	3,950	1,906	3	477 D	37.2%	42.3%	20.4%
34,020	PARKER	27,494	10,321	7,934	9,148	91	1,173 R	37.5%	28.9%	33.3%
3,861	PARMER	3,033	1,829	637	564	3	1,192 R	60.3%	21.0%	18.6%
7,323	PECOS	4,523	1,836	1,778	895	14	58 R	40.6%	39.3%	19.8%
20,799	POLK	14,254	5,390	5,942	2,884	38	552 D	37.8%	41.7%	20.2%
36,395	POTTER	27,775	13,510	9,527	4,655	83	3,983 R	48.6%	34.3%	16.8%
3,050	PRESIDIO	1,891	400	1,189	290	12	789 D	21.2%	62.9%	15.3%
3,941	RAINS	2,983	975	1,108	890	10	133 D	32.7%	37.1%	29.8%
49,960	RANDALL	40,537	24,971	9,119	6,340	107	15,852 R	61.6%	22.5%	15.6%
1,840	REAGAN	1,250	651	337	259	3	314 R	52.1%	27.0%	20.7%
2,123	REAL	1,640	787	463	386	4	324 R	48.0%	28.2%	23.5%
8,544	RED RIVER	5,655	1,735	2,686	1,228	6	951 D	30.7%	47.5%	21.7%
7,371	REEVES	4,557	1,244	2,569	734	10	1,325 D	27.3%	56.4%	16.1%
5,201	REFUGIO	3,732	1,469	1,531	716	16	62 D	39.4%	41.0%	19.2%
781	ROBERTS	617	391	126	99	1	265 R	63.4%	20.4%	16.0%
8,968	ROBERTSON	5,604	1,707	2,927	963	7	1,220 D	30.5%	52.2%	17.2%
16,277	ROCKWALL	13,269	6,427	2,397	4,393	52	2,034 R	48.4%	18.1%	33.1%
6,278	RUNNELS	4,340	1,653	1,401	1,279	7	252 R	38.1%	32.3%	29.5%
25,103	RUSK	16,574	7,560	5,391	3,575	48	2,169 R	45.6%	32.5%	21.6%
6,699	SABINE	4,678	1,490	2,288	894	6	798 D	31.9%	48.9%	19.1%
6,109	SAN AUGUSTINE	3,649	1,243	1,737	667	2	494 D	34.1%	47.6%	18.3%
9,784	SAN JACINTO	7,011	2,494	2,846	1,653	18	352 D	35.6%	40.6%	23.6%
30,302	SAN PATRICIO	18,887	7,456	8,202	3,178	51	746 D	39.5%	43.4%	16.8%
3,167	SAN SABA	2,103	723	716	660	4	7 R	34.4%	34.0%	31.4%
1,669	SCHLEICHER	1,231	452	420	355	4	32 R	36.7%	34.1%	28.8%
8,724	SCURRY	6,121	2,670	1,609	1,826	16	844 R	43.6%	26.3%	29.8%
2,362	SHACKELFORD	1,533	623	484	422	4	139 R	40.6%	31.6%	27.5%
13,616	SHELBY	8,705	3,217	3,986	1,487	15	769 D	37.0%	45.8%	17.1%
1,704	SHERMAN	1,369	851	261	256	1	590 R	62.2%	19.1%	18.7%
79,968	SMITH	59,006	27,753	17,514	13,569	170	10,239 R	47.0%	29.7%	23.0%
3,495	SOMERVELL	2,568	872	782	903	11	31 P	34.0%	30.5%	35.2%
17,030	STARR	9,261	1,209	7,668	345	39	6,459 D	13.1%	82.8%	3.7%
5,349	STEPHENS	3,756	1,573	1,115	1,062	6	458 R	41.9%	29.7%	28.3%
838	STERLING	634	322	127	182	3	140 R	50.8%	20.0%	28.7%
1,441	STONEWALL	1,125	242	561	322		239 D	21.5%	49.9%	28.6%
2,317	SUTTON	1,598	687	524	387		163 R	43.0%	32.8%	24.2%
4,315	SWISHER	2,949	989	1,413	541	6	424 D	33.5%	47.9%	18.3%
596,958	TARRANT	471,396	183,387	156,230	129,998	1,781	27,157 R	38.9%	33.1%	27.6%
58,096	TAYLOR	45,454	22,614	12,382	10,331	127	10,232 R	49.8%	27.2%	22.7%
896	TERRELL	631	176	325	128	2	149 D	27.9%	51.5%	20.3%
6,998	TERRY	4,395	2,309	1,461	619	6	848 R	52.5%	33.2%	14.1%
1,347	THROCKMORTON	1,018	389	401	228		12 D	38.2%	39.4%	22.4%
12,283	TITUS	8,810	3,024	3,625	2,146	15	601 D	34.3%	41.1%	24.4%
47,892	TOM GREEN	36,739	14,989	11,437	10,244	69	3,552 R	40.8%	31.1%	27.9%
352,737	TRAVIS	276,235	88,105	130,546	56,158	1,426	42,441 D	31.9%	47.3%	20.3%
8,791	TRINITY	5,909	1,988	2,784	1,133	4	796 D	33.6%	47.1%	19.2%
10,749	TYLER	7,360	2,357	3,465	1,529	9	1,108 D	32.0%	47.1%	20.8%
17,348	UPSHUR	12,208	4,511	4,776	2,896	25	265 D	37.0%	39.1%	23.7%
2,419	UPTON	1,756	908	489	313	46	419 R	51.7%	27.8%	17.8%
13,279	UVALDE	8,543	3,635	3,482	1,387	39	153 R	42.5%	40.8%	16.2%
15,545	VAL VERDE	10,996	4,102	4,748	2,093	53	646 D	37.3%	43.2%	19.0%
23,102	VAN ZANDT	16,396	5,810	5,310	5,239	37	500 R	35.4%	32.4%	32.0%
37,179	VICTORIA	26,037	13,086	7,604	5,136	211	5,482 R	50.3%	29.2%	19.7%
21,558	WALKER	15,924	6,662	5,619	3,619	24	1,043 R	41.8%	35.3%	22.7%
15,041	WALLER	9,058	3,065	4,270	1,692	31	1,205 D	33.8%	47.1%	18.7%
6,261	WARD	4,422	1,769	1,695	948	10	74 R	40.0%	38.3%	21.4%
14,899	WASHINGTON	10,853	5,817	3,283	1,738	15	2,534 R	53.6%	30.2%	16.0%
52,178	WEBB	24,866	7,789	14,509	2,517	51	6,720 D	31.3%	58.3%	10.1%

TEXAS

PRESIDENT 1992

Registration	County	Total Vote	Republican	Democratic	Perot	Other	Plurality	Percentage Total Vote		
								Rep.	Dem.	Perot
19,017	WHARTON	12,797	5,503	4,643	2,624	27	860 R	43.0%	36.3%	20.5%
3,822	WHEELER	2,767	1,458	938	367	4	520 R	52.7%	33.9%	13.3%
59,926	WICHITA	46,608	17,956	17,021	11,478	153	935 R	38.5%	36.5%	24.6%
7,586	WILBARGER	5,340	1,959	1,924	1,453	4	35 R	36.7%	36.0%	27.2%
9,158	WILLACY	5,510	1,490	3,359	652	9	1,869 D	27.0%	61.0%	11.8%
72,005	WILLIAMSON	61,254	26,208	19,437	15,415	194	6,771 R	42.8%	31.7%	25.2%
13,666	WILSON	9,625	3,766	3,711	2,105	43	55 R	39.1%	38.6%	21.9%
3,990	WINKLER	2,702	1,173	942	582	5	231 R	43.4%	34.9%	21.5%
17,895	WISE	13,568	4,555	4,478	4,485	50	70 R	33.6%	33.0%	33.1%
16,378	WOOD	12,318	4,708	4,084	3,494	32	624 R	38.2%	33.2%	28.4%
3,572	YOAKUM	2,575	1,486	595	484	10	891 R	57.7%	23.1%	18.8%
10,379	YOUNG	7,675	2,894	2,464	2,302	15	430 R	37.7%	32.1%	30.0%
5,342	ZAPATA	3,249	866	2,052	326	5	1,186 D	26.7%	63.2%	10.0%
7,128	ZAVALA	3,868	571	3,058	237	2	2,487 D	14.8%	79.1%	6.1%
8,440,143	TOTAL	6,154,018	2,496,071	2,281,815	1,354,781	21,351	214,256 R	40.6%	37.1%	22.0%

HARRIS COUNTY

PRESIDENT 1992

Registration	District	Total Vote	Republican	Democratic	Perot	Other	Plurality	Percentage Total Vote		
								Rep.	Dem.	Perot
63,032	DISTRICT 126	52,526	31,694	9,890	10,829	113	20,865 R	60.3%	18.8%	20.6%
66,234	DISTRICT 127	54,176	31,010	11,377	11,658	131	19,352 R	57.2%	21.0%	21.5%
46,887	DISTRICT 128	32,871	12,371	13,162	7,275	63	791 D	37.6%	40.0%	22.1%
64,721	DISTRICT 129	53,349	27,237	13,112	12,851	149	14,125 R	51.1%	24.6%	24.1%
60,202	DISTRICT 130	51,370	29,038	10,241	11,974	117	17,064 R	56.5%	19.9%	23.3%
47,938	DISTRICT 131	32,611	8,041	20,763	3,722	85	12,722 D	24.7%	63.7%	11.4%
60,526	DISTRICT 132	46,605	17,247	22,708	6,472	178	5,461 D	37.0%	48.7%	13.9%
66,615	DISTRICT 133	54,868	32,832	12,103	9,773	160	20,729 R	59.8%	22.1%	17.8%
46,106	DISTRICT 134	36,582	16,864	13,252	6,332	134	3,612 R	46.1%	36.2%	17.3%
57,704	DISTRICT 135	48,513	27,458	10,146	10,800	109	16,658 R	56.6%	20.9%	22.3%
70,000	DISTRICT 136	56,773	34,165	12,457	9,989	162	21,708 R	60.2%	21.9%	17.6%
46,514	DISTRICT 137	35,880	12,120	17,267	6,276	217	5,147 D	33.8%	48.1%	17.5%
49,561	DISTRICT 138	33,888	13,027	14,682	6,073	106	1,655 D	38.4%	43.3%	17.9%
40,237	DISTRICT 139	26,219	6,095	16,693	3,363	68	10,598 D	23.2%	63.7%	12.8%
36,003	DISTRICT 140	20,347	6,680	9,866	3,743	58	3,186 D	32.8%	48.5%	18.4%
54,912	DISTRICT 141	32,870	6,351	22,698	3,740	81	16,347 D	19.3%	69.1%	11.4%
52,870	DISTRICT 142	31,195	5,540	22,322	3,265	68	16,782 D	17.8%	71.6%	10.5%
39,085	DISTRICT 143	22,820	6,821	11,925	3,972	102	5,104 D	29.9%	52.3%	17.4%
41,147	DISTRICT 144	28,762	11,462	10,315	6,888	97	1,147 R	39.9%	35.9%	23.9%
33,020	DISTRICT 145	19,662	6,719	9,127	3,745	71	2,408 D	34.2%	46.4%	19.0%
63,320	DISTRICT 146	40,386	9,660	25,743	4,877	106	16,083 D	23.9%	63.7%	12.1%
48,298	DISTRICT 147	29,537	6,314	19,486	3,649	88	13,172 D	21.4%	66.0%	12.4%
35,651	DISTRICT 148	21,496	6,814	11,009	3,587	86	4,195 D	31.7%	51.2%	16.7%
44,454	DISTRICT 149	34,570	16,882	10,137	7,449	102	6,745 R	48.8%	29.3%	21.5%
55,507	DISTRICT 150	44,760	24,336	9,690	10,620	114	13,716 R	54.4%	21.6%	23.7%
1,290,544	TOTAL	942,947	406,778	360,171	172,922	3,076	46,607 R	43.1%	38.2%	18.3%

TEXAS

CONGRESS

CD	Year	Total Vote	Republican Vote	Republican Candidate	Democratic Vote	Democratic Candidate	Other Vote	Rep.-Dem. Plurality	Total Vote Rep.	Total Vote Dem.	Major Vote Rep.	Major Vote Dem.
1	1992	152,209			152,209	CHAPMAN, JAMES L.		152,209 D		100.0%		100.0%
2	1992	211,350	92,176	PETERSON, DONNA	118,625	WILSON, CHARLES	549	26,449 D	43.6%	56.1%	43.7%	56.3%
3	1992	234,139	201,569	JOHNSON, SAM			32,570	201,569 R	86.1%		100.0%	
4	1992	220,333	83,875	BRIDGES, DAVID L.	128,008	HALL, RALPH M.	8,450	44,133 D	38.1%	58.1%	39.6%	60.4%
5	1992	167,330	62,419	STOKLEY, RICHARD	98,567	BRYANT, JOHN	6,344	36,148 D	37.3%	58.9%	38.8%	61.2%
6	1992	263,073	189,140	BARTON, JOE L.	73,933	DIETRICH, JOHN E.		115,207 R	71.9%	28.1%	71.9%	28.1%
7	1992	169,407	169,407	ARCHER, W. R.				169,407 R	100.0%		100.0%	
8	1992	232,822	179,349	FIELDS, JACK	53,473	ROBINSON, CHARLES E.		125,876 R	77.0%	23.0%	77.0%	23.0%
9	1992	221,361	96,270	STOCKMAN, STEVE	118,690	BROOKS, JACK B.	6,401	22,420 D	43.5%	53.6%	44.8%	55.2%
10	1992	261,892	68,646	SPIRO, HERBERT	177,233	PICKLE, JAKE	16,013	108,587 D	26.2%	67.7%	27.9%	72.1%
11	1992	178,032	58,033	BROYLES, JAMES W.	119,999	EDWARDS, CHET		61,966 D	32.6%	67.4%	32.6%	67.4%
12	1992	199,924	74,432	HOBBS, DAVID	125,492	GEREN, PETE		51,060 D	37.2%	62.8%	37.2%	62.8%
13	1992	195,406	77,514	BOULTER, BEAU	117,892	SARPALIUS, BILL		40,378 D	39.7%	60.3%	39.7%	60.3%
14	1992	199,671	54,412	GARZA, HUMBERTO J.	135,930	LAUGHLIN, GREG	9,329	81,518 D	27.3%	68.1%	28.6%	71.4%
15	1992	142,900	56,549	HAUGHEY, TOM	86,351	DE LA GARZA, ELIGIO		29,802 D	39.6%	60.4%	39.6%	60.4%
16	1992	128,601	61,870	TABERSKI, CHIP	66,731	COLEMAN, RONALD		4,861 D	48.1%	51.9%	48.1%	51.9%
17	1992	206,171	69,958	SADOWSKI, JEANNIE	136,213	STENHOLM, CHARLES W.		66,255 D	33.9%	66.1%	33.9%	66.1%
18	1992	172,208	56,080	BLUM, EDWARD	111,422	WASHINGTON, CRAIG A.	4,706	55,342 D	32.6%	64.7%	33.5%	66.5%
19	1992	209,382	162,057	COMBEST, LARRY	47,325	MOSER, TERRY L.		114,732 R	77.4%	22.6%	77.4%	22.6%
20	1992	103,755			103,755	GONZALEZ, HENRY B.		103,755 D		100.0%		100.0%
21	1992	264,653	190,979	SMITH, LAMAR	62,827	GADDY, JAMES M.	10,847	128,152 R	72.2%	23.7%	75.2%	24.8%
22	1992	218,033	150,221	DELAY, THOMAS D.	67,812	KONRAD, RICHARD		82,409 R	68.9%	31.1%	68.9%	31.1%
23	1992	166,347	98,259	BONILLA, HENRY	63,797	BUSTAMANTE, ALBERT G.	4,291	34,462 R	59.1%	38.4%	60.6%	39.4%
24	1992	174,216	70,042	MASTERSON, STEVE	104,174	FROST, MARTIN		34,132 D	40.2%	59.8%	40.2%	59.8%
25	1992	176,877	73,192	MCKENNA, DOLLY M.	98,975	ANDREWS, MIKE	4,710	25,783 D	41.4%	56.0%	42.5%	57.5%
26	1992	205,531	150,209	ARMEY, DICK	55,237	CATON, JOHN W.	85	94,972 R	73.1%	26.9%	73.1%	26.9%
27	1992	156,844	66,853	KIMBROUGH, JAY	87,022	ORTIZ, SOLOMON P.	2,969	20,169 D	42.6%	55.5%	43.4%	56.6%
28	1992	140,585			122,457	TEJEDA, FRANK M.	18,128	122,457 D		87.1%		100.0%
29	1992	98,673	34,609	ERVIN, CLARK K.	64,064	GREEN, GENE		29,455 D	35.1%	64.9%	35.1%	64.9%
30	1992	150,747	37,853	CAIN, LUCY	107,831	JOHNSON, EDDIE B.	5,063	69,978 D	25.1%	71.5%	26.0%	74.0%

TEXAS

1992 GENERAL ELECTION

President Other vote was 19,699 Libertarian (Marrou); 505 Gritz (write-in); 359 Phillips (write-in); 301 Fulani (write-in); 217 Hagelin (write-in); 169 LaRouche (write-in); 78 Brisben (write-in); 23 scattered write-in.

Congress Other vote was Northern (write-in) in CD 2; Libertarian (Kopala) in CD 3; Libertarian (Rothacker) in CD 4; Libertarian (Walker) in CD 5; Libertarian (Crawford) in CD 9; 6,353 Libertarian (Blum), 6,056 Independent (Davis), 3,510 Hopkins (write-in) and 94 Shaw (write-in) in CD 10; Independent (Vreeland) in CD 14; Libertarian (Lassen) in CD 18; Libertarian (Grisham) in CD 21; Libertarian (Alter) in CD 23; Libertarian (Mauk) in CD 25; Love (write-in) in CD 26; Libertarian (Schoonover) in CD 27; Libertarian (Slatter) in CD 28; Libertarian (Ashby) in CD 30.

HARRIS COUNTY

President Other vote was 2,765 Libertarian (Marrou) and 311 write-ins. The write-in votes are included in the total of the other vote column but are not available by district. The registration for Harris county reported on the state return (1,315,010) differs from the data provided by the Harris county clerk. The county clerk's figures are used in the Harris county table.

1992 PRIMARIES

MARCH 10 REPUBLICAN

Congress Unopposed in thirteen CD's. In CD 1 Robert E. Lee, the unopposed candidate, withdrew after the primary and no substitution was made. No candidate in CD's 20 and 28. Contested as follows:

CD 2 7,916 Donna Peterson; 1,866 D. J. Fillippa.
CD 3 44,920 Sam Johnson; 9,107 David Corley.
CD 4 13,661 David L. Bridges; 9,583 Tim McCord.
CD 5 6,784 Richard Stokley; 5,592 Farrell Ray.
CD 6 34,366 Joe L. Barton; 9,089 Mike McGinn.
CD 12 15,452 David Hobbs; 4,575 Terry L. Hicks.
CD 13 13,285 Beau Boulter; 4,532 Robert Price; 3,692 Ernie Houdashell; 1,438 Ray Powell.
CD 16 6,795 Chip Taberski; 5,001 Pat O'Rourke; 2,605 Michael G. White; 610 Walt E. Woelper.
CD 18 7,214 Edward Blum; 2,518 C. L. Kennedy.
CD 23 9,013 Henry Bonilla; 5,216 Dick Bowen.
CD 24 7,056 Steve Masterson; 3,674 Phillip Bielamowicz; 3,090 Reby Cary; 3,080 Duane McGuffey.
CD 25 10,402 Dolly M. McKenna; 8,532 Esther L. Yao.
CD 27 8,019 Jay Kimbrough; 3,305 Henry Kosling.
CD 29 3,614 Clark K. Ervin; 2,952 Freddy Rios.
CD 30 4,758 Lucy Cain; 4,382 Kelvin Malone.

MARCH 10 DEMOCRATIC

Congress Unopposed in eighteen CD's. No candidate in CD's 3 and 7. Contested as follows:

CD 2 74,674 Charles Wilson; 16,938 Stuart F. Williamson; 13,912 Edgar J. Groce.
CD 4 36,837 Ralph M. Hall; 18,833 Roger Sanders.
CD 6 11,603 John E. Dietrich; 9,977 Frank E. Smith.
CD 8 10,687 Charles E. Robinson; 6,774 Donald M. Guillory.
CD 10 55,703 Jake Pickle; 12,034 John Longsworth.
CD 16 27,562 Ronald Coleman; 11,104 Charles Ponzio; 2,704 Robert K. Jones; 1,856 Jorge Artalejo.
CD 23 44,856 Albert G. Bustamante; 20,934 Clayton H. Mulvaney.
CD 25 25,291 Mike Andrews; 5,371 Mary R. Whipple.
CD 29 10,504 Ben Reyes; 8,533 Gene Green; 6,487 Sylvia R. Garcia; 4,661 Albert Luna; 804 Andrew C. Burks.
CD 30 41,587 Eddie B. Johnson; 3,794 Adolph Hauntz.

TEXAS

APRIL 14 REPUBLICAN RUN-OFF

Congress   Contested as follows:

CD 16   7,229 Chip Taberski; 2,231 Pat O'Rourke.
CD 24   2,268 Steve Masterson; 1,634 Phillip Bielamowicz.

APRIL 14 DEMOCRATIC RUN-OFF

Congress   Contested as follows:

CD 29   15,844 Gene Green; 15,664 Ben Reyes. There was a court-ordered second run-off primary held July 28 due to illegal crossover voting by voters who had participated in the Republican primary in March and voted in the April Democratic run-off primary. The results of this second run-off were as follows: 18,927 Gene Green; 17,795 Ben Reyes.

UTAH

GOVERNOR
Mike Leavitt (R). Elected 1992 to a four-year term.

SENATORS
Robert F. Bennett (R). Elected 1992 to a six-year term.

Orrin G. Hatch (R). Re-elected 1988 to a six-year term. Previously elected 1982, 1976.

REPRESENTATIVES
1. James V. Hansen (R)   2. Karen Shepherd (D)   3. Bill Orton (D)

POSTWAR VOTE FOR PRESIDENT

Year	Total Vote	Republican Vote	Republican Candidate	Democratic Vote	Democratic Candidate	Other Vote	Plurality	Total Vote Rep.	Total Vote Dem.	Major Vote Rep.	Major Vote Dem.
1992 **	743,999	322,632	Bush, George	183,429	Clinton, Bill	237,938	119,232 R	43.4%	24.7%	63.8%	36.2%
1988	647,008	428,442	Bush, George	207,343	Dukakis, Michael S.	11,223	221,099 R	66.2%	32.0%	67.4%	32.6%
1984	629,656	469,105	Reagan, Ronald	155,369	Mondale, Walter F.	5,182	313,736 R	74.5%	24.7%	75.1%	24.9%
1980	604,222	439,687	Reagan, Ronald	124,266	Carter, Jimmy	40,269	315,421 R	72.8%	20.6%	78.0%	22.0%
1976	541,198	337,908	Ford, Gerald R.	182,110	Carter, Jimmy	21,180	155,798 R	62.4%	33.6%	65.0%	35.0%
1972	478,476	323,643	Nixon, Richard M.	126,284	McGovern, George S.	28,549	197,359 R	67.6%	26.4%	71.9%	28.1%
1968	422,568	238,728	Nixon, Richard M.	156,665	Humphrey, Hubert H.	27,175	82,063 R	56.5%	37.1%	60.4%	39.6%
1964	401,413	181,785	Goldwater, Barry M.	219,628	Johnson, Lyndon B.		37,843 D	45.3%	54.7%	45.3%	54.7%
1960	374,709	205,361	Nixon, Richard M.	169,248	Kennedy, John F.	100	36,113 R	54.8%	45.2%	54.8%	45.2%
1956	333,995	215,631	Eisenhower, Dwight D.	118,364	Stevenson, Adlai E.		97,267 R	64.6%	35.4%	64.6%	35.4%
1952	329,554	194,190	Eisenhower, Dwight D.	135,364	Stevenson, Adlai E.		58,826 R	58.9%	41.1%	58.9%	41.1%
1948	276,306	124,402	Dewey, Thomas E.	149,151	Truman, Harry S.	2,753	24,749 D	45.0%	54.0%	45.5%	54.5%

In 1992 the other vote column includes 203,400 votes cast for Perot who came in second.

POSTWAR VOTE FOR GOVERNOR

Year	Total Vote	Republican Vote	Republican Candidate	Democratic Vote	Democratic Candidate	Other Vote	Rep.-Dem. Plurality	Total Vote Rep.	Total Vote Dem.	Major Vote Rep.	Major Vote Dem.
1992 **	762,549	321,713	Leavitt, Mike	177,181	Hanson, Stewart	263,655	144,532 R	42.2%	23.2%	64.5%	35.5%
1988 **	649,114	260,462	Bangerter, Norman H.	249,321	Wilson, Ted	139,331	11,141 R	40.1%	38.4%	51.1%	48.9%
1984	629,619	351,792	Bangerter, Norman H.	275,669	Owens, Wayne	2,158	76,123 R	55.9%	43.8%	56.1%	43.9%
1980	600,019	266,578	Wright, Bob	330,974	Matheson, Scott M.	2,467	64,396 D	44.4%	55.2%	44.6%	55.4%
1976	539,649	248,027	Romney, Vernon B.	280,706	Matheson, Scott M.	10,916	32,679 D	46.0%	52.0%	46.9%	53.1%
1972	476,447	144,449	Strike, Nicholas L.	331,998	Rampton, Calvin L.		187,549 D	30.3%	69.7%	30.3%	69.7%
1968	421,012	131,729	Buehner, Carl W.	289,283	Rampton, Calvin L.		157,554 D	31.3%	68.7%	31.3%	68.7%
1964	398,256	171,300	Melich, Mitchell	226,956	Rampton, Calvin L.		55,656 D	43.0%	57.0%	43.0%	57.0%
1960	371,489	195,634	Clyde, George D.	175,855	Barlocker, W. A.		19,779 R	52.7%	47.3%	52.7%	47.3%
1956 **	332,889	127,164	Clyde, George D.	111,297	Romney, L. C.	94,428	15,867 R	38.2%	33.4%	53.3%	46.7%
1952	327,704	180,516	Lee, J. Bracken	147,188	Glade, Earl J.		33,328 R	55.1%	44.9%	55.1%	44.9%
1948	275,067	151,253	Lee, J. Bracken	123,814	Maw, Herbert B.		27,439 R	55.0%	45.0%	55.0%	45.0%

In 1992 other vote was 255,753 Independent (Cook); 3,593 Populist (Gum); 1,492 American (Van Horn); 1,158 Socialist Workers (Garcia); 917 Independent (Metzger-Agin); 729 Independent American (Richins) and 13 scattered. In 1988 other vote was 136,651 Independent (Cook); 1,661 Libertarian (Burton) and 1,019 American (Pedersen). In 1956 other vote was Independent (Lee).

UTAH

POSTWAR VOTE FOR SENATOR

Year	Total Vote	Republican Vote	Republican Candidate	Democratic Vote	Democratic Candidate	Other Vote	Rep.-Dem. Plurality	Percentage Total Vote Rep.	Percentage Total Vote Dem.	Percentage Major Vote Rep.	Percentage Major Vote Dem.
1992	758,479	420,069	Bennett, Robert F.	301,228	Owens, Wayne	37,182	118,841 R	55.4%	39.7%	58.2%	41.8%
1988	640,702	430,089	Hatch, Orrin G.	203,364	Moss, Brian H.	7,249	226,725 R	67.1%	31.7%	67.9%	32.1%
1986	435,111	314,608	Garn, E. J.	115,523	Oliver, Craig	4,980	199,085 R	72.3%	26.6%	73.1%	26.9%
1982	530,802	309,332	Hatch, Orrin G.	219,482	Wilson, Ted	1,988	89,850 R	58.3%	41.3%	58.5%	41.5%
1980	594,298	437,675	Garn, E. J.	151,454	Berman, Dan	5,169	286,221 R	73.6%	25.5%	74.3%	25.7%
1976	540,108	290,221	Hatch, Orrin G.	241,948	Moss, Frank E.	7,939	48,273 R	53.7%	44.8%	54.5%	45.5%
1974	420,642	210,299	Garn, E. J.	185,377	Owens, Wayne	24,966	24,922 R	50.0%	44.1%	53.1%	46.9%
1970	374,303	159,004	Burton, Laurence J.	210,207	Moss, Frank E.	5,092	51,203 D	42.5%	56.2%	43.1%	56.9%
1968	419,262	225,075	Bennett, Wallace F.	192,168	Weilenmann, Milton	2,019	32,907 R	53.7%	45.8%	53.9%	46.1%
1964	397,384	169,562	Wilkinson, Ernest L.	227,822	Moss, Frank E.		58,260 D	42.7%	57.3%	42.7%	57.3%
1962	318,411	166,755	Bennett, Wallace F.	151,656	King, David S.		15,099 R	52.4%	47.6%	52.4%	47.6%
1958 **	291,311	101,471	Watkins, Arthur V.	112,827	Moss, Frank E.	77,013	11,356 D	34.8%	38.7%	47.4%	52.6%
1956	330,381	178,261	Bennett, Wallace F.	152,120	Hopkin, Alonzo F.		26,141 R	54.0%	46.0%	54.0%	46.0%
1952	327,033	177,435	Watkins, Arthur V.	149,598	Granger, Walter K.		27,837 R	54.3%	45.7%	54.3%	45.7%
1950	264,440	142,427	Bennett, Wallace F.	121,198	Thomas, Elbert D.	815	21,229 R	53.9%	45.8%	54.0%	46.0%
1946	197,399	101,142	Watkins, Arthur V.	96,257	Murdock, Abe		4,885 R	51.2%	48.8%	51.2%	48.8%

In 1958 other vote was Independent (Lee).

UTAH

Districts Established January 1, 1992

UTAH

PRESIDENT 1992

Registration	County	Total Vote	Republican	Democratic	Perot	Other	Plurality	Percentage Total Vote		
								Rep.	Dem.	Perot
2,694	BEAVER	2,111	1,040	668	330	73	372 R	49.3%	31.6%	15.6%
20,025	BOX ELDER	15,555	7,712	2,186	4,507	1,150	3,205 R	49.6%	14.1%	29.0%
44,330	CACHE	30,725	15,971	4,973	8,032	1,749	7,939 R	52.0%	16.2%	26.1%
11,447	CARBON	8,817	2,038	4,480	2,002	297	2,442 D	23.1%	50.8%	22.7%
542	DAGGETT	442	172	122	117	31	50 R	38.9%	27.6%	26.5%
99,935	DAVIS	81,350	39,087	14,924	24,105	3,234	14,982 R	48.0%	18.3%	29.6%
6,288	DUCHESNE	4,565	1,983	772	1,229	581	754 R	43.4%	16.9%	26.9%
5,816	EMERY	4,510	1,643	1,349	1,138	380	294 R	36.4%	29.9%	25.2%
2,263	GARFIELD	1,983	1,235	309	355	84	880 R	62.3%	15.6%	17.9%
4,688	GRAND	3,342	1,100	1,160	991	91	60 D	32.9%	34.7%	29.7%
13,118	IRON	9,378	5,616	1,537	1,693	532	3,923 R	59.9%	16.4%	18.1%
3,422	JUAB	2,895	1,237	823	616	219	414 R	42.7%	28.4%	21.3%
2,881	KANE	2,172	1,241	295	534	102	707 R	57.1%	13.6%	24.6%
6,248	MILLARD	4,770	2,496	742	1,064	468	1,432 R	52.3%	15.6%	22.3%
3,238	MORGAN	2,940	1,339	520	851	230	488 R	45.5%	17.7%	28.9%
901	PIUTE	753	429	169	146	9	260 R	57.0%	22.4%	19.4%
1,091	RICH	876	525	154	187	10	338 R	59.9%	17.6%	21.3%
397,534	SALT LAKE	318,661	117,247	100,082	91,968	9,364	17,165 R	36.8%	31.4%	28.9%
6,720	SAN JUAN	4,335	2,004	1,639	576	116	365 R	46.2%	37.8%	13.3%
9,431	SANPETE	6,685	2,995	1,302	1,742	646	1,253 R	44.8%	19.5%	26.1%
8,235	SEVIER	6,258	3,160	1,039	1,671	388	1,489 R	50.5%	16.6%	26.7%
11,921	SUMMIT	9,399	3,133	3,013	3,060	193	73 R	33.3%	32.1%	32.6%
14,113	TOOELE	10,271	3,676	3,270	3,011	314	406 R	35.8%	31.8%	29.3%
11,406	UINTAH	7,774	3,505	1,374	2,250	645	1,255 R	45.1%	17.7%	28.9%
145,465	UTAH	108,178	61,398	14,090	24,558	8,132	36,840 R	56.8%	13.0%	22.7%
6,172	WASATCH	4,336	1,822	1,042	1,234	238	588 R	42.0%	24.0%	28.5%
29,081	WASHINGTON	21,476	11,310	3,364	4,623	2,179	6,687 R	52.7%	15.7%	21.5%
1,466	WAYNE	1,225	706	236	251	32	455 R	57.6%	19.3%	20.5%
94,740	WEBER	68,216	26,812	17,795	20,559	3,050	6,253 R	39.3%	26.1%	30.1%
965,211	TOTAL	743,999	322,632	183,429	203,400	34,538	119,232 R	43.4%	24.7%	27.3%

UTAH

GOVERNOR 1992

Registration	County	Total Vote	Republican	Democratic	Independent	Other	Plurality	Percentage Total Vote		
								Rep.	Dem.	Ind.
2,694	BEAVER	2,175	1,121	547	502	5	574 R	51.5%	25.1%	23.1%
20,025	BOX ELDER	16,040	7,863	2,005	5,994	178	1,869 R	49.0%	12.5%	37.4%
44,330	CACHE	31,548	17,251	4,736	9,199	362	8,052 R	54.7%	15.0%	29.2%
11,447	CARBON	9,039	2,149	3,850	2,956	84	894 D	23.8%	42.6%	32.7%
542	DAGGETT	423	189	124	108	2	65 R	44.7%	29.3%	25.5%
99,935	DAVIS	82,989	37,921	14,359	29,949	760	7,972 R	45.7%	17.3%	36.1%
6,288	DUCHESNE	4,688	2,144	755	1,735	54	409 R	45.7%	16.1%	37.0%
5,816	EMERY	4,454	1,941	1,076	1,376	61	565 R	43.6%	24.2%	30.9%
2,263	GARFIELD	1,956	1,289	248	409	10	880 R	65.9%	12.7%	20.9%
4,688	GRAND	3,376	1,163	1,117	1,057	39	46 R	34.4%	33.1%	31.3%
13,118	IRON	9,635	6,167	1,241	2,125	102	4,042 R	64.0%	12.9%	22.1%
3,422	JUAB	2,862	1,225	597	1,009	31	216 R	42.8%	20.9%	35.3%
2,881	KANE	2,233	1,253	300	660	20	593 R	56.1%	13.4%	29.6%
6,248	MILLARD	4,902	2,510	644	1,703	45	807 R	51.2%	13.1%	34.7%
3,238	MORGAN	2,890	1,354	470	1,029	37	325 R	46.9%	16.3%	35.6%
901	PIUTE	747	444	109	191	3	253 R	59.4%	14.6%	25.6%
1,091	RICH	869	485	173	208	3	277 R	55.8%	19.9%	23.9%
397,534	SALT LAKE	326,308	115,583	100,570	107,549	2,606	8,034 R	35.4%	30.8%	33.0%
6,720	SAN JUAN	4,208	2,020	1,596	563	29	424 R	48.0%	37.9%	13.4%
9,431	SANPETE	6,919	3,233	1,072	2,511	103	722 R	46.7%	15.5%	36.3%
8,235	SEVIER	6,464	3,389	754	2,275	46	1,114 R	52.4%	11.7%	35.2%
11,921	SUMMIT	9,537	3,194	3,645	2,629	69	451 D	33.5%	38.2%	27.6%
14,113	TOOELE	10,598	3,712	2,785	4,017	84	305 I	35.0%	26.3%	37.9%
11,406	UINTAH	7,959	3,328	1,308	3,224	99	104 R	41.8%	16.4%	40.5%
145,465	UTAH	110,780	59,933	12,414	37,067	1,366	22,866 R	54.1%	11.2%	33.5%
6,172	WASATCH	4,578	1,952	1,063	1,521	42	431 R	42.6%	23.2%	33.2%
29,081	WASHINGTON	22,130	12,113	3,037	6,590	390	5,523 R	54.7%	13.7%	29.8%
1,466	WAYNE	1,208	773	191	243	1	530 R	64.0%	15.8%	20.1%
94,740	WEBER	71,021	26,014	16,395	27,354	1,258	1,340 I	36.6%	23.1%	38.5%
965,211	TOTAL	762,549	321,713	177,181	255,753	7,902	65,960 R	42.2%	23.2%	33.5%

UTAH

SENATOR 1992

Registration	County	Total Vote	Republican	Democratic	Other	Rep.-Dem. Plurality	Percentage			
							Total Vote		Major Vote	
							Rep.	Dem.	Rep.	Dem.
2,694	BEAVER	2,209	1,351	802	56	549 R	61.2%	36.3%	62.7%	37.3%
20,025	BOX ELDER	15,970	9,777	5,171	1,022	4,606 R	61.2%	32.4%	65.4%	34.6%
44,330	CACHE	31,368	19,575	10,212	1,581	9,363 R	62.4%	32.6%	65.7%	34.3%
11,447	CARBON	9,087	3,449	5,249	389	1,800 D	38.0%	57.8%	39.7%	60.3%
542	DAGGETT	406	224	164	18	60 R	55.2%	40.4%	57.7%	42.3%
99,935	DAVIS	82,092	49,415	28,318	4,359	21,097 R	60.2%	34.5%	63.6%	36.4%
6,288	DUCHESNE	4,678	3,132	1,292	254	1,840 R	67.0%	27.6%	70.8%	29.2%
5,816	EMERY	4,216	2,846	1,167	203	1,679 R	67.5%	27.7%	70.9%	29.1%
2,263	GARFIELD	1,875	1,457	377	41	1,080 R	77.7%	20.1%	79.4%	20.6%
4,688	GRAND	3,375	1,803	1,413	159	390 R	53.4%	41.9%	56.1%	43.9%
13,118	IRON	9,591	6,908	2,293	390	4,615 R	72.0%	23.9%	75.1%	24.9%
3,422	JUAB	2,755	1,639	1,022	94	617 R	59.5%	37.1%	61.6%	38.4%
2,881	KANE	2,070	1,601	371	98	1,230 R	77.3%	17.9%	81.2%	18.8%
6,248	MILLARD	4,892	3,383	1,249	260	2,134 R	69.2%	25.5%	73.0%	27.0%
3,238	MORGAN	2,717	1,588	981	148	607 R	58.4%	36.1%	61.8%	38.2%
901	PIUTE	721	537	171	13	366 R	74.5%	23.7%	75.8%	24.2%
1,091	RICH	825	602	202	21	400 R	73.0%	24.5%	74.9%	25.1%
397,534	SALT LAKE	325,922	157,781	153,714	14,427	4,067 R	48.4%	47.2%	50.7%	49.3%
6,720	SAN JUAN	4,146	2,304	1,794	48	510 R	55.6%	43.3%	56.2%	43.8%
9,431	SANPETE	6,890	4,308	2,205	377	2,103 R	62.5%	32.0%	66.1%	33.9%
8,235	SEVIER	6,438	4,485	1,654	299	2,831 R	69.7%	25.7%	73.1%	26.9%
11,921	SUMMIT	9,506	4,437	4,680	389	243 D	46.7%	49.2%	48.7%	51.3%
14,113	TOOELE	10,616	4,877	5,180	559	303 D	45.9%	48.8%	48.5%	51.5%
11,406	UINTAH	8,042	4,983	2,492	567	2,491 R	62.0%	31.0%	66.7%	33.3%
145,465	UTAH	109,961	74,545	30,487	4,929	44,058 R	67.8%	27.7%	71.0%	29.0%
6,172	WASATCH	4,530	2,526	1,870	134	656 R	55.8%	41.3%	57.5%	42.5%
29,081	WASHINGTON	21,926	14,953	5,555	1,418	9,398 R	68.2%	25.3%	72.9%	27.1%
1,466	WAYNE	1,169	960	195	14	765 R	82.1%	16.7%	83.1%	16.9%
94,740	WEBER	70,486	34,623	30,948	4,915	3,675 R	49.1%	43.9%	52.8%	47.2%
965,211	TOTAL	758,479	420,069	301,228	37,182	118,841 R	55.4%	39.7%	58.2%	41.8%

UTAH

CONGRESS

CD	Year	Total Vote	Republican Vote	Republican Candidate	Democratic Vote	Democratic Candidate	Other Vote	Rep.-Dem. Plurality	Percentage Total Vote Rep.	Percentage Total Vote Dem.	Percentage Major Vote Rep.	Percentage Major Vote Dem.
1	1992	245,254	160,037	HANSEN, JAMES V.	68,712	HOLT, RON	16,505	91,325 R	65.3%	28.0%	70.0%	30.0%
2	1992	252,969	118,307	GREENE, ENID	127,738	SHEPHERD, KAREN	6,924	9,431 D	46.8%	50.5%	48.1%	51.9%
3	1992	229,061	84,019	HARRINGTON, RICHARD R.	135,029	ORTON, BILL	10,013	51,010 D	36.7%	58.9%	38.4%	61.6%

UTAH

1992 GENERAL ELECTION

President   Other vote was 28,602 Populist (Gritz); 1,900 Libertarian (Marrou); 1,319 Natural Law (Hagelin); 1,089 Independent for Economic Recovery (LaRouche); 414 New Alliance (Fulani); 393 Taxpayers (Phillips); 292 American (Smith); 200 Socialist Workers (Warren); 177 Campaign for a New Tomorrow (Daniels); 151 Socialist (Brisben); 1 scattered write-in.

Governor   The data for Governor are presented in a four column (Republican, Democratic, Independent and Other) tabulation and the plurality figures are calculated on a first-second party basis. Merrill Cook, the Independent candidate, carried two counties and ran second statewide and in many counties. Other vote was 3,593 Populist (Gum); 1,492 American (Van Horn); 1,158 Socialist Workers (Garcia); 917 Independent (Metzger-Agin); 729 Independent American (Richins); 13 scattered write-ins not available by county.

Senator   Other vote was 17,549 Populist (Morrow); 14,341 Libertarian (Modine); 5,292 Socialist Workers (Grogan).

Congress   Other vote was Independent Party (Lawrence) in CD 1; 6,274 Independent Party (Crane) and 650 Socialist Workers (Koschak) in CD 2; 5,764 Independent Party (Hill), 2,068 Independent (Wilson); 1,797 Libertarian (Jones) and 384 Socialist Workers (Anthony) in CD 3.

1992 PRIMARIES

Candidates in Utah are nominated by convention. If a candidate receives seventy percent or more of the convention vote, no primary is held.

SEPTEMBER 8 REPUBLICAN

Governor   143,514 Mike Leavitt; 112,881 Richard M. Eyre. Uncorrected returns gave the Leavitt vote as 143,647.

Senator   135,514 Robert F. Bennett; 128,125 Joe Cannon.

Congress   Nominated by convention in CD's 1 and 3. Contested as follows:

    CD   2   50,280 Enid Greene; 25,832 Jim Bartleson.

SEPTEMBER 8 DEMOCRATIC

Governor   64,084 Stewart Hanson; 48,758 Patrick Shea.

Senator   74,124 Wayne Owens; 46,622 Doug Anderson.

Congress   Nominated by convention in all three CD's.

VERMONT

GOVERNOR
Howard B. Dean (D). Elected 1992 to a two year term; had been elected Lt. Governor 1990 and became Governor August 1991 upon the death of Richard A. Snelling (R).

SENATORS
James M. Jeffords (R). Elected 1988 to a six-year term.

Patrick J. Leahy (D). Re-elected 1992 to a six-year term. Previously elected 1986, 1980, 1974.

REPRESENTATIVE
At-Large. Bernard Sanders (I)

POSTWAR VOTE FOR PRESIDENT

Year	Total Vote	Republican		Democratic		Other Vote	Plurality	Percentage			
								Total Vote		Major Vote	
		Vote	Candidate	Vote	Candidate			Rep.	Dem.	Rep.	Dem.
1992 **	289,701	88,122	Bush, George	133,592	Clinton, Bill	67,987	45,470 D	30.4%	46.1%	39.7%	60.3%
1988	243,328	124,331	Bush, George	115,775	Dukakis, Michael S.	3,222	8,556 R	51.1%	47.6%	51.8%	48.2%
1984	234,561	135,865	Reagan, Ronald	95,730	Mondale, Walter F.	2,966	40,135 R	57.9%	40.8%	58.7%	41.3%
1980	213,299	94,628	Reagan, Ronald	81,952	Carter, Jimmy	36,719	12,676 R	44.4%	38.4%	53.6%	46.4%
1976	187,765	102,085	Ford, Gerald R.	80,954	Carter, Jimmy	4,726	21,131 R	54.4%	43.1%	55.8%	44.2%
1972	186,947	117,149	Nixon, Richard M.	68,174	McGovern, George S.	1,624	48,975 R	62.7%	36.5%	63.2%	36.8%
1968	161,404	85,142	Nixon, Richard M.	70,255	Humphrey, Hubert H.	6,007	14,887 R	52.8%	43.5%	54.8%	45.2%
1964	163,089	54,942	Goldwater, Barry M.	108,127	Johnson, Lyndon B.	20	53,185 D	33.7%	66.3%	33.7%	66.3%
1960	167,324	98,131	Nixon, Richard M.	69,186	Kennedy, John F.	7	28,945 R	58.6%	41.3%	58.6%	41.4%
1956	152,978	110,390	Eisenhower, Dwight D.	42,549	Stevenson, Adlai E.	39	67,841 R	72.2%	27.8%	72.2%	27.8%
1952	153,557	109,717	Eisenhower, Dwight D.	43,355	Stevenson, Adlai E.	485	66,362 R	71.5%	28.2%	71.7%	28.3%
1948	123,382	75,926	Dewey, Thomas E.	45,557	Truman, Harry S.	1,899	30,369 R	61.5%	36.9%	62.5%	37.5%

In 1992 the other vote column includes 65,991 votes cast for Perot.

VERMONT

POSTWAR VOTE FOR GOVERNOR

Year	Total Vote	Republican		Democratic		Other Vote	Rep.-Dem. Plurality	Percentage			
								Total Vote		Major Vote	
		Vote	Candidate	Vote	Candidate			Rep.	Dem.	Rep.	Dem.
1992	285,728	65,837	McClaughry, John	213,523	Dean, Howard B.	6,368	147,686 D	23.0%	74.7%	23.6%	76.4%
1990	211,422	109,540	Snelling, Richard A.	97,321	Welch, Peter	4,561	12,219 R	51.8%	46.0%	53.0%	47.0%
1988	243,130	105,319	Bernhardt, Michael	134,594	Kunin, Madeleine M.	3,253	29,275 D	43.3%	55.4%	43.9%	56.1%
1986 **	196,716	75,162	Smith, Peter	92,379	Kunin, Madeleine M.	29,175	17,217 D	38.2%	47.0%	44.9%	55.1%
1984	233,753	113,264	Easton, John J.	116,938	Kunin, Madeleine M.	3,551	3,674 D	48.5%	50.0%	49.2%	50.8%
1982	169,251	93,111	Snelling, Richard A.	74,394	Kunin, Madeleine M.	1,746	18,717 R	55.0%	44.0%	55.6%	44.4%
1980	210,381	123,229	Snelling, Richard A.	77,363	Diamond, J. Jerome	9,789	45,866 R	58.6%	36.8%	61.4%	38.6%
1978	124,482	78,181	Snelling, Richard A.	42,482	Granai, Edwin C.	3,819	35,699 R	62.8%	34.1%	64.8%	35.2%
1976	185,929	99,268	Snelling, Richard A.	75,262	Hackel, Stella B.	11,399	24,006 R	53.4%	40.5%	56.9%	43.1%
1974	141,156	53,672	Kennedy, Walter L.	79,842	Salmon, Thomas P.	7,642	26,170 D	38.0%	56.6%	40.2%	59.8%
1972	189,237	82,491	Hackett, Luther F.	104,533	Salmon, Thomas P.	2,213	22,042 D	43.6%	55.2%	44.1%	55.9%
1970	153,528	87,458	Davis, Deane C.	66,028	O'Brien, Leo	42	21,430 R	57.0%	43.0%	57.0%	43.0%
1968	161,089	89,387	Davis, Deane C.	71,656	Daley, John J.	46	17,731 R	55.5%	44.5%	55.5%	44.5%
1966	136,262	57,577	Snelling, Richard A.	78,669	Hoff, Philip H.	16	21,092 D	42.3%	57.7%	42.3%	57.7%
1964	164,199	57,576	Foote, Ralph A.	106,611	Hoff, Philip H.	12	49,035 D	35.1%	64.9%	35.1%	64.9%
1962	121,422	60,035	Keyser, F. Ray	61,383	Hoff, Philip H.	4	1,348 D	49.4%	50.6%	49.4%	50.6%
1960	164,632	92,861	Keyser, F. Ray	71,755	Niquette, Russell F.	16	21,106 R	56.4%	43.6%	56.4%	43.6%
1958	123,728	62,222	Stafford, Robert T.	61,503	Leddy, Bernard J.	3	719 R	50.3%	49.7%	50.3%	49.7%
1956	153,809	88,379	Johnson, Joseph B.	65,420	Branon, E. Frank	10	22,959 R	57.5%	42.5%	57.5%	42.5%
1954	114,360	59,778	Johnson, Joseph B.	54,554	Branon, E. Frank	28	5,224 R	52.3%	47.7%	52.3%	47.7%
1952	150,862	78,338	Emerson, Lee E.	60,051	Larrow, Robert W.	12,473	18,287 R	51.9%	39.8%	56.6%	43.4%
1950	87,155	64,915	Emerson, Lee E.	22,227	Moran, J. Edward	13	42,688 R	74.5%	25.5%	74.5%	25.5%
1948	120,183	86,394	Gibson, Ernest W., Jr.	33,588	Ryan, Charles F.	201	52,806 R	71.9%	27.9%	72.0%	28.0%
1946	72,044	57,849	Gibson, Ernest W., Jr.	14,096	Coburn, Berthold	99	43,753 R	80.3%	19.6%	80.4%	19.6%

In 1986, in the absence of a majority for any candidate, the State Legislature elected Madeleine M. Kunin to a two-year term.

POSTWAR VOTE FOR SENATOR

Year	Total Vote	Republican		Democratic		Other Vote	Rep.-Dem. Plurality	Percentage			
								Total Vote		Major Vote	
		Vote	Candidate	Vote	Candidate			Rep.	Dem.	Rep.	Dem.
1992	285,739	123,854	Douglas, James H.	154,762	Leahy, Patrick J.	7,123	30,908 D	43.3%	54.2%	44.5%	55.5%
1988	240,111	163,203	Jeffords, James M.	71,469	Gray, William	5,439	91,736 R	68.0%	29.8%	69.5%	30.5%
1986	196,532	67,798	Snelling, Richard A.	124,123	Leahy, Patrick J.	4,611	56,325 D	34.5%	63.2%	35.3%	64.7%
1982	168,003	84,450	Stafford, Robert T.	79,340	Guest, James A.	4,213	5,110 R	50.3%	47.2%	51.6%	48.4%
1980	209,124	101,421	Ledbetter, Stewart M.	104,176	Leahy, Patrick J.	3,527	2,755 D	48.5%	49.8%	49.3%	50.7%
1976	189,060	94,481	Stafford, Robert T.	85,682	Salmon, Thomas P.	8,897	8,799 R	50.0%	45.3%	52.4%	47.6%
1974	142,772	66,223	Mallary, Richard W.	70,629	Leahy, Patrick J.	5,920	4,406 D	46.4%	49.5%	48.4%	51.6%
1972 S	71,348	45,888	Stafford, Robert T.	23,842	Major, Randolph T.	1,618	22,046 R	64.3%	33.4%	65.8%	34.2%
1970	154,899	91,198	Prouty, Winston L.	62,271	Hoff, Philip H.	1,430	28,927 R	58.9%	40.2%	59.4%	40.6%
1968 **	157,375	157,154	Aiken, George D.	—		221	157,154 R	99.9%	0.0%	100.0%	
1964	164,350	87,879	Prouty, Winston L.	76,457	Fayette, Frederick J.	14	11,422 R	53.5%	46.5%	53.5%	46.5%
1962	121,571	81,241	Aiken, George D.	40,134	Johnson, W. Robert	196	41,107 R	66.8%	33.0%	66.9%	33.1%
1958	124,442	64,900	Prouty, Winston L.	59,536	Fayette, Frederick J.	6	5,364 R	52.2%	47.8%	52.2%	47.8%
1956	155,289	103,101	Aiken, George D.	52,184	O'Shea, Bernard G.	4	50,917 R	66.4%	33.6%	66.4%	33.6%
1952	154,052	111,406	Flanders, Ralph E.	42,630	Johnston, Allan R.	16	68,776 R	72.3%	27.7%	72.3%	27.7%
1950	89,171	69,543	Aiken, George D.	19,608	Bigelow, James E.	20	49,935 R	78.0%	22.0%	78.0%	22.0%
1946	73,340	54,729	Flanders, Ralph E.	18,594	McDevitt, Charles P.	17	36,135 R	74.6%	25.4%	74.6%	25.4%

In 1968 the Republican candidate won both major party nominations. The January 1972 election was for a short term to fill a vacancy.

VERMONT

One At Large

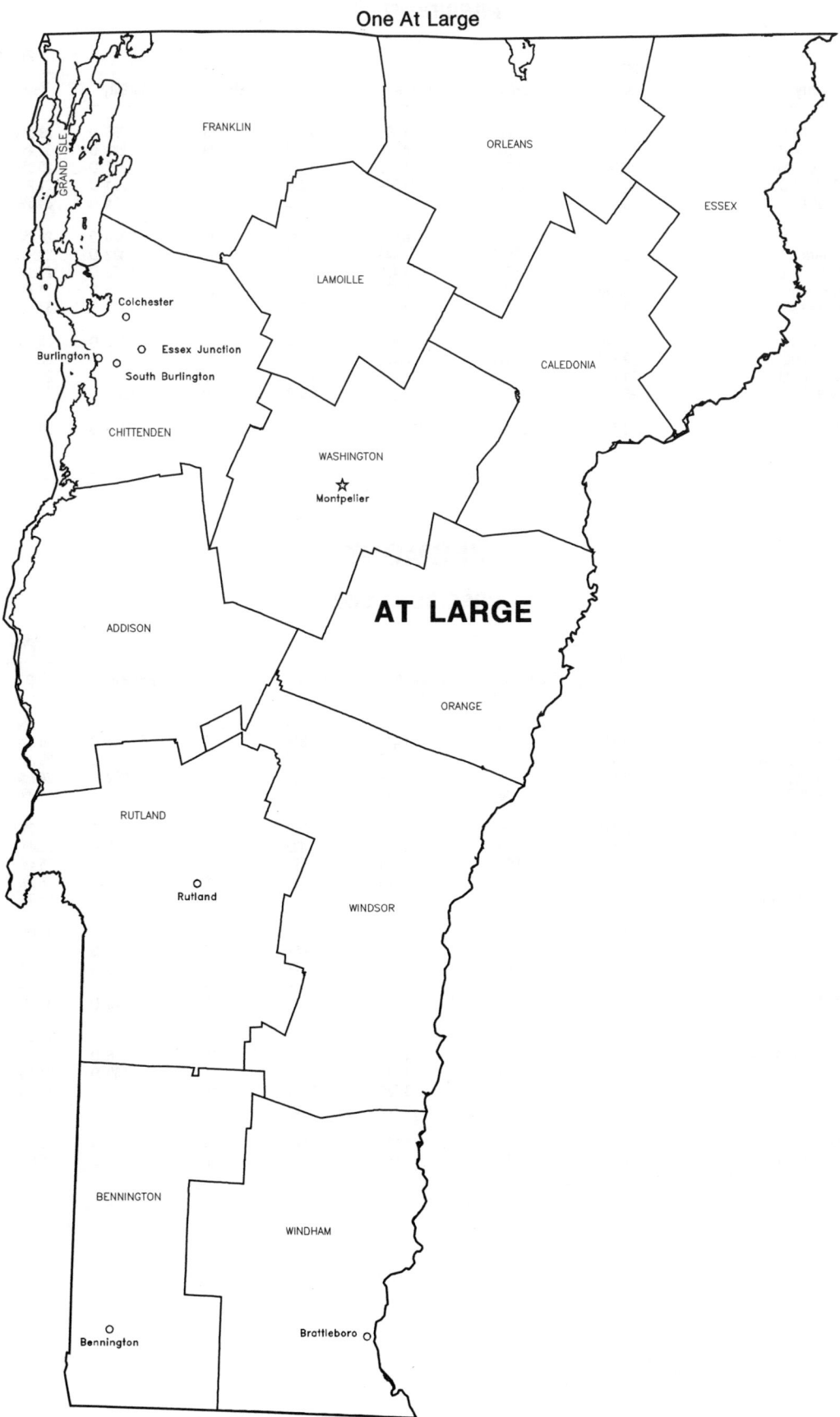

FRANKLIN

GRAND ISLE

ORLEANS

ESSEX

LAMOILLE

Colchester

Essex Junction

Burlington

South Burlington

CHITTENDEN

CALEDONIA

WASHINGTON

☆
Montpelier

AT LARGE

ADDISON

ORANGE

RUTLAND

Rutland

WINDSOR

BENNINGTON

WINDHAM

Bennington

Brattleboro

VERMONT

PRESIDENT 1992

Registration	County	Total Vote	Republican	Democratic	Perot	Other	Plurality	Percentage Total Vote		
								Rep.	Dem.	Perot
21,479	ADDISON	17,026	5,034	8,092	3,777	123	3,058 D	29.6%	47.5%	22.2%
24,189	BENNINGTON	18,216	5,895	8,178	4,023	120	2,283 D	32.4%	44.9%	22.1%
17,304	CALEDONIA	13,062	4,571	4,948	3,458	85	377 D	35.0%	37.9%	26.5%
94,842	CHITTENDEN	70,121	19,093	35,314	15,202	512	16,221 D	27.2%	50.4%	21.7%
3,826	ESSEX	2,996	1,038	1,092	845	21	54 D	34.6%	36.4%	28.2%
27,286	FRANKLIN	18,751	5,484	8,004	5,146	117	2,520 D	29.2%	42.7%	27.4%
4,054	GRAND ISLE	3,379	1,012	1,444	893	30	432 D	29.9%	42.7%	26.4%
13,324	LAMOILLE	10,142	2,936	4,459	2,674	73	1,523 D	28.9%	44.0%	26.4%
17,649	ORANGE	13,410	4,249	5,774	3,283	104	1,525 D	31.7%	43.1%	24.5%
14,702	ORLEANS	11,513	3,572	4,721	3,135	85	1,149 D	31.0%	41.0%	27.2%
40,720	RUTLAND	31,144	10,963	12,829	7,190	162	1,866 D	35.2%	41.2%	23.1%
37,760	WASHINGTON	29,338	9,424	13,452	6,274	188	4,028 D	32.1%	45.9%	21.4%
27,798	WINDHAM	21,411	5,816	11,414	4,014	167	5,598 D	27.2%	53.3%	18.7%
38,438	WINDSOR	29,192	9,035	13,871	6,077	209	4,836 D	31.0%	47.5%	20.8%
383,371	TOTAL	289,701	88,122	133,592	65,991	1,996	45,470 D	30.4%	46.1%	22.8%

VERMONT

PRESIDENT 1992

Registration	City/Town	Total Vote	Republican	Democratic	Perot	Other	Plurality	Percentage Total Vote		
								Rep.	Dem.	Perot
6,042	BARRE CITY	4,363	1,508	1,807	1,035	13	299 D	34.6%	41.4%	23.7%
4,606	BARRE TOWN	3,843	1,568	1,412	855	8	156 R	40.8%	36.7%	22.2%
10,514	BENNINGTON TOWN	7,372	2,151	3,646	1,536	39	1,495 D	29.2%	49.5%	20.8%
7,640	BRATTLEBORO	5,858	1,447	3,519	847	45	2,072 D	24.7%	60.1%	14.5%
29,516	BURLINGTON	20,401	4,462	12,510	3,241	188	8,048 D	21.9%	61.3%	15.9%
8,738	COLCHESTER	6,737	1,997	2,966	1,739	35	969 D	29.6%	44.0%	25.8%
12,893	ESSEX TOWN	9,132	2,960	3,825	2,302	45	865 D	32.4%	41.9%	25.2%
6,517	HARTFORD	4,422	1,564	2,034	793	31	470 D	35.4%	46.0%	17.9%
2,834	LYNDON	2,136	817	726	584	9	91 R	38.2%	34.0%	27.3%
5,407	MIDDLEBURY	3,837	1,021	2,176	612	28	1,155 D	26.6%	56.7%	15.9%
4,826	MILTON	3,762	1,188	1,357	1,194	23	163 D	31.6%	36.1%	31.7%
5,946	MONTPELIER	4,592	1,407	2,490	657	38	1,083 D	30.6%	54.2%	14.3%
3,792	NORTHFIELD	2,716	1,024	996	677	19	28 R	37.7%	36.7%	24.9%
3,946	ROCKINGHAM	2,434	630	1,338	454	12	708 D	25.9%	55.0%	18.7%
12,138	RUTLAND CITY	8,560	2,915	3,888	1,722	35	973 D	34.1%	45.4%	20.1%
7,631	ST. ALBANS CITY	3,120	887	1,455	744	34	568 D	28.4%	46.6%	23.8%
4,790	ST. JOHNSBURY	3,344	1,243	1,249	836	16	6 D	37.2%	37.4%	25.0%
4,327	SHELBURNE	3,787	1,202	1,841	723	21	639 D	31.7%	48.6%	19.1%
9,217	SOUTH BURLINGTON	7,278	2,131	3,730	1,359	58	1,599 D	29.3%	51.3%	18.7%
6,287	SPRINGFIELD	4,767	1,468	2,179	1,091	29	711 D	30.8%	45.7%	22.9%
3,636	SWANTON	2,505	764	1,115	622	4	351 D	30.5%	44.5%	24.8%
4,899	WINOOSKI	2,868	733	1,462	646	27	729 D	25.6%	51.0%	22.5%

VERMONT

GOVERNOR 1992

| | | | | | | | Percentage | | | |
| | | | | | | | Total Vote | | Major Vote | |
Registration	County	Total Vote	Republican	Democratic	Other	Rep.-Dem. Plurality	Rep.	Dem.	Rep.	Dem.
21,479	ADDISON	16,796	3,413	13,058	325	9,645 D	20.3%	77.7%	20.7%	79.3%
24,189	BENNINGTON	17,813	4,776	12,640	397	7,864 D	26.8%	71.0%	27.4%	72.6%
17,304	CALEDONIA	12,934	5,665	7,027	242	1,362 D	43.8%	54.3%	44.6%	55.4%
94,842	CHITTENDEN	69,067	13,047	54,818	1,202	41,771 D	18.9%	79.4%	19.2%	80.8%
3,826	ESSEX	2,956	1,138	1,738	80	600 D	38.5%	58.8%	39.6%	60.4%
27,286	FRANKLIN	18,616	4,045	14,258	313	10,213 D	21.7%	76.6%	22.1%	77.9%
4,054	GRAND ISLE	3,351	743	2,548	60	1,805 D	22.2%	76.0%	22.6%	77.4%
13,324	LAMOILLE	10,012	2,242	7,564	206	6,279 D	32.5%	95.2%	25.4%	74.6%
17,649	ORANGE	13,229	3,253	9,532	444	4,836 D	23.8%	60.4%	28.3%	71.7%
14,702	ORLEANS	11,406	3,154	7,990	262	4,836 D	27.7%	70.1%	28.3%	71.7%
40,720	RUTLAND	30,783	7,360	22,907	516	15,547 D	23.9%	74.4%	24.3%	75.7%
37,760	WASHINGTON	29,009	6,724	21,584	701	14,860 D	23.2%	74.4%	23.8%	76.2%
27,798	WINDHAM	20,957	4,312	15,698	947	11,386 D	20.6%	74.9%	21.5%	78.5%
38,438	WINDSOR	28,799	5,965	22,161	673	16,196 D	20.7%	77.0%	21.2%	78.8%
383,371	TOTAL	285,728	65,837	213,523	6,368	147,686 D	23.0%	74.7%	23.6%	76.4%

VERMONT

GOVERNOR 1992

| | | | | | | | Percentage | | | |
| | | | | | | | Total Vote | | Major Vote | |
Registration	City/Town	Total Vote	Republican	Democratic	Other	Rep.-Dem. Plurality	Rep.	Dem.	Rep.	Dem.
6,042	BARRE CITY	4,378	1,133	3,176	69	2,043 D	25.9%	72.5%	26.3%	73.7%
4,606	BARRE TOWN	3,826	1,115	2,676	35	1,561 D	29.1%	69.9%	29.4%	70.6%
10,514	BENNINGTON TOWN	7,189	1,602	5,451	136	3,849 D	22.3%	75.8%	22.7%	77.3%
7,640	BRATTLEBORO	5,705	905	4,551	249	3,646 D	15.9%	79.8%	16.6%	83.4%
29,516	BURLINGTON	19,884	2,798	16,506	580	13,708 D	14.1%	83.0%	14.5%	85.5%
8,738	COLCHESTER	6,648	1,299	5,292	57	3,993 D	19.5%	79.6%	19.7%	80.3%
12,893	ESSEX TOWN	9,017	2,157	6,778	82	4,621 D	23.9%	75.2%	24.1%	75.9%
6,517	HARTFORD	4,373	978	3,317	78	2,339 D	22.4%	75.9%	22.8%	77.2%
2,834	LYNDON	2,117	1018	1065	34	47 D	48.1%	50.3%	48.9%	51.1%
5,407	MIDDLEBURY	3,708	626	3,010	72	2,384 D	16.9%	81.2%	17.2%	82.8%
4,826	MILTON	3,724	858	2,822	44	1,964 D	23.0%	75.8%	23.3%	76.7%
5,946	MONTPELIER	4,457	878	3,454	125	2,576 D	19.7%	77.5%	20.3%	79.7%
3,792	NORTHFIELD	2,666	670	1,954	42	1,284 D	25.1%	73.3%	25.5%	74.5%
3,946	ROCKINGHAM	2,407	426	1,913	68	1,487 D	17.7%	79.5%	18.2%	81.8%
12,138	RUTLAND CITY	8,508	1,766	6,639	103	4,873 D	20.8%	78.0%	21.0%	79.0%
7,631	ST. ALBANS CITY	3,100	674	2,372	54	1,698 D	21.7%	76.5%	22.1%	77.9%
4,790	ST. JOHNSBURY	3,310	1,622	1,637	51	15 D	49.0%	49.5%	49.8%	50.2%
4,327	SHELBURNE	3,751	681	3,031	39	2,350 D	18.2%	80.8%	18.3%	81.7%
9,217	SOUTH BURLINGTON	7,208	1,330	5,783	95	4,453 D	18.5%	80.2%	18.7%	81.3%
6,287	SPRINGFIELD	4,726	919	3,725	82	2,806 D	19.4%	78.8%	19.8%	80.2%
3,636	SWANTON	2,489	516	1,932	41	1,416 D	20.7%	77.6%	21.1%	78.9%
4,899	WINOOSKI	2,783	469	2,271	43	1,802 D	16.9%	81.6%	17.1%	82.9%

VERMONT

SENATOR 1992

| | | | | | | | Percentage | | | |
| | | | | | | | Total Vote | | Major Vote | |
Registration	County	Total Vote	Republican	Democratic	Other	Rep.-Dem. Plurality	Rep.	Dem.	Rep.	Dem.
21,479	ADDISON	16,866	8,103	8,414	349	311 D	48.0%	49.9%	49.1%	50.9%
24,189	BENNINGTON	17,787	7,713	9,489	585	1,776 D	43.4%	53.3%	44.8%	55.2%
17,304	CALEDONIA	12,880	6,495	6,090	295	405 R	50.4%	47.3%	51.6%	48.4%
94,842	CHITTENDEN	69,154	26,582	41,448	1,124	14,866 D	38.4%	59.9%	39.1%	60.9%
3,826	ESSEX	2,952	1,377	1,485	90	108 D	46.6%	50.3%	48.1%	51.9%
27,286	FRANKLIN	18,574	7,812	10,304	458	2,492 D	42.1%	55.5%	43.1%	56.9%
4,054	GRAND ISLE	3,347	1,478	1,792	77	314 D	44.2%	53.5%	45.2%	54.8%
13,324	LAMOILLE	10,019	4,301	5,475	243	1,174 D	42.9%	54.6%	44.0%	56.0%
17,649	ORANGE	13,218	6,045	6,831	342	786 D	45.7%	51.7%	46.9%	53.1%
14,702	ORLEANS	11,400	4,941	6,171	288	1,230 D	43.3%	54.1%	44.5%	55.5%
40,720	RUTLAND	30,747	14,946	15,067	734	121 D	48.6%	49.0%	49.8%	50.2%
37,760	WASHINGTON	29,012	12,794	15,576	642	2,782 D	44.1%	53.7%	45.1%	54.9%
27,798	WINDHAM	21,011	8,332	11,576	1,103	3,244 D	39.7%	55.1%	41.9%	58.1%
38,438	WINDSOR	28,772	12,935	15,044	793	2,109 D	45.0%	52.3%	46.2%	53.8%
383,371	TOTAL	285,739	123,854	154,762	7,123	30,908 D	43.3%	54.2%	44.5%	55.5%

VERMONT

SENATOR 1992

| | | | | | | | Percentage | | | |
| | | | | | | | Total Vote | | Major Vote | |
Registration	City/Town	Total Vote	Republican	Democratic	Other	Rep.-Dem. Plurality	Rep.	Dem.	Rep.	Dem.
6,042	BARRE CITY	4,371	2,097	2,189	85	92 D	48.0%	50.1%	48.9%	51.1%
4,606	BARRE TOWN	3,818	2,031	1,725	62	306 R	48.0%	45.2%	54.1%	45.9%
10,514	BENNINGTON TOWN	7,106	2,664	4,229	213	1,565 D	53.2%	59.5%	38.6%	61.4%
7,640	BRATTLEBORO	5,752	2,029	3,426	297	1,397 D	37.5%	59.6%	37.2%	62.8%
29,516	BURLINGTON	20,032	5,635	13,955	442	8,320 D	35.3%	69.7%	28.8%	71.2%
8,738	COLCHESTER	6,575	2,818	3,669	88	851 D	28.1%	55.8%	43.4%	56.6%
12,893	ESSEX TOWN	9,026	4,224	4,705	97	481 D	42.9%	52.1%	47.3%	52.7%
6,517	HARTFORD	4,373	2,017	2,273	83	256 D	46.8%	52.0%	47.0%	53.0%
2,834	LYNDON	2,102	1134	932	36	202 R	46.1%	44.3%	54.9%	45.1%
5,407	MIDDLEBURY	3,741	1,641	2,056	44	415 D	53.9%	55.0%	44.4%	55.6%
4,826	MILTON	3,723	1,775	1,876	72	101 D	43.9%	50.4%	48.6%	51.4%
5,946	MONTPELIER	4,486	1,802	2,592	92	790 D	47.7%	57.8%	41.0%	59.0%
3,792	NORTHFIELD	2,671	1,327	1,279	65	48 R	40.2%	47.9%	50.9%	49.1%
3,946	ROCKINGHAM	2,397	934	1,344	119	410 D	49.7%	56.1%	41.0%	59.0%
12,138	RUTLAND CITY	8,497	3,708	4,641	148	933 D	39.0%	54.6%	44.4%	55.6%
7,631	ST. ALBANS CITY	3,084	1,163	1,825	96	662 D	43.6%	59.2%	38.9%	61.1%
4,790	ST. JOHNSBURY	3,295	1,803	1,413	79	390 R	37.7%	42.9%	56.1%	43.9%
4,327	SHELBURNE	3,756	1,613	2,108	35	495 D	54.7%	56.1%	43.3%	56.7%
9,217	SOUTH BURLINGTON	7,200	2,832	4,288	80	1,456 D	42.9%	59.6%	39.8%	60.2%
6,287	SPRINGFIELD	4,704	2,203	2,355	146	152 D	39.3%	50.1%	48.3%	51.7%
3,636	SWANTON	2,480	1,051	1,376	53	325 D	46.8%	55.5%	43.3%	56.7%
4,899	WINOOSKI	2,804	1,011	1,745	48	734 D	42.4%	62.2%	36.7%	63.3%

VERMONT

CONGRESS

			Republican			Democratic		Other	Rep.-Dem.	Percentage			
										Total Vote		Major Vote	
CD	Year	Total Vote	Vote	Candidate	Vote	Candidate		Vote	Plurality	Rep.	Dem.	Rep.	Dem.
AL	1992	281,626	86,901	PHILBIN, TIMOTHY	22,279	YOUNG, LEWIS E.		172,446	64,622 R	30.9%	7.9%	79.6%	20.4%
AL	1990	209,856	82,938	SMITH, PETER	6,315	SANDOVAL, DOLORES		120,603	76,623 R	39.5%	3.0%	92.9%	7.1%
AL	1988	240,131	98,937	SMITH, PETER	45,330	POIRIER, PAUL N		95,864	53,607 R	41.2%	18.9%	68.6%	31.4%
AL	1986	188,954	168,403 *	JEFFORDS, JAMES M.				20,551	168,403 R	89.1%		100.0%	
AL	1984	226,297	148,025	JEFFORDS, JAMES M.	60,360	POLLINA, ANTHONY		17,912	87,665 R	65.4%	26.7%	71.0%	29.0%
AL	1982	164,951	114,191	JEFFORDS, JAMES M.	38,296	KAPLAN, MARK A.		12,464	75,895 R	69.2%	23.2%	74.9%	25.1%
AL	1980	194,697	154,274	JEFFORDS, JAMES M.				40,423	154,274 R	79.2%		100.0%	
AL	1978	120,502	90,688	JEFFORDS, JAMES M.	23,228	DIETZ, S. MARIE		6,586	67,460 R	75.3%	19.3%	79.6%	20.4%
AL	1976	184,783	124,458	JEFFORDS, JAMES M.	60,202 *	BURGESS, JOHN A.		123	64,256 R	67.4%	32.6%	67.4%	32.6%
AL	1974	140,899	74,561	JEFFORDS, JAMES M.	56,342 *	CAIN, FRANCIS J.		9,996	18,219 R	52.9%	40.0%	57.0%	43.0%
AL	1972	186,028	120,924	MALLARY, RICHARD W.	65,062	MEYER, WILLIAM H.		42	55,862 R	65.0%	35.0%	65.0%	35.0%
AL	1970	152,557	103,806	STAFFORD, ROBERT T.	44,415	O'SHEA, BERNARD G.		4,336	59,391 R	68.0%	29.1%	70.0%	30.0%
AL	1968	157,133	156,956 *	STAFFORD, ROBERT T.				177	156,956 R	99.9%		100.0%	
AL	1966	135,748	89,097	STAFFORD, ROBERT T.	46,643	RYAN, WILLIAM J.		8	42,454 R	65.6%	34.4%	65.6%	34.4%
AL	1964	163,452	92,252	STAFFORD, ROBERT T.	71,193	O'SHEA, BERNARD G.		7	21,059 R	56.4%	43.6%	56.4%	43.6%
AL	1962	121,381	68,822	STAFFORD, ROBERT T.	52,535	RAYNOLDS, HAROLD		24	16,287 R	56.7%	43.3%	56.7%	43.3%
AL	1960	166,035	94,905	STAFFORD, ROBERT T.	71,111	MEYER, WILLIAM H.		19	23,794 R	57.2%	42.8%	57.2%	42.8%
AL	1958	122,702	59,536	ARTHUR, HAROLD J.	63,131	MEYER, WILLIAM H.		35	3,595 D	48.5%	51.5%	48.5%	51.5%
AL	1956	154,536	103,736	PROUTY, WINSTON L.	50,797	ST. AMOUR, CAMILLE		3	52,939 R	67.1%	32.9%	67.1%	32.9%
AL	1954	114,289	70,143	PROUTY, WINSTON L.	44,141	BOYLAN, JOHN J.		5	26,002 R	61.4%	38.6%	61.4%	38.6%
AL	1952	153,060	109,871	PROUTY, WINSTON L.	43,187	COMINGS, HERBERT B.		2	66,684 R	71.8%	28.2%	71.8%	28.2%
AL	1950	88,851	65,248	PROUTY, WINSTON L.	22,709	COMINGS, HERBERT B.		894	42,539 R	73.4%	25.6%	74.2%	25.8%
AL	1948	121,968	74,076	PLUMLEY, CHARLES A.	47,767	READY, ROBERT W.		125	26,309 R	60.7%	39.2%	60.8%	39.2%
AL	1946	73,066	46,985	PLUMLEY, CHARLES A.	26,056	CALDBECK, MATTHEW J.		25	20,929 R	64.3%	35.7%	64.3%	35.7%

VERMONT

1992 GENERAL ELECTION

In addition to the county-by-county figures, data are presented for selected Vermont communities. Since not all jurisdictions of the state are listed in this tabulation, state-wide totals are shown only with the county-by-county statistics.

President   Other vote was 501 Libertarian (Marrou); 429 Liberty Union/New Alliance (Fulani); 315 Natural Law (Hagelin); 124 Taxpayers (Phillips); 82 Socialist Workers (Warren); 57 Freedom for LaRouche (La-Rouche); 488 scattered write-in.

Governor   Other vote was 3,120 Liberty Union (Gottlieb); 2,834 Natural Law/New Alliance (Jaccaci); 414 scattered write-in.

Senator   Other vote was 5,121 Liberty Union (Levy); 1,780 Freedom for LaRouche (Godeck); 222 scattered write-in.

Congress   An asterisk in the Congressional table indicates a candidate received votes from another party endorsing his/her candidacy. Other vote at-large was 162,724 Independent (Sanders); 3,660 Liberty Union (Diamondstone); 3,549 Natural Law/New Alliance (Dewey); 2,049 Freedom for LaRouche (Miller); 464 scattered write-in. Bernard Sanders, the Independent candidate, received 57.8% of the total vote and won the election with a 75,823 plurality.

1992 PRIMARIES

SEPTEMBER 8 REPUBLICAN

Governor   John McClaughry, unopposed.

Senator   28,693 James H. Douglas; 7,395 John L. Gropper; 586 scattered write-in.

Congress   Contested as follows:

AL   18,489 Timothy Philbin; 14,881 Jeff Wennberg; 3,250 Ralph H. Sinclair; 203 scattered write-in.

SEPTEMBER 8 DEMOCRATIC

Governor   Howard B. Dean, unopposed.

Senator   Patrick J. Leahy, unopposed.

Congress   Unopposed at-large.

SEPTEMBER 8 LIBERTY UNION

Governor   Richard F. Gottlieb, unopposed.

Senator   Jerry Levy, unopposed.

Congress   Unopposed at-large.

VIRGINIA

GOVERNOR
L. Douglas Wilder (D). Elected 1989 to a four-year term.

SENATORS
Charles S. Robb (D). Elected 1988 to a six-year term.

John Warner (R). Re-elected 1990 to a six-year term. Previously elected 1984, 1978.

REPRESENTATIVES
1. Herbert H. Bateman (R)
2. Owen B. Pickett (D)
3. Robert C. Scott (D)
4. Norman Sisisky (D)
5. L. F. Payne (D)
6. Robert W. Goodlatte (R)
7. Thomas J. Bliley (R)
8. James P. Moran (D)
9. Frederick C. Boucher (D)
10. Frank R. Wolf (R)
11. Leslie L. Byrne (D)

POSTWAR VOTE FOR PRESIDENT

| | | Republican | | Democratic | | Other | | Percentage | | | |
| | Total | | | | | | | Total Vote | | Major Vote | |
Year	Vote	Vote	Candidate	Vote	Candidate	Vote	Plurality	Rep.	Dem.	Rep.	Dem.
1992 * *	2,558,665	1,150,517	Bush, George	1,038,650	Clinton, Bill	369,498	111,867 R	45.0%	40.6%	52.6%	47.4%
1988	2,191,609	1,309,162	Bush, George	859,799	Dukakis, Michael S.	22,648	449,363 R	59.7%	39.2%	60.4%	39.6%
1984	2,146,635	1,337,078	Reagan, Ronald	796,250	Mondale, Walter F.	13,307	540,828 R	62.3%	37.1%	62.7%	37.3%
1980	1,866,032	989,609	Reagan, Ronald	752,174	Carter, Jimmy	124,249	237,435 R	53.0%	40.3%	56.8%	43.2%
1976	1,697,094	836,554	Ford, Gerald R.	813,896	Carter, Jimmy	46,644	22,658 R	49.3%	48.0%	50.7%	49.3%
1972	1,457,019	988,493	Nixon, Richard M.	438,887	McGovern, George S.	29,639	549,606 R	67.8%	30.1%	69.3%	30.7%
1968 * *	1,361,491	590,319	Nixon, Richard M.	442,387	Humphrey, Hubert H.	328,785	147,932 R	43.4%	32.5%	57.2%	42.8%
1964	1,042,267	481,334	Goldwater, Barry M.	558,038	Johnson, Lyndon B.	2,895	76,704 D	46.2%	53.5%	46.3%	53.7%
1960	771,449	404,521	Nixon, Richard M.	362,327	Kennedy, John F.	4,601	42,194 R	52.4%	47.0%	52.8%	47.2%
1956	697,978	386,459	Eisenhower, Dwight D.	267,760	Stevenson, Adlai E.	43,759	118,699 R	55.4%	38.4%	59.1%	40.9%
1952	619,689	349,037	Eisenhower, Dwight D.	268,677	Stevenson, Adlai E.	1,975	80,360 R	56.3%	43.4%	56.5%	43.5%
1948	419,256	172,070	Dewey, Thomas E.	200,786	Truman, Harry S.	46,400	28,716 D	41.0%	47.9%	46.1%	53.9%

In 1992 the other vote column includes 348,639 votes cast for Perot. In 1968 other vote was 321,833 American Independent (Wallace); 4,671 Socialist Labor; 1,680 Peace and Freedom and 601 Prohibition.

POSTWAR VOTE FOR GOVERNOR

| | | Republican | | Democratic | | Other | Rep.-Dem. | Percentage | | | |
| | Total | | | | | | | Total Vote | | Major Vote | |
Year	Vote	Vote	Candidate	Vote	Candidate	Vote	Plurality	Rep.	Dem.	Rep.	Dem.
1989	1,789,078	890,195	Coleman, J. Marshall	896,936	Wilder, L. Douglas	1,947	6,741 D	49.8%	50.1%	49.8%	50.2%
1985	1,343,243	601,652	Durrette, Wyatt B.	741,438	Baliles, Gerald L.	153	139,786 D	44.8%	55.2%	44.8%	55.2%
1981	1,420,611	659,398	Coleman, J. Marshall	760,357	Robb, Charles S.	856	100,959 D	46.4%	53.5%	46.4%	53.6%
1977	1,250,940	699,302	Dalton, John	541,319	Howell, Henry	10,319	157,983 R	55.9%	43.3%	56.4%	43.6%
1973 * *	1,035,495	525,075	Godwin, Mills E.	—		510,420	525,075 R	50.7%		100.0%	
1969	915,764	480,869	Holton, Linwood	415,695	Battle, William C.	19,200	65,174 R	52.5%	45.4%	53.6%	46.4%
1965	562,789	212,207	Holton, Linwood	269,526	Godwin, Mills E.	81,056	57,319 D	37.7%	47.9%	44.1%	55.9%
1961	394,490	142,567	Pearson, H. Clyde	251,861	Harrison, Albertis	62	109,294 D	36.1%	63.8%	36.1%	63.9%
1957	517,655	188,628	Dalton, Ted	326,921	Almond, J. Lindsay	2,106	138,293 D	36.4%	63.2%	36.6%	63.4%
1953	414,025	183,328	Dalton, Ted	226,998	Stanley, Thomas B.	3,699	43,670 D	44.3%	54.8%	44.7%	55.3%
1949	262,350	71,991	Johnson, Walter	184,772	Battle, John S.	5,587	112,781 D	27.4%	70.4%	28.0%	72.0%
1945	168,783	52,386	Landreth, S. Floyd	112,355	Tuck, William M.	4,042	59,969 D	31.0%	66.6%	31.8%	68.2%

In 1973 other vote was 510,103 Independent (Howell) and 317 scattered.

VIRGINIA

POSTWAR VOTE FOR SENATOR

Year	Total Vote	Republican		Democratic		Other Vote	Rep.-Dem. Plurality	Percentage			
								Total Vote		Major Vote	
		Vote	Candidate	Vote	Candidate			Rep.	Dem.	Rep.	Dem.
1990	1,083,690	876,782	Warner, John		—	206,908	876,782 R	80.9%		100.0%	
1988	2,068,897	593,652	Dawkins, Maurice A.	1,474,086	Robb, Charles S.	1,159	880,434 D	28.7%	71.2%	28.7%	71.3%
1984	2,007,487	1,406,194	Warner, John	601,142	Harrison, Edythe C.	151	805,052 R	70.0%	29.9%	70.1%	29.9%
1982	1,415,622	724,571	Trible, Paul	690,839	Davis, Richard	212	33,732 R	51.2%	48.8%	51.2%	48.8%
1978	1,222,256	613,232	Warner, John	608,511	Miller, Andrew P.	513	4,721 R	50.2%	49.8%	50.2%	49.8%
1976 * *	1,557,500		—	596,009	Zumwalt, Elmo R.	961,491	596,009 D		38.3%		100.0%
1972	1,396,268	718,337	Scott, William L.	643,963	Spong, William B.	33,968	74,374 R	51.4%	46.1%	52.7%	47.3%
1970 * *	946,751	145,031	Garland, Ray	295,057	Rawlings, George C.	506,663	150,026 D	15.3%	31.2%	33.0%	67.0%
1966	733,879	245,681	Ould, James P.	429,855	Spong, William B.	58,343	184,174 D	33.5%	58.6%	36.4%	63.6%
1966 S	729,839	272,804	Traylor, Lawrence M.	389,028	Byrd, Harry Flood, Jr.	68,007	116,224 D	37.4%	53.3%	41.2%	58.8%
1964	928,363	176,624	May, Richard A.	592,260	Byrd, Harry Flood	159,479	415,636 D	19.0%	63.8%	23.0%	77.0%
1960	622,820		—	506,169	Robertson, A. Willis	116,651	506,169 D		81.3%		100.0%
1958	457,640		—	317,221	Byrd, Harry Flood	140,419	317,221 D		69.3%		100.0%
1954	306,510		—	244,844	Robertson, A. Willis	61,666	244,844 D		79.9%		100.0%
1952	543,516		—	398,677	Byrd, Harry Flood	144,839	398,677 D		73.4%		100.0%
1948	386,178	118,546	Woods, Robert	253,865	Robertson, A. Willis	13,767	135,319 D	30.7%	65.7%	31.8%	68.2%
1946	252,863	77,005	Parsons, Lester S.	163,960	Byrd, Harry Flood	11,898	86,955 D	30.5%	64.8%	32.0%	68.0%
1946 S	248,962	72,253	Woods, Robert	169,680	Robertson, A. Willis	7,029	97,427 D	29.0%	68.2%	29.9%	70.1%

One each of the 1966 and 1946 elections was for a short term to fill a vacancy. In 1970 Harry Flood Byrd, Jr., the Independent candidate, polled 506,633 votes (53.5% of the total vote) and won the election with a 211,576 plurality. In 1976 Harry Flood Byrd, Jr., polled 890,778 votes as an Independent candidate (57.2% of the total vote) and won the election with a 294,769 plurality.

VIRGINIA

Districts Established April 15, 1992

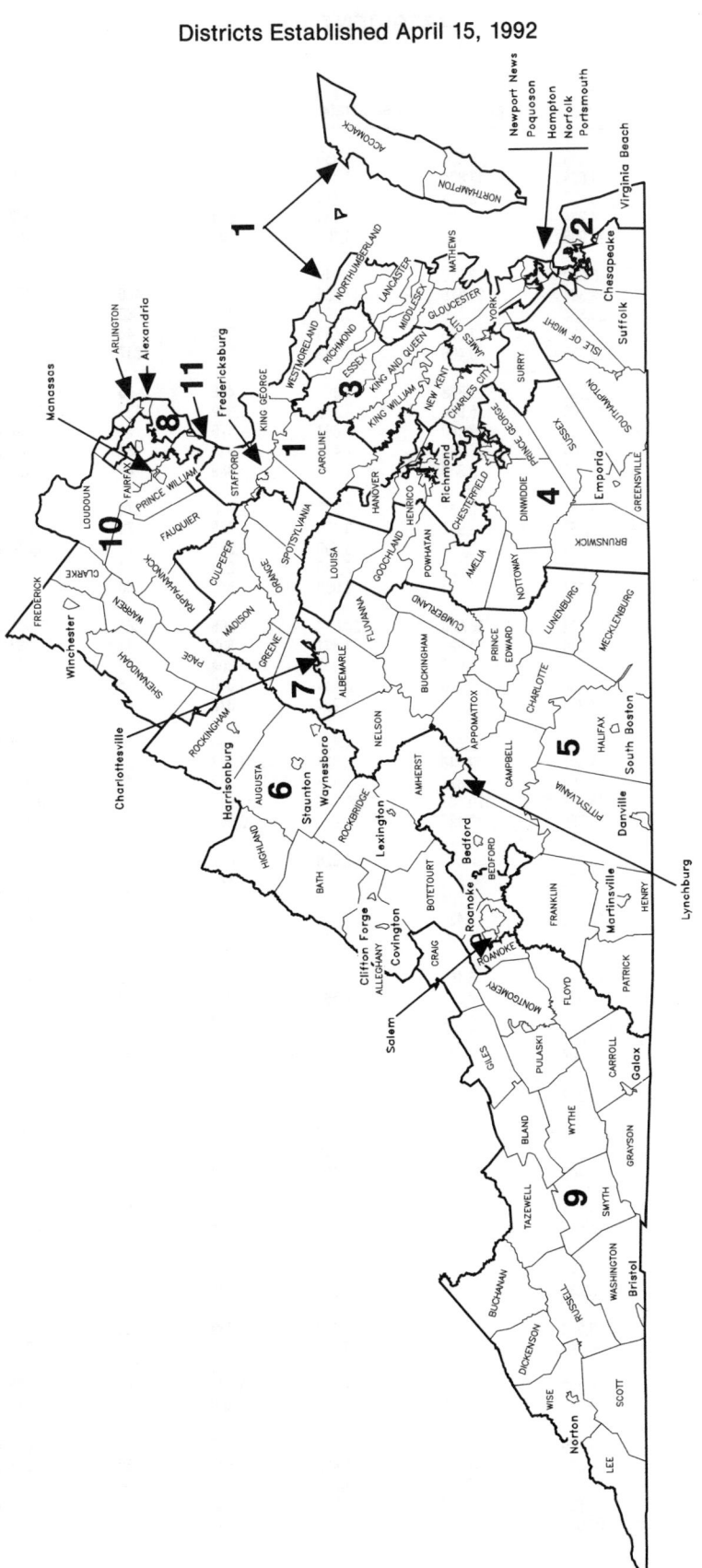

VIRGINIA

PRESIDENT 1992

Registration	County	Total Vote	Republican	Democratic	Perot	Other	Plurality	Percentage Total Vote Rep.	Dem.	Perot
16,131	ACCOMACK	13,125	5,666	4,950	2,304	205	716 R	43.2%	37.7%	17.6%
37,298	ALBEMARLE	31,804	13,894	13,886	3,855	169	8 R	43.7%	43.7%	12.1%
6,495	ALLEGHANY	5,657	2,294	2,396	926	41	102 D	40.6%	42.4%	16.4%
5,011	AMELIA	4,224	2,062	1,534	574	54	528 R	48.8%	36.3%	13.6%
12,919	AMHERST	10,908	5,482	4,101	1,268	57	1,381 R	50.3%	37.6%	11.6%
7,026	APPOMATTOX	5,620	2,830	1,919	801	70	911 R	50.4%	34.1%	14.3%
97,902	ARLINGTON	82,584	26,376	47,756	7,992	460	21,380 D	31.9%	57.8%	9.7%
24,749	AUGUSTA	21,866	12,896	5,190	3,397	383	7,706 R	59.0%	23.7%	15.5%
2,835	BATH	2,330	1,075	855	354	46	220 R	46.1%	36.7%	15.2%
23,929	BEDFORD COUNTY	20,756	10,496	6,792	3,251	217	3,704 R	50.6%	32.7%	15.7%
3,486	BLAND	2,832	1,368	1,001	408	55	367 R	48.3%	35.3%	14.4%
14,112	BOTETOURT	12,209	5,904	4,349	1,819	137	1,555 R	48.4%	35.6%	14.9%
8,744	BRUNSWICK	6,718	2,480	3,687	479	72	1,207 D	36.9%	54.9%	7.1%
15,178	BUCHANAN	11,704	3,297	7,405	815	187	4,108 D	28.2%	63.3%	7.0%
6,263	BUCKINGHAM	5,103	2,368	2,193	459	83	175 R	46.4%	43.0%	9.0%
24,333	CAMPBELL	19,757	10,931	5,999	2,553	274	4,932 R	55.3%	30.4%	12.9%
9,416	CAROLINE	7,753	2,947	3,770	965	71	823 D	38.0%	48.6%	12.4%
12,798	CARROLL	10,915	5,664	3,790	1,388	73	1,874 R	51.9%	34.7%	12.7%
3,614	CHARLES CITY	3,014	729	2,010	251	24	1,281 D	24.2%	66.7%	8.3%
6,353	CHARLOTTE	5,111	2,293	2,098	640	80	195 R	44.9%	41.0%	12.5%
118,963	CHESTERFIELD	101,933	56,626	28,028	16,898	381	28,598 R	55.6%	27.5%	16.6%
5,344	CLARKE	4,648	1,994	1,811	802	41	183 R	42.9%	39.0%	17.3%
2,636	CRAIG	2,297	1,008	965	304	20	43 R	43.9%	42.0%	13.2%
12,511	CULPEPER	10,466	5,226	3,444	1,640	156	1,782 R	49.9%	32.9%	15.7%
4,264	CUMBERLAND	3,384	1,643	1,284	372	85	359 R	48.6%	37.9%	11.0%
10,287	DICKENSON	8,143	2,574	4,839	660	70	2,265 D	31.6%	59.4%	8.1%
10,110	DINWIDDIE	8,597	3,648	3,624	1,198	127	24 R	42.4%	42.2%	13.9%
4,494	ESSEX	3,904	1,897	1,583	382	42	314 R	48.6%	40.5%	9.8%
459,118	FAIRFAX COUNTY	385,218	170,488	160,186	53,012	1,532	10,302 R	44.3%	41.6%	13.8%
23,211	FAUQUIER	20,759	10,497	6,600	3,464	198	3,897 R	50.6%	31.8%	16.7%
6,219	FLOYD	5,316	2,575	2,026	672	43	549 R	48.4%	38.1%	12.6%
6,718	FLUVANNA	5,852	2,811	2,134	871	36	677 R	48.0%	36.5%	14.9%
17,943	FRANKLIN COUNTY	15,701	6,724	6,590	2,232	155	134 R	42.8%	42.0%	14.2%
20,939	FREDERICK	17,468	9,425	4,942	2,981	120	4,483 R	54.0%	28.3%	17.1%
9,155	GILES	7,632	3,023	3,346	1,142	121	323 D	39.6%	43.8%	15.0%
15,552	GLOUCESTER	13,345	6,461	4,058	2,640	186	2,403 R	48.4%	30.4%	19.8%
8,269	GOOCHLAND	7,479	3,834	2,589	994	62	1,245 R	51.3%	34.6%	13.3%
8,463	GRAYSON	6,939	3,378	2,615	860	86	763 R	48.7%	37.7%	12.4%
5,239	GREENE	4,331	2,265	1,353	627	86	912 R	52.3%	31.2%	14.5%
5,030	GREENSVILLE	3,986	1,335	2,237	360	54	902 D	33.5%	56.1%	9.0%
13,716	HALIFAX	11,262	5,199	4,752	1,140	171	447 R	46.2%	42.2%	10.1%
37,597	HANOVER	34,261	20,336	8,021	5,674	230	12,315 R	59.4%	23.4%	16.6%
122,698	HENRICO	108,868	56,910	36,807	14,720	431	20,103 R	52.3%	33.8%	13.5%
26,574	HENRY	21,825	9,005	9,296	3,212	312	291 D	41.3%	42.6%	14.7%
1,598	HIGHLAND	1,400	686	494	212	8	192 R	49.0%	35.3%	15.1%
13,520	ISLE OF WIGHT	11,387	5,370	4,380	1,536	101	990 R	47.2%	38.5%	13.5%
20,911	JAMES CITY	18,221	8,781	6,536	2,675	229	2,245 R	48.2%	35.9%	14.7%
3,463	KING AND QUEEN	2,917	1,206	1,363	323	25	157 D	41.3%	46.7%	11.1%
6,148	KING GEORGE	5,324	2,570	1,811	918	25	759 R	48.3%	34.0%	17.2%
6,134	KING WILLIAM	5,230	2,591	1,822	758	59	769 R	49.5%	34.8%	14.5%
6,370	LANCASTER	5,528	2,841	1,812	739	136	1,029 R	51.4%	32.8%	13.4%
12,896	LEE	9,796	3,504	5,215	1,002	75	1,711 D	35.8%	53.2%	10.2%
49,040	LOUDOUN	41,574	19,290	14,462	7,391	431	4,828 R	46.4%	34.8%	17.8%
9,607	LOUISA	8,307	3,461	3,399	1,381	66	62 R	41.7%	40.9%	16.6%
5,976	LUNENBURG	4,912	2,227	2,082	505	98	145 R	45.3%	42.4%	10.3%
5,600	MADISON	4,779	2,341	1,700	653	85	641 R	49.0%	35.6%	13.7%
5,224	MATHEWS	4,525	2,179	1,402	884	60	777 R	48.2%	31.0%	19.5%
13,457	MECKLENBURG	10,970	5,401	4,273	1,128	168	1,128 R	49.2%	39.0%	10.3%
5,407	MIDDLESEX	4,685	2,224	1,597	768	96	627 R	47.5%	34.1%	16.4%
29,343	MONTGOMERY	24,935	10,606	10,658	3,449	222	52 D	42.5%	42.7%	13.8%

VIRGINIA

PRESIDENT 1992

Registration	County	Total Vote	Republican	Democratic	Perot	Other	Plurality	Percentage Total Vote		
								Rep.	Dem.	Perot
6,677	NELSON	5,538	2,159	2,586	748	45	427 D	39.0%	46.7%	13.5%
6,214	NEW KENT	5,483	2,708	1,738	1,017	20	970 R	49.4%	31.7%	18.5%
7,083	NORTHAMPTON	5,618	2,088	2,568	844	118	480 D	37.2%	45.7%	15.0%
6,278	NORTHUMBERLAND	5,334	2,667	1,862	729	76	805 R	50.0%	34.9%	13.7%
6,893	NOTTOWAY	5,743	2,610	2,411	606	116	199 R	45.4%	42.0%	10.6%
10,369	ORANGE	8,966	4,092	3,348	1,425	101	744 R	45.6%	37.3%	15.9%
10,357	PAGE	8,460	4,203	3,010	1,163	84	1,193 R	49.7%	35.6%	13.7%
8,507	PATRICK	7,189	3,521	2,465	1,026	177	1,056 R	49.0%	34.3%	14.3%
26,088	PITTSYLVANIA	21,894	11,467	7,675	2,296	456	3,792 R	52.4%	35.1%	10.5%
7,903	POWHATAN	7,086	3,832	1,950	1,232	72	1,882 R	54.1%	27.5%	17.4%
7,696	PRINCE EDWARD	6,383	2,858	2,775	635	115	83 R	44.8%	43.5%	9.9%
10,799	PRINCE GEORGE	9,412	4,799	3,087	1,459	67	1,712 R	51.0%	32.8%	15.5%
85,512	PRINCE WILLIAM	75,680	35,432	26,486	13,190	572	8,946 R	46.8%	35.0%	17.4%
16,761	PULASKI	13,987	6,148	5,633	2,066	140	515 R	44.0%	40.3%	14.8%
3,621	RAPPAHANNOCK	3,181	1,410	1,273	487	11	137 R	44.3%	40.0%	15.3%
3,518	RICHMOND COUNTY	3,050	1,609	1,034	366	41	575 R	52.8%	33.9%	12.0%
45,448	ROANOKE COUNTY	41,080	20,667	14,704	5,477	232	5,963 R	50.3%	35.8%	13.3%
8,617	ROCKBRIDGE	7,503	3,228	2,908	1,254	113	320 R	43.0%	38.8%	16.7%
24,378	ROCKINGHAM	21,493	13,016	5,407	2,839	231	7,609 R	60.6%	25.2%	13.2%
14,423	RUSSELL	11,484	3,891	6,480	958	155	2,589 D	33.9%	56.4%	8.3%
11,987	SCOTT	9,690	4,515	3,979	957	239	536 R	46.6%	41.1%	9.9%
15,697	SHENANDOAH	13,896	7,746	3,956	2,063	131	3,790 R	55.7%	28.5%	14.8%
15,258	SMYTH	12,931	6,128	4,924	1,618	261	1,204 R	47.4%	38.1%	12.5%
8,254	SOUTHAMPTON	6,874	2,844	3,199	754	77	355 D	41.4%	46.5%	11.0%
27,585	SPOTSYLVANIA	24,014	11,829	8,133	3,918	134	3,696 R	49.3%	33.9%	16.3%
29,113	STAFFORD	24,871	12,528	7,718	4,481	144	4,810 R	50.4%	31.0%	18.0%
3,977	SURRY	3,275	1,046	1,823	364	42	777 D	31.9%	55.7%	11.1%
5,530	SUSSEX	4,253	1,527	2,193	446	87	666 D	35.9%	51.6%	10.5%
21,034	TAZEWELL	17,056	6,375	8,586	1,872	223	2,211 D	37.4%	50.3%	11.0%
11,226	WARREN	9,676	4,319	3,554	1,650	153	765 R	44.6%	36.7%	17.1%
22,585	WASHINGTON	18,995	9,150	7,269	2,288	288	1,881 R	48.2%	38.3%	12.0%
7,564	WESTMORELAND	6,223	2,554	2,758	818	93	204 D	41.0%	44.3%	13.1%
18,717	WISE	14,857	5,144	7,681	1,835	197	2,537 D	34.6%	51.7%	12.4%
12,382	WYTHE	10,492	5,121	3,616	1,557	198	1,505 R	48.8%	34.5%	14.8%
22,714	YORK	19,966	10,197	6,218	3,426	125	3,979 R	51.1%	31.1%	17.2%
	City									
67,596	ALEXANDRIA	52,675	16,700	30,784	4,934	257	14,084 D	31.7%	58.4%	9.4%
2,949	BEDFORD CITY	2,409	1,091	963	313	42	128 R	45.3%	40.0%	13.0%
9,020	BRISTOL	7,462	3,616	2,948	851	47	668 R	48.5%	39.5%	11.4%
2,697	BUENA VISTA	2,200	849	1,023	291	37	174 D	38.6%	46.5%	13.2%
17,147	CHARLOTTESVILLE	14,899	4,705	8,685	1,397	112	3,980 D	31.6%	58.3%	9.4%
77,883	CHESAPEAKE	61,868	28,909	23,495	9,237	227	5,414 R	46.7%	38.0%	14.9%
2,275	CLIFTON FORGE	1,873	632	958	251	32	326 D	33.7%	51.1%	13.4%
9,892	COLONIAL HEIGHTS	8,400	5,298	1,721	1,312	69	3,577 R	63.1%	20.5%	15.6%
3,482	COVINGTON	2,869	995	1,442	402	30	447 D	34.7%	50.3%	14.0%
23,470	DANVILLE	19,661	9,584	8,134	1,679	264	1,450 R	48.7%	41.4%	8.5%
2,880	EMPORIA	2,319	1,094	1,048	157	20	46 R	47.2%	45.2%	6.8%
10,955	FAIRFAX CITY	9,693	4,333	3,884	1,439	37	449 R	44.7%	40.1%	14.8%
5,829	FALLS CHURCH	5,404	1,912	2,864	599	29	952 D	35.4%	53.0%	11.1%
4,219	FRANKLIN CITY	3,339	1,347	1,696	272	24	349 D	40.3%	50.8%	8.1%
8,294	FREDERICKSBURG	6,879	2,819	3,266	738	56	447 D	41.0%	47.5%	10.7%
2,881	GALAX	2,344	1,087	957	276	24	130 R	46.4%	40.8%	11.8%
60,715	HAMPTON	49,878	19,219	23,395	6,581	683	4,176 D	38.5%	46.9%	13.2%
11,622	HARRISONBURG	9,632	4,935	3,414	1,162	121	1,521 R	51.2%	35.4%	12.1%
9,835	HOPEWELL	8,042	3,818	2,863	1,227	134	955 R	47.5%	35.6%	15.3%
2,665	LEXINGTON	2,277	894	1,128	228	27	234 D	39.3%	49.5%	10.0%

VIRGINIA

PRESIDENT 1992

Registration	County	Total Vote	Republican	Democratic	Perot	Other	Plurality	Percentage Total Vote		
								Rep.	Dem.	Perot
30,804	LYNCHBURG	24,969	12,518	9,587	2,545	319	2,931 R	50.1%	38.4%	10.2%
13,253	MANASSAS	11,154	5,453	3,647	1,971	83	1,806 R	48.9%	32.7%	17.7%
2,031	MANASSAS PARK	1,720	792	567	356	5	225 R	46.0%	33.0%	20.7%
8,180	MARTINSVILLE	6,617	2,690	3,073	748	106	383 D	40.7%	46.4%	11.3%
74,942	NEWPORT NEWS	61,091	26,779	25,743	8,217	352	1,036 R	43.8%	42.1%	13.5%
92,304	NORFOLK	69,027	22,362	37,602	8,732	331	15,240 D	32.4%	54.5%	12.7%
1,930	NORTON	1,548	472	871	182	23	399 D	30.5%	56.3%	11.8%
16,107	PETERSBURG	12,717	3,125	8,671	834	87	5,546 D	24.6%	68.2%	6.6%
6,252	POQUOSON	5,437	3,354	1,086	960	37	2,268 R	61.7%	20.0%	17.7%
46,396	PORTSMOUTH	37,599	12,575	20,416	4,360	248	7,841 D	33.4%	54.3%	11.6%
5,706	RADFORD	4,785	1,996	2,183	582	24	187 D	41.7%	45.6%	12.2%
96,283	RICHMOND CITY	79,735	24,341	47,642	6,992	760	23,301 D	30.5%	59.8%	8.8%
42,915	ROANOKE CITY	35,181	13,443	17,724	3,753	261	4,281 D	38.2%	50.4%	10.7%
12,191	SALEM	10,669	5,143	4,028	1,430	68	1,115 R	48.2%	37.8%	13.4%
3,380	SOUTH BOSTON	2,757	1,435	1,051	252	19	384 R	52.0%	38.1%	9.1%
10,861	STAUNTON	9,232	4,989	2,851	1,146	246	2,138 R	54.0%	30.9%	12.4%
24,573	SUFFOLK	20,223	8,697	9,196	2,150	180	499 D	43.0%	45.5%	10.6%
169,556	VIRGINIA BEACH	137,785	68,936	44,294	24,087	468	24,642 R	50.0%	32.1%	17.5%
8,196	WAYNESBORO	7,149	3,758	2,302	961	128	1,456 R	52.6%	32.2%	13.4%
4,401	WILLIAMSBURG	3,719	1,349	1,856	445	69	507 D	36.3%	49.9%	12.0%
8,994	WINCHESTER	7,701	3,833	2,768	1,048	52	1,065 R	49.8%	35.9%	13.6%
3,054,662	TOTAL	2,558,665	1,150,517	1,038,650	348,639	20,859	111,867 R	45.0%	40.6%	13.6%

VIRGINIA

CONGRESS

CD	Year	Total Vote	Republican Vote	Republican Candidate	Democratic Vote	Democratic Candidate	Other Vote	Rep.-Dem. Plurality	Total Vote Rep.	Total Vote Dem.	Major Vote Rep.	Major Vote Dem.
1	1992	232,051	133,537	BATEMAN, HERBERT H.	89,814	FOX, ANDREW H.	8,700	43,723 R	57.5%	38.7%	59.8%	40.2%
2	1992	177,133	77,797	CHAPMAN, J. L.	99,253	PICKETT, OWEN B.	83	21,456 D	43.9%	56.0%	43.9%	56.1%
3	1992	168,473	35,780	JENKINS, DANIEL	132,432	SCOTT, ROBERT C.	261	96,652 D	21.2%	78.6%	21.3%	78.7%
4	1992	215,960	68,286	ZEVGOLIS, A. J.	147,649	SISISKY, NORMAN	25	79,363 D	31.6%	68.4%	31.6%	68.4%
5	1992	193,084	60,030	HURLBURT, W. A.	133,031	PAYNE, L. F.	23	73,001 D	31.1%	68.9%	31.1%	68.9%
6	1992	212,087	127,309	GOODLATTE, ROBERT W.	84,618	MUSSELWHITE, STEPHEN A.	160	42,691 R	60.0%	39.9%	60.1%	39.9%
7	1992	255,375	211,618	BLILEY, THOMAS J.			43,757	211,618 R	82.9%		100.0%	
8	1992	247,126	102,717	MCSLARROW, KYLE E.	138,542	MORAN, JAMES P.	5,867	35,825 D	41.6%	56.1%	42.6%	57.4%
9	1992	211,295	77,985	WEDDLE, L. GARRETT	133,284	BOUCHER, FREDERICK C.	26	55,299 D	36.9%	63.1%	36.9%	63.1%
10	1992	227,191	144,471	WOLF, FRANK R.	75,775	VICKERY, RAYMOND E.	6,945	68,696 R	63.6%	33.4%	65.6%	34.4%
11	1992	228,272	103,119	BUTLER, HENRY N.	114,172	BYRNE, LESLIE L.	10,981	11,053 D	45.2%	50.0%	47.5%	52.5%

VIRGINIA

Under Virginia's local government system a number of urban areas - 41 since 1977 - are organized as cities independent of county authority.

1992 GENERAL ELECTION

President   Other vote was 11,937 Independent (LaRouche); 5,730 Libertarian (Marrou); 3,192 Independent (Fulani).

Congress   Other vote was 8,677 Independent (Macleay) and 23 scattered write-in in CD 1; 43,267 Independent (Berg) and 490 scattered write-in in CD 7; 5,601 Independent (West) and 266 scattered write-in in CD 8; 6,874 Independent (Ogden) and 71 scattered write-in in CD 10; 6,681 Independent (Narro), 4,155 Independent (Mitchell) and 145 scattered write-in in CD 11; scattered write-in in all other CD's.

1992 PRIMARIES

In Virginia, local party committees have the option of holding a primary election to select candidates or nominating candidates by convention.

JUNE 9 REPUBLICAN

Congress   Candidates nominated by convention in all CD's except the following:

CD 8   9,320 Kyle E. McSlarrow; 4,885 William C. Cleveland; 3,096 J. V. Vasapoli.
CD 11   9,058 Henry N. Butler; 6,130 Mark D. Siljander; 5,491 J. A. Rollison; 4,605 Jay W. Khim; 3,181 A. L. Schlafly.

JUNE 9 DEMOCRATIC

Congress   No candidate in CD 7. Candidates nominated by convention in all other CD's except CD 3 as follows:

CD 3   23,381 Robert C. Scott; 7,520 Jean W. Cunningham; 4,003 Jacqueline G. Epps.

WASHINGTON

GOVERNOR
Mike Lowry (D). Elected 1992 to a four-year term.

SENATORS
Slade Gorton (R). Elected 1988 to a six-year term. Previously elected 1980.

Patty Murray (D). Elected 1992 to a six-year term.

REPRESENTATIVES
1. Maria Cantwell (D)
2. Al Swift (D)
3. Jolene Unsoeld (D)
4. Jay Inslee (D)
5. Thomas S. Foley (D)
6. Norman D. Dicks (D)
7. Jim McDermott (D)
8. Jennifer Dunn (R)
9. Mike Kreidler (D)

POSTWAR VOTE FOR PRESIDENT

Year	Total Vote	Republican Vote	Republican Candidate	Democratic Vote	Democratic Candidate	Other Vote	Plurality	Total Vote Rep.	Total Vote Dem.	Major Vote Rep.	Major Vote Dem.
1992 **	2,288,230	731,234	Bush, George	993,037	Clinton, Bill	563,959	261,803 D	32.0%	43.4%	42.4%	57.6%
1988	1,865,253	903,835	Bush, George	933,516	Dukakis, Michael S.	27,902	29,681 D	48.5%	50.0%	49.2%	50.8%
1984	1,883,910	1,051,670	Reagan, Ronald	807,352	Mondale, Walter F.	24,888	244,318 R	55.8%	42.9%	56.6%	43.4%
1980	1,742,394	865,244	Reagan, Ronald	650,193	Carter, Jimmy	226,957	215,051 R	49.7%	37.3%	57.1%	42.9%
1976	1,555,534	777,732	Ford, Gerald R.	717,323	Carter, Jimmy	60,479	60,409 R	50.0%	46.1%	52.0%	48.0%
1972	1,470,847	837,135	Nixon, Richard M.	568,334	McGovern, George S.	65,378	268,801 R	56.9%	38.6%	59.6%	40.4%
1968	1,304,281	588,510	Nixon, Richard M.	616,037	Humphrey, Hubert H.	99,734	27,527 D	45.1%	47.2%	48.9%	51.1%
1964	1,258,556	470,366	Goldwater, Barry M.	779,881	Johnson, Lyndon B.	8,309	309,515 D	37.4%	62.0%	37.6%	62.4%
1960	1,241,572	629,273	Nixon, Richard M.	599,298	Kennedy, John F.	13,001	29,975 R	50.7%	48.3%	51.2%	48.8%
1956	1,150,889	620,430	Eisenhower, Dwight D.	523,002	Stevenson, Adlai E.	7,457	97,428 R	53.9%	45.4%	54.3%	45.7%
1952	1,102,708	599,107	Eisenhower, Dwight D.	492,845	Stevenson, Adlai E.	10,756	106,262 R	54.3%	44.7%	54.9%	45.1%
1948	905,058	386,314	Dewey, Thomas E.	476,165	Truman, Harry S.	42,579	89,851 D	42.7%	52.6%	44.8%	55.2%

In 1992 the other vote column includes 541,780 votes cast for Perot.

POSTWAR VOTE FOR GOVERNOR

Year	Total Vote	Republican Vote	Republican Candidate	Democratic Vote	Democratic Candidate	Other Vote	Rep.-Dem. Plurality	Total Vote Rep.	Total Vote Dem.	Major Vote Rep.	Major Vote Dem.
1992	2,270,826	1,086,216	Eikenberry, Ken	1,184,315	Lowry, Mike	295	98,099 D	47.8%	52.2%	47.8%	52.2%
1988	1,874,929	708,481	Williams, Bob	1,166,448	Gardner, Booth		457,967 D	37.8%	62.2%	37.8%	62.2%
1984	1,888,987	881,994	Spellman, John D.	1,006,993	Gardner, Booth		124,999 D	46.7%	53.3%	46.7%	53.3%
1980	1,730,896	981,083	Spellman, John D.	749,813	McDermott, James A.		231,270 R	56.7%	43.3%	56.7%	43.3%
1976	1,546,382	687,039	Spellman, John D.	821,797	Ray, Dixy Lee	37,546	134,758 D	44.4%	53.1%	45.5%	54.5%
1972	1,472,542	747,825	Evans, Daniel J.	630,613	Rosellini, Albert D.	94,104	117,212 R	50.8%	42.8%	54.3%	45.7%
1968	1,265,355	692,378	Evans, Daniel J.	560,262	O'Connell, John J.	12,715	132,116 R	54.7%	44.3%	55.3%	44.7%
1964	1,250,274	697,256	Evans, Daniel J.	548,692	Rosellini, Albert D.	4,326	148,564 R	55.8%	43.9%	56.0%	44.0%
1960	1,215,748	594,122	Andrews, Lloyd J.	611,987	Rosellini, Albert D.	9,639	17,865 D	48.9%	50.3%	49.3%	50.7%
1956	1,128,977	508,041	Anderson, Emmett T.	616,773	Rosellini, Albert D.	4,163	108,732 D	45.0%	54.6%	45.2%	54.8%
1952	1,078,497	567,822	Langlie, Arthur B.	510,675	Mitchell, Hugh B.		57,147 R	52.6%	47.4%	52.6%	47.4%
1948	883,141	445,958	Langlie, Arthur B.	417,035	Wallgren, Mon C.	20,148	28,923 R	50.5%	47.2%	51.7%	48.3%

WASHINGTON

POSTWAR VOTE FOR SENATOR

Year	Total Vote	Republican Vote	Republican Candidate	Democratic Vote	Democratic Candidate	Other Vote	Rep.-Dem. Plurality	Percentage Total Vote Rep.	Percentage Total Vote Dem.	Percentage Major Vote Rep.	Percentage Major Vote Dem.
1992	2,219,162	1,020,829	Chandler, Rod	1,197,973	Murray, Patty	360	177,144 D	46.0%	54.0%	46.0%	54.0%
1988	1,848,542	944,359	Gorton, Slade	904,183	Lowry, Mike		40,176 R	51.1%	48.9%	51.1%	48.9%
1986	1,337,367	650,931	Gorton, Slade	677,471	Adams, Brock	8,965	26,540 D	48.7%	50.7%	49.0%	51.0%
1983 S	1,213,307	672,326	Evans, Daniel J.	540,981	Lowry, Mike		131,345 R	55.4%	44.6%	55.4%	44.6%
1982	1,368,476	332,273	Jewett, Doug	943,655	Jackson, Henry M.	92,548	611,382 D	24.3%	69.0%	26.0%	74.0%
1980	1,728,369	936,317	Gorton, Slade	792,052	Magnuson, Warren G.		144,265 R	54.2%	45.8%	54.2%	45.8%
1976	1,491,111	361,546	Brown, George M.	1,071,219	Jackson, Henry M.	58,346	709,673 D	24.2%	71.8%	25.2%	74.8%
1974	1,007,847	363,626	Metcalf, Jack	611,811	Magnuson, Warren G.	32,410	248,185 D	36.1%	60.7%	37.3%	62.7%
1970	1,066,807	170,790	Elicker, Charles W.	879,385	Jackson, Henry M.	16,632	708,595 D	16.0%	82.4%	16.3%	83.7%
1968	1,236,063	435,894	Metcalf, Jack	796,183	Magnuson, Warren G.	3,986	360,289 D	35.3%	64.4%	35.4%	64.6%
1964	1,213,088	337,138	Andrews, Lloyd J.	875,950	Jackson, Henry M.		538,812 D	27.8%	72.2%	27.8%	72.2%
1962	943,229	446,204	Christensen, Richard G.	491,365	Magnuson, Warren G.	5,660	45,161 D	47.3%	52.1%	47.6%	52.4%
1958	886,822	278,271	Bantz, William B.	597,040	Jackson, Henry M.	11,511	318,769 D	31.4%	67.3%	31.8%	68.2%
1956	1,122,217	436,652	Langlie, Arthur B.	685,565	Magnuson, Warren G.		248,913 D	38.9%	61.1%	38.9%	61.1%
1952	1,058,735	460,884	Cain, Harry P.	595,288	Jackson, Henry M.	2,563	134,404 D	43.5%	56.2%	43.6%	56.4%
1950	744,783	342,464	Williams, Walter	397,719	Magnuson, Warren G.	4,600	55,255 D	46.0%	53.4%	46.3%	53.7%
1946	660,342	358,847	Cain, Harry P.	298,683	Mitchell, Hugh B.	2,812	60,164 R	54.3%	45.2%	54.6%	45.4%

The 1983 election was for a short term to fill a vacancy.

WASHINGTON

Districts Established February 12, 1992

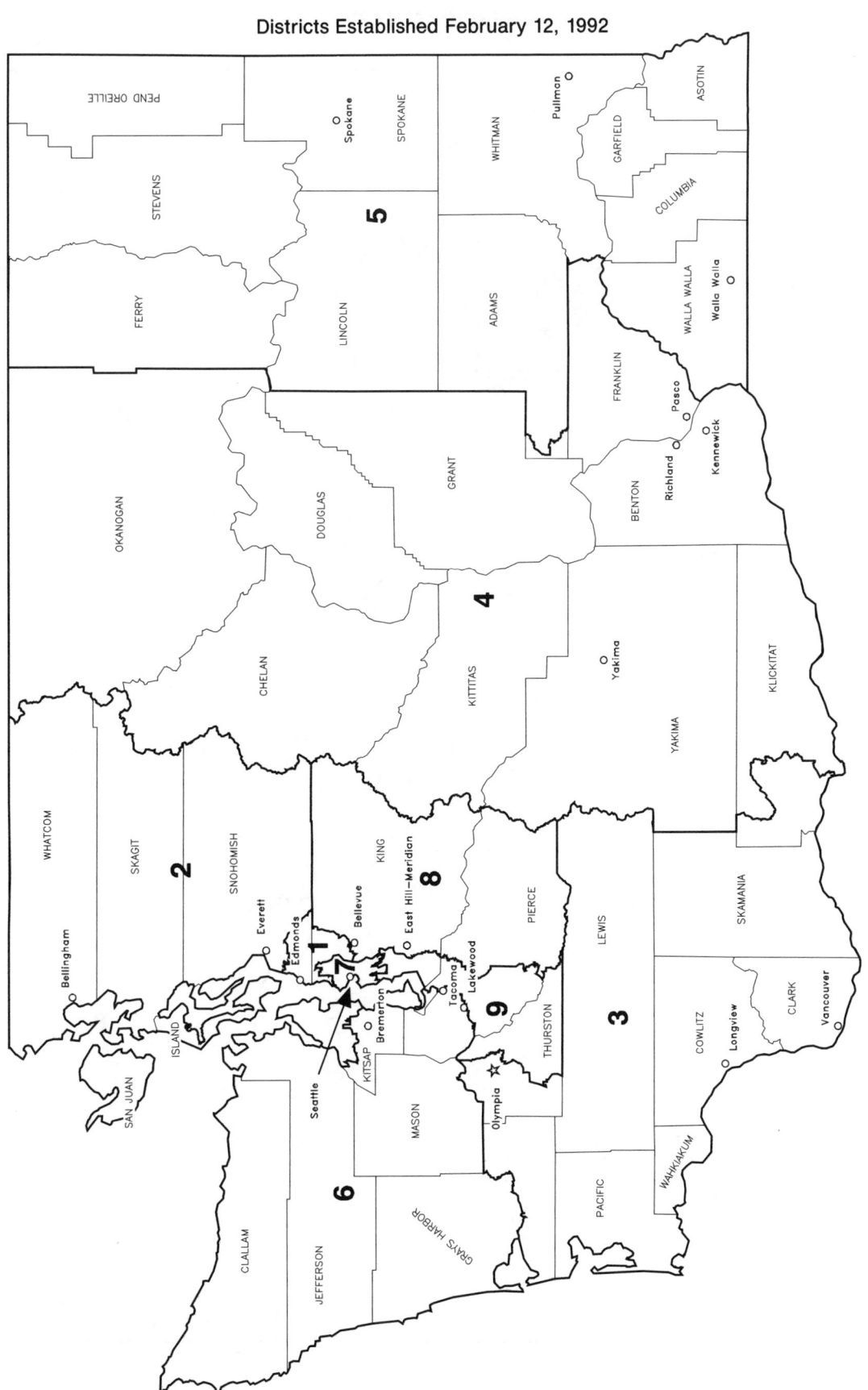

SEATTLE/PUGET SOUND AREA

CONGRESSIONAL DISTRICTS

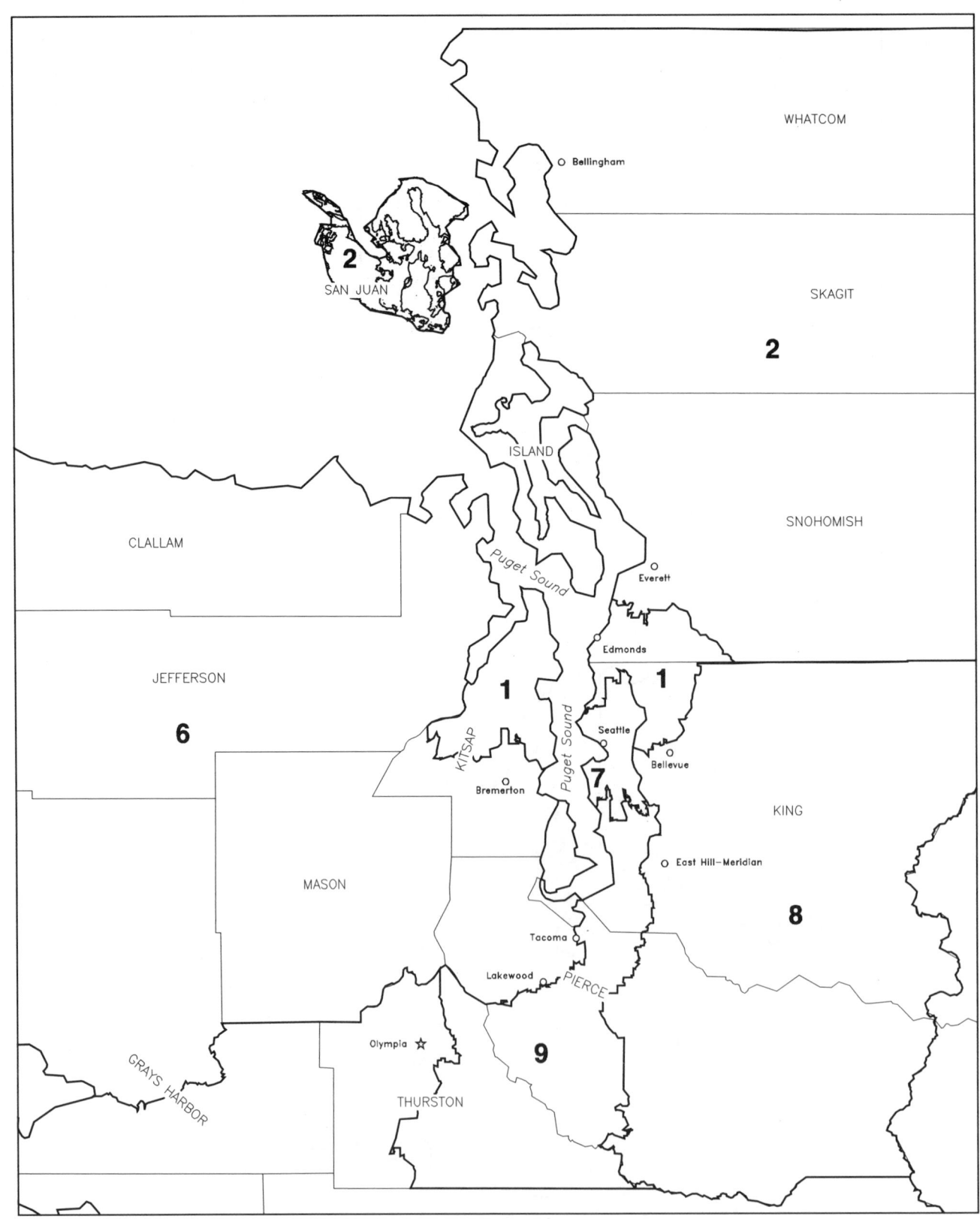

WASHINGTON

PRESIDENT 1992

Registration	County	Total Vote	Republican	Democratic	Perot	Other	Plurality	Percentage Total Vote		
								Rep.	Dem.	Perot
5,886	ADAMS	4,585	2,087	1,449	1,010	39	638 R	45.5%	31.6%	22.0%
9,729	ASOTIN	7,596	2,425	3,239	1,849	83	814 D	31.9%	42.6%	24.3%
65,475	BENTON	52,602	22,883	16,459	12,878	382	6,424 R	43.5%	31.3%	24.5%
28,505	CHELAN	23,476	10,716	7,860	4,606	294	2,856 R	45.6%	33.5%	19.6%
34,667	CLALLAM	28,673	9,765	10,820	7,775	313	1,055 D	34.1%	37.7%	27.1%
129,869	CLARK	106,536	36,906	42,648	26,163	819	5,742 D	34.6%	40.0%	24.6%
2,452	COLUMBIA	1,914	761	668	466	19	93 R	39.8%	34.9%	24.3%
42,360	COWLITZ	34,529	10,000	15,052	9,246	231	5,052 D	29.0%	43.6%	26.8%
13,561	DOUGLAS	11,048	4,920	3,731	2,315	82	1,189 R	44.5%	33.8%	21.0%
3,313	FERRY	2,557	773	963	762	59	190 D	30.2%	37.7%	29.8%
15,483	FRANKLIN	10,937	4,486	3,743	2,597	111	743 R	41.0%	34.2%	23.7%
1,572	GARFIELD	1,321	620	473	222	6	147 R	46.9%	35.8%	16.8%
26,805	GRANT	21,921	9,503	7,278	4,898	242	2,225 R	43.4%	33.2%	22.3%
33,060	GRAYS HARBOR	27,238	6,904	12,599	7,460	275	5,139 D	25.3%	46.3%	27.4%
33,014	ISLAND	27,168	9,526	9,555	7,889	198	29 D	35.1%	35.2%	29.0%
15,136	JEFFERSON	12,942	3,467	6,148	3,168	159	2,681 D	26.8%	47.5%	24.5%
943,396	KING	778,593	212,986	391,050	167,216	7,341	178,064 D	27.4%	50.2%	21.5%
108,470	KITSAP	88,568	29,340	34,442	23,873	913	5,102 D	33.1%	38.9%	27.0%
15,366	KITTITAS	12,385	4,078	5,432	2,778	97	1,354 D	32.9%	43.9%	22.4%
8,843	KLICKITAT	6,849	2,085	2,758	1,938	68	673 D	30.4%	40.3%	28.3%
33,696	LEWIS	27,168	12,316	7,810	6,684	358	4,506 R	45.3%	28.7%	24.6%
5,891	LINCOLN	4,937	2,152	1,653	1,098	34	499 R	43.6%	33.5%	22.2%
23,613	MASON	19,626	5,776	8,076	5,577	197	2,300 D	29.4%	41.1%	28.4%
16,720	OKANOGAN	13,033	4,265	5,015	3,541	212	750 D	32.7%	38.5%	27.2%
11,248	PACIFIC	9,252	2,243	4,587	2,351	71	2,236 D	24.2%	49.6%	25.4%
5,986	PEND OREILLE	4,716	1,528	1,798	1,340	50	270 D	32.4%	38.1%	28.4%
314,777	PIERCE	241,149	77,410	102,243	59,523	1,973	24,833 D	32.1%	42.4%	24.7%
7,932	SAN JUAN	7,117	1,901	3,353	1,776	87	1,452 D	26.7%	47.1%	25.0%
48,737	SKAGIT	40,728	13,388	15,936	10,973	431	2,548 D	32.9%	39.1%	26.9%
4,626	SKAMANIA	3,680	1,102	1,474	1,050	54	372 D	29.9%	40.1%	28.5%
272,621	SNOHOMISH	225,430	69,137	88,643	65,838	1,812	19,506 D	30.7%	39.3%	29.2%
207,167	SPOKANE	169,132	59,984	69,526	38,251	1,371	9,542 D	35.5%	41.1%	22.6%
18,309	STEVENS	14,787	5,706	4,960	3,769	352	746 R	38.6%	33.5%	25.5%
95,998	THURSTON	84,569	25,643	38,293	19,551	1,082	12,650 D	30.3%	45.3%	23.1%
2,220	WAHKIAKUM	1,796	488	696	584	28	112 D	27.2%	38.8%	32.5%
25,062	WALLA WALLA	19,881	7,894	7,325	4,507	155	569 R	39.7%	36.8%	22.7%
79,501	WHATCOM	63,679	23,801	26,619	12,455	804	2,818 D	37.4%	41.8%	19.6%
23,424	WHITMAN	17,478	6,428	7,637	3,220	193	1,209 D	36.8%	43.7%	18.4%
80,190	YAKIMA	57,969	25,841	21,026	10,583	519	4,815 R	44.6%	36.3%	18.3%
2,814,680	TOTAL	2,288,230	731,234	993,037	541,780	22,179	261,803 D	32.0%	43.4%	23.7%

WASHINGTON

GOVERNOR 1992

Registration	County	Total Vote	Republican	Democratic	Other	Rep.-Dem. Plurality	Percentage			
							Total Vote		Major Vote	
							Rep.	Dem.	Rep.	Dem.
5,886	ADAMS	4,557	2,807	1,750		1,057 R	61.6%	38.4%	61.6%	38.4%
9,729	ASOTIN	7,471	4,035	3,436		599 R	54.0%	46.0%	54.0%	46.0%
65,475	BENTON	51,486	29,614	21,872		7,742 R	57.5%	42.5%	57.5%	42.5%
28,505	CHELAN	23,045	14,379	8,666		5,713 R	62.4%	37.6%	62.4%	37.6%
34,667	CLALLAM	28,379	16,330	12,049		4,281 R	57.5%	42.5%	57.5%	42.5%
129,869	CLARK	104,072	55,780	48,292		7,488 R	53.6%	46.4%	53.6%	46.4%
2,452	COLUMBIA	1,912	1,313	599		714 R	68.7%	31.3%	68.7%	31.3%
42,360	COWLITZ	34,058	17,381	16,677		704 R	51.0%	49.0%	51.0%	49.0%
13,561	DOUGLAS	10,924	6,785	4,139		2,646 R	62.1%	37.9%	62.1%	37.9%
3,313	FERRY	2,521	1,459	1,062		397 R	57.9%	42.1%	57.9%	42.1%
15,483	FRANKLIN	12,005	6,531	5,474		1,057 R	54.4%	45.6%	54.4%	45.6%
1,572	GARFIELD	1,304	878	426		452 R	67.3%	32.7%	67.3%	32.7%
26,805	GRANT	21,679	13,688	7,991		5,697 R	63.1%	36.9%	63.1%	36.9%
33,060	GRAYS HARBOR	27,046	12,060	14,986		2,926 D	44.6%	55.4%	44.6%	55.4%
33,014	ISLAND	27,133	14,704	12,429		2,275 R	54.2%	45.8%	54.2%	45.8%
15,136	JEFFERSON	12,867	5,820	7,047		1,227 D	45.2%	54.8%	45.2%	54.8%
943,396	KING	771,832	305,326	466,506		161,180 D	39.6%	60.4%	39.6%	60.4%
108,470	KITSAP	87,414	44,852	42,562		2,290 R	51.3%	48.7%	51.3%	48.7%
15,366	KITTITAS	12,210	5,978	6,232		254 D	49.0%	51.0%	49.0%	51.0%
8,843	KLICKITAT	6,635	3,752	2,883		869 R	56.5%	43.5%	56.5%	43.5%
33,696	LEWIS	26,941	19,003	7,938		11,065 R	70.5%	29.5%	70.5%	29.5%
5,891	LINCOLN	4,940	3,223	1,717		1,506 R	65.2%	34.8%	65.2%	34.8%
23,613	MASON	19,659	10,111	9,548		563 R	51.4%	48.6%	51.4%	48.6%
16,720	OKANOGAN	12,851	7,712	5,139		2,573 R	60.0%	40.0%	60.0%	40.0%
11,248	PACIFIC	9,187	4,254	4,933		679 D	46.3%	53.7%	46.3%	53.7%
5,986	PEND OREILLE	4,645	2,726	1,919		807 R	58.7%	41.3%	58.7%	41.3%
314,777	PIERCE	238,591	117,623	120,968		3,345 D	49.3%	50.7%	49.3%	50.7%
7,932	SAN JUAN	6,881	3,123	3,758		635 D	45.4%	54.6%	45.4%	54.6%
48,737	SKAGIT	40,344	21,560	18,784		2,776 R	53.4%	46.6%	53.4%	46.6%
4,626	SKAMANIA	3,540	1,883	1,657		226 R	53.2%	46.8%	53.2%	46.8%
272,621	SNOHOMISH	223,196	106,196	117,000		10,804 D	47.6%	52.4%	47.6%	52.4%
207,167	SPOKANE	167,531	93,269	74,262		19,007 R	55.7%	44.3%	55.7%	44.3%
18,309	STEVENS	14,664	9,217	5,447		3,770 R	62.9%	37.1%	62.9%	37.1%
95,998	THURSTON	83,704	37,038	46,666		9,628 D	44.2%	55.8%	44.2%	55.8%
2,220	WAHKIAKUM	1,741	966	775		191 R	55.5%	44.5%	55.5%	44.5%
25,062	WALLA WALLA	19,663	11,333	8,330		3,003 R	57.6%	42.4%	57.6%	42.4%
79,501	WHATCOM	62,869	31,756	31,113		643 R	50.5%	49.5%	50.5%	49.5%
23,424	WHITMAN	17,342	8,883	8,459		424 R	51.2%	48.8%	51.2%	48.8%
80,190	YAKIMA	63,692	32,868	30,824		2,044 R	51.6%	48.4%	51.6%	48.4%
2,814,680	TOTAL	2,270,826	1,086,216	1,184,315	295	98,099 D	47.8%	52.2%	47.8%	52.2%

WASHINGTON

CONGRESS

Total Vote	Republican Vote	Republican Candidate	Democratic Vote	Democratic Candidate	Other Vote	Rep.-Dem. Plurality	Percentage Total Vote Rep.	Total Vote Dem.	Major Vote Rep.	Major Vote Dem.
71,278	113,897	NELSON, GARY	148,844	CANTWELL, MARIA	8,537	34,947 D	42.0%	54.9%	43.3%	56.7%
55,926	107,365	METCALF, JACK	133,207	SWIFT, AL	15,354	25,842 D	42.0%	52.0%	44.6%	55.4%
46,644	108,583	FISKE, PAT	138,043	UNSOELD, JOLENE	18	29,460 D	44.0%	56.0%	44.0%	56.0%
09,604	103,028	HASTINGS, RICHARD	106,556	INSLEE, JAY	20	3,528 D	49.2%	50.8%	49.2%	50.8%
246,413	110,443	SONNELAND, JOHN	135,965	FOLEY, THOMAS S.	5	25,522 D	44.8%	55.2%	44.8%	55.2%
238,182	66,664	PHILLIPS, LAURI J.	152,933	DICKS, NORMAN D.	18,585	86,269 D	28.0%	64.2%	30.4%	69.6%
283,992	54,149	HAMPSON, GLENN C.	222,604	MCDERMOTT, JIM	7,239	168,455 D	19.1%	78.4%	19.6%	80.4%
258,188	155,874	DUNN, JENNIFER	87,611	TAMBLYN, GOERGE O.	14,703	68,263 R	60.4%	33.9%	64.0%	36.0%
212,931	91,910	VON REICHBAUER, PETER	110,902	KREIDLER, MIKE	10,119	18,992 D	43.2%	52.1%	45.3%	54.7%

WASHINGTON

SENATOR 1992

Registration	County	Total Vote	Republican	Democratic	Other	Rep.-Dem. Plurality		CD	Year
5,886	ADAMS	4,535	2,879	1,656		1,223 R			
9,729	ASOTIN	7,389	3,703	3,686		17 R		1	1992
65,475	BENTON	51,722	32,542	19,180		13,362 R			
28,505	CHELAN	22,369	13,195	9,174		4,021 R		2	1992
34,667	CLALLAM	28,164	14,268	13,896		372 R			
								3	1992
129,869	CLARK	103,690	45,923	57,767		11,844 D			
2,452	COLUMBIA	1,856	1,128	728		400 R		4	1992
42,360	COWLITZ	33,412	14,457	18,955		4,498 D			
13,561	DOUGLAS	10,823	6,416	4,407		2,009 R		5	1992
3,313	FERRY	2,491	1,278	1,213		65 R			
15,483	FRANKLIN	11,894	7,042	4,852		2,190 R		6	1992
1,572	GARFIELD	1,290	822	468		354 R			
26,805	GRANT	21,226	12,741	8,485		4,256 R		7	1992
33,060	GRAYS HARBOR	26,760	11,495	15,265		3,770 D			
33,014	ISLAND	27,041	13,320	13,721		401 D		8	1992
15,136	JEFFERSON	12,600	5,218	7,382		2,164 D			
943,396	KING	768,191	310,014	458,177		148,163 D		9	1992
108,470	KITSAP	86,960	43,547	43,413		134 R			
15,366	KITTITAS	12,155	5,789	6,366		577 D			
8,843	KLICKITAT	6,553	3,006	3,547		541 D			
33,696	LEWIS	26,639	16,573	10,066		6,507 R	6		
5,891	LINCOLN	4,890	3,108	1,782		1,326 R	6		
23,613	MASON	19,496	8,890	10,606		1,716 D	4		
16,720	OKANOGAN	12,687	6,832	5,855		977 D	5		
11,248	PACIFIC	9,043	3,579	5,464		1,885 D	3		
5,986	PEND OREILLE	4,529	2,371	2,158		213 R	5		
314,777	PIERCE	234,027	105,346	128,681		23,335 D	4		
7,932	SAN JUAN	6,835	2,827	4,008		1,181 D	4		
48,737	SKAGIT	40,029	18,992	21,037		2,045 D	4		
4,626	SKAMANIA	3,465	1,406	2,059		653 D	4		
272,621	SNOHOMISH	196,906	89,689	107,217		17,528 D	4		
207,167	SPOKANE	166,442	88,857	77,585		11,272 R	5		
18,309	STEVENS	14,061	8,214	5,847		2,367 R	5		
95,998	THURSTON	83,375	36,038	47,337		11,299 D	4		
2,220	WAHKIAKUM	1,707	775	932		157 D	4		
25,062	WALLA WALLA	19,160	10,067	9,093		974 R	52		
79,501	WHATCOM	56,786	26,950	29,836		2,886 D	47		
23,424	WHITMAN	14,408	7,798	6,610		1,188 R	54		
80,190	YAKIMA	63,196	33,734	29,462		4,272 R	53		
2,814,680	TOTAL	2,219,162	1,020,829	1,197,973	360	177,144 D	46.		

WASHINGTON

1992 GENERAL ELECTION

President   Other vote was 7,533 Libertarian (Marrou); 4,854 Populist (Gritz); 2,456 Natural Law (Hagelin); 2,354 Taxpayers (Phillips); 1,776 New Alliance (Fulani); 1,171 Independent (Daniels); 855 Independent (LaRouche); 515 Socialist Workers (Warren); 665 scattered write-in. The total of the other vote column includes the 665 write-in votes not available by county.

Governor   Other vote was scattered write-in. The total line for the other vote column represents these 295 write-in votes not available by county.

Senator   Other vote was scattered write-in. The total line for the other vote column represents these 360 write-in votes not available by county.

Congress   Other vote was 4,322 Independent (Ruckert), 4,211 Natural Law (Fleming) and 4 scattered write-in in CD 1; 8,702 Independent (Dexter), 6,646 Natural Law (Leibrant) and 6 scattered write-in in CD 2; scattered write-in in CD's 3, 4 and 5; 14,490 Independent (Donnelly), 4,075 Libertarian (Horrigan) and 20 scattered write-in in CD 6; 7,197 Independent (Glumaz) and 42 scattered write-in in CD 7; 14,686 Independent (Adams) and 17 scattered write-in in CD 8; 6,585 Independent (Wilson), 3,522 Independent (Brill) and 12 scattered write-in in CD 9.

1992 PRIMARIES

Washington's primaries are completely open, with all candidates for an office carried on the ballot together; thus a voter may vote for a Republican for Governor, a Democrat for Senator, and so on. In this so-called "jungle primary," nominations go to the highest party candidate, providing the winner receives a minimum of one percent of the total votes cast for the office. Independents qualify for a place on the general election ballot by polling the same minimum requirement.

SEPTEMBER 15 REPUBLICAN

Governor   258,553 Ken Eikenberry; 250,418 Sid Morrison; 144,050 Dan McDonald; 8,103 Bob Tharp.

Senator   228,083 Rod Chandler; 184,498 Leo K. Thorsness; 128,232 Tim Hill.

Congress   Contested as follows:

CD 1   32,348 Gary Nelson; 17,698 Mark Gardner; 6,885 John K. Dahl.
CD 2   31,661 Jack Metcalf; 13,114 Tim Erwin; 9,856 Doug Smith; 5,123 David Montgomery.
CD 3   22,848 Pat Fiske; 16,737 Bill Hughes; 5,575 Gary L. Snell.
CD 4   28,952 Richard Hastings; 13,605 Alex McLean; 12,074 Jeffrey C. Sullivan; 9,168 Bill Almon.
CD 5   27,384 John Sonneland; 20,110 Duane Sommers; 10,833 Marlyn A. Derby; 3,077 William Johns.
CD 6   34,325 Lauri J. Phillips (only Republican candidate).
CD 7   26,042 Glenn C. Hampson (only Republican candidate).
CD 8   39,405 Jennifer Dunn; 35,387 Pam Roach; 8,832 Roy A. Ferguson; 8,166 Michael Campbell.
CD 9   25,917 Peter Von Reichbauer; 22,856 Paul Barden.

SEPTEMBER 15 DEMOCRATIC

Governor   337,783 Mike Lowry; 96,480 Joe King; 31,175 Sally McQuown; 8,470 Richard B. Short; 7,860 Wayne Madsen.

Senator   318,455 Patty Murray; 208,321 Don Bonker; 15,894 Gene D. Hart; 11,659 Marshall; 7,259 Jeffrey B. Venezia.

WASHINGTON

Congress   Contested as follows:

CD 1   67,727 Maria Cantwell (only Democratic candidate).
CD 2   56,290 Al Swift; 6,344 Frank D. Sadowski.
CD 3   59,510 Jolene Unsoeld; 10,495 Chuck O'Reilly.
CD 4   27,429 Jay Inslee; 26,320 Jim Jesernig; 3,774 Joe Walkenhauer.
CD 5   68,536 Thomas S. Foley (only Democratic candidate).
CD 6   73,832 Norman D. Dicks; 10,306 Dennis Christiani.
CD 7   102,818 Jim McDermott; 8,741 Ken Yeager.
CD 8   28,213 George O. Tamblyn (only Democratic candidate).
CD 9   23,687 Mike Kreidler; 14,387 Tim McConnell; 9,382 Dick Hill.

SEPTEMBER 15 MINOR PARTIES/INDEPENDENTS

Governor   6,645 Mike the Mover (Independent); 6,068 Kathleen Wheeler (Socialist Workers). Neither candidate qualified for the general election ballot.

Senator   10,877 William C. Goodloe (Taxpayers); 7,044 LaPriel C. Barnes (Independent); 3,309 Mark Severs (Socialist Workers). None of these candidates qualified for the general election ballot.

Congress   Contested as follows:

CD 1   2,366 Anne Fleming (Natural Law); 1,967 Patrick L. Ruckert (Independent). Both candidates qualified for the general election ballot.
CD 2   3,814 Karen Leibrant (Natural Law); 2,076 R. M. Dexter (Independent); 1,173 Nico M. DeGroot (Independent Urgent). Leibrant and Dexter qualified for the general election ballot.
CD 6   6,968 Tom Donnelly (Independent); 1,882 Jim Horrigan (Libertarian); 808 Eric H. Hoffman (Natural Law). Donnelly and Horrigan qualified for the general election ballot.
CD 7   3,288 Paul Glumaz (Independent). Glumaz qualified for the general election ballot.
CD 8   3,671 Bob Adams (Independent). Adams qualified for the general election ballot.
CD 9   3,263 Brian Wilson (Independent); 1,606 Timothy J. Brill (Independent). Both candidates qualified for the general election ballot.

WEST VIRGINIA

GOVERNOR
Gaston Caperton (D). Re-elected 1992 to a four-year term. Previously elected 1988.

SENATORS
Robert C. Byrd (D). Re-elected 1988 to a six-year term. Previously elected 1982, 1976, 1970, 1964, 1958.

John D. Rockefeller (D). Re-elected 1990 to a six-year term. Previously elected 1984.

REPRESENTATIVES
1. Alan B. Mollohan (D)   2. Robert E. Wise (D)   3. Nick J. Rahall (D)

POSTWAR VOTE FOR PRESIDENT

| | | Republican | | Democratic | | Other | | Percentage Total Vote | | Major Vote | |
| | Total | | | | | | | | | | |
Year	Vote	Vote	Candidate	Vote	Candidate	Vote	Plurality	Rep.	Dem.	Rep.	Dem.
1992 **	683,762	241,974	Bush, George	331,001	Clinton, Bill	110,787	89,027 D	35.4%	48.4%	42.2%	57.8%
1988	653,311	310,065	Bush, George	341,016	Dukakis, Michael S.	2,230	30,951 D	47.5%	52.2%	47.6%	52.4%
1984	735,742	405,483	Reagan, Ronald	328,125	Mondale, Walter F.	2,134	77,358 R	55.1%	44.6%	55.3%	44.7%
1980	737,715	334,206	Reagan, Ronald	367,462	Carter, Jimmy	36,047	33,256 D	45.3%	49.8%	47.6%	52.4%
1976	750,964	314,760	Ford, Gerald R.	435,914	Carter, Jimmy	290	121,154 D	41.9%	58.0%	41.9%	58.1%
1972	762,399	484,964	Nixon, Richard M.	277,435	McGovern, George S.		207,529 R	63.6%	36.4%	63.6%	36.4%
1968	754,206	307,555	Nixon, Richard M.	374,091	Humphrey, Hubert H.	72,560	66,536 D	40.8%	49.6%	45.1%	54.9%
1964	792,040	253,953	Goldwater, Barry M.	538,087	Johnson, Lyndon B.		284,134 D	32.1%	67.9%	32.1%	67.9%
1960	837,781	395,995	Nixon, Richard M.	441,786	Kennedy, John F.		45,791 D	47.3%	52.7%	47.3%	52.7%
1956	830,831	449,297	Eisenhower, Dwight D.	381,534	Stevenson, Adlai E.		67,763 R	54.1%	45.9%	54.1%	45.9%
1952	873,548	419,970	Eisenhower, Dwight D.	453,578	Stevenson, Adlai E.		33,608 D	48.1%	51.9%	48.1%	51.9%
1948	748,750	316,251	Dewey, Thomas E.	429,188	Truman, Harry S.	3,311	112,937 D	42.2%	57.3%	42.4%	57.6%

In 1992 the other vote column includes 108,829 votes cast for Perot.

POSTWAR VOTE FOR GOVERNOR

| | | Republican | | Democratic | | Other | Rep.-Dem. | Percentage Total Vote | | Major Vote | |
| | Total | | | | | | | | | | |
Year	Vote	Vote	Candidate	Vote	Candidate	Vote	Plurality	Rep.	Dem.	Rep.	Dem.
1992	657,193	240,390	Benedict, Cleveland K.	368,302	Caperton, Gaston	48,501	127,912 D	36.6%	56.0%	39.5%	60.5%
1988	649,593	267,172	Moore, Arch A.	382,421	Caperton, Gaston		115,249 D	41.1%	58.9%	41.1%	58.9%
1984	741,502	394,937	Moore, Arch A.	346,565	See, Clyde M.		48,372 R	53.3%	46.7%	53.3%	46.7%
1980	742,150	337,240	Moore, Arch A.	401,863	Rockefeller, John D.	3,047	64,623 D	45.4%	54.1%	45.6%	54.4%
1976	749,270	253,420	Underwood, Cecil H.	495,661	Rockefeller, John D.	189	242,241 D	33.8%	66.2%	33.8%	66.2%
1972	774,279	423,817	Moore, Arch A.	350,462	Rockefeller, John D.		73,355 R	54.7%	45.3%	54.7%	45.3%
1968	743,845	378,315	Moore, Arch A.	365,530	Sprouse, James M.		12,785 R	50.9%	49.1%	50.9%	49.1%
1964	788,582	355,559	Underwood, Cecil H.	433,023	Smith, Hulett C.		77,464 D	45.1%	54.9%	45.1%	54.9%
1960	827,420	380,665	Neely, Harold E.	446,755	Barron, W. W.		66,090 D	46.0%	54.0%	46.0%	54.0%
1956	817,623	440,502	Underwood, Cecil H.	377,121	Mollohan, Robert H.		63,381 R	53.9%	46.1%	53.9%	46.1%
1952	882,527	427,629	Holt, Rush D.	454,898	Marland, William C.		27,269 D	48.5%	51.5%	48.5%	51.5%
1948	768,061	329,309	Boreman, Herbert	438,752	Patteson, Okey L.		109,443 D	42.9%	57.1%	42.9%	57.1%

WEST VIRGINIA

POSTWAR VOTE FOR SENATOR

Year	Total Vote	Republican Vote	Republican Candidate	Democratic Vote	Democratic Candidate	Other Vote	Rep.-Dem. Plurality		Total Vote Rep.	Total Vote Dem.	Major Vote Rep.	Major Vote Dem.
1990	404,305	128,071	Yoder, John	276,234	Rockefeller, John D.		148,163	D	31.7%	68.3%	31.7%	68.3%
1988	634,547	223,564	Wolfe, M. Jay	410,983	Byrd, Robert C.		187,419	D	35.2%	64.8%	35.2%	64.8%
1984	722,212	344,680	Raese, John R.	374,233	Rockefeller, John D.	3,299	29,553	D	47.7%	51.8%	47.9%	52.1%
1982	565,314	173,910	Benedict, Cleveland K.	387,170	Byrd, Robert C.	4,234	213,260	D	30.8%	68.5%	31.0%	69.0%
1978	493,351	244,317	Moore, Arch A.	249,034	Randolph, Jennings		4,717	D	49.5%	50.5%	49.5%	50.5%
1976	566,790		—	566,423	Byrd, Robert C.	367	566,423	D		99.9%		100.0%
1972	731,841	245,531	Leonard, Louise	486,310	Randolph, Jennings		240,779	D	33.5%	66.5%	33.5%	66.5%
1970	445,623	99,658	Dodson, Elmer H.	345,965	Byrd, Robert C.		246,307	D	22.4%	77.6%	22.4%	77.6%
1966	491,216	198,891	Love, Francis J.	292,325	Randolph, Jennings		93,434	D	40.5%	59.5%	40.5%	59.5%
1964	761,087	246,072	Benedict, Cooper P.	515,015	Byrd, Robert C.		268,943	D	32.3%	67.7%	32.3%	67.7%
1960	828,292	369,935	Underwood, Cecil H.	458,355	Randolph, Jennings	2	88,420	D	44.7%	55.3%	44.7%	55.3%
1958	644,917	263,172	Revercomb, Chapman	381,745	Byrd, Robert C.		118,573	D	40.8%	59.2%	40.8%	59.2%
1958 S	630,677	256,510	Hoblitzell, John D.	374,167	Randolph, Jennings		117,657	D	40.7%	59.3%	40.7%	59.3%
1956 S	805,174	432,123	Revercomb, Chapman	373,051	Marland, William C.		59,072	R	53.7%	46.3%	53.7%	46.3%
1954	593,329	268,066	Sweeney, Tom	325,263	Neely, Matthew M.		57,197	D	45.2%	54.8%	45.2%	54.8%
1952	876,573	406,554	Revercomb, Chapman	470,019	Kilgore, Harley M.		63,465	D	46.4%	53.6%	46.4%	53.6%
1948	763,888	328,534	Revercomb, Chapman	435,354	Neely, Matthew M.		106,820	D	43.0%	57.0%	43.0%	57.0%
1946	542,768	269,617	Sweeney, Tom	273,151	Kilgore, Harley M.		3,534	D	49.7%	50.3%	49.7%	50.3%

One of the 1958 elections and the 1956 election were for short terms to fill vacancies.

WEST VIRGINIA

Districts Established October 17, 1991

WEST VIRGINIA

PRESIDENT 1992

Registration	County	Total Vote	Republican	Democratic	Perot	Other	Plurality	Percentage Total Vote		
								Rep.	Dem.	Perot
9,115	BARBOUR	6,954	2,322	3,467	1,153	12	1,145 D	33.4%	49.9%	16.6%
27,937	BERKELEY	20,029	9,134	7,159	3,645	91	1,975 R	45.6%	35.7%	18.2%
14,477	BOONE	9,658	2,021	6,576	1,037	24	4,555 D	20.9%	68.1%	10.7%
7,778	BRAXTON	5,765	1,535	3,396	823	11	1,861 D	26.6%	58.9%	14.3%
13,919	BROOKE	10,415	2,582	5,693	2,103	37	3,111 D	24.8%	54.7%	20.2%
49,310	CABELL	33,725	13,203	15,111	5,311	100	1,908 D	39.1%	44.8%	15.7%
4,678	CALHOUN	3,268	1,095	1,627	537	9	532 D	33.5%	49.8%	16.4%
5,678	CLAY	3,657	1,255	1,928	462	12	673 D	34.3%	52.7%	12.6%
3,937	DODDRIDGE	2,992	1,500	968	515	9	532 R	50.1%	32.4%	17.2%
22,215	FAYETTE	15,608	3,991	9,574	2,002	41	5,583 D	25.6%	61.3%	12.8%
4,361	GILMER	3,154	1,085	1,576	484	9	491 D	34.4%	50.0%	15.3%
5,964	GRANT	4,298	2,762	1,011	519	6	1,751 R	64.3%	23.5%	12.1%
16,308	GREENBRIER	12,187	4,442	5,784	1,898	63	1,342 D	36.4%	47.5%	15.6%
7,773	HAMPSHIRE	6,171	2,767	2,365	1,022	17	402 R	44.8%	38.3%	16.6%
18,772	HANCOCK	15,046	3,897	7,830	3,267	52	3,933 D	25.9%	52.0%	21.7%
6,067	HARDY	4,671	2,144	1,917	602	8	227 R	45.9%	41.0%	12.9%
40,691	HARRISON	30,341	9,687	15,480	5,131	43	5,793 D	31.9%	51.0%	16.9%
14,506	JACKSON	11,229	4,192	5,102	1,908	27	910 D	37.3%	45.4%	17.0%
16,506	JEFFERSON	12,189	4,656	5,363	2,114	56	707 D	38.2%	44.0%	17.3%
117,569	KANAWHA	81,683	31,358	38,315	11,778	232	6,957 D	38.4%	46.9%	14.4%
8,527	LEWIS	6,563	2,413	2,931	1,197	22	518 D	36.8%	44.7%	18.2%
14,525	LINCOLN	7,984	2,637	4,502	787	58	1,865 D	33.0%	56.4%	9.9%
26,547	LOGAN	16,297	3,336	11,095	1,835	31	7,759 D	20.5%	68.1%	11.3%
15,682	MCDOWELL	9,781	1,941	7,019	803	18	5,078 D	19.8%	71.8%	8.2%
32,866	MARION	25,194	6,380	14,042	4,736	36	7,662 D	25.3%	55.7%	18.8%
19,981	MARSHALL	15,219	4,463	7,298	3,402	56	2,835 D	29.3%	48.0%	22.4%
15,162	MASON	11,200	3,808	5,331	2,045	16	1,523 D	34.0%	47.6%	18.3%
28,047	MERCER	20,290	7,888	9,511	2,817	74	1,623 D	38.9%	46.9%	13.9%
14,548	MINERAL	10,728	4,837	3,992	1,884	15	845 R	45.1%	37.2%	17.6%
19,292	MINGO	10,873	2,584	7,342	915	32	4,758 D	23.8%	67.5%	8.4%
37,760	MONONGALIA	28,634	9,831	14,142	4,576	85	4,311 D	34.3%	49.4%	16.0%
7,775	MONROE	5,420	2,311	2,418	685	6	107 D	42.6%	44.6%	12.6%
6,703	MORGAN	5,346	2,585	1,854	886	21	731 R	48.4%	34.7%	16.6%
13,982	NICHOLAS	9,531	2,959	5,042	1,495	35	2,083 D	31.0%	52.9%	15.7%
26,732	OHIO	20,633	7,421	9,522	3,632	58	2,101 D	36.0%	46.1%	17.6%
4,644	PENDLETON	3,583	1,589	1,626	362	6	37 D	44.3%	45.4%	10.1%
4,225	PLEASANTS	3,376	1,248	1,387	731	10	139 D	37.0%	41.1%	21.7%
4,916	POCAHONTAS	3,781	1,401	1,741	627	12	340 D	37.1%	46.0%	16.6%
13,585	PRESTON	10,495	4,429	3,933	2,109	24	496 R	42.2%	37.5%	20.1%
23,742	PUTNAM	17,428	7,653	6,817	2,910	48	836 R	43.9%	39.1%	16.7%
38,096	RALEIGH	25,214	8,700	13,171	3,247	96	4,471 D	34.5%	52.2%	12.9%
14,871	RANDOLPH	10,222	3,496	5,097	1,582	47	1,601 D	34.2%	49.9%	15.5%
5,919	RITCHIE	4,416	2,184	1,474	745	13	710 R	49.5%	33.4%	16.9%
8,178	ROANE	5,857	2,207	2,607	1,009	34	400 D	37.7%	44.5%	17.2%
7,202	SUMMERS	4,882	1,652	2,650	565	15	998 D	33.8%	54.3%	11.6%
7,711	TAYLOR	6,117	2,022	2,843	1,242	10	821 D	33.1%	46.5%	20.3%
5,177	TUCKER	3,625	1,261	1,805	550	9	544 D	34.8%	49.8%	15.2%
5,512	TYLER	4,203	1,593	1,587	1,013	10	6 R	37.9%	37.8%	24.1%
11,647	UPSHUR	8,253	3,505	3,161	1,558	29	344 R	42.5%	38.3%	18.9%
24,260	WAYNE	16,347	5,729	8,392	2,199	27	2,663 D	35.0%	51.3%	13.5%
5,110	WEBSTER	3,576	811	2,320	436	9	1,509 D	22.7%	64.9%	12.2%
10,903	WETZEL	7,597	2,271	3,753	1,550	23	1,482 D	29.9%	49.4%	20.4%
3,188	WIRT	2,382	939	1,043	394	6	104 D	39.4%	43.8%	16.5%
46,889	WOOD	36,068	15,441	13,529	6,998	100	1,912 R	42.8%	37.5%	19.4%
14,707	WYOMING	9,607	2,821	5,782	996	8	2,961 D	29.4%	60.2%	10.4%
956,172	TOTAL	683,762	241,974	331,001	108,829	1,958	89,027 D	35.4%	48.4%	15.9%

WEST VIRGINIA

GOVERNOR 1992

Registration	County	Total Vote	Republican	Democratic	Other	Rep.-Dem. Plurality	Percentage Total Vote Rep.	Dem.	Major Vote Rep.	Dem.
9,115	BARBOUR	6,830	2,699	3,805	326	1,106 D	39.5%	55.7%	41.5%	58.5%
27,937	BERKELEY	18,912	8,605	9,969	338	1,364 D	45.5%	52.7%	46.3%	53.7%
14,477	BOONE	9,273	2,069	6,543	661	4,474 D	22.3%	70.6%	24.0%	76.0%
7,778	BRAXTON	5,604	1,872	3,316	416	1,444 D	33.4%	59.2%	36.1%	63.9%
13,919	BROOKE	9,917	3,190	6,322	405	3,132 D	32.2%	63.7%	33.5%	66.5%
49,310	CABELL	32,404	10,746	18,674	2,984	7,928 D	33.2%	57.6%	36.5%	63.5%
4,678	CALHOUN	3,128	1,333	1,464	331	131 D	42.6%	46.8%	47.7%	52.3%
5,678	CLAY	3,550	1,386	1,814	350	428 D	39.0%	51.1%	43.3%	56.7%
3,937	DODDRIDGE	2,918	1,512	1,161	245	351 R	51.8%	39.8%	56.6%	43.4%
22,215	FAYETTE	15,100	4,395	8,908	1,797	4,513 D	29.1%	59.0%	33.0%	67.0%
4,361	GILMER	3,076	1,250	1,554	272	304 D	40.6%	50.5%	44.6%	55.4%
5,964	GRANT	4,148	2,739	1,356	53	1,383 R	66.0%	32.7%	66.9%	33.1%
16,308	GREENBRIER	11,646	5,683	5,159	804	524 R	48.8%	44.3%	52.4%	47.6%
7,773	HAMPSHIRE	5,963	2,990	2,850	123	140 R	50.1%	47.8%	51.2%	48.8%
18,772	HANCOCK	14,047	4,927	8,700	420	3,773 D	35.1%	61.9%	36.2%	63.8%
6,067	HARDY	4,533	2,032	2,456	45	424 D	44.8%	54.2%	45.3%	54.7%
40,691	HARRISON	29,314	8,195	18,335	2,784	10,140 D	28.0%	62.5%	30.9%	69.1%
14,506	JACKSON	10,928	4,559	5,307	1,062	748 D	41.7%	48.6%	46.2%	53.8%
16,506	JEFFERSON	11,475	4,887	6,391	197	1,504 D	42.6%	55.7%	43.3%	56.7%
117,569	KANAWHA	78,748	29,802	40,285	8,661	10,483 D	37.8%	51.2%	42.5%	57.5%
8,527	LEWIS	6,447	2,175	4,009	263	1,834 D	33.7%	62.2%	35.2%	64.8%
14,525	LINCOLN	7,706	2,857	4,158	691	1,301 D	37.1%	54.0%	40.7%	59.3%
26,547	LOGAN	15,220	3,378	10,460	1,382	7,082 D	22.2%	68.7%	24.4%	75.6%
15,682	MCDOWELL	9,286	1,685	7,227	374	5,542 D	18.1%	77.8%	18.9%	81.1%
32,866	MARION	24,659	6,098	15,989	2,572	9,891 D	24.7%	64.8%	27.6%	72.4%
19,981	MARSHALL	14,478	5,459	8,299	720	2,840 D	37.7%	57.3%	39.7%	60.3%
15,162	MASON	10,878	3,445	6,040	1,393	2,595 D	31.7%	55.5%	36.3%	63.7%
28,047	MERCER	19,231	6,952	10,925	1,354	3,973 D	36.1%	56.8%	38.9%	61.1%
14,548	MINERAL	10,560	5,241	5,278	41	37 D	49.6%	50.0%	49.8%	50.2%
19,292	MINGO	10,355	2,257	7,823	275	5,566 D	21.8%	75.5%	22.4%	77.6%
37,760	MONONGALIA	27,911	8,535	17,365	2,011	8,830 D	30.6%	62.2%	33.0%	67.0%
7,775	MONROE	5,293	2,456	2,590	247	134 D	46.4%	48.9%	48.7%	51.3%
6,703	MORGAN	5,163	2,867	2,166	130	701 R	55.5%	42.0%	57.0%	43.0%
13,982	NICHOLAS	9,147	3,271	4,812	1,064	1,541 D	35.8%	52.6%	40.5%	59.5%
26,732	OHIO	20,121	7,196	12,148	777	4,952 D	35.8%	60.4%	37.2%	62.8%
4,644	PENDLETON	3,477	1,610	1,834	33	224 D	46.3%	52.7%	46.7%	53.3%
4,225	PLEASANTS	3,264	1,481	1,580	203	99 D	45.4%	48.4%	48.4%	51.6%
4,916	POCAHONTAS	3,696	1,806	1,535	355	271 R	48.9%	41.5%	54.1%	45.9%
13,585	PRESTON	10,232	4,866	4,995	371	129 D	47.6%	48.8%	49.3%	50.7%
23,742	PUTNAM	16,932	7,538	7,567	1,827	29 D	44.5%	44.7%	49.9%	50.1%
38,096	RALEIGH	23,605	8,281	12,840	2,484	4,559 D	35.1%	54.4%	39.2%	60.8%
14,871	RANDOLPH	9,848	3,583	5,908	357	2,325 D	36.4%	60.0%	37.8%	62.2%
5,919	RITCHIE	4,280	2,122	1,784	374	338 R	49.6%	41.7%	54.3%	45.7%
8,178	ROANE	5,569	2,305	2,568	696	263 D	41.4%	46.1%	47.3%	52.7%
7,202	SUMMERS	4,231	1,727	2,504		777 D	40.8%	59.2%	40.8%	59.2%
7,711	TAYLOR	6,074	2,275	3,477	322	1,202 D	37.5%	57.2%	39.6%	60.4%
5,177	TUCKER	3,542	1,460	1,959	123	499 D	41.2%	55.3%	42.7%	57.3%
5,512	TYLER	4,111	1,735	2,108	268	373 D	42.2%	51.3%	45.1%	54.9%
11,647	UPSHUR	8,056	3,677	3,904	475	227 D	45.6%	48.5%	48.5%	51.5%
24,260	WAYNE	15,312	5,256	8,959	1,097	3,703 D	34.3%	58.5%	37.0%	63.0%
5,110	WEBSTER	3,496	1,005	2,081	410	1,076 D	28.7%	59.5%	32.6%	67.4%
10,903	WETZEL	7,359	2,489	4,622	248	2,133 D	33.8%	62.8%	35.0%	65.0%
3,188	WIRT	2,303	909	1,202	192	293 D	39.5%	52.2%	43.1%	56.9%
46,889	WOOD	34,503	14,834	17,781	1,888	2,947 D	43.0%	51.5%	45.5%	54.5%
14,707	WYOMING	9,334	2,688	5,436	1,210	2,748 D	28.8%	58.2%	33.1%	66.9%
956,172	TOTAL	657,193	240,390	368,302	48,501	127,912 D	36.6%	56.0%	39.5%	60.5%

WEST VIRGINIA

CONGRESS

CD	Year	Total Vote	Republican Vote	Republican Candidate	Democratic Vote	Democratic Candidate	Other Vote	Rep.-Dem. Plurality	Percentage Total Vote Rep.	Total Vote Dem.	Major Vote Rep.	Major Vote Dem.
1	1992	172,924			172,924	MOLLOHAN, ALAN B.		172,924 D		100.0%		100.0%
2	1992	203,090	59,102	CRAVOTTA, SAMUEL A.	143,988	WISE, ROBERT E.		84,886 D	29.1%	70.9%	29.1%	70.9%
3	1992	186,291	64,012	WALDMAN, BEN	122,279	RAHALL, NICK J.		58,267 D	34.4%	65.6%	34.4%	65.6%

WEST VIRGINIA

1992 GENERAL ELECTION

President Other vote was 1,873 Libertarian (Marrou); 34 Gritz (write-in); 6 Fulani (write-in); 6 Warren (write-in); 2 Hagelin (write-in); 2 Phillips (write-in); 35 scattered write-in.

Governor Other vote was Pritt (write-in). Charlotte Pritt came in second in the Democratic primary with 34.7% of the total vote.

Congress

1992 PRIMARIES

MAY 12 REPUBLICAN

Governor 104,169 Cleveland K. Benedict; 16,350 Vernon Criss.

Congress Unopposed in CD's 2 and 3. In CD 2 Ron Foster, the unopposed candidate, withdrew after the primary and Samuel A. Cravotta was substituted by the local party committee. No candidate in CD 1.

MAY 12 DEMOCRATIC

Governor 142,261 Gaston Caperton; 115,498 Charlotte Pritt; 66,984 Mario J. Palumbo; 4,994 Larry E. Butcher; 3,590 Rodger Belknap.

Congress Unopposed in CD's 2 and 3. Contested as follows:

CD 1 57,568 Alan B. Mollohan; 36,038 Harley O. Staggers, Jr.

WISCONSIN

GOVERNOR
Tommy G. Thompson (R). Re-elected 1990 to a four-year term. Previously elected 1986.

SENATORS
Russell D. Feingold (D). Elected 1992 to a six-year term.

Herbert H. Kohl (D). Elected 1988 to a six-year term.

REPRESENTATIVES
1. Les Aspin (D) (see page 1)
2. Scott L. Klug (R)
3. Steven Gunderson (R)
4. Gerald D. Kleczka (D)
5. Thomas M. Barrett (D)
6. Thomas E. Petri (R)
7. David R. Obey (D)
8. Toby Roth (R)
9. F. James Sensenbrenner (R)

POSTWAR VOTE FOR PRESIDENT

Year	Total Vote	Republican Vote	Republican Candidate	Democratic Vote	Democratic Candidate	Other Vote	Plurality	Total Vote Rep.	Total Vote Dem.	Major Vote Rep.	Major Vote Dem.
1992 **	2,531,114	930,855	Bush, George	1,041,066	Clinton, Bill	559,193	110,211 D	36.8%	41.1%	47.2%	52.8%
1988	2,191,608	1,047,499	Bush, George	1,126,794	Dukakis, Michael S.	17,315	79,295 D	47.8%	51.4%	48.2%	51.8%
1984	2,211,689	1,198,584	Reagan, Ronald	995,740	Mondale, Walter F.	17,365	202,844 R	54.2%	45.0%	54.6%	45.4%
1980	2,273,221	1,088,845	Reagan, Ronald	981,584	Carter, Jimmy	202,792	107,261 R	47.9%	43.2%	52.6%	47.4%
1976	2,104,175	1,004,987	Ford, Gerald R.	1,040,232	Carter, Jimmy	58,956	35,245 D	47.8%	49.4%	49.1%	50.9%
1972	1,852,890	989,430	Nixon, Richard M.	810,174	McGovern, George S.	53,286	179,256 R	53.4%	43.7%	55.0%	45.0%
1968	1,691,538	809,997	Nixon, Richard M.	748,804	Humphrey, Hubert H.	132,737	61,193 R	47.9%	44.3%	52.0%	48.0%
1964	1,691,815	638,495	Goldwater, Barry M.	1,050,424	Johnson, Lyndon B.	2,896	411,929 D	37.7%	62.1%	37.8%	62.2%
1960	1,729,082	895,175	Nixon, Richard M.	830,805	Kennedy, John F.	3,102	64,370 R	51.8%	48.0%	51.9%	48.1%
1956	1,550,558	954,844	Eisenhower, Dwight D.	586,768	Stevenson, Adlai E.	8,946	368,076 R	61.6%	37.8%	61.9%	38.1%
1952	1,607,370	979,744	Eisenhower, Dwight D.	622,175	Stevenson, Adlai E.	5,451	357,569 R	61.0%	38.7%	61.2%	38.8%
1948	1,276,800	590,959	Dewey, Thomas E.	647,310	Truman, Harry S.	38,531	56,351 D	46.3%	50.7%	47.7%	52.3%

In 1992 the other vote column includes 544,479 votes cast for Perot.

WISCONSIN

POSTWAR VOTE FOR GOVERNOR

Year	Total Vote	Republican Vote	Republican Candidate	Democratic Vote	Democratic Candidate	Other Vote	Rep.-Dem. Plurality	Total Vote Rep.	Total Vote Dem.	Major Vote Rep.	Major Vote Dem.
1990	1,379,727	802,321	Thompson, Tommy G.	576,280	Loftus, Thomas	1,126	226,041 R	58.2%	41.8%	58.2%	41.8%
1986	1,526,960	805,090	Thompson, Tommy G.	705,578	Earl, Anthony S.	16,292	99,512 R	52.7%	46.2%	53.3%	46.7%
1982	1,580,344	662,838	Kohler, Terry J.	896,812	Earl, Anthony S.	20,694	233,974 D	41.9%	56.7%	42.5%	57.5%
1978	1,500,996	816,056	Dreyfus, Lee S.	673,813	Schreiber, Martin J.	11,127	142,243 D	54.4%	44.9%	54.8%	45.2%
1974	1,181,976	497,195	Dyke, William D.	628,639	Lucey, Patrick J.	56,142	131,444 D	42.1%	53.2%	44.2%	55.8%
1970 **	1,343,160	602,617	Olson, Jack B.	728,403	Lucey, Patrick J.	12,140	125,786 D	44.9%	54.2%	45.3%	54.7%
1968	1,689,738	893,463	Knowles, Warren P.	791,100	LaFollette, Bronson C.	5,175	102,363 R	52.9%	46.8%	53.0%	47.0%
1966	1,170,173	626,041	Knowles, Warren P.	539,258	Lucey, Patrick J.	4,874	86,783 R	53.5%	46.1%	53.7%	46.3%
1964	1,694,887	856,779	Knowles, Warren P.	837,901	Reynolds, John W.	207	18,878 R	50.6%	49.4%	50.6%	49.4%
1962	1,265,900	625,536	Kuehn, Philip G.	637,491	Reynolds, John W.	2,873	11,955 D	49.4%	50.4%	49.5%	50.5%
1960	1,728,009	837,123	Kuehn, Philip G.	890,868	Nelson, Gaylord A.	18	53,745 D	48.4%	51.6%	48.4%	51.6%
1958	1,202,219	556,391	Thomson, Vernon W.	644,296	Nelson, Gaylord A.	1,532	87,905 D	46.3%	53.6%	46.3%	53.7%
1956	1,557,788	808,273	Thomson, Vernon W.	749,421	Proxmire, William	94	58,852 R	51.9%	48.1%	51.9%	48.1%
1954	1,158,666	596,158	Kohler, Walter J.	560,747	Proxmire, William	1,761	35,411 R	51.5%	48.4%	51.5%	48.5%
1952	1,615,214	1,009,171	Kohler, Walter J.	601,844	Proxmire, William	4,199	407,327 R	62.5%	37.3%	62.6%	37.4%
1950	1,138,148	605,649	Kohler, Walter J.	525,319	Thompson, Carl W.	7,180	80,330 R	53.2%	46.2%	53.6%	46.4%
1948	1,266,139	684,839	Rennebohm, Oscar	558,497	Thompson, Carl W.	22,803	126,342 R	54.1%	44.1%	55.1%	44.9%
1946	1,040,444	621,970	Goodland, Walter	406,499	Hoan, Daniel W.	11,975	215,471 R	59.8%	39.1%	60.5%	39.5%

The term of office of Wisconsin's Governor was increased from two to four years effective with the 1970 election.

POSTWAR VOTE FOR SENATOR

Year	Total Vote	Republican Vote	Republican Candidate	Democratic Vote	Democratic Candidate	Other Vote	Rep.-Dem. Plurality	Total Vote Rep.	Total Vote Dem.	Major Vote Rep.	Major Vote Dem.
1992	2,455,124	1,129,599	Kasten, Robert W.	1,290,662	Feingold, Russell D.	34,863	161,063 D	46.0%	52.6%	46.7%	53.3%
1988	2,168,190	1,030,440	Engeleiter, Susan	1,128,625	Kohl, Herbert H.	9,125	98,185 D	47.5%	52.1%	47.7%	52.3%
1986	1,483,174	754,573	Kasten, Robert W.	702,963	Garvey, Edward R.	25,638	51,610 R	50.9%	47.4%	51.8%	48.2%
1982	1,544,981	527,355	McCallum, Scott	983,311	Proxmire, William	34,315	455,956 D	34.1%	63.6%	34.9%	65.1%
1980	2,204,202	1,106,311	Kasten, Robert W.	1,065,487	Nelson, Gaylord A.	32,404	40,824 R	50.2%	48.3%	50.9%	49.1%
1976	1,935,183	521,902	York, Stanley	1,396,970	Proxmire, William	16,311	875,068 D	27.0%	72.2%	27.2%	72.8%
1974	1,199,495	429,327	Petri, Thomas E.	740,700	Nelson, Gaylord A.	29,468	311,373 D	35.8%	61.8%	36.7%	63.3%
1970	1,338,967	381,297	Erickson, John E.	948,445	Proxmire, William	9,225	567,148 D	28.5%	70.8%	28.7%	71.3%
1968	1,654,861	633,910	Leonard, Jerris	1,020,931	Nelson, Gaylord A.	20	387,021 D	38.3%	61.7%	38.3%	61.7%
1964	1,673,776	780,116	Renk, Wilbur N.	892,013	Proxmire, William	1,647	111,897 D	46.6%	53.3%	46.7%	53.3%
1962	1,260,168	594,846	Wiley, Alexander	662,342	Nelson, Gaylord A.	2,980	67,496 D	47.2%	52.6%	47.3%	52.7%
1958	1,194,678	510,398	Steinle, Roland J.	682,440	Proxmire, William	1,840	172,042 D	42.7%	57.1%	42.8%	57.2%
1957 S	772,620	312,931	Kohler, Walter J.	435,985	Proxmire, William	23,704	123,054 D	40.5%	56.4%	41.8%	58.2%
1956	1,523,356	892,473	Wiley, Alexander	627,903	Maier, Henry W.	2,980	264,570 R	58.6%	41.2%	58.7%	41.3%
1952	1,605,228	870,444	McCarthy, Joseph R.	731,402	Fairchild, Thomas E.	3,382	139,042 R	54.2%	45.6%	54.3%	45.7%
1950	1,116,135	595,283	Wiley, Alexander	515,539	Fairchild, Thomas E.	5,313	79,744 R	53.3%	46.2%	53.6%	46.4%
1946	1,014,594	620,430	McCarthy, Joseph R.	378,772	McMurray, Howard J.	15,392	241,658 R	61.2%	37.3%	62.1%	37.9%

The August 1957 election was for a short term to fill a vacancy.

WISCONSIN

Districts Established May 12, 1992

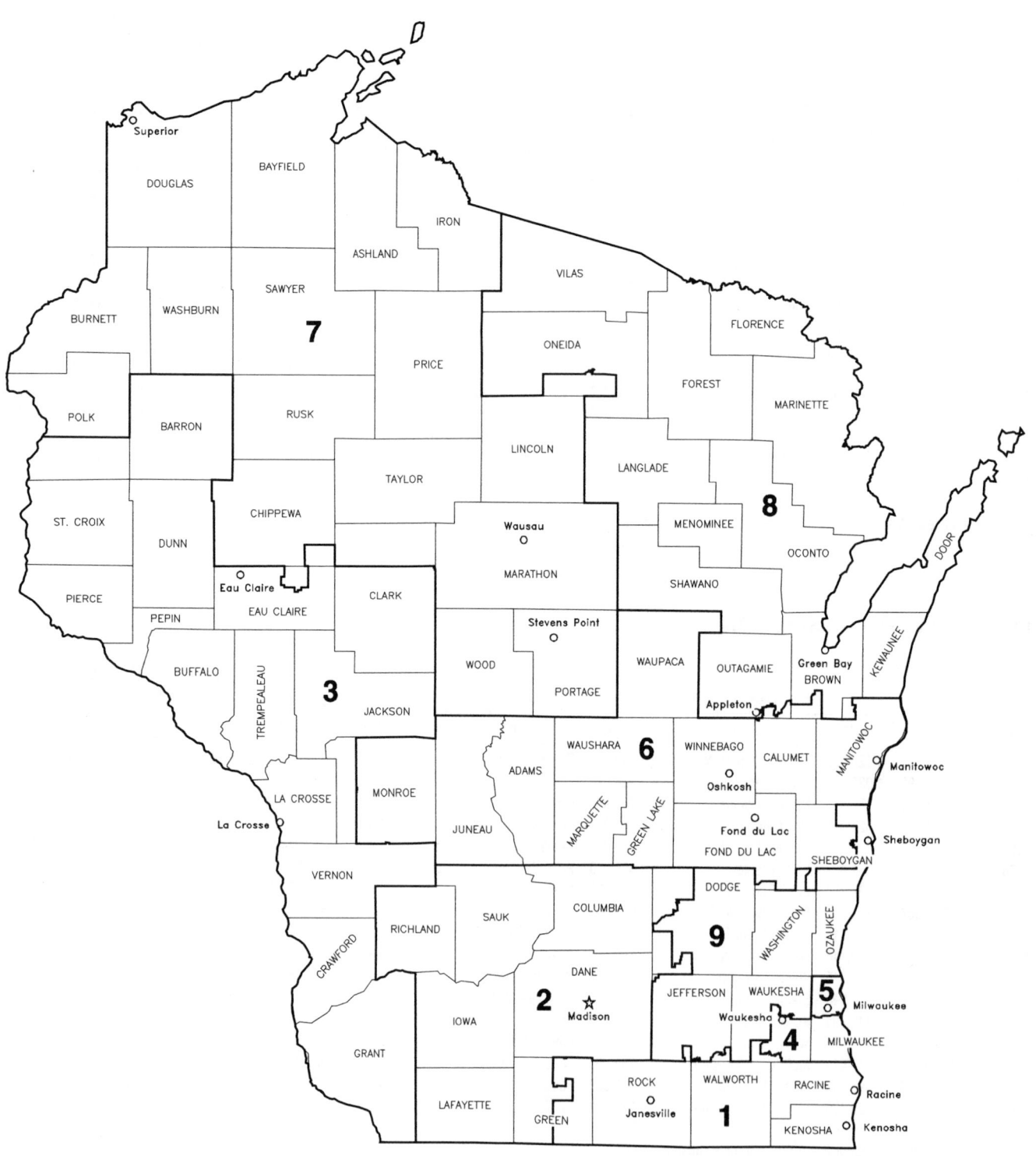

WISCONSIN

PRESIDENT 1992

1990 Voting Age Population	County	Total Vote	Republican	Democratic	Perot	Other	Plurality	Percentage Total Vote Rep.	Dem.	Perot
12,378	ADAMS	8,048	2,465	3,539	2,003	41	1,074 D	30.6%	44.0%	24.9%
11,890	ASHLAND	8,393	2,372	4,213	1,746	62	1,841 D	28.3%	50.2%	20.8%
29,450	BARRON	20,230	6,572	8,063	5,479	116	1,491 D	32.5%	39.9%	27.1%
10,280	BAYFIELD	8,112	2,393	3,873	1,786	60	1,480 D	29.5%	47.7%	22.0%
141,943	BROWN	102,701	42,352	37,513	22,395	441	4,839 R	41.2%	36.5%	21.8%
9,912	BUFFALO	6,950	2,029	2,996	1,889	36	967 D	29.2%	43.1%	27.2%
9,811	BURNETT	7,436	2,340	3,172	1,855	69	832 D	31.5%	42.7%	24.9%
23,798	CALUMET	18,401	7,541	5,701	5,055	104	1,840 R	41.0%	31.0%	27.5%
37,530	CHIPPEWA	25,230	8,215	10,487	6,408	120	2,272 D	32.6%	41.6%	25.4%
22,078	CLARK	14,885	4,977	5,540	4,284	84	563 D	33.4%	37.2%	28.8%
33,211	COLUMBIA	23,984	9,099	9,348	5,439	98	249 D	37.9%	39.0%	22.7%
11,319	CRAWFORD	7,812	2,390	3,540	1,797	85	1,150 D	30.6%	45.3%	23.0%
283,748	DANE	210,122	61,957	114,724	31,874	1,567	52,767 D	29.5%	54.6%	15.2%
56,109	DODGE	35,709	14,971	11,438	9,136	164	3,533 R	41.9%	32.0%	25.6%
19,031	DOOR	13,777	5,468	4,735	3,506	68	733 R	39.7%	34.4%	25.4%
31,077	DOUGLAS	22,253	5,679	12,319	4,150	105	6,640 D	25.5%	55.4%	18.6%
27,062	DUNN	18,218	5,283	7,965	4,809	161	2,682 D	29.0%	43.7%	26.4%
64,088	EAU CLAIRE	47,076	15,915	21,221	9,783	157	5,306 D	33.8%	45.1%	20.8%
3,368	FLORENCE	2,646	942	978	719	7	36 D	35.6%	37.0%	27.2%
65,514	FOND DU LAC	44,506	19,785	13,757	10,660	304	6,028 R	44.5%	30.9%	24.0%
6,395	FOREST	4,368	1,393	1,904	1,062	9	511 D	31.9%	43.6%	24.3%
36,088	GRANT	23,157	7,678	8,914	6,405	160	1,236 D	33.2%	38.5%	27.7%
22,070	GREEN	14,183	4,887	5,467	3,735	94	580 D	34.5%	38.5%	26.3%
13,805	GREEN LAKE	9,540	3,897	2,772	2,827	44	1,070 R	40.8%	29.1%	29.6%
14,389	IOWA	10,151	3,288	4,467	2,341	55	1,179 D	32.4%	44.0%	23.1%
4,842	IRON	3,891	1,273	1,762	835	21	489 D	32.7%	45.3%	21.5%
12,086	JACKSON	8,418	2,644	3,681	2,040	53	1,037 D	31.4%	43.7%	24.2%
50,211	JEFFERSON	32,802	13,072	11,593	7,960	177	1,479 R	39.9%	35.3%	24.3%
15,736	JUNEAU	10,993	4,051	4,177	2,670	95	126 D	36.9%	38.0%	24.3%
93,848	KENOSHA	61,837	19,854	27,341	14,232	410	7,487 D	32.1%	44.2%	23.0%
13,563	KEWAUNEE	10,377	3,570	4,050	2,700	57	480 D	34.4%	39.0%	26.0%
73,794	LA CROSSE	52,273	18,891	22,838	10,224	320	3,947 D	36.1%	43.7%	19.6%
11,384	LAFAYETTE	7,859	2,582	3,143	2,079	55	561 D	32.9%	40.0%	26.5%
14,302	LANGLADE	10,042	3,890	3,630	2,444	78	260 R	38.7%	36.1%	24.3%
19,722	LINCOLN	13,304	4,321	5,297	3,605	81	976 D	32.5%	39.8%	27.1%
59,085	MANITOWOC	41,268	14,008	15,903	11,179	178	1,895 D	33.9%	38.5%	27.1%
82,947	MARATHON	57,378	20,948	21,482	14,600	348	534 D	36.5%	37.4%	25.4%
29,650	MARINETTE	21,093	7,984	7,626	5,412	71	358 R	37.9%	36.2%	25.7%
9,296	MARQUETTE	6,720	2,322	2,533	1,818	47	211 D	34.6%	37.7%	27.1%
2,290	MENOMINEE	1,160	244	691	221	4	447 D	21.0%	59.6%	19.1%
712,973	MILWAUKEE	465,496	151,314	235,521	76,039	2,622	84,207 D	32.5%	50.6%	16.3%
25,941	MONROE	16,805	6,118	6,427	4,183	77	309 D	36.4%	38.2%	24.9%
21,995	OCONTO	16,073	5,720	5,898	4,405	50	178 D	35.6%	36.7%	27.4%
24,155	ONEIDA	18,714	6,725	7,160	4,782	47	435 D	35.9%	38.3%	25.6%
100,590	OUTAGAMIE	72,911	30,370	23,735	18,479	327	6,635 R	41.7%	32.6%	25.3%
53,146	OZAUKEE	42,910	22,805	11,879	8,002	224	10,926 R	53.1%	27.7%	18.6%
5,057	PEPIN	3,572	1,098	1,673	781	20	575 D	30.7%	46.8%	21.9%
23,917	PIERCE	17,272	4,844	7,824	4,492	112	2,980 D	28.0%	45.3%	26.0%
24,845	POLK	18,071	5,446	7,746	4,753	126	2,300 D	30.1%	42.9%	26.3%
45,661	PORTAGE	33,716	10,914	15,553	7,083	166	4,639 D	32.4%	46.1%	21.0%
11,467	PRICE	8,550	2,654	3,575	2,286	35	921 D	31.0%	41.8%	26.7%
126,413	RACINE	87,819	32,310	34,875	20,227	407	2,565 D	36.8%	39.7%	23.0%
12,761	RICHLAND	8,540	3,144	3,458	1,899	39	314 D	36.8%	40.5%	22.2%
101,651	ROCK	69,025	21,942	31,154	15,700	229	9,212 D	31.8%	45.1%	22.7%
10,919	RUSK	7,967	2,430	3,376	2,085	76	946 D	30.5%	42.4%	26.2%
35,134	ST. CROIX	25,676	8,114	10,281	7,125	156	2,167 D	31.6%	40.0%	27.7%
34,203	SAUK	23,422	8,886	9,128	5,280	128	242 D	37.9%	39.0%	22.5%
10,465	SAWYER	7,365	2,658	2,796	1,861	50	138 D	36.1%	38.0%	25.3%
27,177	SHAWANO	17,952	7,253	6,062	4,540	97	1,191 R	40.4%	33.8%	25.3%
76,022	SHEBOYGAN	54,559	22,526	20,568	11,295	170	1,958 R	41.3%	37.7%	20.7%

WISCONSIN

PRESIDENT 1992

1990 Voting Age Population	County	Total Vote	Republican	Democratic	Perot	Other	Plurality	Percentage Total Vote		
								Rep.	Dem.	Perot
13,191	TAYLOR	9,359	3,415	3,305	2,590	49	110 R	36.5%	35.3%	27.7%
18,670	TREMPEALEAU	13,012	3,577	6,218	3,160	57	2,641 D	27.5%	47.8%	24.3%
18,590	VERNON	12,716	4,072	5,673	2,890	81	1,601 D	32.0%	44.6%	22.7%
13,772	VILAS	11,262	4,616	3,764	2,827	55	852 R	41.0%	33.4%	25.1%
57,021	WALWORTH	36,796	15,727	11,825	9,029	215	3,902 R	42.7%	32.1%	24.5%
10,155	WASHBURN	7,686	2,586	3,080	1,978	42	494 D	33.6%	40.1%	25.7%
68,285	WASHINGTON	50,073	22,739	13,339	13,045	950	9,400 R	45.4%	26.6%	26.1%
221,605	WAUKESHA	179,182	91,461	50,270	36,622	829	41,191 R	51.0%	28.1%	20.4%
33,721	WAUPACA	23,159	10,252	6,666	6,088	153	3,586 R	44.3%	28.8%	26.3%
14,589	WAUSHARA	10,329	4,045	3,402	2,829	53	643 R	39.2%	32.9%	27.4%
106,523	WINNEBAGO	77,386	33,709	27,234	16,140	303	6,475 R	43.6%	35.2%	20.9%
53,073	WOOD	36,436	13,843	13,208	8,822	563	635 R	38.0%	36.2%	24.2%
3,602,787	TOTAL	2,531,114	930,855	1,041,066	544,479	14,714	110,211 D	36.8%	41.1%	21.5%

WISCONSIN

SENATOR 1992

1990 Voting Age Population	County	Total Vote	Republican	Democratic	Other	Rep.-Dem. Plurality	Percentage Total Vote Rep.	Dem.	Major Vote Rep.	Dem.
12,378	ADAMS	7,529	3,491	3,979	59	488 D	46.4%	52.8%	46.7%	53.3%
11,890	ASHLAND	7,868	3,153	4,650	65	1,497 D	40.1%	59.1%	40.4%	59.6%
29,450	BARRON	19,150	9,138	9,867	145	729 D	47.7%	51.5%	48.1%	51.9%
10,280	BAYFIELD	7,657	3,112	4,487	58	1,375 D	40.6%	58.6%	41.0%	59.0%
141,943	BROWN	101,455	49,487	50,125	1,843	638 D	48.8%	49.4%	49.7%	50.3%
9,912	BUFFALO	6,683	3,181	3,429	73	248 D	47.6%	51.3%	48.1%	51.9%
9,811	BURNETT	6,924	3,052	3,627	245	575 D	44.1%	52.4%	45.7%	54.3%
23,798	CALUMET	17,788	9,424	8,128	236	1,296 R	53.0%	45.7%	53.7%	46.3%
37,530	CHIPPEWA	24,565	11,209	12,976	380	1,767 D	45.6%	52.8%	46.3%	53.7%
22,078	CLARK	14,034	7,152	6,778	104	374 R	51.0%	48.3%	51.3%	48.7%
33,211	COLUMBIA	23,447	10,183	13,000	264	2,817 D	43.4%	55.4%	43.9%	56.1%
11,319	CRAWFORD	7,118	3,431	3,620	67	189 D	48.2%	50.9%	48.7%	51.3%
283,748	DANE	202,788	68,076	132,512	2,200	64,436 D	33.6%	65.3%	33.9%	66.1%
56,109	DODGE	35,616	19,025	15,904	687	3,121 R	53.4%	44.7%	54.5%	45.5%
19,031	DOOR	13,829	7,364	6,276	189	1,088 R	53.3%	45.4%	54.0%	46.0%
31,077	DOUGLAS	20,990	7,083	13,502	405	6,419 D	33.7%	64.3%	34.4%	65.6%
27,062	DUNN	16,418	7,334	8,801	283	1,467 D	44.7%	53.6%	45.5%	54.5%
64,088	EAU CLAIRE	45,944	19,495	25,846	603	6,351 D	42.4%	56.3%	43.0%	57.0%
3,368	FLORENCE	2,382	1,324	1,038	20	286 R	55.6%	43.6%	56.1%	43.9%
65,514	FOND DU LAC	44,710	23,425	20,583	702	2,842 R	52.4%	46.0%	53.2%	46.8%
6,395	FOREST	4,050	1,915	2,120	15	205 D	47.3%	52.3%	47.5%	52.5%
36,088	GRANT	21,892	12,034	9,664	194	2,370 R	55.0%	44.1%	55.5%	44.5%
22,070	GREEN	14,148	6,696	7,171	281	475 D	47.3%	50.7%	48.3%	51.7%
13,805	GREEN LAKE	9,210	5,066	4,017	127	1,049 R	55.0%	43.6%	55.8%	44.2%
14,389	IOWA	9,652	4,413	5,169	70	756 D	45.7%	53.6%	46.1%	53.9%
4,842	IRON	3,609	1,666	1,912	31	246 D	46.2%	53.0%	46.6%	53.4%
12,086	JACKSON	7,971	3,436	4,447	88	1,011 D	43.1%	55.8%	43.6%	56.4%
50,211	JEFFERSON	32,722	16,315	15,852	555	463 R	49.9%	48.4%	50.7%	49.3%
15,736	JUNEAU	10,395	5,355	4,955	85	400 R	51.5%	47.7%	51.9%	48.1%
93,848	KENOSHA	59,080	25,413	31,920	1,747	6,507 D	43.0%	54.0%	44.3%	55.7%
13,563	KEWAUNEE	9,903	4,755	4,957	191	202 D	48.0%	50.1%	49.0%	51.0%
73,794	LA CROSSE	50,608	22,010	27,935	663	5,925 D	43.5%	55.2%	44.1%	55.9%
11,384	LAFAYETTE	7,170	3,576	3,553	41	23 R	49.9%	49.6%	50.2%	49.8%
14,302	LANGLADE	9,647	5,370	4,193	84	1,177 R	55.7%	43.5%	56.2%	43.8%
19,722	LINCOLN	13,115	6,159	6,742	214	583 D	47.0%	51.4%	47.7%	52.3%
59,085	MANITOWOC	39,622	16,745	22,309	568	5,564 D	42.3%	56.3%	42.9%	57.1%
82,947	MARATHON	56,374	28,237	27,308	829	929 R	50.1%	48.4%	50.8%	49.2%
29,650	MARINETTE	19,517	10,187	9,159	171	1,028 R	52.2%	46.9%	52.7%	47.3%
9,296	MARQUETTE	6,305	3,049	3,196	60	147 D	48.4%	50.7%	48.8%	51.2%
2,290	MENOMINEE	783	300	476	7	176 D	38.3%	60.8%	38.7%	61.3%
712,973	MILWAUKEE	455,301	175,676	273,748	5,877	98,072 D	38.6%	60.1%	39.1%	60.9%
25,941	MONROE	16,271	8,195	7,935	141	260 R	50.4%	48.8%	50.8%	49.2%
21,995	OCONTO	14,678	7,391	7,151	136	240 R	50.4%	48.7%	50.8%	49.2%
24,155	ONEIDA	18,243	9,389	8,702	152	687 R	51.5%	47.7%	51.9%	48.1%
100,590	OUTAGAMIE	71,218	35,880	34,109	1,229	1,771 R	50.4%	47.9%	51.3%	48.7%
53,146	OZAUKEE	43,011	25,563	16,825	623	8,738 R	59.4%	39.1%	60.3%	39.7%
5,057	PEPIN	3,332	1,498	1,795	39	297 D	45.0%	53.9%	45.5%	54.5%
23,917	PIERCE	16,269	7,462	8,481	326	1,019 D	45.9%	52.1%	46.8%	53.2%
24,845	POLK	17,099	7,752	9,031	316	1,279 D	45.3%	52.8%	46.2%	53.8%
45,661	PORTAGE	32,275	13,190	18,750	335	5,560 D	40.9%	58.1%	41.3%	58.7%
11,467	PRICE	8,203	3,946	4,215	42	269 D	48.1%	51.4%	48.4%	51.6%
126,413	RACINE	83,256	38,208	43,551	1,497	5,343 D	45.9%	52.3%	46.7%	53.3%
12,761	RICHLAND	7,909	4,154	3,722	33	432 R	52.5%	47.1%	52.7%	47.3%
101,651	ROCK	65,845	26,739	38,067	1,039	11,328 D	40.6%	57.8%	41.3%	58.7%
10,919	RUSK	7,633	3,612	3,948	73	336 D	47.3%	51.7%	47.8%	52.2%
35,134	ST. CROIX	24,788	11,873	12,065	850	192 D	47.9%	48.7%	49.6%	50.4%
34,203	SAUK	23,323	11,270	11,772	281	502 D	48.3%	50.5%	48.9%	51.1%
10,465	SAWYER	7,024	3,748	3,193	83	555 R	53.4%	45.5%	54.0%	46.0%
27,177	SHAWANO	16,977	9,830	7,059	88	2,771 R	57.9%	41.6%	58.2%	41.8%
76,022	SHEBOYGAN	53,264	25,371	27,185	708	1,814 D	47.6%	51.0%	48.3%	51.7%

524

WISCONSIN

SENATOR 1992

1990 Voting Age Population	County	Total Vote	Republican	Democratic	Other	Rep.-Dem. Plurality	Percentage			
							Total Vote		Major Vote	
							Rep.	Dem.	Rep.	Dem.
13,191	TAYLOR	8,918	4,644	4,191	83	453 R	52.1%	47.0%	52.6%	47.4%
18,670	TREMPEALEAU	12,179	5,085	6,986	108	1,901 D	41.8%	57.4%	42.1%	57.9%
18,590	VERNON	12,242	5,662	6,433	147	771 D	46.3%	52.5%	46.8%	53.2%
13,772	VILAS	10,885	6,147	4,634	104	1,513 R	56.5%	42.6%	57.0%	43.0%
57,021	WALWORTH	36,688	19,318	16,552	818	2,766 R	52.7%	45.1%	53.9%	46.1%
10,155	WASHBURN	7,212	3,489	3,657	66	168 D	48.4%	50.7%	48.8%	51.2%
68,285	WASHINGTON	49,834	27,498	21,477	859	6,021 R	55.2%	43.1%	56.1%	43.9%
221,605	WAUKESHA	175,720	101,903	71,839	1,978	30,064 R	58.0%	40.9%	58.7%	41.3%
33,721	WAUPACA	21,909	12,068	9,530	311	2,538 R	55.1%	43.5%	55.9%	44.1%
14,589	WAUSHARA	9,783	5,424	4,247	112	1,177 R	55.4%	43.4%	56.1%	43.9%
106,523	WINNEBAGO	75,006	37,440	36,372	1,194	1,068 R	49.9%	48.5%	50.7%	49.3%
53,073	WOOD	36,161	18,338	17,257	566	1,081 R	50.7%	47.7%	51.5%	48.5%
3,602,787	TOTAL	2,455,124	1,129,599	1,290,662	34,863	161,063 D	46.0%	52.6%	46.7%	53.3%

WISCONSIN

CONGRESS

CD	Year	Total Vote	Republican Vote	Republican Candidate	Democratic Vote	Democratic Candidate	Other Vote	Rep.-Dem. Plurality	Total Vote Rep.	Total Vote Dem.	Major Vote Rep.	Major Vote Dem.
1	1992	256,280	104,352	NEUMANN, MARK W.	147,495	ASPIN, LES	4,433	43,143 D	40.7%	57.6%	41.4%	58.6%
2	1992	292,898	183,366	KLUG, SCOTT L.	108,291	DEER, ADA E.	1,241	75,075 R	62.6%	37.0%	62.9%	37.1%
3	1992	260,335	146,903	GUNDERSON, STEVEN	108,664	SACIA, PAUL	4,768	38,239 R	56.4%	41.7%	57.5%	42.5%
4	1992	263,803	84,872	COOK, JOSEPH L.	173,482	KLECZKA, GERALD D.	5,449	88,610 D	32.2%	65.8%	32.9%	67.1%
5	1992	234,176	71,085	HAMMERSMITH, DONALDA A.	162,344	BARRETT, THOMAS M.	747	91,259 D	30.4%	69.3%	30.5%	69.5%
6	1992	272,137	143,875	PETRI, THOMAS E.	128,232	LAUTENSCHLAGER, PEGGY A.	30	15,643 R	52.9%	47.1%	52.9%	47.1%
7	1992	257,982	91,772	VANNES, DALE R.	166,200	OBEY, DAVID R.	10	74,428 D	35.6%	64.4%	35.6%	64.4%
8	1992	273,532	191,704	ROTH, TOBY	81,792	HELMS, CATHERINE L.	36	109,912 R	70.1%	29.9%	70.1%	29.9%
9	1992	276,787	192,898	SENSENBRENNER, F. JAMES	77,362	BUXTON, INGRID K.	6,527	115,536 R	69.7%	28.0%	71.4%	28.6%

WISCONSIN

1992 GENERAL ELECTION

Wisconsin has no statewide registration system; only jurisdictions of over 5,000 population require voters to register and voters are allowed to register on election day. The data presented in the registration column in the tables are for the 1990 Voting-Age Population.

President   Other vote was 2,877 Libertarian (Marrou); 2,311 America First (Gritz); 1,883 Labor-Farm (Daniels); 1,772 Taxpayers (Phillips); 1,211 Socialist (Brisben); 1,070 Natural Law (Hagelin); 654 New Alliance (Fulani); 633 Independent for Economic Recovery (LaRouche); 405 Third Party (Hem); 390 Socialist Workers (Warren); 547 Grassroots (Herer); 961 scattered write-in.

Senator   Other vote was 16,513 Independent (Johnson); 9,147 Libertarian (Bittner); 3,264 Independent (Hanson); 2,747 Grassroots (Kundert); 2,733 Independent Populist (Selliken); 459 scattered write-in.

Congress   Other vote was 4,391 Independent (Graf) and 42 scattered write-in in CD 1; 1,140 Independent (Schumacher) and 101 scattered write-in in CD 2; 4,736 Independent (Evenson) and 32 scattered write-in in CD 3; 2,803 Independent (Slak), 2,488 Libertarian (Washburn) and 158 scattered write-in in CD 4; scattered write-in in CD's 5, 6, 7 and 8; 4,619 Independent (Marlow), 1,881 Libertarian (Millikin) and 27 scattered write-in in CD 9.

1992 PRIMARIES

SEPTEMBER 8 REPUBLICAN

Senator   197,488 Robert W. Kasten; 47,804 Roger W. Faulkner; 79 scattered write-in. Early uncorrected returns gave the Kasten vote as 194,799 and the Faulkner vote as 47,254.

Congress   Unopposed in seven CD's. Contested as follows:

CD 1   16,547 Mark W. Neumann; 3,364 Kenneth Elmer.
CD 5   6,756 Donalda A. Hammersmith; 3,938 Robert Day; 3,576 Sidney Shindell; 2,341 Fred J. Barbian.

SEPTEMBER 8 DEMOCRATIC

Senator   367,746 Russell D. Feingold; 74,472 Jim Moody; 71,570 Joseph W. Checota; 8,678 Thomas Keller; 5,019 Edmond Hou-Seye; 359 scattered write-in.

Congress   Unopposed in six CD's. Contested as follows:

CD 2   47,777 Ada E. Deer; 31,961 David Clarenbach.
CD 3   16,338 Paul Sacia; 12,771 James L. Ziegeweid; 5,806 Donald B. Schultz.
CD 5   34,301 Thomas M. Barrett; 18,928 Terrance L. Pitts; 15,729 Frederick P. Kessler; 13,411 Marc J. Marotta; 662 Roman R. Blenski; 483 Gerald D. Wilson.

WYOMING

GOVERNOR
Mike Sullivan (D). Re-elected 1990 to a four-year term. Previously elected 1986.

SENATORS
Alan K. Simpson (R). Re-elected 1990 to a six-year term. Previously elected 1984, 1978.

Malcolm Wallop (R). Re-elected 1988 to a six-year term. Previously elected 1982, 1976.

REPRESENTATIVE
At-Large. Craig Thomas (R)

POSTWAR VOTE FOR PRESIDENT

Year	Total Vote	Republican Vote	Republican Candidate	Democratic Vote	Democratic Candidate	Other Vote	Plurality	Total Vote Rep.	Total Vote Dem.	Major Vote Rep.	Major Vote Dem.
1992 **	200,598	79,347	Bush, George	68,160	Clinton, Bill	53,091	11,187 R	39.6%	34.0%	53.8%	46.2%
1988	176,551	106,867	Bush, George	67,113	Dukakis, Michael S.	2,571	39,754 R	60.5%	38.0%	61.4%	38.6%
1984	188,968	133,241	Reagan, Ronald	53,370	Mondale, Walter F.	2,357	79,871 R	70.5%	28.2%	71.4%	28.6%
1980	176,713	110,700	Reagan, Ronald	49,427	Carter, Jimmy	16,586	61,273 R	62.6%	28.0%	69.1%	30.9%
1976	156,343	92,717	Ford, Gerald R.	62,239	Carter, Jimmy	1,387	30,478 R	59.3%	39.8%	59.8%	40.2%
1972	145,570	100,464	Nixon, Richard M.	44,358	McGovern, George S.	748	56,106 R	69.0%	30.5%	69.4%	30.6%
1968	127,205	70,927	Nixon, Richard M.	45,173	Humphrey, Hubert H.	11,105	25,754 R	55.8%	35.5%	61.1%	38.9%
1964	142,716	61,998	Goldwater, Barry M.	80,718	Johnson, Lyndon B.		18,720 D	43.4%	56.6%	43.4%	56.6%
1960	140,782	77,451	Nixon, Richard M.	63,331	Kennedy, John F.		14,120 R	55.0%	45.0%	55.0%	45.0%
1956	124,127	74,573	Eisenhower, Dwight D.	49,554	Stevenson, Adlai E.		25,019 R	60.1%	39.9%	60.1%	39.9%
1952	129,253	81,049	Eisenhower, Dwight D.	47,934	Stevenson, Adlai E.	270	33,115 R	62.7%	37.1%	62.8%	37.2%
1948	101,425	47,947	Dewey, Thomas E.	52,354	Truman, Harry S.	1,124	4,407 D	47.3%	51.6%	47.8%	52.2%

In 1992 the other vote column includes 51,263 votes cast for Perot.

POSTWAR VOTE FOR GOVERNOR

Year	Total Vote	Republican Vote	Republican Candidate	Democratic Vote	Democratic Candidate	Other Vote	Rep.-Dem. Plurality	Total Vote Rep.	Total Vote Dem.	Major Vote Rep.	Major Vote Dem.
1990	160,109	55,471	Mead, Mary	104,638	Sullivan, Mike		49,167 D	34.6%	65.4%	34.6%	65.4%
1986	164,720	75,841	Simpson, Peter	88,879	Sullivan, Mike		13,038 D	46.0%	54.0%	46.0%	54.0%
1982	168,555	62,128	Morton, Warren A.	106,427	Herschler, Ed		44,299 D	36.9%	63.1%	36.9%	63.1%
1978	137,567	67,595	Ostlund, John C.	69,972	Herschler, Ed		2,377 D	49.1%	50.9%	49.1%	50.9%
1974	128,386	56,645	Jones, Dick	71,741	Herschler, Ed		15,096 D	44.1%	55.9%	44.1%	55.9%
1970	118,257	74,249	Hathaway, Stan	44,008	Rooney, John J.		30,241 R	62.8%	37.2%	62.8%	37.2%
1966	120,873	65,624	Hathaway, Stan	55,249	Wilkerson, Ernest		10,375 R	54.3%	45.7%	54.3%	45.7%
1962	119,268	64,970	Hansen, Clifford P.	54,298	Gage, Jack R.		10,672 R	54.5%	45.5%	54.5%	45.5%
1958	112,537	52,488	Simpson, Milward L.	55,070	Hickey, J. J.	4,979	2,582 D	46.6%	48.9%	48.8%	51.2%
1954	111,438	56,275	Simpson, Milward L.	55,163	Jack, William		1,112 R	50.5%	49.5%	50.5%	49.5%
1950	96,959	54,441	Barrett, Frank A.	42,518	McIntyre, John J.		11,923 R	56.1%	43.9%	56.1%	43.9%
1946	81,353	38,333	Wright, Earl	43,020	Hunt, Lester C.		4,687 D	47.1%	52.9%	47.1%	52.9%

WYOMING

POSTWAR VOTE FOR SENATOR

Year	Total Vote	Republican Vote	Republican Candidate	Democratic Vote	Democratic Candidate	Other Vote	Rep.-Dem. Plurality	Percentage Total Vote Rep.	Percentage Total Vote Dem.	Percentage Major Vote Rep.	Percentage Major Vote Dem.
1990	157,632	100,784	Simpson, Alan K.	56,848	Helling, Kathy		43,936 R	63.9%	36.1%	63.9%	36.1%
1988	180,964	91,143	Wallop, Malcolm	89,821	Vinich, John P.		1,322 R	50.4%	49.6%	50.4%	49.6%
1984	186,898	146,373	Simpson, Alan K.	40,525	Ryan, Victor A.		105,848 R	78.3%	21.7%	78.3%	21.7%
1982	167,191	94,725	Wallop, Malcolm	72,466	McDaniel, Rodger		22,259 R	56.7%	43.3%	56.7%	43.3%
1978	133,364	82,908	Simpson, Alan K.	50,456	Whitaker, Raymond B.		32,452 R	62.2%	37.8%	62.2%	37.8%
1976	155,368	84,810	Wallop, Malcolm	70,558	McGee, Gale		14,252 R	54.6%	45.4%	54.6%	45.4%
1972	142,067	101,314	Hansen, Clifford P.	40,753	Vinich, Mike		60,561 R	71.3%	28.7%	71.3%	28.7%
1970	120,486	53,279	Wold, John S.	67,207	McGee, Gale		13,928 D	44.2%	55.8%	44.2%	55.8%
1966	122,689	63,548	Hansen, Clifford P.	59,141	Roncalio, Teno		4,407 R	51.8%	48.2%	51.8%	48.2%
1964	141,670	65,185	Wold, John S.	76,485	McGee, Gale		11,300 D	46.0%	54.0%	46.0%	54.0%
1962 S	119,372	69,043	Simpson, Milward L.	50,329	Hickey, J. J.		18,714 R	57.8%	42.2%	57.8%	42.2%
1960	138,550	78,103	Thomson, E. Keith	60,447	Whitaker, Ray		17,656 R	56.4%	43.6%	56.4%	43.6%
1958	114,157	56,122	Barrett, Frank A.	58,035	McGee, Gale		1,913 D	49.2%	50.8%	49.2%	50.8%
1954	112,252	54,407	Harrison, William H.	57,845	O'Mahoney, Joseph C.		3,438 D	48.5%	51.5%	48.5%	51.5%
1952	130,097	67,176	Barrett, Frank A.	62,921	O'Mahoney, Joseph C.		4,255 R	51.6%	48.4%	51.6%	48.4%
1948	101,480	43,527	Robertson, Edward V.	57,953	Hunt, Lester C.		14,426 D	42.9%	57.1%	42.9%	57.1%
1946	81,557	35,714	Henderson, Harry B.	45,843	O'Mahoney, Joseph C.		10,129 D	43.8%	56.2%	43.8%	56.2%

The 1962 election was for a short term to fill a vacancy.

WYOMING

One At Large

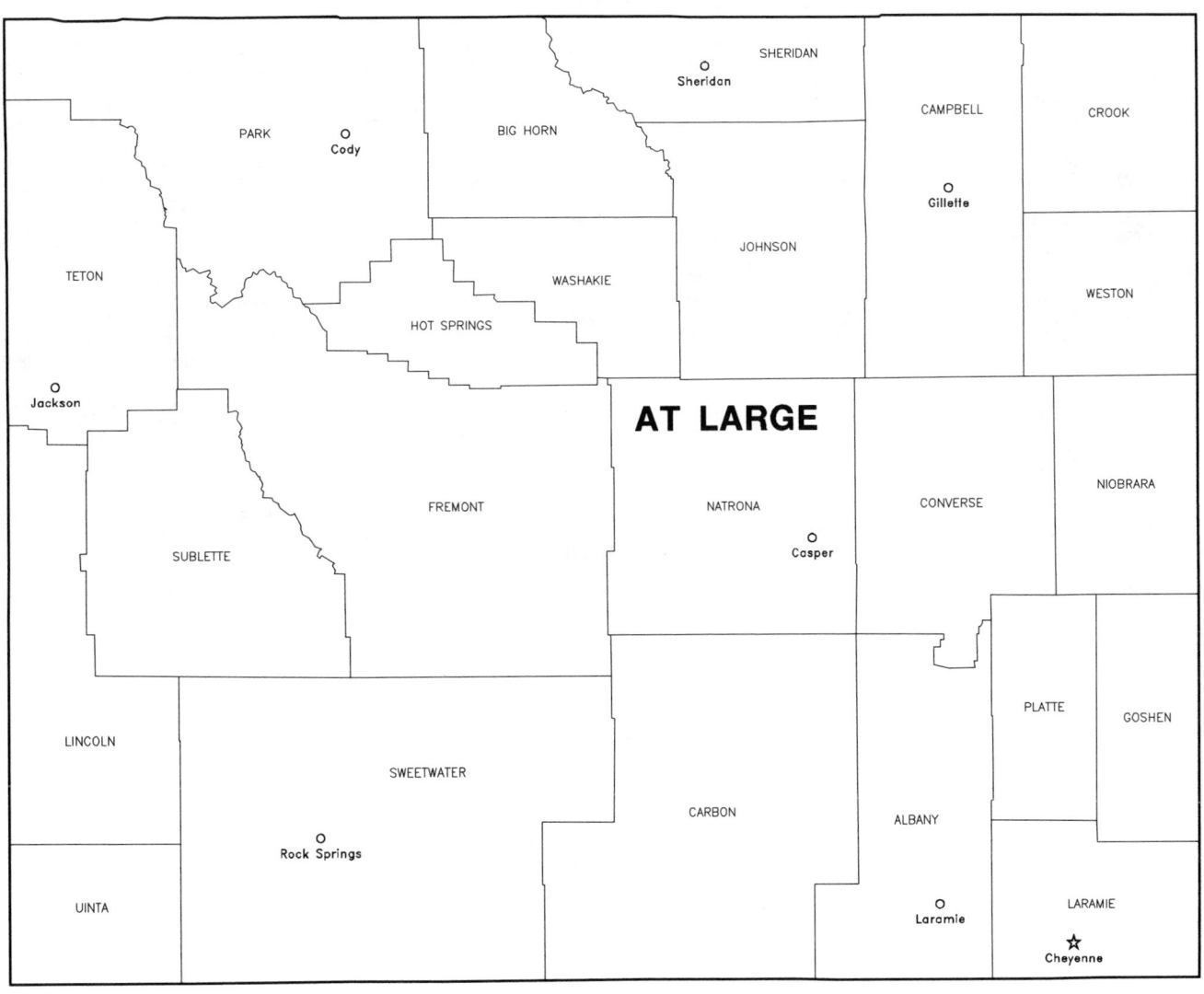

SHERIDAN
○ Sheridan

PARK
○ Cody

BIG HORN

CAMPBELL

CROOK

○ Gillette

TETON

WASHAKIE

JOHNSON

HOT SPRINGS

WESTON

○
Jackson

AT LARGE

FREMONT

NATRONA

CONVERSE

NIOBRARA

SUBLETTE

○
Casper

LINCOLN

PLATTE

GOSHEN

SWEETWATER

CARBON

ALBANY

○
Rock Springs

UINTA

○
Laramie

LARAMIE

☆
Cheyenne

WYOMING

PRESIDENT 1992

Registration	County	Total Vote	Republican	Democratic	Perot	Other	Plurality	Percentage Total Vote		
								Rep.	Dem.	Perot
15,082	ALBANY	12,867	4,176	5,713	2,862	116	1,537 D	32.5%	44.4%	22.2%
5,889	BIG HORN	4,762	2,216	1,216	1,236	94	980 R	46.5%	25.5%	26.0%
12,935	CAMPBELL	11,219	5,315	2,709	3,133	62	2,182 R	47.4%	24.1%	27.9%
8,107	CARBON	6,678	2,320	2,737	1,579	42	417 D	34.7%	41.0%	23.6%
5,554	CONVERSE	4,751	2,159	1,307	1,260	25	852 R	45.4%	27.5%	26.5%
3,148	CROOK	2,683	1,377	568	718	20	659 R	51.3%	21.2%	26.8%
16,429	FREEMONT	13,894	5,387	4,765	3,594	148	622 R	38.8%	34.3%	25.9%
6,317	GOSHEN	5,318	2,395	1,754	1,144	25	641 R	45.0%	33.0%	21.5%
2,787	HOT SPRINGS	2,399	978	740	652	29	238 R	40.8%	30.8%	27.2%
3,656	JOHNSON	3,146	1,614	656	844	32	770 R	51.3%	20.9%	26.8%
37,193	LARAMIE	31,855	12,890	12,177	6,607	181	713 R	40.5%	38.2%	20.7%
7,089	LINCOLN	5,757	2,595	1,430	1,495	237	1,100 R	45.1%	24.8%	26.0%
31,732	NATRONA	27,400	9,717	9,817	7,647	219	100 D	35.5%	35.8%	27.9%
1,591	NIOBRARA	1,299	635	298	355	11	280 R	48.9%	22.9%	27.3%
12,988	PARK	11,209	5,218	2,771	3,145	75	2,073 R	46.6%	24.7%	28.1%
4,699	PLATTE	4,051	1,668	1,398	956	29	270 R	41.2%	34.5%	23.6%
13,028	SHERIDAN	11,559	4,303	4,139	3,035	82	164 R	37.2%	35.8%	26.3%
3,185	SUBLETTE	2,573	1,168	536	828	41	340 R	45.4%	20.8%	32.2%
17,197	SWEETWATER	14,891	4,476	6,417	3,879	119	1,941 D	30.1%	43.1%	26.0%
9,689	TETON	8,382	2,854	3,120	2,340	68	266 D	34.0%	37.2%	27.9%
7,932	UINTA	6,896	2,701	2,047	2,041	107	654 R	39.2%	29.7%	29.6%
4,579	WASHAKIE	3,982	1,720	1,118	1,084	60	602 R	43.2%	28.1%	27.2%
3,454	WESTON	3,027	1,465	727	829	6	636 R	48.4%	24.0%	27.4%
234,260	TOTAL	200,598	79,347	68,160	51,263	1,828	11,187 R	39.6%	34.0%	25.6%

WYOMING

CONGRESS

CD	Year	Total Vote	Republican Vote	Republican Candidate	Democratic Vote	Democratic Candidate	Other Vote	Rep.-Dem. Plurality	Total Vote Rep.	Total Vote Dem.	Major Vote Rep.	Major Vote Dem.
AL	1992	196,977	113,882	THOMAS, CRAIG	77,418	HERSCHLER, JON	5,677	36,464 R	57.8%	39.3%	59.5%	40.5%
AL	1990	158,055	87,078	THOMAS, CRAIG	70,977	MAXFIELD, PETE		16,101 R	55.1%	44.9%	55.1%	44.9%
AL	1988	177,651	118,350	CHENEY, RICHARD	56,527	SHARRATT, BRYAN	2,774	61,823 R	66.6%	31.8%	67.7%	32.3%
AL	1986	159,787	111,007	CHENEY, RICHARD	48,780	GILMORE, RICK		62,227 R	69.5%	30.5%	69.5%	30.5%
AL	1984	187,904	138,234	CHENEY, RICHARD	45,857	MCFADDEN, HUGH B.	3,813	92,377 R	73.6%	24.4%	75.1%	24.9%
AL	1982	159,277	113,236	CHENEY, RICHARD	46,041	HOMMEL, THEODORE H.		67,195 R	71.1%	28.9%	71.1%	28.9%
AL	1980	169,699	116,361	CHENEY, RICHARD	53,338	ROGERS, JIM		63,023 R	68.6%	31.4%	68.6%	31.4%
AL	1978	129,377	75,855	CHENEY, RICHARD	53,522	BAGLEY, BILL		22,333 R	58.6%	41.4%	58.6%	41.4%
AL	1976	151,868	66,147	HART, LARRY	85,721	RONCALIO, TENO		19,574 D	43.6%	56.4%	43.6%	56.4%
AL	1974	126,933	57,499	STROOCK, TOM	69,434	RONCALIO, TENO		11,935 D	45.3%	54.7%	45.3%	54.7%
AL	1972	146,299	70,667	KIDD, WILLIAM	75,632	RONCALIO, TENO		4,965 D	48.3%	51.7%	48.3%	51.7%
AL	1970	116,304	57,848	ROBERTS, HARRY	58,456	RONCALIO, TENO		608 D	49.7%	50.3%	49.7%	50.3%
AL	1968	123,313	77,363	WOLD, JOHN S.	45,950	LINFORD, VELMA		31,413 R	62.7%	37.3%	62.7%	37.3%
AL	1966	119,426	62,984	HARRISON, WILLIAM H.	56,442	CHRISTIAN, AL	6,542	6,542 R	52.7%	47.3%	52.7%	47.3%
AL	1964	139,175	68,482	HARRISON, WILLIAM H.	70,693	RONCALIO, TENO		2,211 D	49.2%	50.8%	49.2%	50.8%
AL	1962	116,474	71,489	HARRISON, WILLIAM H.	44,985	MANKUS, LOUIS A.		26,504 R	61.4%	38.6%	61.4%	38.6%
AL	1960	134,331	70,241	HARRISON, WILLIAM H.	64,090	ARMSTRONG, H. T		6,151 R	52.3%	47.7%	52.3%	47.7%
AL	1958	111,780	59,894	THOMSON, E. KEITH	51,886	WHITAKER, RAY		8,008 R	53.6%	46.4%	53.6%	46.4%
AL	1956	120,128	69,903	THOMSON, E. KEITH	50,225	O'CALLAGHAN, JERRY		19,678 R	58.2%	41.8%	58.2%	41.8%
AL	1954	108,771	61,111	THOMSON, E. KEITH	47,660	TULLY, SAM		13,451 R	56.2%	43.8%	56.2%	43.8%
AL	1952	126,720	76,161	HARRISON, WILLIAM H.	50,559	ROSE, ROBERT R		25,602 R	60.1%	39.9%	60.1%	39.9%
AL	1950	93,348	50,865	HARRISON, WILLIAM H.	42,483	CLARK, JOHN B.		8,382 R	54.5%	45.5%	54.5%	45.5%
AL	1948	97,464	50,218	BARRETT, FRANK A.	47,246	FLANNERY, L. G.		2,972 R	51.5%	48.5%	51.5%	48.5%
AL	1946	79,438	44,482	BARRETT, FRANK A.	34,956	MCINTYRE, JOHN J.		9,526 R	56.0%	44.0%	56.0%	44.0%

WYOMING

1992 GENERAL ELECTION

President   Other vote was 844 Libertarian (Marrou); 569 Gritz (write-in); 270 Independent (Fulani); 11 Hagelin (write-in); 7 Phillips (write-in); 127 scattered write-in.

Congress   Other vote was Libertarian (McCune).

1992 PRIMARIES

AUGUST 18 REPUBLICAN

Congress   Unopposed at-large.

AUGUST 18 DEMOCRATIC

Congress   Contested as follows:

AL   26,407 Jon Herschler; 11,007 Jim Huidekoper; 3,864 Charles Carroll; 2,188 Emmett Jones; 1,575 Michael S. Daizell.

DISTRICT OF COLUMBIA

GOVERNMENT
The District of Columbia is governed by a Mayor and City Council of thirteen.

MAYOR
Sharon Pratt Dixon (D). Elected 1990 to a four year term.

DELEGATE
Eleanor Holmes Norton (D)

POSTWAR VOTE FOR PRESIDENT

Year	Total Vote	Republican Vote	Republican Candidate	Democratic Vote	Democratic Candidate	Other Vote	Plurality	Total Vote Rep.	Total Vote Dem.	Major Vote Rep.	Major Vote Dem.
1992 **	227,572	20,698	Bush, George	192,619	Clinton, Bill	14,255	171,921 D	9.1%	84.6%	9.7%	90.3%
1988	192,877	27,590	Bush, George	159,407	Dukakis, Michael S.	5,880	131,817 D	14.3%	82.6%	14.8%	85.2%
1984	211,288	29,009	Reagan, Ronald	180,408	Mondale, Walter F.	1,871	151,399 D	13.7%	85.4%	13.9%	86.1%
1980	175,237	23,545	Reagan, Ronald	131,113	Carter, Jimmy	20,579	107,568 D	13.4%	74.8%	15.2%	84.8%
1976	168,830	27,873	Ford, Gerald R.	137,818	Carter, Jimmy	3,139	109,945 D	16.5%	81.6%	16.8%	83.2%
1972	163,421	35,226	Nixon, Richard M.	127,627	McGovern, George S.	568	92,401 D	21.6%	78.1%	21.6%	78.4%
1968	170,578	31,012	Nixon, Richard M.	139,566	Humphrey, Hubert H.		108,554 D	18.2%	81.8%	18.2%	81.8%
1964 **	198,597	28,801	Goldwater, Barry M.	169,796	Johnson, Lyndon B.		140,995 D	14.5%	85.5%	14.5%	85.5%

In 1992 the other vote column includes 9,681 votes cast for Perot. Under the 23rd Amendment to the Constitution, the District of Columbia became entitled to choose Electors beginning with the 1964 election.

POSTWAR VOTE FOR MAYOR

Year	Total Vote	Republican Vote	Republican Candidate	Democratic Vote	Democratic Candidate	Other Vote	Rep.-Dem. Plurality	Total Vote Rep.	Total Vote Dem.	Major Vote Rep.	Major Vote Dem.
1990	169,066	19,764	Turner, Maurice T.	144,701	Dixon, Sharon Pratt	4,601	124,937 D	11.7%	85.6%	12.0%	88.0%
1986	131,802	43,676	Schwartz, Carol	80,666	Barry, Marion	7,460	36,990 D	33.1%	61.2%	35.1%	64.9%
1982	117,623	16,501	Lee, E. Brooke	95,007	Barry, Marion	6,115	78,506 D	14.0%	80.8%	14.8%	85.2%
1978	100,861	28,032	Fletcher, Arthur	69,888	Barry, Marion	2,941	41,856 D	27.8%	69.3%	28.6%	71.4%
1974	105,183	3,703	Champion, Jackson R.	84,676	Washington, Walter E.	16,804	80,973 D	3.5%	80.5%	4.2%	95.8%

DISTRICT OF COLUMBIA

POSTWAR VOTE FOR DELEGATE

Year	Total Vote	Republican		Democratic		Other Vote	Rep.-Dem. Plurality	Percentage			
		Vote	Candidate	Vote	Candidate			Total Vote		Major Vote	
								Rep.	Dem.	Rep.	Dem.
1992	196,754	20,108	Emerson, Susan	166,808	Norton, Eleanor Holmes	9,838	146,700 D	10.2%	84.8%	10.8%	89.2%
1990	159,627	41,999	Singleton, Harry M.	98,442	Norton, Eleanor Holmes	19,186	56,443 D	26.3%	61.7%	29.9%	70.1%
1988	170,933	22,936	Reed, William	121,817	Fauntroy, Walter E.	26,180	98,881 D	13.4%	71.3%	15.8%	84.2%
1986	126,855	17,643	King, Mary L. H.	101,604	Fauntroy, Walter E.	7,608	83,961 D	13.9%	80.1%	14.8%	85.2%
1984 **	161,771		—	154,583	Fauntroy, Walter E.	7,188	154,583 D		95.6%		100.0%
1982	112,543	17,242	West, John	93,422	Fauntroy, Walter E.	1,879	76,180 D	15.3%	83.0%	15.6%	84.4%
1980	151,046	21,245	Roehr, Robert J.	112,339	Fauntroy, Walter E.	17,462	91,094 D	14.1%	74.4%	15.9%	84.1%
1978	96,306	11,677	Champion, Jackson R.	76,557	Fauntroy, Walter E.	8,072	64,880 D	12.1%	79.5%	13.2%	86.8%
1976	159,790	21,699	Hall, Daniel L.	123,464	Fauntroy, Walter E.	14,627	101,765 D	13.6%	77.3%	14.9%	85.1%
1974	104,014	9,166	Phillips, William R.	66,337	Fauntroy, Walter E.	28,511	57,171 D	8.8%	63.8%	12.1%	87.9%
1972	159,612	39,487	Chin-Lee, William	95,300	Fauntroy, Walter E.	24,825	55,813 D	24.7%	59.7%	29.3%	70.7%
1971 S	116,635	29,249	Nevius, John A.	68,166	Fauntroy, Walter E.	19,220	38,917 D	25.1%	58.4%	30.0%	70.0%

The 1971 election was held in March for a short term to the end of the 92nd Congress. In 1984 the Democratic candidate was also the nominee of the Republican and Statehood parties.

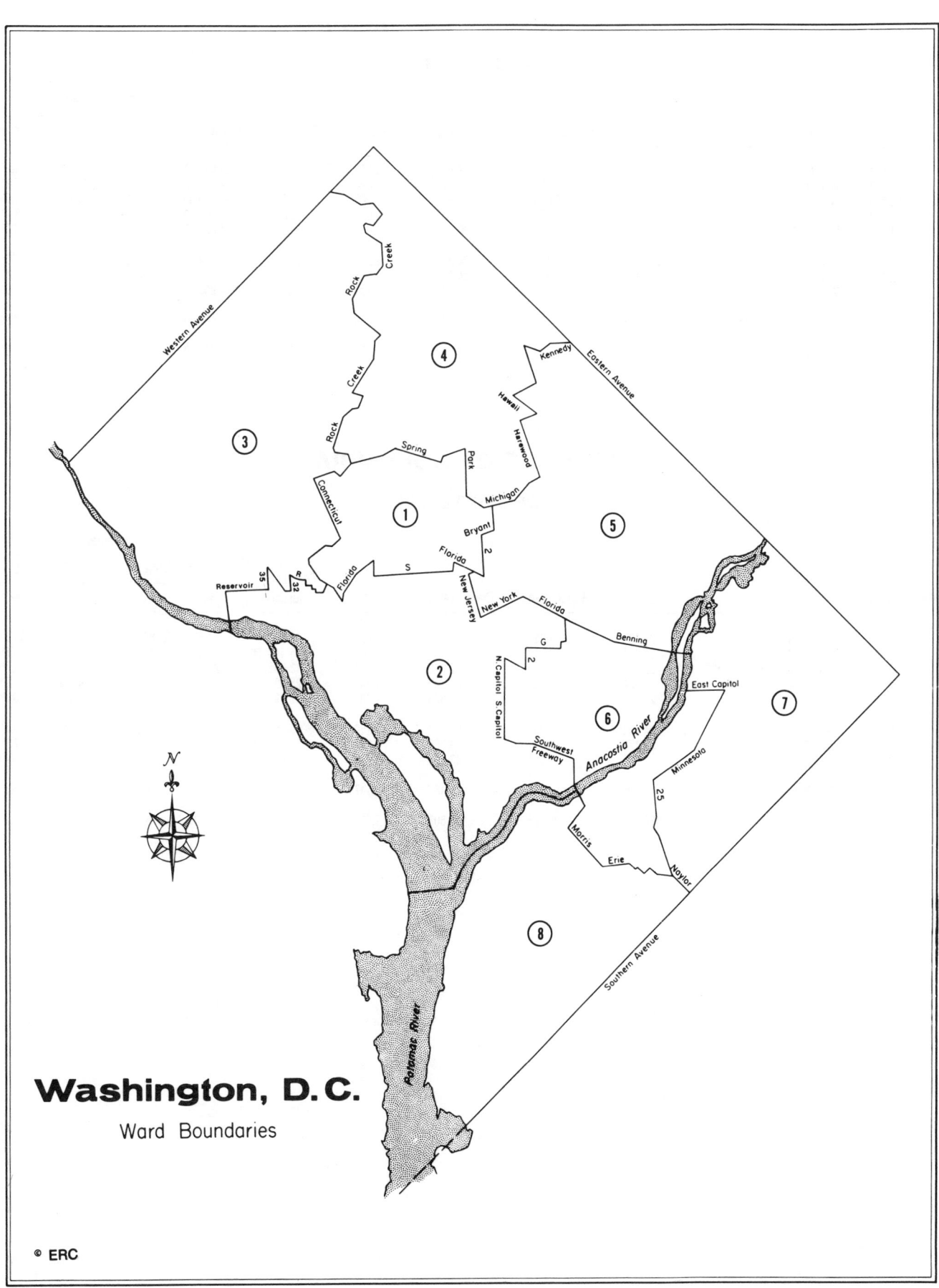

Washington, D.C.

Ward Boundaries

DISTRICT OF COLUMBIA

PRESIDENT 1992

Registration	Ward	Total Vote	Republican	Democratic	Perot	Other	Plurality	Percentage Total Vote Rep.	Dem.	Perot
42,114	WARD 1	26,488	1,892	22,832	1,112	652	20,940 D	7.1%	86.2%	4.2%
41,492	WARD 2	28,512	4,157	22,143	1,692	520	17,986 D	14.6%	77.7%	5.9%
48,225	WARD 3	38,007	8,001	26,906	2,606	494	18,905 D	21.1%	70.8%	6.9%
47,158	WARD 4	32,932	1,650	29,457	1,068	757	27,807 D	5.0%	89.4%	3.2%
44,891	WARD 5	29,034	1,352	26,243	814	625	24,891 D	4.7%	90.4%	2.8%
43,911	WARD 6	28,360	2,115	24,329	1,294	622	22,214 D	7.5%	85.8%	4.6%
42,189	WARD 7	26,985	924	24,882	638	541	23,958 D	3.4%	92.2%	2.4%
30,973	WARD 8	16,819	546	15,484	431	358	14,938 D	3.2%	92.1%	2.6%
	FEDERAL BALLOTS	435	61	343	26	5	282 D	14.0%	78.9%	6.0%
340,953	TOTAL	227,572	20,698	192,619	9,681	4,574	171,921 D	9.1%	84.6%	4.3%

DISTRICT OF COLUMBIA

DELEGATE 1992

Registration	Ward	Total Vote	Republican	Democratic	Other	Rep.-Dem. Plurality	Percentage Total Vote Rep.	Dem.	Major Vote Rep.	Dem.
42,114	WARD 1	22,891	1,937	19,520	1,434	17,583 D	8.5%	85.3%	9.0%	91.0%
41,492	WARD 2	24,984	4,572	19,018	1,394	14,446 D	18.3%	76.1%	19.4%	80.6%
48,225	WARD 3	32,980	8,840	22,345	1,795	13,505 D	26.8%	67.8%	28.3%	71.7%
47,158	WARD 4	28,884	1,103	26,640	1,141	25,537 D	3.8%	92.2%	4.0%	96.0%
44,891	WARD 5	24,792	779	22,876	1,137	22,097 D	3.1%	92.3%	3.3%	96.7%
43,911	WARD 6	24,613	2,143	21,210	1,260	19,067 D	8.7%	86.2%	9.2%	90.8%
42,189	WARD 7	23,179	477	21,755	947	21,278 D	2.1%	93.9%	2.1%	97.9%
30,973	WARD 8	14,235	215	13,307	713	13,092 D	1.5%	93.5%	1.6%	98.4%
	FEDERAL BALLOTS	196	42	137	17	95 D	21.4%	69.9%	23.5%	76.5%
340,953	TOTAL	196,754	20,108	166,808	9,838	146,700 D	10.2%	84.8%	10.8%	89.2%

DISTRICT OF COLUMBIA

1992 GENERAL ELECTION

President Other vote was 1,459 New Alliance (Fulani); 1,186 Independent (Daniels); 467 Libertarian (Marrou); 260 Independent (LaRouche); 230 Natural Law (Hagelin); 191 Socialist (Brisben); 105 Socialist Workers (Warren); 676 scattered write-in.

Delegate Other vote was 7,253 Statehood (Griffin); 1,840 Socialist Workers (Manuel); 745 scattered write-in.

1992 PRIMARIES

MAY 5 REPUBLICAN

Delegate No Republican candidate. Susan Emerson received the nomination by write-in vote.

MAY 5 DEMOCRATIC

Delegate Eleanor Holmes Norton, unopposed.

MAY 5 STATEHOOD

Delegate No Statehood candidate. Susan Griffin received the nomination by write-in vote.